A HISTORY OF THE MUSLIM WORLD

A HISTORY OF THE MUSLIM WORLD

From its origins to the dawn of modernity

MICHAEL COOK

PRINCETON UNIVERSITY PRESS
PRINCETON & OXFORD

Published by Princeton University Press
41 William Street, Princeton, New Jersey 08540
99 Banbury Road, Oxford OX2 6JX

press.princeton.edu

Library of Congress Cataloging-in-Publication Data

Names: Cook, Michael, 1940– author.
Title: A history of the Muslim world: from its origins to the dawn of modernity / Michael Cook.
Description: Princeton : Princeton University Press, [2024] | Includes bibliographical references and index.
Identifiers: LCCN 2023009577 (print) | LCCN 2023009578 (ebook) | ISBN 9780691236575 | ISBN 9780691236582 (ebook)
Subjects: LCSH: Islamic countries—History. | Islamic Empire—History.
Classification: LCC DS35.63 .C66 2024 (print) | LCC DS35.63 (ebook) | DDC 909/.09767—dc23/eng/20230302
LC record available at https://lccn.loc.gov/2023009577
LC ebook record available at https://lccn.loc.gov/2023009578

British Library Cataloging-in-Publication Data is available

Editorial: Priya Nelson and Emma Wagh
Production Editorial: Kathleen Cioffi
Text Design: Karl Spurzem
Jacket Design: Katie Osborne
Production: Danielle Amatucci
Publicity: Alyssa Sanford and Carmen Jimenez
Copyeditor: Hanna Siurua

Jacket image: Chorna_L / Adobe Stock

This book has been composed in Adobe Text Pro with Bely

Printed on acid-free paper. ∞

Printed in the United States of America

10 9 8 7 6 5 4 3 2 1

In memory of Ed Cordes

1951–2020

CONTENTS

PART II. The Muslim world from the eleventh century to the eighteenth

MAPS

PREFACE

Humans are an interesting species, even if their long-term viability is questionable. One reason they are interesting is that they are able to build exotically different cultures on more or less the same biological and material foundations. This book is about a substantial slice of human history delimited by a particular cultural characteristic: adherence to Islam in some form or other. Religious adherence is, of course, only one among a number of criteria by which the history of the world can be divided up. One could, for example, cut the slices by period, geography, or ethnicity. In fact, all three play roles in the internal organization of this book. It is divided into three parts by period, with six chapters covering the emergence of the Muslim world and its history down to the eleventh century, eight chapters covering the centuries from the eleventh to the eighteenth, and finally, by way of epilogue, a single chapter that is largely devoted to outlining how the Muslim world of the later eighteenth century became what it is today. Within the first two parts, most chapters are explicitly or implicitly limited in scope to particular geographical regions—India, Africa, and the like. And at certain points I have made more use of ethnic distinction as an organizing principle than many of my colleagues might have done by, for example, devoting a chapter to the history of the Arabs between the eleventh and eighteenth centuries. But my overarching choice has been to write a history of the *Muslim* world, and while this is by no means the only defensible choice, it has its rewards. A commitment to Islam makes a difference: wherever a society and its rulers have come to be Muslim, sooner or later this has led to a major discontinuity with the society's pre-Islamic past and a significant expansion of its relations with the wider Muslim world. It is also worth noting that the very existence of a Muslim world depends on historical contingencies that in any secular perspective could easily have turned out differently, so it does not take much strain to imagine a counterfactual history in which it never emerged. What exactly a world without Islam would have looked like is impossible to say, but it would assuredly have been markedly different from the one we actually inhabit.

Coverage

I should say something about what this book does and does not cover to supplement what is already apparent from its title and table of contents. How does one write a single volume about a history that extends in time over fourteen centuries and in space from Morocco to Mindanao? The answer, of course, is by leaving most of it out. This is especially true for the period since 1800, which I take account of only in an epilogue. But it applies also to the period before 1800, for which my coverage is intended to be reasonably systematic. Here we are helped by the ravages of time, which have brought about the extinction of memory and destruction of evidence on a vast scale. The fraction of past humans whom we know even by name is exiguous, and the proportion of named individuals whose lives are known to us in any fullness is tiny. And yet the body of surviving source material for the history of the Muslim world is far greater than a single historian could ever hope to handle. For most of the ground covered in this book I am accordingly dependent on the work of historians who have grappled directly with the sources. I do, of course, make extensive use of my professional judgment in tacitly picking and choosing between the interpretations they present, but that still leaves me substantially at their mercy; if they err, I am likely to follow them in error. This is, naturally, a two-way street, in that they are also at my mercy—I may have misunderstood them or misused the information they provide. What I can say is that the outlines I present in this book are, for the most part, reasonably well agreed on among scholars. In the more flagrant cases where they are not, I have sometimes drawn attention to the fact in the footnotes, suggesting where the reader might go for a different view. The outlines I provide are also fairly comprehensive; it is not the case that there are vast regions or periods that I have simply ignored. But outlining is not the only way in which the author of a book such as this decides what to omit. I have tried throughout to combine broad outlines with close-ups, zooming in and out. It is here that my choices of what to include or exclude are likely to be most idiosyncratic. They are not entirely arbitrary in that I do have my reasons, but undoubtedly any other historian writing this book would have made a very different selection, and it would probably be at least equally valid if not more so.

I have also made choices, though fairly conventional ones, about what *kinds* of history to cover or leave out. Broadly speaking, I give systematic attention to two things: the making and unmaking of states, and really major cultural shifts that affect large populations. There are two reasons for doing this. One is that these things matter historically, and the other is that they are fairly well documented and studied across the history of the Muslim world. There are other kinds of history that arguably matter just as much, such as economic and social history,[1] and perhaps it will one day be possible to survey them in the same way. But at this point this is not yet possible, or if it is I don't know how to do it. Another historical genre that I leave aside is intellectual history; as it happens, this is the field in which I did much of my previous work, but it is not what this book is about. Nor do I make any attempt at systematic coverage of the non-Muslims who found themselves under Muslim rule and not infrequently constituted the majority of the population. All these kinds of history, and others, make incidental appearances in this book, sometimes frequent or sustained ones, but they are not its core. In short, this book is neither as grand in scale nor as thematically broad as Marshall Hodgson's classic three-volume *Venture of Islam*, a history of an entire civilization published half a century ago.[2]

The job of a historian is to make the past intelligible to the present, and although I have tried to do this as objectively as I can, there can be no doubt that the values I hold in the present have a way of coloring the way I see the past. So readers will probably not have much trouble figuring out that I like some of the people I write about more than I like others. But I have not made it my business to express opinions about the relative moral standing of the Walrus and the Carpenter—two figures who, between them, engross a large share of human history. In fact, the single most consistent and pervasive bias in this book is of a different kind: it gives disproportionate voice to the articulate and the opinionated to the virtual exclusion of the silent, the tongue-tied, and the anonymous mass of the population. Given the character of our sources this is more or less inevitable, but the reader should be aware of it.

Terminology

There are a number of points about terminology that I should note for the record, though the reader who wants to proceed to the substance of the book will lose little by skipping them.

"Middle East" versus "Near East": These terms originally referred to rather different regions. Roughly speaking, the "Near East" was what one reached coming from the west across the Mediterranean, whereas the "Middle East" was what one reached coming from the east across the Indian Ocean. In effect the two have coalesced geographically, with usage depending on the period one is concerned with: the region called the "Near East" by historians of the ancient world is much the same as that called the "Middle East" by those writing about its recent past and present. For the long period in between, usage is unsettled. This situation does not

1. For the latter, note the bold title of I. M. Lapidus, *A history of Islamic societies*, Cambridge 1988.
2. M. G. S. Hodgson, *The venture of Islam*, Chicago 1974.

make much sense, so I have steeled myself to use "Middle East" rather than "Near East" except in occasional references to the "Ancient Near East."[3] But I have also referred to the Middle East in many places as the "heartlands" of the Muslim world.

"Secular": "Secularism" is a modern Western phenomenon, but "secular" is a medieval Christian term, applied to matters of this world as opposed to the next. Medieval Muslims made the same distinction, the key term being *dunyā*—this world, the Latin *saeculum*, as opposed to the world to come. Alternatives to "secular" would be "worldly" or "profane," but all three have irrelevant connotations, and I have chosen to use "secular."[4] It does not mean "secularist."

"Muslim" versus "Islamic": Hodgson in his *Venture of Islam* made a distinction between "Islamic" (intrinsic to the religion of Islam) and "Islamicate" (contingently associated with the religion of Islam). In this usage fasting prescribed by the Qur'ān would be Islamic, whereas fasting prescribed by a Muslim physician working in the Greek medical tradition of the medieval Muslim world would be Islamicate. As with many distinctions, there is a gray area between the cases to which the terms apply unambiguously; compare our everyday distinction between red and green, where there is an intervening "gray" area of reddish green or greenish red. But as with red and green, Hodgson's distinction is to my mind a sensible and useful one.[5] Yet I have always been somewhat allergic to his neologism "Islamicate," so rather than grit my teeth and use it, I have tended to map his distinction onto two words that everyone uses: "Islamic" and "Muslim." Thus Qur'ānic fasting is Islamic, whereas medical fasting when done by Muslims is just Muslim. This is a distinction that Hodgson himself considered and judged to possess "some advantage." It also lies behind the wording of the title of this book: *A history of the Muslim world*, not *A history of the Islamic world*. In the same vein I talk regularly about Muslim states, meaning states ruled by Muslims in whatever fashion, and only rarely of Islamic states—that is, states constituted by Muslims in some intrinsically Islamic fashion. On the other hand, I have gone along with general chronological usage in speaking of, say, "pre-Islamic Arabia" rather than "pre-Muslim Arabia."

3. I take courage from J. Tannous, *The making of the medieval Middle East*, Princeton 2018.

4. For what is at stake see Rushain Abbasi's forthcoming monograph tentatively entitled *Islam and the dissolution of the secular*.

5. Shahab Ahmed vigorously attacked this distinction, but a close reading of his argument shows that he was not rejecting it in principle: "To my mind, when Muslims claim to be speaking and acting *as Muslims*, that is, to be speaking and acting *in Islam* we need, as an analytical and conceptual matter, to take them *at their word*" (S. Ahmed, *What is Islam?*, Princeton 2016, 303, italics in the original). The tacit implication is that there exists a domain in which Muslims do not act "as Muslims" or "in Islam"; it is this domain that Hodgson labels "Islamicate." The dispute is thus about the extent of the domain, not its existence. Incidentally, any reader interested in the phenomenon known as Islamic civilization should read at least the first chapter of Ahmed's book.

"Turkish" versus "Turkic": Like everyone else, I use the term "Turks" in two different ways: to refer to a broad grouping of peoples who are to be found from Siberia to the Balkans, and to pick out one particular people—the core population of what is now Turkey. But when it comes to forming an adjective, I distinguish the two, using "Turkic" for the broad sense and "Turkish" for the narrow sense. I did not invent this distinction, which is widely used by linguists, but I probably adhere to it more than is usual among historians.

"Tunisia" versus "Ifrīqiya" and the like: What is now Tunisia was known in the early centuries of Islam as "Ifrīqiya," from the Latin "Africa." I have referred to this territory as "Tunisia" throughout, partly because of the advantage of using terms likely to be familiar to anyone who reads English, and partly to avoid using different terms for the same territory at different times. This is not a perfect solution because "Ifrīqiya" as understood by medieval Muslim authors included more territory than Tunisia does today, but that is a cost I have chosen to incur. In the same way I refer to the entire Iberian Peninsula as "Spain," echoing the Latin "Hispania" and distinguishing the part ruled by Muslims as "Muslim Spain." The alternative is to use the Arabic term "al-Andalus" in place of "Muslim Spain," and there is much to be said for it; but I have preferred "Spain" for the same reasons for which I have chosen "Tunisia." The cost here is that in the aftermath of the Christian reconquest, Spain becomes the name of a state distinct from Portugal. Overall, I have applied the same reasoning across the Muslim world. Another point that is worth noting is that "Syria" in this book refers to geographical Syria—including the small countries of the modern Levant and excluding the northeastern extension of the modern state of Syria into the region known as the Jazīra, roughly northern Mesopotamia.

"Pagan" and "paganism": In this book we often encounter situations in which monotheism contrasts with other forms of religious belief that vary greatly among themselves in their content. Today there is a feeling that "pagan" is a derogatory term—and indeed as used by committed monotheists it is—and that the euphemism "animism" should be substituted for it. The trouble with "animism" is that it implies a specific belief in souls that may or may not be a relevant feature of a given form of paganism. "Pagan" is convenient because it lacks any such implication and because it can still be used neutrally in a way that its archaic synonym "heathen" cannot.

Technical matters

With regard to diacritics, my policy is to give them in full for words and names from non-European languages that do not have well-known anglicized forms. It is for readers to decide how much, if any, attention to pay to them, depending on how far it matters to them to pronounce such items in a passably authentic way.

Anyone aiming for a minimally acceptable pronunciation, but no more, could attend to the macrons and ignore the rest. A macron is a bar over a vowel showing lengthening: *ā* as in "father" (not as in "fat"), *ī* as in "leap" (not as in "lip"), *ū* as in "food" (not as in "foot"). Other diacritics, such as underdots, ʿ (*ʿayn*), and ʾ (*hamza*), will be meaningful and useful mainly to people with some knowledge of Arabic. In a book with the scope of this one Arabic is, of course, not the only language in play, but here again, readers are free to ignore diacritics that don't mean anything to them. With regard to Turkish, I am painfully aware that I have not found a good solution to the problems arising from the confluence of the "three languages" and the transition from the Arabic to the Latin script.

A word about the footnotes included in this book may be in order. My working draft contained a myriad of them, representing my efforts to keep track of where exactly I had come by each bit of information I included in the text. My intention had been to discard all this in the published text as mere scaffolding. But in response to the comments I received when the typescript was reviewed I have opted for something less than total elimination. Those footnotes that have survived the triage serve four main purposes: to identify some of the main secondary sources I depend on; to indicate where a curious reader might go for further information; to alert the reader that the view I express in the text is not the only one that has standing in the field and may indeed be an outlier; and in the great majority of cases, to give references for direct quotations that go back to primary sources.[6] I also give references to the Bible and the Qurʾān in the text itself for anyone interested in following them up. That leaves a large amount of information derived from many sources, primary and more frequently secondary, that is not covered in the footnotes. Some of the information conveyed in this book derives from my own research, and some of the thoughts expressed in it are my own original ideas, but the reader's default assumption should be that I am drawing on a secondary source. Anyone who needs a reference for this detail or that is welcome to contact me.

As indicated, the reader who wishes to delve further into the scholarly literature will find some leads in my footnotes. But it may be more useful to outline a basic strategy here for readers of English with an interest in learning about the history of the Muslim world. In the first place I would recommend anyone approaching the topic for the first time and in need of a bird's-eye view to start with the first chapter of A. J. Silverstein, *Islamic history: A very short introduction*, Oxford

6. In giving the sources of quotations I veer between purist references to primary sources in the original language and pragmatic references to secondary sources in English that the average reader can follow up; it is often to such secondary sources that I owe my knowledge of these quotations. Where I use the translations of other scholars for such quotations I have felt at liberty to make minor changes to the wording.

2010. Second, there are three indispensable reference works to be used as needed: C. E. Bosworth, *The new Islamic dynasties*, New York 1996, with tables of Muslim rulers and their dates; H. Kennedy, *An historical atlas of Islam*, Leiden 2002; and *The encyclopaedia of Islam*, second edition, Leiden 1960–2009, together with the new online edition, *Encyclopaedia of Islam three*, Leiden 2007–. Also useful and often fuller is the *Encyclopædia Iranica*, London 1985–. Third, the history of the Muslim world is covered systematically in six volumes by *The new Cambridge history of Islam*, Cambridge 2010, and several other multivolume Cambridge histories cover parts of the same ground (*The Cambridge history of Iran*, *The Cambridge history of Turkey*, *The Cambridge history of Egypt*, *The Cambridge history of Africa*, *The Cambridge history of (early) Inner Asia*, and *The Cambridge history of Southeast Asia*). Fourth, each volume in the series Makers of the Muslim World covers the life and times of a historically significant personality of the Muslim past, so there are volumes devoted to the Umayyad caliph ʿAbd al-Malik, the Moroccan sultan Aḥmad al-Manṣūr, the Najdī reformer Ibn ʿAbd al-Wahhāb, and many others. Any reader making regular use of these resources needs no further guidance from me.

The reader will notice sooner or later that there are many dates in this book of the form "1208–9," and may be puzzled by this. Such spans occur mainly because Muslim historians often tell us that an event took place in, say, AH 605, that is to say, in the year 605 of the Muslim calendar, without specifying precisely when in that year it took place. As it happens, the first half of AH 605 corresponds to the last half of 1208, and the second half of AH 605 to the first half of 1209, so that AH 605 overlaps with parts of both 1208 and 1209. Hence we have to hedge and say "1208–9." The extent of the overlap varies over time because the Muslim calendar is strictly lunar, and twelve lunar months fall short of a solar year by about eleven days. This, in turn, makes the calendar a somewhat inconvenient one to live by, since there is no correlation between the Muslim months and the seasons of the year. It is nevertheless a boon for historians: a single era used across the Muslim world largely replaced the chaos of regional calendars that characterized the ancient world. In references to ancient history I occasionally use the abbreviations "BC" and "AD" to avoid ambiguity; I do so in the same spirit as I speak of "Wednesday" or "Thursday" without implying a belief in the pagan gods these days are named for.

With regard to "black" versus "Black," I use "Black" where the term refers to an ethnic community. The prime example, and the case on which the discussion has largely focused, is the use of the term as a synonym for "African American" in the United States. There is one other context in which I have used "Black," together with its antonym "White"—namely, in translating Arabic color terms that are used to refer to something more like a caste than an ethnic group and that are not in fact focused on skin color. Most of the time, however, I use "black" to render a color term, widespread in the Arabic sources for African history, that serves as little more than a catchall for a wide range of dark-skinned peoples whose ethnic identities are rarely specified.

Caveats

First, a caveat about reading this book. It is fairly dense, and I would not advise anyone to try to get through it in one sitting. Nor would I expect any but the most intrepid to read all of it. Here a relevant feature of the book is the italicized passage preceding the substance of each chapter, an idea I owe to Tony Kronman. Each of these provides a selective road map for the chapter in question, indicating what it will cover and identifying its major themes. These passages can be used by readers in either of two ways. Those who do not propose to read the chapter can obtain from them a sense of what they are missing, while those who do intend to read the chapter can get a sense of what to expect. At the same time, I have been liberal with headings and subheadings within chapters; these, too, are intended to help readers decide what they want to read and, by the same token, what they want to skip.

Second, a caveat about the historical phenomenon of Islam. I remarked earlier that the populations covered in this book are characterized by adherence to Islam *in some form or other*. This wording reflects the fact that any world religion is bound to change over time and vary over space—and also, though I will not take this up here, to take different forms in different parts of the same society, be it elite and masses or cities and villages.

As to change over time, it has aptly been suggested that Islam can be seen as a discursive tradition[7]—the locus of continuing talk in which new things can be said and old things can be repeated in new contexts. But Islam is not *merely* a discursive tradition. If it were, it could easily develop in such a way that its current state would have nothing in common with its initial state. Islam, however, is a religion heavily invested in its foundational texts and in practices closely associated with them. This means that it is a tradition with an anchor. Some Muslims may be comfortable drifting away from the earlier forms of their faith, but they are always vulnerable to challenge by reformers seeking to pull them back.

Turning to variation over space, a world religion, like any tradition extending over a wide area, is liable to be exposed to conflicting pulls. On the one hand, there

7. For this suggestion of Talal Asad's, see his pamphlet "The idea of an anthropology of Islam," Center for Contemporary Arab Studies, Georgetown University, Occasional Papers Series, Washington, DC 1986, 14. Asad was not denying that Islam is more than a discursive tradition. Alongside the discursive tradition he speaks of the established practices that the tradition addresses, and in this context he uses the phrase "Islamic practice." Such practices are thus clearly part of Islam, and at the same time distinct from the discursive tradition that addresses them.

will be centrifugal forces making for the emergence of variant regional forms of the religion, often in response to divergent regional traditions that preexist its advent. And on the other hand, there are likely to be centripetal forces reflecting a sense among followers of the religion that some forms are more authoritative than others and that divergent forms should be brought into line with the mainstream, however defined. In the Islamic case this tends to be seen as some form of the religion prevalent among the urban elite of the heartlands of the Muslim world. Modern communications have greatly strengthened the centripetal forces at the expense of the centrifugal ones, but in the Islamic case the centripetal forces were already conspicuous in premodern times. Under the conditions obtaining then, as not today, it was indeed possible for regional adaptations of Islam to survive for long periods without serious challenge. But they, too, were vulnerable to the attacks of reformers who saw such adaptations as unacceptable deviations, and sometimes, as we will see, these reformers triumphed. A historian of the Muslim world accordingly has to do justice to the historical reality of both the centrifugal and the centripetal pulls. Doing justice to them will often mean bringing out the differences between one form of Islam and another, including ways in which forms of the religion practiced in outlying parts of the Muslim world differed from those found in the central regions. This does not mean that historians have to privilege any particular form of the religion as more authentic. Here Western academics typically counsel their readers against putting a metropolitan form of Islam on a pedestal. To the limited extent that their works are read by Muslims with a fundamentalist bias against the regional adaptations, they are making a significant point. But for the most part such counsel is preaching to the converted. The works of Western scholars are mainly read by people with a Western cultural background who share a bias against what they tend to see as the unprovoked interference of intolerant and puritanical busybodies. Indeed, it would be disingenuous of me to claim that I am myself entirely free of this bias. But historians have to keep it in check.

Third, a caveat about the truth status of many of the details—as opposed to the outlines—included in this book, a caveat that would apply even if neither I nor the modern scholars on whose work I regularly depend ever made mistakes. A few years ago some researchers at the Massachusetts Institute of Technology examined the flow of stories on Twitter. They found that false claims were 70 percent more likely to be shared than true ones were. The suggested explanation was simple: people prefer false news. If that is what people are like in our time, they were probably much the same in the past, and we have to reckon with the possibility that a considerable portion of the news conveyed by our primary sources may be false. Historians do have ways of separating the wheat from the chaff, but these methods go only so far. In sum, while the outlines conveyed in this book have a good chance of being sound, it could well be that many of the sometimes colorful details I have included are not. They are perhaps best seen in the light of a remark that Giordano Bruno (d. 1600) famously put in the mouth of one of his characters: "Se non è vero è molto ben trovato"—"If it's not true, it's very aptly invented." Even if invented, such details often have something valuable to tell us about the past, and I can at least say that in choosing them I have put a lot of effort into assessing their aptness.

Finally, I should perhaps mention that the last time I taught undergraduates, one of the course evaluations I received described my teaching as "old-fashioned in a good way." The description is probably correct, but whether the evaluation is right is for readers of this book to decide.

Michael Cook

ACKNOWLEDGMENTS

This book is the product of the best part of a lifetime spent in teaching and researching the history of the Muslim world. A full acknowledgment of the sources of the information and thinking that have gone into it would accordingly stretch over many pages. Generations of undergraduates taking my courses have forced me to read widely and think boldly in the hope of presenting Muslim history in an adequate and intelligible fashion. If any of them happen to dip into this book, they are likely to encounter many echoes of the lectures they heard and the readings I assigned to them. My graduate student teaching likewise informs much of the book, and graduate students who served as my teaching assistants have made significant contributions to it, as have the many dissertations in the writing of which I have played a role over the decades. All this has added up to a continuing education program without which I would long ago have lapsed into obsolescence. I have also learned recondite facts and picked up valuable ideas from numerous colleagues over the years. The same goes for the young scholars who were involved in the Holberg Seminar from 2015 to 2018, and those who are currently members of the Balzan Seminar on the Formation, Maintenance, and Failure of States in the Muslim World before 1800. I have no doubt that much of what I unthinkingly credit to myself had its origin in interactions with students and colleagues that I no longer recollect. As a gesture toward acknowledging what I owe, here is a list of some of the people who I know I am in debt to in one way or another because I have kept a record of it: Rushain Abbasi, Ahmad Al-Jallad, Javier Albarrán, Ahmed Almaazmi, Roger Bagnall, Tommy Benfey, Lorenzo Bondioli, Antoine Borrut, Houchang Chehabi, Edith Chen, Duygu Coşkuntuna, John Dunn, Tamer El-Leithy, Khaled El-Rouayheb, Shohreh Gholsorkhi, Alessandro Gori, Simcha Gross, John Haldon, Colin Heywood, Hugh Kennedy, Bilal Khadim, Shaya Landa, Ella Landau-Tasseron, Tommi Lankila, Marie Legendre, Christian Mauder, Naveena Naqvi, M'hamed Oualdi, Cecilia Palombo, Kate Pukhovaia, Eugénie Rébillard, Merle Ricklefs, Dan Sheffield, Petra Sijpesteijn, Shivaji Sondhi, Matt Steele, Lindsey Stephenson, Dan Stolz, Jimmy Yu, and Aron Zysow. Some of these kindly responded to my inquries, but many simply said things in my hearing that stuck in my memory. My most recent debt is to Karen Bauer and Ben Green for checking a reference to a rare book in the library of Magdalen College, Oxford.

Let me add that no one has helped me more during my years at Princeton than my colleague Hossein Modarressi.

One of my most fundamental debts is, of course, to the many scholars whose published works I have drawn on so extensively in writing this book. Since their books and articles are in the public domain, I have preferred not to burden this already prolix work with full references to their publications. But if I were to try to do so, I suspect that one scholar would stand out as my most-cited author: Edmund Bosworth. Without his numerous contributions to our knowledge of Muslim history this book would have been far harder to write and much the poorer.

Very fresh in my mind is the benefit I have derived from colleagues who read the draft typescript, or parts of it, whether at my request or that of Princeton University Press. Three scholars heroically reported on the whole typescript and supplied generous comments on it: Maribel Fierro, whose remarks saved me from several mistakes about the western Muslim world and sent me to valuable further reading; Roy Mottahedeh, who did the same for the central Muslim world; and Ulrich Rebstock, who in addition to wide-ranging comments and suggestions supplied me with a mass of additional material that has enriched the book. Several scholars helped me with comments on particular chapters: Matthew Gordon on chapter 6, Peter Golden on chapter 7, Ali Yaycıoğlu on chapter 10 (where the last section is his suggestion), Michael Laffan on chapter 12, an anonymous reader on chapter 12, and another on chapter 13 (where the last section arises from a comment on what the draft was missing). Frank Stewart read and commented on several passages concerned with nomads, as well as supplying me with valuable references. All this helped me both avoid mistakes and improve my coverage. One of my regrets is that I wrote this book too late to benefit from the sharp eye of Patricia Crone.

I would particularly like to thank Owen Fiss and Anthony Kronman for organizing a workshop at the Kamel Center at Yale Law School on April 11–12, 2018, at which chapters 12 and 13 were discussed. I am grateful to them and to all the participants for their comments.

For the maps I am very much in debt to two people: Tsering Wangyal Shawa of Princeton University Library, who succeeded in the uphill task of teaching me enough about the workings of QGIS to enable me to prepare rough drafts of my maps, and Rob McCaleb, the cartographer who turned my inelegant work into something presentable.

At Princeton University Press I owe a great debt to Priya Nelson for liking the project and at the same time providing me with firm guidance. My thanks also go to her successive assistants Barbara Shi and Emma Wagh for their good-natured efficiency, and to Dimitri Karetnikov for his advice on the maps. I should also mention an older debt, to Marigold Acland of Cambridge University Press. I had originally promised the book to her on the condition that she had not retired by the time I was ready to submit it. In the event she did not keep her end of that bargain, but my conversations with her helped shape the project in its initial stages. In its final stages it benefited greatly from the superb copyediting of Hanna Siurua. My thanks go to Scott Smiley for undertaking the formidable task of indexing the book, and to Amairah Islam for many helpful suggestions in this regard.

I could not have written the book without massive use of Princeton University Library over a long period, and the continuing assistance of its staff. My last full year of writing coincided with the onset of the pandemic; the constructive and helpful ways in which the library responded to the situation minimized the inevitable disruption and made it possible for me to continue my work almost unimpeded.

Everyone acknowledged here, by name or otherwise, has helped me make this book a better one. They are not responsible for my temerity in undertaking the project, or the many imperfections that remain.

Finally, I could not have written the book at all without the support of my wife, Kim, who has helped me in ways so numerous and far-reaching that I could not begin to describe them.

MAPS

In a work of history, a map can be designed to provide a snapshot of a region as it was in some particular period; the maps in *An historical atlas of Islam* mentioned in the preface are of this kind. By contrast, the intention behind most of my maps in this book is a modest one: to show where as many as possible of the places I mention in the text were located (it is not always possible to do this—sometimes we do not know the location of a place, and sometimes parts of the maps become so crowded that a name or two has to be sacrificed). As a result, my maps often include names from a variety of periods. But some elements on some of the maps are more time-specific, notably the boundaries of empires. The reader should be aware that these are at best approximate.

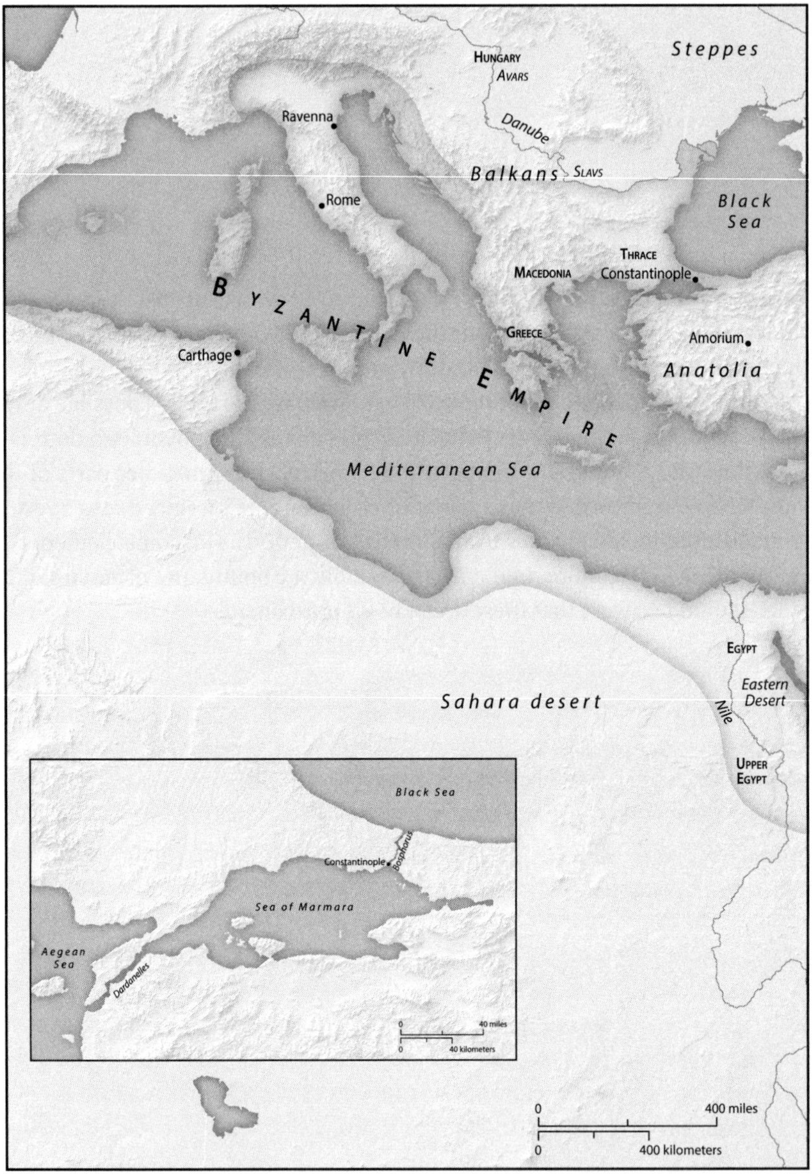

MAP 1. Arabia and the empires in late antiquity (west). Inset: The Straits. *Note*: With the replacement of Constantinople by Istanbul, this map remains good into modern times.

Boundaries of the Byzantine Empire adapted from *The new Cambridge history of Islam*, Cambridge 2010, vol. 1, xxviii, map 2.

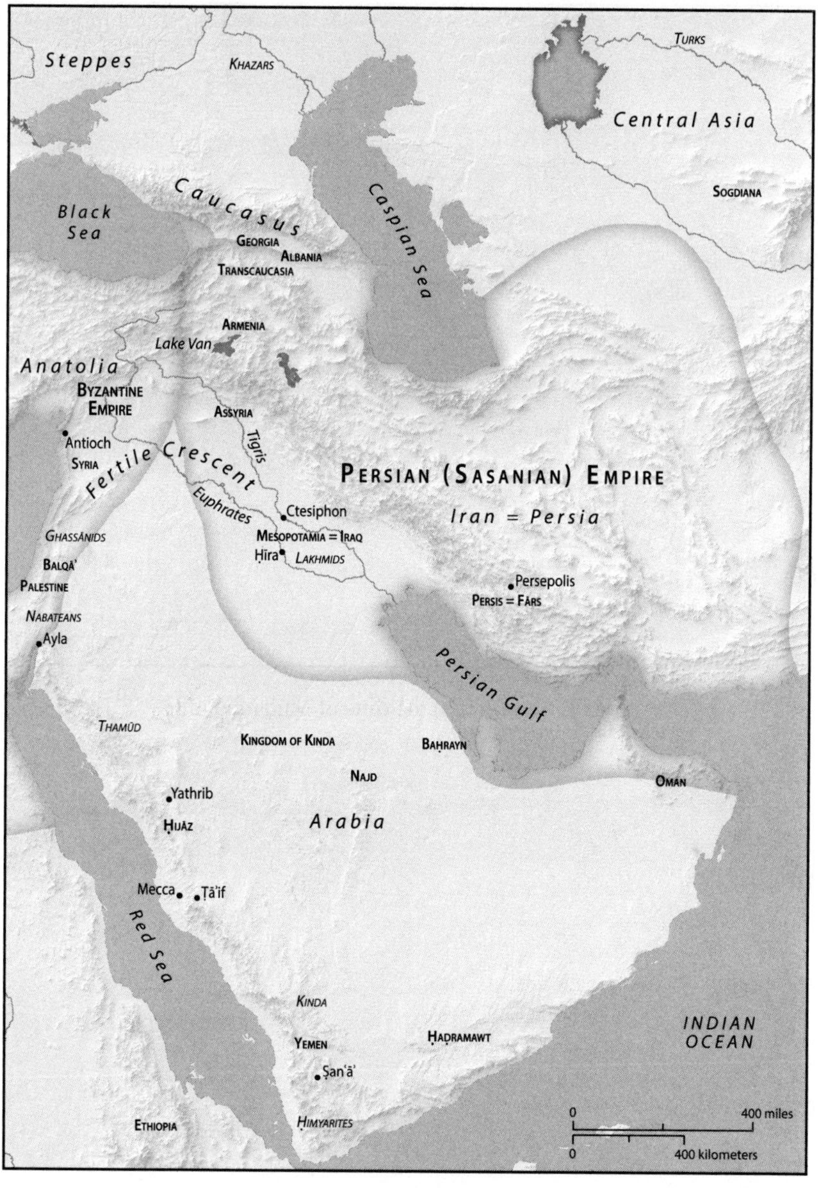

MAP 2. Arabia and the empires in late antiquity (east).

Boundaries of the Persian Empire adapted from K. Rezakhani, *Reorienting the Sasanians*, Edinburgh 2017, xi.

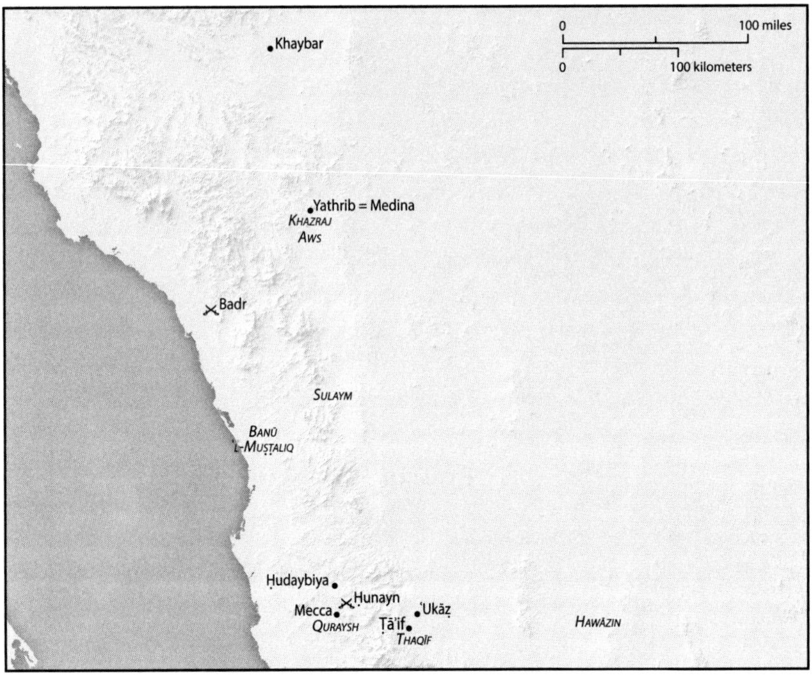

MAP 3. The Ḥijāz in the time of Muḥammad.

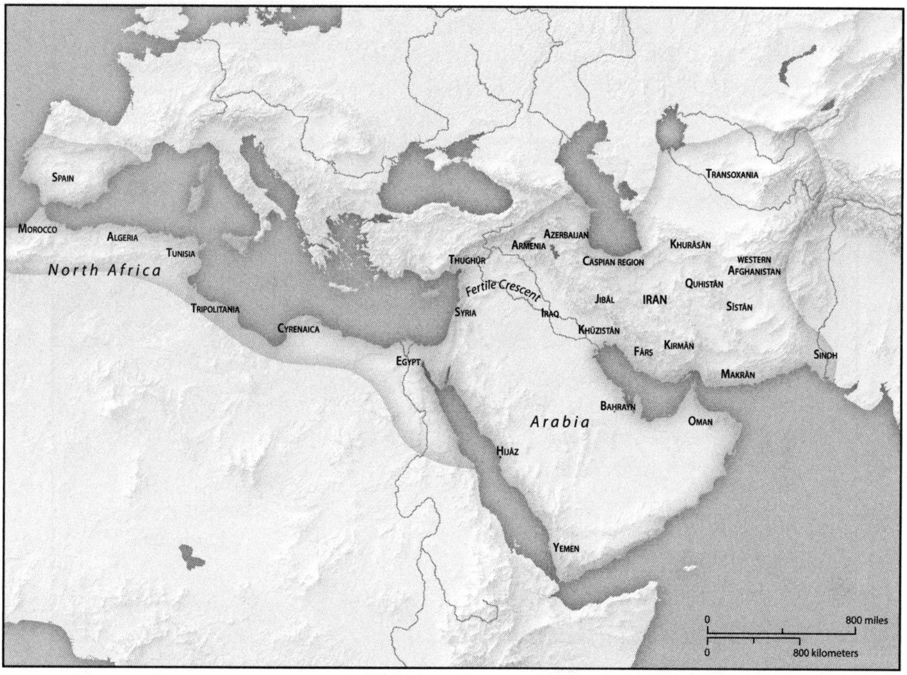

MAP 4. The provinces of the Caliphate.

Boundaries of the Caliphate adapted from *The new Cambridge history of Islam*, Cambridge 2010, vol. 1, xxxi, map 5.

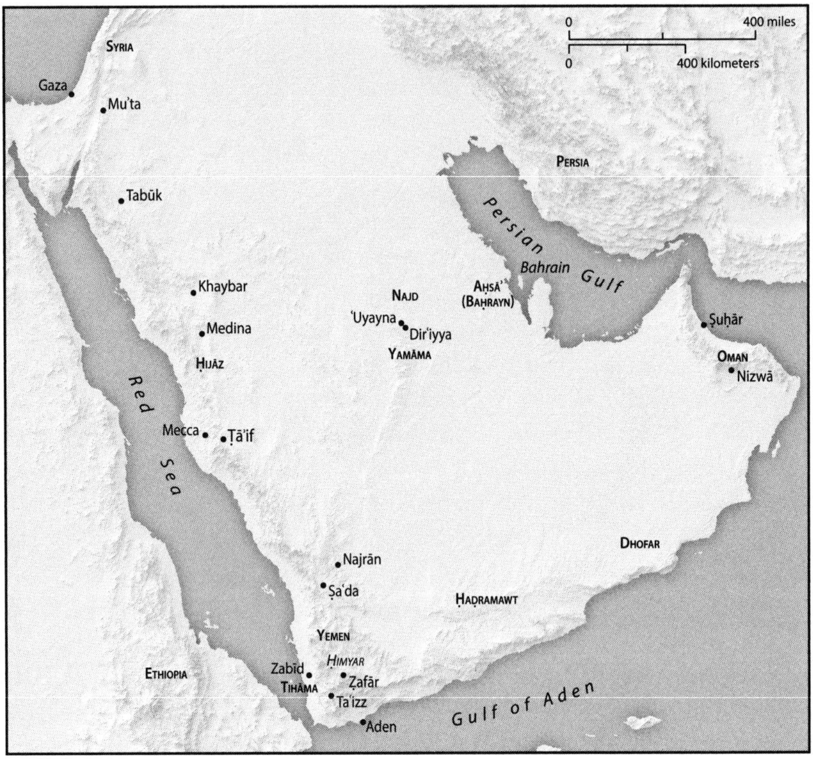
0
400 miles
0
400 kilometers
Syria
Gaza
Mu'ta
Tabūk
Persia
Persian Gulf
Bahrain
Khaybar
Najd
Aḥsā'
(Baḥrayn)
'Uyayna
Dir'iyya
Medina
Yamāma
Ṣuḥār
Oman
Nizwā
Ḥijāz
Red Sea
Mecca
Ṭā'if
Dhofar
Najrān
Ṣa'da
Ḥadramawt
Yemen
Ḥimyar
Ethiopia
Zabīd
Ẓafār
Tihāma
Ta'izz
Aden
Gulf of Aden

MAP 5. Arabia.

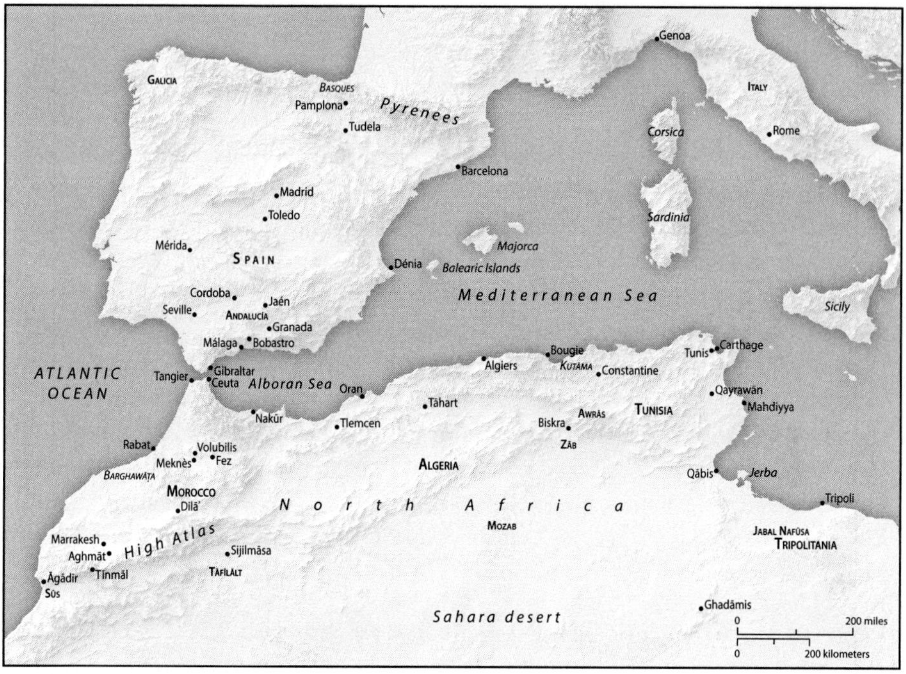

MAP 6. Spain and North Africa.

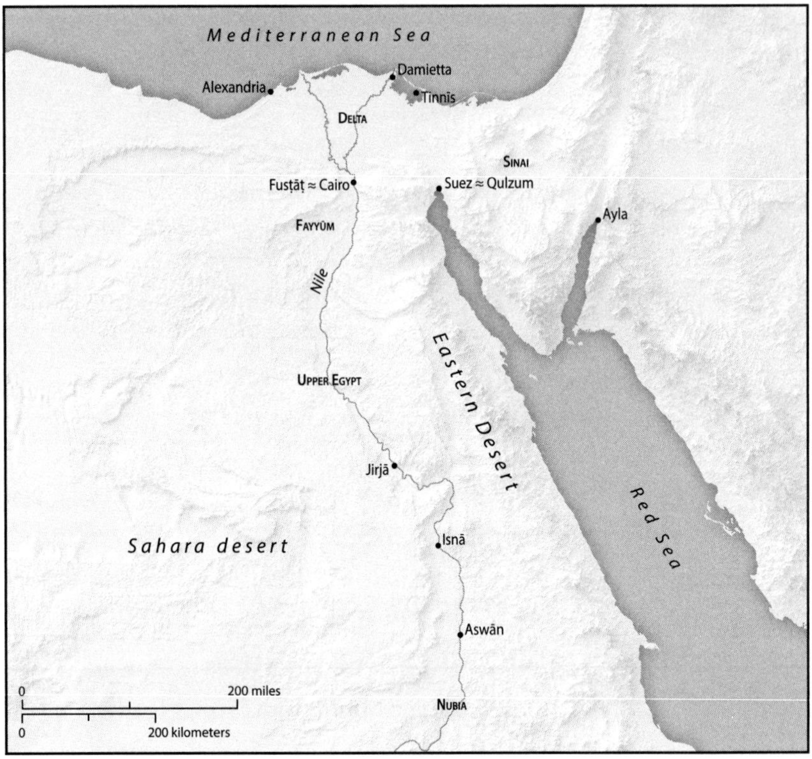
Mediterranean Sea
Alexandria
Damietta
Tinnīs
Delta
Sinai
Fusṭāṭ ≈ Cairo
Suez ≈ Qulzum
Ayla
Fayyūm
Nile
Eastern Desert
Upper Egypt
Jirjā
Red Sea
Sahara desert
Isnā
Aswān
0
200 miles
0
200 kilometers
Nubia

MAP 7. Egypt.

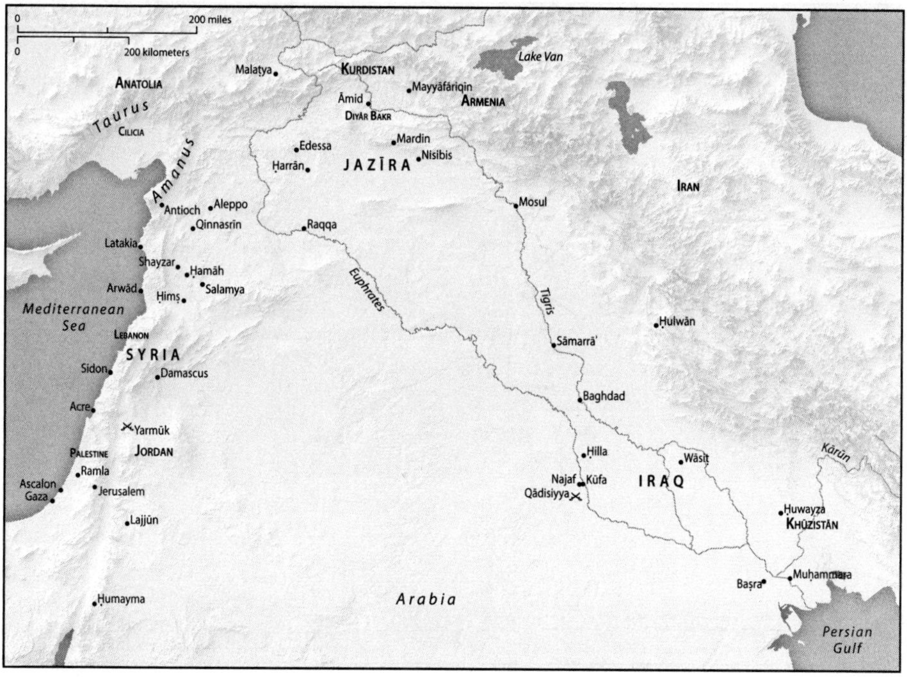

MAP 8. The Fertile Crescent.

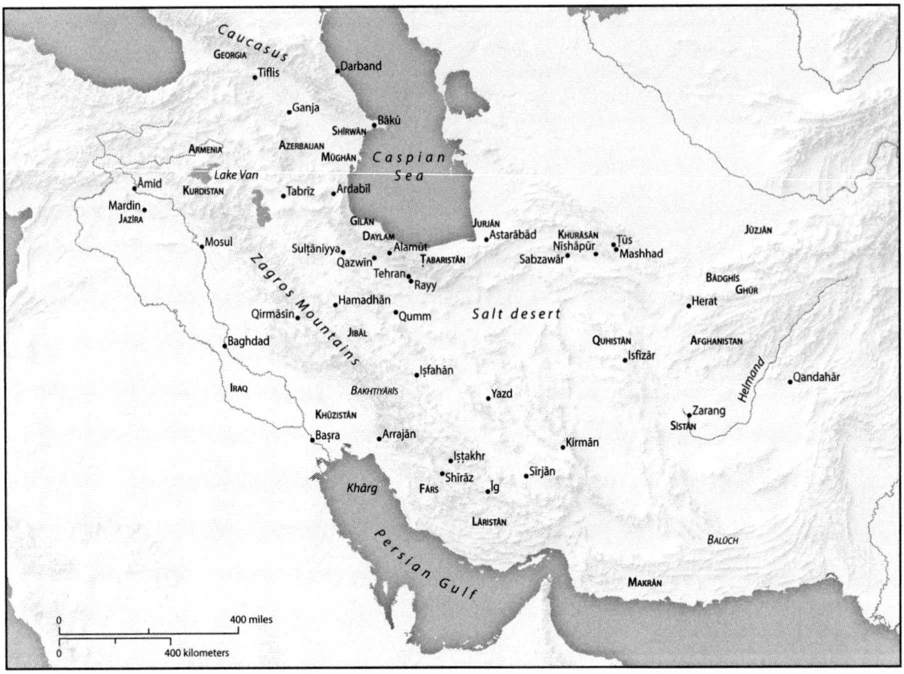
Caucasus
Georgia
Tiflis
Darband
Ganja
Bākū
Shīrwān
Armenia
Azerbaijan
Mūghān
Caspian Sea
Lake Van
Āmid
Kurdistan
Tabrīz
Ardabīl
Mardin
Jazīra
Gīlān
Daylam
Jurjān
Astarābād
Khurāsān
Nīshāpūr
Ṭūs
Mashhad
Jūzjān
Mosul
Sulṭāniyya
Alamūt
Qazwīn
Ṭabaristān
Sabzawār
Zagros Mountains
Tehran
Rayy
Bādghīs
Ghūr
Hamadhān
Herat
Qirmāsīn
Qumm
Salt desert
Jibāl
Baghdad
Quhistān
Isfizār
Afghanistan
Iṣfahān
Helmand
Qandahār
Iraq
Bakhtiyārīs
Yazd
Zarang
Sīstān
Khūzistān
Baṣra
Arrajān
Kirmān
Iṣṭakhr
Shīrāz
Sīrjān
Khārg
Fārs
Īg
Lāristān
Balūch
Persian Gulf
Makrān
0
400 miles
0
400 kilometers

MAP 9. Iran.

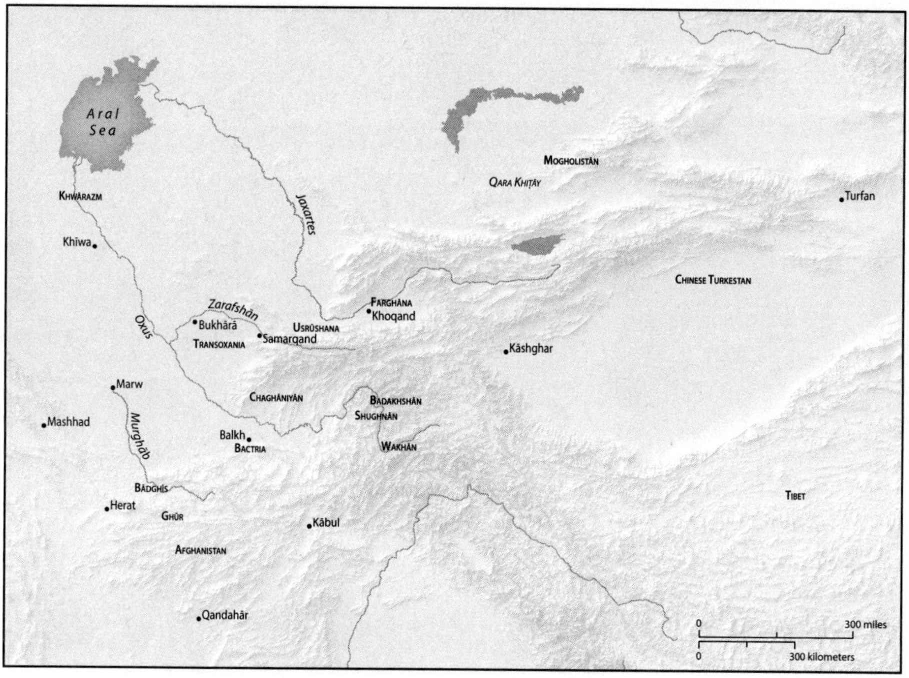

MAP 10. Central Asia.

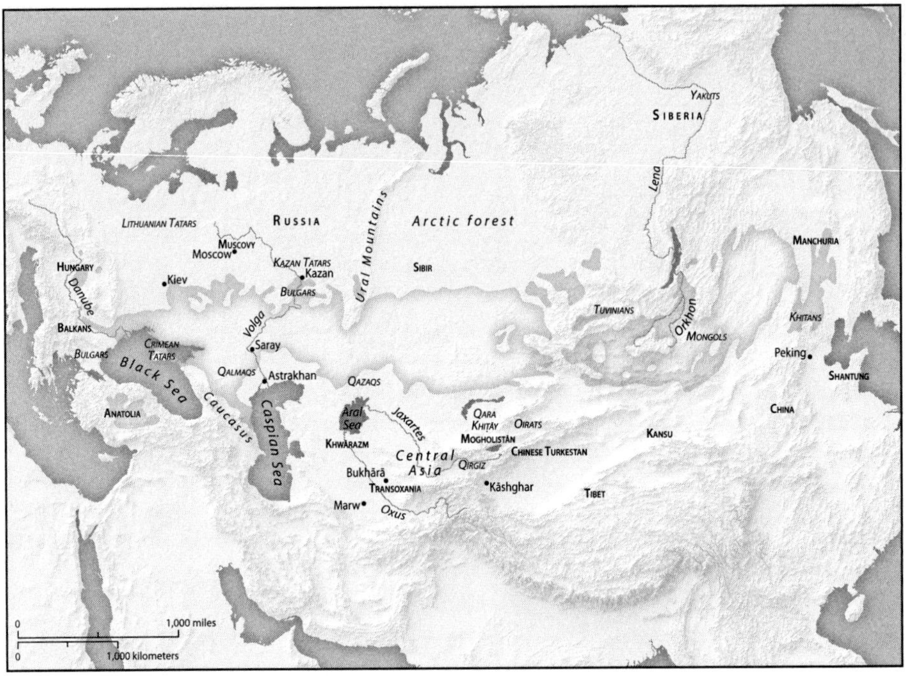

MAP 11. The steppes.

Boundaries of the steppes adapted from *Encyclopaedia Britannica*, online edition, art. "The Steppe."

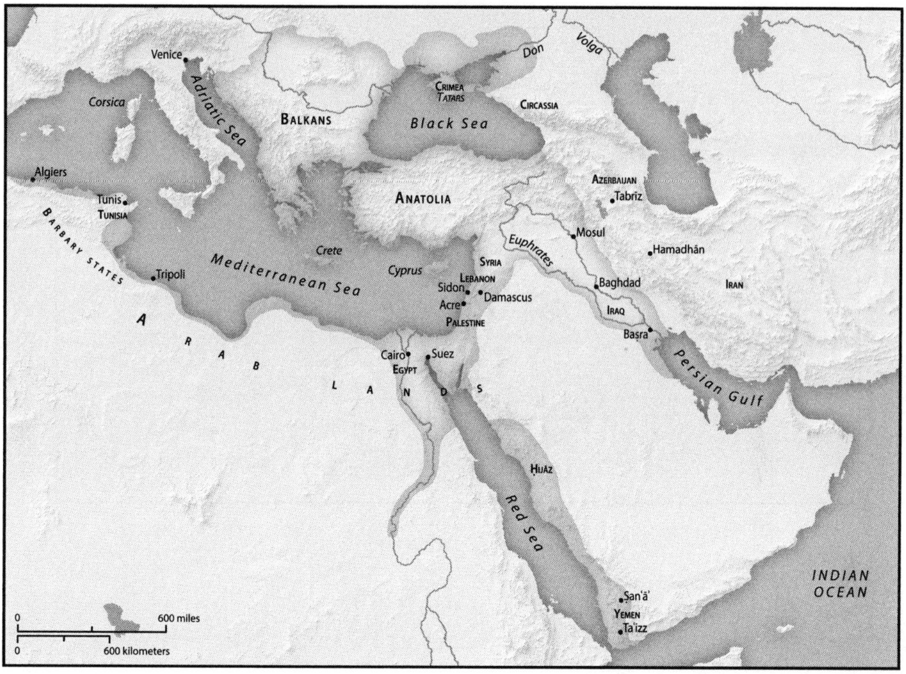

MAP 12. The Ottoman Empire.

Boundaries of the empire adapted from *The new Cambridge history of Islam*, Cambridge 2010, vol. 2, xlv, map 8.

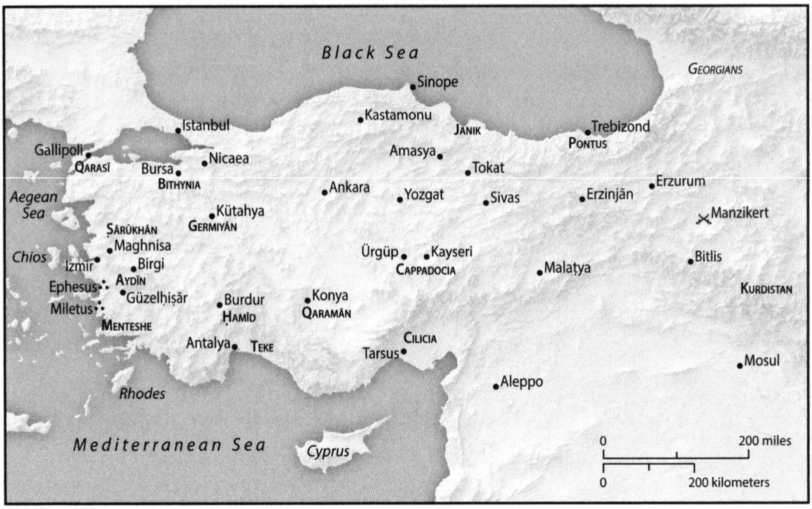

MAP 13. Anatolia.

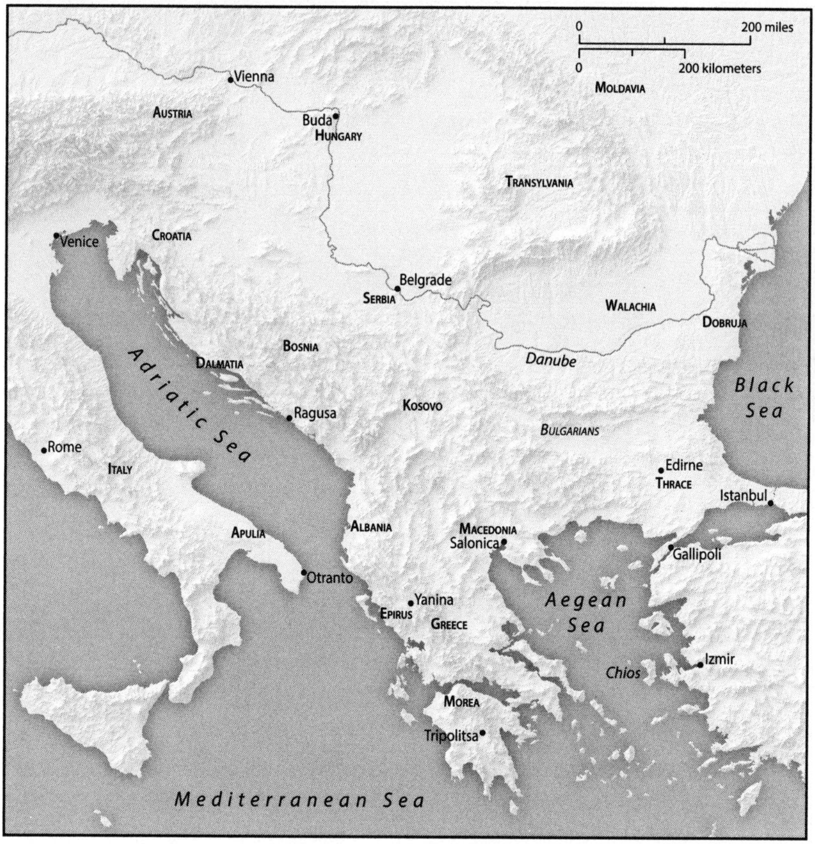

MAP 14. The Balkans.

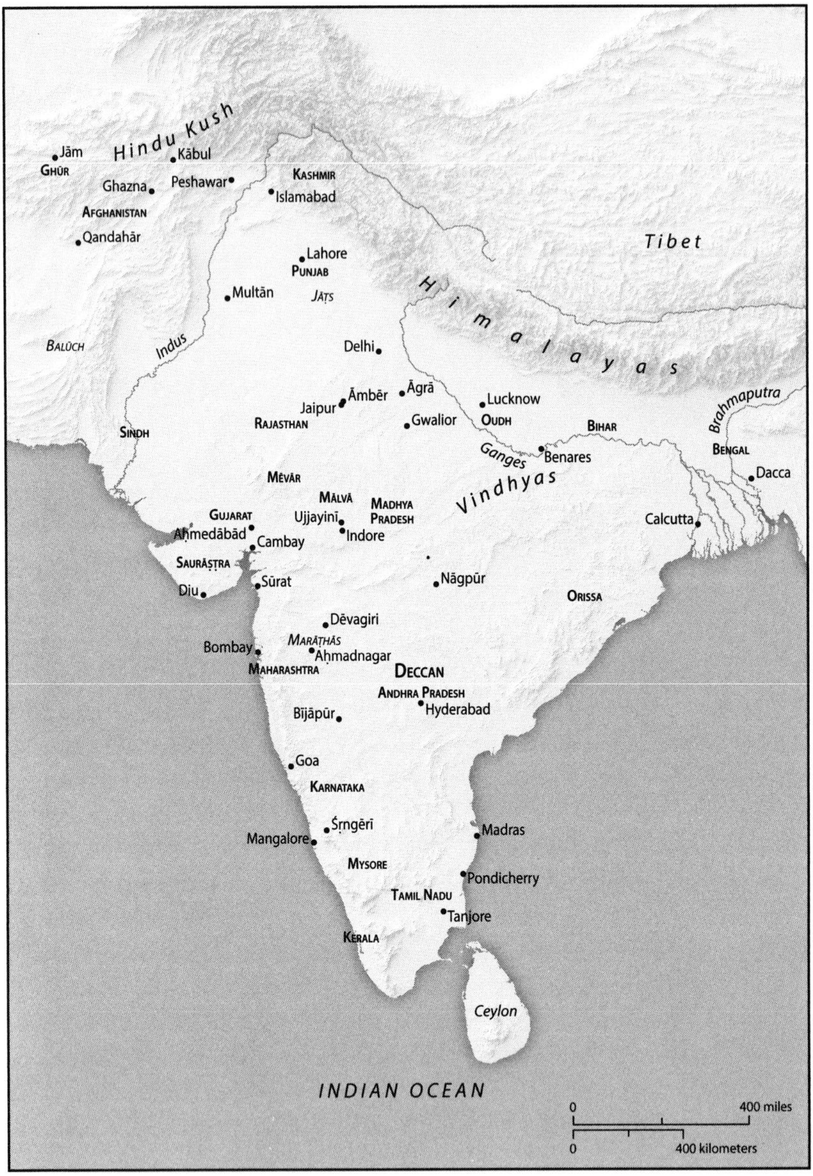

MAP 15. India. *Note:* But for the crowding of place-names the Vindyas would be centered farther to the west.

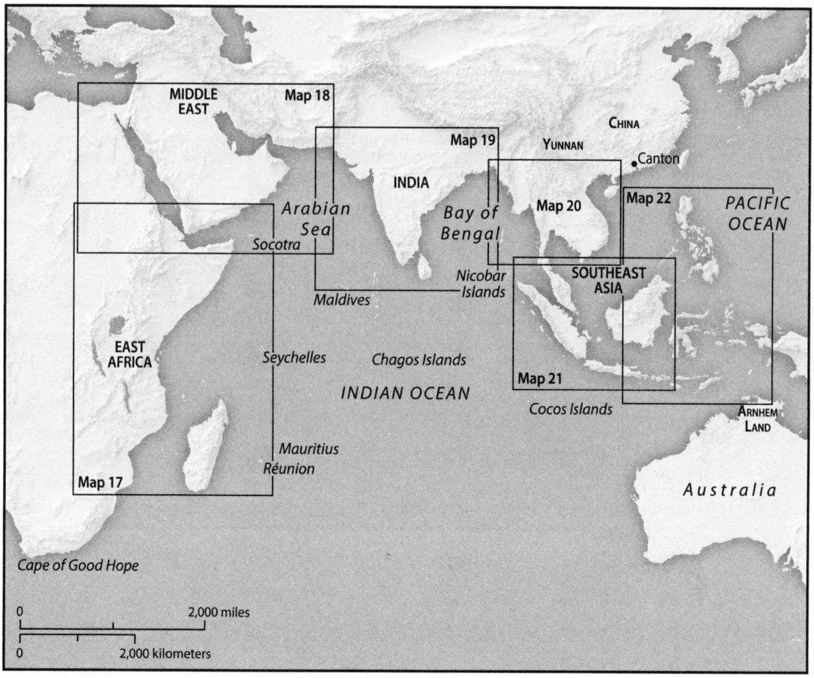

MAP 16. The Indian Ocean.

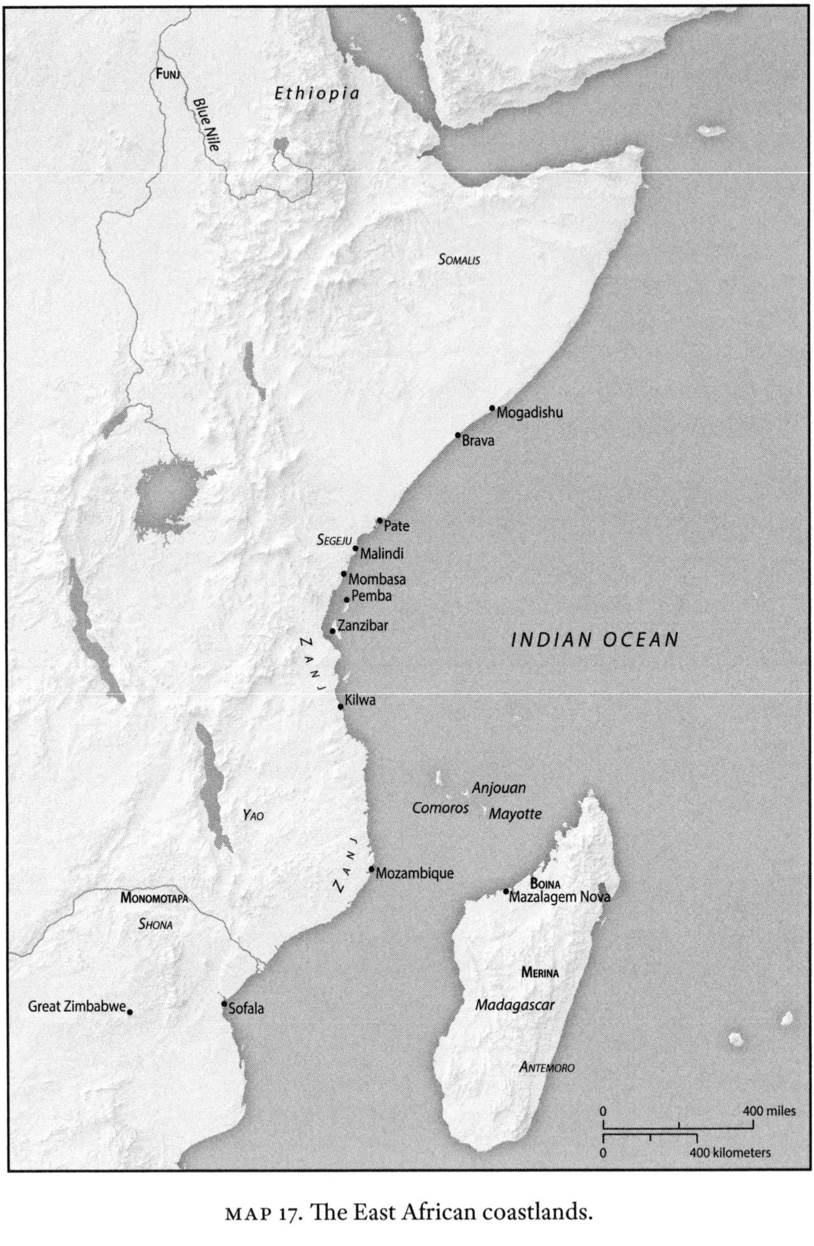

MAP 17. The East African coastlands.

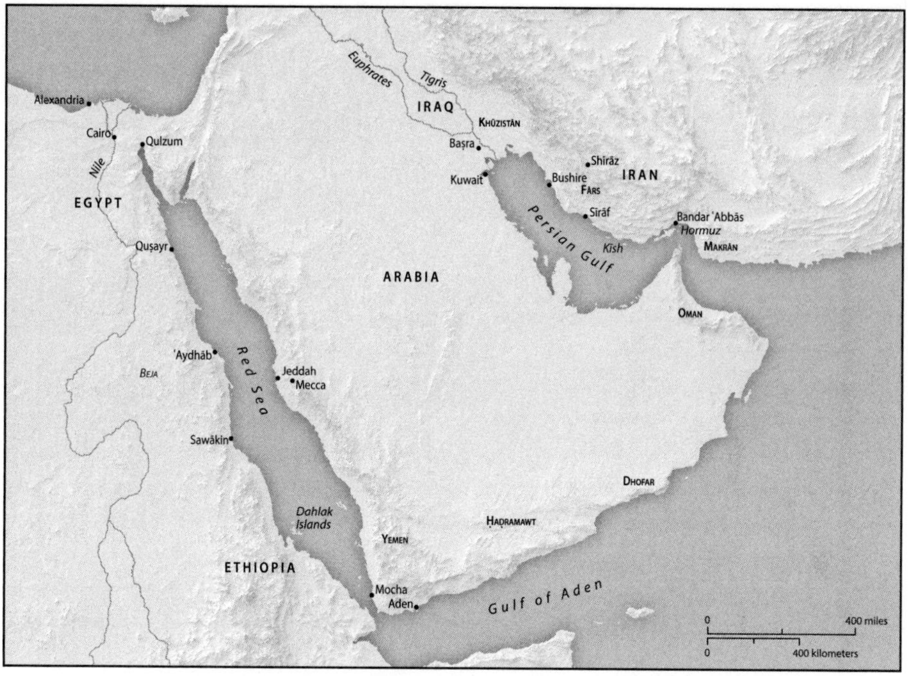

MAP 18. The southeastern coastlands of the Middle East.

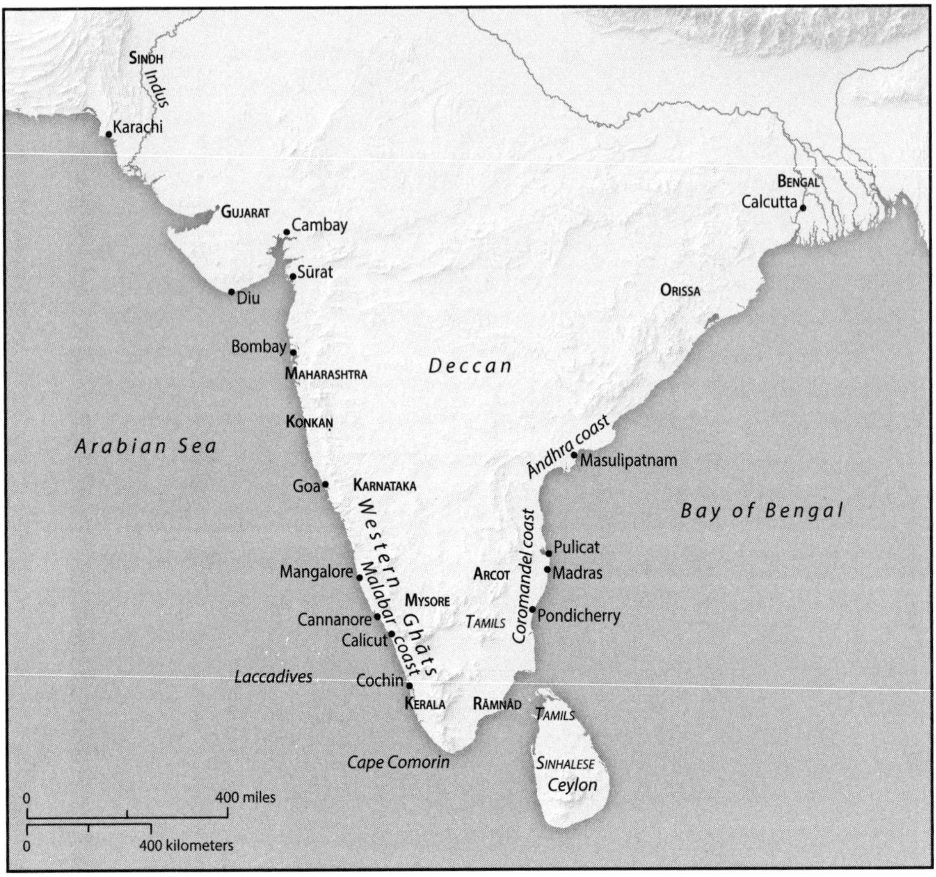

SINDH
Indus
Karachi
GUJARAT
Cambay
Sūrat
Diu
Bombay
MAHARASHTRA
Deccan
KONKAṆ
Arabian Sea
Goa
KARNATAKA
Western Ghāts
Mangalore
Malabar coast
MYSORE
Cannanore
Calicut
Laccadives
Cochin
KERALA
Cape Comorin
RĀMNĀD
TAMILS
ARCOT
Coromandel coast
Pulicat
Madras
Pondicherry
Āndhra coast
Masulipatnam
Bay of Bengal
ORISSA
BENGAL
Calcutta
TAMILS
SINHALESE
Ceylon
0
400 miles
0
400 kilometers

MAP 19. The Indian coastlands.

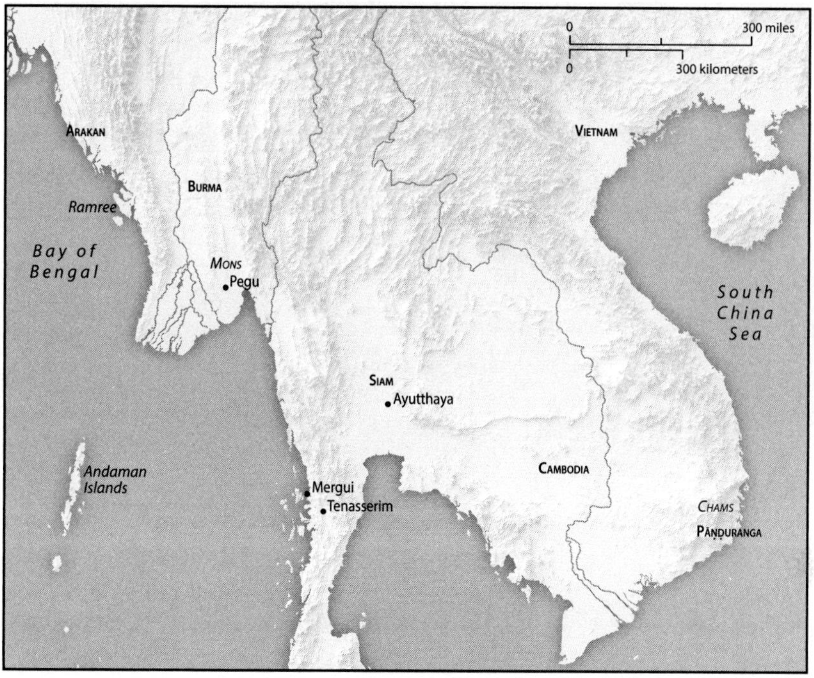

MAP 20. Continental Southeast Asia.

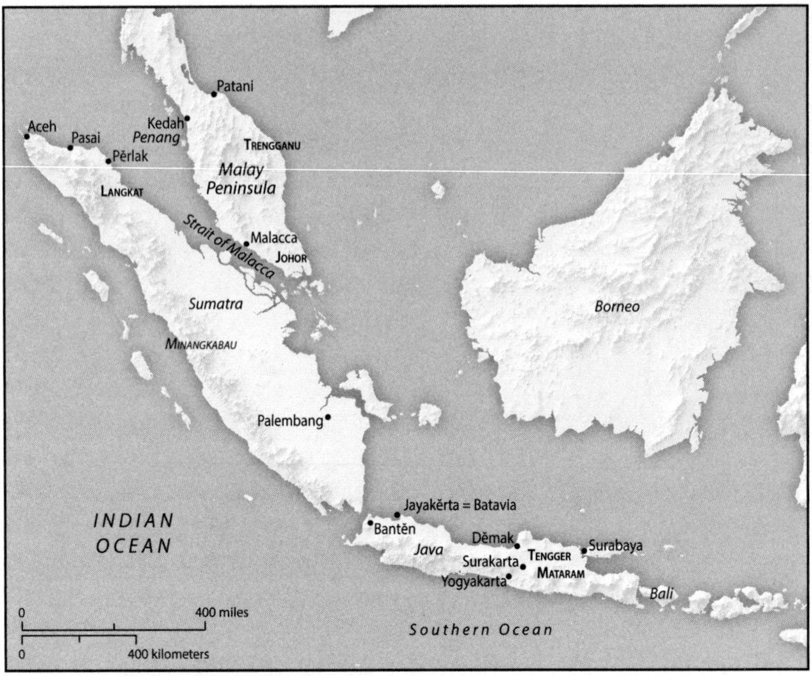

MAP 21. Maritime Southeast Asia (west). *Note:* The term "Southern Ocean" is used in a traditional Javanese sense here.

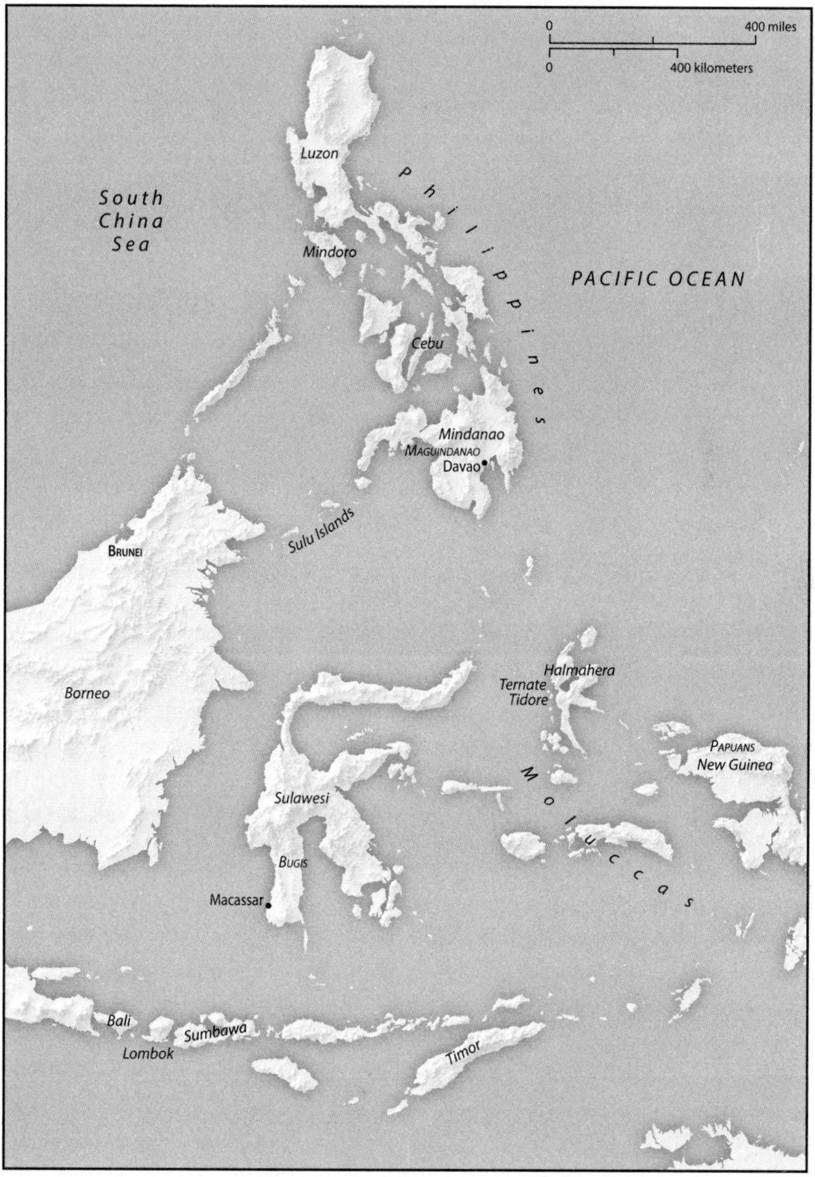

MAP 22. Maritime Southeast Asia (east).

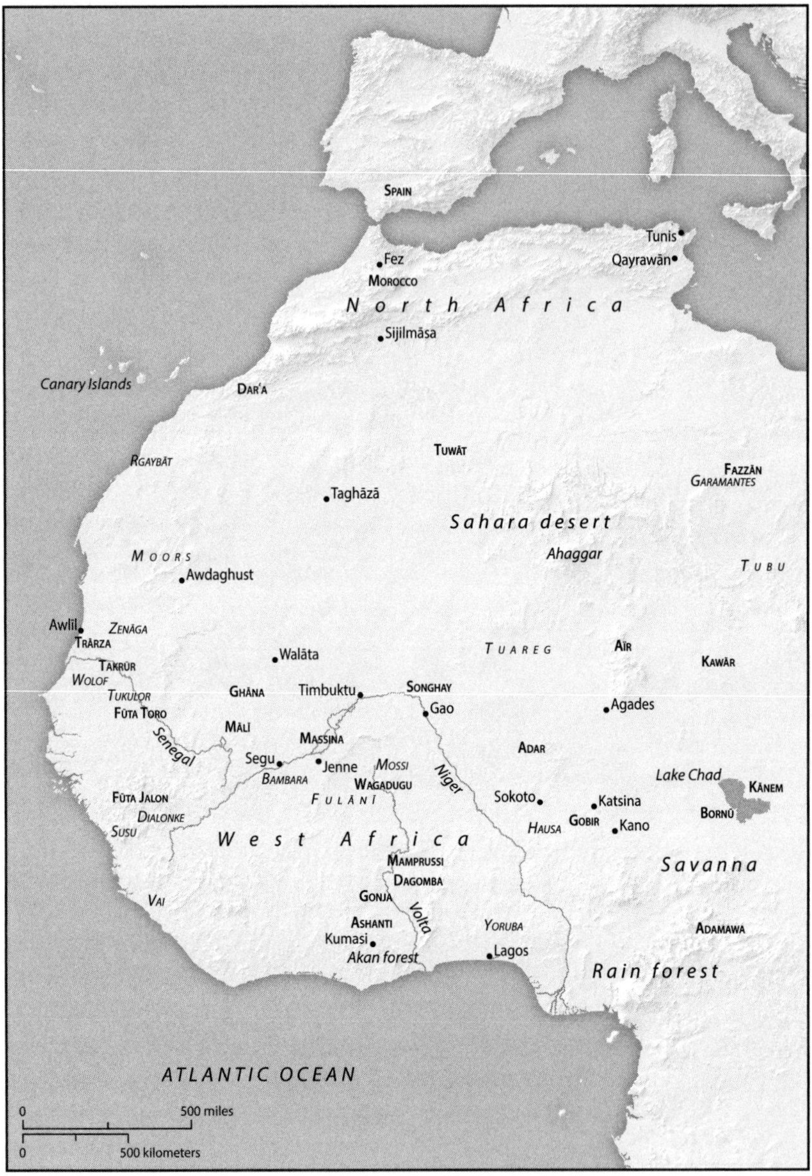

MAP 23. Africa north of the equator (west).

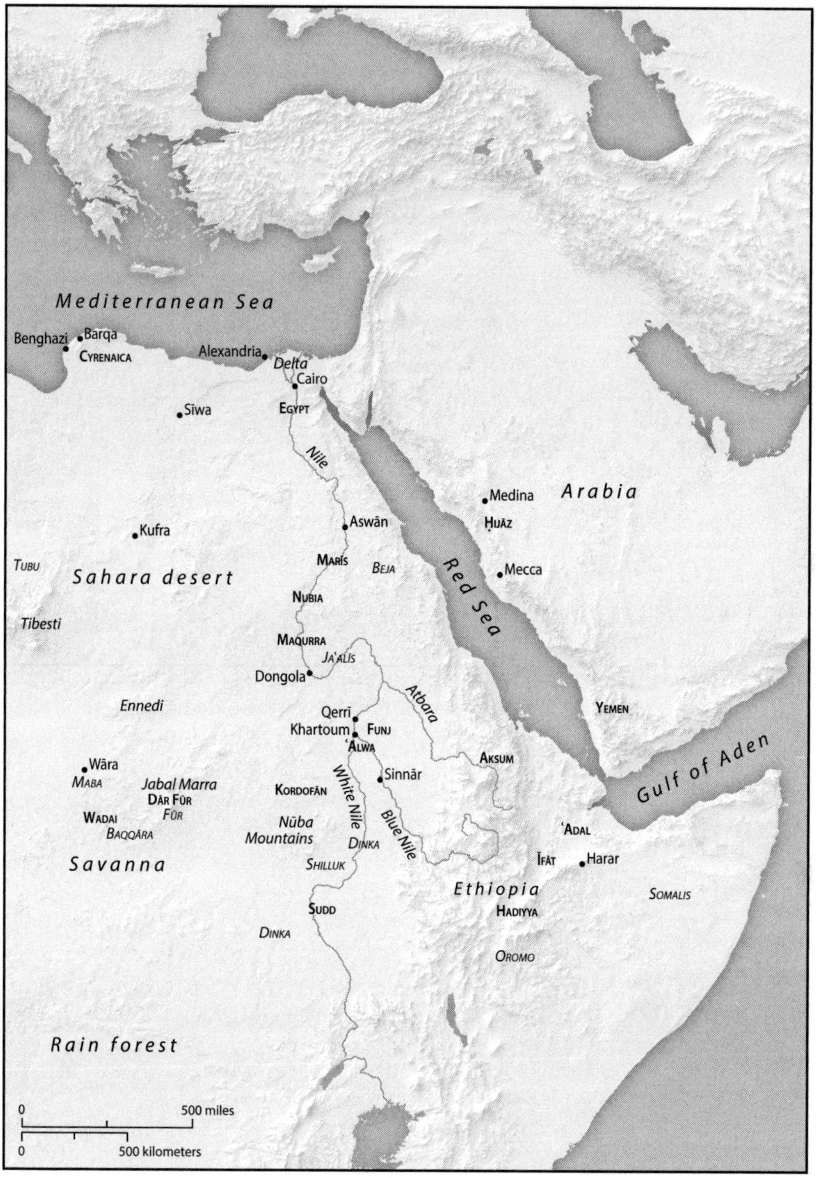

MAP 24. Africa north of the equator (east).

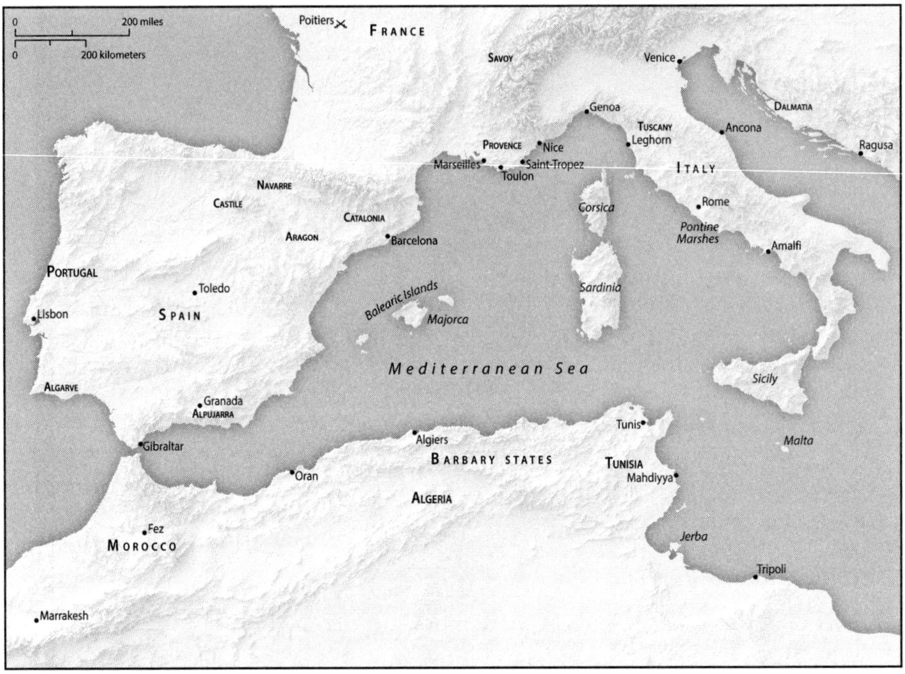

MAP 25. Muslim-Christian relations in the western Mediterranean.

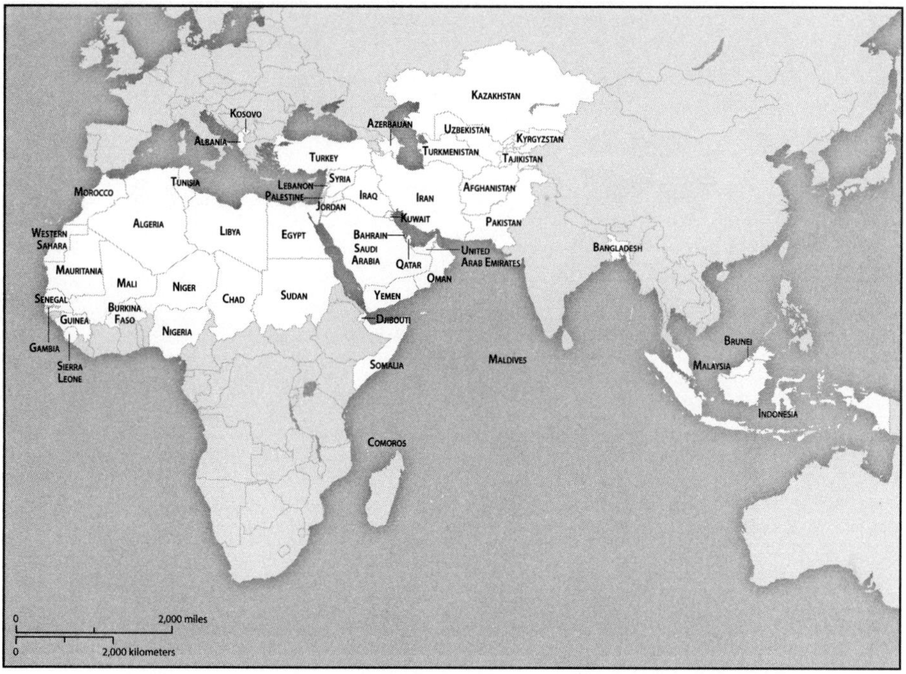

MAP 26. States and their boundaries in the Muslim world at the present day. *Note*: "Palestine" here refers to the West Bank and the Gaza Strip, whereas on maps 2, 8, and 12 it marks the historical Palestine.

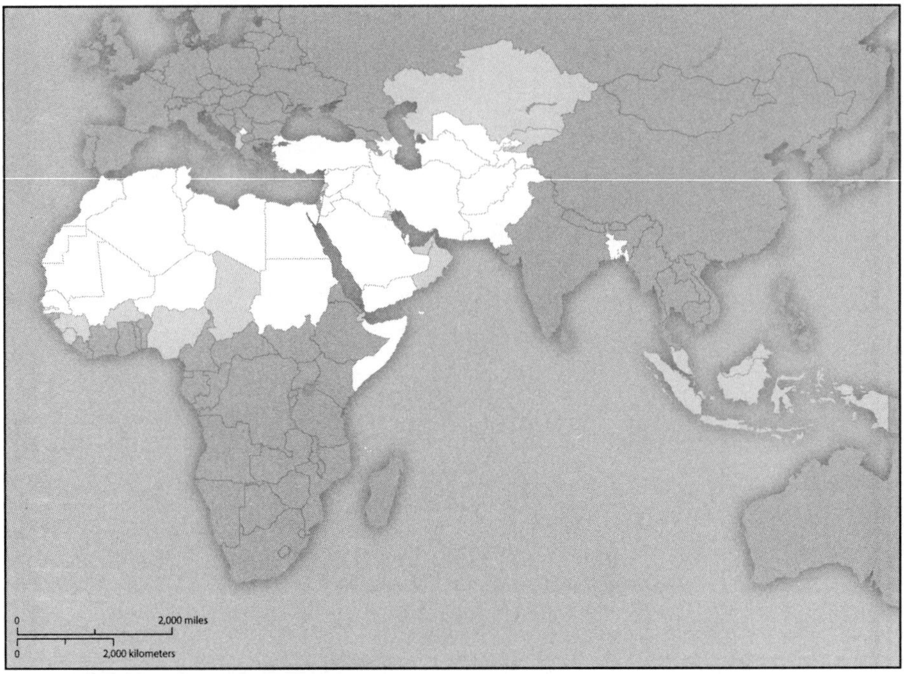

MAP 27. Countries where Muslims are a majority at the present day. *Note*: Countries in which Muslims account for 90% or more of the population are in white, countries in which they account for between 50% and 90% are lightly shaded, and countries in which they account for less than 50% are heavily shaded. Note that several large countries include both Muslim and non-Muslim populations in significant numbers, usually with concentrations in different parts of the country. Thus Russia has three Muslim-majority regions, one in the south; China has one in the west; India has one in the north; Ethiopia has one in the east; and both Chad and Nigeria have them in the north. Indonesia has a non-Muslim concentration in the east. Sudan was a similar case until the southern part of the country broke away to become an independent non-Muslim state.

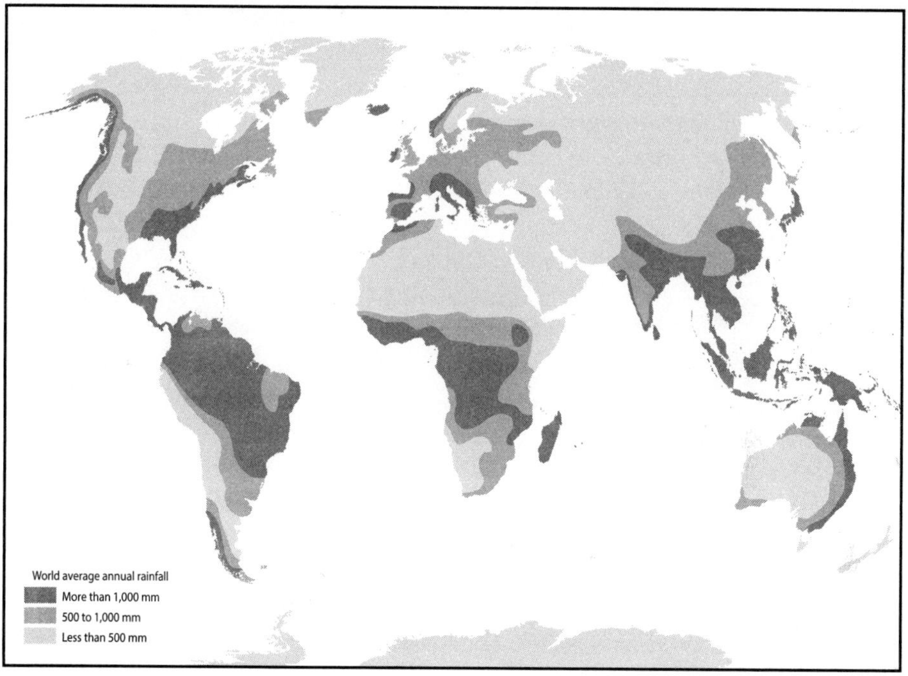

MAP 28. Where the world's rain falls. *Note*: As a rough approximation, notice that the western and central regions of the Muslim world have less than their fair share of rainfall, in some regions far less, whereas the eastern regions have more than their share.

PART I

The emergence of the Muslim world

1

The Middle East in late antiquity

To understand the rise of Islam requires some familiarity with the state of the Middle East in late antiquity—roughly the period from the fourth century to the early seventh. What was it about the pre-Islamic Middle East of that time that led to the rise of Islam or, if that is too much to ask, made it possible? Here we have to distinguish three geographically very different scenes.

We will start in the Arabian interior, in the region where Islam was to be born in the early seventh century. What we see there is a stateless, tribal society, much of it nomadic. Its nature will be apparent in the style of warfare between the tribes, the character of their internal politics, and their identity, language, and culture. How did the environment in which they lived shape a lifestyle so remote from urban civilization?

We will then move north to the two empires, Byzantine and Persian, that dominated the rest of the Middle East. This was a very different world, one of teeming cities and tax-paying peasantries living in an environment that favored the formation of powerful states. However, this two-empire configuration, stable for centuries despite frequent hostilities, came under serious strain in the early seventh century thanks to a war of unprecedented duration between the two. At the same time their geopolitical rivalry was exacerbated by a religious difference: the Byzantine Empire was Christian, whereas the Persian Empire was Zoroastrian. Yet they had coexisted for centuries in the past, so why not in the future?

Farther to the north, beyond the boundaries of the Middle East, lived the nomadic peoples of the steppes. Unlike the Arab tribes, these northern nomads had a track record of threatening the empires, and we will see two steppe rulers intervening in the war between them. If any external force was to overthrow one or both of the warring empires, would it not be these steppe nomads?

The main call on our attention, however, will be relations between the empires and the Arabs. In political and military terms the empires had a number of options, of which the most significant was outsourcing the task of keeping order among the tribes of the borderlands to a cooperative Arab chief. As we will see, by the late sixth century this practice was in abeyance—a fact of some significance for our story.

In religious terms the key change of late antiquity was the rise of monotheism in its Christian form, including a strong presence on the fringes of Arabia, which already had Jewish populations in the interior. This meant that the paganism of the Arab tribes looked increasingly out of place in the wider world. Did that matter?

All these questions focus on late antiquity, but in the last section of the chapter we will reach deeper into the past to ground our understanding of two things: how the existence of states in the Middle East related to its resources, and how old-fashioned paganism was giving way to something else.

We will end by asking what the future of the Middle East might have looked like to an early seventh-century observer who lacked what we have: the wisdom of hindsight.

The Fijār wars and the Arabian interior

Sometime in the later sixth century, the wilderness of western Arabia was the scene of four successive wars.[1] They were concentrated around Mecca, in the region of the Ḥijāz, and were known as the "Fijārs." The name suggests that there was something immoral about them (*fujūr* means depravity), and the explanation given is that they took place during a sacred month when people were not supposed to fight each other. Each of these wars is a colorful story in itself, but we will have to be content with looking closely at just one of them and making some reference to another. Here, then, is what happened in the "Third Fijār," as narrated in an Arabic book by a ninth-century author, Ibn Ḥabīb (d. 860), with occasional details drawn from other sources. Despite the passage of more than a millennium since he composed his book, most of the narrative flows easily enough in the twenty-first century. But from time to time a word of explanation is needed, and where that is so, I put it in parentheses. Also, at a couple of points we are given more names than most readers today would know what to do with; I will come back to this profusion of names a little further on.

The story of the Third Fijār

The trouble began when an Arab woman came to ʿUkāẓ, not far from Mecca, to do some shopping. (The reference to her being an Arab suggests that she belonged to a nomadic tribe rather than to the sedentary population of the oases; ʿUkāẓ was

1. E. Landau-Tasseron, "The sinful wars," *Jerusalem Studies in Arabic and Islam*, 8 (1986). For a wider survey of the pre-Islamic Arabian past see R. G. Hoyland, *Arabia and the Arabs*, London 2001, and for the whole sweep of the history of the Arabs see T. Mackintosh-Smith, *Arabs*, New Haven 2019.

the site of an annual fair at which people from different tribes would gather to buy and sell.) The woman belonged to the Banū ʿĀmir ibn Ṣaʿṣaʿa (the sons of ʿĀmir son of Ṣaʿṣaʿa), who in turn were part of a larger tribal group, the descendants of ʿIkrima ibn Khaṣafa ibn Qays. (For now the only name to remember here is Qays; we can think of Qays as her tribe, named after its common ancestor.) The woman was tall and attractive, and her presence soon drew the attention of some young men from Mecca. She was wearing a striped veil that concealed all of her face but her eyes. Cheekily, the young men suggested she remove it, but she did not oblige them. Now in those days, our narrator explains, women wore only a single garment. So when she sat down to negotiate some purchases, one of the young men came up behind her and pinned the end of her dress to her back. This young man was Abū ʾl-Ghashim ibn ʿAbd al-ʿUzzā ibn ʿĀmir ibn al-Ḥārith ibn Ḥāritha ibn Saʿd ibn Taym ibn Murra. (There is no need to attend to any of these names at this point; what an insider learns from them is that the young man belonged to a certain Qurashī clan, Quraysh being the tribe that dominated Mecca.) This practical joke was a success: when the woman had completed her purchases and stood up, her lower body was stripped naked. This greatly amused the young men, who taunted her, "You wouldn't show us your face, and now you've shown us your buttocks!" She responded by unveiling her face (now an appeal for aid) and shouting, "Help, O Qays! Look what they've done to me!"[2] A crowd gathered, and members of her tribe rallied around her. The fellow tribesmen of the young men must have responded similarly, and there was a skirmish between the two sides. But there was no serious fighting, and the opponents soon separated. There, in this account, the war ended; but other accounts have it that the fighting, whether described as light or heavy, did lead to injuries. A prominent member of Quraysh then took it upon himself to pay the requisite blood money, thereby resolving the matter before it could lead to further trouble.

This story gives us several things to think about. Perhaps the most obvious question it invites is why, in a book devoted to the grand narrative of fourteen centuries of Muslim history, we should be bothering with an incident as trivial as this. But we had best defer that question till we have tackled some more pedestrian ones.

Should we believe the story?

The first and most pedestrian question is whether we are to believe this story. Well over two centuries intervened between the time when the incident allegedly took place in the Arabian desert and the time when Ibn Ḥabīb was composing his book in the sophisticated urban milieu of Baghdad. Two things might nevertheless be said to shore up his credibility. One is that he was an expert on the lore of

2. Ibn Ḥabīb, *Munammaq*, Hyderabad 1964, 189–90.

pre-Islamic Arabia, and indeed one of many such experts. By the ninth century this was a well-developed scholarly discipline with a significant readership among the cultural elite of the day—or perhaps we should say audience, since this was a society whose elite absorbed much of its literary heritage in oral settings. The other is that he did not compose his book out of thin air; he used earlier sources, and he tells us what—or rather who—they were. He had his account of the Third Fijār from an earlier expert in the same field who hailed from Medina in western Arabia but moved to Baghdad, where he died in 815–16. He, in turn, had the story from another resident of Medina, who died in 768–69 and incidentally belonged to the same clan of Quraysh as the youth who caused the woman such distress. He had a reputation for unreliability among experts on the transmission of traditions about the sayings and doings of the Prophet Muḥammad, but that was a different discipline from the study of pre-Islamic Arabian lore, so perhaps it did not matter. This man, in turn, had the account from a Medinese poet who died in 747–48. There the chain of transmission ends. So even if we believe in the accuracy of this chain of transmission and accept that the account as we have it today is pretty much as it left the hands—or the mouth—of the eighth-century poet, we still have a gap of more than a century between the event and the poet's lifetime. We have no idea how the information was transmitted—or alternatively invented—over that period.

Another consideration is that stories like this one are often told in variant forms. For example, one key feature of our story is unstable: depending on the account, the fighting is said to have been insignificant or severe. Obviously two such variants cannot both be right. Yet another phenomenon that could incline us to skepticism is the way elements of a story can appear in more than one narrative context. Thus we encounter the same practical joke in Yathrib or, to use its Islamic name, Medina in 624; this time the joker is a Jew, and the incident leads to the expulsion of his tribe from the oasis. Either the trick was a popular one among young men at the time, or the story has migrated within the literary tradition. A further problem could be that accounts of the past are liable to be distorted to serve the purposes of the present, but this is not apparent in the case at hand.

Very occasionally we are able to check such memories of pre-Islamic Arabia against sources external to the Arabic literary tradition. For example, the Arabic sources tell us that Muḥammad's great-grandfather Hāshim, who must have lived around the year 500, met the Byzantine emperor in Syria. We can say with assurance that this is wrong, because we know from the Byzantine sources, which are fairly extensive, that no emperor visited Syria between the fourth century and the seventh. But consider another example. The literary tradition preserves the testimony of a contemporary poet to the effect that his eastern Arabian tribe fought on the side of Abraha, a mid-sixth-century Ethiopian ruler of Yemen, in the course of a campaign in western Arabia. This sounds unlikely, but it finds startling confirmation in a contemporary inscription that we owe to the Ethiopian ruler. As these examples show, external checks can go either way. But in the case of the Third Fijār there are no sources external to the tradition that we could bring to bear. Are we then to say that we have no reason to believe this account? Or should we rather say that we have no reason to doubt it? The issue arises with regard to much of what the Islamic sources have to tell us about pre-Islamic Arabia, and often, as in this case, there is no clear resolution.

A possible compromise, and one we will adopt here more because it is fruitful than because it is demonstrably right, is to say that irrespective of whether the details of a narrative are true, the narrators of the early Islamic period still retained a good sense of the realities of life in pre-Islamic Arabia, despite the distance that already separated their world from the one they described. They were certainly aware of this distance. As we saw, our narrator—presumably the eighth-century poet—knows that he has to explain to his audience that in those days women wore only a single garment; in his own time they obviously wore more than one. Read in this vein, what does our story have to tell us about the character of the society in which it is set?

The marginality of states

When reading a historical source, it often pays to ask what is *not* there. One thing that is conspicuously absent from the background assumed by the story is any sign of activity on the part of a state or its agents. A ruler whose territories included ʿUkāẓ would have had reason to maintain a presence there during the fair. This concentration of commerce would have provided an opportunity for him to collect some taxes, and that, in turn, would have given him a motive for reining in any conflict likely to disrupt the buying and selling. Such an authority might, of course, have missed this particular incident, which does not seem to have been very serious; but in fact there is no trace of a ruler or his agents in any of these wars bar the fourth and last. There the ruler in question was indeed an Arab king, but he was located far away to the north in the town of Ḥīra, on the edge of Mesopotamia—the region we will know in Islamic times by its Arabic name, Iraq. This king had organized a caravan that was to bring goods to ʿUkāẓ, and to ensure its safe passage through the territories of the tribes he was looking for someone with the right local connections to guard it. Clearly he had no permanent agents in place in western Arabia. Meanwhile, rulers based beyond the frontiers of Arabia do not even appear on the horizon.

For the most part the impression we get from the accounts of the Fijārs fits well with the wider picture of the Arabian interior in this period that we gather from our sources, such as they are. We hear of occasional kings who ruled there, but they were unimpressive figures by the royal standards of the outside world—we could call them kinglets. In general the Arabian interior was stateless. Thus in the Ḥijāz, the region of western Arabia that included Mecca and Yathrib, there was no king in sight on the eve of the rise of Islam. Neither the Ḥijāz as a whole, nor any of its oases, nor any of its nomadic populations were then ruled by kings. In Yathrib there was a tribal leader who had hopes of making himself king but did not succeed, and there were recollections of men who had ruled as kings there in bygone days. One was appointed king by his clan but was then attacked and injured by one of his subjects, a man whose inheritance he wanted to appropriate part of. Unable to get even with his assailant because members of the clan were protecting him, the king went on strike by sitting in the sun and vowing not to enter a house till the score was settled. A little girl collecting firewood happened to pass by and asked him what he was doing sitting in the sun, so he told her his hard-luck story in verse. She passed it on to his fellow clansmen, who then bound the assailant and brought him to the king, who thereupon forgave the clan. He did, in the event, get some of the inheritance, but the story is hardly redolent of the pomp and power of kingship as it was understood outside Arabia. The Ḥijāzī tribe of Sulaym, which was partly nomadic and partly settled, likewise had traditions about kings in the past. We are told of one man who was about to become king when a cousin slapped him in the face, after which he left the tribal territory in humiliation. Another was deposed when he acted contrary to the wishes of the tribesmen in some matter—when it came to the crunch he did not have enough kinsmen in the tribe to support him.

This absence of states in most of Arabia is not hard to understand, once we think away our modern assumption that outside Antarctica the world's land surface is partitioned into territories each ruled by a state. In a premodern context such as this, we can usually think of a state as an enterprise that made a living by collecting taxes from its subjects and delivering security in exchange; this security, in turn, encouraged the economic activity without which there would be nothing to tax. Such an enterprise was worth mounting only in an environment in which a decent amount of tax could be collected without too much difficulty. Egypt is a prime example of a premodern tax collector's paradise: a country in which rich agricultural land was cultivated by humble peasants and laid out along a river system that ensured easy access for the agents of the state. The Arabian interior, by contrast, was a tax collector's hell: a wilderness in which agricultural land was scarce and widely dispersed, with a population of refractory and often nomadic tribesmen. This Arabian landscape forms part of an extended band of desert that stretches to the Atlantic in the west and spills over into northwestern India in the east. So Arabian agriculture was largely confined to the oases. Rare in the Ḥijāz, they were somewhat more common in the eastern region known as Najd and culminated in Arabia's largest oasis in Baḥrayn near the coast of the Persian Gulf (here Baḥrayn refers to the mainland opposite the island we know today as

Bahrain). But most of Arabia was too poor in agricultural resources to provide adequate returns to would-be state builders, and this was particularly true of the Ḥijāz. A fifteenth-century navigator summed it up: "The Ḥijāz is barren with little food. . . . The winter rains never reach it except a little."[3] A Syrian Jew who settled in Yathrib in pre-Islamic times is described as contrasting his former abode—"a land of bread and wine" with his new one—"a land of hardship and hunger."[4] Farther south, in Mecca, we have the derisive response of some pagans who were resistant to the message brought to them by Muḥammad: "Well, Muḥammad," they are said to have mocked their prophet, "you know that no people are more short of land and water, and live a harder life than we, so ask your Lord who has sent you . . . to straighten out our country for us, and to open up in it rivers like those of Syria and Iraq." Without rivers, drought meant famine, particularly for the nomads whose animals had nothing to eat when the vegetation did not grow. Accounts of a drought that struck Medina and the region around it in 639 preserve a vignette of a nomadic group who prevailed on their reluctant chief to slaughter a sheep for them: it turned out to be nothing but skin and bones. It certainly helped that there was, as we have seen, some trade in the pre-Islamic Arabian interior. But the fair at ʿUkāẓ clearly did not offer sufficient resources for state building. One reason for this was that between the decline of the frankincense trade in late antiquity and the rise of the Yemeni coffee trade in the seventeenth century, no part of Arabia grew a cash crop valuable enough to be of serious interest to the world outside it.

The corners of the peninsula, the Yemen and Oman, were better provided with rainfall. Here let us concentrate on the Yemen, which played a more prominent role in Arabian affairs than Oman did. It was not for nothing that the ancients knew it as Arabia Felix, as opposed to Arabia Deserta. The Yemen had a long tradition of state formation associated with a culture of Ancient Near Eastern vintage, and in late antiquity, between the third and sixth centuries, the Ḥimyarites united the region for the first time and maintained a significant kingdom there. Yet even in the Yemen the supply of water was far from generous. A Roman military expedition to the Yemen led by Aelius Gallus in 25–24 BC failed to take the capital city for lack of water. Moreover, such water as the country possessed was associated with a mountainous terrain, the result of the rifting that produced the Red Sea. Mountains help bring down rainfall, but they are also one of nature's devices for making life difficult for states and their tax collectors. Thus any state in the Yemeni interior was condemned to float uneasily on a sea of recalcitrant mountain tribes.

3. Ibn Mājid in G. R. Tibbetts, *Arab navigation in the Indian Ocean before the coming of the Portuguese*, London 1971, 264.

4. For this and the next quotation see Ibn Isḥāq, *The life of Muhammad*, trans. A. Guillaume, Oxford 1955, 94, 134.

Of course commercial revenues helped, since the Yemen, like Oman, had Indian Ocean frontage. But by the time of the Fijārs the Yemeni tradition of state formation was over, as was the larger culture that went with it. Ḥimyarite rule had ended in the later 520s thanks to an Ethiopian military intervention against a background of debilitating drought. Thereafter, the Ethiopian Abraha ruled a successor state for a few decades, but after about 570 even that came to an end.

Meanwhile, the tribesmen of the Arabian interior did not just lack rulers; they showed themselves positively allergic to them. A self-respecting tribe would set a high value on being what was called *laqāḥ*, a status it could claim if and only if it had never given allegiance to a king and never paid tribute to one. Thus the story goes that a member of Quraysh sought to become king of Mecca. But one of his fellow tribesmen quickly killed the idea, declaring that "Quraysh is *laqāḥ*; it neither wields royal power nor is subject to it."[5] This defiant attitude to kings is vividly illustrated in a story about a pre-Islamic poet who killed one. The king in question—a king of Ḥīra—had attempted to trap the poet's mother into the servile act of passing a plate to his own mother. The poet's mother at once called out to her tribe for help, and the poet promptly killed the king. In a poem he boasts on behalf of his fellow tribesmen that "we rebelled against the king, and would not serve him." He asks the king why they should "be underlings to your chosen princelet" and when they were ever "your mother's domestics"; he describes how they returned from a raid "leading the kings in fetters."[6] Another story recounts that a tribe responded to the arrival of a would-be tax collector sent by the king of Ḥīra by throwing him into a well.

Unfriendly as the Arabian environment may have been for the nurturing of states, are we to say that the interior had always been as lacking in large-scale political organization as it appears to have been on the eve of the rise of Islam? This is a good question, but one that is best deferred until we have brought the two largest and most powerful states of the Middle East into the picture. Before we do that, we should pay some further attention to the society and culture of the Arab tribes.

The centrality of tribes

If this Arabian society lacked states, what did it have instead? The answer is easily detected in our story of the Third Fijār: a form of tribalism based on patrilineal descent that embraced the entire free population, nomadic and sedentary. Each of the two main actors in the story—the woman and the young man who humiliated her—is given a tribal identity expressed by the naming of a string of male

5. Muṣʿab al-Zubayrī, *Nasab Quraysh*, Cairo 1976, 210.
6. A. J. Arberry (trans.), *The seven odes*, London 1957, 204–9.

ancestors. In the case of the woman, her own name is not even mentioned; it is enough that we know that she belonged to the Banū ʿĀmir ibn Ṣaʿṣaʿa, who in turn were among the descendants of ʿIkrima ibn Khaṣafa ibn Qays (*ibn*, again, means "son of," and *banū* is its plural). The reader is expected to make this connection when she uses a set form (*yā la-Qays*) to call upon any members of Qays within hearing to come to her aid. By addressing herself to all those descended from this distant ancestor, she is casting her net very wide; a variant version has her call out *yā la-ʿĀmir*, thereby limiting her appeal to the Banū ʿĀmir ibn Ṣaʿṣaʿa. In the case of the young man, we are given a full recital of his male ancestors back to a certain Murra: Abū 'l-Ghashim ibn ʿAbd al-ʿUzzā ibn ʿĀmir ibn al-Ḥārith ibn Ḥāritha ibn Saʿd ibn Taym ibn Murra. As already indicated, the reader is expected to know that Taym ibn Murra is the ancestor who gave his name to a well-known clan within the tribe of Quraysh. In both cases, we see that Arab genealogy is about men. Of course everyone knew perfectly well that women had a role to play in the process by which men begat men, but no need was felt to provide comparably systematic information about female lines of descent—which is not to say that they didn't matter.

But why so many ancestors? Why not simply say that the young woman belonged to Qays and the young man to Quraysh? This, indeed, is all we need to know to make sense of the story as told above. But in other contexts other ancestors could come to the fore. Thus in a variant version of the story the woman's side is identified with the tribe of Hawāzin—Hawāzin being an intermediate ancestor, a grandson of ʿIkrima and great-grandfather of Ṣaʿṣaʿa. In some other conflict the Banū ʿĀmir ibn Ṣaʿṣaʿa might find themselves pitted against another Qaysī group that did not descend from ʿĀmir. Or Qays and Quraysh, both descended from a certain Muḍar, might even find themselves on the same side against a group that did not share that ancestry. Some of these genealogical nodes are more important than others, so that in practice we can often think of the pre-Islamic Arabs as divided into a fixed set of tribes—Hawāzin, Quraysh, and so forth. But in any given situation the operative group might be larger or smaller, bringing different ancestors into play.

This salience of patrilineal genealogy does not mean that the structure of Arabian society was based *exclusively* on extended kinship. Two men could create a formal relationship whereby one became the client or ally (*ḥalīf*) of the other; the agreement would likely include the kinsmen of each party. Such supplementation of the kinship system was in fact an ancient feature of Arabian society. Herodotus, the Greek historian of the fifth century BC, has this to say:

> No nation regards the sanctity of a pledge more seriously than the Arabs. When two men wish to make a solemn compact, they get the service of a third, who stands between them and with a sharp stone cuts the palms of their hands near

> the base of the thumb; then he takes a little tuft of wool from their clothes, dips it in the blood and smears the blood on seven stones which lie between them, invoking, as he does so, the names of Dionysus and Urania; then the person who is giving the pledge commends the stranger—or fellow-citizen, as the case may be—to his friends, who in their turn consider themselves equally bound to honor it.[7]

By the time of the Fijārs this ritual had been forgotten, and instead we hear of one involving fire. But the basic social building block described by Herodotus was still in play, and we will soon see an example of it in the context of the Fourth Fijār. Like extended kinship, this institution helps a tribal society function in the absence of a state.

To an extent, then, we can see Arabian society as having tribes *instead* of states. One aspect of this can perhaps be seen in our story. In her distress, the woman calls upon the members of her tribe for help. What would a woman subjected to comparable sexual harassment do in our own society? Depending on the context, she might call upon her immediate family members, her friends, bystanders, the campus authorities, or those in charge at her workplace. In terms of kinship, the options of a woman today are much narrower than those of the woman in the story; few Americans, for example, maintain bonds of kinship with relatives more distant than their cousins. But as far as authorities independent of the kinship system are concerned, her options today are considerably wider. Moreover, if the incident were to take place at her workplace, it could end up in court; if it led to violence, the police might be involved. But Arabian society, lacking rulers, did without such authorities. In one version of the story, as we have seen, the hostilities ceased when a prominent member of Quraysh took it upon himself to pay blood money.

We can perceive more clearly how the tribal structure substituted for the state—as we would see it—if we shift our attention briefly from the Third to the Fourth Fijār, where the key event was a murder. When the king of Ḥīra was looking for someone to secure the safe passage of his caravan, there were two candidates for the job. One was a certain Barrāḍ, a drunkard and a troublemaker who had moved to Mecca after being disowned by his own tribe; there he obtained the protection of a leading member of Quraysh by becoming his client (*ḥalīf*). Because he continued to make trouble his patron soon wanted to end the relationship, but against his better judgment he was persuaded to continue it on condition that his client left Mecca. Barrāḍ then went to Ḥīra, where he offered himself to the king as an escort for the caravan, though quite unsuited for the role. Instead, the king gave the job to a rival, a certain ʿUrwa; as it happened, ʿUrwa belonged to the same tribal

7. Herodotus, *The histories*, trans. A. de Selincourt, Harmondsworth 1955, 176–77 (3.8).

group as the woman at the center of the Third Fijār, the Banū ʿĀmir ibn Ṣaʿṣaʿa. Barrāḍ then followed the caravan, killed his rival, and went off with the goods. He did at least have the grace to notify his patron and other leaders of Quraysh, who were at ʿUkāẓ at the time; they immediately left for the security of Mecca—its security arising from the fact that the town was located within a widely recognized sanctuary. Their problem was that the Banū ʿĀmir ibn Ṣaʿṣaʿa would want revenge for the murder of their fellow tribesman. Killing the murderer himself would not have satisfied them, since as an outlaw Barrāḍ could not rank as the equal of a man like ʿUrwa. Killing members of Barrāḍ's own tribe was against the rules because they had already disowned him and so bore no responsibility for anything he did. But the continuing relationship of clientage that bound him to his patron made members of Quraysh a suitable target to avenge the murder. In short, we can see revenge killing as a game with rules that took the place of our criminal justice system—or more accurately, our criminal justice system is a development that has replaced practices of revenge killing that were no doubt more or less universal in human societies prior to the emergence of states.

This is not to imply that the Arabs lacked a judicial system. They had one, and here is a rare anecdote that gives some idea how it worked:

> Murattiʿ . . . married a woman of Ḥaḍramawt; her father imposed on him the condition that he take no further wife in addition to her and that she give birth only in the abode of her own people. But Murattiʿ did not observe the condition. So they made Afʿā ibn al-Ḥuṣayn the Jurhumite their judge . . . the Arabs being in the habit of having recourse to him in their disputes. At the hearing the fact that the condition had been imposed was established, and Afʿā gave the verdict "The condition is binding." He was the first to use this maxim. So the Ḥaḍramīs took the woman and the son she had had by Murattiʿ.[8]

Here, then, we have a judicial system, but the judge is not appointed by a ruler who gives him the authority to try cases within a certain jurisdiction; instead, the judge is chosen by the agreement of the parties concerned, and the authority he derives from this is limited to the particular case. Thus Afʿā in the anecdote had a continuing role as a judge only in the sense that the Arabs made a practice of submitting cases to him, presumably because he had established a reputation as a fair and insightful judge. If the parties to a dispute did not agree on taking it before a judge, it was likely to be resolved, if at all, by violence.

That brings us to the character of tribal warfare. According to Ibn Ḥabīb's version—and not his alone—the fighting in the Third Fijār was limited to a brief skirmish. In fact, of the four Fijārs, the only one in which anyone was actually killed

8. Balādhurī, *Ansāb al-ashrāf*, vol. 1, ed. M. Ḥamīd Allāh, Cairo 1959, 9.

was the last. In this case the need for the tribe of the murdered man to avenge the killing led to a series of one-day battles at exact intervals of a year. To us that sounds peculiar, not to say quaint; yet such anniversary battles are a standard ingredient of accounts of pre-Islamic Arabian warfare. The fourth battle was the last, but it was followed by some further killings on both sides. In due course there were calls for a peace settlement, as without one the killings might have continued indefinitely, an unenticing prospect. It was now suggested that the party that had suffered the most killings should receive blood money to make up for the difference; we are told that the side of the murdered man had lost twenty more men than their enemies had. The first time this deal was proposed it was torpedoed by a leading figure from the town of Ṭā'if, an oasis to the east of Mecca, but the second time it held, and the war was brought to an end. Appropriately, the blood money was paid by Barrāḍ's patron—incidentally the same prominent member of Quraysh who in some versions had paid the blood money to settle the Third Fijār. All this could, of course, have been avoided had the patron had the good sense to end his relationship with his troublesome client before the damage was done. But the level of violence in the Fourth Fijār need not surprise us. This was a society in which any adult male who was sound in mind and body would bear arms and know how to use them; among adult males there was no distinction to be made between soldiers and civilians. Thus warfare was an endemic feature of Arabian society. The poem composed by the killer of the king of Ḥīra is accordingly full of bellicosity. He boasts of white banners taken into battle and brought back crimson, of youths "who deem death in battle a glory" and graybeards "long tested in warfare."[9] Such sentiments are typical of the warlike ethos of pre-Islamic Arabian poetry. "Not one chief of ours ever died a natural death, nor was any slain man of ours ever left where he lay unavenged," as another poet puts it.[10] Here, then, was a society with an abundance of military energy. But the energy was dissipated in small-scale hostilities, not channeled into total war aimed at the subjection or elimination of a rival group. Warfare had its rules and could be tied to a schedule that in today's world we might associate more readily with football than with war.

Someone who thought hard about the nature of the tribal society of the Arabs was the historian Ibn Khaldūn (d. 1406), a North African of Spanish origin who settled in Egypt. His ideas have a certain affinity to the thinking behind Second Amendment fundamentalism in the United States today. He saw two groups as polar opposites: the nomads of the deserts—above all the camel nomads—on the one hand, and the sedentary populations—above all those of the

9. Arberry, *The seven odes*, 206.
10. A. J. Arberry, *Arabic poetry*, Cambridge 1965, 30 verse 10.

cities—on the other. Sedentary people are "sunk in well-being and luxury."[11] They have "entrusted defense of their property and their lives to the governor and ruler who rules them, and to the militia that has the task of guarding them." Accordingly, they "have ceased to carry weapons" and have "become like women and children"; in another passage he compares their inability to defend themselves to that of students. Their fortitude is broken by the domination of the state, with the result that they grow up in fear and docility, losing their power of resistance as a result of "the inertness that develops in the souls of the oppressed." Camel nomads, by contrast, make do with the bare necessities of life. They are "the most savage human beings that exist," and they have the virtues that go with that condition. They do not outsource their self-defense to rulers and their armies. Instead they are self-reliant; they always carry weapons and have developed a character marked by fortitude and courage. Their way of life also means that they are held together by "group feeling" (*ʿaṣabiyya*): only "a closely knit group of common descent" can hope to defend itself successfully—though bonds of clientage and alliance can amount to the same thing. But this group feeling is in one crucial way limited in what it can achieve. These desert Arabs are rude, proud, and ambitious, each one eager to be the leader. They are reluctant to subordinate themselves to their chiefs, who have to avoid antagonizing them. That is why these Arabs could form only tribes and not states. Altogether, Ibn Khaldūn's analysis is insightful, and it does much to explain why the warlike energy of the Arab tribes was mostly expended on small-scale conflicts among themselves, between and within the tribes.

The culture of a tribal people

A key part of the culture of a people is its sense of its own identity. Did the society of the Arabian interior see itself as Arab? As we saw, ethnic identity is not a prominent theme in the Fijārs. The young woman in the Third Fijār is described as an Arab, probably reflecting a sense that the nomads of Arabia were the Arabs par excellence. Yet the word was readily used in sources of the early Islamic period to include the settled but fully tribal population of the oases, and the general absence of reference to ethnicity in our story may reflect no more than the fact that all those involved were Arabs and spoke Arabic. There is reason to think that a sense of Arab identity was old.[12] In the first half of the first millennium BC we encounter forms of the word "Arab" in texts from three different linguistic regions on the borders of Arabia: Assyria in the northeast, Israel in the northwest, and

11. For this and the quotations that follow see Ibn Khaldûn, *The Muqaddimah*, Princeton 1967, 1:252, 257, 259, 261, 263.

12. For a very different perspective on the history of Arab ethnic identity see P. Webb, *Imagining the Arabs*, Edinburgh 2016, arguing that Arab identity emerged only after the rise of Islam.

the Yemen in the south (the people of the ancient Yemen were not Arabs, and they spoke languages quite distinct from Arabic). It is in the Assyrian records that we meet the first Arab whom we know by name, a certain Gindibu, who appears in 853 BC with a thousand camel riders from Arabia fighting for a king with whom the Assyrian monarch was at war. The name Gindibu means "cricket," one of many words for animals that were used as personal names among the Arabs; it was still common as a name in the form Jundab around the time of the rise of Islam. That the ethnonym "Arab" should appear in the records of three distinct neighboring regions strongly suggests that a people identifying itself as Arab had already spread over a large part of Arabia more than a millennium before the rise of Islam. But for direct evidence of the indigenous use of the ethnonym we have to wait till around AD 200. A particularly striking instance is found in an inscription marking the grave of an Arab king who died in 328; he describes himself, with royal exaggeration, as the "king of all the Arabs" (*malik al-ʿArab kullihā*).[13] By contrast, in late antiquity outsiders on the northern frontiers of Arabia took to calling the Arabs by other names, Saracens in Greek and Ṭayyāyē in Syriac. The fact that the Arabs of Islamic times nevertheless called themselves Arabs is a clear indication of the continuous existence of this identity among the Arabs themselves. This survival need not, of course, mean that nothing about Arab identity had changed over the centuries, but it clearly had staying power. It is worth noting that, just like Greek identity before the rise of Macedonia, Arab identity did not owe its emergence and persistence prior to the rise of Islam to the homogenizing activities of a state. It must have been helped by the fact that Arabia—like Greece and unlike the Sahara—is a peninsula with the sea on three sides, and by the mobility of much of the population in the open desert environment.

An important part of the culture of the Arabs was their language. Unlike the other major languages of the Middle East today—Persian and Turkish—Arabic has a good claim to be indigenous to the region. It belongs to the Semitic language family, which is attested in Syria and Mesopotamia already in the third millennium BC (no language can be attested much earlier than that, since writing was not developed till toward 3000 BC). Semitic is the close-knit family that includes such ancient languages of the Fertile Crescent as Akkadian, Hebrew, and Aramaic, together with the languages of pre-Islamic South Arabia and their African offshoot, Ethiopic. Any reader with a knowledge of Arabic or Hebrew should have no trouble deciphering most of the following Ethiopic sequence: *aḥadu, kelʾētu, shalastu, arbāʿtu*; the catch is the second word, which is as if the Ethiopians said "both" in place of "two." Arabic shares with its sister Semitic languages a pattern of triconsonantal roots. Thus words from the root *k-t-b* will usually refer in one

13. A.F.L. Beeston, "Nemara and Fau," *Bulletin of the School of Oriental and African Studies*, 42 (1979), 3, 6.

way or another to writing: *kataba* is "he wrote," *yaktubu* is "he writes," *kātib* is "someone who writes" or "a scribe," and *maktūb* is "something written." Given this information and the fact that *qatala* means "he killed," no attentive reader should have much trouble figuring out the meaning of *yaqtulu*, *qātil*, and *maqtūl*. But despite the indigenous status of Arabic, as we have seen it is not till the early first millennium BC that we begin to hear of the Arabs. And though Arabian inscriptions written in dialects related to Arabic are found in large numbers before the rise of Islam, they are usually frustratingly brief—more in the nature of graffiti than of texts. It is only in late antiquity that we have significant numbers of inscriptions that are unambiguously in Arabic and written in what we know as the Arabic script; currently more than thirty such inscriptions are known. Among the more significant is the inscription of the "king of all the Arabs" dating from 328. But the only substantial body of pre-Islamic material we possess in Arabic is the tribal poetry that was transmitted into Islamic times. Though its transmission can be problematic, there is little doubt that much of this material is authentically pre-Islamic. Nevertheless, the first book we possess in Arabic, and to the best of our knowledge the first ever to be written in the language, is the Qurʾān, the collection of Muḥammad's revelations. In that respect, at least, there is some truth in the saying attributed to Muḥammad: "We are an illiterate people; we neither write nor count."[14]

Arabic was and is the language of the Arabs. But in late antiquity the geographical distribution of the Arabs and their language was much more limited than it is today. The Arabs of that time were primarily the people of the Arabian Peninsula—bar the south—and the Syrian desert, and they had to an extent spread into Mesopotamia, Syria, and the Eastern Desert of Egypt. But the mass of the rural population in Mesopotamia and Syria still spoke dialects of Aramaic, just as the mass of the Egyptian peasantry spoke dialects of Coptic, a late form of the language of the Pharaohs. Both Coptic and Aramaic had written forms; in the case of Aramaic the most widely used was Syriac. These languages coexisted with the relevant imperial language, Persian in Mesopotamia and Greek in Syria and Egypt. We know that Greek had made very considerable inroads in Syria and Egypt, particularly in the cities, and it is likely enough that Persian had done the same in Mesopotamia. Meanwhile in the Yemen, the South Arabian linguistic heritage still prevailed. A story that amused people in the early centuries of Islam had it that an Arab came to visit the Ḥimyarite king, who greeted his visitor with the command "*Thib!*"[15]—the Ḥimyarite for "Sit down!" (from the same Semitic root as "yeshiva"). But "*Thib!*" in Arabic means "Jump!"—which the Arab did, in one version of the story tumbling over a precipice.

14. See, for example, Ibn Ḥanbal, *Musnad*, ed. A. M. Shākir, Cairo 1949–, nos. 5017, 5137.
15. See, for example, Samʿānī, *Ansāb*, Hyderabad 1962–82, 4:264.

A significant aspect of the culture of any society is its religion. It does not, however, play much part in our stories of the Fijārs. In one way this is typical of the wars of the pre-Islamic Arab tribes as a whole. Whatever else they may have been about, they were not about religion, and their protagonists were not the sort of men whom we can readily imagine throwing themselves into religious warfare. There are nevertheless two religious elements in the stories. One is the idea that the Fijārs were immoral because they occurred during a sacred month, and the other is the fact that Quraysh felt safer in Mecca because it was located within a sanctuary. This is the sanctuary at the center of which lay the Kaʿba, the temple into which was built the sacred Black Stone. According to tradition, five generations before Muḥammad an enterprising Qurashī had taken over the sanctuary from another tribe and settled his fellow tribesmen there. Both the sacred months and the sanctuary are examples of Arab paganism providing amenities that made life somewhat less dangerous and more predictable for all concerned. But these elements are incidental to stories that focus on other matters.

What the Fijār narratives do not reveal to us is the abiding core of Arab paganism: idol worship. It was of hoary antiquity. We get a vivid picture of it as early as the seventh century BC, when the Assyrian ruler Esarhaddon (ruled 680–669 BC) tells us that his father Sennacherib (ruled 704–681 BC) had raided an oasis in northern Arabia and taken its idols as booty. After Esarhaddon's accession, an Arab king had come and kissed his feet, begging for the return of his idols. Esarhaddon in his mercy had the idols—there were six of them—repaired and handed over to the Arab king, after taking the opportunity to inscribe on them a message proclaiming the superior might of the Assyrian god Ashur, together with his own name. One god among the six was Ruldaiu, still remembered in early Islamic times as Ruḍā; a leading genealogist recorded sixteen men who bore the name "Slave of Ruḍā" (ʿAbd Ruḍā) before the rise of Islam. A couple of centuries after Esarhaddon, when Herodotus identified the deities the Arabs invoked in making a solemn compact as the Greek gods Dionysus and Urania, he went on to explain that the Arabs themselves called them something like Orotalt and Alilat. Orotalt would seem to be a garbled form of Ruḍā, while Alilat is readily identifiable as the goddess Allāt, who was still widely worshipped by the pagans of Arabia in Muḥammad's day. At that time we find Yathrib chockablock with idols. Some were closely connected to the tribal system; it seems that each clan had its idol, and above these clan idols an entire tribe might have one. Below them were the ones people kept in their homes. Mecca, too, had a large population of idols. One of them was the idol of the god Hubal, which had the privilege of being placed inside the Kaʿba. There were 360 more surrounding the Kaʿba, and as in Yathrib there were idols in people's homes—we are told that every Qurashī had one in his house. A Meccan several centuries before the rise of Islam is credited with bringing Hubal to Mecca:

> ʿAmr ibn Luḥayy left Mecca for Syria on business. When he got to Moab in the Balqāʾ, then inhabited by the Amalekites, . . . he saw them worshipping idols, and said to them, "What are these idols I see you worshipping?" They said, "These are idols that we worship. We ask them for rain, and they make it rain; we ask them for victory, and they give us victory." He said to them, "Do you think you could spare me one to take back to the land of the Arabs for them to worship?" So they gave him an idol called Hubal. He took it back to Mecca and set it up there, telling people to worship and venerate it.[16]

Whatever the historical value of this story, it conveys a good sense of what idols were for—and by implication what they were not for. Insofar as the pre-Islamic Arabs thought about the meaning of life, Hubal had nothing to do with it. He did not offer cosmic mystery, spiritual sustenance, or redemption from the burden of sin. Any deeper reflections the Arabs might have on the human condition came rather in the context of their heroic poetry: "The days of a man are numbered to him, and through them all / The snares of death lurk by the warrior as he travels perilous ways."[17] The poets rarely had much to say about idols.

Finally, the story of the Third Fijār, though not the Fourth, can tell us something about women in pre-Islamic Arabia. The woman in the story is veiled, which we should probably take to mean that she has class—were she a mere slave girl it would be presumptuous of her to give herself such airs. She nevertheless moves freely at the fair to do her shopping, with no sign of the presence of a kinsman to escort her and watch her back. Moreover, in another version of the story she has no inhibitions about chatting to amorous young men who manifestly find her sexually attractive. To use a term that was later to become widespread among the Muslims of India, she is not in purdah. This picture fits the fact that we find occasional references in our sources to Arab queens. Sennacherib's booty included a "queen of the Arabs," and in the fourth century the Byzantines were using troops contributed by one. On the other hand, the way in which the woman in the story is identified by a recital of her male ancestors finds a telling parallel in the case of the mother of the regicide poet. The king asks his companions why she would disdain to be of service, and they answer by pointing not to *her* character but to those of her father, uncle, husband, and son.

That leaves us with the question deferred at the start of this discussion: Why should we be bothering ourselves with an event as historically trivial as the Third Fijār? Even the Fourth Fijār hardly sounds like the stuff of world history, and the same goes for events in Arabia as far back as we can peer. But as we will see in the

16. Ibn Hishām, *al-Sīra al-nabawiyya*, Cairo 1955, 1–2:77; for the context see Ibn Isḥāq, *The life of Muhammad*, 701.

17. ʿAbīd ibn al-Abraṣ in H. Ringgren, *Studies in Arabian fatalism*, Uppsala 1955, 67.

next chapter, the story does something to frame a major explanatory problem regarding the history of state formation in Arabia. And in the meantime it helps point up the drastic contrast between the tribal society of the Arabian interior and the two empires that ruled the Middle East outside it.

The last war between the empires

A summer night in 626

For ten days in the summer of 626 the Avars laid siege to Constantinople, the capital city of the Byzantine Empire.[18] They were nomads from the steppes of Eurasia who had occupied the grasslands we know today as Hungary. The Byzantine forces defending the city included some twelve thousand cavalry, but the attackers numbered around eighty thousand. On the evening of Saturday, August 2, the Avar ruler—the Kagan, as they called him—invited the defenders to send him a delegation. When the members of this delegation arrived, they found three silk-clad Persian envoys seated comfortably in the presence of the Kagan, while they were left to stand. These envoys had been sent by the Persian general whose army was encamped on the opposite side of the Bosphorus—the narrow waterway that separates Europe from Asia. The Kagan's message to the Byzantine delegation was all too clear: with the Avars at the walls of their city and the Persians just across the water in a position to send him reinforcements, the situation of the defenders was hopeless. As he put it, unless they could turn themselves into birds or fish they had no way to escape. But he did make them an offer of sorts: if they left their city and their property behind them, each of them could take with him a cloak, a shirt, and his family. With these they could cross the Bosphorus to the Asian side, where the Kagan would generously arrange for his Persian allies not to harm them. Presumably Constantinople would then become an Avar city. But the Byzantine delegation responded in no uncertain terms that they would never relinquish it.

That night the Persian envoys attempted to cross back to the Asian side, but this time they were out of luck. The Byzantines captured them in transit. They found one of them hiding in the bottom of a skiff, killed him, and cut off his head. The other two they captured alive. They cut off the hands of one of them, hung the severed head of the first envoy around his neck, and in this state sent him back to the Kagan. The remaining envoy they threw in a skiff that they took close enough to the Asian shore for the Persians to be able to see him. There they proceeded to behead him and throw his head to the Persians, accompanied by a written message designed to make them think that the Kagan had double-crossed

18. J. Howard-Johnston, "The siege of Constantinople in 626," in his *East Rome, Sasanian Persia and the end of antiquity*, Aldershot 2006, art. VII.

them. Five days later the Kagan abandoned the siege, burned the twelve massive siege towers with which he had attacked the city, and went home. The Persians likewise abandoned their positions on the Asian side of the Bosphorus. The Byzantines had survived, and they duly gave thanks to the Mother of God for protecting her city from its enemies.

It is immediately obvious from this narrative that we are in a different world from that of the tribesmen of the Arabian interior. For a start, we can pinpoint the exact date of an event—Saturday, August 2, 626—whereas all we can say of the Fijārs is that they must have taken place sometime in the later sixth century. This difference reflects the fact that the Byzantines chronicled historical events in a way that the pre-Islamic Arabs did not. Thus most of the details of the siege given above derive from a Greek chronicle written by an inhabitant of Constantinople who lived through it. This leads to another contrast. Constantinople, where the anonymous chronicler wrote, was a massively fortified city; in western Arabia Ṭā'if was unusual in being a walled town, and with the possible exception of Ṣanʿā' in the Yemeni highlands, there was nothing anywhere in the peninsula that could have been called a city. We also meet a ruler, the Avar Kagan, who was far more powerful than the king of Ḥīra. There were, of course, other major rulers with a stake in the outcome, but in this story, as it happens, we do not meet either the Byzantine emperor Heraclius (ruled 610–41) or his Persian counterpart Khusraw II (ruled 591–628). Both were otherwise engaged far to the east, in the heartlands of the Persian Empire. At the same time, we hear nothing of tribes. There were none among the Byzantines or the Persians, though they no doubt existed among the Avars. Particularly striking is the very different character of warfare as it appears in the two settings. At the siege of Constantinople we encounter armies that were far larger than any tribal forces that might gather in western Arabia, and quite different in kind. Likewise the siege equipment brought to bear by the Avars would have been unheard of among the Arabs; a sixth-century Byzantine historian describes them as adept in plundering but incapable of storming a wall.

These contrasts reflect two things: the much greater fiscal resources available to the parties involved in the siege of Constantinople, and the much higher stakes of the conflict. None of the Fijārs were about seizing territory from the enemy, let alone expelling a whole population from its abode. The high stakes in turn help explain the vein of calculated atrocity that we see in the Byzantine treatment of the Persian envoys. All in all, we have left the wilds of Arabia for the charms of civilization.

During the siege of 626, large numbers of Byzantines, Persians, and Avars were crowded together within a few square miles in and around Constantinople. But they were not usually to be found in such close proximity, and they had very different histories and destinies. We need to look separately at each of them, and at the states of which they were the core populations.

The Byzantine Empire

Byzantium was a Greek colony founded in the seventh century BC on the site of the future Constantinople, known today by its Turkish name as Istanbul. During the thousand years in which it was called Byzantium it was never an imperial capital; that dignity came to it only when the Roman emperor Constantine (ruled 306–37) refounded it as his "New Rome" in 330, following which the city soon came to be known after him as Constantinople. For the next millennium it served as a capital for emperors belonging to a succession of dynasties, though in its last two or three centuries there was not much of an empire left. Calling this empire "Byzantine" and its people "Byzantines" is a modern anachronism. At the time, its rulers and subjects identified it as the Roman Empire and themselves as Romans. Despite the fact that Rome itself usually lay beyond its borders, this usage made some sense. What we call the Byzantine Empire was what remained of the Roman Empire after its division into an eastern and a western half in 395 and the demise of the western half in 476. This territorial displacement had a significant linguistic implication: the demographic base of the empire was now a population that spoke Greek rather than Latin, the language historically associated with Rome and its imperial role. The emperor Justinian (ruled 527–65) still had his monumental codification of Roman law prepared in Latin, but increasingly the language of his "Roman" empire was to be Greek. A ninth-century pope was ill-mannered enough to tell the Byzantine emperor that it was ridiculous to call oneself emperor of the Romans without knowing the Roman language. And yet the name "Roman" stuck, and this is why even today the Turkish word "Rum" means "Greek." So to speak of the "Byzantines" and their empire, though anachronistic, avoids a certain confusion.[19]

Even if we ignore the last centuries of Byzantine history, when this state was only a shadow of its former self, the fact that an empire centered on Constantinople lasted from the fourth century to the twelfth would suggest that in choosing his new capital Constantine had done something right. And the fact that the Ottomans were able to repeat the imperial achievement from the fifteenth century to the early twentieth is strong confirmation. What, then, was so advantageous about Constantinople? In microgeographical terms, its location on a peninsula that could be defended with a massive land wall was a major strategic asset, enhanced by its possession of an adjoining harbor, the Golden Horn, that could be closed off from the sea with a chain. In macrogeographical terms the city had two things going for it. On the sea, it had easy access both to the Black Sea at the northern

19. For a survey of the history of the empire see A. A. Vasiliev, *History of the Byzantine Empire*, Madison 1958; for its history before the rise of Islam see A. Cameron, *The Mediterranean world in late antiquity*, London 1993.

end of the Bosphorus and to the Aegean, and hence the Mediterranean, through the Dardanelles at the western end of the Sea of Marmara. This latter linked it to what in this period was perhaps the most commercially active maritime scene to be found anywhere in the world, together with the agricultural wealth of Egypt. Meanwhile on land, Constantinople was close to the fertile river valleys of western Anatolia and the southeastern Balkans. ("Anatolia" is a convenient—because ethnically neutral—term for what is now the Asian part of Turkey.) This combination of advantages meant more than just rich potential for collecting taxes, crucial as that was. It also made it easy to supply the imperial capital with an abundance of grain, the commodity without which large urban populations could not be sustained. All in all, Constantinople made a fine capital for an eastern Mediterranean empire, whether in late antiquity or in Ottoman times.

But these advantages of the location of Constantinople were not the whole story. Polybius, a Greek historian of the second century BC, drew a sharp contrast between land and sea when he sized up the location of the city: "The site of Byzantium is as regards the sea more favorable to security and prosperity than that of any other city in the world known to us, but as regards the land it is most disadvantageous in both respects."[20] He saw the city's maritime advantage as its control over entry to the Black Sea: no one could sail into or out of it without the consent of the Byzantines. But the disadvantage on land was that for all its fertility the city's agricultural territory was exposed to the raids of the neighboring Thracian chieftains. Given their number the Byzantines could hope neither to subdue them nor to reach an agreement with them. Not that things were any better when the Thracian chieftains were replaced for a while by a single Celtic ruler—they then found themselves paying an onerous tribute to him. Polybius's analysis of this disadvantage related to the time before the city was the capital of an empire, but we can easily update it. To be successful, an eastern Mediterranean empire based in Constantinople had to have undisputed control of the good agricultural land of the southwestern Balkans, western Anatolia, and if possible Egypt. But Egypt was some way across the sea, Anatolia was exposed to invasion from the east, and the Balkans were open to invasion from the north. This predicament was a key part of the background to the siege of 626. The Avars had invaded the Balkans from the north and reached the walls of Constantinople, while the Persians had taken possession of Egypt and overrun Anatolia from the east. Had the city held out without being able to recover at least some of its agricultural territory, it would in effect have regressed to being the Byzantium described by Polybius.

At the same time we should add a qualification to Polybius's favorable assessment of the maritime situation of the city. His analysis rested on the assumption

20. Polybius, *The histories*, trans. W. R. Paton, Cambridge, MA 2010–12, 2:431 (4.38.1–2).

that the naval technology available to the Byzantines was as good as anyone else's. For a long time this was indeed so. The Avars ruled a large Slav population in the Balkans, and although most of them were agriculturalists, those living along the banks of the Danube were adept at navigating the river in canoes. In 626 the Kagan brought a large number of Slavs with their boats to the siege of Constantinople and used them as a navy. However, a combination of Byzantine naval resources, trickery, and bad weather sufficed to parry this threat, which explains why communications between the Avars and the Persians worked out so badly. But what if the navy of the incumbent imperial power was no longer state-of-the-art? This came to be a serious problem for the Byzantines from the eleventh century onward, just as it was to be for the Ottomans from the seventeenth century. In the period that concerns us here, however, these developments were still far in the future.

Before we leave the Byzantines we should say something about their religion. They were Christians; like the population of the Roman Empire in general, they had abandoned paganism for Christianity following the conversion of the emperor Constantine in the early fourth century. More specifically, they were Orthodox, as the term is conventionally used. This distinguished them from a number of other Christian groups that had emerged in the fourth and fifth centuries and were regarded by the Orthodox as heretical in their Christological doctrines. There were the Arians, for whom God had not always had a son; the Nestorians, for whom God did not have a mother; and the Monophysites, for whom God died on the cross. Eventually, in the Orthodox view, these heretics would be joined by the Catholics of western and central Europe over a doctrinal issue of such nuance that we can ignore it. This fissiparous tendency arose at least in part from the imposition of the abstract categories of Greek thought on a myth in Ancient Near Eastern style about a god and his son. One can get a sense of what this doctrinal hairsplitting involved from a tortured passage in the Athanasian Creed, a fourth-century document that came to form part of the traditional prayer book of the Church of England: "For the right Faith is that we believe and confess: that our Lord Jesus Christ, the Son of God, is God and Man . . . Who although he be God and Man: yet he is not two, but one Christ; One, not by conversion of the Godhead into flesh: but by taking of the Manhood into God; One altogether, not by confusion of Substance: but by unity of Person. . . . This is the Catholick Faith: which except a man believe faithfully, he cannot be saved."[21] This suggests that despite some theological trickle-down, large numbers of ordinary people must have suffered eternal damnation because of their inability to understand just what it was they were being told to believe. A prominent fourth-century churchman visiting Constantinople

21. *The book of common prayer*, London n.d., 29–30.

gave a vivid account of the resulting chaos: "If you ask about your change, the shopkeeper talks theology to you, on the Begotten and the Unbegotten; if you inquire the price of a loaf, the reply is: 'The Father is greater and the Son is inferior'; and if you say, 'Is the bath ready?' the attendant affirms that the Son is of nothing."[22] In the sixth century we hear of thousands chanting Christological slogans at the emperor Justinian; they did not have to understand the issues to know which side they were on. Such scenes help explain why the Byzantine emperors of late antiquity got so little joy out of their efforts to get everyone on the same theological page by holding large church councils to resolve contentious issues—in marked contrast to the way in which Justinian was able to codify Roman law to his own satisfaction without serious challenge from anyone. By the time of the rise of Islam a fairly clear geographical pattern had emerged: the core of the empire was Orthodox, whereas the eastern and southern fringes—Armenia, Syria, and Egypt—were Monophysite, and the Nestorians were yet farther to the east, in the Persian Empire.

In 626, however, theological nitpicking was not at the forefront. Instead, just as in the case of the Third Fijār, a woman played a key part in the story—but in a very different role. Before the siege began the patriarch Sergius, the head of the Byzantine church, placed icons of the Virgin Mary at the gates of the city to ensure that she would protect them. At one of the gates he addressed himself to the enemy who was threatening the city: "A woman, the Mother of God, will quell all your boldness and boasting with one command, for she is truly the Mother of Him who drowned Pharaoh with all his army in the Red Sea."[23] The rout of the Slavs in their canoes was likewise attributed to "the intercession of our Lady the Mother of God," and the pagan Kagan was quoted as having seen "a woman in stately dress rushing about on the wall all alone"[24]—obviously the Virgin defending her city from his infidel hordes. Such stories may not reveal much about relations between Byzantine men and women on the street—for that we might do marginally better to turn to Theodora (d. 548), the actress whom Justinian made his empress and who looks us straight in the eye, without a face veil and in mixed company, in the mosaics of San Vitale in Ravenna. But the role of the Virgin in 626 certainly tells us something about the development of Byzantine religion. In pagan times the patron deities of cities might well be female, as in the case of Ephesus, where the preaching of Saint Paul elicited the angry response "Great is Diana of the Ephesians!" (Acts 19:28). Thanks to the rise of the cult of the Virgin in late antiquity, the people of Constantinople had in effect found for themselves a Christian counterpart of such a pagan goddess.

22. Quoted in P. Brown, *Power and persuasion in late antiquity*, Madison 1992, 89–90.
23. Quoted in A. Cameron, "Images of authority," *Past & Present*, 84 (1979), 20–21.
24. *Chronicon Paschale*, trans. M. Whitby and M. Whitby, Liverpool 1989, 178, 180.

The Persian Empire

Whereas the rulers of the Byzantine Empire belonged to a whole series of different families, the Persian Empire from its inception in 224 to its demise in 651 was almost the exclusive possession of the Sasanian dynasty.[25] The second ruler of this dynasty was Shāhpuhr I (ruled 240–70). To burnish his image he had a long account of his glorious deeds inscribed on a rock surface near the site of Persepolis in southwestern Iran, and to get his message out he made the inscription trilingual. One text was written in his own language, Persian. Another was in Parthian, the closely related language of the Arsacids, the Parthian dynasty that had ruled Iran from the third century BC until displaced by the Sasanians in 224. The third was in Greek, a language widely known in the Middle East ever since its conquest by the Macedonian Alexander the Great (ruled 336–323 BC) had opened it up to Greek colonization. That conquest had ended the rule of the Achaemenids, the Persian dynasty that dominated the Middle East from the sixth to the fourth century BC and likewise celebrated itself in inscriptions in Persian.

As all this makes clear, Persian has had a long history, and as might be expected it has changed over the course of it. Unlike Arabic, it belongs to the Indo-European family, which in contrast to Semitic cannot have originated in the Middle East. Within this family Persian belongs to the Indo-Iranian branch, speakers of which are likely to have arrived in Iran from the steppes in the second millennium BC. The oldest Iranian text we possess is the Gāthās, composed in an archaic Iranian language quite close to the Sanskrit of the Vēdas. We first hear of the Persians in the ninth century BC, but the oldest specifically Persian texts are the Achaemenid inscriptions, composed in a form of the language known as "Old Persian." There is then a silence of several centuries until the early Sasanian inscriptions, which are in "Middle Persian," as is a body of literature preserved by Zoroastrian priests (we will come to Zoroastrianism shortly). The fact that both Persian and English (like Latin and Greek) are Indo-European languages is not, in general, of much help to English speakers, but the following words for close relatives should be fairly transparent: *pidar*, *mādar*, *birādar*. As cited here, these words are in "New Persian," a form of the language that emerged only after the rise of Islam. Persian was originally the language of the Persians in a narrow sense—that is, the people of Persis or Fārs, the region in southwestern Iran from which both the Achaemenids and the Sasanians stemmed. But as the imperial language of both these dynasties its use naturally spread well beyond its original homeland, particularly among the elite. Today it is recognized without contestation as the national language of Iran,

25. For surveys of the history of the empire see R. N. Frye, "The political history of Iran under the Sasanians," in *The Cambridge history of Iran*, Cambridge 1968–91, vol. 3; J. Wiesehöfer, "The late Sasanian Near East," in *The new Cambridge history of Islam*, Cambridge 2010, vol. 1.

but there are still dialects in the north of the country that are closer to Parthian than to Persian.

Returning to Shāhpuhr's inscription in its Middle Persian version, he introduces himself as follows: "I, the Mazdā-worshipping god Shāhpuhr, King of Kings of Ērān and Anērān, of the seed of the gods . . . am the sovereign of Ērānshahr."[26] Several things in this short passage are worth a comment.

First, the passage tells us something about Persian identity in this period. The key word is Ērān. If we go forward in time, we can see in it the name of the modern country of Iran, but in Shāhpuhr's usage it is rather the name of a people, the Iranians, who are contrasted with Anērān, the non-Iranians ("an-" is the same negative prefix as that found in Greek words such as "anarchy"). The kingdom that the Iranians possess is Ērānshahr, "the kingdom of the Iranians," and an inscription of the later third century stresses the role of the reigning monarch in keeping Ērānshahr "in peace and confident" and ensuring its well-being.[27] If instead of going forward we go back in time, we can make a further connection. The people called Ērān in the Middle Persian text are referred to as Aryān in the Parthian version and as Arians (not to be confused with the Christian heretics of the same name) in the Greek. This is a very ancient but also very familiar ethnic term. It is well attested not just in the Avesta, the body of religious texts of which the Gāthās form part, but also in the form Ārya in the oldest Sanskrit texts; from there it eventually made its way to the Nazis. In its third-century context Shāhpuhr's use of the term Ērān seems to aim at pitching a big tent—big enough to include Persians, Parthians, and no doubt other Iranian ethnic groups. Thus the rarity of references to Persians in the third-century Sasanian inscriptions could be deliberate. In this they contrast sharply with the Achaemenid inscriptions, where references to Persia and Persians abound; thus in an inscription at Persepolis, Darius I (ruled 522–486 BC) speaks proudly of "this country Persia which Ahura Mazdā bestowed upon me, good, possessed of good horses, possessed of good men,"[28] and he affirms that thanks to his god, Ahura Mazdā, and himself, it does not fear any other country. He rarely uses the word Aryan, though at one point he describes himself as "a Persian, son of a Persian, an Aryan, having Aryan lineage."[29] By the time of Shāhpuhr, Persians and Parthians had long been rubbing off on each other. The very name Shāhpuhr, "son (*puhr*) of the king (*shāh*)," is an example, since the form of the word for "son" used here is Parthian, not Persian. By Islamic times the Parthians seem to have disappeared as an ethnic group. A tenth-century Iranian

26. A. Maricq, "Res gestae divi Saporis," *Syria*, 35 (1958), 304–5.

27. H. Humbach and P. O. Skjærvø, *The Sassanian inscription of Paikuli*, Wiesbaden 1978–83, part 3.1, 60–61.

28. R. G. Kent, *Old Persian*, New Haven 1953, 136a §2.

29. Kent, *Old Persian*, 138a §2.

writer still knew the Parthian form "Aryān" as the name of a people, but he equated this people with the Persians.

Second, the passage tells us something about Persian religion. As in the paganism of ancient Greece and Rome, there are many gods, and the line between gods and humans is not sharply drawn—Shāhpuhr is descended from the gods and is himself a god. He does, however, tie himself closely to the cult of one particular god, namely Mazdā. This is Ahura Mazdā, the good god of Zoroastrianism, the ancient dualistic religion of Iran that was closely tied to Iranian ethnic identity. The linkage between Ahura Mazdā and Persian kingship was an old one, already conspicuous under the Achaemenids. Darius, boasting of his deeds in a famous trilingual rock inscription of his own, gives credit to this god: "By the favor of Ahura Mazdā I am King; Ahura Mazdā bestowed the kingdom upon me."[30] But Zoroastrianism was considerably older than the Achaemenids. Indeed, its oldest text, the Gāthās, could easily date from around 1000 BC. The religion flourished until the rise of Islam, though thereafter its adherents were gradually reduced to small communities in Iran and western India. In Shāhpuhr's time Zoroastrianism was heavily backed by the state; as one Middle Persian text puts it, the helpmate of the Good Religion is kingship. Kerdīr, whom Shāhpuhr put in charge of religious affairs, celebrated himself in an inscription just like his patron. He boasted about his closeness to Shāhpuhr and his successors and described how he had ensured that the cult flourished from Mesopotamia to Peshawar, protecting it outside the empire wherever Shāhpuhr's armies burned and pillaged. He tormented heretics until he "made them better," and converted many unbelievers. Jews, Buddhists, Hindus, Nazarenes, Christians, Baptists, and Manichaeans were all of them, he proudly declared, "smitten in the empire."[31]

Third, Shāhpuhr lays claim to a characteristic Iranian royal title, "King of Kings." This title, too, was old. Darius used it in introducing himself at the beginning of his long and boastful inscription: "I am Darius the Great King, King of Kings, King in Persia, King of countries."[32] The Arsacid rulers of the Parthian Empire frequently included the title (in Greek) on their coins. It likewise had a distinguished future: it was to be revived in Islamic times in the form Shāhanshāh and seen as a key symbol in a continuing tradition of Persian statecraft. Occasionally it was matched by the female equivalent, "Queen of Queens." A couple of the luckless rulers at the tail end of the Sasanian dynasty were women, allegedly prompting the Prophet Muḥammad to observe that "a people who appoint a woman as their ruler will not prosper."[33]

30. Kent, *Old Persian*, 119b §5.

31. D. N. Mackenzie, *Kerdir's inscription*, in *Iranische Denkmäler*, Lieferung 13, Reihe II, Berlin 1989, 58–59 §11, §16. For a different perspective see R. E. Payne, *A state of mixture*, Oakland 2015, ch. 1, "The myth of Zoroastrian intolerance."

32. Kent, *Old Persian*, 119a §1.

33. Bukhārī, *Ṣaḥīḥ*, Beirut 1987, 7–8:687 no. 1923.

After the third century the Persians seem to have lost the habit of inscribing their deeds on stone. This means that for the subsequent history of their empire we depend largely on books. But whose books? For us to possess a society's record of its own history, two conditions must be satisfied. The first is that its members should have written about it. This cannot be taken for granted; even societies that possess the skill of writing may not choose to use it to record their history. The second is that the books, or at least a few of them, should survive into our time. But unless books are preserved archaeologically—in caves, deserts, or waterlogged tombs—they will survive only if people think them worth preserving throughout the intervening generations. Here a number of interrelated historical variables come into play. One is political: other things being equal, the literary heritage of an elite culture that is disestablished by unsympathetic conquerors is in danger of disappearing. Another is religious: where religious truth is understood as a zero-sum game, the books of a sect or faith that goes extinct have little chance of survival. Yet another is institutional: a book that has found its way into something like a monastic library has a better chance of survival than does one in private circulation. In the case of Middle Persian literature, the prospects for the survival of historical works, though not hopeless, were dim. Middle Persian books reach us in their original language only if they were continuously transmitted by Zoroastrian priests, and these priests were not much interested in history. By contrast, some Muslim scholars of the early Islamic period were very interested in the history of pre-Islamic Iran, and they made use of Arabic translations of a late Sasanian chronicle known as the *Khwadāy-nāmag*, the "Book of sovereigns" (*khwadāy* is the same word as that used by Shāhpuhr when he described himself as "the sovereign of Ērānshahr"). But the accounts of Sasanian history given by these scholars are divergent enough that we have only a rather fuzzy notion of what the Sasanian chronicle originally said. We also have the works of contemporary historians writing in Syriac, Armenian, Greek, and Latin to fall back on. They can tell us a lot about the wars between the empires, but their knowledge of the internal history of the Persian Empire tends to be sketchy, particularly in the case of the Greek and Latin sources.

What, then, can we say if we turn to the sinews, as opposed to the symbols, of empire? Fortunately the broad outlines are clear enough. The foundation of imperial power was an ethnic division of labor, or more precisely a geographical one, that went back to the sixth century BC. According to Herodotus, the Persians once suggested to Cyrus (ruled 560–530 BC), the founder of the Achaemenid Empire, that they should leave their "small and barren country" and take possession of a better one. Cyrus warned them that if they did so they should expect to be ruled by others rather than be rulers themselves. "Soft countries," he told them in an anticipation of Ibn Khaldūn, "breed soft men; it is not the property of any one soil to produce fine fruits and good soldiers too." The Persians listened to the wisdom of their ruler and "chose rather to live in a rugged land and rule than to cultivate rich plains and be slaves."[34] In other words, the military manpower that created and sustained the empire was recruited from the Persian highlands, the land Darius praised as "possessed of good horses, possessed of good men." But this did not mean that the rich plains with their fine fruits and servile cultivators were of no consequence. On the contrary, it was the lowlands of Mesopotamia, irrigated by the Tigris and the Euphrates and inhabited by Aramaic-speaking peasants, that provided the empire with its fiscal sinews—its tax power. Mesopotamia lived on borrowed rainfall brought to it by rivers rising in eastern Anatolia. As long as it lasted, this combination of highland manpower and lowland tax power provided a firm foundation for an empire based in the eastern region of the Middle East. It worked for the Achaemenids, the Arsacids, and the Sasanians. What became of it in the Islamic period, and what that meant for the geopolitics of the Middle East, we will see in a later chapter.

The Avars

North of the Byzantine and Persian Empires lay the world of the steppes, the grasslands extending across northern Eurasia from Manchuria to Hungary. This band of territory was the natural habitat of the horse, whose domestication a few thousand years earlier had made possible the spread of nomadic pastoralism throughout the region. Economically these nomads may have been more dependent on sheep than on horses, but it was their horses that made them so formidable for the civilizations to the south. In an age in which the horse was crucial to military power, the nomads of the steppes were habituated to riding from childhood. As a fifth-century European writer put it in describing the Huns, "You would think the limbs of man and beast were born together, so firmly does the rider always stick to the horse."[35] These people, he added, were not just transported on horseback; they lived there. Their mobility made them almost impossible for settled empires to conquer. As Herodotus observed of the Scythians in the region north of the Black Sea,

> Such is their manner of life that no one who invades their country can escape destruction, and if they wish to avoid engaging with an enemy, that enemy cannot by any possibility come to grips with them. A people without fortified towns, living, as the Scythians do, in wagons which they take with them wherever they go, accustomed, one and all, to fight on horseback with bows and arrows, and dependent for their food not upon agriculture but upon their cattle:

34. Herodotus, *The histories*, 599 (9.122).
35. Sidonius, *Poems [and] letters*, trans. W. B. Anderson, London 1936–65, 1:31.

> How can such a people fail to defeat the attempt of an invader not only to subdue them, but even to make contact with them?[36]

More ominously, their equestrian skills made it possible for these nomads not just to evade empires but to conquer them, or at least subject them to severe military damage. As late as the seventeenth century Manchu nomads were to conquer the whole of China. The Middle East had some protection thanks to the Black Sea, the Caucasus, and the Caspian, but a nomad army could easily avoid these barriers by taking a route to the east of the Caspian, or to the west of the Black Sea if it could succeed in crossing the Danube, or even along the narrow coastal route on the eastern side of the Caucasus. Only the development of modern warfare gradually rendered steppe nomads militarily obsolete.

How did these steppe nomads of the north compare with the desert nomads of the south? In some ways they were very similar. Seen from the viewpoint of the sedentary agrarian civilizations, both were wild, mobile, and dangerous tribal societies in which almost every adult male was well armed. But there were a couple of differences that tended to make steppe nomads much more threatening. One was their access to unlimited supplies of horses—whereas desert nomads, as Ibn Khaldūn emphasized, tended to depend on the camel, an animal of American origin that had considerable military potential for transport but was of little use on the battlefield. Consider even just the awkwardness of riding on a camel: do you place your saddle in front of the hump (the solution adopted by the Tuareg in the Sahara) or behind it (a southeast Arabian solution), or do you construct an elevated saddle that can go on top of it (the most widespread Arabian solution)? The other difference was that as pastoralists go, steppe nomads were relatively affluent. They thus had resources that favored a steeper social hierarchy than was seen among the nomads of the desert. The peoples of the steppes were typically divided into nobles and commoners, whereas the nomadic society of the Arabian desert tended to be rather flat—"All alike are warriors of equal rank," as a fourth-century Roman observer said of the Saracens.[37] Furthermore, steppe nomads had rulers who could amass power on an imperial scale, and they were thus in a different league from the petty kings of Arabia.

These advantages do not, however, mean that steppe empires could compare with sedentary empires in terms of political economy. While a state built on grass is likely to be more robust than one built on sand, it is likely to be much flimsier than one built on rich plains with fine fruits. This explains why, on average, steppe empires did not last as long as sedentary ones did—unless, like the Manchus, they were able to conquer and hold a sedentary empire. In comparison to the states that

36. Herodotus, *The histories*, 257 (4.46).

37. Ammianus Marcellinus, [*History*], trans. J. C. Rolfe, Cambridge, MA 1940–52, 1:27 (14.4.3).

ruled the world's sedentary civilizations, steppe empires seemed to appear out of nowhere and disappear into nowhere. Partly this impression arises from the fact that nomads are slow to write books, so we are often dependent on scraps of information from external sources for our knowledge of their history. But it also reflects the fact that steppe empires lacked the staying power of sedentary ones.

The Avars are a case in point. They arrived in Europe in 558 from somewhere to the east; back there they seem to have been closely connected to the Turks, another nomadic people of the steppes, who claimed that the Avars had been their slaves. Like the Turks, the Avars were no doubt a tribal people, and they seem to have practiced a similar form of paganism. As among the Turks, the ruler bore the title Kagan. Once in Europe the Avars soon established a state based in the grasslands of what was later to be Hungary. They also came to rule over a large Slav population, some of whom we encountered as the naval wing of the Avar forces at the siege of Constantinople in 626. The Avar state was then at its peak and displayed an alarming proficiency in the art of siege warfare. Yet as we saw, the Kagan called off the siege after only ten days. The reason he gave the Byzantine defenders for this surprising withdrawal was that he had not made sufficient arrangements to provision his army. Alternative explanations might be unrest in the Avar heartland or dissension within his forces—at one point Avars were killing Slavs who had fled from the naval disaster. Either way, this failure suggests the limits of Avar state building. Their polity nevertheless survived in a diminished form till destroyed by Charlemagne around 800. Thereafter the Avars disappeared as a people; today no population claims descent from them or speaks their language (the Avars of the northern Caucasus are not related to them).

As their fate suggests, the Avars themselves will play no further part in our story. But they have been worth meeting because steppe nomads similar to them in character repeatedly disturbed the peace of the sedentary empires. A famous example is the threat posed by the Huns. They were already making trouble in the steppes to the north of the Caucasus in the later fourth century, and in 395 they bypassed the mountains on the east to overrun parts of both the Byzantine and Persian Empires. In the 440s, under the leadership of their famous king Attila, they invaded the Balkans before moving on to western Europe; his plans also extended to the Persian Empire but were frustrated by his death in 453 and the collapse of his kingdom. Like the Avars, the Huns subsequently ceased to exist as a people. A later example of a steppe empire is that of the Turks, much farther to the east, which we will take up in a later chapter. Here it is enough to note their role, or that of their subordinates, the Khazars, in the final war between the two sedentary empires. In the 620s Heraclius reached out to them, persuading them to help him against the Persians by invading their empire along the same route that the Huns had taken. Just as the Persians were in league with one steppe empire against the Byzantines, so the Byzantines were in league with another steppe empire against the Persians. A nomadic empire on your doorstep was bad news, but on your enemy's doorstep it was reassuringly good news.

Relations between the empires

Byzantine and Persian rulers had good reason to lose some sleep over the intermittent threats posed by nomadic empires on their northern borders. But for each of the two sedentary empires the primary danger was the other empire. An imperial state is most secure if it is surrounded by a lot of loose packaging—in physical terms by mountains, deserts, or seas; in political terms by no-man's-lands, subservient client states, clusters of small city-states, or anarchic tribes whose unruliness poses only a local threat. For most of its history the Achaemenid Empire had had the benefit of such circumstances, as in general did empires based in northern India and northern China. But the Byzantine and Persian Empires of late antiquity conspicuously failed to enjoy them. This was a case of two empires eyeball to eyeball, glowering at each other across the mountains of Armenia and the plains of Mesopotamia. There were, admittedly, some mitigating factors in the situation. Most obviously, the fact that the Mediterranean and the Indian Ocean did not interconnect made naval conflict between the empires difficult, though by the same token it was bad for trade. At the same time the mountains of Armenia did something to impede hostilities and could encourage the formation of client states, though these proved to be of limited duration. But the lowlands of Mesopotamia had the opposite effect. Add to this the fact that the Persian capital, Ctesiphon, was located in the plains less than three hundred miles from the border between the two empires, and we have a recipe for endless, destabilizing wars.

The surprise is that down to the end of the sixth century the wars, though fairly frequent, did not in fact prove destabilizing. In the third century, for example, wars broke out in or around 230, 238, 243, 256, 283, and 297; after forty years of peace they resumed in the fourth century, almost disappeared in the fifth, and flared up again in the sixth. These wars could be brutal. The Persians took the major Roman city of Antioch in northwestern Syria in 256, deporting much of its population, and again in 540, when they sacked it. The Romans (we cannot yet call them Byzantines) took Ctesiphon in 283. But sooner or later the balance would be restored, and there could be long periods of peace. Indeed, from time to time there were notably cooperative interactions. In the early fifth century a Byzantine emperor appointed his counterpart the guardian of his son and successor, a responsibility the Sasanian ruler took very seriously. The last major Sasanian ruler, Khusraw II, owed his throne to the assistance he received against a dangerous rebel from the Byzantine emperor Maurice (ruled 582–602), and it is reported that the Persian court went into mourning on receiving news of Maurice's execution in a Byzantine coup d'état in 602.

This balance of power rested on the existence of two distinct imperial heartlands in the Middle East, each of which provided a foundation for both economic and military strength. There were nevertheless significant asymmetries between the two empires. In military terms the Persian Empire was more muscular. Its very salient aristocracy was military rather than civilian, and the culture of the empire was more insistently warlike than that of the Byzantines was. This is how Bahrām I (ruled 271–74) berated Mani, the founder of Manichaeism, after telling him he was not welcome: "Eh, what are you good for, since you go neither fighting nor hunting?"[38] Our fourth-century Roman observer remarked of the art of the Persians that "nothing in their country is painted or sculptured except slaughter in diverse forms and scenes of war."[39] But in economic terms the Byzantine Empire had the edge. In comparison with its rival it had a more pronounced maritime character. It was an eastern Mediterranean empire, whereas large parts of the Persian Empire were effectively landlocked—too much so for it to count as an Indian Ocean empire. The coasts of the Persian Gulf and southeastern Iran were for the most part thinly populated desert; the Mediterranean parallel to this was the southern shore between Egypt and North Africa, a long stretch but not one that denied maritime access to any densely populated region behind it. This contrast between the empires matters because communications by sea were easier and cheaper than communications by land, especially when it came to moving bulk goods over any distance. In the days when Rome ruled the Mediterranean it was less expensive to transport grain by sea from one end of the Mediterranean to the other than it was to move it seventy-five miles overland by cart. It is not surprising, then, that the Persian Empire seems to have been less urbanized, and also less centralized. Thus Sasanian rulers might appoint their sons as sub-kings of particular territories, a practice unheard of in the Byzantine Empire. Also noteworthy is the fact that the Sasanians used their invasions of Byzantine territory to seize large numbers of captives, whom they took back to their empire and resettled there; the Byzantines showed no interest in doing likewise when invading Persian territory. The disparity between the military and economic balances surfaces in a recurrent theme in the relations between the two empires: it was the Byzantine rulers who would grease the wheels of peacemaking by providing substantial amounts of cash for their Persian counterparts.

In the early seventh century this remarkably stable coexistence of the two empires came to an end. The final war between them lasted for a whole generation, from 603 to 628, and the stakes went well beyond the apportionment of the borderlands between the two empires. It was precipitated by a concern hardly

38. Translated in W. B. Henning, "Mani's last journey," *Bulletin of the School of Oriental and African Studies*, 10 (1942), 951.

39. Ammianus Marcellinus, [*History*], 2:457 (XXIV, 6, 3).

commensurate with its outcome: Khusraw II wanted to pursue vengeance against the Byzantine usurper Phocas (ruled 602–10) for overthrowing and executing Khusraw's benefactor, the emperor Maurice. But when as a result of an internal upheaval Phocas was overthrown and executed in turn, Khusraw declined to make peace with the new emperor, Heraclius. He then went on to extend his territories in a way that no previous Sasanian ruler had done. Between 611 and 619 his armies conquered Syria and Egypt, ravaged Anatolia, and reached the Bosphorus more than a decade before we meet them there again in the context of the siege of 626. At this point it looked as if the Persian Empire was set to become the sole empire in the Middle East, a return to the situation that had obtained in Achaemenid times. But in the face of imminent catastrophe Heraclius adopted an extraordinarily daring strategy that explains his absence from his capital when the Avars were laying siege to it. Instead of concentrating on the defense of what was left of his territories, he invaded the Persian Empire from the northwest, thereby posing a threat to its heartlands that soon brought him within striking distance of Ctesiphon. The reaction at the Persian court was dramatic. A conspiracy against Khusraw was mounted with the full knowledge of Heraclius. In 628 Khusraw was overthrown and executed, and the new ruler promptly offered to restore all captured Byzantine territory in return for peace. Having obtained what he wanted through regime change, Heraclius turned round and went home; he showed no interest in conquering the Persian Empire. Left to themselves, the two empires might now have licked their wounds and reverted to the old balance of power.

The empires and Arabia

Imperial options

In comparison with the steppes to the north and the deserts to the south, the lands ruled by the two empires of the Middle East were a densely populated band of agrarian civilization. These empires had peasantries, aristocracies, bureaucracies, professional armies, and cities, and such resources naturally gave them disproportionate power in the region. But they could also make them the ham in the sandwich, victims of the rapacity of their warlike nomadic neighbors on both sides. Yet there was a wide gap between the northern and southern threats. To the north the steppes gave rise to nomadic empires like that of the Avars; they came and went, but while they lasted they could be very dangerous. To the south the desert was home to petty kings and stateless tribes who might raid imperial territory but spent most of their energies on small-scale warfare among themselves. That they too might be geopolitically dangerous were they to unite would have seemed idle speculation, since nothing in the track record of the Arabs suggested that they were likely to do that. It was accordingly the northern nomads, not those of the south, that caused the rulers of the empires to lie awake at night. A book about the military affairs of the Byzantine Empire, plausibly attributed to the emperor Maurice, includes a very practical chapter about fighting various troublesome peoples. As we would expect, he starts with the disciplined Persians before going on to the hardy nomads of the steppes—the Avars and the Turks. He then concerns himself with the impetuous Franks and Lombards and ends up with the anarchic Slavs. He does not even mention the Arabs—unlike Leo VI (ruled 886–912), who, thanks to the rise of Islam, has a lot to say about them in his own book on military tactics. This neglect would, of course, turn out to be an illustration of the danger of expecting the future to be like the past. If we factor in our knowledge of what was about to happen a few decades into the seventh century, we can see that in fact the empires faced acute danger on both sides. In this they were in a situation that was unique among the major Eurasian civilizations. Other civilizations also had to contend with steppe nomads, but none of them faced desert nomads in addition. In the case of India and China there were none, and in the European case the Mediterranean blocked invasion from the desert.

How, then, did the empires relate to Arabia? The parts of the peninsula where the water supply was best could be worth owning, and as a result the Sasanians had long had a presence on the southern coast of the Persian Gulf, in Baḥrayn and Oman. But when Khusraw I (ruled 531–79) wanted to send a punitive force against a tribe in the interior, he gave up the idea on being told that "their land is a bad land, made up of deserts and wastes, with tracks that cannot be followed."[40] This did not stop the Persians' sending an expedition by sea to Yemen around 570, thereby establishing a foothold in a region with sufficient resources to have already attracted invasion from Ethiopia in the third and sixth centuries. The Byzantines, by contrast, made no attempt to repeat the expedition of Aelius Gallus. They had possession of a small island at the southern end of the Sinai Peninsula but seem to have maintained no presence along the Arabian coast of the Red Sea. Nor did they have one in the interior of the northern Ḥijāz southeast of Ayla—in contrast to the situation in the second century after the Romans annexed the Nabatean kingdom in 106. The emperor Justinian was the nominal owner of some palm groves in the interior, but a sixth-century Byzantine historian explains that for him to take effective possession of this territory was out of the question: over a distance of ten days' journey the land between Byzantine Palestine and the palm groves was "completely destitute of human presence and absolutely dry."[41] Indeed, in economic terms most of northern and central Arabia was not worth bothering with. It was, as a derogatory Middle Persian text had it, a hot, dry desert whose people ate insects, rats, and snakes. Given its lack of resources and the refractory

40. *The history of al-Ṭabarī*, Albany 1985–2007 (hereafter Ṭabarī, *History*), 5:290.

41. Prokopios, *The wars of Justinian*, trans. H. B. Dewing, Indianapolis 2014, 50 (1.19.13).

character of its population, the cost of providing government to such a wilderness would have been greater than any fiscal benefit that could have accrued from the enterprise. But the catch was security. Left to themselves, the Arab tribes would take to raiding imperial territory, degrading fiscally valuable resources by disrupting agriculture and carrying off captives as slaves. Thus in the fourth century Arabs from the southern coast of the Persian Gulf are recorded to have raided Fārs: "They seized the local people's herds of cattle, their cultivated lands, and their means of subsistence, and did a great deal of damage in those regions."[42] Then in Mesopotamia in 484, according to a local bishop, drought led to an influx of Arab tribes from the south that devastated the villages, even in the mountains. In 501 it was the turn of Syria: the Arabs appeared "like a hurricane"[43] and quickly disappeared with their booty before Byzantine troops could engage them. In 610 raiders from Arabia entered Syria and "pillaged and laid waste many lands, committed many massacres of men and burned without compassion or pity."[44] The imperial response in the first case was savage though delayed retaliation; in the second case it was coordination between the empires; in the third it was a diplomatic mission that issued in a peace the following year; and in the last case, in the middle of the long war with the Persians, no response is recorded. Provided the empires were reasonably strong such incursions were the worst that could be expected. Centuries earlier, in an age of imperial weakness under Arsacid rule around the turn of our era, the most the Arabs had done was establish a set of minor principalities in Syria and Mesopotamia—evidence that Ibn Khaldūn somewhat exaggerated the inability of the Arabs to form states. In late antiquity such seizure of imperial territory was no longer an option for the Arabs, but raiding was still on the cards. Ad hoc responses apart, what were imperial rulers to do about it?

In general, rulers had a variety of options in dealing with their Arab problem, all of them requiring some expenditure. They could build a barrier to keep the nomads out, dispatch occasional punitive expeditions to teach the nomads a lesson, station troops in forts along the frontier, co-opt the nomads by recruiting them into imperial armies, or outsource the problem by picking one nomad chief and rewarding him for keeping the rest in check. Of these options, anti-nomad barriers appear occasionally in the history of the Middle East, but never on a Chinese scale. Punitive expeditions are more common, and we have already encountered ones mounted by both the Byzantines and the Persians. The fortified and garrisoned frontier was the classic strategy of imperial Rome in the Syrian borderlands from the second century down to the early fifth. Recruiting Arabs into the army

42. Ṭabarī, *History*, 5:51–52, no doubt deriving from a Middle Persian source.
43. *The chronicle of Theophanes the Confessor*, trans. C. Mango and R. Scott, Oxford 1997, 222.
44. *Theophilus of Edessa's chronicle*, trans. R. Hoyland, Liverpool 2011, 63–64.

was a practice of some antiquity—Gindibu and his thousand camel riders could well have been such mercenaries. Herodotus describes Arab archers, some on foot and some on camels, who formed part of the massive army assembled by the Achaemenid king Xerxes (ruled 486–465 BC) for his ill-starred invasion of Greece. Likewise, the Seleucid ruler of the Fertile Crescent had ten thousand Arabs fighting for him when he lost a key battle against the army of Egypt in 217 BC. Such recruitment was common in late antiquity; for example, the Arab troops who were sent by an Arab queen to fight for the Byzantines in Thrace in 378 are said to have struck terror into the hearts of the Goths. In this period recruitment came to be combined with outsourcing, whereby the empires provided the resources to maintain client Arab states in the northern borderlands of Arabia. This last option will repay a closer look in the context of the Arabian interior.

The Arabian interior

Given the imperial presence on the fringes of Arabia, it is not unreasonable to suppose that the empires would occasionally intervene directly in the interior. But it is hard to say how much faith we should put in the rare attestations of such intervention in the later Arabic sources. We read that when Quraysh took over Mecca they had the help of the Byzantine emperor. Similarly, in the story about the Qurashī who sought to make himself king of Mecca, we are told that he did so as a Byzantine client. In the same way we hear about a Persian role in appointing kings and collecting taxes in sixth-century Yathrib, however geographically unlikely that might seem. In none of these cases is there any indication that a military expedition was involved, and the only evidence we have in Byzantine sources for imperial involvement in the interior relates to diplomatic missions in the first third of the sixth century. All these reports contrast with the hard evidence we possess of military interventions in the politics of the Arabian desert mounted by the rulers of the Yemen. As their inscriptions show, the Ḥimyarite kingdom and its successor state under Ethiopian rule made considerable efforts to project their power to the north. They had diplomatic contact with Arabian actors as far away as the northern edge of the peninsula, and more significantly, they mounted military expeditions to northern Arabia in the fourth, fifth, and sixth centuries. The obvious question about such expeditions is what they achieved: did they conquer territory on a long-term basis, were they just temporary interventions, or was the outcome something in between? The inscriptions are, of course, royal propaganda and so to be taken with a pinch of salt; if we went by the coins that the kings of England minted down to the late eighteenth century, we would think that they also ruled France. But leaving that aside, if we parse the details the inscriptions supply, the answer to our question is mixed. On one occasion we hear of pledges or hostages being taken by Abraha, including a son of a prominent northern figure who had been defeated—a measure clearly intended to ensure continuing good behavior. Yet the same person is then appointed as the victor's deputy, suggesting a face-saving arrangement that left things much as they were before. At the same time Abraha speaks of this expedition as his fourth against the same enemy, which indicates that the first three had achieved no lasting effect. It is also telling that none of these inscriptions mentions the bottom line of successful conquest: tribute. In short, what we have here could have more to do with outsourcing than with territorial expansion.

Outsourcing is in fact a prominent pattern in the handling of the Arab tribes by the settled states on their borders—the two empires and the Ḥimyarite kingdom. The most enduring arrangement of this kind was the relationship between the Persian Empire and the Lakhmids. This dynasty came to be based in Ḥīra on the border of Mesopotamia, and it ruled from around 300 to around 600. The "king of all the Arabs" was a Lakhmid, as was the king who was killed by the poet. The Lakhmids' autonomy was limited by the stationing of Persian troops in their capital and by its geographical location close to the settled lands directly ruled by the Persians. The Byzantines likewise had their "phylarchs," tribal chiefs on whom they relied for stability on their Arabian border. The palm groves that Justinian supposedly owned in the northern Ḥijāz were billed as a gift from a prominent tribal chief in the region; it was the thought that counted, and in return Justinian appointed this chief phylarch over the Arabs of Palestine. In that capacity "he preserved the land intact from plunder"[45]—something he was well qualified to do, being fearsome and energetic. This was a small-scale local arrangement, but around 528 the Byzantines picked one particular family usually known as the Ghassānids to defend their Syrian frontier against the Lakhmids but also, no doubt, to keep order among the tribes; unlike the Lakhmids, the Ghassānids were desert dwellers.

The Ḥimyarites played the same game, insofar as we can reconstruct it. Here we have to go on isolated scraps of hard evidence together with an abundance of soft evidence provided by the later Arabic sources, reporting traditions that are often confused. Among the neighbors of the Ḥimyarites in southwestern Arabia was the Arab tribe of Kinda, first mentioned in a South Arabian inscription of 220. Toward the middle of the fourth century a Kindī came to rule over what we know as the kingdom of Kinda in central Arabia. This does not mean that the tribe had migrated northward en masse. Rather, the founder, Ḥujr ibn ʿAmr, seems to have established his rule over the tribes of the region with the help of the Ḥimyarites. Unfortunately the one brief inscription that mentions him says only "Ḥujr son of

45. Prokopios, *The wars of Justinian*, 50 (1.19.11).

ʿAmr king of Kinda,"[46] but that at least guarantees his historicity. His son and successor was far less successful despite the continuing theme of Ḥimyarite support in the Arabic traditions about the kingdom. But his grandson Ḥārith son of ʿAmr revived the kingdom, which then enjoyed its finest days till his death in 528. Again the traditions stress the Ḥimyarites' role in supporting him, and they present him as ruling over a vast territory in central Arabia. He was also throwing his weight around as far afield as the northern borders of Arabia. If some teasing identifications are correct, he was behind the Arab raid on Syria in 501 and was the ruler with whom the Byzantines made peace in 502. What is for sure is that toward the end of his life he attacked and seized the Lakhmid capital of Ḥīra, taking up residence there for a while. But after he was killed in obscure circumstances his kingdom fell apart, never to be restored. His grandson Imru'u 'l-Qays (d. ca. 550), as well as being a great poet, spent his life seeking to avenge his grandfather's death and to revive his kingdom, but without success; the vivid traditions that were handed down about his travails would make a good film but bad history. He, too, is said to have looked to the Ḥimyarites for support. Other members of the family took refuge in the old southern homeland of the tribe of Kinda. As to the structure of the kingdom, the one indication we have is that Ḥārith is said to have assigned particular tribes to each of his several sons. There is also a mention of tribute owed by a certain tribe to one of them—being good Arabs, the tribesmen rebelled and killed him rather than pay it. As we might expect, there is no sign of bureaucracy. Outsourcing also extended to Oman, where the role of Arab client was played by a family known as the Julandās. They did not, however, figure in the affairs of Arabia at large.

It is clear from this discussion that the age of the Lakhmids, the Ghassānids, and the kings of Kinda was marked by a scale of political activity that the Arab tribes would not have developed if left to themselves. Earlier in this chapter we raised the question whether the Arabian desert was always as lacking in large-scale political organization as it was on the eve of the rise of Islam, and we can now answer the question in the negative. But this does not mean that outsourcing had changed the dispositions of Arab tribesmen in any drastic way. Back in the eighth century BC the Assyrian ruler Sargon (ruled 722–705 BC) had mounted an attack on "the Arabs who live, far away, in the desert and who know neither overseers nor officials and who had not yet brought their tribute to any king."[47] This characterization would have been immediately recognizable at any time in late antiquity. There were nevertheless significant changes in the decades immediately preceding the rise of Islam. One was the tightening of the Persian encirclement of Arabia with the expedition to the Yemen around 570 and the conquest of Syria

46. C. Robin, "Le royaume ḥujride," *Comptes rendus des séances de l'Académie des Inscriptions et Belles-Lettres*, 140 (1996), 694.

47. J. B. Pritchard (ed.), *Ancient Near Eastern texts*, Princeton 1969, 286a.

and Egypt in 611–19. This development was not, however, as threatening as it might seem. The expedition to the Yemen established a Persian presence there, but by the time of Muḥammad its rule was limited to Ṣanʿāʾ; in other words, there was no longer a state in the Yemen, be it Ḥimyarite, Ethiopian, or Persian. Meanwhile, the exigencies of the long war between the empires meant that the Persians on the Syrian frontier were unlikely to be paying much attention to palm groves in the Arabian interior. The other change was that the client Arab rulers disappeared—the kings of Kinda effectively in 528, the Ghassānids in 582, and the Lakhmids in 602. Of their patrons, the Yemeni state had fallen apart in the 570s, the Byzantine Empire lost its Arabian frontier to the Persians in 614, and the Persians placed one of themselves in Ḥīra as "frontier governor" (*marzbān*) alongside a tribal chief, thus replicating a pattern they had already established along the Arabian coast of the Persian Gulf. This second change was more drastic. In its heyday outsourcing had involved the Arab client states in the projection of political ambition and military activity over long distances across the Arabian Peninsula, creating an environment in which it was unlikely that any actor lacking the support of one or other of the settled societies could compete on a comparable scale. In Muḥammad's time, by contrast, the client states had faded out.

Monotheism in Arabia

As we have seen, from a geopolitical angle it was the Persian Empire, not the Byzantine, that was coming to encircle Arabia in late antiquity. But from a religious angle it was Christianity, not Zoroastrianism, that did so. By the sixth century the population of the Byzantine Empire was overwhelmingly Christian, and there was a substantial Christian minority in the Persian Empire, not least in the lowlands of Mesopotamia; by the mid-seventh century it was large enough to be divided between almost a hundred bishoprics. This, in turn, led to the conversion of considerable numbers of Arabs to Christianity on the imperial periphery of Arabia—in the Syrian desert, in Ḥīra, along the coast of the Persian Gulf, and in Oman. Persian rule may have slowed the advance of Christianity, but it certainly did not stop it in its tracks. Christianity was also making headway in the Yemen and among the Arabs in the region immediately north of it; for several decades in the sixth century the Yemen was ruled by Christians. But north of it, on the eastern side of the Red Sea, there was no coastal scene to compare with the southern shore of the Persian Gulf, a region about which, despite the desert environment, a fourth-century Roman author could write that "all along the coast is a throng of cities and villages, and many ships sail to and fro."[48] By contrast, a Greek author of the first century described setting a course along the west coast of Arabia as thoroughly

48. Quoted in Hoyland, *Arabia and the Arabs*, 28.

risky owing to the lack of good anchorage, the rocky stretches, and the unapproachable cliffs—a coast "fearsome in every respect."[49] Along this coast Christian communities were not to be found, and they likewise did not exist in the interior of the Ḥijāz, around Mecca and Yathrib; in Mecca our sources mention only a few individuals who were Christians. This region was nevertheless in touch with the Christian world outside Arabia, if only through trade. The later Arabic sources lay particular emphasis on the dependence of Quraysh on trade with Syria. The claim is credible, as they may have been helping meet the apparently insatiable demand of the Roman army for leather. A significant point here is that the merchants of Arabia were the Arabs themselves. There was no parallel here to the role of the Sogdians of Transoxania as traders among the Turks in the steppe region between the Persian Empire and China. As we will see, early sources tell us that Muḥammad himself had been involved in trade with Syria before embarking on his mission as a prophet.

Christianity was not, however, the only form of monotheism in play. There was a substantial Jewish population in the Yemen, which led to a remarkable spread of monotheism among the Ḥimyarites. This is attested by Ḥimyarite inscriptions starting in the fourth century. In interpreting these inscriptions it can be hard to tell how far we are dealing with an actual conversion of Ḥimyarites to Judaism as opposed to a gentile monotheism under strong Jewish influence. But that there was a religious transformation is clear, and after the beginning of the fifth century polytheistic inscriptions are no longer to be found. In the early sixth century the phenomenon extended to a persecution of Christians by a Ḥimyarite ruler. Judaism had also won converts from the Arab tribe of Kinda. At the same time many of the inhabitants of the Ḥijāzī oases were Jewish. From later Arabic sources we learn that of the five tribes that lived in Yathrib on the eve of the rise of Islam, three were Jewish. There were also numerous smaller groups of Jewish clients of Arab clans in Yathrib, and some of the Arab population had converted to Judaism. The Arabic sources also speak of generic monotheists who had not converted to either Christianity or Judaism. Unlike their Ḥimyarite counterparts, these Ḥanīfs, as they were called, appear in the tradition as a scattering of individuals, and they are not as closely associated with the Jews. That the phenomenon was real has some epigraphic support from a monotheistic inscription of the period found in the neighborhood of Ṭā'if.

The result of all this was to create an atmosphere far more conducive to the spread of monotheism in Arabia than had existed in antiquity. At a time when monotheism was no more than a parochial persuasion of the Israelites, Herodotus could effortlessly identify Arabian gods with their Greek counterparts. But such

49. Quoted in Hoyland, *Arabia and the Arabs*, 58.

equivalences were no longer available once the Greeks had turned Christian in late antiquity. The Arabian interior was still the largest reservoir of old-fashioned paganism to be found in the Middle East, but for anyone with an awareness of wider horizons—anyone who had traveled to Syria as a merchant, for example—Arab paganism must by now have appeared at odds with the prevailing ideas of right religion in the world at large. Under such conditions it must have seemed only a matter of time before the Arabs would complete their conversion to monotheism. The main retardant was no doubt the absence of powerful rulers in the Arabian interior. Clovis, the king of the Franks who reputedly became a Christian in 496 after the Christian God had won him a battle, and King Ethelbert of Kent, who decided to extend a cautious welcome to the mission of Saint Augustine in 597, are both examples of influential decision-makers who delivered their peoples to monotheism. Arabia lacked such rulers, or in many parts of the peninsula any rulers at all. But if the conversion of the Arabs to monotheism was likely to be slow, it could be expected to be sure. The obvious alternatives were the local Judaism and the Christianity of the outside world. But Judaism had been present in the oases of the Ḥijāz for centuries without provoking the conversion of its inhabitants at large; it was the Christian encirclement of Arabia that was new. Why wouldn't the Arabs follow the example of so many other peoples of the time and convert to Christianity?

The broader background

So far in this chapter our focus has been on Arabia and the empires at the end of late antiquity. This has involved many incidental references to a deeper past. It may therefore be helpful at this point to present a more systematic outline of that past, however briefly and schematically. After that we can move on to two larger topics that arise in that framework. One has to do with the continuing character of states, and the other with a discontinuity in the character of religion.

The long-term perspective

In a long-term perspective, the first event to take note of would be the agricultural revolution, which turned hunter-gatherers into cultivators and pastoralists. In the Middle East this transformation began around 10,000 BC, earlier than anywhere else in the world, and was so thoroughgoing that in historical times we have no record of the presence of hunter-gatherers anywhere in the region. The agricultural revolution in turn laid the foundation for the emergence of civilization—a syndrome marked by a combination of monumental architecture, writing, and states—in Mesopotamia and Egypt around 3000 BC, again earlier than elsewhere.

The next two and a half millennia are the age of the Ancient Near East. During this extended period the first-generation civilizations of the Middle East, those of the Sumerians and the Egyptians, evolved without major discontinuity. They already displayed the basic elements that were to characterize the much later empires of our period—villages, cities, peasantries, aristocracies, professional armies, and not least bureaucracies. Thus Egypt under the New Kingdom of the sixteenth to eleventh centuries BC possessed a literary genre devoted to celebrating the job satisfaction that went with being a scribe: as a bureaucrat he was spared the grind of manual labor. Meanwhile a variety of less durable cultures came and went in Syria and elsewhere. One of them was that of ancient Israel, relatively unimportant at the time but of great significance to posterity; it developed rather late in the period and is known to us mainly from a book that was to acquire a remarkably wide readership—the Bible. Its significance for us is that this is the origin of the monotheistic tradition. Another culture of this vintage emerged in South Arabia and especially the Yemen, again rather late in the period, and lasted into the sixth century of our era. As might be expected, the syndrome is largely absent from Arabia outside the south.

We come next to a messy transitional period of a millennium or so, lasting from around 500 BC to around 600. The most obvious feature of this period is that what had been the Ancient Near East was now under the almost continuous military and political domination of conquerors from outside it—Persians and Parthians from the northeast, Greeks and Romans from the northwest. In late antiquity these two sets of invaders were represented by the Persian and Byzantine Empires. This foreign domination led, in turn, to the slow demise of the Ancient Near Eastern civilizations, now starved of resources and marginalized by new forms of elite culture. Well before the end of the period the ancient civilizations were extinct in both Mesopotamia and Egypt. Of course, it is only in retrospect that we know that by 600 the period was about to end, and that it was a transition to something very different.

Resources and states

The resource that makes all the difference in the Middle East, whether by its presence, scarcity, or absence, is freshwater. But if we want to understand its distribution, we need to start with salt water, since it is evaporation from the seas that contributes the bulk of the world's freshwater supply. An obvious fact about the Middle East is that it is far from being a landlocked region like Central Asia: it has the Mediterranean to the west and the Indian Ocean to the southeast. Moreover, the maritime penetration of the Middle East is enhanced by the smaller seas that branch off from each of the larger ones. The Mediterranean connects with the Black Sea and the Indian Ocean with the Red Sea and the Persian Gulf, leaving only the Caspian isolated. But there is a significant limitation to this penetration. Despite the presence of all this sea, the Middle East is squeezed between the world's two largest landmasses, Eurasia and Africa, and this location has major climatic implications. Arctic winds do a lot to make the northern Middle East cold in winter, while Saharan winds do as much to make the southern Middle East hot in summer. But winds that blow for thousands of miles overland are unlikely to bring rain. Only small fringes of the Middle East—the southeastern coast of the Black Sea and the southern coast of the Caspian—have levels of rainfall comparable to those of northwestern Europe or monsoon Asia. This may seem paradoxical given that to the southeast the region backs onto the Indian Ocean, where evaporation in the tropics produces enormous amounts of rainfall. The explanation lies in the prevailing winds, which bypass the Middle East to take the rainfall to India in summer and East Africa in winter. The result is that only the Mediterranean, a much smaller body of water well to the north of the tropics, makes a direct contribution to Middle Eastern rainfall on a significant scale; here at least the prevailing winds blow onto the Middle East in winter. Once the rain clouds reach the Middle East one of the main things that causes them to release their moisture is the presence of mountains. This gives the northern highlands of the Middle East—roughly today's Turkey and western Iran—an advantage over the southern lowlands—roughly the Arab lands with the partial exception of Syria and the Yemen, which owe their less formidable mountains to rifting. The advantage is nevertheless qualified by the fact that both Turkey and Iran are plateaus with a salt desert in the middle—relatively small in the Anatolian case, much larger in the case of Iran.

Putting all this together, the approximate result is an aridity gradient running across the Middle East from the wet northwest to the dry southeast. If we take two of the largest Middle Eastern countries today, only a small fraction of the surface area of Turkey is desert, whereas only a small fraction of that of Saudi Arabia is not. Overall, these conditions impose a relatively low ceiling on the agricultural productivity of the Middle East, and that, in turn, constrains the size of the population, the scale of economic activity, and the viability of states. There is, however, one vital phenomenon that this analysis has so far left aside—namely, the role of rivers in delivering secondhand rainfall to arid lands where it can be used to practice irrigation. In Mesopotamia the Euphrates and Tigris played this part, and in Egypt the Nile. The Egyptian case is particularly striking: Egypt, thanks to the Nile, is the only part of the Middle East that gets a generous supply of freshwater deriving from the Indian Ocean. Arabia, by contrast, is riverless.

Such were the conditions under which states in the premodern Middle East were obliged to make a living. These states were in many respects different from the states we are used to today. Their populations, for example, would have been smaller by at least an order of magnitude, and overwhelmingly rural. We should also keep in mind that communication over long distances was much more difficult then than it is now. Whether we are concerned with information, people, or goods, moving them was slower, harder, and more expensive than it is in the modern world. If the governor of Syria in, say, the second century sent an urgent message to the emperor in Rome, he could not expect to get a reply in less than two months. If in the meantime an invader was ravaging his province he was effectively on his own. There are two obvious inferences one might draw from the slow pace of communications. The first is that under such conditions states would not be large, and the second is that their ability to control events on the ground outside their capital cities would be limited.

The first inference, interestingly enough, is false, as we already know. It is not that premodern states of small to moderate size are rare; for example, we find them in abundance in the Ancient Near East and again in the medieval Middle East, not to mention in India, Southeast Asia, and post-Roman Europe. But empires were manifestly possible. Indeed, one such state may have emerged in the Middle East as early as the twenty-third century BC. In late antiquity, as we have seen, empires were the norm in a Middle East that was distinctly inhospitable to smaller states. They existed, but only in mountainous regions such as the Yemen and Transcaucasia. Thus the Ḥimyarites had their kingdom in the Yemen, and in Transcaucasia the Armenians, the Georgians, and the Caucasian Albanians each possessed monarchies that maintained their existence as client states of one empire or the other. Yet in the course of late antiquity all these minor monarchies disappeared.

The second inference—that states would have only limited ability to control events on the ground—holds up better, though even here there was enormous variation. This variation was not just between states. The same state would exercise a much greater degree of control in its good lands than it did in its bad lands—more in the rich and fertile plains, less in the mountains, and least in the deserts. This was no small matter, since both mountains and deserts were by global standards more than usually abundant in the Middle East, mountains more in the north and deserts more in the south. Two examples taken from the ancient history of the Middle East may help convey something of the range of state presence.

The first relates to Egypt under Roman rule. As mentioned earlier, Egypt was a tax collector's paradise, and tax collectors need to know who their taxpayers are. From the first to the third century, the Romans would accordingly organize a house-by-house census of the population every fourteen years, and the dry climate of Egypt has preserved some three hundred of the declarations that heads of households were obliged to submit to the authorities. One of them, from a village in Upper Egypt and dating from 119, reads as follows:

> From Harpokration son of Dioskoros son of Harmais and of Senorsenouphis daughter of Psenanouphis, from Tanyaithis: I declare for the house-by-house

> census of the second year of Hadrian Caesar the lord . . . : myself, a scribe, aged seventy, scar on the shank of the left leg; Dioskoros, my son, his mother being Senpachoumis daughter of Anompis, without scar, doctor, aged seventeen; Senpachoumis, my daughter by Anompis, wife of Harpokration, aged thirty-nine; Tazbes the Younger, a daughter, aged fifteen. And I swear by the fortune of the emperor . . . Hadrian . . . that I have honestly and truthfully presented the above return, and that I have left no one unregistered, or may I be liable on my oath.[50]

Here, then, was a state that knew about the scar on the left leg of a seventy-year old scribe in an Upper Egyptian village and had a record of the names of his father, his paternal grandfather, his mother, his maternal grandmother, his son, his wife, his mother-in-law, and his two daughters—though the name of the mother of the second daughter is not specified—together with the ages of the scribe and his children. This is high-resolution data collection. That the state could collect this kind of information across the country also implies that it had formidable coercive powers, for as the last sentence of the declaration presupposes, it was not at all in Harpokration's interest that a tax-greedy state should learn so much about him and his family.

At the other extreme, take the experience of ten thousand Greek mercenaries in 401 BC. These foot soldiers had been hired by a rebel Achaemenid prince who sought to take the place of his brother on the Persian throne. In the battle that ensued on the plains of Mesopotamia the mercenaries acquitted themselves well, but their prince was killed, the rebellion collapsed, and the Greeks were left to be picked off by the Persian cavalry. Where were they to go? Their prospects on the plains were poor, and going south into the Arabian desert would have been worse, so they decided to head north into the mountains of Carduchia—the region to the south of Lake Van that would later be part of Kurdistan. The mercenaries had secured one piece of intelligence about this region, and it was not encouraging: at some time in the past the Persians had dispatched a large army into these mountains, and it had never returned. By following in the footsteps of that ill-fated army the Greeks had at least put the Persians behind them, but they now had to fight the Carduchians every inch of the way, even though all they wanted from them was safe passage. This was par for the course. People who live in remote and rugged mountains tend to be hardy and self-reliant; think of William Tell. It was not until a week later that the mercenaries emerged on the other side of the mountains. They had reached the Persian province of Armenia. In front of them

50. Papyrus Giessen 43; Greek text in J. Schwartz, *Papyri variae Alexandrinae et Gissenses*, Brussels 1969, 27–28 no. 14; thanks to Petra Sijpesteijn for bibliographical guidance and to Roger Bagnall for revising the translation I had from an anonymous handout.

was a river, and beyond it a plain, a beautiful sight after the forbidding landscapes of Carduchia. The only fly in the ointment was what they saw on the plain: a Persian army. Their adventure—and the fact that they lived to record it—enables us to see something we could otherwise only have guessed at: in the middle of the Persian Empire was a large hole in which the presence of the imperial authorities was zero. No doubt there were many others that we do not get to hear about.

These two examples represent the extremes. For most places most of the time we should probably imagine something in between. For example, the Armenia that the mercenaries had reached at such cost was part of the Persian Empire and doubtless ruled by the Persians through Armenian intermediaries rooted in the local society—including the "village chiefs" that the Greek mercenaries were to encounter. Centuries later, in the days when the Byzantines and the Persians shared the Middle East, our sources are more plentiful, and we see a powerful Armenian aristocracy occupying much of the space between the imperial rulers and the mass of the local population; whether or not there happened to be an Armenian king, the imperial rulers had to work with the aristocrats. Since each party had different interests their relations might be troubled, but no empire of the time could afford to alienate all of the Armenian aristocracy all of the time. There can, of course, be many variants on the aristocratic theme, but we can think of some such intermediate elite as the default in premodern agrarian societies.

In addition to this variation over space, the strength of states could also vary considerably over time. For example, under conditions of demographic and economic growth a state would have more to tax and wax stronger, whereas under conditions of demographic and economic decline it would find itself living off a diminished fiscal base and its strength would wane. There is some evidence that the latter was happening in the Middle East toward the end of late antiquity—that the population was contracting, that levels of production were falling, that irrigation systems were being disrupted, that urban infrastructure was not being maintained, and the like. The problem is that there is also evidence suggesting that this demographic and economic downturn may have begun only after the end of late antiquity, or indeed that it did not take place at all. In the nature of things, we cannot hope to have the statistical data that would give us certainty one way or the other. There are, however, a couple of major historical events that lend some plausibility to the hypothesis of declining resources and population, though the impact of the first of them has been challenged. This is the pandemic of bubonic plague that reached the Middle East in 541 and while sparing Arabia continued to flare up on and off for the next two centuries. Our direct evidence for its impact is not very good. But although it is hard to prove that it had an impact comparable to that of the Black Death in fourteenth-century Europe, it is also hard to prove that it did not, and whatever impact it did have would undoubtedly have been negative. The other major event was the last war between the empires. This long period of highly destructive warfare must have meant a lot of disruption for the population and economy of the Middle East. In cases of rapid conquest, as with the Persian seizure of Syria and Egypt, the pain, though sharp, may be short; but where armies maraud over an extended period, as in Anatolia, the result can be catastrophic. Such sustained stress would have made the Middle Eastern empires more vulnerable to invasion and conquest. There is one other factor that we should take into consideration here: the very real possibility of adverse climate change. At this point there is already a considerable body of findings regarding historical shifts in climate, but discussions of their relationship to major historical trends have a tendency to be either too speculative to be believed or too cautious to say anything useful. However, a study published in 2022 makes a rather convincing case for the role of drought in the decline of the Ḥimyarite kingdom, noting also that the effect could have been exacerbated by the global cooling that is in evidence from the 530s. We live in hope of more evidence of this kind.

Paganism and its discontents

Paganism is a loose but useful term for forms of religion that are historically the human default. Such religions are typically polytheistic, which is to say that they involve the worship of many gods, usually grouping them in some kind of pantheon, as in ancient Egypt, Greece, Mesopotamia, India, and elsewhere. In western Eurasia—the Middle East and Europe—paganism was on its way out by late antiquity. By contrast, in eastern Eurasia—India and China—it suffered no such decline. This suggests that it was not the nature of paganism as such that ensured its demise farther to the west. Yet at a certain point in the development of civilization paganism did come to seem inadequate, at least among a substantial part of the cultural elite, in both east and west. Anyone coming from a monotheistic background has an intuitive understanding of some of this. What a monotheistic perspective obscures is the fact that the normal reaction to this discontent was not to reject paganism outright but to rise above it. When the dying Roman emperor Vespasian (ruled 69–79) displayed his sense of humor with the sardonic remark "Woe is me. Methinks I'm turning into a god,"[51] what he showed was that he did not take gods too seriously. The same could be said, in different ways and without the humor, of Confucius, the Buddha, Epicurus, and many others; it was not that they were steadfastly opposed to gods but rather that in their different ways they had more important things to talk about. Something analogous could also be said of the Zoroastrians. As we have seen, they readily spoke of the gods in the plural, but what mattered to them was their grand unified myth of a cosmic struggle

51. Suetonius, [*Lives of the Caesars*], trans. J. C. Rolfe, Cambridge, MA 1997–98, 2:305 (8.23).

between a single good god and his demonic adversary. In a way even the pagan Arabs fit into this pattern, ignoring gods by rising above them in their heroic poetry.

Monotheists, by contrast, set out to abolish paganism, not to rise above it. For them it is not just inadequate; it is an abomination. It was the ancient Israelites, a minor people of the Ancient Near East, who first developed this unusual attitude in a lasting form, bequeathing it to their Jewish descendants in Palestine and the diaspora, the milieu in which Christianity eventually emerged and began to spread. Crucially, the early Christians decided to seek converts among the gentiles. But even then, their monotheism remained the religion of a socially inferior minority until the conversion of the emperor Constantine. The aftermath of this momentous event showed the extent of the power and patronage at the disposal of a Roman emperor in this period. By making Christianity the state's favorite religion, Constantine set in motion a bandwagon effect that sooner or later brought even the educated aristocracy on board and overcame the powerful combination of cultural inertia and vested interests that had seemed to assure the indefinite future of paganism. There is even a story about the last pagan philosophers of antiquity taking refuge in the Persian Empire to escape the intolerance of the emperor Justinian. Meanwhile, the conversion of the Roman Empire to Christianity set in motion a similar effect involving whole peoples in the regions around it. Just as in the Roman case, the key decision-makers were rulers. To the west of Iran, conversion came sooner or later for most of these peoples; the Lithuanians, who held fast to their paganism into the fourteenth century, were the outlier. Even some ethnic groups that lived in the shadow of Iran—the Armenians, the Georgians, and the Caucasian Albanians—became Christian. The only people that bucked the trend in pre-Islamic times by converting to a form of monotheism other than Christianity were the Ḥimyarites, who as we have seen adopted a monotheism that was Jewish, or of Jewish inspiration. The Ḥimyarites apart, down to the seventh century the story was consistently one of the triumph of Christianity.

There were nevertheless limits to this triumph. One was on the pagan front. The inadequacy of paganism did not mean that it was dispensable. If polytheism rather than monotheism was the default religion of the human race, we can plausibly infer that it was well attuned to basic human needs. That is why Christianity—and not just Christianity—has a perennial tendency to recreate within itself the comforts and conveniences of paganism. The example we encountered earlier was the cult of the Virgin Mary as in effect the tutelary goddess of Constantinople, a development that goes with a wider phenomenon of the worship of saints and images that was to become very controversial in the Byzantine Empire after the rise of Islam.

Another limit was on the Persian front. Here the Persian Empire posed a formidable barrier to Christian dominance in a large part of the Middle East. Kingship, far from being an agent of Christianization, remained the committed helpmate of the Good Religion, Zoroastrianism. This intimate link between Zoroastrianism and the Persian state, vaunted from both sides in the third-century inscriptions, was accompanied by a deep suspicion of Christianity as the religion of the Byzantine enemy. A Persian official is reported to have advised Bahrām V (ruled 420–38) that he should "give orders that the Christians convert from their religion, for they hold the same faith as the Romans, and they are in entire agreement together; should a war interpose between the two empires these Christians will turn out to be defectors from our side in any fighting, and through their playing false they will bring down your power."[52] Or as Shāhpuhr II (ruled 309–79) put it to a Christian who was protesting his loyalty to him, "How can you consider me to be King of Kings, mighty and powerful, when you have had the effrontery to say in my presence that you are a Christian?"[53] In practice, of course, there had to be a large measure of accommodation, and it was helped by the fact that most of the Christians of the Persian Empire regarded Byzantine Orthodoxy as heretical. As Khusraw II observed, the empire could not endure "if we cause the Christians and adherents of other faiths, who differ in belief from ourselves, to become hostile to us."[54] But Christians were never more than a minority of the empire's population. This in turn stymied their missionary efforts farther east. Christian communities were to be found as far as China, but east of Iran it was usually the Buddhist bandwagon, not the Christian one, that rolled.

Finally, it was only when and where Christians had the backing of the state that they could hope to put rival religious entrepreneurs out of business. In the absence of such backing the Middle East in the early centuries of our era had been fertile soil for religious innovators. This was the golden age of Gnostic speculation in both empires. Kerdīr, as we saw, included the Manichaeans among those whose persecution he rejoiced in. These were the followers of Mani, a third-century Babylonian prophet who considered his new religion superior to those of his predecessors, among other things because it was to be propagated "in every land and in all languages."[55] He reckoned his predecessors to be the Buddha, Zoroaster, and Jesus, and despite identifying himself as coming from Babylon, he made no mention of its pagan gods. But nowhere in the Middle East did Manichaeism have the support of a state, and with the Persian turn to a more zealous Zoroastrianism and the Byzantine espousal of Christianity the space for it was severely limited by persecution. It was not until 763, after the Uighur ruler met Sogdian Manichaeans in China and converted to Manichaeism, that the religion had a state behind it.

52. Quoted in S. P. Brock, "Christians in the Sasanian empire," *Studies in Church History*, 18 (1982), 8.

53. Brock, "Christians in the Sasanian empire," 14.

54. Quoted in Payne, *A state of mixture*, 167.

55. See F. C. Andreas, *Mitteliranische Manichaica aus Chinesisch-Turkestan*, Berlin 1932–34, 2:295.

Now, at last, after five centuries of being persecuted, the Manichaeans were in the happy position of being able to turn their attention to persecuting pagan Uighurs and imposing vegetarianism on them. But to return to the Middle East, on the eve of the rise of Islam the region was markedly inhospitable to Gnostics and Manichaeans. Yet even on the Byzantine side of the imperial border it remained some way from religious homogeneity. Quite apart from the sectarian divisions of the Christians, there were still, for example, Jews and sun worshippers in sixth-century Syria. And in the Arabian interior there was no state to back Christianity.

In the immediate aftermath of the last war between the empires, even a well-informed observer would not have had much reason to anticipate a drastic discontinuity in the history of the Middle East. The crisis had been a major one, but it was over. With the Persian Empire under new and more prudent management and the Byzantine emperor on his way home, it looked as if the long-lasting balance of power between the two empires was at last being restored. If anything were to upset this applecart, it would surely be the sudden emergence of some fearsome new force among the nomads of the steppes. Meanwhile the tribes of Arabia could be expected to continue to feud among themselves. They might well pose local threats to the southern borderlands of the empires at a time when both were exhausted. But the Arabs were manifestly not in the same league as the nomads of the north. In any event, sooner or later the Arabs would surely follow the path taken by so many other peoples and convert to Christianity, as indeed a fair number of them had already done. If there was an open question about the future of religion in the Middle East, it was whether in the long run the Persian Empire could continue to stand out against the Christian tide. Beside that question, anything that happened in Arabia would be a sideshow. All this sounds very reasonable, and indeed it would have been. But it is not what happened.

Can we come up with any good reasons it didn't happen beyond simply telling the story we are about to relate in the next chapter? It is, of course, possible that our observer might have heard rumors of the formation of a new state governed by a religious leader in the Arabian interior, but the obvious reaction would have been to dismiss it as unlikely to last. Yet why should such a state have emerged there in the first place? What we can take from our survey in this chapter is two faint opportunities. One was religious. In contrast to most of the lands in and around the Mediterranean, Arabia in late antiquity hosted forms of monotheism that may not have been confined to Judaism and Christianity. In other words, there were indications of a third way. The other faint opportunity was geopolitical. Although it seemed unlikely that anything like a state could arise in the Arabian interior independent of the patronage of one or other of the settled societies, the early seventh century provided a window of opportunity for anyone brave enough to try.

2

Muḥammad

Two things were central to Muḥammad's career in early seventh-century Arabia: his monotheistic message and his state. There was something very unusual about each of them.

First, his message. In seeking to spread monotheism among the Arabs, why did Muḥammad not do what almost everybody else did in the western part of the Old World—that is to say, adopt monotheism in the form of Christianity? Why did he take the quite unusual step of providing the Arabs with a monotheism of their own?

To see how he did this we have to look hard at his scripture, the Qur'ān. There his role as a messenger appears in three distinct frames: as a warner sent to deliver an ultimatum to a polytheistic community that God was about to destroy; as the reviver of the monotheistic religion of the patriarch Abraham; and as the successor of Moses and Jesus. The first was a dead end, though it explains why his message could be very offensive to his pagan contemporaries. The third would be crucial for the future of Islam as a universal religion. But it was the second, Abrahamic revivalism, that was the key to the emergence of a specifically Arab form of monotheism. How did that work?

The other surprising feature of Muḥammad's career was that he founded a polity in a region whose lack of resources seemed inimical to state formation. How did he do it? It was the offensiveness of his denunciation of paganism that set in motion the process by which he made his risky move from his native Mecca to the oasis of Yathrib. But that does not explain how he succeeded in leveraging the chaotic politics of the oasis, together with his limited initial support there, in such a way as to found a state. How did he combine his monotheistic message with the institutions of an anarchic tribal society to create this monotheistic polity? Here our key source will be the document known as the Constitution of Medina.

Once established in one part of Medina, Muḥammad set about expanding his power not just within the oasis but also outside it. So we find him dispatching numerous military expeditions and leading some of them himself; we will sample one of them in some detail. What can these raids tell us about the character of Muḥammad's state and the way he ran it? And what light does his scripture shed on the nature of his state?

Finally, we will again try to reconstruct how things might have looked to contemporary observers. If we place one in the Arabian interior at the start of the seventh century, what reason, if any, would such an observer have had to anticipate the imminent emergence of a new religion and a new state? And later, in Medina at the time of Muḥammad's death, what reason would an observer have had to expect the long-term survival of either the religion or the state that Muḥammad had founded?

Let us begin this chapter with a very brief outline of Muḥammad's life.[1] He was born in Mecca around 570 into the tribe of Quraysh, specifically the clan of the Banū Hāshim. Since Mecca lacked agricultural land, Quraysh made much of their living from commerce; Muḥammad was involved in this activity in his youth, and as a result had traveled to Syria. About 610 he received the first of the revelations that would eventually constitute the Qur'ān. This moment marked the beginning of his role as the prophet of Islam, a new monotheistic religion that was to spread widely among the Arabs of his day. Then, in 622, he moved from Mecca to Yathrib, since then better known as Medina. The move marked the start of his role as the founder of a state that already in his lifetime came to exercise some degree of influence, if not hegemony, over a large part of Arabia. After he died in 632, his successors did not just ensure the survival of his state; they launched a series of conquests that extended its sway over territories stretching far beyond the borders of Arabia and led to the emergence of a new civilization.

We will come back to some of this in more detail, but for now it is all we need. Two things are worth saying about this narrative. First, it follows the account of Muḥammad's career given in the traditional Muslim sources. This chapter is based squarely on them, together with the Qur'ān, though at a couple of points other sources will contribute to the picture. This is not to say that the traditional sources are reliable. In the previous chapter we saw how problems arise with regard to what they tell us about pre-Islamic Arabia, and the situation is not radically different when we enter the early Islamic period.[2] But consider the reports in the Arabic sources that Muḥammad in his youth accompanied an uncle who was traveling as a merchant to Syria and that he later returned there in partnership with the merchant woman who became his first wife—he did the traveling, while she supplied the capital and stayed at home in Mecca. This matters historically because it means that Muḥammad had exposure to a wider horizon, and it finds confirmation in the

1. For short accounts of his life see W. M. Watt, *Muḥammad: Prophet and statesman*, London 1961; J.A.C. Brown, *Muhammad: A very short introduction*, Oxford 2011.

2. A few decades ago a radical skepticism toward the Arabic sources for the life of Muḥammad was widespread in some parts of the Western academy, and in my youth I played a part in this turn. Anyone curious about how my views have changed in the meantime could glance at an article I published not so long ago: M. Cook, "Muḥammad's deputies in Medina," *Al-ʿUṣūr al-Wusṭā*, 23 (2015).

earliest preserved account of his career, that of an Armenian Christian chronicler writing in the 660s who describes him as a merchant. We likewise have an impressive fit in connection with an incident from near the end of Muḥammad's career. The standard biography of the Prophet lists the members of a tribal delegation that came to see him from the region of Najrān in 631, and we now have an early inscription commemorating one of them by name. What this chapter accordingly assumes is that the outline of Muḥammad's life as given in the Muslim sources is largely reliable, and that the colorful details they supply, whether or not they are accurate, are not out of place in the society they describe. A more intractable problem is the poor fit between the content of the Qur'ānic polemic against Muḥammad's opponents and what the Muslim sources tell us about them. But we will simply leave that issue aside.

Second, this outline gives us some surprising things to think about, three in particular. One is that the Arabs, though no different from many other peoples of western Eurasia in converting to monotheism, were unique in that instead of accepting it in an existing form—the normal choice, as we have seen, being Christianity—they adopted it in the form of Islam, a monotheistic religion very much their own. Another is that by the last years of Muḥammad's life many Arabs belonged to a state far larger in extent than anything they had previously possessed, despite the fact that it was based in a region of the peninsula that seemed particularly unfavorable for state formation. Finally, the Arabs went on to conquer for themselves one of the largest empires in history, with enduring religious and cultural consequences, even though they had never done such a thing before and would never do it again.

These three surprising developments were obviously linked. But this is not to say that there was any inevitability about the sequence. Muḥammad could have created a new monotheistic religion in Arabia without founding a state, in which case his religion would very likely have disappeared without trace. And he could have founded a state in Arabia without it going on to acquire an empire, in which case we would most probably never have heard of it. Yet if we think in terms of necessary rather than sufficient conditions, the linkage between the three developments is unquestionable. As we will see, without his role as a prophet it is very hard to imagine Muḥammad becoming a ruler, and without the existence of his state it is just as hard to imagine the Arabs conquering themselves an empire. In this sense these three unlikely developments hang together, and we can think of them as jointly constituting one of the great Black Swan Events of history. As elaborated a few years ago by the financier Nassim Nicholas Taleb, this metaphor applies to events that combine three features. The first is unpredictability—nobody could have seen them coming. The second is extreme impact—they changed the course of history. And the third is that in retrospect we try to make sense of them by concocting spurious explanations. As might be expected, Taleb categorizes the rise of Islam as a Black Swan Event, noting its "full unpredictability."[3] Of his three definitional features, the unpredictability of Muḥammad's enterprise will occupy us in this chapter, and its massive impact throughout the rest of this book. As to concocting spurious explanations after the event, that is what historians do for a living.

We can best begin by going to the Qur'ān to get a sense of Muḥammad's monotheistic message. We can then ask why his possession of that message led him to found a state in a remote and unpromising part of the Arabian wilderness. But we can leave to the next chapter the question of why his founding of this state should have led to the creation of an empire and the formation of a civilization.

Muḥammad's message

The central message of Muḥammad's scripture, the Qur'ān, is a relentless monotheism. But his role in delivering this message appears in three distinct frames, and each of them has something to tell us about how the Arabs came to possess a monotheistic religion of their own.

Every nation has its messenger

The Qur'ān tells us that "every nation (*umma*) has its messenger (*rasūl*)" (Q10:47). As to the message, at one point God says, "We sent forth among every nation a messenger [who said to them]: 'Serve you God, and eschew idols'" (Q16:36). The rest of the verse explains that some would respond to the call, while others would not; the deniers would then suffer a dire fate, the traces of which can be seen by travelers even today. Here God trades on the ready visibility of ancient ruins in the arid climate of Arabia—we are not in the Mayan jungle. Although in essence the message is always the same, a call to monotheism, there is a measure of ethnic and linguistic customization. All messengers deliver the message in the language of the people they are sent to, and it is often specified that in selecting their messenger God chooses one of their own number. Thus to 'Ād He sends "their brother Hūd" and to Thamūd "their brother Ṣāliḥ" (Q7:65, 73)—both 'Ād and Thamūd being ancient Arabian peoples, 'Ād doubtless mythical but Thamūd historically well attested. The Qur'ān devotes numerous passages to recounting particular instances of this pattern in Arabia. Thus Hūd addresses 'Ād: "O my people, serve God! You have no god other than Him" (Q7:65). They respond: "Why, hast thou come to us that we may serve God alone, and forsake that which our fathers served?"

3. N. N. Taleb, *The Black Swan*, New York 2010, 11.

(Q7:70). In another passage they tell Hūd that they are not about to abandon their gods on his say-so. Hūd responds by declaring himself quit of what his people associate with God—in other words, what they worship alongside Him. The upshot is that God saves Hūd and those who listen to him and destroys the rest. The stories of the various messengers differ in their details, but they are unmistakably variants on a theme. For example, Ṣāliḥ addresses Thamūd just as Hūd addresses ʿĀd: "O my people, serve God! You have no god other than Him" (Q7:73). In each case the dramatic destruction marks the end of the story; no doubt the messenger and those of his people who believed in him lived happily ever after, but we hear nothing further about them. What makes these stories relevant to Muḥammad is the fact that he clearly sees himself as just such a messenger. In one verse God says of him, "This is a warner, of the warners of old" (Q53:56). He has been sent to warn a people to whom no previous warner has come.

If we think of Muḥammad in this frame, how close is he to endowing the Arabs with a new monotheistic religion of their own? Not at all close. The ethnic and linguistic customization is real insofar as Muḥammad is a member of the community he is sent to and speaks its language. But that does not make this community in any way special, for as we have seen God sends such a messenger to *every* nation; what He did for the Arabs He would, by implication, be just as ready to do for the Estonians. But why, in fact, should we think that God sent Muḥammad to the Arabs at large? His mission, it seems, was in fact a much more local one, limited to those living in and around Mecca. Moreover, his task on this showing would appear to have been limited to bringing them a warning. Although it is unclear how figures such as Hūd and Ṣāliḥ relate to the established forms of monotheism—Judaism and Christianity—there is nothing to indicate that either of them was bringing a new religion to his people. In any case the warner model suggests that most of Muḥammad's intended audience would be unlikely to listen to him and that God would accordingly bring his mission to an abrupt end by destroying them. The script makes no provision for success.

How, then, do these Arabian figures relate to the wider monotheistic tradition? What is clear is that the Qur'ān narrates their stories on a par with those of such Biblical figures as Noah and Lot. Indeed, the Qur'ānic story of Noah displays an interesting twist that brings him into line with Hūd and Ṣāliḥ and, by implication, Muḥammad. God sends Noah to his people as a warner who admonishes them that they should worship none but God; he, too, addresses his people with the words "O my people, serve God! You have no god other than Him" (Q23:23). This will surprise attentive Bible readers, because it is not at all how the Bible tells the story: there Noah is not sent to anyone, and the "wickedness of man" that leads to the Flood is not related to polytheism (Gen. 6:5). The warner model has pulled the Noah of the Qur'ān into line with Muḥammad.

Muḥammad as an Abrahamic revivalist

As we saw, Hūd's people responded to his warning by asking, "Why, hast thou come to us that we may serve God alone, and forsake that which our fathers served?" In other words, they rejected the call to monotheism because it would mean breaking faith with their ancestors. The Qur'ān places this sentiment in the mouths of numerous polytheists of the past, including Noah's people, Abraham's father and people, Pharaoh and his council, ʿĀd, Thamūd, and the Midianites. Characteristically, it is also expressed by the people Muḥammad himself is addressing: "We found our fathers practicing a religion (*umma*), and we are guided upon their traces." God then tells Muḥammad that He has never sent "any warner to any city" without his meeting with just this response (Q43:22–23). The wording tends to be stereotyped, but the sentiment behind the response is real, and as widespread as the human race. To pick an example contemporary with Muḥammad's lifetime, here is what the pagan King Ethelbert of Kent in southeastern England told the Christian missionary Saint Augustine in 597: "The words and promises you bring are fair indeed, but since they are new to us and doubtful, I cannot consent to accept them and forsake those beliefs that I and the whole English race have held so long."[4] Humans do sometimes break with what their whole people have long held, as Ethelbert himself would do in due course. But they do not do it lightly.

In his struggle against the desire of his people to keep faith with their ancestors, Muḥammad had one advantage that was denied to Saint Augustine. To see what it was, we need to go back to the Bible. According to the Book of Genesis, the patriarch Abraham had two sons, Isaac and Ishmael; Isaac, the younger son, was the ancestor of the Israelites, whereas Ishmael, the elder son, was the ancestor of the Ishmaelites. This is typical of the way in which Genesis seeks to identify the peoples within its horizon and relate them to each other in genealogical terms. With the passage of time the schema naturally came to need updating; the Samaritans apart, by late antiquity the Israelites had been reduced to the Jews, while everyone at the time understood the Ishmaelites to be the Arabs. So Isaac and Ishmael stood for Jews and Arabs. The Arabs were thus fortunate in having a clear Biblical identity that gave them Abraham as an ancestor—something the English and many other peoples had to do without.

What did this identity imply in religious terms? Here the Bible is rather discouraging. At one point God speaks to Abraham as follows: "Sarah thy wife shall bear thee a son indeed; and thou shalt call his name Isaac: and I will establish my cov-

4. Bede, *The ecclesiastical history of the English people*, Oxford 1994, 40 (1.25).

enant with him for an everlasting covenant, and with his seed after him." God then addresses Abraham's concern about the future of his elder son, whose mother was the Egyptian concubine Hagar: "And as for Ishmael, I have heard thee: Behold, I have blessed him, and will make him fruitful, and will multiply him exceedingly; twelve princes shall he beget, and I will make him a great nation. But my covenant will I establish with Isaac" (Gen. 17:19–21). Thus for all their worldly success, and despite their descent from Abraham, the Bible sees the monotheistic high road as bypassing the Arabs.

Arab descent from Abraham was nevertheless a potential asset, and by late antiquity it had begun to be exploited. Sozomenus, a Christian from a village near Gaza writing in the first half of the fifth century, has an interesting account of the Saracens, one of the names by which the Arabs were widely known at the time. They descended from Ishmael, after whom they were also called Ishmaelites. "Such being their origin, they practice circumcision like the Jews, refrain from the use of pork, and observe many other Jewish rites and customs." Of course this ancient heritage of the Arabs was only imperfectly preserved, but that was not hard to explain: "The inhabitants of the neighboring countries, being strongly addicted to superstition, probably soon corrupted the laws imposed upon them by their forefather Ishmael." They thus came to serve "the same gods as the neighboring nations." But eventually the damage was repaired: "Some of their tribe, afterwards happening to come in contact with the Jews, gathered from them the facts of their true origin, returned to their kinsmen, and inclined to the Hebrew customs and laws." Finally Sozomenus comes back to his own time: "From that time on, until now, many of them regulate their lives according to the Jewish precepts."[5] For Sozomenus, then, the Arabs had originally shared with the Israelites the heritage of their common ancestor Abraham, though under the influence of their pagan neighbors they had later lost this precious ancestral heritage and fallen into paganism. This is not just how Sozomenus sees it himself; he is also telling us in this passage that some Arabs had learned of their Ishmaelite ancestry through contact with Jews and had then returned to the heritage of their ancestors. In doing so they were discarding the errors of their recent ancestors in order to recover their original ancestral heritage. Rather than a betrayal of their ancestry their embrace of Abraham's legacy was the height of fidelity to it.

Two centuries later a similar idea figures prominently in the Qur'ān. Muḥammad is to follow and preach "the religion of Abraham" (*millat Ibrāhīm*). Thus when he and his followers are urged to become Jews or Christians, he should respond, "Nay, rather the religion of Abraham" (Q2:135), for Abraham was "not a Jew, neither a

5. Translated in F. Millar, "Hagar, Ishmael, Josephus, and the origins of Islam," in his *Rome, the Greek world, and the East*, Chapel Hill 2002–6, 3:374–75.

Christian" (Q3:67), the Torah and the Gospel not yet having been revealed in his time. Genealogy is central here: in one passage the faith of the Muslims is identified as "the religion of your father Abraham" (Q22:78). But we also find in the Qur'ān developments that go far beyond anything Sozomenus mentions. Ishmael has been promoted and is now one of God's messengers and a prophet. Moreover, we learn that Abraham and Ishmael together built the House—a temple to serve as a cultic center and a place of pilgrimage (*ḥajj*). Associated with this House is a territory that Abraham twice asks God to make secure, and in one of these passages he tells God, "I have made some of my seed to dwell in a valley where there is no sown land by Thy Holy House" (Q14:37). The Qur'ān tells us that this House was located in a place called Bakka, and the Islamic tradition is unanimous in identifying Bakka as Mecca. In other words, the religion of Abraham was not just a form of Arab monotheism; it also provided a monotheistic charter for the Meccan sanctuary and the associated pilgrimage of Muḥammad's own day. Nor is this the only way in which the Abrahamic past links to Muḥammad's present. In their prayer Abraham and Ishmael ask God to "make us submissive (*muslim*) to Thee, and of our seed a nation submissive (*umma muslima*) to Thee" (Q2:128); this is tantamount to an Abrahamic justification for calling Muḥammad's religion "Islam." Abraham and Ishmael then go on to make another request for the benefit of their descendants: "And, our Lord, do Thou send among them a messenger, one of them, who shall recite to them Thy signs, and teach them the Book and the Wisdom, and purify them" (Q2:129). Here, then, is an Abrahamic anticipation of the mission of Muḥammad. Crucially, it presents his monotheism as an ancestral truth, not a foreign one. Monotheism in this vision is the birthright of the Arabs.

There is nothing in the Qur'ānic account of the religion of Abraham that explicitly presents its espousal by Muḥammad as a message addressed to the Arabs at large, rather than to a local community living around the House. But there is equally nothing that prevents understanding it as directed to all Arabs, and it soon came to be taken that way. Here two elements of the warner model contribute to the Arab appeal of Islam. First, the messenger, as we saw, is always a member of the community to which he is sent, and this applies to Muḥammad as much as to his predecessors; we have just seen Abraham and Ishmael asking God to send to their descendants a messenger who would be "one of them." If we think of the messenger as sent to Quraysh, this means that he would be a Qurashī, but if we think of him as sent to the Arabs at large, then it means that he would be an Arab. Second, the messenger always delivers the message in the language of the people to whom he is sent, which for Muḥammad means Arabic. A feature of the revelation that is stressed in the Qur'ān is precisely that it is in Arabic. For example, a verse according to which Muḥammad was sent to warn the Mother of Cities (understood as Mecca) states that to this end, "We have revealed to thee an Arabic Qur'ān"

(Q42:7). Here the significance of this linguistic fact would seem to be local, but it is fully compatible with a mission to the Arabs at large. As a later tradition has Muḥammad say, "I am an Arab, the Qur'ān is Arabic, and the language of the people of Paradise is Arabic."[6]

Muḥammad as the successor of Moses and Jesus

If Muḥammad is only a warner or an Abrahamic revivalist sent to a particular ethnic community, then his mission lies outside the mainstream of monotheistic history. In that perspective the careers of ethnic warners are little more than sideshows. The same is true of Abrahamic revivalism: at most it opens up a new line of monotheistic history on behalf of the Arabs, but it does not challenge the centrality of the line that runs through Moses and Jesus. And indeed the Qur'ān accepts the authority of that line, albeit with strong reservations about the fidelity of latter-day Jews and Christians to the messages of their respective founders. But this is not to say that Islam is just a sideshow. It is God's religion, not just one of a number of acceptable religions: "The religion with God is Islam" (Q3:19).

In this context Muḥammad appears as the successor of Moses and Jesus. Thus in a passage concerned with the legal content of successive revelations, we are presented with three of them: first, God says, "We sent down the Torah," obviously to Moses; then came Jesus, to whom God gave the Gospel, which confirmed the Torah; and finally, addressing Muḥammad, God says, "We have sent down to thee the Book with the truth, confirming the Book that was before it" (Q5:44–48). This succession of three great scriptural prophets is confirmed by the Qur'ānic Jesus, the middle link in the chain, when he says to the Israelites, "I am indeed the messenger of God to you, confirming the Torah that is before me, and giving good tidings of a messenger who shall come after me, whose name shall be Aḥmad" (Q61:6). As we might expect, the Islamic tradition understands Aḥmad as another name of Muḥammad. This puts him fully in the mainstream of the monotheistic tradition, the third of three major prophets and the last of them, "the Seal of the Prophets" (Q33:40). Here Muḥammad's role transcends those of the ethnic warner and the Abrahamic revivalist, and Islam emerges as a new religion completing and superseding those that preceded it. This view links up with indications that Muḥammad's mission is a universal one, as when God tells him that He has sent him to "humankind entire" (Q34:28) and as "a mercy unto all beings" (Q21:107).

6. Ṭabarānī, *al-Muʿjam al-awsaṭ*, Cairo 1995, 9:69 no. 9147.

Strong monotheism

In principle the proposition that there is only one god sounds clear-cut: either you believe it or you don't. Historically, however, there have been gray areas. For example, is one still a monotheist if one believes God to have a son—"that our Lord Jesus Christ, the Son of God, is God and Man," as the Athanasian Creed has it? Or if one believes in the doctrine of the Trinity? This means, as the same creed expresses it, "that we worship one God in Trinity, and Trinity in Unity; neither confounding the Persons: nor dividing the Substance. . . . So the Father is God, the Son is God: and the Holy Ghost is God. And yet they are not three Gods: but one God."[7] Or what if one venerates lesser beings such as saints or angels in an effort to get through to God, saying, "We only serve them that they may bring us nigh in nearness to God" (Q39:3)? Without getting tied up in such theological issues we can make a historically useful distinction between weaker and stronger forms of monotheism—with the qualification that from the point of view of strong monotheists, what they believe is simply monotheism, weak monotheism being no more than a euphemism for creeping polytheism.

Muḥammad's message as embodied in the Qur'ān is a classic example of strong monotheism. Shock is expressed at the idea that God should have a son: Jesus was only a messenger, not God's son, and those who say "God is the Messiah, Mary's son" are unbelievers (Q5:17). One might have expected that the Jews would be in the clear on this point, but in fact they are accused of believing Ezra to be the son of God. Belief in a Trinity is likewise condemned: "They are unbelievers who say, 'God is the Third of Three.' No god is there but One God" (Q5:73). Nor is it acceptable to try to approach God through lesser beings; those who take protectors other than God are not redeemed by their claim that they serve them only to get closer to Him. It is in fact a historically puzzling feature of Qur'ānic polemic, even when not directed against Jews and Christians, that it often seems to take aim at weak monotheists rather than the outright pagans described in our non-Qur'ānic sources. For example, we are told that these opponents will affirm that the earth belongs to God, that He is "the Lord of the seven heavens," and that "the dominion of everything" is in His hands (Q23:84–89). The point is that even this is not enough to make them true monotheists.

This discussion of Muḥammad's message yields several points that are of particular historical importance for us. The first is that the message was offensive. Denouncing "the abomination of idols" (Q22:30) and putting down the immediate

7. *The book of common prayer*, London n.d., 27–28, 29.

ancestors of those one is seeking to convert as having had "knowledge of naught" (Q5:104) does not make for popularity; monotheist incivility is part of the job description of a monotheistic prophet, but as we will see it has consequences. The second point is that despite his monotheist incivility, Muḥammad's message was in another way notably accommodating—far more so than Christianity. It showed a pronounced respect for the language and ethnic identity of the people to whom it was addressed, it assured them that monotheism was in fact the original religion of their ancestors, and it provided a monotheistic charter for their effectively pagan sanctuary. The third point is that although the message was addressed in the first instance to a particular community, Muḥammad's claim to be the successor of Moses and Jesus could easily be read to imply a message to all humankind, despite that fact that non-Arabs would not get the same degree of accommodation as Arabs would. A final point worth adding is the intensity of Muḥammad's focus on the Judeo-Christian tradition. The Zoroastrians are mentioned only once, and as no more than an item in a list of religious persuasions, good and bad. It is the Christian, not the Persian, encirclement of the Arabian Peninsula that is reflected in the concerns of the Qur'ān.

Muḥammad's state

The message, then, was uncompromising monotheism. But why would a monotheistic messenger consider it his business to establish a state? Was it something about the message, or something about the context in which the message was delivered?

The political consequences of the message

If we go back to the Bible, we do not find a strong correlation between monotheism and state formation. For example, Abraham was not the founder of any kind of state, and later there was a long period between the time of Joshua and the time of Samuel in which the Israelites did without a ruler. Eventually, we are told, this came to be seen as a problem by the elders of Israel, who wanted the Israelites to have a king in the same way as other peoples did; but the absence of a ruler was not seen as a problem by God, who made it very clear that He did not welcome the creation of the monarchy. If we move on to the New Testament, Jesus does not deny that he is in some sense a king, but as he puts it to Pilate, "My kingdom is not of this world" (John 18:33–36). There is, of course, one major Biblical precedent for a monotheistic prophet who rules some kind of polity: Moses. Indeed, our earliest datable account of the career of Muḥammad, that given by the Armenian chronicler of the 660s, describes him as "learned and informed in the history of Moses,"[8] and the Qur'ān's repeated references to Moses seem to bear this out. But while the book has a lot to say about Moses, its interest in his role as a ruler is rather limited. Moreover, state formation forms no part of the agenda of the warners whose stories are told in the Qur'ān, nor of the self-consciously Ishmaelite community described by Sozomenus. In short, there was no intrinsic link between monotheism and state formation, no inner logic leading directly from the content of Muḥammad's message to the creation of his state.

There was nevertheless a feature of his message that was indirectly relevant: its offensiveness. Like many pagans, those of Mecca were not by nature religiously intolerant; one of them is quoted by Ibn Isḥāq (d. 767–68), the author of the standard life of Muḥammad, as asking rhetorically, "Why shouldn't a man choose a religion for himself?"[9] Ibn Isḥāq accordingly tells us that people did not turn against Muḥammad until he spoke disparagingly of their gods. It was only at that point that "they took great offense and resolved unanimously to treat him as an enemy," with the exception of a small and despised minority of converts to Islam. As a pagan delegation protested to Abū Ṭālib, an uncle of Muḥammad who was protecting him though himself a pagan, "Your nephew has cursed our gods, insulted our religion, mocked our way of life, and accused our forefathers of error." They accordingly demanded that Abū Ṭālib either put an end to Muḥammad's activities or stop protecting him. Yet even after that they were willing to make an agreement to live and let live: "Let him have his religion and we will have ours." The intransigence was on Muḥammad's side. Once, in a moment of weakness, we are told that he compromised by inserting into the text of the revelation verses that accorded to three pagan goddesses (one of them Allāt) the role of intercessors with God. That lapse apart, he stayed true to his mission, with rather predictable results.

Muḥammad's need for protection

The pagans now began to persecute the Muslims. Here is how Ibn Isḥāq describes it: "Then Quraysh incited one another against the followers of the Prophet in each clan. . . . So each clan fell upon those of its members who were Muslims, tormenting them and seducing them from their religion. But God protected His Messenger from them through his uncle Abū Ṭālib. When he saw Quraysh behaving in this way toward the Banū Hāshim . . . , he called on them [the Banū Hāshim]

8. *The Armenian history attributed to Sebeos*, trans. R. W. Thomson, Liverpool 1999, 95.

9. For the quotations in this paragraph see Ibn Isḥāq, *The life of Muhammad*, trans. A. Guillaume, Oxford 1955, 118, 119, 158, 191.

to join him in protecting the Messenger."[10] They did so, with one exception. As this narrative makes clear, one could not go around persecuting people in Mecca without taking the tribal structure into account. For a clan to persecute its own Muslims was not a problem, but an attempt to persecute Muslims of another clan would have led to trouble between the two clans. Moreover, the idea that each clan should persecute its own Muslims did not work in the case of Muḥammad himself, since his uncle was able to secure the commitment of his clan, the Banū Hāshim, to join him in protecting Muḥammad. The upshot was that whereas Muḥammad's own position was secure enough as long as Abū Ṭālib was alive, that of his followers in most clans was not. Finding protection for these vulnerable followers was now a major practical problem for Muḥammad, and unless he was prepared to compromise his message, he clearly could not solve it within Mecca itself.

Hence he started to look for protection outside Mecca. Gaining the patronage of a king, much as Martin Luther did with the elector of Saxony, would have solved his problem. He would then have been a religious leader working in concert with a secular ruler. We find such a duo in the Biblical account of ancient Israel, where at one time Samuel was the religious leader and Saul the political leader—an arrangement referred to in the Qur'ānic account of Saul. A later parallel would be the collaboration of the eighteenth-century religious reformer Muḥammad ibn 'Abd al-Wahhāb with the Saudi ruler in eastern Arabia. But for Muḥammad this was not an option, since as we have seen there was no king to be found in the Ḥijāz. The nearest sympathetic ruler was the Negus of Christian Ethiopia, who was willing to provide a refuge for persecuted Muslims who could make their way there (the two empires of late antiquity play no part in this story). As Ibn Isḥāq tells it, "When the Prophet saw how his followers were suffering, while he himself was quite safe thanks to the support of God and his uncle Abū Ṭālib, and that he could do nothing to protect them from the trials they were exposed to, he said to them: 'I suggest you go off to Ethiopia, for there's a king there under whose rule no one is wronged.'"[11] More than eighty Muslims took this course. But Muḥammad himself did not go. If he wanted Islam to have a future in the Ḥijāz, he needed to find protection closer to home.

In the absence of a local king, that meant looking for a tribe to act as protector, and the search was made all the more urgent by the death of Abū Ṭālib in 619. Muḥammad first tried a tribe, Thaqīf, that was sedentary like his own and that dominated the agricultural town of Ṭā'if much as Quraysh dominated Mecca. This

10. Ibn Hishām, *al-Sīra al-nabawiyya*, Cairo 1955, 1–2:268–69; for the context see Ibn Isḥāq, *The life of Muhammad*, 120.

11. Ibn Hishām, *al-Sīra al-nabawiyya*, 1–2:321; for the context see Ibn Isḥāq, *The life of Muhammad*, 146.

tribe was by Arabian standards unusually cohesive. One indication of this was the fact that the town was surrounded by a wall, a construction requiring large-scale collective effort for the public good. Another was the small number of the town's poets, for as a ninth-century scholar explains, in pre-Islamic Arabia poets with their fighting words flourished only where there was conflict. So Thaqīf would have been an effective protector. But when Muḥammad went there alone to speak to the leaders of the tribe, he was rebuffed, and one of them asked derisively, "Couldn't God have found someone else to send?"[12]

Muḥammad then widened his quest, making apt use of a pre-Islamic Arabian institution with which we are already familiar. As Ibn Isḥāq explains, "The Prophet used to present himself to the Arab tribes at fairs, as the opportunity arose, calling them to God and telling them that he was a prophet sent with a message, and asking them to believe in him and protect him until such time as God should make his mission plain."[13] He names four of these tribes and records that in each case Muḥammad was unsuccessful in his efforts. Had he been successful, he would presumably have found himself working with the existing leadership of the tribe. In one case we are told that the sticking point was the question whether the tribe would inherit Muḥammad's political power after his death; as he was not prepared to promise this, the negotiations fell through. We should notice one significant silence: Muḥammad did not approach any Jewish tribes.

The breakthrough

Finally, at a fair near Mecca where Muḥammad was presenting himself to the tribes in his usual way, he met with a positive response from some men of the tribe of Khazraj. Here we need a bit of background. Khazraj, along with Aws, was one of the two main Arab tribes of the large agricultural oasis of Yathrib and lived there alongside the three Jewish tribes of the oasis. These Jewish tribes were no less warlike than the Arab tribes were; an early source describes them as people with weapons and fortresses. That five tribes shared a single sprawling settlement made Yathrib far less cohesive than Mecca or Ṭā'if. Relations between Arab and Jewish tribal groups could be good, with cross-cutting alliances, but they could also be bad, and when they were bad, Ibn Isḥāq says, the Jews would threaten the Arabs with the coming of a prophet at whose hands the Arabs would be killed. As Ibn Isḥāq tells it, when Muḥammad encountered the Khazrajīs and learned who they were, he asked them whether they were allies of the Jews. They said they were, and he then invited them to sit with him so he could talk to them. They agreed,

12. Ibn Isḥāq, *The life of Muhammad*, 192.

13. Ibn Hishām, *al-Sīra al-nabawiyya*, 1–2:422; for the context see Ibn Isḥāq, *The life of Muhammad*, 194.

and he set out his message. Their reaction was to say to one another, "He must be the prophet the Jews have been threatening us with. Don't let them get to him first!" So they accepted Muḥammad's message, believing in him and in Islam as he had presented it to them. Speaking of Yathrib, they told him, "When we set out, our people were more riven by enmity and wrongdoing than any other. Maybe God will unite them through you. We'll go to them and call them to your cause. . . . If God unites them in it, there will be no man more powerful than you!"[14] In other words, Ibn Isḥāq is stressing two factors that account for the positive response of the Khazrajīs, such as it was. One was their exposure to the Jews, which gave them a religious awareness that most pagan Arabs would have lacked, and the other was the dire straits in which their oasis currently found itself. Here it is characteristic of the thinking of the pagan Arabs as represented in Muslim sources—and quite likely as it was in real life—that in each case the calculation that led them to accept Muḥammad's message was concerned solely with their interests in this world. To these points we can add something Ibn Isḥāq does not say. For a prophet in search of protection, what the Khazrajīs were offering was hardly reassuring. Rather than obtaining the ready-made protection of a single powerful and cohesive tribe, Muḥammad would be free to walk into a hornets' nest and contrive his protection for himself. Once in Yathrib he would get some local support, but it was not clear how much, and it would be up to him to make what he could of the contentious politics of the oasis. As one might expect, Muḥammad was in no hurry to accept such a risky deal; that he accepted it at all is an indication of the seriousness of the problem he confronted.

A year after this encounter with the Khazrajīs, Muḥammad met with twelve men from Yathrib, this time drawn from both the Arab tribes—but not the Jewish ones. They agreed to abide by a simple religious code, but not as yet to fight to protect him. When they returned to Yathrib, Muḥammad sent one of his trusted companions with them to instruct them in their new religion. The presence of this companion also solved a problem of tribal rivalry in the nascent Muslim community of Yathrib: neither the Awsīs nor the Khazrajīs could abide having a member of the other tribe lead the prayer.

The year after that, seventy-three men and two women of Aws and Khazraj met with Muḥammad. This time the agenda was to reach an agreement under which he would move to Yathrib. He accordingly asked the tribesmen to undertake to protect him as they would their women and children. While one of them was expressing agreement with this proposal, another interrupted with a tough question. Suppose they were to cut their ties with the Jews for his sake, and Muḥammad were to triumph over his enemies; could it be that he would then abandon them

14. Ibn Hishām, *al-Sīra al-nabawiyya*, 1–2:429; for the context see Ibn Isḥāq, *The life of Muhammad*, 198.

and go back to his own people? Muḥammad smiled and reassured them on this point, adding, "I will make war against those on whom you make war, and make peace with those with whom you make peace."[15] He then asked them to designate twelve leaders who would take charge of the affairs of their people. They did so, naming nine from Khazraj and three from Aws. Soon the matter was settled. Those members of Aws and Khazraj who accepted Islam and supported Muḥammad came to be known as the Anṣār, the "helpers."

Muḥammad now told his Meccan followers to leave for Yathrib, and in due course, as Ibn Isḥāq tells us, God gave him permission to follow suit. This removal from Mecca to Yathrib was the Hijra, the "emigration." Those of Muḥammad's Meccan followers who made the Hijra were the Muhājirs, the "emigrants." His own Hijra took place in the fall of 622, and the lunar year in which it fell was later adopted as year 1 of the Muslim era.

Ibn Isḥāq's account of the way in which Muḥammad came to found a state has a tight logic to it. But he does not present it as the unfolding of a grand design that was there from the start; rather, the state was a by-product of a process in which one thing led to another. Monotheist incivility led to a backlash, the backlash led to a need for protection, and in the absence of a king or a tribe that would provide it, the quest for protection led to Yathrib—or as we can now start to call it, Medina. There, for lack of a political order, Muḥammad had to create one himself. Given the union of political and religious authority in the person of Muḥammad that characterized his decade in Medina and became a paradigmatic feature of the Islamic vision of politics, we might have expected the tradition represented by Ibn Isḥāq to retroject this union to the very beginnings of Islam. That it did not do so says something in favor of the general credibility of the tradition.

The "Constitution of Medina"

A delicate question faced by Muḥammad once he had reached Medina was where in the oasis he should establish himself. Any decision he made would show favoritism toward one tribal group and thereby alienate others. His solution was to let his camel wander as it chose—or as God chose—while he refused numerous offers of hospitality on the way. Eventually the camel came to a halt and lay down, as it happened in the territory of the Banū Mālik ibn al-Najjār, one of the Khazrajī clans. There Muḥammad stayed in the house of a friendly tribesman, gave audience to his new neighbors, and built his mosque. This was a walled complex combining two things: a largely open-air public space that was used for a variety of purposes, not just religious but also social and political; and private dwellings for

15. Ibn Hishām, *al-Sīra al-nabawiyya*, 1–2:442; for the context see Ibn Isḥāq, *The life of Muhammad*, 204.

his wives. He now had to set about establishing a political order within which he and his followers would be secure, and in a fragmented tribal setting this was an even more troublesome issue than deciding where to live.

Some light on this process is shed by an archaic and often obscure document that Western scholars have dubbed the "Constitution of Medina." It is widely accepted as genuine, and as reflecting conditions early in Muḥammad's decade in Medina. It begins: "This is a document (*hādhā kitāb*) from Muḥammad the Prophet between the Believers and Muslims of Quraysh and Yathrib and those who follow them, join with them, and wage jihad (*jāhada*) alongside them."[16] What follows is a remarkable combination of elements old and new.

The old elements are tribal. Numerous tribal groups are mentioned in the document, for example the Banū 'l-Najjār, named alongside many other clans; the Jews of the Banū 'l-Najjār, presumably clients of the clan, named alongside many other such Jewish groups; Quraysh, seen as the enemy; and the Muhājirs of Quraysh. Several tribal institutions also appear: vengeance, blood money, ransom, alliance, clientage. An example of both types of element is the following clause (one among many): "The Banū 'l-Najjār keep to their tribal organization and leadership, continuing to cooperate with each other in accordance with their former mutual aid agreements regarding blood money, and every subgroup ransoms its captives according to what is customary and equitable among the believers."[17] Not everything in this translation is certain, but the continuing role of long-established tribal groups and practices in Muḥammad's polity is manifest.

Alongside these old elements there are three significant features of the document that are new. First, there now exists a community that constitutes "one people to the exclusion of others," defined, rather cumbersomely, as "the Believers and Muslims of Quraysh and Yathrib and those who follow them, join with them, and wage jihad alongside them."[18] The wording allows for the possibility that non-Muslims might be part of this community, and indeed they are: "The Jews have their religion and the Muslims have theirs," and the Jews "share expenditure with the believers as long as they are at war." However, this religiously plural character of the early community did not last.[19] What did last was the idea that the community is indivisible in ways that a tribe, with its multiple genealogical nodes, is not. Thus "a believer will not kill a believer in retaliation for an unbeliever and will not

16. M. Lecker, *The "Constitution of Medina,"* Princeton 2004, 32 (with a slightly different translation).

17. Translation based on Lecker, *The "Constitution of Medina,"* 32–33; for the context see Ibn Isḥāq, *The life of Muhammad*, 232.

18. This and the quotations that follow are based on the translations in Lecker, *The "Constitution of Medina,"* 32–35.

19. See F. M. Donner, *Muhammad and the believers*, Cambridge, MA 2010, for the argument that it lasted considerably longer than has been thought.

aid an unbeliever against a believer." Likewise, "the believers are each other's allies to the exclusion of other people," and "the peace of the believers is one"—meaning that "a believer will not make peace to the exclusion of another believer in fighting in the way of God." The second new element in the document is the supreme authority that regulates the community, though its role as it appears here is rather passive: "Whatever you are in dispute about should be referred to God and Muḥammad." Another clause speaks of such referral in cases of violence likely to cause dissension. Here the supreme authority is religious—God and His Prophet—but its scope is not limited to religious matters. The third new element is jihad, religious war; we have already seen references to it.

What we have here is a document in which old and new elements appear side by side. On the one hand, old tribal loyalties and institutions are recognized and endorsed, with the result that Muḥammad's polity is deeply embedded in the existing tribal society. But on the other hand, some key features of this polity are new and closely linked to Muḥammad's monotheism. Where the two orders conflict, the old order tends to be constrained by the new. Thus vengeance continues, and the believers will avenge deaths and injuries sustained by fellow believers in the course of fighting in the way of God, but a believer will not kill a fellow believer in retaliation for an unbeliever.

Muḥammad's military activity

As Ibn Isḥāq tells us, up to the point at which he reached his agreement with the Anṣār to move to Medina, Muḥammad's mission had been solely to call people to God and to put up with the unpleasant consequences this led to. Only now did God give him permission to fight those who wronged and attacked him and his followers. But once he was established in Medina warfare became an increasingly prominent part of his activities. During his decade there, Ibn Isḥāq tells us, he mounted no fewer than sixty-four military expeditions against unbelievers—another early source says seventy-nine—and of these he commanded twenty-seven in person. Some were offensive, some defensive. Many were minor forays involving small numbers of men engaged in more or less irregular warfare. But others, though modest by the standards of the outside world, were large by those of Arabia. Here is a list of Muḥammad's most famous expeditions (the figure on the left is the date, and the number of men on the Muslim side is as given by Ibn Isḥāq):

624	Battle of Badr	314 men
625	Battle of Uḥud	700 men
627	Battle of the Khandaq	3,000 men
628	Truce of Ḥudaybiya	700 or 1,400 men
630	Conquest of Mecca	10,000 men
630	Battle of Ḥunayn	12,000 men

This list reflects the centrality of Muḥammad's struggle with his hometown of Mecca. Badr was a successful attack on a Meccan force; Uḥud and the Battle of the Khandaq involved defense against Meccan attacks on Medina, the first a defeat and the second a victory; the truce made at Ḥudaybiya was likewise with the Meccans and was supposed to be good for ten years, but in fact lasted for less than two. The struggle finally ended with a "conquest" of Mecca that was almost bloodless. In this list only the Battle of Ḥunayn against the tribe of Hawāzin in the southern Ḥijāz takes us outside the framework of the confrontation with Mecca. Of these events, the Battle of Badr, as Muḥammad's first victory, was so significant in Muslim retrospect that Ibn Isḥāq gives us a complete listing of those who fought on the Muslim side, clan by clan. The 314 men present were made up of 83 Muhājirs and 231 Anṣār, 170 of the Anṣār being Khazrajīs and 61 being Awsīs. These numbers suggest that in the year and a half since his arrival in Medina Muḥammad had obtained a significant amount of local backing. Thereafter, if we can set any store by the figures, we see a rapid growth in the number of men Muḥammad could recruit for an expedition. What the list leaves out is a set of three expeditions in the direction of Syria—now back under Byzantine rule—that Muḥammad mounted toward the end of his life. Though they achieved little at the time, they were a prelude to the conquests that were to follow in the years after his death:

629	Battle of Mu'ta	3,000 men
630	Expedition to Tabūk	30,000 men
632	Raid on Ubnā	3,000 men

The first of these three expeditions was engaged by a Byzantine force and defeated to the east of the southern end of the Dead Sea, in what is now Jordan. Significantly, this defeat at Mu'ta remained the only major military engagement outside the Ḥijāz during Muḥammad's lifetime, and he was not present there himself. The second, led by the Prophet in person, in the event stopped at Tabūk, well short of entering Byzantine territory. The third was set to head for the same region as the first and eventually did so, but it had not yet left when Muḥammad died. To an outside observer the ventures of 629 and 632 would have looked like the usual Arab raids, the first firmly repulsed and the second of no great consequence. It is clear from the record of his raids that Muḥammad's expeditions often met with local opposition, but nobody else in Arabia at the time was engaged in a comparably far-flung enterprise.

If we think of these events as the top tier of Muḥammad's military activities, what should we reckon as the second tier? An obvious theme here would be his hostilities with the Jews, who proved unreceptive to his mission. No major battles were involved. First came his confrontations with the three Jewish tribes of Medina in 624–27; the outcome was that two of them were expelled, while the fate of the third was the execution of the men and the enslavement of the women and children. Then in 628 it was the turn of the two Jewish oases of the northern Ḥijāz, Khaybar and Fadak. Besieged by Muḥammad in their fortresses, the Jews of Khaybar surrendered; the terms were that they should continue to cultivate the land but hand over half the produce of the oasis each year. Seeing what had happened to their coreligionists, the Jews of Fadak immediately agreed to a similar arrangement. The importance of these hostilities from Muḥammad's point of view was twofold. They ended any threat from hostile Jewish tribes in the Ḥijāz, and they provided him with spoils, land, and produce that he could use to support and reward his followers, especially the Muhājirs who had left their livelihoods behind them when they migrated to Medina.

What, then, did the bottom tier look like? Of course every raid is different. But let us pick out one that, while it has something to tell us about Muḥammad's warfare, is even more revealing about his domestic problems—domestic in more than one sense.

The raid on the Banū 'l-Muṣṭaliq

The Banū 'l-Muṣṭaliq were nomads of the southwestern Ḥijāz with links to Mecca. Ibn Isḥāq recounts that Muḥammad had intelligence that they were gathering against him under their chief, so he decided on a preemptive strike. This must have been around 627. The site of the encounter was a watering place, and Muḥammad won an easy victory: the Banū 'l-Muṣṭaliq fled, some were killed, and he took possession of their wives, children, and property as booty. Later he distributed the captives among his followers. But for a series of complications, this would have been a straightforward case of mission accomplished.

The first complication was an instance of friendly fire. In the fog of war, a Khazrajī had mistaken a Meccan Muslim for one of the enemy and killed him. The slain man's brother was still in Mecca and now came to Muḥammad purporting to be a Muslim. He accepted the blood money that was due to him under Islamic rules but then reverted to pagan rules, killing his brother's killer and fleeing back to Mecca. In a manner characteristic of Arab culture then and later, he celebrated this escapade in verse, boasting that "I gave free vent to my vengeance / and was the first to return to the idols."[20] We see here the seventh-century Arabian version of a selfie; since then the technology has improved, but the psychology remains the same. Muḥammad did not forgive or forget this incident, and when he occupied Mecca in 630, this man was among the small number of people he had killed.

But there was worse to come in the aftermath of the raid—much worse. In the press around the watering place two men got into a fight. Neither the men nor the

20. Ibn Isḥāq, *The life of Muhammad*, 492.

tribes they belonged to were in themselves of much consequence for Muḥammad's enterprise, but both men were well connected: one was an ally of a Khazrajī clan and the other a hireling of a prominent Qurashī, no less than the future caliph 'Umar ibn al-Khaṭṭāb (d. 644). The first man called upon the Anṣār to come to his aid, and the second countered by appealing to the Muhājirs. The conflict threatened to split Muḥammad's constituency along its most dangerous fault line, the division between his Meccan and Medinese followers. Moreover, the incident caught the attention of 'Abdallāh ibn Ubayy, the influential chief of a Khazrajī clan. This man secretly—or not so secretly—detested Muḥammad, whose arrival in Medina had frustrated his hopes of making himself king there. Ibn Ubayy now gave vent to a vein of paranoia latent in the thinking of the Anṣār: they had only themselves to blame, he said, for foolishly agreeing to let those Meccans move into their oasis and sharing their property with them; now the intruders were taking over. His rant was overheard by a Khazrajī boy who went and told Muḥammad about it. 'Umar was with Muḥammad at the time, and in his characteristic headstrong way he wanted Muḥammad to have Ibn Ubayy killed. This Muḥammad was not about to do; as he explained to 'Umar, he did not want the public relations disaster of having people say that he was killing his own companions—a category to which Ibn Ubayy nominally belonged. Instead, Muḥammad ordered his men to set out for home even though it was the most unpleasant time of the day, and he kept them moving until they were utterly exhausted. This had the desired effect of distracting them from the dissension that the incident might otherwise have caused.

In the meantime Ibn Ubayy's son was worrying that Muḥammad would want to have his father killed. Unlike the father, the son was a good Muslim. So he went to Muḥammad and told him, "If you must do it, then order me to do it and I will bring you his head."[21] He added that among Khazraj there was no man more loyal to his father than he was, and that he feared that if Muḥammad had someone else kill Ibn Ubayy he would be unable to restrain himself: he would kill the killer, thereby killing a believer for an unbeliever and ending up in hell. This was an astute move. Had Muḥammad wanted to have Ibn Ubayy killed, he would now have been in a distinctly awkward situation. As God's Prophet he could hardly order a son to kill his own father, but having someone else do the deed would assuredly have led to a politically disruptive blood feud.

There was one final complication, though not an entirely unwelcome one. The chief of the Banū 'l-Muṣṭaliq had a daughter named Juwayriya who was now among the captives. She was a very attractive young woman, and fully aware of it. According to the story as told by 'Ā'isha, Muḥammad's favorite wife, the man to whose

21. Ibn Isḥāq, *The life of Muhammad*, 492.

lot she had fallen had a rare capacity for delayed gratification. Instead of exercising his sexual rights as her owner, he was prepared to let her ransom herself if she could raise the money. So she came to Muḥammad asking for his help in this endeavor. ʿĀʾisha, who had taken a dislike to Juwayriya the moment she walked in, tells us that she knew exactly how this scene was going to play out. She was not mistaken. In a moment Muḥammad was offering to pay Juwayriya's ransom and marry her. This domestic drama had an interesting repercussion, or maybe two. The first concerned the captives. These hard-won slaves of Muḥammad's followers had now become the in-laws of their Prophet, which meant that the Muslims could not decently keep them in slavery. The result was that a hundred families of the Banū ʾl-Muṣṭaliq were set free. As ʿĀʾisha conceded—perhaps through clenched teeth—"I do not know a woman who was a greater blessing to her people than she was."[22] The other possible repercussion is more speculative. Was it mere coincidence that it was on the way home from this raid that an incident occurred which raised doubts about ʿĀʾisha's fidelity to her husband? Some advised him to get rid of her; as his cousin ʿAlī bluntly told him, "Women are plentiful, and you can easily change one for another." In the end it took a special Qurʾānic revelation to clear ʿĀʾisha's name and restore her to her husband's favor.

Anyone who expects the life of Muḥammad to read like the Gospels will be taken aback by the story of the raid on the Banū ʾl-Muṣṭaliq, and not just by the military activity that figures briefly at the beginning of the narrative. The storytelling is inspired by a vivid sense of what politics is like—that everything has a way of happening at once, that foreign affairs are easily swamped by domestic tensions, that scandal is never far below the surface, and that we should appreciate political astuteness—whether it be Muḥammad deflecting the imprudent advice of ʿUmar and wearing out his men with a forced march, or Ibn Ubayy's son deftly maneuvering to protect the life of his father, or the panache with which Juwayriya plays her cards. All this may have something to do with how things actually were, but it could also tell us a lot about the audience for whom the story was intended: not a community of otherworldly pietists like the early Christian audience of the Gospels, but rather an imperial military and political elite, men for whom, most of the time, this world bulked larger than the next.

The extent of Muḥammad's state

As we have seen, Muḥammad was able to project real military force within the Ḥijāz. But once he had demonstrated the ability to use it he did not always need to deploy it. Hence it was that after Muḥammad had conquered Khaybar, Fadak

22. For this and the quotation that follows see Ibn Isḥāq, *The life of Muhammad*, 493, 496.

submitted without hostilities, and when he later advanced on his hometown with ten thousand men, the Meccans gave up almost without a fight. Likewise, after he had defeated the nomads of Hawāzin, the nearby town of Ṭā'if grudgingly came to terms. So without going into his relations with all the tribes of the Ḥijāz, we can think of Muḥammad as acquiring a fairly strong grip on the region. This is confirmed by what happened after his death, when many Arab tribes rebelled against his successor in a set of events known as the Ridda (Apostasy): those in the vicinity of Medina remained loyal, most of those between Medina and Mecca did not rebel, the nomadic Hawāzin did nothing worse than sit on the fence, and Thaqīf was steadfast. Only Sulaym played a prominent role in the rebellions. But what of the rest of Arabia with its thankless landscapes and ungovernable tribes?

Outside the Ḥijāz, as we have seen, the only part of the peninsula to which Muḥammad dispatched sizeable military expeditions was the northwest, no doubt because it was on the borders of Syria, with its combination of the "Holy Land" (Q5:21) and relative agricultural wealth. That apart, he sent a few relatively small expeditions to the southwest, and none at all to the rest of Arabia. Nor did he have any naval presence on the Red Sea, let alone in the Gulf of Aden or the Persian Gulf. And yet our sources report delegations sent by a considerable number of Arabian tribes. They tell us that he was able to assert some degree of authority over most of the peninsula, appointing governors and collecting taxes as far afield as the Yemen, Oman, Yamāma (south of Najd), and the part of the mainland known as Baḥrayn. The probability is that his authority outside the Ḥijāz, insofar as it existed, was weak and geographically uneven. This supposition finds a measure of support in the fact that Muḥammad would often appoint as his agent over a tribe someone from the same region, or even a member of the tribe in question. There was also a pattern whereby the weaker of two tribal factions would ally with Muḥammad against the stronger. Many tribes contained only enclaves of Muslims, or none at all. In short, we have the impression that the expansion of Muḥammad's state outside the Ḥijāz was thin and patchy—but at the same time that it left no major region of Arabia untouched.

If this picture is correct, it would be hard to explain it in purely material terms. Clearly religious factors played a key part in the spread of Islam in Arabia; Muḥammad, for all his activity as a politician during his years in Medina, was in the first instance a prophet. Two points in particular are worth making here. The first is that the reception of his message is more than likely to have been aided by its appeal to Arab identity. The Muslim sources are unhelpful here, but it is worth going back to the Armenian chronicler who described Muḥammad as very well acquainted with the story of Moses. He also tells us that when Muḥammad presented himself to the Ishmaelites he "taught them to recognize the God of Abraham." He goes on to say that "now because the command was from on high, at a single order they all came together in unity of religion. Abandoning their vain cults, they turned to the living God who had appeared to their father Abraham."[23] For this chronicler, or more precisely for the prisoners of war who were his sources, the Abrahamic ancestry of the Arabs was clearly central to the appeal of Muḥammad's preaching to them. The second point is that we have indirect but telling evidence of the imaginative impact of Muḥammad's religion on the Arabs. After his death, and perhaps even before, one form taken by the short-lived rejection of Islam in Arabia was the appearance of no fewer than five false prophets—false, that is to say, in the eyes of our Muslim sources. There was one in the Yemen, one in Yamāma, two—including a woman—among the nomads of Najd, and one in Oman. This epidemic of copycat prophets is a backhanded compliment to the wide appeal of Muḥammad's mission in Arabia.

The character of Muḥammad's state

What did Muḥammad's state consist of? This is one of those occasions when it pays to notice what is *not* there. What is conspicuously missing from the narratives we have been looking at is any formal structure of power mediating relations between Muḥammad and the people he led. The one exception we have encountered is only apparent. As we saw, in the negotiations that led to his move to Medina, Muḥammad asked the Anṣār to designate twelve leaders who would take charge of the affairs of their people. We might have expected to encounter this institution repeatedly in the course of his time in Medina, but instead it simply disappears from the narrative. Another innovation introduced by Muḥammad, this one dating from soon after the Hijra, was "brothering": He told his followers to form pairs of brothers in God, and typically one of the Muhājirs would pair with one of the Anṣār. But again, this system seems to have had very little continuing role in the structure of Muhammad's state.

It was not that more centralized structures emerged to replace these early experiments as Muḥammad consolidated his power. He did indeed have men who wrote for him—the tradition has it that he himself was illiterate—but we have nothing to indicate the emergence of an incipient bureaucracy. Likewise, each time Muḥammad sent out an expedition he recruited men for the occasion, but apart from a small body of guards with a rotating commandership that we hear of once, we see no sign of the development of a standing army with a continuing existence between expeditions. In the same way Muḥammad talked to many people but had no formal council with a defined membership. He would sometimes consult his followers informally before a major battle. Thus in the consultation (*shūrā*) preceding the Battle of Uḥud in 625 he was persuaded against his better judgment into

23. *The Armenian history attributed to Sebeos*, 95–96.

taking a course of action that led to disaster. The consultation before the Battle of the Khandaq in 627 was more fruitful: in one account Salmān al-Fārisī, who was Muḥammad's Persian companion, drew on his experience of warfare in his homeland to suggest digging a trench (*khandaq*, an Arabic word of Persian origin) that would prevent enemy cavalry from entering the oasis through a gap in its natural defenses. (This figures—a Byzantine strategist of the period describes how the Persians would dig ditches when preparing for a battle.) Muḥammad adopted the idea and joined with his men in the hard work of excavation. Yet another context that highlights the absence of structure is the pattern of access to Muḥammad. Like many of his followers, he would spend much of his time sitting and talking in his mosque, so that was the place to look for him. The mosque had a gate—in fact several—but there were no guards posted there, and no requirement that a visitor should deposit his arms before entering. Once inside the mosque, there was no chamberlain to decide whether and when the visitor would be permitted to speak to Muḥammad. It was for the visitor to pick him out and approach him—which could be a problem if he did not already know Muḥammad by sight, as there was nothing to distinguish the Prophet from any of his companions. Having approached him, the visitor would greet him, sit down in front of him, and transact his business. It fits with this informal setting that the Qur'ān finds it necessary to urge the believers not to shout at the Prophet as they do at one another. Indeed, though inconvenient, it would not be unreasonable to insist on calling Muḥammad's polity something other than a state.

There is an interesting comparison to be made here with Moses as he is depicted in the Bible, and it may help us in thinking about Muḥammad. When Moses's father-in-law Jethro came to visit him, he found Moses sitting in judgment over the disputes of his people from morning to night. Jethro warned him that this was not sustainable—he was wearing himself out with a burden that he could not bear alone. So Jethro told Moses that he should seek out able and trustworthy men and put them in charge of thousands, hundreds, fifties, and tens. These officers should then judge small matters and refer only hard cases to Moses himself. Moses listened to his father-in-law and did exactly as he said (Exod. 18:14–26). In other words, he gave up micromanaging and started to delegate.

Muḥammad, by contrast, was never much of a delegator. This makes it interesting to see what he did on occasions when he had no choice but to delegate. He faced such a situation each time he decided on a military expedition. If he led it himself he had to appoint a deputy to look after Medina while he was away, and if he stayed at home he had to appoint a commander to lead the expedition. Let us concentrate on the commanders. Here, according to a list of expeditions given by the scholar Wāqidī (d. 823), are the commanders Muḥammad appointed for the nine expeditions he sent out in year 8 of the Hijra, the lunar year that began in May 629 and ended in April 630:

	Name of expedition	Name of commander	Other commands
1.	al-Kadīd	Ghālib ibn ʿAbdallāh al-Laythī	1
2.	al-Siyy	Shujāʿ ibn Wahb al-Asadī	0
3.	Dhāt Aṭlāḥ	Kaʿb ibn ʿUmayr al-Ghifārī	0
4	Mu'ta	Zayd ibn Ḥāritha al-Kalbī	7
5.	Dhāt al-Salāsil	ʿAmr ibn al-ʿĀṣ al-Sahmī	0
6.	al-Khabaṭ	Abū ʿUbayda ibn al-Jarrāḥ al-Fihrī	1
7.	Khaḍira	Abū Qatāda ibn Ribʿī al-Salamī	1
8.	Iḍam	Abū Qatāda ibn Ribʿī al-Salamī	1
9.	Banū Jadhīma	Khālid ibn al-Walīd al-Makhzūmī	2

What does this list tell us? The names of the expeditions are there just to identify them; they refer to the place to which the expedition went or in one instance to the tribe against which it was directed. The names of the commanders are more interesting for our purposes, since with some coaxing they reveal tribal affiliations. We look first for members of Muḥammad's core constituencies. From his own tribe of Quraysh we find three (nos. 5, 6, and 9), all of them well-known figures with military talent. Then we move to the Anṣār and find one, a Khazrajī known as "the knight of the Messenger of God,"[24] which again suggests military talent; he commands two expeditions in the course of the year (nos. 7 and 8). But these figures account for only half the commanders that year. Of the remaining four, two belong to small tribal groups closely associated with Mecca (nos. 1 and 2), and one stems from a small tribe living between Mecca and Medina (no. 3). That leaves one, number 4, whose original tribal affiliation is of no consequence. This Zayd was a former slave of Muḥammad's who became his freedman and was entirely dependent on him. These pieces of information already tell us something: Meccans are disproportionately represented vis-à-vis Medinese, as are groups outside these core constituencies. Now let us turn to the figures in the final column, which show the number of times Muḥammad appointed each man as the commander of an expedition in other years. What we see is that with one exception, they were not serial commanders. Two other commands are the maximum (no. 9), and one or none is standard. The only exception (no. 4), tellingly, is the man who had been, and in a significant sense remained, a wholly owned subsidiary of Muḥammad's. If we extended the sample to the entire set of expeditions Muḥammad sent out during the decade when he ruled in Medina, the results would be very similar.

Here again, it is worth noting what Muḥammad did *not* do. He did not choose for himself a favorite general, or a select group of generals, distinguished by a combination of military ability and political standing in the community. He did indeed use a few people of such stature in year 8, but as we see he made little use

24. Ibn ʿAbd al-Barr, *al-Istīʿāb fī maʿrifat al-aṣḥāb*, Cairo n.d., 1731.

of these individuals in other years. In general, it is obvious that in selecting commanders he was not prioritizing either tribal standing or military experience. The simplest explanation for this pattern is that he wished to avoid letting any of his followers acquire a power base that might rival his own. In a society with an unusually high rate of political participation this made sense. Muḥammad was ready to delegate when he had to, but he was not prepared to build up any one of his followers as his right-hand man. It fits well with this perspective that his only serial commander should have been his former slave—a choice that may have suited Muḥammad very well but does not seem to have appealed to his followers.

If one notable feature of Muḥammad's state was the lack of intermediate powers, another was the fusion of political and religious authority in his person. This aspect of his rule was highlighted by the physical arrangements he made when establishing his base in Medina. His mosque, as we have seen, was a place of worship where his followers could also spend time socially and confer politically. As such it had a close parallel in Mecca, where the enclosed space around the Kaʿba, likewise known as the "mosque," met the same needs. But Mecca had something else adjoining this sacred space: a kind of town hall (the Dār al-Nadwa) whose functions were purely secular. When Muḥammad moved to Medina he recreated the mosque but left the town hall behind. Yet despite his authority to decide both secular and religious issues affecting his community, there was a major asymmetry here. What Muḥammad knew best about was religious questions—he was, after all, God's Prophet. But this did not mean that he knew best about secular matters. In preparing his men for the Battle of Badr in 624 he halted them in an ill-chosen position. One of his companions politely asked him whether this decision was pursuant to a command from God or just a matter of military judgment. On being told it was the second, this companion pointed out a much better location, one where the Muslims would have access to a water supply and at the same time deny it to the enemy. Muḥammad took his advice and won the battle. Essentially the same point is made in a famous story about his interactions with some cultivators of date palms. Thinking he knew best, he gave them advice that resulted in a failed harvest. At that point he recognized his mistake and told them that they were better informed about their worldly affairs than he was.

If we can trust Ibn Isḥāq, the nature of Muḥammad's authority was something his contemporaries thought about quite a lot. The question they asked themselves was whether he was a king or a prophet. To those who already believed in him he was, of course, a prophet; his followers addressed him as "Messenger of God." To those who did not like him, by contrast, he was a king; an unsympathetic Jew in Khaybar accused his wife of having a crush on "Muḥammad the king of the Ḥijāz."[25] Others were more open-minded. There is a long story about a major Christian

25. Ibn Isḥāq, *The life of Muhammad*, 515.

tribal chief from north Arabia, ʿAdī ibn Ḥātim (d. 687–88), who paid Muḥammad a visit after an astute female relative had advised him to get on Muḥammad's bandwagon irrespective of whether he was a prophet or a king. ʿAdī thereupon came to Medina and sought out Muḥammad at his mosque. Appreciating the importance of his visitor, Muḥammad suggested that they repair to his house and talk there. On the way they were delayed by an encounter with a frail old woman, who had a problem and wanted to talk to Muḥammad about it. He spent a considerable amount of time with her, from which ʿAdī drew the inference that he could not be a king—kings don't spend time on the needs of old women. When they eventually reached the house, which can only have been a stone's throw away, Muḥammad threw a cushion to ʿAdī and told him to sit on it. There was apparently no other cushion in the house, so after first politely refusing, ʿAdī sat on the cushion while Muḥammad sat on the ground. ʿAdī again remarked to himself that this was not the way a king would behave, and in due course he reached the conclusion that Muḥammad had to be a prophet.

Someone who thought about the same question in more sophisticated terms several centuries later was Ibn Khaldūn. "The Arabs," he said, "are of all nations the one most remote from royal leadership."[26] He attributed this characteristic to their rootedness in desert life, which made them "the least willing of nations to subordinate themselves to each other." Religion, however, provided a way around this obstacle. Whether in the form of prophecy or of sainthood, it could exercise a restraining influence on the Arabs, overriding their haughtiness and jealousy. "It is, then, easy for them to subordinate themselves and to unite," this being "achieved by the common religion they now have"—a judgment reminiscent of the account given by our Armenian chronicler. Hence it is that "Arabs can obtain royal authority only by making use of some religious coloring." In short, to use a metaphor that would not have meant much to Ibn Khaldūn, religion makes possible an end run around the refractoriness of Arab tribalism and thereby opens the door to Arab state formation. In fact, Ibn Khaldūn was wrong to deny altogether the ability of Arab tribes to engage in nonreligious state formation on a limited scale; there had been examples of it before the rise of Islam, and there would be more after it. But he put his finger on a mode of religious state formation in a tribal society of which we have no historical attestations before the rise of Islam, though we have many in the centuries that followed it. This mode seems to be something that Muḥammad discovered for himself as one thing led to another in the course of his career as a monotheistic prophet. The repetition of the pattern in later centuries shows Muḥammad's continuing success in inspiring lesser imitators.

26. For this and the quotations that follow see Ibn Khaldûn, *The Muqaddimah*, Princeton 1967, 1:305–6.

Messages about the state

During his decade in Medina Muḥammad continued to receive revelations from on high, and we can easily find in the Qur'ān themes relating to his political and military career in the oasis. We should at least glance at some of them, not just because they shed light on the nature of Muḥammad's state, but also because they are central to what one might call his political legacy, the set of ideas that were part of the mix available to Muslims engaged in political thought and action in subsequent centuries. In this they differ from the Constitution of Medina, which despite its preservation in the sources had little resonance in later Muslim politics.

Following the sequence of Muḥammad's career, we can start with the term Hijra, "emigration." Although the Qur'ān does not use the word, it makes frequent use of related forms, including the term Muhājir, "emigrant." The core of the idea is putting physical and moral distance between oneself and the unbelievers. Doing so, the Qur'ān insists, should not be a practical problem: "Whoso emigrates in the way of God will find in the earth many refuges" (Q4:100). By contrast, those who merely believe but do not emigrate are assigned a distinctly inferior status. Emigration may be no more than a matter of finding a refuge, as in the case of the early Muslims who were granted religious asylum if they made the journey to Ethiopia; that too was a Hijra. But it may also lead to something more active: Hijra and jihad are often mentioned in the same breath. Thus we read that "the believers and those who emigrate (*hājarū*) and struggle (*jāhadū*) in God's way" may expect divine mercy (Q2:218).

Moving on to jihad, warfare against the unbelievers is a theme with a strong presence in the Qur'ān. One verse announces: "Leave is granted to those who fight because they have been wronged"; in the next verse they are described as having been "expelled from their habitations without right" (Q22:39–40). These verses form part of a passage that is said to have been revealed to Muḥammad at the moment when God gave him permission to fight. Another verse tells the believers that just as soon as the sacred months are over they should "slay the idolaters wherever you find them, and take them, and confine them, and lie in wait for them at every place of ambush" (Q9:5). Yet another states that "God has bought from the believers their selves and their possessions against the gift of Paradise; they fight in the way of God; they kill and are killed" (Q9:111). They should accordingly fight the unbelievers until "the religion is God's entirely" (Q8:39). There was, however, a crucial qualification to all this: certain unbelievers could be tolerated on suitable terms. The key verse runs: "Fight those who believe not in God and the Last Day and do not forbid what God and His Messenger have forbidden—such men as practice not the religion of truth, being of those who have been given the Book—until they pay the poll tax (*jizya*) out of hand and have been humbled" (Q9:29). Despite the obscurity of the wording, this verse was read as divine approval for the toleration of a set of unbelievers that included Jews and Christians and was extended to others, notably Zoroastrians.

The Qur'ān has less to say about the nature of Muḥammad's polity, but it still has a few things to tell us. It calls repeatedly for obedience to God and His Messenger—which suggests, of course, that securing obedience was proving something of a problem, as might be expected in an Arabian society. Thus God tells Muḥammad to say "Obey God and the Messenger," but the verse anticipates noncompliance by adding that "if they turn their backs, God loves not the unbelievers" (Q3:32). We read that "it is not for any believer, man or woman, when God and His Messenger have decreed a matter, to have the choice in the affair" (Q33:36). One verse adds to the list of those who are to be obeyed the rather vague phrase "those in authority among you." It then goes on to a stipulation familiar to us from the Constitution of Medina: "If you should quarrel on anything, refer it to God and the Messenger" (Q4:59). Here, too, the commandment betrays a problem: as we learn from another passage, there are people who claim to believe in God and His Messenger, but "when they are called to God and His Messenger that he may judge between them, lo, a party of them are swerving aside" (Q24:47–48). Yet there is also a recognition that relations between Muḥammad and his followers are a two-way street. In one verse God congratulates him on having avoided a harshness that would have alienated them and tells him to be forgiving and "take counsel with them in the affair" (Q3:159). In other ways, however, the Qur'ān puts some distance between Muḥammad and his followers. His domestic life provides a striking example. His wives have a special status among the believers and are subject to restrictions the Qur'ān does not otherwise impose on women. They are the "mothers" of the believers (Q33:6) and "are not as other women" (Q33:32). "Remain in your houses," they are told; they should not flaunt their sexuality in the ancient pagan manner (Q33:33), and the believers should address them only "from behind a curtain" (Q33:53). Indeed, in the event of indecent behavior on their part, "the chastisement shall be doubled" (Q33:30). Muḥammad also has the exclusive privilege of taking in marriage any woman who "gives herself to the Prophet" (Q33:50). Apart from the continued existence of slavery and the subordination of women to men, this is perhaps the single most inegalitarian aspect of Muḥammad's polity.

A significant feature of the Qur'ānic language of politics is its marked tendency to prefer ideological phrases to proper names. Thus on one side we find "those who believe," "the friends of God," "the party of God" (*ḥizb Allāh*), while on the other are "those who disbelieve," "the enemies of God," "the party of Satan." The Bible, by contrast, ranges the "Children of Israel" against the "Philistines," the "Canaanites," the "Amorites," and the like. In a similar way the idea of Hijra is ideologically loaded; it is as if in an American context the term "immigration" could be used only of the Puritans and not of the Blacks, the Irish, the Poles, or the Latinos. Jihad is another case in point: unlike "warfare," it refers to something Muslims do, to the exclusion of comparable activities on the part of non-Muslims. This makes the Qur'ānic articulation of Muḥammad's politics very different in texture from the story of Moses as told in the Bible, and it makes it easy to transfer the vocabulary of Qur'ānic politics from the context in which it originated to any number of other contexts, medieval and modern.

There is a final aspect of Muḥammad's activity in Medina that we should look for in the Qur'ān: legislation. As we have already noted in passing, in the Qur'ānic conception successive revelations have legal content. Thus the Torah contains "God's judgment," including the prescription "a life for a life, an eye for an eye, a nose for a nose, an ear for an ear" (Q5:43, 45); likewise the "people of the Gospel" should judge in accordance with its provisions (Q5:47). Now that God has revealed a scripture to Muḥammad, he too should judge "according to what God has sent down" (Q5:48). The Qur'ān is not in fact a law code, and its coverage of legal matters is uneven, but it does contain a considerable amount of legal material. Some of the topics dealt with are religious in a narrow sense, such as the daily ritual prayers, fasting in the lunar month of Ramaḍān, almsgiving, and the pilgrimage to Mecca; conspicuously absent here is any kind of role for a priesthood. Some topics pertain to family or household law, as with marriage, divorce, inheritance, and slavery. Some are commercial, as with rules regarding the recording of debts. Yet others are penal, as with the prohibitions of usury, wine drinking, and adultery. This list is by no means exhaustive, but it should be enough to make it clear that Islam—like Judaism and unlike Christianity—is a law-centered religion. This legal orientation is taken much further in two bodies of material that we leave aside here: the traditions about the sayings and doings of Muḥammad, and the voluminous writings of the later Islamic jurists.

As a substantive example of Qur'ānic legislation we can take something that looks unfamiliar in the modern West but fits well with the Arabian tribal background: the law of homicide. The key verse reads: "O believers, prescribed for you is retaliation, touching the slain: freeman for freeman, slave for slave, female for female" (Q2:178). This is the same idea that we find in the tribal society of ancient Israel: "life for life" (Exod. 21:23, Deut. 19:21). The Qur'ānic verse then goes on to mention a payment (that is to say, of blood money) that may be accepted in place of the retaliatory killing. But what if one believer slays another in error? The slayer must then manumit a believing slave to appease God and pay blood money to compensate the family; recall the case of friendly fire during the raid on the Banū 'l-Muṣṭaliq, though we heard nothing of a slave being manumitted on that occasion. What if the slayer acts deliberately? Then "his recompense is Gehenna, therein dwelling forever" (Q4:92–93). That settles his fate in the next world, but for the consequences in this world we have to turn to another verse: "Whosoever is slain unjustly, We have appointed to his next of kin authority; but let him not exceed in slaying" (Q17:33). What is striking from a modern Western perspective is that it is the next of kin, not the ruler, who is entitled to act, and he does so to avenge, not to punish, the killing. The bottom line is that in the society for which God and His Prophet were legislating, homicide was a tort, not a crime.

At this point we can pause to look back on the ground we have covered in this chapter and forward to what lies ahead. To look back let us return to the metaphor of the black swan. Putting ourselves in the shoes of an observer of the Arabian interior at the beginning of the seventh century, there would be two ways in which we could try to anticipate the future. One is straightforward extrapolation from the past, on the assumption that, other things being equal, the future can be expected to resemble it. The other is more sophisticated: by analyzing the causal structure of the present, we can attempt to anticipate how things could change in the future. If we apply these methods to estimating the likelihood of the emergence of a viable state in the early seventh-century Ḥijāz, the result is clear. There had been no such state in the past, and causality in the guise of the scarcity of resources carried a strong implication that there would be none in the future. The fact that neither outside powers nor their Arab clients were active in the Arabian interior in this period was significant, but it was hardly enough to tip the balance toward state formation in the Ḥijāz.

With Muḥammad's new religion the case is similar. If we extrapolate from the past, no previous people had reacted to the rise of monotheism by adopting it in a form that was distinctively their own, and to the best of our knowledge no new religion, monotheistic or otherwise, had emerged from any part of Arabia prior to the rise of Islam. The argument from causality is similar. The Arabian interior certainly provided elbow room for a religious entrepreneur, and this is an important point. By the time of Muḥammad the religious life of the Byzantine Empire was regimented to a degree that made it an uninviting terrain for the development of new religions. As we have seen, there was diversity there, but it was subject to considerable pressure from the state and mostly contained within the narrow limits of the Christological disputes of late antiquity. Conditions were far from what they had been in pagan times, before the Roman state adopted Christianity. Back then, according to a second-century observer, Syria was awash in prophets with messages of this type: "I am God or the Son of God or a divine spirit. And I have come. Already the world is being destroyed. And you, O men, are to perish because of your iniquities. But I wish to save you. And you shall see me returning again with heavenly power. Blessed is he who has worshiped me now! But I will cast everlasting fire upon all the rest."[27] By the time of Muḥammad, however, Syria was no

27. Origen, *Contra Celsum*, trans. H. Chadwick, Cambridge 1953, 402, from Celsus (7.9).

longer fertile soil for such ventures. The Arabian interior, by contrast, still lay outside the constraints that now limited religious innovation in Syria, ironically thanks to the fact that it was literally stony ground and so unenticing to imperial rulers. But this argument says only that there was more room for religious innovation in Arabia than there was outside it, without indicating the form it might take, if any. Yet there were a few things that pointed, if only vaguely, in the direction of what was about to happen. One was that in religious terms Arabia in late antiquity was subject to increasing Christian encirclement; this meant that any significant religious innovation in the interior was likely to be at least in part a reaction to that pressure. Another was that the idea of a third monotheist way—one that was neither Judaism nor Christianity—seems already to have been present in Arabia. First, there is a real possibility that the Ḥimyarites, or many of them, were Judaic monotheists without exactly being Jews. Second, the later reports about the Ḥanīfs of the Ḥijāz may point to a significant, if limited, monotheistic trend among individual Arabs. Third, thanks to Sozomenus an Ishmaelite monotheism is attested in northwestern Arabia. To this we can add that the presence of Judaism and the spread of Christianity made the idea of Abrahamic descent widely available to the Arabs at large. But at most such thinking tells us why the emergence of Islam was a possibility—why it *might* just happen, not why it *had* to happen.

Turning to the ground that lies ahead, let us reposition our observer in Medina at the time of the death of Muḥammad in 632. One who knew the Bible would know that when God informed Moses that he would soon die, Moses asked Him to appoint a successor "that the congregation of the Lord be not as sheep which have no shepherd" (Num. 27:17). God then told him to take Joshua and lay his hands on him in front of the entire congregation, transferring some of his authority to him so that the people would obey him. Moses did so, and by this very public procedure installed Joshua as his successor. At the time Joshua already had a track record as Moses's assistant. After Moses died, Joshua succeeded without a hitch and went on to issue his first orders to the people through their officers. As this suggests, delegating during one's lifetime and arranging for the succession after one's death are related activities. What historical truth this account may contain we cannot tell, but it provides us with one way to imagine a smooth succession in a desert polity established by a prophet.

The succession to Muḥammad was unlikely to be so smooth. As we would expect from his record as a delegator, he left no designated successor ready to assume the leadership of the community when he died. There were other reasons too. There was the dearth of intermediate structures that could provide continuity while a successor emerged and assumed the reins of power; and alongside the usual rivalries, personal and tribal, there was the perilous fault line between the Meccan Muhājirs and the Medinese Anṣār. Nor were the prospects encouraging outside Medina. Muḥammad's decade in the oasis had had a considerable impact on the tribes of the surrounding region, but as we have seen, even one as close to Medina as Sulaym made a significant contribution to the Arabian backlash that followed his death. In the rest of Arabia the presence of Muḥammad's state was even more recent, and it was not secured by any serious military presence. Altogether, it is hard to see how so flimsy a construction could be expected to survive the death of its originator.

If Muḥammad's state had foundered, what are the chances that his religion would have lived on? When in later chapters we look at the history of Arabia as it actually developed within the wider Muslim framework, we will see that sectarian forms of Islam were able to perpetuate themselves for long periods in the Arabian environment. But they did so only in the economically more favored parts of the peninsula, and in each case they were aided by one of two circumstances: either they enjoyed at least the intermittent protection of a local state identified with the sectarian community in question, or they were anchored by having a significant presence somewhere outside Arabia. This suggests that the chances for an isolated survival of Islam in its Ḥijāzī homeland would not have been good, particularly given the likelihood of an increasing penetration of Arabia by Christianity. Perhaps a small Muslim community in the remoteness of the Ḥijāz might have preserved the Qurʾān into modern times, much as the Mandaeans preserved their scripture in the marshes of lower Mesopotamia. But it seems unlikely; marshes provide more protection for a small and idiosyncratic religious community than open desert does.

In fact, of course, both Muḥammad's state and his religion not only survived but spread over large parts of the known world and transformed it in fundamental ways. How that could be is a question to be taken up in the next chapter. Thereafter we will find the history of the Muslim world to be dominated overwhelmingly by white swans.

3

The Caliphate from the seventh to the ninth century

This chapter starts in 632, at a point at which the future of the Muslim community seemed anything but assured, and ends in the later ninth century, at a time when the Muslim world was a solid reality extending from Spain to Sindh. One thing that made this survival and expansion possible was the continuing existence of the state that Muḥammad had formed in Medina. By the time this state began to disintegrate in the later ninth century, the Muslim world was sufficiently firmly established to do without it.

The first three sections of this chapter accordingly provide a narrative of the history of this state, the Caliphate. They begin with the immediate successors of the Prophet, who were based in Medina; move on to the Umayyads, based in Syria; and end with the 'Abbāsids, based in Iraq. They show how the changes in the geographical location of the central government had pronounced geopolitical implications. Another major theme of these sections is the remarkable success of the conquests initiated by the caliphs, and the way in which their state evolved to handle the resources thus made available to them. But this is not to say that the caliphs ruled unchallenged. There were no fewer than four periods of civil war, each extending over several years, and there were numerous other rebellions posing varying degrees of threat to the ruler of the day. An obvious question is why such outbreaks did not lead to the early demise of the Caliphate, either through domestic subversion or at the hands of foreign invaders.

The first three sections thus present the history of the period from the vantage point of the center. The fourth section seeks to complement that perspective with a geographical survey of the Muslim world, going province by province from Spain to Sindh. It covers all regions other than the Fertile Crescent—that is to say, the central region from which the Umayyads and the 'Abbāsids ruled. As will become apparent, each province had its own, more or less distinctive profile.

The final section takes up the major cultural development of the period: the emergence of Islamic civilization. It shows how unusual this was as a historical event and identifies some of the preconditions for its occurrence. It begins with the spread of

Arabic and Islam among the non-Arab populations of the conquered territories; without such spread it would be hard to imagine the formation of a new civilization around the Arabs and their religion. It then seeks to shed at least an indirect light on the process of this formation by focusing on the books that came to be available to Muslims literate in Arabic in three fields: the Arabian heritage, the legacies of the Greeks and the Persians, and the new Islamic sciences. For the formation of the new civilization the crucial field is the third one. Here my purpose is to show, or at least suggest, a close relationship between the way Arabic and Islam spread in the early period and the way these sciences were formed.

After this chapter and until we reach the final chapter of the book, we will no longer be looking at the Muslim world as a whole. Instead we will examine it by regions, reflecting both its political breakup and its continuing expansion.

The early Caliphate

The succession to the Prophet in 632

Our sources tell us that Muḥammad died on a Monday in the third month of year 11—that would be in the early summer of 632—and was buried the next day. On that same Tuesday, the Muslims assembled in the mosque and pledged their allegiance to Abū Bakr (ruled 632–34) as caliph. This seemed to make a lot of sense. Abū Bakr was a leading figure among the Muhājirs: a Qurashī and a very early convert, he had been the trusted friend who had accompanied Muḥammad during his Hijra, and most recently he had been appointed by the ailing Muḥammad to lead the prayer in the mosque. On that Tuesday he made a brief accession speech that we will have occasion to come back to. He also took a step that highlighted the continuity of the Muslim polity in a purposive way. Before his death Muḥammad had been assembling an expedition directed at the Syrian borderlands, and he had appointed as its commander Usāma ibn Zayd, the son of the Zayd ibn Ḥāritha whom we met as Muḥammad's favorite commander. The expedition had turned back on hearing the news of Muḥammad's death, but Abū Bakr now insisted that it proceed, and against vocal opposition he confirmed Muḥammad's appointment of Usāma to command it. Altogether, what we see here has all the appearance of a smooth succession, and it established the Caliphate, the central political institution of the Muslim community after the death of its prophet.

But was the succession really so smooth? Our sources also tell us things that point to considerable disarray. For a start, ʿUmar's initial response to the situation was to hold forth in the mosque denying that Muḥammad was dead and insisting that he would return—an extravagant belief of a kind that would later be associated with Shīʿism. This was serious, since ʿUmar was one of the leading members of the community. It was Abū Bakr who calmed him down. But there was worse to come. Now that Muḥammad was undeniably dead, his community split three ways. One group consisted of Muḥammad's close kin, who went off and gathered in the house of Fāṭima, the daughter of Muḥammad and wife of his cousin ʿAlī. Another group comprised the Anṣār, who congregated around the leading Khazrajī chief, Saʿd ibn ʿUbāda, in a tribal hall belonging to one of the clans of Khazraj. The rest of the Muhājirs gathered around Abū Bakr and ʿUmar—we are not told where. Hearing about the gathering of the Anṣār, Abū Bakr and ʿUmar hastened to intervene and were confronted with a proposal that the Muhājirs and the Anṣār should each choose a leader (*amīr*) for themselves: "A leader from us and a leader from you."[1] ʿUmar was nevertheless able to persuade them to accept Abū Bakr. Meanwhile the mosque, the public space of the Muslim community and its political center, was apparently left deserted. It was only the next day that the formal accession of Abū Bakr took place there. And even then, not everything was made whole: the kinsfolk of Muḥammad, and in particular his cousin ʿAlī, were conspicuously absent. In all this, the fact that Muḥammad appears not to have designated a successor cast a long shadow. Smoldering resentment among the two losing groups, the close kin of Muḥammad and the Anṣār, later fused and fed into the civil war of 656–61.

But that was still a quarter of a century in the future, and by then several things had happened that, taken together, would do a lot to ensure the survival of the Muslim community despite the stresses and strains that threatened to disrupt it. Abū Bakr's insistence on dispatching the expedition to Syria leads us straight into one of them.

The conquests

The Arab conquests were by any standards a momentous happening.[2] Against the track record of Arab history before and after, they were more than a little surprising. And at the same time they were a necessary—though not a sufficient—condition for the formation of a Muslim world.

The accounts of the conquests in the extant Muslim sources, which as we have them date from the ninth century onward, tend to be generous in the amount of narrative they provide, but quite often they contradict each other, even on basic questions such as the year in which a major battle took place. Thus the Battle of

1. Ibn Hishām, *al-Sīra al-nabawiyya*, Cairo 1955, 3–4:660; for the context see Ibn Isḥāq, *The life of Muhammad*, trans. A. Guillaume, Oxford 1955, 686.

2. For surveys of the conquests see H. Kennedy, *The great Arab conquests*, London 2007; R. G. Hoyland, *In God's path*, Oxford 2015. For the conquest of the Fertile Crescent see F. M. Donner, *The early Islamic conquests*, Princeton 1981. For a broad survey of early Muslim history in the period covered by this chapter and beyond, see H. Kennedy, *The Prophet and the age of the caliphates*, London 1986.

Qādisiyya was a crucial event in the conquest of Iraq, and it took place sometime around 636, but we have no way of pinning down the exact date—it could have been that year, or the year before, or the year after. The non-Muslim sources in Greek and Syriac are much skimpier than the Muslim sources and leave large parts of the territory conquered by the Arabs uncovered. But many of them are independent of the Muslim sources, particularly if they are early. What happens, then, when we put the two together? The findings of two detailed case studies are worth contrasting. One concerns Arwād, a small island off the Syrian coast. Here it is hard to resist the conclusion that the accounts preserved by the Muslim sources are of almost no historical value, and that if we want to learn what actually happened our only option is to go by the non-Muslim testimony. The other study concerns Khūzistān, the region of southeastern Iraq that today forms part of Iran. Here there is basic common ground between the Muslim sources and a near-contemporary Syriac chronicle, and this chronicle enables us to identify some elements in the Muslim sources as more historically trustworthy than others. Given that a major region such as Khūzistān provides a better test than a small island, the case of Khūzistān is perhaps more likely to be typical than that of Arwād. We accordingly have reason to believe that the Muslim sources contain a good measure of historical truth; but unless independent non-Muslim sources are to hand, and usually they are not, we have to accept that when we pick and choose between one Muslim account and another it is likely that we quite often go wrong. So while the broad outline that follows is reasonably secure, a fair amount of the detail could well be false. With that caveat in mind, let us see how the conquests came about.

As in the case of Muḥammad's establishment of a state, we may well be looking at a process whereby one thing led to another, rather than at the implementation of a grand design. Despite Abū Bakr's insistence on carrying on with Muḥammad's planned expedition to the borderlands of Syria, the immediate military agenda of his reign was not conquest outside Arabia. Priority went to the more modest goal of restoring the hegemony of the Muslim state within it. As we have seen, for the most part the tribes of the Ḥijāz remained loyal. But elsewhere in Arabia the news of Muḥammad's death provoked widespread defection, or as loyal Muslims saw it, apostasy (Ridda). They had a point: in several cases the rebels were led by would-be prophets—an indirect testimony to the power of Muḥammad's example. The followers of one of these prophets, who is known to us as Musaylima, proposed a deal to the Muslims, who promptly rejected it: "A prophet from us and a prophet from you!"[3] Crucial for the Muslim victory was the fact that rebellion, though widespread, was by no means ubiquitous. Most expeditions sent against the rebels were able to recruit troops from friendly tribes along the way, and many

3. Khalīfa ibn Khayyāṭ, *Ta'rīkh*, Damascus 1968, 86.

pagan tribes contained Muslim enclaves—weaker sections of the tribe that were glad to have external support against stronger sections. It must also have helped that Arabia outside the south was uniformly Arab, without any appearance of sharp ethnic fault lines to solidify resistance, and even in the south the sense of a non-Arab identity seems to have been fading out. The Muslim state nevertheless faced very real difficulties despite its success in suppressing the rebellions. Outside the imperial fringes, statehood in Arabia was nowhere more than ten years old, so most Arabs at the time had grown up in a stateless society and could easily revert to its ways. And at this point the state had few material resources with which to dissuade them from doing so. Such resources did exist beyond the northern border of Arabia, but they were in the hands of the empires. Without access to them the chances for the long-term survival of the Muslim state looked distinctly poor.

Having dealt with these rebels, the Muslims went on to raid the borderlands of Syria and Iraq in 633–34. Booty apart, their main concern was very likely to secure the conversion to Islam of the Arab tribesmen of these regions, rather than to annex territory from the empires. But whether or not expansion into the settled lands of the Fertile Crescent was planned from the start, it soon happened. At first it must have taken considerable courage. The only previous Muslim engagement with an imperial force, the expedition to Muʾta in 629, had been a disaster, and when Muḥammad led a large force to Tabūk the following year, there were doubters who posed the rhetorical question "Do you think that fighting the Byzantines is like the Arabs fighting among themselves?"[4] Yet the Arabs now showed themselves ready to attack two empires simultaneously. The pattern was the same in both Syria and Iraq: following initial raiding there was a phase in which the Arabs overran the territory and won most of a series of minor battles; then came a serious imperial attempt to recover the lost territories, issuing in a major battle that the Arabs won handsomely. In the case of Syria this was the Battle of the Yarmūk River in 636, and in that of Iraq it was the Battle of Qādisiyya around the same date. The Arabs also rounded out their possession of the southern lowlands of the Middle East in two directions. In the east, we have already noted the conquest of Khūzistān, which took place at about the same time as those of Syria and the main part of Iraq. In the west, Egypt was conquered a bit later by a force led by ʿAmr ibn al-ʿĀṣ, whom we met as one of the Prophet's commanders in year 8; the conquest spanned the years 639–42 and was perhaps undertaken on his own initiative.

What happened next broke the symmetry that had hitherto been apparent. In the east the Arabs, having secured their possession of Iraq, went on to conquer Iran in the 640s, frustrating the attempt of the last Persian king to rally the ethnic

4. Ibn Hishām, *al-Sīra al-nabawiyya*, 3–4:525; for the context see Ibn Isḥāq, *The life of Muhammad*, 606.

heartland of his empire against them. By the middle of the century the Persian Empire had been destroyed; the son of the last ruler was reduced to setting up a court in exile in China. This victory completed the first wave of conquests, but as we will see later it was by no means the last of them. The Byzantine Empire, however, was a different story, though not for lack of effort on the part of the Arabs. On land they were active in Anatolia in the 640s, and they remained a mortal threat to the empire there for the next two centuries. At the same time they took the obvious but by no means easy step of developing a navy, winning a major sea battle against the Byzantines in the early 650s and establishing a degree of hegemony over Cyprus. But they did not take Constantinople.

This bare outline of the conquests leaves aside the mass of colorful—and often unreliable—detail that is to be found in the Muslim sources. To sample this material, let us pick out a single moment for a closer look: the negotiations between the Arabs and the Persians on the eve of the Battle of Qādisiyya. The opposing armies were camped within a few miles of each other a bit south of Najaf in Iraq. The Persian general, Rustam, asked the Arabs to send him an emissary, and they did—in fact a series of emissaries. One was a scruffy Bedouin—a desert Arab—who arrived on horseback. While awaiting his arrival, the Persians had been discussing how best to receive him and had decided to overwhelm him with a display of Persian magnificence. Rustam accordingly sat on a throne surrounded by carpets and cushions (cushions in this culture being a sign of royal authority). But when he reached the edge of the carpets, the Bedouin rode right onto them, dismounting only when he chose to. He then advanced toward Rustam using his sharp-pointed spear as a walking stick, jabbing holes in the carpets and cushions. Another emissary made his point just as vividly: when he got to Rustam on his throne, he sat down on it beside him. This upset the Persians, and there was a scuffle, but the emissary had his answer ready: "We Arabs are equals,"[5] he explained, enslaving each other only in warfare. He went on to say with mock innocence that he had assumed that the Persians treated each other in the same way; how was he to know that some of them were the owners of others? The Persian audience was ominously divided in its response to this incident. The common people warmed to what the Arab had said, whereas the nobles remarked that this was what their slaves had always wanted to hear. Once such preliminaries were over, the time came for an exchange of views between Rustam and the emissary. When Rustam asked the first emissary what had brought the Arabs to Iraq, the reply was that God had sent them to deliver those who so wished from being ser-

5. For this and the next quotation see *The history of al-Ṭabarī*, Albany 1985–2007 (hereafter Ṭabarī, *History*), 12:67, 70 (translation modified; see Ṭabarī, *Ta'rīkh al-rusul wa'l-mulūk*, Leiden 1879–1901, series 1, 2271, 2274). Ṭabarī's work in this translation provides an abundance of primary-source material on the first three centuries of Muslim history.

vants of God's servants to being servants of God—an expression of the same egalitarian theme. Another emissary similarly summed up Islam for Rustam in a few basic points, among them a commitment to "deliver whoever so wishes from the service of servants to the service of God" and a belief in the full brotherhood of men, all alike descended from Adam and Eve. The outcome was a three-day truce between the two armies. When it was over, the battle was duly fought. The austere and egalitarian Arabs won, as they deserved, and the luxurious and hierarchical Persians lost, as they deserved. The story may not be true, but as an articulation of some of the values of early Islam in its Arab tribal environment it was "molto ben trovato," "very aptly invented." Slavery apart, these emissaries were saying, only God had the right to push people around—an attitude that promised trouble for rulers, Muslim and non-Muslim alike.

A less colorful and more demanding task is to explain the extraordinary success of the Arabs in conquering the world for the first and last time. With regard to the conquests as a whole, some of the answer is obvious enough. The second quarter of the seventh century was an exceptional period in the Middle East for two reasons. First, the empires were unusually weak as a result of the damage they had inflicted on each other in the course of their unprecedented war to the death, likely compounded by adverse climatic change and the plague. The Persian Empire was now in chaos. The ruler who came to the throne in 628 when the Byzantine emperor Heraclius (ruled 610–41) demanded a change of regime began by executing some seventeen of his brothers and soon died leaving an infant successor; in the absence of plausible male rulers two queens reigned briefly in this period. Meanwhile the Byzantine Empire, though politically stable, was at the end of its tether. When a Byzantine eunuch arrived in southern Palestine to pay the soldiers in the region their wages, the neighboring Arabs came to him expecting to receive their usual small subsidies. The eunuch drove them away with the remark "The emperor can barely pay his soldiers their wages, much less these dogs!"[6] The rejected Arabs then went over to the Muslims. Second, the Arabs at large were unusually strong because for once they had a state that held some kind of sway over most of Arabia. Thus the military energy of the Arabs, hitherto dissipated in low-level conflicts between tribal groups, could now be redirected to the conquest of the vastly richer lands beyond the Arabian borders, catching the empires at a time when they were least able to parry this threat. In short, if the Arabs were ever to conquer themselves an empire, this was when it had to happen. But that it happened is still surprising. Given their historical track record, one might have expected it to be the steppe peoples who would take advantage of the imperial disarray. Indeed they had done so: we saw the Avars besieging

6. *The chronicle of Theophanes the Confessor*, trans. C. Mango and R. Scott, Oxford 1997, 466.

Constantinople with their siege towers in alliance with the Persians, and the Turks joining Heraclius in his advance toward Ctesiphon. But both went home, the Avars for reasons obscure to us and the Turks because they apparently disliked the weather. By contrast, the Arabs, rather than cautiously seek an alliance with one empire against the other, invaded both, and despite their limited knowledge of siegecraft they did not go home.

There is a further point that relates to premodern history in general, and not just the Middle East in the second quarter of the seventh century. In modern times military power is tightly linked to economic resources, for two reasons: armies have to be paid, and sophisticated military technology is expensive. In premodern times, by and large, the first constraint applied but the second did not. That is to say, the technology that it took to make an effective professional soldier was equally available to tribesmen: the swords of the Arabs were no less sharp than those of the Byzantines and Persians. Instead, the chronic weakness imposed on the Arabs by the poverty of their environment arose from the difficulty of getting significant numbers of them together on the same side. Very likely the largest bodies of Arab troops ever raised prior to Islamic times were those recruited by the empires, who unlike the tribal chiefs of Arabia usually had the resources to pay them. But there was a possible way around this. If the Arab state could, in effect, organize large armies on credit—by giving the tribesmen a realistic expectation of substantial material rewards from the rich territories they would conquer—then the organizational deficit of the Arabs could be overcome for a limited period. By the end of that period, if they were successful, they would have taken possession of the resources they needed to pay themselves stipends at least as good as those of an imperial army.

A more specific explanatory question relates to what the Arabs did and didn't conquer. They showed themselves best at conquering territory of a kind already familiar to them: the lowlands of the southern Middle East. As we have seen, by the early 640s they held all of this territory from Khūzistān to Egypt. By contrast, the northern Middle East, with its high altitudes and bitter winter weather, was alien to them. Why, then, did they conquer Iran but not Anatolia? This question was posed and answered long ago by Ibn Khaldūn. As he pointed out, the Persian capital was located in Iraq, not Iran, and it was thus close to Arabia and surrounded by the kind of territory the Arabs were used to. Once they had taken Iraq, they had, so to speak, decapitated the Persian Empire, making it harder for the last Persian king to organize effective resistance in Iran. But the Byzantine capital was located not in Syria but far away on the other side of Anatolia. By conquering Syria and Egypt the Arabs had lopped off a couple of the limbs of the empire, depriving it of considerable revenue and a large supply of grain; but they had not decapitated it. So despite continued Arab invasions of Anatolia and two attempts to take Constantinople by laying siege to it, the Byzantine Empire was able to survive in a much-reduced form. Meanwhile in the south, the Arabs showed little interest in crossing the Red Sea to attack Ethiopia. In 641 a failed expedition against Ethiopia is said to have led the caliph ʿUmar (ruled 634–44) to forswear naval attacks.

What was it like to be on the receiving end of the Arab conquests? Being conquered is always dangerous and usually unpleasant, and in this instance there was a reason to expect it to be particularly so. The Arab nomads, who provided the armies of conquest with much of their rank and file, had a long record of ruthless raiding of settled societies. It would have been surprising if the rise of Islam had changed their habits overnight, and indeed their later history suggests that it may not have changed them much even in the long run. As we will see in a later chapter, in the mid-eleventh century Arab nomads then living in the region of Upper Egypt moved west and overran Tunisia. In the course of this incursion, with no state in a position to rein them in, they brought about what a contemporary described as the ruin of the country. There was nothing unusual about that event except its scale. If we look for similar testimony about the Arab conquests in the seventh-century sources, we have no trouble finding it. Contemporary non-Muslim accounts speak of extensive violence and devastation: one Syrian chronicler mentions the killing of four thousand villagers in Palestine, while another Syrian observer speaks of the ravaging of numerous villages, with many people slain or taken captive. Such testimony seems too consistent to be set aside. But it is not the whole story. If we switch our attention from the villages to the cities we tend to see a different pattern. Here Muslim sources even tell us of urban populations that came out to welcome the Arab armies. It would be a mistake to read this welcome as an expression of their enthusiasm for their new masters. People who come out to meet an invader in this way are taking a calculated risk. If all goes well they establish a stable relationship with the newcomers, but if it goes badly they are the first to be slaughtered. What such behavior crucially reveals is a belief that the invaders are probably people one can do business with; such a belief would have dissipated very quickly if news had spread that the Arabs engaged in the indiscriminate destruction of cities that submitted to them, massacring whole populations. Whether or not the processions were real, the early sources show cities surrendering to the Arabs on terms, which means that they must have had a realistic expectation that those terms would be honored.

Behind the contrast between these early rural and urban experiences lie the differing interests of nomads and states. Marauding nomads who enter a territory to pillage it have no reason to consider the long-term welfare of its inhabitants. In the classic Biblical account of the menace of the Midianite camel nomads, we read that the Israelites would sow their crops, whereupon the Midianites would descend on them like locusts with their cattle and their tents; together with their innumerable camels "they entered into the land to destroy it," leaving the impoverished

Israelites without sustenance (Judg. 6:1–6). By contrast, a state that conquers territory and aspires to hold it has good reason to pay some attention to the interests of its inhabitants, since a thriving economy will mean more taxes. Of course, states can vary enormously in how they see and pursue their interests, and in any case surgical precision is always elusive. But a relevant distinction here is between conquerors—as opposed to marauders—of two kinds: those who desire to possess the land together with its population (like the British in India), and those who want the land without its population (like the British in Australia). Conquerors of the second kind are likely to engage in activities inimical to the native population, and we have already seen examples of this in the case of Muḥammad's treatment of the Jewish tribes of Medina. There was a recurrence of this pattern when the caliph ʿUmar decided to terminate the arrangements Muḥammad had made with the Jews of Khaybar and Fadak and to expel them from Arabia. But these Jews were allowed to settle in southern Syria, and there is little sign of such measures outside Arabia. Doctrinally this was unproblematic since, as we have seen, the Qurʾān contains a verse that opens the door to the toleration of non-Muslims who submit to Muslim rule. What we see in the story of the conquests is thus that in the urban context the interests of the state were predominant from the start, whereas in the countryside it took more time for them to be asserted effectively. But asserted they were. A bishop chronicling the Arab conquest of Egypt describes the Muslim invaders as absconding with a large number of sheep and goats without the knowledge of their owners. Yet as early as 643, the year following the completion of the conquest, bureaucracy was making itself felt: a papyrus document shows an Arab commander formally acknowledging the receipt of sixty-five requisitioned sheep. Soon the complaint of the subject populations of the conquered territories was less that they were being raided without mercy and more that they were being taxed to excess. The same bishop speaks of the taxes paid by the Egyptians being doubled and trebled. Later he tells us that ʿAmr, the conqueror and governor of Egypt, "became stronger every day in every field of his activity"; he "exacted the taxes that had been determined upon" but "committed no act of spoliation or plunder."[7] Yet another indication of the relative success of the state in asserting its interests is the fact that not a single independent Arab warlord emerged from the conquests. In sum, a crucial factor in the story was the role of the Muslim state under its first three caliphs, Abū Bakr, ʿUmar, and ʿUthmān (ruled 644–56)—the three who together with ʿAlī (ruled 656–61) make up the Rightly Guided Caliphs in the retrospective view of the Sunnī Muslim majority. This was a state that could rein in nomadic predation and give the rural population a chance to recover from the initial trauma of the conquest.

7. *The chronicle of John, Bishop of Nikiu*, trans. R. H. Charles, London 1916, 200 §3.

The state

The role of the Muslim state in organizing the conquests outside Arabia begins with Abū Bakr's insistence that the expedition to Syria should go ahead. This does not, of course, mean that the caliph in Medina was in any position to micromanage the progress of the Arab armies; commanders had to be allowed to respond flexibly to changing local circumstances, not least because communications in premodern times were so slow. But if we set any store by the Arabic sources, it was typically the caliph who decided whom to appoint as commanders and assigned them their missions, and he could terminate their commands when it seemed politic to him to do so. It fits with this evidence that the commanders who played major roles in the early conquests were typically Medinese appointed from Medina. An exception was a north Arabian tribal chief, Muthannā ibn Ḥāritha, who had a significant role in the early stages of the conquest of Iraq. One might have expected many other such locals to have played prominent parts in the conquest of the Fertile Crescent, but our sources give little indication that this was so—a remarkable fact considering that Arabs with experience of service in the Byzantine or Persian armies and familiarity with their style of warfare must have been numerous in these frontier areas. The early governors of provinces follow the same pattern: they, too, tend to be Medinese appointed from Medina. One can certainly suspect that the later Muslim sources would tend to exaggerate the extent of central control, but they cannot be entirely wrong about it. For one thing, our Armenian chronicler of the 660s conveys the same picture. For another, if the central government had not been in control, the outcome of the conquests would have looked more like eleventh-century Tunisia or the Fertile Crescent of Arsacid times. In that event, the central government in Medina would not have reaped the benefits of the conquests, and its survival would have been very much in question.

The structure of the central government in Medina was nevertheless a simple one. At the top was of course the caliph. The first three caliphs were all leading companions of Muḥammad from among the Muhājirs, and they were not closely related to each other. We already know how Abū Bakr came to be caliph, and who resented his election. When he was dying he appointed ʿUmar his successor. This happened after some uneasy private consultation, and the choice did not please all the leading figures of the community—as Abū Bakr is said to have put it, each one's nose was out of joint because he wanted the succession to be his and not ʿUmar's. At least, as Abū Bakr pointed out in self-defense, he had not chosen one of his own kinsmen. When ʿUmar was on his deathbed as a result of being stabbed repeatedly by a Persian slave, he responded to the same problem with a hard-headed institutional device: he appointed a committee of half a dozen leading figures and tasked them with choosing one of their own number to be his successor; they had to do so within three days, under threat of dire consequences if their deliberations failed to issue in a consensus. The outcome was the appointment of ʿUthmān. He, too, was killed, in his case without being able to make any arrangement for the succession. As we will see later in this chapter, what followed was a long civil war. So the question of the succession was tense and problematic, but stability was nevertheless maintained from 632 to 656.

The caliph in turn appointed a small number of officials to serve him in Medina. Let us take the example of ʿUmar. One ninth-century source lists those appointed by him as follows:

(1) a secretary, Zayd ibn Thābit, a young but highly literate and numerate member of the Anṣār
(2) a chamberlain, Yarfaʾ, a client of ʿUmar's
(3) a steward (*khāzin*), Yasār, again a client of ʿUmar's
(4) a treasurer entrusted with the administration of public funds, ʿAbdallāh ibn al-Arqam, a member of one of the clans of Quraysh

This list is quite telling. First, it is short: ʿUmar was not being served by an elaborate bureaucracy in Byzantine or Persian style. But second, none of these men were prominent in their own right. They held their offices because ʿUmar wanted their services, not because they were the socially prestigious representatives of constituencies that ʿUmar needed to cultivate. This is obvious with the two clients, Yarfaʾ and Yasār, the names of whose fathers our source does not bother to mention. That they are shorn of the dignity of ancestors in this way means that they must have been of servile origin, and so mere instruments of their patron. Zayd and ʿAbdallāh, by contrast, were freeborn Arabs. But Zayd was an orphan, and still in his twenties; the Prophet and his first three successors clearly liked having him around because of his skills, and his role in the politics of the period suggests that he was not close to his fellow Anṣār. Lastly, ʿAbdallāh ibn al-Arqam was a member of the tribe of Quraysh and as such on the inside track in a way that Zayd and the two clients could not be. Moreover, his unimpeachable tribal background was appropriate to an office that required the trust of the community—he was in charge of a public institution, "the treasury of the Muslims," and it was fitting that he piously refused to accept even a modest stipend for his work. But he had a serious weakness: he was a late convert to Islam. Had it not been for this, ʿUmar once told him, he would have been promoted much higher. When ʿUmar left Medina—say, on pilgrimage to Mecca or on a journey to Syria—he would appoint Zayd or some other person of no great consequence as his deputy. In sum, with officers like these the caliph owned his administration and was already much more than a first among equals. But he still had a long way to go before he was in any danger of becoming a despot. There are traditions that tell us that there were as yet no prisons in the days of the first three caliphs, or at least not until the time of the third, who is also said to have been the first to institute a security force (*shurṭa*)—something like a police force but more formidable. And indeed the early caliphs do not seem to have had much military force available to them locally when they needed it. ʿUthmān lost his life in 656 when several hundred malcontents arrived from Egypt and he lacked the troops to face them down.

The same source also informs us about provincial administration. Here the key figure was the governor, who was normally appointed by ʿUmar and frequently fired by him. For example, in nearby Mecca he appointed four successive governors, firing the first three of them; in Kūfa, which was, along with Baṣra, one of the major garrison cities of Iraq, he appointed five successive governors and fired three of them, one before he had even traveled to Kūfa. But appointments were not invariably made from the center. A governor who had reason to leave his province or knew himself to be dying would appoint his own successor. When bubonic plague struck southern Syria in 639, such transfers of authority happened three times in rapid succession; the third time, the dying governor, a member of the Umayyad clan, appointed his brother, Muʿāwiya, and ʿUmar then confirmed him. He did not always change his governors as rapidly as these details might suggest. At ʿUmar's death Muʿāwiya had been governing Syria for five years, and ʿAmr, who had conquered Egypt, was governor there for a comparable period. But ʿUmar did not simply leave governors to administer their provinces on their own. In Baṣra and Kūfa he also hired and fired judges, and for each city he appointed a secretary to superintend the payment of allowances. We also learn from a Christian source that ʿUmar ordered a census to be taken of all the inhabited territory under his rule; it was to cover people, animals, and plants.

That brings us to a fundamental issue that arises in any conquest situation: what the conquerors do with the resources now at their disposal. One could imagine those who participated in the conquest of a given region simply helping themselves, without any role being played by a state authority, local or central. But booty apart, this is not how our sources describe the arrangements made by the Arabs. We are told that when the rich agricultural land of Iraq was conquered there was a move to divide it up among the conquerors as private property. ʿUmar, however, asserted the public interest by asking what would then be left for future generations of Muslims. So he left the land in the hands of its existing inhabitants and imposed taxes—specifically a poll tax and a land tax. What, then, was to be done with the revenue from these taxes? Here we come to another major decision that the sources ascribe to ʿUmar, acting in consultation with the leading figures in Medina. This was the creation of the Dīwān in the winter of 640–41. The term refers to a register recording the names of those entitled to stipends (above all soldiers) and the amounts that were due to them. There was, for example, a Dīwān in Baṣra and a Dīwān in Kūfa, and as we have seen ʿUmar appointed secretaries to oversee each of them. Nothing of this kind had existed under Muḥammad or Abū Bakr. ʿUmar thereby ensured that a large part of the flow of resources from the conquered population to the conquerors passed through the hands of the state. This decision had a very significant implication for the shape of the conquest society, though not one that could be implemented universally or sustained indefinitely: the conquerors were to draw stipends rather than become rural landowners. This principle was reinforced where the Arab armies were housed in newly built garrison cities, as with Baṣra and Kūfa in Iraq and Fusṭāṭ in Egypt. In Syria, by contrast, the conquerors were spread out in the form of several geographically defined troops known as Junds. There ʿUmar is said to have ordered the burning of crops that had been planted by Muslims. That the exclusion of the Arabs from landownership was not, however, sustained is evident from an eschatological tradition describing the land reform that would be carried out in Syria by the Mahdī—the future messianic leader who is to set the world to rights: he would restore every inch of land to the Christians (*ahl al-dhimma*) and every Muslim to jihad. Yet to the extent that it worked, the stipend system did a lot to enhance the power of the state. For example, it gave the authorities the ability to make deductions from salaries, and in a practice introduced by Muʿāwiya (ruled 661–80) this was applied to payments of blood money. When such payments had been made in the course of the pre-Islamic Fijār wars no state had played any part in them, but now the state was inserting itself into the process by making the payment and recovering the outlay through deductions from the salaries of those who were liable. This change pointed to a radical transformation in the character of the conquest society. We should nevertheless note that the Dīwān system did not mean that all revenue passed through the hands of the central government. For the most part the role of each Dīwān was a local one, in the sense that revenue raised in Iraq was largely spent there. Of course the central government, too, needed funding to cover its costs, notably the allowances it was now paying in Medina, including the considerable sums that went to Muḥammad's widows. Given the relative poverty of the Ḥijāz, the upshot was that there had to be a transfer of resources to it from the richer provinces. This was not popular in the provinces affected. One of the demands put to ʿUthmān by the malcontents from Egypt was that the people of Medina should not receive stipends; the wealth of Egypt should go to those who had fought for it—together, they piously added, with the aged companions of Muḥammad. But it was not just cash that Egypt was supplying to the Ḥijāz; it was also grain. For this purpose a major infrastructural project was undertaken on the orders of ʿUmar in 643–44: the reopening of the seasonal canal linking the Nile to the Red Sea, a facility that had existed intermittently since Achaemenid times.

All this points to a relatively powerful central government in Medina that could make decisions and impose them on the provinces. There were undoubtedly local initiatives, but at least during ʿUmar's reign we do not see them being taken in open defiance of the center. That was to change under the third caliph, ʿUthmān. At first he seemed powerful enough—four years into his caliphate he fired ʿAmr, the well-rooted governor of Egypt, and in Kūfa he hired and fired governors with abandon. But then the Kūfans took it upon themselves to expel 'Uthmān's governor from their city and appoint another in his place; tellingly, 'Uthmān went along with this, after failing in an attempt to reimpose his own governor. The following year the Egyptian malcontents killed him. But this disorder appears in our sources as a new development, very likely related to the lack of fresh conquests in the latter part of 'Uthmān's reign. Overall, for most of the quarter century during which the caliphs ruled from Medina, they appear to be firmly in control. Modern historians have expressed doubts about this picture of strong central government, and not without reason. But as the dust settles on the outcome of the conquests, it becomes very clear that we are not looking at the results of a tribal free-for-all, nor are we witnessing the emergence of autonomous principalities.

So far we have concerned ourselves with the commanding heights of administration. What about the lower levels, particularly in the provinces? The short answer is that the administrative structures inherited from the defeated empires continued to function much as before, usually conducting their business in Greek or Persian; it was not till the end of the seventh century that that a highly symbolic switch to Arabic began. For example, we have Coptic documents from Egypt reminiscent of Roman census returns in which village headmen and other locals swear by God and the well-being of 'Amr—the governor—that they have not omitted anyone in their village. Yet the short answer is a little too short. We have a bilingual papyrus document from Egypt dating from 643, soon after the conquest of the country, in which a Greek text is matched by an Arabic text. But the Arabic version does not look like a translation of the Greek into a language not previously used for such purposes. This and similar texts indicate that the Arabs must have brought with them a preexisting documentary tradition of their own. We will come back to this, but for now we need to return to the narrative of events.

The first civil war

The first civil war of Muslim history lasted for five years, from 656 to 661. Significantly, it took place after the initial wave of conquests was over. It began with the killing of 'Uthmān by the malcontents from Egypt against a background of widespread discontent among the Arab troops in the provinces. As we have seen, 'Uthmān had no opportunity to provide for his succession, so it was up for grabs. The struggle began in Medina. By now the resentments of the Anṣār and the close kin of Muḥammad had fused, giving 'Alī his chance to assume the caliphate. But there were others strongly opposed to him, notably two senior companions of Muḥammad, Ṭalḥa and Zubayr, and one of Muḥammad's widows, 'Ā'isha. At this point, instead of continuing the struggle in Medina, both sides moved to Iraq: 'Alī's opponents went to Baṣra while 'Alī himself sought the support of the Kūfans. There was a battle between the two sides in 656, the first to be fought between Muslims, and ʿAlī's victory over his opponents was definitive. But that was not the end of the matter. Up to this point it seems to have been accepted that it was the elite in Medina that would provide the Muslims with their caliphs. But ʿAlī now found he had a more dangerous rival, Muʿāwiya, who was based in Syria. Again there was a battle, in 657, but this time the outcome was a stalemate that led to an inconclusive arbitration. Meanwhile ʿAmr, now an ally of Muʿāwiya, had an opportunity to do something he must have wanted to do ever since he was fired by ʿUthmān: he invaded Egypt and made himself its governor again. But there was worse news for ʿAlī in Iraq itself. There an obstinately principled opposition had emerged that condemned him for submitting his cause to mere human arbitration. These were the Khārijites, those who "walked out," and ʿAlī was able to defeat them in a battle in 658. But they had their revenge: in the twilight of ʿAlī's failing reign he was assassinated by a Khārijite in 661. The Syrians had already given their allegiance to Muʿāwiya as caliph in 658, and with the death of ʿAlī he was soon able to take over Iraq without having to fight a battle, thereby bringing the civil war to an end. This, finally, was the "year of unity." Muʿāwiya had triumphed despite what in the eyes of the pious was a serious strike against him. Like ʿAbdallāh ibn al-Arqam, and indeed like most of his Umayyad clan, he was a late convert.

The Muslim sources relate these events with a profusion of confusing detail, but there is one story there that is too good to miss: the assassination of ʿAlī. As told in the massive history of Ṭabarī (d. 923), it combines synchronized terrorism with romance—a combination that could well be the result of two originally distinct narratives being fused into one. The story begins with three Khārijites who wanted revenge agreeing that each of them would assassinate one of the "leaders of error" on a certain day, these leaders being ʿAlī, Muʿāwiya, and ʿAmr. Of the three would-be assassins, only one, a certain Ibn Muljam, was successful, his target being ʿAlī. Yet at one point he had come close to abandoning his mission. After reaching Kūfa he fell in love with a beautiful Khārijite woman, a certain Qaṭām, and wanted to marry her. As it happened, her father and brother had been killed when ʿAlī defeated the Khārijites, so she too wanted revenge. But killing caliphs was men's work. She accordingly told Ibn Muljam her conditions for marrying him: "Three thousand silver coins, a slave, a singing girl, and the killing of ʿAlī."[8] His rather crestfallen response was to accuse her of not really loving him. To this she replied brusquely that if he killed ʿAlī and got away he would get her, and if he was caught he would get Paradise, so what was the problem? Shamed into renewing his mission, Ibn Muljam went ahead, and as it happened, he was caught and had to settle for Paradise. The story is remarkable and also instructive. We—the audience—are

8. Ṭabarī, *History*, 17:213, 214.

presumably good Sunnīs, so we regard Khārijites as damnable heretics and revere ʿAlī as the fourth of the Rightly Guided Caliphs. Presumably we are also men, and accustomed to the idea that women pursue their nefarious purposes with cunning and guile. And yet Qaṭām is not exactly demonized. Her motive is revenge—a natural reaction to the killing of her father and brother that we can all understand. And while she certainly benefits from her good looks, she is no Delilah; she plays it absolutely straight with Ibn Muljam. Unquestionably she is headed for hellfire, and yet on the way she gets a certain respect from us. Religion is a big thing, but it isn't everything.

So what should we take away from the taut narrative of the first civil war? The most obvious point is a geopolitical one. For an empire ruling rich agricultural provinces to have its capital in the wilderness of western Arabia was unsustainable. It was no longer possible to raise a serious army there, and we can see the consequences of this in ʿUthmān's inability to confront the violence of the Egyptian malcontents, as also in the speed with which the initial contenders in the civil war abandoned the Ḥijāz for Iraq. Up to this point the center had still been the center: the Egyptians had chosen to bring their grievances to the caliph in Medina rather than to stay at home and ignore him, and the initial move to appoint a new caliph likewise took place in Medina. But once the civil war had started Medina was no longer the center. The rise of Islam could give Arabia a brief moment of power, but there was no way this political dominance could become permanent. So the question was whether the provinces would go their separate ways or hold together—and if the latter, which province would now be the site of the central government. The answer was that the empire would be reunited around Syria, and there were reasons for that. One was geopolitical: Syria, though by no means as rich as Egypt or Iraq, had a military advantage. It was located on the crucial frontier with the Byzantine Empire, and it accordingly needed to maintain a large and effective army, not to mention a navy. By contrast, Egypt was not situated on a dangerous frontier and so maintained only a limited army. Iraq was no longer on a frontier at all—the conquest of Iran had shifted the border to the Caucasus and Central Asia. Another reason was that the Arabs of Syria held together better than those of Iraq did. Qurashīs, who were the dominant tribe of the Muslim state, had settled disproportionately in Syria, and the Umayyads had good relations with the locally dominant tribe of Kalb. Meanwhile, Iraq was divided between two rival centers, Kūfa and Baṣra, both more heterogeneous than Syria in tribal terms, Kūfa especially so. There was also a more personal factor having to do with the career of Muʿāwiya. As we saw, a rather fortuitous chain of events during the plague of 639 had established him as governor in Syria, and no subsequent caliph had fired him. By the time of the civil war he was more deeply entrenched in his province than any other governors were in theirs. Both ʿAlī and his Medinese opponents, by contrast, began the civil war by moving into Iraq, where their newcomer status showed in the ricketiness of the coalitions they put together. If Syria had been like the other provinces, disintegration would have been the most likely outcome of the civil war.

That that is not what happened had a significant implication for the processes of assimilation at work between conquerors and conquered. Imagine that the empire that had once been ruled from Medina had fragmented into a plurality of mutually independent and competing states, as the empire conquered by Alexander the Great had done a millennium earlier. The Arabs of each region would then have set less store by maintaining their bonds with their fellow Arabs elsewhere and more by developing bonds with their local subjects. The Armenian chronicler tells us that during the civil war fifteen thousand Arabs in Egypt converted to Christianity. This claim is not supported by the Arabic sources, but it is the kind of thing that would probably have happened on a large scale if the fragmentation of those years had proved permanent so early in Muslim history.

By way of contrast, consider the changing attitudes of the early Visigothic king Athaulf (ruled 410–15), who came to rule Roman territory in Gaul and Spain. At first, we are told, "he ardently desired to blot out the Roman name and to make all the Roman territory a Gothic empire in fact as well as in name, so that, to use the popular expressions, *Gothia* should take the place of *Romania*." But from his long experience of his people he had learned that "the Goths, because of their unbridled barbarism, were utterly incapable of obeying laws." So "he chose to seek for himself at least the glory of restoring and increasing the renown of the Roman name by the power of the Goths, wishing to be looked upon by posterity as the restorer of the Roman Empire, since he could not be its transformer." His attempts at good government were much indebted to the advice of his wife Placidia, a sister of the Roman emperor and "a woman of the keenest intelligence and of exceptional piety."[9] The Arabs, like the younger Athaulf, desired to blot out the Roman name. But unlike Athaulf they never looked back and did not depend on the advice of any sister of the Byzantine emperor.

The Umayyad dynasty

With Muʿāwiya taking firm control of a reunited empire and establishing the Umayyad dynasty (661–750),[10] we finally leave behind the black-swan terrain of the emergence of Islam and the Muslim state. Of course the history of the Muslim world, like any history, would see the occasional incidence of unlikely events. But from this moment on the very existence of the Muslim world was never as

9. Orosius, *Seven books of history against the pagans*, New York 1936, 396 (7.43).

10. For the history of this dynasty see G. R. Hawting, *The first dynasty of Islam*, London 1986; J. Wellhausen, *The Arab kingdom and its fall*, Calcutta 1927.

precarious as it had been at several critical points prior to the consolidation of Muʿāwiya's power.

Muʿāwiya's achievement was to reestablish the empire created by the conquests on a foundation sufficiently viable for it to last for two full centuries. As we have seen, the key geopolitical change was that the state was now ruled from a center outside Arabia, from one of the conquered territories where fiscal and military power were concentrated. This shift accelerated a gradual evolution in the character of the state that had already begun under the caliphs in Medina, as it became less like the polity that Muḥammad had ruled and more like the imperial states that the Muslims had defeated. For example, the caliphs who ruled before Muʿāwiya, though all members of the tribe of Quraysh, were not a dynasty in the conventional English usage of the term: they did not belong to a single ruling family. This and other features of the early Caliphate resonated with the egalitarian values articulated by the emissaries sent to Rustam, as also with modern republican values. "By God," as ʿUmar is reported to have said in his role as caliph, "I am not a king so that I should enslave you; I am only a servant of God to whom a trust was offered."[11] But such attitudes did not make for stability in the premodern world. So Muʿāwiya set about establishing dynastic rule, albeit in the face of considerable opposition; practices of this kind came to be condemned as Persian and Byzantine—"Khusrawism" and "Caesarism." Muʿāwiya's success did not, however, mean that his reign ushered in two centuries of *unbroken* political stability. On average, between 656 and 861, stable dynastic rule prevailed for about nine-tenths of the time, while the other tenth was spent in a series of civil wars. After the first civil war of 656–61, there was to be a second in 684–92, a third in 744–50, and a fourth in 811–19. Of these the second resulted in a dynastic shift within the Umayyad clan to which Muʿāwiya belonged, from the Sufyānids to the Marwānids, whereas the third led to a more drastic change in which the Umayyads were replaced by the ʿAbbāsids, members of the same Qurashī clan as the Prophet. At the same time the center of the empire moved from Syria to Iraq. Yet none of these civil wars brought about the breakup of the empire. That was to come only with the disorders that beset the ʿAbbāsid dynasty in the later ninth and early tenth centuries, after which there would never again be any question of the Muslim world being ruled by a single state. The relative stability of the Caliphate in its first couple of centuries is also evident in the decline in the proportion of caliphs meeting violent deaths and in the consensus that the realm they ruled was indivisible. These precious centuries before political disintegration set in were crucial for the future of the Muslim world. As we will see, they provided a framework conducive to the spread of Islam and Arabic and to the formation of Islamic civilization around them. By the time the initial political unity of the Caliphate came to an end, this

11. Ṭabarī, *History*, 12:151.

new civilization was already firmly in place, its future as secure as anything can be in human affairs.

With this bird's-eye view of the whole imperial phase of Muslim history in mind, let us look a little more closely at what happened in the course of it. We will now begin to move faster than we did while covering the first crucial decades of Muslim history. But there is a fresh caveat about the sources: the Arabic historiographical tradition as we have it regarding these two centuries is mainly a product of Iraq, for which we accordingly have an abundance of detail that we lack for Syria, despite its central role in Umayyad politics.

Umayyad rule

In all, there were fourteen Umayyad rulers spanning the period from 661 to 750. Let us concentrate on three of them: Muʿāwiya (ruled 661–80), ʿAbd al-Malik (ruled 685–705), and Hishām (ruled 724–43). Their reigns were not just the longest, but also the most significant.

What was special about Muʿāwiya?[12] Like ʿUthmān, he belonged to the Umayyad clan. They were a leading clan of Quraysh, and perhaps for that reason had been slow to convert to Islam. In this respect ʿUthmān had been an exception, but Muʿāwiya could not match his claim to religious merit, having converted only in 630. He was nevertheless a very successful ruler. We can take our cue from a Christian author writing in the Jazīra—northern Mesopotamia—in the 690s. He usually recounts the events of recent decades with a long face; for example, he characterizes the Arab conquerors as a people "whose comfort lies in blood that is shed without reason, whose pleasure is to dominate everyone, whose wish it is to take captives and to deport." He uses the same tone in speaking of the continuing Muslim expeditions beyond the frontiers under Muʿāwiya: "Their robber bands went annually to distant parts and to the islands, bringing back captives from all the peoples under the heavens." Yet when he comments on the governance of the empire under Muʿāwiya, his tone is remarkably sunny. Muʿāwiya's reign, he tells us, was one of justice and peace; indeed, once he had come to power, "the peace throughout the world was such that we have never heard, either from our fathers or from our grandparents, or seen that there had ever been any like it."[13] This unprecedented peace was naturally good for the economy: crops were plentiful and commerce doubled. How did Muʿāwiya manage to earn such an extraordinary accolade?

12. On Muʿāwiya see R. S. Humphreys, *Muʿawiya ibn Abi Sufyan*, Oxford 2006.

13. S. P. Brock, "North Mesopotamia in the late seventh century," *Jerusalem Studies in Arabic and Islam*, 9 (1987), 60–61.

This is a real question because there were serious limits to Muʿāwiya's power. By now the Arabs in the conquered territories were more used to living with government than their fathers had been, but they were still members of an Arab tribal society with all the unruliness that went with it. Take the Kūfans in 671. Muʿāwiya's governor of Kūfa, Baṣra, and the East, Ziyād ibn Abīh (d. 673), was trying to arrest a certain ʿAbdallāh ibn Khalīfa, a member of the tribe of Ṭayyiʾ who had been involved in subversive activities. He sent his security force to bring him in, but when ʿAbdallāh's sister appealed to her fellow tribesmen for help they rescued him and beat up the security force, which went back to the governor empty-handed. The governor then accosted ʿAdī ibn Ḥātim, the chief of Ṭayyiʾ, in the mosque, demanding that he deliver ʿAbdallāh to him. ʿAdī would not hear of it; did the governor expect him to hand over his own kinsman to be killed? The governor then arrested the chief, provoking extensive protests. In response to the backlash he soon released him, but on the understanding that the chief would send ʿAbdallāh into exile, which he did. Yet it is clear from this story of provincial dissidence that being Muʿāwiya's governor was not an easy job. In particular, Ziyād had no body of loyal Syrian troops to fall back on when he faced trouble in his province. In 661 Muʿāwiya had come to Kūfa with a Syrian army, but he did not leave it behind when he returned to Syria. This in turn meant that he could exert only limited pressure on the Kūfans and on the provinces in general. Likewise Ziyād may have been an energetic and determined governor, but he was, for example, in no position to cream off a substantial portion of the revenue of his province and send it to the central government. At one point, we are told, he did dispatch such a payment from Baṣra, whereupon the tribesmen of the city complained to Mālik ibn Mismaʿ, a major tribal leader there: "He's sending the money, and we'll be left without stipends!"[14] Mālik then led a force that recovered the money, from which he paid the tribesmen's stipends in full; he did not object to the remainder going to Muʿāwiya. Ziyād had no choice but to take this quietly. In effect it was the same story with the revenues of Egypt, where ʿAmr was disinclined to send anything to Muʿāwiya. We are told that Muʿāwiya's staff would urge him to write to ʿAmr about this, but he demurred on the ground that ʿAmr was a willful, greedy, and grasping man. It was left to his staff to write—which they did, but to no avail. Once ʿAmr had died and Muʿāwiya was free to appoint a governor of his choice, he was in a better position to extract some revenue from Egypt, but it was still not very much. He thus had to lean heavily on taxes collected in Syria. In short, Muʿāwiya's was a strange and unusual empire, one that has been described as a federation of regional armies. There were no imperial troops in the provinces to keep them obedient, and the provinces in turn seem to have contributed little to the imperial

14. Abū 'l-Faraj al-Iṣbahānī, *Aghānī*, Cairo 1927–74, 22:339.

treasury. Rather than prove stable, we would expect such a configuration to give way either to a real empire with the center exploiting its provinces or to a set of independent states. Eventually both these outcomes would be realized, first one and then the other.

What, then, did Muʿāwiya have going for him that enabled him to keep such an empire together? For one thing, he had at his disposal the Syrian army, which was by far the most cohesive.[15] It was a tribal army like all Muslim armies at the time, but it held together thanks to the preponderant role played in it by the Syrian tribe of Kalb, with which Muʿāwiya had close relations. There could be some continuity here with the Arab troops recruited by the Byzantines; when the eunuch denounced as "dogs" the Arabs whom the emperor could not afford to pay, his comment was likely a pun on the name of this tribe, *kalb* being the Arabic for dog. That Muʿāwiya had such an army at his command must have given him leverage, which meant that he rarely had to use this army to subdue a rebellious province; most of the time the iron fist could be kept inside the velvet glove. Alongside this military foundation of his power Muʿāwiya had administrators he could depend on. Most of his governors were members of the Arab elite, but he was powerful enough to be able employ useful people who lacked independent social standing. Ziyād was a telling example. He was known as Ziyād ibn Abīh, "Ziyād son of his father," because it was unclear who his father was—a genealogical catastrophe in a patrilineal society. His mother was a slave, which did not make things any better. But despite this social stigma Ziyād had talent, both technical and political, and his superiors recognized it. ʿUmar gave him a thousand dirhams, which he used to buy the freedom of either his mother or his putative father. In 665 Muʿāwiya did his best to erase the scandal of Ziyād's illegitimate birth by recognizing him as his natural brother. He then appointed him governor of Baṣra and the East, to which he added Kūfa. So as with the Prophet's former slave Zayd ibn Ḥāritha, we can think of Ziyād as a wholly owned subsidiary of his powerful patron. We can also see the security force that served Ziyād as somewhat analogous. Its members were not Syrian Arabs, but neither were they local Kūfan Arabs. They instead belonged to the Ḥamrā', a group of Persian soldiers who had gone over to the Muslim side at the time of the conquests. Something else that worked to Muʿāwiya's advantage in the provinces was the Dīwān, the fiscal system established by ʿUmar thanks to which the taxes raised in a province passed through the hands of the caliph's administrators before being paid out to the local Arab soldiery as stipends. Finally, the very fractiousness of the tribal society could be advantageous through the opportunities it provided for a governor to divide and rule.

15. For the Muslim armies of the first three and a half centuries see H. Kennedy, *The armies of the Caliphs*, London 2001.

The result of all this was that Muʿāwiya and his governors had a considerable ability to shape what happened in the provinces. For example, in Kūfa the army had been divided into administrative groupings of tribes, with each tribal unit assigned to a particular group. Ziyād was able to reorganize this system, reducing the number of groups from seven to four and even breaking up some larger tribal groupings. He was also able to move some fifty thousand tribesmen and their families from Iraq to Khurāsān in northeastern Iran in 671. And as we have seen, if he did not succeed in arresting ʿAbdallāh ibn Khalīfa, let alone killing him, he could at least lean hard enough on ʿAbdallāh's tribal leader to secure the exile of the dissident from Kūfa. Such tribal leaders were an essential part of the system, interacting with their tribesmen on the one hand and with the caliph's representatives on the other. In short, Muʿāwiya and his governors were by no means powerless. Yet the balance of caliphal order and tribal disorder was precarious. Success turned on Muʿāwiya's consummate political skill. He was famous for a quality known by a single Arabic word, *ḥilm*, that has no single English equivalent—roughly the ability to handle noisy, difficult, and excitable people with a calm and purposive patience. Not surprisingly, after Muʿāwiya's death and the short reign of his son Yazīd I (ruled 680–83), there was a second civil war. We will return to it when we survey the opposition that the Umayyads faced.

The second in our selection of Umayyad caliphs is ʿAbd al-Malik,[16] the first Marwānid to rule for any length of time. However, he spent the initial third of his reign—from 685 to 692—in the cauldron of the second civil war. What concerns us here is the period from 692 to 705, during which ʿAbd al-Malik's power extended over the entire empire, just as Muʿāwiya's had done. Despite the intervening civil war, there were significant similarities between their reigns. Syria was once again the center of power thanks to its Kalbī troops, and once again an Umayyad was caliph, though one stemming from a different branch of the clan. There was also a familiar division of labor: just as Muʿāwiya had delegated power over Iraq and the East to his trusted governor Ziyād, so now ʿAbd al-Malik did the same with Ḥajjāj, a schoolmaster from Ṭā'if who displayed unusual political and administrative talent. Thanks to this he served as the caliph's viceroy in the East from 694 to 714. But there were some profound differences between the two reigns, three of which are worth picking out.

The first concerns the use of disciplined Syrian troops—still the best in the empire—in establishing and maintaining the grip of the central government on its provinces, especially Iraq with its unruly tribesmen. As we have seen, Muʿāwiya had brought along a Syrian army when he came to Kūfa after the assassination of ʿAlī in 661, but he did not use it to fight any battles and took it back with him when

16. For whom see C. F. Robinson, *ʿAbd al-Malik*, Oxford 2005.

he left; for the rest of his reign Syrian troops had no presence in the provinces. Under ʿAbd al-Malik, by contrast, Syrian troops had to fight a major battle in 691 in order to recover possession of Iraq, and more Syrian troops were sent there in response to two subsequent emergencies. The second of these was the rebellion of Ibn al-Ashʿath, a Kūfan leader of the kind that had flourished in the good old days of Muʿāwiya. In 699 Ibn al-Ashʿath was sent with an Iraqi army to campaign in what is now Afghanistan. His troops were discontented because their stipends had been cut, with the result that they were being paid less than Syrian troops were, and Ibn al-Ashʿath himself was infuriated by the hectoring and micromanaging he experienced from Ḥajjāj. In response, he and his army rebelled and returned in force to Iraq, shaking the foundations of Umayyad rule there to the point that ʿAbd al-Malik was willing to appease them by increasing their pay and firing Ḥajjāj. But they refused the offer, and their rebellion was crushed in 701. Ḥajjāj now created the new garrison city of Wāsiṭ, built in 702 to accommodate a permanent Syrian military presence in Iraq. In short, the iron fist was no longer concealed in a velvet glove, and Ḥajjāj's notoriously abrasive style did nothing to assuage the humiliation and resentment of the Iraqi troops.

A second feature of ʿAbd al-Malik's reign was the increasing prominence of a pattern of tribal factionalism that was to last till the end of the Umayyad period and even beyond, pitting northern Arabs against southern Arabs—we can call them Northerners and Southerners. The conquerors had naturally brought their tribal identities with them from Arabia, and these identities had persisted in the conquered territories, despite a measure of administrative repackaging. But as we saw when we first encountered the Arab tribes, the genealogical system made it possible to define a larger or smaller tribal group by selecting a more distant or recent common ancestor. Beginning in the second civil war and continuing through the reigns of ʿAbd al-Malik and his successors, this led to the emergence of what was effectively a new form of tribal alignment. The change began in Syria and spread from there. The Northerners would usually be known as Qays or Muḍar, depending on the precise selection of a distant ancestor, and the Southerners as Yaman. The tribes that belonged to Yaman had not necessarily migrated to the conquered territories directly from the Yemen, but they were ultimately of Yemeni origin, or at least were believed to be. Northerners and Southerners displayed a high level of mutual hostility, raiding and killing each other; we even hear of the slaughter of female captives. Much of the conflict revolved around competition for the spoils of office. If a Southerner was appointed to a major governorship, he would pick his subordinates overwhelmingly from his own faction. If replaced by a Northerner, he could expect his successor to torture him to extract his ill-gotten gains and to replace his subordinates with Northerners. The struggle was powered by factional chauvinism, not by any higher ethical or religious principle. One Northerner took his followers on an expedition that was supposed to collect taxes, but his plan was in fact to kill as many members of a southern tribe as he could. In abruptly announcing this mission creep to his band, he made no bones about the ethics of his plan: "You have the choice between hell, if you follow me, and disgrace if you don't."[17] They chose hell. Meanwhile the caliph's task—as also that of Ḥajjāj—was to balance the factions as best they could. For the caliph in Syria this meant securing the loyalty of the troops of northern Syria and the Jazīra, who were Northerners, without thereby alienating the Kalbī core of the Umayyad army, the Kalbīs being Southerners.

The third feature of ʿAbd al-Malik's reign shows the political authorities in a more proactive role. This period saw the state take a series of measures that dramatized the advent of a new Arab and Islamic order in a way that Muʿāwiya had not done. In several provinces the language of administration was changed to Arabic in this period, ending the use of Greek in former Byzantine territories and of Middle Persian in former Sasanian territories. The evidence does not support the idea that this reform was implemented at the local level overnight, but whatever the exact trajectory the change did indeed happen—not that this meant the end of the employment of Christians or other non-Muslims in the bureaucracy. As a tangible example of the very public use of Arabic we can cite the milestones erected in Palestine in ʿAbd al-Malik's reign. He was also a builder, as shown by a highly symbolic edifice of his that survives to this day: the Dome of the Rock, which he erected on the Temple Mount in Jerusalem. It is an enigmatic building whose purpose has been much discussed, and the rituals performed inside it were curious, but its Qurʾānic inscriptions convey a strongly Islamic message. Just as striking is what is known as the "reform coinage." Instituted under ʿAbd al-Malik, it was first issued in 696 and then imposed on the entire Muslim world in a drastic standardization, though one that was not matched in the anarchic field of weights and measures. We will return to the new coinage in the last section of this chapter, but here it is enough to note a conspicuous absence: neither the image nor the name of the caliph appears on these coins. This caliphal self-effacement was part of a wider pattern. For example, we hear no reports of dead caliphs being seen off with elaborate public funerals or buried in imposing tombs.

From ʿAbd al-Malik's death in 705 until 743, all the caliphs but one were his sons, the exception being the pious ʿUmar II (ruled 717–20). Hishām, whose reign began in 724, was the fourth and last of them. This sequence points to a degree of long-term stability in the political system that had not existed previously, and this stability was especially pronounced in Hishām's reign. There had not been a major revolt in Iraq since 720, when a former governor of the East, Yazīd ibn al-Muhallab, had rebelled and been defeated. As we will see later, there was significant

17. Quoted in Wellhausen, *The Arab kingdom and its fall*, 207–8.

trouble on the frontiers of distant provinces in Hishām's time, but in the central regions of the empire there were only minor rebellions. His reign was in fact a somewhat prosaic one. Like his two illustrious predecessors, he had his loyal and efficient right-hand man in Iraq, Khālid al-Qasrī, who governed it from 724 to 738. But whereas Muʿāwiya and ʿAbd al-Malik exemplify the high drama of doing things for the first time and the imagination that goes with it, Hishām spent his reign maintaining an established routine in a thoroughgoing and competent fashion. For example, he continued the reform coinage unchanged, and his primary concern and his greatest talent seem to have lain in extracting revenue from his empire. This did not make him popular, but it made for a strong central government. At his death Hishām passed on to his successor what looked like a robust and durable state.

In fact, however, what lay ahead was a third civil war. If we look back on Hishām's reign with that outcome in mind, there are perhaps a couple of features of it that in retrospect signal danger. One of them starts with Khālid al-Qasrī. Whereas Ziyād and Ḥajjāj had each held office until dying a natural death, Khālid's fate was to be dismissed in 738 and tortured by his successor; the treatment eventually killed him. His fall does not seem to have been prompted by any suspicions entertained by Hishām regarding his loyalty. More likely it was related to the conflict between Northerners and Southerners: Khālid had come to be seen as a Southerner, whereas his successor was an ardent Northerner. The virulence of the factional conflict that we see here had become a structural weakness of the Caliphate, and one that would play a central role in the third civil war. From the appointments he made, it is clear that Hishām himself sought to balance the factions rather than to align himself with one against the other, but this caliphal neutrality would scarcely survive his death. The other potentially dangerous feature of the reign was the succession arrangement that had been in place since its beginning. Hishām's predecessor had designated him as his successor but had stipulated that after Hishām his own son Walīd should rule. Although Hishām was unhappy with this provision, he was not able to generate a consensus among the key players to overturn it, so Walīd duly became caliph on Hishām's death. The problems were that this Walīd II (ruled 743–44) was personally unsuited to the role and that the politically alienated life he had led under Hishām had denied him the opportunity to build up a following that could have stood by him on his accession. Looming behind these developments was a fiscal imbalance that had been there all along. As mentioned earlier, Syria was far less wealthy than Iraq. If we take the figures given by our sources for the time around the second civil war, we see that Iraq—including the Jazīra and Khūzistān—provided more than half the revenues of the Caliphate, and Syria less than a twentieth. If we bring Egypt and Iran into the picture, the tilt to the east remains: Egypt provided a tenth, Iran a quarter.

A combination of these structural weaknesses and dynastic bad luck would lead to the fall of the Umayyad dynasty.

The non-Muslim enemies of the Umayyads

The Umayyads were not short of enemies. We can divide them into three categories: hostile non-Muslim states beyond the imperial frontiers, hostile non-Muslim populations within the frontiers, and hostile Muslims whose primary motives were variously religious or secular. The challenges posed by all these enemies are worth attention, but it was the Muslim enemies of the caliphs that brought down the dynasty.

The Middle East of late antiquity had been a geopolitically tense region owing to the existence of two empires of roughly equal power in close proximity, not to mention the threats posed to each by the nomads of the northern steppes. By contrast, the Caliphate of the early centuries of Muslim history found itself in a much more comfortable strategic situation. The nomads were still there, but nowhere on its frontiers did the Caliphate march with a state that was its equal in military power. To the south the Muslim world of the day was largely bounded by the Indian Ocean and the Sahara; states on the far side of either of these barriers were too remote for military interaction. Only in northeastern Africa was the situation more complex because of the existence of the Christian kingdoms of Nubia and Ethiopia. The Nubians, who lived on the upper Nile south of Egypt, held out against the Muslim conquerors of this period thanks to their skill in archery—it was said that the aim of a Nubian archer was so accurate that he could hit the pupil of his enemy's eye. But Nubia did not pose a serious military threat to the Muslim possession of Egypt, and the two sides struck a deal whereby the Nubians were to pay an annual tribute of slaves; they did so, though in a somewhat desultory fashion. The Ethiopians lived in the mountainous interior of the horn of Africa, where their highlands were the counterpart of those of the Yemen on the other side of the Red Sea. The terrain in itself was enough to discourage attempts at Muslim conquest in this period, and at the same time its inhabitants showed only limited interest in attacking Muslims outside their homeland. The Muslims would eventually overthrow the Nubian kingdoms and almost conquer Ethiopia, but in the period we are concerned with here these events still lay centuries in the future.

The most active borders of the Caliphate were accordingly to the west, north, and east, rather than to the south. During the Umayyad period the story here was mostly one of the continuing expansion of the Caliphate, though not at the same rate as in the first wave of conquest. In the west that wave had temporarily taken Arab troops from Egypt as far as Tunisia by 647. They subsequently returned to Tunisia and from 670 clearly intended to stay there, setting up the garrison city of Qayrawān in the Tunisian interior and eventually evicting the Byzantines from

North Africa altogether. Farther to the west an expedition in 681–83 even reached the Atlantic, but it ended badly, and the conquest of the far west and its Berber tribal population, to the extent that it happened at all, was a difficult one not accomplished till the beginning of the eighth century. This was followed in 711 by the invasion of Spain and its relatively easy conquest over the next few years. Perhaps the same year saw the conquest of Sindh in northwestern India; never before or since has the same state ruled over both Spain and Sindh. Meanwhile, the conquest of Transoxania and Khwārazm in Central Asia took place between 705 and 715. Where the Muslims were less successful was on the Byzantine front. They raided freely and frequently in Anatolia, devastating what had been one of the heartlands of the Byzantine Empire. What they failed to do was to take Constantinople, despite sustained attacks by both land and sea in the 670s and again in the course of a long siege in 716–17. They were somewhat more successful in Armenia, though they never had a solid grip on that mountainous land.

This expansion still left the Caliphate with a number of enemies on its frontiers. In western Europe the Carolingians were a rising power that by end of the eighth century would be encroaching on northeastern Spain. Farther to the east the Byzantine Empire, though shorn of its southern provinces, starved of Egyptian grain, and overrun by the Muslims in Anatolia and the Slavs and Bulgars in the Balkans, still had a military potential that could not be ignored.[18] At the same time two steppe peoples posed significant threats to the Caliphate, the Khazars to the north of the Caucasus and the Turks to the northeast of Iran. None of these four states was powerful enough to pose an existential threat to the Caliphate, but each of them defeated a Muslim army at some point in the reign of Hishām and thus posed at least a regional threat to Muslim territory. As far as the central government was concerned, the Carolingians were a long way away. But the other three were closer to home. In the event the threats posed by the Khazars and the Turks ended in 737, but the Byzantine Empire remained menacing. And as we will see, the confrontations with these three states were to have a crucial implication for the domestic politics of the Caliphate in the last years of Umayyad rule: the three frontiers on which there were major Muslim armies were precisely those of the Byzantines, the Khazars, and the Turks, and the central story of the third civil war is how the competition between these armies played out. Yet overall the geopolitical situation of the Caliphate was a rather relaxed one, despite the fact that the days of easy conquests were over. The most telling illustration of this relative comfort is the fact that the Muslims could safely take time off from their hostilities with foreign states to concentrate on their domestic civil wars. This was not, of course, cost-free. In the first civil war Muʿāwiya had to reach an accommodation

18. For the Byzantine response to the threat posed by the Caliphate see J. Haldon, *The empire that would not die*, Cambridge, MA 2016.

with the Byzantine emperor under which he paid tribute to the infidel ruler; ʿAbd al-Malik did the same in the second. In the third the Byzantines took advantage of the situation to push their frontier farther to the east. But no non-Muslim state took a Muslim civil war as an invitation to invade the Caliphate and take over.

We turn now to those enemies of Umayyad rule who lived within the borders of the empire, and in the first instance the non-Muslim ones. Conquering foreign peoples and subjecting them to heavy and very likely increased burdens of taxation could be seen as an invitation to rebellion, particularly given the initial demographic disparity between the two populations—the small number of Arab Muslim conquerors as against the vast subject population. But by and large rebellion among non-Muslims was rare, and at no point could it be said to have threatened to overturn the rule of the caliphs. This is remarkable; matters are not always so easy for conquerors. Led by the founder of the Ming dynasty, Chinese rebels in 1368 ended Mongol rule in their country by expelling the Mongols, who returned disconsolately to their homeland in the steppes. But there was no comparable attempt to send the Arabs back to Arabia.

Such rebellions as there were can be divided into two categories according to the kind of population involved in them. Among the peasants and city dwellers of the plains, who were accustomed to being ruled by people of a different ethnicity and often religion, rebellion was virtually absent except in one setting: among the Copts of the Egyptian countryside. The Copts apart, such populations seem to have come to terms with their new rulers much as they had done with their old ones. Indeed, they sometimes saw the newcomers in a distinctly favorable light—we witnessed a Christian in the Jazīra wax lyrical about the rule of Muʿāwiya. If instead they were impatient for Muslim rule to end, they made do with eschatological fantasy rather than actual insurrection. For example, there was a belief that the king of the Greeks would turn the tables on the Arabs and inflict on them what they had inflicted on the Christians, but a hundred times over. The Egyptian exception most likely arose from the fact that in a tax collector's paradise it is sorely tempting for the state to binge on extracting resources from its subjects (though it is not obvious why the taxation of the irrigated agriculture of Iraq should not have had the same effect). Coptic rebellions began in the late seventh century; the first major revolt was in 725–26, and the last major one was suppressed in 832. This last revolt was notable inasmuch as the Copts in question lived in the coastal marshes, an environment into which a state could have trouble projecting its power (though again one might have expected the same effect in the much larger marshland of lower Iraq).

We come now to the mountain peoples. Highlanders are in general more likely to engage in dissident behavior than are inhabitants of the plains, since the terrain makes them harder for the state to control and encourages them to rely on themselves for their security. And yet we do not find many examples of rebellious mountaineers among the non-Muslim populations of the early Caliphate. One such population, attested from the later seventh century to the early ninth, was the Jarājima—alias Mardaites—of the Amanus range in northwestern Syria. They were Christians, and in that respect closer to the Byzantines than to the Muslims, but they performed military service for both sides. They alarmed ʿAbd al-Malik by overrunning Lebanon. The caliphs nevertheless found them useful and handled them with a mixture of repression and co-option; for example, they were allowed to remain Christian but dress as Muslims. In short, they were serious troublemakers but not exactly rebels. Another example takes us to western Iran, or Media, as our Armenian chronicler calls it. Here, he tells us, the "Medes" rebelled in 654 in response to overtaxation and killed the chief of the tax collectors appointed by the caliph. The chronicler comments on how the rebels were helped by the "fastnesses" of Media—the deep valleys, the precipices, the rocks, and the rugged, difficult terrain. The Arab attempt to suppress the rebellion was a failure. But at the time of these events Muʿāwiya was not yet caliph. Undoubtedly the most conspicuous example of rebellious mountaineers anywhere in the empire was to be found among the Berber population of North Africa. As non-Muslims they mounted large-scale resistance to being conquered, but the rapidity with which they adopted Islam meant that when they later rebelled they did so as Muslims. In short, when we look for cases of rebellion among non-Muslim peoples in the Umayyad period we find ourselves scraping the barrel. This makes the Coptic exception to the general quiescence all the more noteworthy.

The Muslim enemies of the Umayyads

By contrast, when we turn to Muslim rebels the barrel overflows. A surfeit of rebellions is by its nature a somewhat chaotic phenomenon, and we have to do what we can to reduce it to some kind of order. We can start with the fact that royal families can be their own worst enemies. Rebellion within the family—or in the Umayyad case we should perhaps say within the clan—is a familiar hazard of monarchical polities, often centered on disputed successions. Such revolts were in fact less common in the Umayyad case than among many other dynasties. Thus the transition from the Sufyānids to the Marwānids in 684 did not involve a rebellion; Sufyānid rule had already petered out before the new branch of the family claimed the caliphate. One member of yet another branch did mount a minor rebellion in 689, but thereafter the Umayyads were free of this problem until after the death of Hishām in 743. As we saw, the accession of his predecessor's son, Walīd II, did not augur well for the stability of the state, and the years 743–44 saw three short Umayyad reigns and four rebellions mounted by Umayyads in quick succession. The third of these rebellions brought the last Umayyad ruler, Marwān II (ruled 744–50), to power, and as we will see his accession meant a radical discontinuity in the history of the dynasty.

Just as familiar up and down history are rebellions on the part of members of the wider political elite who for one reason or another turn dissident. In the first civil war, as we saw, these dissidents were prominent Qurashī companions of the Prophet. In the second civil war the central figure was the son of one of these companions, Ibn al-Zubayr. Following the death of Yazīd I in 683, he claimed the caliphate and ruled from Mecca till he was killed in 692. This was a geopolitically perverse choice of location, but his brother Muṣʿab was doing the hard work as his governor in Iraq, and at first Ibn al-Zubayr was far more widely recognized as caliph than his Umayyad competitors were. He was not the only son of a leading companion to rebel in this period. Another was ʿAlī's son Ḥusayn, who, like Ibn al-Zubayr, belonged to the last generation with childhood memories of the Prophet; but his poorly supported rebellion of 680 against Yazīd I was no more than a sideshow at the time, though it became central in later retrospect, especially among Shīʿites. By late Umayyad times any such childhood memories were long gone, and the original political elite of the Muslim state had lost such coherence as it had once had. Insofar as it survived, it had in effect been reduced to two key clans of Quraysh: the Banū Umayya or Umayyads, and the Banū Hāshim or Hāshimites. The latter were the descendants of the Prophet's great-grandfather Hāshim, the Qurashī who had reputedly met the Byzantine emperor in Syria. Since Muḥammad himself was an only child and had no descendants in the male line, the ancestors of the later Hāshimites were his uncles, notably Abū Ṭālib and al-ʿAbbās. In a broad sense the set of these descendants made up the family of Muḥammad, but among them there was a subset that could be seen as closer to him than the rest. ʿAlī ibn Abī Ṭālib had married Muḥammad's daughter Fāṭima, and their issue—including Ḥusayn—could accordingly claim descent from the Prophet himself, albeit in the female line; so genealogically they were at once ʿAlids and Fāṭimids. We are already familiar with the Umayyad contenders in the third civil war, and we will take up the Hāshimite contenders below, using the term Hāshimiyya for the associated movement that eventually brought the ʿAbbāsid dynasty to power. A final type of insurgent that belongs in the wider typology of rebellion is the disaffected provincial governor or general. Here Muʿāwiya is of course the prime example, and the only successful one in Umayyad times. We have encountered two failed rebellions of this kind that occurred between the second and third civil wars, those of Ibn al-Ashʿath and Yazīd ibn al-Muhallab.

This picture is complicated by the way in which the various types of rebellion intersected with three kinds of hostility that were prominent for much of the Umayyad period: that between Syrians and Iraqis, that between Northerners and Southerners, and that between Arabs and non-Arabs. As to Syrians and Iraqis, in each civil war Syria and Iraq aligned differently; whatever side the Iraqis were on—and they tended to be divided between several sides—it was not that of the Umayyads. The rebellions of Ibn al-Ashʿath and Yazīd ibn al-Muhallab were variations on the same theme.

The factional conflict between Northerners and Southerners, once it had taken shape, had a way of seeping into everything. By way of example, the revolt of the Southerner Yazīd ibn al-Muhallab in 720 intensified the factional conflict, and we have seen how it swallowed up Hishām's governor of the East, Khālid al-Qasrī. More ominously, in the years following the death of Hishām the conflict engulfed Syria. As long as the factions had existed, there had been hostility between the Kalbī Southerners of central and southern Syria and the Qaysī Northerners of northern Syria and the Jazīra; both factions contributed heavily to the Umayyad armies. To manage the tension the caliphs needed to be above the fray, but in those last years of the dynasty they turned partisan. Walīd II took actions that marked him as partial to the Northerners. The rebel who overthrew him, Yazīd III, was aligned with the Southerners. And Marwān II was the leader of an army of Northerners from the Jazīra.

Turning to ethnic conflict, the Arabs were not the only Muslims of the Umayyad period who were discontented: numerous non-Arab converts to Islam were if anything even more so. We will leave aside for now what made them both numerous and discontented and glance instead at some of the contexts in which they participated in rebellion. In 685–87, at a time when Iraq was under Zubayrid rule, there was a rebellion in Kūfa. The leader, Mukhtār, was an Arab, a member of the tribe of Thaqīf and so a distant relative of Ḥajjāj. But his followers, including his personal bodyguard, were disproportionately non-Arab, most likely Iranian. The Arabs of Kūfa were not pleased by this, and after a while many of the tribal leaders rebelled against Mukhtār—a rebellion within a rebellion within a rebellion. Unsurprisingly, it is said that the reason for their dissatisfaction was Mukhtār's partiality for non-Arabs. So far, we see non-Arab rebels who nevertheless accept Arab leadership. But then, according to a contemporary Syriac source, a group of these rebels found themselves in Nisibis, where they decided that they wanted to be led by one of their own. They killed their Arab leader and appointed one of themselves commander. Another context of such tension in this period was the rebellion of the Azāriqa, a ferocious Khārijite sect that took shape in Baṣra around the start of the second civil war, retreated into Iran under strong military pressure, and was finally defeated only in the late 690s by Muhallab ibn Abī Ṣufra, the father of Yazīd ibn al-Muhallab. At some point in Iran the sect split. What makes this split relevant here is its ethnic character: the Arabs and the non-Arabs went their separate ways, with the non-Arabs being defeated two or three years before the Arabs. As a final example let us take the rebellion of the pious Ḥārith ibn Surayj in Khurāsān and the East; it lasted, with intervals, from 734 to his death in 746. Ḥārith belonged to the tribe of Tamīm, so he was as much an Arab as Mukhtār. But again his followers included non-Arabs, in this instance native Sogdian converts to Islam, and he championed their sense of grievance against the Arabs. What we see in these examples is a pattern in which non-Arab Muslim rebels, despite their ethnic grievances, normally continued to accept Arab leadership even when they rebelled. Yet they had sufficient clout that it was wise for rebel Arab leaders to pay at least some attention to their concerns, and on occasion the non-Arabs dispensed with Arab leadership altogether.

Another complicating factor was religion, which was more salient than appears from the account given above. This salience was almost inevitable given the way the Muslim polity had come into being. The central issue at stake in Umayyad politics was who should be caliph (*khalīfa*), and this was an intrinsically religious issue inasmuch as the title, whether understood as "Deputy of God" or "Successor of the Messenger of God," identified an intrinsically religious office, as did another common caliphal title, "Commander of the Faithful" or more literally "Commander of the Believers." This meant that political rhetoric was to a large extent religious rhetoric. The caliphs had their version of it. A letter sent out by the ill-fated Walīd II reminded recipients that "the caliphs of God followed one another, in charge of that which God had caused them to inherit from His prophets and over which He had deputed them." His optimistic inference from this was that no one could dispute the rights of God's caliphs without God casting him down. To this, rebels—including the Umayyad rebel Yazīd III—predictably responded with religious rhetoric of their own. Our contemporary Syriac source noticed this in the case of Ibn al-Zubayr: "He made it known about himself that he had come out of zeal for the house of God," and he denounced the "westerners"—the Umayyads and their followers—as "transgressors of the law."[19] Ibn al-Ash'ath's troops, announcing their decision to rebel with him, used a markedly religious language about Ḥajjāj: "We will not obey the enemy of God, who like a Pharaoh coerces us to the farthest campaigns and keeps us here so that we can never see our wives and children."[20] These rebels had a readily intelligible worldly grievance, but that did not stop them from embellishing it with religious rhetoric. Similarly, Yazīd ibn al-Muhallab in 720 called the Baṣrans to the Qur'ān and the practice of the Prophet—boilerplate rebel rhetoric of Umayyad times—and told them that jihad against the Syrians would win a greater reward from God than would jihad against such infidel peoples as the Turks and the Daylamites of northern Iran. None of this is to say that religion was everything. Boilerplate religious rhetoric can be skin-deep, and it was certainly not the case that all Muslim rebels affected it all of the time. Moreover, the whole phenomenon of factional conflict between Northerners and Southerners lay in the domain of secular politics, as was tacitly acknowledged by the leader who gave his followers the choice of hell or disgrace.

19. Brock, "North Mesopotamia in the late seventh century," 64.
20. Quoted in Wellhausen, *The Arab kingdom and its fall*, 233–34.

There was nevertheless a form of religious politics where the suspicion of mere rhetorical embellishment would be out of place: sectarian rebellion. Already in the first civil war we saw the Khārijite movement take shape. Its adherents were characterized by a zealous and puritanical adherence to principles, which helps explain why they divided into numerous subsects; the split among the Baṣran Khārijites that gave rise to the Azāriqa is the classic example of this fissiparousness. Over the decades several of these subsects became well-defined communities with beliefs and practices that set them off from each other and from the Muslim mainstream that would later be identified as Sunnī. Khārijite subsects were prone to rebellion, particularly in times of civil war when the cat was away. Thus the Azāriqa, as we saw in passing, were a product of the second civil war, though it was not until several years after it ended that they were finally suppressed. Another Khārijite subsect, the Ṣufriyya, was apparently the product of the same Khārijite split but did not rebel until 695–97; it took root in the Jazīra, where it was endemic among the Arab tribes for the next two centuries. The third civil war was the occasion for a major Ṣufrī rebellion in 744–46, and it was briefly successful in taking Kūfa and Wāsiṭ. One thing people found noteworthy, and perhaps somewhat unnerving, about these Ṣufrī rebels was the presence of 150 female fighters in their ranks. It was in tune with this that the mother of the Ṣufrī leader, who was later killed in battle, gave a speech from the pulpit of the mosque in Kūfa. Some say these sectarians held the highly unusual view that a woman could serve as imam—in other words caliph—provided she administered the affairs of the believers and went forth to fight their opponents. (Of course, not all violent women were principled: we also hear of female bandits.) Meanwhile, the Ṣufrīs were also active far away among the Berber tribes of North Africa. Yet another Khārijite subsect that is said to have arisen in the course of the same split was the Ibāḍiyya, the only one that survives to this day, with the result that we know about its doctrines and fortunes from internal sources. The Ibāḍīs were amphibious: their beliefs allowed them to live peaceably alongside non-Ibāḍī Muslims in good conscience, or alternatively to go forth and rebel to establish an Ibāḍī imamate. In the urban setting of Baṣra they took the first course, living quietly among their neighbors while preparing the way for insurrection among the Arab tribes of Oman and the Berber tribes of North Africa. In other words, they were mounting a long-term, long-distance conspiracy that would eventually issue in rebellion and statehood in lands remote from the center of Umayyad power. We will take up the outcome of this strategy in later chapters.

In the last years of Umayyad rule, the Ibāḍīs had an opportunity to set up an imamate in Ḥaḍramawt. From there Ibāḍī troops advanced westward to the Yemen and then northward to the Ḥijāz; we can only guess where they might have gone next had they not been defeated by a Syrian force. While these Ibāḍīs were in the Ḥijāz, sometime around 747, their leader, Abū Ḥamza, delivered an oration in

Mecca or Medina in which he reviewed the history of the Muslim state from his sectarian standpoint. What he had to say about the first four caliphs was the standard Khārijite view: Abū Bakr and ʿUmar were good, ʿUthmān was not much good and became even worse, and ʿAlī started good but went bad with his acceptance of arbitration between himself and Muʿāwiya. Abū Ḥamza then went on to speak about the Umayyads, whom he denounced as unbelievers; even the pietist ʿUmar II was dismissed as having had good intentions but failing to implement them. Two themes dominate his account of the other Umayyad rulers. One expresses the puritanical streak of Khārijism: he condemns Yazīd I as "a sinner in respect of his belly and his private parts"[21] and says much the same about three subsequent rulers, with lurid details of the depravity of one of them. The other theme is the injustice of Umayyad rule. Here the accusations he levels at the rulers indirectly reveal what just rule would have looked like for Abū Ḥamza. Muʿāwiya, he tells us, "made the servants of God slaves" and "the property of God something to be taken by turns." The Marwānids "shed forbidden blood and devoured forbidden property." With regard to Yazīd II (ruled 720–24) he quotes a Qurʾānic verse about giving orphans their possessions and observes that "the matter of Muḥammad's nation is of greater moment than the property of the orphan." A measure taken by Hishām "made the rich among you richer and the poor poorer," and Marwān II "abraded faces, put out eyes, and cut off hands and feet." He ends with a sweeping comment about the Umayyads at large: "Their might is self-magnification. They arrest on suspicion, make decrees capriciously, kill in anger, and judge by passing over crimes without punishment." He sums up their vicious attitude by putting into their mouths the boast "The land is our land, the property is our property, and the people are our slaves." In another age Abū Ḥamza might have been an ardent constitutionalist.

The Khārijites were not the only sectarians to rebel in Umayyad times. If we think of the mainstream that would one day be Sunnism, we can see it as flanked by two mutually hostile sectarian streams: Khārijism on the left and Shīʿism on the right. The two differed in several ways. First, where the Khārijites respected principles, the Shīʿites respected persons, notably ʿAlī and the other members of the family of the Prophet, however defined or left undefined. This difference had a significant bearing on how each group saw the genealogical qualifications for the imamate: there were none among the Khārijites, but Shīʿite imams had to belong to the Prophet's family. Second, Khārijism, though extreme by mainstream standards, was sober and austere, whereas Shīʿism had space for wild ideas and tempestuous emotions. Third, no Khārijite subsect was quietist, whereas among the Shīʿites the Imāmīs—the subsect that seems to have crystallized earliest and

21. For this and the quotations that follow see P. Crone and M. Hinds, *God's caliph*, Cambridge 1986, 130–32.

was to have the largest share of the Shīʿite future—had renounced rebellion, thus adapting in a way that enabled them to survive as an urban population in the central Muslim world. The point was further underlined when this subsect adopted the doctrine that in 874 its twelfth and last imam had gone into hiding, from which he has yet to return; what had been a very real if apolitical imamate, complete with disputed successions and financial scandals, now became a focus of eschatological hope. Finally, Khārijism at an early stage congealed in the form of a sharp-edged sect or set of sects, whereas Shīʿism overall remained more fluid into the late Umayyad period and even beyond. In the first civil war we can speak of the role of ʿAlī and his supporters in a political and military conflict, but not of a sect comparable to the Khārijites. In the second civil war Mukhtār's largely non-Arab following in Kūfa was clearly responsive to his ideas, which included identifying Muḥammad ibn al-Ḥanafiyya—a son of ʿAlī, but not by Fāṭima—as the Mahdī. But the revolt was too transitory for us to think of Mukhtār's followers as a sect. Their heritage would nevertheless bulk large in a plethora of more or less extremist Shīʿite groups that survived into the second half of the eighth century and are conveniently subsumed under the term Kaysāniyya. Thus the third civil war saw the rebellion of ʿAbdallāh ibn Muʿāwiya, a descendant of Abū Ṭālib but not through ʿAlī. It began in Kūfa in 744; easily defeated, the rebels moved into western Iran, where they held a large territory until defeated once again in 747. These rebels were very mixed, but they included many who subscribed to the extreme ideas of the Kaysānīs, such as the transmigration of souls—a mainstream doctrine in Indian religions but highly heterodox in the Islamic context. As with Mukhtār, it would be hard to see ʿAbdallāh ibn Muʿāwiya's adherents as a well-defined sect. But from a historical perspective what matters most about the Kaysānī milieu we encounter here is that the Hāshimiyya—the movement that was to bring the ʿAbbāsids to power in 749—emerged from it. Just how it emerged is a good question, but one narrative has it that the imamate passed from Muḥammad ibn al-Ḥanafiyya to his son Abū Hāshim, who at his death bequeathed it to the leading member of the ʿAbbāsid family, Muḥammad ibn ʿAlī.

From the Umayyads to the ʿAbbāsids

The ʿAbbāsid revolution was unquestionably the most successful rebellion of the entire Umayyad period,[22] and it brings together many of the threads we have been following. A good starting point is the distribution of military power in late Umayyad times. As we have seen, it was the location of the main hostile states bordering on the empire that determined the placing of the major Muslim armies:

22. On the ʿAbbāsid revolution see M. Sharon, *Black banners from the east*, Jerusalem 1983.

one in Syria, one in the Jazīra, and one in Khurāsān. Since the second civil war the Syrian army had been a tense combination of Northerners and Southerners, and the partisanship of the last caliphs in this factional conflict meant that it now fell apart. This, as we saw, was Marwān II's opportunity to move in with his own army of Northerners from the Jazīra in 744. What followed did irreparable damage to his relationship with Syria. After he moved the capital to Ḥarrān—his base in the Jazīra—there were two major Syrian rebellions, which he defeated, demolishing the walls of the Syrian cities in 746 and returning again to Ḥarrān. Having dealt in this fashion with Syria, he was able to gain control of Iraq and some other provinces. Thanks to his energy, his determination, and his military resources Marwān was now well on the way to restoring Umayyad power, albeit on a different geographical and military basis. He had survived the years when it was most vulnerable, the chaos of 743–44 and the Syrian rebellions of 745–46, and he was now firmly in the saddle.

But there was a third army in the wings, that of Khurāsān, and in 748 it set out on the road to Iraq. On its way it won four successive military engagements against Umayyad forces, culminating in the definitive defeat of Marwān near Mosul in 750. The rest was mopping up. Marwān fled to Egypt, where he was tracked down and killed that same year. Numerous members of the Umayyad family were massacred in Syria and elsewhere, while the tombs of the Umayyad caliphs were destroyed, their bodies whipped and burned, and the ashes scattered. The Khurāsānī troops had not started with any obvious military superiority over those of Marwān, and winning four victories in a row does suggest a run of good luck. But however far from inevitable, the triumph of the Khurāsānīs was hardly mysterious.

What is harder to explain is how the soldiers of Khurāsān had come to be assembled into the militarily and politically coherent force that enthroned the ʿAbbāsids. Until 743 the Syrian army was held together by a powerful caliph, Hishām, and that of the Jazīra by a powerful governor, Marwān. But in his later years Naṣr ibn Sayyār, the last Umayyad governor of Khurāsān, was trying to hold together a province whose army was fragmenting. Appointed in 738, he was a Northerner, in contrast to his predecessor, who had been a Southerner. By 744 the Southerners were in open revolt against Naṣr, and the Northerners of Khurāsān may not have been particularly well disposed toward Umayyad rule since they had come there from Iraq, not Syria. In 746 the Southerners allied with the rebel Ḥārith ibn Surayj and his following, and this alliance lasted long enough for their combined forces to expel Naṣr from Marw, the main city of Khurāsān. He fled westwards to Nīshāpūr, where the presence of his fellow Northerners increased his chances of a soft landing. He returned in 747 and succeeded in reoccupying Marw, but only because he was now in alliance with his former enemies, the Southerners. This new and unlikely alignment was a response to the sudden appearance of a common enemy that same year: the Hāshimiyya, led by a certain Abū Muslim, a ruthlessly effective leader of obscure origin. In 748 Abū Muslim, now allied in his turn with the Southerners, was strong enough to occupy Marw. He then proceeded to take over Khurāsān in a way that Naṣr had been unable to do, disposing of the leader of the Southerners once he had no further use for him. Out of the fragmented army of Khurāsān Abū Muslim put together the cohesive force that was to bring the ʿAbbāsids to power. Meanwhile Naṣr once again fled westward, dying in western Iran in 748. Obviously there was no inevitability about the triumph of Abū Muslim in Khurāsān, but given his strong following and his unusual talents that, too, is hardly mysterious.

The real issue, then, is how Abū Muslim came to have such a following. This is the most interesting and also the murkiest question about the ʿAbbāsid revolution—murky not because we lack sources, but because what the sources tell us does not add up. A fairly standard account would run as follows. Over the course of three decades the Hāshimiyya developed as a clandestine movement aiming to bring to power a member of the ʿAbbāsid family—that is to say, one of the descendants of the Prophet's uncle ʿAbbās. The movement emerged from the Kaysāniyya, itself part of the wider Shīʿite trend. Its operations were divided between three far-flung locations. The family itself, including its leader, lived inconspicuously at Ḥumayma, to the north of Ayla, today's ʿAqaba in southern Jordan; a small group of organizers resided in Kūfa, the main center of Shīʿism; and the field in which they were secretly laying the foundations for their eventual rebellion was Khurāsān. There the agents of the movement recruited both Arabs and non-Arabs (here, as often, we see non-Arabs rebels accepting Arab leadership). In the meantime, the ʿAbbāsid leader Muḥammad ibn ʿAlī had died, and his son, known as Ibrāhīm al-Imām, had succeeded him. He now dispatched Abū Muslim to Khurāsān to take over the leadership of the movement there. Abū Muslim did so in 746 or 747, eventually having the previous leader killed. If we stand back from these details, we have here something analogous to the Ibāḍī movement of late Umayyad times, with its headquarters in Baṣra and its operations in Oman and North Africa. Of course there were differences. The Ibāḍīs, being Khārijites, worked for their principles, not for a member of the family of Muḥammad in Shīʿite style. And though they succeeded in establishing states in both Oman and North Africa, they failed to take over the Muslim world as a whole; unlike the Hāshimiyya, they did not link their fortunes to one of the three centers of Muslim military strength at the time. But however different, the two groups had in common a very distinctive pattern of political conspiracy sustained over space and time. We will encounter it one last time in the ninth century, in the early history of the Shīʿite sect known as the Ismāʿīlīs.

Yet as indicated, our sources present us with problems. The most fundamental concerns the relationship of the Hāshimiyya to the ʿAbbāsids. The movement's agents in Khurāsān did not make propaganda specifically on behalf of a member of the ʿAbbāsid family; rather, they called for the caliphate to go to "an agreed member (*al-riḍā*) of the family of Muḥammad," with agreement presumably to be reached by a process of wide consultation (*shūrā*). This phrasing could, of course, have been a tactical move to maximize recruitment. But if so, it is odd that several ʿAbbāsids were among the rebel ʿAbdallāh ibn Muʿāwiya's diverse following in western Iran, including the future ʿAbbāsid caliph al-Manṣūr (ruled 754–75). Could they really have been unaware that they had a movement of their own not so far away in Khurāsān? Just as odd is what is said to have happened when the Khurāsānī army reached Kūfa in 749 and was joined there by members of the ʿAbbāsid family. Abū Salama, who was in charge of the movement in the city, kept their arrival secret and wanted to appoint a non-ʿAbbāsid to the caliphate. Or as another account has it, he resolved to have the question of the imamate decided through a consultation between the ʿAlids and the ʿAbbāsids. What sense can we make of this? By way of background, we need to note that there are two very different conceptions of appointment to the imamate in play here: designation by the previous imam, as Muḥammad ibn ʿAlī is said to have been designated by the dying Abū Hāshim; and election through consultation. One explanation of Abū Salama's behavior would be that Ibrāhīm al-Imām, who had recently died or been killed in one of Marwān II's prisons, had been unable to appoint a successor. As Abū Salama put it to Abū ʾl-ʿAbbās, the ʿAbbāsid who in the event became caliph, "I think that the imam to whom we owe obedience is dead."[23] This perplexing situation could have meant disarray at the very moment of military triumph, so that in the absence of a designated successor Abū Salama could have turned to the idea of a consultation among the family of Muḥammad as the only way forward. Another, more drastic, explanation would be that the call for an agreed member of the family of Muḥammad had never disguised a secret purpose but rather was what the Hāshimiyya had been about all along. This would mean that the switch to an ʿAbbāsid imam took place only at the last minute. There is nothing we can do to solve the puzzle here.

What we can do is get some sense of what the clandestine movement may have been like from an inside source describing the instructions allegedly given by the predecessor of Ibrāhīm al-Imām, Muḥammad ibn ʿAlī, to Abū ʿIkrima, a non-Arab saddler who acted as one of his secret agents. He was instructed to call himself Abū Muḥammad—a name that would not stand out, unlike the rare Abū ʿIkrima. He was to pose as a merchant—an excellent cover, since it is natural for merchants to travel around and talk to numerous people in the course of their business. He was to communicate as little as possible with Muḥammad ibn ʿAlī, and to keep the latter's identity secret except from those he could trust absolutely. To others

23. Quoted in M. Sharon, *Revolt*, Jerusalem 1990, 251.

he was to speak in his propaganda of an agreed member of the family of Muḥammad. He was not to encourage anyone to draw a sword; the time for that would come later. Once he reached Marw he was to live among the Southerners and be wary of the Northerners, though enlisting those of them whom he could trust. At the same time he was to recruit as many Persians as he could, since God would support the movement through them. Here, then, we have backing for the view that the call for an agreed member of the family of Muḥammad was a pretense.

One thing that emerges from this whole survey of the rebels of Umayyad times is that the political culture of both rulers and rebels was permeated by religion to an unusual extent. The key word here is "extent." Not all Muslim politics was Islamic; as we have seen, the factional conflict between Northerners and Southerners was emphatically a matter of this world, not of the next—like the clashes between the Byzantine circus factions known as the Blues and the Greens. At the same time, in the non-Muslim states of premodern times it was likewise normal for religion to play a significant part in politics. It takes the doctrinaire secularism of the modern world to attempt to evict religion from politics, not always successfully. But the extent of the permeation of politics by religion in the early Muslim case was decidedly above the average, particularly as religion was to a marked degree constitutive of Muslim politics.

A couple of comparisons with the Byzantine and Persian Empires of pre-Islamic times may help highlight the difference and its limits. The first and clearest concerns the office of the ruler. The caliphate, as we have seen, was conceived in intrinsically religious terms, with the caliph defined as the Deputy of God, the Successor of His Messenger, or the Commander of the Faithful. By contrast, the Byzantine emperor inherited his office in an unbroken chain stretching back to the emperors of pagan Rome, while the word "king" in the Persian title "King of Kings" was a term used for rulers irrespective of their religious or ethnic affiliations. In the Sasanian conception, religion and kingship were very close to each other—in one wording they were twins. But as that metaphor implies, they were not the same thing. A second comparison concerns the role of sects. They were a conspicuous phenomenon on both sides of the transition from Byzantine late antiquity to early Islam and the cause of much hostility and disorder in both settings. Yet in contrast to the Muslim case, sectarian rebellion is not a widespread phenomenon in Byzantine politics. A large part of the explanation for this is a variant of the first contrast: whereas the Christian sects of late antiquity were mostly about issues of Christological doctrine, the Islamic sects that concern us were in the first instance about who should rule and how, questions that had very direct practical and political implications. A twelfth-century Muslim heresiographer aptly observed that the disagreement over the imamate—in other words the caliphate—was the most serious in the Muslim community, for in all ages the sword had never been unsheathed in Islam for any religious principle as it had been for the imamate. An Islamic sect of this kind aspired to rule. Another factor in the background was no doubt the high level of political participation that the Arabs had brought with them from Arabia. In his accession speech Abū Bakr told his subjects that they should help him if he did right but correct him if he did wrong. His successor, ʿUmar, is likewise said to have requested that anyone who detected crookedness in him should tell him; a leading companion reassured him that in such an event, "we will straighten you out with our swords."[24] This was not the style of late antique Constantinople or Ctesiphon. But neither were these contrasts hard and fast. Though Byzantine rebels did not revolt in the name of Christian political values, some of them were partisan in terms of the Christological disputes of the day. Meanwhile in the Persian case there seems to have been an instance—though only one—in which rebels justified their conduct by invoking Zoroastrian values: the revolt of Mazdak in the 530s. But the contrasts are nonetheless real and may give us a clue as to why the phenomenon of long-term, long-distance conspiracy should have been exclusively Muslim in premodern times. For a man to devote his life to such a conspiracy called for a willingness to endure the deferral of political gratification to an extent that in premodern times perhaps only religious faith could adequately motivate. When Muḥammad ibn ʿAlī gave Abū ʿIkrima his instructions for his dangerous mission, he told him: "I am not guaranteeing that you will live, but I do guarantee you'll have the divine reward that is better for you than this world and everything in it."[25] Abū ʿIkrima's mission did indeed come to an end when he was cut in two by order of the governor of Khurāsān, but whether he got the promised reward in heaven is not recorded.

Before we leave the Umayyads, we should pause to review the larger record of Arab and Muslim state formation in the century and more that ended with the ʿAbbāsid revolution. Here it is worth returning to the contrast between the outcomes of the Arab invasion of the Persian and Byzantine Empires, on the one hand, and the Germanic invasions of the Western Roman Empire, on the other. The most obvious contrast here, and a very significant one, is the survival of government on an imperial scale in the east as against its demise in the west. But there is another contrast, less striking but no less revealing. The basic form of government instituted by the caliphs was one in which the state collected taxes and used them to pay for the cost of maintaining the state apparatus, especially the army. This seems unremarkable, inasmuch as it is how we usually think of states making a living—taxes being what they eat. But that was not how things worked out in what had been the Western Roman Empire. There the fiscal system atrophied in the early Middle Ages and the agents of government, above all armies, were supported by

24. Tatāʾī, *Tanwīr al-maqāla fī ḥall alfāẓ al-Risāla*, n.p. 1988, 1:370.
25. *Akhbār al-dawla al-ʿAbbāsiyya*, ed. ʿA. al-Dūrī and ʿA. al-Muṭṭalibī, Beirut 1971, 203.

grants of land.[26] As we have seen, the Arabic sources did not regard such an outcome as unthinkable. Rather, they saw it as the option that ʿUmar had decided against, though attesting that it did happen to an extent. That it should happen is not surprising. Taxing is hard work, and the commitment of the caliphs to tax collection was not a foregone conclusion, particularly in view of the constraints under which they operated. They had to build a state using the manpower of a tribal people that until recently had been accustomed to life in a stateless society, and they had to do so in the face of strong provincial reluctance to fund the central government, a constraint that forced them to fall back on the rather limited resources of Syria. Some of the overall contrast between the fiscal east and the tax-free west could be put down to the greater depletion of material resources in the west; there is no eastern parallel to the disappearance of the potter's wheel and the absence of coin minting in post-Roman Britain. But much of the contrast was down to political will, as dramatized in ʿUmar's decision. Where we could nevertheless see the caliphs as taking the line of least resistance was the overwhelmingly military character of the political elite that their taxation paid for. In this respect the Caliphate aligned with the traditions of the Persian Empire and broke with those of the Byzantine Empire, which in late antiquity still preserved a civilian aristocracy in Roman imperial style—a rarity in the premodern world.

The ʿAbbāsid dynasty

The ʿAbbāsids reigned in Iraq for five centuries, from 749 to 1258.[27] But reigning is not the same as ruling, and ruling Iraq, or some part of it, is not the same as ruling an empire. In outline, the ʿAbbāsids were at first fairly successful imperial rulers, but they sustained this role only for a bit over a century. They then found themselves in trouble for several decades, at the end of which they had been reduced to reigning rather than ruling. Later they recovered sufficiently to become a modest power within Iraq, and they continued as such until the Mongols put an end to their rule. Even after that the Mamlūk rulers of Egypt maintained a token ʿAbbāsid caliphate from 1261 to 1517. But all that concerns us in this chapter is the period of imperial rule from the inception of the dynasty in 749 to the beginning of its time of troubles in 861. This period falls into three parts: before, during, and after the fourth civil war of 811–19. Let us take each in turn.

26. This contrast between east and west is a prominent theme of C. Wickham, *Framing the early Middle Ages*, Oxford 2005 (see, for example, 56).

27. For surveys of ʿAbbāsid history in the period covered in this chapter, see the relevant chapters of Kennedy, *The Prophet and the age of the caliphates*, and T. El-Hibri, *The Abbasid caliphate*, Cambridge 2021.

The ʿAbbāsids from 749 to 811

Despite the triumph of the Khurāsānī army, the beginnings of ʿAbbāsid rule were far from smooth. The members of the family arrived in Kūfa without their leader, the recently deceased Ibrāhīm al-Imām, without being able to rely on Abū Salama, and without any of them having participated in the rising in Khurāsān or the epic victories won on the way to Iraq. We have already seen the disarray that ensued in Kūfa. In the event it was the forceful intervention of the leaders of the army that installed Abū ʾl-ʿAbbās al-Saffāḥ (ruled 749–54) as the first ʿAbbāsid caliph. His public speech at his accession was not an auspicious occasion: he was taken ill, and an uncle had to complete the performance on his behalf. Within a few years he was dead, and so, too, were some of the key figures of the movement. First Abū Muslim had Abū Salama killed. Then the uncle who had completed the speech of Abū ʾl-ʿAbbās rebelled on his nephew's death, suffered defeat at the hands of Abū Muslim, and was eventually killed. And finally the caliph al-Manṣūr, the successor of Abū ʾl-ʿAbbās, had Abū Muslim killed and his body thrown into the Tigris. Characteristically, each of these killings involved treachery.

Thereafter the ship of state was on a somewhat more even keel for several decades. This undoubtedly had something to do with the ways in which ʿAbbāsid rule differed from that of the Umayyads. One major difference was that the ʿAbbāsids were based in Iraq, not Syria, giving them the full benefit of Iraqi tax power. The irrigated agriculture of lowland Iraq—the Sawād, as the Arabs called it—made Iraq far wealthier and more populous than Syria with its uneven terrain and Mediterranean agriculture. So Iraq now underpinned the finances of the ʿAbbāsid Caliphate just as it had done for the pre-Islamic Iranian empires. Another difference that helped stabilize the new dynasty was that the ʿAbbāsids, like the Iranian imperial rulers of the past, were able to combine the tax power of Iraq with the manpower of Iran, in this instance that of Khurāsān. Whereas in Syria the tribal configuration that had given the region a transient military advantage was a casualty of the last years of Umayyad rule, in Iraq the Khurāsānī troops that had assured the accession of Abū ʾl-ʿAbbās became a long-term pillar of ʿAbbāsid rule. After the construction of the new capital of Baghdad was undertaken in 762, the city became their home, and their descendants were known as the "Sons of the Dynasty," Abnāʾ al-Dawla, or Abnāʾ for short. Their presence offered welcome support and was much needed even in Baghdad. One might have expected that the population of such a purpose-built capital would have been solidly in favor of its founding dynasty, but a ninth-century Muslim author who regarded the city as ruler-friendly stressed not the loyalty of the population but rather its heterogeneity: all the various religiopolitical trends were represented there, and the net effect was that they canceled each other out. Yet the ʿAbbāsids could not afford to be wholly dependent on their Khurāsānī army. Already in their first years in power they recruited extensively from the remnants of Marwān II's Qaysī army, and in the mid-790s they raised fifty thousand fresh troops in Khurāsān.

A further feature that may have helped stabilize the state was a gradual institutional development: the emergence of the office of the vizier (*wazīr*), in other words the chief minister of the caliph. The term itself is Qur'ānic—Aaron was the vizier of Moses (Q25:35)—and it had been taken up by the Hāshimiyya, with the result that Abū Salama was styled "vizier of the family of Muḥammad." No office of chief minister had existed under the Umayyads, and even in the first century of ʿAbbāsid rule it did not become as institutionally well defined as the office of caliph; the word vizier could be used for persons close to the caliph who held no formal office, and the authority of the chief minister might or might not extend to military affairs. But from the reign of al-Mahdī (ruled 775–85) the vizierate gradually became a normal part of the state apparatus. Perhaps the most celebrated vizier of all time was Yaḥyā ibn Khālid (d. 805), the leading figure of the Barmakid family (alias the Barmecides), an elite Iranian lineage from Balkh that had played a part in the ʿAbbāsid revolution. For seventeen years Yaḥyā was the vizier of Hārūn al-Rashīd (ruled 786–809), with his sons joining him in playing prominent roles in the administration of the empire. This continued until the caliph suddenly turned on the family in 803. We do not know what lay behind their dramatic fall from power, but it demonstrates the inherent insecurity of the office. Other things being equal a caliph had tenure for life, but a vizier definitely did not. The next vizier held the office for the rest of al-Rashīd's reign, but the authority delegated to him was more limited. The overall trend was nevertheless toward institutionalization of the vizierate, and it was linked to the rise of a secretarial class associated with increased centralization. The bureaucrats had, of course, been there all along, but they were probably more numerous than they had been in Umayyad times, and unquestionably more powerful. What is more, they were now strong enough for tension between them and the military to become a structural feature of the ʿAbbāsid state in this period. In the end, of course, the two parties needed each other: without bureaucrats to raise taxes the soldiers did not get paid, and without soldiers to defend them the bureaucrats could not collect taxes. But a key weakness of the Barmakids was that they did not have reliable military support at their disposal.

Yet another feature of early ʿAbbāsid rule that sets it apart from Umayyad practice is the assumption of individual regnal titles by the rulers, though whether this contributed to the stability of the dynasty is hard to say—political legitimacy is an elusive good. To this day we know Umayyad rulers by their personal names: Muʿāwiya, ʿAbd al-Malik, Hishām. By contrast, it takes erudition to recollect that the third ʿAbbāsid caliph was named Muḥammad; instead, this ruler is always known by his regnal title, the epithet al-Mahdī, "the rightly guided one." That observation leads to another point about the regnal titles of the early ʿAbbāsids.

We have already encountered the Mahdī, the messianic figure with whom the Kūfan rebel Mukhtār identified Muḥammad ibn al-Ḥanafiyya. The epithet al-Mahdī is the most transparently apocalyptic of the regnal titles of the early ʿAbbāsid rulers, but it is by no means isolated. Meanwhile, if we go by a much later source describing ʿAbbāsid court protocol, the personal name of the ruler was granted a peculiar protection: "It is not the custom for anyone to be mentioned in the presence of the caliph . . . by the name of the caliph, if his name happens to be his."[28] In other words, if the caliph's name was Jaʿfar, you could not use that name in the caliph's presence to refer to anyone else whose name was Jaʿfar, yourself included—which could be a problem if the caliph happened to ask you your name. What we have here is a mild version of a taboo system that was much more highly developed in imperial China; whatever its origins, it has nothing to do with Islam.

Though the ʿAbbāsid state was fairly strong in its first six decades, it was beset by frequent rebellions, so numerous that we will leave many of them aside. Some were of a broadly familiar character. As among the Umayyads, trouble could come from within the ruling family. In 754 there was the failed rebellion of the uncle of the first ʿAbbāsid caliph, and in 786 the accession of al-Rashīd was the product of a successful coup coinciding with the suspicious death of his brother al-Hādī (ruled 785–86). Meanwhile, sectarian rebellions continued as before. There were a couple of ʿAlid risings in the Ḥijāz, a major one in 762 and a minor one in 786. Such rebellions were in a broad sense Shīʿite, but they could still attract mainstream support. What made the first one serious was that it repeated the Zubayrid pattern: the claimant to the caliphate had a brother who posed a much more acute military threat in Iraq. These rebellions were part of a long story of ʿAbbāsid oscillation between repressing the ʿAlids and conciliating them. Likewise, Khārijites continued to rebel from time to time, as in eastern Iran, the Jazīra, and North Africa. But just as in Umayyad times, discontent was not necessarily articulated in religious terms. A case in point is a major rebellion that broke out in Samarqand in 806 and spread widely in the region. Its leader was Rāfiʿ ibn Layth, a grandson of Naṣr ibn Sayyār, whom we met as the last Umayyad governor of Khurāsān. This rising was provoked by the fiscal overreach of the governor of the day, ʿAlī ibn ʿĪsā ibn Māhān, and it seems to have lacked any religious dimension. Again as in Umayyad times, straightforwardly non-Muslim rebellion remained rare outside Egypt, but it did occur. In Iran in 755 a Zoroastrian rebel named Sunbādh declared that the dominion of the Arabs was over and proceeded to persecute Muslims, killing them in large numbers. In Lebanon in 759 Christian peasants rebelled under a leader who styled himself king.

28. Hilāl al-Ṣābiʾ, *Rusūm Dār al-Khilāfa*, Baghdad 1964, 57.

The landscape of rebellion was nevertheless changing significantly in geographical, factional, and ethnic terms. Geographically, Syria was a troublesome province for the ʿAbbāsids just as Iraq had been for the Umayyads. It had its rebellions, though rather fewer of them; here there was some benefit from the ʿAbbāsid co-option of much of Marwān II's Qaysī army. In any case Syria was not as wealthy as Iraq, with the result that it mattered somewhat less to the ʿAbbāsids than Iraq had mattered to the Umayyads. Turning to the factional conflict between Northerners and Southerners, it was still alive, not least in Syria, where we encounter it in 776, 793, 796–97, 803, and 806. It is noteworthy that in the case of the events of 793, which took place in or near Damascus, we hear of villages identified as belonging to one faction or the other, showing that the antagonism had permeated rural society. Indeed, this pattern of factionalism was to remain a feature of Syrian life down to modern times. But from the point of view of the central government, the factional conflict inherited from the Umayyad period was no longer as politically salient across the empire as it had been. To an extent the same was probably true of the ethnic tension between Arabs and non-Arabs. Thanks to intermarriage and assimilation there was bound to be an eventual blurring of what had once been a sharp ethnic boundary between the conquerors and the conquered, and in ʿAbbāsid times non-Arabs could more easily rise to elite positions. Another significant development affecting the character of rebellion was a shift among the religious scholars of the emergent Sunnī mainstream toward rejecting the idea of insurrection against unjust rule. In this milieu subversive notions were either forgotten or took on a harmless academic form. Thus around 790 the governor of Tunisia wanted to appoint a certain scholar, ʿAbdallāh ibn Farrūkh, as judge, but he was worried because he had heard that Ibn Farrūkh believed in rebellion against the authorities. Ibn Farrūkh confirmed this, but he added that he would rebel only if he had the support of as many men as fought for the Prophet at the Battle of Badr, each of them better than himself. "In that case," the governor responded with relief and a touch of humor, "we need have no fear that you'll ever rebel against us."[29] A contemporary Iraqi scholar of this ilk was al-Ḥasan ibn Ṣāliḥ ibn Ḥayy (d. 784–85), who likewise approved of armed rebellion; as one of his colleagues quipped, "This Ibn Ḥayy has been asking to be crucified for a long time, but we can't find anyone to do it for him."[30]

At the same time, a new kind of religious rebellion was to emerge in Iran on the fringes of Islam and beyond.[31] It had a background in the heterodoxy of the Umayyad period. As we have seen, wild ideas of flagrantly non-Muslim origin had played a part in the turmoil of the age, notably among the followers of Mukhtār,

29. Abū ʾl-ʿArab al-Tamīmī, *Ṭabaqāt ʿulamāʾ Ifrīqiya wa-Tūnis*, Tunis 1968, 108.
30. Mizzī, *Tahdhīb al-Kamāl*, Beirut 1985–92, 6:184.
31. For these rebellions see P. Crone, *The nativist prophets of early Islamic Iran*, Cambridge 2012.

ʿAbdallāh ibn Muʿāwiya, and the Hāshimiyya. The revolution through which the ʿAbbāsids took power thus brought the beliefs of some of their less respectable followers into public view. A dramatic incident of this kind took place around 754–59 in Iraq, in a transitory city that served as the ʿAbbāsid capital at the time. The group in question was known as the Rāwandiyya, and its members were Khurāsānīs belonging to the Hāshimiyya; they combined devotion to the ʿAbbāsid cause with highly heterodox beliefs. Several hundred of them now came to al-Manṣūr's palace and circumambulated it, acclaiming him as their god. This was embarrassing for al-Manṣūr. He responded by having some of them imprisoned and told the rest not to gather together, but they ignored him, stormed the prison, and released their fellows. By this point they were hostile to al-Manṣūr, and outright dangerous—he came close to losing his life, and in a supreme irony it is said that it was a former Umayyad general who emerged from hiding and came to his rescue. Such heterodoxy played no further part in the metropolitan politics of the ʿAbbāsid state, and for the most part the dynasty came to be characterized by a decorous Sunnism. But the heterodoxy from which the Hāshimiyya had emerged had a colorful future in Iran.

There a series of religious leaders, most of them rebels, were making their appearance, on occasion mixing Islamic and non-Islamic elements in what by mainstream Islamic standards were bizarre syncretisms. The first of them, Bihāfarīdh, was a Zoroastrian who set himself up as a prophet near Nīshāpūr. It is not sure that he rebelled, and he did not live into the ʿAbbāsid period, since Abū Muslim had him and his disciples killed in 748–49 at the request of the local Zoroastrian clergy. Despite his Zoroastrian background, his religion bore the unmistakable imprint of Islam. He claimed to be the messenger of God, he had a Persian scripture, he prohibited wine and the close-kin marriages encouraged by Zoroastrianism, and he prescribed five (or maybe seven) daily prayers, the first of which was in praise of the unity of God. In short, he was someone who had no wish to convert to Islam but was only too well aware of its prestige as a model of right religion, and his response was to set about reforming his own religion to bring it into line. He must have struck a chord, for in the 760s his followers were numerous enough to mount a major rebellion with its epicenter in Bādghīs near Herat. The next rising of this ilk was that of a follower of Abū Muslim known as al-Muqannaʿ, the "Veiled One." His rebellion began in Transoxania in or before 773–74, and it ended with his dramatic suicide at some time between 779 and 784. His followers were Sogdian villagers and Turkic nomads. As to his doctrine, he held that from time to time God would enter the body of a man, and his list of those who had hosted the deity in this way shows his religion to have had a significant Islamic component: Adam, Noah, Abraham, Moses, Jesus, Muḥammad, Abū Muslim, and, last but by no means least, himself. The non-Islamic component of his religion does not, however, seem to have derived from Zoroastrianism; Transoxania, on the eastern fringe of the

Iranian world, was religiously mixed, and al-Muqannaʿ may have owed more to Buddhism. Later we will touch on the last—and most long-lasting—rebellion of this kind, that of Bābak from 816–17 to 837 in western Iran. Of these movements, the most interesting is that of Bihāfarīdh. It has no parallel among the Christians subject to Muslim rule, perhaps because their clergy had more of a grip on the laity than their Zoroastrian counterparts did. There was nevertheless an analogous phenomenon in the Byzantine Empire of the eighth and ninth centuries: iconoclasm. We have already encountered the iconoclastic streak in early Islam, and the Byzantine version looks like a grudging admission that to be so successful the Muslims must have been doing something right; as the Roman poet Ovid had said long before, "It is proper to learn even from an enemy."[32] Yet we see nothing of the kind among the Coptic rebels of Umayyad and early ʿAbbāsid Egypt, whose rebellions, as we saw, continued until 832. To find a Bihāfarīd outside Iran we have to go as far west as the Atlantic coast of Morocco.

The fourth civil war, 811–19

Nothing causes more contention within royal families than rivalries over the succession to the throne. As we saw, al-Manṣūr's accession was challenged by an uncle, but more commonly the problem would be a brother. In 785 there was serious fraternal tension when al-Hādī came to the throne, and the process by which his brother al-Rashīd replaced him only a year later may well have involved foul play. So it is not surprising that there was trouble when al-Rashīd in turn left two sons in line for the succession. We can call them by their regnal titles: al-Amīn (ruled 809–13) and al-Maʾmūn (ruled 813–33). In 802 al-Rashīd had imposed a solemn agreement on them whereby al-Amīn was to become caliph on his death, while al-Maʾmūn would rule Khurāsān as an autonomous principality; then, on al-Amīn's death, al-Maʾmūn would succeed him. Things got off to a promising start, since at the time of al-Rashīd's death in 809 al-Amīn was in Baghdad and al-Maʾmūn was in Marw. But quite apart from the mix of aspirations, fears, and mistrust in the relationship between the brothers, there was a basic flaw in the design of the settlement: the Abnāʾ al-Dawla—the Khurāsānī troops in Baghdad—depended for their stipends on the revenues of Khurāsān. This pitted their interests against those of the inhabitants of Khurāsān. ʿAlī ibn ʿĪsā ibn Māhān, the governor whose fiscal overreach had provoked the rebellion of 806, was a leading figure among the Abnāʾ, and it was doubtless for their sakes that he had been determined to extract as much revenue as he could. Now they were faced with the prospect of losing that revenue to al-Maʾmūn and his supporters. What made things worse was that the tensions between the brothers aligned with the diverging interests of the military and

32. Ovid, *Metamorphoses*, trans. F. J. Miller, 1977–84, 1:209 (4.428).

the bureaucracy: al-Amīn had close links to the military, whereas al-Ma'mūn's ties were with the bureaucrats. Nor did it help that the two young brothers—at this point in their early twenties—were both in the hands of hard-line advisers. So in Baghdad the war party prevailed, and in Marw al-Ma'mūn's vizier persuaded him to strengthen his position by allying with local interests that did not want to be exploited by Baghdad.

A massive army of Abnā' now left Baghdad for Khurāsān, while al-Ma'mūn and his bureaucrats could only dispatch a force a fraction of its size to oppose it. When the two forces met at Rayy in 811 the outcome seemed a foregone conclusion. But battles are chancy, and against all odds the Abnā' suffered a disastrous defeat. Perhaps it was simply that their commander happened to be killed, whereupon his soldiers panicked—a pattern attested elsewhere in the history of warfare. In any case the Abnā' went on to lose the war. The end came in 813, after a prolonged siege of Baghdad in which many of the Abnā' defected to al-Ma'mūn's side and al-Amīn's strongest supporters were the populace of the city. It is in this context that we first hear of the urban militiamen known as the 'Ayyārs. But the resistance was in vain: al-Amīn was executed, and the first phase of the civil war was over.

At this stage one might have expected al-Ma'mūn to arrive in Baghdad and take up residence as caliph—as indeed he eventually did, but not until 819. Instead, under the influence of his vizier, he turned his back on Baghdad and tried to govern the Caliphate from Marw. This suited local Khurāsānī interests very well, but elsewhere it did not work, and it was unacceptable to the Abnā' and the 'Abbāsid family in Iraq. In 817 al-Ma'mūn alienated his family in yet another way. In a strange symbolic gesture he appointed 'Alī al-Riḍā, the imam of the quietist Imāmī Shī'ites, heir to the throne; he apparently believed a prophecy that as the seventh 'Abbāsid ruler he would also be the last. Appointing an 'Alid heir could also have been a response to a major 'Alid rebellion in Iraq in 815. But the effect was to provoke an 'Abbāsid rebellion in Baghdad, where a son of al-Mahdī was installed as caliph. Elsewhere the civil war had seen large parts of the empire fall into disorder. Thus in 811–13 there was a rebellion in Syria led by an elderly Umayyad—more specifically a Sufyānid—who took over Damascus and claimed the Caliphate. His supporters were mainly Southerners, and the rising was suppressed by the Northerners of the region, who at one stage had an Umayyad caliph of their own, a Marwānid; the logic of factional conflict did not, however, stop the Northerners fighting a brief civil war among themselves. The 'Abbāsid authorities had ceased to play any part in these events: early in the revolt their governor of Damascus, a son of the caliph al-Manṣūr, had fled to Iraq. As a Christian chronicler remarked, "All of Syria was without a king for fifteen years."[33] Meanwhile, a confusing struggle in Egypt led by 813 to a configuration reminiscent of the intermediate periods of Pharaonic

33. Quoted in P. M. Cobb, *White banners*, Albany 2001, 95.

times, with one ruler in the north and another in the south. These rulers did not claim to be caliphs, but when they both died in 820 they were succeeded by their respective sons. In Azerbaijan the rebellion of Bābak, a man of humble origins, began in 816–17 and was not over till 837. He claimed to be "the spirit of the prophets" and to be divine, but also saw himself more straightforwardly as a king. Once al-Ma'mūn became aware of the extent of the disaster he was courting, he took action by having his vizier killed and moving back to Baghdad. In the course of this, his Shī'ite heir conveniently died—it is said poisoned—and in 819 al-Ma'mūn was in Baghdad, picking up the pieces.

There is one other actor in the drama of the civil war whose role was historically significant both at the time and for the future: Ṭāhir ibn al-Ḥusayn (d. 822). He belonged to a Khurāsānī family of Persian descent that had played a part in the 'Abbāsid revolution and been rewarded with the governorship of a town a day's journey from Herat. He had military experience, having participated in the suppression of the rebellion of Rāfi' ibn Layth. It was he who in 811 led the small force that defeated the much larger army sent by al-Amīn, and he played the central role in winning the war for al-Ma'mūn. His troops included several hundred men from Khwārazm and some from Bukhārā in Transoxania, but it is not clear whether he was put in charge of them only at the start of the campaign or had already recruited them before it as a kind of private army. The second scenario would fit a pattern: it seems that al-Ma'mūn did not possess a sizeable body of troops on which he could rely and instead had to depend on what one might call military entrepreneurs. Ṭāhir could have been the first, and we will encounter others in the years following the civil war.

A final point is that as in previous civil wars, the Muslims were still free to spend several years in conflict among themselves without running a serious risk of foreign intervention. In fact the fourth civil war was the most extreme case of the four; this time there was no loss of territory on the frontiers, and no tribute paid to a foreign ruler. In short, the overall geopolitical situation of the empire continued to be an enviable one, with the only worrisome state on the frontiers being the Byzantine Empire. On the Byzantine side the opportunity of the early years of the Muslim civil war was wasted in a succession of failed reigns and disastrous defeats at the hands of the Bulgars. Leo V (ruled 813–20) was an able general who made peace with the Bulgars, but he did not take any dramatic action on the Muslim front.

The 'Abbāsids from 819 to 861

When it came to picking up the pieces following the civil war, a prominent part was played in several regions by Ṭāhir and his family. In 820 he assumed the sensitive role of security force chief of Baghdad, and in 822 he was succeeded in that position by a cousin; thereafter members of the family held it continuously till 891, at a time when the security forces in Iraq extended their originally urban territory to include the countryside. The arrangement worked well for two reasons. Ṭāhir had good relations with those of the Abnāʾ who had defected to him during the siege of the city, and as we will see, from 836 the caliphs were absent from Baghdad for several decades. Meanwhile, in 821 Ṭāhir had been appointed governor of Khurāsān, another sensitive position. He died there the next year, having shown signs of aspiration to independence, but he was succeeded by one of his sons, and the family continued to rule this large and revenue-rich province till 873. The emergence of a regional dynasty of this kind within the Caliphate was something significantly new, but as yet the phenomenon did not involve anything like secession; the Ṭāhirids continued to remit a handsome tribute to the caliphs. To the west of Iraq there was no comparable entrenchment of Ṭāhirid power. Instead, Ṭāhir's son ʿAbdallāh was the first of a succession of military leaders who came and went with their troops. He led the military force that began the restoration of ʿAbbāsid rule in Syria in 823 and in Egypt in 826. His army included Abnāʾ from Baghdad, no doubt thanks to his father's good relationship with them. But he returned to Baghdad as early as 827, which meant that he did not venture farther west to North Africa, where Tunisia had become effectively independent already in 800. Instead, in 828 he went east to Khurāsān, succeeding his brother there and ruling it until his death in 844. Responsibility for the western provinces now passed to a brother of al-Ma'mūn, the future caliph al-Muʿtaṣim (ruled 833–42). He sought to delegate his authority in Egypt to a governor, but the fiscal exactions of an alien ʿAbbāsid regime riding roughshod over the local elite led to widespread rebellions in which his governor perished in 830. At this point al-Muʿtaṣim visited Egypt in person with a small though formidable force, but after he left a fresh rebellion broke out in 831. This one was suppressed by the Afshīn, the hereditary ruler of the eastern Iranian principality of Usrūshana in the mountains of Central Asia. His Usrūshanī troops were thus part of his ancestral heritage, though during his stay in Egypt he took the opportunity to recruit Arab tribesmen for al-Muʿtaṣim.

The takeaway from these complicated events is that the four military leaders involved—Ṭāhir, his son ʿAbdallāh, al-Muʿtaṣim, and the Afshīn—had something significant in common. In different ways they were there to fill the vacuum left by the fact that al-Ma'mūn was short of dependable military support to replace the defeated Abnāʾ, the foundation of ʿAbbāsid military power before the civil war. In fact, al-Ma'mūn was fortunate that none of the four ever mounted a rebellion against him. Among them al-Muʿtaṣim stands out: he was a future caliph, and the manner in which he recruited his troops provided a new military foundation for the state. What he did was to purchase Turkic slaves originating from the steppes, and these slaves, whether subsequently manumitted or not, then served him as soldiers.[34] He was already doing this during the civil war, and by the time he became caliph he had three thousand such soldiers, a very effective force. What made them so effective is no mystery. As we saw when we first met the nomads of the Eurasian steppes, they had the incomparable advantage of being nature's cavalry. They used their equestrian skills in combination with the steadying effect of the stirrup to develop a style of highly mobile mounted archery that their opponents experienced as devastating. These Turks were a valuable commodity, and al-Muʿtaṣim quartered them with care, physically isolating them and forbidding them to intermarry with the rest of the population. He provided them with mosques, baths, a market, and essential shops. As the reference to mosques suggests, they were now Muslims, but a telling incident points to a retention of pagan customs from the steppes: when a leading Turkic commander was killed in 870, the Turks broke a thousand swords over his grave, and the chronicler explains that this was what they would do on the death of one of their chiefs. The caliph also supplied his Turks with slave girls "so that when their children grew up they would marry among themselves."[35] In other words, what he had in mind seems to have been the nurturing of a hereditary Turkish military caste, though this particular feature of the institution of military slavery did not have a future. The effect was nevertheless to increase the ethnic and linguistic distance between the military and the bureaucrats, and between the military and society at large. What we have here is thus the opposite of a citizen army, and it is no coincidence that it was in the reign of al-Muʿtaṣim that the descendants of the Arab conquerors were dropped from the payroll in Egypt. As we will see, military slavery was already quite widespread in the Muslim world of the ninth century. Slave soldiers of various ethnic or racial groups—Slavs, blacks, Greeks, Turks—were to be found in Muslim Spain, Tunisia, and Egypt, as well as Iraq. The numbers exploded in this period, but the military use of slaves went back to the third civil war and perhaps even the second. At the same time the institution had a long future ahead of it in Muslim lands. It can readily be seen as an instance of a wider phenomenon: it often makes sense for states to retain the services of people drawn from marginal groups that do not share the interests of the major stakeholders of the society they rule, since such groups will be less responsive to the society and more dependent on the ruler. The puzzle, which we will not attempt to solve here, is that although arming slaves had a long past both inside and outside the Muslim world, cases in which the core of an army was formed in this fashion are barely to be found outside it.

The purpose-built quarters in which al-Muʿtaṣim settled his Turks were not located in Baghdad. He had a serious problem in that city: it was still the home of the Abnāʾ, who did not warm to the presence of his new and alien troops.

34. On the early history of the Turkic military in Iraq see M. Gordon, *The breaking of a thousand swords*, Albany 2001.

35. Yaʿqūbī, *Kitāb al-buldān*, Leiden 1967, 259.

The Turkish slaves, it was said, would gallop through the streets, knocking down men and women and trampling children underfoot. Some of these soldiers lost their lives in the resulting clashes. The solution al-Muʿtaṣim adopted was to move out of Baghdad with his court and his army to a newly built capital at Sāmarrāʾ, some seventy-five miles farther up the Tigris. Sāmarrāʾ served as the caliphs' capital from 836 until their return to Baghdad in 892; thereafter Baghdad would remain the ʿAbbāsid capital until the Mongols sacked it in 1258. Both Baghdad and Sāmarrāʾ were the invention of rulers, but whereas Baghdad had no trouble surviving the absence of the caliphs, Sāmarrāʾ after 892 was a failure in that respect—though for that very reason a gift to archaeologists. As we will see in later chapters, for states to move their capitals was not uncommon in the history of the Muslim world, and quite often it involved the construction of new cities in the middle of nowhere. Three other ʿAbbāsid caliphs undertook such moves. One was al-Rashīd, who effectively made the twin cities of Raqqa and Rāfiqa in the Jazīra his capital from 796 to 808. Raqqa was an ancient city, but nearby Rāfiqa was a new foundation of the early ʿAbbāsid period. The second, of course, was al-Maʾmūn, who tried to govern the empire from Marw. The third was al-Mutawakkil (ruled 847–61), who at the end of his reign was building himself a brand-new city not far from Sāmarrāʾ. There might have been push factors promoting such geographical instability, as in the case of the hostility of Baghdad to al-Muʿtaṣim's Turks, but there were also pull factors. There was the real estate boom that would be generated by constructing a new city in a rural area, where the caliph could acquire land cheaply and then distribute portions of this increasingly valuable asset to his followers. There was also the appeal to the ruler's vanity of the opportunity to plan an urban landscape that was not cluttered with buildings erected by his predecessors.

The caliph al-Maʾmūn was not immune to vanity, but his was of a different kind. If any of the first seven ʿAbbāsid caliphs could be described as an intellectual, it would be him. When he spent a few weeks in Egypt in 832, he paid a visit to the pyramids. One medieval account of the visit starts by stressing his thirst for arcane knowledge and backs this up with a reference to the translations of Greek philosophical works made in his time. Naturally al-Maʾmūn was intensely curious about what might be inside the pyramids, and he insisted on having an opening made into the largest of them. One does not, of course, have to be an intellectual to wonder about the interior of an Egyptian pyramid, but al-Maʾmūn went well beyond that: he also had a local expert translate ancient Egyptian inscriptions for him. It was not his fault that the expert was undoubtedly a fraud. This was not the only manifestation of al-Maʾmūn's interest in pre-Islamic antiquity. In his youth he is said to have "worked hard at reading ancient books."[36] He is reputed to have

36. Quoted in D. Gutas, *Greek thought, Arabic culture*, London 1998, 77.

dreamed of Aristotle (d. 322 BC), who offered him some banalities in response to a question about the best speech or alternatively answered a question about the good in a somewhat Islamizing fashion. We are told that following this dream al-Ma'mūn was in touch with the Byzantine emperor and obtained books from him, some of which he then had translated; indeed, patronage at his court extended to organized teams of translators of Greek philosophical works. One notable member of his circle was Abū Yūsuf al-Kindī, an authentic member of the tribe of Kinda and the first Muslim philosopher in the Greek tradition. Already known in the tenth century as "the philosopher of the Arabs,"[37] he was credited with command of the whole range of the ancient sciences.

A caliph with such wide intellectual interests was clearly unlikely to leave religion alone, and we have already seen how al-Ma'mūn made waves by appointing 'Alī al-Riḍā as his heir. However politically counterproductive, this ploy made some sense. It was al-Ma'mūn who bestowed the title al-Riḍā on his heir, and in doing so he was harking back to the call of the Hāshimiyya for "an agreed member (*al-riḍā*) of the family of Muḥammad." Then, in the last few months of his reign, he took a step that showed that he still had the capacity to surprise. This time the issue was strictly theological: Was God's speech—the Qur'ān—created or uncreated? For our purposes we do not need to understand the doctrinal issue any more than we needed to comprehend the Christological hairsplitting of late antiquity. Indeed, there must have been many at the time who found such matters entirely above their heads, as did a leading Turkic general who remarked in Persian: "I wouldn't know anything about that stuff, except the words 'There is no god but God and Muḥammad is His Prophet,' and the caliph being a kinsman of the Prophet."[38] In this vein it is enough for us to note that the question of God's speech was linked to a wider dispute about His nature. Should we be anthropomorphists and imagine Him as a glorified human, as the Book of Genesis would suggest when it tells us that "God created man in His own image" (Genesis 1:27)? Or should we be transcendentalists and think of Him as utterly unlike anything we experience? The Qur'ān provides proof texts for both sides of the argument, and the issue became a very contentious one in the early centuries of Islam. What is more, there was a pronounced social gravitation in play: anthropomorphism was for the common people, whose religion abounded in myths and superstitions, whereas transcendentalism, with its austerely abstract and conceptual approach, was for the elite. In pagan antiquity such cognitive disparity between elite and masses would have been accepted as normal, but with the rise of monotheism it became intensely problematic. Every member of a monotheistic community is supposed to believe the same thing—whence the ecclesiastical councils and creeds of late antique

37. Ibn al-Nadīm, *Fihrist*, Tehran n.d., 315.
38. Ṣāliḥ ibn Aḥmad ibn Ḥanbal, *Sīrat al-imām Aḥmad ibn Ḥanbal*, Beirut 1997, 36.

Christianity. As one would expect, al-Ma'mūn was an intransigent elitist who regarded the beliefs of the common people with utter contempt; cosmopolitanism and snobbery readily go together. He described the masses as rabble who lacked the faculty of reason. Everywhere they were ignorant of God, unable to know Him properly "because of the feebleness of their judgment" and "the deficiency of their intellects."[39] But this did not inhibit them from expressing their views. A ninth-century observer remarks that if a scholar holds forth about a theological issue in the street or the marketplace, "there will be no fool of a porter, no down-and-out wretch, no tongue-tied idiot or ignorant blockhead who will not stop and argue"[40]—just as in fourth-century Constantinople. Moreover, there were many religious scholars in the ninth century who were closer to the way of thinking of the common people than to that of the elite associates of al-Ma'mūn. One of them, Ibn Qutayba (d. 889), put it like this: "Take your cue from the common people in every city and every age, for it is one of the signs of the truth that their hearts are together in according with it."[41] So in 833, to bring refractory scholars to heel, al-Ma'mūn instituted a kind of inquisition known as the Miḥna, and a prominent role in implementing it was played by his chief judge, Ibn Abī Du'ād (d. 854). The procedure was applied both in the capital and in the provinces. Suspect scholars could tell the inquisitors what they wanted to hear—that the Qur'ān was created—or they could be flogged; sooner or later most of them caved in.

The most celebrated case was that of Ibn Ḥanbal (d. 855), a humble but learned scholar who was imprisoned, interrogated, and flogged early in the reign of al-Mu'taṣim. The sources differ as to whether he gave lip service to the official doctrine at some point in the process. But he refused to support an abortive rebellion in 846 stirred up by a report that the authorities were proposing to indoctrinate schoolchildren with the doctrine of the created Qur'ān. The Miḥna was continued by al-Mu'taṣim's immediate successor, but later al-Mutawakkil gradually abandoned it over the years 847–52, forbidding further argument about the issue. That was not, however, the end of Ibn Ḥanbal's ordeal. It now became a matter of caliphal public relations strategy to lionize Ibn Ḥanbal, and he had to endure the unwanted but persistent attentions of the agents of the state; he saw their blandishments as corrupting his own family, who valued the goods of this world more than those of the next. As he summed up his unhappy relations with the state, "I've been spared these people for sixty years, and now at the end of my life I'm afflicted with them."[42] It would be hard to imagine a stronger contrast to the way in which the third-century Zoroastrian high priest Kerdīr had boasted about his close

39. Ṭabarī, *History*, 32:200–201.

40. See C. Pellat, *The life and works of Jāḥiẓ*, Berkeley 1969, 79.

41. Ibn Qutayba, *Ta'wīl mukhtalif al-ḥadīth*, Cairo 1326 *hijrī*, 20.

42. Abū Nu'aym al-Iṣbahānī, *Ḥilyat al-awliyā'*, Cairo 1932–38, 9:209.

relations with his royal patrons. But it was not just Ibn Ḥanbal and his likes who suffered as a result of the Miḥna. The caliphs did not do so well out of it either, and later Muslim rulers showed little interest in repeating such inquisitions. Altogether, the episode confirmed a fait accompli, the emergence of an Islamic religious leadership made up of scholars (*'ulamā'*) who had no official position and who acquired their learning outside any formal institutional structure. There were no priests, and perhaps just as importantly from the viewpoint of the ruler, no bishops. King James I of England (ruled 1603–25), who in 1604 famously remarked "No bishop, no King,"[43] would have taken a very dim view of this state of affairs. The 'Abbāsid caliphs did indeed patronize—or as Ibn Ḥanbal would have seen it, corrupt—religious scholars on a significant scale, but it was not till the eleventh century that Muslim states found a reliable institutional mechanism for co-opting and controlling their religious scholars. The Miḥna was no solution to this problem. Like al-Ma'mūn's attempt to rule from Marw and his appointment of an 'Alid heir, it was a political liability that gave rise to much bad blood for little gain—in short, another bad idea.

Meanwhile, wars and rebellions made their less cerebral contribution to caliphal history. On the frontiers, the only major activity was a resumption of raids into Byzantine Anatolia. These had been a feature of the early 'Abbāsid period, when at times they were mounted almost every summer, on occasion led by the caliph himself. Such raids reached the Bosphorus in 780 and climaxed in al-Mu'taṣim's sacking of Amorium in western Anatolia in 838, but they did not add new territory to the Caliphate. As to rebellions within the empire, we have already noted those of the Copts in Egypt and Bābak in Azerbaijan. A very different Iranian rebellion was that of Māzyār in 839–40. It took place in Ṭabaristān, at the eastern end of the mountain range to the south of the Caspian Sea. Here the Qārinid dynasty had been ruling since pre-Islamic times. Though it recognized the overlordship of the caliphs, Māzyār's grandfather had mounted a rebellion and reputedly massacred all Muslims in Ṭabaristān in 783. Māzyār himself converted to Islam while a refugee at the court of the caliph in 816–17, but later he mounted an unsuccessful rebellion. A curious detail of his revolt was his encouragement of the peasants of the neighboring lowlands to seize the estates and womenfolk of the local landlords; something the two Iranian rebellions may have shared was an allergic response to the presence of Arab settlers in both regions. Meanwhile, in 840 southern Syria saw the last revolt to evoke the idea of an Umayyad restoration. The pretender was a local outlaw with a peasant following. This is an indication that Umayyad loyalties now meant something at the level of the village, but also that the elite had moved on.

43. D. H. Willson, *James VI and I*, New York 1956, 207.

For the most part these insurrections were variations on familiar themes, but the last rebellion of the period was something new: a military coup at the center that terminated the reign of al-Mutawakkil in 861. He was not, of course, the first ʿAbbāsid to suffer a violent death, but the events surrounding the probable murder of al-Hādī in 786 amounted to a civilian rather than a military coup, and al-Amīn in 813 was executed after losing a civil war. The background to the coup of 861 was an alliance of two parties, Turkic slave soldiers and a son of al-Mutawakkil. Both seem to have been on the defensive. The caliph had been broadening recruitment to the army to balance the Turks, and his son, the heir apparent, had reason to think that he was being eased out of the line of succession. With the coup of 861 the imperial phase of ʿAbbāsid history was more or less at an end.

The provinces

So far in this chapter, the story of the Muslim state has been told from the perspective of the central government. Provinces from Spain to Sindh have figured at various points in the narrative, but without sustained focus. This section will do something to compensate for that. We will start with Spain in the west and end with Sindh in the east but bypass the Fertile Crescent—Syria, the Jazīra, and Iraq—since they have already received frequent attention. The purpose of this survey is to trace the history of each province no further than the second half of the ninth century, stopping at the point at which the regional chapters of this book take over.

Spain

The period of Spanish history that concerns us here is particularly short.[44] It runs from the Muslim invasion in 711 to the early 740s, covering the three decades when the country was under Umayyad rule from Syria—it was fated never to be part of the ʿAbbāsid Empire. Spain was relatively well endowed with agricultural and other resources. At the time of the Muslim conquest it was heavily Romanized. Of its pre-Roman population only the Basques in the north still held out in medieval times, as they do to this day. But the rulers of Spain in late antiquity were Visigoths; that is to say, they belonged to one of the Germanic peoples that had moved into the Roman Empire. It was in the fifth century that the Visigoths had come to rule most of Spain, and they went on to establish a kingdom there that ended only with the Muslim conquest. On balance it was a fairly robust state, but one thing making for Muslim success in 711 was the fact that there had been a Visigothic civil war over the succession the previous year. The central event of the conquest was a

44. For the history of Muslim Spain see H. Kennedy, *Muslim Spain and Portugal*, London 1996.

decisive Muslim victory on the battlefield; the rest was largely mopping up. The key leaders of the Muslim troops were the Berber Ṭāriq ibn Ziyād, who was the governor of Tangier and led the invasion of 711, and his superior the governor of Tunisia, Mūsā ibn Nuṣayr, who joined him in Spain in 712. In the early years the Muslims went as far as the north coast, but they did not retain their grip on it. To the northeast their penetration of France was dramatic but ultimately inconsequential.

Despite the distances involved, Spain in the decades that followed was ruled from Syria, with Egypt and Tunisia serving as intermediate centers of power. There was nothing inherently impossible about such a configuration: for several decades in the fourth century Spain had been ruled from Constantinople. The reality of Umayyad rule is confirmed by the fact that when Ṭāriq and Mūsā received orders to report in person to the caliph, they complied and left for Syria in 714. There was then a succession of Umayyad governors appointed from outside, the last of them in 743. We are told that when discontent with one of these governors boiled over, the troops in Spain would on occasion appeal to the caliph, rather than take direct action on the spot. Moreover, these governors were soon minting coins in conformity with the standard imposed by the central government. From 720–21 on the coins of Spain were almost identical with those of Balkh in what is now Afghanistan.

Yet distance inevitably took its toll, and the conquest itself is an example. Ṭāriq seems to have been acting on his own initiative, not on instructions from the east. In this he may have resembled ʿAmr ibn al-ʿĀṣ, the conqueror of Egypt, but ʿAmr was a powerful member of the Qurashī elite, whereas Ṭāriq was just a Berber client of Mūsā's. By contrast, the commanders who led the contemporary conquests of Transoxania and Sindh were Arabs. In this respect Ṭāriq was the tip of an ethnic iceberg. In North Africa, the source of the invasion, Berbers were plentiful whereas Arabs were scarce, and many Berbers were converting to Islam and enlisting in Muslim armies. Hence much of the early Muslim presence in Spain was Berber. As in North Africa, the Berbers tended to feel that they were getting a bad deal from the Arabs; there was a minor Berber rebellion around 730 and another, much more serious, in 741. It was thus a real question whether the Arabs in Spain would be swamped by this resentful Berber population and lose their political power to them, but as we will see in the next chapter, two events of the 740s and 750s determined otherwise. The situation of the Umayyad governors of Spain likewise betrays the effects of distance. They tended to come and go, lacking any local power base, and we have no reason to think that they sent the central government any revenue. A governor appointed by the caliph in 718 was an exception, arriving with a substantial army; he started to make waves but died in 721. All in all, the Arabs of Spain were a small minority a long way from home, and as such they also faced a danger that was in a way more threatening than being submerged by the Berbers: going native. The Visigothic aristocracy did not immediately disappear, and there was intermarriage between the two elites. Thus when Mūsā departed for the east he left a son of his in charge. This son married the widow of the last Visigothic king, and she persuaded him to act like one; he even wore a crown. That, however, was going too far, and it got him killed. How all this would play out we will see in later chapters.

North Africa

The conquest of North Africa, though completed before that of Spain began, was a much more extended and difficult affair.[45] This was mainly due to the character of the native population, which in turn reflected the nature of the terrain. What lay between Egypt and Tunisia was mostly desert, with limited agricultural regions hugging the Mediterranean coasts of Cyrenaica and Tripolitania. Tunisia had rich agricultural plains, and the same was true of the Atlantic coast of Morocco. But the intervening terrain—in Morocco and what is now Algeria—was mountainous, and to the south lay the Sahara desert. When the Arabs arrived some of this territory was ruled by the Byzantine Empire. Tunisia had been a Byzantine possession since 534, with its capital at Carthage, and elsewhere there was some Byzantine presence on parts of the coast. But the bulk of North Africa was in the hands of its Berber tribal population. Immediately after the conquest of Egypt the Arabs had reached out to take Barqa in Cyrenaica, a region that powerful rulers of Egypt often control, and they even sacked Tripoli in what is today western Libya. Farther west, the first Arab raid to reach Tunisia took place in 647, but it was not till 670 that the Arabs established a permanent settlement there—the garrison city of Qayrawān in the Tunisian interior. Even then their possession of it was subject to interruption until the end of the seventh century, and again in early ʿAbbāsid times. It is significant that on the occasions when they were constrained to abandon it the threat came not from the Byzantines but from the Berber tribes, though Byzantine troops did sometimes operate in the interior. Only at the beginning of the eighth century could the Arabs even begin to feel secure in Qayrawān. The Berber tribes of the region had now been pacified, and the Byzantines had been evicted from Carthage and other footholds on the coast.

The conquest of North Africa to the west of Tunisia was a different story. Here there was no large and powerful state to reckon with, either imperial or indigenous; we can think of the region as populated by Berber tribes among which some relatively local states had emerged. The conquest of this region did not involve the establishment of any further garrison cities. Instead, the decades from the 670s

45. For the conquest of this region see W. E. Kaegi, *Muslim expansion and Byzantine collapse in North Africa*, Cambridge 2010.

to the 690s saw armies come and go, their campaigns marked more by distance than by depth. As we have seen, there was even an expedition that reached the Atlantic in the early 680s, though it ended in disaster. The basic problem was that too few Arabs were trying to conquer too many Berbers. This meant that the Arabs could win only by enlisting large numbers of Berbers in their armies and using them to fight those who resisted. In itself this was not too difficult a task, since the Berbers lacked solidarity, readily converted to Islam, and jumped at military opportunity. The issue was the terms of the partnership, and here the early governors of Tunisia varied considerably in their policies. One governor won over a prominent Berber chieftain from what is now eastern Morocco, a certain Kusayla, who converted to Islam and joined him. But the next governor took Kusayla prisoner and humiliated him, so when Kusayla escaped he mounted a rebellion, defeating and killing the hated governor in 683 and going on to occupy Qayrawān for several years. After Kusayla, in turn, was defeated and killed, Berber resistance was led by a woman known as the Kāhina, an Arabic word for a female soothsayer. She won one battle but lost the next, and with it her life. Her two sons converted to Islam and joined the Arabs. After Mūsā ibn Nuṣayr was appointed governor in 698 or so, he completed the pacification of the west in some fashion over the next few years. Thereafter the situation seems to have been stable for the first four decades of the eighth century, though just what that meant on the ground is hard to say. The extent of Arab dominance no doubt varied from region to region, and even at its strongest it can hardly have taken the form of an administration such as that found in Tunisia, let alone Egypt. But to an extent it was real—real enough that the Berber tribes resented its oppressiveness, not least the number of their children whom the Arabs enslaved and sent to the east. As to the Berbers who enlisted in the Muslim armies, they resented Arab discrimination. There is a telling anecdote about one governor of Tunisia: he set about tattooing the hands of his Berber guards with their names, which was clearly felt as humiliating, and soon one of them killed him. So there is nothing puzzling about the explosion of Berber Khārijite rebellion in the 740s; if anything is surprising, it is that it had not erupted earlier. Thereafter North Africa west of Tunisia was no longer part of the Caliphate, as we will see in the following chapter.

The waves of Berber rebellion in the 740s also washed over Tunisia, and Berber rebels seized Qayrawān in 757, in 758, and again in 771. But unlike the territory to the west, Tunisia in 761 emerged from the turmoil of the mid-eighth century as an ʿAbbāsid province, and it continued as such until one of its governors was able to establish an effectively independent dynasty, that of the Aghlabids (800–909), whose fortunes we will take up in the next chapter. In the meantime, two things are noteworthy about the history of the province in the second half of the eighth century. One is its Muhallabid governors. We encountered a member of this family, Yazīd ibn al-Muhallab, in an Umayyad context; he served as governor of the East and later rebelled. The family was remarkable for its capacity for survival. Yazīd's father, an Omani, had been a general in the service of Ibn al-Zubayr's brother Muṣʿab and so on the losing side of the second civil war, but when the Umayyads were back in control they found him indispensable and kept him on. In due course the ʿAbbāsids followed suit, and in the first decades of ʿAbbāsid rule members of the family held governorships as far afield as Sindh and Tunisia; some of them governed both these provinces at different times in their careers. In Tunisia, where they served as governors from 771 to 793, it looked for a while as if they might anticipate the Aghlabids in establishing an autonomous dynasty. That they were unsuccessful had more to do with the political incompetence of the last Muhallabids than it did with any structural obstacle. The other noteworthy aspect of the history of the province in this period is the willingness of the ʿAbbāsids, following Umayyad precedent, to pour large numbers of troops into Tunisia in the face of the threat from the Berber Khārijites. One massive army was sent by al-Manṣūr in 761, and another arrived in 772. This response may have been commensurate with the Berber threat, but not with the resources of Tunisia. The result was unreliable pay for the troops, whose discontent then posed a major problem for the governors and their Aghlabid successors.

East of Tunisia, the Sahara desert either reaches the Mediterranean or comes uncomfortably close to it. There are nevertheless two regions on this coast where a rather narrow band of territory between the desert and the sea receives enough rainfall to support a measure of agriculture: Tripolitania and Cyrenaica. As we have seen, the Arabs conquered both regions. Today they are parts of Libya, but in premodern times Tripolitania gravitated toward Tunisia and Cyrenaica toward Egypt; neither was ever a major center of power. We will encounter both of these coastal bands from time to time. Of course, the medieval Muslim world did not stop at the southern edge of the Mediterranean. Not just Spain but also several of the larger islands, and even the far south of Italy, were subject to Muslim rule at one time or another. But of these territories only Spain and to an extent Cyprus were ever part of the Caliphate.

Egypt

The period of Egyptian history that concerns us here is a long one, from the Arab conquest in 639–42 to the beginnings of an effectively independent dynasty, the Ṭūlūnids, in 868. One thing this long history obviously reflects is the proximity of Egypt to the center of caliphal power in the Fertile Crescent. Another is the desirability of the country in terms of its agricultural and commercial resources. The irrigated agriculture made possible by the Nile endowed Egypt with unusual agricultural wealth, and thanks to the Red Sea its commercial potential was enhanced by its possession of the shortest land route linking the Mediterranean to the Indian Ocean. Add the ease of riverine transport and a high level of urbanization, and Egypt was well worth owning. It makes sense that it was conquered long before North Africa and Spain and remained a province of the Caliphate long after them.

The conquest of Egypt was a relatively easy one. By taking Syria the Arabs had already cut off Egypt from the rest of the Byzantine Empire by land. Moreover, Byzantine Egypt was not a militarized frontier province, and the quality of its troops is accordingly likely to have been low. When the Persians withdrew in 629 after their decade-long occupation of the country, their departure required no military effort on the part of the Byzantines, who are therefore unlikely to have positioned elite troops in Egypt at that point. It fits with this that the major actor on the Byzantine side during the conquest was not a general but rather an ecclesiastic, the patriarch of Alexandria. So as ʿAmr is said to have put it to ʿUmar, Egypt was not just the richest of countries; it was also militarily the weakest. This did not change. Egypt was not a heavily militarized province under the Arabs; as we saw, already at the time of the conquest they began pushing their frontier farther to the west. There was indeed a border to the south, where Egypt marched with Nubia. But the Nubians, though well able to defend themselves in this period, were not a threat to the Muslim possession of Egypt. High-quality troops from Syria or Khurāsān did occasionally make an appearance on the banks of the Nile, but their presence was usually temporary. Once their mission was accomplished they would return home or continue on their way to the battlefields of North Africa. The troops permanently stationed in Egypt were those who made up the Jund, the descendants of the Arab conquerors. They were the military and political elite of early Muslim Egypt, but they were not a battle-hardened army that could stand up to more formidable forces from the east. In the competition between armies that decided the fate of the Umayyads, the Egyptian Jund was not a player.

Yet for some two centuries the members of the Jund were in effect the owners of the country, and they were strongly opposed to anyone who threatened to take it away from them—for example, by creaming off a large share of Egypt's revenue for the central government.[46] They lived mainly in Fusṭāṭ, today part of the southern suburbs of Cairo. Two things were noteworthy about Fusṭāṭ. Like Baṣra, Kūfa, and Qayrawān it was a purpose-built garrison city, and again like Qayrawān it was an inland city, in contrast to the Byzantine provincial capitals of Alexandria and Carthage. The Dīwān of Egypt was located in Fusṭāṭ, and those whose names were recorded in it received their stipends or protested violently if they did not. How the provincial elite centered on the Jund related to the imperial government based in Syria or Iraq was the decisive variable in Egyptian politics in this period.

46. For what follows see H. Kennedy, "Egypt as a province in the Islamic caliphate," in *The Cambridge history of Egypt*, Cambridge 1998, vol. 1.

Here one key office was that of the security force chief; he was nearly always a prominent member of the provincial elite. The governor, by contrast, was usually, though not always, an outsider. As such he could be a powerful figure like ʿAmr, who as we have seen made no contribution to the finances of the central government, or he might be a lightweight without significant local support. Either way, the crucial thing from the point of view of the provincial elite was how respectful he was of their interests.

The most critical junctures in the relationship between the provincial elite and the central government tended to be the civil wars of the period. This illustrates a certain passivity in the political role of Egypt in the wider Muslim world. Despite the initial role of the Egyptian malcontents in killing ʿUthmān, thereafter it was civil wars fought elsewhere that spilled over into Egypt, not the other way around. In the first civil war the Jund split, with a battle in 657; Muʿāwiya intervened twice, once in person and once by unleashing ʿAmr on Egypt with Syrian troops. But the outcome was to the general satisfaction of the provincial elite. The second civil war likewise saw a split in Egypt, but fighting broke out only with another intervention from Syria, this time by the Umayyad caliph Marwān against a governor appointed by Ibn al-Zubayr. Again the outcome suited most of the Jund. By the time of the third civil war matters had been complicated by the factional dispute between Northerners and Southerners: the Jund were Southerners, whereas recent arrivals in the eastern Nile delta and Upper Egypt were Northerners. This contention came to play a far larger role in Egyptian politics than did the sectarian alignments that were so prominent in other parts of the Muslim world in this period. The ensuing disorder led as usual to a Syrian intervention, with Marwān II sending a Syrian army to Egypt in 745. This time the intervention was brutal, but it also proved a failure: in 750 the ʿAbbāsids took over Egypt and Marwān was killed there. The outcome was the restoration of the old pattern, with outsiders as governors and locals as chiefs of the security force. There was no settling of Khurāsānī troops in Egypt at this stage, and as before the new authorities worked with the provincial elite, which had thus weathered three civil wars. But the fourth was to be a game changer, and it brought about the downfall of the Egyptian elite. The process was adumbrated already in the reign of al-Rashīd. Because the Jund was proving ineffective against the rebellious Arabs of the eastern fringe of the delta, Abnāʾ were dispatched from Baghdad, thus further diluting the military weight of the Jund. As we have seen, the fourth civil war then saw Egypt divided: Fusṭāṭ and the south were controlled by one of the Abnāʾ while the north was in the hands of a Southerner, and the Jund in Fusṭāṭ lost out. It was not till 826–32 that drastic military interventions from the east restored the unity of Egypt and caliphal authority over it, and they did so in a very different style. The security force chiefs were now outsiders like the governors, and worse yet, in 833 "the Arabs"—meaning the provincial elite of the Jund—ceased to be paid their stipends. Instead, power in Egypt was increasingly in the hands of Turks from Sāmarrā'. In the 860s a rebellion broke out in the north, and survivors of the provincial elite were still among those who joined it. But theirs was now a hopelessly lost cause. Much later, when the Fāṭimid caliph al-Ḥākim (ruled 996–1021) was visiting Fusṭāṭ in 1013, thirteen descendants of ʿAmr ibn al-ʿĀṣ introduced themselves and complained of the state of poverty to which they had been reduced. The caliph was kind enough to provide each of them with a thousand dirhams and some clothing.

A leitmotif in all this is the heavy burden of taxation. A governor appointed in 705 decreed that if you were dead you could not be buried till your taxes had been paid. The fiscal policies of another, appointed in 784, had the remarkable effect of uniting Northerners and Southerners against him; the Jund, too, was happy to collude with the rebels, who killed the hated governor. At the same time, it was overtaxation that led to the Coptic revolts. Much of the fiscal pressure provoking them originated outside Egypt. The first major revolt, in 725–26, was a reaction to the methods of a new superintendent of taxation installed by Hishām—methods that included a census in which men were forced to wear numbered badges. Fiscal pressure was likewise a factor in Coptic conversion to Islam, and the major Christian chronicle of the period speaks of Copts converting to escape the heavy taxation imposed on non-Muslims. The accounts of Muslim geographers show that by the tenth century the penetration of Islam in the Egyptian countryside was extensive, though far from universal, and this spread is likely to reflect Coptic conversion as well as Arab settlement. There was nevertheless a vein of sympathy for the Copts among the provincial elite that is reflected in the traditions they handed down. According to one transmitted by an eighth-century Egyptian scholar, the Prophet on his deathbed kept losing consciousness and then regaining it. Three times on coming to he commended to his followers "the swarthy people with curly hair." This puzzled them, and when he next came to they asked him who these people were. The answer was unambiguous: "The Copts of Egypt, for they are your maternal uncles and in-laws; they are your helpers against your enemy and your helpers in your religion."[47] The reference to maternal uncles and in-laws points to the Copts' twofold kinship with the Arabs—through Abraham's Egyptian concubine Hagar, the mother of Ishmael and hence of the Arabs, and through Muḥammad's Egyptian concubine Māriya, by whom he had a son, Ibrāhīm, who died in infancy. Another tradition has it that had this Ibrāhīm lived, no Copt would have been obliged to pay the poll tax due from non-Muslims. But how could the Copts, as Christians, be the helpers of the Muslims with regard to their religion? The Prophet was asked this next time he came to, and he answered that the Copts

47. Ibn ʿAbd al-Ḥakam, *The history of the conquest of Egypt*, New Haven 1922, 3.

would take care of the worldly needs of the Muslims, thus leaving them free to serve God; he added a warning against maltreating them. ʿAmr, in turn, was remembered to have echoed the Prophet's deathbed commendation of the Copts in a sermon he gave in Egypt, telling the assembled Muslims to treat their Coptic clients well. The scholars of Egypt likewise quoted a son of ʿAmr praising the Copts to the skies: "The Copts of Egypt are the noblest of all the non-Arabs, the most generous of them, the most excellent in lineage, and the closest in kinship to the Arabs at large and to Quraysh in particular."[48] Of course the tone was not always so respectful. Thus one of Egypt's earliest historians, Yazīd ibn Abī Ḥabīb (d. 745–46), remarked that no Copt would buy or sell anything without saying "I'll check with my wife"[49]—incidentally an attestation of the marketing skills of Egyptian women that has parallels as early as Herodotus and as late as modern ethnography. But the contrast between the sympathetic attitude to the Copts in the early Islamic period and the hatred we will see in late medieval times is remarkable.

Before we move on, there is another side to Egypt that calls for attention: the relative abundance of documents—in Greek, Coptic, and Arabic—that survive from its two centuries and more as a province of the Caliphate.[50] Like most literate peoples, the Egyptians wrote a lot on perishable materials. From at least the time of the pyramid builder Cheops some 4,500 years ago they used papyrus, after which they switched rapidly to paper in the first half of the tenth century. What was special about Egypt was not the production of these documents but their survival in large numbers when discarded on the arid desert fringes of the country. Such documents have also been found in some other parts of the Caliphate, but in much smaller quantities. The Egyptian documents can nevertheless be very frustrating. The conditions that made their survival possible render them a geographically unbalanced source: they are hardly found at all in the delta and are rare in cities. On top of that they are often badly written, badly damaged, and incomplete; just deciphering them requires formidable expertise. One specialist once edited a fragment of papyrus that he identified as part of an official letter, but another scholar then showed that it was in fact a passage from the Qurʾān. And even when we know what the documents say, their fragmentation and disorder mean that it is often hard to make convincing historical sense of them. Working on such papyri is thus very different from studying orderly files of documents continuously preserved in an archive. Yet we should not complain—we are lucky that we have these documents at all. And unlike our literary sources, which typically reach us through chains of editing and copying, they have the great virtue of being time capsules: what we have in front of us is exactly what the author

48. Ibn ʿAbd al-Ḥakam, *The history of the conquest of Egypt*, 5.
49. Ibn ʿAbd al-Ḥakam, *The history of the conquest of Egypt*, 28.
50. For what follows see P. M. Sijpesteijn, *Shaping a Muslim state*, Oxford 2013.

wrote. So what can these documents tell us? Many things, but one is of particular interest for our purposes. Let us approach it indirectly by returning to the history of Muslim coinage.

Coins, like documents, are time capsules, and in the context of the early Muslim state they show us a clear evolution. It starts from zero: the Prophet minted no coins whatsoever. This did not mean that coins were unknown in the Arabian interior, since those minted by the empires could easily find their way there, and indeed the Qur'ān mentions both silver and gold coins. But there was no living tradition of Arabian coinage at this time. The next step, taken by the Arabs as they were conquering the Sasanian Empire, was to continue minting Sasanian coins there without change. This was very practical. People trust the money they are used to, and the Muslim state now needed cash to pay its stipends. So up to this point the Arabs, having no model of their own to offer, simply replicated the ways of the empire they had overthrown. The next stage involved adding short Arabic inscriptions in the margins of coins, still leaving their general look reassuringly unchanged. Only decades later, after a period of experimentation, did they make the drastic shift to the fully Islamic "reform coinage," starting in 696. We have hard evidence for this whole evolution, and it makes good sense. We might therefore expect the case of administration in the conquered territories to run parallel to it. Coming from a society that until recently had been stateless, the Arabs would lack any administrative tradition of their own and would simply take over the bureaucratic machinery of the conquered territories as they found it. Later, of course, they might reform it; as we have seen, the literary sources credit 'Abd al-Malik with changing the language of administration to Arabic, and some such change undoubtedly took place. Thus the numismatic record provides us with an obvious hypothesis, and we would expect the documents from the Egyptian desert to back it up.

To an extent they do. For example, Byzantine Egypt was made up of four regions, each under an official known as a "duke" (*dux*), and it was further divided into some sixty districts each controlled by a "pagarch." When the Arabs arrived the dukes and pagarchs were of course Christian, and they remained so for several decades; only gradually, toward the end of the seventh century, did the new rulers begin to appoint Muslim dukes and pagarchs. This, then, is a clear example of continuity in administration. But other things go against this pattern. Soon after the conquest the Arabs made a major change in the fiscal system by introducing a poll tax. This is doubtless the tax that the Copts would have been exempt from if only Muḥammad's son Ibrāhīm had lived. Moreover, the Arabs had their own ideas about how to draw up a document from the start. Early Arabic documents from Khurāsān show conventions also found in those from Egypt, conventions that were at variance with the local administrative tradition of either region. Thus a papyrus of 643 that we have already met is actually bilingual, with the Greek and

Arabic versions saying essentially the same thing: that an Arab commander acknowledges requisitioning sixty-five sheep. Yet the Arabic is not a translation of the Greek. For example, the Greek begins: "[From] the commander Abdellas to you, Christopher . . ." By contrast, the Arabic starts: "This is what (*hādhā mā*) 'Abdallāh ibn Jābir and his companions have taken . . ."[51] The initial "This is what . . ." in the Arabic version is characteristic of the early Arabic documentary style; it also appears in Arabic documents of the mid-eighth century from Khurāsān, and in early inscriptions. Other such documents begin slightly differently, but with the same "This": "This is a document (*hādhā kitāb*) . . ."[52] In short, it is clear that the Arabs brought some kind of documentary tradition with them to the territories they conquered. The obvious inference would be that this tradition, whatever its ultimate origins, was already practiced by the earliest rulers of the Muslim state in Medina. And indeed, as we saw, the Constitution of Medina begins with just such a formula: "This is a document (*hādhā kitāb*) . . ." There is, however, one problem that remains to be solved. It seems that what the Arabs brought with them was not limited to Arabic: Greek documents from early Islamic Egypt contain Greek technical terms that had not been used there in Byzantine times. Taken with the Arabic documentary tradition, these terms point to a background in a bilingual environment, and on its own a tradition shaped or adopted in the Ḥijāz would not explain them.

Arabia

There are four regions of Arabia for which our sources make it possible to write a more or less continuous history in the period that concerns us: Oman, the Yemen, Baḥrayn, and the Ḥijāz.[53] Of course the data vary in quality, being best for the Ḥijāz and worst for Baḥrayn. We will in any case limit ourselves to these four. That is not to say that they are representative. It is no coincidence that these regions stood out for having better resources than the rest of Arabia, and for that reason they were more conducive to the rule of states and the writing of history. Initially the state in question was the Caliphate, but all of them eventually developed states of their own. In the cases of Oman, the Yemen, and Baḥrayn we will stop at the point at which such states began to take shape, but in the case of the Ḥijāz we will hand over to a later chapter well before it. In each case the later discussion will be more substantial than this one.

51. G. Khan, "The opening formula and witness clauses in Arabic legal documents from the early Islamic period," *Journal of the American Oriental Society*, 139 (2019), 24.

52. Khan, "The opening formula and witness clauses," 26.

53. For Arabia in this period see E. Landau-Tasseron, "Arabia," in *The new Cambridge history of Islam*, Cambridge 2010, vol. 1.

We have already encountered Oman in passing. It combined agricultural resources thanks to its mountains with commercial resources thanks to the Indian Ocean. Before the rise of Islam it was under the sway of a Persian coastal presence and an Arab client dynasty in the interior known as the Julandās. As we saw, the sources tell us that the Muslim state was already active in Oman in the time of Muḥammad and that the rebellion that followed his death was duly suppressed. Thereafter authority in Oman seems to have been divided for a while between the same client dynasty and caliphal governors appointed from outside. But the dynasty showed more staying power than did the governors, who disappeared following the first civil war and remained absent until Oman was reconquered by troops sent from Iraq by Ḥajjāj. After that there were Umayyad governors in Oman, but the Julandās were still entrenched there. When the activity of Ibāḍī agents from Baṣra issued in the establishment of an Ibāḍī imamate in the early 750s, it was a Julandā who briefly became the first imam. The ʿAbbāsids then sent troops to overthrow him, and they invaded Oman again in 805 and 893, but what they failed to do was to establish lasting provincial government there. Thanks to this failure a more durable Ibāḍī imamate was set up in 793, but even then the Julandās could still make trouble for the imams.

Like Oman, the Yemen combined agricultural and commercial resources. Its agricultural resources were more abundant because of its larger share of mountains, but this also posed a serious obstacle to the power of states. So far in this book we have spent more time on the Yemen than on Oman in recognition of the Yemen's ancient tradition of culture and state formation as well as its closer relations with the peninsula at large. But by early Islamic times this Yemeni tradition, if not already dead, was moribund, though we can say little about the process of its demise. Part of the change was linguistic: at some point the language of the Ḥimyarites died out, replaced by Arabic; by the tenth century only a few pockets of it survived. With it disappeared knowledge of Sabaean, the related but distinct language used by the Ḥimyarites in their inscriptions. A tenth-century Yemeni author could still read the script, but the language itself was beyond him. At the same time, such memory as survived of Ḥimyarite history was surprisingly confused and threadbare. Another part of the change was political: the Yemen was no longer what it had been in late antiquity, the site of a state strong enough to dominate the region and project its power far to the north. As we saw, the Persians had sent an expedition to the Yemen around 570, but half a century later such power as their descendants retained was limited to Ṣanʿāʾ. It was not that the Ḥimyarite kingdom was forgotten. Ḥimyarite restorationist sentiment is attested among Yemenis who settled in Syria in early Islamic times. One tradition transmitted there affects to predict a succession of rulers of Ẓafār, the Ḥimyarite capital: first the good Ḥimyarites, then the evil Ethiopians, then the noble Persians, and then the mercantile Quraysh (a disparaging reference to the rulers of the Muslim state, who were of course Qurashīs). At this point the tradition ventures a real prediction, as it turned out a false one: from Quraysh dominion would return to Ḥimyar. Such subversive hopes may also have been behind a rebellion that took place in the Yemen in 725–26. Later we hear of a governor appointed by al-Ma'mūn in 827–28 who was hostile to everything Ḥimyarite, suggesting that restorationist aspirations could still have been in evidence in the Yemen of his day. But these too died out, though leaving behind some continuing pride in Ḥimyarite antiquities and ancestry. Strikingly, there does not seem to have been any dispute in early Islamic times about the standing of Ḥimyarites as Arabs—southern Arabs, of course, but Arabs nonetheless. As a ninth-century cultural luminary put it, the Arabs, despite their original lack of common ancestry, had been poured into a single mold.

The Yemen of Islamic times was thus a land of rebellious Arab tribes. Just as in Oman, the sources describe some activity on the part of adherents of Muḥammad in the Yemen, followed by rebellion after his death. For the next two or three centuries the caliphal governors appointed to the region were usually outsiders, though occasionally Yemenis held the office. They often struggled to exert authority, but the caliph could send in troops if he really wanted to, as Muʿāwiya did in 660 or so, and al-Ma'mūn in 820. On balance the governors of the Yemen were more successful, or at least more persistent, than their peers in Oman. As we will see in a later chapter, they were still trying to exert some influence in the late ninth century, at a time when the first regional dynasties were already several decades old and aspiring Shīʿite sectarians were hard at work among the tribes. Altogether, power in the Yemen was located in the tribal countryside, not in the urban centers, such as they were.

Like Oman and the Yemen, Baḥrayn combined agricultural resources—here in the form of a vast oasis—with the commercial opportunities arising from access to the Persian Gulf. We know that under the caliphs the region was to prove a source of considerable revenue when they could control it, and this helps explain why the Sasanians had found it worth taking possession of in pre-Islamic times. As usual the sources describe the penetration of the area by Muḥammad's state, with widespread rebellions following his death. Thereafter we see the rule of caliphal governors pitted against local rebellions and sectarian state formation. Thus the early ʿAbbāsids were able to suppress revolts, and their successors retained their hold on the province into the ninth century—we even hear of an ʿAbbāsid governor in 893 under the rule of the vigorous caliph al-Muʿtaḍid (ruled 892–902). Sectarian state formation began with the Khārijites in the second civil war. The subsect in question was the Najdiyya, named for its leader Najda ibn ʿĀmir. Though based in Baḥrayn, its forces ranged as far afield as Oman, the Yemen, and the Ḥijāz. Zubayrid attempts to suppress the sect had no success, and the revolt was ended only by the dispatch of Umayyad troops in 692. This Khārijite rebellion lasted for some eight years, and another that started in 723 is said to have lasted for nineteen. Thereafter it was the turn of the Shīʿites. An ʿAlid claimant, one ʿAlī ibn Muḥammad, made an attempt to take over the region in 863 but was driven out by the local tribes, though he went on to organize a devastating rebellion among the East African slaves—the Zanj—in the marshes of Iraq. Then, in 886–87, an Ismāʿīlī agent went to work in Baḥrayn, and his labor bore fruit with the emergence of a Qarmaṭī state in 899. These Qarmaṭīs—members of an Ismāʿīlī subsect—were to prove every bit as aggressive as the Najdiyya.

That leaves the Ḥijāz. As we saw, on the eve of the rise of Islam this region was not a promising part of the world for state formation, and Muḥammad's unlikely success in this endeavor was remarkable. The Ḥijāz did, of course, have maritime frontage on the Red Sea, but in the absence of significant ports or an agricultural hinterland, that was not worth much. Things changed with the rise of Islam. Medina was now briefly the capital of an expanding empire, and as such it had a claim—albeit a disputed one—on the resources of the lands the Arabs were so rapidly conquering. That meant grain from Egypt to feed the growing urban populations of Mecca and Medina and to pay stipends to the elite there. When ʿUmar set up the Dīwān, for example, we are told that he awarded each of Muḥammad's widows ten thousand dirhams a year, while some soldiers received as little as two hundred. A large part of the lavish stipends of the elite must surely have trickled down to their social inferiors through purchases and patronage. And yet the speed with which the competitors for the Caliphate abandoned Medina at the start of the first civil war was ominous; at that point a pessimist might have anticipated that the Ḥijāz would revert to its condition at the time of the Fijār wars. But this did not happen, despite the failure of Ibn al-Zubayr's attempt to rule from Mecca in the second civil war. Instead, the sanctity of Mecca and Medina proved enough to ensure that grain and stipends continued to make life pleasant for the inhabitants of the holy cities and that pilgrims continued to visit them. The cities were now, of course, more vulnerable. When an ʿAlid rebelled in Medina in 762, the caliph al-Manṣūr responded by interrupting the supply of Egyptian grain. But in normal times the Ḥijāz could still rely on generous external support. What this meant was that the interests of the Ḥijāz were now dependent on the strength of the central government in Syria or Iraq; as long as it was strong, it usually honored its commitment to the welfare of the Ḥijāz. This commitment was confirmed by the high standing of the governors appointed, often members of the ruling dynasty. It was also evident in the scale of the investments the caliphs made to improve the infrastructure of the Ḥijāz and to develop agriculture there with a slave labor force—an activity in which the elite of the holy cities likewise participated. No doubt much of this agriculture would have been unprofitable but for the increase in effective demand through the payment of stipends.

Despite their dependence on external largesse, the members of the Ḥijāzī elite were by no means docile. They rebelled against Yazīd I, dramatically throwing off their turbans in the mosque as they threw off their allegiance to him but losing the battle against his forces in 683. Under the ʿAbbāsids there were ʿAlid revolts from time to time, the first in 762 and others in 786, 815, and 865; they were invariably defeated. By contrast, the Ḥijāzī elite had no taste for Khārijite rebellion, despite the presence of Ibāḍīs in the holy cities and the unwelcome intrusion of Khārijite rebels in the second and third civil wars. Such disturbances apart, the region continued to be administered by the governors appointed by the caliphs. But from the first half of the ninth century the ʿAbbāsid grip on the Ḥijāz was weakening, which meant that conditions there deteriorated. After the reign of al-Rashīd we no longer hear of stipends being paid. At the same time the Bedouin became more of a threat to the cities, though in the 840s the caliph was still powerful enough to send a prominent Turkic general with an army to deal with them. But eventually, as we will see, it was the ʿAlids who inherited a much-diminished Ḥijāz.

Altogether, the first two centuries of the Caliphate, for all their disorder, mark the high tide of imperial rule over Arabia. No earlier or later empire could compare in the extent of its sway over the interior of the peninsula. Perhaps the most telling example of this tide is the existence until the mid-eighth century of large areas of inner Arabian pastureland that had been confiscated from the tribes and reserved for the use of the state.

On the borders of the Fertile Crescent

As indicated, we will not revisit Syria and Iraq, nor the intervening Jazīra, since they have already figured prominently in this chapter. Instead, our concern at this point is with some less significant regions on the borders of the Fertile Crescent: the Thughūr to the northwest, Armenia to the north, and Khūzistān to the east. They vary a lot in character and history.

To the northwest of Syria lay a chain of mountains, the Taurus, forming a natural barrier between Syria and the Anatolian plateau.[54] The routes leading through the mountains were the Thughūr proper, the "gaps" through which armies could move. To the south of the mountains a string of towns stretched some 250 miles from Tarsus in the west to Malaṭya in the east, and these settlements came to be identified with the Thughūr. In Umayyad times this region was not in the stable possession of either the Arabs or the Byzantines, but the ʿAbbāsids, after some initial chaos, took possession of it and were sufficiently secure there to build up

54. For what follows see M. Bonner, *Aristocratic violence and holy war*, New Haven 1996.

the towns as forward bases for their raids into Anatolia. Large numbers of raiders now lived, or at least wintered, in these settlements. They included volunteers from lands as far afield as Sīstān in southeastern Iran, the Yemen, and North Africa; every great city had its hostel in Tarsus where its fighters would stay. Pious scholars likewise flocked to the Thughūr to participate in jihad. In short, there was an element of what today would be called jihad tourism. By now, however, the conquest of Constantinople was no longer a plausible objective. It is true that al-Ma'mūn, imaginative as ever, revived this aspiration, complete with the idea of planting settlements of Arab tribesmen along the way. In practice, however, the raids of the early 'Abbāsid period were no longer attempts to extend the Muslim frontier. In material terms they were not useless, since they served to amass booty and weaken a rival state by disrupting its agricultural production and tax collection. In more exalted terms they enabled everyone concerned to engage in the conspicuous performance of the religious duty of making war on the infidel. This included the troops, the volunteers, the scholars, and not least the caliph himself, who on occasion would lead the raid in person. The Thughūr were thus yoked to the duty of jihad as the Ḥijāz was to that of pilgrimage. This role in generating religious merit was not the only thing the two regions had in common. Another was that in each case the operation was very expensive. For the Thughūr it involved the caliph's spending large sums of money to build and rebuild the towns and their fortifications. In terms of hard cash, maintaining the Thughūr was thus no more profitable than was maintaining the Ḥijāz. A further similarity between the Thughūr and the Ḥijāz was that those who depended on this largesse were not noticeably grateful for it. And like the Ḥijāz, the Thughūr went to rack and ruin when the 'Abbāsids were no longer in a position to continue their military and financial support. The people of the Thughūr had their first taste of this during the fourth civil war, and by 897 the inhabitants of Tarsus were complaining to the caliph because they had no governor. And though the Thughūr were free of the 'Alids and Bedouin who preyed on the people of the Ḥijāz, from 863 the resurgent Byzantines more than made up for that. Moreover, the dependence of the people of the Thughūr on the central government seems to have been accentuated by the absence on the Muslim side of marcher lords of the kind that often dominate frontier areas, as they did, for example, in the marches of Muslim Spain. In this respect the Muslim side of the Thughūr seems to have been very different from the Byzantine side, where great aristocratic families were a conspicuous presence.

We come now to Armenia, an ancient kingdom in the region between the northern arc of the Fertile Crescent and the Caucasus. It was ruled from the first century to the fifth by a branch of the Arsacids, a dynasty we already encountered in Iran. This kingdom had two obvious vulnerabilities. One was internal: the mountainous terrain predisposed the region to political fragmentation. The other was external: Armenia was in frequent danger of being crushed by larger and more powerful neighbors. Here the mountains had some defensive value, but not enough. In late antiquity the overbearing neighbors were the Byzantine and Persian Empires. In 387 or so they had formally partitioned Armenia, and as a fifth-century Armenian historian put it, the kingdom of Armenia was now "diminished, divided, and scattered."[55] Only vestiges of the dynasty survived for a few years on the Byzantine side of the border and until 428–29 on the Persian side. Nevertheless, the Armenian aristocrats were still in place; indeed, it was they who had pressed the Sasanian ruler to put an end to the kingdom. In cultural terms, as might be expected, their imperial neighbors left a heavy imprint on the Armenians. Looking east, the most obvious residue of this influence in Islamic times was linguistic. Armenian is an Indo-European language on its own, not part of the Iranian family, but its vocabulary has a wide range of Iranian loanwords dating from antiquity, for the most part Parthian rather than Persian. These borrowings reflect a period when the Armenian aristocracy was culturally Iranian and Zoroastrianism was well established in the country. Looking west, the key development was the adoption of Christianity by the Armenian kingdom in the early fourth century, leading eventually to the development of an Armenian literary language more open to the west than to the east. Yet the relationship with the west was fractured when the Armenians and the Byzantines placed themselves on different sides of the Christological disputes that raged in late antiquity. If we take the Byzantines to be Orthodox, the Armenians were Monophysite sectarians like the Ethiopians, the Copts, and many of the Syrians. Alongside the Armenians, there were two smaller peoples to their north, but still to the south of the Caucasus, with broadly similar histories: the Georgians, who are there to this day, and the Caucasian Albanians, who disappeared long ago. We can leave them aside and concentrate on the Armenians.[56]

In the 640s and 650s the Arabs and the Byzantines competed for the possession of Armenia, and it was only after the first civil war that the Arabs prevailed. They appointed governors to administer the province in their usual fashion. But the mountainous terrain favored the survival of the Christian Armenian aristocrats, and at first they continued to exercise full power on the ground. From the late seventh century, however, the pressure on them increased. Muslim garrisons were installed in Armenia, a mass killing of the aristocracy is reported in 705, and taxes increased sharply in 724–25. There were failed rebellions, notably in 784–85; governors brought Arab tribesmen to settle in the country, and minor Muslim states were formed. Yet a ninth-century Muslim historian quotes a telling description of the Armenian magnates in the early decades of ʿAbbāsid rule: they remained in their lands, each defending his own region, and when a new governor arrived they

55. *The epic histories attributed to Pʿawstos Buzand*, trans. N. G. Garsoïan, Cambridge, MA 1989, 234.
56. For what follows see A. Vacca, *Non-Muslim provinces under early Islam*, Cambridge 2017.

would humor him while they sized him up; if they found him to be tough, they would pay the tribute that was due from them and obey him, but if they found him to be weak they would not take him seriously. In the ninth century enough of this aristocracy survived to benefit from the disruptions of the fourth civil war and the distractions of the prolonged revolt of Bābak in neighboring Azerbaijan. The revival of caliphal power that followed saw a major rebellion that issued in an attempt at the forced conversion of the aristocrats in 852. But the subsequent weakening of ʿAbbāsid rule enabled the leading member of an Armenian princely family, the Bagratids, to expand his power and eventually revive the Armenian monarchy in 884. This is significant: it is the only case of the restoration of a non-Muslim monarchy in a province of the Caliphate in this period. Though Bagratid rule suffered from the usual tendency to fragmentation, enhanced by the presence of the small Muslim states, it survived until 1045. What led to its demise was a Byzantine intervention, but within a few years of that the Turks had arrived, and their impact on the history of Armenia was to prove far greater than that of the Byzantines or the Arabs.

We now move to Khūzistān at the eastern end of the Fertile Crescent. This, too, was once an ancient kingdom, or rather a part of the ancient kingdom of Elam, which in its day extended eastward into the highlands of Fārs. This state was far more ancient than that of Armenia and had disappeared a millennium earlier. There had nevertheless been a kingdom of Elymais within the Arsacid Empire, though it, too, had come to an end under the more centralized rule of the Sasanians. The one residue of ancient Elam that may have survived into Islamic times was its language, Elamite: a tenth-century geographer describes the Khūzīs as having an unintelligible tongue that the Prophet is said to have disparaged as the language of the devils. The reputation of the Khūzīs themselves was no better than that of their language. As this geographer puts it, commenting on the wealth and amenities of Khūzistān, "What a fine region it would be were it not for its people!"[57] This wealth arose from the fact that Khūzistān was effectively an extension of the lowlands of Iraq, except that the rivers watering it—the Kārūn and its affluents—rose in the nearby highlands of Iran. The Arabs took possession of this revenue-rich region as part of their first wave of conquests, and thereafter it was administered by provincial governors. Rebel forces from elsewhere washed over it from time to time. Thus the Khārijite insurgents of 695–97 were from the Jazīra, but their leader met his death by drowning in the Kārūn. Likewise Ibn al-Ashʿath's revolt of 699–701 had nothing to do with Khūzistān, except that two of the three battles that decided its outcome were fought there. This pattern was repeated when ʿAbbāsid power began to weaken and rebellions had more of a chance of leading

57. Muqaddasī, *Aḥsan al-taqāsīm*, Leiden 1967, 403.

to the formation of states. Yaʿqūb the Coppersmith was the founder of an early independent dynasty in eastern Iran, the Ṣaffārids. After failing to extend his rule to Baghdad and Sāmarrā' in 876 he died in Khūzistān in 879. But it would be centuries into Islamic times before we find anyone engaged in forming a state in Khūzistān itself, and even then what emerged was unimpressive by the standards of ancient Elam. In short, it seems that what had been a viable setting for a powerful state in much of antiquity was no longer so. Just why this had changed is worth thinking about. It was undoubtedly related to a long-term northward shift in the center of political gravity in the Middle East. That shift had begun as early as the seventh century BC with the formation of the first of the Iranian empires of antiquity. Thereafter northern dominance was temporarily interrupted by the Arab conquests in the seventh century, partially reaffirmed by the role of northern armies in the power struggles of the mid-eighth, and definitively reestablished by the arrival of the Turks in the eleventh.

Iran

We come now to a region too large and diverse to be treated as a whole, despite its shared imperial history and a certain degree of ethnic and cultural homogeneity. As a first approximation, it pays to think of Iran as a right-angled triangle, with the right angle located in the northeast, in Khurāsān. The hypotenuse stretches from Makrān in the southeast through Kirmān, Fārs, and the Jibāl to Azerbaijan in the northwest. Its main physical feature is a wide band of mountains that starts in Kirmān and ends by merging with the Armenian highlands; this band is the Zagros. To the north and south of the Zagros the terrain is relatively flat, with the central desert of Iran to the north and the lowlands of Iraq and the shallow waters of the Persian Gulf to the south. One term here calls for special comment: the Jibāl (literally "the mountains"). This is a region for which there is no name that is stable over time—it was Media in antiquity, the Jibāl in early medieval times, and Persian Iraq in the later Middle Ages; it lacks a convenient name today. Let us call it the Jibāl. The northern leg of the triangle runs from Azerbaijan in the west to Khurāsān in the east, and between them lies a high but narrow band of mountains, the Elburz, together with a coastal plain flanking it on the north; we can refer to the mountains and plain together as the Caspian region. Farther to the north lie the mountains of the Caucasus, the Caspian Sea, and the desert of what is now Turkmenistan. To the south lies the central desert. The eastern leg of the triangle runs from Khurāsān south to Makrān and is a patchwork of deserts, highlands, and depressions that we will pass over fairly rapidly. For the purposes of this survey of Iran we will start in Fārs, roughly in the middle of the hypotenuse, and then proceed clockwise. But first, a general point about the social history of Iran after the Arab conquest. The pre-Islamic society of Iran had been dominated by an aristocratic elite for whom the Arab conquest was not good news. But the overall pattern was that the news was worse for the higher aristocracy. The lower aristocracy (generally known as the *dihqāns*) survived, preserving Iranian traditions while sooner or later converting to Islam.

Fārs, the ancient Persis, possesses an arid coastal plain of varying width, but its heart is in the highlands. Here the physical geography is in one way advantageous for agriculture: unlike the Jibāl with its narrow valleys, the highlands of Fārs include several basins suitable for cultivation. On the other hand, there is a falling off of rainfall in the Zagros as one goes southeast. In this respect Fārs is not as good as the Jibāl, though better than Kirmān—its southeastern basins are too dry for agriculture. Like Khūzistān, Fārs was taken by the Arabs in the first wave of conquests. Attacks across the Persian Gulf from Baḥrayn began as early as 635 but took only the coastal plain; the conquest of the highlands required the use of troops from Baṣra in 650. The region thus conquered had a glorious pre-Islamic past, having been the homeland of two of the three imperial dynasties of Iran, the Achaemenids and the Sasanians. But there was a difference between the two. The Achaemenids made much of their devotion to Persis and the Persian people and maintained what was probably a summer capital at Persepolis in their homeland. Under the Sasanians the principal city of Fārs was Iṣṭakhr, not far from Persepolis, but it was not an imperial capital, and as we saw, the Sasanians seem to have avoided talk of Persis and its people. Though they could not be said to have neglected Fārs, the effect was nevertheless a certain downgrading of the political standing of the region that continued into Islamic times, reinforced by the fact that in fiscal terms Fārs was worth far less than the Jibāl. In the period that concerns us here Fārs was a province of the Caliphate, and from time to time we hear about its governors. There was a rebellion in Iṣṭakhr early in the first civil war, but major insurrections affecting Fārs tended to begin and end elsewhere, as in the case of the Azāriqa in the second civil war and of ʿAbdallāh ibn Muʿāwiya in the third. Though the downgrading of Fārs would eventually prove more open to reversal than that of Khūzistān, its experience of Iranian state formation in the later ninth century was similar: Yaʿqūb the Coppersmith swept in from the east in 875, after which he and his successors had somewhat discontinuous possession of Fārs for the next thirty-six years. They based themselves not in Iṣṭakhr but rather in the upstart city of Shīrāz. Despite entrenched local power—there were said to be five thousand castles in tenth-century Fārs—it was not until the thirteenth century that indigenous actors would play a significant role there in state formation, and even then they did so on a much smaller scale than their pre-Islamic ancestors.

Moving northwest from Fārs into the Jibāl, we are in a region that contains two of Iran's major cities, Iṣfahān in the southeast and Hamadhān in the northwest. It is said that the caliph ʿUmar once consulted a captive Persian general about where best to begin the conquest of Iran. The general's response likened Iran to a bird:

Iṣfahān was its head, while Fārs and Azerbaijan were its wings, so that if the head was cut off, the wings would fall. The crucial campaign in the Arab conquest was indeed an invasion of the Jibāl, though the key battle in 642 or so was fought much closer to Hamadhān than to Iṣfahān. As no doubt in Fārs, the main cities of the Jibāl now had Arab garrisons, but once the frontier of conquest had moved on there was no need to station a large army there. The appointments and firings of provincial governors find frequent mention in the sources throughout our period, whether they be governors of Iṣfahān, Hamadhān, the Jibāl as a whole, or yet larger regions including the Jibāl. There was money in these appointments. When ʿAbd al-Malik was trying to win over the tribal leaders of Kūfa and Baṣra toward the end of the second civil war, we are told that no fewer than forty of them wrote to ask him for the governorship of Iṣfahān. They clearly knew what they were doing: the Jibāl in this period supplied the lion's share of the revenues of Iran. Of course we rarely get much sense of what this looked like on the ground, but events in Hamadhān in 696–97 give us a taste. Ḥajjāj, as viceroy of the East, wanted to be rid of a governor he could no longer trust—the man's brother had rebelled. So he wrote to appoint the chief of the governor's security force in his place, instructing him to put his predecessor in irons and throw him into prison. The chief was in a position to do so because he belonged to the Arab tribe of ʿIjl, which was well represented in Hamadhān, as a result of which he had fellow tribesmen he could rely on. After taking over the governorship he amply rewarded them, choosing all his officials from his own tribe and sending them out to collect the land tax. None of this is surprising, but the account is refreshingly concrete. Meanwhile, the Jibāl was particularly vulnerable to passing armies, rebel and other, because unlike Fārs it lay athwart the busy route from Iraq to Khurāsān. It was overrun by the Azāriqa in the second civil war and by the forces of ʿAbdallāh ibn Muʿāwiya in the third, and it was trampled on by rival armies in the course of the third and fourth civil wars.

In the Jibāl, as in Fārs, we hear relatively little of local initiatives, but there are a couple worth noting. One was the rising of Sunbādh, the rebel of 755 who declared the end of the rule of the Arabs; he did not come from the Jibāl himself, but many of his followers did, and it was there that he was defeated. The other was the rebellion of the Khurramīs in 833–34, in which many people of the Jibāl banded together in the region of Hamadhān. We are told that large numbers of them were killed, while the rest fled to the Byzantine Empire, where they reappeared a few years later as a military force fighting for the Byzantines. Though we lack information about the beliefs of these particular rebels, the general character of Khurramism is known. Its followers were villagers, and they were found in many parts of Iran, but most of all in the Jibāl. They believed in incarnation, the idea of a divine being's taking up residence in a human body. They also held with a broad acceptance of the good faith of other people's religions and—rebellions apart—

considered it wrong to harm any living being. Meanwhile, the weakening of 'Abbāsid rule was reflected in the emergence of a semi-independent dynasty in the ninth-century Jibāl, the Dulafids. Like the Ṭāhirids, but on a smaller scale, the Dulafids succeeded more by serving the 'Abbāsids than by rebelling against them. Abū Dulaf (d. 839–40), the founder of the dynasty, was an accomplished courtier and general whom al-Rashīd appointed governor of the Jibāl, an office he held on to despite being on the losing side in the fourth civil war. But he was not an outsider to the region: either his grandfather or his father had moved to the Jibāl, and he too was a member of the tribe of 'Ijl, which as we have seen had a significant presence in Hamadhān. In the event, despite cutthroat competition, three generations of the family held the office of governor until their tenure was ended by the caliph al-Mu'taḍid in the 890s.

Azerbaijan, like Fārs and the Jibāl, was conquered in the first wave of the Arab expansion, but in the period that now concerns us it comes across as something of a poor relation in comparison to its neighbors. It had agricultural resources, but they were concentrated in the valleys of the highlands; the uplands and, absent large-scale irrigation works, the lowlands of Mūghān were more suitable for pastoralists. In its mountain valleys Azerbaijan was similar to Armenia, yet it seems to have lacked the entrenched aristocracy that played so prominent a role in Armenian history. Azerbaijan was likewise not so different from the Jibāl, but it lacked major cities and cultural centers like Iṣfahān and Hamadhān. The difference is apparent in what we know of the provincial government of the region. We hear of many governors of Azerbaijan at large. Sometimes they are assigned the province on its own, sometimes it is combined with Armenia, and sometimes it forms part of even larger agglomerations. But we almost never hear of governors of cities or regions within Azerbaijan, as we often do with regard to the Jibāl. Like Khurāsān, Azerbaijan mattered because it was close to a militarily dangerous frontier. Beyond Darband—known to the Arabs as Bāb al-Abwāb, the "Gate of Gates" guarding the eastern flank of the Caucasus—lay the land of the Khazar nomads whose invasions could wreak havoc if unchecked. But this does not appear to have led to the stationing of a field army in Azerbaijan itself. For the most part the relevant military forces seem to have been based either to the south in the northern Jazīra or to the north in Darband. Rather than a field army, what Azerbaijan had in perhaps unusual abundance was men whose loyalties, if any, were shifting and whose way of making a living was informal and opportunistic violence. The principled violence of the Khārijites could also be found there, for example in the context of the third civil war, but not on the same scale. Many of those living by unprincipled violence were Arabs, but the native population they preyed on was hardly passive. In 807–8 some of our sources report a Khurramī rebellion in Azerbaijan, troublesome enough that the caliph's response was to dispatch an army of ten thousand cavalrymen—incidentally an indication that such a force was not available locally. This army took large numbers of Khurramīs captive, after which al-Rashīd ordered the killing of the men and the selling of the women and children into slavery. So it fits that Azerbaijan was soon to be the scene of an indigenous disturbance far larger in scale than anything mounted by the natives of Fārs or the Jibāl. This was the twenty-year rebellion of Bābak that began in 816–17 and ended in 837. Given the level of disorder that marks the history of Azerbaijan in this period, it is somewhat surprising that the emergence of a quasi-independent dynasty founded by a provincial governor was delayed until 889. There were nevertheless a couple of early developments on a smaller scale to the northeast of Azerbaijan. One was the formation of the principality of the Shīrwān-Shāhs, the rulers of Shīrwān near Bākū; they descended from a governor of Azerbaijan appointed in 799 and did not finally disappear until the early seventeenth century. The other took place yet farther north, in Darband, where the Hāshimids (869–1075) seem to have been a local family that achieved power in the city.

From Azerbaijan we move east into the Caspian region.[58] Here, as already indicated, the dominant physical feature is a long and narrow chain of mountains running from west to east, the Elburz; these are the highest mountains in Iran. To the north is a coastal plain of varying width, and to the south lies the plateau. As usual, the combination of sea and mountains means rainfall, and the coastal plain receives more of it than any other part of Iran. The rain that falls on the mountains likewise makes some agriculture possible there, and it indirectly supplies water to the northern fringe of the plateau—hence the presence of cities in locations just south of the mountains, notably Rayy, today effectively a suburb of Tehran. In our period this fringe was very much part of the world of large and powerful states, and it is in line with this that Rayy was reckoned part of the Jibāl. But whatever authority such states could exercise on the plateau, the Elburz chain was enough to stop them in their tracks and at the same time to impede their access to the coastal plain in the north. The main qualification to this simple picture is that the mountains are lower in the east than in the west, petering out in the region of Jurjān; moreover, they do not close off access to the eastern end of the coastal plain. This made Ṭabaristān, and especially its lowlands, significantly easier for the states of the plateau to penetrate than the western part of the Caspian region was.

The history of the region was strongly shaped by this geography. There was no Arab conquest until 759–61, and even then it was only the eastern coastal plain that was won by the armies of the caliph. The eastern mountains were still ruled by two Iranian dynasties, the Qārinids (ca. 665–840) and the Bāwandids (665–1074). These and other kingdoms of the Elburz chain were small in comparison with those of the plateau, but in compensation they had a fair chance of maintaining their

58. For the history of this region in the early centuries of Islam see W. Madelung, "The minor dynasties of northern Iran," in *The Cambridge history of Iran*, Cambridge 1968–91, vol. 4.

independent existence much longer than states battling for survival on the windy plains. Some of these mountain kingdoms are likely to go back to Sasanian times, and some persisted long after the period that concerns us here. It fits well with this political history that except at the eastern end of the region, Arab settlement was notably absent. In an environment without Muslim domination, either political or social, conversion to Islam came late. As we have seen, in 720 the Daylamites were mentioned as paradigmatic infidels on a level with the Turks, and in Ṭabaristān the rebels of 783 massacred Muslims when revolting against the overlordship of the caliph. In the reign of al-Rashīd the rulers of Ṭabaristān were still not allowing any Muslim to be buried in the territories they ruled. It was not till Māzyār was a refugee at the court of the caliph in 816–17 that he had the grace to convert to Islam. The help he received in reward enabled him to conquer the entire highland part of Ṭabaristān, where he dutifully built mosques and, less dutifully, set about expanding his rule into the lowlands. It was his disrespect for the Ṭāhirids that was his undoing, leading to his failed rebellion in 839 and a Ṭāhirid conquest; but it did not help that his enemies accused him of reverting to Zoroastrianism, and he did indeed have Zoroastrian supporters. The other of the two kingdoms of the eastern highlands, that of the Bāwandids, survived the cataclysm by cooperating with the Ṭāhirids, and in 842 its ruler converted to Islam just as Māzyār had done. Meanwhile, the western half of the Caspian region was still something of a world apart, despite Arab attacks on it. It was there that the lowlands of Gīlān produced an adventurer who ruled much of Iran in the 930s, and as we will see, he was conspicuously hostile to Islam. When conversion did come to the western part of the Caspian region, it owed a lot to missionary activity. In particular, ʿAlids belonging to the politically activist Zaydī Shīʿite sect could escape their enemies in the plains by taking refuge in the mountains, and once there they would set about converting the pagan mountaineers. This was a significant development of the second half of the ninth century, not least because the ʿAlids did something Christian missionaries do not usually do: they used their followings to establish miniature states. Even then it was not until the tenth century that the western mountaineers began to play a prominent role in the affairs of the plains.

Moving east from the Caspian region we soon find ourselves in Khurāsān. The term is geographically vague. Etymologically it simply means "sunrise" or "east," and historically it has been used for a territory of greatly varying extent. This territory does, however, have a stable core, made up of two components. The first lies within the modern borders of Iran. Although the Elburz chain peters out in the east, the baton is soon picked up by a less formidable set of mountain ranges running from northwest to southeast in the direction of the highlands of what is now Afghanistan. These mountains attract some rainfall, the direct or indirect use of which makes possible significant agriculture. In our period the major city of this western part of Khurāsān was Nīshāpūr. The other core component, lying beyond the current Iranian frontier, is an expanse of steppe and desert to the east of the mountains; today it is part of Turkmenistan. Here agriculture depends mainly on rivers. Some of their water is contributed by the same mountains, but the greater part of it comes from the highlands of Afghanistan. In this region of Khurāsān the major city was Marw on the river Murghāb, with a cluster of villages around it. Marw had been the provincial capital in Sasanian times, and it retained this role under the Arabs, who conquered Khurāsān in the early 650s. What lay behind much of the subsequent prominence of Khurāsān and accounts for the frequency of our references to it was its military importance in protecting Iran from the incursions of steppe nomads, who in this period were Turks. This role required settling large numbers of Arab tribesmen in Khurāsān—far more than in western Iran. In 714–15, if we can trust the figures we are given, there were the best part of fifty thousand Arab soldiers there. Hence the centrality of Khurāsān to the ʿAbbāsid revolution, the key role of the Khurāsānī supporters of the new dynasty in the first decades of its rule, and the part played by the province in the fourth civil war. These developments in turn led to the early emergence of a semiautonomous regional dynasty. There is no need for us to return to these themes here or to review the record of rebellions in this tumultuous province. What is worth adding is that a ninth-century Balkhī scholar tells us that in his day most of the population in the Khurāsānī countryside was already Muslim, in contrast to the Iraqi countryside a century earlier.

From Khurāsān we turn south toward the shore of the Indian Ocean, keeping largely within what is now the eastern border of Iran. Most of what lies between western Khurāsān and the Indian Ocean is desert, but there are three exceptions we should pause for on the way. The first is Quhistān, a highland area surrounded on all sides by salt desert; thanks to its mountains some cultivation is possible in places. Its isolation made it a region where followers of unorthodox creeds could find refuge—first the Zoroastrians and later, as we will see, the Ismāʿīlīs. Farther to the south we come to Sīstān, a depression now shared with Afghanistan that would be desert but for an unreliable river. The Arabs conquered it in the mid-seventh century, and some of them settled there, bringing with them, as they often did, their familiar tribal feuds. The caliphs and later the Ṭāhirids appointed governors who tried to administer Sīstān from its main town, Zarang, the last such governor being expelled in 854. Khārijites were active in the region from the late seventh century, whether fighting non-Khārijites or each other. Their most successful leader held power in the early ninth century and wrote a cheeky letter to al-Rashīd. But Sīstān, though less isolated than Quhistān, was not usually a significant player in the larger history of Iran. The exception was the career of Yaʿqūb the Coppersmith in the second half of the ninth century. This upstart craftsman and leader of an anti-Khārijite vigilante movement succeeded in creating an empire that briefly embraced much of Iran and threatened the caliph in Iraq. South of Sīstān lies Makrān, now better known as Balūchistān, straddling the border between Iran and Pakistan. This was an arid region in which agricultural areas were few and far between, the population was thin and tribal, and not much happened on the coast. It, too, was Khārijite country. We will encounter it only as a bad option for those seeking a route by which to invade or leave India.

To complete our circuit of Iran we now move northwest into Kirmān, a region of transition from the deserts of Makrān to the highlands of Fārs. Like Fārs, Kirmān has deserts to the north and south—namely, a part of the desert that occupies the interior of the Iranian triangle to the north and the barren coastal plain to the south. But here too the territory in between was of some value. Its main city in our period was Sīrjān in the middle of the mountains, not the town near the great desert that later came to be known as the city of Kirmān. Though the region was reckoned to be rich, its arable land was scattered, and the terrain was difficult and fragmented. Its history mixed provincial governors, Khārijites, and untamed Iranian tribes. Only from the tenth century would there be occasional dynasties that set up in the region, though originating elsewhere. For a native son to rise to power we have to wait even longer, perhaps until the eighteenth century, when we will encounter a charcoal seller who briefly made himself master of the city of Kirmān.

The eastern fringe

We are now left with the eastern fringe of the Muslim world of our period, a set of territories to the northeast, east, and southeast of the eastern frontier of modern Iran. Two of these regions are fairly large, and at the same time relatively straightforward in geographical and historical terms: Transoxania in the northeast and Sindh in the southeast. Located roughly between them was a medley of smaller territories where neither the geography nor the history was simple. We will start with Transoxania, then move south through the smaller territories, and end up in Sindh.

Transoxania means what it says: it is the land on the far side of the Oxus, the major river rising in the mountains of Central Asia and discharging into the southern end of the Aral Sea. The other borders of Transoxania were less sharply defined, but it certainly did not reach beyond the Jaxartes to the northeast, and to the northwest the delta of the Oxus was a distinct region, Khwārazm. The major cities of Transoxania were Bukhārā and Samarqand, both located on the Zarafshān, a river between the Oxus and the Jaxartes that disappears into the desert downstream of Bukhārā. The region had not been part of the Sasanian Empire, but it had been subject to marked Persian influence; for example, Sasanian coins provided the prototype for those of Bukhārā. Moreover, it seems that Persian must already have been in use in the city before the arrival of the Arabs, since it is related that following the conquest people were using the language to recite the Qur'ān in the vernacular. The indigenous language of the region was nevertheless Sogdian, an Eastern Iranian tongue very different from Persian. A dialect of it is still spoken by a few thousand people in the mountains where the Zarafshān rises. Politically Transoxania was divided among numerous Sogdian principalities. From the point of view of a prospective conqueror this was mixed news. On the one hand, no one Sogdian ruler would be really formidable—there was no counterpart here to the Byzantine emperor—and any alliance of Sogdian rulers against the invader was liable to fragment. But on the other hand, such rulers, once conquered, could not be relied on to stay conquered, and they could seek support from the Turks or the Chinese. This made the definitive conquest of Transoxania an elusive goal. It is true enough that the Arabs conquered Transoxania in 705–14, built mosques, and, it is said, paid the people of Bukhārā two dirhams each to show up at the congregational prayers held on Fridays, one of the most significant public rituals of Islam. But in a rebellion in 728 they lost all but two cities, with their losses including Bukhārā, and had to put effort into making up the lost ground. Muslim rule became stronger in the early ʿAbbāsid period once the Turks and Chinese were no longer a serious threat; yet there were still native rulers, even one in Bukhārā in the 770s. And as we have seen, the history of Transoxania in the decades that followed abounded in rebellions. The region was, however, rich enough in resources and far enough away from the center to support the emergence of a virtually independent Transoxanian dynasty over the course of the ninth century. This was the Sāmānids, a local family that had made itself useful to the caliph and whose members were consequently appointed to provincial governorships.

We come now to the smaller territories of the eastern fringe, located in or close to what is now western Afghanistan. Here the terrain is fragmented and the information we have about its history in our period is more fragmentary still. To frame our discussion it is worth looking back at a part of Iran whose geography is simpler and history better known—namely, the Caspian region south of the coastal plain. There we had three distinct zones: the plains south of the Elburz, where cities such as Rayy lay wide open to the prevailing states of the lowlands; the mountains of the western Elburz, which were beyond the reach of such powers; and the mountains of the eastern Elburz, which were somewhere in between. With that tripartite schema in mind let us turn to the eastern fringe. A counterpart of Rayy would be Balkh. Though it took time, by the late Umayyad period the Arabs had a firm grip on the city and used it as a military base. In the course of the ʿAbbāsid revolution it was in dispute between Umayyad and ʿAbbāsid forces, with the local princes playing only a secondary role as allies on the Umayyad side. Counterparts of the western Elburz would be regions deep in the mountains such as Shughnān and Wakhān to the east of Badakhshān, or Ghūr in what is now northwestern Afghanistan. But most of the territories we are concerned with here would be somewhere in between, variations on what we saw in the eastern Elburz. Here Arab raids were widespread, but conquests, especially lasting ones, were less common. Military pressure could elicit tribute, but the willingness to pay it might not last. In some parts governors were installed by the ʿAbbāsids or their regional successors, but we tend to hear more about the continued existence of native dynasties. A good many of these lasted into ʿAbbāsid times; that of Khwārazm endured until 995. Most of these dynasties would convert to Islam sooner or later, often later. One dynasty, the Zunbīls of what is now southwestern Afghanistan, did not convert at all and did more than any other to check the advance of the Arabs and their religion until its reign was ended by Yaʿqūb the Coppersmith. Overall, it is clear that the long-term trend was toward the extension of Muslim power and the spread of Islam, but the process was uneven, and as of the middle of the ninth century there was still a long way to go.

Finally we come to Sindh. The Arabs, as we saw, conquered it in the early eighth century. They entered through Makrān and extended their rule to the northeast to include Multān in the Punjab. Unlike most of India, this territory was of a kind already familiar to them. It belonged to the arid lowlands of northwestern India, a desert like those of Egypt and Iraq that owed its agricultural potential to its rivers, in this case the Indus and—in the Punjab—its tributaries. The very names of these regions reflect the centrality of rivers to human habitation. The Sanskrit "Sindhu" is the original form behind our "Indus," and it names both the region and the river, while "Punjab" is the Persian for "five rivers," referring to the five tributaries of the Indus. The number of Arabs settling in this region must have been very small in comparison to the native population, and it is in line with this that we hear of no dramatic expansion of their territory after the initial conquest; but neither did they suffer any dramatic loss to hostile Indian states or rebellious subjects. Instead, the Arabs of Sindh seem to have felt secure enough to occupy themselves with their familiar factional conflict between Northerners and Southerners. How they related to the non-Muslim population is a question we will take up in a later chapter, but it is worth noting that here, too, there seems to have been some persistence of native rulers under Muslim overlordship. The central government continued to dispatch governors to administer Sindh into the 830s, and as in Tunisia the Muhallabids were prominent as governors for the ʿAbbāsids. Indeed, here too they looked like obvious candidates to found a more or less independent dynasty in the period when ʿAbbāsid power was on the wane. But this did not happen, nor did any counterpart of the Aghlabids emerge in Sindh. Instead the province seems to have disintegrated into a number of principalities under Arab rulers, not to mention native rulers and an Ismāʿīlī polity in Multān to which we will return in a later chapter. With this we end our survey of the provinces of the Caliphate, some 4,500 miles from where we started.

The formation of Islamic civilization

The emergence of a civilization is a rare event. In the time of Muḥammad there were only three core cases in the Old World: those of the Chinese, the Indians, and the Greeks. They had not, of course, been the first to appear. Two earlier civilizations had emerged in the Ancient Near East at the dawn of history, one among the Egyptians and the other among the Sumerians. But by now both were long extinct—though the last distant offshoot of Ancient Near Eastern civilization, the culture of pre-Islamic southwestern Arabia, had only recently disintegrated. Even if we factor in these extinct civilizations, we are left with a total of no more than five. Yet if pioneering a civilization was rare, adopting one already in existence was common. Thus the civilization of northern China spread to the peoples of southern China, Vietnam, Korea, and Japan; the civilization of northern India reached the peoples of southern India, Central Asia, Tibet, and Southeast Asia; and the civilization of the Greeks passed to the Romans and through them to the Germanic peoples and others. Gradually it came to be the case that almost any people with the material basis to support a civilization would adopt one or another of those on offer. The process could be accelerated when those without a civilization were conquered by those who had one, as in the case of the Koreans in relation to the Chinese. But often those who adopted a civilization did so of their own free will, as was the case with the Romans—indeed it was they who were to conquer the Greeks. Moreover, the adoption of a foreign civilization did not have to be slavish, particularly for those not subject to conquest. They had considerable latitude in choosing the terms on which they joined. Thus the Romans adopted much of the high culture of the Greeks but transposed it into their own language, Latin. And they were selective: they adopted Greek philosophy but did not feel obliged to replace Roman law with some form of Greek law. Still less did they come to regard themselves as Greeks.

A particularly relevant case for us is the Germanic conquest of the Western Roman Empire in late antiquity. Here peoples who lacked a civilization came to dominate people who had one. As we have seen, the Gothic ruler Athaulf at first aspired to blot out the Roman name and replace Romania with Gothia, but in the light of long and bitter experience and the wise counsels of his Roman wife, this reconstructed barbarian ruler came to see his role as restoring the renown of the Roman name through the power of the Goths. Yet the cultural capitulation of the Germanic peoples to Romania was by no means unconditional. Like the Romans they preserved their ethnic legal heritages, albeit mostly in Latin. What they did not do was create a new Germanic civilization. We might accordingly have expected the Arabs to take a similar course. The pre-Islamic Arabs, like the early Goths, were a people unburdened by a civilization, living in an environment too poor to support one. As we saw, the Prophet is said to have remarked, though with considerable exaggeration, "We are an illiterate people; we neither write nor count." Then, in the seventh century, they conquered the very lands that had been civilized for longest in the history of the world. So it does not seem extravagant to suppose that they would now adopt the civilization of their subjects.

To a significant degree that is just what the Arabs did. Take the decision to institute the Dīwān. We are told that during the consultation that led to it, one of those present recalled seeing such a system in operation in Syria and recommended that the Muslims adopt it. A related borrowing was the idea of an era. Our sources tell us that in pre-Islamic times the Arabs would count the years from some fairly recent event for a while, then switch to some new event as memory of the earlier one faded. This practice was no longer convenient for a state that operated a Dīwān system. One account has a man come to ʿUmar and tell him, "You should date things." ʿUmar asked him what he meant and received the reply "It's something the non-Arabs do—they write 'month this of year that.'" ʿUmar responded, "That sounds good. Do it."[59] So far, as with the Dīwān, this was a straightforward case of the adoption of a practice from a more advanced society. But now a question arose: What year was the era to start from? The simplest course would have been to adopt the Seleucid era, which was in wide use at the time, but our account makes no mention of this option. Instead, those present made various suggestions—the year when Muḥammad was called to be a prophet, the year of his Hijra from Mecca to Medina, or the year of his death. They settled on the Hijra, which is why the Muslim calendar is known as the Hijrī calendar and starts in 622. Here, then, we see the freedom the Arabs enjoyed in choosing the terms of adoption. They borrowed a foreign practice but gave it a distinctively Muslim stamp. A third case concerns nothing less than the text of the Qurʾān. We are told that in the time of ʿUthmān disputes arose over its wording. ʿUthmān wisely appointed a committee to look into the matter, and the result was a more or less standard text of the Qurʾān in the form of a codex—or as we would say, a book. So far as we know, there had been no book written in Arabic prior to the Qurʾān; books were a feature of the cultures prevailing outside Arabia.

The cases just discussed are known to us primarily through later literary sources, but we can also see the processes of adoption and appropriation at work if we return to the hard evidence of contemporary coins. In the Old World west of China there was a standard notion of what a coin should look like: a disk of metal with the ruler's head on one side and some religious symbol on the other. In the early decades of Muslim rule this pattern continued. One coin known from this period is so Persian in style that on the evidence of its obverse we would identify it as a

59. ʿAbd al-Malik ibn Ḥabīb, *Kitāb al-taʾrīkh*, Madrid 1991, 104 no. 291.

coin of the Sasanian emperor Khusraw II (ruled 591–628). The image is his, and he is named in the Middle Persian inscription. The image on the reverse continues the illusion, showing a Zoroastrian fire temple with attendants on either side. Only the Middle Persian inscription on the reverse gives the game away: "Year one of Yazīt," presumably Yazīd I (ruled 680–83).[60] Even here, the practice of dating by regnal years was a Sasanian one. In short, if we went by this coin it would look as if Yazīd were engaged in restoring the renown of the Persian name through the power of the Arabs. Some other coins minted in former Sasanian lands in the early decades of Arab rule have brief Arabic inscriptions in the margins, but the general appearance of these coins is still that of Sasanian times. Then, as we have seen, starting in 696 we have ʿAbd al-Malik's reform coinage. His coins still took the familiar form of metal disks, but everything else was breathtakingly different. He did not replace the head of the Persian king with his own, or the Zoroastrian symbol with an Islamic one. Instead, in line with the marked streak of hostility to images that was already apparent in Islam, he substituted Arabic inscriptions for the head and the symbol. Thus on the silver coinage one inscription says where and when the coin was minted, but the rest of its surface is made over to Qurʾānic articulations of God's message. One affirms that "there is no god but God, alone, without companion." Another brings in Muḥammad: "Muḥammad is the messenger of God; He sent him with the guidance and the religion of truth, that He may uplift it above every religion, though the unbelievers be averse."[61] In short, where the coin of Yazīd I suggests that the Arabs were perpetuating an old world, the reform coinage announces an almost complete break with it. Here, then, we catch a rare glimpse of a new civilization in formation.

As so often, reality mostly fell somewhere in between. Here we can make a rough and ready distinction. In terms of the material foundations of civilization very little had changed: the basics of agriculture, crafts, cities, ships, and the like were no different, and coins retained their familiar shape. But in terms of worldview the change was dramatic. By the ninth century, or even earlier, a whole new order of thought and expression had come into being in line with ʿAbd al-Malik's reform coinage, persuasive to its inhabitants in both its general character and its myriad details. In short, it was a world they could live in and take for granted. How are we to explain the emergence of such a new world? Let us start with two preconditions for this outcome, the spread of Arabic and that of Islam. Though both these developments are crucial, for lack of adequate data they are known to us only in outline.

60. M. I. Mochiri, "A Sasanian-type coin of Yazīd b. Muʿāwiya," *Journal of the Royal Asiatic Society*, 1982, 137–38.

61. See S. Heidemann, "Numismatics," in *The new Cambridge history of Islam*, 1:656 and plate 16.13.

The spread of Arabic

A conquest brings together two populations that have previously lived apart, with the result that they now start to rub off on each other. One aspect of this potentially unstable situation is inevitably linguistic. In general, the more the two populations interact, the sooner they are likely to end up speaking the same language—but which one? In the case of the Roman conquest of Gaul it was the Latin of the conquerors that prevailed, not the Gaulish of the natives, whereas in the case of the Norman conquest of England it was the English of the natives that won out, not the French of the conquerors. In our case Arabic had some obvious advantages in the postconquest competition. An eighth-century Shīʿite polemist who was doubtless writing in Iraq wished to advance an argument for the superiority of the family of the Prophet, one that not everyone might be about to accept. So he paved the way by pointing to cases of superiority that no one would think of denying. One was the superiority of the language of the Arabs to other languages; no non-Arab, he tells us, converts to Islam without abandoning the language of his own people and speaking that of the Arabs. He makes it clear that he sees the superiority of Arabic as God-given, but in the context of eighth-century Iraq we can easily understand it in more human terms. As the language of the conquerors, Arabic was the language of power and prestige, and sooner or later it became the language of opportunity for anyone aspiring to political, military, bureaucratic, cultural, or commercial success. And yet at first it was only the language of a small minority in comparison to the masses speaking Persian, Aramaic, Coptic, and the like.

How this linguistic competition played out varied greatly in geographical terms. In the southern Middle East—the Fertile Crescent and Egypt—the spread of Arabic seems to have been far-reaching already in the early centuries, though we know for a fact that it was not universal. A Jewish scholar in Iraq who died in 1038 remarks that "still in all the smaller towns everyone is using Aramaic and Chaldaic, both Jews and Gentiles."[62] In the case of Egypt the earliest testimonies to the loss of Coptic seem to come from the eleventh century, but it is suggestive that Coptic documents almost disappear after 800. In Iran, by contrast, Persian and related vernaculars did not give way in everyday life, even in the cities. Arabic made more inroads in Khurāsān than it did in western Iran—a disparity readily explained by the greater density of Arab settlement in the northeast—but even there the sources give us glimpses of the troops that brought the ʿAbbāsids to power speaking to each other in Persian. That outcome is likely connected with the fact that in Khurāsān the Arabs tended to settle in the villages. Meanwhile in North Africa

62. Quoted in J. Blau, *The emergence and linguistic background of Judaeo-Arabic*, Jerusalem 1981, 20 note 1.

Arabic seems to have made no serious headway against Berber outside the cities until the coming of the Arab nomads in the eleventh century. This, in turn, may suggest an explanation for the contrast between Iran and the southern Middle East: sooner or later the Fertile Crescent and Egypt attracted an influx of Arab nomads and their livestock, whereas for climatic reasons the Iranian plateau was harder for them to adapt to. As ʿUmar is said to have observed, "Arab tribesmen flourish only in regions where their camels and sheep do well."[63] Thus to the extent that the Arab armies of conquest settled in garrison cities, with only a light presence in the countryside, we can see Arab armies and Arab nomads in the southern Middle East as complementary. Without the nomads the Arabs might have done no better than the Greeks following the Macedonian conquest of the Middle East in the fourth century BC, disproportionately implanting their language in the cities of Egypt and the Fertile Crescent rather than in the countryside. But the qualification "to the extent" matters here. There was no real garrison city in Syria, where the Arabs mostly settled in the existing urban centers, and in Egypt there was a custom whereby each spring the troops of the Jund would go out from Fusṭāṭ into the countryside, which led some of them to settle there.

What was uniform across the entire Muslim world of the time was that Arabic became the standard written language, eventually taking on a canonical form—what we call classical Arabic—that was to match Sanskrit and Attic Greek in its standards of linguistic purism. By the tenth century it was common even for Jews and Christians to write in Arabic among themselves. For example, the Jewish scholar Saʿadya Gaon (d. 942) wrote extensively in Arabic and translated the Pentateuch into that language, while an earlier Jewish author may have written several works in Arabic a century before. Earlier still a Christian churchman who served as bishop of Ḥarrān and died around 820 was writing some of his works in Arabic, and among the Christians of Palestine the phenomenon goes back to the late eighth century. In short, both spoken and written Arabic had become the property of society at large, including large numbers of non-Muslims. It had not been relegated to the position of a decaying linguistic heritage surviving only among the descendants of the conquerors, as Manchu had among the ruling ethnic group of late imperial China. Sooner or later, this spread of Arabic posed an awkward question: If you were descended from non-Arab ancestors but Arabic was your mother tongue, did you count as an Arab? From the viewpoint of Arabs who took pride in their tribal genealogies the answer could only be negative, but there was also a pious view that whoever spoke Arabic was an Arab, and this was ascribed to the Prophet. Be that as it may, in the early spread of Arabic we have one precondition for the emergence of Islamic civilization.

63. Ṭabarī, *History*, 13:65; cf. 63.

The spread of Islam

The other crucial phenomenon was the spread of Islam.[64] What we can take for granted with only marginal qualification is the acceptance of Islam among the great majority of the Arabs themselves. For many of them this could have been a hazy acceptance, particularly for those whose conversion was collective and above all for those who continued to nomadize in the deserts of Arabia. But it is striking that we have no unambiguous evidence for the survival of Arab paganism into the first decades of Islam. At the same time there was grudging acceptance of the fact that some Arab tribesmen who had been Christians before the rise of Islam were reluctant to part with their faith, though one tribal chief was told by the caliph Walīd I (ruled 705–15) that his adoration of the cross was a disgrace for all Arabs. But overwhelmingly the converts of Umayyad and ʿAbbāsid times were non-Arabs. Here Islam and Arabic did, of course, have a tendency to go together, as in the statement of the Shīʿite polemist that any non-Arab who had converted to Islam would now speak Arabic. But Arabic could spread ahead of conversion, as with our Jewish and Christian authors, and Islam could spread ahead of Arabic, as with the Bukhāran converts who for lack of knowledge of the language were permitted to recite the Qurʾān in Persian. In what follows our concern is solely with the early spread of Islam among non-Arabs.

At least three things must have worked in favor of this spread. One was the phenomenal military success of the Muslims, which strongly suggested that God was on their side. Of course the Christian clergy vigorously denied this, maintaining that God was merely using the Muslims to punish the Christians for their sins, but among the laity this could have sounded like special pleading on the part of a group whose material interests were at stake. A second factor was the ease of conversion. Despite the partiality of Islam for Arab ethnicity, the bottom line was that non-Arabs could become Muslims just as Arabs could. The Prophet, after all, had had a Persian companion, not to mention Greek and Ethiopian ones. A third factor was the fiscal incentive. Converts had a right—not always honored—to exemption from the burden of the poll tax payable by tolerated non-Muslims. The amounts involved were not trivial: soon after the conquest of Egypt a local administrator expressed his fear that the new tax would cause the population to flee. But what did the process of conversion actually look like in this early period? Our starting point is that whether or not they lived in garrison cities, the Arabs of the armies of conquest were surrounded by large numbers of non-Arabs. Many of these people were there involuntarily, since in the course of their conquests the Arabs continued the practice of their ancestors on a much larger scale, enslaving large

64. On conversion to Islam in this period see J. Tannous, *The making of the medieval Middle East*, Princeton 2018.

numbers of captives—male and female—and thereby prizing them loose from their families and communities. Unless used as a mass labor force in such projects as infrastructural investment or agricultural development in Arabia, these captives would be the personal slaves of their Arab masters and mistresses until such time as they might be manumitted, after which they would remain tied to them as their clients. In this situation it could almost be taken for granted that most such slaves would convert to the religion of their owners. Other non-Arabs sought to make a living by voluntarily hanging around Arabs, and in this context they were more than likely to engage in strategic conversion. The way to do that was to seek out an Arab patron and convert at his hands, thereby becoming his client. As a result, although conversion could occur in any context where Arabs and non-Arabs interacted, this particular locus of conversion was unusually salient in the decades following the conquests. The result was that any large concentration of Arabs in the conquered territories—as in Kūfa or Baṣra—was a vortex sucking in non-Arabs and converting them to Islam. Such converts were often known as Mawālī. This curiously ambiguous term could mean not just "clients" but also "patrons" or "kinsfolk," and it was not always limited to Muslims, but the rule of thumb is that Mawālī are non-Arab Muslims.

The inequality of the relationship between Arabs and Mawālī generated strong social tensions in early Muslim society. Having put considerable effort into conquering the world, the Arabs were naturally unenthusiastic about sharing their gains with others. More precisely, they tended to be more willing to share the next world than this one. A tradition spoke of the Mawālī as people dragged to Paradise in chains—a favor for which the Arabs thought the Mawālī should have been more grateful than they apparently were. But in this world the Arabs discriminated against the Mawālī and denied them the respect they showed to each other. We are told that one did not walk side by side with Mawālī or allow them to be at the head of a procession. If present at a meal, they stood while Arabs sat. If for some reason one of them was permitted to eat, he would be seated in a place that made it clear that he was not an Arab. This was not to deny that they were useful people for their Arab patrons; indeed, they were indispensable. As one Arab put it, "They sweep our roads, sew our boots, and weave our clothes."[65] They also served in less menial roles. They might appear in administrative capacities as fiscal agents and even governors. They might serve as secretaries for their patrons. They figured prominently in cultural roles, as tutors of the children of the elite, as scholars in a variety of disciplines, and as musicians. Perhaps most strikingly, Umayyad caliphs entrusted their lives to them. The chief of the caliph's bodyguard, and so presumably the men he commanded, would be recruited from the Mawālī; obviously

65. Ibn ʿAbd Rabbih, translated in B. Lewis, *Islam from the Prophet Muhammad to the capture of Constantinople*, New York 1987, 2:205.

the caliphs felt that these ethnic strangers were less likely to betray them than their fellow Arabs were. All this, in turn, could provoke Arab resentment of upstart Mawālī. Nor was this all. So far we have been thinking primarily of male Mawālī, but among those enslaved in warfare were large numbers of women. Thanks to their role as concubines, many of these women came to occupy a much more intimate position within the conquest society than their male counterparts did. The anxiety this gave rise to among conservative Arabs finds expression in a saying ascribed, like so many other forthright statements, to ʿUmar: "The Arabs will be lost when the sons of the daughters of Persia come of age."[66] In other words, the Arabs might have won on the battlefield, but the cost of their success was that Arab society was now being corrupted in the most intimate of settings. For example, it was said that Arabic grammar had to be invented because the Arab sons of Persian concubines couldn't speak the language properly.

A couple of examples will convey a sense of how the Arabs felt about what to them could appear as the invasion of their space by the foreigners they ruled. We are told of Sufyān al-Thawrī (d. 778), a distinguished Arab scholar, that his countenance would change when he saw Nabateans writing away in class. The Nabateans in this context were the native Aramaic-speaking population of Iraq, who were held in low esteem; the most provocative thing you could say to your wife was that you had discovered that her mother was a Nabatean. When queried about his reaction to the presence of Nabatean students, Sufyān's comment was somber: "Scholarship used to be in the hands of the Arabs and the cream of society. When they lose it and these people take it up the faith becomes corrupted."[67] In a similar vein, the alarming prominence of Mawālī in the ranks of the religious scholars as early as ʿAbd al-Malik's day is dramatized—perhaps overdramatized—in a dialogue that is said to have taken place between him and the well-known scholar Zuhrī (d. 742). The caliph asks Zuhrī to name the leading scholar in each of a succession of provinces, and each time he inquires whether the scholar is an Arab or one of the Mawālī. In this fashion they cover Mecca, the Yemen, Egypt, Syria, the Jazīra, Khurāsān, and Baṣra, and in each case Zuhrī informs the dismayed caliph that the leading scholar is one of the Mawālī. Finally ʿAbd al-Malik asks about Kūfa, and this time, to his relief, the answer is an Arab. Yet overall the picture is grim; as he goes on to remark, "The Mawālī are going to lord it over the Arabs to the point that they will address them from the pulpits, with the Arabs down below them." Zuhrī, himself an Arab, responds to the caliph, "Commander of the Faithful, it's all a matter of religion. Whoever secures it comes out on top, and whoever neglects it drops out."[68]

66. Ibn Abī Shayba, *Muṣannaf*, ed. K. Y. al-Ḥūt, Beirut 1989, 7:506 no. 37,591.
67. Ṭurṭūshī, *al-Ḥawādith wa'l-bidaʿ*, Beirut 1990, 178 no. 126.
68. Abū Ḥayyān al-Tawḥīdī, *al-Baṣā'ir wa'l-dhakhā'ir*, Beirut 1988, 8:85 no. 288.

This early spread of Islam is a second precondition for the emergence of Islamic civilization. Things would have been very different had Islam been the religion of the Arabs in the way that Arianism was the religion of the Visigoths in Spain—that is to say, a religious persuasion confined to the ruling ethnic group and eventually abandoned by it. The mere fact that large-scale conversion of non-Arabs to Islam began early and continued apace is enough to establish the contrast. Eventually, of course, people began to convert in huge numbers where they were, in their towns and villages and within their families and communities; the Egyptian documentary record gives us occasional glimpses of this. There can be little doubt that in the long run most of those who converted to Islam in the lands ruled by the caliphs did so in this way, and in the countryside the process may well have been helped by the presence of Arab nomads. But initially, as we have seen, conversion took place through a process whereby non-Arabs left their abodes, whether voluntarily or otherwise, and went to live with the Arabs, often in their garrison cities. As we will see, the initial salience of this form of conversion may in itself have been a precondition for the formation of a new civilization.

The Arab heritage

As already mentioned, the Qur'ān is to the best of our knowledge the first book ever written in Arabic. So in 600 there would have been none. It would be satisfying to be able draw a graph showing the subsequent rise in the number of Arabic books, but we lack the data to do that. What we can do is consult a catalog prepared by Ibn al-Nadīm, a Shīʿite bookseller in Baghdad, in 987–88, a date by which Arabic already had a long track record as a full-fledged literary language. Ibn al-Nadīm set out to list the books of all nations that existed in the Arabic language and script, whether their authors were Arabs or not, but blank spaces in one of the manuscripts suggest that he hoped to add more titles than he had to hand. As we might expect, he knew Ibn Isḥāq's work on the life of the Prophet, yet it seems that the ninth-century Egyptian recension in which we possess it today had not come his way, and we can easily find other gaps in his coverage; for example, he has no works written in Muslim Spain, despite the fact that by his time several hundred had been composed there. So we cannot take his listing of Arabic books as comprehensive, let alone as an inventory of the whole culture, written and oral. But that the total number of works covered in his catalog is some eight thousand is nevertheless significant as a minimum. What, then, could you read about if you had access to all these works, only a fraction of which survive today? Ibn al-Nadīm's book is a subject catalog, with the books distributed between ten fields and thirty-two subfields. But for our purposes it will be enough to divide them into three major categories.

The first is works preserving the Arab heritage, particularly that of pre-Islamic Arabia. We have already met a book of this kind composed by a ninth-century author, Ibn Ḥabīb, from whom we took an account of the events of the Third Fijār. He himself was one of the Mawālī, and a tutor. Ibn al-Nadīm lists more than thirty works by Ibn Ḥabīb, many of which may have been quite short. But one, devoted to tribes and their battles, was enormous—Ibn al-Nadīm had seen only part of it, but he estimated that the complete work must have run to more than eight thousand leaves. Another major field in which Ibn Ḥabīb had several works was genealogy—which of course meant the genealogy of the Arab tribes. He was also a transmitter of a large genealogical work by one of his teachers, a work that survives to this day. A minor field to which he contributed was the study of an Arabian practice that used the risings and settings of stars to forecast the weather and mark the passage of time. The work in question does not survive, but we have one on the same subject by Ibn Qutayba, whom we met in the role of a religious populist. A striking feature of Ibn Qutayba's presentation of the topic is that he starts by asserting the superiority of this Arab folk tradition to the sciences of the non-Arabs. What the Arabs know is "knowledge that is plain to sight, true when put to the test, and useful to the traveler by land and sea,"[69] in contrast to the abstruse philosophy and mathematics of the non-Arabs.

Last but far from least, Ibn Ḥabīb was very active in the field of Arabic poetry and poets. For Arabs poetry, like genealogy, was an aspect of their heritage in which they took enormous pride. Ibn Qutayba, in a book on the excellence of the Arabs, declares them to be unrivaled in their poetry; it is the source of their learning, "the basis of their wisdom, the archive of their history, and the repository of their battle lore."[70] Another ninth-century authority avers that "There is no Arab who is unable to compose poetry, which is a natural trait of theirs, whether they make little or much of it."[71] Or more vulgarly, as a Bedouin is said to have expressed it to a Persian poet, "Poetry belongs to the Arabs; every one of you who composes poetry does it only because one of us has mounted his mother!" Poetry was indeed highly developed in pre-Islamic Arabia, partly because it did not depend on the material infrastructure of urban civilization, but also because it played a central role in everyday Arabian life, a role that has no counterpart in modern Western culture. Thus in the context of Muḥammad's raid on the Banū 'l-Muṣṭaliq we saw how a nefarious Meccan, absconding with blood money after killing the slayer of his brother, congratulated himself in verse. As on this occasion, poetic words were often fighting words, vicious attacks "burning like a mark made with

69. Quoted in Gutas, *Greek thought, Arabic culture*, 165.

70. Ibn Qutaybah, *The excellence of the Arabs*, New York 2017, 151.

71. For this and the quotation that follows see G. J. van Gelder, "*Mawālī* and Arabic poetry," in M. Bernards and J. Nawas (eds.), *Patronate and patronage in early and classical Islam*, Leiden 2005, 356.

hot coal"[72] that invited violent retaliation in the course of intertribal conflicts. The other side of this coin is manifest in the remark of a ninth-century scholar who was seeking to explain the scarcity of poets in pre-Islamic Ṭā'if, where the level of internal conflict was low: "Poetry abounded only through the wars that took place between tribes."[73] In this view a civil society was no place for a poet.

All told, the Muslim elite of the early centuries consumed a vast amount of literature on the genealogies, doings, sayings, and poetry of the pagan Arabs. But it should be understood that reading books of this kind was not expected to get anyone to heaven. Because Islam had originated in Arabia, any extended discussion of the Arab heritage was naturally bound to touch on religious matters from time to time. Yet this literature was overwhelmingly focused on the concerns of this world, not those of the next. Indeed there was a vein of pietism that put an outright condemnation of poetry in the mouth of the Prophet: "It is better for a man that his body be full of pus than that it be full of poems!"[74] Muḥammad, however, was also adduced as speaking and acting in a more accommodating vein, and in any case people liked poetry too much to pass up the temptation. One pious poet—incidentally a black slave—found an elegant compromise: he would recite poetry, but never on Fridays.

An anecdote that aptly dramatizes the Arab addiction to poetry involves the attitude of the Azāriqa, who were Khārijite extremists in their violence and their piety alike. Muhallab ibn Abī Ṣufra was campaigning against them in Fārs when one evening there was a commotion in his camp. It turned out to be a heated argument among his men about who was the better poet, Jarīr or Farazdaq; these were two Baṣran poets of the day who belonged to rival tribal groups and could cause riots in the city by tossing poetic grenades at each other. The soldiers wanted Muhallab to arbitrate their dispute. But Muhallab was far too sensible to fall for this, knowing well that whichever poet he pronounced against would take his revenge by shredding him in his next poem. He did nevertheless make a practical suggestion to his men: ask the Azāriqa. These sectarians, he pointed out, were indifferent to the poetic insults of Jarīr and Farazdaq, but at the same time they were Arabs who knew about poetry and would give an honest answer. The next day the battle lines were drawn up and one of the Azāriqa, a certain ʿUbayda ibn Hilāl, came out and challenged any of Muhallab's men with the stomach for it to single combat. One soldier went out to him, but instead of fighting him to the death he asked politely if ʿUbayda would answer a question. ʿUbayda said he would respond if he knew the answer. The soldier then put the question to him: "Is Jarīr the better poet or Farazdaq?" The response expressed the full puritanical piety of

72. Quoted in I. Goldziher, *Muslim studies*, London 1967–71, 1:50.
73. Ibn Sallām, *Ṭabaqāt fuḥūl al-shuʿarā'*, Cairo 1952, 217.
74. Quoted in Goldziher, *Muslim studies*, 1:56.

the Azāriqa: "God damn you! You leave aside the Qur'ān and knowledge of religion, and ask me about poetry?"[75] The soldier explained that he and his fellows were in dispute about the issue and had agreed on 'Ubayda as their umpire. Without so much as a pause 'Ubayda now spoke as an Arab, quoting a line of verse with a particularly striking image, and asked: "Who said that?" The soldier immediately recognized the verse and acknowledged that it was Jarīr's. 'Ubayda then delivered his verdict: "Of the two men, he's the better poet." So even a Khārijite extremist on the battlefield could savor a fine line of verse and knew what good poetry was about. The story ends there; presumably the soldier was able to return to his fellows with the electrifying news of the verdict before the daily grind of battle began. There can be few armies at the present day with such a lively interest in poetry.

The Arabs were not in fact doing anything unique in proudly preserving a heritage dating back to the time before they succumbed to the charms and corruptions of civilization. In different ways, the Irish, the Icelanders, and the Japanese were doing the same thing in roughly the same period. Perhaps the Arabs had the edge in sheer volume, but not in any other respect. The comparison is significant because the Irish, Icelanders, and Japanese adopted civilizations that already existed, and they used the technologies that came with them to make and maintain records of their own uncivilized past. In other words, the preservation of the Arab heritage, however significant for Muslim culture, was not in itself enough to bring a new civilization into existence. For that we have to look elsewhere. But before we do that, we need to sketch the non-Arab heritage that likewise filled many of the volumes cataloged by Ibn al-Nadīm.

The non-Arab heritage

If you want access to the books of a high culture that is foreign to you, there are two ways to go about it. One is to learn the literary language of that culture and make acquiring it a regular part of the educational curriculum of your society. Thus educated Romans of antiquity knew Greek, educated Germans of medieval times knew Latin, and educated Koreans of medieval and early modern times knew Chinese. The other option is to translate foreign books into a literary language of your own, if necessary developing or adapting a literary form of your vernacular for the purpose. The Arab elite in the early centuries was clearly disinclined to learn a foreign literary language, and indeed this barely changed until modern times. So the solution was translation, and in the first century and a half of 'Abbāsid rule there was a lot of it, taking off in the reign of al-Rashīd and climaxing in that of

75. Abū 'l-Faraj al-Iṣbahānī, *Aghānī*, 8:43.

al-Ma'mūn. This is why Ibn al-Nadīm could announce that his catalog would cover the books of *all* nations, provided of course that they were available in Arabic. But the books of two nations in particular bulked larger than any others in this activity of translation: those of the Greeks and the Persians. The Greeks here are the ancient Greeks, whom the Arabs referred to as the Yūnān, literally the Ionians, as opposed to the contemporary Byzantines, who were the Rūm or Romans, both in their own eyes and in those of the Arabs. We will consider the works of the Greeks and the Persians in turn, since if we compare those translated from Greek with those translated from Persian a significant difference in profile emerges.

First the Greeks. One thing that creates a seller's market for translations of the books of a foreign culture is the belief that they contain *useful* information. Medical works are an obvious example. We all want to enjoy good health, and non-Arab peoples—such as the Indians and the Persians, but above all the Greeks—had sophisticated medical literatures with which the folk medicine of pre-Islamic Arabia could not compete. Here, then, was something the Arab elite very much needed, or at least thought they did (we can leave aside the question of the extent to which all medicine before the nineteenth century was malpractice). Most of the laborious process of translation took place in the ninth century, and it involved extensive elite and official patronage. The result was the rendering of hundreds of medical works into Arabic, some from Middle Persian and Sanskrit but most of them from Greek, whether directly or through Syriac. These Greek works included more than a hundred by Galen, the famous second-century physician from western Anatolia. The outcome was that Greek medicine in its Galenic version became standard in the Muslim world, and it was overwhelmingly to this tradition that Muslim authors of medical works subsequently contributed.

Greek medicine, if one accepted its claims, could do a lot for one's welfare in this world, but like Arabic poetry it did not help much with the next. So again there were tensions with Islamic piety. In its Greek form the Hippocratic oath has the physician swear by "all the gods and goddesses"; in Arabic this became "the saints of God, be they men or women,"[76] excising the polytheism of the original while retaining its inclusive reference to male and female. There was also a substantive issue: the status of medical remedies attributed to the Prophet. Were these part of God's revelation to humankind, and so to be preferred to the remedies prescribed by the infidel Greeks? Or were they just folk medicine that Muḥammad had picked up from his Arabian environment? Ibn Khaldūn, for one, thought the second, and expressed the corollary in no uncertain terms: "Muḥammad was sent to teach us the religious law. He was not sent to teach us medicine or any other

76. M. Ullmann, *Islamic medicine*, Edinburgh 1978, 30.

ordinary matter."[77] And without question, the form of medicine that was in general use in the Muslim world was Greek and Galenic, not Arabian and Prophetic. According to one famous jurist, if books were taken as booty from the unbelievers in the course of making war on them, the ruler should summon someone who could read them; and whereas polytheistic books had to be ripped up, unobjectionable books on subjects such as medicine could be preserved. This, of course, was theory. In practice we find that even an objectionable book on the medicinal uses of wine found its way into Arabic literature.

Medicine was not the only form of useful knowledge that merited translation. Another was alchemy, the science whose objective was to manufacture gold and silver from base metals (that it did not attain its objective is again not our concern). Alchemy, too, was first and foremost a Greek science—the Byzantine emperor Heraclius had found time to write about it. Given the anticipated rewards, alchemical texts seemed well worth the effort and expense of translation. Significant numbers of Greek works on the subject were accordingly rendered into Arabic, most likely in the late eighth and ninth centuries. The process did not get the same attention in our sources as the translation of medical works, no doubt because alchemy was somewhat disreputable—it was to come under strong attack from religious scholars. But this did not deter Muslim alchemists from going on to produce a large Arabic literature of their own. Another example of useful but religiously controversial knowledge was astrology, the science that relied on astronomical data to predict the future of human affairs (again, we need not inquire about the success rate of astrological prediction). Astrology was in fact a belief system so widespread in the Old World that it made religions like Buddhism, Christianity, and Islam look parochial. Rulers depended on their astrologers as much as they did on their spies to let them know what was coming their way; it was not for nothing that the ʿAbbāsid caliphs had their court astrologers. In the western part of the Old World the fundamental text of this science was the *Tetrabiblos* of the second-century Egyptian astrologer Ptolemy. It was duly translated from Greek into Arabic, and a court astrologer who flourished around the time of al-Rashīd wrote a commentary on it.

A rather different field in which there was extensive translation from Greek was philosophy. Philosophical knowledge was not as straightforwardly useful as medicine or alchemy. Depending on one's perspective, what it offered was either sublime illumination of the nature of the cosmos or an unconscionable subversion of right religion. But it enjoyed high prestige with much of the elite at the time when Greek works were being translated; its fans included Kindī, whom we encountered as "the philosopher of the Arabs." The biggest name in this field was,

77. Ibn Khaldûn, *The Muqaddimah*, trans. F. Rosenthal, Princeton 1967, 3:150.

of course, the ancient philosopher Aristotle, and a large corpus of his writings became available in Arabic.

As the preceding survey may suggest, the relationship of the Arabs with Greek learning tended to be at once highbrow and somewhat distant. Even if the caliph reached out to the Byzantine emperor for books, he does not seem to have ruled over any significant population of Greek-speaking Muslims, and the intermediaries who transmitted these books to the Arabs were mainly Aramaic-speaking Christians. Moreover, there seems to have been little interest among the Arabs in the history of either the ancient Greeks or their Byzantine heirs. The historian Ṭabarī has a list of Roman and Byzantine rulers covering the six centuries from Tiberius to Heraclius, but it is a bare list of names and reign lengths salted with a few brief references to events of significance for the history of monotheism—and these do not even include the conversion of Constantine. About the history of the ancient Greeks he has nothing to say. Altogether the Arab relationship with Greek culture was a serious one, but in the absence of a significant number of Muslims whose first language was Greek there was nothing intimate about it. The Prophet in his day had three ethnic companions, each the first of his people to enter Islam; as he is said to have put it, "Ṣuhayb is the pioneer of the Greeks, Salmān is the pioneer of the Persians, and Bilāl is the pioneer of the Ethiopians."[78] But Ṣuhayb, unlike the other two, did not have much of a role to play as an ethnic representative after his death, and instead the story went that he was born into an Arab tribe and was then captured and enslaved as a child by the Byzantines, with the result that he learned Greek and lost the ability to speak good Arabic.

Translations from Middle Persian were similar to those from Greek in including works of medicine, astrology, and philosophy—the philosophical texts in particular being Middle Persian translations of Greek works. But the translation of Persian books may well have begun earlier than that of Greek ones, and it had less of the character of a grand official project. These translations also had a much wider range, from the highbrow as already mentioned to the downright frivolous—narratives of the wiles of women and sexy stories. In other words, translation was not confined to delivering knowledge, whether useful or sublime; at least some translators from Persian were in the business of providing entertainment, as those of Aristotle's works were not. A further contrast is that the translations from Persian included an early rendering of a late Sasanian chronicle, the *Khwadāy-nāmag*. It was thanks to the translation of this chronicle that Ṭabarī was in a position to give about two hundred times more space to Sasanian history than he did to that of the pre-Islamic Roman and Byzantine Empires. At the same time it is not hard to see why Ṭabarī and his readers would like it this way. Iraq, where he

78. Ibn ʿAbd al-Barr, *al-Istīʿāb fī maʿrifat al-aṣḥāb*, Cairo n.d., 729.

lived for half a century, had been the political heartland of the Sasanian Empire. It had not been its ethnic heartland—that was the plateau—but alongside its native Aramaic-speaking population, Iraq was home to numerous Persians, of whom Ṭabarī himself was very likely one. Thus many people in Iraq, not to mention Iran, were interested in the Persian past. Some were unashamedly proud of it, like the members of the largely Persian Shuʿūbī movement of the eighth and ninth centuries. Theirs was a cultural milieu that disparaged the claims of the lizard-eating Arabs to superiority over the civilized peoples they had conquered. Were not all the great kings of the past non-Arabs? Were not all but four of the prophets non-Arabs? What did the Arabs ever achieve in the arts and crafts, what mark did they make in philosophy? Their only achievement was poetry, and non-Arabs had that too. Worse yet, what was Arab genealogy worth when their womenfolk were "trampled like a paved road" in the course of intertribal raids?[79] Such arguments were, of course, distinctly risqué from an Islamic point of view. A safer course was to play up the Prophet's Persian companion Salmān. Like Ṣuhayb, he had had a hard life before joining Muḥammad (both had suffered enslavement), but in contrast to Ṣuhayb's case, there are no stories seeking to endow Salmān with an Arab ancestry.

As with the creation of a literature on Arabian antiquities, the translation of books from Greek and Middle Persian—and to a lesser extent from Sanskrit—did not entail the creation of a new civilization. Indeed, the reverse was true. Despite suggestions that the Greeks had plagiarized their wisdom from the Arabs, material from other civilizations was regularly appropriated in a manner that continued to advertise its foreign origin, prompting complaints from the pious that the names of these alien authors and the titles of their books were unpronounceable for the true believers. Nor was this spate of translations unparalleled. The rendering of Indian Buddhist texts into Chinese was likewise a massive effort, and a highly organized one. In our case the process certainly enriched the new civilization, but again we have to look elsewhere for what made the civilization new. As far as books are concerned, the answer lies in a vast literature that we can broadly categorize as devoted to specifically Islamic learning.

The Islamic component

When new civilizations appear, they usually do so in regions where they have no predecessors, or at least no immediate ones.[80] There may be links to other civilizations, as when the Greeks borrowed the Phoenician alphabet and the Chinese came by the western Asian chariot. But Islamic civilization constitutes the only

79. Ibn ʿAbd Rabbih, translated in Lewis, *Islam from the Prophet Muhammad to the capture of Constantinople*, 2:203.

80. I don't think the views I express in this subsection are mainstream, but I'm not sure what is.

case of one civilization arising on top of another—a feature that goes with its being the most recent to emerge, and the one that emerged most rapidly. This meant that the makers of the new civilization had no need to reinvent the wheel, literally or figuratively; the necessary infrastructure was already in place. In such a situation it is obvious that the Islamic sciences would not come into existence by parthenogenesis. What we might therefore have expected is the wholesale adoption by the Muslims of what was already there, resulting in a set of Islamic disciplines that were straightforward adaptations of the religious literatures of the conquered territories, be they Jewish, Christian, or Zoroastrian. This, however, was conspicuously not the case. It is quite possible to identify specific elements of the Islamic sciences that look very much like borrowings from these earlier literatures, and that is probably what they were. But these elements are typically isolated, meaning that the wider contexts in which they appear on the two sides of the fence do not match each other.

A good example is the science of dialectical theology, this phrase being a clumsy rendering of the Arabic term Kalām. In terms of method, Kalām was a disciplined and sophisticated way of arguing, particularly of engaging in disputation with those who held beliefs opposed to one's own. In terms of subject matter, it covered questions about God but also extended to a wide range of issues regarding the world—for example, is matter made up of atoms? In terms of beliefs, Kalām was emphatically not a single coherent system. Different practitioners held different beliefs, often ones they were saddled with through their inherited religious affiliations. Thus a Khārijite practitioner of Kalām would use it to defend his Khārijite beliefs, a Shīʿite to defend his Shīʿite beliefs, and so on—"his" because those who practiced Kalām were almost always men, though we do encounter one notably aggressive woman in the role. In a broad cross-cultural perspective we could classify Kalām as a form of philosophy, since it looks and sounds quite similar to what we call philosophy in a Greek or Indian context. But in properly Islamic terms Kalām was something else; philosophy (*falsafa*) was what the Greeks did, and educated Muslims were well aware of the difference. So what can we say of the origins of this ramified system of Kalām? The fact that it emerged in a part of the world in which philosophy already existed—mainly Greek, but perhaps in some measure Indian too—is clearly no accident. Sophisticated intellectual practices like Kalām do not arise at random across space and time, and if the Middle East at the time of the rise of Islam had not known philosophy, it is unlikely that the Muslims would have invented Kalām within a century of the conquests. But just as clear is the fact that Kalām is not a simple transposition of Greek—or for that matter Indian—philosophy into Arabic. And yet certain elements of it look more or less convincingly like borrowings.

One such element is a genre of instructions for those about to engage in the dialectical equivalent of single combat, most likely in the presence of a doctrinally mixed audience. Your mission is to reduce to incoherence a champion of an opposing view. The instructions tell you to confront your opponent with a dilemma: Do you say X or do you say Y? The instructions then provide for either eventuality, telling you how to respond depending on which horn of the dilemma your opponent opts for. After a few such moves he is trapped, forced into either contradicting himself or accepting your view. This is a simple exercise in Kalām, and it appears early on the Muslim side. Intriguingly, the same genre is well attested on the Christian side in late antiquity, so it looks uncommonly like a borrowing from Christianity into Islam. Another example, less secure but in a way more interesting, concerns epistemology. The Murji'ites were an early Islamic school of thought that suspended judgment on the rights and wrongs of the first civil war—a stance that, had everyone subscribed to it, would have worked wonders for civility in early Muslim society. They justified their position in terms of an epistemological doctrine according to which there are two sources you can rely on to make a judgment: your own experience and the unanimous testimony of others. If you have neither, as was the case for the early Murji'a with reference to the first civil war, then you are obliged to suspend judgment. This is a neat little doctrine, and it has a precedent in antiquity, though in a quite different field: the sources of medical knowledge. Here there was disagreement between rival schools of thought, and one view was that there were three valid sources: one's own experience, the testimony of others, and a form of analogical reasoning. The testimony of others had to be unanimous. The issue was one that Galen had written about, and his works were widely read in late antiquity. The Murji'a are missing one feature of the position, but the resemblance is still intriguing. That the doctrine appears in quite different contexts on the two sides of the fence should make us pause before asserting a connection, but it is also what makes the connection, if real, a particularly interesting one. Yet early Murji'ite epistemology is just a minor theme in the larger field of Kalām.

Another major Islamic science was the study of law, that is to say Islamic law, alias the Sharīʿa. The foundation of this law was a revelation in two parts. One was scripture, the very words of God as recorded in the Qur'ān, and the other was an oral tradition, the corpus of Ḥadīth, the core of which was a mass of accounts of the sayings and doings of Muḥammad and his companions. Ḥadīth, too, eventually became as much a written tradition as the Qur'ān, but in principle it remained oral. This is not the way the foundations of law are commonly conceived in human societies; as the early Christian apologist Tertullian remarked, Roman law "did not come down from heaven."[81] There is in fact only one other full parallel, namely Jewish law, where we likewise find the conception of a two-part revelation, written and oral. This parallel is unlikely to be accidental, and if we put together the

81. Tertullian, *Apology*, trans. T. R. Glover, Cambridge, MA 1931, 25.

fact that Jewish law is centuries older than Islamic law and the evidence of early interactions between Muslims and Jews, including Jewish conversion to Islam, it is a plausible inference that the Muslims owed the general conception to Judaism. We can then go on to find elements in the Islamic edifice that look like specific borrowings from Judaism. One is an Arabic technical term for analogical thinking, *qiyās*, that derives from Jewish Aramaic. Another is the chain of transmitters that accompanies an oral account, known on the Muslim side as the *isnād*, as in "Muḥammad ibn Yūsuf informed us from Sufyān from Abū 'l-Zinād from Mūsā ibn Abī 'Uthmān from his father from Abū Hurayra from the Prophet who said . . ."[82] The only other religious culture in which we find such a style of attribution is Judaism, as in "Rabbi Zeriqa said: Rabbi Ammi said: Rabbi Simeon ben Laqish said: . . . "[83] What was different was that once adopted in Islam the practice was developed much more systematically and applied to a much wider range of material. For example, if we take the somewhat frivolous story in which a Khārijite champion settles the dispute about the relative merits of the poets Jarīr and Farazdaq, we find it preceded by a chain of transmitters. Likewise Ṭabarī's history is full of such chains. The practice became so pervasive that it invited parody: "Ḥiryāq related to me from Yiqāq from Riyāq: 'The rain in spring is all water.'"[84] Here, as often, we see a wide gap between what the early Muslims appear to have taken from other cultures—or brought with them as converts—and what they made of these imports in constructing their own culture. We could easily illustrate this from the substance of Islamic law, but perhaps the most striking example would be the development in Islam of a uniquely elaborate and sophisticated *theory* of law.

These examples cover only a small part of the Islamic sciences, but they suggest a pattern that may have a wider validity. The similarities between these sciences and earlier forms of religious scholarship in the same region tend to be either very general or very particular. There is a parallel to this in the case of one of the linguistic sciences, Arabic lexicography—a discipline that ministered to the central place of Arabic in the new culture. Lexicography had already been developed in the Greek context, showing a similarity of the general kind. But Arabic lexicography also yields a similarity of the particular kind, and here, interestingly enough, the link is not with Greek lexicography but rather with Sanskrit phonetics. The oldest surviving work of Arabic lexicography is a dictionary by the eighth-century Baṣran philologist Khalīl ibn Aḥmad al-Farāhīdī. The way it is organized is unusual: rather than employing the conventional order of the Arabic alphabet, Khalīl makes use of a phonetic order, starting from the back of the throat and

82. Dārimī, *Sunan*, Medina 1966, 1:344 no. 1728.
83. *Babylonian Talmud*, Vilnius 1880–86, Berakhot f. 11b.
84. Subkī, *Ṭabaqāt al-Shāfiʿiyya al-kubrā*, Cairo 1964–76, 7:56.

proceeding to the front of the mouth. It is unlikely to be a coincidence that this is the principle behind the order of the Sanskrit alphabet. In this case the idea did not really catch on, though a major tenth-century dictionary was still arranged in this way. Another example, in a quite different field, would be Ṣūfism. Ṣūfism is a form of Islamic pietism—including mysticism—that took shape by the ninth century. It did so in a world in which pietism and mysticism were already well developed in the Greek and Syriac Christianity of late antiquity. Given that Muslims in the early centuries of Islam lived alongside large numbers of Christians and absorbed many of them as converts, it would be implausible to see the emergence of Ṣūfism as unrelated to this Christian environment. But here again, what Muslims made of it is something else. One major and early change was a refocusing on the wording and imagery of the Qur'ān. A later and far-reaching change, beginning in the twelfth century, was the formation of the Ṣūfī orders that came to anchor the religious life of large numbers of Muslims; we will encounter some of these orders from time to time in later chapters, together with the dervishes who spread them at a popular level. And here again, alongside the very general similarity, we have a very specific one: the perverse form of piety that consists in leading a life of secret virtue while misleading others through an outward impression of vice. This phenomenon is well attested in late antique Christianity, and it reappears on the Muslim side in a Ṣūfī movement known as the Malāmatiyya, again with a Qur'ānic focus. If we now step back from these particular examples, we can see that a crucial feature of the overall pattern was the existence of a vast middle ground between the very general similarities and the very particular ones. Within this middle ground those who created the new sciences took great liberties, or to put it another way, they were busy transforming their raw materials into a new civilization.

What made this outcome possible? Let us focus on Iraq, which more than anywhere else seems to have been the site where the new civilization was formed. First, there is an obvious point about the Arabs. Though they arrived in Iraq with a script, they came with little in the way of high-cultural baggage. But they did bring with them a lot in the way of identity, both ethnic and religious. It would be wrong to describe this identity as nonnegotiable, but it certainly tended that way. Second, there is a point about the non-Arabs. Far from being a homogeneous population with a single cultural tradition, they were very diverse, much more so than the Arabs. They might speak Aramaic or Iranian dialects, and in religious terms they might be Zoroastrians, Christians, Jews, or followers of more obscure faiths. Only the Persians had been members of a politically hegemonic community in the recent past. So the Persians apart, the non-Arabs were low in identity and high in cultural baggage—in both respects the opposite of the Arabs. It could have been a very different story if instead of conquering the Middle East the Arabs had conquered a region where cultural homogeneity and a sense of identity went hand in hand, as by premodern standards was to a significant extent the case in China. Third, the context in which the Arabs and the local populations interacted in early Islamic times was arguably crucial. As we saw, large numbers of non-Arabs were sucked into the vortex of the garrison cities and emerged there in servile roles, as slaves of Arab masters and clients of Arab patrons. Cut loose from their families and communities and subordinated to the social structures of the Arab elite, they likely brought with them little more than what they carried in their heads—which were often, no doubt, the heads of laymen rather than of the relevant cultural specialists. Under these conditions the raw materials of the emerging culture were unusually plastic, making possible the formation of cultural edifices that departed dramatically from those of late antiquity. The contributions of the Mawālī came in at the bottom, so to speak, and in due course Kalām, Islamic law, Arabic grammar, and Ṣūfism developed in ways that made their origins almost unrecognizable, while many other ideas that the Mawālī must have brought with them were no doubt simply ignored. For example, despite the conversion of large numbers of Christians, the Islam that took shape in the early centuries had no sacraments, no priests, and no monasteries; and despite both Christian and Jewish converts, it is not until the tenth century that we begin to see the institutionalization of education in the form of Muslim colleges (*madrasas*) comparable to the Christian School of Nisibis or the Jewish academies of Babylonia. By contrast, Greek philosophy in Arabic translation came in at the top, which meant that it could not be filtered in such a cavalier fashion, and despite its Arabic dress it never ceased to be *Greek* philosophy. These three points—one about the Arabs, one about the non-Arabs, and one about how they came together—can be seen as necessary conditions for the formation of Islamic civilization. What would count as sufficient conditions would be much harder to say.

A final point about Islamic civilization is not directly concerned with its origins and relates rather to the degree to which it was Islamic. The justification for calling it Islamic is not just that it owes its existence to the rise of Islam, but also that Islam lies unambiguously at its core. What is more, this is a core that includes matters whose counterparts in a Christian context would be reckoned as secular, notably law and the caliphate. But this view of things is not to be exaggerated. We noted above that the Qurʾān is the first book we know to have been written in Arabic, and its centrality to the emerging civilization is indisputable. Yet it was far from being fully adopted as the model for classical Arabic, the literary language that gradually assumed a canonical form in Iraq under significant influence from the dialects of eastern Arabia—dialects that must have predominated among the Arabs who settled in Kūfa and Baṣra. Indeed, there is considerable evidence that some features of the eastern dialects came to be imposed on the text of the Qurʾān itself. More generally, there is a broad domain of the secular under the Islamic dispensation, and we have encountered a number of examples of it. Some are covert. We have seen how the concerns of a worldly elite audience shape the way in which the life of the Prophet is narrated, and how the same audience can appreciate the role of the Khārijite Qaṭām in setting up the otherwise shocking assassination of ʿAlī. Another example is the appeal of the oration of the Ibāḍī Abū Ḥamza. Damnable heretic though he may have been, most of the compilers who preserve the text of his speech were Sunnīs or others who did not share his heresy. The reason they opened their pages to him is simple: while they may have detested his doctrines, they loved his rhetorical panache. Other examples are overt. Two major components of the wider culture, the Arab and non-Arab heritages, are inherently distinct from the Islamic core and in that sense secular matters. Another telling case, though one we have not taken up in the preceding discussion, is the field of Arabic belles lettres (*adab*). Writers in this genre, which was closely associated with the assimilated non-Arab bureaucrats of ʿAbbāsid times, may discourse on just about anything, but their primary focus is on how people behave, or should or shouldn't behave, in polite society in this world, not on what will get them saved or damned in the next. A story told in a tenth-century work of this kind describes a visit by the caliph al-Mutawakkil to a cluster of churches in Syria. One might have expected God's caliph to see such churches as dens of polytheism, and indeed this particular caliph had a track record of taking hard-line measures against Christians. But on this occasion al-Mutawakkil was off duty and approached the churches much as a modern tourist might do: he wanted to look at them, to go for a walk in pleasant surroundings, to eye the local talent, and to get passably drunk. Soon it all came together for him in a room with a beautiful view, drinking in the company of a charming and accomplished Christian girl. The end of the story is that the al-Mutawakkil married her and she became his favorite wife. But before that he had taken the trouble to persuade her to convert to Islam; though tipsy and off duty, he had at least rescued an infidel soul from eternal damnation. This, however, is the only feature of the story that could elicit the approval of a pietist. In terms of its appeal to the sophisticated worldling, the story about the zealous Khārijite sectarian settling the dispute over the relative merits of the two poets belongs in the same genre.

4

The breakup of the Caliphate in the West

The next three chapters are about the fragmentation of the Caliphate in the west, the east, and the center, and its outcome in each case. In all three regions the basic story was the same: a single empire gave way to numerous smaller states. The unity of the Caliphate was now irredeemably lost, and the Muslim world would never again be united in a single polity. What complicates the story is that the smaller states were also very diverse. Was the diversity just chaotic, or can we find larger patterns that make some sense of it?

At the same time, political fragmentation provided opportunities for peoples and cultures that had been subjected by the Caliphate to reassert themselves within a Muslim world that was no longer a single polity. Who, then, took advantage of these opportunities, and who did not?

The focus of the present chapter is on the West—that is to say, the region to the west of Egypt whose main centers of population were in North Africa and Spain. The history of this part of the Muslim world in the eighth to eleventh centuries alternates between two phenomena. There are relatively brief periods of upheaval—waves of rebellion or conquest sweeping over the region, or large parts of it. And there are longer periods of relative stability—the troughs between the waves. Somewhat counterintuitively, we will start with one of the troughs, roughly the long ninth century, and examine the ethnic, religious, and political character of the smaller states into which the region was divided. We will then reach back to the preceding wave, the epidemic of Berber rebellion in the mid-eighth century, to see how that convulsion shaped the states that emerged from it. After that we will move on to the next wave, the Fāṭimid conquest of the early tenth century, together with the long trough that followed it and lasted well into the eleventh. This second trough was in one way similar to the first: the robust states of the period, while they lasted, were in Tunisia and Spain. But what was happening in the territory between them?

The trajectory of Muslim Spain stands somewhat apart from that of North Africa, sharing the Berber rebellion but not the Fāṭimid conquest and exposed at the end of the period to the beginnings of a wave of its own, Christian reconquest from the north. What accounts for its distinctive trajectory?

Meanwhile in North Africa, the Berbers had reasserted themselves politically on a large scale. But how far had they matched this self-assertion in religious and cultural terms?

From the viewpoint of an empire based in or near Baghdad, the most salient feature of the Muslim West was its remoteness. We can define the region as North Africa, Sicily, and Spain, with North Africa extending from Tripolitania, now in western Libya, to the Atlantic coast of Morocco. Even Tripoli was farther from Baghdad than were the major cities of the eastern ʿAbbāsid territories, such as Samarqand in Transoxania or Multān in Sindh. To the west of Tripoli, Qayrawān, the capital established by the Arab conquerors of North Africa, was the best part of two thousand miles from Baghdad, while the coast of the region of the Sūs in southwestern Morocco was over three thousand miles from it. Such distances meant much more then than they do today. A tenth-century geographer estimated that it took twelve days to travel from the Sūs to Sijilmāsa in southern Morocco, and two months from Sijilmāsa to Qayrawān. At the same time, the effects of distance were exacerbated by some specific features of the geography of the region. The terrain between Egypt and Tunisia was mostly desert; although Arab tribesmen could cross it with relative ease, it inevitably meant a weakening of the sinews of empire. Moreover, the region between the plains of eastern Tunisia and those of the Atlantic coast of Morocco was dominated by mountain ranges, to the advantage of tribes and the disadvantage of states. Spain, too, combined its agricultural plains with a generous supply of mountains, and in addition it could not be reached without a sea crossing. The distance at the Strait of Gibraltar was a mere ten miles, not in itself a formidable barrier as long as sea power on the Mediterranean was largely in Muslim hands, but strong currents could make the crossing a difficult one, and this obstacle was enough to weaken the projection of power—and at the same time to block, or at least impede, the spread of North African nomads in Spain. It is significant that until the Muslim conquest brought the Berbers across the Strait of Gibraltar, we have no record of Spain having been invaded by any Moroccan population or Morocco by any Spanish population. Only the Carthaginians in the third century BC had ever begun a conquest of Spain from the south.

The region was by no means devoid of resources. The coastal strip of Tripolitania, though fertile, was narrow, but the ancient province of Africa—whence the Arabic "Ifrīqiya," roughly Tunisia—had been the granary of ancient Rome, or one of them, until it was conquered by the Germanic Vandals in 439. Similarly, the plains of western Morocco—the ancient Mauretania—and of Spain offered significant agricultural wealth. What lay between the two was less privileged. The alternating bands of mountain ranges and high plains were poor environments for agriculture. Yet the richer parts of the wider region had resources sufficient to attract a succession of foreign conquerors and settlers, particularly in the case of Tunisia. Here the Arabs had been preceded by the Phoenicians, the Romans, the Vandals, and the resurgent Byzantine Empire of the sixth century—a pattern of foreign interest that continued to mark the history of the region after the Arab conquest. But in general the resources of North Africa were far from stellar. This region, it could be said, lay on the right side of the Sahara but the wrong side of the Mediterranean. It had no water supply that could compare with the rivers of Iraq or Egypt, so its agriculture depended overwhelmingly on rainfall. And if we look for territory with an adequate supply of it on a large-scale rainfall map, the broad band we see running across the northern Middle East dwarfs the narrow strip that hugs the coast of North Africa. The recipe is the same—winter winds from the west encountering mountains—but the scale is very different.

We can think of the history of the Muslim West between the seventh and eleventh centuries as made up of periods of two kinds, waves and troughs. In periods of the first kind massive human waves crested and broke over the region as a whole, or the greater part of it. In the troughs between the waves, by contrast, the various parts of the region were more likely to be left to make their own history.

The first wave was of course the Arab conquest of North Africa and Spain in the later seventh and early eighth centuries. As we have seen, it took the Arabs prolonged military operations to effect their conquest of North Africa, and although the conquest of Spain was in some ways easier, it faced the added burden of the sea crossing. Thereafter, between the seventh and eleventh centuries, the region experienced further waves. The second was the Berber rebellion of the mid-eighth century; this insurrection and its immediate aftermath were followed by a long trough marked by relative stability. The third wave was the rise of the Fāṭimid dynasty (909–1171) in the early tenth century, which was followed by a trough of an increasingly chaotic character. The next waves came in the mid-eleventh century, the later eleventh, and the twelfth.

In this chapter we will approach this complicated history in a somewhat unconventional way. The next section provides a survey of the Muslim West as it was in the period of relative stability between the Berber rebellion and the rise of the Fāṭimids, the trough of what we might call the long ninth century. Thereafter we will deal with the two waves either side of it. One section will treat the Berber rebellion and its aftermath to show how the ninth-century Muslim West emerged, and another will turn to the rise of the Fāṭimids and its aftermath. The section following that will survey the trough of the later tenth and early eleventh centuries. Finally, the concluding section will make some reference to the new waves that were to follow in the eleventh century. These brought the arrival of the Hilālī Arabs in Tunisia and the subsequent spread of Arab tribes to Morocco and beyond; the religious movement that established the Almoravid dynasty

(1062–1147), to be followed in the next century by that of the Almohads (1130–1269); and the beginnings of Christian reconquest—this latter largely limited to Spain. But a more sustained account of these later developments will come in subsequent chapters.

The Muslim West around the ninth century

Tunisia

A tenth-century source tells the story of a minor crisis of orthopraxy set in Qayrawān in the later eighth century. A certain Buhlūl ibn Rāshid (d. 799–800), a scholar of exemplary piety, was asked by his family to see to something, perhaps a purchase in the market. Fearing he might forget, Buhlūl tied a thread around his little finger as a reminder. But then he started to worry. Could it be that in doing this he was committing an innovation, an offense the Prophet had denounced to his followers as a sure path to hellfire? Deeply concerned, he appeared before his friends with his little finger concealed in his sleeve and whispered to one of them to go and consult a particularly trustworthy scholar who had migrated to Tunisia from the east. The mission proved successful: word came back that the dour but deeply respected pietist ʿAbdallāh ibn ʿUmar (d. 693), the son of the second caliph, was known to have used the same mnemonic technique. If ʿAbdallāh ibn ʿUmar did it, it had to be acceptable. Buhlūl accordingly removed his little finger from its hiding place and exclaimed in relief: "Praise be to God, who has not made me an innovator in Islam!"[1]

We can see this punctilious regard for the norms of a distant but authoritative eastern Islam as setting the tone for ninth-century Tunisia, or more particularly the city of Qayrawān. The scholars who appear in our sources as representing its society in the ninth and tenth centuries were overwhelmingly Mālikī. That is to say, they were followers of the jurist Mālik ibn Anas (d. 795), the Medinese founder of a Sunnī school of legal doctrine whose central claim was to represent the authentic tradition of Medina as passed down from the days of the Prophet. Buhlūl himself had traveled to the east and studied with Mālik. One could hardly be more metropolitan than that, and the austere works of the Mālikī jurists of Tunisia, such as the celebrated *Mudawwana* of Saḥnūn (d. 854), have little to show in the way of local color. In fact this strongly eastern orientation was shared by both society and state, the difference being that where the society was fixated on the Ḥijāz, the state was fixated on Iraq. Thus the personnel of the state tended to be Ḥanafīs, followers of a law school that in its early history was as closely identified with the Iraqi city of Kūfa as the Mālikīs were with Medina. After the ʿAbbāsid caliphs in the east instituted the Miḥna to impose the doctrine of the created Qurʾān, the ruler

1. Abū ʾl-ʿArab al-Tamīmī, *Ṭabaqāt ʿulamāʾ Ifrīqiya wa-Tūnis*, Tunis 1968, 128.

of Tunisia followed suit, despite the fact that the dynasty to which he belonged was effectively independent of the ʿAbbāsids. So in 846 Saḥnūn—the local Mālikī counterpart of Ibn Ḥanbal—was arrested and tried in a court presided over by the judge Ibn Abī ʾl-Jawād—the local counterpart of Ibn Abī Duʾād. Nor was such easternizing limited to Muslims. The Jews of ninth-century Qayrawān showed the same deference to the centers of Rabbinic Judaism in Iraq, with the earliest evidence for this dating from around the beginning of the century.

Effective or full independence of Baghdad was nothing remarkable in the ninth-century Muslim West; it was shared by all rulers in the region. What was distinctive about the Aghlabid dynasty (800–909) was the path they took to their autonomy.[2] They did not achieve it by rebelling against the central government in a manifestation of political or religious dissidence. Instead they secured it by a mutually advantageous agreement. The caliph in effect gave Ibrāhīm ibn al-Aghlab (ruled 800–12), the founder of the dynasty, a permanent right to rule Tunisia and even pass it on to his descendants, while Ibn al-Aghlab in turn undertook to pay an annual tribute to the caliph. Characteristically, when the first Aghlabid ruler built himself a new capital a few miles from Qayrawān, he called it ʿAbbāsiyya; only in 876 was it replaced by a fresh capital, the nearby Raqqāda, and later by the more distant city of Tunis. It fits well with this that the ceramics excavated at the site of Raqqāda resemble those of the ʿAbbāsid capital of Sāmarrāʾ in Iraq. Indeed, it appears that the ʿAbbāsid caliph could still have some say in Aghlabid affairs as late as 902. This political continuity from caliphal to Aghlabid rule is of a piece with the strongly eastern religious and cultural orientation of Tunisia.

The Aghlabids' connection to the east also correlates with a couple of features of Tunisian society not otherwise replicated in North Africa, though they have significant parallels in Spain. The first was the survival of a military institution inherited from the eighth century: the Jund, with its Arab troops quartered in the urban centers of Tunisia. The revolts of these often disgruntled Arabs were a prominent theme of Aghlabid history, and the institution was still there under the early Fāṭimids. On one occasion, in 824, the ruler somewhat paradoxically suppressed the revolt of the Jund by calling in the Berbers of the south. Or perhaps it was not so paradoxical: the Aghlabids also purchased large numbers of slave soldiers to balance the Jund. Some were black slaves imported from across the Sahara, whose number is said at one point to have reached five thousand. Others were Slavs from across the Mediterranean; Ibrāhīm II (ruled 875–902) is said to have been able to speak Slavonic. The one thing one would not want to be in the polite society of Qayrawān was Berber. On an occasion when Buhlūl received assurances that despite his anxieties he was not of Berber origin, he was so relieved that he threw a party for his friends.

2. For the background to the Aghlabids see H. Kennedy, "The origins of the Aghlabids," in G. D. Anderson and others (eds.), *The Aghlabids and their neighbors*, Leiden 2018.

The second feature was the presence of an indigenous non-Berber and initially Christian population, the Afāriqa ("Africans"). They now spoke a Romance dialect comparable to those of Spain, France, and Italy, rather than the Punic of the Phoenician settlers who had founded Carthage, though this Semitic tongue was still very much alive in the early fifth century and perhaps even into the sixth. A twelfth-century geographer characterized the language of a population in what is today the southern Tunisian interior as "Ifrīqiyan Latin," the Latin of Tunisia. To the extent that they remained Christian, the Afāriqa were the counterpart of the Copts in Egypt and of other eastern Christian populations who for some time retained their ancestral languages under Muslim rule. But unlike the Copts they seem to have been politically invisible, and they disappeared long ago.

Altogether, ninth-century Tunisia appears as a remote but remarkably faithful outpost of the ʿAbbāsid Caliphate and Sunnī Islam. Even the leader of the heterodox Ismāʿīlī movement, who after fleeing from Syria in the early tenth century had seen more than he might have wanted of North Africa, recognized the people of Qayrawān as true representatives of eastern civilization: "It's as if we were looking at city dwellers of the east,"[3] he exclaimed admiringly, whereas the North Africans he had previously encountered were uncultured rustics. At the same time, the resources of Tunisia made possible what by the standards of the day was a real state, and even to an extent an expansive one. In 839 the Aghlabids conquered southern Tunisia, and between 827 and 902 they almost completed a long, slow conquest of Sicily. The latter was a naval as well as a military achievement: Sicily is about a hundred miles from the North African coast, whereas it is only a couple of miles from the Italian mainland. Its conquest was also fiscally advantageous. It seems that the early ʿAbbāsids had created a major problem for anyone ruling Tunisia by flooding it with far more troops that its revenue could support, with the result that governors of ʿAbbāsid Tunisia could pay the soldiers their stipends only with the help of a subsidy from Egypt. Now Sicily, another of the granaries of ancient Rome, became the Aghlabid substitute for this subsidy. The island almost marked the limit of Muslim conquest—but not quite, for there was also a Muslim presence on the mainland in the heel and toe of Italy.

The land of Berber heresy

North Africa to the west of the Aghlabid state was a very different story. Beyond the plains of Tunisia we enter a vast and largely mountainous territory populated by Berber tribes making a living from agriculture or animal husbandry, no doubt often in combination.[4] To the north much of this territory was poorly integrated into the maritime world of the Mediterranean; coastal plains that might have

3. Quoted in H. Halm, *The empire of the Mahdi*, Leiden 1996, 146.
4. For the history of the Berbers see M. Brett and E. Fentress, *The Berbers*, Oxford 1996.

facilitated interaction were scarce. To the south conditions were more open. Here the Berbers were by no means confined to the highlands: they also dominated the southern foothills, together with much of the vast Sahara desert as far east as the borders of Egypt. The rulers of Tunisia were thus liable to find themselves confronting a wild south as well as a wild west. How far they could project some semblance of government into such territories depended on the vicissitudes of military and political power. In the ninth century much of the region was probably stateless, but by no means all of it. Four states in particular stand out in the sea of tribes, each ruled by its dynasty. The Rustamids (778–909) were based in Tāhart, in what is now western Algeria. At its height their state stretched from Tlemcen in the far west of Algeria to Tripolitania in western Libya, hemming in the Aghlabids on both the west and the south, but the Aghlabid conquest of southern Tunisia in 839 split the Rustamid territories into two noncontiguous parts. The Midrārids (772–977) ruled from Sijilmāsa in the region of the Tāfīlālt, on the edge of the Sahara in southern Morocco. The Idrīsids (789–985) ruled in northern and western Morocco, their main center being the city of Fez, though after 828 their territories were divided among members of the family who were often in conflict with each other. Finally, the Ṣāliḥids (709–917) founded the town of Nakūr, near the coast of northeastern Morocco, and from there ruled a state of modest size.

Several features were widely shared among these states. The first was that the populations they ruled were overwhelmingly made up of Berber tribesmen. Of course any reasonably successful state in such a tribal backland could be expected to attract enterprising foreigners, and we know that they were present in considerable numbers in Tāhart, Sijilmāsa, and Fez. But in this period the core populations of these regions were solidly Berber.

Against this background, the second feature might seem paradoxical: the rulers of these states tended to be of non-Berber extraction. As indicated by their name, the Rustamids were originally Persian and claimed descent from the Sasanians; the Idrīsids were descended from the Prophet, which made them Arabs; and the Ṣāliḥids had at least a claim to South Arabian ancestry. Only the Midrārids were unambiguously indigenous. The Berbers were thus a population that easily accommodated rulers of foreign origin, somewhat in the manner of the early medieval Slavs. Perhaps the Berbers had a liking for such rulers because they could exercise an authority that transcended local tribal conflicts, but the tribes of Arabia showed no such partiality to non-Arabs.

A third feature was a widespread adoption of sectarian forms of Islam that from a Sunnī point of view were manifestly heretical. As we saw, the seventh-century split established two sects, the Shīʿites and the Khārijites, each of which subsequently splintered into many subsects. In North Africa the Rustamids were Ibāḍī Khārijites, the Midrārids were Ṣufrī Khārijites, and the Idrīsids were Shīʿites of some kind, very likely Zaydīs. Only the Ṣāliḥids were Sunnīs, specifically Mālikīs, though one Midrārid ruler of the mid-tenth century converted to Mālikī Sunnism.

In the Rustamid case the dynasty's authority originally extended on a sectarian basis to the considerable Ibāḍī populations found in other parts of North Africa, as far east as what is now Libya, but both the Aghlabid expansion to the south and schism within the Ibāḍī community soon curtailed this reach. In any case, none of these sectarians had a use for the orthodox Mālikism of Qayrawān. The Mālikī Saḥnūn's *Mudawwana*, "the Compiled," elicited so little respect from them that one ninth-century Ibāḍī referred to it as the *Mudawwada*, "the Worm-eaten."

A fourth feature was strong linkage of one kind or another with the wider world. The Rustamids had well-attested religious links with their fellow Ibāḍīs in the east, together with robust commercial ties to the Sahara and the lands to the south of it; in the mid-ninth century they dispatched an embassy to a king who ruled the blacks on the far side of the desert. The Midrārids likewise played a prominent role in trans-Saharan commerce and very likely kept in contact with their eastern Ṣufrī brethren—the lack of any surviving Ṣufrī literary heritage denies us information on this. The Ṣāliḥid case was different. Like the Idrīsids, and unlike the Rustamids and Midrārids, they lived rather close to one of the major powers of the region, the offshoot of the Umayyad dynasty that ruled in Spain (756–1031). In the Ṣāliḥid case the resulting relationship was a cooperative one. This fits well with the Sunnism of the Ṣāliḥids, and also with the Spanish provenance of much of their imported pottery as found by archaeologists. Of all these dynasties, the one most weakly connected to the outside world may have been the Idrīsids. Archaeological evidence from Fez does not suggest that the local artisans were in communication with the east, in contrast to those of Raqqāda in Tunisia, and a tenth-century geographer remarks that in Fez scholars were few.

Overall, one would expect that a state acceptable to a Berber tribal society would govern with a comparatively light touch. In the case we know best, the Rustamids of Tāhart, there are indications that this expectation was at times correct. We are told that the reason the first Rustamid ruler, the Persian ʿAbd al-Raḥmān ibn Rustam (ruled 778–88), was chosen as imam was that he lacked a tribal constituency; in other words, he would not be in a position to bully his subjects, and he could be neutral among the tribes. Before his death he piously appointed a council to decide on a new imam, just as the caliph ʿUmar had done on his deathbed in 644. His lifestyle was suitably simple. At one point he received news of the unexpected arrival of emissaries from the eastern Ibāḍīs. At the time he and his slave were engaged in repairing the roofs of his home in Tāhart, with the slave handing up clay to him, so he had to come down and wash off the clay before he could greet his guests. Nothing like that could have befallen the Aghlabid ruler of Tunisia in his palace. On the other hand, ʿAbd al-Raḥmān's son and successor ʿAbd al-Wahhāb (ruled 788–824) is described by a Sunnī chronicler of the late ninth century as having built up such extensive power as to become a king rather than an imam. This was a ruler who could spend a thousand gold coins on procuring books from the east. His reign accordingly saw a schism within the Ibāḍī movement, with his opponents seeking to limit the powers of the imam by requiring him to make decisions only in the presence of an assembly of known membership. These constitutionalist schismatics formed an Ibāḍī subsect known as the Nukkār, which fought two battles against the imam and lost. (Relations between Ibāḍī subsects were usually bad, though we know of a case in Tripolitania in the first half of the tenth century when they were extraordinarily good.) These defeats did not put an end to the Nukkār. In the next century a Nukkārī leader, Abū Yazīd, mounted a major rebellion against the Fāṭimids, and the same themes reappear. At first he established a council of twelve to rule with him and led a simple life—he was "the man on the donkey" (*ṣāḥib al-ḥimār*). But after taking Qayrawān in 944, he alienated his followers by riding a thoroughbred horse and wearing garments of silk. Only when he repented and returned to his former ways did his followers once again rally to his cause. Whether things were like this in the Midrārid and Idrīsid states, too, is hard to know for lack of sources. In the Midrārid case a ruler of the late eighth and early ninth centuries is described as particularly violent and despotic, but he is also said to have equipped Sijilmāsa with a city wall at his own expense; both reports perhaps reflect an abundance of revenue from trans-Saharan commerce. But the ruler was not the only political actor in this polity. Around 867 we find the people of Sijilmāsa intervening forcefully in the choice of a new ruler, and in the decades that follow they were significant—and violent—participants in the politics of the city. The Ṣāliḥids, by contrast, look more like a small-scale version of the Aghlabids—or perhaps rather of the Umayyads of Spain. A striking feature they had in common with their Umayyad neighbors across the Alboran Sea was the use of Slav military slaves, an institution we would not expect to encounter in a Berber tribal polity.

This survey of the land of Berber heresy has focused on states and their sectarian allegiances. But Shīʿite sects, unlike those of the Khārijites, were not necessarily interested in state formation, though the ones we hear most about certainly were. As to those that were not, there is a report that in 762–63 the seventh imam of the Imāmī Shīʿites sent two emissaries to North Africa with instructions to settle among the Berbers. They made converts, but there is no suggestion that their mission aimed to raise the tribes and form a state. Somewhat later a subsect of the Imāmīs spread in two widely separated parts of North Africa, again without political fanfare. This was a group that believed the imamate to have come to an end with the death of the eighth imam in 799. It seems that they were already established in southern Tunisia in the ninth century, and in the same century they spread to the Sūs thanks to the missionary activity of a certain Ibn Warsand al-Bajalī, after whom they were known as the Bajaliyya. But it is only in the tenth century that these sectarians come into focus, when a geographer describes them as sharing the Friday mosque of the main city of the Sūs with the local Mālikīs—though they also fought them constantly. Politically they were subject to Idrīsid rule.

The land of Berber unbelief

To the west of the Idrīsids, on the Atlantic plains of northwestern Morocco, heretical Islam gave way to something more unusual. The Barghawāṭa were Berbers with not just a polity but also a religion of their own. It was clearly modeled on Islam and gave Islam a significant place in its genealogy, but it was not Islam. At its core was a belief in the mission of a Berber prophet, a certain Ṣāliḥ ibn Ṭarīf, to whom a scripture had been revealed in Berber. Like his father, he bore an Arab name, in his case one that had a place in the Qur'ān. The Qur'ānic phrase *ṣāliḥ al-mu'minīn* (Q66:4), meaning "the righteous among the believers," was taken by some to refer to the first two caliphs, but Ṣāliḥ's followers saw in it a reference to their prophet. He was, they said, descended from Sham'ūn ibn Ya'qūb ibn Isḥāq—in other words, Simeon son of Jacob son of Isaac, the ancestor of the lost Israelite tribe of Simeon; this suggests Jewish influence. As to their rituals, they fasted in the month of Rajab—the Arab month that comes two months before the Muslim fasting month of Ramaḍān—while eating freely in Ramaḍān itself. Like Muslims they prayed five times a day, but also five times a night. Their annual sacrifice was in Muḥarram, a month after the Muslim sacrifice in Dhū 'l-Ḥijja. Their weekly prayer gathering was on Thursdays, not Fridays. They had borrowed the Muslim affirmation "God is great" (*Allāhu akbar*), but they said it in Berber. Their religious law was likewise different from that of the Muslims. Their bloodwite for the slaying of a man was a hundred cows, not a hundred camels. They held that it was not permissible to eat fish unless they had been ritually slaughtered, and they deemed eggs forbidden. Much of our account of the Barghawāṭa comes from an eleventh-century author who derived part of his information from a certain Zammūr ibn Mūsā, an ambassador sent from the Barghawāṭa to the Umayyad court in Spain in 963. We can thus have no assurance that the details he gives us are valid for the ninth century, but the general character of the religion is clear enough.

There were other examples of Berber prophets in North Africa in the early centuries of Islam. In the 920s a prophet called Ḥā-mīm (another name derived from the Qur'ān) appeared with a Berber scripture in northern Morocco, not far from the Strait of Gibraltar. In the previous decade there had been a Berber prophet among the Kutāma tribesmen in what is now northeastern Algeria, and there was one near Ceuta as late as the thirteenth century. It could indeed be said that the Qur'ān invited such ventures in ethnic prophecy with its declaration "We have sent no messenger save in the language of his people, that he might make all clear to them" (Q14:4). So why not in Berber? But only in the case of the Barghawāṭa does such a venture appear to have stood the test of time: according to our main source it originated in the eighth century, and we know that it lasted into the eleventh. Yet it seems to have had no significant appeal outside its homeland.

This phenomenon of Berber prophethood completes our survey of mainland North Africa in a telling way. It shows that from one end of the region to the other, Islam was the only significant source of religious ideas. What varied was the form in which these ideas were adopted: fidelity to orthodox Islam in Tunisia, adhesion to sectarian forms of Islam farther west, and in the far west a Berber remaking of Islam. At the same time it seems likely that the spread of Islam among the Berbers had netted many more of them than Christianity had ever done, especially in the south, beyond the frontiers of Roman imperial rule. This effect was no doubt accelerated by the development of trans-Saharan trade, but at the same time it surely had something to do with a certain elective affinity between Berbers and Arabs, both of them tribal populations hitherto on the margins of civilization.

The one Berber population of North Africa that was untouched by Islam, and presumably practiced a paganism of ancient origins in our period, was that of the Canary Islands off the southwestern coast of Morocco. In fact, we hear nothing of the religion of these islanders until the late twelfth or early thirteenth century, when a Ṣūfī from southern Morocco who died in 1208–9 is reputed to have traveled there; finding the inhabitants entirely ignorant of Islam he set about converting them, both men and women. But this conversion, if it happened, left no trace, and the account does not tell us anything of the character of Canarian paganism. For that we have to wait till the fourteenth century. It is then that Ibn Khaldūn (d. 1406) recounts that Frankish ships—most likely Majorcan—had reached the Canaries around the middle of the century. They had taken native Canarians captive and then sold them into slavery on the Moroccan coast. Once these slaves had learned enough Arabic to explain themselves, they revealed that their worship had consisted of prostrating themselves to the rising sun. They had known no religion—meaning revealed religion—and had not been reached by any missionary activity. A later Italian source confirms the existence of sun worship but shows it to have been just one among many cults. No doubt that was also true in our period.

Muslim Spain

Of all the western Muslim lands, Spain was the most remote.[5] It was as distant from Baghdad as Morocco was, and in addition required crossing the sea. A large part of the country was averted from the Mediterranean, with rivers draining into the Atlantic, and it has been suggested that the Spanish interior may have been

5. For its history under Muslim rule see H. Kennedy, *Muslim Spain and Portugal*, London 1996.

the most isolated region of the entire late Roman world. Given its remoteness, we could easily imagine the Muslim conquest having either of two outcomes. One would have been a rapid Christian resurgence issuing in the expulsion of the invaders. Some Muslims did indeed anticipate this. A tradition preserved in a ninth-century source foretells the exodus of the Muslims from the peninsula, complete with a parting of the waves such as God had arranged for the Children of Israel on their departure from Egypt. And in the long run, of course, all of Spain would become Christian once more, though this reconquest was not to begin until the eleventh century; around the ninth century Christian rule was still confined to the northern fringe of the peninsula. The other outcome might have been some Spanish analog of the Barghawāṭa, seizing on Islamic ideas and tempering them with Hispanic pride, but the native population of Spain, unlike that of Morocco, may have been too deeply Christianized for that to happen. What one would not have expected is what actually happened: in cultural and religious terms, despite its remoteness, the elite of Muslim Spain was as fixated on the east as was that of Tunisia. This is all the more surprising in that Spain never came under ʿAbbāsid rule. Two things nonetheless help explain this trajectory. One is a chain of events in the mid-eighth century that led, improbably, to the strengthening of the Arab presence in Spain and the establishment of a long-lasting dynasty of Umayyad descent there; we will see how this happened in the next section. The other relevant factor was the potential of the agricultural resources of the plains of southern and central Spain. These consisted of a set of rich river valleys, and though separated from each other by mountain ranges, they provided the best basis for a powerful state anywhere in the Muslim world west of Egypt. Not surprisingly, we find the Umayyads importing slave soldiers just as their eastern peers did. Indeed, since ʿAbd al-Raḥmān I (ruled 756–88) was already buying himself black slave soldiers, presumably from across the Sahara, the Umayyads of Spain seem to have been the pioneers in this development.

The resources of Muslim Spain were not, however, enough to support a reliably strong state, still less an imperial one. The expansion of the Muslims beyond the Pyrenees was minimal. Although they had taken the city of Narbonne in 719, they lost it to the Christians in 759 and thereafter ruled no territory north of the mountains. Their raids penetrated far into France but ended with defeat at the hands of the Carolingians at the Battle of Poitiers in 732. The Arabs had successfully co-opted the Berbers for the conquest of Spain, but they failed to co-opt the Basques—the next wild mountain people in their path—for the conquest of France. Meanwhile, a sizeable part of northwestern Spain was to escape their rule, perhaps starting as soon as 717, and there were likewise some early losses in the northeast—Pamplona and Barcelona around 800—that pulled parts of the northeastern frontier well back from the Pyrenees. Raids into Christian Spain continued, sometimes vigorously, but they did not result in territorial gains. This meant that the long-term strategic viability of Muslim Spain was already in doubt from early in its history. The other direction in which the Umayyad state might have expanded was southward, but on the Moroccan side of the Strait of Gibraltar it had no presence until the tenth century. And even within the Spanish territory held by Muslims, Umayyad rule was uneven over both space and time.

In terms of space, the presence of Christian rule in the north had a knock-on effect on the Muslim territory adjoining the border. It led to the emergence of a wide band made up of three marches in which powerful families could build up largely autonomous principalities, paying little or nothing in the way of taxes to the state and often rebelling against it. The Lower March was centered on Mérida in the southwest, the Middle March on Toledo in the center, and the Upper March on Tudela in the east. The Lower March was held from 884 to 930 by a family of Galician origin that first appears there in the early ninth century. The founder of this local dynasty, Ibn al-Jillīqī, reached a tacit accommodation with the Umayyads after repeated rebellions and passed on his principality to his descendants. The Middle March did not have a family of this kind until the Umayyad state fragmented in the eleventh century. But the city of Toledo had a record of persistent rebellion, and in a settlement of 873 we find the Umayyads granting the people of the city the right to choose their own governor. In the Upper March the Banū Qasī were long the main family. Like their counterparts in the Lower March, they were indigenous; their fortunes can be traced from the late eighth century to the early tenth. One powerful ninth-century member of the family took to styling himself "the third king in Spain." They also formed long-lasting bonds with a powerful Basque family on the Christian side of the frontier—an unholy alliance of a kind that is familiar in premodern frontier history but was hardly in the best interests of the Umayyad state. That so much territory on the northern frontier was so often effectively denied to the central government was a serious structural weakness for it, exacerbated by the atrophied fiscal system it inherited from the Visigoths. It also helps explain why the Umayyad center of gravity remained firmly fixed in the south. It was the southern city of Cordoba that became the Muslim capital, in contrast to the Visigothic capital of Toledo in the center of the peninsula. The denial of territory to the Umayyad state consequent on the existence of the Marches lies behind the evolution that gives us the term "Andalucía" as the name of the southern province of Spain in which Cordoba is located. Here a Germanic term that must have been used by the Visigoths to refer to the territory of their kingdom became the Arabic "al-Andalus," a name that might be applied to the whole peninsula or limited to the part of it under Muslim rule. As Muslim rule contracted, al-Andalus in this latter usage was pushed farther and farther to the south.

In terms of time, periods of relatively strong central government contrasted with periods of massive disorder. Thus the Umayyad dynasty was fairly successful until the later ninth century, despite many disturbances, including a serious rebellion in

Cordoba itself in 818. This willingness of the Cordoban populace to involve itself in the violent politics of the day was not isolated. In the mid-sixth century they had mounted a major uprising against their Visigothic ruler, in 805 they conspired to depose their Umayyad ruler, and in 891 volunteers from the city were to play a key part in fending off the attack of a dangerous rebel. It was in this latter period, the later ninth century, that the Umayyad dynasty entered several decades of disarray that lasted well into the tenth century. This phase was marked by a strong tendency for the border regions to escape Umayyad control, but its highlight was a long-lasting insurrection well away from the frontier, in the mountains of southeastern Spain. It began in 878 and even threatened Cordoba in 891. Its leader was a certain Ibn Ḥafṣūn (d. 918), whose rhetoric pitted the indigenous population, both Muslim and Christian, against their Arab oppressors. The Arabs, he told these natives (*muwalladūn*), had long humiliated and enslaved them, and his only wish was to deliver them from their slavery. The political and military salience of Christians in this insurrection is in striking contrast to their invisibility in the turbulent history of North Africa in the same period, although in the long run Christianity may well have come close to disappearing from Muslim Spain, to return with the Christian reconquest. Meanwhile, there was also trouble in Seville, a major center where a king set himself up with a court of his own; it was over twenty years before the Umayyads retook the city. As if that was not enough, violent conflicts broke out within the Umayyad family. But if the Umayyad state had serious problems, it also had considerable resources, and in due course it recovered from the disarray and entered another period in which the state was relatively strong.

The combination of an increased Arab presence and an Umayyad state does much to explain the strongly eastern orientation of Muslim Spain, even if relations between the two components were by no means smooth. This orientation was reinforced by an archaic feature of Muslim society in Spain—namely, the continued prestige that accrued to Arab aristocrats long after they had largely lost it elsewhere. But thanks to the provenance of our sources the milieu in which deference to the east is most obvious is that of scholars, not aristocrats. As in Tunisia, a characteristic aspect of this orientation was the early reception of the Mālikī law school. Here the pioneering figure was a certain ʿĪsā ibn Dīnār al-Ghāfiqī (d. 827). Born in Toledo, he traveled all the way to Egypt and on to Medina in the hope of meeting with Mālik himself, but he arrived too late—Mālik was already dead. So instead ʿĪsā went back to Egypt, where he studied with a distinguished pupil of Mālik's before returning to a career in Cordoba. He composed a book in which he put together his knowledge of Mālikī law, and it seems that at least part of this book reached Medina, where it impressed a prominent member of the school. A somewhat later contemporary of ʿĪsā's, a Cordoban scholar of Berber descent named Yaḥyā ibn Yaḥyā al-Laythī (d. 848), introduced Mālik's prime work, the

Muwaṭṭa', to Spain. Remarkably, it was to be his version that became the standard text among Mālikīs at large, not the version of some leading scholar of Medina, Iraq, Egypt, or Tunisia. Spain had its sectarians, Khārijite and even Shī'ite, but Sunnism in its Mālikī form was unquestionably dominant, and there was no counterpart in Spain to the role of Ḥanafism in Tunisia. "We recognize only the Book of God and the *Muwaṭṭa'* of Mālik," as a geographer of the later tenth century has the Muslims of Spain declare.[6] He adds that they would expel members of other law schools from the country, not to speak of Shī'ites. A strong indication of the absence of a significant sectarian population is the fact that when Muslim Spain broke up into the best part of forty petty states in the eleventh century, not one of them was ruled by a Khārijite or a Shī'ite.

An analogous eastern orientation is evident in the worldly culture of the Umayyad court, and it is encapsulated in the story of Ziryāb.[7] A brilliant young musician in Iraq, his promising career at the 'Abbāsid court ended prematurely, it is said as a result of professional jealousy. At some point he moved to Qayrawān, where he was employed by the Aghlabid ruler, but this too ended badly. He was then welcomed to Cordoba by the Umayyad ruler in 822 and remained in his service till both died in 852. Ziryāb was much more than just a musician. He was highly educated, and he introduced the Umayyad court to the latest forms of eastern sophistication in food, clothing, hairstyles, and etiquette. The story shows that the Umayyad ruler was lucky: had it not been for Ziryāb's troubles in Baghdad and Qayrawān, he would never have entertained the idea of migrating to a land as remote as Spain. But it also indicates that the ruler, and no doubt his court, were sensible of their own provinciality and hungry for the refinements of the east. Ziryāb and his Umayyad patron were thus the key agents in a process of easternization. Unlike the Aghlabids, the Umayyads ignored the Miḥna, being close to the local Mālikīs, but in other respects they took catching up with the 'Abbāsids very seriously. That included importing large numbers of books from the east.

As in Qayrawān, it was not just the Muslims who were attracted by eastern models. In the mid-ninth century a pious and intransigent Christian, Alvarus of Cordoba, complained bitterly about the cultural treason of the Christian laity, especially the young. Where today could you find a layman who read the Latin commentaries on the Bible? Hardly one in a thousand could write a letter to a friend in correct Latin. Instead, these Christians delighted in reading Islamic texts, not in order to refute them, but to acquire an elegant Arabic style. Many of them, he tells us, could write Arabic of the greatest eloquence and compose poems in

6. Muqaddasī, *Aḥsan al-taqāsīm*, Leiden 1967, 236.

7. For what follows see D. Reynolds, "Ziryab in the Aghlabid court," in G. D. Anderson and others (eds.), *The Aghlabids and their neighbors*, Leiden 2018.

Arabic superior to those of the Arabs themselves. A metrical rendering of the Psalms into Arabic produced at the end of the ninth century may reflect this literary taste. Likewise the Jews of Muslim Spain were easternizers in the same manner as their coreligionists in Qayrawān, certainly in the ninth century and perhaps as early as the late eighth.

Such, then, was the Muslim West around the ninth century. It was marked by a dramatic cultural gradient running across North Africa, from the orthodoxy of Qayrawān through the heterodoxy of the Berber highlands to the unbelief of the Atlantic plains and the intact paganism of the Canaries. This gradient highlights an asymmetry that also characterizes the political geography of the period. As we have seen, the prime agricultural resources of North Africa were concentrated at either end, in Tunisia and Morocco. Tunisia, as we might expect, became the site of a fairly robust state; yet Morocco in this period did not. The contrast antedated Islam, in the sense that the power of the state under the Romans and their successors had been much stronger in what was then called Africa than it was in what was then Mauretania Tingitana.[8] The Romans had held onto this troubled province in the far west for a couple of centuries, even ruling it from Volubilis deep in the interior, but in the late third century they abandoned all but the northwestern corner of it. Against that background it is perhaps unsurprising that Morocco from the later eighth century to the middle of the eleventh was characterized by political fragmentation. There were the Barghawāṭa; there were the Idrīsids, who themselves were fragmented for much of the time; there were the Midrārids; and there were the Ṣāliḥids—but there was no overarching political structure or religious orthodoxy. And yet the combination of a relatively strong state and religious orthodoxy was found to the north of Morocco in Spain.

This picture is, of course, a simplification; it ignores some of what we do know and a great deal that we don't know. For example, in the last years of the ninth century there was a new religious and political development in what is now northeastern Algeria, one that brought to power a new and famous dynasty, the Fāṭimids (909–1171). Had it not done that—had it remained a local phenomenon—we would most likely know nothing about it. By the same token, there may have been numerous no less interesting local scenes scattered across North Africa of which we have no record. But the simple picture of the ninth-century Muslim West outlined in this section is adequate for our purposes, and our task in the next section is to see how it emerged.

8. Note the difference between Mauretania, the ancient country of the Mauri in western North Africa, and Mauritania, the modern country southwest of Morocco.

Back to the Berber rebellion and its aftermath

The Berber rebellion

The Berbers had no tradition of political unity, but like the ancient Greeks and the Arabs they nonetheless came to count as a people. The Arabs certainly saw the Berbers that way. In fact it seems that it was the Arabs who gave them their name, since nobody had called their ancestors Berbers before the rise of Islam—in late antiquity they were known as Moors (Mauri or Maurousioi). It seems likely that the Arabs were applying to a population they were meeting for the first time a name already known to them in connection with a quite different people, one living on the south side of the Gulf of Aden. But despite this complexity there can be little doubt that the Moors of late antiquity and the Berbers of early Islamic times were the same population.[9] Indeed, the Arabs inherited from the Byzantines the legend that this population was originally from Palestine and fled westward to escape from the Israelites. Moreover, the Berbers themselves accepted the name, and their shared experiences at the hands of the Arabs may well have pushed them to develop a stronger sense of identity in association with it. Thus there came to be experts on the genealogy of the Berbers; an eleventh-century Spanish scholar quotes two of them by name, and significantly both were Ibāḍīs. What the Berbers spoke, though not a single language, was a group of manifestly related languages. They shared a word for God—Yākush—that is widely attested in one form or another as far east as the hinterland of Tripolitania and as far west as Spain and the Atlantic plains of Morocco. Something else that came to be widely shared at an early date was a core vocabulary of distinctive Berber renderings of Arabic religious terms, such as "to pray," "to fast," and "mosque." A word for "Arabs" may also have been widely used: they were called "Saracens" (*Iserghinen*) and their language "Saracen" (*Taserghint*). At the same time, the Berbers, like the Arabs, were divided into numerous different tribes, some of which we will have reason to mention; tribal divisions were as fundamental to Berber politics as they were to Arab politics. The Berbers also had intermediate ethnic categories between the people as a whole and the individual tribes, denoted by terms such as Zanāta, Ṣanhāja, and Maṣmūda. These can be compared to the division of the Arabs into Northerners and Southerners, or the Greek distinction between Dorians, Ionians, and Aeolians. They clearly meant something to the Berbers, but for our purposes we can leave them aside.

By the beginning of the eighth century the Arabs had conquered the Berber tribes in some fashion. There was, however, no way they could rule them as they did the peasants of eastern Tunisia. And yet the Arab presence seems to have been

9. For a different view see R. Rouighi, *Inventing the Berbers*, Philadelphia 2019.

real enough—and oppressive enough—to elicit massive discontent among the Berbers. Among their various grievances, the enslavement of Berber girls by the Arabs for export to the east was no doubt particularly galling. That this resentment should flare up in a violent form is hardly surprising in the case of a warlike tribal population like the Berbers; such a people might be conquered, but it was unlikely to stay that way for long. Yet it was not until the 740s that Berber rebellion became epidemic in the Muslim West. It was encouraged by the weakening of the central government in the east around the middle of the eighth century, when the last tumultuous years of Umayyad rule gave way to revolution and the first unsteady years of ʿAbbāsid rule. As we will see, the Berber rebels did not possess any overarching leadership, but we can think of them as participants in a single historical phenomenon, and their activities often involved movement over long distances.

Before we come to the rebellion itself, we need to go back to the religious proclivities of the Berbers. On the eve of the Arab conquest we can assume the presence of three religions among them: Judaism, Christianity, and paganism. We know that all three were present among the Berbers of northern Morocco in the late eighth century, since the founder of the Idrīsid dynasty encountered them among the neighboring tribes. Judaism is not of much concern to us here, though it continued to be present down to modern times. Christianity had been prominent in North Africa for centuries, and it was not just the religion of the Mediterranean coastal population; we have evidence that in the mid-seventh century it retained a vigorous presence in the towns of the interior. What we don't know is how deeply it had penetrated the countryside in the hinterland. Yet Christianity was fated to disappear altogether from the region, though it took a long time doing so. The last attestations of the existence of indigenous Christians come from Tunis toward the end of the fourteenth century, and perhaps even later. But references to Christians in the Berber interior in Islamic times are scarce, and they may not be to Berbers. Altogether, for the period that concerns us here we have no indication that Christianity had a strong presence among the Berbers tribes at large, and there was no North African equivalent of Christian Nubia or the Christian kingdoms of northern Spain. Indeed, the Arabic sources give the impression that at the time of the conquest Berber paganism was more salient than Berber Christianity. Thus we find Muslim jurists classifying the Berbers as Magians, in other words Zoroastrians; this is an odd application of the term, but enough to make it clear that these jurists did not regard them as Christians. A bold hypothesis to account for the discrepancy between the late antique and early Islamic sources would be that late antiquity had seen a migration of pagan Berbers from the Sahara into the North African hinterland, and there is some archaeological evidence that could support this. Yet paganism, like Christianity, faded out among the North African Berbers. As late as the eleventh century we hear, for example, of a ram cult in southwestern Morocco, but thereafter we know of no Berber population on the

North African mainland that continued to practice a paganism untouched by Islam. In any case, it is clear that even before the ninth century the only religion that was making history in North Africa was Islam. As early as 754 a provincial governor of Tunisia was explaining to the caliph that he could not send him slaves because "Ifrīqiya today is all converts (*islāmiyya*)."[10]

What that left in play was Muslim sectarianism, together with Berber prophethood on the Islamic model. In other words, at the center of the early Berber response to the Arab conquest was a paradox that made considerable sense: by distinguishing the persons from the beliefs of their conquerors, the Berbers could at the same time hate the Arabs and love Islam. Such a spirit is evident in an old theme that we encounter in North African Ibāḍī literature. There are a couple of Qur'ānic verses in which the believers are warned that if they are remiss in the struggle in the way of God, He will "substitute a people other than you" (Q9:39, Q47:38). One way to understand this divine threat was to see it as directed against the Arabs: if they did not perform as they should, God would turn instead to some other ethnic group. Some saw the Persians or the Yemenis as the group in question. But in an Ibāḍī work from ninth-century North Africa, we read that Ibn Mas'ūd—a distinguished Arab companion of the Prophet—told the people of Mecca and Medina that the Berbers would "come to you with God's religion from the west,"[11] and that they were the ones whom God would substitute in accordance with the Qur'ānic threat. Whether or not Berbers were already thinking like this in the eighth century, espousing the new religion in a dissident form was a bold and effective way to accept Islam while rejecting Arab domination. This the Berbers did by adopting Khārijism in both its Ibāḍī and Ṣufrī forms. The two sects had sent missionaries to North Africa in the early eighth century; one account has it that the first Ibāḍī and the first Ṣufrī reached the region riding on the same camel. Of course not all Berber rebels need have been affiliated to these sects, and not all Berbers responded to the challenge of the Arabs by rebelling against them. There were Berber groups who themselves developed claims to be of Arab, specifically Yemeni, descent. But it was Islam as resistance that made Berber history. The sectarian violence it brought with it was nothing new in North African history. The Circumcellion bands that championed the cause of the Donatist schismatics of the fourth and fifth centuries must to a considerable extent have been made up of what in Islamic times would be called Berbers. But Islamic sectarianism brought to the fray something that Christian sectarianism lacked: the objective of state formation.

10. Quoted in M. Talbi, *L'Émirat aghlabide*, Paris 1966, 36, from Ibn 'Idhārī, *al-Bayān al-mughrib*, Leiden 1948–51, 1:67.

11. Ibn Sallām al-Ibāḍī, *Kitāb fīhi bad' al-islām wa-sharā'i' al-dīn*, Wiesbaden 1986, 124.

One scene of rebellion, Ṣufrī in inspiration, was located far to the west in Morocco. In 740 the insurgent tribes of the region were led by a certain Maysara, who belonged to one of them. Like many of the rebels mentioned in the sources he bore an Arab name, and he had spent time in Qayrawān, albeit only as a water seller in the market. He seized Tangier and the Sūs, and the rebels went on to inflict crushing defeats on two Arab armies sent against them, the second dispatched from Syria. Meanwhile in 741 a major Berber rebellion broke out in Spain. The rebels were clearly influenced by their Moroccan counterparts; like them, they shaved their heads before going into battle. It took desperate measures on the part of the Arabs to defeat them, and a tenth-century chronicler comments on the resulting hatred between Arabs and Berbers in Spain as an enmity that would endure till the Day of Judgment. Much farther to the east there was a Ṣufrī rebellion in Tunisia itself beginning in the late 740s, and in 757 some Berber tribesmen seized Qayrawān, though these may not have been Ṣufrīs. The Ibāḍīs, too, were active in eastern North Africa. They had been successful in converting the tribes of Tripolitania, and at midcentury there was an Ibāḍī state there; it briefly invaded southeastern Tunisia, but soon collapsed. A new Ibāḍī state was formed in the late 750s, with Tripoli as its capital. This time an invasion of Tunisia led in 758 to the capture of Qayrawān from the Berber tribe that had occupied it the year before. The result of this expansion was an Ibāḍī state that ruled not just Tripolitania but also Tunisia as far west as the Kutāma country. But this state, too, did not last for long. In 761 an army led by the ʿAbbāsid governor of Egypt destroyed it and took Qayrawān. The Ibāḍīs, however, were persistent, and in 768 there was a fresh Ibāḍī revolt that was also joined by Ṣufrīs, and in 771 they again took Qayrawān. Four years later the rebels were once more defeated by ʿAbbāsid forces, and with that this last phase of the Berber rebellion was over. In the event it was the Ibāḍīs, not the Ṣufrīs, who survived into modern times. Both represented a form of Islam that was oriented to the east—but a dissident east.

The aftermath of the rebellion in North Africa

It naturally took time for the dust to settle, but the aftermath of the rebellion saw the emergence and consolidation of the ninth-century scene that we surveyed in the first section of this chapter. In Tunisia, Qayrawān had fallen to the Berber rebels more than once, but ʿAbbāsid armies had succeeded in recovering it, and the region remained a province of the ʿAbbāsid Empire until in 800 its governor secured autonomy through negotiation. That the Berber rebels failed in Tunisia is not surprising: its plains and peasants made it relatively easy to conquer, and its agricultural resources made it worth holding onto. But as we will see, Qayrawān would once again fall to Berber rebels in the tenth century.

The ʿAbbāsid recovery of Tunisia did not, of course, mean that the North African Khārijites were reduced to statelessness. They did, however, shift their political activities to more remote areas where the writ of the ʿAbbāsid governors of Qayrawān and their Aghlabid successors did not run. Some Ibāḍīs moved south from Tripolitania into the region of the Fazzān in the south of today's Libya; we know of an Ibāḍī principality in the Fazzān in the tenth century. Others moved west to Tāhart, which became the main Ibāḍī center in North Africa. Among them was ʿAbd al-Raḥmān ibn Rustam. As we have seen, he was of Persian origin, but he had lived in Qayrawān since childhood and had served as its governor when the Ibāḍīs occupied it. He had also spent time in Baṣra, where the Ibāḍī leadership still resided in this period. In Tāhart he and his companions established an imamate that he ruled for a decade (778–88) before passing it on to his descendants. The Ṣufrīs, too, showed a tendency to move westward, and after failing to sustain a state based in Tlemcen, they shifted their center to the Tāfīlālt in southeastern Morocco, where the Midrārid dynasty ruled from 772. Once again a high level of mobility is in evidence: Samghū ibn Wāsūl, the Berber who in one account was the first ruler of the dynasty, is said to have studied in Qayrawān and to have played a part in Maysara's revolt.

Undoubtedly the most curious phenomenon to arise from the rebellion was the Berber religion of the Barghawāṭa. According to our eleventh-century account, Ṭarīf—the father of the prophet Ṣāliḥ—had been a follower of Maysara, and Ṣāliḥ himself had been present among the rebels as a child. He would thus have been born in the 730s. After the rebellion was over, Ṭarīf settled in the Barghawāṭa region, founding a dynasty and remaining a Muslim till his death. When his son Ṣāliḥ devised the new religion, instead of proclaiming it he bequeathed it in secret to his son Ilyās, instructing him to wait till he was strong enough to make it public and kill those who opposed it. Ilyās then ruled for fifty years, outwardly professing Islam and keeping the religion secret. It was his son Yūnus who finally revealed the religion, summoning his subjects to it and killing large numbers of opponents. This would have been around the middle of the ninth century. Yūnus was also the only member of the dynasty to perform the pilgrimage to Mecca; the fact that there seems to have been no Berber sanctuary to replace that of the Muslims is an indication of the degree to which the new religion retained its links to Islam. Just what we should make of the details of this whole story is hard to say, but a link to the Berber rebellion of the mid-eighth century is certainly plausible.

The aftermath of the rebellion in Spain

That leaves Spain. Given that the Berbers were a major component of the Muslim presence there in the years following the conquest, the Berber rebellion was bound to pose a serious challenge to Arab rule. Indeed, the outcome could easily have been the downfall of the Arabs and the emergence of a state run by Ṣufrī Berbers. But any such prospect was averted through a serendipitous chain of events that took place on the North African side of the Strait of Gibraltar. The sequence began with the Arab army sent from Syria against Maysara in 740. It was known as the army of Balj, after the name of one of its commanders, and was made up of Syrian cavalry. After this force was crushingly defeated by the Berbers, Balj with some seven thousand men fled to Ceuta on the northern tip of Morocco. Besieged by the Berbers and in desperate straits, they appealed for help to the Qurashī governor of Spain, who was after all a fellow Arab. But at this point the Arabs of Spain had no wish to see the Syrians cross the Strait and share in their patrimony. That changed in 741 when the Berber rebellion broke out in Spain. The Arabs of Spain now found that they needed the Syrians as much as the Syrians needed them. Though neither group trusted the other, a deal was done, and in 742 the Syrians were brought over to Spain to help in the struggle against the Berber rebels; it was part of the deal that once victory was achieved they would leave. Thus reinforced, the Arabs prevailed against the Berbers. But the deal came unstuck, the governor ended up crucified by the bridge in Cordoba, and the Syrians stayed on. The way they then settled on the land mapped the geography of Syria onto Spain: the Jund of Jordan settled around Málaga, that of Qinnasrīn around Jaén, and so forth. They were now a powerful military force in Spain. Moreover, among their number were some hundreds of clients of the Umayyads.

In 756 serendipity was again at work, and this time it had nothing to do with Berber insurrection. Spain had effectively come adrift from the Umayyad Caliphate in the 740s, and unlike Tunisia it was never to be possessed by their ʿAbbāsid successors, despite a somewhat halfhearted attempt in 763. This made Spain a potential refuge for an Umayyad prince fleeing westward to escape the massacre of his family by the victorious ʿAbbāsids. The young prince, ʿAbd al-Raḥmān I—known as ʿAbd al-Raḥmān al-Dākhil ("ʿAbd al-Raḥmān the immigrant")—reached Spain in 755 after a hair-raising journey from Syria. He owed his survival to a combination of luck, daring, and connections. One connection paid off handsomely in North Africa: his mother was Berber, so when he found himself unwelcome in Tunisia he was able to take refuge with her tribe. The other crucial connection was, of course, the presence of those clients of his family in Spain. A further feature of the Spanish political landscape that will have looked very familiar to him was the factional conflict between Northerners and Southerners; when turned down by the leader of the Northerners, he proceeded to ally with the Southerners. Thanks to such deft political and military moves, he became the founder of a new Umayyad dynasty in Spain, holding power there from 756 till his death in 788. After the first year he ceased to give any recognition to the ʿAbbāsid caliph, but he did not claim to be caliph himself. His success in consolidating his rule in

Spain naturally encouraged other members of his family and its supporters to come to join him.

The key to the emergence of the Muslim Spain that we surveyed in the previous section was thus a combination of factors: good agricultural resources, the reinforcement of the Arab presence through the coming of the Syrians, and the establishment of a refugee Umayyad dynasty that was to last the best part of three centuries. These factors decisively shaped the character of Muslim Spain. Though the new Umayyad dynasty was politically independent virtually from the start, Spain shared with Tunisia its strong commitment to the religious and cultural norms prevailing in the east.

The coming of Shīʿism

The coming of Shīʿism to the western Muslim world was the major novelty of the trough between the Berber rebellion and the rise of the Fāṭimids. There is no indication of a Shīʿite presence among the Berbers before 762–63, and the main contribution of the rebellion to the spread of Shīʿism was simply the extinction of caliphal power west of Tunisia. It would have been odd if Shīʿites had not ventured into this tempting terrain of dissident Berber tribes.

How much we know about the arrival of various forms of Shīʿism in the West depends largely on the extent to which its bearers were making political and military history. As we have seen, the Bajaliyya were not doing so, and we know nothing of the process by which their spiritual forebears had reached North Africa.

The Idrīsids, by contrast, were a by-product of a well-known historical event that took place in the Ḥijāz. There in 786 an ʿAlid rebelled against the ʿAbbāsids. As usual the rising was a failure, with the rebels being slaughtered in a battle at Fakhkh near Mecca. One of those who escaped was an ʿAlid named Idrīs. He mingled with the pilgrims who were in Mecca at the time and so avoided detection. Like ʿAbd al-Raḥmān al-Dākhil, he then fled westward, ending his journey two years later in Walīla, the Roman Volubilis, to the west of the future city of Fez in Morocco. There he had the protection of the chief of a Berber tribe, the Awraba. Thanks to this chief, in 789 the Awraba and other tribes of the area recognized him as imam. But he died soon after, in 791. The story goes that he was poisoned by a Zaydī Shīʿite agent who was sent for the purpose by the ʿAbbāsid caliph Hārūn al-Rashīd (ruled 786–809). We are told that the agent used his sectarian allegiance to win the trust of Idrīs, which suggests that Idrīs may have been a Zaydī himself; indeed, later Zaydīs in the east recognized him as one of their imams. But it did not augur well for the future of the dynasty that he died after so short a reign and left no heir bar a fetus in the womb of a Berber concubine—thus opening the door to doubts about whether his successor, Idrīs II (ruled 803–28), was really his son. The dynasty nevertheless survived. Meanwhile, we know that the Idrīsids were not the only ʿAlids to engage in politics among the Berber tribes in this period: a ninth-century author mentions ʿAlid principalities in what is now northern Algeria.

The presence of Shīʿism in Spain was much more limited. The first sign of it was the rebellion of a certain Shaqyā, a schoolmaster, that began in 768 and continued for almost a decade. He claimed to be an ʿAlid, but other than that we know nothing about his sectarian affiliation. Shaqyā apart, there is little evidence of Shīʿites in Spain before the rise of the Fāṭimids, and not much even then.

By contrast, we know a lot about the development that led to Fāṭimid rule in North Africa. That constituted the next wave to break over the Muslim West.

On to the rise of the Fāṭimids and its aftermath

How the Fāṭimids came to power

Early Ismāʿīlism was, among other things, a far-flung conspiracy to bring about revolution in the Muslim world.[12] Its secret headquarters at Salamya in Syria accordingly dispatched agents to test the waters in many different regions. By far the most successful of these agents was a certain Abū ʿAbdallāh al-Shīʿī (d. 911), a native of Kūfa. After joining the Ismāʿīlīs he was sent to serve an apprenticeship in the Yemen under a more experienced agent to prepare him to set about spreading the movement elsewhere. His apprenticeship completed, he went on pilgrimage to Mecca. This was not a vacation. The pilgrimage scene provided excellent cover for subversive activity, since a skilled agent could make contact with Muslims from almost any part of the Muslim world and do so in crowded conditions that must have made the work of the caliph's intelligence agents very difficult. While roaming the area where the pilgrims were camped at Minā near Mecca, he chanced on a group of Kutāma tribesmen; the homeland of these Berbers was the region to the west of Constantine in northeastern Algeria. Two of them were Shīʿites thanks to the missionary work of one of the emissaries sent by the seventh imam back in the eighth century, so Abū ʿAbdallāh easily got talking to them—presumably in Arabic, though this was a language the Kutāma were later said to have spoken very badly. Soon the whole group took a shine to him, and when the pilgrimage was over and he said he was traveling to Egypt they accompanied him on his journey.

The trip gave him ample opportunity to ply the tribesmen with questions about their homeland, which he did as if he was just making conversation. Their answers

12. For the rise of the Fāṭimids see Halm, *The empire of the Mahdi*.

convinced him that he had found what he was looking for. They told him that the ruler—meaning the Aghlabid ruler of Tunisia—had no power over them and had no governors in the urban centers within their territory. Nor did they have any ruler of their own: "Every man among us is his own master."[13] They did have elders, and schoolmasters with some slight knowledge of Islam whom they would consult on religious questions; these men would also arbitrate disputes among the tribesmen. The Kutāma, they said, were a single people, but divided into tribes, clans, and families. Groups of them would fight each other and then make peace and fight other groups. Abū ʿAbdallāh wanted to know whether they would unite if attacked by outsiders. This was a question to which they had no answer—they explained that it had never happened to them on account of the inaccessibility of their territory and their large numbers. He inquired how many of them there were, but they had no idea. They were better able to respond when he asked them whether they had horses and weapons: "Those are most of what we do for a living; they're what we take pride in; we prepare them because we need them in the wars we fight between ourselves."[14] Abū ʿAbdallāh had indeed struck gold. Here was a warlike people remote from any state that could obstruct his activities and with no significant political leadership of its own that would get in his way. Moreover, the Kutāma already had a pattern of deference to men of religion that would give him an entrée to their society. And if their warlike energies could be turned outward, he would have a formidable military force at his disposal.

Once Abū ʿAbdallāh and his Kutāma pilgrims reached Egypt, he gave them to understand that he planned to stay there to make a living as a schoolmaster. He then deftly allowed them to persuade him to forget about Egypt and accompany them to their homeland instead. Nowhere, they assured him, were schoolmasters more respected and better rewarded than in their country; if he wanted, they would pay him a year or two's salary in advance. All this was very clever. Schoolmastering was a role in which a literate foreigner could insert himself into a tribal society without attracting suspicion; we know of another early Ismāʿīlī agent who used this cover with an Arab tribe in Egypt. After Abū ʿAbdallāh and the returning pilgrims reached the Kutāma homeland in 893, he set about establishing his position among the tribesmen and organizing them into a political and military force under his command. His style of state formation echoed that of the Prophet: he set himself up in an "abode of Hijra" (*dār hijra*), and those who came to join him there were Muhājirs. Eventually the Aghlabid ruler caught wind of Abū ʿAbdallāh's activities and sent two expeditions against him in 902–3, but they failed to eliminate him. After this it was Abū ʿAbdallāh's turn to attack. In the course of the following years he conquered Tunisia, and in 909 he entered the capital city

13. Qāḍī Nuʿmān, *Risālat iftitāḥ al-daʿwa*, Beirut 1970, 65.
14. Qāḍī Nuʿmān, *Risālat iftitāḥ al-daʿwa*, 66.

of Raqqāda, from which the Aghlabids had already fled, marking the end of Aghlabid rule. "Easternizing" (*tasharruq*) now meant adopting Ismāʿīlism.

At this time the Ismāʿīlī leadership in the east was in crisis, and the leader of the sect, ʿAbdallāh al-Mahdī, had fled his home in Syria in 902. He then made his way through Egypt to North Africa, but rather than joining Abū ʿAbdallāh he continued westward all the way to Sijilmāsa, where he spent four years posing as a merchant. Once his conquest of Tunisia was complete, Abū ʿAbdallāh arrived in force and brought al-Mahdī back with him to Tunisia in triumph, thus inaugurating the Fāṭimid Caliphate (909–1171).

The Fāṭimids in Tunisia

Two contrasting themes are worth noting in the aftermath of the change of dynasties. One is a certain continuity. Two successive states based on the same territory are likely to be largely dependent of the same set of resources, including human resources. This did not just mean keeping the peasants on the land; it was also important to retain the services of at least some of the bureaucrats who knew how to tax them, particularly as the Aghlabid financial archives had been destroyed in the course of the transition. Here a seasoned Aghlabid administrator played a leading role in the initial phase of Fāṭimid rule. Nor was such continuity limited to financial officials: we also find a secretary, a court poet, and a doctor who weathered the change of employers. Even the military forces of the fallen dynasty could be co-opted. In this way al-Mahdī took over and expanded the Aghlabid corps of Slav military slaves, and likewise the old Arab Jund—still Arab and, what is more, Sunnī—entered the service of the Fāṭimid rulers. What dynasty would want to be entirely dependent on the unruly and rapacious Kutāma?

Pitted against this continuity was the messianic expectation, widespread among those who had helped bring al-Mahdī to power, that everything would now be completely different, and that all who had participated in the enterprise would get whatever they wanted in reward. Politicians who seek support in order to come to power are always likely to promise more than they can deliver, and when they do so in an idiom of messianic enthusiasm the gap is apt to be spectacular. So as postrevolutionary disillusion began to take its toll, al-Mahdī found himself being called out by one of the Kutāma chiefs: "We have doubts about your cause! Perform a miracle for us, if you really are the Mahdī, as you have maintained."[15] Some of al-Mahdī's young and mischievous Sunnī subjects had the clever idea of having an anonymous note delivered to him challenging him to identify the senders: "O you who claim to know all secrets, who is it who wrote this note?" Of course

15. For this and the quotations that follow see Halm, *The empire of the Mahdi*, 160, 164, 165, 173.

he did not know the answer. Worst of all, Abū ʿAbdallāh himself was led by al-Mahdī's conduct to conclude that the man to whom he had devoted his life's work was a fraud: "His deeds are shameful and have no resemblance whatsoever to the deeds of the Mahdī, for whom I recruited among you." His triumph now turned to dust and ashes, and in 911 al-Mahdī proceeded to have him killed—much as Abū Muslim al-Khurāsānī, the architect of the ʿAbbāsid revolution, had perished at the hands of the caliph al-Manṣūr. In fact Abū ʿAbdallāh was far from being the only such casualty. Meanwhile, al-Mahdī sought to buy time by building up his son and heir rather than himself as the future messiah; he gave him the title al-Qāʾim, a term with powerful resonance in Shīʿite eschatology that had usually been applied to the Mahdī. But the very idea that the Mahdī would have a successor invited protest against eschatological dilution: "You are the Mahdī; after you there will not be another!" In any case, the son showed himself no more plausible than the father. As we will see, already in al-Mahdī's lifetime the two expeditions led by al-Qāʾim to conquer Egypt were embarrassing failures. It was perhaps this demoralizing experience of starring in the role of the Qāʾim and falling short that led him to spend almost his entire reign (934–46) in seclusion, with the result that his successor had no trouble concealing his death for over a year. Just as telling was the inability of al-Mahdī to come up with a plausible genealogy linking himself and his son to the family of the Prophet—an indication that his claim to ʿAlid descent was very likely spurious.

Despite all this unpleasantness, the Fāṭimids ruled in Tunisia from 910 to 972. But the discomfort they felt there, especially in their first decades, is reflected in the location of the new capital city inaugurated by al-Mahdī in 921, Mahdiyya. The Aghlabids, in part no doubt to put some daylight between their Ḥanafī supporters and the surly Mālikīs of Qayrawān, had built themselves capitals elsewhere, but none of them were actually on the coast—even Tunis is set back from it. By contrast, Mahdiyya was situated on a spur jutting out about a mile from the coast, approached by a road that is described as having been as narrow as a shoelace. This choice to perch on the very edge of Tunisia did not arise from the pull of maritime commerce, as with some of the world's coastal capitals in later centuries. Instead, it reflected the insecurity of a sectarian ruler who in religious terms was profoundly at odds with the great majority of his subjects—far more so than the Aghlabids had been. For the intransigent Mālikīs of Qayrawān, al-Mahdī was the Commander of the Polytheists, not the Commander of the Faithful. In this context the imposition of the Shīʿite call to prayer, with its slightly different wording, might seem like a detail, but to the Mālikīs it was an insufferable deviation from orthopraxy. The Fāṭimid authorities took it just as seriously. One muezzin who refused to use it had his tongue cut out and was then paraded around Qayrawān with his tongue attached to his forehead. All told, this was a fairly toxic relationship, though it did not exclude a measure of pragmatism and coexistence. On one occasion when the Mālikī scholars of Qayrawān were challenged as to why they did not simply emigrate to escape Fāṭimid rule, they responded with some irritation, and perhaps embarrassment, that they had chosen the lesser of two evils: were they to leave Tunisia, the laity they left behind would convert to Ismāʿīlism in their thousands. It is always fortunate when the most convenient thing to do is also the principled choice.

The enemy with regard to whom the adoption of Mahdiyya as the Fāṭimid capital paid off most handsomely was not in fact the Mālikīs. In the 940s the Fāṭimids faced an initially devastating rebellion of schismatic Ibāḍī Berbers from the mountains of the Awrās in what is now eastern Algeria. This insurrection, which could easily have brought down the dynasty, was led by the onetime Berber schoolmaster whom we have already encountered, Abū Yazīd al-Nukkārī; as we have seen before, it can be a mistake to think of schoolmastering as a dead-end profession. He began his rebellion in 943. In 944 he took Qayrawān, where the Mālikīs decided that for the time being they should hold their noses and side with the Ibāḍīs against the Fāṭimids. From there the rebels went on to subject Mahdiyya to a prolonged siege in 945. It proved impregnable, but only in 947 was the rebellion finally defeated.

The impregnability of Mahdiyya from the land was not, however, the only reason the Fāṭimids survived the insurrection of Abū Yazīd. The other was a marked upturn in the quality of Fāṭimid leadership. The Fāṭimid caliph al-Manṣūr (ruled 946–53), unlike his reclusive father al-Qā'im, cut a fine figure in the public domain. On one occasion we see him hoisting a kid from the street onto his saddle as he rode through a triumphal gateway. He personally led the campaigns that broke the power of Abū Yazīd, and it was to celebrate this victory that he took the title al-Manṣūr, meaning the one to whom God gives victory. In pursuing the fugitive Abū Yazīd, he took his troops into the Sahara "where no army had ever yet set foot,"[16] and into mountains where he trod narrow paths on his own two feet. He was conspicuously courageous on the battlefield. He could also echo the Prophetic paradigm to good effect. On one occasion he found it necessary to dig a ditch to protect his troops from the enemy, a task involving them in manual labor of a kind they considered beneath their dignity. He pointed out that the Prophet had dug such a ditch when defending Medina against a Meccan attack, and like Muḥammad he himself joined in the digging. It went well with this common touch that he did not allow people to prostrate themselves in front of him, kissing the ground—something his grandfather had tolerated. In addition, he had political nerve. Instead of perching defensively in Mahdiyya, he built himself a new capital, Manṣūriyya, on the outskirts of Qayrawān. He even preached in the Great Mosque

16. Quoted in Halm, *The empire of the Mahdi*, 318.

of Qayrawān, the citadel of North African Mālikism, and despite his heterodoxy he seems to have been popular with the common people of the city. All this went with a lively mind. He showed a marked curiosity about the ancient monuments he saw around him and asked for Latin inscriptions to be translated. Much impressed by the ruins of Carthage, he spent several days there and posed questions that may not have been historically well informed but were sharply intelligent. Had a single ruler built all this, he wondered, and if so, how had he been able to do it? Or had a succession of rulers been at work, and if so, how was it that they had all devoted their efforts to a single site, given the tendency for kings to have divergent views as to where cities should be located? Thereupon he had a dream in which the ruler who had built the city (it turned out there was just one of them) appeared before him. He asked this ruler if he hadn't had an enemy he had to wage war on, distracting him from the building work. To this the ruler replied that he had had many enemies—who doesn't? In addition to all this, al-Manṣūr was an author. His son once encountered him sitting under a tree on a hot summer's day, bareheaded and streaming with sweat; he was scribbling away to record his ideas and reacted with irritation to having his train of thought interrupted. But despite all this he was unlucky. He suffered from serious ill health that clouded the last years of his reign, and he died at the age of thirty-nine.

His successor was his son al-Muʿizz (ruled 953–75). This ruler was not a recluse like his grandfather. He made formal public appearances to lead the prayer and preach every Friday, and on his many excursions he would be surrounded by people seeking to hand him their petitions. In 962 he organized a massive, very public, and fantastically expensive circumcision ceremony; for a month, thousands of his subjects were circumcised each day, and all received gifts. He, too, had a lively mind: he invented the fountain pen. But he was not a born military leader like his father. For example, we find him going out on campaign in 969 but soon handing over command of the expedition to his subordinates. In 956 he was at Mahdiyya supervising the preparation of a fleet, but when he tried going out to sea on a ship he did not enjoy it and never did it again. Likewise he did not accompany his troops when they set out for the conquest of Egypt. The general he put in charge of the operation nevertheless served him well.

The Fāṭimids beyond Tunisia

Fāṭimid efforts were not, of course, limited to Tunisia. To the northwest lay the island of Sicily, and the Fāṭimids soon moved to take over this Aghlabid territory in the face of considerable Sunnī resistance. But in 948 they entrusted the administration of the island to a governor who proved to be the founder of a dynasty, the Kalbids (948–1055). The autonomy of this dynasty was strengthened by the Fāṭimid departure for Egypt in 972. We are not well informed about Sicilian society in this period, but the spread of Arabic and Islam there seems to have been quite extensive. A Muslim geographer who visited the island in 973 gives us two contrasting snapshots. One is his estimate of the size of the congregation he saw in the main mosque of the capital city, Palermo: thirty-six rows of 200 men each, for a total of more than 7,000. Factor in women, children, and slaves, and we have a substantial Muslim population in the city. The other snapshot takes us out into the countryside, where we catch a glimpse of a community somewhere between Christianity and Islam. This large population, which our geographer calls the Mushaʿmidhūn, clearly purported to be Muslim but for the most part did not observe the basic duties of Islam. The men intermarried with Christian women, which in itself was perfectly legal for Muslim men, but their practice was that sons would follow the religion of their fathers and daughters that of their mothers. This kind of halfway house between Christianity and Islam was not unique, as we will see in later chapters. But the Islamization of the island, however imperfect, was reversed after its loss to the Normans in the later eleventh century.

The projection of Fāṭimid power to the west—the wild Berber west—was a different story. In 909 it was not just the Aghlabid dynasty that fell victim to the onslaught of the Kutāma led by Abū ʿAbdallāh; with very little effort he also put an end to the disintegrating Rustamid imamate of Tāhart in the same year. Yet despite his expedition to Sijilmāsa to free al-Mahdī and his violent seizure of that city, he did not succeed in destroying the Midrārid state. Nor did he tangle with the Idrīsids. Moreover, subsequent Fāṭimid experience reinforced the point that the subjugation of Berber tribes was rarely definitive. Two years after the fall of the Rustamids a revolt broke out and Tāhart had to be taken afresh—and not for the last time. Sijilmāsa was repossessed in 921. Fez, the Idrīsid capital, was taken in 920 and retaken twice in the years that followed. Finally a Fāṭimid expedition of 958–60 took Tāhart, Fez, and Sijilmāsa, reaching the Atlantic. But this victory, too, was transitory, and in 979 we find the Zīrids—the successors of the departed Fāṭimids in Tunisia—taking Fez and Sijilmāsa yet again; within a few years they had given up on campaigns in the west. It was around this time that both the Midrārid and Idrīsid dynasties came to an end, but not at the hands of the Fāṭimids or the Zīrids. In general, the Fāṭimids did not try to impose direct rule west of Tāhart, preferring to hand over whatever authority they had to powerful tribal leaders.

Unlike Morocco, Spain and its Umayyad rulers were beyond the military reach of the Fāṭimids in Tunisia. As the two major powers of the Muslim West, with strongly antithetical religious orientations, the Umayyads and the Fāṭimids were bitter rivals. Apart from a couple of naval attacks on each other's coasts in 955–56, this enmity played out in three main arenas. The first was the intervening territory. The Umayyads in this period took possession of a few ports on the Moroccan coast, but for the most part they competed with the Fāṭimids by exercising their influence farther afield and waging proxy wars. Thus the later Idrīsids found themselves having to recognize the overlordship of one state or the other, and we likewise find both allegiances among the rulers of Sijilmāsa. The Fāṭimids responded to the Umayyads in kind, but as we have seen they also mounted repeated military expeditions to the west. The second arena was promoting subversion within the core territory of the enemy state, though in each case the initiative seems to have come from the local rebels. In Spain, Ibn Ḥafṣūn was in contact with the Fāṭimids. He is said to have recognized al-Mahdī in 909, he adopted the Shīʿite form of the call to prayer, and he may have received provisions from Fāṭimid territory. Two Fāṭimid agents joined him and participated in his campaigns. Conversely, Abū Yazīd al-Nukkārī appealed to the Umayyads for support, and they sent a naval expedition in response—but it arrived too late. The third arena was symbolic: contending claims to the caliphate. The ʿAbbāsids, of course, were widely acknowledged as caliphs in the Muslim world until the dynasty met its end in 1258, but as we have seen, the Umayyads of Spain soon stopped recognizing them. Yet despite being descended from the Umayyad caliphs of the east, until well into the tenth century they did not claim the status for themselves. The Fāṭimids, however, did so from the inception of their rule in 909, and in 929 ʿAbd al-Raḥmān III (ruled 912–61) followed suit, announcing his own claim to be caliph.

By far the greatest success of the Fāṭimids outside Tunisia was the conquest of Egypt, which they finally achieved in 969. Egypt has been successfully invaded many times, but this was the only occasion in history when it was conquered from North Africa. Despite the absence at this point of a strong state in Egypt, where resistance to the Fāṭimid takeover was minimal, such a conquest was a logistically difficult enterprise. In fact, three earlier attempts, in 913–15, 919–21, and 935–36, had failed, though they did leave the Fāṭimids in possession of Barqa in Cyrenaica. The final and successful attack involved the advance placement of provisions and the digging of wells along the route, and it proved alarmingly expensive. That the Fāṭimids nevertheless persisted and eventually succeeded points to the grandeur of their ambition. Not content with the role of a provincial dynasty like the Aghlabids, they aspired to take the place of the ʿAbbāsids as the rulers of the Muslim world. For them Tunisia was just a stepping-stone on the way to something much bigger: they had their eyes on Iraq, and even Khurāsān. So in 972 al-Muʿizz left Tunisia behind him, and in 973 he took up residence in Cairo, the palace city newly constructed for him by the general who had conquered Egypt.

The resurgence of Umayyad Spain

As we have seen, the reign of ʿAbd al-Raḥmān III was a rather successful one, despite the fact that it coincided with the menace of the Fāṭimid presence in Tunisia. ʿAbd al-Raḥmān acquired a few possessions and considerable influence in

Morocco, he held his own against the Fāṭimids, and like them he claimed the caliphate. In addition, he built himself a magnificent new capital a few miles west of Cordoba, Madīnat al-Zahrā'. All in all, this was a dramatic resurgence of Umayyad rule. But a glance at other aspects of the history of the period should dispel any tendency to hyperbole on this score. The reign of ʿAbd al-Raḥmān was a mercilessly uphill struggle, fought with a steady combination of persistence and pragmatism.

Creating and sustaining a centralized government can be a labor of Sisyphus under premodern conditions. Geographically Spain had the resources to make it possible, but also the mountains to make it difficult. The situation was made worse by two historical factors. First, whereas under the Romans and Visigoths the conquerors of Spain had belonged to a single ethnic group, in the case of the Muslims there were deep ethnic divisions among them. There was little love lost between Arabs and Berbers, or among the Arabs between Northerners and Southerners. These enmities affected not just politics but also the core of the army. In the later Umayyad period Berbers recruited from North Africa came to replace rather than complement the Arab troops of the Junds, as the role of Berbers—not to mention that of Slavs imported from Europe—became more obtrusive. These Berbers from North Africa now constituted the core of the army. The second historical factor was that, as we have seen, the Muslims had failed to conquer the whole peninsula. Perhaps that was because Spain was so remote from the center, or perhaps because the sea crossing reduced the influx of manpower from south of the Strait. In addition, the cavalrymen of Muslim Spain are reported by an eastern observer of the mid-tenth century to have been notably archaic in one respect: they made no use of the stirrup—though it is attested early in the next century. Whatever the reasons, the failure to conquer the entire peninsula mattered. Had the Muslims succeeded, their sole land frontier would have coincided with a formidable natural barrier, the Pyrenees. Instead, the Muslims came to face an extended land frontier stretching from the Mediterranean to the Atlantic. This had two adverse consequences. The first was direct: a long frontier had to be defended against the Christian kingdoms of northern Spain and their allies from north of the Pyrenees. The second was indirect: as already mentioned, a vast band of territory on the Muslim side of the frontier consisted of marches, and their existence worked to deprive the central government of resources and limit its control. Mérida, at the center of the Lower March, had been one of the great cities of Roman and Visigothic Spain and was the location of its most prolific mint in late Visigothic times, which went well with the outstanding fertility of the region surrounding it. Toledo, the former Visigothic capital, was likewise a major city. It is thus telling that a tenth-century Muslim geographer, while remarking that Mérida and Toledo were among the greatest cities of Spain, went on to note their effective independence: no Umayyad governor was present in either of them.

Against this background, it is easy to see why creating a durably centralized state could be so difficult for the Umayyads. ʿAbd al-Raḥmān began his reign by reestablishing the power of his state in the territories close to Cordoba. Once this modest objective had been attained, he turned to more distant and more serious enemies: Ibn Ḥafṣūn, the marcher lords, and the Christians of the north. Uprooting Ibn Ḥafṣūn, his supporters, and his progeny from their castles in the mountains of the southeast was a thankless task. It took ʿAbd al-Raḥmān many years to accomplish it, and it was not till 928 that the key fortress of Bobastro fell. It likewise took him years to deal with the dissidence of the marcher lords, and even then he could not entirely eliminate them; especially in the Upper March, he made accommodations that gave them considerable autonomy in return for a show of allegiance. With the Christians of the north it was largely a matter of running to stay in the same place. There were the usual raids into the Christian kingdoms, but rather than attempting to expand his territory, ʿAbd al-Raḥmān was satisfied with maintaining the status quo. Worse yet, in 939 he suffered a disconcerting defeat. Neither in Spain to the north nor in Morocco to the south did he show any interest in building an empire, and talk of recovering the Umayyad patrimony in the east was just that. It was not until the sixteenth century that Spain became for the first time in history an imperial center, and by then the country was ruled and largely inhabited by Christians. Altogether, it is not surprising that when ʿAbd al-Raḥmān's diaries were examined after his death, it was found that of the nearly eighteen thousand days of his reign, he had experienced only eighteen as happy ones. And within half a century of his death the state he had so painstakingly rebuilt was in terminal decay.

The rest of the story

The rest of the story: Tunisia

We now come to a phase that lasted the best part of a century, a time when good news was scarce for states in the Muslim West.

The Fāṭimid departure to the east in 972 once more reduced Tunisia to the status of a province. To rule it on their behalf, the Fāṭimids left behind them a Berber dynasty of governors, the Zīrids (972–1148)—an ordinary dynasty free of messianic pretensions. Never before or since has a state based in Egypt controlled Tunisia across the intervening desert, and the Zīrids were Berber tribal chiefs and military leaders in their own right. Thus it was just a matter of time before they became effectively independent. The second Zīrid ruler was already boasting that he was not the sort than can be appointed and dismissed by the stroke of a pen and that he had inherited his kingdom from his father and his ancestors. Yet it was several decades before the Zīrids made the break a formal one. In the 1040s they repudiated their allegiance to the Fāṭimids and instead recognized the even more distant ʿAbbāsid caliph as their overlord. It must have been a richly symbolic moment when the Zīrid ruler at the time of the break donated to the Great Mosque of Qayrawān a Qurʾān in which he had written in his own hand the affirmation that the best of men after Muḥammad are Abū Bakr, then ʿUmar, then ʿUthmān, and only then ʿAlī, at the same time cursing the Fāṭimids. Politically this made good sense. What the ʿAbbāsid allegiance had to offer the Zīrids was absolution from the charge of heresy, given the failure of the Fāṭimids to convert the mass of the population of Tunisia to their doctrine. This stigma had damned Ismāʿīlī rule in Tunisia in the eyes of many of its Sunnī subjects, as vicious anti-Shīʿite riots in 1016 made clear. The rioters were encouraged by scholars who assured them that if they happened to kill a fellow Sunnī by mistake, that just meant that the victim would get to paradise all the sooner. If there is a puzzle, it is that the Zīrid break with the Fāṭimids had not come before the 1040s. By then the Zīrid rulers had long ago lost interest in rendering any substantive services to their Fāṭimid overlords. The first Zīrid ruler, Buluggīn (ruled 972–84), had made a serious effort to sustain the Fāṭimid claim to rule the west; in the course of his last great expedition to Morocco in 979, he had taken Fez and Sijilmāsa and had gone on to campaign against the Barghawāṭa. But his successor al-Manṣūr (ruled 984–96) soon gave up on western campaigns. The Zīrids, in short, settled down to be just another Sunnī dynasty ruling Tunisia. But even this was not to last. Their former Fāṭimid overlords in Egypt were not doing particularly well in the later 1040s and were in no condition to dispatch an army to punish the Zīrids. But if our sources are to be believed, they had their revenge. Killing two birds with one stone, they encouraged a couple of troublesome Arab tribes in Upper Egypt, Hilāl and Sulaym, to move to Tunisia. The tribes did so, inflicting a catastrophic defeat on the Zīrid ruler in 1052 and reducing the Zīrid state to a shadow of its former self. According to our sources, both contemporary and later, they devastated the country;[17] it was apparently from this time on that what had been the breadbasket of Rome ceased to be an exporter of grain. After 1057 the Zīrids were reduced to perching in Mahdiyya as the Fāṭimids had once done, ruling only the coastal strip. By now there was no longer an effective state in possession of Tunisia.

The Zīrids nevertheless continued to reign in some fashion until 1148, when a fleet dispatched by the Norman king of Sicily took Mahdiyya. All good dynasties have to end, and bad ones too, but for what had once been a respectable Muslim dynasty this was an undignified finale, a testimony to the weakness of the Zīrid state after the arrival of the Arab tribes. It was also significant in another way. The very fact that Sicily was now in the possession of Norman adventurers from the

17. For the mainstream view that the Arab tribes did not in fact cause serious damage in Tunisia, see S. Garnier, *Histoires hafsides*, Leiden 2022, 331–35.

north was a telling example of the growing military power of the Christians of Europe. The demise of the Kalbid dynasty around 1055 and the weakness of the Zīrids offered an opportunity that the Normans had seized, conquering the island over the decades from 1061 to 1091. The fact that they now mounted a naval expedition that put an end to a Muslim dynasty on the North African mainland was likewise an ominous development. The Fāṭimids had never had to face such a threat when they took refuge in Mahdiyya. Indeed, in 934–35 their fleet had been able to seize Genoa, leaving it plundered and burned, and it was not until 1087 that the Genoese had returned the compliment. The balance of power was finally shifting.

The rest of the story: Spain

Meanwhile in Spain, the Umayyad state had collapsed. In the last decades of the tenth century, in fact down to 1008, it had still been doing well, but much had changed since the days of ʿAbd al-Raḥmān III. The most conspicuous novelty was the emergence of what might be called a shogunate. Though the dynasty limped on until 1031, the last effective Umayyad caliph was ʿAbd al-Raḥmān's son and successor, al-Ḥakam II (ruled 961–976). In the succession struggle that followed his death, the key figure was a very astute Arab known as Ibn Abī ʿĀmir. Under al-Ḥakam II he had been appointed a judge on the Moroccan side of the Strait, and he became in effect an intermediary between the caliph and the Berbers of the region. Finding himself in Cordoba at the time of al-Ḥakam's death, he soon amassed all real power and exercised it until his own death in 1002. In this respect the caliph no longer mattered. For a few years in the early eleventh century it looked as if Ibn Abī ʿĀmir would prove to have been the founder of a dynasty. One of his sons succeeded him in his role and did tolerably well, but when a second son, ʿAbd al-Raḥmān ibn Abī ʿĀmir, inherited the position in 1008 the result was disaster. His most striking mistake was to cross a symbolic red line by forcing the Umayyad caliph to name him as his heir.

Another source of tension had been building up over the years thanks to the policies of Ibn Abī ʿĀmir, but also of the caliphs before him. As we have seen, from being a significant component of the army the Berbers were becoming the core element, and they tended to be raw Berbers newly recruited from North Africa, not acculturated Berbers long resident in Spain. Adding sectarian to ethnic tension, some few hundred of those who arrived in the reign of al-Ḥakam II were Ibāḍīs. The result was a strong sense in Spain of the alien character of the Berber army, particularly among the populace of Cordoba. This resentment was not assuaged by Ibn Abī ʿĀmir's assiduous pursuit of jihad—he mounted more than fifty expeditions against the Christian kingdoms of the north. His son ʿAbd al-Raḥmān's behavior further exacerbated the sense of a Berber takeover of the army. So while he was away from the capital on campaign, his enemies seized power there and set about recruiting a militia among the Cordobans. ʿAbd al-Raḥmān was abandoned by his troops and killed in 1009.

The state was now falling apart, and the last two decades of the Umayyad dynasty were a time of political and military chaos. The end came in 1031 when the Cordobans themselves decided that they had had enough of the Umayyad Caliphate and abolished it. Meanwhile Spain was breaking up into some three dozen small states, each ruled by its own petty dynasty. In a way this development was nothing new. The Umayyad state had fallen into disarray before, notably in the later ninth century, as had the Visigothic kingdom in the mid-sixth. But this time the disintegration was more extreme—unparalleled since the Roman conquest—and, crucially, on this occasion there would be no recovery for Muslim Spain. Whatever its ultimate causes, the disintegration was not the result of Christian pressure from the north, but much as in the case of Sicily it was a clear invitation to Christian invasion. Thus Toledo, for centuries a dissident outpost of Muslim rule, once again became a Christian possession in 1085. This loss of territory in the heart of Spain exacerbated the long-term threat to Muslim rule in the south and east of the peninsula. But for now, even more catastrophic losses to hostile invaders from the north were held in check by supposedly friendly invaders from the south, the Berber Almoravids from the western Sahara. They crossed the Strait into Spain in 1086.

Despite the rather grim political and military context, the period was one of a remarkable cultural efflorescence in Muslim Spain, and one that was recognized even in the east. Back in the reign of ʿAbd al-Raḥmān III, one of his court poets, Ibn ʿAbd Rabbih (d. 940), had produced a large literary anthology. A highly cultured vizier in Iran, known as the Ṣāḥib ibn ʿAbbād (d. 995), was later curious to see it, but after taking a look at it his tart response was a quotation from the Qurʾān: "This is our own goods returned to us" (Q12:65). He had been hoping to learn about a distant land, but instead all he found in the book was accounts of his own region. In the next century, Spanish scholars were not so easily brushed aside. For example, Ḥumaydī (d. 1095), who traveled to the east and settled in Baghdad, was asked there to put together a work on the scholars and other cultural luminaries of his country, which he did. A contemporary of his in Baghdad then made extensive use of this book in a work of his own in which he mentioned more than two hundred Spanish scholars. At the same time, scholars in Spain were now writing books on subjects such as the text of the Qurʾān and the biographies of the companions of the Prophet that were to become standard works in the east, and it was thanks to the account of an eleventh-century Spanish historian that extensive information about the history of Muslim Spain—the kind that the Ṣāḥib ibn ʿAbbād had sought in vain—eventually became available in the east. It was also in this period that the accomplished Spanish scholar Ibn Ḥazm (d. 1064) wrote an epistle on the excellences of Muslim Spain in which he argued that its literary productivity in the fields of the religious sciences, linguistics, poetry, history, genealogy, medicine, philosophy, and the like could compare favorably with that of the lands of the east. He was not denying that Spain was located at a great distance from Iraq, the fount of learning and abode of the learned; in other words, he accepted that Spain was culturally provincial. But the fact was, he argued, that if anyone were to look for the likes of the works of the Spanish Muslim authors in Persia, Khūzistān, the Jazīra, the Yemen, or Syria, he would fail to find them, despite the proximity of these lands to the Iraqi metropolis (*dār hijra*) of culture. We may add to what he says something he would have taken for granted—namely, that nobody in Morocco could have claimed such stature in this period.

The other side of the coin was that the Romance language of Muslim Spain did not become a literary language till long after the end of our period. That it was widely spoken is not in doubt. Ibn Ḥazm noted as a point of interest about the members of the Arab tribe of Balī living in Spain that they spoke only Arabic; even the women were ignorant of Romance—or as he called it, Latin. Clearly this was unusual (and the implication that women were more likely than men were to speak Romance is interesting). But the oral use of the Romance vernacular did not carry over into literature, with one very minor exception. In our period a new Arabic poetic genre emerged in Spain and later spread to the east; its characteristic feature was the "seasoning" of the poem with a last line in the vernacular—usually vernacular Arabic, occasionally mixed with Romance, and very occasionally in Romance alone. But that was all.

Another aspect of the culture of Muslim Spain at the end of our period is worth a glance for its social and political significance. As we have seen, ill feeling between Arabs and native Spaniards was very real, and in everyday life it must have generated torrents of derogatory remarks on both sides. We hear of a judge in the time of ʿAbd al-Raḥmān III who was highly partisan, strongly aligned with the natives and full of disparagement of the Arabs. But so far as we know, in Spain—in contrast to the east—being rude about the Arabs was not as yet a literary genre. That changed after the decline of the Umayyad dynasty with the disintegration of Muslim Spain into a large number of petty states, most of them ruled by non-Arab dynasties. It was in this context that a Muslim of Basque origin, a certain Abū ʿĀmir ibn Gharsiyya (García in its Spanish spelling), wrote an epistle in which he asserted the superiority of the non-Arabs over the Arabs. In yet another testimony to the eastern orientation of the culture of Muslim Spain, he borrowed the old themes of eastern Shuʿūbism while making no reference to the particular ethnic and cultural heritage of the non-Arabs of Spain. He nevertheless succeeded in causing great offense, spawning no fewer than seven refutations. A twelfth-century Spanish scholar linked to the tribe of Balī expressed his amazement that Ibn Gharsiyya had been allowed to get away with what he did—why didn't they stone him? The answer was actually rather simple: Ibn Gharsiyya was making a living at the court of a Slav ruler in Dénia.

The rest of the story: The Berber tribes

Where did the disintegration of the state in Tunisia and Spain leave the Berbers of North Africa in the period prior to the arrival of the Almoravids? The two major states that had long framed their territory had effectively disappeared, leaving the Berbers west of Tunisia and south of Spain to their own devices. By this time few of the states that had appeared within this region in earlier times were still in existence. Abū ʿAbdallāh al-Shīʿī had destroyed the Rustamid state in 909. The last Midrārid ruler, who had recognized Fāṭimid overlordship, was killed around 977 by a tribal chief allied with the Umayyads. The last Idrīsid ruler, who likewise had Fāṭimid support, was killed in 985 by the Umayyad general who had captured him. Of the states we have considered, that left only those of the Barghawāṭa and the Ṣāliḥids. With both the Zīrids and the Umayyads out of the picture, we would expect that some new Berber states would now emerge in place of the old ones. But if we are looking for states as prominent as those of the ninth century, that does not seem to have happened. The one new Berber dynasty in this league, that of the Ḥammādids (1015–1152) of northeastern Algeria, was an offshoot of the Zīrids; like them, it lost the battle against the Arab nomads and took refuge on the coast, in this case in Bougie. So at this level, Berber North Africa was once again little more than a sea of tribes. But if we want to have a sense of the political realities on the ground, we need to dip below this level.

Under premodern conditions there is often a stratum of more or less autonomous political organization beneath the level of those states that are prominent enough to find a place in our handbooks. In fact, two of the states we have already looked at, the Barghawāṭa and the Ṣāliḥid dynasty, fall into this category. Just how many of these second-tier entities it makes sense to call states is a good question, but one to which we can rarely give an informed answer because we tend to know rather little about them. We could call them petty states.

In the region and period that concern us here—and before it, and after it—a widespread feature of Berber North Africa was the proliferation of petty states ruled by dynasties belonging to the Maghrāwa,[18] the Berber tribe to which the killer of the last Midrārid ruler belonged. This tribe may already be attested in ancient times, and its homeland seems to have been in what is now northern Algeria, to the west of Algiers. In our period, however, we already find it widely dispersed over North Africa from Tripolitania to Morocco. The Maghrāwa were

18. For these states see T. Lewicki, "Maghrāwa," in *The encyclopaedia of Islam*, 2nd ed., Leiden 1960–2009, 5:1173–83.

predominantly Sunnī but included significant numbers of Ibāḍīs. The founders of the Maghrāwī dynasties stemmed from a single lineage, the Khazarids; their ancestor, Khazar ibn Ḥafṣ, had lived in the first half of the eighth century and had taken advantage of the Berber rebellion to extend his power over the nomads of central North Africa. In the period when the region was overshadowed by major powers based in Tunisia and Spain, these Khazarids would ally with one power or the other. Thereafter they had much of North Africa to themselves until the intrusions of the Arab nomads in the east and the Almoravids in the west. In their heyday Khazarid dynasties are attested in Fez from the late tenth century to 1069–70, in Sijilmāsa from around 977 to 1053–54, in Aghmāt from around 971 to 1059, in Tlemcen from the early eleventh century to 1080–81, and in Tripolitania from 1000–1001 to 1145. The first four went down to Almoravid conquest, while the last was battered by the Hilālīs and terminated by the intervention of the Normans of Sicily.

Of course, not all the petty Berber states of the period were founded by Khazarids. Take, for example, the tribe of Īfran, which like the Maghrāwa was to be encountered from Tripolitania to Morocco. We know of an Īfranī state based in Tlemcen in the later ninth century, and another somewhat farther to the east in the tenth. Both were short-lived, but one on the Atlantic coast lasted from about 1000 until the Almoravid conquest around 1057. Or take the Hawwāra, a tribe with a presence from Spain to Egypt: in the ninth century some members of the tribe were in rebellion against the second Rustamid ruler and had a small state of their own northwest of Tāhart. One thing all these examples make clear is that there was a high level of geographical mobility among Berber tribes. Altogether, this pattern of minor Berber state formation was nothing new; matters were essentially no different in late antiquity.

We will leave a sustained discussion of subsequent waves to later chapters and content ourselves here with a quick look ahead. In a sense the second half of the eleventh century saw not one but three waves. One was the wave of nomadic Arab tribes from the east that engulfed Tunisia and in the course of the next few centuries spread all the way westward to Morocco. From there it continued southward into what is now Mauritania, and even to an extent northward into Spain despite the sea crossing. Another was the incipient Christian wave from the north that broke over Muslim Spain, though largely sparing North Africa, at least in part thanks to the same sea crossing; in Spain it was staved off by intervention from North Africa, but only for a couple of centuries. And last but not least, there was the Berber wave from the Sahara that established the Almoravid dynasty. This latter was a notable event in two ways. It was the only time in recorded history when Saharan nomads conquered a significant agrarian territory in northern Africa—neither Tunisia nor Egypt ever experienced such a conquest. And it created the first major state to be based in Morocco since antiquity, or perhaps we could say the first ever. With a single exception, all the Muslim waves mentioned in this chapter had a strongly religious character and involved the formation of states. It was the Arab nomads who diverged on both counts: they made no pretense of fighting for God, and they demolished other people's states without building their own. It would seem that they introduced into North Africa a pattern of sustained raiding that led to the long-term attrition of the economy of the settled population.

Absent from the entire history of our period was any dream of reviving an ancient imperial heritage, be it Roman or Berber, in a Muslim context. In the Roman case the lack of interest was no different from what we see in the east. In the Berber case the silence was overdetermined. In historical fact the Berbers had no ancient imperial tradition, and what they did have—kings such as Masinissa and Jugurtha, rebels such as Tacfarinas—had long been forgotten. This was undoubtedly related to the lack of a Berber literary heritage. When the Arabs began minting coins in North Africa in the years following the conquest, they inscribed on some of them a non-Arabic version of the first part of the Islamic profession of faith, the affirmation that there is no god but God; but they did so in Latin, not Berber. Unquestionably Berber was written in our period, for as we have seen there were prophets with Berber scriptures, and within Islam an old Berber commentary on a work of Ibāḍī law could date from the tenth century, though so early a date is not assured for it. Yet we know of no significant development of a Berber literature. Speaking of the Zanāta, to which the petty dynasties of the Maghrāwa belonged, Ibn Khaldūn attributed this absence to the political and religious dominance of Arabic, with the result that the Berber language did not develop. All this, as we will see in the next chapter, contrasts strongly with what was to happen in Iran.

One major consequence of the coming of the Almoravids is worth highlighting here. Before the eleventh century the Sunnī population of the Muslim West was concentrated in Tunisia and Spain. There were certainly Sunnīs in the Berber country. We met them as enemies of the local Shīʿites in the Sūs, we noted a Midrārid ruler who embraced Sunnism, the Ṣāliḥids were Sunnīs, and as we have just seen the Maghrāwa were mainly Sunnī, as were some of the Īfran. In the first two cases, and very likely in the others, the Sunnīs in question were Mālikīs, like the populations of Tunisia and Spain. Perhaps Mālikism would eventually have triumphed in the Berber lands without any external assistance. But even if that was so, it is likely that the process was greatly accelerated by the coming of the Almoravids, whose religion was a zealous Mālikism. In this context it was ironic but historically crucial that the wildest of the Berber nomads from the Sahara should have shared the same religious affiliation as the sophisticated urbanites of Qayrawān. The outcome was that Mālikism came to predominate almost everywhere in North Africa and Muslim Spain, as also to the south in the western Sahara and Muslim West Africa. On the political level dynasties came and went, with their various religious allegiances, but on the social level Mālikism persisted forever—in North Africa, at least, though not of course in Spain. By contrast, Shīʿism disappeared entirely, while Khārijism came to be confined to small Ibāḍī communities on the southern fringes of North Africa; they are still to be found in the Mozab in southern Algeria, on the island of Jerba in Tunisia, and in the Jabal Nafūsa in western Libya. This eclipse of heterodoxy matters. If North Africa had remained predominantly non-Sunnī, as it seems to have been in the period we have been concerned with in this chapter, it would very likely have taken much of the Sahara and sub-Saharan Africa with it, and the Muslim world today would be a significantly different place.

5

The breakup of the Caliphate in the East

Between the ninth and eleventh centuries the political fragmentation of the East—effectively Iran—was more extreme than at any other time in its history. This was not for lack of unifying ideas. In Iran as in North Africa, sectarians were in principle as committed to recreating a single Muslim polity as Sunnīs were. Moreover Iran, unlike North Africa, nurtured a memory of past imperial greatness, and the idea of a restoration of the Persian Empire was current. So what happened to these ideas in practice?

As in North Africa, the smaller states into which the East was divided in this period were diverse in character. Some themes echo what we saw in North Africa: provincial governors entrenching their power and founding dynasties, mountain tribesmen engaging in state formation. But there were differences. Why, for example, do we see some mountain tribesmen come to form states through serving as mercenaries in the armies of the rulers of the plains? This is a phenomenon that we do not encounter in the Muslim West. And how do we make sense of a highly unusual case in which a powerful if short-lived state arose from popular mobilization in an apparently nontribal society? At the same time, some phenomena we encountered in the Muslim West have no counterpart in the East. No Umayyad refugee established a state there, and there was no lasting Iranian counterpart of the Barghawāṭa. An obvious point here is that Iran is less remote than North Africa is from the center.

As in the West, fragmentation provided opportunities for peoples who had been conquered by the Arabs to reassert themselves within a Muslim context. The Persians did not just play a role in the formation of states in this period; they also turned a form of their vernacular into a prestigious literary language and began composing a large literature in it. Among the Berbers we saw only faint signs of such a development, and even those have no parallel in the central region of the Muslim world. What made the Persians in the East so different?

This chapter covers the history of Iran from the mid-ninth to the mid-eleventh century, the first of several periods of disunity that were to mark its history in Islamic times. These chronological limits, though approximate, need no further comment. The geographical limits of the chapter, however, are not so easy to set out. The Iran we are concerned with here extends considerably farther than the country we know by that name today, both to the east, where it includes parts of Central Asia and what is now Afghanistan, and to the west, where it includes territory that is now in eastern Turkey. We can think of this greater Iran as the Iranian plateau together with the mountainous regions that frame it on all sides, though with gaps in the northeast and southeast. But this version of Iran does not coincide with the Iranian empires of pre-Islamic times in that it excludes the adjoining lowlands—Iraq in the southwest and Sindh in the southeast.

The mountains as such did not provide a promising terrain for state formation. Their inhabitants were hardy mountaineers, organized in clans or tribes and resistant to the fiscal aspirations of the rulers of the plains; a good number of them are likely to have been nomadic or seminomadic pastoralists. At the same time, much of the plateau itself is desert, and in this sense Iran could be said to suffer from a hole-in-the-heart syndrome marked by the presence of a central salt desert, a wilderness whose few and impoverished inhabitants were said to kill people with stones in order to conserve their sword blades. Nor is this the only unrewarding territory to form part of our region. There is more desert to the north of the mountains in Central Asia and to their south in the Iranian coastlands of the Persian Gulf and Indian Ocean. But despite all this there were significant urban and peasant populations. Some lived in enclaves in the mountains where conditions favored agriculture and urban life; prime examples are the cities of Hamadhān and Shīrāz. Many more hugged the inner rim of the mountains; such were the cities of Rayy, Iṣfahān, and Yazd. These populations owed their water supplies to mountain rainfall, and the means by which it reached them often took the form of extended underground channels. Meanwhile, in Central Asia such cities as Marw, Bukhārā, and Samarqand depended on rivers for their supply of mountain rainfall. All such resource-rich regions provided some basis for the formation of aristocracies and states, but the geography of Iran meant that there was no obvious imperial center. As we saw, what had made possible the great Iranian empires of pre-Islamic times was the availability to their rulers of the easily accessible agricultural wealth of Iraq, and it was no accident that Ctesiphon, the Sasanian capital, was located there and not in the Persian ethnic heartland. A key feature of the period we are now concerned with was that from the later ninth century onward the old Iraqi resource base was no longer there, a fact that was to prove of central importance for the political history of Iran. But before we come to that, we need some sense of the ethnic and religious makeup of the region. Our focus here is roughly on the ninth century, as the period in which the breakup of the Caliphate began. What we see then is an elusive mix of unity and diversity.

The simplest way to approach the ethnic makeup of Iran is to take language as a proxy for it. Here the unity consisted in the fact that, applying a modern linguistic classification, the spoken languages of Iran were overwhelmingly Iranian, with non-Iranian languages other than Arabic appearing only on its periphery. The diversity lay in the marked differentiation of these languages, already apparent in pre-Islamic times in the case of those with written forms. But this, of course, is too simple, since it does not tell us whether the speakers of the various Iranian languages had any sense of a larger Iranian identity. Scattered evidence indicates that at least some of them did. As examples we can take two figures we will come to later in this chapter. A ninth-century Sogdian ruler, the Afshīn, manifested a clear sense of a wider Iranian loyalty, despite the fact that the Sogdians spoke an Eastern Iranian language very different from those of Iranians farther west. Likewise Mardāwīj, a tenth-century Gīlite from the region of Gīlān southwest of the Caspian, identified strongly enough with the Persian imperial tradition to seek to revive it, despite the fact that the Gīlites counted as a distinct people both before and after the rise of Islam.

This brings us to a significant aspect of the history of Iran: the linguistic residues of vanished states. The Arsacid Empire was overthrown four centuries before the Arab conquest, but in medieval times the dialects of northwestern Iran were still known by a term that originally meant "Parthian" (*Fahlawī*), and in referring to the Iranians a tenth-century author in the region could still use the archaic Parthian form of the ethnonym (*Aryān* as against the Persian *Ērān*, later *Īrān*). Meanwhile Persian, originally the dialect of Fārs, had spread more widely thanks to its association with the imperial rule of the Sasanians, and it had a written form known to us as Middle Persian. A more recent state to have left a linguistic residue in Iran was the Caliphate. Arab settlement was particularly dense in the northeast, where large numbers of Arab soldiers were deployed in Umayyad times to man the frontier with the Turks. As a result, pockets of Arabic dialect survived down to modern times in parts of eastern Iran and Central Asia. They were doubtless reinforced by those Arab nomads who succeeded in coming to terms with to the harsh Central Asian climate. Thus in an anonymous geographical work composed in the region in 973–74, we read that in the steppes of Jūzjān, located southwest of Balkh in the north of today's Afghanistan, there were some twenty thousand Arabs with numerous sheep and camels; they are described as richer than the other Arabs scattered throughout Khurāsān. But Persian soon began to make inroads among the sedentary Arabs of the region, and Arabic did not become the vernacular of any sizeable part of Iran—a failure deplored by the opinionated Damascene scholar Ibn Taymiyya (d. 1328), who lamented that after a good start, the Muslim settlers in Khurāsān "became easygoing in the matter of language," with the result that "for many of them Arabic became a dead language."[1] This was crucial for the preservation of Iranian identity. As Ibn Taymiyya correctly remarked, "languages are among the most powerful symbols of nations (*umam*), through which they are distinguished from one another."[2] That Arabic did not spread to the population of Iran at large is likely to reflect the limited extent of Arab tribal—as opposed to military—migration to a region of frigid winters; this was an environment that Arab nomads and their livestock could not easily adapt to.

What did spread extensively in Iran was Islam. For a religion that had only recently arrived there, it was perhaps surprisingly diverse:[3] there were Khārijites and Shīʿites of various kinds, not to mention a variety of people who would come to be known as Sunnīs. But in the ninth century Muslims still coexisted with a large Zoroastrian population. Here, too, we have evidence of diversity, which given the antiquity of the religion is what we would expect. Thus Sogdian Zoroastrianism seems to have differed markedly from what was found farther west, and in much of Iran we sense a considerable gap between popular forms of the religion and the learned Zoroastrianism known to us from its literary heritage. Between the adherents of the two ongoing religious traditions, Islamic and Zoroastrian, there would obviously be tension. Abū Isḥāq al-Kāzarūnī (d. 1033), the founder of the Kāzarūnī Ṣūfī order in Fārs, is said in one source to have been continuously getting into fights with the local Zoroastrians. As we have seen, the tension also stimulated an intermediate phenomenon: rebellious movements led by nativist prophets who in at least one case created a form of Iranian religion deeply shaped by the encounter with Islam. On top of all this there were other religions that survived for a while in Iran, notably Christianity and Buddhism, but they were fading out.

Political history: Grand designs

At the time the ʿAbbāsid Caliphate was breaking up, there were at least two grand designs that might have inspired a new order to replace it. One was religious: a counter-caliphate. The other was ethnic: a revived Iranian empire. Neither issued in the establishment of a viable new order extending over Iran as a whole. These projects nevertheless deserve our attention because they were interwoven with the political fragmentation that actually ensued. In addition, we will take a moment to look back at the nativist prophets, though the failure of their rebellions meant that any long-term political contribution they might have made was stillborn.

1. Ibn Taymiyya, *Iqtiḍāʾ al-ṣirāṭ al-mustaqīm*, Cairo 1979, 206.
2. Ibn Taymiyya, *Iqtiḍāʾ al-ṣirāṭ al-mustaqīm*, 203.
3. For the Islamic sects and schools of Iran in our period see W. Madelung, *Religious trends in early Islamic Iran*, Albany 1988.

Counter-caliphs

In the political tradition initiated by Muḥammad it was almost axiomatic that the Muslim community was a single polity and as such to be ruled by a single leader, the caliph or imam. With the passage of time this conception came to be modified somewhat in theory and wholly disregarded in practice. But as of the ninth century it was still the case that in religious terms the alternative to a failed or illegitimate caliphate was a legitimate counter-caliphate. The Umayyad caliphate had been overthrown by the ʿAbbāsids; who then would overthrow and replace the ʿAbbāsid caliphate?

The most successful competitor here was the Ismāʿīlī movement. It was active in many parts of the Muslim world, including Iran, seeking to overthrow the existing order and institute a new one. But its only major political success, the formation of the Fāṭimid Caliphate (909–1171), was achieved far to the west, and even when established in Egypt the Fāṭimids did not attempt to conquer Iran. The local agents of the movement did achieve some scattered political successes there, occasionally converting a local governor or dynastic ruler. But it was not until the late eleventh century that their efforts issued in the consolidation of an Ismāʿīlī state, and even then it was to be confined to the northern mountains. In short, Ismāʿīlī imams provided no antidote to the fragmentation of Iran.

There were, of course, other claimants to the imamate. Some were Khārijites. In the eastern Iranian region of Sīstān, endemic Khārijite activity culminated in the imamate of Ḥamza ibn Ādharak (d. 828). The name of his father takes us to a feature of Khārijism that may have been attractive to Iranians. Ādharak is a manifestly Iranian name, indeed one suggesting that its bearer was a Zoroastrian, so Ḥamza was not an Arab. That a non-Arab should be imam would have been inadmissible for Sunnīs and Shīʿites, but it was no problem for the ethnically egalitarian Khārijites. This Ḥamza defied ʿAbbāsid rule for some thirty years, making a point of killing tax collectors. The ʿAbbāsid caliph Hārūn al-Rashīd (ruled 786–809) decided near the end of his reign that something had to be done about him, and he started with a polite letter beginning as follows: "From the servant of God Hārūn, Commander of the Faithful, to Ḥamza son of ʿAbdallāh, peace be upon you!" The response began: "From the servant of God Ḥamza, Commander of the Faithful, peace be upon the friends of God!"[4] Ḥamza then went on to make it painfully obvious that he did not reckon Hārūn among God's friends. Yet despite this uncompromising claim that he, and not Hārūn, was the legitimate ruler of the Muslim community, there was never the slightest prospect of his extending his sectarian polity to the Muslim world as a whole. In fact Ḥamza was as active in waging war on neighboring Khārijite communities as he was in resisting the

4. *Tārīkh-i Sīstān*, ed. Malik al-Shuʿarāʾ Bahār, Tehran 1314 *shamsī*, 162, 164.

ʿAbbāsids. The polity he ruled was thus very much a regional phenomenon; he was not the first Khārijite leader in this part of Iran, nor was he the last. And though the military power of the Khārijites of Sīstān was to be broken within a few decades of his death, the community was still in existence in the tenth century. In many other regions of Iran we likewise encounter Khārijites at one time or another: in Fārs, Khurāsān, and Azerbaijan, for example. Thus in Azerbaijan, as we will see, a tenth-century Kurdish Khārijite commander played a role in the struggle for power following the demise of the state he served. But nowhere outside Sīstān do we find a Khārijite state maintaining its existence over generations. The Ibāḍīs, whom we have seen establishing quite long-lived imamates in North Africa and Arabia, did not do so in Iran, though Ibāḍī communities existed into the early ninth century in some regions, including eastern Fārs and Khurāsān.

Other sectarians active in Iran were Shīʿites. Of these we have already discussed the Ismāʿīlīs. The Imāmīs, who are today the major Shīʿite community of Iran, had an early presence there, especially in Qumm, but they were not in the business of state formation. That leaves us with the Zaydīs, who as we will see in the next chapter were also active in the Yemen. In Iran, as in the Yemen, the Zaydīs went for the mountains, specifically those of the Elburz to the south of the Caspian Sea. Their affinity for remote and inaccessible terrain is reflected in the lament of a sympathetic author of a work on the misfortunes of the ʿAlids written in Baghdad in 925: he knew that there were ʿAlids currently active in the Yemen and Ṭabaristān, but no further information about them had reached him. In fact, the Zaydīs of the Caspian region had a continuous existence from the second half of the ninth century to the first half of the sixteenth—far longer than the Khārijites on the plains of eastern Iran. They were ruled by their imams for much of the tenth and eleventh centuries, and again in the later fourteenth. Owing to an internal religious and ethnic split there could be two imams at a time, an arrangement favored by the mountainous terrain. On one occasion in the late eleventh century the forces of the two imams were about to clash when the conflict was averted through the deft sabotage of a bridge; the two then agreed to divide the Zaydī territory and rule simultaneously. Much as with Ḥamza's Khārijite imamate, these miniature Zaydī states had no prospect of large-scale expansion. They could seize and hold neighboring urban centers in the plains for a while, but they lacked the resources to do more than that. Instead, they made a virtue of necessity by highlighting austerity as the basis of their simple but righteous style of governance. One imam mended his own shirt, carried fish home from the market, and compensated the treasury for paper his scribes had wasted by leaving too much blank space between the lines of letters to important people. Altogether, the spirit of this tradition of miniature state formation is captured in the prescription that the imam is obliged to fight to establish his imamate once he has as many men supporting him as were with the Prophet at the Battle of Badr; as we saw, that was a mere 314. Just as Imāmī quietism was a good adaption to the cities of the central Islamic world, so Zaydī activism went well with the mountains of the periphery.

Imperial restorationists

The other grand design that had some traction in Iran in this period was a restored Iranian empire. Unlike the counter-caliphate, this was an idea with no parallel in the rest of the Muslim world. It came in two versions, hard and soft. Roughly speaking, the hard version sought both an ethnic and a religious restoration, whereas the soft one was content with an ethnic restoration.

The appeal of the hard version was largely limited to the Zoroastrian population of Iran, which in the ninth and tenth centuries was still a considerable one, though likely in rapid decline. The sense of grievance that Zoroastrians could feel is vividly expressed in a Persian poem preserved in their literature, perhaps dating from the ninth century, in which they lament their sufferings at the hands of the Arabs. Their complaint against them is not just that they had "killed the princes," "taken from men their wives, their private property, their orchards and gardens," and imposed the poll tax; the Arabs had also "enfeebled the Religion." The future was accordingly to see a reversal of the Islamization of Iran in which "we shall pull down their mosques and set up again the sacred fires"—the fires, that is, of the Zoroastrian cult. This, then, was an outright rejection of both the Arabs and Islam, and it carried with it a strong political aspiration. The demonic Arabs had "seized royal power from the Khusraws"—Khusraw being the name of two major Sasanian rulers, Khusraw I (ruled 531–79) and Khusraw II (ruled 591–628). This wrong was to be righted at the hands of "Shāh Bahrām from the family of the Kayānids"; Bahrām had been the name of no fewer than five Sasanian rulers, whereas the Kayānids belonged to an earlier and more mythical Iranian epoch. This Shāh Bahrām was to arrive from India, accompanied by a thousand elephants each of whose drivers "holds unfurled a standard in the manner of the Khusraws."[5]

Talk is cheap, and there may have been quite a lot of it in this period. A Zoroastrian apocalypse foretold that the Arabs would rule Iran for 382 years, nine months, seven days, and four hours; that would take us to about 1034, suggesting that the apocalypse was composed or revised shortly before that date. Thereafter, it affirmed, the religion—Zoroastrianism—would be put back on a sound footing. Earlier, perhaps in the late ninth or early tenth century, a certain Abū ʿAbdallāh al-ʿĀdī had predicted that "a man will come forward who will restore the rule of Zoroastrianism; he will occupy the whole world, he will do away with the rule of the Arabs and others, and he will unite all humankind in one religion and under

5. For these quotations see F. de Blois, "A Persian poem lamenting the Arab conquest," in C. Hillenbrand (ed.), *Studies in honour of Clifford Edmund Bosworth*, vol. 2, Leiden 2000, 92.

one rule."[6] Yet another case we happen to hear about concerns two brothers who belonged to the ruling family of Usrūshana, an Iranian kingdom in the mountain valleys of what is now roughly northern Tajikistan. By the first half of the ninth century its politics had become deeply entangled with those of the Caliphate. Its ruler, known by his title as the Afshīn, played a prominent role in ʿAbbāsid military politics and at least passed as a Muslim, though uncircumcised. But eventually he fell from grace and was put through an interrogation at which dirty linen was washed, leading soon after to his death in 841. Prior to that interrogation his house had been raided, and among his effects were idols and numerous books relating to his religion, one of them described specifically as a Zoroastrian work. During his interrogation he mentioned that he had spoken in confidence to a Zoroastrian priest about "Iranianness" (*al-Aʿjamiyya*) and his sympathy for those who shared it. Worse yet, a witness quoted a letter written by his brother identifying himself with the cause of "this white religion" and outlining a course of rebellion that would lead to the return of the religion to what it had been in the days of the Iranians (*ʿAjam*). Just what political form this restoration would take was not specified.

In the event, all such dreams came to nothing. But if we are looking for a historical figure to play the part of the mythical Shāh Bahrām, the closest approximation would be the Gīlite Mardāwīj ibn Ziyār (ruled 931–35). We have already encountered the Gīlites of the coastal plain on the southwestern shore of the Caspian. They were closely associated with a better-known people, the Daylamites, who lived in the mountains of Daylam immediately to the east of them. Thanks to the terrain both peoples were protected against states based in the plains to the south of the mountains. As the sixth-century Byzantine historian Procopius says of the Daylamites, "they inhabit sheer mountainsides that are altogether inaccessible," and in consequence they "have never been subject to the king of the Persians."[7] The Gīlites themselves were lowlanders, but their marshy plain was isolated and protected by the mountains, as a result of which they had continued to be an independent tribal people like their Daylamite neighbors; exceptionally, Gīlān was a lowland region the Arabs did not conquer. But these peoples did contribute in one crucial way to the states ruling the plateau. Both before and after the rise of Islam we find them emerging from the mountains to serve as mercenary infantry. To quote Procopius again, "they always march with the Persians as mercenaries when they go against their enemies." All of them, he adds, are foot soldiers. In a battle fought in 867 the Daylamites are described as standing in serried ranks, their shields impenetrable to the arrows of the enemy archers. In the

6. Bīrūnī, *The chronology of ancient nations*, London 1879, 197.

7. For these and the quotation that follows see Prokopios, *The wars of Justinian*, trans. H. B. Dewing, Indianapolis 2014, 493 (8.14.6–7).

tenth and eleventh centuries they were employed in the armies of many different rulers, rather like the Swiss mountaineers who served as mercenaries in Renaissance Europe; they were hired by dynasties as far afield as the Ghaznawids (977–1186) in what is now Afghanistan and the Fāṭimids in Egypt. But they also did something the Swiss did not do: they showed a pronounced interest in taking over from their employers and ruling in their place. In this Mardāwīj was briefly successful, taking possession of a large part of northern Iran and threatening to expand into Iraq.

Though initially he was content to pose as a governor on behalf of the caliph, once established in Iṣfahān Mardāwīj changed his tune. He did, after all, have some claim to kingly status as a member of the royal clan of the Gīlites. His purpose was now to march on Baghdad, overthrow the Caliphate, and appoint his own governors over all the cities of Islam, whether in the east or the west. He put on his head an elaborate crown, seated himself on a splendid throne, and made it very clear what he meant by this: "I shall restore the empire of the Persians (*al-ʿAjam*) and destroy the empire of the Arabs."[8] Indeed, his crown was modeled on that of the Sasanian Khusraw I, and his imperial residence was to be the restored Hall of Khusraw in the former Sasanian capital of Ctesiphon in Iraq. Once all this was achieved, he would be addressed by the traditional Iranian title "King of Kings" (Shāhanshāh). A prophecy current among his entourage indicated that he would in due course be succeeded by no fewer than forty kings—a recipe for a dynasty that could have lasted even longer than the Sasanians. But was he proposing to restore the hegemony of Zoroastrianism? It is clear is that Mardāwīj was no friend of Islam, and his troops made a point of massacring the Muslim religious elite. It is not recorded that he cast down mosques, though a Daylamite leader of the day did just that in Qazwīn, forbidding the performance of Muslim prayer and having the muezzin of the main mosque thrown from the minaret. At the time of his death Mardāwīj was preparing for a spectacular celebration of a Zoroastrian festival, albeit one that Iranian Muslims, too, had a weakness for, and a subsequent poem congratulating the caliph on Mardāwīj's death spoke of his demise as extinguishing the fire of the Zoroastrians. But the sources are not consistent: there is also talk of a new religion due to appear in Iṣfahān, and of Mardāwīj as having converted at some point to Ismāʿīlism. How all this might have played out if Mardāwīj had not been killed by his Turkic slave soldiers in 935 is impossible to say; as it was, his plans came to nothing.

Restorationist ideas of the soft kind were more widespread. One of the most powerful rulers of Iran in this period was Yaʿqūb the Coppersmith (ruled 861–79), the founder of the Ṣaffārid dynasty (861–1003). He came from humble beginnings in Sīstān, which as we have seen was full of Khārijites, and he first made his mark

8. Quoted in W. Madelung, "The assumption of the title Shāhānshāh by the Būyids," in his *Religious and ethnic movements in medieval Islam*, Aldershot 1992, art. VIII, 86.

fighting against them as a leader in a Sunnī vigilante movement. In other words, he was unquestionably a Muslim, even a pious one. But once he had become a powerful ruler it would have been unthinkable for him not to have poets in his entourage, and one of them, an Iṣfahānī, composed a remarkable poem for him. Here the poet has Yaʿqūb pose as the heir of the Iranian kings; this fits to the extent that we know from another source that Sasanian ancestry was claimed for him. Likewise Yaʿqūb declares in the poem that he possesses the imperial banner of the Sasanians, by which he hopes to rule the peoples, mounting the throne of the kings. The poem makes no secret of the identity of the enemy in all this: "all the sons of Hāshim"—in this context the ʿAbbāsids—are invited to abdicate without further ado and go home to the Ḥijāz to eat lizards and tend sheep.[9] (Persians would mock the Arabs for eating lizards much as the English mock the French for eating frogs.) This, of course, is playing with fire, since one of "the sons of Hāshim" was God's Prophet. But the poem makes no suggestion that the ʿAbbāsids should take Islam with them when they retreat to the Ḥijāz, and indeed at one point it invokes God and the Prophet. It is for that reason that we can call the sentiments attributed to Yaʿqūb by the poet a soft restorationism. Apart from the reference to his Sasanian ancestry the poem has no parallel elsewhere in what we know of Yaʿqūb's self-image, but it is an eloquent statement of ideas that were in circulation at the time.

Typically, the ideas associated with such restorationism took less overtly confrontational forms. One such form was an epidemic among ruling dynasties of claims to descent from the Sasanian kings or other grandees of the Iranian past. Many of the dynasties we will meet in this chapter exemplified this trend, albeit without going so far as to call for vengeance as the poet had Yaʿqūb do. Thus the Ṭāhirids (821–73) chose descent from the Iranian hero Rustam, though also claiming Arab ancestry. The Sāmānids (819–1005) elected to descend from Bahrām Chōbīn (ruled 590–91), who was not himself a Sasanian but rather a member of a family claiming descent from the Arsacids, the royal house of the earlier Parthian Empire whose rule he allegedly sought to restore. The Ziyārids (931 to ca. 1090), the relatively modest dynasty founded by a brother of Mardāwīj, likewise claimed Sasanian descent, though in a maternal line; they took as their ancestor a brother of "Anūshirwān the Just," better known as Khusraw I. Even the Ghaznawids, a dynasty of manifestly Turkic origin, acquired a Sasanian genealogy, as did the Būyids (932–1062). The Shīrwān-Shāhs of eastern Transcaucasia are a particularly striking example. They were originally provincial governors of unquestioned Arab ancestry, yet by the tenth century they had traded it in for Sasanian descent. It

9. Translated in S. M. Stern, "Yaʿqūb the Coppersmith and Persian national sentiment," in C. E. Bosworth (ed.), *Iran and Islam*, Edinburgh 1971, 541f.

would be hard to find a parallel to this exchange elsewhere in the non-Arab Muslim world.

More directly restorationist was the revival of the pre-Islamic Iranian imperial title "King of Kings," or Shāhanshāh. We have already encountered it as an aspiration of Mardāwīj, and thereafter it was used by the Būyids, the Sāmānids, and the Ghaznawids. In Azerbaijan Qaṭrān, an eleventh-century poet, praised even the minor rulers of the region as the Shāhanshāhs of Iran. But it is the Būyid use of the title that is most richly attested. The first Būyid ruler, ʿAlī ibn Būya (ruled 934–49), is said to have adopted it as early as 936–37, and the most powerful ruler of the dynasty, ʿAḍud al-Dawla (ruled 978–83), laid particular emphasis on it. Mardāwīj apart, these rulers were without any question Muslims, but their adoption of the title can hardly be reckoned innocent. On two occasions—on a coin of 962 and a medallion of 969–70—it was written in Middle Persian script, highlighting its Zoroastrian associations. However, not everyone approved of such extravagances. There were traditions from the Prophet explicitly condemning the use of the title, and in Baghdad in 1038 its unprecedented inclusion in the titulature of the Būyid ruler at the Friday prayer was greeted with a hail of mud bricks from the congregation (mud bricks being the nearest thing to stones on the alluvial plain of Iraq). The caliph then referred the issue to a group of prominent jurists, only one of whom had the courage to declare the title illicit. The Būyid ruler complimented him handsomely on his integrity, but the next time the title was used in the Friday prayer there were armed guards present to deal with any opposition.

Nativist prophets

Before we end this treatment of grand designs, we should pause for a moment to bring the nativist prophets back into the discussion. As we saw, all but one of these movements began and ended within a few years in the second half of the eighth century, at a time when the Caliphate was still militarily strong. The exception was the revolt of Bābak in northern Azerbaijan, which lasted for some twenty years before its suppression in 837. But even this was too early to benefit from the weakening of the Caliphate. So we can only speculate as to what a lasting polity founded by Bābak or one of his predecessors might have looked like; the analogy of the Barghawāṭa on the Atlantic coast of Morocco is relevant but does not take us very far. The most prominent feature of Bābak's political vision seems to have been his raw personal ambition to play the part of a king. That raises the question whether he saw his kingship as a restoration of that of the Sasanians. There is little evidence that he did, except perhaps the fact that at some point he assumed the name Bābak, having previously been called Ḥasan. Bābak was not a very common name, and it sounds like an evocation of Pāpak, the father of the first Sasanian ruler.

Beyond that, Bābak's political assignment was pitched as being to "possess the earth, slay the tyrants," and "make the humble among you mighty and the lowly high." As to who were the tyrants to be slain, there was talk of the "wickedness of the Arabs."[10] But there is no indication in the twenty years of warfare waged by Bābak that he was interested in extending his power to Iran at large, let alone beyond it. If there was a grand design here, it has eluded us.

Political history: Petty states

Although grand designs undoubtedly colored the history of Iran in the aftermath of the breakup of the ʿAbbāsid Caliphate, the basic political reality of the period was fragmentation. Indeed, at no other time in its recorded history was Iran divided into so many different states; more than a score of them qualify for inclusion in the standard handbook of Muslim dynasties. We can conveniently arrange most of them under a limited number of headings. There were heterodox religious figures who formed imamates in remote regions comparable to those of the Idrīsids, Midrārids, and Rustamids in North Africa, though none were in the same league as the Fāṭimids; we have already covered these sectarian ventures and will not return to them in this section. Then there were the dynasties established by ʿAbbāsid provincial governors who found opportunities to entrench themselves permanently in their provinces. This process is already familiar to us from the case of the Aghlabids in Tunisia, and we will see it again with the Ṭūlūnids and Ikhshīdids in Egypt. Next come the martial mountaineers who formed states in the plains by going into service as mercenaries and then taking over from their employers. As we have seen, Gīlites and Daylamites played this game, which had no parallel in the western Muslim world. At the same time another mountain people, the Kurds, engaged in nonsectarian state formation of a geographically more limited kind, comparable perhaps to the petty states established in North Africa by the Maghrāwa. That leaves three historically significant cases that do not fit any of these categories. In what follows we will look at examples under each of these headings.

Provincial governors who dig in

There are half a dozen clear-cut cases of provincial governors who in effect overstayed their appointments, and as we might expect, they are usually found in regions distant from the center of the Caliphate. One such region was Azerbaijan in northwestern Iran, where we have already encountered the Shīrwān-Shāhs (799

10. Quoted in P. Crone, *The nativist prophets of early Islamic Iran*, Cambridge 2012, 61, 72.

to ca. 1382) who gave up their Arab genealogy for a Sasanian one. A shorter-lived dynasty in this part of Iran was that of the Sājids (889–929), descended from a Sogdian named Dēwdād who hailed from the same part of the world as the Afshīn; in fact one member of the dynasty adopted this eastern Iranian title for himself. The relationship between the Sājids and the ʿAbbāsids was an uneasy one, despite the fact that the Sājids acknowledged the caliphs on their coins. At one point the caliph sent an army against the incumbent Sājid, but a few years later he was able to recall him and send him on what proved a fatal military mission to lower Iraq. The other region in which governors entrenched themselves was northeastern Iran. We have already met both the dynasties in question, the Ṭāhirids (821–73) and the Sāmānids (819–1005). The relationship of the Ṭāhirids to the caliphs was close. They had played a part in the ʿAbbāsid revolution, and while some members of the family were governors of Khurāsān, others were in charge of Baghdad. Yet there could still be tension, and shortly before his death in 822 the founder of the dynasty in Khurāsān took the ominous step of omitting the name of the caliph from the Friday prayer and the coinage; but his successors did not repeat it.[11] That leaves the Sāmānids, and they deserve a closer look as the only dynasty in this category to rule a substantial territory for over a century.[12]

Their ancestor, the Sāmān-khudā, was a member of the Iranian landed elite who had converted to Islam in the late Umayyad period. In 819 the caliph had four grandsons of this rather shadowy figure appointed to subgovernorships of parts of Khurāsān in reward for their loyalty during a dangerous rebellion in the region. A little over twenty years later only two of the four brothers remained, and they were appointed by the Ṭāhirid ruler to governorships in Transoxania. Soon after only one brother was left, and he was succeeded by a son. When the Ṭāhirid dynasty in Khurāsān was overthrown by Yaʿqūb the Coppersmith in 873, this son found himself ruling Transoxania with no superior bar the caliph. By now this meant only a distantly formal relationship requiring little more than acknowledging the caliph in the Friday prayer and on the coinage. But this son was in turn marginalized by a brother, Ismāʿīl I (ruled 892–907), who established the Sāmānid capital in Bukhārā and from whom all subsequent rulers of the dynasty were descended. This complicated sequence shows how large a part luck, both good and bad, could play in the process whereby a governor might found a dynasty. It also illustrates the point that the process could be a serial one: we see the Ṭāhirids doing for the Sāmānids what the ʿAbbāsids had done for the Ṭāhirids. Until their last two decades the Sāmānids were a rather successful dynasty, especially when in addition to Transoxania they also ruled Khurāsān. They are complimented by the

11. For the Ṭāhirids see C. E. Bosworth, "The Ṭāhirids and Ṣaffārids," in *The Cambridge history of Iran*, Cambridge 1968–91, vol. 4.

12. For the Sāmānids see R. N. Frye, "The Sāmānids," in *The Cambridge history of Iran*, vol. 4.

sources on their good governance, and apart from one ruler's flirtation with Ismāʿīlism around 940 they remained more or less within the Sunnī fold. But they were located on a dangerous frontier of the Muslim world, one beyond which roamed the Turkic nomads of the steppes. This location did, of course, have a silver lining: when recruiting troops for their armies, they had first choice of captured or imported Turkic military slaves. But these slaves were not always reliable—in 914, for example, a Sāmānid ruler was murdered by them, anticipating the fate of Mardāwīj. And in the end the Sāmānid territories were to be partitioned by two groups of Turks: the Qarakhānids (992–1212) moving in from the north and the Ghaznawids (977–1186) moving in from the south. Of these the Qarakhānids were free Turks from the steppes. The Ghaznawids, by contrast, were a spin-off from the Sāmānids' own slave troops, a group of whom had at one point absconded to Ghazna in what is now Afghanistan and established their rule there.

Mercenaries who take over

The mountains of Daylam, and those that stretched along the southern coast of the Caspian in general, were discouraging to outsiders, but this did not preclude the formation of minor kingdoms among the native population. There was one such dynasty in Daylam, the Justānids.[13] We first happen to hear of them in the late eighth century, but they could have been there long before. We know little of their history, but one thing is clear: unlike most of the dynasties we are concerned with in this chapter, they did not owe their existence to the disintegration of the ʿAbbāsid Caliphate. They had mixed relations with the Zaydī ʿAlids, suffered from the rise of the rival Sallārid dynasty, and disappeared from view in the eleventh century. Meanwhile in Ṭabaristān, at the eastern end of the mountain range, another dynasty of equal or greater antiquity held sway: the Bāwandids (665–1074). In the later eighth century they were involved in violent resistance to Muslim settlement in the highlands. They claimed Sasanian descent, and at least some of them were Imāmī Shīʿites. In short, the mountaineers did not hail from an entirely stateless society. So it is perhaps not surprising that on descending from their mountains to serve in the armies of the rulers of the plains they soon showed a propensity to form states of their own. We have already seen the meteoric rise and fall of Mardāwīj in an Iran awash with Gīlite and Daylamite mercenaries. Three dynasties emerged from this upheaval. The Ziyārids (931 to ca. 1090) set up a state to the east of their homeland, the Būyids (932–1062) established a set of states to the south, and the Sallārids (alias Musāfirids, 941–84) expanded to the west. We will look at all three but give most of our attention to the Būyids.

13. For this and the other dynasties of the region (but not the Būyids) see W. Madelung, "The minor dynasties of northern Iran," in *The Cambridge history of Iran*, vol. 4.

The Ziyārid state was the residue of Mardāwīj's domains. It was his brother Wushmgīr (ruled 935–67) who succeeded him and from whom all subsequent rulers of the dynasty were descended. After the speedy loss of most of the territories overrun by Mardāwīj, what was left was a relatively small state which in good times comprised the highlands of Ṭabaristān together with the lowlands of Jurjān to the southeast of the Caspian. The mountains were at least somewhat secure, but the plains—economically the best part of the Ziyārid territory—were wide open to intruders, including nomads from the steppes to the north. The Ziyārid achievement was accordingly to survive, though discontinuously, for well over a century. To do this they maneuvered as best they could and acknowledged as necessary the overlordship of more powerful dynasties: the Sāmānids, the Būyids, the Ghaznawids, and finally the Seljuqs (1040–1194) with their following of Turkic nomads.

Unlike the Ziyārids, the Būyids did not belong to a royal clan. Būya, the ancestor of the dynasty, was a Daylamite fisherman. Despite not being born to rule they did better than the Ziyārids, establishing a group of states that ruled central and southern Iran together with Iraq and competing with other states of the day on considerably more advantageous terms.[14]

The key figure in the creation of these states was ʿAlī ibn Būya (ruled 934–49), also known as ʿImād al-Dawla from the title bestowed on him by the caliph. As a Daylamite mercenary he served a rapidly changing cast of patrons: first the Sāmānid ruler Naṣr II (ruled 914–43), then a Gīlite leader named Mākān ibn Kākī, then Mardāwīj, and finally, if only formally, the caliph. Two episodes in this adventurous trajectory convey the flavor of these relationships. One was the shift from Mākān to Mardāwīj. Mardāwīj had just defeated Mākān, so the move made sense, though in a society that set a high value on gratitude for favors, it was a little awkward. ʿAlī, together with one of his brothers, negotiated the awkwardness by asking Mākān for permission to join the winner; they assured him that "if you become powerful again, we will return to you."[15] The other episode took place after Mardāwīj had soured on ʿAlī, who then moved south and in 934 seized Shīrāz, the main city of Fārs, ruling it until his death. His concern was now to legitimize his position in Shīrāz by persuading the caliph to appoint him governor of the province, in return for which he promised a suitably large sum of money. The caliph's vizier duly sent an envoy with the appropriate insignia—robes of honor and the ʿAbbāsid banner—but instructed him to make sure he was paid cash in advance. ʿAlī, however, forced the envoy to hand over the insignia immediately and then kept fobbing him off whenever he requested payment; the luckless envoy died in

14. On the Būyids see H. Busse, "Iran under the Būyids," in *The Cambridge history of Iran*, vol. 4.

15. Quoted in R. P. Mottahedeh, *Loyalty and leadership in an early Islamic society*, Princeton 1980, 80.

Shīrāz a year later without having received anything. In short, loyalty and trust were in short supply in ʿAlī's relationships with his patrons, and in this respect he was typical of the Daylamites of his day—which is why he in turn never felt secure among his own generals.

By contrast, ʿAlī's relationship with his two brothers was a model of family values. He described them as "by blood my brothers, by upbringing my sons, and by what they are invested to govern, my protégés."[16] He brought both of them into his enterprise and enabled them to conquer principalities of their own. He sent one brother, Ḥasan (also known by his title as Rukn al-Dawla), to take Iṣfahān, giving him the opportunity to found a subdynasty that lasted until 1029. In the same way he sent his youngest brother, Aḥmad (also known by his title as Muʿizz al-Dawla), to Khūzistān, whence he went on to take Baghdad in 945. Aḥmad and after him his son ʿIzz al-Dawla then ruled Iraq until 978. It was not that ʿAlī had ordered Aḥmad to go beyond Khūzistān and conquer Iraq, but neither did he seek to prevent him. In other words, ʿAlī was comfortable with a plurality of Būyid states, provided his younger brothers recognized his primacy; Aḥmad explicitly accepted it, and Ḥasan does not seem to have contested it. After ʿAlī's death Ḥasan (ruled 947–77) inherited his position of leadership, together with his family values, as dramatized by the events that unfolded in 975. Ḥasan had a son, Fanā Khusraw, better known by his title as ʿAḍud al-Dawla. This son succeeded ʿAlī, who was childless, as ruler of Fārs. In 975 his father sent him to Iraq to help his cousin ʿIzz al-Dawla (ruled 967–78) against a dangerous rebellion, but instead of helping his cousin, ʿAḍud al-Dawla deposed him and assumed power over Iraq himself. Ḥasan, greatly distressed, now intervened to support his nephew against his own son, who was constrained to restore his cousin to power and return to Fārs. But not for long. When Ḥasan died in 977, ʿAḍud al-Dawla repeated his invasion of Iraq, and this time there was no one to stop him. ʿIzz al-Dawla was defeated and killed, and ʿAḍud al-Dawla then ruled Iraq together with his other domains from 978 to his death in 983. He was, without question, the single most powerful ruler of the dynasty, and he ruled more territory than any other. But from this point on the Būyids were a dysfunctional family, and it would be unrewarding to follow the details of their political and military fortunes in their last decades.

There are nevertheless some larger points that emerge from the history of the dynasty. One concerns the fact that ʿAlī was content to remain in Fārs while his younger brother conquered Iraq. This certainly says something about fraternal relations among the early Būyids, but it also highlights the changing geographical basis of power. For three centuries major rulers and rebels might pass through Fārs in one direction or another, but no one before Būyid times had paused to establish

16. Quoted in Mottahedeh, *Loyalty and leadership*, 197 note 56.

a state there. Now times had changed, though the change had taken place in Iraq rather than in Fārs: as we have seen, Iraq could no longer provide the fiscal foundation for an empire. Thus it was Fārs, not Iraq, that was the jewel in the Būyid crown for ʿAlī at the start of the dynasty and again for ʿAḍud al-Dawla's son Bahāʾ al-Dawla (ruled 989–1012). This ruler neglected Iraq and lost much of his territory there, but he spent a decade struggling to take Fārs and never left it once he had secured possession of Shīrāz. The only exception, though not a trivial one, was ʿAḍud al-Dawla himself, who after his second conquest of Iraq did not return to Fārs. But he very likely intended to, for he left his main administrative offices in Shīrāz. "I want Iraq for the sake of its name," he is reported to have said, "but I want Arrajān for its revenue";[17] Arrajān was at that time a flourishing city on the western border of Fārs. In the good old days such a judgment would have made no sense.

Another significant point about the Būyids concerns their armies. The Daylamites were infantry. They had been so already before the rise of Islam, and they remained so thereafter. This had two consequences, one immediate and one long-term. As to the immediate consequence, we are in a period when infantry still mattered on the battlefield, but cavalry were indispensable. This meant that even a Daylamite ruler could not make do with an army composed only of fellow Daylamites: he needed to complement his Daylamite infantry with Turkic cavalry. We saw this already when Mardāwīj was killed by his Turkic slave soldiers in 935, after which many of them found employment with ʿAlī. It perhaps says something for the abilities of the Būyids as rulers that at no point did their Turkic troops take over any of their states. But complementarity did not preclude conflict, and friction between Daylamites and Turks in Būyid armies was a recurrent theme, particularly in Baghdad. It was no doubt made worse by the fact that the Daylamites were Shīʿites while the Turks were Sunnīs. We could see this fault line as one of the weaknesses of the Būyid states, though that might not be the way contemporaries looked at it: one chronicler condemns ʿIzz al-Dawla, the second Būyid ruler of Iraq, for allowing his Turks and Daylamites to cooperate against him. The long-term consequence of being infantry was that as the cavalry became more dominant in warfare, the Daylamites lost the capacity to form states outside their homeland. As we will see in a later chapter, two contenders for power in eighteenth-century Iran were Iranian tribesmen from the hills—but they were not from the Caspian region, and unlike the Daylamites they fought as cavalry. Back in the tenth century the infantry could still make history.

A further point that Būyid history highlights is the continuing centrality of the practice and culture of the bureaucratic tradition that Iran inherited from the ʿAbbāsids. The Būyids brought no administrative tradition with them from their

17. Quoted in H. Busse, "Iran under the Buyids," 282.

homeland; when the Daylamites descended from their mountains with their long, unkempt hair, they were rough and uncultured. In this they resembled the Gīlites. We get a sense of how these peoples appeared to the cultured elite from the shock expressed by an envoy sent to Gīlān to persuade Wushmgīr to come and join his brother Mardāwīj. Like his brother, Wushmgīr was a member of a royal clan, but this did not do much for his lifestyle. The envoy found him in a rice paddy amid a group of men who were barefoot and half-naked, dressed in patched pants and tattered garments. Worse yet, Wushmgīr's immediate reaction to his brother's message was vulgarly contemptuous. He did not like the fact that Mardāwīj, at this point in his career formally a governor on behalf of the caliph, had donned the black uniform of the ʿAbbāsids, and he showed what he thought of it by simulating a fart with his lips, intending it for his brother's beard. The unfortunate envoy did succeed in persuading Wushmgīr to accompany him to Qazwīn, but he professed to be too embarrassed to describe the boorish behavior he had witnessed. With such men as their rulers, the bureaucrats obviously had a problem, but they did their best, and the envoy conceded that even Wushmgīr subsequently improved. One bureaucrat, Ibn al-ʿAmīd (d. 970), served for three decades as Ḥasan's vizier and regarded him as a cut above the general run of his Daylamite peers. Yet even Ibn al-ʿAmīd was unable to put through much-needed reforms because Ḥasan still had the predatory mentality of a soldier in a hurry for plunder, with no regard for his long-term interests or those of his subjects. Ḥasan nevertheless had the wisdom to retain Ibn al-ʿAmīd to tutor his son ʿAḍud al-Dawla in statecraft, so that with the coming to power of the second generation of Būyid rulers the cultural gap between them and their viziers had narrowed. Thus the Ṣāḥib ibn ʿAbbād (d. 995), a disciple of Ibn al-ʿAmīd who served as vizier to two of Ḥasan's successors, does not seem to have suffered the same level of frustration. A third vizier we might mention is Ibn Sīnā (d. 1037), who entered Būyid service as a physician but went on to act as vizier to a Būyid ruler for a few years prior to the latter's death in 1021. Then from about 1024 till his own death he served a Daylamite dynasty that had emerged out of a Būyid provincial governorship in Iṣfahān, the Kākawayhids (ca. 1008 to 1051). As a disciple of Ibn Sīnā's wrote, this ruler gave him "the respect and esteem that someone like him deserved."[18] Even Daylamites could eventually learn the ways of polite society.

Significantly, all three of these viziers were at the same time masters and patrons of high culture. Ibn al-ʿAmīd regarded himself as a partisan of Socrates, Plato, and Aristotle and was a patron of the famous Arab poet Mutanabbī (d. 965). The Ṣāḥib ibn ʿAbbād was a prolific author whose writings on a variety of topics we still possess; he too was a patron of poets. Ibn Sīnā was of course the

18. Quoted in D. Gutas, "Avicenna ii. Biography," in *Encyclopædia Iranica*, London 1985–, 3:70a.

most famous of the Muslim philosophers. He transmitted and refined the Greek philosophical heritage, becoming known in Christian Europe as Avicenna. Some of this culture rubbed off onto the rulers served by these viziers. At the request of his appreciative Kākawayhid employer, Ibn Sīnā wrote an encyclopedia of the sciences for the ruler's followers. It was an introductory work written in a simple Persian accessible to laymen, not in the elaborate Arabic appropriate for scholars, but it nevertheless suggests that since leaving their mountains some Daylamites at least had acquired the ability to benefit from such a book. In this respect, however, one Gīlite did even better. The Ziyārid Qābūs (ruled 978–81 and 997–402), a son of the coarse and vulgar Wushmgīr, earned a reputation as a scholar and poet in both Persian and Arabic and became a patron of the arts and sciences. He would have decorated his court with Ibn Sīnā had he not had the misfortune to die shortly before the philosopher arrived. Qābūs had come a long way from his father's rice paddy.

We should not, however, think that victory in this process of assimilation went entirely to the bureaucrats. The Būyid period saw the spread of a practice that seems to have dated from the late ʿAbbāsid period. States live off taxes and can collect them in either of two ways: directly or indirectly. Direct collection means that bureaucrats employed by the state take what is due directly from the taxpayers. Indirect collection in this context means that the bureaucracy outsources the collection of taxes to those who are to be paid from them. The Būyid period saw a marked intensification of such indirect collection. It became increasingly common for a military officer to be assigned a source of revenue—a village, for example—and left to collect the tax it owed for himself. The technical term for such an assignment in this period was *iqṭāʿ*, but under various names the institution was to be a widespread one in the Muslim world of later centuries. If we are not too fussy about terminology we can call an *iqṭāʿ* a fief. What matters is that it marked a major retrenchment in the role of the bureaucracy. One historian of the day wrote that most of the alluvial land of Iraq had become inaccessible to tax collectors, with the result that the majority of the financial departments became superfluous and were amalgamated. The effects on the ground could be very disruptive. The same historian describes how soldiers would strip the assets of their assignments and move on to others, taking no steps to ensure cultivation or maintain essential infrastructure. The caliph ʿUmar, who had instituted the Dīwān, would not have approved.

Before leaving the Būyids we should return to the symbolic aspects of their rule. We are dealing here with rhetoric, verbal and visual, but as we have seen rhetoric can give rise to something as concrete as a hail of mud bricks. Claiming Sasanian ancestry and the title Shāhanshāh were not the only ways in which the Būyids appealed to Iranian loyalties. Also significant was the appearance of a telling phrase stressing the Daylamite ethnicity of the Būyid polity: "the reign of the Daylamites" or "the Daylamite state" (*al-dawla al-Daylamiyya*). There is some reason to think that the Būyids played a part in giving currency to this phrase. Another example of playing to the Iranian gallery can be seen in the visits of Būyid rulers and princes to the ancient imperial site of Persepolis in Fārs, recorded in three elegant inscriptions. Two of them mention that in 955 ʿAḍud al-Dawla had the nearby inscriptions at the site read out to him. These were in Old and Middle Persian, and he drew on the services of a Zoroastrian priest, at least for the Middle Persian. The Būyids also came to share with other ruling families of Iran at the time a taste for Iranian names, often ones associated with the Iranian past. Thus one Ziyārid ruler was called Anūshirwān after Khusraw I, and his successor was Dārā (Darius), a throwback to the mythical Kayānid dynasty or more historically to the Achaemenids. Among the Būyids themselves, the first generation of rulers had Arabic names: ʿAlī, Ḥasan, and Aḥmad. In the second generation, by contrast, there was only one Arabic name, ʿAlī, and the other three were Iranian: Fanā Khusraw, Būya, and Bakhtiyār. Thereafter Iranian names are about twice as common as Arabic ones. This Daylamite fashion for conspicuously Iranian names was not confined to royalty. Shīrawayh ibn Shahrdār ibn Fanā Khusraw of Hamadhān (d. 1115) was a taciturn Daylamite scholar who wrote a history of the city and a collection of traditions from the Prophet. All three names—his own, his father's, and his grandfather's—are Iranian, and he clearly had no problem with this, since he in turn named a son Shahrdār after his father.

Of course the Būyids could not ignore Islam. We have seen that after taking possession of Fārs, ʿAlī recognized the ʿAbbāsid caliph by seeking investiture as a provincial governor—and proceeded to cheat him of the money he had promised in return. At least two things were likely in play here. One was the recent spread of Zaydī Shīʿism among the Daylamites, which gave them no reason to think of the ʿAbbāsid caliphate as religiously legitimate; we can compare ʿAlī's failure to pay to Wushmgīr's discourteous reaction to his brother's wearing black. That, as well as the general unreliability of Daylamite leaders, could account for the shamelessness of the cheating. The other factor that may have been at work was a realization that the Muslim world outside the mountains of Daylam was more Sunnī than Shīʿite and that recognizing the ʿAbbāsid caliphate, however insincerely, was sound politics. The moment of truth came when Aḥmad took Baghdad and had the caliph in his power. He had him dragged from his throne by two Daylamite soldiers and according to one account was about to appoint a Zaydī ʿAlid in his place. We are told that he was dissuaded by the Machiavellian counsel of his vizier: in the event of a confrontation with the titular caliph, Aḥmad's Daylamite followers could be relied on to obey his commands even if it meant killing an ʿAbbāsid, whereas they would take orders from an ʿAlid even if it meant killing Aḥmad himself. Thereafter the Būyids remained Shīʿites, and no doubt Zaydīs, but formally they recognized the authority of the ʿAbbāsids. It wasn't logical, but it made sense.

The most striking tensions arose at the intersections of the two orders, the Iranian and the Islamic. As noted earlier, we have two instances of the title Shāhanshāh being written in Middle Persian; the second of these is a gold medallion produced for ʿAḍud al-Dawla in 969–70. Here the Middle Persian inscription accompanies an image of this ruler, crowned and dressed as a king—so much for the objections of the pious to images of human beings. And yet the Iranian order is complemented by the Islamic order thanks to an Arabic inscription with the Muslim confession of faith. The most acute tensions naturally arose in Baghdad, where the caliph had to coexist with a Būyid ruler who had the power to depose him and used it at the time of the initial conquest of Iraq, and again in 991. Under these conditions the caliph was not his own master. But neither was he was a mere puppet. When ʿAḍud al-Dawla, who was used to getting his way, was arranging an audience with the caliph, he laid down two conditions. One was that he should ride into the audience chamber on horseback, and the other was that a curtain should be hung such that none of his entourage could see him kiss the ground at the caliph's feet. Both accommodations were denied to him, and he prostrated himself in front of the caliph as required. The caliph then performed his side of the transaction, handing over the government of the Caliphate to ʿAḍud al-Dawla, excepting only his private possessions, his wealth, and his palace. The caliph may have been effectively powerless, but being the fount of Islamic political legitimacy still left him with a certain leverage.

That leaves us to glance at the Sallārids and their westward extension of Daylamite power in 941–84. In contrast to the Ziyārids and Būyids, the Sallārids were already an established dynasty in Daylam before they began to play a role outside their homeland; one branch of the family mostly remained there, while the other sought its fortune in Azerbaijan. But for better or worse the two branches remained closely connected. A couple of things provided the window of opportunity for this move into Azerbaijan. One was the demise of the Sājid dynasty in 929. The other was the presence of Daylamite mercenaries in the army of the Sallārids' main competitor, an ill-starred but resilient Kurd named Daysam who had risen to prominence in the service of the Sājids and was also a Khārijite. At first his troops had been Kurdish, but because of their unruliness he started hiring Daylamites to balance them. This turned out to be a mistake. When the Sallārid prince Marzubān (ruled 941–57) invaded Azerbaijan in 941–42, the ground had been carefully prepared, and Daysam's Daylamites deserted him and joined Marzubān. So this was a case in which mercenaries were crucial but did not in fact take over. Marzubān then had to contend with a variety of enemies, including the ever-persistent Daysam, the infidel Scandinavian raiders known as the Rūs who launched repeated attacks down the Volga, and the Arab Ḥamdānids to the south. Despite these challenges, Marzubān held out and eventually got the better of Daysam, but things did not go well under the rule of his successors. It was now the turn of another

Kurdish competitor, the Rawwādids, so it is with some reason that at this point we turn to the Kurds.

The Kurds

The term "Kurd" is ancient, though just how ancient is hard to say. Today it is a reasonably precise term, referring to a people living in the adjoining parts of Iran, Iraq, and Turkey that make up Kurdistan. Medieval usage was less stable, and sometimes the term seems to function less as the name of a specific ethnic group than as a general label for wild nomadic tribesmen. One tenth-century expert on Iranian history informs us that the Persians used to call the Daylamites the Kurds of Ṭabaristān, just as they called the Arabs the Kurds of Khūzistān. We could take this as metaphor, but in 873 we hear of Kurds nomadizing in the steppes around Isfizār, a town in what is now western Afghanistan, and a geographer of the same period speaks of them yet farther to the east in Jūzjān. It seems unlikely that these were Kurds in our ethnic sense of the term, though it is not impossible. The Balūchīs would be a parallel. Today they live in southeastern Iran, western Pakistan, and southwestern Afghanistan, but they speak a northwestern Iranian language akin to Parthian, implying a long-distance migration that seems to have been mostly completed by the time our Arab sources begin to speak of them. But one thing at least is clear: in the context of tenth-century Azerbaijan, people knew the difference between Kurds and Daylamites, and the two groups easily came into conflict with each other. In practice, the simplest thing is to go along with the sources. If they speak of Kurds, we will.

The Kurds and Daylamites were both mountaineers, but they differed in the character of their mountains. The Daylamites, as Procopius put it, dwelled on "sheer mountainsides," whereas the terrain where the Kurds lived tended to be considerably less forbidding. The downside of this for the Kurds was that powerful states in the plains did not find their mountains as impenetrable as those of the Daylamites. This effect is particularly clear in the case of Ḥasanawayh (ruled 961–79), the founder of a Kurdish dynasty we will come to shortly. When he stopped making the payments he used to send to one of the Būyid rulers, he faced a punitive expedition in 969–70, which he defeated, followed by a larger one, which led to a negotiated settlement in which he agreed to pay a substantial sum. After his death ʿAḍud al-Dawla sent an even more formidable expedition through which he imposed his will on Ḥasanawayh's sons, appointing one of them to rule as his vassal and killing the rest. The upside of the Kurdish mountains was that the terrain was more suitable than that of the Daylamites for horses, with the result that unlike them the Kurds could field cavalry. One might have expected this to give them the edge over the Daylamites in state formation, but that did not prove to be the case. Five Kurdish states emerged in this period that were significant enough to find a place in the standard handbook of Muslim dynasties, but not one of them was in the same league as the Būyids. Instead, their expansion tended to be limited to the territories surrounding their ancestral habitat. This in turn made them less visible in our sources than the Būyids were; often we know about their history only through the parts they played in other people's affairs.

Of the five dynasties, two were located in Azerbaijan: the Shaddādids (ca. 951 to 1075) with their center to the north in the city of Ganja, and the Rawwādids (early tenth century to 1071) with their center the best part of two hundred miles to the south in the city of Tabrīz. Some three hundred miles farther to the south, the Ḥasanawayhids (ca. 961 to 1015) emerged in the region of Qirmāsīn (the modern Kirmānshāh) on the highway from Baghdad to Khurāsān. About a hundred miles to the west, on the same highway, the ʿAnnāzids (991–1055) appeared in the region of Ḥulwān. Finally, the fifth Kurdish dynasty, the Marwānids (983–1085), arose in Diyār Bakr and the mountainous territory to the north of it; its center was the city of Mayyāfāriqīn, nearly four hundred miles to the northwest of Ḥulwān. A number of features of these states are worth attention.

The first arises from their geographical distribution. Of the five Kurdish states only the Ḥasanawayhids and the ʿAnnāzids were uncomfortably close to each other; their rivalry was an old one and ended in the victory of the ʿAnnāzids and the demise of the Ḥasanawayhids. By contrast, the Shaddādids and the Rawwādids did not interact much with each other, since each was preoccupied with other enemies, notably non-Muslims. Likewise the Marwānids were geographically too much of an outlier to have dealings with the other Kurdish dynasties. As this implies, although the period marked the high point of Kurdish state formation and some Kurdish groups were busily engaged in it, most of the tribes of Kurdistan were clearly not involved, or not on a scale large enough to be visible in our sources. Kurdish state formation at this time nevertheless contrasts positively with the track record of the contemporary mountain populations of eastern Iran, where we find no counterparts of the five Kurdish dynasties. The Afshīn's kingdom of Usrūshana had ceased to exist in 893. The Ghūrids (early eleventh century to 1215), ruling in what is now central Afghanistan, held sway over a population that remained pagan well into the eleventh century, living in isolation from the Muslim world in a way the Kurds and even the Daylamites did not. Only in the middle of the twelfth century did this dynasty begin to have an impact beyond its mountains.

The second feature of the Kurdish dynasties is their varied relationships with cities. The Shaddādids had close ties to the people of Ganja and were wanted by the townspeople. The Rawwādids likewise built a wall around Tabrīz, adopting it as their capital, and after an earthquake in 1042, the ruler put great effort into rebuilding it. For the Ḥasanawayhids, by contrast, what mattered seems to have been the possession of castles, not cities, though we hear of one ruler of the dynasty who used his influence to establish a market in Hamadhān. The founder of the ʿAnnāzid dynasty ruled from Ḥulwān, at the foot of the pass leading up to the Iranian plateau, and the town continued to have some significance in the later history of the dynasty. Being closer to the plains of Iraq likely meant that the ʿAnnāzids were somewhat more urban than their Ḥasanawayhid enemies. The Marwānids were thoroughly urban and very much at home in their capital city, Mayyāfāriqīn, where their court boasted viziers and cultural luminaries. This degree of refined urbanity is untypical of the Kurdish dynasties, though both the Shaddādids and the Rawwādids were patrons of Qaṭrān, the first Persian poet of Azerbaijan.

The third feature of these dynasties is their more or less tribal character. We hear of the "tribe" (*ʿashīra*) of the first Shaddādid ruler, and it still mattered toward the end of the dynasty—though we are not told its name. The Rawwādids, very likely of Arab origin, were by the tenth century considered to be Kurds, and they were closely associated with the Hadhbānī tribe. The Ḥasanawayhids belonged to the Barzikānī tribe; when the Būyid ʿAḍud al-Dawla appointed Ḥasanawayh's son Badr as successor to his father, he described the appointment as entrusting "leadership over the Barzikānī Kurds" to him. The ʿAnnāzid dynasty was based on the seminomadic Shādhinjān tribe. A later ruler was accused of neglecting the tribe, but his successor's troops were Shādhinjānīs. In the case of the Marwānids we hear of a tribe to which they belonged, but it does not appear to have played much of a part in the history of the dynasty. The ethnicity of the dynasty nevertheless seems to have mattered in the process whereby the region they ruled acquired a large Kurdish population from farther east.

Other ventures in state formation

To complete our survey, we come to three cases that do not fit the categories used above. The first is the Ṣaffārid dynasty (861–1003) in Sīstān; the second is the Ghaznawid dynasty (977–1186) in what is now Afghanistan; and the third is the line of the Khwārazm-Shāhs (from pre-Islamic times to 1231), who were in fact a succession of dynasties that ruled in Khwārazm to the south of the Aral Sea. Though they do not fit, these cases matter, for each of them issued in a short-lived empire. We will concentrate here on the Ṣaffārids, treating the others only briefly but taking them up again in later chapters.

The formation of the Ṣaffārid state in Sīstān is not something we would expect.[19] For one thing, Sīstān seems an unlikely part of Iran for such a development. So far as we know, no strong state had ever emerged there in earlier times, and for sure none did later. This, then, was a unique event in the history of the region, and just why it should have happened is not obvious. The plains of Sīstān

19. For the Ṣaffārids see C. E. Bosworth, *The history of the Saffarids of Sistan and the Maliks of Nimruz*, Costa Mesa CA, 1994, or more briefly Bosworth, "The Ṭāhirids and Ṣaffārids."

were arid, and they were swept by merciless winds that repeatedly threatened habitable areas with invasive sand. But Sīstān, like Egypt, was the gift of a river, in this case the Helmand, which rises in the mountains of Afghanistan, and the irrigation this made possible could generate agricultural wealth. The gift, however, was a qualified one. The amount of water could vary enormously, ranging from the river running dry, as in 835, to intense flooding, as in 1244. At the same time, the water supply required a lot of human management. This was just the kind of activity that was likely to be neglected under the conditions of insecurity that were a chronic feature of life in Sīstān. So how rich was Sīstān? Sources from the period that concerns us suggest that the revenue of the province was around four million dirhams per annum; by way of comparison, one source gives the total revenue of Khurāsān—including Sīstān—as forty-five million dirhams. In other words, the contribution of the province was about a tenth of the total revenue of Khurāsān, which is not very impressive. Another feature of Sīstān, and an elusive one, is the character of its population. If we go by the geographical setting—a river valley with irrigated land—we would expect to find peasants, and there is indeed a reference to them. But if instead we go by the bellicosity of the population as attested in the historical record, we would expect to find tribes, just as we do in the mountains and deserts of the Middle East. Yet there is no indication that the population was tribal. Whatever we make of these issues, the evidence for bellicosity is overwhelming—and it goes back to the fourth century, when a Roman historian described the warriors of Sīstān as the most ardent of all.

By the middle of the ninth century a three-cornered conflict had developed in Sīstān. There was the provincial governor representing the ʿAbbāsids, or in practice rather the Ṭāhirids; one was appointed in 840 and held on until 854. There were the Khārijites. The first Khārijites to arrive were naturally outsiders, but there must have been intensive local recruitment into their forces. This Khārijite mobilization then triggered the formation of anti-Khārijite militias among the urban Sunnī populace. These fighters were known as the ʿAyyārs, and they were part of a wider phenomenon that comes most sharply into focus in Sīstān.[20] In 854 the provincial governor lost out, but the Khārijites had not exactly won. The successors of Ḥamza ibn Ādharak were not leaders of the same caliber, and the conflict between them and the ʿAyyārs looked set to continue indefinitely. The two militarized populations were divided by sectarian animus, as so often a deadly serious matter. And yet they had something significant in common: they shared a dislike of the efforts of outsiders such as the ʿAbbāsids to dominate Sīstān and collect taxes from its people, the Sagzīs. There was thus a sense that the Sagzīs belonged together against malign outsiders seeking to govern and tax them.

20. On this phenomenon see D. G. Tor, *Violent order*, Würzburg 2007.

Something else that was notable about the rise of the Ṣaffārids was their humble origin. No other dynasty ever emerged from the ʿAyyārs. The founder, Yaʿqūb ibn Layth (ruled 861–79), was a coppersmith (*ṣaffār*) who joined an anti-Khārijite militia. Now an ʿAyyār, he rose to be a commander, and in 861 he was acclaimed as ruler (*amīr*) of Sīstān. But he did not see his popular roots as an embarrassment to be overcome. He kept faith with them by maintaining a simple lifestyle, sleeping on an old saddlecloth and eating the plain food of Sīstān: barley bread, rice, leeks, onions, fish, and asafetida (a resinous gum widely consumed there). As might be expected, much of his rise was a matter of blood and gore. But he also had political imagination. He set about not just defeating his Khārijite rivals but also winning them over. Thus he wrote to the current Khārijite leader praising Ḥamza, who "never harmed any of the people of Sīstān." At a time when "the governorship of Sīstān was in the hands of outsiders," he said, Ḥamza's quarrel had been with the outsiders, not with "the Sagzī people."[21] The outsiders were in the first instance the ʿAbbāsids, whose track record of treachery toward their own followers Yaʿqūb excoriated. He accordingly invited the Khārijite imam to "come and link your army with us," presenting his program as in effect a continuation of Ḥamza's—"we shall never deliver Sīstān into anyone else's hands again"—and promising to "promote the interests and prosperity of Sīstān." In the event the Khārijite leader did not accept the invitation, and in due course Yaʿqūb inflicted a gruesome death on him. But despite his Sunnī partisanship, Yaʿqūb energetically recruited Khārijites into his army, and we are told that most of them joined him; the incentives included promotion, as from foot soldier to horseman. In welcoming one Khārijite leader who submitted to him, Yaʿqūb told him that "the greater part of my army and of my commanders are Khārijites too, and you will not feel strange among them." In this way Yaʿqūb reaped the harvest of the dual militarization of Sagzī society, welding ʿAyyārs and Khārijites into a single force. As the reference to promotion makes clear, a significant part of this force consisted of cavalry. Sīstān was not the best country for horses, but the Sagzīs had a fair number of them.

With the force he had collected, Yaʿqūb set about conquering himself an empire larger than any of the emerging states we have so far considered in this chapter. He expanded eastward deep into non-Muslim territory in what is now Afghanistan, northward to extinguish the Ṭāhirids, and westward into Kirmān, Fārs, Khūzistān, and even Iraq—he came within fifty miles of Baghdad before suffering an uncharacteristic defeat in 876. Not surprisingly, the sources stress the efficiency with which his army was managed. When Yaʿqūb died in 879 his successor was his brother ʿAmr ibn Layth (ruled 879–900), who continued the

21. For this and the quotations that follow see C. E. Bosworth, "The armies of the Ṣaffārids," *Bulletin of the School of Oriental and African Studies*, 31 (1968), 542–43.

enterprise with considerable success but came to grief when he went up against the Sāmānids. He did not just lose the battle; he was captured and later killed. Within a dozen years of this defeat the Ṣaffārids no longer reigned over an empire, or even Sīstān, which passed under Sāmānid rule in 911.

This was not quite the end of the story. Sāmānid fiscal exactions soon provoked the Sagzīs to rebel, and there was a restoration of Ṣaffārid rule in 923. In contrast to the popular origins of the dynasty, the two main rulers of this period were recognized cultural patrons; one of them was praised by Rūdakī, a famous Persian poet of the day, as "the pride of Iran . . . of the stock of Sāsān."[22] But they were just local potentates in Sīstān, not imperial rulers, and their reign lasted only until the Ghaznawids conquered Sīstān in 1003. This, of course, led to more rebellion. It was said of the Ghaznawid governor who served for over a decade from 1010 that during his entire governorship there were always a thousand men in revolt. Subsequently a new local dynasty, the Naṣrids, emerged in the 1030s and lasted until 1225, but these rulers did not stand out and tended to be vassals of the major power of the day. Yet the memory of the family did not disappear. As late as the middle of the eighteenth century an alleged Ṣaffārid was still making trouble.

This leaves us to deal briefly with the Ghaznawids and the Khwārazm-Shāhs. As we have already noted, the Ghaznawids were a spin-off from the Sāmānid state. The basis of Sāmānid rule was their possession of extensive lowlands in Transoxania and Khurāsān, but there was no lack of mountainous country in the region. We would not therefore expect the Sāmānids to have ruled directly throughout the territory they claimed, and indeed they had a variety of vassals. There were the Banījūrids, a line of rulers in the region of Balkh who were probably of Iranian origin. There were the Muḥtājids, probably also Iranian, in Chaghāniyān a bit to the north. There were the Ilyāsids, a Sogdian line that established itself in distant Kirmān after backing the wrong horse in a rebellion of Sāmānid princes in Bukhārā. And there were the Sīmjūrids, a line of Turkic slave-soldier origin that acquired a territorial base in Quhistān, an isolated mountainous region of Khurāsān. The emergence of the Ghaznawids combines some of these themes. Like the Sīmjūrids, they began as slave soldiers of the Sāmānids. Like the Ilyāsids, they backed a wrong horse in Sāmānid politics—in their case in a succession struggle of 961. Like them, they needed to put distance between themselves and the Sāmānid capital, which they did by removing to Ghazna in the south, deep in the mountains of what is now Afghanistan. Like the other vassals, they acted as governors for the Sāmānids—or such was the pretense. In other words, they did not diverge greatly from the overall pattern of Sāmānid vassals, though benefiting

22. Bosworth, "The Ṭāhirids and Ṣaffārids," 132.

more from the relative security of their mountainous terrain. Yet they had a far greater historical impact than any of the others did.

For now we can content ourselves with a very brief account of the expansion of the Ghaznawid dynasty. The essence of it is that in the early eleventh century, under the rule of Maḥmūd of Ghazna (ruled 998–1030), the Ghaznawid state became an expansive military power on two fronts, in Iran and India. On the Iranian front Maḥmūd conquered the Sāmānid territories in Khurāsān, adding Khwārazm and invading western Iran. On the Indian front his persistent raiding generated enormous amounts of booty that funded his Iranian campaigns. He thereby created an empire larger even than that of Yaʿqūb the Coppersmith. But the Ghaznawid empire in Iran was transitory, collapsing with the arrival of the Seljuqs and their Turkic nomads; the crucial battle against the Seljuqs took place in 1040, and the Ghaznawids lost it. Their future now lay in India, and it is in that context that we will return to them.

The story of the Khwārazm-Shāhs was initially very different. Khwārazm—Chorasmia—was at one time a rich plain, essentially the delta of the Oxus as it flowed into the Aral Sea from the south. But the desert on either side could isolate it, while exposing it to the attacks of nomads. In the early centuries of Islam its population still spoke an Eastern Iranian language of its own and was ruled by an indigenous dynasty, the Afrīghids of Kāth. This dynasty may have been established in 305, and it lasted till 995; its rulers bore the title Khwārazm-Shāh. Around the early ninth century they converted to Islam. But in 995 they were deposed by a rival family, the Ma'mūnids of Gurganj (995–1017), to whom the title now passed. This may have represented something more than politics as usual. Kāth and Gurganj, both of them close to Khīwa, lay on opposite sides of the Oxus and differed in that Gurganj, and not Kāth, was the commercial capital of Khwārazm, linked to the long-distance trade with the north; moreover, the two cities came to have separate political leaderships. So the overthrow of the Afrīghids by the Ma'mūnids may have been the triumph of an outward-looking, commercial Khwārazm over an inward-looking, traditional one. The next discontinuity was more drastic: a Ghaznawid conquest in 1017, followed until 1041 by a series of Ghaznawid governors who likewise bore the title Khwārazm-Shāh. From this point on only Turks were to hold the title. In 1097 a line of governors was installed by the Seljuqs and held power until 1231, again with the title Khwārazm-Shāh. They were a classic example of provincial governors who entrench themselves and become independent rulers. Eventually they acquired a transient empire, but that development lies outside the period covered in this chapter.

To pull together the threads of this survey, of some twenty-two dynasties discussed in this section, the majority lasted for over a century. So fragmentation, though it meant considerable instability and widespread insecurity, did not mean chaos. The immediate cause of most of the fragmentation was of course the disintegration of the ʿAbbāsid Caliphate. But the underlying reason none of the fragments proved capable of establishing a lasting imperial state to replace that of the ʿAbbāsids was the fact that Iraq could no longer play its traditional fiscal role in supporting an Iranian empire. While Iraq had flourished, the Sasanian Empire had held Iran together for four centuries; but now things were different. Given the extent of the fragmentation, it is not surprising that the various fragments should also have been diverse. As we have seen, states were formed by sectarian imams, by entrenched provincial governors, by insubordinate mercenaries, by Kurdish tribesmen, and through an unusual popular upwelling in Sīstān. As to how these dynasties came to an end, diversity again prevailed. The single most salient cause of dynastic extinction was the coming of the Seljuqs and the Turkic nomads who accompanied them: they had a hand in the demise of up to eight of the dynasties they encountered in Iran. There was, however, no lack of dynastic mortality before their arrival, and a small number of peripheral dynasties succeeded in surviving it. That the number of these survivors was so small reflects the fact that it was the Seljuq Turks, rather than any of the predominantly Iranian actors we have considered in this chapter, who would come closest to a geopolitical restoration of the Sasanian Empire.

The emergence of a Muslim Persian culture

The medium

As we saw in a previous chapter, the emergence of classical Arabic played a central role in the formation of Islamic civilization. Across the Muslim world of the ninth to eleventh centuries, it was the literary language of educated Muslims, the standard language of their high culture and administration. In the central Muslim world from Egypt to Iraq, where the mass of the population gradually came to speak Arabic, this monopoly was unchallenged; neither Coptic nor the various forms of Aramaic current in the Fertile Crescent became Muslim literary languages. In the far west Berber did to an extent achieve that status, but if we can judge from what survives and from the character of Berber society at the time, it can only have played that role on a limited scale. A far greater exception to the literary monopoly of Arabic was Persian, which in the same period became a Muslim literary language with a rich body of literature, a significant part of which has reached us across a millennium.

The emergence of Persian as a Muslim literary language was, of course, an exception only at the time. Today the Muslim world possesses a large number of literary languages alongside Arabic, and many of these have existed for centuries. This is not surprising. In a situation in which a literary language coexists with a vernacular that is not closely related to it, there is always a likelihood that people will sooner or later succumb to the convenience of writing in the vernacular. Though this trend has been intensified in modern times, it is abundantly attested in the premodern linguistic history of the world—in Europe, in India, and elsewhere. But just how soon or how late such promotion of the vernacular takes place naturally depends on other things.

Here one major factor is the role of religion. Religious traditions may invest great energy in translating their canonical texts into the languages of their adherents: Buddhists and Christians did this on a large scale in the early centuries of their respective expansions. This meant either adopting existing literary forms of these languages or, if none existed, creating them. But the guardians of a canon may equally prefer to remain faithful to the original language of their texts. The Brahmins of premodern India never translated the Vēdas for their followers, the Thēravāda Buddhists of Ceylon (today's Sri Lanka) and Southeast Asia kept their canon in Pali, and the Catholic Christians stayed with Latin until the twentieth century. Islam is by and large a religion of this second kind, in the sense that the language of Qur'ānic recitation and ritual prayer was and remains overwhelmingly Arabic. Exceptions can be found, but they are rare. The Islamic profession of faith appears in a Middle Persian version on a coin of 691–92, and as we have seen the early Muslim coinage of North Africa had it in Latin. Likewise near the beginning of the history of Islam in Bukhārā there is evidence of the Qur'ān being recited in a vernacular tongue during prayer. Later the Ḥanafīs, one of the four Sunnī schools of Islamic law, acquired a large Persian-speaking following and took the view that reciting the Qur'ān in a non-Arabic language in the course of the ritual prayers might be permissible. But this was an idiosyncratic doctrine of the Ḥanafīs, and it does not seem to have been much invoked in practice. Worse yet, it invited ridicule. The Ḥanafīs lost a debate with the Shāfi'ites in the early eleventh century when a Shāfi'ite performed a parody of Ḥanafī prayer in which he included a short Qur'ānic verse in Persian. It just sounded silly. There was therefore no compelling religious need for the Muslims either to adopt the Middle Persian literary language that prevailed in Iran at the time of the conquest or to develop a new form of literary Persian. This meant that the process was likely to take place later rather than sooner.

The countervailing factor was the Sasanian legacy. It is actually somewhat misleading to characterize Persian as the vernacular of early Islamic Iran: we are talking about a large region, and despite the prevalence of Iranian languages throughout, it was linguistically diverse. As we have already seen, the dialects of northwestern Iran were more akin to Parthian than they were to Persian. To the east there were Iranian languages that were very different from either Persian or Parthian; thus Khwārazmian was the language of Khwārazm, Sogdian that of the plains of Transoxania and the mountains of Usrūshana, and Bactrian that of the region of Balkh. In a way Persian, too, was a regional language, the speech of the people of Fārs (whence the Persian name for the language, *Fārsī*). But thanks to the fact that the Sasanians came from Fārs and ruled for four centuries, Persian had come to be more than a regional language and must have become widely known across Iran. Even then, it was not the same language everywhere. By the end of the Sasanian period there seem to have been two major dialects. One was a southern dialect centered on Fārs and extending westward into Khūzistān and eastward into Sīstān, and the other was a northern dialect best attested in Khurāsān. Yet it was still recognizably the same language. In principle we could imagine the Arab conquest ending this imperial role of Persian; in practice what seems to have happened is that even where it was not the mother tongue of the population, Persian lived on as the lingua franca by which the Arabs and their Iranian subjects communicated with each other. Indeed, the use of Persian seems to have expanded under alien rule (compare the spread of Quechua in the Andes after the Spanish conquest). Transoxania in pre-Islamic times was Sogdian-speaking, but by the later tenth century it appears that the cities at least were Persian-speaking. Thus it was thanks to the Sasanians that Iran possessed a single overarching Iranian language that coexisted with the diversity of vernaculars. The Berbers in North Africa had no counterpart to this.

Another part of the Sasanian legacy was the Aramaic script in which Middle Persian was written. One way in which Persian Muslims could have acquired a literary language other than Arabic would have been to continue the use of Middle Persian and its script but to purge it of its more obviously Zoroastrian features and introduce Islamic ones, especially Arabic loanwords. But this did not happen in early Islamic Iran, where Middle Persian became a literary language used only by Zoroastrians, and above all by priests, notably those of Fārs. Two reasons might be suggested for this. One, which may not have counted for much, is that Middle Persian as written was an inconveniently archaic language, with a script that was often ambiguous and full of Arameograms (the word for "king" would be written in Aramaic as *malkā* but read in Persian as *shāh*). The other reason, which may have counted for more, was a tendency in this part of the world to link choice of script with religious affiliation, no doubt reflecting a pattern whereby the acquisition of literacy took place within religious communities. Sogdian, for example, was written in three different scripts by Christians, Manichaeans, and Buddhists, and from at least the eighth century Jews wrote Persian in the Hebrew script. By the same token we could expect Muslims to write Persian in the Arabic script and thereby Islamize it. This was the path actually taken. A new Persian literary language developed, based on contemporary spoken Persian and written in the Arabic script. This language is New Persian in contradistinction to Old and Middle Persian, but today it is over a thousand years old, and in most contexts we can simply call it Persian. We can now turn to how it emerged.

Our sources tell us, quite credibly, that the first major innovation took place in the second half of the ninth century and consisted in the use of Persian in formal poetry (oral folk poetry in Persian had no doubt existed all along). There is a story about Yaʿqūb the Coppersmith preserved in a proud local history of Sīstān that, whether or not it is true, is undoubtedly apt. As we have seen, a successful ruler such as Yaʿqūb the Coppersmith had to have an entourage of poets to eulogize him. They naturally did so in Arabic, the only respectable language of royal eulogy at the time. But there was a problem: Yaʿqūb did not understand Arabic—unlike a later Ṣaffārid, who knew enough Arabic to teach Prophetic traditions on Fridays. Listening to the panegyrics of the poets, like the one composed by the poet from Iṣfahān, must have been excruciatingly boring for Yaʿqūb, and he did not have a sufficient sense of *noblesse oblige* to put up with it. "Why," he demanded, "do you compose verses which I don't understand?"[23] This was an embarrassing moment of truth, and something now had to be done about it. Fortunately one of Yaʿqūb's secretaries came up with a solution: he composed panegyrics in Persian, and the idea caught on. Another account has it that the first Persian poet was in fact a contemporary of this secretary in Bādghīs, north of Herat. We are told that in 875 two lines of his Persian poetry inspired an adventurer to rebel and take over Khurāsān. All in all, what we have of this poet's work adds up to no more than four lines. Yet despite the fact that the early record remains fragmentary, from this point on we can sketch a more or less continuous history of Persian poetry culminating in the celebrated *Shāhnāma* of Firdawsī, completed in 1010. Of his epic we possess not four but some fifty thousand lines, and we will shortly take up its content.

Prose developed more slowly than poetry, with its beginnings in the tenth century rather than the ninth. But by the 1030s there was an extensive Persian prose literature, and a dozen works from this period survive to the present day. These books covered a range of topics about which literate people needed or desired to be informed—history, geography, Qurʾān commentary, dogmatics, mysticism, medicine, pharmacology, astronomy, astrology, and philosophy (the latter the topic on which Ibn Sīnā wrote in Persian for his last patron). In all this there was a large element of free translation from texts already existing in Arabic. When the authors of these works give their reasons for writing in Persian rather than Arabic, they are eminently practical ones. As the author of a work on astronomy composed in 1073–74 remarks about his predecessors, "when they write a book in Persian, they state that they have adopted this language in order that those who

23. Quoted in G. Lazard, "The rise of the New Persian language," in *The Cambridge history of Iran*, 4:595.

do not know Arabic may be able to use the book."[24] A Sāmānid vizier who made a very free translation of a major Arabic history of the world in 963–64 offers just such a statement: "I have translated this book," he writes, "in order that all, princes and subjects alike, may have access to it, so as to read it and know it."[25] The author of a medical work written about 980 (actually composed in didactic verse, a genre too prosaic to count as poetry) tells us that he wanted to achieve as wide a circulation as he could, and wondered whether to write the book in Arabic (*Tāzī*) or Persian (*Pārsī*); in the end he said to himself that "our land is Iran, so most of its people know Persian."[26] Many of the people of Iran may not in fact have spoken Persian as their mother tongue, but as this author says, they knew it, and most of those who were literate could doubtless read it more comfortably than they did Arabic. This Persian prose literature was not intended for professional scholars, nor as yet for cultural luminaries—one reason early Persian prose tends to be written in a simpler style than that of later centuries. But taken with the rise of Persian poetry, the emergence of this prose literature represents a significant structural modification of the monolingualism of early Islamic civilization. Not that everyone thought this change a good thing. Bīrūnī, a major scholar from Khwārazm who must have died sometime after 1050, describes himself as originally a stranger to both Arabic and Persian but avers that it is better to be disparaged in Arabic than to be praised in Persian. A book translated into Persian, he tells us, becomes lackluster and useless, for Persian is a language good only for tales of the Persian kings and evening entertainment. Yet in due course New Persian would become a vehicle of high culture as far west as the Balkans and as far east as Bengal.

If Persian was now an acceptable language of literature, an obvious question was whether it would also become the language of administration. It seems that both the Sāmānids and the Ghaznawids used it but then at some point went back to Arabic. In the Sāmānid case, we are told, the return to Arabic did not go down well and had to be reversed. In the Ghaznawid case an elitist comment of the contemporary historian ʿUtbī (d. 1036 or 1040) reveals something of what was at stake. When Persian was used, he tells us, "the bazaar of eloquence suffered loss" with the result that "capable and incapable became equal."[27] Needless to say, ʿUtbī wrote his history in Arabic, demonstrating his capability with a prose style so ornate that commentaries had to be written to explicate it, something almost unheard of for works of history. But in the long run the incapable had their revenge:

24. Quoted in Lazard, "The rise of the New Persian language," 632.

25. Quoted in Lazard, "The rise of the New Persian language," 630.

26. Quoted in L. Richter-Bernburg, "Linguistic shuʿūbīya and early Neo-Persian prose," *Journal of the American Oriental Society*, 94 (1974), 57b.

27. Quoted in W. Barthold, *Turkestan down to the Mongol invasion*, London 1928, 291.

the book was translated several times into Persian for their benefit. In fact something similar was already happening with official documents in ʿUtbī's day. When diplomatic communications written in Arabic were received at the Ghaznawid court, they would be translated into Persian for the benefit of the incapable courtiers.

Such, in outline, is the story of the rise of New Persian and the literature written in it. What we have so far left implicit is a striking geographical asymmetry. This language emerged not in the homeland of Persian in southwestern Iran, but rather in the northeast—in Khurāsān, where a few centuries earlier the prevalent language may have been Parthian, and in Transoxania, where the mother tongue of the population was still Sogdian in early Islamic times. In other words, the new literary language was based on the northern dialect, not the southern one. From the northeast it only gradually spread westward, and for much of the period covered in this chapter the Muslims of western Iran were still adhering to a monolingual Arabic high culture. An interesting moment in the story concerns Qaṭrān of Tabrīz. We met him above as the first poet to compose Persian verse in Azerbaijan. By eastern standards he was a rather late figure to be a pioneer of this kind—he had patrons who ruled in the mid-eleventh century, and we know that he was still active in 1088. Back in 1045 he had received a visit from an eastern traveler, who commented that Qaṭrān was "a good poet, but one who did not know Persian very well."[28] He had come to this traveler with copies of the collected poems of two well-known eastern poets and asked him to explain passages he did not understand. It is hard to imagine how someone who did not know Persian well could have composed good poetry in the language, and it seems more likely that Qaṭrān's problem was that early New Persian bore a strong imprint of its northeastern origin. For example, the Persian word *mul*, meaning wine, is a Sogdian loanword that would have meant nothing to Persian speakers west of Transoxania when they first encountered it. As this suggests, it was not just Qaṭrān who had a problem. The earliest extant New Persian dictionary, which likewise dates from the mid-eleventh century, was written by a certain Asadī who hailed from the city of Ṭūs in Khurāsān, and it aimed to explain such words to readers in western Iran. It duly glosses *mul* and illustrates its use with a couplet from an eastern poet. So there is no real doubt that New Persian was a product of the northeast. That leaves us with the intriguing question why it should have emerged there, rather than in some other part of Iran such as Fārs. The answer is by no means clear; paradoxically, the northeast was precisely the region where Arab settlement had been densest.

28. Lazard, "The rise of the New Persian language," 606.

Before we leave the medium and turn to the message, there was one choice the initiators of the New Persian literary language had to face that was perhaps more than just a matter of practicality. How open was this language to be to Arabic loanwords? A couple of points are worth noting here. One is that such loanwords were much less in evidence in accounts of the pre-Islamic history of Iran than they were in the general run of New Persian texts. Perhaps this arose from a sense that Arabic was out of place in so Iranian a context, or perhaps it was simply a natural consequence of the use of material inherited from the Iranian past. The other point is that there were two very different approaches to the problem of rendering technical terms in New Persian. When translating a scientific or philosophical text from Arabic, one could simply retain the Arabic words for things that had no names in Persian as commonly spoken. Or one could set about replacing them with purely Persian words, either revived Middle Persian forms or newly invented ones. Both tendencies are found, but the Arabizing trend prevailed. The author who noted that his predecessors would say that they wrote in Persian for the benefit of those who did not know Arabic went on to complain that they had recourse to "words of pure Persian that are more difficult than Arabic."[29] He himself professed to use Arabic terms that could be learned by anyone in five days. But he did not say whether those earlier authors used pure Persian out of a false sense of practicality or in pursuit of some kind of authenticity. In any case, New Persian was deeply influenced by Arabic. For example, in older New Persian we find the language called *Pārsī*, retaining the initial *p* of Old and Middle Persian. But later the Arabic form of the name was adopted into Persian and became *Fārsī*; unlike Persian, Arabic has no *p*, and in borrowing foreign words it replaces a *p* with an *f* or a *b*.

The message

There were any number of messages in the poetry and prose composed in New Persian, but the one we will take up here concerns the relevance of the Iranian past for Muslim Iranians of the ninth to eleventh centuries. How far did New Persian serve as a vehicle for the cultivation of memories of this past? It did not have to. Much information about the history of Iran had been rendered into Arabic through early translations of Middle Persian sources, so that to a large extent the Muslim discussion of Iranian antiquity could be conducted in Arabic. In fact, instances of the translation of material from Middle Persian into New Persian are surprisingly rare. But if significant numbers of Iranians valued their past despite the fact that they were now Muslims, and if they now possessed a Muslim literary language of their own and often had a hard time coping with

29. Lazard, "The rise of the New Persian language," 632.

Arabic, then it was almost inevitable that New Persian would come to serve as a medium for an Iranian message. Thus we find the poet Farrukhī, who was in the service of Maḥmūd of Ghazna, referring to Iran with the archaic term "Ērānshahr," Middle Persian for "the kingdom of the Iranians." Asadī, whom we met above as the author a Persian dictionary, also wrote a short account in verse of a disputation in which he engaged with a group of Arabs in the course of a banquet at which everyone got cheerfully drunk. The Arabs claimed to be superior to the Iranians and in making their case mentioned twenty-three famous Arabs of the past; Asadī then hit back in kind, naming twenty-six famous Iranians of the past—most of them rulers, heroes, or poets—while at the same time disparaging the Arabs as lizard eaters. Thumbing one's nose at the Arabs in this way was risqué but not irreligious, since it was well known that Muḥammad did not eat lizard himself.

There were substantial works of both poetry and prose dedicated to recounting the story of the Iranian past before Islam. An early poet of Marw composed a work in this vein of which we possess only three couplets. Later Daqīqī, an eastern Iranian poet of the mid-tenth century, began composing a *Shāhnāma* ("Book of kings") of which a thousand couplets were to be adopted by Firdawsī into his own *Shāhnāma*. A Balkhī active in the later tenth century turned to prose to write a bulky *Shāhnāma* of which we have only fragments, and his was not the only one. The culmination of these efforts was the fifty thousand lines of Firdawsī's *Shāhnāma*, composed between 975 and 1010. For Persian posterity this became the definitive account of the Iranian past, largely driving other accounts out of circulation and becoming a prominent feature of the Iranian cultural landscape. Thus in 1089 a poet composed a long epic about the wars of ʿAlī, the cousin of the Prophet. In it he denounced the *Shāhnāma* as untruthful and disparaged it as a *Mughnāma*, a "Book of Magi," the Magi being the Zoroastrian priests. Yet in a backhanded compliment to the *Shāhnāma* he borrowed its meter, echoed its verses, and made references to one of its heroes, Rustam. He obviously did not like the book, but he had to relate to it. Later a rare compliment, entirely free of backhandedness, came to the *Shāhnāma* from an unexpected source: a literary critic who was not an Iranian at all, Ḍiyāʾ al-Dīn ibn al-Athīr of Mosul (d. 1239). His point was that there was one thing in which the Persians outdid the Arabs, and that was the composition of epics. Inevitably he illustrated this point with the *Shāhnāma*, observing that it "contains the whole history of the Persians" and adding that it was "the Qurʾān of the nation" (*Qurʾān al-qawm*), accomplished Persians being in agreement that "there is nothing in their literature to exceed this work in eloquence."[30]

30. Quoted in I. Goldziher, *Muslim studies*, London 1967–71, 1:160 note 2.

As the dismissal of the *Shāhnāma* as a *Mughnāma* suggests, the difficulty in all this was to find a plausible accommodation between Islam and Zoroastrianism. Once the nativist prophets had come and gone, most Muslim Iranians had no easy way around the plain fact that Islam was true and Zoroastrianism was false. Of course they could always try. There was a well-known Islamic tradition in which ʿAlī explained that the Zoroastrians had once possessed a genuine revelation, but their memories had been wiped clean of it after their king got drunk and made love to his sister or daughter; better to have once had a revelation and lost it than never to have had one at all. There was likewise a tendency to create links between Zoroastrianism and the Biblical narrative, for example by having the Persians join the Jews and Arabs in being descended from Abraham. Meanwhile, poets had license to make naughty Zoroastrian references that pietists would not have approved of, and Daqīqī for one was known for doing this. He has a poem that ends by listing the only four things in the world that he needs: "The ruby-colored lip, the harp's lament / The blood-red wine, and Zoroaster's creed."[31]

Perhaps the most arresting attempt to align the two religions is a story told by the Seljuq vizier Niẓām al-Mulk (d. 1092) in his book of advice for rulers. This Iranian vizier was a somewhat paranoid Sunnī confronting what he deemed the irreligion and sedition of the Ismāʿīlīs. His paranoia may in fact have been well judged: there is reason to believe that it was the Ismāʿīlīs who were responsible for assassinating him. But the story in question is not about the Ismāʿīlīs, or not directly. Instead it is about Mazdak, the Zoroastrian heretic of the late fifth or early sixth century, and about how after his prolonged efforts to subvert the Iranian polity and its social basis he and his followers got their just deserts, which consisted in being stripped naked and buried head down in pits, with their legs in the air. This auspicious outcome, we learn, was largely owed to the courageous and astute conduct of the eighteen-year-old prince Anūshirwān, the future Khusraw I, acting in league with a wise old Zoroastrian priest from Fārs. So what was it all about? In Niẓām al-Mulk's view there was a key thing that the Mazdakites of those days and the Ismāʿīlīs of his own day shared: a vicious and subversive denial of the property rights of individual males in wealth and wives. If these heretics had their way, wealth and women would be shared by all and sundry—all men, that is. By contrast, what orthodox Zoroastrianism and orthodox Islam had in common was the uncompromising affirmation of male property rights. In this perspective, what mattered about a religion, in this world at least, was not so much whether it was true as whether it was a good thing, and orthodox Zoroastrianism, it seems, had proved itself every bit as good a thing as orthodox Islam. At a certain level, one could say, they were functionally interchangeable. That it had become acceptable

31. Quoted in E. G. Browne, *A literary history of Persia*, Cambridge 1956, 1:459.

to articulate such a view in a work on good governance written for a Muslim audience no doubt reflects the fact that by the later eleventh century there were far fewer Zoroastrians than there had been, even in the mountains, so the dominance of Islam could now be taken for granted. Given the dominance of the true religion, recognizing that a false religion could have been socially beneficial in its day hardly amounted to unbelief. Yet the thinking behind the story veers surprisingly close to the idea ascribed to the English playwright Christopher Marlowe (d. 1593) that religion is no more than "a device of policy."[32]

As this story suggests, the figure of Khusraw I was a crucial one for the relationship between Muslim Iranians and a past that was ethnically theirs but religiously alien. Was he really "Anūshirwān the Just," as he was often known in Persian? For sure he had a relatively good press in ninth-century Arabic texts, and there was even a saying of the Prophet that was understood to refer to him: "I was born in the time of the just king."[33] If this seemed to open the door too wide, a variant form of the tradition added that the rest of the Sasanian rulers were unjust. But could Muḥammad really have endorsed even one Sasanian ruler as just? Here we encounter a sharp reaction at the Islamic end of the spectrum. The Prophet, we are told, took the trouble of appearing to someone in a dream to assure him that he had never said such a thing. The Transoxanian scholar Ḥalīmī (d. 1012) concurs: How could God's Prophet possibly have called someone just who judged by a law other than God's? This stance fits well with Ḥalīmī's general condemnation of the cultivation of the Iranian past. In a somewhat repetitive passage he says that one should not read, like, memorize, or talk about the books of the Iranians (*al-Aʿājim*), nor should one discuss their contents in social gatherings. One should not spend time on memorizing such accounts or money on copying them, and one should not treat such material as worth reading, hearing, copying, purchasing, or taking seriously. All this, Ḥalīmī says, is subject to the strongest religious condemnation. We have here the language of the pietist side of a medieval Muslim culture war. As to the other extreme, an Ismāʿīlī source gives us a vivid account of a group of heretics from Azerbaijan who had infiltrated the Ismāʿīlī fold and in 1141–42 went on to manifest their abominable beliefs. The source calls them "Mazdakites" but informs us that they called themselves "Persians" (*Pārsīs*). Their leader told them that Muḥammad, ʿAlī, and Muḥammad's Persian companion Salmān were all three of them God. In terms of the persons included in this trinity, we are here at least on the outer fringes of Islam. In particular, it was perfectly respectable for Persians to take pride in Salmān as *their* companion; no adoration without representation, one might say. Asadī, disputing

32. Quoted in P. Crone, "Oral transmission of subversive ideas from the Islamic world to Europe," in her *Collected studies in three volumes*, Leiden 2016, 3:234.

33. Quoted in S. B. Savant, *The new Muslims of post-conquest Iran*, Cambridge 2013, 132.

with the Arabs at the banquet, boasted that "Salmān the Chosen" was a Persian (*Pārsī*). But the "Persians" described by our Ismāʿīlī source believed something more: that the pre-Islamic Iranian kings had been rightful imams. From them the imamate had passed to Muḥammad, ʿAlī, and eventually a grandson of Abū Muslim, returning us again to the fringes of Islam. So in this view Anūshirwān was not merely just; he was a legitimate imam.

But what might have been the view of someone who was not attracted to either of these extremes? The Ziyārid Kay Kāʾūs ibn Iskandar (ruled 1049 to ca. 1087) wrote a book of advice for his favorite son and included in it a chapter made up of some forty-odd sayings of Anūshirwān, from whose brother he reputedly descended. It is, he says in advance, obligatory to practice these counsels, and after listing them he adds that they exude "the fragrance of wisdom and kingly dignity."[34] He is not, however, committed to them as one might be to a scripture. He notes that these counsels are for the young, whereas those who have grown old no longer need them, since experience has taught them all they need to know. Yet he obviously does not regard the Zoroastrian polity ruled by the brother of his ancestor as an evil empire. This accords with his overall tendency to moderation. Though not a pietist, he was certainly not impious. Thus he would indeed have preferred his son not to drink, but knowing that he would, if only through peer pressure, he counseled him on how to manage the habit. You should do your best to repent, he advised; you should start drinking only after performing the afternoon prayer, and you should never drink on Fridays in deference to the holiness of the day (compare the black poet who abstained from reciting poetry on Fridays). In fact, not drinking on Fridays is a particularly good move: if you do that nobody will criticize you for drinking during the rest of the week, and you will earn yourself a reward in heaven. What we see here is perhaps an attitude that was widely shared among ordinary people, though rarely articulated by them in forms that have reached us: Islam is a fine religion, but it should not become more than a religion, so it should leave plenty of room for other things. Some of the responses of the Afshīn to his interrogators were in this vein. Thus he told them that he had inherited a non-Muslim book from his father that contained both wise counsels and blasphemies and that he had enjoyed the wise counsels and ignored the rest. "I did not think," he added, "that this was in any way going outside Islam."[35]

This response might not have pleased the pietists, but it was better than some of the reprehensible things laypeople were apparently saying in Central Asia around the twelfth century. The jurists discussed such sayings in scholarly Arabic, but they quoted them in the vernacular language of the laity—that is to say, in Persian. The issue for the jurists was in each case whether a person saying such a

34. Kai Kāʾūs ibn Iskandar, *Mirror for princes*, London 1951, 48.
35. *The history of al-Ṭabarī*, Albany 1985–2007, 33:188.

thing thereby became an unbeliever. Thanks to their concerns we gain a vivid picture of the sentiments ordinary people may have given vent to in unguarded—or perhaps not so unguarded—moments. We see a dismissive attitude to the basic duties of a Muslim: "I'm so tired of fasting and praying!"[36] "It's great not to pray!" "Man, performing prayers is a real drag!" Someone who is asked to contribute to the repair of a mosque or to show up there to pray responds, "I won't come to the mosque, I won't give a dirham; what is the mosque to me?" Such statements go with a cavalier attitude to the Sharīʿa, the holy law of Islam. One man responds to being informed by a jurist that he is divorced from his wife by exclaiming, "What do I know about divorce and all that? The mother of the kids has to stay in the house." Another man declines to go to court: "I've got a club; what do I want with the Sharīʿa?" Then again there are inappropriate attitudes to unbelievers. A woman says to her husband, "Better to be an unbeliever than to be with you!" In response to the celebration of the Persian New Year by the Zoroastrians, people make comments such as "They put on a good show!" Someone is puzzled by a conversion to Islam and asks the convert, "What harm did you suffer from your own religion?" Responses to reminders about the afterlife are dismissive or downright skeptical. One man says, "I don't care about hell!" Another, urged not to sin because there is another world, answers, "Who has come back from that world and told us about it?" On top of all this we have the man who says, "I'm fed up with Islam!" The material is unusual, but it is a salutary reminder that even in an age of faith no religion can hope to secure the commitment of all of the people all of the time.

36. For this and the quotations that follow see R. Jaʿfarīyān, "Adabīyāt-i alfāẓ-i kufr dar fiqh-i Ḥanafī," *Mutūn-i Īrānī*, 2 (2012), 138, 140, 142, 146, 149, 150, 151, 152, 153.

6

The breakup of the Caliphate in the central Muslim world

In the two chapters preceding this one we took for granted a fundamental change: the decline in the power of the central government of the Caliphate. In this chapter we begin with a closer look at that decline. Why did it happen?

Just as consequential as the decline itself is the fact that no one replaced the declining ʿAbbāsids in their imperial role as rulers of the Muslim world. It was the Ismāʿīlī sectarians, and the Fāṭimid dynasty they brought to power, who came closest to success. Why, then, did they fail?

The decline of the ʿAbbāsids and the failure of the Fāṭimids meant that political fragmentation would prevail in the central Muslim world, just as it did in the regions to the west and to the east. Much of this chapter will therefore be devoted to surveying the smaller states of the central region from roughly the ninth to the eleventh century. We will start in the Fertile Crescent, move south to Arabia, and end with Egypt. These are three very different environments; how far did their contrasting resource endowments shape the outcome in each of the three?

In the Fertile Crescent the Ḥamdānids were quite similar to some of the states we have already looked at in the two preceding chapters. What was different in Syria and Iraq was the prominent role of Arab tribes in forming states, and the most interesting aspect of the way they did this was the irrelevance of religion. In other words, these tribesmen departed conspicuously from the Ibn Khaldūnian model.

In Arabia, by contrast, the Ibn Khaldūnian model was alive and well in the three parts of the peninsula best provided with natural resources. The Yemen and Oman were the sites of long-lived sectarian imamates, though both could also sustain normal secular states. Meanwhile Baḥrayn saw the formation of the most extravagantly heterodox sectarian polity of them all, and the Ḥijāz supported a uniquely hybrid state.

The wealth of Egypt promised the fiscal resources for a major imperial power in the Middle East, yet it was never quite to deliver on this promise—or not until the first half of the nineteenth century. Why not? Here we are back with the Fāṭimid dynasty, its successes and its failures.

In conclusion we will pick up three themes that arise implicitly or explicitly in the chapter: the role of Arab nomads in the history of the region, the fade-out of Iraq as a center of power, and the absence of any significant reassertion of a non-Arab identity within a Muslim framework.

In the previous two chapters we have seen the emergence of independent or autonomous states in the western and eastern territories formerly ruled by the Caliphate. That leaves us to account for a core region made up of the Fertile Crescent, Arabia, and Egypt, and a major theme of this chapter will be the formation of similar states in these central territories and the extent of their political and military success in the same period, from the ninth to the eleventh century. But before we come to this there are two other themes we need to take up, themes that underlie the breakup of the Caliphate in all parts of the Muslim world. One is something that happened: the once imperial power of the ʿAbbāsid central government diminished to the point that it was virtually extinguished in 945, despite the survival of the dynasty until 1258 and a modest revival of its power in the twelfth century. The other theme is something that did not happen: no new imperial dynasty emerged to replace the ʿAbbāsids as they had replaced the Umayyads. These, then, are the three main themes of this chapter.

The decline of the ʿAbbāsid central government

The decline of the ʿAbbāsid central government in Iraq resembles many historical processes that take place over an extended period:[1] it involved the complex interaction of a variety of factors over time. But rather than attempt to tell the story as it unfolded, we will simplify it by considering its main aspects one by one, focusing first on developments at the center and then on the role of the provinces in the story.

The central government

In any monarchical system changes in the quality of successive rulers are likely to correlate in some degree with historical outcomes. Until the middle of the ninth century this had not been a major problem for the ʿAbbāsids. But as we have seen, in 861 the caliph al-Mutawakkil (ruled 847–61), who had bad relations with his Turkic troops, was killed by a group of Turkic conspirators, and over the next decade no fewer than four caliphs reigned under conditions so anarchic that they could hardly be said to have ruled. "The Turks have become master of the realm;

1. For surveys of ʿAbbāsid history see H. Kennedy, *The Prophet and the age of the caliphates*, London 1986, and T. El-Hibri, *The Abbasid caliphate*, Cambridge 2021.

the world must fall silent and obey," as a poet lamented when another caliph met his death at the hands of the Turks in 868.[2] In other words, the caliphs were no longer in control of their own army. Stability returned to the center only with the accession of al-Muʿtamid (ruled 870–92). He himself was not notably able, but he unwillingly shared power with his brother al-Muwaffaq, who was a strong leader, an effective general, and on good terms with the Turks. On al-Muʿtamid's death it was al-Muwaffaq's son al-Muʿtaḍid (ruled 892–902) who became caliph. He had already shown himself a contender of the same kind as his father. He was also notable in that the beginning of his reign saw the final abandonment of Sāmarrāʾ in favor of Baghdad, the traditional ʿAbbāsid capital. His son al-Muktafī (ruled 902–8) was an adequate ruler, but when he was succeeded by another son of al-Muʿtaḍid, al-Muqtadir (ruled 908–32), the result proved disastrous. Unlike his father, al-Muqtadir was a weak ruler. He was also no military leader: he never led his army when it went out on campaign until the final act of his reign, when he sallied forth to do battle against his own troops and was killed by them. His luckless successors were a varied lot, but by this point what they were like no longer mattered much. At this level, then, what we see is a sharp downturn in rulership in the 860s, an upturn from 870 to 908, and a terminal downturn from then till 945.

Even a downturn in the performance of the rulers of a state does not necessarily lead to an eclipse of the state as such. It is always possible for power to be transferred to an alternative locus within the state—to a mayor of the palace (as in the case of the Merovingians in early medieval France) or a shogun (as in medieval and early modern Japan). There was indeed a development of this kind in the ʿAbbāsid state. In 936 the caliph invited Ibn Rāʾiq, then governor of Wāsiṭ, to come to Baghdad and take power; he was given the grandiose title "Commander of Commanders." Crucially, he brought his own troops with him and disbanded those of the ʿAbbāsids, so they no longer had an army of their own. He did much the same with the ʿAbbāsid bureaucracy. Yet these drastic measures did not lead to stability. Ibn Rāʾiq had several successors in the chaotic years that followed, until in 945 the Būyids (932–1062) finally assumed the role, taking over Iraq and ruling it till 1055. But unlike Ibn Rāʾiq, the Būyids did not emerge from within the ʿAbbāsid state. Instead, as we have seen, they were intruders, already possessed of states of their own.

Prior to this development the ʿAbbāsids still had a bureaucracy and an army, indispensable instruments for any ruler seeking to exercise power. Neither could be described as a cohesive unit. The bureaucracy was divided into factions, while the army comprised a variety of ethnic and other groups. But such divisions were

2. Quoted in M. Gordon, *The breaking of a thousand swords*, Albany 2001, 134.

nothing unusual, and only if they got out of hand would they pose an existential threat to the state. One way they could get out of hand was fiscal. If the bureaucracy failed to raise enough taxes to pay the army, there was bound to be trouble—nothing causes soldiers to run amok like not being paid. This is what happened, or one thing that happened, in the caliphal capital of Sāmarrā' in the 860s. Another route to trouble was factional. When factions compete, they tend to put factional interests above those of the state as a whole, and one form this can take is pushing for the accession of a weak ruler whom the faction hopes to control. This was not so much a vice of the soldiers, who liked having strong military leaders like al-Muwaffaq and al-Muʿtaḍid, but it made its appearance among the bureaucrats. On one account at least, it was a senior bureaucrat who recommended the enthronement of al-Muqtadir. "Why," he asked the vizier, "should you appoint a man who will govern, who knows our resources, who will administer affairs himself and regard himself as independent? Why do you not entrust this matter to someone who will leave *you* to manage it?"[3]

The provinces

Alongside these factors, the decline of the power of the central government was closely linked to the loss of provinces through regional state formation, irrespective of whether the new rulers gave formal recognition to the ʿAbbāsids or rejected their authority in principle. Either way, there was a vicious circle at work: the weaker the central government, the easier it was for provinces to break away, and the more provinces broke away, the less revenue accrued to the central government and the weaker it became. At this point it may be helpful to anticipate in brief the developments we will cover in later sections of this chapter. To start with Egypt and the Fertile Crescent, the richest province, Egypt, was first lost to the Ṭūlūnids (868–905), then recovered for a while, and then allowed to drift away again under the Ikhshīdids (935–69), only to be conquered by the Fāṭimids (969–1171). Each time, whoever ruled Egypt also had a presence in Syria. In northern Syria and the Jazīra, however, the Ḥamdānids (906–1004) entrenched their power, to be followed in the later tenth century by a set of Arab tribal dynasties spread around the Fertile Crescent. In Arabia ʿAbbāsid rule was moribund. Oman effectively escaped from caliphal control in the eighth century and the Yemen in the ninth, with new regional states appearing in each case. A more malign development from the point of view of the central government was the appearance of an aggressively hostile state in Baḥrayn. Founded by an Ismāʿīlī agent, it posed a direct

3. Quoted in H. Kennedy, "The reign of al-Muqtadir," in M. van Berkel and others (eds.), *Crisis and continuity at the Abbasid court*, Leiden 2013, 18.

threat to the Ḥijāz and the Fertile Crescent. Meanwhile, a period of disorder in the Ḥijāz issued in the establishment of ʿAlid dynasties in Mecca and Medina. We will consider these polities in their own right later in this chapter; the point here is to highlight the contracting horizons of ʿAbbāsid power.

At the same time there were threats to the position of the ʿAbbāsids in Iraq itself that did not result in the permanent loss of territory but still cost them dearly. In 869 a massive rebellion broke out near Baṣra among the Zanj—East African agricultural slaves who were used to reclaim land in the marshy lowlands of Iraq. It was led by a certain ʿAlī ibn Muḥammad whom we have already encountered in Baḥrayn. This alleged ʿAlid from Iran was a failed poet turned religiopolitical entrepreneur. In this capacity he had tried his luck in eastern Arabia, failed again, wearied of the desert, and moved to Baṣra, where did no better. But his luck turned when he fortuitously discovered the Zanj and proceeded to recruit them, promising them slaves, money, and homes of their own and setting them to flog their masters. These rebels were pitiless, and their attacks included a traumatic sacking of Baṣra in 871. But there was also incipient state formation when ʿAlī founded a capital named Mukhtāra and minted coins there. The insurrection was not finally suppressed till 883, after the ʿAbbāsid army fought the rebels in the streets of Mukhtāra. Meanwhile, Yaʿqūb the Coppersmith (ruled 861–79), who as we have seen had created a large but short-lived state in eastern Iran, mounted an invasion of Iraq in 876, but before he could reach Baghdad and Sāmarrāʾ he was defeated, and it was not until the arrival of the Būyids that the heartland of the ʿAbbāsid Empire would succumb to conquest from this direction. Yet both the Zanj rebellion and Yaʿqūb's invasion were major crises for the ʿAbbāsids, diverting resources that could have been used to recover control of their provinces.

The problem was not simply that the weakening of the central government encouraged provinces to go their own way. In addition, something had changed about the situation of the provinces themselves. As late as the mid-eighth century, around the time of the ʿAbbāsid revolution, we are doubtless justified in imagining the world's Muslim population outside Arabia as made up of relatively small minorities ruling over large non-Muslim majorities. But between then and the late ninth century these Muslim minorities must have grown a lot through conversion, and they had developed strong local roots. One aspect of this is that the old rivalry of Northerners and Southerners, despite some local survival, had ceased to provide an overall framework linking factional conflict across the Caliphate. Another aspect, directly relevant here, is that the prospect of non-Muslim rebellion was now less of a threat. Muslim populations were increasingly able to take their continued existence for granted, even in the absence of an overarching Muslim state. This opened up an expanding space for local actors to engage in political and military activities without regard for the interests of a central government on which they no longer depended.

The fundamental change

Among the various factors that contributed to the decline of the power of the central government, perhaps the single most important one was that the ʿAbbāsid state in this period was seriously short of money. The main reason for this seems to have been a catastrophic decline in revenue in the second half of the ninth century. Such a decline could have happened in two ways. It could be that the state was getting a smaller proportion of the economic pie owing to diminishing territory or deteriorating administrative reach. Or it could be that the pie itself was contracting, above all in Iraq, where the Sawād was the fiscal core of the ʿAbbāsid Empire, as it had been of the Achaemenid, Arsacid, and Sasanian Empires before it. The first may well have been a factor, but the second seems to have been more fundamental. So far as we know, the downturn in the agricultural economy of Iraq that began in the later ninth century was not to be reversed at any time before the twentieth; it led to the transformation of Iraq from a state-friendly land of tax-paying peasants to a state-hostile land of tax-resistant tribesmen. The result was an Iraq that could no longer provide the economic foundation for a large and lasting empire. This negative outcome is undoubtedly related to the fact that the Iraqi irrigation system was much more vulnerable to human neglect and abuse than that of Egypt: bad drainage meant loss of fertility though salinization, and good drainage required good government. But just why the definitive downturn should have come in the later ninth century, and not earlier or later, is far from obvious.

The end of ʿAbbāsid imperial rule attracted sharp comments from contemporaries. The historian Masʿūdī (d. 956), writing in the last year of his life, compared the current state of affairs to the political fragmentation that followed the death of Alexander the Great and prevailed until the establishment of the Sasanian dynasty. Each ruler was defending the territory he had seized and seeking to expand it, to the accompaniment of depopulation, the interruption of communications, the ruin of numerous regions, and the loss of frontier territory to the Byzantines and others. Likewise the astrologers—experts whose views were taken very seriously by elite society—made a tart comment on the transfer of power from the ʿAbbāsids to the Būyids. All that was now left to the ʿAbbāsids, they said, was a religious (*dīnī iʿtiqādī*) authority to the exclusion of a secular (*mulkī dunyāwī*) one. They added to the humiliation by comparing the residual role of the Muslim caliph to that of the Jewish exilarch, who had only religious primacy without sovereignty or state. In short, the incumbent ʿAbbāsid caliph was merely the head of Islam (*raʾīs al-islām*), not a king. We have here a fitting epitaph for the ʿAbbāsid Empire and, incidentally, a clear example of the fact—alluded to in the preface of this book—that the distinction between religious and secular authority was perfectly intelligible to medieval Muslims. Nevertheless, the religious prestige that went with being the head of Islam was still an asset, as the sense of desolation with which Sunnīs would react to the final demise of their caliphate at the hands of the Mongols in 1258 would make clear. In the meantime, the Sunnī religious scholars were too concerned with saving the appearances to share the sneering tone of the astrologers. In the eleventh century we find them elaborating theories of the caliphate that sought to reconcile the lofty conception they had inherited with the prevailing disarray. The best known of them, Ghazālī (d. 1111), was essentially in agreement with the astrologers: he held that the caliph was primarily a religious figurehead.

No new imperial order

Ismāʿīlī ambitions

If the demise of the ʿAbbāsid Empire had issued in a new imperial order, rather than the fragmentation that actually ensued, its creators would most likely have been the Ismāʿīlīs.[4] No other sectarian group, Shīʿite or Khārijite, was a serious contender, and no dream of restoring a pre-Islamic empire had any appeal to Muslims outside Iran. The early Ismāʿīlīs defined themselves in terms of the controversial succession to the sixth imam of the Imāmī Shīʿites, Jaʿfar al-Ṣādiq (d. 765). His son Ismāʿīl had died before him but left a son of his own named Muḥammad. The Ismāʿīlīs were those who, in contrast to the mainstream of Imāmī Shīʿism, adopted the doctrine that this Muḥammad ibn Ismāʿīl was the seventh and last imam, that he was alive and in hiding, and that he would return as the Mahdī. It is not, however, till 875, or maybe 878, that we have evidence that this sect was active, or even existed; the timing of its appearance may reflect the dispiriting impact on many Imāmīs of the confusion that followed the death of their eleventh imam in 874. At this stage the Ismāʿīlīs clearly expected the reappearance of Muḥammad ibn Ismāʿīl as an imminent messianic consummation of history, and they were actively preparing for it.

The manner in which they went about their preparations was in significant ways a reenactment of the pattern of long-term, long-distance conspiracy that had characterized the ʿAbbāsid and Ibāḍī movements of the mid-eighth century. It was in fact the last such movement of premodern Muslim history, and by far the most elaborate. There was a clandestine headquarters that came to be located in the town of Salamya (now Salamiyya) in Syria. From there missions were organized that went to work in well over a dozen different parts of the Muslim world—not just in one as in the ʿAbbāsid case, and in many more than in the Ibāḍī case. Geograph-

4. The early development of Ismāʿīlism is covered in the first chapter of H. Halm, *The empire of the Mahdi*, Leiden 1996; this remarkable book covers Fāṭimid history to the establishment of the dynasty in Egypt.

ically, Ismāʿīlī agents were active from one end of the Muslim world to the other. In Spain, as we have seen, Fāṭimid agents joined the rebellion of Ibn Ḥafṣūn. Among the Kutāma tribesmen Abū ʿAbdallāh created the military force that brought the Fāṭimids to power. In Egypt Ismāʿīlī agents were quietly present: one agent took care of the leader of the movement while he was in Fusṭāṭ during his flight through Egypt to the West, while another struck up a relationship with an Egyptian tribe, though this venture does not seem to have come to anything. In Syria, as we just saw, the leader of the movement resided in Salamya, and Iraq was an early hotbed of Ismāʿīlī activity. In Iran and Central Asia agents were at work in several different regions—Rayy, Daylam, Azerbaijan, Fārs, Sīstān, Khurāsān, Transoxania. In Arabia the Yemen and Baḥrayn were centers of Ismāʿīlī activity. And in India, as we will shortly see, there was a lively Ismāʿīlī polity in Sindh. This survey shows an impressive geographical range, but it is by no means comprehensive. The social and political contexts in which the agents went to work were likewise very varied, extending to the peasants of lower Iraq, the elites of major cities, the rulers of established dynasties, and the tribes of Arabia and North Africa. Particularly striking here is the appeal to the nontribal peasantry in Iraq. An Ismāʿīlī agent on his way to a village there explained his mission as "to cure the people of this village, to make them rich, to save them, and to take the kingdoms of the world out of the hands of those who now control them, and place them under their rule."[5] Such mobilization of peasants for social revolution is familiar from the histories of Europe and China but surprisingly rare in a Muslim context. Altogether, this was a movement of remarkable scale and vision, and it was clearly looking to take over the entire Muslim world. Why, then, was it not successful?

Why did the Ismāʿīlīs fail?

Any far-flung and clandestine messianic movement inevitably has problems relating to both space and time. One is geographical dispersal. Each field of activity in which an agent is at work has its own distinctive local opportunities and constraints, and responding to these successfully requires local initiative and creativity. Meanwhile the headquarters of the sect is far away and may be further hampered in its attempts to control its agents by the need to keep its activities secret. Lines of communication are long and uncertain: "Most disasters are caused by unreliable couriers," as an Ismāʿīlī author of the later tenth century remarked.[6] That agents in the field had to be allowed considerable freedom of action was to some degree recognized by the center; the same author says that the imam does not interfere with the work of his agents, giving only general

5. Quoted in Halm, *The empire of the Mahdi*, 29.
6. Quoted in H. Halm, *The Fatimids and their traditions of learning*, London 1997, 65.

direction and guidance. A vivid illustration of the way things could nevertheless go wrong is provided by events in Sindh, where an Ismāʿīlī agent from the Yemen had begun work soon after 883, leading to the establishment of an Ismāʿīlī community in Multān. In the time of the Fāṭimid caliph al-Muʿizz (ruled 953–75), the agent in Sindh was a very successful and locally well-regarded figure who had even succeeded in converting a ruler to the cause. But unfortunately he owed some of his popularity to his easy way with converts. He allowed them to retain un-Islamic practices and permitted them violations of Islamic dietary and marriage laws. This was embarrassing, but al-Muʿizz, some 3,500 miles away in Tunisia, recognized that he was not in a position to dismiss the offending agent. Instead he sent secret letters to a more orthodox member of the community asking him to resort to trickery to eliminate this enemy of God. In the event his powers of intrigue were moot. The agent died thanks to a riding accident, and his orthodox rival took his place—and set a new tone when he destroyed the idol of Multān, building a mosque on the site.

Another problem for such a movement is temporal. The passage of time inevitably forces an acute messianic dilemma on its leadership. Staging the apocalypse now plays well to the excitement of the moment but risks subsequent disillusion as disappointed believers begin asking, "Is that all?" Recollect the Kutāma chief who heckled al-Mahdī in Tunisia: "Perform a miracle for us, if you really are the Mahdī." But repeatedly postponing the apocalypse invites disillusion of another kind, as disappointed believers respond, "Not again?" Ibn Ḥawshab (d. 914), born an Imāmī Shīʿite but later an Ismāʿīlī agent in the Yemen, eloquently describes the disillusion he experienced as a young man waiting endlessly for the return of the twelfth imam: "Time dragged on, the wait grew long, and the pondering and brooding grew ever stronger."[7] But now his beloved Mahdī, in a letter to the Ismāʿīlīs of the Yemen, was propounding a doctrinal hairpin bend that postponed the apocalyptic moment indefinitely: there could be "as many imams as God wills" before the promised dawn of the messianic age. This time the aging Ibn Ḥawshab did not change his allegiance. But just how far into the future the dreary succession of imam after imam might stretch before the promised eschatological drama finally unfolded was made clear by a leading Ismāʿīlī agent of the early eleventh century: he anticipated the rule of the hundredth imam of the line. A little mental arithmetic suggests that we could be talking about the second half of the third millennium of our era, a time that even in our own day is still centuries in the future. Of course, any imperial order needs a dynasty, but postponement of messianic expectations on this scale carries a heavy cost once the adrenalin starts to drain away.

7. For this and the next quotation see Halm, *The empire of the Mahdi*, 32, 194.

Other problems were more specific to the Muslim world of the ninth to eleventh centuries. One concerned the axiom that the Islamic community (*umma*) was a single polity to be ruled by a single ruler. At a certain doctrinal level this axiom remained more or less intact; "One God, one imam," as a Fāṭimid agent put it. But as we have seen, the reinforcement that the axiom could derive from the historical conditions of the time had considerably diminished. The other problem was that arguably by the ninth century, and increasingly thereafter, a mainstream, if not quite an orthodoxy, was emerging in the Muslim world. This was, roughly speaking, a Sunnism that by the later ninth century no longer lent itself as freely to the support of ʿAlid rebellions as it had done earlier, let alone to long-term, long-distance conspiracies. The result was that any such conspiracy could be articulated only in a sectarian idiom that to Sunnīs would have seemed shockingly heretical. We have seen the Mālikīs of Qayrawān decide that even the Ibāḍī heretic Abū Yazīd al-Nukkārī was preferable to the Ismāʿīlīs. In fact, nowhere in the Muslim world did the Ismāʿīlīs succeed in converting the masses to their faith, even where they held political power. We have seen this in Tunisia, and we will see it again in Egypt.

Given these problems it is not surprising that the first moment of crisis came early in the history of Ismāʿīlī activism. In 899 the leader of the movement in Salamya propounded a strange new doctrine to his followers: he himself, he claimed, was the imam. The result of this self-promotion was a deep split in the movement. The new doctrine was accepted by Abū ʿAbdallāh al-Shīʿī in North Africa, for example, and as we have seen it was under his aegis that the Ismāʿīlī leader came to power in Tunisia as the caliph al-Mahdī (ruled 909–34). But in the east many Ismāʿīlīs stuck with the old teaching. Among them was a group in southern Iraq known as the Qarmaṭīs whose activities included establishing a state in Baḥrayn. It was only several decades later that the Fāṭimid caliph al-Muʿizz was able to repair relations with some of the eastern Ismāʿīlīs, partly by adopting a Neoplatonism that had recently become popular among them. In the meantime, the most militarily active of the Ismāʿīlīs in the east, the Qarmaṭīs of Baḥrayn, were sworn enemies of the Fāṭimids and long remained so despite the efforts of al-Muʿizz. Those eastern Ismāʿīlīs who did return to the fold, like those who had never left it, were no doubt an asset for the Fāṭimids, enabling them to have fingers in pies as far away as Sindh. But they were largely a soft-power asset and did nothing to enlarge the territory the Fāṭimids actually ruled.

Even if the movement had been able to hold together despite its problems, there was another reason—one directly related to hard power—why the Ismāʿīlī ambition to inherit the Muslim world as a single apocalyptic polity was doomed. For such a goal peasants and urban elites were irrelevant; what counted was martial populations. In the mid-eighth century the ʿAbbāsids had succeeded where the Ibāḍīs had failed by recruiting some of the best troops of the day, the professional

Arab soldiers of Khurāsān. In the period when the Ismāʿīlīs were active, Arab armies of this kind were to be found only in the west, in Tunisia and Spain, and by eastern standards they were no longer state-of-the-art. The soldiers that now won wars in the central and eastern Muslim world were Turks. But it was the Arabs and the Berbers, not the Turks, that Ismāʿīlī agents successfully mobilized. In hard-power terms, the Arabs did not in the end do much for the Fāṭimids, but the Berbers served them well, enabling them to conquer both Tunisia and Egypt. Yet as we will see, the Fāṭimids soon got bogged down in Syria and never made it to Iraq, let alone Iran. They did at this point begin to acquire Turkic slave soldiers, but the experiment eventually ended badly for them. What to our knowledge the Fāṭimids, and the Ismāʿīlīs in general, did not do was focus on recruiting Turks into the sect by going directly to the nomadic tribes of Central Asia. Nor did they succeed in taking over the polity that had the easiest access to them—the Sāmānid state in Khurāsān. Here, toward the end of the reign of the Sāmānid Naṣr II (ruled 914–43), an Ismāʿīlī agent successfully penetrated the court, to the point of converting the ruler himself. The result was a showdown in which a coalition of Sunnī religious scholars and—significantly—the Turkic military succeeded in forcing a return to orthodoxy. Abū ʿAbdallāh undoubtedly made history with his Kutāma, but in the end they were the wrong choice. So no new imperial order replaced that of the ʿAbbāsids, and we turn instead to the regional states into which the Caliphate fragmented—states that made no attempt to bring about a grand reunification of the Muslim world.

New states in the Fertile Crescent

As long as the Fertile Crescent served as a base for a strong imperial state, as in the Umayyad and early ʿAbbāsid periods, it was in no danger of invasion from outside. But in the second half of the ninth century this was changing, and older geopolitical configurations were reemerging. To the west the ancient pattern of Egyptian domination extending into Syria reasserted itself, first with the Ṭūlūnids and later with the Ikhshīdids and the Fāṭimids. To the east the familiar pattern of Iranian domination of Iraq resurfaced, first with the abortive incursion of Yaʿqūb the Coppersmith and then on a more lasting basis with the Būyid conquest. To the north the tenth century saw a Byzantine reconquest extending into northern Syria. Unlike the other threats to the Fertile Crescent, this one came from outside the lands of Islam and marked the end of a long period in which the Muslim world faced no formidable enemy beyond its borders. The turning of the tables began with a gradual Byzantine reconquest of the frontier regions from which the Muslims had so persistently raided Anatolia. Thus Malaṭya, already much weakened, was taken by the Byzantines in 934, and Cilicia in the 960s. The retreat was not just political but also demographic, involving the expulsion of Muslim populations.

Meanwhile to the south, the Arab tribes were once more pressing on the settled lands of the Fertile Crescent. Some were long resident in the region, but others were recent arrivals from Arabia; the first third of the tenth century saw a large influx of such nomads from the peninsula. In short, times had changed, and in no uncertain way.

Since the most obvious beneficiaries of the weakening of the ʿAbbāsid state in the Fertile Crescent were outsiders, there was little room for large-scale state formation on the part of the population of the region itself. The closest thing to an exception was the Ḥamdānid dynasty, or rather pair of dynasties: one branch ruled in Mosul (906–89) and the other in Aleppo (944–1004). These were Arab tribal dynasties in origin, but not in their mature character. Their ancestor, Ḥamdān, was a tribal chief in the Jazīra in the later ninth century. Despite the fact that at one point he joined the Khārijites, who were still endemic in the Jazīra, his son Ḥusayn succeeded in doing a deal with the ʿAbbāsids, who gave him funds to recruit a military force for them from his fellow Taghlibī tribesmen. By 907 he and his troops were a significant component of the ʿAbbāsid army. Meanwhile, in 905 his brother Abū ʾl-Hayjāʾ (ruled 906–29) had been appointed governor of Mosul and was able to weather the storm when Ḥusayn got involved in a rebellion and was executed in 918. In 929 Abū ʾl-Hayjāʾ in turn lost his life through backing a losing horse in ʿAbbāsid politics, but by now the family was sufficiently well entrenched in Mosul that his son Ḥasan, better known by his later title Nāṣir al-Dawla (ruled 929–67), was able to hold on there. Yet Ḥasan's very title—"Helper of the (ʿAbbāsid) State"—illustrates the dynasty's continuing links with Baghdad. It was around this time that the Ḥamdānid army ceased to be tribal. Much of Taghlib, a traditionally Christian tribe, crossed over into Byzantine territory, and the Ḥamdānids, though continuing to include Arabs in their armies, came to rely mainly on Turkic slave soldiers and other non-Arabs. This, of course, was much more expensive, and contributed to heavy taxation. So, too, did the tribute that the Ḥamdānids intermittently paid to whoever held power in Baghdad, especially to stave off attacks from the more powerful Būyids. When the Būyids nevertheless invaded their territory, the Ḥamdānids would abandon Mosul and retreat to the mountains—an apt strategy for survival, but one manifestly predicated on military weakness. Eventually one of these attacks, mounted by the aggressive Būyid ruler ʿAḍud al-Dawla (ruled 978–83), effectively ended the Ḥamdānid dynasty of Mosul in 979, despite a bit of a comeback in the 980s. That it had been possible for the Ḥamdānids to establish a relatively weak state in Mosul just a couple of hundred miles upstream from Baghdad and to maintain it there for some decades is nevertheless a clear indication of the debility of the central government. The weakness of the Ḥamdānids in the face of repeated Būyid invasions also illustrates the lack of a foundation for a robust state in the Mosul region—in contrast, for example, to Egypt or Tunisia. Though beyond the reach of Byzantine or Fāṭimid armies, the Ḥamdānids of Mosul were just too close to Baghdad, as their tangled relations with its rulers make clear.

The Ḥamdānid dynasty of Aleppo was a rather different story. Nāṣir al-Dawla had an energetic younger brother, Sayf al-Dawla (ruled 944–67)—"Sword of the State," again a title won in the service of the ʿAbbāsids. He was to be the major patron of the celebrated Arab poet Mutanabbī (d. 965), who lamented that Arabs ruled by non-Arabs do not prosper and complained of the rule of slaves. In need of a principality to support himself and his followers, Sayf al-Dawla was fortunate enough to secure Aleppo in 944. Kilāb, the local Arab tribe, supported him, and the then ruler of Egypt, the Ikhshīd, does not seem to have objected—though he drew the line at a Ḥamdānid takeover of Damascus. Like his brother in Mosul, Sayf al-Dawla recruited slave soldiers and other non-Arabs for his army. At first the main enemy he confronted was the Arab tribes, whose rebellion against him he successfully crushed in 955. But this was the period in which pressure from the reinvigorated Byzantine Empire was increasing, and northern Syria was not spared. In the old days the Caliphate could have mustered large forces to confront such a threat, but a state ruling just a small part of Syria had no way to do that, and widely shared Muslim indignation against the Byzantine expansion did little to help. So when the Byzantine army attacked Aleppo in 962, Sayf al-Dawla opted to abandon his city, just as his brother used to abandon Mosul in the face of Būyid attacks. This could have been the end for the Ḥamdānid dynasty of Aleppo, but it survived thanks to the limited territorial ambitions of the Byzantines: having taken Antioch and occupied Aleppo in 969, they did a deal by which Aleppo became a Byzantine client state, paying tribute but also receiving protection. After 991 the dynasty entered a twilight of which we can ignore the details. The basic point is that the continued existence of the Ḥamdānid state of Aleppo turned on the fact that it was out of reach of the Būyids, accepted by the rulers of Egypt as a convenient buffer, and protected in the same role by the Byzantines. There was clearly no possibility of major state formation on such a site.

Meanwhile, the Arab tribesmen of both the Fertile Crescent and Arabia were active in the military and political affairs of the Fertile Crescent. The local tribesmen played a significant role in two rebellions organized by Ismāʿīlī agents in the early tenth century—rebellions that, had they been successful, could well have led to state formation. In both cases the rebels belonged to the Kalb tribe of central Syria. The first rebellion took place in 902–3, when the tribesmen besieged Damascus for several months before being defeated by an ʿAbbāsid army. This insurrection was mounted on behalf of the leader of the Ismāʿīlī movement and future caliph al-Mahdī, but the rebels' commitment to him turned sour when instead of joining them he fled from Salamya, ultimately to North Africa. The second rebellion followed in 906–7, and during it the rebels raided southern Syria, attacked

Kūfa, and plundered a caravan of Iraqi pilgrims before again being defeated by ʿAbbāsid troops. Thereafter the source of the action shifted deep into Arabia, to the Qarmaṭīs of Baḥrayn, but for now we need note only their impact on the Fertile Crescent. Their raids had already begun before 913 but became particularly vigorous in the 920s, when they sacked Baṣra and Kūfa, plundered pilgrim caravans, and threatened Baghdad. Later, in the 960s and 970s, their attention was focused on southern Syria, where they repeatedly occupied Damascus and Ramla in opposition to the hated Fāṭimids. Then in the 980s they again turned their attention to Iraq, attacking Baṣra and occupying Kūfa. But the only state they established in all of this was their base in Baḥrayn. In this respect they missed their window of maximum opportunity in the Fertile Crescent—namely, the period between 908 and 945, when ʿAbbāsid rule was weak and the Būyids had not yet moved into Iraq.

Finally, there was the formation of the Arab tribal states of the Fertile Crescent in the later tenth century. This was a three-stage process, initially involving the northward migration of Bedouin tribes from Arabia in the first third of the century, very likely to escape the disruption caused by the Qarmaṭī state from its base in Baḥrayn. Once established in their new northern territories, the tribes were drawn into military service as auxiliaries in the armies of the states of the Fertile Crescent, thereby gaining experience of the way settled societies conducted their military and political affairs. Thereafter these tribes—or some of them—used their experience to develop veritable states of their own in their territories, typically obtaining a neighboring city as their capital at the invitation of its inhabitants. Such invitations presuppose that in the eyes of urban populations Bedouin domination, however undesirable in itself, could provide protection on terms better than those offered by the militaries of the weak and unstable sedentary states of the region. Of course there were variations. The Khafāja in the neighborhood of Kūfa engaged in extensive predatory activities but never tried to form a state, while the Ṭayy in Palestine tried to do so repeatedly and failed. For all these groups, raiding and levying protection money were alternative means to much the same end. What is striking overall is that the process did not involve the formation of Bedouin states deep in the desert that would then conquer settled territory in the Fertile Crescent, and likewise that it had no Ibn Khaldūnian dimension. These dynasties tended to be Shīʿite—in this, in fact, they resembled the Ḥamdānids—but they did not exist to further a religious cause and had no pretensions to be sectarian imamates. Where they differed from the Ḥamdānids was in their relationship to the Arab tribal milieu. Like the Ḥamdānids they were born into a tribal environment, but unlike them they never left it, and their armies were made up of Arab tribesmen to the end. Such is the general character of these tribal states, but we will come back to them in somewhat more detail in a later chapter.

New states in Arabia

There were only limited parts of Arabia whose resources were sufficient to make government a viable enterprise—and by the same token to invite invasion. The combination of mountains attracting modest rainfall and coastal lowlands well positioned to benefit from Indian Ocean commerce meant that the two corners of Arabia, Oman and the Yemen, were perennial sites of state formation, though the mountains that attracted the rain also impeded government, especially in the Yemen. But whatever might be the case commercially, in military terms the horizons of the states formed in these two regions tended to be local. This was almost always the case for the Yemen, though from the seventeenth century on it would change for Oman. Two other regions of Arabia had some potential for state formation. One was Baḥrayn—a term that in medieval times referred primarily to the mainland opposite the island we know as Bahrain today. Here, too, there was agriculture together with maritime frontage onto a waterway linked to the commerce of the Indian Ocean, but in this case the basis of the region's agricultural productivity was not direct rainfall but rather the presence of Arabia's largest oasis. Unlike the Yemen or Oman, Baḥrayn gave rise to a highly aggressive state in our period—a surprising development that had a precedent in the Najdiyya but was not to be repeated. The other region with a certain potential was the Ḥijāz. Of course, the days when it was the seat of a state that was expanding to become one of the world's largest empires were long gone. Far from giving rise to aggressive states, the Ḥijāz could now thrive only in the presence of a measure of foreign rule. These four regions—Oman, the Yemen, Baḥrayn, and the Ḥijāz—were thus the preeminent sites of state formation in Arabia; we could add others, like Ḥaḍramawt, but we would be scraping the barrel.[8]

Oman

Oman, our first port of call, was geographically less forbidding than the Yemen was.[9] Its mountains took the form of a relatively narrow band separating the coastal plain from the interior; they did not match those of the Yemen in either height or extent. This in turn meant less rainfall, though still enough to support an agricultural economy that was respectable by Arabian standards. It also meant that the human action took place not so much in the mountains themselves as on either side of them. Thus the highlands of Oman were not, as in the Yemeni case, the demographic core of the country. The lion's share of the water flowed to the

8. For the history of these regions in the period covered in this chapter see E. Landau-Tasseron, "Arabia," in *The new Cambridge history of Islam*, Cambridge 2010, vol. 1.

9. For its history see J. C. Wilkinson, *The Imamate tradition of Oman*, Cambridge 1987.

coastal plain, confusingly known as the Bāṭina or "interior," thereby making it the prime agricultural land of Oman. But some water also went to the interior, just as confusingly known as the Ẓāhira or "exterior." This made possible the existence of a settled society there, with its main center in the oasis of Nizwā. The very labor-intensive investment that made Omani agriculture possible was the construction and maintenance of subterranean channels (*aflāj*) that brought the rainfall of the mountains to the plains with minimal loss through evaporation. In addition to its agricultural resources, Oman was similar to the Yemen in benefiting from its location at the entrance to a commercially crucial waterway, in this case the Persian Gulf; the chief port of Oman in our period was Ṣuḥār. The combination of these agricultural and commercial assets made Oman a viable site for Arabian state formation. But these assets were also liable to attract the interest of foreign states, and here it is significant that Oman was far more accessible from the center of ʿAbbāsid power in Iraq than the Yemen was, a point that also applies to any powerful state based in Mesopotamia since the third millennium BC. Thus the Sasanians were far more solidly entrenched on the coastal plain of Oman, and for longer, than they were in the Yemen, and they should probably receive a large share of the credit for the underground water channels that are so crucial for Omani agriculture. In short, Oman, or at least its coast, looks like a plausible candidate for the role of a long-term province of a regional empire, be it Sasanian, ʿAbbāsid, or other.

Yet Oman can hardly be described as a province of the ʿAbbāsid Empire. In 752 the ʿAbbāsids sent an army to subdue the country. Despite suffering heavy casualties, these troops succeeded in defeating and killing a recently elected Ibāḍī imam, the Julandā ibn Masʿūd (ruled 750–52). But the outcome does not seem to have been a regular succession of ʿAbbāsid governors, though one is mentioned in 785–86. This curious pattern was to be replicated twice. The second ʿAbbāsid invasion came in 805, and again it had no lasting effects. The third and last was mounted by the governor of Baḥrayn in 893 with the involvement of the caliph al-Muʿtaḍid; the invading force left a governor to administer Oman, or as much of it as had been conquered, but again this arrangement does not seem to have endured. Thus for most of the period down to the Būyid takeover of Baghdad in 945, the ʿAbbāsids were conspicuous by their absence from the Omani scene. By contrast, a variety of external powers became active on the coastal plain as the ʿAbbāsid central government weakened—the Qarmaṭīs of Baḥrayn, the Ṣaffārids of Sīstān, and above all the Būyids, who invaded Oman in 966 and stayed long enough for a brief dynasty of governors to entrench itself and become autonomous. These were the Mukramids, who from 1003 ruled the coast for the best part of half a century. But the Būyids were back in the 1040s. As we will soon see, the termination of Būyid rule in Iraq by the Seljuqs created an opening for the Omanis, but it did not last long: in 1063 the Seljuqs invaded Oman. In sum, no foreign dominations of Oman lasted as long as those that were to characterize the Yemen from the twelfth century onward, but incursions were much more frequent than in the Yemeni case. This record makes it all the more puzzling that the ʿAbbāsids, even at their height, had only an intermittent presence in Oman.

What we have seen so far is just one of the two very different sides of Oman: the cosmopolitan coast or Bāṭina. This was a land where Indian and African music was to be heard, and armies included troops imported from India and East Africa. We hear, for example, of badly behaved Indian mercenaries, and of six thousand Zanj soldiers who were paid at half the rate of their white counterparts; they did not like this, and there was fighting between the two racial groups. Likewise the major port on this coast, Ṣuḥār, was a place where merchants probably felt more at home than tribesmen did, not least because the spoken language of the city was Persian. Polytheistic merchants—most likely from India—were permitted to reside there. Overseas there were Omani communities as far afield as the port of Daybul in Sindh, and—given the presence of Zanj in Oman—very likely on the East African coast. The other side of Oman was the interior or Ẓāhira. Foreign states ruling the coast had relatively little reason to concern themselves with it. They might venture there for punitive purposes, but they made little attempt to establish any continuing administration. Thus the third ʿAbbāsid invasion, which was brutally destructive, left behind a subgovernor in the interior who was responsible to the governor on the coast, but he was soon killed, and once again the Omanis had the interior to themselves. Sometime in the years following 966 a Būyid army chased an Ibāḍī imam out of Nizwā, but again there is no indication of lasting change.

This left room for an Ibāḍī imamate in the interior. After the Julandā ibn Masʿūd was killed by the ʿAbbāsid invaders in 752, the Ibāḍīs of Oman did not make another attempt until 793. But in contrast to the Julandā's two-year reign, the new imamate lasted a century, till in 893 it was swept away by the third ʿAbbāsid invasion. Even after that, the long-term tradition of an Ibāḍī imamate endured on and off until 1955. But unlike the Rustamid imamate of Tāhart (778–909), the Omani imamate in our period was not the possession of a single family. This was a significant difference. That the Rustamid imams were foreigners meant that as a family they could claim to be neutral with regard to the Berber tribes; in that respect they were comparable to the Zaydī ʿAlids of the Yemen, who were northern Arabs in a sea of southern tribes. But the genealogical egalitarianism of the Ibāḍīs precluded the Zaydī pattern of embedding the imamate in an aristocracy of descendants of the Prophet, and the imams of ninth-century Oman were very much native tribesmen. In fact, with a single exception they were members of one clan or another of the same southern Arab tribe, the Yaḥmad of central Oman. This meant that some mechanism was needed to prevent the imamate from degenerating (or evolving) into the continuing dominance of a single Yaḥmadī clan over everyone else. Three features of the way the imamate was linked to the tribal politics of Oman are relevant here. The first was that although the imam was almost always a Yaḥmadī, his successor was never from the same clan, let alone the same family; there could thus be no consolidation of an ongoing dynastic structure of power. The second feature was that while the imam would be a Yaḥmadī, the people who were crucial in choosing him were not. They belonged rather to the Banū Sāma, an offshoot of the northern Arab tribe of Quraysh. The third feature was that the imam was under an obligation to reside in Nizwā, a settlement with a mixed tribal population that was situated well outside the territory of the Yaḥmad. This was not just an informal understanding. A highly regarded ninth-century scholar, one whose reputation spread not just in Oman but even in North Africa, gave it formal legal status: an imam who failed to reside in Nizwā thereby forfeited the imamate. The imamate as practiced in Oman was thus a form of limited government appropriate for a tribal society.

Limited government is typically a device for containing strong tensions, and it is only to be expected that it does not always succeed. In the Omani case the crunch came in 886. Toward the end of his long reign, Imam Ṣalt ibn Mālik al-Kharūṣī (ruled 851–86) was showing signs of senility, and at the instigation of a leading scholar of the Banū Sāma, Mūsā ibn Mūsā, he was deposed and retired to his tribal homeland. A new imam, Rāshid ibn al-Naẓr al-Fajḥī (ruled 886–90), was then elected in his place, with Mūsā again playing a prominent role. (Both Kharūṣ and Fajḥ were Yaḥmadī clans.) These events led to a civil war that ended only in 893. In the course of it the losing side—the deposers, prominent among them members of the Banū Sāma—appealed for ʿAbbāsid intervention. The result was the third ʿAbbāsid invasion and the end of what is known as the First Imamate. These were traumatic events, and deeply divisive, but one might have anticipated that with the passing of generations, time would have healed the wounds. That it did not do so is revealing of the doctrinaire and self-righteous style in which Omani Ibāḍīs argued about politics, at least in the polemical record that survives. There were those who thought the deposition of Ṣalt ibn Mālik was unconscionable; there were those who thought it fully justified; and there were moderates who suspended judgment on the rights and wrongs of the case. At one point in the tenth century it seemed that the community was coming back together on a platform of suspension of judgment, but this was not to be. In 1052 a powerful imam, Rāshid ibn Saʿīd, declared for the first view, excommunicating those who thought otherwise and consigning them to the fires of hell. Since the protagonists of the second view were concentrated in the non-Yaḥmadī north of Oman, this sectarian attitude is likely to have played a part in furthering the conversion of the north from Ibāḍism to Sunnism. The deposition thus cast a long shadow on the history of Oman.

Beyond all this, the Ibāḍī polity in Oman faced a deeper structural problem, this one not of its own making. As we have seen, invaders on the coast did not have much reason to involve themselves in the interior, but the reverse was not the case.

The coast was a source not just of invaders but also of agricultural and commercial wealth—and thus a temptation hard to resist. With only the resources of the interior to draw on, the imamate tended to be threadbare, so any imam seriously interested in building up his state had to be eyeing the coast. The stronger imams of the First Imamate were very much aware of this, moving to take possession of the coast and make use of its resources. Thus in 816 Imam Ghassān ibn ʿAbdallāh (ruled 808–23) installed himself for five years in Ṣuḥār (and not, problematically, in Nizwā). There he started developing a navy and dealt with the pirates who preyed on maritime commerce. Likewise Imam Muhannā ibn Jayfar (ruled 841–51) built up a navy of three hundred ships and a standing army of ten thousand men. Presumably before the onset of his senility, Imam Ṣalt ibn Mālik sent a large expedition—reputedly a hundred and one ships—to the island of Socotra near the entrance to the Gulf of Aden, bringing it under Omani rule. Such imams could be very successful, but by the standards of the tribal polity of the interior they were also alarmingly strong. After the fall of the First Imamate there was no sign of imams of this caliber for the next century and a half, and the imamate seems to have been intermittent and weak. Thus we hear of an imam in the years after 934 that he did well enough at first but was then deserted by his followers. In 1050–51, with the reign of Rāshid ibn Saʿīd, there was finally an imam powerful enough to expel the Būyids from the coastal plain and reoccupy Ṣuḥār, but this was the only time such a thing had happened since the fall of the First Imamate. In any case Rāshid died in 1053, and his success proved transitory. His rule was nevertheless revealingly colored by the cosmopolitan world of the coast: he was unusual among the Ibāḍī imams of our period in issuing coins, and those he minted showed the influence of Būyid models.

A teasing chronological point is that the Omani imamate of 794–893 was contemporaneous with that of the Rustamids in North Africa. Though they were separated by over three thousand miles, their coexistence could have been doctrinally problematic in view of the principle that the Islamic community should have a single ruler. Yet in contrast to what we will find among the Zaydīs, a plurality of imams does not seem to have been much of an issue among the Ibāḍīs. One ninth-century scholar, an Omani, held that two imams could rule at the same time provided their territories were not contiguous; neither of them, however, was to be addressed as "Commander of the Faithful," since this was a title reserved for a ruler of the entire Muslim world.

The Yemen

The mountains of the Yemen were more formidable than those of Oman, and it was there that the agricultural resources of the country were concentrated, together with the bulk of the population. In contrast to Oman, the key infrastructural investment in the Yemen was terracing the hillsides of the highlands. The rewards of ruling such a territory were unlikely to be very high, particularly from the point of view of a state based in Iraq for which access to the Yemen involved either a crossing of the Arabian desert or a circuitous voyage by sea. Nevertheless, the ʿAbbāsids were still playing an active role there in the first half of the ninth century and may have retained a degree of control in Ṣanʿāʾ for some time thereafter; we hear of the presence of a governor with Turkic troops as late as the 890s. But this was in the reign of the formidable caliph al-Muʿtaḍid, who as we saw also intervened in Oman.

Well before the end of the ninth century local dynasties had begun to emerge in the Yemen. The earliest was that of the Ziyādids (818–1018) on the western coastal plain, ruling from their city of Zabīd. The founder was an outsider dispatched by the caliph to suppress a tribal rebellion, and the dynasty he established was autonomous rather than independent, adhering to Sunnism and recognizing the ʿAbbāsid caliphs in the manner of the Aghlabids, Ṭūlūnids, and Sāmānids. At its height it ruled most of the Yemen in some fashion, but this did not last, and in any case the Ziyādids came to be dominated by their own black slaves. Their state nevertheless outlived the end of the dynasty in 1018, with one of these slaves founding a new dynasty, the Najāḥids (1022–1158), who continued the Sunnī and ʿAbbāsid allegiance of their former masters. Meanwhile the Yuʿfirid dynasty (847–997) had emerged in the highland interior, much of which it came to rule. In contrast to the Ziyādids the Yuʿfirids were indigenous, being Ḥimyarites, and so related to the last native rulers of the pre-Islamic Yemen. Though Sunnī, they were opposed to direct ʿAbbāsid control. After twenty years of conflict with the ʿAbbāsid governors of Ṣanʿāʾ they took the city in 847 and were recognized by the ʿAbbāsids in 870. In fact, all three of these dynasties were Sunnī, and none of them came to power through religious mobilization in Ibn Khaldūnian style.

Sectarian politics were nevertheless prominent in the history of the Yemen. By far its most enduring political tradition in Muslim times was the Zaydī imamate. First established in 897, it lasted somewhat discontinuously until 1962. The founder was a Medinese descendant of the Prophet, Yaḥyā ibn al-Ḥusayn, known by his regnal title as al-Hādī ilā ʾl-Ḥaqq (ruled 897–911). The Zaydīs, as we have seen, were a politically activist Shīʿite sect that from the second half of the ninth century was engaged in state formation in the mountains to the south of the Caspian. But when Yaḥyā visited that region, he found no opening there. He then tried the Yemen, but again had no luck. Yet he was nothing if not persistent, and a second attempt in the Yemen in 897 proved more successful: he was able to establish himself as the imam of a small Zaydī state based in Ṣaʿda in the northern highlands of the country. Like the Prophet he had his Muhājirs, some fifty of them, though in his case they were Ṭabarīs from the northern outpost of Zaydism; alongside these Muhājirs, we find one of his sons speaking of the local Anṣār. The state al-Hādī thus created ruled over a territory of variable extent, but never anything approaching the whole of the Yemen. The secret of his success, such as it was, is portrayed in our Zaydī account of his life as his awesomeness (*hayba*)—his capacity to inspire veneration and respect. Thanks to it, we are told, he was able to make peace between the two warring tribes of Ṣaʿda whose quarrels, in combination with a drought and a bad harvest, had made life miserable for all concerned. This was a task that a Yuʿfirid general, with thousands of men at his disposal, had been unable to accomplish. But once al-Hādī intervened, it was as though there had never been any enmity between the two tribes, the rain fell, and the harvest was abundant. He went on to do the same around Najrān, putting an end to tribal animosities so that people could return to their homes, cultivate their fields, and travel in safety. We have here advertisements for the potency of religious charisma as against the brute force of secular authority. Not that al-Hādī was a pacifist of any kind: to fight for him was jihad, and those killed by the evildoers were martyrs. He himself at one point challenged an opponent to a duel—that, too, was part of the image of a Zaydī imam. His charisma was personal, but it was also in considerable part genealogical. As an ʿAlid—or as he preferred to put it on a gold coin he minted in 910–11, a "son of the Messenger of God"[10]—he was a northern Arab, reinforcing his position as a prestigious and neutral outsider among the squabbles of the southern Arab tribes of the Yemen.

The fact that the Zaydīs were simultaneously active in the mountains of both Iran and the Yemen raises the question how the two communities would relate to each other. In practical terms the relationship between the northern and southern Zaydīs could not be a close one, since they were some 1,500 miles apart. But it existed. As might be expected, the flow was mostly from the north to the south. The Iranian Zaydīs had established themselves earlier than had those of the Yemen, and they had easy access to a major intellectual and cultural center, the city of Rayy—a facility the Yemen could not match. One thing the north could offer in limited quantities was manpower. As we have seen, al-Hādī had his Ṭabarī Muhājirs with him in the Yemen. But after his death one of his sons complained bitterly that when he appealed to the north for more such help, few responded, and those who did acted like mercenaries, behaving abusively and leaving him in the lurch. The other major commodity the north could offer was learning, or more concretely books. Following a period in which there were almost no links between the two communities, the early twelfth century saw the northern ruler dispatch to the Yemen a judge who brought with him a library that is said to have contained twelve thousand works. In fact, almost all the northern Zaydī literature we possess survived in the Yemen, not in Iran. The south, by contrast,

10. See S. Lane Poole, *Catalogue of Oriental coins in the British Museum*, London 1875–90, 10:74.

had relatively little to offer the north. There were followers of al-Hādī in the north, and a grandson of his tried and failed to establish an imamate among the Daylamites. But he did at least succeed in transmitting his grandfather's legal teachings among the northern Zaydīs.

At a more theoretical level the issue was the propriety of the existence of more than one imamate at the same time. As we have seen, this issue arose even within the northern community, and it was prominent in relations between north and south. The Zaydīs developed no settled doctrine in response to this awkward question. The principle that the Muslim community should have a single ruler was not to be set aside lightly. It was presupposed by al-Hādī when he swore by God that if he knew of anyone better qualified for the imamate than himself, he would join him wherever he might be and fight under his orders (naturally he knew of no such person). The Zaydīs of the north could be no less intransigent. The northern imam al-Mu'ayyad bi'llāh (d. 1020) held that all believers had to recognize the imam irrespective of distance; on no account were they to follow other pretenders. Just like al-Hādī, he averred that if he knew of anyone better qualified for the imamate he would hand over power to him (and just like al-Hādī he knew of no such person). Likewise in 1117 the northern imam, a great-grandson of al-Mu'ayyad, sent a message to the Yemen, demanding to be recognized as the imam. Surprisingly, a descendant of al-Hādī's who was in control of Ṣa'da accepted the demand, and for a few years the northern and southern Zaydīs were formally united in a single polity; this was the context of the major transfusion of learning from the north to the south. But not everyone was so doctrinaire. We are told that an early northern imam, al-Nāṣir al-Uṭrūsh (d. 917), held that anyone in the north should follow him, whereas anyone in the south should follow al-Hādī. A southern imam who died in 1003 held that there could be a plurality of imams even in the same country, though not in the same village. So despite the prestige of the one-imam principle, practicality did get a hearing among the Zaydīs.

The other sectarians who engaged in state formation in the Yemen were the Ismā'īlīs. As we have seen, it was here that Abū 'Abdallāh al-Shī'ī learned his tradecraft. The agent he learned it from was Ibn Ḥawshab, one of two agents who arrived in the Yemen in 881. Like Abū 'Abdallāh al-Shī'ī he had his Muhājirs in the manner of the Prophet, and likewise his Anṣār. The other agent was 'Alī ibn al-Faḍl (d. 915). The two went to work in different regions of the Yemen, but their mutual relations were tense. In 911 Ibn al-Faḍl broke with the Fāṭimids and declared the Sharī'a abolished, and after this the two agents waged war against each other. Ibn al-Faḍl's movement imploded after his death, while Ibn Ḥawshab's remained loyal to the Fāṭimids but did not last long. The Fāṭimid cause did better in the last decade of the tenth century thanks to the support of the Yu'firid ruler of the day, but it was not until 1047 that an Ismā'īlī dynasty was established—in this case by a local Ismā'īlī, not an agent sent from outside. This was the Ṣulayḥid dynasty (1047–1138), which gave its allegiance to the Fāṭimids and ruled a large part of the Yemen, including the southern port of Aden; we will take it up in a later chapter.

What was notably absent from the history of the Yemen in this period was foreign invasion. As we have seen, foreign incursions were a considerable hazard for Oman at this time. Moreover, the Yemen had been invaded by the Ethiopians and the Persians before the rise of Islam and would suffer the same fate at the hands of the Ayyūbids and others from the twelfth century onward. If we leave aside the period when the Yemen was part of the Caliphate, the explanation for the lack of invaders between the sixth and the twelfth centuries is perhaps the remoteness of the Yemen from the more expansive states of the eastern Middle East, at a time when comparable states were largely lacking in the western Middle East.

Baḥrayn

We turn now to Baḥrayn in its medieval sense, the mainland region later known more often as Aḥsāʾ.[11] We hear of an ʿAbbāsid governor of this large, low-lying oasis as late as 893, and there is little history of local state formation in Islamic times prior to 899. In that year a Qarmaṭī agent from the Persian coast of the Gulf, Abū Saʿīd al-Jannābī (d. 913), established a polity in Baḥrayn; he had gone to work there in 886–87. It was his son Abū Ṭāhir al-Jannābī (d. 944) who in the 920s unleashed the military energies of this state on Iraq. Then in 930 he took Mecca, slaughtering the pilgrims and the local population alike, throwing corpses into the sacred well of Zamzam, plundering the Kaʿba, and carrying off its revered Black Stone to Baḥrayn. There he reused the two fragments into which it had now been broken as steps to his toilet. This attack may have been a traumatic event for Muslim world at large, but it was a good fit for a movement that had been looking forward to the end of the era of Islam. It was around this time, however, and perhaps in connection with these events, that Abū Ṭāhir made a terrible mistake. A striking young man called Abū ʾl-Faḍl the Zoroastrian had been taken captive in Iraq and brought to Baḥrayn. There Abū Ṭāhir imprudently recognized him as the Mahdī, or more extravagantly as God, and handed over power to him. The young man, he told his followers, was "my god and your god; we are all his slaves!"[12] This was accompanied by the cursing of Moses, Jesus, and Muḥammad, who were denounced as swindlers, cheats, and liars, and by the restoration of the religion of Adam. The Qarmaṭīs now went wild, openly burning Qurʾāns and worshipping their god with no clothes on. At the same time this newfound god turned out to be disruptive and singularly bloodthirsty. Within three months Abū Ṭāhir had to

11. Much of what follows is covered in Halm, *The empire of the Mahdi*.
12. For this and the quotations that follow see Halm, *The empire of the Mahdi*, 258, 262, 263.

allow him to be killed and admitted that he had been taken in by a fraud—a vivid illustration of the hazards of messianic politics. "This was a huge mistake that we made!" as one leading Qarmaṭī lamented. The message was now a return to the old teaching, "namely, that we are companions of the Mahdī and recruiters for the Mahdī, and that we are believers and Shīʿites." Small wonder that people complained: "Every day you tell us something different!" This disastrous episode was not just shocking to Muslims in general; it was also deeply demoralizing for the Qarmaṭīs themselves, especially those in Baḥrayn. The Iraqi Qarmaṭīs who had migrated there to witness the apocalypse now left, and many of them abandoned the movement altogether, spilling its secrets—to the great advantage of historians. Meanwhile, the Bedouin who had been a key component of the Qarmaṭī armies were instead going into service as mercenaries with the dynasties of the day. Abū Ṭāhir still conducted some raids on a smaller scale, but in 939 he reached an agreement with the ʿAbbāsids whereby he turned gamekeeper, undertaking to protect the pilgrimage caravans instead of attacking them. In return he got a subsidy from the ʿAbbāsids and a fee from the pilgrims. It was in this period of détente, in 951, that the Qarmaṭīs relinquished the Black Stone in return for an extortionate ransom.

There was, however, a resumption of the old militancy in the face of the Fāṭimid conquest of Egypt and expansion into Syria. Most of the action was in southern Syria, but at one point in 971 the Qarmaṭīs even laid siege to Cairo. Thus the violence of the Qarmaṭīs was now directed against the Fāṭimids, formerly their fellow sectarians, so much so that they even recognized the authority of the powerless ʿAbbāsids. These hostilities ended in 978, and in the mid-980s the Qarmaṭīs were back to attacking Baṣra and occupying Kūfa. This time, however, they had more than a taste of their own medicine. After being worsted by the Būyids in Iraq, they were attacked in 988 by the chief of the tribe of Muntafiq. He defeated, besieged, and pillaged them, reversing the normal flow of booty by taking the spoils of Baḥrayn to Baṣra, and he further deprived them of their ability to prosper through the protection of the pilgrim caravans by taking over this lucrative business for his tribe. A few years later we even see the Qarmaṭīs acknowledging the Fāṭimids. Their state nonetheless survived in Baḥrayn until 1077–78, though it was only in the tenth century that it counted as a serious military force.

Two further features of this state stand out in our sources. One is a commitment to the key role in government of a council of fixed membership; leaders like the two Jannābīs could not just decide for themselves who to consult with. This feature is well attested for both the tenth and eleventh centuries. The other is the distribution of wealth by the state to its Qarmaṭī citizens—the "believers," as they were called. This, too, is attested for both centuries, but most elaborately for the eleventh, as we will see in a later chapter.

The Ḥijāz

Finally in this survey of Arabian state formation we come to the Ḥijāz.[13] Here, too, Islam played a central role in the process, but in a quite different way. Like the other Arabian sites where states could be formed, the Ḥijāz consisted of a seacoast and its hinterland. The difference was that the hinterlands of the Yemen, Oman, and Baḥrayn were sufficiently well watered to support significant agricultural production, whereas that of the Ḥijāz was not. The populations of the first three, had they been deprived of the commercial resources of their coasts, might have found life noticeably harder, but they would not normally have been in danger of mass starvation. By contrast, the urban populations of Mecca and Medina had no such safety net. What was special about the Ḥijāz, and gave value to what was otherwise a wilderness, was its sanctity. Mecca had the Kaʿba, Medina had the Mosque of the Prophet with his tomb, and both were intimately connected with his career; they accordingly served as Islam's prime centers of pilgrimage down the centuries. Yet in crude material terms neither Mecca nor Medina could even survive as a city without being supplied with grain from Egypt—a supply that the caliph al-Manṣūr (ruled 754–75) ruthlessly cut off in 762 to deflate a rebellion mounted against him in Medina. So it was crucial that the Muslim lands outside Arabia should recognize that they owed the Ḥijāz a living. Once this living was assured through the largesse of distant but richer regions of the Muslim world, the sanctuary cities could flourish. But one cannot eat sanctity, and the arrangement worked only if those who owed the Ḥijāz its living did not default on their obligations. All was well as long as large numbers of Muslims, especially wealthy ones, were eager to honor the Qurʾānic command to undertake the pilgrimage if they were able to do so, and as long as outside powers contributed by facilitating safe travel through the parched Arabian desert, by showering patronage on the holy cities, and by providing the requisite grain supply from Egypt to feed their populations. The Ḥijāz could then afford to live far beyond its natural means. But unfortunately those who owe cannot always be relied on to pay, and in bad times the Ḥijāz could find itself left to fend for itself. As we saw, in 930 the Qarmaṭīs of Baḥrayn were able to enter Mecca with impunity and reduce it to the abomination of desolation. Fortunately for the Ḥijāz this was as bad as it ever got, but as late as the mid-eleventh century a traveler reported extensive ruins in Mecca and a population of a mere two and a half thousand. At this point one might have wondered whether the whole phenomenon of a world religion situating its major pilgrimage site deep in the Arabian desert was impractical to the point of being unsustainable. That it was in fact sustained is a striking demonstration of the limits of purely material factors in determining historical outcomes.

13. See Landau-Tasseron, "Arabia," 398–413.

In the period we are concerned with in this chapter the Ḥijāz did well as long as the Caliphate was strong. Food arrived from Egypt as early as the reign of ʿUmar (ruled 634–44), slaves captured in the wars of conquest were used to exploit such local agricultural resources as there were, and extensive investments were made in infrastructure. All this and the stipends paid by the government provided the basis for a wealthy and culturally sophisticated elite, including considerable numbers of ʿAlids. But the caliphs of this period had no desire to see their power diluted by the formation of any kind of state in the Ḥijāz. Instead they sent governors to administer the region directly and continued to do so into the second half of the ninth century. From time to time there were rebellions against the caliphs. Under the ʿAbbāsids the rebel leaders were typically ʿAlids, as in 762, 786, 815–16, and 865. But as long as the ʿAbbāsids were firmly in the saddle, these rebellions were regularly suppressed—as indeed was that of Ismāʿīl ibn Yūsuf in 865, despite the fact that it came during a decade of political chaos in Iraq.

By this time, however, the Ḥijāz was no longer doing well. The reason was the disintegration of the ʿAbbāsid Empire and the absence of a comparable successor state to assume its role in the Ḥijāz. This created an unstable situation in which multiple rulers were involving themselves in the affairs of the region. Thus Mecca in 882 was the scene of a clash between troops of the ruler of Egypt, Ibn Ṭūlūn (ruled 868–84), and those of the ruler of eastern Iran, ʿAmr ibn Layth (ruled 879–900). Peaceful competition between rival patrons could, of course, be advantageous to the inhabitants of the Ḥijāz if it stimulated greater generosity on their part, but violent hostilities are unlikely to have been helpful. The outcome was that no one outside power took over the role of the ʿAbbāsids until the Fāṭimids conquered Egypt in 969. At the same time the local actors in the Ḥijāz were behaving badly. The absence of firm government was a prime opportunity for the Bedouin to engage in predation—nobody would have expected anything else. More jarring was delinquent conduct among the ʿAlids, despite their descent from God's Prophet. The ʿAlid rebel of 865 was hardly playing the part of a saint on the way to a dignified martyrdom: he had no compunction about exposing the Meccans to starvation when he besieged their city, robbed the Kaʿba, and massacred large numbers of pilgrims. The resulting economic downturn led many Meccans to emigrate. Indeed, this whole period was one of agricultural decline, depopulation, and Bedouinization. Meanwhile, this vicious ʿAlid of Mecca had a colorful if somewhat later contemporary in Medina. He drank wine in the Mosque of the Prophet in broad daylight, made love to someone else's singing girl while in the mosque, and never performed the Friday prayer; he, too, starved and slaughtered the urban population. All this was bad enough, but there was worse to come in 930 when the Qarmaṭīs of Baḥrayn carried out their devastating attack on Mecca. Thereafter conditions were chaotic, and for several years there was no pilgrimage—or such pilgrimage as there was would be led by local figures, not by dignitaries sent by the caliph in the traditional fashion. In short, the holy city was reduced to anarchy.

From the point of view of ʿAlids interested in seizing power these conditions had the disadvantage that there was not much left to seize, but they also meant that no ruler was likely to step in to stop them seizing it. So in place of the old pattern of ʿAlid revolts, we now see the emergence of ʿAlid dynasties. The first was that of the Banū Muhannā, who established their rule in Medina sometime before 940. The second was the Mūsāwid dynasty, which took over Mecca around 967. The two dynasties now added to the general confusion by fighting each other, and from time to time the Meccan dynasty was able to take over Medina. But from now on, whichever outside power exercised hegemony in the Ḥijāz took the existence of at least one of these ʿAlid dynasties for granted, thereby giving rise to a form of dual rule that in Mecca continued into the early twentieth century. This framework was, however, still loose enough to leave the ʿAlids room to play their political games. A Meccan ʿAlid who ruled from 994 to 1038 first recognized the Fāṭimid caliph, then claimed the caliphate for himself, then returned to his Fāṭimid allegiance, and then switched to the ʿAbbāsids. What was exceptional and unsustainable here was his passing claim to be caliph himself; no one could hope to consolidate his rule in the Ḥijāz without some degree of recognition of an external overlord. An autarkic sectarian imamate might be a good adaption to the isolation of the Yemeni highlands or the Omani interior, but it would have been severely dysfunctional in a region as dependent on the generosity and goodwill of the outside world as was the Ḥijāz.

New dynasties in Egypt

Despite its easily taxable wealth, the interest of the caliphs in Egypt seems to have been somewhat limited. In the days when they still ruled an empire with Egypt as a firmly controlled province, only two of them visited the country. One was the Umayyad Marwān I (ruled 684–85), who spent two or three months there in the context of the second civil war, and the other was the ʿAbbāsid al-Maʾmūn (ruled 813–33), who was there in 832 for rather less than two months following a massive rebellion of Arabs and Copts. Even when Iraq no longer provided the fiscal support for an empire, the caliphs seem rarely to have entertained the idea of relocating to Egypt. In 882 al-Muʿtamid tried unsuccessfully to escape from the control of his brother al-Muwaffaq and take refuge with Ibn Ṭūlūn, who would have installed him in Egypt—which in terms of personal power might not have been much of an improvement for the caliph. In 944 the luckless caliph al-Muttaqī (ruled 940–44) was encouraged by the Ikhshīdid ruler of Egypt to leave Iraq and join him, but he turned down the offer and returned to Baghdad, only to be blinded and deposed a few months later. In military terms the lack of high-level interest made some sense. Egypt did not have a large army, partly because in the absence of a major enemy on its borders it did not need one, and partly because in the age of the cavalry it lacked good pastureland. This meant that it was unlikely to be a source of existential threats to the central government; even the largest rebellions in Egypt stayed within the borders of the country. So from this point of view it was enough to maintain administrative control through the organs of provincial government and to send troops to suppress rebellions when local forces were insufficient. But given the unusual wealth of Egypt, the ʿAbbāsid attitude to it might seem a little shortsighted. It meant that once the central government weakened in Iraq, the wealth of Egypt was ripe for the picking. The question was who would pick it, and how.

From Ibn Ṭūlūn to renewed ʿAbbāsid rule

What happened in Egypt in the later ninth century was a classic case of a provincial governor who was dispatched from the center but then dug himself into his province and became effectively autonomous. The governor in question—initially the deputy of a governor who continued to reside in Iraq—was Aḥmad ibn Ṭūlūn (ruled 868–84). The son of a Turkic soldier, he founded the short-lived Ṭūlūnid dynasty (868–905). Given the disorder then prevailing in Sāmarrāʾ, the 860s were a good time to embark on such a venture, and the dire threats that kept al-Muwaffaq focused on Iraq in the 870s favored its continuation; though he made a move to eliminate Ibn Ṭūlūn in 877, it came to nothing. But being governor of Egypt did not in itself mean that Ibn Ṭūlūn had access to its wealth. The central government had cleverly divided authority there: on the one hand there was the governor, now Ibn Ṭūlūn, but on the other hand there was the superintendent of finances, a certain Ibn al-Mudabbir. It took four years of intrigue, much of it conducted in Sāmarrāʾ, for Ibn Ṭūlūn to sideline him. The fact that a lot of the action still took place in Sāmarrāʾ shows that up to this point Egypt remained to a significant extent a province controlled by the central government.

That changed once Ibn Ṭūlūn had his hands on the money, which he could now use to fund a much-expanded army. Quite apart from its other military disadvantages, Egypt was not in the best geographical position for military recruitment, not having easy access to a supply of Turkic slave soldiers. But Ibn Ṭūlūn used his resources to reasonably good effect, acquiring considerable numbers of Turks together with military slaves of other kinds, be they blacks from the south or Greeks from the north. His efforts were facilitated by his good fortune in not being encumbered by the survival of a Jund of the kind that still existed farther to the west, in Tunisia and Spain; its Egyptian equivalent had already been discontinued under the caliph al-Muʿtaṣim (ruled 833–42). Thanks to his expanded army Ibn Ṭūlūn's position was strengthened both within Egypt and outside it. He was able to expand his domains to include all of Syria in some fashion and to assert his authority in Cyrenaica, though his attempt to add the Ḥijāz in 882 was a failure. None of this implied a renunciation of his allegiance to the caliph—indeed, as we have seen, he would have been happy to host him in Egypt. Yet for the first time since the Ptolemies (305–30 BC), the fiscal resources of Egypt were at the disposal of a state that was based inside the country. This did not of course mean Egypt for the Egyptians, though we do encounter a hint of that: there is an anecdote according to which Ibn Ṭūlūn preferred an Egyptian to an Iraqi secretary because the Egyptian's family and interests were located within the country, not in a distant homeland to which he hoped one day to return.

With better luck, this could have been a long-lasting dynasty. But two developments brought it to an end in less than forty years. One was the poor quality of its later rulers. Ibn Ṭūlūn's son Khumārawayh (ruled 884–96) was profligate—he had an elaborate garden in which there were representations of his favorite concubines and singing girls—but he was relatively successful. After the failure of an attempt by al-Muwaffaq to dispossess him in 885, he extended his father's Syrian domains northeastward into the Jazīra and northwestward into Cilicia and did deals with the caliphs that secured autonomy in return for tribute—much as the founder of the Aghlabid dynasty had done in Tunisia the best part of a century earlier. But Khumārawayh's reign ended badly when he was killed by one of his own slaves—as always one of the hazards of slave ownership. He was succeeded by his sons, of whom the first, a teenage drunkard, was soon deposed and the second was killed by his uncles while likewise inebriated, leading to the last brief reign of one of the uncles.

The other adverse development for the Ṭūlūnids was the limited but real ʿAbbāsid recovery that continued into the first decade of the tenth century. This was a period in which, as we have seen, ʿAbbāsid armies suppressed two Ismāʿīlī insurrections in Syria, and in between they reconquered Egypt in 905, massacring the black troops of the Ṭūlūnid army. For the next thirty years the ʿAbbāsids ruled Egypt directly, but they did so on the horns of a dilemma. If they allowed their provincial governors to wax strong, they risked a repetition of Ibn Ṭūlūn's bid for autonomy. But if they kept their governors weak, they risked a Fāṭimid conquest from Tunisia. In effect they chose the second option, parrying the Fāṭimid threat by sending the eunuch Muʾnis to bolster the defense of Egypt in 915 and 920—Muʾnis being the leading ʿAbbāsid general from 908 to 933, and an able one. But weak provincial government inevitably carried costs for Egypt, with the result that this was a period of general insecurity in the country. And as the power of the Caliphate finally drained away, both horns of the dilemma came to pass: the governor appointed in 935 founded a second short-lived dynasty, and the Fāṭimids ended it with their conquest of Egypt in 969.

The Ikhshīdids

The founder of the Ikhshīdid dynasty (935–69) was Muḥammad ibn Ṭughj, known by a royal title of Sogdian origin as the Ikhshīd (ruled 935–46). His grandfather stemmed from the Central Asian region of Farghāna and had entered the service of the ʿAbbāsids, followed by a son and grandson. Since the Ikhshīd had a genealogy that ran to six ancestors and mixed apparently Iranian and Turkic names, we can assume that he belonged to an aristocratic lineage, very likely one of mixed blood. He himself was born in Baghdad, served in Syria, and in 935 was appointed governor of Egypt. The context combined threat and opportunity. It was in 935–36 that the Fāṭimids made their third attempt to conquer the country, and the Ikhshīd successfully repulsed them. This gave him a strong position in Egypt and may have helped him to obtain his title from the caliph in 939. Like Ibn Ṭūlūn, he coupled careful financial administration with recruiting an effective army, composed mainly of Turks and blacks. Like Khumārawayh he made an agreement with the caliph that gave him security of tenure. And as with the Ṭūlūnids, his objective was autonomy, not formal independence. He differed from Ibn Ṭūlūn in having a less forward Syrian policy: despite reaching Aleppo he proved content with southern Syria, leaving the north to the Ḥamdānids.

The dynastic successors of the Ikhshīd may have been no better than those of Khumārawayh, but if so, this hardly mattered. From 946 to 966 they reigned rather than ruled because power was firmly in the hands of Kāfūr, a talented black eunuch from Nubia who had risen as a general in the army of the Ikhshīd. Fāṭimid propaganda used his color to disparage him as a "black crow," but from 966 he ruled in his own right, and only after his death in 968 was an eleven-year-old grandson of the Ikhshīd put on the throne. The grandson's reign was short, as the Fāṭimids conquered Egypt the year after his accession.

The Fāṭimids: A modest empire

The Fāṭimids (909–1171) are perhaps the major victim of the structure of this book.[14] Their origins in a clandestine sectarian movement have been discussed earlier in this chapter, their rule in North Africa (909–72) was outlined in a previous chapter, the first century of their time in Egypt (973–1074) will occupy us now, and their second Egyptian century (1074–1171) is covered in a later chapter. In one way this dispersal is a tribute to the geographical and chronological extent of their activity, but it also reflects the failure of their larger aspirations.

14. For their history see M. Brett, *The Fatimid Empire*, Edinburgh 2017.

In 973 the Fāṭimids arrived in Egypt and took up residence in Cairo, the palace city that had been prepared for them in the years since their army had conquered the country in 969. But to call Cairo a city at this early stage is really a misnomer. It was a walled rectangle enclosing a space of less than half a square mile, providing room for the caliph, his numerous servants, at least part of his central administration, and his army. It originally lacked an urban facility as basic as a market. For that one had to go to Fusṭāṭ, a couple of miles to the south. And yet Cairo was to become one of the major cities of the Muslim world, effectively swallowing up the former capital Fusṭāṭ as a suburb; a wall built in the twelfth century would surround both. Once established in Cairo, the Fāṭimid caliphs rarely ventured far from it, settling down there to rule their empire. Their stationary habit was linked to the fact that unlike the earlier Fāṭimid caliph al-Manṣūr (ruled 946–53), and unusually for rulers in the Muslim world at the time, they did not often act as military leaders. Among the Fāṭimid rulers in Egypt, only one ever led his troops in battle as caliph; this was al-ʿAzīz (ruled 975–96) in 978.

The Fāṭimids were accordingly fortunate in that for the most part the frontiers of their empire were not strongly contested. To the west, as we have seen, they made over their North African territory to the Zīrids, a dynasty that was at first autonomous but later became fully independent. Cyrenaica seems to have become the western limit of Fāṭimid power: they had a garrison in Barqa, as we learn from the events of 1005–6, when a certain Abū Rakwa—a Spanish schoolmaster claiming Umayyad descent—fomented a tribal rebellion, besieged the garrison, and went on to invade Egypt in a significant threat to Fāṭimid rule. But no state threatened Egypt on the west. To the south, apart from an Egyptian raid in 1066, the Fāṭimid period was an unusually quiet one in relations between Egypt and Nubia—in contrast, for example, to the years immediately preceding and following Fāṭimid rule. To the southeast they threw a lot of money and some troops at the Ḥijāz, starting as early as 969, and became the incumbent power there for most of the next century, alongside the local ʿAlid dynasties. This was to be expected. With the demise of the ʿAbbāsid Empire, any reasonably strong state based in Egypt was well placed to assume its role, since in this period the food supplies on which Mecca and Medina depended could only come from Egypt. Such allegiance as the Fāṭimids received from elsewhere in Arabia was nominal, be it from the Qarmaṭīs of Baḥrayn in the later tenth century or the Ṣulayḥids of the Yemen in the mid-eleventh. The Qarmaṭīs, of course, were normally a sworn enemy, but they were too small and distant a state to pose a sustained threat to the Fāṭimids in Egypt.

It was to the northeast that the only seriously contentious frontier of the Fāṭimid Empire lay, and it was there that the Fāṭimids were tested. They were not, of course, destined to realize their aspirations to conquer Iraq and Khurāsān. The nearest they came to this was a curious escapade that took place in 1059 against the background of the confused politics of Iraq in the middle years of the century. A Turkic general in the service of the Būyids known as Basāsīrī had decided to transfer his loyalty to the Fāṭimids, and after occupying Baghdad he had the Fāṭimid caliph al-Mustanṣir (ruled 1036–94) recognized in the Friday prayers for about a year. But while al-Mustanṣir supported Basāsīrī with funding and supplies, it is telling that he sent him no troops. So there was no prospect of a Fāṭimid conquest of Iraq, let alone Khurāsān, and even the Jazīra was usually beyond their reach. On the other hand, threats to Egypt itself from the northeast were limited until the twelfth century. There were Qarmaṭī invasions in 971 and 974, the first of which involved a siege of Cairo, and a Turcoman invasion in 1076–77, but these incursions had no lasting effects.

The issue was rather how much of Syria the Fāṭimids could bring under their rule. Would it be a greater Syria in the style of Ibn Ṭūlūn, or a lesser Syria—southern Syria—on the Ikhshīdid model? The second option meant a comfortable northern frontier with a minor Muslim dynasty, the Ḥamdānids of Aleppo (944–1004) or their Mirdāsid successors (1024–80). The first meant something very different: a border with the resurgent Byzantine Empire, a Christian polity that at the time was more powerful than any Muslim state, that of the Fāṭimids included. In 969 the Byzantines had shown their teeth by taking Antioch, which they then held for over a century, and in 975 they came as far south as northern Palestine. Meanwhile the Ḥamdānid state in Aleppo had become a Byzantine vassal. Sharing a frontier with the Byzantines in this period would thus have given the Fāṭimids an opportunity to wage a glorious war against the infidel—a theme they had emphasized in their propaganda, disparaging the ʿAbbāsids for their failure to step up to the plate. There was, however, a serious risk of humiliating defeat, and it is characteristic of the Fāṭimids that on balance they preferred not to run it. So like the Byzantines they were willing to live with the Ḥamdānids. As a Fāṭimid vizier advised on his deathbed in 991, "Leave the Byzantines in peace as long as they leave you in peace."[15] In 995, near the end of his reign, the caliph al-ʿAzīz did make the momentous decision to go out on campaign against them in person. It took seventy camels just to carry his caliphal tent, and he brought with him the coffins of his ancestors. But he died well before reaching the borders of Egypt, let alone those of the Byzantine Empire. And when the Fāṭimids did provoke the Byzantines, things tended to go badly for them. In 995 the formidable emperor Basil II (ruled 976–1025) appeared in northern Syria and obliged the Fāṭimid army to retreat to the south; he was back in force in 999. Yet the Fāṭimids did hold Aleppo in some fashion in the years 1015–23, and they defeated a Byzantine force in 1041, though to little effect. The overall result was that despite their failure to get a firm grip on Syria, the Fāṭimids enjoyed a relatively relaxed strategic environment. They had

15. Quoted in H. Halm, *Die Kalifen von Kairo*, Munich 2003, 157.

no permanent frontier with a major power, and their worst enemies turned out to be Arabs of one kind or another—the Cyrenaican rebels led by Abū Rakwa, the Qarmaṭīs of Baḥrayn, and the local Arab tribes of Syria. These were enemies with a sting, but they were not in the same league as the professional armies of powerful states. Indeed, the inability of the Fāṭimids to suppress such relatively weak enemies is a reflection of the inferior quality of their army. The military force that had established an empire in Africa was not competitive in Asia.

In this mix of forces eroding the Fāṭimid position in Syria, there is one other element that is of interest in a way that goes beyond its limited effect on historical outcomes: the popular militias (*aḥdāth*, literally "young men"). They were urban, though their recruits might be of rural origin. The phenomenon seems to be circumscribed in both space and time. It is limited to Syria and the Jazīra, and it does not appear before the later tenth century or after the mid-twelfth. Within these limits, it is best known in two cases, Damascus from the later tenth century to the mid-twelfth and Aleppo from the first half of the eleventh century, again to the mid-twelfth. We can leave Aleppo to a later chapter and concentrate here on Damascus, where the militia was staunchly Sunnī and strongly opposed to the Fāṭimids, particularly their Kutāma soldiery. It is clear from the sources that we are dealing with an institution. The young men were divided into regular units, each with its leader, banners, and trumpets. They evidently belonged to the lower levels of Damascene society, and their bellicosity worried the notables of the city. There was also a leader of the militia as a whole, at first a certain Ibn al-Māward and later a certain Qassām. Ibn al-Māward had a fairly strong position in the city. He could take the decision to invite Alp Tegin, an unemployed Turkic commander with three hundred men, to establish himself in Damascus in 975 (the notables, too, welcomed the newcomers, asking them to rid them of the militia). Later Ibn al-Māward accompanied Alp Tegin on a mission to the Byzantine emperor, then in Syria; this was a dazzling opportunity for the leader of a popular militia, but it ended badly when the commander prevailed on the emperor to detain Ibn al-Māward. Qassām, who reputedly made a living by collecting dung, fared better as leader of the militia once Alp Tegin was out of the picture, and for five years he held the city in his grip. In 983 we see him repairing its walls and gates, and setting up mangonels to defend it against an approaching Fāṭimid army. But his support inside the city crumbled, and the notables, fed up with all the mayhem and destruction, prevailed on him to give up the fight. He was sent to Cairo in chains. But if this was the end of his career, it was not the end of the Damascene militia. In 997 they were still pitted against the Berbers, joining the Turkic troops in attacking them. In the same year a new governor was appointed to Damascus, and he took the militia very seriously. He plied its leaders with gifts, invited them to dinner, and even sent one of them to Cairo to be invested with a robe of honor. But the last of these convivial dinners ended with a massacre of the militia leaders. The rank and file were then apprehended or killed, and the corpses of the leaders were crucified. Even this was not the end of the institution in Damascus, since the militia reappears in 1019–21, 1066, 1069, and 1076, and as we will see in a later chapter it was still very much alive in the first half of the twelfth century. But the closest the militia came to state formation was during the five-year domination of the city by Qassām the dung collector. Outside Damascus we might compare this with a brief episode in Ascalon, where in 997 a sailor led a rebellion against Fāṭimid rule and went so far as to mint self-congratulatory coins—a clear manifestation of a short-lived aspiration to sovereignty. But it was the Arab tribes of the Fertile Crescent, not its urban militias, that showed a real capacity for state formation in this period.

The outcome of all this was that instead of straining to conquer the world, the Fāṭimids for the most part settled down to cultivate their own garden—which they did with considerable success. Egypt was indeed the richest garden in the Middle East of the day, and for much of the first century of Fāṭimid rule it seems to have been relatively well run and prosperous, despite the famines that tore into the population when the Nile failed to rise. "Nowhere have I seen such prosperity as I saw here," wrote a Persian traveler who was in Egypt in the late 1040s[16]—though as a devotee of the Fāṭimids he may have been biased. As we will shortly see, there were two Fāṭimid reigns that departed from this relatively benign pattern, but neither involved large-scale military adventure beyond the frontiers. Arguably this meant that rather more of the history of the Fāṭimid state was made by bureaucrats than was the case with the average Muslim polity of the period. Ya'qūb ibn Killis (d. 991), a Jewish convert to Islam born in Baghdad, was inherited by the Fāṭimids from Kāfūr and served as vizier almost continuously from 973 till his death. Another successful and long-lasting vizier, a Muslim of Iraqi origin, was Jarjarā'ī, who despite having lost his hands in a political mishap held the position from 1027 until his death in 1045. Remarkably, both men died in office of natural causes. As the case of Ibn Killis suggests, Fāṭimid viziers could be quite diverse—some were even unconverted Christians. These were expert administrators whose religious affiliation meant that they could not pose a political threat to their masters, but by the same token they could expose the Fāṭimids to a Muslim backlash.

The Fāṭimids and their problems

Of the two disruptive reigns of the first Fāṭimid century in Egypt, one was that of al-Ḥākim (ruled 996–1021), and the other that of al-Mustanṣir. What was wrong with al-Ḥākim would seem to have been that he was mad;[17] but madness in its

16. Quoted in I. Hrbek, "Egypt, Nubia and the eastern deserts," in *The Cambridge history of Africa*, Cambridge 1975–84, 3:16.

17. For a contrary view see Halm, *Die Kalifen von Kairo*, 169, 184, 303.

more articulate forms can be strongly shaped by the ambient culture, and in al-Ḥākim's case this reflected a problematic religious heritage. What was wrong with al-Mustanṣir, by contrast, was that he was weak, and his weakness eventually threw into relief the divisive ethnic structure of the Fāṭimid army. Let us take each of these problems in turn.

As we have already seen in the North African context, the Fāṭimids were the bearers of a sectarian tradition that was anathema to most Muslims. In the pithy formulation of a Damascene popular preacher, if he had ten arrows he would shoot nine of them at the "Westerners"—the Kutāma—and only one at the Byzantines. For this spirited remark he was sent to Cairo in a cage to become the first Sunnī martyr of the new order. One option for a ruling group hoping to dodge the nine arrows in such a situation is to abandon its heritage and adopt that of the majority of its subjects. This was what the ʿAbbāsids had done in the decades after they came to power. Another option is for the ruling group to force some version of its heritage on its subjects. This was roughly what the Ṣafawids (1501–1722) would do after conquering Iran. But the Fāṭimids in Egypt, as in Tunisia, did neither. They were no doubt too heavily invested in Ismāʿīlism to follow the ʿAbbāsid precedent. As a dynasty they did not merely happen to be Ismāʿīlīs; they were the leaders of a sect with well-developed institutions and beliefs, in effect its owners. In addition, a key component of their army, the Kutāma tribesmen, were with them thanks to a process of strongly sectarian mobilization, unlike troops that give allegiance to a state merely because it buys them or pays them. Beyond their eastern frontiers, moreover, the Fāṭimids were able to exercise an unusual degree of soft power thanks to the presence of Ismāʿīlī groups that had never broken with them or had returned to the fold through the religious diplomacy of al-Muʿizz—even if he greatly exaggerated its scope when he claimed in a letter to a Qarmaṭī leader that there was no part of the world where his agents were not active. The Fāṭimids accordingly remained Ismāʿīlīs to the end, and in some ways they made Ismāʿīlism their state religion: Ismāʿīlī law was applied in the courts, at least in the first century of Fāṭimid rule in Egypt, and Ismāʿīlī ritual was observed in public, at least in the major centers. This could cause friction. But at the same time the Fāṭimids did not force Ismāʿīlism on the generality of their subjects, and few of them converted to it. Perhaps this was simply realism on the part of the Fāṭimids. Short of a catastrophic foreign invasion, nothing would have been more likely to disrupt the cultivation of their garden than mass persecution of their subjects. The result was that when Fāṭimid rule came to an end, it left behind it only a small Ismāʿīlī population. We are told that the town of Isnā in Upper Egypt was still "stuffed full" of Ismāʿīlīs far into the thirteenth century, this being due to its remoteness from Cairo.[18] But subsequently even they disappeared.

18. Isnawī, *Ṭabaqāt al-Shāfiʿiyya*, Baghdad 1970–71, 2:331–32.

What the Fāṭimids did tend to do was suppress the most outrageous elements of their heritage, or at least keep them out of public view. This involved two heresies in particular. One was antinomianism, the idea that in the new messianic era the divine law brought by Muḥammad would become—or already was—null and void. Though a familiar feature of Christianity thanks to Saint Paul, for whom Christians are "not under the law, but under grace" (Rom. 6:14), antinomianism had no foothold in mainstream Islam. Yet it was allegedly the message of ʿAlī ibn al-Faḍl in the Yemen after he broke with the Fāṭimids in 911, and there was a well-attested outbreak of it in Tunisia in 921, in the reign of al-Mahdī. Those concerned held that all things previously forbidden were now permitted, and they made their point by eating pork and drinking wine in Ramaḍān. This became embarrassing for the regime, and al-Mahdī rather tardily had the offenders rounded up and put in prison, where most of them died. Such antinomianism was also to be found among the Qarmaṭīs of Baḥrayn; as they proclaimed during one of their raids on Iraq in 927, "We have come not to establish a dynasty, but rather to put an end to the Sharīʿa!"[19] And as we will see in a later chapter, in 1164 antinomianism was to resurface among the Nizārīs, an Ismāʿīlī subsect in Iran. Against such wild thinking, the Fāṭimids punctiliously insisted on the continuing validity of the law, and Qāḍī Nuʿmān (d. 974), the influential chief jurist of al-Muʿizz, produced a set of works laying out an Ismāʿīlī version of it. The other outrageous idea was incarnation. Like antinomianism, this was mainstream in Christianity—"the Word was made flesh, and dwelt among us" (John 1:14)—but in Islam it was beyond the pale. Again the Fāṭimids tried to keep clear of it: with perhaps one exception their caliphs made no claim to divinity. But again the idea was part of their wider heritage. One of the Tunisian antinomians used to pray toward whichever city—be it Raqqāda or Mahdiyya—was the residence of al-Mahdī at the time, explaining that he was not about to offer his prayers to an invisible god. Again, as we have seen, the Qarmaṭīs of Baḥrayn provided a lurid parallel. Both of these heady ideas resurfaced in Egypt toward the end of the reign of al-Ḥākim.

By no means everything al-Ḥākim did was linked to his Ismāʿīlī heritage. His whimsical tendency to strike down people around him, starting in 1000 with the murder of his tutor when he was fifteen and including the mishap that cost Jarjarāʾī his hands, had no particular sectarian resonance. His attacks on Jews and Christians—not least the numerous Christian bureaucrats who served the state—showed a marked religious animus but hardly a sectarian one. His decree forbidding the manufacture of shoes for women was unconventional, and punishing women who went out to the baths by walling them up there was even more so, but these measures did speak to a widespread Muslim sentiment that a woman's place was in the home. On the other hand, his prohibition of the eating of fish

19. Quoted in Halm, *The empire of the Mahdi*, 254.

without scales was diagnostically Shīʿite, as was the cursing of the first two caliphs. His more extreme followers went much further. One of them said of him, "Our Lord has completely abrogated the Sharīʿa of Muḥammad,"[20] while others decried the Sharīʿa as no more than "superstitions, husks, and mere stuffing." According to a contemporary Christian source, his devotees cursed the prophets, including Muḥammad, defecated in mosques, and urinated on Qurʾāns. And when some of these followers began to put it about that al-Ḥākim was God—as the phrase "our Lord" already suggests—he does not seem to have minded. In 1019 a document headed "In the name of God, al-Ḥākim, the Merciful, the Compassionate"[21] not surprisingly started a riot in the main Sunnī mosque of Fusṭāṭ. These heterodox followers of al-Ḥākim have left an abiding residue in the form of the Druze religion; though extinct in Egypt, it survives to this day in Syria, Lebanon, and Israel. Meanwhile in 1021 al-Ḥākim had disappeared—or more likely, someone had arranged his disappearance. It could have been his half sister, who was now in control of the state, but it could equally have been any number of people who feared that the longer al-Ḥākim survived, the more likely he was to kill them. Those who had believed him divine were now persecuted, but not entirely silenced. It was very likely one of them—a Druze, we could say—who appeared in Mecca in 1023 armed with a sword and a club and set about smashing the Black Stone, denouncing it as an object of idolatry. The man was eventually killed and the stone, now in three pieces, repaired. The movement now went underground, and outside Syria it still had adherents in Upper Egypt into the fourteenth century. But to return to al-Ḥākim, its bizarre quality aside, two things are remarkable about his reign. One is the limited extent of opposition, though it is notable that the Turks played a part in what opposition there was. The other is the absence of external attack. The first is perhaps an indication of the general prosperity of Egypt at the time, and the second of its rather fortunate geopolitical situation.

Geopolitical good fortune was also apparent in the fact that there was no foreign conquest of Egypt in the years of the reign of al-Mustanṣir when ethnic tensions in the army boiled over into civil war. Though the Fāṭimids had already done something to diversify their army while still in Tunisia, the Kutāma tribesmen still constituted the cavalry at its core, and next to the dynasty, they seem to have felt themselves to be the owners of the state. This was a problem for a number of reasons. First, the Fāṭimids were no different from the average dynasty of their day in not wishing to put all their military eggs in one ethnic basket, despite the fact that diversity inevitably meant tensions within the army—tensions that Muslim rulers of the time were normally able to keep within

20. For this and the next quotation see D.R.W. Bryer, "The origins of the Druze religion," *Der Islam*, 52 (1975), 68, 250.

21. See Halm, *Die Kalifen von Kairo*, 290.

limits. Second, the undisciplined Kutāma were alien to the civilian populations the Fāṭimids ruled, and this caused serious friction in Syria, just as the increasingly Berber makeup of the army did in late Umayyad Spain. Third, in the central Muslim lands Berbers were not the best troops in the field; the Turks had the edge on them. So once the Fāṭimids had encountered Turks after their arrival in Egypt, they set about acquiring them as military slaves. Thus in 975 a group of three hundred Turks from Baghdad found themselves at a loose end in Syria after fleeing from the Būyids. As we have seen, the Damascenes, who hated the Kutāma, invited them in, and they took possession of the city to the satisfaction of its inhabitants. They then allied with the Qarmaṭīs and proceeded to cause the Fāṭimids a remarkable amount of military grief till defeated in a major campaign in 978. At that point the Fāṭimids took the opportunity to incorporate these Turks into their army. A fourteenth-century historian describes the process as building "an army on the Iraqi model."[22]

In military terms this made good sense, but it was to prove politically toxic when ethnic tensions within the army escalated into civil war. At first it was the Kutāma who reacted badly to the competition from the new Turkic cavalry, and early in the reign of al-Ḥākim—at a time when he was still a minor—there was fighting between them. However, an element of method apparent in his madness was that once he assumed power he kept a balance between the two groups. But in 1029, some years after his disappearance, there was trouble again, with large numbers of Turks being killed in Cairo and many leaving Egypt. There was more trouble between Turks and Berbers in 1047. Yet in 1058 and thereafter the alignment was different, and the trouble was now between the Turks and the black slave infantry. There was another clash between them in 1062, followed by full-scale civil war in 1066–68. Berbers and Turks now joined together to defeat the black slave infantry, whose numbers had been increasing thanks to the power and partisanship of the black mother of al-Mustanṣir. In the course of all this the palace was plundered and stripped of its treasures, with the Turks playing the leading role. These events were accompanied by acute political instability in which the office of vizier changed hands more than thirty times between 1063 and 1067. A further indignity was that in some cities of the Nile delta the ʿAbbāsids were being acknowledged in the Friday prayer; worse still, the same thing seemed likely to happen in Cairo itself. The anarchy had also disrupted agriculture, causing famine followed by epidemic disease. Meanwhile, the caliph al-Mustanṣir was destitute. In 1072 we see him sitting on a mat amid the wreckage of his palace attended by three servants. These three were what was left of the twelve thousand servants—not to mention their wives and slave girls—who had staffed his palace a quarter of a century earlier.

22. Quoted in Y. Lev, *State and society in Fatimid Egypt*, Leiden 1991, 89.

The chaos ended only in 1074 after al-Mustanṣir did something uncharacteristic: he made a decision of his own, calling on Badr al-Jamālī (d. 1094) to come to Cairo to take over the floundering ship of state. This Badr was a Muslim Armenian slave who had risen high in Fāṭimid service in Syria. He had troops of his own who were loyal to him, a significant number of them being Armenians like himself. He duly arrived in Cairo with his army, and one of the first things he did was to kill off the Turkic military leadership. Thereafter Armenian Christians played a key role in the Fāṭimid forces. In effect, the dynasty had decided to do without Turks, thereby embracing military obsolescence as the price of political stability. This meant that they no longer had the strength to hold Syria against militarily more capable forces, which in turn put Egypt itself at serious risk. In fact, it is remarkable that the Fāṭimids were able to continue to cultivate their Egyptian garden in some fashion until 1171.

The history we have covered in the last three chapters is varied and complex, but we can end by highlighting two aspects of it, together with a silence. The first concerns the relationship between states, nomads, and agriculture. A strong and well-organized state that delivers security provides an environment in which an agricultural economy is likely to expand. By contrast, large and well-armed nomadic groups that raid settled populations in the absence of strong states create conditions in which an agricultural economy is liable to contract. The period we have been concerned with is one in which states became less powerful and nomads more so, and there is some evidence that this development was indeed associated with a significant degradation of the agricultural economy, notably in the Fertile Crescent and North Africa. Speaking of a region in the northern Jazīra, the tenth-century geographer Ibn Ḥawqal mentions that many of its districts had been invaded by nomads who now dominated the original inhabitants. "When a powerful prince rules on the Euphrates," he says, "they enjoy security, but when the state weakens in their districts, their lot is destruction and pillage."[23] Ibn Khaldūn described the same effect in a grander perspective, and without mincing words. "It is their nature," he wrote of the nomadic Arabs, "to plunder whatever other people possess." They create anarchy, "which destroys humankind and ruins civilization."[24] In a survey of regions where depopulation had attended their dominance, he mentions the Yemen, Syria, Tunisia, and Morocco, the latter two as regions where the plains had been completely ruined. In the last few decades modern scholarship has tended to be reluctant to follow Ibn Khaldūn in this view, preferring to entertain a rosier picture of symbiotic relations between nomadic and settled populations. The two populations do indeed have things to offer each other, so that

23. Ibn Ḥawqal, *Ṣūrat al-arḍ*, Leiden 1967, 211.
24. Ibn Khaldûn, *The Muqaddimah*, trans. F. Rosenthal, Princeton 1967, 1:303, 304.

mutually advantageous relations are quite possible. But their interests also diverge, and in the absence of a strong state the inequality of power between them tips the balance in favor of the nomads. Ibn Ḥawqal and Ibn Khaldūn understood this very well, although in the end they may have made too much of human agency: there is some evidence from the Fertile Crescent of a long-term increase in aridity that could have played a part in destabilizing relations between nomads and peasants. On the other hand, the changes they describe did not take place everywhere in our period, or not to the same extent. Thus Egypt was perhaps something of an exception. Here there was no shortage of Arab tribes; several are already attested in the desert of Upper Egypt in the ninth century. But at this date they seem to have been less powerful in Egypt than they were in the Fertile Crescent. The Egyptian tribes might well rebel against the state, but in contrast to their counterparts in the Fertile Crescent they did not engage in state formation, even in Upper Egypt. The one arguable exception could be the Banū 'l-Kanz in the far south, where the clan had control of valuable gold mines. It held considerable local power in the eleventh century but was not in the same league as the Arab dynasties of the Fertile Crescent. At the same time, when adverse changes took place, they were not necessarily permanent. There are indications that things improved in the Fertile Crescent with the advent of the Seljuqs and their successors.

The second aspect of the history of the period is what it meant for the future of the Muslim world. The key point here is a matter of material resources. Now that Iraq was no longer able to provide the fiscal foundation for an imperial polity, the only site for such a state between Iraq and Morocco was Egypt, and as we have seen even Egypt had its limits. The modesty of the Fāṭimid Empire was also typical of the states that succeeded it there. From the eleventh century onward the Muslim world was thus a significantly different place: it was now the northern Middle East that played the dominant role in empire building. This, in turn, had a consequence for the role of religion in politics. The Ibn Khaldūnian mode of state formation worked with Arab and Berber tribes, but not in general with Turkic ones. From Arabia to North Africa it became harder to create empires in this way, and that of the Almohads (1130–1269) turned out to be the last. With the exception of the Ṣafawids, whom we will come to in a later chapter, new imperial states emerging in the Muslim world owed nothing to the process so perceptively analyzed by Ibn Khaldūn.

Finally, the silence. In the preceding chapter we saw the Persians reassert their identity within the Muslim world. They proudly remembered their pre-Islamic imperial glory, even reviving some of its trappings, and they created for themselves a new literary language that already by the eleventh century possessed a substantial literature. There were also some slight stirrings in that direction among the Berbers. But we have seen nothing of the kind among the non-Arab Muslims of

Egypt or the Fertile Crescent. Nowhere there did a Muslim population emerge that identified itself ethnically and historically with a pre-Islamic people. In the case of Egypt the Arabic word for Egyptians at the time of the Arab conquest was the etymologically related term "Qibṭ," whence the English form "Copt." The term was thus in origin an ethnic label, not a religious one, and in medieval Arabic usage the polytheists of ancient Egypt were as much Copts as their Christian descendants were. If there could be polytheistic and Christian Copts, there was no reason in principle why the process of conversion to Islam in the period that concerns us should not have given rise to a population of Muslim Copts—at once Copts by ethnicity and Muslims by faith. Had there been such a population, it would no doubt have found something to say for itself. But the fact is that when Copts converted to Islam they left their ethnic identity behind them. One factor here was no doubt the rapid spread of Arabic in Egypt, as also in the Fertile Crescent, in contrast to the large-scale survival of Berber into at least the eleventh century and of Persian to this day. Another was that the Jews apart, the populations of Egypt and the Fertile Crescent had for the most part lost touch with their ancient heritages long before the rise of Islam, so their traditions no longer amounted to much more than Christianity and a language. With the spread of Arabic erasing Coptic and Aramaic and conversion to Islam erasing Christianity, there was not much left for them to hold on to. There was one unusual milieu in which a continuity with ancient Assyria was cultivated among Aramaic speakers in late antiquity, but this tradition was not retained by converts to Islam. In Egypt there was certainly interest in the Pharaonic past among medieval Muslims, but they did not see it as an ancestral heritage.

In fact, the only region in the lands considered in this chapter where we find such an identification among a Muslim population is the Yemen. Here the Ḥimyarites lost their language to Arabization, and as we have seen they found their place in the Arab ethnic community as Southerners. But Ḥimyarites in the city of Ḥimṣ in eighth-century Syria still indulged in the fantasy that the power held by the Qurashī caliphs would return to Ḥimyar, and there were people in the medieval Yemen who, without seeking a Ḥimyarite restoration, still retained a sense of the pre-Islamic past of the country as *their* past.

PART II

The Muslim world from the eleventh century to the eighteenth

7

The Turks, the Mongols, and Islam in the steppes

Pastoral nomads have been significant actors in our story, but so far the lion's share of our attention has gone to those of the Arabian desert. It is now time to redress the balance and concentrate on those of the Eurasian steppes. How did these nomads of the north differ from those of the south, and why?

The steppe nomads matter to us for two reasons: the conversion of many of them to Islam, and their impact on the wider Muslim world in India, the Middle East, and even farther afield. But for the most part we will leave that expansion to later chapters and confine ourselves here to the nomads who remained broadly within the world of the steppes.

The steppe people—or rather set of peoples—that most concerns us is the Turks. We will begin by looking at two early ventures in state formation that took place among Turkic peoples who were still pagan. This will take us to regions as far apart as present-day Bulgaria and Mongolia. The second venture will also give us a vivid sense of both the reality and the fragility of a steppe empire, not to mention its tense relations with a neighboring settled empire, in this case China.

We will then move on to the early spread of Islam among the Turkic peoples, notably the Oghuz on the northeastern frontier of the Muslim world. How did they come to convert, and how did they see their Turkic identity in relation to Islam?

Our Turkic story will be interrupted halfway through by a couple of non-Turkic steppe peoples who subjected Muslim populations to non-Muslim rule. This raises an interesting question that is by no means new to us: What are the options for rulers who find themselves holding sway over populations whose religions they do not share? One of these steppe peoples was the Qara Khiṭāy, who ruled only in Central Asia, and in a rather benign fashion. The other was the Mongols, who conquered an empire on a vast scale, and in a manner that was not in the least benign. But as we will see, the Qara Khiṭāy never converted to Islam, whereas the Mongols in Muslim lands eventually did.

Once Mongol power had disintegrated we are back with the Turks of the steppes, by now overwhelmingly Muslim. Here the writings of a seventeenth-century ruler provide an occasion to return to a question raised earlier: How did Turks see the relationship between being a Muslim and being a Turk?

We are now reaching a period in which the military threat posed by the Eurasian nomads to the armies of settled societies was on the wane, and the steppes would in effect be partitioned between two major agrarian powers, Russia and China. But before we leave the region behind us, we will take a hard look at a feature of the political culture of the nomads that was at once characteristic and disruptive: qazaqlïq.

Insofar as Islam reached China, it did so mainly through the steppes, thanks to the employment of Muslims by its Mongol conquerors. The resulting Muslim minority is of great historical interest. Because it does not fit anywhere else in this book, we will treat it in an excursus to this chapter.

As we saw in the first chapter of this book, the agriculturally productive and densely settled territories of the Middle East were sandwiched between two domains of nomadic pastoralism: the deserts to the south and the steppes to the north. In this the Middle East was unique among the Old World's lands of ancient civilization. China, for example, was threatened by nomads on its northern border, as was Europe on its eastern frontier, but neither faced the dual threat that did so much to shape the history of the Middle East and hence, to a significant extent, of the Muslim world. It is no accident that all three major ethnic identities of the Middle East today—those of the Arabs, the Iranians, and the Turks—originated in nomadic populations, that of the Arabs in the nomads of the south, and those of the Turks and Iranians in the nomads of the north.

Yet as we also saw, this appearance of symmetry between the nomads to the north and to the south is somewhat misleading. The two nomadic domains were very different. Unlike Arabia, a peninsula of limited size bounded on three sides by the sea, the steppes were vast; this meant that, like the Sahara desert, they would not be the land of a single people. In combination with the mobility of nomads, the sheer extent of the steppes made for an ethnic landscape that was both complex and shifting. While nothing is forever, there is no doubt that the half-life of a nomadic people in the steppes was considerably shorter than that of a settled agrarian people. And unlike the deserts of Arabia and the Sahara, the steppes were grasslands, making possible a pastoral economy that by Arabian standards was affluent and could often be supplemented by agriculture. There were also significant trade routes running through the steppes, and these could reach far to the north, since the furs of the Arctic forests were coveted by the elites of the urban civilizations to the south. There were indeed desert areas immediately to the south of the steppes, a fact of some historical significance. But the nomads of the grasslands were endowed with a far richer resource base than the nomads of the Arabian desert were, and they had a virtually unlimited supply not just of sheep but also of horses that they rode from childhood—no small matter in the age of the cavalry. This abundance did not, of course, mean affluence by the standards of the elites of settled societies. In 1260 a Syrian prince was a worried guest at the camp of the Mongol ruler of Iran, where he was assigned a goatskin tent with a sheep, a pot, and some firewood. He was unnerved by this treatment until it was explained to him that it was not a deliberate slight—it was simply "the best way of life that the Mongols know."[1] At the same time, the nomads of the steppes were more vulnerable than settled populations were to the vagaries of the weather. Settled populations produce grain, which can be stored over long periods without needing further nourishment; not so the livestock of nomads. Yet the resources of the steppes, miserable though they might appear to a Syrian prince, could support stratified societies in which nobles and commoners were distinct, and by the same token they could provide a basis for state formation. The resulting kingdoms might be flimsy by the standards of settled societies, but they were far stronger than any that could emerge among Arabian nomads, even when catalyzed by the oasis dwellers. In sum, there was no need of a prophet to establish a militarily powerful state in the steppes; here Ibn Khaldūn was irrelevant.

All—or most—of this is already familiar. What we need to do now is look more closely at the history of a particular subset of steppe peoples, above all the Turks.[2] If the Arabs drove the first phase of the history of the Muslim world, the Turks drove much of the second phase. Non-Turkic nomads—notably the Mongols—will eventually intrude to complicate the picture, but for the moment we can leave them aside.

The Turks before the Mongols

The emergence of the Turks

The story of nomadic pastoral societies in the steppes divides into two broad periods. In the first the action was driven from the west, and the nomads were speakers of Indo-European languages, later specifically Iranians such as the Scythians. In the second period, the action was driven from the east, and the nomads, whatever their exact ethnic character, were of eastern origin. Most of the steppe peoples we met earlier, including the Huns, Avars, and Turks, belonged to this second period. Some, though by no means all, of these eastern peoples were Turkic in the sense that we know them to have called themselves Turks or to have spoken languages belonging to the Turkic linguistic family. But our first

1. Quoted in B. Lewis, *Islam from the Prophet Muhammad to the capture of Constantinople*, New York 1987, 1:95.

2. For the history of the Turks in the steppes see P. B. Golden, *An introduction to the history of the Turkic peoples*, Wiesbaden 1992, and for this chapter as a whole see his *Central Asia in world history*, New York 2011.

unassailable historical references to Turks come only in the mid-sixth century, and as yet without any solid information about their languages. For that we have to wait till the seventh or eighth century, when it reaches us through two widely separated regions.

One is Bulgaria. We have a list of Bulgar rulers dating from the eighth century and transmitted in two versions of a medieval Russian chronicle. The Bulgars were a Turkic people who entered the Balkans from the steppes in the later seventh century. Once there they eventually adopted Christianity and gave their name to the Slavic people we know as the Bulgarians. The list as we have it is in Old Russian, but it contains accession dates in the language of the Bulgars. For example:[3]

> Irnik lived 100 years and 5 years, his tribe Dulo, and his year *DILOM tvirem.*
> Gostun as regent 2 years, his tribe Ermi, and his year *DOKHS tvirem.*
> Kurt reigned 60 years, his tribe Dulo, and his year *SHEGOR vechem.*

The words in italics are the Bulgar dates: the uppercase word gives the year and the lowercase word the month. The three year-names translate as "snake," "pig," and "ox," respectively. They are part of the twelve-year animal cycle that Westerners usually know as Chinese; the Bulgars had no doubt brought the cycle with them from somewhere much farther to the east. Of more immediate relevance is the fact that to the philological eye the year-names are recognizably Turkic (the equivalents in modern Turkish would be *yılan, domuz,* and *sığır*). So, too, are the month-names, but very much to the philological eye; they are simply ordinals ("ninth" and "second"; the modern Turkish would be *dokuzuncu* and *ikinci*). Beyond the data of this list, our knowledge of the language of these Bulgars is slight, though a ninth-century inscription written in Greek seems to give us their word for god: *tangra*. This language must also have been spoken by another group of Bulgars who lived around the bend in the Volga, but there our earliest textual attestation comes only with Muslim tombstones of the thirteenth and fourteenth centuries. The language still survives today, but it is restricted to a small Christian people of the region, the Chuvash. Yet loanwords deriving from Bulgar or closely related languages are attested as far afield as Mongol in the east and Hungarian in the west—the Hungarians being a steppe people who in the ninth century settled in what thereby became Hungary.

The other region from which we have serious attestation of a Turkic language in this period is centered on the Orkhon valley in what is now Mongolia. Here our record comes to us directly in the form of inscriptions, and it is much more gener-

3. Quoted in S. Runciman, *A history of the first Bulgarian empire*, London 1930, 273.

ous: it includes three from the first half of the eighth century that are of considerable length. These inscriptions are the work of a Turkic empire that ruled in the eastern steppes from 552 to 630 and again, after an intermission of half a century, from 682 to 744. This time it does not take a philological eye to see that the language is Turkic—the fact is obvious to anyone who knows some modern Turkish (for example, "ninth" here is *toquzunch*, much closer to the modern Turkish *dokuzuncu* than to the Bulgar *tvirem*). These inscriptions use the same dating system as the Bulgar document does. For example, one of the inscriptions records that it was finished in the seventh month of the Year of the Monkey.

That we should encounter two eighth-century Turkic languages that are geographically so far apart and linguistically so different from each other has implications for the earlier history of the Turks. Since the two languages belong to the same family, they must go back to a parent language once spoken by a single Turkic-speaking community. But since we find them so far apart both geographically and linguistically, some centuries must surely have passed between the breakup of the original community and our eighth-century records. As often happens in such situations, we have no direct attestation of the historical existence of that community, or of the cause of its subsequent breakup. All we can say with confidence, on the basis of historical sources, is that by the sixth century the Turks had already spread out over a large part of the Eurasian steppes.

The world according to Bilgä Qaghan

Later we will return to the Bulgars—those of the Volga, not those of the Balkans—because in the early tenth century Ibn Faḍlān, a Muslim emissary sent by the caliph, penned a vivid account of their conversion to Islam. The Turks of the Orkhon, however, were still pagan when their empire came to an end toward 744, overthrown by another Turkic people of the eastern steppes, the Uighurs. Yet their inscriptions are well worth our attention for what they can tell us about the early Turks. Whereas most accounts of steppe peoples are the work of outsiders, these inscriptions give us an internal view.

Historically the most interesting of the Orkhon inscriptions is also the longest. It was the work of the ruler Bilgä Qaghan (ruled 716–34—"Qaghan" being a title we already encountered among the Avars as "Kagan"), but it may include an addition by a slightly later ruler. Bilgä Qaghan had it inscribed in 732 on the occasion of the death of a younger brother, and it is a remarkable document. The ruler addresses the "Turkic lords and people" and does so in a style that often verges on the conversational. He narrates the history of the state he ruled, particularly his own glorious deeds and those of his deceased brother, while acknowledging the assistance of supernatural forces—"the Turkic god above and the Turkic holy earth and water."[4] (The word for "god" is *tängri*, close to the Bulgar *tangra* and the modern Turkish *tanrı*.) Not least, he underlines the lessons his subjects should learn from these events. His perspective is very much that of the ruler. We hear the voices of his subjects only as and when he chooses to include them. There are two main themes in these reminiscences: the internal affairs of the Turkic state and its foreign relations.

With regard to internal affairs, one point worth noting is that the Turks are made up of lords (*bägs*) and people (*bodun*); the latter are also referred to as the "black people" (*qara . . . bodun*). The two orders of society are not always in accord, and at one point we find them slandering one another, resulting in the ruin of their state. Another point is Bilgä Qaghan's strong feeling that the Turks must stick together in order to establish and maintain a state of their own. At one point the ruler ascribes this view to "all the Turkic black people," who lament as follows: "We used to be a people with a state (*illig bodun*). Where is our own state now? . . . We used to be a people with its own Qaghan (*qaghanlïgh bodun*). Where is our own Qaghan now?"[5] This, then, is a state that can easily fall apart through the waywardness of its nomadic subjects: "O Turkic people, regret and repent! Because of your unruliness, you yourselves betrayed your wise Qaghan who had nourished you." Against these powerful forces of disorder we find a persistent emphasis on organizing the state and implementing its law (*törü*). In short, this is a society in which state formation is possible but precarious—hence that fifty-year gap in the continuity of Turkic rule. Indeed, the inscription gives us a graphic account of the process by which Bilgä Qaghan's father Ilterish brought the gap to an end. He launched the struggle by going out with a mere seventeen men; then others heard the news and joined him, so that seventeen became seventy. Thereafter things went well—his troops were like wolves while his enemies were like sheep—and he was able to bring the number up to seven hundred men. One other detail that emerges from the inscription is worth adding here because it hints at something significant about steppe society. In the accounts of heroic deeds there is frequent reference to horses, and here it is as if there is an unspoken rule: you never mention a horse without stating its color. You can speak of a gray horse, a bay horse, a white horse; you can even leave out the word for horse (*at*) altogether, mentioning only its color, and any Turk will understand you. But you cannot just say "a horse."

Turning to the wider geopolitical scene, the only state outside the steppes that figures seriously in Bilgä Qaghan's worldview is China. He knew of the Byzantine Empire (*Purum*), and another inscription mentions the Arabs (*Täzik*). This is not

4. See the translation of the inscription in T. Tekin, *A grammar of Orkhon Turkic*, Bloomington 1968, 261–73, here 262, 265; for a more recent translation of the inscription see H. Chen, *A history of the second Türk empire*, Leiden 2021, 199–205.

5. For this and the next quotation see Tekin, *A grammar of Orkhon Turkic*, 264–65, 267.

surprising, since his empire was one of a pair ruled by the same Turkic people in the sixth to eighth centuries, and the other empire, which lasted from 552 to 659 and then from 699 to the 740s, was located far enough to the west to engage in hostilities with the Persian Empire, ally with the Byzantine Empire against it, and then go on to fight the Arabs. Yet it is China that is most prominent in the inscription, and in two antithetical ways. On the one hand, the Chinese are the source of much that is desirable. They dispense gold, silver, and silk in abundance. They are wizards at the art of painting, which is why Bilgä Qaghan was happy to have craftsmen sent from the Chinese court to construct a mausoleum for his brother. But on the other hand, the Chinese are a mortal danger for the Turks. Their words are sweet just as their materials are soft, yet they are wily and deceitful, and their intentions can be genocidal. Those who succumb to their blandishments and move too close to China end up getting killed—or, less drastically, their sons become slaves of the Chinese and their daughters their servants. The solution is to stay far away from the Chinese and send caravans to them. As is evident, these contrasting sentiments have a lot in common with those of modern nationalists. On the one hand, there is deep resentment of the imperial power of China and the threat it poses, along with a determination to ensure that "the name and fame of the Turkic people" does not perish.[6] But on the other hand, there is an unmistakable fascination with the economic, technological, and artistic superiority of the Chinese.

Chinese sources shed further light on this conflicted relationship with their country. They tell us that Bilgä Qaghan had once entertained the idea of settling his people and building a Chinese-style walled city as his capital. This would have made the Turks a sitting target for a Chinese army, as Herodotus would have told him on the basis of his observation of the Scythians. In the event the Qaghan was dissuaded from his foolish assimilationist plan by the advice of a Turkic adviser who had himself been educated in China, then ruled by the T'ang dynasty (618–906). His argument was as follows:

> The reason why the Turks can always stand against the T'ang is that we move about in search of grass and water, our abode always changes, we hunt for a living, and also we all learn how to fight. When we are strong, we send soldiers to plunder. When we are weak, we hide in mountains and forests. Even if the T'ang soldiers are numerous, they are useless. If we build a fortress and reside in it, we are changing our old custom. We will lose our advantage all of a sudden. Then we will certainly become incorporated into the T'ang in the future.[7]

6. Tekin, *A grammar of Orkhon Turkic*, 267.

7. Quoted in J.-Y. Lee, *Qazaqlïq or ambitious brigandage, and the formation of the Qazaqs*, Leiden 2016, 57.

The Chinese sources also tell us that Bilgä Qaghan had repeatedly asked for a Chinese princess in marriage but was never granted this privilege. Compounding the irony, if one goes round to the back of his nationalistic inscription, there is a Chinese inscription placed there by the imperial delegation that was sent with condolences on the death of the Qaghan's brother. In it the Chinese emperor speaks of Bilgä Qaghan's younger brother as having sought to "keep a close relationship with the T'ang," likens the Qaghan himself to an adopted son, and speaks of "cementing a father-son relationship."[8] For the Chinese emperor to adopt the Turkic Qaghan as a son was not an expression of pure benevolence: it meant that the Qaghan was expected to obey the emperor in accordance with Chinese norms of filial piety. As Mencius had said long before, "The richest fruit of benevolence is this: the service of one's parents."[9]

This unusual window onto the worldview of the ruler of a nomadic state in the steppes does two things for us. First, it confirms from the inside the rather abstract understanding of the character of such states that we developed earlier. Second, it makes it abundantly clear that the relationship of a nomadic state to a sedentary imperial power is not reducible to nomadic military superiority. That superiority was potentially there, but by no means assured. Moreover, a sedentary empire could always deploy soft power to control and disrupt nomad polities. No wonder the Turks appear at times like a moth in the Chinese flame—and no wonder Bilgä Qaghan seems so thoroughly mixed up.

The spread of Islam among the Turks

The default religious orientation of the Turks was paganism. As we have seen, Bilgä Qaghan speaks of "the Turkic god above and the Turkic holy earth and water." But like many pagan populations, the Turks tended not to be strongly resistant to the religions that were spreading in the settled world outside the steppes—Buddhism, Christianity, Manichaeism, and Islam. As might be expected, the early spread of Islam to the Turks took place in regions adjoining the northern frontiers of the Muslim world, from Transoxania in the east to the Caucasus in the west. While there was persistent military activity on this frontier in the early centuries of Islam, in territorial terms the result was broadly a stalemate: neither side conquered the other. The standoff was nicely expressed in a piece of advice attributed to Muḥammad: "Leave the Turks alone as long as they leave you alone."[10] The existence of this stalemate meant that the extension of Muslim rule by conquest did not play much part in the conversion of the Turks. Nor do we have evidence of Muslim

8. Chen, *A history of the second Türk empire*, 230.
9. *The works of Mencius*, trans. J. Legge, New York 1970, 313 (4.1.27).
10. Ibn Ḥassūl, *Tafḍīl al-Atrāk*, Istanbul 1940, 42.

missionaries. But Muslim merchants were certainly active among Turkic populations, just as Sogdian merchants had been earlier. Unlike the pre-Islamic Arabs, the Turks were thus habituated to the presence of foreign merchants among them. Although this meant that the Turks were exposed to Islam through military interaction on the frontiers of the Muslim world and the activities of merchants beyond them, they were not under significant pressure to accept it.

Yet to some extent they did. North of the Caucasus the Khazar state held sway on the lower Volga roughly from the seventh century to the tenth. Its ruling stratum distanced itself from both the Byzantine Empire and the Caliphate by adopting Judaism, perhaps sometime around 800. In 837–38 the Khazars were going so far as to mint coins with the Arabic legend "Moses is the messenger of God"[11]—a declaration that must have made Muslims uncomfortable. A tenth-century source nevertheless tells us that some members of the Khazar royal family were Muslims, and for that reason barred from accession to the throne. Meanwhile to the northeast of Transoxania, a ramified though little-known Turkic dynasty—usually referred to by modern scholars as the Qarakhānids—was well established in the tenth century, and around the middle of the century it converted to Islam, accompanied, it seems, by its considerable tribal following. When half a century later the Qarakhānids conquered Transoxania, the fact that they were already Muslims no doubt made the experience less traumatic for their new subjects. We can also credit Qarakhānid rule with facilitating the spread of Islam to regions some hundreds of miles farther east than it had previously extended, such as the western part of Chinese Turkestan (today's Xinjiang). In the eastern part of this region Buddhism was still predominant in the thirteenth century under the rule of an Uighur Buddhist dynasty, and its full incorporation into the Muslim world came only in the fifteenth century or later. But by far the most important conversion of a Turkic people to Islam was that of the Oghuz—or as we will eventually, following our sources, start to call these converts, the Turcomans.

In the tenth century the Oghuz nomadized between the Khazars and the Qarakhānids. They were made up of twenty-four (or twenty-two) clans. It was they who in the eleventh century would invade the Muslim world and establish the power of the Seljuq dynasty; by that time, it seems, they had already converted to Islam. One significant feature of their location was that unlike the Khazars they in fact had little opportunity to consider adopting religions other than Islam. We have some vivid details of the beginnings of the process thanks to the fact that in 922 Ibn Faḍlān, the emissary sent to the Bulgars, had to travel through Oghuz territory on his way to them. He describes the Oghuz as having no religion. They do not submit to God, he says, and they do not worship anything—though oddly

11. See P. B. Golden, "The conversion of the Khazars to Judaism," in his *Turks and Khazars*, Farnham 2010, art. XI, 34.

enough he goes on to give us their word for god (*tankrī*, the same word as the Bulgar *tangra* and the *tängri* of Bilgä Qaghan's inscription). It is true that they could be heard to recite the Muslim confession of faith, "There is no god but God; Muḥammad is the messenger of God." But Ibn Faḍlān tells us that they did this not because they believed in it, but rather to curry favor with Muslims visiting their country. They were nevertheless curious about Islam. One of them heard the emissary reciting the Qur'ān, liked it, and asked the interpreter to tell him not to stop. One day the same man wanted to know whether God has a wife. The emissary was shocked and expressed his consternation with suitable Arabic formulae, which the man then parroted in the way that Turks were wont to do. The emissary did meet one tribal chief who had converted to Islam, but his fellow tribesmen had told him that if he was a Muslim he could not be their chief, so he returned to paganism. The funerary practices the emissary describes are thoroughly pagan: the dead were buried with grave goods. Over the course of the next century these halting beginnings of Islam among the Oghuz must have blossomed into a general—if often superficial—acceptance of the religion, but our sources tell us very little about how this happened. Muslim merchants very likely played a part; no doubt it was usually merchants with whom the Oghuz liked to curry favor. Raids mounted by the incumbent Muslim dynasty of Transoxania, the Sāmānids, may also have been a factor. But the general conversion of the Oghuz did not mean that no trace of their former paganism survived. In 1098 Turkish soldiers in Syria were still burying their fallen comrades with an array of grave goods, though they now did so at a mosque. This ancient custom survived into modern times among such Turkic peoples as the superficially Christianized Chuvash of the Volga region and the superficially Islamized Qirgiz of Central Asia.

Meanwhile Islam was making some headway well beyond the borderlands of the Muslim world. The case best known to us is that of the tent-dwelling Bulgars of the Volga. A twelfth-century traveler tells us that their conversion began when a Muslim merchant cured the king and queen of an illness on condition that they accept Islam. They duly converted, as did their people, provoking a Khazar attack that they repulsed with the war cry "God is great" and the help of the angels. There is a strong dose of legend here, but that a merchant should have had a part in bringing word of Islam to the Bulgars is very plausible, since the Arctic forests to the north were a source of furs for the markets of the Middle East. Just as plausible is the interest in medicine: everyone wants to get well. But a much better source, and a contemporary one, is our emissary Ibn Faḍlān.[12] Although his account says nothing about merchants, he, too, mentions medicine—the king had requested some drugs—and he underlines the geopolitical aspect of the conversion. As the

12. His account is edited and translated by J. E. Montgomery under the title "Mission to the Volga" in *Two Arabic travel books*, New York 2015.

Bulgar ruler pointed out to him, the caliph could not bring military pressure to bear on the Bulgars. He was too far away, and there were too many infidel tribes in between. But they did have a common enemy, the Khazars, and an alliance accordingly made sense. From this alliance the Bulgar ruler expected financial support that would enable him to construct a fortress to protect him from the Jews who had "enslaved" him—he was referring, of course, to the Khazars. It was in this context that the Bulgar conversion took place. But that need not mean that it was insincere. The ruler showed himself anxious to learn the right Islamic way of doing things, though he could relapse into error if displeased. When it came to the practice of naming the ruler during the Friday prayer, he was punctilious in changing his given name to Jaʿfar (the name of al-Muqtadir, the caliph of the day) and substituting ʿAbdallāh for that of his non-Muslim father. Moreover, it was not just the ruler who converted but also, it seems, the people at large. Yet there were limits to the extent of their conversion. For example, the Bulgars, like steppe dwellers in general, do not seem to have felt that public interaction between men and women was a problem. Thus the practice of the king and queen was to sit side by side in front of their people, and at one point Ibn Faḍlān found himself in the awkward position of having to confer a robe of honor on the queen. Another of their customs was for men and women to bathe together naked in the Volga; Ibn Faḍlān tried hard to change that but had no success. We have here an illustration of a common theme: peoples who live far from the central lands of the Muslim world and who convert to Islam very much of their own volition are often reluctant to abandon customs that from a more metropolitan viewpoint appear as grossly un-Islamic.

There was another outpost of Islam, though a small one, at the western extremity of the steppes. This was the Muslim minority that lived in Hungary between the tenth and fourteenth centuries. Though they are not said to have practiced mixed bathing in the Danube, they are described as dressing like Christians and shaving their beards. They must have entered Hungary from the western steppes, suggesting that Islam already had some presence there—though down to the fourteenth century the major nomadic peoples of this region, as in much of the eastern steppes, were still predominantly non-Muslim. Meanwhile, the settled peoples of eastern Europe opted for Christianity. We are told that in 986 the Bulgars sent an embassy to persuade the grand prince of Kievan Russia, Vladimir I (ruled 980–1015), to adopt Islam. He liked the houris, but their attractions were outweighed by some obvious downsides of the religion: circumcision, the prohibition of pork, and above all the ban on liquor. Soon afterward Vladimir converted to Christianity, which awarded him the bonus of posthumous sainthood. Anyone with a taste for the counterfactual is free to wonder what the history of the world would have been like had sobriety been a Russian value for the last thousand years. But let us return to the Turks.

How do being a Turk and being a Muslim go together?

In converting to Islam, the Turks, like the Persians, were espousing a religion that was not ethnically their own and was in palpable ways the inalienable property of another people, the Arabs. Bīrūnī (d. ca. 1050), a celebrated scholar from Khwārazm, remarked in one of his many works that "our religion and the state are both Arab" (*dīnunā wa'l-dawla 'Arabiyyān*).[13] What he says about the state was by his time a bit theoretical, but the Arab character of the religion was not in any doubt: Islam began among the Arabs, its prophet was an Arab, its sanctuary was in Arabia, its sacred language was Arabic, and its language of scholarship was Arabic. We have seen something of the ways in which the Persians squared this circle; what then of the Turks? Here the record is much thinner, perhaps for a couple of reasons. First, unlike the Persians, the Turks had not endured the humiliation of being conquered by the Arabs. Instead, as we have seen, the Prophet had reputedly warned his followers to leave them alone. Second, the Turks possessed no traditions comparable to those of the Persians that were in need of reconciliation with Islam. They came to Islam as pagans, and so far as we can tell they had no historical memory of the Turkic imperial record of the sixth to eighth centuries. A certain Yūsuf Khāṣṣ Ḥājib completed a Turkic mirror for princes in Kāshghar in 1069. In it he appeals repeatedly to the authority of Turkic rulers and statesmen of the past, but despite these formal invocations the substance of his work is Persian and Islamic. The solidarity he urges on the ruler is accordingly religious, not ethnic. He is to direct all his weapons and troops against the infidel: "Burn his house and hall, break his idol, and put a mosque and Muslim congregation in their place. Take captive his son and daughter, his male and female slaves. . . . Open a way for Islam. Spread abroad the Sharī'a." But the ruler should not attack other Muslims: "Muslims are brothers to one another: do not quarrel with your brother."[14] So it is unsurprising that we do not possess a literature written by the Turks about their pre-Islamic past, one reflecting the early stages of their encounter with Islam in the way that texts written by Muslim Persians do. If ever there was such a literature, it seems that the Turks of later centuries were unconcerned about preserving it.

There is nevertheless one eleventh-century spokesman for the Turks who has something to tell us. Maḥmūd al-Kāshgharī, a Turk from what is now Kyrgyzstan, came to Baghdad, where in 1072 he started compiling a dictionary of the Turkic languages. It is an unusual work and we possess only a single manuscript of it, copied in 1266. This, then, is a book that has survived by the skin of its teeth, which says something about the limited interest of subsequent generations in Turkic antiquities. In his preface Kāshgharī sets out the purpose of the book in high Ara-

13. Bīrūnī, *al-Ṣaydana fī 'l-ṭibb*, Tehran 1370 *shamsī*, 14.

14. Yūsuf Khāṣṣ Ḥājib, *Wisdom of royal glory*, Chicago 1983, 218.

bic rhyming prose, but his message to his non-Turkic readers is a simple one: Since the Turks now rule you, you are going to have to come to terms with them, and the best way to do that is to get acquainted with their language. He backs up this advice with an alleged saying of the Prophet: "Learn the language of the Turks, for they will have a long reign."[15] He is, however, aware that the authenticity of this saying is doubtful, so he adds that in any case reason requires learning their language.

One thing that Kāshgharī intimates about the Turks in his preface is that God is behind them: "He called them Turks, He conferred sovereignty on them, and He made them the rulers of the age." Later in the work he devotes an entry of a couple of pages to the word "Türk." It is, he tells us, the name of a son of Noah; it is also the name by which God called the descendants of this son. In another passage he makes Türk a son of Japheth and so a grandson of Noah. Although such a son or grandson is unknown either to the Bible or to the early Islamic tradition, the practice of identifying upstart peoples by slotting them into the genealogical schema of the Book of Genesis was common in medieval times (compare the idea of the Arabs as Ishmaelites), and making him a son of Japheth went well with the consensus that this Biblical figure was the ancestor of the Turks and other northern peoples. But how was it that God Himself named the Turks, as Kāshgharī has told us twice? The answer lies in another tradition that he proceeds to quote, this one purporting to give the actual words of God: "I have an army whom I have named 'the Turks' and placed in the east; when I am angry with a people, I give them [the Turks] dominion over them." This time Kāshgharī does not allude to the dubious authenticity of the tradition. Nor does he note that it ascribes no intrinsic virtue to the Turks but rather presents them as a people so unpleasant that to be ruled by them constitutes divine punishment. Instead he argues that this tradition makes the Turks superior to everyone else. After all, it informs us that God personally saw to their naming and called them His very own army. Here Kāshgharī cannot resist adding a list of further excellences of the Turks, such as their good looks, good breeding, respect for elders, fidelity to their undertakings, and—perhaps a little jarringly in this context—abstention from boasting. He has clearly worked hard with unpromising resources to find a special place for the Turks in Islam. Incidentally, he also informs us that Turks identified as such: you ask a Turk, "Who are you?" and he replies, "I'm a Turk." We should not be surprised to find such a geographically extended ethnic identity among steppe nomads, even if the steppes lack the peninsular borders of Arabia. Nomads are highly mobile, and so better placed than peasants to keep in touch with each other. This sense of common ethnicity extended to Turkic slave soldiers.

15. For this and the quotations that follow see Kāshgharī, *Dīwān lughāt al-Turk*, Istanbul 1333–35 *hijrī*, 1:2–3, 294.

The expansion of the Turks outside the steppes

There were three main processes through which the Turks spread outside the steppes. One was being enslaved. Turkic slaves were a highly valued commodity in the slave markets of the Muslim world, particularly those who from the ninth century onward were imported to serve as soldiers. We have already encountered this influx of Turks in previous chapters, and it was to continue for centuries; as we will see, it brought considerable numbers of Turks to India as well as the Middle East. A second process was the spread of Turks into settled areas immediately adjoining those in which they nomadized, whether by conquest or otherwise. This could lead to the linguistic assimilation of the indigenous populations, in which case the boundaries of the Turkic-speaking world were permanently extended. We are ill informed about the chronology of this second process, but sooner or later it led to the Turkification of such regions as Khwārazm, Transoxania, and Chinese Turkestan, none of which were originally Turkic-speaking. Khwārazm, for example, had lost its ancient Iranian language and become Turkic-speaking by the sixteenth century. In Chinese Turkestan the process began with an influx of Uighurs fleeing the collapse of their state in 840. By the sixteenth century the ethnonym "Uighur" had been forgotten there, but it was to be revived in 1921. The third process through which the Turks spread was more dramatic: the conquest of regions far removed from their steppe homeland. We saw an abortive case of this kind in the establishment of a Bulgar state in the southeastern Balkans—abortive because in the event the Bulgars were linguistically assimilated by their Slavic subjects, with the result that despite their Turkic ethnonym the modern Bulgarians have no sense of being a Turkic people. On a far larger scale, and of far greater historical importance, was the Turkic—specifically Oghuz—conquest of much of the Middle East in the eleventh century. As we will see in a later chapter, this is how there came to be a country called "Turkey" so far removed from the Turkic homeland.

Our purpose here is simply to note the existence and broad significance of the processes by which Turks spread beyond the steppes. How each of them affected the regions into which the Turks were moving is a theme to be taken up in later chapters.

Non-Turkic nomads from the East

The Qara Khiṭāy

Given the mobility of nomads, it is to be expected that from time to time in our period peoples from the eastern steppes would involve themselves in the affairs of the lands to the west. A relevant example is the Khitans, a people whose language seems to have been related to Mongol. In the early tenth century they took over northern China, ruling it as the Liao dynasty (907–1125). When they in turn were overthrown by a rival people from the eastern steppes, a group of them fled west, establishing a large Central Asian kingdom at the expense of the Qarakhānids and Seljuqs. Their domains included Transoxania. This state, which lasted from 1131 to 1218, was known to the Chinese as the Western Liao and to later Muslim scholars as the Qara Khiṭāy.[16]

Perhaps the most interesting thing about the Qara Khiṭāy was their relationship with their Muslim subjects, who in all probability were the majority of the population they ruled, alongside Buddhists and Christians. As long as their state lasted they never converted to Islam, yet they seem not to have experienced any serious tension with the Muslims they ruled, despite the strong commitment of the Islamic tradition to the maintenance of Muslim rule over Muslim societies. This lack of tension clearly had a lot to do with the attitudes of the Qara Khiṭāy: they were tolerant, they respected the Muslim scholars and local Muslim structures of authority, and in return they were regarded as a bulwark protecting Islam against infidel enemies to the east. It may also have helped that they were just a remnant of a people fleeing from disaster, so the demographic pressure they exerted on their new subjects was probably rather slight.

This raises an issue with wider application, and one that will be of considerable importance when we come to the regional states into which the Mongol Empire was to be divided. In general terms, invaders who conquer a large population adhering to a religion different from their own are likely to be pulled in two directions. On the one hand, they have an interest in maintaining the unity of the ruling group by emphasizing its distinctiveness. But on the other hand, it makes sense for them to avoid tensions with their subjects by getting everyone, rulers and ruled, on the same page. If they give priority to the first consideration, they are likely to keep things as they are; thus the Fāṭimid rulers of Egypt (969–1171) retained their Ismāʿīlī Shīʿism to the end, despite the fact that the overwhelming majority of their subjects were Sunnīs. If instead they set more store by the second consideration, then they are more likely to seek to bring their religion and that of their subjects into line. There are two very different ways in which they can do this. One is to force their own religion on their subjects, which is more or less what the Ṣafawid dynasty (1501–1722) was to do in Iran. The other is to abandon their religious allegiance for that of their subjects, and this is what the Zīrids (972–1148)—the dynasty of governors left behind by the Fāṭimids in Sunnī Tunisia—elected to do in the middle of the eleventh century. Such abandonment may not be cost-free, since there is always the risk of a backlash among members of the ruling group who remain attached to their traditional faith. Pragmatic thinking along

16. For the history of this state see M. Biran, *The empire of the Qara Khitai in Eurasian history*, Cambridge 2005.

these lines was not alien to people at the time. A thirteenth-century Syrian Christian author represents the Seljuqs as sizing up Iran and saying to each other that if they did not "enter the faith of the people of the country," then "no man will cleave to us, and we shall be a small and solitary people."[17]

In terms of this schema, the Qara Khiṭāy would seem to belong with the Fāṭimids in Egypt. But despite the fact that they made no attempt either to change or to adopt the beliefs of their subjects, they do not quite fit there. Though they no doubt brought some religious traditions with them from the east—elements of their ancestral paganism and of Chinese Buddhism—they do not seem to have established anything resembling a state religion in their domains. The key thing about the Qara Khiṭāy was perhaps the fact that they had ruled in northern China for over two centuries, with the result that included in their cultural baggage was a Chinese heritage to which they remained attached even in exile, just as their rulers had Chinese regnal titles and their officials bore Chinese designations. This meant two things. First, despite their nomadic traditions they were not simply unlettered pagans. They possessed a high culture that was in no way Islamic, and we can readily imagine that they were reluctant to part with it. Second, this culture did not include a commitment to a single revealed truth beside which all else was error; whatever their religious beliefs, they were not like those of Christians or Muslims. Tolerance thus came easily to the Qara Khiṭāy, and in a style that did not preclude respect for the religions of others.

There is one other feature of the Qara Khiṭāy state that is worth mentioning here. If in religious terms the majority of their subjects were Muslims, in ethnic terms they were doubtless Turks of various kinds. By a similar logic we might have expected the Qara Khiṭāy either to Khitanize the Turks or to become Turkified themselves. The first definitely did not happen, and it seems that the second did not either, with the result that they continued to be set apart by their distinctive ethnicity to the end. This point is not as assured as their persistence in not converting to Islam, and if correct may not be surprising, but it is worth bearing in mind when we come to the aftermath of the Mongol expansion.

The Mongols

As we saw, Bilgä Qaghan ruled an empire based in what is now Mongolia. Since the fall of his empire in the mid-eighth century we have not been concerned with this region, which never became part of the Muslim world. But we now need to return to it. At some time between the ninth century and the twelfth it came to be inhabited by a non-Turkic steppe people, the Mongols—which is why we know

17. Quoted in A.C.S. Peacock, *Early Seljūq history*, London 2010, 123.

it as Mongolia. More precisely, the Mongols were initially just one of a set of peoples, some of them in fact Turkic, that occupied the region and came to be known collectively as Mongols in the course of their subsequent expansion.[18] Even those who were not Turkic lived very much as Turkic nomads did. They spoke a language that had clearly been deeply influenced by Turkic (although despite considerable efforts on the part of philologists it does not demonstrably belong to the same family of languages). They shared with the Turks such lexical items as their word for "god" (*tenggeri*) and the term Qaghan; and like the Turks, they associated the color black with the common people. Mongol roots nevertheless lay farther to the east than did those of the Turks, and historians of East Asia tend to link them to a variety of peoples of the eastern steppes who appeared from time to time on the northern borders of China. We might thus have expected the Mongols, like Bilgä Qaghan, to concern themselves overwhelmingly with China and to leave the rest of the world to its own devices. But we would be wrong. The Mongol expansion was in fact the mother of all nomad conquests. It illustrates once again the military potential of steppe nomads, but on a larger scale than ever before or after.

The story of how this potential was realized also illustrates the extent to which history can be contingent on the actions of a single individual, in this case Chingiz Khān (ruled 1206–27), to call him by the title he assumed.[19] The narrative of his early life is set in a part of Mongolia so far to the east that its rivers drain into the Pacific. He was of noble birth, but his family had fallen upon hard times. He was still a child when his father was killed by a rival tribe and his mother Hö'elün fled with him and his siblings into the wilderness. Not that he had the temperament of a victim—when one of his half brothers took to bullying him, he and his full brother killed him, to the great displeasure of their formidable mother. Later in life he dissented from the view that hunting was the greatest joy in life, holding that it lay rather in utterly destroying one's enemies and seizing their property, above all their horses and their womenfolk, kissing the cheeks and sucking the lips of their ladies. As a young adult he engaged in a process of vicious tribal infighting, making and breaking alliances. Though it is not part of the standard biography, a credible Chinese source states that the ups and downs of his early life included a decade as a slave in northern China. Eventually he built up a sufficient military following to have himself proclaimed the ruler of the "peoples of the felt tent" (the kind of tent in which the nomads of the steppes typically lived). This took place at an assembly (*qurïltay*) convened in 1206.

18. For the Mongols and their expansion see D. Morgan, *The Mongols*, 2nd ed., Malden, MA 2007, and T. Allsen, "The rise of the Mongolian empire and Mongolian rule in north China," in *The Cambridge history of China*, Cambridge 1978–, vol. 6.

19. On him see M. Biran, *Chinggis Khan*, Oxford 2007.

Having consolidated his power in the eastern steppes, Chingiz Khān embarked on a career of conquest further afield. As we would expect, the initial focus was on East Asia. Here the conquest of northern China began in 1211, though it was not until 1279 that the whole of China came under Mongol rule. In the meantime, following a gratuitous provocation on the part of a Muslim ruler, the Khwārazm-Shāh, Chingiz Khān's forces had invaded the Muslim world in 1219. A by-product of this campaign was a reconnaissance of the eastern European steppes in 1221–24. However, serious attention to eastern Europe, including Russia, came only in 1237–42, a decade after the death of Chingiz Khān. In the end there were limits, of course, even to the Mongol expansion. In the west, Hungary with its grasslands was occupied by the Mongols in 1241, but they soon left and did not return. In the east, they twice attacked Japan by sea, in 1274 and 1281, but both expeditions met with disaster. The sea was not the Mongols' strong point.

The most conspicuous feature of the Mongol conquests was their savagely destructive character and the enormous numbers of people slaughtered in the course of them. This may be linked to the fact that the Mongols were what we might call deep-steppe nomads; they knew and related to other nomads as well as merchants, but peasants and city dwellers were so alien to them as to be beyond the range of empathy. There is an illuminating distinction that has been made between two kinds of bandit: the "roving bandit," who, having no interest in the future wealth of his victims, takes it all regardless of the consequences for them, and the "stationary bandit," who stands to benefit from their future productivity and therefore contents himself with a cut. The Mongols seem to have begun as an archetypal case of roving banditry and to have been somewhat slow to shift their strategy to stationary banditry. An anecdote about the Mongols and the Chinese peasantry sets the tone. In a debate that took place early in the reign of Chingiz Khān's successor, the Great Khān Ögedei (ruled 1229–41), one Mongol official proposed exterminating the population of northern China and turning the land into pasture for Mongol livestock. Mercifully the argument was won by a Khitan adviser who pointed out the benefits to the Mongol conquerors of keeping the Chinese alive to pay taxes. But in Iran this lesson still needed to be taught in the reign of Ghāzān (ruled 1295–1304). He assured the leading Mongols of the region that in principle he had nothing against joining with them in robbing the peasantry; it was just that if the livelihood of the peasants was destroyed for immediate gain, the Mongols would be unable to secure provisions from them in the future. Changing tune, he went on to encourage them to be a bit more empathetic: "You must think, too, when you beat and torture their wives and children, that just as our wives and children are dear to our hearts, so are theirs to them. They are human beings, just as we are."[20] But long before that the rulers of the empire had begun

20. Quoted in Morgan, *The Mongols*, 146.

to invest in the future of their peasantries by conducting censuses of the population—something a roving bandit has no reason to bother with. The first census was conducted in northern China in the 1230s; in the 1240s the idea was extended to Iran and Russia; and in the 1250s, as we will see, the whole empire was covered.

A basic fact about this empire was that, even more than that of the Arabs, it was too large to be geopolitically sustainable. It also suffered from another problem it shared with the Arab empire: the best of the resources and the armies they supported were located in the conquered peripheries, not in the homeland. For a while the central government in Mongolia held on to the reins of power, and when a ruler died the Mongols would assemble there to choose the next Great Khān from among the sons and grandsons of Chingiz Khān. Such assemblies performed their task in 1229, two years after the death of Chingiz Khān, and again in 1246, five years after the death of his son and successor Ögedei. But on the death of Ögedei's successor, his son Güyüg (ruled 1246–48), it took two assemblies, held in 1250 and 1251, to complete the installation of Möngke (ruled 1251–59), another grandson of Chingiz Khān. Moreover, Möngke's accession was greeted by a failed attempt to assassinate him; his response was a massive purge in which numerous members of the Chingizid family were killed. Despite the breakdown of consensus his authority was real, to such an extent that the central government was able to carry out a census of the population and resources of the entire empire, starting with China and ending with Russia. When Möngke died in 1259, however, what followed was a four-year civil war, the Mongol analog of the first Muslim civil war. In contrast to the outcome in the Muslim case, the upshot was that the Mongol Empire no longer possessed a central government, and whatever the pretenses, the days of Mongol imperial unity under the Great Khāns were over. Those Mongols who remained in the homeland now faced frequent hardship and impoverishment. We even find them selling their children to Uighurs and Chinese as slaves. But this did not mean the end of Mongol power in the conquered territories. Rather, the empire was now divided into a set of regional states that were effectively independent of one another. It is these regional states—the Mongol Khānates—that are our main concern.

The Mongol regional states

There were four of these regional states that mattered, each ruled by a descendant of Chingiz Khān. All four had roots in the period before the breakup of the empire. Two of them went back to arrangements made by Chingiz Khān for his eldest sons, whereby he laid the foundations of what became the Golden Horde and the Chaghatay Khānate. The other two were the work of Möngke, who in effect assigned China to one of his brothers and Iran to another, though keeping both on a tight rein. After the dissolution of the empire these regional states soon went their separate ways, though the Mongols of Iran and China kept up close relations for some decades. Let us take these states from east to west. The Yuan dynasty, to call it by its Chinese name, ruled over China from 1260 till its expulsion by the native Ming dynasty in 1368. The same branch of the family also held power in Mongolia, where it continued to reign into the seventeenth century. The Chaghatay Khānate, named for Chingiz Khān's son Chaghatay, held sway in Central Asia, where from 1227 to 1363 it was in possession of roughly the same territories as had once been ruled by the Qarakhānids and Qara Khiṭāy. In 1363 it lost Transoxania, but down to 1678 it still clung to power in its eastern lands, including the nomad country that now came to be known as Mogholistān. The Īlkhāns ruled Iran and Iraq from 1256 to 1335; we will take them up in the next chapter in the context of the history of Iran. The Golden Horde, as it later came to be called, ruled Russia and the adjoining steppes from 1227 to 1357 and continued to exist in some fashion until 1502. But by the middle of the fifteenth century it was fragmenting and had manifestly lost its grip on Russia to the rising power of the principality of Muscovy. There were also some minor Chingizid Khānates in the steppes to the east and south of the Golden Horde, including a branch line in the Crimea that lasted from the mid-fifteenth century until 1787. Its troops were notorious for raiding the Christians of eastern Europe and returning with large numbers of slaves. Within this jumble of dates and places there is a significant pattern to be discerned. Each of the four regional states initially comprised territories of two kinds: on the one hand, there were grasslands suitable for nomadic pastoralism (Mongolia, Mogholistān, the grassier parts of Iran, and the steppes of eastern Europe), and on the other hand, there were rich agricultural lands with tax-paying peasantries (China, parts of Transoxania, the more fertile parts of Iran, and Russia). Except in Iran, these were clearly distinct zones, and the regional states became inconsequential after they had lost possession of their agricultural zones. Thus the basic structural problem of the Mongol successor states was that those who believed in Chingizid rule lived mainly in the steppes, whereas those who produced the wealth lived in the agricultural lands, and where the two were geographically separate, they were liable to come apart. The main qualification to this simple analysis is commercial revenue, the role of which was probably greatest in the case of the Golden Horde.

Our interest here lies in what these states meant for Islam and for the Turks. To start with Islam, the Mongols at the time of their conquests were not Muslims but pagans, despite some prior exposure to Muslim merchants. Moreover, their paganism was not like that of the Qara Khiṭāy; it was an unsophisticated paganism straight from the steppes of Mongolia. There was therefore reason to expect that sooner or later the Mongols would succumb to one or other of the world religions whose representatives they were now encountering in large numbers. In the case of the Yuan dynasty they chose Buddhism, though perversely they adopted it in its Tibetan, not its Chinese form. But the Mongols did do something for Islam in China: numerous Muslim migrants from the west entered their service, and the result was a small but energetic Muslim minority in southern and eastern China that from the sixteenth century onward developed an unusual rapport with the Confucian tradition. Though it will take us far outside the steppes, we will come back to it in an excursus at the end of this chapter.

The other three regional states all adopted Islam, though not with any alacrity. In the Chaghatay case the dynasty ruled over a solidly Muslim population in Transoxania but confronted a much more mixed one in its eastern lands, where Buddhism was still strong and many of the nomads were pagan. The effect was to delay the definitive conversion of the dynasty far into the fourteenth century, and even when it did convert the spread of Islam in the east remained slow, despite strong encouragement on the part of some of the rulers. Under one of them, for example, we are told that if a Mongol did not wear a turban—as a Muslim could be expected to do—then "a horseshoe nail was driven into his head."[21] Despite such incentives, Islam finally prevailed in the eastern region only in the seventeenth and eighteenth centuries. The case of the Īlkhāns was very different. Here the ruler converted in 1295, and thereafter the dynasty was Muslim. This outcome was almost inevitable, given that Islam was already the religion of the great majority of the population, nomad and settled alike. For the Golden Horde there was more of an issue than for the Īlkhāns. While the settled population of Russia was solidly Christian, the nomads of the western steppes were divided, with both Christianity and Islam making inroads into their traditional paganism. In the end the decisive role may have been played by the rulers. Two of the Horde's thirteenth-century Khāns were Muslims, and despite the opposition he faced the third Muslim ruler, Özbeg (ruled 1313–41), seems to have tipped the balance. Why, then, did the Horde opt for Islam? We do not know enough about its history to answer the question, but one relevant point is that the interaction between the Christian population of Russia and the nomads of the steppes was weak. To a much greater extent than in China or even Iran, Mongol rule in Russia, however abrasive and extortionate, was at least somewhat indirect, being exercised in considerable measure through indigenous Russian princes. The separation was also geographical. The Īlkhāns located their capitals in Azerbaijan, well inside the settled lands of Iran, and the Yuan dynasty ruled from Peking, close to the border between the settled land and the steppes. The Horde, by contrast, had its capital, Saray, deep in the steppes of the lower Volga. This meant that however important the material resources of Russia may have been to the Horde in its heyday, they did not do much to pull it toward Christianity. The result was a division in which religion coincided

21. Quoted in Golden, *An introduction to the history of the Turkic peoples*, 314–15.

sharply with way of life: the Russian word for "peasant" is *krest'yánin*, a form of the word "Christian."

Let us turn now to what the Mongol successor states meant for the Turks. Here, too, we can quickly dismiss the Yuan dynasty. Many individual Turks migrated east to seek their fortunes in the service of the Mongols in China, but nowhere within China did this result in a dense Turkic population. The other three regional states are again a different story—the story of how a limited number of Mongol conquerors disappeared into the much larger Turkic populations of Central Asia, Iran, and the eastern European steppes. Thus in Central Asia Tīmūr (ruled 1370–1405) was a member of the Mongol tribe of Barlas, but his language was Turkic, as was that of the dynasty he established, the Tīmūrids (1370–1507). When Bābur (ruled 1526–30), a dispossessed Tīmūrid prince, founded a dynasty in India, its rulers came to be known as the Mughals (1526–1858), in other words the Mongols, but the language they brought with them from Central Asia was again Turkic. It is telling that although Chingiz Khān's son Chaghatay was very much a Mongol, his name came to be used for a Turkic literary language, one that flourished in Central Asia in the fourteenth century and after. In Iran the Mongols were in due course absorbed by the Turkic nomads, many of whom had been there since the eleventh century, though we still have a decree written in Mongol from 1320. Among the Golden Horde we find Turkic replacing Mongol on coins as early as the 1280s, though Mongol remained in use far into the fourteenth century. A Syro-Egyptian author writing toward the middle of the fourteenth century gives us some insight into the process, describing how the Mongols mixed with the Qipchaqs, intermarrying with them and becoming like them "as if they were of one stock (*jins*)."[22] Altogether, whereas Turkey came to be a country on the Mediterranean, Mongolia remains where it had been before the Mongol conquests began.

This is not to say that the Mongols did nothing for Islam and the Turks other than melt into them. In religious terms, the Turkic populations of the eastern European steppes before the Mongol expansion had been predominantly non-Muslim, whereas after the conversion of the Golden Horde it was increasingly Islam that prevailed among them. In ethnic terms, the Mongol upheaval involved much movement of populations in and around the Eurasian steppes, and it is likely that one result of this was to add new elements to the Turkic nomadic presence in all three of the regional states to the west of China. In the eastern European steppes this meant the increased prominence of the Qipchaq Turks; though they were not newcomers to the region, their homeland was in the steppes to the east of the Urals. These Qipchaq speakers tended to be known in Europe as Tatars. Those of the Volga were doubtless in large measure descendants of the Bulgars,

22. Quoted in Golden, *An introduction to the history of the Turkic peoples*, 292.

but their language was now a form of Qipchaq, not Bulgar. Moreover, the Mongols were not absorbed without trace. For example, in the steppes and even in the settled lands of Central Asia they left behind the idea that only Chingizids—descendants of Chingiz Khān—were entitled to rule. This could mean some embarrassment for non-Chingizid contenders such as Tīmūr, who for a long time sought to legitimate his rule by recourse to the device of enthroning a Chingizid puppet. The Chingizid claim to rulership could also give offense to the pious: Shāh Ismāʿīl (ruled 1501–24), the first Ṣafawid ruler of Iran, denounced the idea as "a branch of the tree of Chingizian unbelief."[23] And yet it had resonance even in Christian Russia. For a year, in 1575–76, Ivan the Terrible (ruled 1533–84) formally installed a Christian Chingizid to reign over Russia in his place.

The Turks after the Mongols

The Turks in the post-Mongol period

The world of the steppes as it took shape in the aftermath of the Mongol explosion was marked by an increasing tendency for Turks to be Muslims and Muslims to be Turks.

As for Turks being Muslims, today it almost takes erudition to find non-Muslim Turkic peoples, though they do exist—for example, there are the Christian Gagauz of the eastern Balkans, the Christian Chuvash of the Volga region, the Buddhist Tuvinians who live just to the north of western Mongolia, and the Christian Yakuts who dwell in the valley of the Lena, far to the northeast of Mongolia. The Muslim preponderance is nevertheless a product of recent centuries. As late as the early sixteenth century the Qazaqs—a Qipchaq people living in the steppes to the east of the Urals—were still largely pagan, and ironically their conversion was carried through at the grassroots level only after they had passed under Russian hegemony in the later eighteenth and early nineteenth centuries. The Qirgiz, another people with a partially Qipchaq background, were a similar case. In the first half of the sixteenth century they are described as still being unbelievers, and much of their conversion took place in the late seventeenth and eighteenth centuries.

As to steppe Muslims being Turks, there are no significant Muslim populations among the non-Turkic peoples in or near the steppes, other than those of the settled areas adjoining the Middle East in Central Asia and the Caucasus. Whereas Islam swept the band of desert from the Persian Gulf to the Atlantic, it did not do the same for the steppes. To the east, the Mongols in their homeland were not receptive to Islam. The sixteenth century saw their definitive adoption of Tibetan

23. Quoted in J. E. Woods, *The Aqquyunlu*, rev. ed., Salt Lake City 1999, 169.

Buddhism, and the Mongols' dislike of Islam found lively expression in their Buddhist literature. In this they were in agreement with their Tibetan mentors—one sixteenth-century Tibetan account of the origins of Islam portrays Muḥammad as a renegade Buddhist disciple who composed a barbarian scripture preaching violence. There are Muslim speakers of forms of Mongol in northwestern China, but their numbers are small. The picture is much the same at the western end of the steppes, where no Slav people converted to Islam under the influence of the Golden Horde and where Hungary, though mauled by a Mongol invasion, remained Christian. In the same way the numerous minor peoples of the Arctic forests and the tundra—the coastal plains to the north of them—gravitated to Christianity rather than Islam.

As might be expected, there were occasional upheavals to complicate this simple picture, but overall they did little to upset the status quo. On the eastern border the main destabilizing factor was the rise of the Oirats (alias Dzungars), a Mongol people who formed a powerful state in the steppes in the fifteenth century and again in the seventeenth. Despite some early interest in Islam they adopted Tibetan Buddhism. They caused considerable grief to the Turkic Muslims of Central Asia and the steppes to the north until their state was destroyed by the Manchu rulers of China in 1757. In the meantime some of them, known as the Qalmaqs (or Kalmyks), had migrated west to the lower Volga in the 1620s; they, too, were Buddhists. Though many of them left the Volga in the later eighteenth century, a Buddhist Qalmaq population is still to be found in this region. On the western border of the steppes it was the Ottomans who disturbed things, for a while reintroducing Islam to Hungary, from which it had disappeared in the fourteenth century, and creating conditions in which some Slav and Albanian populations of the Balkans converted to Islam. But the Ottoman expansion in the Balkans had little to do with the steppes, and we will take it up in another chapter.

A minor development that does relate to the steppes was the formation of a small Tatar community in fourteenth-century Lithuania. It appears to have been founded by Turkic Muslim warriors from the east who went into service with the grand dukes of Lithuania, a country later united with Poland. Like the Muslims of medieval Hungary, these Tatars were in some ways very assimilated. Their aristocratic families had coats of arms just like the Polish nobility; some of these included a star and crescent, but others sported images of animals and even humans. At the second Ottoman siege of Vienna in 1683 the Lithuanian Tatars fought on the Christian side (not that this seemed out of place—an army of Hungarian Protestants was fighting on the Muslim side). They lost their Turkic language early in their history, but in their own way they remained faithful to Islam, creating a religious literature in Polish and White Russian written in the Arabic script. They also made practical compromises with their environment: they held that downing a drink or two was not forbidden provided one didn't actually get drunk.

Being a Turk and being a Muslim again

How, if they considered the question at all, did the Turks of the steppes in these later centuries see the relationship between being a Turk and being a Muslim? As before, the evidence is rather thin, but one figure of some interest in this connection is Abū 'l-Ghāzī Bahādur Khān (d. 1663). He was a member of the 'Arabshāhid dynasty, a Chingizid line that ruled in seventeenth-century Khwārazm and had stayed close to its nomad roots. Abū 'l-Ghāzī took a strong interest in the Turkic past, and toward the end of his life he wrote a substantial book about it. This literary project obviously mattered to him. He wanted the book to be widely accessible, so he set about composing it in a Turkic that a five-year-old could understand. He wrote much of it in his own hand, and when he became too ill to write he continued by dictating it. On his deathbed he asked his son to finish the book—which he did.

As a Chingizid Abū 'l-Ghāzī was genealogically a Mongol, but unlike us he had no problem seeing the Mongols as a Turkic people. So in his account Turks and Mongols alike descend from Türk. As in one of Kāshgharī's versions, he makes Türk a son of Japheth. The genealogical line then continues from father to son for five generations during which, Abū 'l-Ghāzī tells us, all descendants of Japheth were Muslims. This may sound surprising, but it actually makes sense—if Noah was a monotheist, then naturally his immediate descendants would have been too. After those five generations Islam disappeared, but not for long. Following two generations of unbelief, the line issued in a key figure for Abū 'l-Ghāzī's conception of Turkic ethnogenesis: Oghuz Khān. As a newborn baby Oghuz refused his mother's milk until she accepted Islam, and as a young man he declined to have conjugal relations with the wives he was given unless they converted—which the first two did not do, but the third one did. When he came to power he ruthlessly imposed Islam on his subjects, killing those who held out and enslaving their children. He then embarked on a glorious career of conquest, subjecting India and much of the Middle East to his rule. After further detail on the life of Oghuz the narrative continues with his descendants, but at this point we can interrupt it.

A plausible way to look at this narrative, and in particular the role of Oghuz, is to see it as developing in two stages. We start with an account celebrating the origins, early history, and glorious deeds of the Turks—or more specifically of the Oghuz, since non-Oghuz Turkic peoples would no doubt have put the spotlight on ancestral figures of their own. This ethnic legend could well be pre-Islamic, or it could have emerged in Islamic times but without reference to Islam. Superimposed on it is a religious legend according to which the Turks were Muslims long before the historical conversion of the Oghuz. The relevant themes here are the descent of the Turks from a grandson of Noah, the residual monotheism that went with this, and the miraculous revival of Islam with Oghuz himself. The best evidence in favor of this reconstruction would be clear attestation of the ethnic legend in a source dating from before the rise of Islam, but this we do not have. What we do have are several versions of the story of Oghuz Khān dating perhaps from around 1300 and after. One of these may date from the fifteenth century. Two things stand out about this particular version. First, it is written in the Uighur script, not in the Arabic script in which pious Muslims typically write their languages. In the Turkic world of the fifteenth century use of the Uighur script sent a message of Turkic authenticity that might have made a Muslim pietist wince. Second, there is a notable absence of Islamic elements in this version of the story. Thus the infant Oghuz has no problem with his mother's milk, and as a youth he has no inhibitions about mating with two successive girls he happens to encounter, both of whom are of course quite extraordinarily beautiful. If we can take this version as broadly representative of the original Oghuz legend, then we are justified in thinking of the Islamization that produced Abū 'l-Ghāzī's version as a secondary overlay. It would in a way complement the work of Kāshgharī: whereas he took the Islamic tradition and reworked it to accommodate the Turks, Abū 'l-Ghāzī's version takes the Turkic tradition and reworks it to accommodate Islam. Abū 'l-Ghāzī himself, however, was no innovator, for all the energy with which he retells the story; the Islamization of the Oghuz legend goes back at least to the early fourteenth century.

Let us now skip to the part of Abū 'l-Ghāzī's book concerned with his own lifetime. Though he talks a lot more about the Turks than he does about Islam, there is no reason to doubt that he was at least a passable Muslim. He does admit to doing one un-Islamic thing, though it was very common: forgetful of the admonitions of moralists such as Yūsuf Khāṣṣ Ḥājib, he busied himself making war on fellow Muslims. But after a final raid on Bukhārā near the end of his life, he decided that enough was enough and resolved that henceforth he would only make war on the Qizilbāsh and the Qalmaqs. The Qizilbāsh were the Turkic Shīʿites of Iran; he had spent ten years living in Iṣfahān, their capital city, but he had good authority for considering them infidels. The Qalmaqs, as Buddhists, were incontrovertibly infidels, and Abū 'l-Ghāzī had fought them more than once—though he had also spent a year among the Volga Qalmaqs as a guest of their ruler. His relations with these two sets of infidels raise an interesting question. On the one hand, he regarded them as unbelievers, so they had no place in the Muslim community; but on the other hand, he thought of them as Turks, so they had an undeniable place in the Turkic community. What did Abū 'l-Ghāzī make of this tension? With regard to the Qizilbāsh he does not tell us. But with regard to the Qalmaqs he makes a brief but interesting observation. In explaining why he is well qualified to write his book, he tells us that during his year among the Qalmaqs he learned their language, customs, and usages. There is no indication that he found the experience distasteful. He clearly had some sense of a Turkic community that could extend beyond the Muslim community. And whereas he gave up raiding fellow Muslims in anticipation of death and the afterlife, he did not give up composing his book about the Turks till death intervened and parted him from it.

Was Abū 'l-Ghāzī just a voice crying in the Khwārazmian wilderness, or was he responding to a wider interest among his fellow Turks? There is one piece of evidence that does something to favor the second possibility. The book we have been concentrating on was not Abū 'l-Ghāzī's first. Previously he had written a shorter one at the request of the Turcoman religious and political elite; the reference is no doubt to the nomads of the desert between Khwārazm and the Caspian Sea, or what is now Turkmenistan. They had heard that Abū 'l-Ghāzī knew history well, so one day they all came to him and complained that while they possessed many accounts of the Oghuz story, none of them were any good—they all contained mistakes, and they diverged from each other. These notables therefore asked him to write something better for them, which he did, again using simple language that avoided Arabic and Persian vocabulary. As he says, if you want all the Turks to understand you, you have to address them in Turkic. So this first book, at least, was not just the work of a maverick but was written in response to Turkic demand.

The passing of the nomad threat

Meanwhile, what had become of the old threat posed by nomadic conquerors to lands of ancient civilization outside the steppes? In the east it remained very much alive: China was conquered by the Manchus in the seventeenth century, and the greatest security nightmare of its Manchu rulers down to 1757 was that they in turn would go down to the Oirats. In the west, however, the threat had dissipated long before. It was the Ottomans, not the nomads of the steppes, who threatened to remake the map of eastern Europe in the fifteenth and sixteenth centuries. It is true that as late as the closing decades of the sixteenth century the Crimean Tatars were still launching major raids on Russia—in 1571 they burned Moscow. But by the eighteenth century they were little more than a nuisance to the Christian powers of the region. The contrast between the eastern and western ends of the steppes was largely due to the fact that the Russians under Peter the Great (ruled 1682–1725) adopted a style of European warfare that gave their armies the advantage against nomadic cavalry, whereas the Manchus did not.

The experience of the central Muslim lands was somewhere in between. There was no major nomadic conquest on the scale of the Oghuz invasion of the eleventh century, let alone the Mongol expansion. But a new horde took shape in western Siberia in the fifteenth century among the Özbegs, who were recently Islamized Qipchaqs. Although their ruler was able to take over northern Khwārazm, he got no further. But his grandson Shībānī Khān (ruled 1500–1510) succeeded in conquering Transoxania in the early years of the sixteenth century, thereby establishing the Shībānid dynasty (1500–1599). It is due to these Özbegs that Transoxania is known today as Uzbekistan. Yet after this initial success they did not go on to take and hold territory in Iran, despite raiding it repeatedly.

There was nevertheless a significant phenomenon in the northern Middle East that had no equivalent in China, or in central and western Europe: the political role of internal nomads. Turkic nomads already living within the settled regions of the Middle East and Central Asia—in Transoxania, Iran, and for a while Anatolia—had come to constitute a key element in the political metabolism of these lands. One prominent example is the Tīmūrid dynasty; the power of the founder, Tīmūr, was based on the nomads of Transoxania. There were many more examples of dynasties rooted in nomad power in western Iran and Anatolia, and we will take up the role of these internal nomads in later chapters.

The story of the Turks and Islam in the steppes was thus broadly one of success for both. But this was not to endure. Attacking from the west, the Russians in 1552 took Kazan, the capital of the Tatar Khānate of Kazan at the bend in the Volga, and set about the forced conversion of the Tatars to Christianity, though with limited success. Four years later it was the turn of the Khānate of Astrakhan to the north of the Caspian to succumb to Russian conquest, and in 1582 the Russians—or Russian Cossacks—conquered the Muslim Khānate of Sibir in western Siberia. What followed was an expansion across Siberia that reached the Pacific shore in the 1650s, bringing geopolitics to the forest region north of the steppes for the first time in its history. Although as late as the first half of the eighteenth century raiders from the steppes were still capturing and enslaving large numbers of Russians, the tide was turning. Starting in 1730 the Russians gradually extended their overlordship over the steppes of what is now Kazakhstan. A few decades later the Manchu rulers of China attacked from the east. Their purpose was to eliminate the menace of the Buddhist Oirats, whose state represented the last major assertion of nomad power in the steppes. This was part of a grand strategy intended to ensure an absence of threats from a vast territory to the north and west of China by securing control of it, and the objective was achieved with the destruction of the Oirat state in 1757. For the most part this drama played out beyond the frontiers of the Muslim world, but a significant by-product of it was the Manchu conquest of what thereby became Chinese Turkestan in 1759. These events marked the onset of a process that increasingly subjected the Turkic Muslims of the steppes and Central Asia to Russian and Manchu imperial rule and, unevenly but more drastically, to Russian and Chinese colonization. But pursuing the partition of the steppes between these two sedentary powers would take us beyond our period. Instead, the next section of this chapter is devoted to a feature of steppe political culture in the centuries before the settled empires moved in.

Qazaqlïq *and the political culture of the steppes*

In the fifteenth and sixteenth centuries we hear a lot about a pattern of political behavior in the steppes that goes more or less as follows. A man—invariably a man—has bad relations with his ruler, so he breaks with him and goes off into the wilderness with a few associates. There they lead a wandering life, living off the land by raiding and robbing wherever they go. This secures the man a reputation, and gradually more and more men come to join him—particularly young men. Eventually he builds up a military following large enough to enable him to conquer a territory and set himself up as its ruler. We do not find every element of this pattern in every case, and no doubt there were many men of this type who failed to achieve power and were forgotten or who never aspired to make the transition from robber to ruler. But there is a family likeness between these roughly contemporaneous tales of exile, pillage, and adventure.

One man who exemplifies the pattern is already familiar: the Özbeg ruler Shībānī Khān. Only at the end of his career was he lucky enough to rule Transoxania; before that he had spent nearly thirty years—from 1471 to 1500—as a freebooter in the wilderness. Initially his band consisted of no more than forty men, but after they had shown their mettle in a daring revenge killing, young and old came to join them, bringing the total to a hundred and fifty men. Then he won a battle, and "from all directions came good kinsmen, men, and braves,"[24] raising the total to four hundred. And so it presumably continued. When he finally made good and conquered Transoxania his companions became core members of the new ruling elite. A pair of rather similar figures whom we have not previously encountered are Jānībeg Khān and Girāy Khān. They were on bad terms with Shībānī's grandfather and fled with a few men to Mogholistān. There they practiced the same freebooting lifestyle around 1450–70, gathering more and more men who shared their political dissidence, and on the death of their enemy they were able to establish their power over the Qipchaq steppe. Thereafter their descendants ruled well into the nineteenth century. Yet another example among many is Bābur, the founder of the Mughal dynasty, who acquired considerable experience in the wilderness before his eventual success in India. In each such case there was a push factor—men of this kind did not adopt such a way of life just because they felt like it. One of them did not like his uncle the Khān, one lost a battle against his brother, one was responding to the killing of his father, one felt that his role at court was

24. Quoted in Lee, *Qazaqlïq or ambitious brigandage*, 113 (this book is my prime source for this section).

too servile, one had tried and failed to seize a city from a relative. But as a way of life this kind of freebootery had its attractions, which is why these fugitive leaders could hope to accumulate significant military followings despite their straitened circumstances.

One thing that makes this phenomenon culturally interesting is that it had a name. Someone who lived in this manner was called a *qazaq*, and his way of life was *qazaqlïq* (*-lïq* being a Turkic suffix that forms abstract nouns). The word *qazaq* appears in the fourteenth century, but in the sense of an unattached individual. It is in the fifteenth century that it comes to be used for the kind of political and military dissident we have just described. Thus we are told that a *qazaq* never spends twenty-four hours in the same place and plunders all that comes to hand. In other words, he is the very model of a roving bandit, like the early Mongols though happily on a smaller scale. Between the lines of the sources one gets the sense that those who lived this style of life felt good about it; there is no sign that they were ashamed of what they were doing, despite the disruption and suffering they were inflicting on the economically productive population. Bābur uses the term in in his autobiography when recounting his youthful adventures and applies it approvingly to a brave young man. In short, we are dealing with an accredited element of the political culture of the steppes.

The *qazaqlïq* phenomenon raises a couple of tricky comparative questions. The first is whether it was more at home in the steppes than elsewhere. Very likely it was, though it would take some research to prove it. A priori there is an obvious precondition for the pattern that is not satisfied in all parts of the world: there must be states, but there must also be livable wildernesses not too far away in which the power of the states is ineffective. The second question is internal to the history of the steppes: What exactly was new in the fifteenth-century phenomenon? Was it the pattern itself, or just the term used to refer to it?

We can certainly find earlier examples—and prominent ones—of behavior that in the fifteenth century would likely have been identified as *qazaqlïq*. Tīmūr went through two suggestive periods of it in the 1360s. A Castilian envoy recounts that in his youth he "was wont to ride out with his four or five companions on foray," making off with a sheep one day and a cow the next and inviting his companions and others to feast on it. Thanks to this liberality newcomers started to join him until he had three hundred men, "and with these he would ride forth through the countryside plundering and robbing all who came his way"—but generously "dividing all he took among those who rode with him."[25] Contemporary sources do not use the term *qazaqlïq* to describe his maraudings, but later ones do. Going

25. Quoted in Lee, *Qazaqlïq or ambitious brigandage*, 67–68.

back a couple of centuries before Tīmūr, Chingiz Khān's early life fits the pattern well enough, and again later sources label it *qazaqlïq*. And five centuries before Chingiz Khān we have Bilgä Qaghan's father Ilterish going out with a mere seventeen men at the start of his quest to restore the eastern Turkic empire.

There is nevertheless one reason we might expect *qazaqlïq* to be practiced more often after the Mongols than before them. Something that became more common among Turkic populations in post-Mongol times was for the names of peoples to be derived from the names of historical individuals, as in the Chaghatay case. It seems that tribal ties were no longer what they had been, and that new political communities were increasingly being established around individual leaders. This would make some sense, since tribal solidarity had been disrupted on a large scale by Chingiz Khān's policy of breaking up and scattering the tribes that were subject to his rule. This, in turn, would have favored the kind of bonding that lies at the heart of successful *qazaqlïq*. Here, as often, we see a contrast with Arabia, where despite the significance of nontribal ties it was tribal bonds that remained fundamental. An Arab outlaw who had broken with his tribe had little chance of building up a substantial following, let alone establishing a state.

Whether or not it was unique, the practice of *qazaqlïq* had consequences for the history of the steppes. As we have just seen, it played a significant role in state formation. Moreover, this role could lead to ethnogenesis. After Jānībeg Khān and Girāy Khān created a polity of their own among the Özbegs in the Qipchaq steppes, the members of this polity were distinguished as the *qazaq* Özbegs, in contradistinction to Shībānī's Özbegs. In time they came to be known simply as Qazaqs or, in contemporary spelling, Kazakhs—the people after whom the country of Kazakhstan is named. The Kazakhs in due course forgot the historical events by which a Qazaq people had come into existence, but their oral tradition transmitted mythical accounts of their origins that nonetheless placed *qazaqlïq* at the center of the story. It is related that Alash, a banished prince, went out into the wilderness. According to one version he did rather well there, and when his father heard about it he wanted his son back, so he sent a hundred men to bring him home, but the men preferred to join the prince. This was repeated until the prince had three hundred men with him. At this point they made him their Khān and thereby became a new people. Unlike the historical record, the myth of Alash Khān has the added merit of explaining the later division of the Kazakhs into three "hundreds."

As might be expected, the *qazaq* habit extended to the eastern European steppes, and we find it in the sixteenth-century Crimean Khānate. But in this part of the steppes it was ceasing to be the exclusive property of Muslims with a nomadic Turkic background. From the Muslim Tatars it spread to the Christian Slavs. Thus Slav peasants would flee from serfdom in the settled lands of eastern Europe and embrace the freedom of the steppes as Kazaks, or in the traditional English rendering of the word, Cossacks. Abū 'l-Ghāzī called them "Qazaq Russians."[26] A Polish source of 1517 describes the Cossacks in these terms: "They live by booty and are not subordinate to anyone, and they roam through the wide and empty steppes in detachments of three, six, ten, twenty, and sixty persons and more."[27] In this context *qazaqlïq* was less about the individual fortunes of unemployed princes and more about the formation of new communities like the Don Cossacks and the Zaporozhian Cossacks. The Don Cossacks stuck to old-fashioned banditry, but their Zaporozhian peers gave a new twist to *qazaqlïq* by taking to boats and raiding the Ottoman lands of the Black Sea coast. Less innovative but historically more important was the role of the Cossacks of the Ukraine in establishing the Hetmanate, a Cossack state that lasted from 1648 to 1783 and whose chronicles made a significant contribution to the development of modern Ukrainian nationalism. Perhaps the most extravagant thought to be found in this literature, and a fine testimony to Cossack identification with the life of the steppes, was the idea that the Ukrainian Cossacks were descendants of the Khazars. Here, too, *qazaqlïq* showed its potential for state formation and ethnogenesis. But there is an interesting Asian asymmetry here: the Russian Cossacks had no Chinese counterpart.

Excursus: The Muslims of China

Islam reached China by two routes.[28] One was maritime and had already brought Muslim merchants to southern China by the eighth century. The other was overland and was in use in the same century, as when a Muslim envoy appeared at the Chinese court in 713. There were likewise Arab soldiers, presumably mercenaries who arrived overland, in eighth-century China. These early contacts do not, however, seem to have led to the formation of a Chinese-speaking Muslim population, and despite a plan entertained by Tīmūr near the end of his life there was never a Muslim conquest of China. Yet as we have seen, the Mongol conquerors of China did something to raise the profile of Islam: they welcomed foreigners from the west, many of whom happened to be Muslims. Numerous immigrants held positions in the state apparatus of the Yuan dynasty. Some of the Muslims became tax collectors, which was profitable but did not make them popular. One particularly successful Muslim immigrant was a descendant of the Prophet, Sayyid-i Ajall

26. Abū 'l-Ghāzī Bahādur Khān, *Shejere-i Türk*, in P. I. Desmaisons, *Histoire des Mongols et des Tatares*, Saint Leonards 1970, 312.

27. Quoted in Lee, *Qazaqlïq or ambitious brigandage*, 44.

28. For Islam in premodern China see Z. Ben-Dor Benite, *The dao of Muhammad*, Cambridge, MA 2005, and more briefly his chapter "Follow the white camel," in *The new Cambridge history of Islam*, Cambridge 2010, vol. 3.

Shams al-Dīn (d. 1279) from Bukhārā. In 1274 he was appointed governor of the southwestern province of Yunnan, newly annexed to China by the Mongols, and his descendants have lived there ever since. One of them may have been Cheng Ho, a celebrated eunuch of the early fifteenth century who led Chinese naval expeditions around the Indian Ocean. Another was Ma Chou, who in 1683–84 sought in vain to obtain from the Chinese imperial authorities the same recognition for the descendants of the Arabian Prophet as they gave to those of Confucius. In 1709 he restored the tomb of his forebear Sayyid-i Ajall with an inscription that quoted Mencius and spoke the language of the Chinese ancestor cult. As this inscription suggests, once these Muslims had settled in China, some degree of assimilation was inevitable as the immigrants lost touch with their homelands and Chinese women and slaves were incorporated into their households. What doubtless accelerated the process was the fall of the Yuan dynasty in 1368, which was not good news for China's Muslims: in a major port city on the mainland opposite Taiwan, "all of the western people were annihilated,"[29] any foreigners with large noses were killed, and the naked corpses of one hated Muslim family were thrown into pig troughs. The next dynasty to rule China, the Ming (1368–1644), was ethnically Chinese, and while it had uses for Muslims it was not reliably well disposed toward them. Nor was the Manchu dynasty (1644–1912), despite its foreign origins in the steppes of Manchuria. Under such conditions the Muslims of China had to live as a small minority amid the massive Chinese population, and without a powerful patron. They were thus under strong pressure to come to terms with their Chinese environment. In effect they became what we can loosely call Chinese Muslims. But they tended not to be regarded—and not to regard themselves—as ethnic Chinese; they were Hui, not Han, though they might also be seen as Han-Hui—Han Muslims as opposed to the Turkic-speaking Muslims of Chinese Turkestan. They stood out for their abstention from pork, but linguistically they had come to be as Chinese as anyone else.

There is nevertheless a significant distinction to be made here. It was one thing to speak Chinese as one's mother tongue, and quite another to participate in mainstream Chinese literary culture. Here there was a marked split within Chinese Islam, and it was in large measure geographical. Kansu, the part of China closest to Chinese Turkestan and so to the wider Muslim world, was home to a dense Chinese-speaking Muslim population that wrote its mother tongue in the Arabic script. In the second half of the eighteenth century these Muslims were bitterly divided by an internal struggle between the adherents of the "New Teaching" and those of the "Old Teaching." What was at issue was a disagreement among Ṣūfīs on a matter of ritual, something that did not usually lead to acute conflict in Muslim

29. Quoted in J. W. Chaffee, *The Muslim merchants of premodern China*, Cambridge 2018, 160.

societies. But the attempts of the Chinese state to restore order led the followers of the "New Teaching" to rebel in 1781 and 1784, and these revolts were bloodily suppressed. Eastern and southern China belonged to a different world. Here the Muslim elite invested heavily in Chinese literary culture. In a later chapter we will encounter a similar contrast in southern India between the alienated Muslims of Kerala and the integrated Muslims of the Tamil country. It is the integrated elite of China's east and south that concerns us in this excursus.

As a representative of this elite we can take Liu Chih (d. 1724), the most prolific of Chinese authors on Islam. His education began with a long study of the Chinese classics. This was followed by extended exposure to Islamic works and topped up with Buddhist, Taoist, and "western" texts—the latter being works written in Chinese by the Jesuits in their attempt to convert China to Christianity. There was a purpose to this cross-cultural eclecticism: "I am indeed a scholar of Islamic learning," Liu explained; "however, it is my opinion that if one does not read the classics, the histories, and the doctrines of the hundred schools, then Islamic scholarship will be confined to one corner and will not become the common learning of the world."[30] All this prepared Liu for his attempt to demonstrate that there was no essential difference between Islam and the Confucianism of the Chinese elite and that consequently neither Muslims nor Confucians had anything to worry about. As he put it in a moment of autobiographical reverie, after spending a decade in the seclusion of a mountain forest—a very traditional Chinese setting—he had the sudden illumination "that the Islamic classics have by and large the same purport as Confucius and Mencius."[31] Moreover, his education put him in a position to articulate his insight in a stylish Chinese. The title of one of his works made it into an imperial bibliographical compendium of 1773–82, with the grudging comment that "his literary style is actually rather elegant."[32]

Another of his works, and perhaps the most central for us, was a biography of Muḥammad. We can best get a sense of its character by focusing on its account of one particular event: a public audience that the Prophet allegedly gave soon after his arrival in Medina. For three days, Liu tells us, he had declined to receive visitors, but now the door was thrown open. Muḥammad ascended a dais and assumed a position facing south—or rather a bit to the east of south, differentiating his position from that of a king. Abū Bakr then announced the visitors one by one. The Prophet had specified the appropriate etiquette: the visitors should kneel and kiss the ground with their lips, but not touch it with their foreheads. They did not enter the audience chamber at random. First came the Anṣār, then the Muhājirs, and soon after the civil and military officials of Medina, the gentry and influential fami-

30. Quoted in Ben-Dor Benite, *The dao of Muhammad*, 148–49.
31. Quoted in S. Murata and others, *The sage learning of Liu Zhi*, Cambridge, MA 2009, 94.
32. Quoted in J. D. Frankel, *Rectifying God's name*, Honolulu 2011, 53.

lies, the village headmen, and finally the common people. All kissed the ground but did not kowtow. All greeted the Prophet with adulation, which he received respectfully. Two things stand out in this account. One is the absence of anything that would remind us of the stateless tribal society of the Arabian desert in the early seventh century and the way Muḥammad interacted with it; what we have here sounds more like the visit of an important person to a Chinese provincial capital. We could easily find parallels to this dissonance in other parts of the work. For example, Liu's Arabia is full of cities, and in preparation for the Battle of the Khandaq the Muslims do not simply dig a trench but also divert a stream into it. The other striking feature of the account is the precision with which it specifies what the visitors do and don't do on entering. Here we see a thin line being drawn to resolve an old conflict of values. The Muslim envoy of 713 had rudely announced to the emperor that "in my country we bow only to God, never to a prince,"[33] and he was nearly killed for his disrespect. From a Chinese point of view, if people did not kowtow to Muḥammad he could not have been a person of importance. But from an Islamic point of view, believers should never prostrate themselves to other human beings. So perhaps it was just enough without being too much that Muḥammad's visitors should kiss the ground without actually touching it with their foreheads, much as some fifteenth-century Muslim emissaries to the Chinese court did. There is a similar balancing act with Muḥammad's humility. His posture during the audience makes a claim to authority but is not quite that of a king. Likewise Liu tells us that in his instructions for the building of his mosque Muḥammad wanted it to be "lofty and spacious," but his adjoining residence was to be "plain and small, simple and without ornamentation."[34] Yet he receives his visitors seated on a dais—unlike the Muḥammad of mainstream Islamic tradition, who threw his only cushion to his visitor and was content to sit on the ground. Alongside such cases where Liu is striking a balance, there are others where the pull of Chinese values is so strong as to issue in outright censorship. In the mainstream Muslim tradition about Muḥammad's wives, ʿĀ'isha alone was a virgin when Muḥammad married her; all the others had been married before. Liu could not abide that his Arabian prophet should be marrying such worthless secondhand women, and he regularly turned them into virgins. More brazenly, the defeat at Uḥud becomes a victory in his retelling. The task of making Muḥammad look good in Chinese was clearly not one that could be left to a mere translator.

There were objective reasons Liu had to pick his way carefully in performing his task. Within the Muslim community he may well have faced headwinds on two sides. One would be hard-line Muslims taking a poor view of the bridge to Chinese elite culture that Liu was trying to build. In the view of one eighteenth-century

33. Quoted in H. Yule, *Cathay and the way thither*, Nendeln 1967, 1:90 and note 4.

34. Liu Chai-lien, *The Arabian prophet*, trans. I. Mason, Shanghai 1921, 138.

Muslim of this kind, "if, while talking to someone, you refer to the true religion with the phrase 'my humble religion' and to another religion with the phrase 'your noble religion,' you will be excluded from Islam—for that is to do honor to other religions and to disparage that of Purity and Truth."[35] In other words, to conform to Chinese ideas of good manners was tantamount to apostasy. At the other end of the spectrum there was the temptation for Muslims to abandon their awkward foreign heritage and assimilate fully to Chinese society. One Muslim family of Fuchien was split over the issue: in 1426 an assimilationist nephew complained about his Muslim uncle, who was "deceived and blinded" by alien customs, causing "his sons and grandsons all to be barbarians."[36] More specifically, Muslims who had studied the Confucian classics would sit for examinations in the hope of obtaining employment in the imperial administration—something that had been so much easier in the good old days of the Yuan dynasty. But if that was one's ambition, it could be attained more smoothly without the baggage of Islam, and there was accordingly a temptation for the elite to abandon their religion for the joys of positions and pork. Whether the numbers of those apostatizing in this way were significant is hard to say; in the early seventeenth century the Jesuit Matteo Ricci thought that they were. Meanwhile in Chinese society at large, anti-Muslim sentiment was not hard to find. The commentator who had noted the elegance of Liu's Chinese style had more to say about the book in question. In the imperial compendium the work was assigned to a class of books that "contained little that was praiseworthy and much that was contemptible," and the commentator went on to say of Liu that "the clever literary ornamentation does him no good" for the simple reason that "Islam is fundamentally far-fetched and absurd."[37] In 1724, the year of Liu's death, a judge in Shantung wrote a memorial in which he had this to say of Islam on the basis of his own experience: "It is a perverse doctrine that deceives the people and should be banned by law. Those who enter it do not respect Heaven and Earth and do not worship the gods."[38] He went on to ask for their mosques to be destroyed. This was nothing unusual. The emperor in 1729 observed that over the years many secret memorials had been submitted to the throne arguing for the state to take action against these "fierce, perverse, and lawless" people with their separate religion, strange clothes, and—implausibly—foreign tongue.

There was nevertheless some blue sky in the Chinese firmament for Liu and those who thought like him. When he responded to the memorial from the judge

35. Quoted in Mission d'Ollone, *Recherches sur les musulmans chinois*, Paris 1911, 401–2.

36. Quoted in Chaffee, *The Muslim merchants of premodern China*, 165–66.

37. Quoted in Frankel, *Rectifying God's name*, 52, 53.

38. For this and the following quotation see in J. N. Lipman, "'A fierce and brutal people,'" in P. K. Crossley and others (eds.), *Empire at the margins*, Berkeley 2005, 89.

in Shantung, the emperor agreed that Islam was a foolish religion but observed that it had come down to its low-class followers from antiquity and was not socially dangerous. In pragmatic terms such an attitude makes sense—other things being equal, persecuting a long-established minority with a track record of relative harmlessness is not a good use of a state's resources. But the emperor could reinforce his imperial pragmatism with a rhetoric of diversity. The point behind this rhetoric was not, as with us today, that diversity is a good thing in itself, but rather that it need not be such a bad thing, provided of course that it stays within limits. The emperor deployed this rhetoric in a response to anti-Muslim memorials in 1729. The people of the Middle Kingdom at large, he pointed out, "vary in their tastes and dialects" according to where in China they come from. He saw the case of the Hui as falling within this ballpark of acceptable Chinese diversity: we all have ancestors, and the Hui, in inheriting their religion, family habits, and local customs from their forebears, conform to the general pattern. Moreover, on this occasion the emperor did not dismiss Islam as a foolish religion. Instead he mused that its substance could not be at variance with "the three relationships and the five constant virtues," in other words with core Confucian values. "Our court," he concluded, looks on the Hui "with the same benevolence as on all."[39] At least some members of the mainstream Chinese elite must have felt the same way, since they agreed to write laudatory prefaces for Liu's works—or at the very least we can infer that for them the public embarrassment of granting the favor was less than the private embarrassment of refusing it.

This conception of different traditions converging on the same ethical substance had a deeper root in Chinese thought. According to a twelfth-century neo-Confucian philosopher, "sages appear in the Eastern Seas, they have the same mind, the same principle; sages appear in the Western Seas, they have the same mind, the same principle."[40] A Chinese Muslim echoed this sentiment and added the obvious rider: "Our teaching is transmitted from the west."[41] A similar line of thinking is apparent in an inscription purporting to date from 742 and recording the building of a mosque in the capital city of the day, but likely in fact to be a forgery of the late Ming period—fake antiquities being a well-developed line in traditional China. According to this text, "the western sage Muḥammad was born later than Confucius, and lived in the country of Arabia . . . ; their language differed, yet their principles agreed. Why was this so? Their minds were as one, therefore their principles were the same."[42] Or as another Chinese Muslim said of Muḥammad,

39. Quoted in D. D. Leslie, *Islam in traditional China*, Belconnen 1986, 123–24. I am making the assumption that the document is not a Muslim forgery.

40. Quoted in Ben-Dor Benite, *The dao of Muhammad*, 166 note 7.

41. Quoted in Ben-Dor Benite, *The dao of Muhammad*, 172.

42. Translated in Liu, *The Arabian prophet*, 278.

he "did not follow the sayings of Confucius and Mencius, but his disposition was upright and his principle pure."[43] Yet another informed some Chinese officials who were inspecting a mosque that "the ethics of our teaching and those of the Confucian teaching are the same. Whoever follows our precepts and laws takes loyalty to rulers and obedience to parents as a duty." He followed this up with a rhetorical question deftly exploiting internal Chinese religious disharmony and in effect proposing a united Muslim-Confucian front against subversive religions: "How can this be compared with fatherless and rulerless ill-behaved Buddhists and Taoists?" Liu in his writings conveyed the same reassuring message. For example, he averred that the sage Muḥammad had sent his minister—that was Saʿd ibn Abī Waqqāṣ—to China with a copy of the Muslim scripture, which teaches "loyalty to rulers and filial piety to parents," just like "our Confucianism." That the mainstream Islamic tradition knows nothing of such a mission did not detract from its relevance for Chinese Muslims.

In real life Liu's enterprise remained pretty much confined to one corner of the wider Chinese literary scene, but it is no less interesting for that. In the Muslim world down to the eighteenth century it was rare for Muslims to find themselves in the position of looking up to a dominant non-Muslim culture, still less seeking to form a close relationship with it. Typically their political power meant that they were well placed to look down on other cultures from a superior eminence. But there were exceptions. The case of the Chinese Muslims is one, and as we will see that of the Tamil Muslims is another. In the nineteenth century and after, what had been exceptional was to become the norm as a result of the rise of Europe. The Chinese and Tamil Muslims thus provide significant precedents for that new normality.

43. For this and the quotations that follow see Ben-Dor Benite, *The dao of Muhammad*, 101, 179, 190.

8

Iran and Central Asia

Now that we are familiar with the Turks and Mongols in the steppes, in the next few chapters we will follow these peoples wherever in the Muslim world they went outside them. The present chapter surveys the history of Turkic and Mongol power in Iran, with a final section on Central Asia and the legacy of the Mongols. But it will also give considerable attention to some of the things Iranians were doing below the level of these imposing states and in the intervals between them.

We start with the invasion of Iran by the Oghuz, and the Seljuq empire that emerged from it, looking at several aspects of the interface between the Seljuqs and the society they had come to dominate. Perhaps the most striking of these is the collision between the manners and customs of the Turks and those of polite society in Baghdad, a clash that dogged the marriage of a Seljuq princess to an 'Abbāsid caliph. But the most historically significant theme here is the symbiosis of Turkic military power and Persian bureaucracy.

We then turn to the period of political fragmentation that ensued between the decline of Seljuq power and the coming of the Mongols. How similar was it to the period of fragmentation of the tenth and early eleventh centuries, and how different?

The next few centuries are marked by a continuing alternation between large-scale states established by Turkic and Mongol players and intervening periods of fragmentation, as we move through a succession of major dynasties: the Īlkhāns, the Qara Qoyunlu and Aq Qoyunlu, the Ṣafawids, and finally the Qājārs. Here the dynasty that doesn't quite fit is the Ṣafawids. What was different about it, and what were the long-term consequences of the difference? At some point in all this we will pause to look into one of Iran's most successful exports in this period: the Persian language.

But what if we were to set aside high-level dynastic history and take a more resolutely local view of things? The result will not just qualify some grand generalizations but also bring us face to face with a world of local political activity so extensive that we can only sample it.

Returning to the higher dynastic level, the main gap in our coverage is Central Asia from the sixteenth to the eighteenth century. After filling that gap, we will look at a theme that is relatively prominent there but also arises elsewhere in the Muslim world:

the legal legacy of the Mongols. If only God is allowed to legislate, how can rulers purport to do so?

In the previous chapter we looked at the Turks—supplemented by the Mongols—in the Eurasian steppes. Now we turn to their interactions with the populations of three major regions outside the steppes. In this chapter our concern is with Iran and the more settled parts of Central Asia from the eleventh century to the eighteenth; in the chapters that follow we will move on first to Anatolia and the lands that came under the eventual sway of the Ottoman Empire and then to India, covering roughly the same period. Although the theme of the military and political impact of the Turks and Mongols is shared by all these regions, the trajectories of their histories turned out very differently.

Our primary concern in this chapter will be Iran, though toward the end we will shift the focus to Central Asia. We can best begin with a first-order approximation of the pattern of Iranian history across the whole period.[1] It has four major features. The first is the survival of something called Iran, as both a cultural and a political entity: Iran is there in the eleventh century, and it is still there in the eighteenth. The second is an alternation between periods when Iran is ruled by a single imperial state and periods in which it breaks up into a number of smaller states. The third feature is steppe nomad power: all imperial states based in Iran in this period are the work of Turkic or Mongol nomads. The fourth is the role of the settled Iranian population, whose lot is to pay taxes and—more rewardingly—to serve as bureaucrats and bearers of a literate culture. With this first-order approximation in mind, we can now move on to a second-order approximation in the form of an outline of the history of Iran over eight centuries that will occupy most of this chapter. At this level we will have enough resolution to qualify some of the first-order generalizations just set out and to bring out the more significant differences between periods and states. Thereafter we will sample—but only sample—a third-order approximation.

Iran from the Seljuqs to the Mongols

The Oghuz invasion and the Seljuq dynasty

The Great Seljuq dynasty (1040–1194) was the first in the succession of imperial states that ruled Iran in the centuries from 1000 to 1800.[2] We can usually dispense with the adjective "Great," but it is useful when we need to distinguish the main

1. For a survey of this history see D. Morgan, *Medieval Persia*, New York 2015.

2. For the history of the Seljuqs see C. E. Bosworth, "The political and dynastic history of the Iranian world," in *The Cambridge history of Iran*, Cambridge 1968–91, vol. 5; A.C.S. Peacock, *The Great Seljuk empire*, Edinburgh 2015.

imperial dynasty from a number of Seljuq branch lines. This dynasty stemmed from the Oghuz, alias the Turcomans, and it came to power in the course of the Oghuz invasion of the settled lands of the Middle East in the middle decades of the eleventh century. The Oghuz were among the Turkic peoples of whom Bilgä Qaghan spoke in his inscription, at a time when they were located far to the east. But they did not stay there, and according to one testimony they migrated to the steppes adjoining the northeastern border of the Muslim world as early as the second half of the eighth century. This was now their homeland, and here, as we have seen, they gradually converted to Islam. They were mainly nomadic; there were some settled Oghuz, but they were looked down on as "lazy ones, ones left behind."[3] They had a ruler, the Yabghu, who likewise converted, yet this Oghuz state, such as it was, played no part in the invasion of the Middle East. The Seljuq family, by contrast, had not been rulers of a state in the steppes prior to the invasion. Insofar as we know anything about their background, they belonged to the Oghuz clan of Qïnïq—one of the twenty-four Oghuz clans. They spent time in the armies of the Khazars and later of dynasties such as the Sāmānids and Qarakhānids. By then the Seljuqs and their Oghuz followers were a significant presence in Transoxania, and from there they moved into Khurāsān in the 1020s and 1030s. In other words, the Oghuz expansion—unlike that of the Mongols two centuries later—was not a case of a state taking shape in the steppes before embarking on a career of conquest.

In fact, the Oghuz invasion was a remarkable demonstration of the geopolitical impact that steppe nomads could have without really trying. Left to themselves, the nomads were primarily interested in pasture and plunder. They raided rather than conquered, moving wherever the grass was good and looting anyone and anything in their path. It was the achievement of the Seljuq family to ride this storm and thereby win themselves an empire. The extent of their empire was considerable. Its core was Iran—the whole of Iran, including parts of the northeastern Iranian world that today we allocate to Central Asia. To that they added Iraq, taking Baghdad in 1055, and farther to the west members of the family were able to establish themselves briefly in Syria and on a lasting basis in Anatolia. They manifestly owed much of their success to the abiding military advantage enjoyed by steppe nomads in the age of the cavalry, but they must have been helped by the fact that the Middle East they were invading lacked any strong imperial state that could have stood in their way. Iran, in particular, was more politically fragmented than at any other time in its known history and had been so for longer than in any subsequent period of disunity.

3. Quoted in P. B. Golden, "The Turkic world in Maḥmûd al-Kâshgharî," in J. Bemmann and M. Schmauder (eds.), *Complexity of interaction along the Eurasian steppe zone*, Bonn 2015, 514.

Given the nomadic background of the dynasty, it is an obvious question how the new rulers would relate to the settled and urban society they now ruled. Would they remain obstinately outside it, or would they assimilate to it? The answer seems to have been a mixture.

One way in which the Seljuq sultans remained true to their nomadic roots was the style of itinerant rulership they practiced. Itinerant rulership in itself is not peculiar to nomads; the Carolingians, for example, made a habit of it, as did the dynasties of medieval North Africa. A ruler moving around with a large entourage can easily exhaust the resources of a relatively undeveloped local economy and need to move on. At the same time, moving around his domains is a good way for him to assert his authority in provinces that might otherwise be tempted to forget him. What was different about the Seljuq pattern was two things. First, reconstructing their movements shows that a lot of what they moved for was pastureland; in this sense they were nomadic rather than just itinerant. Second, although they ruled real cities they did not inhabit them. Instead of maintaining a palace in the middle of a city, a visiting Seljuq ruler would set up camp outside it and remain there for the duration of his visit. This was still the case with the last Seljuq sultan in Iran, Ṭoghrïl III (ruled 1176–94): he would spend the winter in pastureland near Hamadhān, his capital, and then move to more distant pastures in the spring.

By contrast, one way in which the Seljuqs assimilated to their new environment was by entering into the religious disputes of their subjects. Far from remaining indifferent to the concerns of the largely urban sects and schools that generated the religious diversity—and cacophony—of Islam at the time, they often showed themselves highly partisan, if not always consistently so. As a result, they had a significant role in reshaping the religious scene in the territories they ruled. Of the four schools of Muslim law that eventually won out in Sunnī Islam, the Ḥanafī school was particularly strong in the lands adjacent to the Oghuz homeland, where it was associated with a local school of theology known as Māturīdism. The Oghuz thus acquired Ḥanafism and Māturīdism as a package, and they did much to spread that package in the lands they conquered, with notable success in Anatolia. This symbiosis was projected back onto the founding figure of the Ḥanafī school, Abū Ḥanīfa (d. 767), who was reputed to have received a supernatural assurance that his school would not cease as long as "the sword remains in the hands of the Turks."[4]

What of the sinews of the state? Here there are two key institutions that call for our attention: the bureaucracy and the army. The Muslim world of the early eleventh century possessed an elaborate and sophisticated bureaucratic tradition, not least in Iran. Many of the bureaucrats who maintained this tradition were face-

4. Rāwandī, *Rāḥat al-ṣudūr*, Leiden 1921, 17.

less, or at least appear so to us today, but there was one who embodied it in a highly personal way: Niẓām al-Mulk (d. 1092). Previously employed by the Ghaznawids (ruled 977–1186), a dynasty whose base was in what is now Afghanistan, he went over to the Seljuqs and served two sultans as vizier. He was thus an early representative of the continuity of Iranian bureaucracy under Turkic rule. The Seljuqs, like many conquerors, were content to adopt the bureaucratic tradition of Iran as they found it, and unlike the Arabs they showed no interest in appropriating it through cultural transformation. Iranian bureaucracy would accordingly remain Iranian—and despite the prestige of Arabic this meant that sooner or later its language would be Persian. One significant change that took place in this period was to affect the character of bureaucracy in much of the Muslim world. This was the accelerated rise and spread of madrasas, colleges whose primary purpose was religious education. These institutions were closely related to the Seljuq and other states in two ways. First, they were typically founded by rulers and other members of the political elite; Niẓām al-Mulk established several madrasas, the most famous of them in Baghdad. Second, their students included considerable numbers of future bureaucrats, thereby creating a new and structurally significant tie between religious education and governance.

Turning to the army, we see the consequences of the fact that the Seljuqs had ridden the storm, not planned it. The relationship of the Oghuz—or as we can start to call them, the Turcomans—to their Seljuq rulers was not one of disciplined loyalty. This made for somewhat chaotic conquests, but it posed a more serious challenge when the conquests and their easy rewards were over. Could the dynasty still depend on the Turcomans as the foundation of its military power? Or did they need to break with the unruly tribesmen and find an alternative source of recruits for their armies? Already in the eleventh century insurgent princes had no trouble recruiting military followings among the Turcomans, and Sanjar (ruled 1118–57), the last effective Seljuq ruler, spent several years toward the end of his reign as the hapless captive of rebellious Turcomans who proceeded to devastate Khurāsān. And yet, as Niẓām al-Mulk put it, despite the vexation they had caused, the Turcomans still had "a long-standing claim upon this dynasty, because at its inception they served it well and suffered much," and this bond was reinforced by "ties of kinship."[5] But in the meantime, in the years following the conquest of Baghdad in 1055, the Seljuq rulers had adopted another institution from the states they had conquered: slave soldiers. These, too, were generally Turks, but Turks imported direct from the steppes—though there could be fellow feeling between the two kinds. The slave soldiers now supplemented the free Oghuz troops without entirely displacing them.

5. Nizam al-Mulk, *The book of government or Rules for kings*, trans. H. Darke, London 1978, 102.

No such long-standing claim or ties of kinship linked the Seljuqs to their sedentary subjects. Perhaps nothing better illustrates the gap between them than the story of one caliph's unhappy marriage to a Seljuq princess, the daughter of the reigning sultan. The story unfolds in the 1080s; the caliph was al-Muqtadī (ruled 1075–94), and the sultan was Malik Shāh (ruled 1073–92). The marriage was the caliph's idea, and it made sense: given the strength of the sultan and the weakness of the caliph, marital ties to the sultan's court could come in very handy for him. The caliph accordingly dispatched his vizier to the sultan's court, where he was duly received by the sultan's vizier, Niẓām al-Mulk. But for reasons we need not go into, the sultan's vizier was not feeling particularly well disposed toward the caliph. When the caliph's vizier raised the question of the marriage, the sultan's vizier replied that nothing had been settled, and that if he wanted to pursue the matter he would have to talk to the girl's mother. This was not how things were done in the polite society of Baghdad. Worse yet, the girl's mother was the formidable Terken Khātūn (d. 1094), a Qarakhānid princess who, among other things, is said to have commanded a contingent of ten thousand men. When the caliph's vizier spoke to her, she boasted to him about the competition for her daughter's hand from other rulers of the day and explained that the going rate was 400,000 dinars; if the caliph would care to match that, they had a deal. Perhaps the caliph could have come up with such a sum in the glorious days of Hārūn al-Rashīd, but as things stood in the 1080s, what Terken Khātūn was asking for was far beyond the means of a cash-strapped caliph. In the end they settled on 150,000, of which only 50,000 was required for the down payment. But even that was more than the caliph's vizier could come up with, so it was agreed that he should pay 10,000 up front and send the rest from Baghdad once he got home. It then turned out that he could not raise even the 10,000, so that amount was added to the 40,000 he was to send from Baghdad. Meanwhile the girl's mother imposed a final humiliation on the caliph: he was to have no other wives and no concubines alongside her daughter. A few years later the marriage took place in Baghdad. Naturally it was a magnificent occasion, and the sultan himself was present, as were Terken Khātūn and Niẓām al-Mulk. But this is not one of those stories where they all live happily ever after. Things started well enough—the girl was soon pregnant and bore the caliph a son. But her relationship with the caliph turned sour, and after a couple of years she went home to her parents, taking her son with her. As if that wasn't enough, it appears that the sultan blamed the caliph for the mess and now treated him worse than ever. On his last visit to Baghdad he had a disturbing message for the caliph: "You must relinquish Baghdad to me, and depart to any land you choose."[6] The sultan would then adopt Baghdad as his winter capital. This time

6. Quoted in Bosworth, "The political and dynastic history of the Iranian world," 101.

at least, the caliph had a stroke of luck: soon afterward the sultan died, a four-year-old was placed on the throne, civil war broke out among the Seljuqs, and the pressure was taken off the caliph. Terken Khātūn was now fully occupied by the struggle within the family.

If things had mostly tended to go badly for the caliph, from now on they did not go particularly well for the Seljuqs. After the civil war the dynasty never recovered its early strength. There was a partial revival under Sanjar in the east, but not in the west, and after he was taken captive by the Turcoman tribesmen the power of the dynasty was residual—except for its branch lines, notably that in Anatolia. The end came in 1194, when the last Seljuq to rule in Iran lost his throne and his life. Why, then, did the Seljuqs have so much less staying power than the Sasanians, who maintained a large and powerful state for four centuries? One reason comes straight from an earlier chapter: the degradation of Iraqi tax power. From the tenth century onward it was, so to speak, axiomatic that anyone ruling Iran could help himself to Iraq, but the rewards of doing so were far smaller than they had been in Sasanian or early ʿAbbāsid times. Though Malik Shāh had his plan for expelling the caliph from Baghdad and using it as a winter capital, Iraq was now a province, not a metropolis, and in practice the Seljuq sultans merely appointed a governor there; unlike Malik Shāh, Alp Arslan (ruled 1063–73) had never bothered to visit the city. Without the revenues of Iraq the fiscal resources for a large and lasting empire were no longer to be found in the eastern part of the Middle East. Another reason already alluded to in this chapter was the shaky relationship between the Seljuqs and the Turcoman tribesmen. In part this may have been a matter of historical contingency: had the Seljuqs formed a state among the Oghuz before the invasion and directed the conquests from such a base, the bond between them and the tribesmen might have been considerably stronger. That there had not been such a development may in turn be linked to a feature of the Oghuz environment that must have inhibited effective state formation. The region in which they were nomadizing was not the steppe proper but rather the deserts to the south of it. A final factor worth noting relates to Seljuq succession practices. One point here is that according to Turkic custom a brother of a deceased ruler had a better claim to his inheritance than a son did, which went against the grain of accepted practice in the Muslim Middle East. But the main point is that the Seljuqs did not regard their empire as indivisible. The dynasty began with two brothers ruling simultaneously, Chaghrï (ruled 1040–60) in Khurāsān and Ṭoghrïl (ruled 1040–63) farther to the west and south. In the next century Sanjar ruled in Khurāsān while a string of Seljuqs held or disputed power in western Iran. Meanwhile, from 1048 to around 1188 a Seljuq branch line ruled in Kirmān. The empire of a dynasty that starts from the premise that the state is divisible—in contrast, for example, to the Sasanians and ʿAbbāsids—is likely to break up sooner. For all these reasons we have no grounds for surprise that the Seljuqs ruled an imperial state for only half a century.

Before we leave the Seljuqs, we should touch on the demographic consequences of the movement of Turcoman tribesmen into Iran and beyond. Much of the Middle East was too arid to be attractive to steppe nomads and so of little interest to them. For example, they moved into Syria in the course of the eleventh century, appearing as far south as Ramla, but soon abandoned this relatively inhospitable terrain. In the same way much of Iran was not their kind of territory. Although we hear of Turcoman nomads in Fārs and even in Lāristān yet farther to the south and east, their presence in such regions was limited. Azerbaijan was different, and it is likely that Turcoman pastoralists came to be well established there in Seljuq times. Here and elsewhere, it is hard to say how far they were pushing aside existing nomadic populations, how far they were harrying and displacing peasants, and how far they were occupying an ecological niche that had previously been empty; very likely there was a bit of each. But there is a serious case to be made that over the centuries nomadic tribes—and not just Turkic ones—expanded their share of the resources of Iran at the expense of the peasantry. For example, until the improved security that came with the rise of the modern state, the locations of the mountain villages of Khurāsān showed a marked preference for higher and less accessible valleys in response to the threat of Turcoman raids. In Azerbaijan the influx of steppe nomads had the effect of changing its language: whereas hitherto this region had been Iranian-speaking, it now gradually became largely Turkic-speaking. In addition, the coming of the Turcomans correlated with a geopolitical shift: it was only in Seljuq times that Azerbaijan began to matter in Muslim history, providing a potential base for the creation of a strong state in a way that it had not done before. The nomads also found a home from home farther west. Those of eastern Anatolia will concern us later in this chapter, those of western Anatolia mainly in the next. All this very likely led to a marked increase in the number of nomads in the northern Middle East.

Between the Seljuqs and the Mongols

In an earlier chapter we saw how the decline of ʿAbbāsid power led to a period of political fragmentation in Iran that lasted until the coming of the Seljuqs. The ʿAbbāsids continued to reign, but as far as Iran is concerned we can think of that phase of disunity as the post-ʿAbbāsid period. When Seljuq power weakened in turn, again the consequence was fragmentation. It became serious from the 1140s onward and ended definitively only with the Mongol conquest a century later. We can see this effectively as the post-Seljuq period, despite the fact that for much of it the Seljuqs, like the ʿAbbāsids, continued to reign in some fashion. There is an obvious analogy between the post-ʿAbbāsid and post-Seljuq periods, but there were also significant differences.

One major difference concerned the nature of the new dynasties. As we saw, those who took advantage of the weakening of ʿAbbāsid power to fill the political vacuum were very varied in their origins and included many who in one way or another stemmed from the native population of Iran. By contrast, a standard pattern predominated among the contenders for power in what had been the Seljuq empire. Typically the founders of upstart dynasties in this period were Turks, whether free tribesmen or slave soldiers, and they started out in the service of the Seljuqs. Such Turkic dynasties would descend from provincial governors appointed by the Seljuq rulers. A case in point is Khwārazm. Here a governor appointed in the late eleventh century established a line known as the Khwārazm-Shāhs (ca. 1077–1231), who became effectively independent of the Seljuqs in the 1140s and went on to defeat and kill the last Seljuq ruler in 1194 in the course of a rapid expansion into Iran. In a common variant, the founder would be an Atabeg—a Turkic term for a military commander appointed by a Seljuq ruler as the guardian of a child prince who had notionally been appointed to govern a province; sooner or later an ambitious Atabeg might contrive to mislay his ward and govern in his own right. The Eldigüzids (ca. 1145–1225) of Azerbaijan are a major example of an Atabeg dynasty, founded by a Qipchaq slave soldier. This dynasty, too, was able to expand its territories, though not as much as the Khwārazm-Shāhs, and while it did not kill the last Seljuq sultan, it kept him on a short leash for much of his reign. Its ability to do so was, in part at least, a testimony to the increased geopolitical salience of Azerbaijan. A humbler example is the Salghurid dynasty (1148–1282) of Fārs, which was of Turcoman origin. Fārs was not like Azerbaijan; the Salghurids did not expand beyond it, and for much of the time they were vassals of external powers. There were also dynasties in this period that did not conform to this pattern. A case in point was that of the Bāwandids, a minor but remarkably persistent Iranian dynasty that was able to hang on from the later seventh century to the mid-fourteenth in the mountains south of the Caspian. It survived both the Oghuz and Mongol invasions, only to be overthrown by another local Iranian family. But in general, native Iranian states of any size were few and far between, and they were not the ones that mattered.

The other major contrast between the two periods concerned the potential of the successor states for expansion. In the post-ʿAbbāsid phase of disunity no one state ever seemed likely to take over the whole of Iran; it took the coming of the steppe nomads to achieve that. Here, too, as we have seen, the post-Seljuq phase was different. Although the Eldigüzids did not come close to such an achievement, the Khwārazm-Shāhs did, albeit briefly, in the late twelfth and early thirteenth centuries. They thereby created a transitory empire that was soon to be destroyed by the Mongols, but while it lasted it was yet another testimony to the military potential of steppe nomads. Their base in Khwārazm gave them easy access to the steppes, and their ties to the nomads enabled them to recruit Qipchaq cavalrymen in large numbers.

The Mongol invasion

In some respects, as indicated in our first-order approximation at the start of this chapter, the Mongol invasion was a repetition of the Oghuz invasion. The elements of nomadic military prowess, invasion, and state formation were present in both. But there were notable contrasts regarding the making of the invasion.

One major difference concerns the order of the elements. In the Oghuz case state formation did not take place in the steppes but rather accompanied the process of invasion. In the Mongol case, by contrast, state formation did take place in the steppes and preceded the invasions that the state went on to organize. This undoubtedly helped bond the nomads of Mongolia to their rulers more tightly than was the case with the Oghuz and the Seljuqs. Combined with the iron discipline that Chingiz Khān succeeded in imposing on his troops, the result was a set of conquests that were centrally planned as much as, if not more than, those of the early Caliphate. Unlike the Oghuz nomads, Mongol soldiers did not wander off at will in search of pasture and plunder. One is thus tempted to say that if the Oghuz invasion showed what steppe nomads could do without really trying, the Mongol invasion was a dramatic demonstration of what could happen if they did try.

Another contrast concerns the location of the nomadic homeland. The Oghuz nomadized in the immediate neighborhood of the Muslim world, and whatever their military superiority, in matters of culture they were a captive audience. In religious terms, the only real alternative to their ancestral paganism was Islam, and it seems they had already adopted it before the invasion began. Something similar was true in wider cultural terms. When the Oghuz found themselves in need of civilization—meaning the sophisticated ways in which things were done in settled societies with urban elites—they had no choice but to call on their Muslim subjects to supply it. The Mongols, by contrast, nomadized in a region hundreds of miles to the east of the Muslim world. Though not on the borders of China, they were considerably closer to it than they were to the Muslim states of the day, and between the Mongols and the Chinese were steppe peoples who had learned to work with the conveniences of Chinese civilization. So when the Mongols invaded the Muslim world they did so as pagans, and when they needed elements of civilization they had more than one option.

The invasion itself, like the Oghuz invasion though in a different style, was in fact a series of events taking place over several decades. There were three phases. The first, in 1219–23, saw Chingiz Khān organize a devastating punitive raid in response to the killing of emissaries and merchants by the Khwārazm-Shāh. The second, starting in 1229, was more of a conquest but involved no leading figure in the Mongol leadership. The third, in 1256–60, was by Mongol standards a more serious affair. Möngke, as supreme ruler of the Mongol Empire, sent his brother Hülegü (ruled 1256–65) with a large body of troops to Iran. Hülegü took possession of it, evenhandedly destroying the Nizārī Ismāʿīlī state in the northern mountains in 1256 and the ʿAbbāsid Caliphate in Baghdad in 1258, in both cases with large-scale slaughter. Sunnī Muslims responded to the first with marked approval and to the second with consternation, demonstrating the continuing symbolic relevance of the Caliphate even in regions where it had long been politically powerless. Meanwhile, Hülegü became the founder of a Mongol dynasty based in Iran. Its rulers were known as the Īlkhāns (1256–1335), and they held sway over Iran, Iraq, and eastern Anatolia.[7] Hülegü and his successors also sought to conquer Syria, but despite some initial success they failed. They seem to have been frustrated by a combination of the distractions of metropolitan Mongol politics, the poverty of Syrian pastureland, and the tenacity of the decades-long defense mounted by the Mamlūk Sultanate from its base in Egypt.

The Īlkhāns

One way to approach the Īlkhāns is to ask how they compare with the Seljuqs, and more broadly how the Mongols of Iran compare with the Oghuz. In some ways the outcomes of the two invasions were rather similar. The Īlkhāns, like the Seljuqs, practiced itinerant kingship in a nomadic style. Just as with the Seljuqs this pattern can be reconstructed from what the sources tell us of the ruler's movements. Thus Öljeitü (ruled 1304–16) nomadized over considerable distances. He built himself a new capital city, Sulṭāniyya, but it was located amid pastureland in a region that was cool in summer, and when present he camped outside the city. Moreover, in the case of the Īlkhāns we are left in no doubt that a Mongol value, and not just a Mongol habit, was at stake. The Mongols liked to hold their assemblies—*qurīltay*s—in five-star meadows; for one held in 1296 they chose a pasture of such quality that they had given it the place-name "Good." An author writing in the first half of the fourteenth century makes this a matter of law: "It is not the rule for Mongols to reside in a city, and it is contrary to the Yāsā of Chingiz Khān"[8]—the "Yāsā of Chingiz Khān" being his law code, to which we will return at the end of this chapter. Such attitudes were widespread among steppe peoples. To take a mid-fifteenth-century example from Central Asia, some commanders in Mogholistān who had rebelled against their Khān explained to him that they had done so "because the Khān was always trying to make us stay in towns and cities";

7. For the Mongols in Iran see J. A. Boyle, "Dynastic and political history of the Īl-Khāns," in *The Cambridge history of Iran*, vol. 5.

8. Quoted in W. Barthold, *Turkestan down to the Mongol invasion*, London 1928, 461 note 5.

they added that it was "more difficult for us to bear towns and cities than to be in prison."[9] The Khān got the message and desisted from such pressure.

The common steppe heritage of the Mongols and the Oghuz was also reflected in the standing of women in Mongol society. We have already encountered Terken Khātūn among the Oghuz and Chingiz Khān's mother Hö'elün among the Mongols, the former negotiating her daughter's marriage and the latter securing the survival of her family in difficult and dangerous circumstances. In the decades following the death of Chingiz Khān women twice ruled the empire as regents, in 1241–46 and again in 1248–51, pending the election of a new ruler. Of course, one reason for this was that women made more acceptable regents than men because they were less likely to exploit the role to usurp the throne. But such arrangements still meant trusting them with real power. More generally, Chingizid women had independent sources of income and entourages of their own, including armed retainers. It was a powerful Mongol woman who was reputed to have dispatched an expedition northward toward the Arctic Ocean in search of silver, led by three of her commanders. As to how Mongol women interacted with their menfolk, a telling vignette relates to Hülegü's siege of Aleppo in 1260. Our informant is a Turkic slave soldier named Özbeg who was in the service of the Syrian prince whom we met as an unhappy guest of Hülegü. Though on the losing side, Özbeg was a survivor. Thanks to his capacity for improvisation, his cheerful extroversion, his readiness to drink wine, and sheer nerve, he got himself invited to appear before Hülegü and made a very good impression. Just like the Bulgar ruler, Hülegü was sitting side by side with his chief wife Doquz Khātūn, a Christian from Mongolia, and she was not the only woman present. Özbeg quickly sensed that in order to stay alive it paid to keep the women amused, which he did with panache. After a while Hülegü sent Özbeg to fetch his master, the Syrian prince, who was fleeing in terror to Egypt. When summoned before Hülegü, the prince—normally a man of considerable courage—was scared out of his wits. But Hülegü asked him what he would like as a present, and on Özbeg's advice the prince asked for the womenfolk of his family to be released to him when the Mongols captured the tower of the citadel of Aleppo, as by now they were sure to do. This was too much for Hülegü, but as Özbeg very likely anticipated, Doquz Khātūn stepped in and shamed him into granting the prince's request. By her standards this was not a big deal: when Baghdad had fallen to the Mongols two years earlier, it was at her insistence that the Christians of the city had been spared, together with those Muslims who had taken refuge with them. That Özbeg had an intuitive understanding of the role of women in Mongol society is not surprising, given that he, too, came from the steppes. The

9. *Mirza Haydar Dughlat's Tarikh-i-Rashidi*, trans. W. M. Thackston, Cambridge, MA 1996, 51a.

famous Moroccan traveler Ibn Baṭṭūṭa, traveling in the steppes north of the Caucasus in the early 1330s, was struck by the respect shown to women by the Turks. He, too, saw the wife of a grandee sitting beside him in public, and he noted that Turkic women did not veil themselves.

One respect in which the Īlkhāns differed from the Seljuqs is that they were slower to take sides in the religious quarrels of their subjects. There was good reason for this. Though conversion began quite early among the Mongols in Iran, many of them remained pagan till the reign of the Īlkhān Ghāzān (ruled 1295–1304). Thus when Hülegü was laid to rest in 1265, he was accompanied in death by human victims—a widespread practice in human history but unthinkable in an Islamic society. Mongol paganism in Iran was reinforced by the fact that for some decades it was still part of a common heritage shared with Mongols in other parts of the empire. Moreover, the power of the Mongols in Iran was such that they did not initially need to set much store by winning the hearts and minds of their subjects. So despite the fact that they ruled an overwhelmingly Muslim population, they were happy to supplement their paganism by experimenting with the full variety of religions available at their court. As a historian of the time puts it, they picked religions according to their inclinations. The Īlkhān Öljeitü (ruled 1304–16) was baptized a Christian, shifted to Buddhism, and then converted to Islam, giving his allegiance first to Sunnism and then to Shīʿism. But the convenience of sharing the convictions of one's subjects eventually prevailed. Ghāzān converted to Islam in 1295, and two years later, at a ceremony staged in Tabrīz, the Mongol elite exchanged their broad-brimmed Mongol hats for Muslim turbans. The violent resistance of conservative Mongols to the conversion was suppressed, though Ghāzān continued to participate in the White Festival that marked the pagan Mongol new year.

We encounter other similarities and differences between the Mongols and the Oghuz when we turn to the sinews of power. When the Mongols conquered Iran, it was not self-evident that the Persian bureaucratic tradition would survive with a simple change of masters, as had been the case under the Seljuqs. At first the leading administrators employed by the Mongols in Iran were not locals but rather members of steppe peoples who had been exposed to Chinese administrative traditions. But in the end it was more convenient to employ Persian bureaucrats who existed in large numbers and were familiar with local conditions, though even there the Īlkhāns differed from the Seljuqs: whereas the face of Persian bureaucracy in Seljuq times was Niẓām al-Mulk, born and bred a Sunnī Muslim, his counterpart under the Īlkhāns was Rashīd al-Dīn (d. 1318), a Jewish convert to Islam.

There is a much starker contrast to be noted when we turn to the army. As we saw, the Seljuqs initially depended on the Turcoman tribesmen but within a few decades were supplementing or replacing them with slave soldiers imported from the steppes. In that way we can see the Seljuqs as assimilating to a standard pattern of military recruitment in the Muslim world of their time. The Īlkhāns did no such thing, and the nomads continued to provide them with the backbone of their armies to the end. In fact, thanks to the Mongols slave soldiers ceased to be in fashion in Iran, and it was another three centuries before they made a significant comeback, only to disappear again in favor of the nomads.

One might have expected the Īlkhāns to prove more successful than the Seljuqs at creating an enduring empire. Their relations with their Mongol nomads were better, they benefited from the discipline that characterized Mongol armies, and they never accommodated rival candidates for the throne by dividing their empire. But like the Seljuqs they had to make do with a fiscally run-down Iraq, and in the long run it may not have helped them that their Mongol constituency tended to fold into the existing Turkic nomadic population of the northern Middle East. In any case, they had dynastic bad luck: the last effective Īlkhān died in 1335 leaving no plausible successor. Thereafter a variety of ineffective Chingizids made claims to legitimacy, including at one point a woman, but within little more than twenty years even that vestige of Mongol legitimacy had disappeared in Iran. Given that nomad rule was to continue there for centuries, this might seem surprising. The explanation is no doubt that there were too few Mongols to spread their political culture to the large number of Turcomans already established in Iran and Anatolia.

The Mongol legacy in Iran

In the end the impact of the Mongols on Iran and the Middle East at large was far smaller than that of the Oghuz. As already noted, Turkey is located in Anatolia, whereas Mongolia remains more or less where it was before the Mongol expansion began. No part of the Middle East today speaks Mongol, though a dialect of the language survived in western Afghanistan down to modern times. In demographic terms, the most the Mongols are likely to have done is to boost the numbers of Turkic nomads in the Middle East and to be assimilated by them. But they did leave a legacy of their own in the field of law that we will take up at the end of this chapter: the "Yāsā of Chingiz Khān" that allegedly forbade Mongols to live in cities.

There was also an unusual historiographical development that was not the work of the Mongols themselves but that could not have happened without them. The Mongol Empire, while it lasted, reached from eastern Europe to China and created sufficient security for long-distance travel to encourage far-flung contacts between widely separated parts of the Old World. And if for a few decades people could journey from one end of Eurasia to the other, so in principle could books. The realization of this potential was nevertheless limited. Western Europeans did not take the opportunity to see what they might gain from the literary tradition of China, nor did the Chinese show any interest in that of western Europe. But things were somewhat different where Iran was concerned.

One field in which traditional Eurasian cultures had long shown a willingness to import alien literature was science. As we have seen, scientific works translated from Greek, Middle Persian, and even Sanskrit were in demand in the ninth-century Muslim Middle East, just as scientific works translated from Arabic were to be well received in twelfth-century Christian Europe. In the same way the Mongol aegis brought scientific literature from Iran to China and from China to Iran. But whereas science was conceived as a cosmopolitan enterprise, historiography in general was not. The Chinese, for example, showed no interest in accessing Arabic or Persian sources on the history of the Muslim world, and the lack of interest was normally reciprocated. It is under Mongol patronage in Iran that we encounter a major exception to the general rule. In part it turned on the fraternal relations between the two Mongol successor states that ruled Iran and China. But it was also more personal. Taking advantage of the long-term presence in Iran of a highly educated Mongol who had previously pursued a successful career in China, the vizier Rashīd al-Dīn developed a quite unusual appreciation of the broad sweep of Chinese culture. He had come to realize, he says, that the Chinese possessed "rules, niceties of speech, truths, clever sayings, and inventions in all spheres of knowledge and art," and that they were "masters in all fields of knowledge." He accordingly set about the translation of "some of their books and histories."[10]

More than that, at the instance of the Īlkhān Öljeitü, Rashīd al-Dīn embarked on a massive collective project for a world history, completed around 1308. In itself the idea of a world history was nothing new. But world historians of premodern times tended to be patchy in their coverage of alien civilizations. As we have seen, Ṭabarī (d. 923) made extensive use of a Middle Persian chronicle in translation when writing about the history of the Sasanian Empire, but for the Roman Empire he had little more than a list of rulers with their dates, despite the fact that in Iraq he could easily have learned more by consulting the local Christians. Moreover, he had almost nothing to say about the histories of China, India, or western Europe. What made Rashīd al-Dīn's project so unusual was the systematic effort to procure and incorporate information from alien sources. Muslim tradition, he averred, was "the most authentic of all," yet "one cannot rely upon it for the history of others."[11] So the work drew on numerous foreign sources made available by informants, and it was in this way that the histories of the Chinese, the Indians, the Jews, and the Franks were included in a single vast work. He was not entirely evenhanded in his attitude to the various peoples: whereas he was fascinated by

10. Quoted in K. Jahn, "Rashīd al-Dīn and Chinese culture," *Central Asiatic Journal*, 14 (1970), 140, 147.

11. Quoted in T. T. Allsen, *Culture and conquest in Mongol Eurasia*, Cambridge 2001, 84.

Chinese culture, nothing suggests a comparable interest in that of the Franks. But all told, the work was a remarkable historiographical achievement, and one has to wonder how it could have been completed by someone occupied in running an empire. The answer is not far to seek. Without acknowledging it, Rashīd al-Dīn was plagiarizing the work of a certain ʿAbdallāh Qāshānī, a less powerful literary figure at Öljeitü's court. This Qāshānī took his revenge in his historical writing by highlighting Rashīd al-Dīn's Jewish background and insinuating that his conversion to Islam had been insincere.

Iran from the Mongols to the Qājārs

Between the Mongols and the Tīmūrids

We now enter upon a long period of disunity stretching from the fade-out of the Īlkhāns after 1335 to the triumph of the Ṣafawids in 1501. This disunity was, however, punctuated by three transitory imperial moments. The first of these lasted only a couple of decades, from the 1380s to 1405, and was the work of Tīmūr, who was based in Central Asia. But before we come to him, we should glance at the political fragmentation of Iran in the decades from the 1330s to the 1380s.

In some ways this post-Mongol period of disunity was similar to the post-Seljuq period. Again the primary contenders were insiders—that is to say, men who had been closely involved in the imperial state that was now fragmenting. Two of them, known as "Little Ḥasan" and "Big Ḥasan," were Mongol generals contending for the heritage of the Īlkhāns, and both established dynasties. Little Ḥasan founded the short-lived Chobanid dynasty (1335–57)—"Choban" being a Turkic word for "shepherd." Big Ḥasan established the longer-lived Jalāyirid dynasty (1340–1432). Even more than in the post-Seljuq period, the prize at stake in their conflict was Azerbaijan: the Jalāyirids finally won it in 1359 but then lost it to Tīmūr in 1386. Thereafter the Jalāyirids tended to become increasingly irrelevant. For a while their capital was Baghdad, where they do not seem to have been popular, and they ended up as local rulers in southern Iraq. In analogy with the post-Seljuq period, there were also opportunities for non-Mongols who had been in service with the Īlkhāns. The leading example was the Muẓaffarid dynasty (1314–93), which stemmed from an Iranian family claiming Arab descent. They were based in Fārs and ruled much of southern and western Iran; at one point they even took Tabrīz, but they failed to hold it.

As in the post-Seljuq period, there were also some significant outsiders. In eastern Anatolia—very much part of the empire of the Īlkhāns in its heyday—two major dynasties emerged in roughly the same period among the Turcoman nomads of the region. One dynasty was the Qara Qoyunlu (1380–1468) and the other the Aq Qoyunlu (1378–1508); appropriately, the names of these dynasties associate them with black sheep and white sheep, respectively, and we will return to them. But in general, the mix of new dynasties in the post-Mongol period was broadly similar to that found in the post-Seljuq period.

There is, however, a major difference: numbers. In the post-Seljuq period we were looking at something like a score of successor dynasties—almost as many as we encounter in the post-ʿAbbāsid period. In the post-Mongol period the number was down to half a dozen. The count is somewhat arbitrary, as will become evident later in this chapter, but the contrast is unmistakable. It is not immediately obvious to what we should attribute it. What is interesting is that the decrease in the number of states in times of disunity proved to be permanent. Never again, unless perhaps in the early twentieth century, would Iran experience the degree of political fragmentation that characterized the post-ʿAbbāsid and post-Seljuq periods. This perhaps has something to do with the mobility of steppe nomads as opposed to more pedestrian armies, though on that basis one would have expected the change to show up already in the post-Seljuq period.

The Tīmūrids

We come now to the fleeting imperial moment associated with the rise of Tīmūr (ruled 1370–1405).[12] The core of his troops was made up of the nomads of Transoxania, the western part of the Chaghatay Khānate; they included Mongol tribes, like Tīmūr's own tribe of Barlas, though by now they were effectively Turkic. These were very much steppe nomads. Tīmūr's followers still wore pigtails like the heathen Mongols, and his womenfolk would attend banquets unveiled. So from the Iranian point of view, as with the Oghuz and Mongol invasions, we have to do with steppe nomads coming from the northeast. But like the Oghuz they were already Muslim, and unlike either the Oghuz or the Mongols they started from a region with a major settled population, rural and urban, one that had been within the frontiers of the Muslim world for centuries. Thus in a phrase introduced in the previous chapter, these were internal nomads.

As we have seen, the process by which Tīmūr began the recruitment of his military following was what was soon to be called *qazaqlïq*. His first bid for power within his own tribe took place in 1360. By 1370 he was the ruler of Transoxania, with Samarqand as his capital, though his position was an insecure one in the face of the intrigues and defections of the tribal leaders. He solved this problem partly by turning the energies of the nomads outward, initially against other parts of Central Asia, and partly by replacing their leaders with a new and less fractious military elite. In the 1380s he directed much of his attention to the Middle East,

12. For Tīmūr see B. F. Manz, *The rise and rule of Tamerlane*, Cambridge 1989; and for the Tīmūrids see M. E. Subtelny, *Timurids in transition*, Leiden 2007.

including Azerbaijan; in 1387 he was in Kurdistan, as well as Iṣfahān and Shīrāz; in 1393 it was the turn of Baghdad; in 1400–1401 he was in Syria sacking Damascus; and in 1402 he defeated the Ottomans in Anatolia at the battle of Ankara and campaigned as far as Smyrna on the west coast. But his campaigns were by no means confined to Central Asia and the Middle East. A northern campaign of 1394–96 took him to Moscow and an Indian campaign of 1398–99 to Delhi—he sacked Delhi but not Moscow. Back in Samarqand near the end of his life he held a *qurīltay* and prepared for a campaign against China that never took place. The whole performance is reminiscent of Alexander the Great—tourism as world conquest. But his role model was no doubt Chingiz Khān, the world conqueror to whose descendants he still deferred as late as 1402 by maintaining one of them as a puppet Khān and ruling in his name. Like Chingiz Khān he had a loyal and disciplined army once he had sidelined the old tribal leadership. But many of his campaigns, including his excursions to Russia, India, Syria, and Anatolia, were raids rather than conquests. In Anatolia, for example, he inflicted a crushing defeat on the Ottoman sultan but used it not to annex Ottoman territory but rather to return it to the Turcoman dynasties that had previously ruled it. Nevertheless, his invasion of Iran looks like a clear case of empire building.

With all this activity Tīmūr founded a dynasty that lasted until 1507. But it was not quite an imperial dynasty in the manner of the early Seljuqs and the Īlkhāns. The most immediate reason for this was that Tīmūr and his descendants resembled the Seljuqs—and not, for example, the ʿAbbāsids or the Īlkhāns—in their propensity to divide their territories in the course of their struggles with each other. At the time there were two key centers of nomad power in the region, Transoxania in the east and Azerbaijan in the west, but by 1408 Azerbaijan, where Tīmūrid roots were shallower, was for the most part lost to the dynasty. Thereafter the Tīmūrids were firmly established in Transoxania and Khurāsān, where their major cities were respectively Samarqand and Herat. The political cultures of the two cities were somewhat different: in Samarqand we still hear of puppet Chingizid Khāns, but nobody bothered with them in Herat. The Tīmūrids did extend their power to much of western Iran, but here both their failure to hold Azerbaijan and the familiar point about the fiscal degradation of Iraq were significant constraints. A final point concerns the relationship of the dynasty to the nomads on whom it drew for military support. Chingiz Khān had a tight and energizing relationship to a particular ethnic group, the Mongols; he was their leader, they were his people, and for a while at least his successors benefited from this. In Tīmūr's case the relationship was not as strong. His nomadic followers were identified as Chaghatays, and one of them once displayed a fine sense of Chaghatay ethnic pride in an interaction with an Özbeg. But in general membership of the Chaghatay people does not seem to have been a very salient or resilient identity, partly perhaps because Tīmūr had drastically diluted it by deporting militarily useful tribes to

Transoxania from the regions he conquered. For sure there is no Chaghatay people in the world today, though there were still tribes that bore the name at the end of the nineteenth century. In sum, the Tīmūrids were unable to sustain their imperial stature. But that is not to say that they no longer mattered.

One way in which they mattered was cultural. Like the political and military elites of Seljuq and Mongol times, that of the Tīmūrids had its roots among the nomads of the steppes. Tīmūr himself was illiterate, and his son Shāh Rukh (ruled 1405–47) still retained a nomadic lifestyle—when at his capital, Herat, he always stayed in gardens and tents outside the city, not in an urban palace. But by this time the Tīmūrid elite was a culturally sophisticated one, considerably more so than its earlier counterparts had been, and appropriately familiar with the Arabic and Persian literary heritages. Steppe roots and sedentary sophistication now came together in the rise of the Turkic literary language often known as Chaghatay. It was a Muslim language, typically written in the Arabic script and with a generous admixture of Arabic and Persian loanwords. The celebrated poet Nawāʾī (d. 1501) wrote a short work in Persian with the object of making Turks more aware of the riches of their language and freeing them from the taunts of Persian speakers. Turkic, he sought to demonstrate with numerous examples, was more expressive than Persian. He wrote these examples in the Arabic script, but as we have seen, Chaghatay could also be written in the non-Muslim Uighur script, thereby signaling continuity with the pre-Islamic past of the steppes. Half a dozen such texts are extant from the lands ruled by the Tīmūrids, dating from between 1431 and 1493; that of 1493 is dated "Year of the Monkey," followed by more precise details according to the Muslim calendar. This cult of the Uighur script was of a piece with the value attached to *qazaqlïq* and the principle of Chingizid legitimacy. All this bespeaks an assumption that Islam, however much it mattered, was by no means everything one should care about. Bābur (d. 1530), the Tīmūrid who was to found the Mughal Empire in India, left an autobiography in Chaghatay in which he gives vivid sketches of the personal characteristics of some of his many relatives—how much they drank, what kind of sex they preferred, what their wives and concubines were like, and so forth. In the same vein he tells us about their religious proclivities or lack of them. How often did they pray? Did they pray even while drinking? Did they incline to Sunnism or Shīʿism, or were they just irreligious? Typically he does not present these proclivities as politically significant. Instead, he seems to take it for granted that religion, like liquor and sex, is a matter of a man's personal taste, and not something on which he would build his politics. We can plausibly see this as an aspect of the Mongol heritage: Öljeitü's romp through Christianity, Buddhism, and two brands of Islam likewise looks more like a personal than a political odyssey. But religion did intrude into politics—for example, Shāh Rukh was a strong promoter of Sunnism—and it would do so far more with the coming of the Ṣafawids.

The Turcoman dynasties

While Tīmūr and the Tīmūrids dominated in the east, the most significant dynasties in the west were the Qara Qoyunlu (1380–1468) and the Aq Qoyunlu (1378–1508), also known in the context of the history of Iran as the Turcoman dynasties.[13] As already mentioned, they arose among the Turcoman tribes of eastern Anatolia. Thus the Aq Qoyunlu were proud members of Bayïndïr, one of the twenty-four Oghuz clans that had been known since the eleventh century. The basis of the power of these dynasties was a pattern of long-distance nomadism of a kind much more typical of Turcomans than of their more localized Kurdish neighbors. The Qara Qoyunlu spent their summers around Lake Van and their winters in the region of Mosul, while farther to the west the Aq Qoyunlu spent their summers around Erzinjān and their winters in the region of Mardin on the plains of northern Mesopotamia. Had the rule of these dynasties remained confined to these regions, we would have no reason to include them in an account of the history of Iran. But in each case an energetic and aggressive ruler embarked on a process of expansion that won his dynasty an imperial phase. It happened first in 1446–67 with the Qara Qoyunlu, their imperial ruler being Jahān Shāh (ruled 1434–67), and then in 1467–78 with the Aq Qoyunlu, for whom it was Uzun Ḥasan (ruled 1457–78). Each time possession of Azerbaijan was crucial to the expansive effort, and in each case the ruler in question projected his power far enough east to intervene against the Tīmūrids in Khurāsān but not far enough to displace them there, let alone in Transoxania. As their dates make clear, the two Turcoman dynasties were in competition, despite a sense of shared identity strong enough for one Qara Qoyunlu ruler to make a fruitless appeal to it; it was the Aq Qoyunlu who ended the rule of the Qara Qoyunlu after defeating and killing Jahān Shāh in 1467. The imperial expansion of the Aq Qoyunlu, however, was not terminated by a rival nomad dynasty. Instead it was the Ottomans with their infantry and firearms who inflicted a crushing defeat on Uzun Ḥasan in 1473. He nevertheless survived with little loss of territory, and after his death the dynasty continued in some fashion, though fragmenting into three principalities. It was the Ṣafawids who finally put an end to it in 1508.

Like the Tīmūrids, the Qara Qoyunlu and Aq Qoyunlu kept faith with the nomad values of the steppes. As the Aq Qoyunlu ruler Qara Yoluq ʿUthmān (ruled 1403–35) put it in his testament, "Don't let it happen that you become settled. Rulership stays with those who live as Turcomans and nomads."[14] Tīmūr would have agreed. Around 1400 he wrote to a subordinate in western Iran about two rulers in the area: "Aḥmad Jalāyir has acquired the temperament of a Tājīk, so there

13. For the Aq Qoyunlu see J. E. Woods, *The Aqquyunlu*, rev. ed., Salt Lake City 1999.
14. Quoted in J. E. Woods, *The Aqquyunlu*, Minneapolis 1976, 249 note 115.

is little need to worry about him. But keep a close watch on Qara Yūsuf the Turcoman."[15] A Tājīk is a settled Iranian, and as such does not have to be taken seriously in political or military terms; Aḥmad might stem from the Mongol tribe of Jalāyir, but in Tīmūr's view he had gone soft. By contrast, Qara Yūsuf (ruled ca. 1390–1400 and 1406–20) was the reigning member of the Qara Qoyunlu dynasty and an authentic nomad for whom even Tīmūr had a grudging respect. "I am from the Turcoman people," Qara Yūsuf is said to have remarked; "my summer residence is Ala Dagh ("Many-Colored Mountain," northeast of Lake Van) and my winter residence is Diyār Bakr and the banks of the Euphrates."[16] These dynasties showed no tendency to become sedentary with the passage of time. In the late fifteenth century a Persian author still praised the Aq Qoyunlu for not being town dwellers affected by dirty habits. Instead they followed the seasons, wandering in open spaces—winter pastures and summer pastures. (In this connection we should not forget that the nomads had a point: in the absence of modern methods of sewage disposal, urban civilization did not merely stink; it was bad for your health.) As with the Tīmūrids, these nomad values carry the suggestion that Islam may not be everything, but here we lack intimate portraits of the kind Bābur provides for his Tīmūrid relatives. A religious difference can nevertheless be detected between the two dynasties. Whereas the Aq Qoyunlu had a reputation for orthodoxy, the Qara Qoyunlu were known for heterodoxy. Yet the dynasties did not base their politics on these allegiances, and their divergent religious orientations did not figure in the conflicts between them.

Although we lack colorful historical accounts of these dynasties, we are fortunate to possess a fictional substitute—a collection of stories from the right place and time, the "Book of Dede Qorqud." These stories recount the valiant deeds of Oghuz heroes, but our interest is not in the deeds themselves but rather in the character of the society that appears in the background to them. It is not a flat society, still less a stateless society: there are nobles and rulers. This again reflects the relative affluence of steppe nomadism, the presence of "the green field, the beautiful meadow."[17] But the ruler's relationship to his nobles is not that of an autocrat to his minions. One story turns on a custom whereby every three years the ruler would allow his nobles to pillage his tent. Horses are ubiquitous, and as in Bilgä Qaghan's inscription the color of a horse is regularly mentioned. One young hero, Beyrek, addresses a poem to his gray horse, telling him, "I shall not call you 'horse' but 'brother'—and better than any brother." Booty bulks large. And in traditional steppe fashion, women are out in the open. The same young hero,

15. Quoted in F. Sümer, *Kara Koyunlular*, Ankara 1984, 1:67 note 187.

16. Quoted in P. Wing, *The Jalayirids*, Edinburgh 2016, 171.

17. For this and the quotations that follow see *The Book of Dede Korkut*, trans. G. Lewis, London 1974, 64, 74, 188.

while out hunting, has a chivalrous interaction with Lady Chichek, a princess who is camping in a red tent with her female attendants. When Beyrek asks to see the princess, she pretends to be one of her attendants and tells him that "the Lady Chichek is not the sort of person to show herself to you." Instead, she proposes that the two of them ride out together, shooting their bows, racing their horses, and wrestling. "If you beat me in these three, you will beat her too," she tells him. He wins the shooting, the horse racing, and—by the skin of his teeth—the wrestling match. Thrown on her back, she now reveals who she is, whereupon Beyrek kisses her three times and bites her once. At this point Lady Chichek prudently ends the interaction; after all, they are not yet married. All this is not *quite* as risqué as it sounds because the couple had apparently been betrothed in the cradle, but the sensibility displayed here would not have reassured Ibn Faḍlān. Islam is indeed present in this society. There is hostility to unbelievers, and toward the end of the story Beyrek and his thirty-nine warriors destroy a church, kill its priests, and erect a mosque in its place. But religion plays no discernible role in the society's internal politics. People swear oaths on the Qurʾān, but we do not see them opening it or reciting it.

Stepping back for a moment, we notice that in the period of disunity between Tīmūr and the Ṣafawids Iran was dominated by no more than three dynasties—fewer even than in the immediate post-Mongol period. This is a little misleading in that the Tīmūrids had a tendency to divide their territories, so that Transoxania and Khurāsān were often in different hands, and at times when conflict within the dynasty was acute, as in 1457, there might be half a dozen princes ensconced in different cities. But there is no comparison with the degree of fragmentation that characterized the post-ʿAbbāsid and post-Seljuq periods.

The Ṣafawids to the later sixteenth century

We come now to the Ṣafawids (1501–1722).[18] They are not what we might have expected at this juncture in the history of Iran. If we were looking for a new imperial state to arise there, the historical record as of 1500 would lead us to expect a nomadic conquest from the northeast. And sure enough, it was around then that the Özbegs conquered Transoxania and went on to occupy Khurāsān. But they failed to hold it, let alone to expand further into Iran. Instead, their main contribution to Iranian history was a pattern of persistent raiding that continued into the eighteenth century and led in turn to the formation of a considerable population of enslaved Iranians in Central Asia. That left the nomads of eastern Anatolia to step into the breach and create a new imperial state. But as we have seen, they

18. For surveys of their history see R. Savory, *Iran under the Safavids*, Cambridge 1980, and H. R. Roemer, "The Safavid period," in *The Cambridge history of Iran*, vol. 6.

had already failed twice. Moreover, their geopolitical situation, and that of Iran in general, was now deteriorating sharply. From the time when the Oghuz nomads had overrun the Anatolian provinces of the Byzantine Empire in the mid-eleventh century until the rise of the Ottoman Empire some three or four centuries later, there had been no imperial state to the west of Iran. Now there was one, and its armies, with their infantry core and extensive use of firearms on the battlefield, were very different from anything the Middle East had known in the preceding centuries. The age of the cavalry was finally slipping away, and steppe cavalry armies were now at some risk of becoming obsolete. We saw what happened to Uzun Ḥasan in 1473, but that was nothing to what was fated to happen in 1514. In that year the Ottoman army inflicted a crushing defeat on the first Ṣafawid ruler, in the aftermath of which the Ottomans took over eastern Anatolia and effectively put an end to the role of its nomads in state formation. The Ṣafawids had indeed come to power by mobilizing the eastern Anatolian Turcomans in the early years of the sixteenth century, but they did so at what was virtually the last moment in history at which such a strategy could have succeeded, and their success was to be seriously undercut by the Ottoman menace to their west.

If the timing of the rise of the Ṣafawids seems a bit unlikely, the manner in which they mobilized their Turcoman following was by the standards of steppe nomads quite extraordinary. We are familiar with the Ibn Khaldūnian mode of state formation among Arab and Berber tribes, and its prominence there makes sense. As we have seen, it provided a way around the constraints of the resource-poor environment of the arid lands of the southern Middle East and North Africa, a setting in which the normal processes by which powerful kingdoms emerge had less chance of success. This kind of state formation had also been present in remote regions of Iran during the early centuries of Islam; for example, there had been a Khārijite imamate in Sīstān and Shīʿite imamates among the Zaydīs in the mountains south of the Caspian. The Zaydīs, unlike the Khārijites, continued their political tradition in Iran well into late medieval times, and they were joined in the late eleventh century by the Nizārīs. But all such statelets arose among the indigenous Iranian population; so far we have seen no example of Ibn Khaldūnian state formation among steppe nomads. The closest parallel would be a major revolt fomented around 1240 among the Turcomans of Anatolia by a heterodox preacher with claims to prophethood. But this was suppressed, and no state was formed. Thus the Ṣafawids are the only exception among steppe nomads, but a major one.

There was also something unusual about the Ṣafawid family. In contrast to all the steppe nomad dynasties we have been concerned with in this and the previous chapter, the family itself was of sedentary stock. Probably of Kurdish origin, they lived in the town of Ardabīl in the northwest of Azerbaijan. We could describe them as ethnically Iranian—Tājīks, as people would have said at the time—though inasmuch as they claimed descent from the Prophet they were genealogically Arabs. Since the first half of the fourteenth century they had been the hereditary leaders of a Ṣūfī order based in Ardabīl. For a century or so the Ṣafawid order was innocuously Sunnī and showed no signs of dangerous political ambitions. This was unsurprising, since state formation was not something that leaders of Ṣūfī orders normally engaged in, nor was it felt to be appropriate for them. Despite occasional exceptions, if they played politics, they usually did so by exercising influence through their relations with the rulers of already existing states. The powerful Ṣūfī Khwāja Aḥrār (d. 1490) in Tīmūrid Samarqand, for example, saw himself as an intermediary between the people and their rulers. But toward the middle of the fifteenth century the Ṣafawid order took a very different turn. From 1447 to 1459, Junayd, the leader of the order, left Ardabīl and wandered among the Turcoman tribes. In addition to acquiring an Aq Qoyunlu bride, he seems to have achieved success in spreading the order among nomads who very likely had heterodox religious inclinations. From now on the order was associated with extreme religious beliefs of a kind most familiar from the fringes of Shīʿism. For example, we are told that Junayd was regarded by his followers as divine, and that he freed them from the yoke of the religious law. The marker of membership in the movement was a red headgear, and the followers of the Ṣafawid order thus came to be known as Qizilbāsh, Turkic for "Redheads." At the same time the order started to make war—again something leaders of Ṣūfī orders usually left to the rulers of the day. The hostilities were directed in the first instance against the Christians of the Caucasus, but in 1460 Junayd was killed in battle against a Muslim ruler in the region, and the same thing happened to another leader of the order in 1488. To them it was jihad, but had these Ṣafawids been worldly princes we might well have called their lifestyle *qazaqlïq*. Meanwhile, the movement was clearly continuing its efforts to secure the loyalty of a large Turcoman following. These efforts extended far to the west, into central and even western Anatolia, a thousand miles from Ardabīl. All this territory was in the hands of the Qara Qoyunlu, the Aq Qoyunlu, and the Ottomans, and none of them can have been fully aware what was brewing among their subjects.

The disasters of 1460 and 1488 did nothing to diminish the Ṣafawid taste for adventure. The next serious bid for power came in 1499, when the leader of the order was the future Shāh Ismāʿīl I (ruled 1501–24)—though at the time he was still an adolescent, so the key decisions may well have been taken by those around him. He met up with his Turcoman followers near Erzinjān in eastern Anatolia, and in 1501 they seized Azerbaijan—still the key province of western Iran—and Ismāʿīl was duly crowned in Tabrīz. From there he extended his power to the rest of Iran, eastern Anatolia, and Iraq. The dynasty then continued to rule, or at least to reign, until 1722. This certainly sounds like a success story, and in obvious ways it was. No other dynasty since the Sasanians had held Iran together and ruled it for so long. But there were serious limits to the Ṣafawid achievement. To see what they were, let us consider the problems of the first century of Ṣafawid rule.

For much of the sixteenth century their enemies denied the Ṣafawids the enjoyment of two key provinces. One was Khurāsān, formerly the agricultural basis of the Tīmūrid state in Herat. Though it was Ṣafawid territory, it was persistently ravaged and its resources were degraded by Özbeg incursions; between 1524 and 1538, for example, there were no fewer than five Özbeg invasions. Another key province was Azerbaijan, the core territory of most successful states in western Iran since the twelfth century. The Ottomans occupied it in 1514, though not for long, and despite further periods of Ottoman occupation in the late sixteenth and early eighteenth centuries, it remained for the most part in the possession of the rulers of Iran. But again its resources were degraded—this time by the Ṣafawids themselves, seeking to deter Ottoman invasion through a scorched earth policy. It was the Ottoman threat, and their response to it, that led the Ṣafawids to move their capital from Tabrīz to Qazwīn and later to Iṣfahān, five hundred miles to the east and south. A third province worth considering in this context is Iraq, though it no longer mattered much. Initially it formed part of the Ṣafawid domains, the last instance of the old rule of thumb that anyone ruling western Iran could help himself to Iraq. But in 1534–35 the Ottomans conquered Iraq, and apart from an interlude in 1623–38 they held it for the rest of the Ṣafawid period. That a state based far away in Istanbul could take and hold Iraq against its immediate neighbor in Iran says something about Ottoman strength, but it is also a testimony to Ṣafawid weakness. Iran under Ṣafawid rule was still Iran, but it was an Iran with clipped wings.

The weakness of the Ṣafawid state was not just a matter of material deprivation. Its military basis was increasingly dysfunctional in ways reminiscent of the problems of the later Mamlūk Sultanate. One point here was the obsolescence of Ṣafawid armies when pitted against the Ottomans. This was behind the loss of eastern Anatolia and Iraq and the degradation of Azerbaijan. A second point was that the prime territories from which the Ṣafawids had recruited their Turcoman troops were now far away and under the rule of a state that had turned predictably hostile toward a population that it saw as a fifth column loyal to an alien power. Moreover, the Turcoman troops of the Ṣafawids were organized in tribal groupings reflecting their regions of origin to the west: the Tekelü were those who had wintered in the land of Teke on the southern coast of Anatolia, the Shāmlu those who had wintered in northern Syria (Shām), and so on. These groups were bonded to their Ṣafawid rulers by strong religious ties, but they were not bonded to each other. In the aftermath of the death of Shāh Ismāʿīl, the founder of the dynasty, his Turcomans spent the years from 1524 to 1533 in quarrels with each other that degenerated into outright civil war. Eventually Ismāʿīl's successor Ṭahmāsp (ruled 1524–76) was able to stabilize the situation, but there was to be more trouble after his death. Before we continue the story, however, we need to attend to the single largest change that Ṣafawid rule brought to Iran: the conversion of the core population of the country to Shīʿism.

The conversion of Iran to Shīʿism

Iran in 1501 was still predominantly Sunnī, despite the existence here and there of small Shīʿite populations of various kinds. The Ṣafawid conquest thus created a tense situation: a small minority with extreme Shīʿite proclivities was now politically dominant over a large Sunnī majority. One option for the new rulers would have been simply to accept a continuing religious division between rulers and ruled, as the Fāṭimids had once done in Egypt. Another would have been to adopt the Sunnism of the majority. The Ṣafawids did in fact try this at one point, in the brief reign of Ismāʿīl II (ruled 1576–78), but given how central their heterodoxy had been to their rise to power, such a break was unlikely to prove successful—this being one of the inconveniences of the religious mode of state formation. A third option might have been for the Ṣafawids to impose their heterodox beliefs on their subjects. But this would have been a tall order. In one of his Turkic poems, for example, Shāh Ismāʿīl I rejects the divinely revealed scriptures on the ground that all authority is vested in his person. In others he calls for his followers to prostrate themselves before him, describing himself as divine and even as "God Himself." Wisely, the Ṣafawids kept such views to themselves. What they did do, beginning already on the morrow of the capture of Tabrīz, was to adopt a more mainstream form of Shīʿism as the religion of the state and to impose that on their subjects. This was Imāmī or Twelver Shīʿism, the most widespread of the Shīʿite sects. It possessed a well-developed literary tradition that included an essential component of the governance of an Islamic society: a comprehensive version of Islamic law. But to institutionalize Imāmī Shīʿism in Iran required people as well as books, and the Ṣafawids found it necessary to import significant numbers of Imāmī scholars from Syria and Baḥrayn.

We are not well informed about the measures by which the Ṣafawids imposed Imāmī Shīʿism on Iran, but it is clear that they were not gentle, and that by the time the dynasty was overthrown by an Afghan invasion in 1722, they had largely succeeded. The Afghan invaders were Sunnīs, and the years during which they ruled Iran were a time when any remaining Sunnīs in the country could safely stand up and be counted. A few did so; notably, there was still a Persian-speaking Sunnī population in the remote region of Lāristān in the south of Iran, and it is there to this day. There were also Persian-speaking populations to the east of Iran that remained Sunnī, and within Iran there were non-Persian ethnic groups, such as the Kurds in the west and the Balūchīs in the southeast, that likewise retained their Sunnism. But the core Persian-speaking population of the country was by now almost entirely Shīʿite. Iran thus became the first and largest country in which Shīʿites were both politically and demographically dominant. One effect of this was to set it apart from the Muslim world at large, a development that gave Iran a certain coherence at the cost of poisoning its relations with its neighbors. This toxicity was not inevitable. When it suited them, as it did in the later seventeenth century, the Ottomans could treat the Ṣafawids as fellow Muslims. But religious attitudes could have drastic implications: when the Özbegs raided Khurāsān, they claimed an Islamic justification for enslaving their captives. Another effect of the conversion was to raise the profile of sectarian allegiance within Iranian society. It could no longer be a matter of personal taste, as it had been in considerable measure for Bābur's relatives. But Sir John Chardin (d. 1713), a French Protestant who came to know Iran well in the second half of the seventeenth century, still praised the Persians for their religious toleration—though he made an exception for the clergy, "who, as in all other places, hate to a furious degree, all those that differ from their opinions."[19] Here "all other places" certainly included his own country, where Catholic toleration of Protestantism ended in 1685, resulting in a large-scale exodus of French Protestants like himself.

The Ṣafawids from the later sixteenth century

In the face of the troubles of the later sixteenth century, and the material and military problems associated with them, the long-term prospects of the Ṣafawid state looked dim. Indeed, in the later 1570s and 1580s it gave the impression of being on its last legs. In addition to the turmoil within the country, the Ottomans invaded in 1578 and again took Tabrīz, while the Özbegs occupied Khurāsān. But the tide was turned by the long and forceful reign of Shāh ʿAbbās I (ruled 1587–1629). At the core of his success was military reform. While he did not entirely rid himself of the dynasty's traditional Turcoman troops, he sidelined them by forming a new kind of army, or rather reviving an old one. Since the Mongol invasion nobody of consequence in Iran had fought wars using armies composed of military slaves. Moreover, the old practice of importing enslaved steppe nomads was no longer viable, since the spread of Islam in the steppes meant that there were no longer enough non-Muslim nomads within reach. What Shāh ʿAbbās did was to take advantage of a long-established Ṣafawid practice of raiding the Christians of the Caucasus and of the supply of slaves this gave rise to. He set about enrolling Caucasian slaves—notably Georgians—in his armies as cavalry on a large scale. In this way he successfully reduced his dependence on his Turcoman horsemen, though he did not dispense with them altogether; they were still there when the

19. Sir John Chardin, *Travels in Persia*, London 1927, 185.

dynasty fell in 1722. But he was also clearly aware of the role of infantry and firearms in the Ottoman army, and he worked to create equivalent bodies of troops in Iran, retaining the services of an English adventurer. The use of firearms was not unprecedented in the region—there had been some recourse to them as early as the late fifteenth century among the Aq Qoyunlu and even the Ṣafawids. In 1528 such artillery as the Ṣafawids possessed gave them the edge in a battle against the Özbegs. But ʿAbbās's emphasis on firearms was new, and his military reforms led to considerable military success. Exploiting the weakness of his neighbors, including at this time the Ottomans, ʿAbbās slowly recovered much of the territory the Ṣafawids had lost, evicting first the Özbegs from Khurāsān and then the Ottomans from Azerbaijan. He even took the city of Āmid, deep inside Ottoman territory, and for a few years recovered Baghdad, lost to the Ottomans in 1534.

While Shāh ʿAbbās was ruling Iran, one of his bureaucrats, Iskandar Beg Munshī, was quietly composing a history of the Ṣafawids. Its two main components are an account of the earlier history of the dynasty and a year-by-year chronicle of the reign of ʿAbbās. The years are named according to the twelve-year animal cycle—the Turkic years, as he calls them. He chooses to use them because the Hijrī years would be lost on "most of the people of Iran."[20] Indeed, use of the Turkic years continued in Iran into the twentieth century. In between the two components he inserts a section on the personal qualities and achievements of ʿAbbās. Unsurprisingly what he has to say is overwhelmingly positive, not to say eulogistic. But this bias has an incidental reward for us: it lets us know what things this author and his prospective audience valued in a ruler. Many of these turn out to be qualities that any of us would appreciate in a ruler today, including good judgment, the ability to detect liars, knowledge of other rulers and countries, and effectiveness in maintaining order and dealing with bandits. A few of the qualities Iskandar Beg dwells on might surprise us. He values his ruler's powers of innovation, which goes against our image of premodern societies as resolutely conservative. He likewise sets high store by the ability of ʿAbbās to speak to people of all classes in their own idiom—a skill we might have thought of as relatively unimportant in the absence of democratic politics. A number of Iskandar Beg's values would appeal to some more than to others at the present day. If we take as our baseline the contemporary politics of the United States, some of his values would appeal particularly to old-fashioned Republicans: victories over enemies, a good intelligence system, not seizing the inheritances of one's subjects, and tax holidays (though the limitation of these to Shīʿites in the month of Ramaḍān would be problematic). Others would appeal more to Democrats: an emphasis on public works and infrastructure, help-

20. Quoted in R. D. McChesney, "A note on Iskandar Beg's chronology," *Journal of Near Eastern Studies*, 39 (1980), 56.

ing the needy, and a war on poverty (though the limitation of this to the descendants of the Prophet might seem unduly elitist). But while much that looked good in Iran four hundred years ago still looks good in the United States today, there are some significant shifts. First, the supernatural is not what it used to be. Divine inspiration and astrological good fortune mattered a lot to Iskandar Beg but are marginal as qualifications for rulership in most countries today. Second, family values are no longer what they were. We have ceased to look favorably on rewarding faithful service with hereditary offices. Finally, the citizens of advanced countries are significantly less willing today to put up with harsh government for the sake of public order. Despotic behavior, towering rages, and the infliction of cruel and unusual punishments are no longer seen as the price that has to be be paid to keep anarchy at bay. But if we were to take as our baseline the politics of contemporary Russia, we would soon encounter attitudes noticeably closer to those of Iskandar Beg than to our own—attitudes that in context may be fully rational. Four hundred years is not a very long time.

The reforms and campaigns of Shāh ʿAbbās secured a few decades of relative strength for Ṣafawid Iran despite the disadvantages of its situation. But this strength was not sustained, particularly after the death of his namesake ʿAbbās II (ruled 1642–66). One reason for this was a change made by Shāh ʿAbbās himself. Like so many dynastic rulers, he faced a dilemma with regard to his sons. He could send a son out to govern a province, in which case the son would have the opportunity to learn how to govern. Such a prince might in due course be well qualified to succeed to the throne. But given that he now had a political and military base of his own, there was always the danger that he might prematurely seek the throne by rebelling against his father. The alternative for a ruler such as Shāh ʿAbbās was to keep his sons under his watchful eye at court or confined in the harem. That lessened the risk that they would rebel, but depriving them of relevant experience and opportunities made for feeble successors. Shāh ʿAbbās started by taking the first course, but after one of his sons rebelled he switched to the second. That the Ṣafawids nevertheless survived until 1722 is mainly a reflection of the weakness of their foreign enemies and the absence of serious domestic rivals. These circumstances, in turn, would seem to have arisen in large measure from good luck, for as we will see when we come to the eighteenth century there was no lack of hostile forces in and around Iran that were waiting to be unleashed. But before we come to the fall of the Ṣafawid dynasty and the chaos that ensued, we should take a look at Iran's relations with the wider world.

One thing that struck Chardin about the people he encountered in Iran was a marked parochialism. The Persians, he says, are "grossly ignorant of the present state of other nations of the world." He describes this ignorance as extending to the highest levels: "The ministers of state generally speaking, know no more what passes in Europe, than in the world of the moon."[21] Chardin wrote at a time when a traveler could safely describe most foreign peoples without running the risk that they might read what he had written about them. But he was by no means a relentless critic of the Persians, and there were many things for which he praised them. As we have seen, he liked their tolerant attitude toward religions other than their own. His testimony nevertheless stands in striking contrast to the wide horizons of Rashīd al-Dīn's Iran over four centuries earlier. It might also seem surprising in view of the increasing contacts between Iran and a world that was beginning to be globalized. In 1753 a Dutch baron seized Khārg, one of the islands of the Persian Gulf, and created a Dutch settlement with a fort and a village. Armenian merchants came from the mainland, German troops were imported to serve as a garrison, and Chinese peasants were brought to grow vegetables. Yet such cosmopolitan ventures had little impact on the nearby Iranian mainland, and this lack of connection is not hard to explain. Trade with Europe had indeed expanded, its basis being the export of Iranian silk—Iran had no other viable export. This trade went back to Mongol times, but under the Ṣafawids it became a key source of revenue for the state, and by one route or another much of Iran's silk went to Europe, where it had become a hot commodity. Yet the geography of Iran in this period was no friendlier to maritime trade than it had been in Sasanian times. To a much greater extent than appears from a glance at a map, Iran is landlocked: the core population and prime resources of the country are located deep in the interior, far from the arid coastlands of the Persian Gulf. Iran was thus much less well placed to participate in the growth of trade on the Indian Ocean than the Ottoman Empire was to participate in that of the Mediterranean. The country was a victim of geography in that both its silk production and the timber it would have needed to build ships out of its own resources were located in the north of the country. Transporting a high-value commodity like silk from there to the Gulf could make sense, though there was no lack of other routes by which to export it. But to anticipate the events of the eighteenth century, it would take an obsessive militarist like Nādir Shāh (ruled 1732–47) to undertake the transportation of heavy and bulky timber all the way to the Gulf for the purpose of building a navy, and it is quite remarkable that his forces were able to occupy Oman from 1736 to 1744. The outside world also bulked somewhat larger for another eighteenth-century ruler of Iran, Karīm Khān (ruled 1751–79), since the location of his capital in Shīrāz meant that he was closer to the Gulf than the Ṣafawids had been. Yet people in Iran in this period seem to have been less aware of the affairs of the outside world than were the inhabitants of the Comoros, small islands on the Indian Ocean off the coast

21. Chardin, *Travels in Persia*, 194–95.

of East Africa. One factor for isolation that worked in tandem with geography and against commercial integration was no doubt the conversion of Iran to Shīʿism.

The fortunes of Persian beyond the borders of Iran

Against that background it might seem paradoxical that during the rule of the Ṣafawids the role of the Persian language, together with its associated culture, should have been at its height in a predominantly Sunnī region extending from the Ottoman Empire to Central Asia and Mughal India—and even beyond. The appearance of paradox arises from the fact that if you want to spread a language far and wide, history demonstrates that by far the most effective strategy is to yoke it to an empire. There are, of course, other ways it can happen. Your language of governance and culture may be so enviably sophisticated that others adopt it out of emulation, outside any framework of conquest and subjection; the reception of Sanskrit in Southeast Asia in pre-Islamic times is a leading example of such soft power. Alternatively, merchants and mariners involved in long-distance trade may make use of your language as a lingua franca with no pretensions to any bureaucratic or cultural role, as with the original Lingua Franca around the shores of the Mediterranean. But the track record of imperial languages is much more impressive than the results of emulation or commercial convenience. The language in which an empire conducts its affairs—the language of its courtly, bureaucratic, and military elites—acquires enormous prestige in the eyes of its subjects, with the result that a large empire is well placed to spread its language over a vast area. Premodern examples of far-flung imperial languages include Greek, Latin, Chinese, and Arabic, while obvious modern instances are Spanish and English. These examples bring home yet another lesson of history. Although imperial languages by definition originate in the hard power of an empire, they can display remarkable staying power, surviving and thriving long after the empire that initially disseminated them has disappeared. Latin was the prime cultural language of Europe for a millennium following the fall of the Roman Empire in the west, and the case of Arabic after the breakup of the Caliphate was similar. In the same way Spanish and English in the world today are in a sense the linguistic ghosts of vanished empires, but they are nevertheless very much alive on a global scale. We can think of these examples as instances of the imperial model of language spread.

The trajectory of Persian from the eleventh century to the eighteenth does not quite fit this model. In the first place, the bulk of the societies in which Persian came to be cultivated in this period were located far beyond the boundaries of the successive states that ruled Iran; indeed, in the Ottoman and Mughal cases these societies were ruled by empires that were in general much more powerful than those ruling Iran at the time. Second, the role of the Persians themselves in the export of their language was a muted one. They were happy to take advantage of the opportunities it afforded them by seeking their fortunes in regions where Persian was now in demand, but they did not supply the hard power that created those opportunities. There had indeed been powerful and enduring Persian empires in the pre-Islamic past, most recently that of the Sasanians, and no doubt their rule had had the effect of extending the use of Persian—the language of Fārs in southwestern Iran—to other parts of their empires. In the Sasanian case this may have been particularly so in the case of Khurāsān, the region where the New Persian literary language was to emerge in Islamic times. There was also a significant Sasanian presence in Bactria, though it was not a continuous one; whether it led to some spread of Persian among the local population is unclear. However, in Islamic times, apart from the meteoric rise and fall of the Ṣaffārids, there was no Iranian state that could be called a Persian empire. Instead, those who wielded the hard power that spread Persian from the eleventh century onward were Turks—or if not Turks, Mongols. Third, the Persian case deviated from the imperial model in that no single empire stood behind the diffusion of the language. Rather, there were two major chains of Turkic state formation, not all of which was imperial. Both chains started from Khurāsān, where the Muslim form of New Persian had emerged under Sāmānid rule and had been adopted by incoming Turks. One chain led to India through the Ghaznawids, the Ghūrids, the Delhi sultans, and their successors, eventually to be reinforced by the arrival of the Mughals. The other led to Anatolia and the Balkans through the Great Seljuqs, the Seljuqs of Anatolia, the Turcoman dynasties of Anatolia, and the Ottomans (we do not need to concern ourselves here with the dates and histories of the individual dynasties involved; some we have already met, others will come in later chapters). These two chains were not the only routes by which Persian reached distant lands, but historically they were the most conspicuous ones.

Given these complications, together with the variety of the lands where Persian was received, we would not expect its spread to be uniform. We can best survey the differing outcomes by laying them out along a spectrum from stronger to weaker.

The strongest outcome is obviously one in which Persian becomes the mother tongue of an entire population that has ceased to speak its original language. We are not concerned here with this process within the borders of the historical Iran, though it is worth noting that even today it is by no means complete there: quite apart from the presence of such languages as Azeri and Kurdish, there are parts of Iran, particularly in the northwest, where the local dialects are not historically forms of Persian at all, but rather residues of the presence of Parthian, the language of the Arsacid Empire that preceded that of the Sasanians. Beyond the eastern border of modern Iran a significant population at some point abandoned its ancestral Eastern Iranian languages and adopted Persian as its mother tongue in a more or less contiguous territory now divided between Afghanistan, Tajikistan, and Uzbekistan. But there may already have been a significant Sasanian imperial presence in parts of this region, so at least the beginning of the change could antedate the coming of Islam. However, in much of what is now Uzbekistan—the historical Transoxania—Persian was later overlaid by Turkic.

The next outcome is one in which the population retains its vernacular, but the elite adopts Persian as its language of governance and culture. The prime example of this is India, where the public language of the Muslim elite was for centuries Persian. In fact, there are indications that the language was not confined to the elite: when the eighteenth-century scholar Shāh Walī Allāh of Delhi (d. 1762) wanted to make the meaning of the Qur'ān accessible to ordinary Muslims, he opted to translate it into Persian. Nor was the use of the language confined to Muslims. Large numbers of Hindus employed in the Mughal bureaucracy learned it, and many Hindus composed poetry in it. In 1804, when the time had come in Bengal to rethink Hinduism in a modern context, the first reformist pamphlet was written and published in Persian. This Hindu role is a striking development given that New Persian was unquestionably a Muslim language, albeit not one dedicated to Islam in the way Arabic was outside the Arab lands. Nor were the Hindus the only non-Muslims of India who adopted Persian; so, too, did those inveterate enemies of the Muslims, the Sikhs. On a Sikh rupee minted in Lahore in 1771 we find a Persian couplet celebrating "the sword, the bowl, and victory unfailing" that the tenth guru is reputed to have owed to the first guru.[22] Yet for all the success of Persian in these centuries, its displacement by English in the nineteenth century did not leave behind any Indian community speaking Persian as its mother tongue. The role of Persian was similar in the Turkic-speaking parts of western Central Asia. As we have seen, there was an eastern Turkic literary language known as Chaghatay, but Persian retained its dominance into the nineteenth century despite some geographical variation owing to the plurality of states in the region. Thus the rulers of Transoxania were still conducting their administration in Persian in 1920, whereas in Khwārazm, whose culture was in any case more threadbare, Chaghatay had the edge on Persian, as in the works of the seventeenth-century Abū 'l-Ghāzī Bahādur Khān. The early spread of Persian in Anatolia seems initially to have been comparable to what we have seen in India and Central Asia. In Konya, the capital city of the Anatolian Seljuq dynasty, Persian was the language of the court and administration. It fits with this Anatolian Seljuq cultivation of Persian that many of the sultans descended from Qïlïj Arslan II (ruled 1156–92) had names redolent of the mythical past of ancient Iran. And as late as 1324, our oldest Ottoman document is in Persian.

22. See H. Herrli, *The coins of the Sikhs*, New Delhi 2004, 28–29, 34, 172–73.

We now shift to an outcome in which Persian is known to educated people but is not—or no longer—their primary language of governance and culture. This is typically what we find in Anatolia and the Balkans under Ottoman rule. The sixteenth-century Bosnian Aḥmed Sūdī wrote a well-known commentary on the poems of the famous fourteenth-century Persian poet Ḥāfiẓ, but he wrote it in Turkish, the dominant language of the empire. As this suggests, Persian was known and cultivated among the educated elite, who were expected to have a knowledge of "the three languages" (Arabic, Persian, and Turkish), but they found it more congenial to have their Persian poetry explained to them in Turkish than in Persian. A select few, of course, were thoroughly at home in Persian. The Ottoman sultan Selīm I (ruled 1512–20) composed a considerable amount of poetry in the language, and what is more he enjoyed speaking it. More surprisingly, the seventeenth-century Ottoman traveler Evliyā Chelebī describes young men in an Albanian city who seem to have doubled as brigands and warriors for the faith; he tells us that all of them could read Persian. But in general the primacy of Turkish in the Ottoman lands is in sharp contrast to the residual role of Turkic in Mughal India. This incidentally helps explain why the Greeks and Slavs of Ottoman Anatolia and the Balkans did not cultivate Persian in the manner of the Hindus—if they acquired a Muslim language, it was Turkish. In addition to Ottoman Anatolia and the Balkans, there were other regions of the Muslim world where Persian had some role as a language of culture, but not the dominant one. In the Eurasian interior there is good evidence for this in the region of the Volga basin in the eighteenth century, and there are scattered indications that it was nothing new. There is also some evidence that would place part of Siberia in this category, and rather more for Chinese Turkestan. Another case is China itself, where Chinese became the prime literary language of the Muslim elite. Here much of the community's literature was translated from Persian, and some direct study of Persian religious texts continued into modern times. A more surprising case is maritime Southeast Asia, where—to judge by the existence of Malay translations from Persian—the language must at some stage have played a role in the process of Islamization. But despite the region's links to India across the Bay of Bengal and the known presence of Persians in later centuries, this role was not sustained, and Persian manuscripts are not to be found in the region. From the Buddhist kingdom of Arakan, in what is now northwestern Burma, we have an Arakanese-Persian bilingual inscription from 1495, but this reflects the overland influence of Bengal rather than maritime interaction with the coasts of India. The same may be true of the likewise Buddhist kingdom of Burma, where Persian was the language of foreigners, as also of diplomacy. When the East India Company sent an envoy to the Burmese court in 1795, it was both the written and the oral language in which the two parties communicated.

Finally, there are the cases where the presence of Persian was weak to the point of being residual. For example, alongside the two chains of Turkic state formation there was a third, a sideline leading from the Great Seljuqs to the Zangids to the Ayyūbids and on to the Mamlūks. Here, as we will see, some Persian vocabulary survived in the language of the state. Near the very end of the Mamlūk period a translation of the *Shāhnāma* into Ottoman Turkish was made for the last Mamlūk sultan, who had an unusual interest in things Persian. But while he must have wanted his elite to acquire some Persian culture, he obviously took it for granted that they would not be acquiring it in Persian. The language was likewise residual in Ottoman North Africa. What we see here is in part the relative impermeability of the Arab world to Persian and its culture. A seventeenth-century Syrian author who included just a few translations of Persian poetry in his anthology of contemporary poets was going against a steep cultural gradient. Meanwhile, the role of Persian as a maritime lingua franca on the Indian Ocean seems to have been limited. Altogether, in the last two centuries it has been the fate of Persian to become residual wherever in its former domain it was not anchored in large populations speaking it as a mother tongue. Without that anchor it was unable to survive the combined pressure of new imperial languages from above and upstart vernaculars from below. Squeezed between English and Russian, on the one hand, and the likes of Urdu and Uzbek, on the other, Persian retreated into a narrower role as the national language of Iran and Tajikistan and one of the two major languages of Afghanistan. But let us now return to the history of eighteenth-century Iran.

Between the Ṣafawids and the Qājārs

Between the fall of the Ṣafawids in 1722 and the emergence of the Qājārs as rulers of a reunited Iran by 1796, the country went through yet another phase of political disintegration—or at best upheaval. But as in the analogous period before the rise of the Ṣafawids, the number of contenders was limited. As an approximation, we can see the period as a succession of three relatively short-lived dominations: first the Afghans (1722–30), then Nādir Shāh (1732–47), and then Karīm Khān (1751–79). These were followed by the rise of the Qājārs (1779–1925), who were then to rule—or at least reign—into the twentieth century. But as we will see, there was a good deal of overlap between these regimes that is suppressed in this simplification, and there was considerable warfare between them. Let us take a look at each contender in turn and then see what their performances can tell us in the aggregate.

In good times Ṣafawid rule had extended eastward to include the city of Qandahār, now in southwest Afghanistan. But in 1709 times were not good, and the city was taken over by a rebellious Sunnī Afghan group, the Ghalzay. Far from being steppe nomads, these Afghans, also known as Pashtuns, were a population of Iranian hill tribes, an eastern counterpart of the Kurds. The Ghalzay had previously played no part in the history of Iran, but by now they had moved into the region of Qandahār, on the edge of the plains. In 1721–22 they mounted an invasion of Iran, took the capital city of Iṣfahān, and ended Ṣafawid rule. State building was not, however, their strong point. They ruled Iran in a chaotic fashion in the years 1722–30, during which there was a Russian incursion from the northwest, followed by an Ottoman invasion from the west. Though they found an ally in the Sunnīs of Lāristān, the Ghalzay were widely hated.

The next contender was Nādir Khān, or Nādir Shāh as he was to become in 1736.[23] We are now back with steppe nomads, specifically a long-lived Turcoman group known as the Afshārs or Avshars. Like the Bayïndïr, their name appears already in the eleventh century, when they were one of the twenty-four clans that made up the Oghuz, and they still nomadized in the region of Kayseri in Anatolia as late as the second half of the nineteenth century. Some of them came to Iran from eastern Anatolia at the time of the Aq Qoyunlu expansion, and they joined the Ṣafawids soon after the inception of the dynasty. The group from which Nādir stemmed was based in Khurāsān, and it was there that he involved himself in an open-ended struggle for power in the 1720s. One of his rivals was allegedly a Ṣaffārid, a scion of the local family that had come to power in Sīstān in the ninth century. Another was a Qājār, a sign of the shape of things to come. But Nādir was the man of the moment. He won out in Khurāsān, ended the rule of the Afghans, evicted the Ottomans, and briefly made Iran an imperial power again; in 1736 he had himself crowned Shāh. He spent most of his reign making war. He invaded India, sacking Delhi in 1739; he invaded Transoxania, taking Samarqand in 1740; and he invaded Iraq, besieging Baghdad and Mosul in 1743. His armies were largely made up of steppe nomads, though he also recruited heavily among the hill tribes of western Iran and Afghanistan. Among the Afghans he favored the Abdālīs (the future Durrānīs) rather than the Ghalzay. Though originally from the region of Qandahār, the Abdālīs were now established around Herat. Yet in the long run none of this mattered much. Nādir was not just congenitally bloodthirsty; he was also becoming increasingly paranoid. This made him ever more dangerous to be around, and in 1747 some of his subordinates sought safety in conspiring against him and killing him. Significantly, it was a Qājār who dealt his deathblow. His state, such as it was, soon fell apart, and his heterogeneous army scattered. He barely left behind anything that could be called a dynasty, though his grandson Shāh Rukh, despite being blinded in the course of the succession struggle, found himself ruling Khurāsān until 1796 as an Afghan client. This was because one of Nādir's

23. For his career see L. Lockhart, *Nadir Shah*, London 1938; see also E. Tucker, *Nadir Shah's quest for legitimacy in post-Safavid Iran*, Gainesville 2006.

Afghan generals, an Abdālī, had taken advantage of the chaos following the assassination to set up the Durrānī monarchy in Afghanistan.

Nādir's values were straightforward. He is said to have taken a poor view of Paradise as described to him by a religious scholar because there was no fighting to be had there, no thrill of vanquishing one's enemies. He saw himself as a world conqueror in the style of Chingiz Khān and Tīmūr. He called one of his sons after his pagan hero Chingiz Khān, though the name did not do much for the unfortunate child, who was put to death at the age of three in the succession struggle in which Shāh Rukh was blinded. He likewise called one of his grandsons Tīmūr and named Shāh Rukh after one of the original Tīmūr's sons. When he invaded Transoxania and took the city of Samarqand, his booty included a large piece of jade from Tīmūr's tomb. He later respectfully returned it, though not in one piece. His invasion of India and sack of Delhi look like imitation of Tīmūr, though he was able to outdo his model by absconding with the Peacock Throne of the Mughal emperors as part of his loot. When he decided to take the title of Shāh he convened an assembly for the purpose in the steppes of northwestern Iran; it was called a *qurïltay* in the best Mongol tradition. Yet it has to be admitted that he did not fully measure up to the standards set by his role models. Unlike Tīmūr he did not visit Damascus, Smyrna, or Moscow, and he had no plans to invade China. He did, however, have a grandiose ambition that they lacked: to bring about a reconciliation of Sunnīs and Shīʿites. As he told a very uncomfortable Sunnī scholar from Baghdad, who much against his will was involved in these proceedings in 1743, "In my kingdom there are two groups, Turks and Afghans, who say to the Iranians: 'You are unbelievers.' Now unbelief is a bad thing, and it is unfitting that there should be people in my kingdom who call each other infidels."[24] His concern may have centered on his army, in which both Sunnīs and Shīʿites were present in considerable numbers, but foreign relations, too, are likely to have been a consideration. He also showed some loyalty to the Ṣafawid tradition in his earlier years in power, ruling in the name of puppet Ṣafawids much as Tīmūr had ruled in the name of puppet Chingizids. And as we will see, he also identified with Iran.

The next serious contender was Karīm Khān the Zand.[25] Like the Afghan invaders, the Zands were an Iranian hill tribe, but unlike them they were not outsiders. They lived in the mountains to the west of Iṣfahān and were reassuringly Shīʿite. They had been active in the troubles of the 1720s, harassing the Ottomans. Yet they would probably not have made history but for the fact that Nādir, thinking they could be a military asset, had deported some of them to Khurāsān, where in the manner of Tīmūr he was in the habit of collecting tribes. When Nādir's armies

24. Suwaydī, *al-Ḥujaj al-qaṭʿiyya*, Cairo 1323 *hijrī*, 11.
25. For his career see J. R. Perry, *Karim Khan Zand*, Oxford 2006.

dispersed after his death, Karīm Khān and the Zands returned to western Iran after an absence of fifteen years and promptly joined in the local power struggle. Karīm Khān won, taking Iṣfahān in 1750. In 1762–63 he extended his rule to Azerbaijan. But he showed no interest in adding Khurāsān to his possessions, despite the centrality of its steppe nomads to Nādir's imperial venture, and his rule did not extend east of the region of Kirmān. Instead he was happy to base himself in the southern city of Shīrāz in Fārs—not a venue for world conquerors, but a good place to enjoy life; after 1765 he never left the city, showing a degree of sedentariness unheard of among other major Iranian rulers of the time. The lack of military glory went with the fact that more than half his standing army in Fārs stemmed from the western hill tribes. This low military profile was balanced by something unusual in eighteenth-century Iran. Though illiterate, Karīm Khān displayed a certain human decency and a concern for good government, including a serious effort to create security for the sedentary population—peasants, craftsmen, and merchants. There was also a symbolic side to this propensity. Unlike other successful contenders for power in eighteenth-century Iran, Karīm Khān never promoted himself to Karīm Shāh. For a while he ruled in the name of a descendant of the Ṣafawid dynasty who died in 1773—he was in fact the last ruler to do so. But by 1765 he also styled himself the representative of the subject population (*wakīl al-raʿāyā*, translatable as ombudsman). No ruler who shared the contempt of steppe nomads for the sedentary Tājīks would have demeaned himself in this way. Yet when it came to leaving a dynasty behind him, he was no more successful than Nādir. The last member of his family to hold power was killed by the Qājārs in 1794. Their judgment of Karīm Khān was disparaging: he "was not a great king," his court "was not splendid," and he "made few conquests." But they did concede that he was "a wonderful magistrate."[26] All in all, his domains represented the largest state put together in Iran through the agency of Iranians, tribal or other, since the Būyids, if not the Ṣaffārids. It was also the largest ever ruled from Fārs in Islamic times. In this respect the Muẓaffarids had done quite well in their day, but not as well as Karīm Khān.

That leaves us with the Qājārs (1779–1925), the last long-lived dynasty to rule Iran. The Qājārs, or Qachars, were a Turcoman tribe like the Afshārs. Unlike them, they had been among the original tribal groups that established the Ṣafawid state; like them, they were somewhat dispersed. In the fifteenth century the Qājārs were to be found in central Anatolia, and in the eighteenth century there were still some even farther to the west. In Iran some had lived in Azerbaijan since the late fifteenth century, while others were moved to Khurāsān under Shāh ʿAbbās. The ones that concern us inhabited the western part of Khurāsān around Astarābād. They were

26. Quoted in Sir John Malcolm, *The history of Persia*, London 1815, 2:152.

persistent contenders in the struggle for power in eighteenth-century Iran. As we saw, one Qājār was active in the 1720s and another around midcentury. But they were hobbled by the strength of their rivals and by internal conflict within the tribe, and it was not till late in the century that they prevailed. The founder of the dynasty that then came to power was Āqā Muḥammad Khān (ruled 1779–97), who got his chance in 1779 with the death of Karīm Khān, at whose court he had long been a well-treated hostage. In 1785 he took Iṣfahān, and by 1796 he ruled the whole of Iran and had himself crowned. Energetic and unpleasant, as a ruler he was more in the style of Tīmūr and Nādir than in that of Karīm Khān. When he took Kirmān in 1794, he blinded or killed all adult males and gave twenty thousand women and children to his troops as slaves. He himself had no descendants, since he had been emasculated by a nephew of Nādir's at the age of four. However, his nephew and successor Fatḥ-ʿAlī Shāh (ruled 1797–1834) fully made up for this: at his death he left behind some fifty-seven sons and forty-six daughters, and it was his descendants who reigned until 1925. The Qājārs may have lacked the religious charisma of the Ṣafawids, but they perhaps made up for it by being less inclined to binge drinking. It was they who made Tehran the capital city of Iran.

The pattern of Iranian history over eight centuries

From this vantage point we can now look back over the eight centuries of the history of Iran covered in this chapter, revisiting the first-order approximation with which we began.

The first feature of the period we picked out there was the survival of an entity called Iran. On one level this was a geopolitical fact. The Seljuqs had created an empire for themselves in roughly the same location as that of the Sasanians, and a succession of imperial dynasties followed suit down to the end of our period, albeit with intermissions. This in itself is somewhat remarkable. As already noted, in geographical terms Iran suffers from a hole-in-the-heart syndrome: a large area of desert intervenes between the eastern and western parts of the plateau, so that in geopolitical terms there is no obvious reason for its survival as a unit. One aspect of this that has become apparent in this chapter is the lack of a permanent capital city that could survive changes of dynasty. Iṣfahān, which served both the Seljuqs and the Ṣafawids, is the nearest thing, but not close. On another level, the geopolitical survival of Iran was accompanied by the continuing use of the name to identify the territory. As we have seen, back around the turn of the millennium Firdawsī had celebrated the glorious history of pre-Islamic Iran in his *Shāhnāma*, and eleventh-century Persian poets in the service of the Ghaznawids made frequent references to Iran. One poet refers to the ruler (who was actually of Turkic stock) as the *Īrānshāh*, speaks of the land as *Īrānshahr* and *Īrān-zamīn*, and opposes *Īrānī*s to *Tūrānī*s, Tūrān being an ancient Iranian term applied to the Central Asian nomadic enemy. Another poet likewise speaks of *Īrānshahr* and affirms a division of labor in which Iran is to kingship what the Ḥijāz is to religion. A contemporary poet in Azerbaijan uses similar language. So does a historian writing around 1051. So, too, do sources of the Īlkhān and Ṣafawid periods. And in the eighteenth century Nādir Shāh speaks freely of Iran; for the most part he is simply calling the country by its name, but occasionally the tone is more grandiloquent, as when he mints a coin on which he refers to himself as "Nādir of the land of Iran" (*Nādir-i Īrān-zamīn*).[27] A source contemporary with Nādir describes him as having "swiftly cleared the enemy from the soil of Iran."[28] And when Āqā Muḥammad Khān laid siege to Tiflis in 1795, it was reportedly to the accompaniment of the chanting of the *Shāhnāma*. His successor Fatḥ-ʿAlī Shāh had a rock carving of himself done in Sasanian style in 1823, and he called many of his sons after pre-Islamic Iranian kings and heroes. Such attitudes went well with a certain Persian chauvinism. When a sixteenth-century Persian author of a biography of the Prophet reached the Battle of the Khandaq, he told the story in which the Prophet's Persian companion Salmān gets the credit for suggesting the digging of the trench to protect Medina from penetration by enemy cavalry; the biographer then commented that the high standing of Salmān on that day was something that all Persian speakers (*Fārsī-zabānān*) could glory in till the day of the resurrection.

This talk of Iran did not, however, mean that the Turks had forgotten about being Turks. Nādir was intensely aware of his Turcoman identity and deployed a pan-Turcoman rhetoric when seeking to mend relations with other dynasties of steppe nomad origin, notably the Ottomans and the Mughals. He spoke of rulership as hereditary within the exalted Turcoman tribe. After sacking Delhi, he was kind enough to reinstate the defeated Mughal emperor; one reason he gave for this friendly gesture was their allegedly shared Turcoman lineage, and another was the emperor's descent from Tīmūr—something Nādir himself could not claim but nevertheless respected. In short, Iranian and Turcoman rhetoric were not mutually exclusive.

The second feature of our first-order approximation was the alternation between imperial states and political fragmentation. This feature, too, is broadly borne out by the history we have been considering, subject to two significant qualifications. The first is that over the centuries the imperial states became smaller. The Ṣafawids after their initial success and the Qājārs throughout their reign ruled less territory than the Seljuqs or Īlkhāns had done. In particular, the Ottoman conquest of eastern Anatolia proved definitive—which is why this region is today part of Turkey, not of Iran. Thus the great game of tribal politics in Iran was now playing out in a considerably smaller arena. A major factor here was the reemergence

27. See Malcolm, *History of Persia*, 2:66.
28. Quoted in Tucker, *Nadir Shah's quest for legitimacy*, 38–39.

of a rival empire to the west of Iran. The other qualification concerns the periods of fragmentation. These periods were recurrent, but in the long run there was a perceptible decrease in the extent of the fragmentation involved. Though there was still some in the interval between the Ṣafawids and the Qājārs, instability over time was now more marked than was territorial breakup. An obvious explanation would be that the mobility of steppe nomads made it harder for small-scale states to emerge and survive, but as we have seen this does not fit well with what had happened in the post-Seljuq period.

The third feature was the primacy of steppe nomads in large-scale state formation. Originally these were external nomads, but after the Mongols internal ones replaced them. Again the outcome of the eighteenth-century struggle for power bears out this primacy. Most obviously, it was a steppe nomad dynasty, the Qājārs, that finally brought the struggle to an end. Another way to look at it is that of the four main contenders after the fall of the Ṣafawids, two—the Afshārs and the Qājārs—were steppe nomads, and in military terms they were by far the most successful; the performance of the Iranian hill tribes—the Ghalzay and the Zands—lagged well behind. But it is also significant that even they were tribal, not to say nomadic—as something like a third of the population of Iran may have been at the time. Meanwhile, slave soldiers were marginal to the eighteenth-century military scene. Although Karīm Khān had at least three hundred of them, the major effort of Shāh ʿAbbās to recruit them had languished. The primacy of free steppe nomads was thus unchanged to the end of our period, and in the early nineteenth century the standing army was still composed in large measure of Qājār tribesmen.

The fourth and final feature was the low profile of the Tājīks, the settled Iranian population. Despite the military reforms of Shāh ʿAbbās, the rise of the infantry had yet to upend the traditional pattern of cavalry warfare in Iran. This pattern excluded peasants and town dwellers from high-level military activity and hence from serious state formation. Political forces welling up from below thus had little impact on the grander struggle for power. In this perspective the role of the Tājīks was to pay their taxes to the military elites that ruled them and, if suitably educated, to serve these elites as bureaucrats. It is noteworthy that the Ṣafawids, though sorely missed in the decades immediately after the fall of the dynasty in 1722, did not start a fashion for indigenous Sharīfian dynasties such as prevailed in Morocco in the same period. Meanwhile, the Persian bureaucracy maintained its record of surviving every change of ruler since the coming of the Seljuqs. Yet the form it took in the eighteenth century was surprisingly faceless. There was no bureaucratic leader in Iran in this period who shared the prominence and caliber of Niẓām al-Mulk or Rashīd al-Dīn.

All in all, much of what we see here arises from the fact that in Iran—as also in Central Asia—nomadic and settled populations lived side by side. In other words, environmental conditions supported the existence of a large body of internal nomads. By contrast, China could be conquered by steppe nomads, but within China itself the conquerors would leave no continuing nomadic society behind them. This was one reason steppe nomads enjoyed eight centuries of power in Iran.

Sampling a third-order approximation

Qualifications

We have now completed our second-order approximation of the history of Iran from the eleventh century to the eighteenth. Completing a third-order approximation is out of the question—it would fill volumes. But we can at least ask what it might look like. It would in fact make a considerable difference to our understanding of the history of Iran in two overlapping ways. First, it would lead us to qualify some of the general perspectives we have deployed or assumed above. And second, it would give us sight of a whole set of intermediate political structures that we have so far ignored. We begin with the qualifications.

Most obviously, a third-order approximation would retell the same story in much greater detail. For example, we would learn that when Karīm Khān took Iṣfahān in 1750, he was in league with a certain ʿAlī Mardān Khān, a leading figure among the Bakhtiyārīs, yet another hill people of western Iran. In 1751 the two men quarreled, with Karīm Khān finally emerging as the winner in 1753. These details were not visible in our second-order approximation, but knowing them is perhaps worth something: it suggests that Karīm Khān was part of a wider phenomenon among the western hill tribes stirred up by Nādir's efforts to expand his army.

At the same time, greater resolution would lead us to qualify several aspects of the pattern of ethnic differentiation as it has appeared above. One is the image of nomads ruling a settled society without becoming assimilated by it. A lot of the time this is not wrong, thanks to the viability of internal steppe nomadism in Iran. For example, Sanjar, the last major Seljuq ruler in Iran, was still illiterate, and as we have seen the last Seljuq to rule in Iran still moved between summer and winter pastures. We would expect the Ṣafawids to be different, especially once they ceased to be dependent on their Turcoman following for the bulk of their army, and indeed Shāh ʿAbbās does not appear to have been a nomadic monarch, though he was certainly an itinerant one who never spent more than a third of a year in a capital city. But the early Qājārs, who look so traditional in terms of the composition of their army, are more of a surprise. They were much more sedentary than the Seljuqs, if not as much as Karīm Khān. They usually spent their winters in Tehran—not in a camp outside the walls, but rather in a palace within them. Their summers were more varied, but a favorite of the second Qājār ruler, Fatḥ-ʿAlī Shāh, was the old Īlkhān capital of Sulṭāniyya. Although at first he camped there in traditional style, after a while he built himself a palace. Until the end of his life he always left Tehran in summer—everybody did if they could—but the major chronicle of his reign shows that in his last Dragon, Snake, and Horse years (1831–34) he went no farther than a palace situated less than a mile from the walls of the city. As this report makes clear, the twelve-year animal cycle of the steppes was still alive and well, but nomadic rulership was by now in an advanced state of decay.

In a similar way we could qualify the distinction between the Turkic military and the Persian bureaucracy. It is easy to complicate the picture by pointing to examples of Persian bureaucrats leading armies: Niẓām al-Mulk did so in Fārs in a context we will come to, and in 1512 a Persian bureaucrat led a Ṣafawid army to defeat at the hands of the Özbegs. It is harder to find Turks serving as a bureaucrats, but it can happen—there is an example in the Seljuq period.

Yet another theme that gets more complicated is the division of labor between the Turkic rulers and their Tājīk subjects. Turks make war, Tājīks pay taxes; this simple dichotomy is correct in the sense that Tājīks did not normally participate to serious effect in the wars that made the history of the major states. But they were by no means passive, and they were not shy of engaging in armed conflict. The hill tribes, of course, were not passive at all. For example, following the short and unhappy reign of the Ṣafawid Ismāʿīl II, four pretenders claiming to be him appeared in mountainous regions, all of them wandering dervishes whose supporters were drawn from the Iranian hill tribes of the southwest, north, and east. Against this background, what was unusual about Karīm Khān was not that he engaged in military activity but that he did so in a way that made him and his tribal following visible on the larger canvas of Iranian history. Urban Tājīks, however, were not like the hill tribes and had even less ability to shape history. Yet they too could engage in military violence. We have already encountered the ʿAyyārs of pre-Mongol times. Another example of urban warfare is a story told about the people of Balkh in the early eleventh century. Now in northern Afghanistan, the city was then ruled by the Ghaznawids, but the Ghaznawid ruler was away campaigning in India, and in his absence Balkh was taken and briefly held by the Qarakhānids. The response of the people of Balkh was vigorous resistance against the Qarakhānid invaders, with considerable loss of life and property. It is worth noting that this did not get them any thanks from the returning Ghaznawid ruler, some of whose property had been destroyed in the hostilities; he admonished the people of Balkh that warfare was for rulers, not for subjects, and that their duty was to pay their taxes to whoever had them in his power. This indeed was the theory. But other examples of such activism among urban populations are not hard to find. In 1365, for example, the people of Samarqand defended their city against invaders from Mogholistān, and they defended it again in 1410 in the absence of its Chaghatay army. At the time of the fall of the Ṣafawid dynasty the Afghan invaders of Iran were driven out of Qazwīn by the townspeople. Urban society was not, of course, homogeneous. The events of the Mongol invasion suggest that the common people of the cities were more likely to resist invaders than were the notables, who had a greater inclination to negotiate. But these events also indicate that even within a single city the populace hardly seems to have had a capacity for coordination above the level of the quarter. In the countryside peasants likewise engaged in military activity when their villages came under attack. We can probably assume that in the exposed plains their settlements were fortified; we know them to have been in later centuries. No doubt peasants also engaged in fighting against neighboring villages. Near the beginning of our period, the defensive military role of peasants in twelfth-century eastern Iran has been well documented. At the end of it, Sir John Malcolm (d. 1833), who wrote with personal experience of Iran, described the "citizens and cultivators of Persia" as unwarlike—"this part of the population seldom furnished many recruits to an army."[29] But while contrasting them with the nomadic tribes, he too noted their role as militias repelling attacks.

A closely related point is that Tājīks had a part to play as infantry even in the armies of the largest states. Not since the Būyids had come to power in the tenth century had the infantry made history, and steppe nomads regularly made bigger history than the Daylamites had ever done. But the infantry were usually there and could still make trouble. There were Tājīks in Tīmūr's armies. A European observer made a count of an Aq Qoyunlu army in 1474 using beans; he reckoned it to consist of twenty-five thousand horsemen and three thousand footmen, and no doubt the footmen were Tājīks. Shāh ʿAbbās had Persian peasants armed with muskets in his infantry. Sometimes Tājīks would be recruited ad hoc. In a Tīmūrid context we hear of the recruitment of infantry in central Iran to put down a rebellion in 1403–4. Faced with a revolt in 1448, a Tīmūrid governor had so few troops that he had to mobilize the Tājīks. As this implies, there was no comparison between Tājīk and Turkic troops. The general sense of the superiority of Turkic soldiery was underlined in the tense dealings between the Seljuqs and the ʿAbbāsid caliphs. To ensure that the caliphs could not pose a military threat to them, Seljuq rulers twice banned their acquisition of Turkic slaves, once in 1078 and again in 1136. In the latter case the caliph had to make do with buying Greeks and Armenians instead. Yet there was one factor that was to favor infantry in the long run: the coming of firearms. We have seen efforts to adopt them in Iran; Nādir, for example, had good artillery thanks to the assistance of French officers. But Iran lagged well behind the Ottoman Empire in this respect—and Central Asia even farther behind Iran.

29. Malcolm, *History of Persia*, 2:120–21.

Other levels of political activity

All these qualifications are significant, but the most interesting result of shifting to a third-order approximation is that a whole new level of political and military activity comes into view. We have already had glimpses of this level, but it is time to focus on it. Especially but not only in rural settings, we should be wary of thinking of the states we have been concerned with as being in regular interaction with the mass of their subjects. In eastern Iran in the twelfth century—and very likely in other regions and centuries—any town or village would have its headman (*ra'īs*). Here "headman," though apt as a literal translation, is perhaps misleading, and we should think rather of a local notable. This figure might be appointed by the state, but he would be a ranking member of the local society, not someone arbitrarily inserted by the state from outside. Unsurprisingly there was a tendency for the position to be passed down within a family. These notables were not immune to the larger conflicts of Iranian history, and sometimes they had to place risky political bets on their outcomes. A village confronted with demands for taxes from two rival states had to decide with which party to align itself, and in this decision the headman would be the key figure. But in much of Iran for much of the time, the states were not interacting even with these notables: there would be yet another level of political organization—or disorganization—in between. What existed at this intermediate level must have been both varied and changeable. Since under normal circumstances the high historiography that gives us most of our sources tends to concentrate on equally high politics, much of the intermediate level is doubtless beyond our capacity to retrieve with the sources we possess. But let us examine six examples of the kinds of things that come into view once we penetrate the Venusian cloud cover that conceals local communities from us. Three of them are primarily rural, and three are primarily urban. There is no need for us to take them in chronological order.

Our first example comes from Fārs. This province was by no means a remote or inaccessible part of Iran, and in medieval times it was ruled by a respectable series of regional dynasties: the Būyids, the Salghurids, and the Muẓaffarids flourished in the post-ʿAbbāsid, post-Seljuq, and post-Mongol periods, respectively. But if we increase the resolution a bit more, we begin to notice the Shabānkāra, a group of vaguely Kurdish tribes leading a life that mixed pastoralism, hunting, and woodcutting around the town of Īg. In the mid-eleventh century the Būyid dynasty of Fārs had in its employ a certain Faḍlawayh, a military commander who belonged to the Shabānkāra. He took advantage of his position to possess himself of the whole of Fārs and put an end to Būyid rule there in 1062. Had he done this in the previous century, he might well have succeeded in establishing a lasting dynasty; his misfortune was to be a contemporary of the Seljuq expansion. This was not all bad, as it got him romanced by one of the contestants in a Seljuq succession struggle in 1064. Later, however, a force commanded by the arch-bureaucrat Niẓām al-Mulk captured and executed him. For a while after that the Shabānkāra were more of a nuisance than a state. But the post-Seljuq period was a new opportunity for them, and in the early thirteenth century they established a warrior principality that even held Kirmān for a few years. The Shabānkāra rulers of this statelet were quite colorful. They claimed descent from Ardashīr, the first Sasanian ruler, and their troops went into battle chanting the *Shāhnāma*. However, one of their rulers, Muẓaffar al-Dīn Muḥammad (ruled 1227–60), was a strict but somewhat idiosyncratic Sunnī. He was much concerned about public morality and had fairly intrusive ideas about how society should be run: he held that everyone should follow the profession of his father and forbade any but men of the pen to send their sons to school. Despite his religiosity, he got along well enough with the pagan Mongols until he piously refused to send troops to join Hülegü's siege of Baghdad in 1258. When a Mongol force came his way two years later, the then octogenarian ruler opted for martyrdom in battle against the infidel rather than submit. Even at that point the Mongols did not put an end to this polity, but they did put in a tax collector and later a garrison, thereby drastically curbing its autonomy. In 1283 a ruler who was unwise enough to quarrel with the tax collector got himself cut in half for his pains. This was followed by a period of social disorder in which we are told that the common soldiery and the populace were indulging in a variety of nefarious activities, such as seizing the property and women of ancient families, engaging in public copulation, having sons execute their fathers, and dropping cats into the pants of women. The disorder came to an end with the advent of two princes who were accustomed to Mongol ways—one had spent time among the Mongols as a hostage. They delivered security, forbidding people to carry knives and daggers, and society prospered. Both, however, were killed in the 1290s. The narrative continues, but by the middle of the fourteenth century this state had faded out. So too did the Shabānkāra, and in the Tīmūrid period we hear little of them.

For a second example we move to a remote region in southeastern Fārs. This is Lāristān, which we have already encountered as a place where Sunnism survived the Ṣafawids. Situated in the arid hinterland north of the Persian Gulf, it was not a part of Iran that had much to offer to a passing world conqueror. From the late twelfth to the mid-sixteenth century it had some kind of local rulers, but we know little about them beyond their names and dates, and indeed we are lucky to have even that. Outsiders did intrude from time to time. We have already noted the appearance of Turcomans in the region; the thirteenth-century Shabānkāra ruler Muẓaffar al-Dīn Muḥammad is said to have annexed it; and in the next century the Muẓaffarids established a mint there. But the main thing Lāristān can do for us is remind us that government is an enterprise requiring attention to costs and benefits. Around 1360 the Muẓaffarid ruler of Fārs was confronted by a revolt in

Lāristān. His father advised him that it was not worth bothering to suppress it: Lāristān, he told him, was a ruin on which no ruler should waste his attention. One could be forgiven for thinking that such a place would be a cultural wilderness. But as it happens a young aristocrat from Rome, Pietro della Valle, spent half a year there in 1622 recovering from an illness and was warmly received into the local society. He writes that nowhere else had he seen "men so learned or so profound in the sciences."[30] The women, too, were sympathetic to him—he had just lost the Christian wife he had married in Iraq. One of the friends he made was a mathematician and astronomer who wanted to learn some Latin and obtain books from Europe, especially recent ones. Some of his friends belonged to a sect that believed in reincarnation and did not expect its women to veil themselves in the presence of male members of the sect. If Lāristān was a ruin, it was an engaging one.

Our third example concerns two remote regions of Iran that were several hundred miles apart and yet were yoked for a while in their fidelity to an extremist religious doctrine. Together they formed a state established by the Nizārīs,[31] alias the Assassins, a branch of the Ismāʿīlīs that broke with the headquarters of the sect in Cairo over a disputed succession to the Fāṭimid caliphate in 1094. Their polity was a throwback to a pattern of sectarian state formation that had been more prominent in the earlier Islamic centuries, and it lasted from 1090 until the Mongols destroyed it in 1256. It was based on castles perched in the mountains south of the Caspian Sea, most famously Alamūt, an asset that, in a testimony to the commercial sophistication of the medieval Muslim world, the leader of the movement was able to purchase by writing a check. At the same time this state also held territory in the isolated mountainous region of northeastern Iran known as Quhistān. This unusual geographical distribution was the result of a somewhat Darwinian process. Initially there was a widespread Ismāʿīlī rising, in the course of which rebels in more accessible locations were driven out or slaughtered by their Sunnī enemies. There was, for example, an acute struggle in and around Iṣfahān. Within the city this issued in a bloodbath in 1101 to which we will return. Outside it the Ismāʿīlīs had obtained possession of the castle of Shāhdiz, perhaps an hour's walk from the city. This castle held out until 1107, when it was taken by the Seljuq sultan and his forces with the financial support of the local elite and the participation of the local militias. The Nizārī state survived the general failure of this insurrection because it had castles in altogether less accessible regions. Once established there, it engaged in a couple of unusual activities. One was organizing suicide missions to assassinate unfriendly rulers, including a couple of ʿAbbāsid caliphs;

30. Quoted in J. D. Gurney, "Pietro della Valle," *Bulletin of the School of Oriental and African Studies*, 49 (1986), 112.

31. For its history see M.G.S. Hodgson, "The Ismāʿīlī state," in *The Cambridge history of Iran*, vol. 5.

in this respect the Nizārīs qualify as authentic medieval terrorists. Their other pastime was a dizzying series of ideological gyrations. Thus in 1164 they proclaimed the resurrection at Alamūt, and with it the abrogation of the Sharīʿa, the sacred law of Islam. The resurrection continued until 1210, when a new leader ended it, went over to Sunnism, and restored the Sharīʿa. Thereafter the sect found subtle ways to have its cake and eat it, as religious and political movements often do. The end came when the Mongols decided to destroy the Nizārī state in 1256, massacring the men and enslaving the women and children. The sect nevertheless survived and is present in Quhistān to this day.

Following these three rural examples we come now to three urban cases. We start in Sabzawār, a small town in eastern Iran that lies to the west of Mashhad. It was here that the Sarbadār statelet (1337–86) arose,[32] a scruffy phenomenon with populist undertones (*sar ba-dār* means "head in gallows," or as we would say gallows bird). The Sarbadār polity had two components. One was a succession of rulers marked by rapid turnover and sticky ends while the other was a Ṣūfī order with pronounced Shīʿite ideas, and by no means did the two always get along with each other. It all began when the founder rose in rebellion after killing a tax collector and taking to the hills. He did not last long, however, as his own brother killed him in a quarrel over the proper treatment of a woman. Local landowners were involved, but the movement also had a significant following among urban craftsmen. We thus get a rare glimpse of what could lie beneath the surface of the Iranian cauldron. But the story is also a telling indication of the limits of this kind of upwelling in the history of Iran. It was not, so far as we can tell, a peasant revolt. In England in 1381 fiscal grievance issued in a massive rebellion of the peasantry, while in China what began as a peasant revolt became an ethnic Chinese insurrection that led in 1368 to the expulsion of the Mongols and the establishment the Ming dynasty. In like manner, the Sarbadārs may have articulated both social and ethnic grievances. A fifteenth-century historian describes them as Tājīks rebelling against Turkic and other oppressors. But though at their height they were minting coins in cities the best part of four hundred miles apart, they never evolved beyond a regional curiosity, and we encounter nothing comparable in earlier or later periods of political fragmentation in Iran. In fact, peasant revolt is surprisingly marginal to the history of Iran and the Middle East at large. When Niẓām al-Mulk argued that fiscal oppression was a bad idea because it drove peasants to extremes, what he meant was that they would flee from their villages, not that they would engage in insurrection.

Let us now move a rung or two up the urban ladder and take a real city, Kirmān. It was never an imperial capital and was usually ruled from elsewhere, but it had

32. See J. M. Smith, *The history of the Sarbadār dynasty*, The Hague 1970.

the stature to serve as a capital city for occasional regional dynasties. A branch of the Seljuq family ruled there from 1048 to around 1188. Then from 1222 to 1307 a dynasty descended from the Qara Khiṭāy royal family held Kirmān as the Qutlughkhānids; they had implanted themselves there somewhat fortuitously under the aegis of the Khwārazm-Shāhs. Their steppe origins are reflected in the prolonged reign or regency of one woman and the shorter reign of another. In sum, Kirmān was not the kind of place where one would expect a regime to emerge from a populist upwelling. But it happened in the chaos of the eighteenth century.[33] In 1760 Karīm Khān sent a Zand commander to impose his rule on the province. He obtained entrance to the city but did not last long there because he offended a rural charcoal seller, one Taqī Khān Durrānī. Taqī was a crack shot with a musket, using it to hunt while transporting charcoal from his village to sell in the city. One day he shot a large mountain sheep and gave it to the governor's servants as a present for him, expecting the customary reward. Instead all he got was a beating and the seizure of his gun. The day after he appealed to the governor himself for justice, holding fast to his stirrup, and was beaten again. This was too much. Back home he gathered a band of three hundred followers, some of them expert marksmen like himself. He also had the support of workers and artisans within the city. One night he and fifty of his men seized the citadel, and the oppressive governor was shot. The charcoal seller now ruled the city of Kirmān, where he initially enjoyed considerable popularity—he fined the rich to give to the poor. But soon things began to go sour, and Taqī became as extortionate as previous governors. Meanwhile Karīm Khān sent three successive expeditions against him, each of which failed. Finally, in 1766, a fourth attack succeeded, largely because the commander made apt use of the widespread disaffection against Taqī. This led the people of the city to open its gates to the Zand forces, and Taqī was taken to Shīrāz and duly executed.

Let us now go back to Iṣfahān in Seljuq times, a capital city under the nose of the ruling dynasty.[34] If there was ever a time and place at which the Seljuqs might have administered their subjects directly, it would have been here in the first four decades of their rule, between the capture of the city in 1051 and the death of Niẓām al-Mulk in 1092. These were good times for the dynasty, and even if the sultans themselves did not live within the walls of the city, Niẓām al-Mulk did so for much of this period; additionally, one of his sons was in due course installed as governor. As usual, we are poorly served for information, but we do have one remarkable vignette that is at least indirectly relevant. Immediately after the Seljuq sultan took the city, he put in a governor whose task it was to get the local economy back on its feet after years of destructive conflict. This governor set about persuading the

33. For the full story see the vivid account in Perry, *Karim Khan Zand*, 56–59.

34. For what follows see D. Durand-Guédy, *Iranian elites and Turkish rulers*, London 2010.

peasants to return to the land and start cultivating again. A contemporary source tells us that he "called them in one by one to his court and treated them kindly,"[35] giving them the cows and seed they needed to resume agricultural production. Here, then, is a high government official in a city bypassing even the village headmen to deal directly with the peasants of the surrounding countryside. But for one thing, conditions at the time were unusually dire and perhaps demanded a dramatization of the state's concern for the peasants. And for another, our source is a poet praising his patron to the skies, so we should be wary of taking him too literally. Yet even then we can infer one point from this account: the poet takes it for granted that the average governor in average times would not have behaved in such a way. From the time when Niẓām al-Mulk was in residence we have a report that he established patronage relations with every student, transmitter of Prophetic traditions, versifier, author, specialist on any field, and scribe. If this is not just rhetoric, it certainly suggests micromanagement, at least of the urban elite. But the chances are that even at the height of Seljuq power, the governing authorities would not normally have dealt directly with anyone below the level of the headmen of the quarters of the city; that is more or less how it was in sixteenth-century Iṣfahān.

Once the best days of the Seljuqs were over, there was plenty of space between them and their subjects, even in a place like Iṣfahān. Much of this space was filled by factional conflicts in which leading local families were closely involved. Such conflicts divided many Iranian settlements both then and later. Tehran around 1200 is described as a large and rebellious village divided into twelve quarters whose populations did not mix except to make war on each other. The basis of the factionalism could be different in different cities, just as it could vary over time within the same city, as it did in Iṣfahān. As a rule of thumb, we could say that in the early centuries of our period factionalism would be based on some difference of religious allegiance. By contrast, in Ṣafawid and later times there was a widespread division of urban populations into two groups known as Ḥaydarīs and Niʿmatīs, a division that lacked any continuing religious basis, though it may have originated in allegiances to rival Ṣūfī masters. This later form of factionalism also differed from that of earlier centuries in that the fighting, though frequent, was now considerably less lethal. Leading families were likewise a widespread feature of Iranian cities. In the case of Seljuq Iṣfahān they tended to be immigrant families from the east that owed their entry into the city to the Seljuqs but soon became local actors in their own right. The prime example would be the Khujandīs, a Shāfiʿite family from Transoxania brought to Iṣfahān by Niẓām al-Mulk, who was himself a Shāfiʿite—like the majority of the population of the city. This family played a lead-

35. Fakhr ud-Dīn Gurgānī, *Vis and Ramin*, New York 1972, 16.

ing role in the fifteen-year civil war that was fought in and around the city between the Ismāʿīlīs and their opponents from 1092 to 1107. Thus it was the Khujandīs who mobilized the urban militias to massacre the Ismāʿīlīs of Iṣfahān in 1101. The story was that good Sunnīs were mysteriously disappearing and that eventually it came to light that the Ismāʿīlīs were kidnapping and torturing them in a secret underground prison. In response to reports of this atrocity the leading member of the Khujandī family collected a large number of armed men and ordered that trenches be dug and fires lit in them; the mob then went about seizing Ismāʿīlīs and throwing them into the flames. Thanks to the increasing power of the Khujandīs the position of headman (*raʾīs*) of the city became hereditary in the family. When rival Seljuq princes fought each other, it was the Khujandīs who decided which one to back, and they flourished or suffered according to the outcome. No doubt it was their landed wealth that formed the basis of their power, enabling them to be the leading patrons in the city now that Niẓām al-Mulk was gone. The elimination of the Ismāʿīlīs did not, however, mean the end of factional polarization. Instead, a new opposition emerged between the Shāfiʿites in the western part of the city and the Ḥanafīs in the east, where a rival family played the leading role. This too involved armed conflict; it was endemic from the later twelfth century on and still virulent on the eve of the Mongol conquest of 1235–36. In fact it was so virulent that the Shāfiʿites threw open the gates of the city to the Mongols on the understanding that the invaders would slaughter only the Ḥanafīs. In the event the Mongols came up with their own evenhanded solution to the problem of factional conflict in Iṣfahān: they slaughtered everybody, starting with the Shāfiʿites.

Perhaps a comprehensive study of local phenomena of the kind we have illustrated here would yield an illuminating way to classify them and a wider understanding of the reasons they appear when and where they do. But on the basis of these examples alone the main points that stand out are the variety and instability of local scenes.

Central Asia and the legal legacy of the Mongols

Central Asia in brief

In the course our treatment of the steppes and Iran, we have already covered much of the history of the settled lands of Central Asia, and in particular Transoxania. So we have no need to go back over the history of such dynasties as the Qarakhānids, the Qara Khiṭāy, the Khwārazm-Shāhs, the Chaghatayids, or the Tīmūrids, and we can take the Özbeg conquest of Transoxania for granted. But we do need to spend a moment on what happened in the region subsequently, in the period in which Iran and Central Asia had come to lead more or less separate lives, Shīʿite in the case of Iran and Sunnī in that of Central Asia.

The central story is the Özbeg Khānate in Transoxania. Between the Özbeg conquest at the beginning of the sixteenth century and the end of our period there was no lack of either domestic disorder or intrusion from outside, notably raids mounted by the Qalmaqs and other nomads; in 1716–17 such raiders are said to have "stripped the sown fields and orchards bare like locusts."[36] But in the whole period there was only one significant discontinuity: Nādir's forces attacked in 1737, and he himself went on to conquer the Khānate in 1740. Like everything Nādir did, this conquest proved transitory, but it had an impact that we will come to shortly. That apart, the basic character of the Khānate and its Özbeg political and military elite remained much the same well into the nineteenth century. There was a relatively undramatic succession of three dynasties: the Shībānids (1500–99), the Toqay Temürids (1599–1747), and finally the Mangïts (1753–1920)—though the break between the Toqay Temürids and the Mangïts was a significant one, since it involved the end of Chingizid rule in Transoxania. The Özbeg elite was still rooted in nomad power, though dominating a long-settled Tājīk population whose bureaucrats the state continued to employ. So on the one hand, the founder of the dynasty told his chronicler, "Let our capital be our saddle";[37] but on the other hand, Bukhārā and Samarqand vied for the role of capital city of the Khānate. Most of the time government tended to be decentralized. This feature arose from the fact that it was the unruly Özbeg leaders rather than the ruler who controlled most of the revenues, but it may also reflect a certain impoverishment of the region. An Indian who accompanied Nādir's forces commented that Central Asia—Tūrān, as he called it—was poor in contrast to Hindūstān, by which he meant northern India. However, the first half of the eighteenth century may have been a particularly bad time in this respect. Overall, the trajectory of the region diverged considerably from that of Iran. The Mongol heritage proved much more enduring in the history of the three Transoxanian dynasties than it did in Iran, where Chingizid rule was unheard of after the mid-fourteenth century. Both the Shībānids and the Toqay Temürids were Chingizids. The Mangïts, despite descending from a respectable Mongol tribe with a history going back to the time of Chingiz Khān, were not themselves Chingizids, and in Transoxania this was embarrassing. The embarrassment showed in two ways. One was a highly eclectic accession ceremony staged for the first Mangït ruler when he claimed the Khānate for himself in 1756; at one point religious dignitaries joined in the Chingizid ritual of elevating the new ruler on a felt carpet. The other was the retention of puppet Chingizids until 1785 in an attempt to boost Mangït legitimacy. Meanwhile, the heritage of the steppes was also exerting a linguistic pull, with Turkic replacing Persian among most of the settled population of Transoxania, a change that in Iran took place on a large scale

36. Quoted in W. Holzwarth, "Relations between Uzbek Central Asia, the Great Steppe and Iran," in S. Leder and B. Streck (eds.), *Shifts and drifts in nomad-sedentary relations*, Wiesbaden 2005, 192.
37. Quoted in Tucker, *Nadir Shah's quest for legitimacy*, 72.

only in Azerbaijan. Given that nomads may have constituted some 40 percent of the Transoxanian population, the spread of Turkic is not surprising. Yet another divergence between the Khānate and Iran concerns military modernization. Iran, as we have seen, lagged well behind the Ottoman Empire in its adoption of firearms, but it was still well ahead of Central Asia. Prior to Nādir's invasion the ruler possessed only a tiny force of a few hundred palace guards that was equipped with firearms and some light artillery mounted on camels. The mass of the Özbeg army still consisted of mounted archers. In a repetition of an old story, it was the use of firearms by Nādir's forces that rendered the Özbeg resistance ineffective. The founder of the Mangït dynasty, who after the invasion spent some years in Nādir's army, learned the lesson and applied it. Yet the old Özbeg elite was still in place, and in the late eighteenth century there was considerable backsliding.

Outside Transoxania there were further regions of Central Asia where the texture of political life was broadly similar, whether or not they were subject to the rule of the Transoxanian dynasties. The main ones were Balkh, Farghāna, and Khwārazm. Balkh to the south tended to be the seat of the Transoxanian crown prince. We have an account dating from the 1630s in which a native of Balkh sets out some of the rules—the Mongol term Yāsā is used—that governed life at an Özbeg court. The author covers the court hierarchy, the reception of ambassadors, and not least the elaborate ritual surrounding the collective drinking of fermented mare's milk, the traditional alcoholic beverage of the Mongols. Here the members of the military elite appear as serious and disciplined drinkers; those who failed to hold their liquor were liable to be reviled and severely punished. To the east in Farghāna the Ming, an Özbeg tribe, built up their power over the course of the eighteenth century, founding the city of Khoqand. There it was a sign of the changing times that in the first decade of the nineteenth century the ruler made a point of recruiting an infantry army of some six thousand Tājīk mountaineers, offending the Özbeg tribesmen by making these Tājīks the core of his military forces. Khwārazm to the northwest had a particularly strong nomadic presence and a Chingizid heritage. We have already met the ʿArabshāhid dynasty of the seventeenth century to which Abū 'l-Ghāzī Bahādur Khān belonged. In the mid-eighteenth century the region was disputed between two Chingizid families. The outcome was the rule of the non-Chingizid Qungrat dynasty (1770–1920), which until 1804 exercised power in the name of puppet Chingizids. This state came to be known from its capital as the Khānate of Khīwa.

There is one further region of Central Asia we should include here: Chinese Turkestan. As we have seen, in the course of the Middle Ages it came to be Turkic-speaking and Muslim. Its location exposed it to political domination from outside, whether by steppe nomad dynasties such as the Qarakhānids and Chaghatay Khāns to the west and north, or by more settled peoples such as the Tibetans and Chinese to the south and east; as we saw, it was the Manchu conquest of 1759 that was eventually to make the region part of China. But there was also a limited amount of state formation within the region. In the seventeenth and eighteenth centuries a family of Ṣūfī leaders belonging to the Naqshbandī order, who were also descendants of the Prophet, came to rule a number of cities, sometimes as clients of foreign overlords and sometimes independently. But their Islamic credentials did not imply a rejection of the Chingizid heritage—indeed they made a point of intermarrying with Chingizids. Nor did they come to power at the head of a militant religious movement, as the Ṣafawids had done. In Turfan they survived into the twentieth century under the aegis of the Manchus.

The legal legacy of the Mongols

Juwaynī (d. 1283) was a cultured Persian bureaucrat who served the Mongol invaders of Iran and wrote a work on their history. At one point in it he discusses the role of Chingiz Khān in the development of Mongol law. He tells us that "he established a rule for every occasion and a regulation for every circumstance, while for every crime he fixed a penalty." Chingiz Khān then had all this written down on rolls, which "are called the *Great Book of Yāsās* and are kept in the treasury of the chief princes."[38] The word *yāsā* here is a Mongol term for a decree or law.

An obvious reading of Juwaynī's statements would be that Chingiz Khān gave his people a code of law. There are, however, problems with this interpretation. Notably, our two best sources for early Mongol affairs say nothing about the promulgation of such a code by Chingiz Khān. But something significant must have happened in 1229, at the start of the reign of Ögedei (ruled 1229–41). According to Juwaynī, the new ruler decreed that the ordinances and commands of his father Chingiz Khān should continue in force without any alteration—and he likewise informs us that Ögedei's son Güyüg (ruled 1246–48) did the same at his accession with regard to Ögedei's ordinances. Meanwhile, according to the Chinese history of the Yuan dynasty of China, completed in 1370, Ögedei promulgated the Great Yāsā, glossed as "the Great Code."[39] Juwaynī does not speak of a code, but this Chinese source certainly does. Yet we have no systematic account of the contents of this code, let alone a copy of it. Two things are nevertheless undeniable. One is that, rightly or wrongly, future generations were in no doubt that Chingiz Khān was the author of a law code, widely known as his Yāsā. The other is that whether or not he actually composed or promulgated such a code, Mongol customary law as shaped by the early Mongol rulers had a long life ahead of it; Juwaynī's reference to Güyüg's confirmation of Ögedei's ordinances already suggests this. It is these two points, not the question what exactly Chingiz Khān did or did not promulgate, that are of interest to us here.

38. Juvaini, *Genghis Khan*, trans. J. A. Boyle, Manchester 1997, 25.

39. I. de Rachewiltz, "Some reflections on Činggis Qan's *Jasay*," *East Asian History*, 6 (1993), 94.

Looking at things from the east, there is nothing remarkable about the idea that Chingiz Khān should have promulgated a code of law. As we saw in the previous chapter, Bilgä Qaghan makes repeated references to law (*törü*) in his inscription; it comes across as a significant part of the glue that holds his state together. Unfortunately he tells us nothing about who made this law, but we are not far from China, and there it was very much in order for each new dynasty to announce itself by promulgating a new code of law. For example, the T'ang (618–907), the Sung (960–1279), and the Ming (1368–1644) did just that. The Chinese tradition of dynastic legislation also wore off on the non-Chinese dynasties of steppe origin that ruled northern China between the T'ang and the Mongols—dynasties such as the Liao, whom we encountered in Central Asia as the Qara Khiṭāy. They, too, promulgated codes of law, though it took them longer to get round to it. So for a Mongol dynasty that was taking over China to follow suit was only to be expected. As the Minister of the Board of Punishments said to the Yuan emperor in 1311, "How could a conscientious holy dynasty like ours have no laws to follow and thus let bureaucrats indulge themselves and people suffer evil?"[40] In fact the Yuan dynasty promulgated several codes. Yet a criticism of the dynasty voiced in China was, ironically, that it never promulgated a *real* law code. As the first Ming emperor put it: "The Yuan alone did not follow this ancient institution, but compiled its regulations on the basis of matters that were current at particular times."[41] When it came to imperial law codes the Chinese clearly had standards that the Mongols had failed to meet.

The view from the west was very different. In the Islamic tradition it is axiomatic that only God is entitled to legislate. As a Qur'ānic verse informs us, "Whosoever judges not according to what God has sent down—they are the unbelievers" (Q5:44). A few verses further on God asks rhetorically, "Is it the judgment of pagandom (*al-Jāhiliyya*) then that they are seeking? Yet who is fairer in judgment than God?" (Q5:50). So human legislation is a pagan abomination. Moreover, Muslims in the early centuries had little historical awareness of the state as a source of legislation. They knew a good deal about the Sasanian Empire, but imperial legislation is not a prominent theme in its history as known either to them or to us. It was, of course, a conspicuous theme in the Byzantine Empire—we need think only of Justinian (ruled 527–65) and his *Digest*. But the Byzantine past had much less purchase on the medieval Muslim historical imagination than did that of the Sasanians. Nor was there a Seljuq precedent. The result was that for many Muslims the Yāsā of Chingiz Khān became the paradigm of legislative activity on the part of the state.

40. Quoted in P. H. Ch'en, *Chinese legal tradition under the Mongols*, Princeton 1979, 24.

41. Quoted in J. D. Langlois, "Law, statecraft, and *The spring and autumn annals* in Yüan political thought," in H. Chan and W. T. de Bary (eds.), *Yüan thought*, New York 1982, 99.

There were thus good Islamic grounds for denouncing the Yāsā as iniquitous. The Damascene Ibn Kathīr (d. 1373) in his commentary on the Qur'ān remarks that in the verse about the judgment of pagandom, one thing God is condemning is the way "the Tatars judge through royal rulings derived from their king Chingiz Khān, who laid down for them the Yāsā, which consists of a book collecting together laws which he borrowed from various legal systems—Judaism, Christianity, Islam, and others—together with many laws that he derived from nothing but his own speculations and fancies." So Chingiz Khān in his lawmaking was guilty of usurping divine authority and thinking for himself. Ibn Kathīr goes on to say that the Yāsā "became a law that was observed among his descendants, and which they preferred to giving judgment according to the Book of God and the practice of God's Messenger." That Ibn Kathīr could express himself so vehemently reflects the fact that he lived in Damascus under the rule of the Mamlūks (1250–1517), who were frequently at war with the Īlkhāns. Thus it cost him nothing to specify the proper treatment of those who engage in such impious disregard of God's law: "Whoever of them does this is an unbeliever who must be fought until he returns to the law of God and His Messenger, so that he does not judge by anything else in matters great or small."[42] Juwaynī, who wrote under Mongol patronage, naturally put things differently. He complimented Chingiz Khān on having abolished "reprehensible customs" among the Mongols, defended his legislation as "praiseworthy from the point of view of reason," and, best of all, affirmed that many of his ordinances were "in conformity with the Sharīʿa."[43] But even Juwaynī did not claim that the entire Yāsā was in such conformity. For example, he tells us that one of its stipulations was indiscriminate toleration: "to consider all sects as one and not to distinguish them from one another." And indeed, if the Mongols left you alive, they were unlikely to make a fuss about your religious beliefs (though they might take exception to some of your practices). Between the lines one suspects that Juwaynī may have liked it that way; but if so, he did not have the nerve to utter so unorthodox a sentiment outright.

If there were good Islamic grounds for denouncing the Yāsā, at least initially there were also good Mongol grounds for denouncing the Sharīʿa. The Chinese history of the Yuan dynasty tells us that the Great Khān Möngke (ruled 1251–59) boasted that he followed the laws of his ancestors and "did not imitate the ways of other countries."[44] Such allergy to "the ways of other countries" was vividly articulated in the aftermath of the Mongol conversion to Islam in Iran, when a certain Qutlugh Shāh Noyan addressed his peers in these terms: "What is this that

42. Ibn Kathīr, *Tafsīr al-Qur'ān al-ʿaẓīm*, Beirut 1990–91, 2:77.

43. For this and the next quotation see Juvaini, *Genghis Khan*, 25, 26.

44. Quoted in T. Allsen, "The rise of the Mongolian empire and Mongolian rule in north China," in *The Cambridge history of China*, Cambridge 1978–, 6:396.

we have done, abandoning the new Yāsā and custom of Chingiz Khān, and taking up the ancient religion of the Arabs . . . ? Let us return to the Yāsā and custom of Chingiz Khān!"[45] Similar sentiments were expressed by the military leaders of the Golden Horde in 1313. Yet as time wore on the ancient religion of the Arabs had to be treated with more respect, while the Yāsā and custom of Chingiz Khān tended to be forgotten. Geographically the process was uneven. Toward the middle of the fourteenth century a Damascene bureaucrat contrasted the persistence of the Yāsā in the Chaghatay Khānate with its decline, as he saw it, in the lands of the Īlkhāns and the Golden Horde. The fourteenth-century Moroccan traveler Ibn Baṭṭūṭa gives a vivid account of how a Chaghatay ruler was deposed for violating the law code of Chingiz Khān; this happened in 1334 at an assembly convened in the eastern part of the Khānate. But by the end of the eighteenth century the prestige of the Yāsā had faded out across the board, even in the lands that had once made up the Chaghatay Khānate.

There was nevertheless a long period—longer in some regions than others—during which Yāsā and Sharīʿa maintained a sometimes tense coexistence, and as we will see in a later chapter that coexistence was to be perpetuated in a modified form in the Ottoman Empire. Both the coexistence and the tensions are strongly in evidence in the Tīmūrid context. Here we can best see the situation from the perspective of a Tīmūrid ruler. On the one hand, he had to keep faith with the Turco-Mongol military elite. They were his kind of people, they were essential to the maintenance of his military power, and he was bonded to many of them by ties formed during his days of *qazaqlïq* in the steppes. To maintain this relationship he had not only to shower this elite with tax-exempt land grants but also to show his continuing loyalty to their legal tradition, the Yāsā of Chingiz Khān and the customary law of Tīmūr (his *törä*, the same word as Bilgä Qaghan's *törü*). But on the other hand, the ruler had to build up the bureaucratic and fiscal infrastructure of his state—how else was he to administer his possessions, collect his taxes, pay for his armies, and balance his budget? For all that he needed good relations with the people who could handle such things: educated urban Tājīks who tended to have close connections to the Islamic scholars of the region. On one level this required reducing the numbers of tax-exempt land grants and generally reining in the share of the available resources going to the military elite; for this, of course, the ruler depended on the bureaucrats. On another level the ruler needed to distance himself from the pagan legal tradition that the military elite held so dear. This in turn meant cultivating the religious scholars, whose commitment to the Sharīʿa was at least as strong as that of the military elite to the legal tradition of Chingiz Khān and Tīmūr.

45. Quoted in D. O. Morgan, "The 'Great *Yāsā* of Chingiz Khān' and Mongol law in the Īlkhānate," *Bulletin of the School of Oriental and African Studies*, 49 (1986), 172.

In the face of this tug of war between the two wings of the elite it was not easy for a Tīmūrid ruler to devise a coherent policy. In 1411 Shāh Rukh abolished Turco-Mongol law and the tribunal that applied it, but there is doubt as to how far this reform was effective. A few decades later Sulṭān-Ḥusayn Bayqara (ruled 1470–1506) would give audience to the religious scholars twice a week and, we are told, would always make decisions in accordance with their views. It went well with this that in 1487 he gave his chief bureaucrat, Majd al-Dīn Khwāfī (d. 1494), sweeping powers to reform the workings of the state in ways that were anathema to the military elite. But in the face of their opposition he allowed his favorite bureaucrat to be arraigned before the very tribunal that Shāh Rukh was supposed to have abolished in 1411. The outcome of the trial and its aftermath was that Majd al-Dīn was killed. But as far as the Tīmūrids are concerned we should perhaps give the last word to Bābur. He comments in his autobiography on the extraordinary respect that his ancestors had shown for Chingizid custom (*törä*). He himself, however, was not a Chingizid fundamentalist: "If someone institutes a good regulation, it should be followed, but if an ancestor leaves behind something bad, then something good should be substituted for it."[46] This position makes a major concession to common sense, but it says nothing about the supremacy of the immutable law of God. Meanwhile in Central Asia, the coexistence of Yāsā and Sharīʿa and the tension between them did not end with the fall of the Tīmūrids. It could still prove a hot topic under the Shībānids and the Toqay Temürids well into the sixteenth and seventeenth centuries. Moreover, the quarrel between Yāsā and Sharīʿa had reverberations far to the west among the fifteenth-century Aq Qoyunlu, not to mention the Ottomans.

Our sources naturally report the extraordinary rather than the ordinary and therefore highlight the tension rather than the coexistence of the two laws. But coexistence there was, and it must have been helped by the capacity of human beings to live with contradictions and get used to what they cannot change. At a somewhat more elevated level, a couple of things might have helped the two sides to get along with each other. On the one hand, the Sharīʿa, like any sophisticated legal system, was not inflexible, and it could extend a certain recognition to human custom that did not derive from divine revelation—though curiously enough this potential does not seem to have been realized in defense of the Yāsā. And on the other hand, Muslims could develop a measure of amnesia with regard to just how irredeemably pagan Chingiz Khān had been. "Even though he was not a Muslim, he had true friendship with God," as a Kurdish historian writing under the later Īlkhāns was to put it.[47] Looking at things in such ways could do something to soften the antagonism between Yāsā and Sharīʿa, though it could never eliminate it.

46. Quoted in Subtelny, *Timurids in transition*, 17–18.
47. Quoted in M. Biran, *Chinggis Khan*, Oxford 2007, 119.

9

The Turks in the western Middle East in medieval times

There were three routes by which the Oghuz Turks moved farther west: northward through the steppes into the Balkans, southwestward from Iran into Syria and Egypt, and westward from Iran into Anatolia. The outcomes of these three ventures were very different.

After dealing briefly with the northern route, we turn to the southern route. Despite some presence of Turkic nomads in Syria, what we see there is a chain of Turkic state formation extending from the eleventh-century Seljuq empire to late medieval Egypt. We will stop to examine the various links in the chain, ending with the Mamlūk Sultanate, its strengths and weaknesses, and in particular its dependence on importing slave soldiers from the Eurasian steppes. How could a state whose prime source of manpower was so distant and whose supply line was so long and exposed hope to survive the vicissitudes of history? Along the way we will encounter the Crusaders, improbable invaders from western Europe who established some small states in Syria. We will also pause to puzzle over an aspect of the domestic history of Egypt: what must have been the final stage of the process whereby the great majority of Egyptians became Muslims.

We will then turn to the process by which Oghuz nomads entered Anatolia and took possession of it. In political terms that meant a series of developments that mirrored the history of Iran on a smaller scale: first a Seljuq sultanate, then the impact of the Mongols, and finally the rise of Turcoman dynasties—the latter at once smaller and more numerous than those that ruled in Iran. Among them was the Ottoman state, whose distinctive historical trajectory we will take up in the next chapter. Meanwhile we will get a glimpse of fourteenth-century Anatolian society thanks to a colorful figure who already appeared in the preceding chapter: the indefatigable Moroccan traveler Ibn Baṭṭūṭa.

The major difference between what happened in Syria and Egypt and what happened in Anatolia was demographic. In Syria and Egypt Turkish power was conspicuous at the top of the state apparatus and in the army, but despite some influx of

Turkic nomads into Syria, it had little effect on the overall makeup of the population, which has remained Arabic-speaking to this day. Anatolia, by contrast, saw a drastic demographic change: for the most part what had long been a Greek-speaking Christian population now became a Turkish-speaking Muslim one, thereby making Anatolia a permanent part of the Muslim world. How do we explain so drastic a shift despite the lack of a comparable spread of Turkish in most of Iran and the Arab lands to the south?

As we saw in the previous chapter, in the middle decades of the eleventh century the Oghuz Turks overran Iran and conquered Iraq. They thereby established themselves in the eastern Middle East. If they were to expand farther to the west, as they did, there were three obvious routes for them to take. One was the northern option, which bypassed Iran entirely: they could migrate westward from their homeland through the steppes that lie to the north of the Caspian and the Black Sea. Another was what we can call the southern option: they could move on from Iran or Iraq into Syria and Egypt. In between there was the western option: they could head westward from Iran into Anatolia. In the event they did all three, but it was the western option that was historically by far the most consequential.

The northern option need not detain us long, despite the fact that it was the most obvious route for steppe nomads to take. The Oghuz had already appeared in the western steppes in the tenth century and remained a presence there in the eleventh as one of a number of nomadic Turkic populations in the region. The Byzantines called them Uzes (*Ouzoi*), whereas the Russians called them Turks (*Torki*). There is no indication that they were Muslims, which is not surprising. There were pagan Oghuz to the east of the Caspian as late as the twelfth century. As usual with steppe nomads, their chances of longevity as a people were poor unless they could take possession of a territory suited to settled life, as the Bulgars and Hungarians had done. But in the event they failed to do that. In 1064, according to one account, "the entire nation of the Uzes crossed the Danube with all their gear,"[1] ravaging Byzantine territory all the way to Salonica and beyond. They were led by their tribal chiefs—the Seljuqs played no part in these events. This was a promising start, but despite their numbers—the figure of six hundred thousand is mentioned—they were forced to retreat by the winter weather, disease, and resistance. Some did settle in Macedonia, while others were recruited into the Byzantine army; at the battle of Manzikert, which the Byzantine emperor lost to the Seljuq sultan in eastern Anatolia in 1071, they defected to their fellow Oghuz. This was always a hazard of armies of mixed ethnicity, as a Byzantine strategist had cautioned around 600: "Long before battle, troops of the same race as

1. Michael Attaleiates, *The history*, Cambridge, MA 2012, 151–53.

the enemy should be separated from the army and sent elsewhere to avoid their going over to the enemy at a critical moment."[2] But however critical the moment in Anatolia, no lasting settlement of the Uzes ensued in the Balkans, and we hear no more of them after the later twelfth century—unless perchance the Gagauz, a Turkic-speaking Christian population that used to live in the Dobruja, should happen to be their descendants, but this is unlikely.

The southern and western options require more extended treatment. Unlike the northern option, they involved Muslim Oghuz, and their migrations led to significant and even, in the case of the western option, momentous historical developments. We can conveniently refer to these Muslim Oghuz as "Turcomans," though many then and now would simply call them Turks.

The Turkic expansion to the southwest

The Turcomans in Syria

As we have seen, there were two features of a territory that would make it inviting to Turcomans: pasture and plunder. Azerbaijan was a Turcoman paradise because it offered both. But the southern Middle East was not. Arabia for the most part offered Turcomans neither pasture nor plunder; consequently they neither conquered it nor roamed it with their flocks, though the Seljuqs at their height could play the role of the major external power. Iraq offered plunder but not pasture. The Seljuqs conquered it with a Turcoman army, taking Baghdad in 1055, but it was not inviting terrain for Turcoman nomads. Likewise in Khūzistān, an eastern extension of Iraq, the Turcoman Shumla set himself up as a local ruler in the second half of the twelfth century, but no Turcoman pastoral economy seems to have been established there. Syria was a more ambiguous case, offering a combination of plunder with mediocre pasture—better in the north, worse in the south. So there the story is more complex.[3]

It begins with a Turcoman adventurer named Atsïz, who in 1071 accepted an invitation from the Fāṭimids to quell Bedouin unrest in Palestine. He went on to carve out a principality for himself, seizing Jerusalem and Damascus but overreaching by attacking Egypt. In the face of an uncharacteristically strong Fāṭimid response, he appealed to the Seljuq sultan Malik Shāh for help. Malik Shāh reacted by sending his brother Tutush (ruled 1078–95) to take over, which he did, disposing of Atsïz in 1079. From then until the death of Tutush in 1095, Syria was under the sway of a Seljuq ruler with a Turcoman army.

2. *Maurice's Stratēgikon*, trans. G. T. Dennis, Philadelphia 1984, 69.

3. For the history of Syria (and Egypt) from the eleventh century to the sixteenth see P. M. Holt, *The age of the Crusades*, London 1986.

But Tutush, like many Seljuq princes, had larger ambitions. When his brother died he moved into Iran in a bid to succeed him, and died in the attempt. He left two sons to inherit his Syrian domains, Riḍwān (ruled 1095–1113) in Aleppo and Duqāq (ruled 1095–1104) in Damascus. Both were military weaklings. The reason was that when attempting to realize his ambitions in Iran, Tutush had taken his Turcomans with him, and after his failure they preferred to remain in the northern Jazīra—that is to say, in the foothills of the northern Middle East. The move made good sense for Turcoman pastoralists, and in fact there was already a considerable Turcoman population in this northern region. This population was to sustain the existence of a long-lasting Turcoman dynasty, the Artuqids (ca. 1101–1409). The founder was initially governor of Palestine and died in Jerusalem, but his sons were unable to sustain his position there and moved instead to the Turcoman-friendly territory of the northern Jazīra. Turcoman power was thus a viable basis for state formation in that region, but not in most of Syria, where the departure of the Turcomans left the Seljuq princes of Aleppo and Damascus high and dry. They had lost their Turcomans, and at the same time they lacked the resources to replace them with significant numbers of Turkic slave soldiers.

This left the princes exposed to many potential enemies, including the Crusaders, most of whom were Franks. The Frankish presence in Syria was the result of the First Crusade (1096–99), which established a Christian kingdom based in Jerusalem (1099–1187) together with three smaller Christian states farther north. In their efforts to survive, the hapless Seljuq princes often had to endure the indignity of accommodating or allying with the Crusaders as a counterweight to their Muslim enemies. Within a few years Seljuq rule in Aleppo collapsed, while in Damascus the Atabeg—the guardian of the Seljuq prince—took over and founded the Būrid dynasty, which lasted until 1154. A telling indication of the weakness of this dynasty is the continuing prominence of the urban militia (*aḥdāth*) of Damascus in its history.

In short, within a few decades of the Seljuq conquest of Syria the Turcomans had left and Seljuq rule had petered out. In the twelfth century we encounter occasional references to Turcomans living in central or southern Syria; then and later they were recruited by rulers as auxiliary troops. Their numbers increased in the second half of the thirteenth century as many Turcomans took refuge in Syria from the Mongols. In the sixteenth century we find Turcoman nomads wintering in northern Syria, but they could also be found as far south as northern Palestine, and even Ramla. As we saw, in the sixteenth century one of the Qizilbāsh tribes was known as Shāmlu, "Syrian." But these Turcoman tribesmen were too few to turn Syria into Turkic-speaking territory, and they were not significant actors in the politics of Syria itself. As far as the making of history is concerned, the story of the Turcomans in Syria was pretty much over by the end of the eleventh century.

There was nevertheless a future for Turks in Syria, though it was not a specifically Turcoman one. It turned on two things. The first was a long-term feature of the military scene, the role of Turkic slave soldiers in the major armies of the Middle East. As we have seen, this phenomenon went back to the ninth century, and it continued in some fashion into the sixteenth. The second was a transitory feature of the decline of the Seljuq state as it affected its peripheral territories. In their better days the Seljuq sultans of Iran could appoint governors to such territories, but as their power waned they could no longer prevent these governors from becoming independent rulers. We saw how this happened in Khwārazm, and there was another such case in Mosul, illustrating the process whereby insiders succeeded to fragments of a failing empire. It is Mosul that concerns us here.

The Zangids and the Ayyūbids

In 1127 a somewhat reluctant Seljuq sultan appointed a certain Zangī governor of Mosul and Atabeg of two Seljuq princes. Zangī (ruled 1127–46) was very much an insider. His father was a Turkic slave soldier, a commander in the army of Malik Shāh, and had served as governor of Aleppo. Though Zangī was ambitious, he made no attempt to expand into Iran, as an aspiring Seljuq prince might have done. Instead he set about extending his territories westward into northern Syria, taking over Aleppo in 1128. He was also involved in Iraq, but it was his activities in Syria that mattered for the future. Here the presence of the Crusaders was both a military obstacle and a rhetorical convenience for Zangī: he could pursue his territorial ambitions in the name of Muslim solidarity against the infidel. In 1144 his capture of Edessa, the northernmost of the Crusader states, gained him a good reputation in this regard.

When Zangī was murdered two years later by one of his slaves, his territories were divided—a reminder that this was a post-Seljuq state. His son Nūr al-Dīn (ruled 1146–74) succeeded to his Syrian lands, and this is the line we need to follow. Nūr al-Dīn continued the rhetoric—and not just the rhetoric—of the counter-Crusade. Fulfilling one of his father's ambitions, he took Damascus in 1154. When in good health Nūr al-Dīn was as strong as the Būrids had been weak, and we hear no more of the involvement of the urban militia in the politics of Damascus. But neither did he rely exclusively on his Turkic slave soldiers. Alongside them he recruited considerable numbers of Kurds, who might be mountaineers but were nevertheless cavalry. Meanwhile in the 1160s a competition developed between Nūr al-Dīn and the Crusaders to take over the decaying Fāṭimid state in Egypt, a struggle that at one point saw a Crusader garrison in Cairo. It was one of his Kurdish officers, Shīrkūh, whom Nūr al-Dīn put in charge of the expeditions he sent to Egypt in 1164, 1167, and 1168–69. The third expedition secured permanent possession of Egypt, but soon after that Shīrkūh died, and his position passed to his nephew Saladin. When Nūr al-Dīn himself died in 1174 leaving only a minor to succeed him, it was Saladin who took over the Zangid lands in the ensuing succession struggle, with the claim that he was the rightful guardian of Nūr al-Dīn's son.

That Saladin was the winner should not surprise us. He was not just a powerful and ambitious military commander; he now had at his disposal something that the Zangids, for all their military mettle, had lacked—the fiscal resources of Egypt. The country had its deficiencies. As an early fourteenth-century Christian author of a tract on how to defeat the Saracens acutely observed, Egypt lacked both iron and timber and depended on foreign trade for supplies of both. But it had the riches of its irrigated agriculture and was ideally placed to take a cut from the transit trade between the Mediterranean and the Indian Ocean. Syria, by contrast, with its Mediterranean agriculture and backbone of mountainous terrain, was not a natural venue for the formation of a strong state. Between the Umayyads and modern times, the Zangids are perhaps the nearest thing to an exception to this rule, and inasmuch as they failed to establish a strong state in Syria on a lasting basis they were not exceptional at all. Yet they did well enough for a few decades to secure possession of Egypt, thereby serving as the stepping-stone by which the Seljuq military tradition reached a land with the wealth to support it. The historical role of the Crusader states in this story was to serve as a catalyst in this process of Turkic state formation.

What needs explaining here is the fact that the Egyptian state, for all its fiscal resources, should have found itself at the mercy of two far less well-endowed Syrian states, to such a degree that the only question was which of them would win the struggle to take it over. In military terms the answer is not far to seek. As we have seen, in the later eleventh century the Fāṭimid state in effect opted for military obsolescence as the price of political stability, and for the next century it stuck to that decision. With neither the mounted archers of the Zangids nor the heavy cavalry of the Crusaders, this meant that they were living on borrowed time. As Nūr al-Dīn put it in a letter to the Fāṭimid caliph, who was understandably nervous about the presence of Nūr al-Dīn's forces in Egypt, the arrows of the Turks were the only thing the Franks with their lances were afraid of. A telling indication of Fāṭimid weakness in the face of these arrows and lances is the fact that in the 1160s a standard Fāṭimid move was to offer either the Crusaders or the Zangids large sums of money as tribute. Meanwhile the dynasty continued until 1171, though of the last six caliphs four came to the throne as children, and their viziers tended to be more powerful than they were themselves. There were also damaging succession disputes in 1094 and 1130–32. That of 1094 was not a momentous event in Egypt itself; it led to a rebellion based in Alexandria but was well enough contained domestically that it did not lead to prolonged civil war. It nevertheless caused a serious rent in the wider Ismāʿīlī community, prompting the formation and secession of the Nizārī subsect, which as we have seen took with it the Ismā'īlīs of Iran, together with many of those of Syria. The dispute of 1130–32 took longer to resolve, and it included a bizarre episode in which the vizier of the day declared the Fāṭimid dynasty deposed in favor of the Hidden Imam of the Imāmī Shī'ites. Domestically this realignment did not last, and the dynasty limped on for another four decades. But the dispute led to the formation of the Ṭayyibī subsect, which took with it the Ismā'īlīs of the Yemen under the rule of the Ṣulayḥids, and probably most if not all those of India. Also significant was the lack of serious resistance to the restoration of Sunnism as the religion of the state when the end came in 1171. This suggests that the traditional sectarian claims of the Fāṭimids had not been doing much to prop up the dynasty even within Egypt. In short, the Fāṭimid state in its last decades was shorn of both soft and hard power, a state asking to be conquered.

With the resources of Egypt and much of Syria at his disposal, Saladin (ruled 1174–93) set about consolidating his rule over both of them. He first laboriously secured the submission of Aleppo and Mosul and then in 1187 dramatically defeated the Crusaders, pretty much reducing their presence in Syria to three coastal cities. The sequence here was not accidental: it was the extension of his territory that gave Saladin the resources and manpower to fight a decisive battle with the Crusaders, perhaps increasing the size of his regular cavalry force from around six thousand to around twelve thousand. This number was still small by the standards of the northern middle East, where a Seljuq army might include several tens of thousands of horsemen, and a Mongol army was likely to exceed a hundred thousand. But a cavalry army of twelve thousand far outmatched the Crusaders, for whom scarcity of manpower in an outpost so distant from their homeland had always been a key problem. The reign of Saladin was accordingly a success story, and despite the initial fiction of his loyalty to Nūr al-Dīn's son, he was in fact the founder of a dynasty known from the name of Saladin's father Ayyūb as the Ayyūbids (1174–1250).[4]

This new dynasty was still in a direct line of derivation from the Seljuq sultanate. Just as the Seljuq-Zangid transition had been a takeover by an insider, so too was the Zangid-Ayyūbid transition. Thus much about Ayyūbid rule was still reminiscent of the Seljuqs. For example, we still hear of Atabegs, and elements of Persian administrative terminology remained in use. More significantly, the Ayyūbids continued the Seljuq and Zangid willingness to divide their territories. Saladin's Syrian lands thus passed into the hands of half a dozen branches of his family. The Seljuq heritage had nevertheless been diluted in two significant ways.

4. For the history of the dynasty see R. S. Humphreys, *From Saladin to the Mongols*, Albany 1977.

The first was the presence of a considerable number of Kurds in the army. Their recruitment had begun already in the reign of Zangī and continued under Nūr al-Dīn and Saladin; under his rule and that of his successors the dynasty itself was now Kurdish. Politically this was remarkable. As we have seen, from time to time Kurds had founded minor dynasties in and around their ancestral lands, but overall they did not have much of a record of state formation. What made the Ayyūbid achievement less remarkable in military terms is that the core of Zangid and Ayyūbid armies seems to have remained the Turkic slave soldiery. Although as late as 1259 there were still Kurdish army commanders of Ayyūbid vintage, it seems that the Kurds had assimilated the Turkic style of warfare. But the numbers of Kurdish soldiers declined under the last effective ruler of the dynasty in Egypt, al-Malik al-Ṣāliḥ (ruled 1240–49), leaving Turkic slave troops, notably Qipchaqs, to dominate the army—and, in the event, to inherit the state. In short, the role of the Kurds was less significant than it looked. The bottom line is that it was Turkic power, not Kurdish power, that had now spread all the way to Egypt. It did not spread far beyond it in the Middle Ages, though as we will see Turkic soldiers reached Morocco in Ayyūbid times, and in the days of the Mamlūk Sultanate they even made an appearance in fourteenth-century West Africa.

The second dilution of the Seljuq heritage was the inclusion of Egypt in the Ayyūbid domains. In military terms this did not make much difference, as the obsolete Fāṭimid army was of no use to the new rulers. Its military elite was replaced by a Turkic and Kurdish one. Meanwhile, the large Fāṭimid infantry force made up of black slaves had rebelled in 1169. At this time Saladin was already in control of Egypt, and his response was ruthless. In the course of the battle he had their quarters set on fire, burning their women, children, and property. The survivors fled to Upper Egypt and made trouble there for a few years. No doubt racial animus was in play here, but what counted most against the black infantry was not that they were black but that they were infantry—a form of military manpower of which the Ayyūbids had only very limited need. So the military role of Egypt was now to provide the revenue to pay for more Turkic and Kurdish troops.

On the civilian side, however, Egypt was bound to play more of a part in shaping its relationship with its new rulers. In the first place, the practice of dividing the dynasty's territories stopped short at the Sinai desert. Unlike Iran, Egypt in Islamic times was a political unit with a more or less fixed capital. As we saw, there was a period of disunity in the ninth century, and there was a long-term tendency for Upper Egypt to become a wild south—but that made it a hotbed of anarchy rather than a site for a rival state. And sure enough, the country retained its unity—together with its capital—under the Ayyūbids. The result was a formidable imbalance of power between Ayyūbid Egypt and the petty principalities of Ayyūbid Syria. In the second place, Egypt had a long-established bureaucratic tradition, and much of it was bound to survive the transition from Fāṭimid to Ayyūbid rule. The documents of the two dynasties can be so similar as to make it hard to tell them apart. Another example is the continuing role of Coptic bureaucrats, especially in the financial administration. There was also continuity at a much higher level: Saladin put at the head of his chancery al-Qāḍī al-Fāḍil, a Palestinian Sunnī but one who had been shaped by a career in the Fāṭimid bureaucracy.

Before we leave the Ayyūbids we should take stock of such efforts as they made to project their power beyond Egypt and Syria. The most obvious direction for expansion—the only direction that did not involve an Egyptian army crossing sea or desert—was southward into Nubia. And indeed, in the winter of 1172–73 Saladin dispatched an expedition to the south under the command of his restless brother Tūrān Shāh. It penetrated Nubia, a land that Tūrān Shāh found unattractive, and after that there were no serious incursions into Nubia in Ayyūbid times. The motive of the attack of 1172–73 was apparently not to build an empire but to have a convenient refuge should Nūr al-Dīn invade Egypt. Just as fruitless was an attempt in the years from 1172 to 1212 to conquer Tunisia, something that has never been done by a state based in Egypt. It was an Armenian slave soldier of a nephew of Saladin who led this effort at the head of a force of "Ghuzz"—the Arabic form of the ethnonym Oghuz. Some of these Turks ended up in Morocco as an elite unit in the army of the Almohad ruler of North Africa. But Saladin did have a presence in Cyrenaica, and his forces had some success in the oases of the Fazzān in what is today southern Libya. A more fruitful venture was another expedition led by Tūrān Shāh in 1173. On this occasion he crossed the Red Sea and conquered the southern Yemen together with its western coastal plain. He himself returned to the north in 1176, but an Ayyūbid dynasty ruled in the Yemen until the last of the line decided to leave for the north in 1229. When he did so he appointed as his deputy a member of a Turcoman family that had long been in the service of the Ayyūbids. Since the departing ruler died on his way north and no other Ayyūbid came to claim his throne, the Turcoman deputy was able to found a dynasty of his own, known as the Rasūlids (1229–1454). While the Yemen itself was not much of a source of revenue, the dynasty had the advantage of a prime location with regard to the commerce of the Indian Ocean, and in territorial terms it did well, expanding as far east as Dhofar, today part of Oman. The Rasūlids were very much in the Ayyūbid tradition, as is evident from their royal titulature; for example, Saladin's title had been al-Malik al-Nāṣir Ṣalāḥ al-Dīn, and it was shared by a Rasūlid ruler of the early fifteenth century. But the Rasūlids did not entirely forget the steppes. One learned ruler, al-Malik al-Afḍal (ruled 1363–77), had enough time on his hands to put together a large compendium of miscellaneous information. Among many other things, it contained vocabularies covering six languages. Not content with Arabic, Persian, Greek, and Armenian, the royal author included Turkic and Mongol (he gives the Turkic for God as *tangrï* or *tengri*, and the Mongol as *tengri*). His father, al-Malik al-Mujāhid (ruled 1321–63), had a military commander called Qubilay, a transparently Mongol name. But to return to the Ayyūbids, the significant point is that despite their Turkic army their state was not an empire, inasmuch as no territory outside Egypt was actually ruled from Cairo.

Meanwhile, the end of Ayyūbid rule and the transition to Mamlūk rule turned out to be a complex process for a couple of reasons. One, which concerns Syria, was the multiplicity of branches of the Ayyūbid dynasty. Here, at least, the ways in which the various branches ended were in themselves simple enough. In one case the dynasty died out, and in the others each branch was terminated in 1260 or later by external forces—be they the Mongols, the Mamlūks, or, in the case of one particularly long-lived branch in the Jazīra, the Aq Qoyunlu.

The other cause of complexity concerns Egypt, where the 1250s were a period of political instability that must have been as confusing for contemporaries as it is for us. Although the decade was bracketed by a Frankish invasion of Egypt and a Mongol invasion of Syria, the transition was essentially an internal one. There were several leading actors in the story. One was a widow, Shajar al-Durr (d. 1257), a Turkic slave who had risen to be the wife of al-Malik al-Ṣāliḥ, the last real Ayyūbid ruler of Egypt till his death in 1249. Then there were a couple of ill-fated members of the Ayyūbid family. And above all, there were the powerful Turkic slave soldiers. The upshot was that the widow was formally installed as ruler, but only for a few months in 1250; the members of the family were killed or exiled; and the most powerful slave soldier won. We can dispense with a detailed narrative of the events, but a few points are worth picking out. One is that in relations between Ayyūbid princes and powerful slave soldiers the old Seljuq figure of the Atabeg was still present. Another is that the rule of a woman was clearly felt by those concerned to be an embarrassment. It invited mocking comments such as that of the ʿAbbāsid caliph, who is reputed to have written to the Egyptians saying, "If you haven't got a man left to appoint as your ruler, just tell us, and we'll send you one."[5] Had not the Prophet remarked on hearing the news of the accession of a princess to the Persian throne that "a people who appoint a woman as their ruler will not prosper"? Perhaps in the same vein, we are told that Shajar al-Durr spent her last hours grinding up her jewelry in a mortar so that no other woman would ever wear it. Finally, the events reveal the salience of a pattern of factionalism among slave soldiers that was to be a structural feature of the politics of the Mamlūk Sultanate: there was solidarity among the slave soldiers purchased by a given commander, matched by tension between those purchased by different commanders. In the 1250s the key group was the Baḥriyya, the slave soldiers purchased by al-Malik al-Ṣāliḥ. They were opposed to any successor with slave soldiers of his own, and it

5. Suyūṭī, *Ḥusn al-muḥāḍara*, Cairo 1967–68, 2:36.

was eventually one of their number, a Qipchaq named Baybars (ruled 1260–77), who held power for long enough to restore stability to the body politic.

The Mamlūks

The Mamlūk Sultanate (1250–1517) was not a dynasty in the conventional sense of a succession of rulers belonging to the same family.[6] Certainly the idea of hereditary succession was present. Sultans tried hard to secure the succession of their sons, though their success in this endeavor tended to be short-lived. Typically a deceased sultan's son would serve as a stopgap until the accession of the next powerful slave soldier—or more precisely, former slave soldier, since by this stage of his career he would have been manumitted. There was nevertheless a prolonged period of not quite continuous hereditary rule from 1279 to 1390. The founder of this dynasty was Qalāwūn (ruled 1279–90), a Qipchaq slave soldier, but the line owed its longevity to the fact that one of his sons turned out to be an unusually astute politician. Yet by and large the most effective sultans were imported slave soldiers. In ethnic terms these soldiers were predominantly Turks until the later fourteenth century. There was then a shift from Turks to Circassians, but also to greater diversity—some recruits were by origin Christians and even Jews from Europe. The Turks were primarily Qipchaqs from the steppes; the Circassian homeland was the mountains and plains of the northwestern Caucasian region. Circassian is a Caucasian language without any relationship to Turkic, yet in our sources the Circassians of Egypt sound very like Turks despite their distinct ethnic identity. They have Turkic names; one of them was named "Aq Qush," Turkic for "White Bird," and another was called "Baybars" like his Qipchaq predecessor. Three of the last Mamlūk sultans wrote Turkic poetry. Even in the Circassian period contemporaries had a tendency to refer to what we call the Mamlūk Sultanate as "the state of the Turks," and the sources give no indication that members of the military were in the habit of transacting their affairs in Circassian. Altogether, the slave soldiers of the Mamlūk period were culturally Turkic even when not ethnically so, and to judge by the prices they fetched, Turkic slaves were still the best on the market.

An interesting point about the descendants of Qalāwūn is the fact that this dynasty won the loyalty of the Cairene populace. One explanation for this would be that the general absence of a royal family among the Mamlūk sultans was seen as a liability. Today the transmission of a public office within a family looks wrong; back then, just as in the Iran of Shāh ʿAbbās, it looked right. This Mamlūk legitimacy deficit perhaps helps explain the fact that from 1261 to 1517 the sultans hosted

6. For the history of the Mamlūk Sultanate to 1382 see R. Irwin, *The Middle East in the Middle Ages*, London 1986.

a refugee line of ʿAbbāsid caliphs in Cairo. These caliphs were figureheads, treated with formal deference and informal contempt. When a failing sultan—Baybars II (ruled 1309–10)—sought to boost his authority with a diploma from the caliph, one of his own commanders made the comment: "Tell him he's stupid. Nobody takes any notice of the caliph."[7] Only once, in 1412, was an unwilling caliph made sultan, raising the possibility that he might rule rather than reign, but he was quickly deposed. Yet the presence of a caliph in Cairo may have helped make Mamlūk rule look a bit more legitimate.

As might be expected, there was much continuity from the Ayyūbids to the Mamlūks. The Seljuq heritage was still palpable. When a four-year-old son of the first major Mamlūk ruler, Baybars, was appointed titular joint sultan in 1264, he was assigned an Atabeg just as a Seljuq princeling would have been. Likewise the Persian administrative terminology was still there; for example, Baybars II had held the office of Jāshnikīr, a thinly Arabized form of the Persian Chāshnīgīr, "taster." But in one major respect the Mamlūks departed from the Seljuq tradition. They never divided their territory—which helps explain why they lasted so much longer than their predecessors did. At the same time, the Egyptian heritage of the Ayyūbids was still very much in evidence. For example, Copts continued to be prominent in the financial administration.

Given the thoroughly military character of the Mamlūk state, one might have expected it to be an expansive military power of the kind we are so familiar with in the northern Middle East. In fact, however, its fundamental military posture was defensive. Based in Egypt, it sought strategic depth by establishing firm control of Syria and the northern approaches to it and defending this territory in the face of repeated invasions mounted by the Īlkhāns between 1260 and 1303. By 1291 the Mamlūks had also ended the Crusader presence on the Syrian coast. But instead of strengthening the fortifications they captured, they demolished them so that no Frankish naval expedition could seize them—a drastic concession to the reality of Christian sea power on the Mediterranean. To the west, in better times they maintained some kind of position in Cyrenaica, a significant source of horses for them. Beyond that they engaged in occasional military activities further afield, mostly in regions where they did not have to confront major military powers. These included the islands of Cyprus and Rhodes, together with Nubia, the Ḥijāz, and the Yemen—this last to counter the naval threat posed by the Portuguese, who rounded the Cape of Good Hope in 1497. In the northern Middle East, where the enemies tended to be more formidable, Mamlūk forces three times penetrated deep enough to reach Kayseri in Cappadocia. But these visits were brief and inconsequential. The reasons for this generally defensive posture are not far to seek.

7. Quoted in Holt, *The age of the Crusades*, 112.

In the age of the cavalry a dearth of steppe-grade pastureland was a serious liability, and if Syrian pasture was mediocre, Egypt's was much worse. Moreover, the Mamlūk army was recruited through a long-distance slave trade, which meant that even at the best of times it was very costly to maintain; contrast the situation that obtained around 1100 in Transcaucasia, where the Georgian monarch could easily bring in fifty thousand Qipchaq warriors from across the mountains to defend his realm against the Turcomans. The result of these factors was to impose a low ceiling on the numbers of the regular cavalry in the Mamlūk army, perhaps no more than twenty thousand. By the standards of the northern Middle East this was a serious constraint, and it meant that the Mamlūk state could not afford to be cavalier in throwing its weight around. Despite these limitations, it survived for over two and a half centuries—longer than any dynasty that ruled Iran in our period.

Yet toward the end the Mamlūks, like the Fāṭimids before them, were living on borrowed time. There were several reasons for this. One was that the Egyptian economy of late Mamlūk times was not what it had been. The most obvious factor at work was the demographic disaster of the Black Death in 1348–49 and the recurrent epidemics of bubonic plague that followed it into the sixteenth century. In its aftermath the sources report a serious degradation of the irrigation system, and we are told that between 1215 and 1517 the land tax of Egypt fell from over nine million dinars to under two million. At the same time, measures such as a heavy-handed pepper monopoly instituted by the sultan in 1438 did not augur well on the commercial front. Toward the end the arrival of the Portuguese on the Indian Ocean posed a new threat to the commercial revenues of the sultans, since the Portuguese were using their naval power in an effort to reroute the trade of the Indian Ocean at Egypt's expense. All this meant less revenue to spend on buying and maintaining slave soldiers. In the first half of the fourteenth century the number of such soldiers owned by the sultan was some twelve thousand; by the fifteenth century it had fallen to less than half that. Not surprisingly, the later Mamlūk rulers had far less control over their territory than their predecessors had, particularly those parts of it that were populated by Arab tribes.

A second reason the later Mamlūks were in trouble arose from the way they recruited their troops. Particularly in the Circassian period, the sons of slave soldiers were typically excluded from the mainstream of the military elite. This meant that the Mamlūks depended heavily on importing slaves to replenish their cavalry in each generation. These imports were not just expensive; they were increasingly insecure. For the system to work it was essential that neither the lands from which the slaves originated nor the route by which they were brought to Egypt should be at the mercy of a hostile power. As long as the relevant states saw the Mamlūks as a potential ally there was no problem, and at first this condition was satisfied. The Golden Horde and the Mamlūks had a common enemy, the Īlkhāns; and the Byzantine Empire, which sat on the sea route out of the Black

Sea, was well disposed toward both. This convergence made it possible for merchants to ply their trade, bringing slaves from the Crimea to Egypt through the Bosphorus or across Anatolia to Syria. But once the residual Byzantine Empire and an increasing amount of Anatolia were swallowed up by a powerful and expansive state, the game was up. By the end of the Mamlūk period the Ottoman Empire controlled both the sea route through the Straits—the Bosphorus and the Dardanelles—and the land route across Anatolia. This stranglehold put the Ottomans in a position to render the Mamlūk model unsustainable.

That was not, however, the only way in which the Mamlūk model was arguably no longer viable. There is reason to think that it was also increasingly obsolete in military terms.[8] The more a ruler could do with artillery, infantry, and handguns, the less he could hope to achieve with an old-fashioned cavalry army. Like the early Ṣafawid Shāhs, the later Mamlūk sultans were well aware of this problem and took steps to address it. One ruler sought to create a troop of black slaves equipped with handguns. This did not go down well with the white slave soldiers, and the crunch came when the sultan decided to dress the commander of his new unit like one of their commanders and to let him marry a white-skinned Circassian slave girl. That was too much for them: they killed the commander and forced the sultan to disband the unit. A later ruler tried again, and harder. But these steps, though prescient, were not enough. The sultans lacked funds, and the slave soldiers were unwilling to change. As a captive Mamlūk commander is reputed to have told the Ottoman sultan with great indignation, using firearms was unmanly cheating. These devices, he is related to have said, were an invention of the European Christians, who stood no chance against a Muslim army without them; even a woman could fire a gun. The outcome was that just as the Ottomans with their infantry and firearms crushed the Ṣafawids in 1514, so, too, they crushed the Mamlūks in 1516.

One more point is perhaps worth adding: the distribution of external attacks on the Mamlūk Sultanate over time. Serious invasions by foreign enemies were heavily bunched in the early decades of Mamlūk rule, when the Īlkhāns were the mortal enemy. Such repeated attacks are a learning experience that can concentrate the military mind. But from then until the Ottoman conquest there was only one invasion of Syria, that of Tīmūr in 1400–1401, and he soon went on his way. In 1485–91 there was a war with the Ottomans, but it was fought in the border areas to the north and west of Syria, not in Syria itself, and the Mamlūks did quite well in it. There was nevertheless an ominous disparity in the effort invested in the conflict by the two sides: the Mamlūks were trying much harder than the Ottomans. The point might have caught the eye of a grand strategist, but probably not of the Mamlūk soldiery at large. So there was no significant learning experience in

8. For a different view see R. Irwin, "Gunpowder and firearms in the Mamluk Sultanate reconsidered," in his *Mamlūks and Crusaders*, Farnham 2010, art. XX.

the decades leading up to the Ottoman conquest. Instead, Mamlūk training and discipline appear to have undergone a long-term degradation.

Except insofar as the Mamlūk elite survived in an eroded form under the Ottomans, the chain that linked the Seljuqs to the Zangids, the Zangids to the Ayyūbids, and the Ayyūbids to the Mamlūks was now broken. This form of Turkic power had nevertheless proved remarkably resilient, despite the false start of the Seljuq conquest of Syria and the lack of any significant Turkic population in this Arabic-speaking region—other than the Turcomans of Syria, who continued to play their minor role as auxiliaries in the armies of the Mamlūks. And while the Ottoman takeover of Syria and Egypt was in no sense an internal transition, what it did was in the end to replace one form of Turkic power with another, and more viable, form. The continuing salience of Turkic power dominates a first and even second approximation of the politics of the region in our period. A third approximation would bring into focus the role of the indigenous Arabic-speaking population, but we will take that up in a later chapter.

The Mamlūk rulers of medieval Egypt were not particularly popular among their Arabic-speaking subjects, but they did receive some thanks for their efforts. In a purple passage eulogizing them, Ibn Khaldūn credited divine providence with saving the Muslims by sending them as their protectors Turks "who are imported as slaves from the lands of heathendom to the lands of Islam." Once arrived there, "they embrace Islam with the determination of true believers, while retaining their nomadic virtues undefiled by vile nature, unmixed with the filth of lustful pleasures, unmarred by the habits of civilization."[9] But such eulogies were uncommon among the scholars, who wrote most of the sources we read. Thus in one work the historian Maqrīzī (d. 1442) vented his spleen indirectly by excoriating the conduct of the ʿAbbāsid caliph al-Muʿtaṣim (ruled 833–42). This ruler, he lamented, had fired the Arabs—the Prophet's own people through whom He had established the religion of Islam—and put an end to Arab power (*al-dawla al-ʿArabiyya*). In their place he had installed the Turks, whom the Prophet had warned the Muslims not to risk attacking—a reference to the Prophet's advice to leave those dangerous Turks alone as long as they left the Muslims alone. The result of this disastrous error was that the Turks came to dominate everywhere, killing al-Muʿtaṣim's son and grandson when they ruled as caliphs after him. But ordinary people seem to have taken a more nuanced view, paying the Turks a backhanded compliment: "Better the injustice of the Turks than the justice of the Arabs."[10] They might even go so far as to say that "the Turk is the salt of Egypt."[11]

9. Quoted in D. Ayalon, "The Great Yāsa of Chingiz Khān," *Studia Islamica*, 36 (1972), 119.

10. Quoted in U. Haarmann, "Rather the injustice of the Turks than the righteousness of the Arabs," *Studia Islamica*, 68 (1988), 71.

11. Quoted in Ṣ. Y. Labīb, "Qudsī's Werk '*Duwal al-Islām aš-šarīfa al-bahiyya*,'" *Der Islam*, 56 (1979), 119.

Copts and Muslims

If the Muslim masses showed a grudging respect for the Turks, they did not extend it to the Copts, the indigenous Egyptian Christians—in sharp contrast to the benevolent attitude found among the Arab elite of early Islamic Egypt.[12] This popular hostility was not unremitting, and as usual in such contexts there must have been many instances of friendly cooperation between Muslims and Copts. In the thirteenth century we hear of Christians regularly attending Muslim weddings in a town in Upper Egypt. But such good relations did not make headlines, and ill feeling was never very far away. According to a piece of allegedly ancient wisdom, there was no people worse than the Copts; "trust them and they cheat you."[13] A specific reason the Copts were disliked was their entrenched position in the fiscal bureaucracy. Here the part they played in enabling the state to extract revenue from its Muslim subjects could be a very visible one, as when Coptic clerks played a prominent part in the fiscal surveys of Egypt carried out in 1298 and 1315. This was part of a larger story.[14] Muslim rulers, like rulers in general, benefited from employing members of groups that were without political power in the society they ruled. Buying foreign slaves was one way to achieve this; hiring members of a subordinate ethnic or religious population was another. The Mamlūk state did both, buying itself Turks as soldiers and employing Copts as bureaucrats. The incumbency of the Copts was reinforced by the fact that they had the know-how that comes with long experience—they knew the arcane details of the fiscal system. As a Mamlūk sultan was told by one of his commanders, "Sire, these men run the financial bureaus. They husband the moneys and the taxes, so that the sultan cannot dispense with their services."[15] But employing Copts carried a cost. It provoked the resentment of Muslims who felt themselves to be suitably qualified and wanted these lucrative jobs for themselves. How, they asked, could people who confused one God with three be trusted to do arithmetic? What made the resentment more than just the articulation of a special interest was a combination of two things: the widespread antipathy of those who pay taxes toward those who collect them and the doctrinal support of the religious scholars, the professional guardians of a tradition that condemned the practice of giving non-Muslims positions of authority in no uncertain terms—or at least the tradition could readily be presented that way. Had not God forbidden Muslims to take Jews and Christians as friends? Had not the Prophet repeatedly refused an offer of assistance from a polytheist before the Battle of Badr, accepting it only when the man professed

12. What follows owes much to unpublished research by Tamer El-Leithy.

13. Ibn al-Nābulusī, *The sword of ambition*, ed. and trans. L. B. Yarbrough, New York 2016, 55.

14. For what follows see L. B. Yarbrough, *Friends of the emir*, Cambridge 2019.

15. Quoted in D. P. Little, "Coptic conversion to Islam under the Baḥrī Mamlūks," *Bulletin of the School of Oriental and African Studies*, 39 (1976), 554.

Islam? More sharply to the point, had not the caliph ʿUmar (ruled 634–44) berated one of the companions of the Prophet for employing a non-Muslim scribe? The alliance of Muslim bureaucrats and Muslim scholars was facilitated by the fact that in post-Fāṭimid Egypt—and not just Egypt—the two groups now overlapped to a significant degree. A sultan could thus find himself embarrassingly vulnerable to the thunderous indignation of a righteous scholar: "You have made the Muslims subject to the Copts and strengthened their religion!"[16]

This tension between the interests of Muslim rulers and those of would-be Muslim bureaucrats was a widespread and long-lasting feature of Muslim states, but it was by no means a constant. It could be in abeyance for long periods and over large regions, or it could suddenly flare up. A flare-up was more likely if the issue caught the attention of a wider Muslim public that already harbored pent-up feelings of hostility toward the group in question. Contagion could also play a part in triggering this effect. A refusal to tolerate the very existence of Jews and Christians had developed in North Africa under the Almohads (1130–1269), and North Africans arriving in Egypt may have stimulated local feelings against non-Muslims. Strong popular sentiment could then put enough pressure on a Muslim ruler to override his interest in employing non-Muslims, if only partially and temporarily, leading him to take measures against non-Muslims at large in an effort to appease Muslim public opinion. The result of the combined hostility of Muslim society and the Muslim state could be catastrophic for the targeted group. So drastic an outcome was rare, but it is more or less what happened in Egypt in the first half of the Mamlūk period.

This period saw a succession of intermittent waves of violence against the Copts. The attacks were widespread in Egypt—not limited to Cairo—and could be very destructive. As a fifteenth-century Muslim historian says, no doubt with some exaggeration, "In all the provinces of Egypt, both north and south, no church remained that had not been razed; on many of those sites mosques were constructed."[17] In this atmosphere minor incidents could provoke major reactions. The wave of 1293 began when a Christian scribe imprudently led a Muslim debtor through the streets at the end of a rope, a vivid violation of the supremacy of Islam. Meanwhile the state would fall into line with public opinion, with the result that the employment of Copts in official positions was repeatedly prohibited. This did not, of course, mean that the practice was actually ended. Copts were still employed in the fiscal bureaucracy when Napoleon arrived in Egypt in 1798, and an Englishman who lived in the country in the 1820s and 1830s speaks of Coptic accountants working in government offices in Cairo and remarks that in "every

16. Quoted in Little, "Coptic conversion to Islam," 560.
17. Quoted in Little, "Coptic conversion to Islam," 568.

village of a moderate size" there was a Copt who kept "the register of the taxes."[18] But to return to medieval times, each explosion of public discontent against the Copts meant that their employment in the administration had to be curtailed for a while, with Coptic bureaucrats pushed to convert in order to keep their jobs. To appease the populace, the sultan at one point ordered that some Coptic clerks should be publicly burned alive, though this order was not in fact carried out. Discriminatory measures that had fallen into disuse were revived, such as obliging Christians to dress differently from Muslims by, for example, wearing blue turbans. This was meant to be humiliating, but it would also have had the effect of rendering Copts obvious targets for abuse in the streets; some sought to attract less hostility by borrowing clothes from the Jews. A more serious blow to the infrastructure of the community, though a silver lining for a state in need of resources, was the confiscation of Coptic endowments and church property. Eventually such waves of persecution would pass and some degree of normality would be restored, but the cumulative effect of the successive waves was predictable: sooner or later large numbers of Copts converted. As the same fifteenth-century historian tells us, "when the Christians' affliction grew great and their incomes small, they decided to embrace Islam."[19] Of course everyone knew that conversion in such circumstances was no guarantee of good faith, and converts were often reported to retain their loyalties to their former coreligionists. Indeed, rumor had it that the Copts were only professing Islam out of malevolent cunning. Many Copts were indeed cunning. There was a practice whereby a Copt would convert while making arrangements for the rest of his family, or the women of the family, to remain Christian. In 1354 the state responded to this stratagem with cunning of its own, requiring that when a Copt adopted Islam his family had to convert with him. But unless a community can develop a stable pattern of crypto-Christianity whereby its members are Muslims in the street but Christians at home, the initial bad faith of such conversions is hard to sustain down the generations. Moreover, the Islamic scholars had no problem recognizing the good faith of some Coptic conversions. A convert whose entire family converted with him, who studiously avoided interacting with his former coreligionists, and who married only Muslim wives had a good chance of gaining their approval; it was said of one who was known for completely avoiding Christians and not even letting them into his house that his Islam turned out to be extremely good. Whether sooner or later, the descendants of Coptic converts would come to be accepted as good Muslims, or at least no worse Muslims than anyone else.

By the nineteenth century Copts were perhaps a tenth of the Egyptian population. Since the fourteenth century they had suffered no major trauma, though the

18. E. W. Lane, *An account of the manners and customs of the modern Egyptians*, Paisley 1895, 552.
19. Quoted in Little, "Coptic conversion to Islam," 568.

French invasion of 1798 predictably increased the tension between Muslims and Copts: a Coptic militia was formed to cooperate with the French, and Muslim revolts against the French in 1798 and 1800 showed strong animus against the Copts, leading to a massacre in the course of the second revolt. But there was nothing comparable to the repeated waves of popular violence abetted by the state that had characterized the first half of the Mamlūk period, so it is not unlikely that the reduction of the Copts to something like a tenth of the total population had already taken place by the time Mamlūk rule was over. A thornier question is what the proportion might have been on the eve of the Mamlūk period. Could the Copts still have been a majority of the population? Or were they already a minority, perhaps even a relatively small one? There had undoubtedly been Coptic conversion in earlier centuries, and it is perhaps significant that there was no serious Coptic resistance to Muslim domination after the ninth century. The most we hear about in the Mamlūk period is an attack on the mosques of Cairo mounted by arsonist monks in 1321 and an epidemic of martyrdoms around 1400 in which Copts quite deliberately went before the Muslim authorities and poured scorn on Islam or, if they had previously converted to it, now abjured it. But if, as was alleged, the Copts still thought of themselves as the rightful owners of Egypt, they did not do much about it. All in all, the chronology of the conversion of the Copts remains in doubt, like that of their loss of Coptic as their mother tongue.

The Turcoman expansion to the west

The Turcomans in Anatolia

The westward expansion of the Turcomans into Anatolia was in one way similar to the migration of the Uzes by the northern route: in addition to plunder, the environment offered abundant pasture. There are several regions of good pastureland in eastern Anatolia and a large block of it in the center of the peninsula. What this meant to the Turcomans was aptly expressed by a Georgian chronicler writing of their intrusion into his own country: "They would settle . . . in all those beautiful winter quarters, where in winter, as in the season of spring, grass is mowed and wood and water are found in abundance." In these regions, he wrote, "they would settle with their tents; of their horses, mules, sheep, and camels there was no reckoning." Thus they passed the winter. "In spring they would begin to ascend the mountains. . . . Thus during summer they would have ease and recreation on the grass and pleasant fields, with springs and flowering meadows." Such was their multitude that you might say, "All Turks of the whole world are here."[20] And yet in another way the Turcoman movement into Anatolia resembled what initially

20. R. W. Thomson, *Rewriting Caucasian history*, Oxford 1996, 323.

happened in Syria: it issued in conquest, much of it under Seljuq leadership. It was this combination of pasture and conquest that made developments in Anatolia momentous. The whole process was facilitated by the fact that the key period—the middle decades of the eleventh century—was one of considerable disarray in the Byzantine Empire. Under Basil II (ruled 976–1025), aptly known as the "Bulgar-slayer," the empire had been stronger than at any time since the rise of Islam, and what was left of it was again to come under firm rule in the reign of Alexius I Comnenus (ruled 1081–1118). But in between there were no fewer than thirteen reigns, and the period was marked by frequent political instability, including the development of a debilitating conflict between military and civilian factions that was resolved only when Alexius I seized the throne. It was a good time for the Turcomans to overrun Anatolia.

The first well-attested Turcoman raid west of Azerbaijan took place in 1029. It was an incursion into Armenia, then under Byzantine domination. Thereafter the pace picked up. By 1048 Turcomans led by a member of the Seljuq family were raiding deep into eastern Anatolia; in 1054–55 the sultan himself led a major raid into the region; and in 1067–68 the raiders were in central Anatolia. But at least up to this point the Turcomans would go back east after their raids. What changed that was a pitched battle fought between the Byzantine and Seljuq armies in 1071, at Manzikert in eastern Anatolia. The outcome was that the Byzantine field army was destroyed, and the Turcomans could now roam the peninsula at will without encountering serious military resistance. From this point on their presence in Anatolia was permanent, and no part of the peninsula was free of their raids. In 1073–74, for example, they were at Miletus on the west coast; in 1081 they were in Smyrna, again on the west coast, and in Nicaea, a mere sixty miles from Constantinople; and around 1090 a certain Tengri-birmish ("God-gave") seized Ephesus. Chaka, the leader of the Turcomans in Smyrna, was not to be stopped even by the sea: he built a fleet and raided the islands of the Aegean. Conspicuously absent from all the activity in the central and western parts of the peninsula were the Seljuq rulers of Iran, whose raids went no farther west than eastern Anatolia. Eventually Malik Shāh was to send two expeditions deeper into the peninsula, one of them far enough to lay siege to Nicaea, but these forces were directed against a Seljuq prince who was making trouble in Anatolia, not against the Byzantines.

For Byzantine Anatolia this looked like the end of the road, but a somewhat fortuitous combination of circumstances in the last years of the century was to afford the battered empire a partial reprieve. The Turcomans, in descending from the plateau to the coastlands, had left behind the steppe environment in which they were at home. The decades of disarray in Constantinople were over, and in the course of a long reign the able Alexius I was picking up the pieces. And not least, the armies of the First Crusade needed to pass through Anatolia on their way from Europe to Syria. They started to arrive at Constantinople at the end of 1096, and

Alexius did his best to minimize the damage they did to his own interests and maximize the grief they caused to the Turcomans. In fact, the Crusaders served him well in their transit across the peninsula, and it was thanks to their military efforts that he was able to restore Byzantine rule over the Anatolian coastlands. But despite some Byzantine expeditions deep into the interior of the peninsula, the recovery of the plateau remained out of reach, and the disastrous defeat of a Byzantine attempt to retake it in 1176 sealed its fate. Then, early in the thirteenth century, the Seljuqs broke through to the south and north coasts, and later in that century the Byzantines lost the west coast with its rich river valleys. Apart from an enclave around Trebizond that had become an independent state under the Comnenid dynasty, the Byzantines now retained only a corner of Anatolian territory close to Constantinople, and in the course of the fourteenth century even that was to disappear.

From Greek-speaking Christians to Turkish-speaking Muslims

We will come back to the political history of Turcoman Anatolia in these centuries; at this point our concern is with the demographic changes that transformed the character of the population. At the start of our period the inhabitants of Anatolia were mainly Greek-speaking Christians, whereas by the later fifteenth century they were mainly Turkish-speaking Muslims. The major exception was eastern Anatolia, where the shift was rather from Armenian-speaking Christians to Kurdish-speaking Muslims. Leaving aside the east, we know the outcome in central and western Anatolia from the fiscal surveys carried out by the Ottoman bureaucracy, the earliest surviving examples of which are from the fifteenth century. These surveys go village by village and, for the urban population, quarter by quarter, and they list the adult male population by name and father's name. Two things stand out in the fifteenth-century registers. One concerns place-names. Many cities and towns retain their pre-Turkish names, so on the west coast Izmir is the Greek Smyrna in Turkish dress, while deep in the interior Kayseri is the Greek Caesarea. By contrast, it is common for the names of villages to be purely Turkish. Thus on the coastal plain around the city of Antalya today, the only pre-Turkish toponym to survive is that of Antalya itself, the Greek Attaleia. We see no such widespread erasure of pre-Turkic toponyms in Iran. The other salient point is that whereas urban populations may include considerable numbers of non-Muslims, the great majority of the rural population is Muslim. For example, in a set of samples of villages in the regions around the cities of Güzelḥiṣār (today's Aydın), Burdur, and Tokat, rural Christians are almost nonexistent in the first two cases and represented only by minorities of Greeks and Armenians in the third. The names of Muslim villagers as they appear in these registers are often generically Muslim, in other words Arabic (Yūsuf, Süleymān, and the like), which tells us nothing about their ethnicity. But where the names are not Arabic, they are overwhelmingly Turkish. Thus in fifteenth-century surveys of villages in the region of Güzelḥiṣār, we find names such as Yakhshï ("Good"), Satïlmïsh ("Sold"), Tengri-vermish ("God-gave"), Sevindük ("We-rejoiced"), and Temür-tash ("Iron-stone"). Some names, like Oghuz and Chaghatay, have deep historical resonance; others refer to recent pre-Ottoman dynasties of southwestern Anatolia, including Menteshe (the founder of the Turcoman dynasty that bears his name), Ṣārūkhān (likewise), and Umur (the most prominent ruler of the Turcoman state of Aydïn). These niceties apart, what all this adds up to is that the major transformation of the character of the Anatolian population had already taken place by the later fifteenth century.

Just how and when did it happen? These are what academics call good questions, meaning that they don't have good answers. As to how it happened, the most plausible guess is that Turkish nomads in Anatolia played the same role there as Arab nomads may have done in the countryside of much of what became the Arab world. That is to say, their depredations eroded the traditional structures of peasant life among the indigenous population and thereby opened the way for linguistic and religious assimilation. There is no lack of complaint on the Christian side about the sufferings of the indigenous population at the hands of the Turcomans. The same Georgian chronicler who gave such a colorful account of the Turcomans in their pastures waxed eloquent about the impact of Turcoman raids: "In those times there was neither sowing nor harvest. The land was ruined and turned into forest; in place of men, beasts and animals of the field made their dwelling there. Insufferable oppression fell on all the inhabitants of the land. . . . For the holy churches were turned into stables for their horses, while the sanctuaries of God became places for their impurities." Priests were put to the sword or taken into captivity, the aged were treated without mercy, virgins were raped, babies were stolen away. "Fire, an unaccustomed adversary, consumed all dwellings; rivers of blood irrigated the land instead of torrents of water."[21] Similarly, an Armenian chronicler reporting on the events of 1079–80 lamented that "famine desolated . . . the lands of the worshippers of the Cross, already ravaged by the ferocious and sanguinary Turkish hordes. Not one province remained protected from their devastations. Everywhere the Christians had been delivered to the sword or into bondage, thus interrupting the cultivation of the fields, so that bread was lacking. The farmers and workers had been massacred or led off into slavery, and famine extended its rigors to all places. Many provinces were depopulated; the Oriental nation [he means the Armenians] no longer existed, and the land of the Greeks was in ruins."[22] The Christian chroniclers may well have exaggerated these

21. Thomson, *Rewriting Caucasian history*, 311.

22. Quoted in S. Vryonis, *The decline of medieval Hellenism in Asia Minor*, Berkeley 1971, 172–73.

traumas, but they are unlikely to have invented them. It was not just Christians who commented negatively on the depredations of the Turcomans. Here, for comparison, is a comment attributed by a fourteenth-century hagiographer to the famous Ṣūfī poet and saint Jalāl al-Dīn Rūmī (d. 1273): God created the Turks "so that they would destroy every building they saw, mercilessly and ruthlessly, and cause it to be demolished. And they are still doing so, and day by day until the Resurrection they will continue to destroy in this manner."[23]

Such rhetoric should not be taken to mean that Turcoman treatment of the indigenous peasantry was always and everywhere destructive. Pastoral and agrarian economies are in part complementary, and it is common for the two parties in such situations to come to terms. But given the superior military force of the nomads, the terms are likely enough to have been unfavorable to the continuing integrity of traditional peasant society. Had they been favorable, after all, the peasants might well have assimilated the nomads to their language and culture. Several further factors no doubt helped shape the outcome. First, the Turcoman invaders of Anatolia were Muslims, not pagans like the Uzes in the Balkans, which made their religious assimilation by the indigenous population much less likely. Second, in most of Anatolia the political authorities, and not just the tribes, were increasingly Muslim, and as such they had more in common with Turkish-speaking nomads than with Greek-speaking peasants. Finally, until the Ottoman conquest of Constantinople ended the Byzantine Empire in 1453, there was still a nearby refuge where Greek-speaking Christians, especially those belonging to the elite, could take shelter, and as the Mālikīs of Qayrawān had pointed out, a population that has lost its elite is more vulnerable to assimilation.

The question when the transformation happened is harder to answer. Europeans had already taken to calling Anatolia "Turkey" (*Turchia*) in the twelfth century. On the other hand, an observant European traveler of the mid-thirteenth century estimated that in Anatolia the native population still outnumbered the Turks by ten to one. The disruption of peasant life by nomads could well have been a more or less continuous phenomenon extending over several centuries, but if we are to pick a single period other than the eleventh century when it is likely to have been at its most intense, we could do worse than choose the century or so following the coming of the Mongols. But this can only be guesswork.

There are nevertheless two bodies of evidence that shed at least an indirect light on the process whereby Anatolia became Turkey. One of them comes again from the study of the Ottoman fiscal surveys, this time those of the sixteenth century. In that century—as still to an extent today—nearly all of the twenty-four Oghuz clans were represented in the names of Anatolian villages, some of them with great

23. Aflākī, *The feats of the knowers of God*, trans. J. O'Kane, Leiden 2002, 502–3.

frequency. Such names extended all the way to the provinces of the west coast. This strongly suggests that at some stage large numbers of Turcomans belonging to these clans had settled down in villages, and that they did so by clans. Thereafter such settlements very likely provided the nuclei around which the assimilation of the indigenous population went forward. The other body of evidence comes from studies of the genetics of the population of Turkey today. These studies indicate that the genetic heritage of the population mostly reflects its geographical surroundings, not its linguistic affiliation. In other words, the Turks of Turkey are genetically closer to their neighbors than they are to their fellow Turkic speakers in Central Asia. One can in fact reach the same conclusion through a simpler and cheaper research technique: eyeballing faces. The average Turk today looks more like a Bulgarian or a Syrian than a native of the eastern steppes. People in the region noticed this long ago. A Turkish author of the first half of the fifteenth century relates that when the Oghuz clans still lived in Türkistān, they looked like Mongols, but when they migrated to Transoxania, Iran, Anatolia, and Syria, they gradually came to look like Tājīks, meaning sedentary Iranians. What all this suggests is that however large the number of Turcomans reaching Anatolia may have been, it was still small in comparison to the size of the indigenous population. It follows that the fundamental process at work was indeed the linguistic and religious assimilation of the existing population by the Turcomans, and not its displacement.

In the abstract, the arrival of Turkic-speaking Muslim nomads in a land populated by settled Greek-speaking Christians could have had a number of outcomes. One would have been the linguistic and religious absorption of the newcomers by the existing population, so that Anatolia would have remained a land of Greek-speaking Christians. And indeed there were parts of Anatolia that retained old Greek-speaking Christian communities into the twentieth century, notably in Cappadocia and the region of Trebizond; the latter was too wet for Turcomans and remained under Christian rule until 1461.

A second outcome would have been the victory of the language of the natives in conjunction with the religion of the nomads, issuing in a population of Greek-speaking Muslims. And here, too, we have an example, the Greek-speaking Muslim population that is still to be found in several districts in the region of Trebizond. But it is a limited example. What did most to preserve Greek here was the unsuitability of the rain-soaked environment for steppe nomads, and there is no comparable example of such a population on the plateau. This absence is worth underlining, since the combination of adopting the religion of Muslim conquerors with retaining one's native language is extremely common in the story of the expansion of Islam. An obvious example is Iran, where, as we saw, a conquest by Muslim Arabs resulted in a population of Persian-speaking Muslims.

A third outcome would have been the victory of the religion of the natives in conjunction with the language of the nomads, producing a population of Turkish-speaking Christians. Again the phenomenon is not just hypothetical. A Turkish-speaking Christian population came to exist in several parts of Anatolia. Such Christians are first mentioned in 1437, later came to be known as the Karamanlis, and likewise survived into the twentieth century. When the Ottoman administration surveyed the province of Kayseri in 1584–85, on average between a fifth and a quarter of the population was Christian. The distribution of Christians was uneven, for of the nine districts making up the province, four had no Christian population whereas one had a Christian majority, though only a slight one. In this latter district the surveyors came to a village called Sarïmsaqlu—a very Turkish name ("[The-place]-with-the-garlic"). The population of this village was by then entirely Muslim and bore names that were either generically Muslim or Turkish. But on its border was another village called something like Enerük—not at all a Turkish name—with an overwhelmingly Christian population, mostly Greek but partly Armenian. Some of these Christians had obviously Christian names such as Manol (Emmanuel), Nikola (Nicholas), or Kirkör (Gregory). But most of them had Turkish names such as Tanrï-verdi ("God-gave"), Qar-yaghdï ("Snow-fell"), or Qara-göz ("Black-eye"). Among the Armenians we also see a trickle-down of historic Muslim names such as Temür (Tīmūr) and Jihān Shāh (Jahān Shāh, the imperial ruler of the Qara Qoyunlu). People with names like these were most likely Turkish-speaking, and the presence of such names is already attested among Christians in Sarïmsaqlu in a survey of 1484. Moreover, since some of the fathers of those listed there likewise had Turkish names, the practice must go back at least to the first half of the fifteenth century. We might compare this pattern to the way in which the English conquest of Ireland eventually led to a population made up mainly of English-speaking Catholics—rather than Gaelic-speaking Catholics or English-speaking Protestants.

Finally, there was what actually happened on a large scale despite the interesting but minor exceptions: the linguistic and religious absorption of the existing population by the newcomers, transforming Anatolia into a land of Turkish-speaking Muslims. This was a remarkable metamorphosis, even given the fact that the invaders were Muslim nomads discovering new pastureland in the steppe country of Anatolia. But for all the force of the transformation, we should not think of it as a clean break. Mixture was the order of the day and long remained so, as we will see in the Ottoman context. One early example stems from a Muslim Turcoman dynasty of twelfth-century Anatolia, the Dānishmendids (1097–1178). A Dānishmendid ruler of the 1150s had a seal in a Byzantine style; it had an Arabic inscription on one side and a bust of Saint Basil on the other. We have nothing quite like that for the Seljuq rulers in Anatolia, but the form taken by their marriage alliances with Christian dynasties is suggestive. An incoming Christian princess would be accompanied by priests and have at her disposal a chapel in the Seljuq palace, a practice similar to one we will encounter in Mughal India. In this context it is no surprise that some—perhaps many—members of the Seljuq dynasty should have been baptized. This was not just a quirk of the dynasty. In the twelfth century baptizing one's children was widespread among the Muslims of Anatolia, and it was centuries before the custom disappeared. Mixed marriages encouraged such practices. In the fourteenth century we hear of a custom that distinguished between the male and female children of such marriages: the boys would become Muslims whereas the girls would either be Christians or have free choice of religion.

The political history of Turcoman Anatolia before the Mongols

As we saw, members of the Seljuq family played a considerable part in leading the early Turcoman expansion into Anatolia. Often these were dissident princes who had fallen out with the Seljuq rulers of Iran and had fled to the Anatolian wild west either to get away from them or to raise Turcoman armies against them. The Seljuq dynasty of Anatolia (1081–1307) had such an origin. The founder, Süleymān (ruled 1081–86), was the son of a prince who had been killed in a succession struggle for the Seljuq sultanate in 1064. He and his brothers escaped to the west, and by 1074 he had acquired a substantial Turcoman following with which he took possession of Nicaea. But his ambitions were in the east, and he died fighting near Aleppo. His son Qïlïj Arslan (ruled 1092–1109) returned to Nicaea for a few years but was deprived of it by the passing Crusaders and then perished in a battle he fought against the forces of the Seljuq sultan far to the east in the Jazīra. It was only after this that these Seljuqs slowly began to reconcile themselves to their lot as a dynasty on the Anatolian plateau and to take the city of Konya (the Byzantine Iconium) seriously as their capital. By the thirteenth century this city had become a respectable Muslim cultural center where scholars of distinction were not ashamed to seek patronage.

In significant ways the Anatolian Seljuqs were broadly similar to those of Iran, despite the smaller scale on which they operated and the very different character of the indigenous population—Greek rather than Iranian. So far as we can tell they reproduced roughly the same pattern in their relationship with the Turcoman population. That is to say, they moved away from their initial dependence on the Turcomans, buying themselves slave soldiers of whom many were Greek and hiring mercenaries, including a good number of European Christians. Yet they retained their ties to the Turcomans. In military terms, the rulers continued to use Turcomans as auxiliaries, and a rebel prince might raise a Turcoman army. In terms of lifestyle, the one Seljuq ruler whose movements we can track, Kay-Qubād I (ruled 1220–37), did as the Turcomans did, spending the summer on the plateau and the winter on the coastal plain to the south, which had recently come under Seljuq rule. While on the plateau, moreover, he spent a considerable amount of time in rural locations where he could interact with the Turcomans. A prime location of this kind was the palace of Qubādābād that he built on the shores of one of the lakes to the west of Konya. A chronicler describes this ruler making the journey down to the coast: "All the way making merry and hunting, he pitched his tent by every lake."[24] In terms of political culture, the rulers continued to invoke traditional Turkic symbols of sovereignty. One example is the emblematic monogram (*ṭughrā*), a device we first hear of in Kāshgharī's dictionary; another is the symbolic use of the bow and arrow. But the Anatolian Seljuqs also resembled the main Seljuq dynasty in their adoption of governmental practices developed in Muslim Iran. Their bureaucracy was essentially an import from the east, and to a considerable extent it was staffed with Iranian immigrants. The Byzantine bureaucratic tradition, which the Uzes might have adopted had they established a state in the Balkans, largely fell by the wayside in Anatolia.

Where the Anatolian Seljuqs differed sharply from their relatives in Iran was in the waxing and waning of their power over time. As we saw, in Iran the trajectory of the dynasty after the first four decades was downhill. In Anatolia, by contrast, the initial decades were not particularly auspicious. One reason was that, as already noted, both of the first two rulers came to grief pursuing their ambitions in the east. Another was that the Byzantine state as revived by Alexius I was still relatively strong; indeed, the third Seljuq ruler was a Byzantine vassal, and in 1146 a Byzantine expedition ravaged the suburbs of Konya. A third reason was that the Seljuqs were not the only Muslim dynasty in twelfth-century Anatolia. The Dānishmendids were a rival Turcoman dynasty ruling considerable territories to the north and east, and they may well have overshadowed the Seljuqs in their first decades. Despite that bust of Saint Basil, they had a reputation as fierce warriors for the faith, yet unlike the Seljuqs they minted coins with Greek inscriptions; one Dānishmendid ruler boasted of being "the great king (*melēkis*, from the Arabic *malik*) of all Romania and Anatolia, Makhamatēs."[25] There were also a couple of minor Turcoman dynasties farther to the east. The Seljuqs nevertheless did better in the second half of the twelfth century than they had done in the first half. They conquered the lands of the Dānishmendids in the 1170s, and the Byzantine threat to their existence ended with their victory of 1176. But this was balanced by a disastrous decision in 1185. Following a familiar Seljuq practice to an extreme degree, the ruler divided his territory between his sons, who happened to number nine or ten. Unsurprisingly there was then a long period of disarray. It was only in the early decades of the thirteenth century, well after the rule of their Iranian relatives had come to an end, that the Seljuqs of Anatolia were at their

24. Quoted in A.C.S. Peacock, "Court and nomadic life in Saljuq Anatolia," in D. Durand-Guédy (ed.), *Turko-Mongol rulers, cities and city life*, Leiden 2013, 205.

25. Vryonis, *The decline of medieval Hellenism*, 473.

height. By now they could intervene in northern Syria and the Jazīra without losing their lives, and after expanding north to the coast they took to the sea and even involved themselves in the affairs of the Crimea. When the Khwārazm-Shāh menaced Anatolia in 1230, a Seljuq-Ayyūbid alliance defeated him. Of course this could not last: for the Seljuqs of Anatolia, as for so many other dynasties, the good times ended with the Mongol invasion. But even then all was not lost, for as we will see the Seljuqs contrived to survive for several decades as a client state of the Īlkhāns.

The Mongols in Anatolia

Anatolia was spared the first phase of the Mongol invasion, but not the second. The Mongols crushingly defeated the Seljuq ruler in a battle fought in 1243 and went on to sack Kayseri. They attacked again in 1256 and 1277. Yet their conquest of Anatolia was by Mongol standards rather shoddy, particularly since unlike Syria it offered good pasture. Eastern Anatolia was indeed properly conquered and in due course ruled directly by the Īlkhāns, though it also served as a base for rebellions by disaffected Mongols. This directly ruled territory extended as far west as the region of Sivas, Tokat, Amasya, and Kayseri. Here there were still significant numbers of Mongols to be found in the later fourteenth century, and their prime concerns remained their livestock, pastures, and migration routes. In central Anatolia, however, conquest was for some time preempted by the submission of the Seljuq state, a delicate diplomatic maneuver contrived by its leading bureaucrats. The degree of Seljuq autonomy was, however, drastically curtailed after 1277, and in 1307 the dynasty finally disappeared. To the west of the Seljuqs Mongol authority was not continuously present in any form, though occasional punitive expeditions were sent against the Turcomans of the region, as in 1262, 1291, and 1326. In 1277 the Īlkhān set his brother the task of restoring order in Anatolia "up to the shore of the western sea."[26] But this was rhetoric; Tīmūr was to outstrip the Īlkhāns with his visit to Izmir in 1402. The problem was that while the Mongols could beat up the Turcomans, the Turcomans were resilient. There was thus an overall gradient across Anatolia, from direct Mongol rule in the east to indirect rule in the center and no rule at all in the west.

Against this background, we would not expect the Mongol impact on Anatolia to have been a profound one, and on the whole it was not. It was, of course, stronger in the east. Here, for example, we still find Ottoman administrators using the word *nöker*, a Mongol term for a companion or retainer of a military leader, but it was clearly unfamiliar to them, since they paused to explain it to be an "eastern" usage and glossed it with a more familiar Ottoman term. Today the word

26. Quoted in C. Melville, "Anatolia under the Mongols," in *The Cambridge history of Turkey*, Cambridge 2006–12, 1:70.

survives in Persian in the sense of "servant," but not in Turkish. Another example is the familiar Mongol term Yāsā in the sense of "law, regulation." When the Ottomans conquered eastern Anatolia following their defeat of the Ṣafawids in 1514, their administrators surveyed several provinces that had once been under the sway of the Aq Qoyunlu ruler Uzun Ḥasan. They reproduced the provincial regulations imposed there in his day, entitling each code "Register of the Yāsās of such-and-such a province" while using the normal Ottoman term Qānūn-nāme ("Book of regulations") in the body of the text.[27] In each case, the Ottoman administrators were clearly encountering long-standing regional usages. Farther to the west the legacy of Mongol terms was thinner, though even there the modern Turkish *yasak*—meaning "forbidden"—is a variant form of Yāsā.

In another way, however, the Mongol presence in eastern Anatolia had a massive indirect impact all the way to the west coast. Although our sources do not really show us this process at work, it is easy to infer what it was. When it came to the exploitation of pastureland, Turcomans and Kurds in eastern Anatolia were perhaps to some degree complementary; but Turcomans and Mongols were alike steppe nomads and so in direct competition with each other. Given their military and political dominance, the Mongols had an obvious advantage, so their armies could help themselves to the best pastures of Azerbaijan and eastern Anatolia. What must have made the situation worse was the arrival of Hülegü in Iran in 1256. At this point Baiju, the incumbent Mongol commander who had defeated the Seljuqs in 1243, was told to move over to the west so that Hülegü could have the use of the best pastureland of Azerbaijan. Baiju did as he was told, asking the Seljuq sultan for new pastureland to support his forces, their livestock, their women, and their children. This must have pushed many Turcomans to move westward, increasing their numbers in central Anatolia, and the figures given in our sources would support that, for what they are worth. This increase in turn must have built up pressure on Turcoman pastoralists to move into the western coastlands. Here, at least, the outcome is well documented: between the 1260s and the first decade of the fourteenth century, the Byzantine Empire lost its rich western Anatolian territory to the Turcomans. They were now back on the coast for good, and western Anatolia, too, was to become a land of Turkish-speaking Muslims—even more solidly so than the center and the east.

The late thirteenth century was also the period in which Anatolian Turkish began to emerge as a literary language. By the early fifteenth century religious works were being composed in Turkish, and the popularity of some of these works would last for centuries. One is a poem by a member of a scholarly family in Bursa, Süleymān Chelebī (d. 1422), that is recited in Turkey to this day as part of the

27. Ö. L. Barkan, *Kanunlar*, Istanbul 1943, 149, 155, 158, 184.

annual celebration of the birth of the Prophet. Another is a much longer versified life of the Prophet by a scholar living in Gallipoli, Yazïjï-oghlu Meḥmed (d. 1451); this work survives in more than three hundred manuscripts and was printed more than forty times in the last decades of the Ottoman Empire. The seventeenth-century Ottoman traveler Evliyā Chelebī tells us that in his day several thousand boys and girls in the region of Kastamonu knew the book by heart. By contrast, there seems to have been relatively little writing about Turkic antiquity. Even the "Book of Dede Qorqud," which we met in the context of the Turcoman dynasties of eastern Anatolia, survives only in two manuscripts, both of them in European libraries.

The Turcoman dynasties of Anatolia

The fourteenth century, and to an extent the fifteenth, is an age of Turcoman dynasties in Anatolia. We have already encountered the Qara Qoyunlu and Aq Qoyunlu of eastern Anatolia because of their role in the history of Iran. Another Turcoman dynasty of eastern Anatolia was Dulghādir (1337–1522), alias Dhū 'l-Qadr, to the west of the Aq Qoyunlu homeland on the plateau northeast of Cilicia. Meanwhile, a score of Turcoman statelets came into being in central and western Anatolia, and it is these latter with which we are concerned here.

There were two preconditions for this phenomenon. One, obvious and already familiar, was the presence of a large Turcoman population of internal nomads across the peninsula. The other was the absence of powerful states in or around Anatolia that would frustrate Turcoman state formation. This second point is worth some elaboration. Let us start with the role of the sea. Because Anatolia is a peninsula, naval powers and pirates could easily attack its coasts, but they had no way to dominate the interior. Of course at the Straits the amount of sea that an army had to cross was minimal, but even that was a barrier. With the help of Alexius I, who was anxious to see them on their way, the armies of the First Crusade made that crossing and traversed Anatolia on their way to Jerusalem. But no state based in the Balkans had expanded in this direction since the days of Alexander the Great. So if any neighboring state was to dominate the politics of the peninsula, it would be one adjoining it by land. One possibility here would be the rulers of Syria and Egypt, but their military posture toward the northern Middle East was fundamentally defensive. It was powerful states in the east that were the real menace. In the late thirteenth century and the first third of the fourteenth, the Īlkhāns were dominant, but even then, as we saw, their presence fell off as one went west. Thereafter there was no serious incursion from the east until Tīmūr's visit in 1402, and he showed himself a friend rather than an enemy toward the Turcoman states. Moreover, the Qara Qoyunlu and Aq Qoyunlu, when they did expand dramatically, mostly did so eastward into Iran rather than westward into central Anatolia.

Meanwhile in Anatolia itself the Seljuq state had faded out, and once the Byzantine Empire had lost the west coast, its residual Anatolian territory was too slight to accord it any significant role in shaping the wider politics of the peninsula. In short, the fourteenth century was a window of opportunity for Turcoman state formation. That window was to be slammed shut by the Ottomans in the late fourteenth century and then dramatically reopened by Tīmūr in 1402, though only for a few decades. But in the account of the Turcoman dynasties that follows we will mostly ignore the Ottomans and the hiatus they caused.

While the window was open, Anatolia was politically more fragmented than at any other time in its history, and as indicated, most of the fragments were small Turcoman states. Some were on the plateau, where the Turcomans had been continuously present since the eleventh century. Here pride of place goes to the Qaramānids (ca. 1256–1475), who were Turcomans from the Taurus mountains southeast of Konya. While the Īlkhāns were still dominant, the Qaramānids repeatedly took and lost Konya, and thereafter it served as their capital, giving them a certain cachet as the heirs of the Seljuqs. They ruled a sizeable territory. To the south they were able to extend their power to the Mediterranean coast opposite Cyprus, though their orientation was always more toward the plateau than toward the sea. To some extent they waged holy war against the infidel by attacking the Cilician Armenian kingdom (1080–1375), but the elimination of this Christian state was the work of the Mamlūks. Initially the Qaramānids seem to have been culturally rather unsophisticated: when they took Konya for the first time in 1277, they announced that from then on only Turkish was to be spoken in the administration and at court—implying that until that point the language of the state had been Persian. But the fifteenth-century ruler Ibrāhīm Beg (ruled 1424–64) was known as a patron of scholars, and these would not have counted as scholars without a conspicuous knowledge of Persian and Arabic. The next most prominent of the Turcoman states of the plateau was Germiyān (from before 1299 to 1428). This state was located on the northwestern part of the plateau, with its capital at Kütahya. Though it initially recognized Seljuq overlordship, in the early decades of the fourteenth century it was the most powerful of the Turcoman states. But it was unable to sustain its power, and in the 1370s it lost much of its territory to the Ottomans and became an Ottoman client; eventually the last ruler bequeathed his principality to the Ottoman sultan. The Qaramānids and Germiyān were by no means the only Turcoman states on the plateau, but we can leave the others aside. Given the existence of a large Turcoman population in a steppe environment, there was in principle no reason nomadic state formation on the plateau could not have continued indefinitely, as it did in Iran, so long as no powerful state intervened from elsewhere to interrupt it.

Some Turcoman dynasties had sway over the coastlands of Anatolia. On the south coast, as we have already seen, the Qaramānids reached the sea. Farther to the west Ḥamīd, another principality formed in the interior, went on to take Antalya and its coastal plain. The dynasty then divided into two branches, one of which, the "sons of Teke," held Antalya most of the time from at least 1321 until 1423; hence the Ṣafawid supporters from this region were to be known in Iran as the Tekelü, the people from Teke. But these dynasties seem not to have made much of their access to the sea. On the north coast matters were only somewhat different. Here the port of Sinope had been in Seljuq hands since 1214. In the early fourteenth century it was held by a certain Ghāzī Chelebī, who had a strong Seljuq connection and waged naval warfare against the Genoese and the Greeks of Trebizond. His tactics were reputed to include an early form of submarine warfare. But he had no successors, and thereafter the port was taken over by a neighboring Turcoman dynasty, the Isfendiyārids (1292–1462). Their primary base was at Kastamonu in the interior, but they nevertheless maintained a navy. However, on both these coasts the steep descent from the plateau to the sea made it hard for a Turcoman state to combine maritime and terrestrial resources effectively.

The west coast, with its combination of maritime frontage and gently descending agricultural river valleys, was another story. There were four Turcoman states on this coast. From south to north, they were Menteshe (late thirteenth century to 1424) in the southwestern corner of Anatolia, Aydïn (1308–1426) in the region of Izmir, Ṣārūkhān (ca. 1313–1410) in the region of Maghnisa, and Qarasï (ca. 1297–ca. 1346) in the northwestern corner. They tended to be based inland rather than on the coast itself, but all four took advantage of their maritime frontage. One prize here was Mediterranean commerce, the alternatives being to tax it or pillage it—or better still, to do both. Another source of wealth was raiding the Aegean islands with their Christian populations, just as Chaka had done a couple of centuries earlier. Such piracy and raiding could of course be celebrated as jihad against the infidel, but this maritime activity required constructing fleets and engaging in naval warfare. In this the Turcoman states proved remarkably adaptive. They were not as adept as their Christian enemies on the sea itself, but once they were able to disembark their troops, their attacks could be devastating. Menteshe took its Aegean raiding far enough to attack Crete, while Aydïn extended its raids to mainland Greece and engaged in military activity in the Balkans in the context of a Byzantine civil war in the 1340s. In fact, its activities were sufficiently vexatious to provoke a couple of naval Crusades against its most energetic ruler, Umur Beg (ruled 1334–48). But when it came to raiding the infidel, Qarasï had an obvious geographical advantage over its peers: there was a vast Christian territory to ravage just on the other side of the Dardanelles. In 1305, five hundred warriors from Qarasï raided Thrace. This, however, was holy war with an interfaith twist—the men of Qarasï mounted the enterprise jointly with some rebellious and no less rapacious Catalans. They raided Thrace again twice on their own in the early 1330s, made another attempt in 1337, carried out two raids in 1341 that also involved Ṣārūkhān, and in 1345 joined Aydïn in its intervention in the Byzantine civil war. They were able to transport their horses across the Dardanelles on their boats.

With this descent to the coastlands, there were now Turcoman dynasties that lived by taking a cut of two resources unavailable to their peers on the plateau: the agricultural wealth of the western river valleys and the commercial wealth of the Mediterranean, which was perhaps still the scene of the most lively maritime commercial exchanges anywhere on the planet. Could a Turcoman dynasty in such an environment continue to be Turcoman in any respect other than ancestry? The scarcity of information about these western dynasties makes the answer to the question elusive. We have an account of the lifestyle of the ruler of Aydïn from Ibn Baṭṭūṭa, a Moroccan traveler who saw a lot of Anatolia in the early 1330s. He tells us that when he arrived at Birgi the ruler was out of town, at his summer quarters on a mountain close by. Once Ibn Baṭṭūṭa reached him, the traveler was supplied with a tent. When the time came to leave, Ibn Baṭṭūṭa accompanied the ruler to his residence in the city. So this ruler was a seminomad. Though we lack information about the habits of his successors, it is hard to imagine a state like Aydïn maintaining its Turcoman character indefinitely.

To complete the picture, we should add that not every Anatolian state in this period was the work of the Turcomans. There were still three Christian states ruling territory on the edges of the peninsula. The residual Byzantine Empire retained some Anatolian territory to the south and east of Constantinople; the diminutive "Empire of Trebizond" (1204–1461) was a separate Byzantine state ruling the eastern part of Anatolia's Black Sea coast; and the Cilician Armenian kingdom lasted till 1375. None of these had much of a future. No Christian state ruled on the plateau, but a significant Mongol successor state emerged there when the Īlkhānate collapsed. Centered on Sivas and Kayseri, it extended from Ankara in the west to Erzinjān in the east. There were no Chingizids to hold sway in Anatolia, and in fact the founder, a certain Eretna (ruled 1336–52), was not himself a Mongol but rather an Uighur with a Buddhist name derived from Sanskrit. He had risen in the service of the Īlkhāns to be their governor of Anatolia and was thus an Anatolian counterpart of insiders such as the Muẓaffarids in post-Mongol Fārs. His descendants ruled after him, though less successfully, till 1380, when the last ruler of the dynasty was deposed by his all-powerful vizier, Burhān al-Dīn, who then reigned till killed at Sivas by the Aq Qoyunlu in 1398. Eretna himself had a reputation among his subjects for delivering a degree of security. If the dynasty as a whole provided some protection against the worst of the Turcoman deluge, this might help explain the survival of significant Christian minorities in the villages of the region, and not just in the urban centers. There may also have been a demographic aspect to the continuity with Mongol rule. When Burhān al-Dīn's biographer explained why he wrote in Persian, he averred that in "the lands of Rūm" (meaning his part of Anatolia) everyone spoke it, suggesting that like Konya the region may have received a substantial number of immigrants from Iran. But not even this Mongol successor state was strong enough to dominate Anatolia as a whole, and this is one reason the great majority of Anatolian states in this period could be established by Turcomans.

There was naturally cutthroat competition among the states of the peninsula. And yet there were surprisingly few cases of dog-eat-dog. If we confine ourselves to the Turcoman states surveyed above, not one of them was terminated by the action of any fellow Turcoman state other than the Ottomans. Had we extended our survey of the plateau states to the minor Turcoman dynasties, we would have come up with one that possibly owed its demise to the Isfendiyārids and a couple whose existence may have been ended by Germiyān. At the same time, none of these dynasties came to an end through endogenous processes—there were no revolutions. Thus until the Ottoman expansion in the later fourteenth century, the whole scene, despite persistent internal and external strife, was relatively stable. It was complex, but it was not kaleidoscopic. To say this is also to imply that none of these states looked as if it was destined for imperial glory. No one of them stood head and shoulders above the rest. Those on the plateau lacked the resources for empire building, though the Qaramānids got far enough to lay siege to Bursa in 1413. Those on the coasts, while benefiting from the wealth that the sea could bring them, were constrained by the difficulty of projecting military power across it. And yet the extreme political fragmentation of Anatolia was historically so untypical that it would seem unlikely to last for long.

Before we leave the Turcoman dynasties, we should return for a moment to Ibn Baṭṭūṭa's experience of Anatolia. He liked it enormously. The food was good, and better still, the locals were eager to treat him to it. He frequently received hospitality and gifts from rulers, something to which he felt himself fully entitled—as we will see in the West African context, his conception of the economics of tourism was very different from ours. But what really entranced him was the hospitality of the Akhīs, the members of the brotherhoods he regularly encountered in the urban centers of Anatolia. These brotherhoods were clearly new to him and his readers, though they were part of an established tradition farther east in the Muslim world that had been brought to Anatolia in the early thirteenth century. The form in which it arrived was directed at the elite, but by the middle of the century a popular form had emerged. In Konya the Akhīs began to participate in the politics of the later Seljuq state, and with its collapse toward the end of the thirteenth century they became prominent political actors. Ibn Baṭṭūṭa explains that the Akhīs were present throughout the Turcoman lands of Anatolia and remarks that "nowhere in the world are there to be found any to compare with them in solicitude for strangers, and in ardor to serve food and satisfy wants."[28] He often enjoyed their lavish hospitality. On one glorious occasion he entered a market to find himself in the middle of an alarming dispute between two groups of men who started to draw knives against each other. When someone was found who could speak Arabic, it turned out that these bellicose characters belonged to two distinct groups of Akhīs and were in competition for the privilege of entertaining Ibn Baṭṭūṭa. Fortunately the dispute was resolved without bloodshed by the time-honored device of casting lots. It was the hospitality of the Akhīs that impressed him most about them, but he also remarked in passing on other aspects of these brotherhoods. Their members might be craftsmen—one was a cobbler—but could also include a judge, and they were ready to kill oppressive agents of the state. This last suggests that it may not have been just in Konya that they were involved in local politics. In fact, Ibn Baṭṭūṭa tells us that in any part of the country that was not the residence of a ruler, it was customary for an Akhī to act as governor. The role of the Anatolian brotherhoods in this period is reminiscent of the social upwelling we have occasionally seen in Iran, including that of the Sarbadārs in the same century and in earlier centuries the role of the ʿAyyārs; it also evokes the activity of the popular militias in the cities of Syria in the tenth to twelfth centuries. This is what popular forces can look like in the absence of strong states. Indeed, in the Anatolian environment we might perhaps have expected to see the emergence of an Akhī state or two. Konya was under the rule of one of its local Akhīs around 1300, and of another a few years later, but when the Qaramānids took the city in 1312, they massacred the Akhīs. In short, no Akhī dynasty was to emerge either there or elsewhere, and in the fifteenth century, as Anatolia passed under the rule of an unusually strong state, the Akhīs disappeared.

A first approximation of the history of the region as we have laid it out above would be that Anatolia in this period was a western extension of Iran, albeit on a smaller scale. In Iran we had a Turcoman invasion and a Great Seljuq dynasty; in Anatolia we have a Turcoman invasion and a little Seljuq dynasty. We then had a Mongol invasion and the rule of the Īlkhāns in Iran, and in the same way we have a Mongol invasion and the rule of the Īlkhāns in a substantial part of Anatolia. Finally we had Turcoman dynasties ruling in Iran, and we now have Turcoman dynasties, albeit smaller ones, ruling in Anatolia. What this comes down to is that Anatolia, like Iran, was at the receiving end of a steppe nomad expansion that first hit Iran and then spilled over into Anatolia.

28. Ibn Baṭṭūṭa, *Travels*, trans. H. A. R. Gibb, Cambridge 1958–2000, 2:419.

There were, of course, major differences. One was the combined ethnic and religious transformation of Anatolia, a process that in scale went far beyond the linguistic impact of the Turcomans on Azerbaijan or the boost they gave to particular religious traditions within Islam. Another was the fact that their invasion of Anatolia sooner or later brought the Turcomans to the shores of the Mediterranean—a far richer sea than any that border on Iran. This second point is in turn closely connected to the massive divergence between the histories of the two regions that was now about to begin. Steppe nomads would continue to dominate the political metabolism of Iran into the nineteenth century. Not so in Anatolia. There we will witness the emergence of something quite different.

10

The Ottoman Empire

The Ottoman state began in a corner of Anatolia but came to include large regions on three continents. Unlike its Asian and African possessions, its European territories had not previously been part of the Muslim world and are accordingly new to us. So we begin by taking a look at the state of southeastern Europe—roughly the Balkans—on the eve of the Ottoman conquest. One question here is whether conditions in the Balkans made the Ottoman conquest easier.

In addition to its territorial extent, the Ottoman state was remarkably long-lived, with a life-span from the early fourteenth century to the early twentieth. We will therefore divide up its history by period: early, middle, and later (though we are not concerned here with its continuing history after about 1800). But how does a state survive for so long?

Two themes dominate the early Ottoman story. One is expansion on two continents, despite a devastating and potentially terminal defeat at the hands of a roving conqueror, Tīmūr. The other is a far-reaching change in the character of the Ottoman polity. In the early fourteenth century it looked like a typical Turcoman state of the kind that prevailed over most of Anatolia. But by the end of the century it had become a massive fiscal and military apparatus like any other large and successful imperial state. Yet the Ottoman state also had some very distinctive features, and perhaps the most notable was that it recruited the core of its army by enslaving the sons of the Balkan peasantry. Why, then, was it the Ottomans, and not one of the many other Turcoman states, that embarked on this idiosyncratic trajectory?

The middle period takes us into the sixteenth century, when the empire was at the height of its extent and power. Again one part of the story is a continuing territorial expansion that, among other things, added extensive territories on the African continent to the empire. This is also a convenient point at which to survey the basic institutions of the Ottoman state in what can be called their classical form. Among them was a habit of deciding the succession to the throne by civil war, a phenomenon that is not uncommon in political history but in the Ottoman context was formally enshrined in the law of fratricide.

The later Ottoman period is characterized by a transformation that in its way was as drastic as the early evolution of the state, but very different in kind. The era of sustained expansion was now over, and the beginnings of contraction were in evidence. At the same time, the power of the central government declined in the face of large-scale insurrection and the eventual emergence of a variety of local power structures. All this was accompanied by extensive disorder and severe economic contraction. The empire nonetheless survived, with the later Ottomans retaining far more control over their provinces than the later ʿAbbāsids had done over theirs. But how do we explain the very real downturn? How did the Ottomans explain it to themselves? And how did the empire survive it?

A major theme in Ottoman history is relations between Muslims and Christians. Here we will look at the geographical distribution of the two populations, the respects in which they rubbed off on each other, and the ways in which the state related to its Christian subjects. There is an interesting comparison in store regarding Muslims and Hindus in India.

We end this survey of Ottoman history by looking at the empire through the eyes of the most famous Ottoman traveler, Evliyā Chelebī.

In the preceding chapter we surveyed three routes by which Oghuz nomads spread westward: the northern route through the steppes to the Balkans, the southwestern route into Syria, and between them the western route into Anatolia. The first proved a dead end, the second extended Turkic power to Syria and Egypt, and the third not only brought Turkic power to Anatolia but also turned the bulk of its population into Turkish-speaking Muslims. Between the later fourteenth century and the early sixteenth all three regions passed under the rule of a single state, the Ottoman Empire. There are two ways to see this remarkable development. We could think of it as the crowning achievement of Oghuz—and more broadly Turkic—state formation; or we could see in it the geopolitical reconstitution of the Byzantine Empire as it had existed before the Arab conquests of the seventh century, with comparable longevity. Either way, the Ottoman story bulks large enough to merit a chapter of its own. We begin the narrative with the emergence of an imperial state over the course of the fourteenth century and end it with its uneasy entry into the nineteenth. But before we come to the story itself, we need to pause for some background on the Balkans, the substantial part of Europe that the Ottomans were to bring under their rule.[1] The rest of their future territory lay in Asia and Africa and is already familiar from earlier chapters.

1. For the history of the pre-Ottoman Balkans see J.V.A. Fine, *The early medieval Balkans*, Ann Arbor 1983, and his sequel *The late medieval Balkans*, Ann Arbor 1987.

Background on the Balkans

Physically, the Balkans are clearly delimited on three sides by water: the Black Sea on the east, the Sea of Marmara, the Aegean, and the Mediterranean on the south, and the Adriatic on the west. To the north, however, there is no such sharply defined border. In the form of the Danube, water does mark what can be a significant frontier, but there is Balkan territory that concerns us to the north of the river, in a region that is perilously open to the Eurasian steppes. Within the space thus defined the distribution of mountains and plains is untidy, but the most consistently mountainous terrain is in the west, stretching from Greece to the borders of Austria, while the most extensive plains are to the east and north.

As usual, mountains are better than plains at preserving archaism, and this shows itself in the ethnic map of the Balkans. Three of the Balkan peoples have been there since antiquity, and all three are strongly associated with mountainous terrain. Most straightforwardly, the Greeks offer a clear case of ethnic and linguistic continuity in their ancient homeland, despite a curious detour in the way they identified themselves between late antiquity and modern times—one that, as we will see, in turn affected the Ottomans. Northwest of the Greeks, the Albanians preserve another ancient Indo-European language, quite likely a descendant of ancient Illyrian, but we begin to hear about them only in the eleventh and twelfth centuries. The third people, today's Romanians, at first sight gives the counterintuitive impression of being an ancient population that has survived in the plains of the northeast, maximally exposed to the ethnic perturbations of late antique and early medieval times, yet retaining a Romance language descended from the Latin of imperial Rome. But the chances are that this apparent territorial continuity is an illusion. The Romance speakers of the Balkans were known in medieval times as the Vlachs. They were a pastoral population and seem to have taken shape as a people in the relatively well-protected mountains of the southern Balkans. If so, there must have been a little-known medieval migration that took some—though by no means all—of them to what is now southern Romania and Moldavia; nineteenth-century nationalism then led them to claim to have been there ever since antiquity. For our period the geographical terms we need for this part of the Balkans are Walachia (Vlach-land, now southern Romania) and again Moldavia.

Elsewhere in the Balkans ethnogenesis was a product of invasion from the north. The invaders were of two kinds: Slavs and steppe nomads. Unlike the equestrian nomads of the steppes, the Slavs were among the pedestrian agriculturalists of eastern Europe. Large numbers of them moved south in the later sixth and seventh centuries, overwhelming the ancient populations outside the mountains. Even Greece, which despite the incursions of the Slavs did not adopt their language, retains many Slavonic place-names implying Slavic settlement. More than four hundred of them are to be found in the very southernmost part of Greece, the Morea—the ancient and modern Peloponnese. Indeed, Slavonic was still spoken in the Morea in the fifteenth century. The steppe nomads included a whole slew of peoples. Most of them left no lasting trace of their incursions—as we might anticipate, given that nomads are demographically more diffuse than peasants. The Huns and Avars are cases in point, and the same very likely goes for those of the Oghuz who entered the Balkans by the northern route. Likewise in the last decades of the thirteenth century the sway of the Golden Horde extended into the northeastern Balkans under a Chingizid commander named Noghay (d. 1299), but again without leaving any ethnic legacy. Yet two steppe peoples did have an enduring impact on the region. The first to arrive were the Bulgars, who as we saw established a state in the southeastern Balkans in the late seventh century. Linguistically their fate was to be assimilated by their Slav subjects, but they gave their name to the Bulgarians, the Slav people that emerged from this ethnic fusion. The second steppe people to leave a lasting mark were the Hungarians, whose legacy was more than nominal. Originally a confederation that included Turkic tribes, in 895–96 they invaded the far western end of the steppes, settling down in an extended territory that included what thereby became Hungary. Unlike the Bulgars they retained their language. No doubt they assimilated whatever native population they found in the region, and at the same time the language of the Turkic tribes died out, leaving Hungarian with a stratum of archaic Turkic loanwords. Processes of fusion analogous to the Bulgarian case may also be behind the ethnogenesis of other Slav peoples, such as the Serbs and the Croats; peoples bearing these names made their appearance in the western Balkans in the seventh century. This survey gives us the major ethnic groups of the Balkans in our period: the survivors from antiquity (the Greeks, Albanians, and Vlachs); the Slav peoples, however they may have come to be individuated (the Bulgarians, Serbs, and Croats); and a former steppe people (the Hungarians).

Mercifully, the religious map of the Balkans on the eve of the Ottoman conquest was considerably simpler. Islam was not yet in the picture, with the exception of the Muslim minority in medieval Hungary. The ancient peoples of the Balkans had duly converted to Christianity in the period following its adoption by the emperor Constantine in the fourth century; that included the Greeks, and no doubt the ancestors of the Albanians and Vlachs, though they are likely to have taken longer to turn Christian than the people of the plains. But the Slavs and the steppe peoples arrived as pagans and had to be converted. Here there was competition between the two geographically most relevant Christian brands: the Orthodoxy of the Byzantine Empire and the Catholicism of western Europe. The rivalry and eventual schism between the two resulted in a sectarian division of the Balkans. For the most part Orthodox Christianity prevailed, especially in the south and east. By and large it was the faith of the Greeks, the Vlachs, the Bulgarians, and the Serbs, and in addition to the Greek liturgy there was now one in Slavonic. But to the north and west Catholicism had the geographical advantage on the Dalmatian coast of the Adriatic, among the Croats, and in Hungary. The Albanians came to be divided. There were a couple of exceptions to this relatively simple picture that deserve a mention. One is the existence of a schismatic church in Bosnia, and the other is scattered evidence of the presence of a dualist religion in the Balkans.

While the mountains offered some security to ancient peoples, it was the plains that provided a more viable basis for state formation. For a long time the major state in the region was the Roman Empire and its Byzantine continuation. But its grip on the northern Balkans was never the same after the coming of the Slavs, and by the fourteenth century little was left of it. The Slavs seem to have lacked large-scale political organization of their own, but they were easily commandeered by more organized peoples such as the Bulgars (compare the role of Scandinavians in the ninth-century Russian ethnogenesis). The Byzantines eventually achieved the definitive destruction of the first Bulgarian empire to rule in the Balkans (681–1018), but because of a downturn in Byzantine power in the late twelfth century they had to live with a second Bulgarian state (1185–1396). This one was at its most successful in the first half of the thirteenth century, but by the second half of the fourteenth century it was fragmented and weak. In the west there was a kingdom of Croatia, but its Croat dynasty came to an end in the late eleventh century, and from the early twelfth it was ruled by the kings of Hungary. Serbia did better. The same downturn in Byzantine power opened a window for a fully independent Serb monarchy, and under Stefan Dushan (ruled 1331–55) Serbia was a powerful state. But after his death it broke up. There was also a Bosnian kingdom, and in the northeast there were two Vlach principalities that emerged in the fourteenth century, Walachia (1330–1715) and Moldavia (1340s-1615). The Albanians were laggards in state formation. A disunited population of mountain tribes, by the late fourteenth century they had local rulers, but there was nothing like an Albanian state until resistance to the Ottoman conquest led to the formation of a transient pan-Albanian league in 1444. To the north of all this the kingdom of Hungary bulked large, much larger than the Hungary we know today. In sum, when the Ottomans moved into the southeastern Balkans there was no strong state south of Hungary to get in their way. And Hungary, thanks to the reluctance of its aristocracy to allow their king to have an effective army at his disposal, was to become yet another weak state in the last decade of the fifteenth century.

The early Ottoman period

Beginnings, expansion, and catastrophe: The Ottomans to 1402

Ibn Khaldūn tells us that Orkhan (ruled 1324–60), the second Ottoman ruler, adopted the city of Bursa in northwest Anatolia as his capital. But, he adds, "he did not abandon tents for palaces, and would camp in his tents in the open country around it."[2] This characterization of Orkhan's lifestyle finds support in other early sources. John VI Cantacuzenus (ruled 1347–54), a sometime Byzantine emperor who knew the Ottomans well, writes that in the spring of 1329 "they were still under tents in the valleys, as the spring was in its middle, in the month of May." He goes on to explain that they were "about to move from the lowlands to higher altitudes, avoiding the heat of the summer; for this was their custom, as they were nomads."[3] Likewise a Greek archbishop captured by the Turks describes Orkhan's surroundings in 1355 as "a hilly place, surrounded by mountains at a distance and beautified by thick-shaded trees"; this, with the cool breezes and the fresh air, he concludes, "is the reason why the greatest ruler of the barbarians was spending his summer there." Of these testimonies, the first states explicitly and the second suggests that Orkhan, unlike the ruler of Aydïn visited by Ibn Baṭṭūṭa, was a full-time nomad. In short, the Ottomans in this early period have all the appearance of being a Turcoman dynasty like any other.

The Ottoman state began its history in Bithynia, in northwestern Anatolia but well to the east of the rival principality of Qarasï.[4] Its homeland was thus in the agricultural plains to the southeast of the Sea of Marmara, bordering on what was left of Byzantine territory on the Asian side of the Bosphorus. Much about the early history of this state is obscure because the Ottoman sources we possess date from the fifteenth century and the external sources are fragmentary. There is even a theory, and some curious pieces of evidence that could support it, that in origin the dynasty stemmed not from the Turcomans but rather from the Mongols of the Golden Horde, whose civil wars encouraged losers to seek refuge in Anatolia, as when Noghay was defeated and killed in 1299. But let us leave that aside to concentrate on the one thing we know the new state to have done with extraordinary persistence and success over the course of the fourteenth century: expanding its territory. In the first instance it did so locally at the expense of the Byzantine Empire. The founder of the dynasty, ʿOthmān, was active in the first quarter of the fourteenth century and most likely died in 1324; we know that he was already attacking and seizing Byzantine territory around 1302. This was enough to attract fighters from outside the Ottoman state to join him. But despite his efforts he was unable to take possession of a major urban center.

That changed under Orkhan, his successor. In 1326 the Ottomans captured their first city, Prusa, or to use the modern Turkish form of the name, Bursa—though

2. Ibn Khaldūn, *ʿIbar*, Būlāq 1284 *hijrī*, 5:562.

3. For these and the quotations that follow see G. G. Arnakis, "Gregory Palamas among the Turks," *Speculum*, 26 (1951), 106–7, 113.

4. For a narrative history of the early Ottoman Empire see C. Imber, *The Ottoman Empire 1300–1481*, Istanbul 1990; for a thematically organized survey see the same author's *The Ottoman Empire, 1300–1650: The structure of power*, Basingstoke 2002.

as we have seen, Orkhan is said to have adopted it as his capital without actually living in it. By 1337 he had possession of all the larger Byzantine towns of Bithynia, and soon he was eyeing the territories of other Anatolian dynasties. In 1354 he took Ankara to the east. But much more momentous was his earlier expansion to the west, absorbing Qarasï; this is likely to have taken place around 1348. Qarasï, as we have seen, was the state that had been making such effective use of its location on the Dardanelles to make war in Thrace. In this respect the Ottomans had been lagging behind. Their homeland was closer to the Bosphorus than it was to the Dardanelles, and the Bosphorus was still dominated by the almost impregnable Byzantine city of Constantinople. By 1337 the Ottomans had possession of some of the coast of the Sea of Marmara and used it to launch a raid on Thrace, but when making the crossing on their light vessels they did not take horses with them and were easily repulsed by the Byzantines. It was only from 1345 on, in the context of the Byzantine civil war of the 1340s, that the Ottoman state began to be a significant actor in Thrace. Orkhan was now sending troops there in large numbers to support a Byzantine ally—the same John VI who described the nomadic lifestyle of the Ottomans. The payoff from this intervention was not just plunder: Ottoman troops got experience of Thrace, and indeed of northern Greece as far west as Salonica. Around the same time the Ottomans moved quickly when in 1354 a major earthquake destroyed the walls of Gallipoli, on the European side of the Dardanelles. They seized the town, brought in settlers from Anatolia, and refortified it, though in 1366 they lost it for a decade. By the time of his death Orkhan had possession of eastern Thrace, roughly the corner of Europe that remains part of Turkey today. He had thus enlarged a minor Turcoman state into one that dominated northwestern Anatolia and the southwestern corner of the Balkans. Constantinople, of course, remained in Byzantine hands, still beyond the reach of the Ottomans despite its dilapidated condition and an attempted siege.

Orkhan's successor was Murād I (ruled 1362–89), who continued to expand Ottoman territory in both Anatolia and the Balkans. In Anatolia, where there was no major state to oppose him, Murād launched a drive to the south, taking over much of Germiyān, conquering Ḥamīd, and possibly seizing Teke with its port of Antalya on the south coast. In the Balkans, Serbia was the one state short of Hungary that might have resisted him effectively, but as we have seen it was weakened by fragmentation at just this time. Here the expansion was more wide-ranging. It was probably in 1369 that Murād took Adrianople, known in Turkish as Edirne, consolidating his rule over eastern Thrace. Thereafter Ottoman armies were active in Bulgaria, Serbia, Bosnia, and northern Greece to the shores of the Adriatic, conquering some territories and raiding others. Typically, local rulers who came to heel would be kept on in the role of vassals for a while, as was the case in Bulgaria. But despite their many successes, the Ottomans were not always victorious. In 1389 both Murād and the Serbian king were killed in a battle that left the two armies leaderless. The result, as a contemporary observer informs us, was that affairs of state in the Ottoman domains became disordered.

But not for long. We come now to the fourth and last of the Ottoman rulers of the fourteenth century, Bāyezīd I (ruled 1389–1402). His nickname was Yïldïrïm, "Thunderbolt," and he lived up to it. In Anatolia he eliminated all the Turcoman dynasties as far east as Sivas and Malaṭya and even took Erzinjān. In the southern Balkans his troops were active in Albania and engaged in repeated attacks on the Morea. Farther north he made the rulers of Serbia his vassals, reasserted Ottoman suzerainty over Bulgaria, and invaded Walachia on the far side of the Danube. He also blockaded Constantinople. By now the only significant enemy that could have countered the Ottoman expansion in the Balkans was the overambitious King Sigismund of Hungary (ruled 1387–1437). Bāyezīd proceeded to invade his lands as far as Buda, his capital city. At the same time the Ottoman fleet dominated at sea. Bāyezīd's reign nevertheless ended badly, for in the east there loomed an enemy far more formidable than the Hungarian monarch. Bāyezīd and Tīmūr were not on good terms: each protected the other's enemies, and Tīmūr's protégés included members of the Turcoman dynasties that the Ottomans had swept away. In 1402 Tīmūr invaded Anatolia, and the inevitable battle was fought near Ankara. A large part of Bāyezīd's army deserted him on the battlefield. We are told that the "Tatars" (most likely the Mongols of central Anatolia) had already made a secret agreement with Tīmūr to do so and that the Anatolian troops of the former Turcoman states did the same when they saw their former lords in Tīmūr's army. The silver lining, if there was one, was that Bāyezīd's infantry—a key component of his army—stayed loyal and fought hard. But in the course of the battle he was taken prisoner, and he died in captivity some seven months later. Meanwhile Tīmūr spent the best part of a year in Anatolia, among other things assiduously setting the clock back by restoring many of the Turcoman dynasties the Ottomans had dispossessed. As Beatrix Potter would say, this looks like the end of the story—but it isn't.

How the Ottoman state changed over the fourteenth century

Before we go any further into the fortunes of the Ottomans in the fifteenth century, we should look back on the fourteenth-century Ottoman trajectory. As we have seen, the Ottoman state entered that century as a minor Turcoman principality and left it as an empire ruling the greater part of Anatolia and the Balkans. It stands to reason that the change the state underwent over the course of the century cannot just have been a matter of scale; its very nature must have changed. But what can we do to back up reason with evidence?

Let us start with the army, for which our evidence for the fourteenth century is best, or perhaps we should say least bad. For the reigns of ʿOthmān and Orkhan the Byzantine sources are suggestive: the failed maritime raid on Thrace in 1337 aside, they tend to describe Ottoman forces as cavalry. In 1402 the cavalry were still there to desert, and they would remain a major component of Ottoman armies, but the core of Bāyezīd's forces, the ones that he commanded in person and who stayed loyal to him in the battle against Tīmūr, now consisted of infantry. These were the famous Janissaries, the "New Army" (*Yeni Cheri*, *yeni* being the Turkish for "new" and *cherīk* a word of Mongol origin for "army"). This force had come into existence at some point in the fourteenth century, most likely under Murād.

Three things mattered about this new army. The first was the very fact that the Janissaries were infantry—a radical break with centuries of Middle Eastern warfare in which cavalry had played the dominant role, but in line with the changing character of late medieval European armies. The second was that they were a standing army of salaried troops. This made them very different from old-fashioned Turcoman cavalry whose reward was plunder, the kind who went home to their winter pastures at the end of a campaign, to return in due course for the next campaign if it suited them. The Janissaries were also unlike the Timariots who were—or became—a prominent feature of fourteenth-century and later Ottoman armies; these were cavalrymen to whom fiefs (in Ottoman parlance, *tīmārs*) were assigned and who returned to their fiefs to collect their revenues when the fighting was over. Being a standing army made for a higher degree of solidarity among the Janissaries and for stronger bonds with the ruler. The third significant feature of the Janissaries was the way they were recruited: they were Christians enslaved and converted to Islam—as indeed were many Timariots in this early period. Their enslavement happened in either of two ways. One was through capture in the course of warfare against the infidel. Ottoman soldiers took large numbers of prisoners when they raided the Balkans, and the ruler would take his cut of them. The fifteenth-century Ottoman chroniclers date the beginning of this practice to the reign of Murād and associate it with the origin of the Janissaries. Up to this point the Janissaries are comparable to the black slave infantry of the Fāṭimids. But already in the fourteenth century an alternative and unprecedented form of recruitment had developed: collecting children from the subject peasant population, again particularly in the Balkans. Known as the Devshirme ("Collection"), this practice was uniquely Ottoman—and, incidentally, irreconcilable with Islamic law. One might think that the Christian origin of these Janissaries would have fomented disloyalty among them, but this would miss the point. Unlike a body of troops recruited from the existing Muslim population, the Janissaries came to the service of the ruler shorn of ethnic or familial ties to other sectors of Ottoman Muslim society. They were therefore uniquely dependent on the ruler and thus likely to be more loyal to him than were troops with wider connections. The conclusion from all this is obvious: a Turcoman dynasty that relies on infantry recruited in such ways as the core of its army can no longer be called a Turcoman dynasty.

We get glimpses of other trends in the character of the Ottoman state that go in the same direction. We find bitter complaints in an Ottoman chronicle of the 1420s regarding the explosion of bureaucracy and the oppressive taxation that went with it. In the good old days, we are told, taxes were low, and "even the unbelievers were not oppressed." Rulers gave away whatever came into their hands; in those days, happily, "they did not know what a treasury was." But the advent of greedy scholars toward the end of the reign of Murād led to drastic change. Presumably in their role as bureaucrats, these nefarious scholars brought oppression and corruption to the Ottoman lands. Before that "nothing was known of keeping account books"; it was again scholars—foreign ones—who introduced this unpleasant habit, together with the pernicious practice of "accumulating money and storing it in a treasury."[5] In this perspective scholars from Qaramān were no less objectionably foreign than Persians were. What we have here is not exactly objective reporting, and it is worth noting that an Ottoman legal document of 1324 is already a respectable bureaucratic product composed in Persian. Yet it makes sense that the Ottoman state at the end of the fourteenth century should have both needed and been able to afford a much larger and more complex bureaucracy than it possessed at the beginning of the century. While any Turcoman ruler is entitled to a measure of bureaucracy, what Bāyezīd had at his disposal in 1400 was clearly more than a measure. It also makes sense that this development was extremely unpopular in certain quarters. One such milieu was that of the dervishes and warriors engaged in jihad (*ghāzīs*) who were associated with the semiautonomous marcher lords of the Balkans. What is remarkable is not so much their discontent as the fact that we hear their voices so loud and clear. We owe this to the fact that a significant part of early Ottoman historiography represents their views, rather than those of the court.[6]

Another fourteenth-century trend that we can dimly discern concerns the ruling family. The early Ottoman sultans faced the usual dilemmas of dynastic rulers with regards to their sons and brothers. If you want your dynasty to continue after you, you had better have sons—more than one, since in a dangerous world just one is too risky—and your sons had better gain experience at an early age of what it is like to wield power. But the more able and experienced they are, the more likely they are to rebel against you rather than politely await your death. And when one of your sons finally succeeds you, what about his brothers? In a society with a deep respect for family values, a ruler's brothers surely have a claim to a share of a dy-

5. Anonymous chronicler translated in B. Lewis, *Islam from the Prophet Muhammad to the capture of Constantinople*, New York 1987, 1:135, 139.

6. For this see C. Kafadar, *Between two worlds*, Berkeley 1995, ch. 2.

nasty's wealth and power. But if they are given that share, they may well use it to subvert the rule of your son. Dynasties are fissiparous. How, then, do the first four Ottoman rulers seem to have managed these dilemmas? We know that ʿOthmān had at least four sons in addition to Orkhan thanks to the legal document of 1324. Here Orkhan as ruler makes a grant of land, and his four brothers appear as witnesses. That tells us that he had not killed them at his accession, and in fact we know that one of them was commanding troops on the battlefield in 1328. As a fifteenth-century Ottoman chronicler comments nostalgically, "brothers consulted each other then; they did not kill one another."[7] From the narrative sources we likewise know that Orkhan had multiple sons, and our earliest Ottoman account tells us that Murād's accession was bloody: "His brothers became enemies to him. The affairs of all of them were ended at his hands. They were all destroyed by his sword."[8] This sounds like a fratricidal civil war. By winning it Murād had solved the problem of his brothers, but there remained that of his sons. One of them rebelled in 1373; the rebellion failed, and the rebel son was blinded. Then, when Murād was killed in battle with the Serbians in 1389, there were apparently two sons in play. According to the narrative sources one of them was promptly executed on the battlefield—the other, of course, being Bāyezīd. What happened on Bāyezīd's death was a saga that we will defer for now. But already a pattern has emerged. In the first place, it seems to have been axiomatic from the start that the state was indivisible. In this respect the Ottomans were more in the tradition of the Īlkhāns than in that of the Seljuqs. In the second place, the accession of one son came in the course of the fourteenth century to mean death for his brothers. The politics of the Ottoman succession had thus become a game played for very high stakes. There is, of course, nothing un-Turcoman about a bit of family mayhem—ʿOthmān had killed an uncle—and there was some precedent for fratricide among the Anatolian Seljuqs, but the systematic cold-bloodedness of the emerging Ottoman practice seems to have been new.

If in the course of the fourteenth century the Ottoman state had moved so far from its beginnings, was there anything left of its original Turcoman heritage? One thing that unquestionably survived was the Turkish language. It was not, of course, the mother tongue of the Janissaries, but the chroniclers tell us that already in the reign of Murād the newly enslaved youths were distributed to Turks in the countryside to facilitate their linguistic assimilation. This Turkish of the Anatolian Turcomans was not the prestigious Chaghatay Turkic associated with the Tīmūrids, though we do possess a magnificent document—the best part of eight yards long—written in eastern Turkic in the Uighur script in which Meḥmed II (ruled 1451–81) announced his victory over Uzun Ḥasan in 1473. But it could still

7. Quoted in Kafadar, *Between two worlds*, 106.

8. Quoted in Imber, *The Ottoman Empire, 1300–1650*, 97.

serve as a marker of identity. Did the dynasty then identify as Turcoman? In the reign of Murād's great-grandson, Murād II (ruled 1421–51), it undoubtedly did. It was then that a certain Yazïjï-oghlu ʿAlī, who probably worked in the chancery in the 1420s, came up with a prestigious genealogy for the dynasty, tracing its descent to the eldest son of the eldest son of Oghuz Khān. This invocation of the Oghuz legend has been argued with some plausibility to have been a recent concoction. Yet we would do well not to throw out the baby with the bathwater. For one thing, if we hear nothing of an Oghuz genealogy of the dynasty in the fourteenth century, the fact is that we do not hear much of anything regarding the Ottoman political culture of that period. For another, the oldest Ottoman narrative source we possess, a poem written by a certain Aḥmedī around 1405, well before the reign of Murād II, has a scene in which the Seljuq sultan goes forth to wage holy war with three heroic companions, one of whom is Ertoghrul, the father of ʿOthmān; with him were "many from the Oghuz."[9] Yazïjï-oghlu ʿAlī may have been creative in elaborating his Oghuz genealogy, but he was not starting from scratch.

Before we move on to the next phase of Ottoman history, there is one basic question we should take up: Why, out of all the Turcoman dynasties, was it the Ottomans who went on to become an imperial power? Two simple ideas may help here. First, between the Turcoman states up on the plateau and their peers down on the coast, it was the coastal states—particularly those of the western lowlands—that had the best chance of transforming themselves into something different. They had left the Eurasian world of the steppes behind them and had entered a maritime one that was also a potential imperial heartland. They now had access to greater agricultural and commercial wealth, and their locations brought them within striking distance of infidel states, giving them standing to recruit from far and wide under the banner of jihad. Second, since in the end it is seizing and holding territory that counts, states close to extensive Christian lands had the advantage over those like Menteshe or Aydïn that could only reach them by sustained seafaring. With these two ideas we can reduce the field of potentially empire-building Turcoman states to a couple of favorites: Qarasï and the Ottomans. The Ottomans had a land frontier with what little was left of the Byzantine Empire in Asia. Qarasï, however, combined maritime frontage on the Mediterranean with unlimited Christian territory just across the Dardanelles, and it was making the crossing to Thrace at a time when the Ottomans were still confined to the Asian side of the Straits. Why, then, did the Ottomans absorb Qarasï and not the other way around? The question is unanswerable because we know even less about Qarasï in the first half of the fourteenth century than we do about the Ottomans. The bottom line is that there was a window of opportunity, and the Ottomans had whatever

9. N. S. Banarlı, "Ahmedi ve Dâsitan-ı tevârih-i mülûk-i Âl-i Osman," *Türkiyat Mecmuası* 6 (1939), 113 verse 34.

it took to jump through it—be it energy, persistence, military and political skill, or even vision.

Recovery and renewed expansion: The Ottomans from 1402 to 1453

We are already accustomed to the idea that Ottoman successions might not be bloodless, but without question none was bloodier than the civil war that followed Tīmūr's intrusion into Anatolia. It lasted for a full decade and involved heavy warfare among four brothers on two continents. But one brother, ʿĪsā, was quickly eliminated, and a second, Mūsā, soon became a prisoner in the hands of a third, Meḥmed, so it seemed that the struggle would be reduced to a straightforward confrontation between two brothers, Meḥmed and Süleymān. Süleymān looked set to win, having a strong position in the Balkans and an army that may well have been superior to the Turcomans and Tatars who constituted the core of Meḥmed's forces. But Meḥmed, based in Anatolia, cleverly released Mūsā from captivity, and with the aid of several of Süleymān's enemies Mūsā crossed to the Balkans, raised an army, failed at first, and then succeeded in defeating his rival. Some say that Süleymān met his end while hopelessly drunk. All Meḥmed now had to do was to eliminate Mūsā, though that took a while. At the end of the day Meḥmed was the only brother left standing. Apart from dramatizing the fact that brotherly love was scarce in the Ottoman setting, the story highlights a key feature of the Ottoman political tradition that we have already noted: the indivisibility of the state, despite occasional proposals to the contrary. "The totality of political power does not admit of division," as Meḥmed is reputed to have written in a letter to a Tīmūrid ruler who had told him that "this manner of acting among dearly beloved brothers is deemed unacceptable."[10] At one point in the civil war Süleymān ruled in the Balkans and Meḥmed in Anatolia, with the Straits tidily separating their territories. In a dynastic culture that accepted division, nothing would have been easier than to take this separation as a basis for a permanent settlement. And indeed, one of the major Ottoman sources implies that such a solution would have been right and proper. Instead, fratricide was the order of the day.

Once he was firmly in control and had suppressed three dangerous rebellions, the basic agenda of the short reign of Meḥmed I (ruled 1413–21) was restoring Ottoman power to what it had been on the eve of Tīmūr's invasion. The same was true of the long reign of his son Murād II (reigned 1421–51), once an initial two-year civil war was over and the two relatives who had separately challenged him for the succession were safely deceased. The upshot of the repeated campaigns of Meḥmed and Murād in the Balkans and Anatolia was the recovery of

10. See the correspondence translated in D. J. Kastritsis, *Sons of Bayezid*, Leiden 2007, 203, 204–5.

the bulk of the lost territories and a limited conquest of new territory, particularly in Albania. There was also a structural change that significantly enhanced the power of the Ottoman state: increasingly these territories were ruled directly, not through unreliable and resentful vassals or marcher lords with entrenched local power. By 1444 Murād felt secure enough to retire—a highly unusual attempt by a member of the Ottoman royal family to shed power rather than acquire it. But this arrangement did not work, and from 1446 to his death in 1451 he was back on the throne.

After this long, slow recovery, the accession of Murād's son Meḥmed II (ruled 1451–81) marked a full-blooded renewal of the aggressive expansionism of the fourteenth century. On this occasion no time was wasted on civil war: one of the first things Meḥmed did on assuming power was to execute an infant who had the misfortune to be his only surviving brother. He then took steps to ensure that there would not be trouble on his more distant borders while he laid siege to Constantinople. Capturing this city was a long-standing Ottoman ambition. Bāyezīd I had blockaded it for the best part of a decade, and Murād II had laid siege to it in 1422. This time, in 1453, the Ottomans finally succeeded. The resistance of the Byzantines was stiff despite the run-down state of their remaining territory and their capital, but by now the Ottomans had artillery powerful enough to open up a breach in the city's defensive wall. The troops then spent three days sacking the city. But Meḥmed had no intention of leaving Constantinople as he found it. For a long time the Byzantines had been sitting on a piece of prime real estate that they no longer had the means to maintain or utilize effectively, resulting, as a contemporary put it, in "a city of ruins, poor, and largely uninhabited."[11] Polybius's account of the disadvantaged situation of the city by land had become painfully relevant. But as of 1453 this problem was solved, and Constantinople was once more the capital of a real empire. Meḥmed now set about refurbishing it in a suitably imperial style, and one of the ways he did this was by encouraging or compelling large numbers of Christians and Muslims from elsewhere to leave their homes and settle in the city. The compulsion gave rise to great bitterness on the part of unwilling migrants, and the whole enterprise was unpopular with the warriors and dervishes of the Balkans. Thus one source rooted in this milieu has it that Meḥmed was warned that the city would never flourish: "However many times you build it, it will fall back into ruin again."[12] The prediction turned out to be resoundingly false, though the western part of Istanbul was to remain more or less empty for decades.

11. Quoted in H. Inalcik, "The policy of Mehmed II toward the Greek population of Istanbul," *Dumbarton Oaks Papers*, 23–24 (1969–70), 231.

12. Quoted in Ç. Kafescioğlu, *Constantinopolis/Istanbul*, University Park 2009, 6b, 174b.

This may be a good moment to pause and take stock before we continue with another century or so of Ottoman expansion. In geopolitical terms, what the Ottomans had done was more or less to reconstitute the Byzantine Empire of better days—not, as yet, the empire as it had been in the sixth century before the Arabs invaded it, but at least the empire of the early eleventh century before the Oghuz invasion. The Ottomans now had Anatolia and the Balkans, they had full possession of the Straits, and they had the imperial capital that went with them. That raises an obvious question: What had made it possible for them to achieve this?

We have already puzzled over the fact that of all the Turcoman states it was the Ottomans who were destined to become an imperial power. The question we should tackle now is somewhat different. Taking all that for granted, what was it about the wider geopolitical environment of the time that made it feasible for an energetic state to reproduce the shape of the Byzantine Empire of several centuries before? The key point here is the absence of any rival states both powerful enough and close enough to prevent the Ottomans from helping themselves to such an empire. In the east, after the ninth century there was never a state in the same league as the Sasanian Empire, and in post-Mongol times the danger from this quarter was reduced to the occasional threat posed by particularly aggressive rulers—Tīmūr, Shāh 'Abbās, and Nādir Shāh. Of these only Tīmūr penetrated deep into Anatolia, and even he left the Balkan possessions of the Ottomans untouched and made no attempt to extinguish the dynasty. In the south, the entrenchment of the Mamlūks in Syria could make for trouble in the extensive borderlands of southeastern Anatolia, but as we have seen they posed no existential threat to the Ottomans. In the west, the monarchies of western Europe were a potential menace insofar as they were a hotbed of military innovation, but they were too far away and too disunited to pose a serious danger at this time. The Crusades that they assembled to attack the Ottomans in the Balkans, in 1396 and 1444, were both failures. Austria was closer, but hardly a formidable military power. And in the north, the migrations of peoples that had so long tormented the Byzantines were over. The most powerful state in the region was Hungary, but by the time of Meḥmed II it was no longer a match for the Ottomans. Meanwhile the days when Russia would menace the empire and even threaten its possession of the Straits were still far in the future.

Meḥmed II and his palaces

One of the most revealing indications of the way Meḥmed saw the world is the palace he had built for himself in his new capital city of Constantinople—or as we can equally call it, following informal Ottoman usage, Istanbul. In fact he built two palaces, known as the Old Palace and the New Palace, both located well inside the city, the second on the promontory at the opposite end of the city from its land walls.[13] He built the Old Palace at great expense in the years immediately after his capture of the city, but for some reason he was dissatisfied with it. As a result it came to be used largely as a facility to which widows were relegated, together with women who had been disgraced or whose presence was no longer desired at court, and for that reason it was known as the "Palace of Tears." The New Palace—the one famous today as the Topkapı Sarayı—was constructed between 1459 and 1478. It seems to have been very much Meḥmed's personal vision, planned "according to his own independent invention," as one chronicler put it.[14] But naturally his vision did not come out of thin air.

In some ways his palace echoed the traditions of the Turcoman dynasties and the Tīmūrids to the east. The fact that the buildings were laid out on the model of a royal encampment fits well with these traditions, and we know that builders were imported from Iran to work on the palace. More pointedly, a well-informed Italian observer tells us that one of the buildings—the Chinili Köshk—was constructed in Persian style and decorated in the mode of the country of Qaramān. But this did not mean that the palace as a whole conformed to this eastern tradition. Indeed, an Aq Qoyunlu prince who had rebelled unsuccessfully against his father, Uzun Ḥasan, and found refuge in Istanbul in 1474 took a rather dim view of Meḥmed's palace. He felt that the right place for a palace was outside a city, where the ruler would be separated from the common people. Meḥmed responded by building a wall to isolate his palace, but he did not go so far as to rebuild it outside Istanbul.

In fact the location of the New Palace was very much in a Byzantine tradition. It sat on the site of the acropolis of the ancient city of Byzantium, close by the ruins of the old Byzantine Great Palace. This was not just the result of geographical factors operating in a cultural vacuum, for Meḥmed was very much aware of the Byzantine past of his new city. He had a history of its rulers and monuments compiled for his use, and in this book the location of his palace in relation to the acropolis and the Great Palace was carefully noted. He also kept a collection of Byzantine antiquities in one of the gardens of his palace and was an admirer of the Athenian acropolis, which he visited in 1458. He went so far as to have a pavilion constructed in Greek style, a counterpart of the eastern style of the Chinili Köshk, though that building, too, had its Byzantine elements. It was not till 1853 that the Ottoman sultans moved into a neoclassical palace that Constantine might have approved of.

Alongside these eastern and local traditions, Meḥmed also drew on skills and tastes from the west, far more than his successors were to do. He invited experts from Italy to work on his palace; they included interior decorators, one of whom

13. For what follows see G. Necipoğlu, *Architecture, ceremonial, and power*, New York 1991.
14. Quoted in Necipoğlu, *Architecture, ceremonial, and power*, 13b.

could have been the artist Gentile Bellini (d. 1507), who painted his famous portrait of Meḥmed while in Istanbul. There was no Italian pavilion in the palace, but its towers were built in "Frankish" style. The eclectic approach to architecture that we see here had a considerable past in the Ottoman context, but only a limited future: between the late fifteenth century and the late sixteenth Ottoman architecture would undergo a far-reaching process of standardization.

Meḥmed was clearly endowed with considerable curiosity about cultures other than his own, and his palace shows a marked appreciation of diversity. But it was not the celebration of diversity that is practiced today, which is intended to erase historical and contemporary disparities of power. To a significant extent the reason Meḥmed liked diversity was that he now owned it—as with his collection of Byzantine antiquities. Pavilions in Persian and Greek style were pleasing reminders of kingdoms he had conquered—which is perhaps why there was no Italian pavilion. In the same way the Ottomans treasured the tents of rulers they had vanquished, and liked to display them. Rulership is a highly competitive sport, and Meḥmed accordingly wanted to know about the competition. That included the great rulers of the past. We know that he possessed a copy of Arrian's second-century life of Alexander the Great in the original Greek, and a Venetian humanist tells us that he would have it read to him every day.

Before we leave Meḥmed's New Palace, the way it was used can tell us a bit more about the continuing evolution of the Ottoman state from a Turcoman principality to something very different. The fifteenth century may have been the period in which the Ottomans were most self-consciously Turcoman. As we have seen, the first half of the century saw the development of an Ottoman claim to a prestigious descent from Oghuz Khān, and Turcoman dynasties were still a conspicuous feature of the political landscape to the east of the Ottomans in the second half of the century. That this Turcoman fashion remained alive in this period is shown by the fact that Meḥmed had grandsons named Oghuz and Qorqud—the latter the name of the wise and cunning Oghuz soothsayer to whom was attributed a prophecy of the rise of the Ottomans. But there was nothing very Turcoman about life in the New Palace. Living in tents lends itself to interaction between the ruler and his elite, whereas the keynote of life in the palace was seclusion. One of its peculiar architectural features was an alcove in which Meḥmed could sit and listen to the deliberations of his ministers from behind a curtain; he did not participate, but he received their petitions four times a week. The frequency of his appearances to his courtiers, his soldiers, and his people likewise diminished. Although matters must have been somewhat different when he was out of town, as he tended to be in the summer, this development of palace life already seems somewhat extreme. But as we will see, a bizarre twist in the sixteenth century was to take it yet further. In the meantime, Turcomans were scarcely to be found at the Ottoman court. As one of Meḥmed's courtiers complained, "If you wish to stand in high honor on the Sultan's threshold, you must be a Jew or a Persian or a Frank."[15]

The middle Ottoman period

Expansion continued: The Ottomans from 1453 to 1566

Meḥmed did not rest on his laurels after taking Constantinople. He maintained a high level of military activity throughout his reign and died a few days into his last campaign. But none of his later conquests was as dramatic. In the Balkans they included Bosnia and the Morea, and in Anatolia the Pontus—the Black Sea coast around Trebizond—in 1461 and Qaramān by 1474. The outcome of an expedition to the Crimea in 1475 was that the Crimean Khānate became and remained a vassal state. However, an Ottoman occupation of Otranto in 1479—and a later raid into Apulia in 1537—did not lead on to a conquest of Italy. We can perhaps see here the incipient revenge effects of successful expansion. One was geopolitical: a pattern of alliances whereby enemies of the Ottomans in the west would seek the cooperation of those in the east—first Qaramān, then the Aq Qoyunlu, and eventually in the next century the Ṣafawids. The other was domestic: the friction that ceaseless campaigning created between Meḥmed and his troops. At one point they refused to fight, at another they threatened to mutiny, and on his death they vented their spleen by spending several days looting Istanbul. Meḥmed had tried the patience of his army, as also that of his taxpayers.

The reign of his successor, Bāyezīd II (ruled 1481–1512), was rather different in tone. Part of the reason was personal. Bāyezīd seems to have been the first Ottoman ruler who did not enjoy making war—a trait one is tempted to link to his grandfather's attempt at retirement. And partly, at least until 1495, the cause was structural. In the fraternal civil war at the start of Bāyezīd's reign, his rival brother Jem, who at one point had proposed a partition of the empire, contrived to get away. He ended up as a pawn in the hands of the Europeans, who were now able to threaten to make the same use of him as Meḥmed I had made of Mūsā. But even after Jem's death in 1495, Bāyezīd showed little appetite for warfare. Crisis came in 1511 when a devastating Shīʿite rebellion broke out in Teke. It was led by a certain Shāh Qulu, who had a track record as an agent of the Ṣafawids. But this upheaval was soon overtaken by a succession struggle in which Bāyezīd lost his throne to his son Selīm. Selīm had found himself in a bind. As governor of Trebizond he was on the outside track with respect to his two brothers, both of whom had been appointed to govern provinces closer to the capital. So he jumped the gun, sailing

15. Quoted in G. Necipoğlu, "Visual cosmopolitanism and creative translation," *Muqarnas*, 29 (2012), 15a.

to the Crimea, where thanks to a strategic marriage he was in a position to borrow troops from his father-in-law, the Khān. He then advanced on Istanbul through the Balkans, and despite an initial defeat this daring maneuver proved successful on a second attempt. In 1513 he disposed of both his brothers.

As the manner of his coming to the throne suggests, Selīm I (ruled 1512–20) was a ruler in the same mold as his grandfather. His short reign had long-term consequences. The first item on his agenda was to confront the Ṣafawid challenge, which he did through a brutal repression of the Qizilbāsh, the pro-Ṣafawid fifth column in Anatolia, followed by an invasion of Ṣafawid territory, during which he won a resounding victory in 1514. He thereupon occupied the Ṣafawid capital, the city of Tabrīz in Azerbaijan, and would have advanced further into Iran the following year but for the fact that the Janissaries refused to winter there—a cussedness already experienced by his grandfather. Then, in 1516, Selīm turned south and conquered Syria, followed by Egypt in the following year. After wintering in Damascus, he planned a new campaign in the east in 1518, but again he was frustrated by the refusal of his troops to comply. His early death meant that Europe was spared his attentions, but one thing he did near the end of his reign was to extend his protection to some Ottoman freebooters who had set up in Tunis and Algiers, thereby making these distant regions—the Barbary states—in some sense parts of his empire. But his most lasting legacy was in the east. Here the defeat of the Ṣafawids led to the permanent absorption of eastern Anatolia into the Ottoman Empire, a process that involved a major effort mounted by Selīm to "win the hearts" of the local Kurdish potentates.[16] The outcome was that today the region, including its large Kurdish population, is part of Turkey, not of Iran or of some third state located in between. The rise of the Ṣafawids and the Ottoman response to it also had profound religious and cultural effects on Anatolian society. Religiously, what could at a pinch have been toleration of diversity hardened into a bitter sectarian division between a self-consciously Sunnī state and a movement on the fringes of Shīʿism whose heirs are the ʿAlevīs of modern Turkey. A European ambassador sent to Istanbul in 1554, Ogier Ghiselin de Busbecq, left some informative letters in which at one point he touches on this animosity. To illustrate "the great dislike which the natives of Asia entertain to the religion and supremacy of the Ottomans," he describes how Selīm's son and successor Süleymān spent a night in a house in Anatolia, the owner of which subsequently proceeded to purify it, regarding it as polluted. Süleymān's response was to have him executed and the house demolished; as Busbecq puts it, the man paid heavily for his "dislike of the Turks and partiality for the Persians."[17] A residual form of this partiality is attested

16. Quoted in V. Genç, *Acem'den Rum'a bir bürokrat ve tarihçi İdris-i Bidlîsî*, Ankara 2019, 307.

17. C. Thornton Forster and F. H. Blackburne Daniell, *The life and letters of Ogier Ghiselin de Busbecq*, London 1881, 1:162.

again in the late nineteenth century, when members of a heterodox community north of Antalya sought to evade military service by claiming to be subjects of the Shāh of Iran. Culturally the dominance of Shīʿism in Iran, Selīm's response to it, and his conquest of the Arab lands ended a long period in which the Ottomans looked to the Persian east and set them looking more to the Arab south.

Selīm's successor was his son Süleymān I (ruled 1520–66), known to Europeans as the Magnificent and to Ottomans as Qānūnī, for reasons we will come to. This was the first uneventful succession since that of Orkhan—Selīm had left no other son to compete with Süleymān. Like Selīm, Süleymān was an assiduous campaigner, though he may have lacked his father's flair. In the first fifteen years or so of his reign he maintained a very respectable rate of expansion. In Europe Belgrade fell to him in 1521, opening the way for his conquest of a share of Hungary, including its capital city of Buda, in 1541; this was soon followed by the acquisition of Transylvania. In Asia he conquered Iraq in 1534, taking Baghdad. With that the Ottomans now held all three of the historic imperial heartlands of the Middle East—their own, Egypt, and Iraq. In later years there were certainly further successes, but they were lesser ones. A naval expedition of 1538 to the Indian Ocean gave the Ottomans some coastal presence in the Yemen, where they subsequently moved inland to take Taʿizz in 1547, followed by Ṣanʿāʾ in the northern highlands a few years later. But the number of fruitless initiatives seemed to increase as the expansive efforts that had yielded such high dividends earlier in Ottoman history encountered diminishing returns. Laying siege to Vienna late in the campaigning season in 1529 and thereby failing to take it did not make much sense, nor did repeatedly occupying Tabrīz and then relinquishing it. For a while, at least, the Ottomans came to terms with this stalemate on the eastern front with the 1555 treaty of Amasya, which confirmed the frontier as it was. It took them longer to do the same on the western front, where Süleymān himself died while on campaign in Hungary. The succession was again a smooth one. Of Süleymān's three sons, Muṣṭafā had been executed for conspiracy in 1553 and Bāyezīd had been killed a couple of years after rebelling unsuccessfully in 1558–59. That left the accession of Selīm II (ruled 1566–74) to pass unchallenged. But at this point we should interrupt our narrative to examine the structure of the empire—a structure that in the reigns ahead would be subject to drastic change.

The structure of the sixteenth-century Ottoman Empire

The heart of the empire was the New Palace, built, as we have seen, by Meḥmed II. His successors, especially Süleymān, did a considerable amount of refurbishing, but they did not change its essential character. They did, however, make two changes to the way it was used. First, whereas Meḥmed could still spend time in summer pastures, later sultans stayed in the palace unless they were out on campaign; for them Turcoman nomadic kingship was now entirely a thing of the past. Second, there was a strange shift in the practice of those inhabitants of the palace who were closest to the sultan. Its origin was apparently accidental. At one point there happened to be two mute brothers serving in the palace, and they communicated with each other in sign language. Süleymān found this behavior very respectful and ordered the pages attached to his private quarters to adopt it. Soon it was thought rude even to whisper in the presence of the sultan. The ruler now spent much of his life enveloped in a cocoon of silence. Idiosyncratic though it was, the cult of silence must have been a good fit with the existing palace culture. This culture contrasted strongly with the ambience of the Ṣafawid court in Iran, and it would not have appealed to a monarch such as Shāh ʿAbbās, who as we have seen could talk to people of all classes in their own idiom. In fact, a generation before ʿAbbās's reign there had been a striking juxtaposition of the two royal cultures when Süleymān's son Bāyezīd fled to Iran in 1559 after the failure of his rebellion against his father. He made a terrible impression on his hosts, who deemed him "arrogant, reticent, and cold natured." He was greeted by Ṭahmāsp, the Ṣafawid ruler at the time, in a warm and friendly fashion, but he nevertheless "maintained his haughty and arrogant demeanor." As our Persian source relates, "He spoke not a word, and did not join in that cultured dialogue which every occasion of this sort demands."[18] A couple of years later Ṭahmāsp allowed an executioner sent by the Ottomans to kill the prince, not to mention four of his sons. There were clear-cut reasons of state for this decision—Ṭahmāsp had already used his possession of Bāyezīd to obtain the concession he wanted from the Ottomans, and in any case he had a ruthless streak. But Bāyezīd's perverse sense of royal decorum may at least have saved the Ṣafawid ruler from a twinge of guilt as he betrayed his guest. It also tells us something about life back in Istanbul: the Ottoman dynasty in this period seems to have been strikingly disconnected from the "cultured dialogue" of high society.

This was not the only way in which the dynasty went against the grain of the values of the society it ruled. Overwhelmingly the sultans had their children by slave concubines, not by wives. There was nothing unlawful about this, since in the eyes of the Sharīʿa such offspring were fully legitimate, but in social terms it was more prestigious to be born of a free mother. The distinctive Ottoman custom was that a concubine would bear the sultan only a single son, and when he was sent out to govern a province, she would accompany him. The practice, however, changed under Süleymān, who had more than one son by his favorite concubine and went so far as to manumit and marry her. In earlier times royal marriages had indeed been part of the system, but they were made with foreign

18. Quoted in Necipoğlu, *Architecture, ceremonial, and power*, 255.

dynasties for political purposes, not to reproduce the dynasty. Ottoman rulers would accordingly marry foreign princesses (whether Christian or Muslim), and Ottoman princesses would marry foreign rulers (but only Muslim ones). Yet this pattern had come to an end around the middle of the fifteenth century, and thereafter Ottoman princesses were married off to leading members of the Ottoman political and military elite, such as the grand vizier. This, too, went against a widespread value of Muslim society, and one that had its place in the Sharīʿa: a woman should not marry down. For an Ottoman princess to marry an actual or former slave—as grand viziers often were—was a clear violation of that value. Not that being on the receiving end of such a marriage was always a privilege; we hear from the seventeenth-century Ottoman traveler Evliyā Chelebī that one of his patrons found himself married against his will to an arrogant, acerbic, and aging princess who had already been through twelve husbands and made extravagant financial demands for the maintenance of her retinue of 1,200 souls. But at least the sultans never parted with their daughters to unbelievers.

In the fratricidal politics of the Ottoman succession we see another aspect of the dynasty that went against the values of the wider society. The Sharīʿa, like most legal systems, takes a dim view of fratricide, as was acknowledged by a fifteenth-century chronicler who, in seeking to justify the killing of the brother of Bāyezīd I in 1389, quoted the maxim "Necessity justifies what is forbidden."[19] A provision in the legal code of Meḥmed II—though it may well be a later insertion—implicitly makes the same admission in different language: if one brother succeeds in his bid for the throne, "it is appropriate that he should kill his brothers for the good order of the world." There is evidence that people outside the dynasty looked askance at Ottoman fratricide, as we have seen in the context of the civil war between the four brothers precipitated by Tīmūr's intervention. We have also noted the nostalgia of the fifteenth-century chronicler for the good old days when brothers did not kill each other. To trespass for a moment into the later sixteenth century, in 1595 a new sultan had his nineteen brothers "dragged from their mothers' knees," as one chronicler puts it, and executed. Another chronicler of this event expressed the pious hope that God would let the angels around His throne "hear the crying and weeping of the people of Istanbul." There was, of course, a reason for all this fratricide. If the axiomatic indivisibility of the empire was to be maintained, and if there was to be no algorithm that determined in advance which prince would be the next ruler, then something had to be done to contain or eliminate the other competitors. Indivisibility was occasionally called into question—Meḥmed I perhaps wished to divide the empire at one point, Jem proposed it to his brother Bāyezīd II, and one of Selīm I's brothers made the same move, but nothing ever

19. For this and the quotations that follow see Imber, *The Ottoman Empire, 1300–1650*, 108–9.

came of such ideas. As to an algorithm, a semblance of one based on seniority was to emerge later, but as yet there was none. What was unusual about the Ottomans in this period was the starkness with which they opted for elimination. Their ruthlessness naturally courted a risk of a different kind: dynastic extinction. In general, this risk ought to be low for royal families whose males can produce legitimate offspring by multiple wives and concubines. The general run of Muslim dynasties thus enjoyed a significant advantage over their European Christian counterparts, whose monogamy meant that the future of a dynasty could turn on the womb of a single woman. But the Ottoman practice of systematic fratricide severely reduced this comparative advantage.

We now descend to the high officers of the state. Typically they were men who, after starting life as Christians, had been enslaved and converted to Islam. For the most part their enslavement took place as before, through capture in warfare or through the Devshirme. We already met this system in the fourteenth century, and it was still integral to the functioning of the state in the sixteenth. From the Christian peasantry of the Balkans it was extended to the Muslim Bosnians, who apparently asked to be included, and to the Christians of Anatolia, who did not. Thus the architect Sinān (d. 1588), a key figure in the standardization of Ottoman architecture, was recruited through an unprecedented "collection" of boys in the Cappadocian province of Kayseri in the reign of Selīm I. Within the ranks of the sultan's slaves, those chosen to become administrators were the cream of the cream. They had first to be selected for education in the palace school and then to be picked out for promotion, initially in the provinces, where governors were subject to rapid rotation, and then back at the center. For those who made it to this level there were a handful of positions at the heart of the administration of the empire, headed by that of the grand vizier, who enjoyed the privilege of one-on-one meetings with the sultan. It was these dignitaries to whose deliberations the sultan might listen from behind a curtain. They were joined in their meetings by some freeborn bureaucrats, but to a large extent the empire was run for the sultan by his slaves. In other words, the Ottoman political and military elite was far from being a hereditary aristocracy. Hence the state felt free to confiscate the property of its servants when they died, something aristocrats would not stand for, and it regularly did so into the nineteenth century, long after most of its servants had ceased to be legally slaves.

It had not always been like this. As we have seen, Orkhan used one of his brothers as a military commander, so he may well have assigned similar responsibilities to the others; this naturally ended when Ottoman rulers no longer had living brothers. Likewise in early Ottoman times prominent families whose power and resources were to some degree independent of the state played a major role at the center. Such families tended to be based in the Balkans, where marcher lords played their part in the early Ottoman expansion, but one Anatolian family, the

Chandarlīs, more or less monopolized the position of grand vizier for some seventy years prior to 1453. In the sixteenth century such families could continue to flourish in the provinces, but they no longer wielded power at the center. Yet another alternative to slave power was rule through scions of royal or aristocratic Christian families that the early Ottoman expansion had reduced to vassalage. Some members of such families converted to Islam and even rose to the rank of grand vizier. But this, too, was a transient phenomenon, no longer encountered after the early sixteenth century. This is not, however, to say that the whole empire was directly ruled by the sultan's slaves. In the European territories there were still vassal states in the sixteenth century, though they were not located where the vassals of the fourteenth century had been. Instead, the phenomenon had moved out to what was now the periphery. There was the vassal Muslim Khān in the Crimea and vassal Christian rulers in Moldavia, Walachia, Transylvania, and for a time in the Ottoman part of Hungary. In Walachia and Moldavia, for example, the local aristocracy often played a part in choosing a new ruler. There was also a vassal polity unlike any of these: the Catholic mercantile republic of Ragusa, which paid tribute to the Ottomans from 1459 to 1804. There were further vassals on the Asian side. A lone Turcoman dynasty, the Ramaḍānids, survived in Cilicia until 1608, and Kurdistan still had an abundance of hereditary potentates, such as the Khān of Bitlis. In the Arab world we see, for example, the continuation of a centuries-old pattern in the Ḥijāz, where local lineages of descendants of the Prophet held power under an Ottoman umbrella. But in Asia by the middle of the sixteenth century all but such remote regions were under the rule of the sultan's slaves. The central authorities also made sure that the slaves they sent out as provincial governors did not entrench themselves and found local dynasties: a governor would spend less than three years in any one province. We have, of course, encountered many Muslim states in which slaves played prominent roles, but the Ottomans arguably took this way of centralizing power to an unprecedented extreme. This had consequences for the character of the Ottoman state. Political systems in which power is diffused, be it to Turcoman chiefs, large landowners, or feudal lords, tend to be less efficient than are those in which it is concentrated at a single central point. But because there is a lot of redundancy built into such decentralized systems, they can also be less fragile and more resilient.

The Ottoman army and navy

The great majority of slaves of the sultan did not, of course, make it all the way to the top. Many spent their lives staffing the palace in a great variety of roles, but most of them were enrolled in one of two military forces. One consisted of six divisions of cavalry attached to the palace; this was the smaller force, but over time its numbers grew, from some 2,300 under Meḥmed II to some 11,000 in 1567. The other was the prime infantry force, the Janissaries. Their numbers likewise grew: around 5,000 in the mid-fifteenth century, by 1567 they had risen to around 13,000. As yet the Janissary infantry made up only a fraction—perhaps a quarter—of an Ottoman field army, which in terms of numbers still consisted mainly of cavalry. But the Janissaries were literally the central component of the army on the battlefield, with the sultan in their midst, and they were also key players in the domestic politics of the empire. For example, it was the Janissaries who forced Bāyezīd II to relinquish the throne to Selīm in 1512, just as it was they who made Selīm abandon Tabrīz after his victory over the Ṣafawids two years later, frustrating his plan to strike deeper into Iran. How much they mattered is also indicated by the fact that the state itself assumed the task of arming them, along with the six divisions of cavalry; the Timariots, by contrast, had to supply their own equipment. In addition, the Janissaries were closely linked to the Ottoman adoption of artillery and handguns on the battlefield—a development that played its part in Ottoman successes against the Aq Qoyunlu in 1473, the Ṣafawids in 1514, and the Mamlūks in 1516.

The Ottoman cavalry in this period was largely made up of fief-holding Timariots. Typically an Ottoman fief was a village that the state had handed over to a Timariot together with the right to collect the taxes due from its peasants. In return he was expected to maintain order locally and to show up for campaigns when required, often with one or two armed retainers. On campaign he would be under the command of the governor of the province in which his fief was situated. If it came to a pitched battle, the Timariots would be on one or other wing of the army. As to recruitment, some Timariots were inherited by the Ottomans from states they had conquered, as with the Christian Timariots of Albania and the former Aq Qoyunlu Timariots of southeastern Anatolia—though these local Timariots would be balanced by ones brought in from elsewhere. Others were products of the palace and thus among the sultan's slaves. But the majority of Timariots were not slaves of the sultan and had inherited their fiefs, or more precisely the right to be assigned a fief, from their fathers. Outsiders were not supposed to receive fiefs, though it was always possible that the state might reward signal service with one or that an outsider might obtain one by fraud. Inevitably mistakes were made, and a bureaucrat's marginal note in a register of 1455 says of one Timariot: "Died. Hanged when he was proved to be a brigand."[20] Like Janissaries, Timariots could act up, but the central government was naturally less immediately vulnerable to their misbehavior. The total number of Timariots in 1525 was around 18,000; to that figure we have to add their armed retainers. In comparative terms what was unusual about the Timariots in the Muslim context was that in general they were

20. Quoted in Imber, *The Ottoman Empire, 1300–1650*, 197.

freeborn without being tribal. Being freeborn set them off from the Mamlūk cavalry, while being nontribal distinguished them from nomadic cavalry. To a European medievalist, of course, both features seem unremarkable.

Other components of the Ottoman army were less central but nonetheless of some comparative interest. There was a kind of low-grade infantry raised by systematic conscription, mainly from the urban population, and known as ʿAzebs—literally "bachelors," though the meaning is irrelevant. When Selīm defeated the Ṣafawids in 1514 he is reported to have had eighteen thousand of them with him, or perhaps it was thirty thousand. The point of interest here is that they were recruited in pretty much the same way as a modern state conscripts its army, and yet in military terms they were as marginal as modern conscript armies are central. There was equally a low-grade cavalry, the Akïnjïs, literally "raiders," and here the meaning of the word is very much in place. These were lightly armed cavalry in the Balkans, and in the words of an order issued by the sultan in 1565, their task in enemy territory was to "raid the abject infidels, enslave their children and wives, plunder and pillage their possessions and properties."[21] Led by the marcher lords, they mounted raids during campaigns on the Balkan frontiers of the empire, but also between campaigns. They sound very like the nomadic Turcomans who ravaged Anatolia in pre-Ottoman times, and like the Turcomans, they were undisciplined, deemed suited only to plundering. But they were not nomads—instead, when they were not raiding they were cultivators. There were indeed Turkish nomads in the Balkans, though fewer than in Anatolia, but their only role in the army was as noncombatants. This leads us to a striking feature of the Ottoman state: the fact that it had no military use for its Turcomans. It did, however, make repeated use of tribal cavalry in another way. The Crimean Tatars were an authentic example of the species, and in return for subsidies they regularly joined Ottoman campaigns in large numbers. Their primary role was naturally on the European front, but they were also present when Selīm defeated the Mamlūks in 1516. This was a clever arrangement that allowed the Ottomans to have the benefit of the military energies of the Tatars while outsourcing to the Khān the headache of dealing with the domestic politics of this "refractory people," as a sixteenth-century Ottoman called them. By contrast, after the triumph of Meḥmed I in the civil war following Tīmūr's invasion, the nomads of Anatolia usually got a share of the military action only during unsuccessful rebellions—a noteworthy exclusion given that even in western Anatolia they made up around 15 percent of the population.

In addition to their land army, the Ottomans had their navy—less important, but historically instructive. That they had one was only to be expected. From early

21. For this and the next quotation see Imber, *The Ottoman Empire, 1300–1650*, 265.

on they found themselves in an inescapably maritime location; as we have seen, they were using boats to transport their troops to Thrace as early as 1337, and in 1354 they took possession of Gallipoli on the European side of the Dardanelles. By 1392 they had a fleet. In this they were hardly being innovative. Although the sea was no part of the ancestral heritage of the Turcomans, as we have seen some of the Turcoman states that came into contact with it quickly adapted to it. The basic instrument of Mediterranean naval warfare in these centuries was the galley, a ship powered by large numbers of rowers and carrying a substantial complement of fighters. Galley warfare was a relatively stable technology, and it was not particularly hard for enterprising newcomers to adopt it and use it for themselves. What the construction and maintenance of a fleet of galleys required was above all resources—large amounts of timber, manpower, biscuit, and the money to pay for it all. These the Ottomans came to possess in abundance, and in a strongly centralized state they could readily mobilize them. As the grand vizier put it to the admiral of the fleet after a major naval defeat off Lepanto in western Greece in 1571, "My dear Pasha, by God, believe me that this empire is such that if it wishes, it can without any difficulty have the whole fleet's anchors made of silver, its rigging of silk, its sails of satin."[22] The sheer scale of their resources thus gave the Ottomans a major advantage over their chief Mediterranean antagonist, Venice, which was no more than a city-state. Where the Ottomans lagged behind the Venetians was in quality, not quantity. This lag was nevertheless significant. Venice was a merchant republic in which commercial and naval activities went hand in hand, reinforcing each other. The Ottoman navy, by contrast, was not an extension of the economic interests of a mercantile polity;[23] instead, Ottoman fleets came into existence by imperial fiat in a context of grand strategy. This meant that if the Ottomans were to confront an enemy yoking commerce and naval power on a scale larger than a city-state, or if they were to suffer a serious diminution in their capacity to mobilize their resources, their navy could be in trouble, and with it the security of Istanbul. But as yet there was no sign of this.

Two phenomena are nevertheless worth noting because they point to the limitations of naval power by imperial fiat. One is the contrast between Ottoman and Portuguese naval activity on the Indian Ocean. Here the intrusion of the ships of a small and remote—but mercantile—Iberian state in 1498 posed a challenge first to the Mamlūks and then to the Ottomans. Despite early efforts to compete that took the Ottomans to the west coast of India in 1538, in the end they did little more than defend the Red Sea and its immediate approaches from the Portuguese. Their performance in the Persian Gulf was more limited still, despite the fact that their

22. Quoted in S. Soucek, *Ottoman maritime wars, 1416–1700*, Istanbul 2015, 112.

23. For a different view see P. Brummett, *Ottoman seapower and Levantine diplomacy in the age of discovery*, Albany 1994.

access to timber there was far better than on the Red Sea thanks to the option of floating it down the Euphrates. All told, the Ottomans were not wholly insensitive to mercantile interests. At one point they contemplated a deal that would have given the Portuguese access to Ottoman ports on the Indian Ocean in return for reciprocal privileges for Ottoman merchants. But mercantile interests did not drive Ottoman naval policies. The other phenomenon is a contrast within the naval forces available to the Ottomans on the Mediterranean. Under normal conditions the western half of this sea was too far away to allow the operation of a regular Ottoman fleet, but in the early sixteenth century some Ottoman freebooters had set up on the North African coast and turned Algiers and Tunis into semiautonomous provinces of the empire. This, as we have seen, was the origin of the Barbary states, nests of corsairs that preyed on Christian shipping. Here no imperial fiat was needed. Like the Venetians and the Portuguese, the corsairs combined naval warfare with the proceeds of trade, though not by engaging in it themselves—they took their cut from it through piracy. What is telling is that the corsairs proved to be by far the most effective component of the Ottoman navy.

Bureaucrats, scholars, law, and identity

In most respects the structure of the Ottoman polity as we have seen it so far looks strangely alien against the background of steppe nomad state formation. But when we turn to the bureaucracy we find ourselves on more familiar ground. Along with the Persian language, the Persian bureaucratic tradition was one of Iran's most successful exports, and it was this tradition that the Ottomans inherited from the earlier Muslim states of Anatolia. As we saw, scholars from Iran and Qaramān were among those blamed for introducing the fourteenth-century Ottomans to such nasty habits as keeping account books. Likewise the Ottoman fiscal surveys are full of Persian. In the survey of the village of Sarïmsaqlu in the province of Kayseri that was carried out in 1584–85, Persian was used, for example, to indicate that one peasant was resident "in the city" (*der shehr*); then a further peasant was mentioned, followed by another who was identified, again in Persian, as "his brother" (*birāder-i ō*). At the same time wheat, the village's major crop, was referred to by a Persian word (*gendüm*)—though for barley the scribe used the Arabic word (*sha'īr*), and when it came to beehives he lapsed into Turkish (*kovan*). Byzantine influence on Ottoman bureaucracy is much less in evidence, though it is there. It lies concealed behind the Ottoman term for a fief, *tīmār*. The word itself is Persian, but it is not being used here in its Persian sense, which is something like "care" or "consideration," not "fief." As it happens, late Byzantine Greek called a fief a *pronoia*, which has the literal meaning of "forethought," so the Ottoman term *tīmār* looks like a loan-translation from Greek. This is a fairly convincing case of Byzantine administrative influence on the Ottomans, but we have to set it against their general indebtedness to Iran for their administrative vocabulary and practice. There is also a lingering structural kinship between Ottoman and Persian bureaucracy in terms of recruitment. Though the dichotomy between Turks and Tājīks does not apply in the Ottoman context, bureaucrats were recruited predominantly from the freeborn Turkish-speaking Muslim families that made up Ottoman civil society, rather than from among the slaves of the sultan. This does not, of course, mean that the bureaucracy was equally open to all such families. Much as with Timariots, a man had a prima facie claim to a bureaucratic position if his father had occupied one. The occupant of one bureaucratic post in the mid-sixteenth century was fired when a better-connected rival denounced him in these terms: "This person's father was not someone entitled to a post; he's the son of a sweet-maker."[24] He was also, as it happened, a lousy speller, yet this orthographic deficit apparently played no part in his dismissal. But to return to the structural comparison of Ottoman and Persian bureaucracy, there was one significant divergence. Where viziers in Iran tended to be civilian bureaucrats, the pattern in the Ottoman case, particularly in this period, was for the grand vizier to be a military man.

The Ottoman bureaucracy at this time was probably more efficient than that of France under the *ancien régime* when it came to getting things done. But as the case of the sweet-maker's son may suggest, we should resist any temptation to think of it as unbendingly Weberian. A low-level Ottoman bureaucrat describing the mishaps of his career in the 1530s states that he was apprenticed to a high treasury official and found himself doing all the work. At a certain point in the saga he asked his boss for a fiscal assignment, in which he could presumably have made himself a tidy profit; when his boss asked for "a little something" to pave the way, the apprentice took out a loan using some of his mother's and sisters' possessions as collateral. At this point he suffered his first stroke of bad luck: his boss died on him. His new boss did not give him the coveted assignment but did give him another that involved collecting some taxes in the east. The apprentice duly did that, taking care to amass a little gift for his boss. But again he was out of luck: while returning with the taxes he was robbed. When he saw his boss again, he humbly kissed his hand, but the response was terse: "What's this? You haven't brought us a present?"[25] This was by no means the end of the story—better luck lay ahead—but it is enough to give us a taste of what life could be like in the Ottoman bureaucracy. To draw another European parallel, what we see here probably has much in common with the English bureaucracy as it was before the reforms of the second half of the seventeenth century. But the very fact that we can tell such stories as this and the one about the sweet-maker's son points to a contrast of a different

24. Quoted in C. H. Fleischer, "Between the lines," in C. Heywood and C. Imber (eds.), *Studies in Ottoman history in honour of Professor V. L. Ménage*, Istanbul 1994, 57.

25. Quoted in Fleischer, "Between the lines," 49, 51.

kind: the Ottoman Empire is the only premodern Muslim state for which archival sources survive in abundance.

Ottoman religious scholars stemmed from the same general background as Ottoman bureaucrats did. They, too, came predominantly from freeborn Turkish-speaking Muslim families, and this was not the only feature the two groups had in common. For both of them an education at a college (*medrese*, the Arabic *madrasa*) was a good start to a career—though combining it with belonging to an established family of bureaucrats or scholars was even better. But the most arresting common feature was that in the Ottoman case many of the religious scholars resembled the bureaucrats in being part of the state apparatus. This was not the case, or not to the same extent, in any of the other states we have looked at so far, except in respect of judges, who had always owed their positions to a combination of religious learning and state appointment. By contrast, the Ottoman religious institution was anchored in a system of education created and funded by the state. Thus the most prestigious Ottoman colleges were foundations associated with two major sultanic mosques in Istanbul, those of Meḥmed II and Süleymān I. Their professors were appointed by the state, which also decided the curriculum. In the same way the state now made official appointments of Müftīs—the jurists people consulted to get expert opinions on points of law. Above them was a supreme Müftī, the Sheykh ül-Islām, who dispensed such opinions for the sultan himself, and for anyone else who cared to ask for them. The holder of this office came to be the leader of the entire Ottoman religious institution. This system was unprecedented in the Muslim world, at least among Sunnīs, and as an innovation it almost ranked with the creation of the Janissaries. Almost, because unlike the Janissaries there was an obvious local precedent for the Ottoman religious institution: the Byzantine church, headed by a patriarch appointed by the emperor. An Ottoman sultan such as Meḥmed II would have been familiar with the Byzantine ecclesiastical system; after all, he appointed a new patriarch to run it in 1454 after conquering Constantinople. He could well have envied the power that a strong Orthodox Christian ruler could exercise over his church and sought to reproduce it on the Muslim side of the fence. But whatever its inspiration may have been, the Ottoman system was in Islamic terms a novelty, and its legitimacy depended less on God's law than on the law of the sultan. That brings us to our next topic: Qānūn.

It would be hard to imagine the Ottomans operating their novel system of government with no explicit rules and regulations other than those of the Sharīʿa. In this respect they adhered to the precedent of the Mongol and post-Mongol states to the east of them, with their combination of Sharīʿa and Yāsā. Like them the Ottomans were bilegal, though for the most part they spoke of Qānūn rather than Yāsā. Sharīʿa and Qānūn were regularly mentioned in tandem, so much so that a delinquent Balkan Timariot in 1572 made the shocking declaration "I recognize neither Sharīʿa nor Qānūn!"[26] In 1630 Qochu Beg, an adviser to Murād IV (ruled 1623–40), wrote him a short work on the evils besetting the empire and the ways in which they could be remedied. In it he told the sultan that "the cause of the good order of state and religion" was holding fast to two things. One was "the firm bond of the Muḥammadan Sharīʿa," and the other was "the Qānūns of the sultans of the past."[27] Likewise a somewhat later man of letters, Ḥüseyn Hezārfenn (d. 1691), explained that the Qānūns of the Ottoman sultans were superior to those of Chingiz Khān, among other things because they were joined to the Sharīʿa of the Prophet of Islam. Indeed, there was an institutional reality to this claim. Thanks to the Ottoman archives, we know a lot about the administration of state-made law in the Ottoman case, and one thing that is clear is that the judges, who as we have seen were by education scholars of religion, played a major role in implementing the Qānūn. In fact, Müftīs might be consulted about matters to which it applied.

In general, whatever tension there might be between the two laws was kept below the surface. A number of things helped here. One was purely verbal: unlike the aggressively pagan Mongol term "Yāsā," "Qānūn" sounded innocuous. Despite its foreign origin (it comes from the same Greek word as the English "canon"), it had long ago been domesticated as an Arabic and even Islamic term. This was, of course, little more than cosmetic, and the term Yāsā still made occasional appearances, as when a late fifteenth-century Ottoman chronicler spoke approvingly of "royal Yāsā" (*yasāgh-i pādishāhī*)[28] and invoked the memory of Chingiz Khān. But cosmetics are not a major industry for nothing. Süleymān I, who, as noted earlier, bore the nickname "Qānūnī," is celebrated in an inscription of 1557 as, among other things, "promulgator of the sultanic Qānūns."[29] To have referred to him as "promulgator of the sultanic Yāsās" would not have been felicitous in the mid-sixteenth-century Ottoman context, though talk of Chingiz Khān and his Yāsā was still respectable among the Crimean Tatar aristocracy. Another thing that helped was a certain complementarity between the two laws, at least in the sense that the areas in which the Qānūn had most to say—matters of land tenure, taxation, and criminal law—were those in which the Sharīʿa, though not silent, tended to be unworkable. At the same time efforts could be made to bring the two laws closer to each other. This could be done by bringing the provisions of the Qānūn into line with those of the Sharīʿa or, failing that, creating at least the illusion of compatibility. In the mid-sixteenth century the Sheykh ül-Islām of the day invested

26. Quoted in M. A. Cook, *Population pressure in rural Anatolia*, London 1972, 36 note 7.

27. Qochï Beg, *Risale*, Istanbul 1303 *hijrī*, 8–9.

28. Quoted in U. Heyd, *Studies in old Ottoman criminal law*, Oxford 1973, 169–70.

29. Quoted in H. İnalcık, "Suleiman the Lawgiver and Ottoman law," *Archivum Ottomanicum*, 1 (1969), 106.

considerable effort in finding ingenious ways to square Ottoman land and tax law with the Sharīʿa without the inconvenience of having to make substantive changes to the Qānūn.

But not everyone was convinced by such attempts to bring principle into line with practice, and sometimes the disparities were just too flagrant to be massaged, as in the case of a punishment prescribed for stabbing under which the offender would be paraded in public with knives stuck into him. The very idea of law made by rulers remained vulnerable to pious objection, as in Egypt in 1521, soon after the Ottoman conquest, when a local scholar imprudently denounced an Ottoman regulation as "the Yāsā of unbelief" (*yasaq al-kufr*).[30] His strident provincial voice was easily silenced—he was thrown into jail. But by the later seventeenth century the metropolitan Ottoman elite was developing a bad conscience about the Qānūn. In 1696 the sultan decreed that in future the Sharīʿa should be the sole basis of imperial orders and that the word "Qānūn" should no longer appear alongside it—a once-standard juxtaposition that he described as perilous and sinful. An Ottoman Sheykh ül-Islām of the early eighteenth century was consulted on the case of a man who insisted on litigating a dispute under the provisions of the Qānūn, not recognizing the Sharīʿa; he responded that the man had to renew his faith and his marriage—in other words, that his stance amounted to apostasy.

Before we end this structural survey and return to the narrative thread, there is one final question to attend to: Ottoman identity. Like many scholars today, I have been using the convenient term "Ottomans" to refer to something between a dynasty and a people, and indeed the Ottomans sometimes spoke in this way themselves. The reason for the convenience of the term is that it avoids a certain awkwardness in calling the Ottomans "Turks." This avoidance is appropriate inasmuch as the Ottomans of the middle period did not usually apply this ethnic label to themselves. This is somewhat surprising. The Oghuz identity of the Ottomans had been in fashion in the early fifteenth century, the elite still called their language Turkish, and their ancestors were in many cases Turks. Moreover, the Ottomans were known as Turks in Morocco and in much of Europe. The Europeans went on from this to argue about whether the Turks were in origin Trojans or Scythians. This made a difference. If the Turks were Trojans, they were relatives of the Italians and Franks and had a valid ethnic claim to the land they now occupied; but if they were Scythians, they were unrelated to them and had no business occupying a territory they had wrongfully seized. Meḥmed II was well aware of this notion of the Trojan descent of the Turks and not above flirting with it in his dealings with western Europeans. But such ideas had no currency among the Ottoman elite at large. For them, in a peculiar shift of ethnic identity, the word "Turk" became a derogatory term for boorish and unruly elements that needed to be kept

30. A.-K. Rafeq, "The Syrian *ʿulamā*, Ottoman law and Islamic *sharīʿa*," *Turcica*, 26 (1994), 12.

out of the state apparatus. Evliyā Chelebī catches this stereotype in a couple of remarks on the inhabitants of the city of Maghnisa. In one place he says that *because* this is Turkish country (Türkistān), their pronunciation of the Qur'ān is defective. In another he observes that *despite* this being a region of Turks, the people are refined and articulate, producing excellent poets. The Turkish-speaking nomads of Anatolia were clearly Turks, and so also were the peasants—and as Evliyā makes clear, not just the peasants. The Ottomans, by contrast, called themselves "Rūmīs," etymologically "Romans." This curious development starts from the fact that what we call the Byzantine Empire was originally the eastern half of the Roman Empire, leading its Greek speakers to identify as Romans, or as the Arabs had it, Rūm. The invading Turcomans then applied the term Rūm as a geographical label to the Anatolian territory they conquered from the Byzantines. In this roundabout way many Turkish-speaking Muslims of Anatolia came to call themselves Rūmīs, people of the land of Rūm. They were not alone in doing so. The term was widely adopted in the rest of the Middle East and in India, and it was taken up by the Portuguese when they spread over the Indian Ocean. Most people, including the Turkish speakers of Anatolia themselves, have long since abandoned this usage, but to this day the term is used in Kurdish to refer to the people whom everyone else calls Turks.

But not all Ottomans rejected the idea that they were Turks. If we stray into the later Ottoman period, the author of a work written in 1679–80 has a remarkable passage expounding the view that when God threatens the believers that He will "substitute for you a different people" (Q9:39) should they prove remiss in performing their duty of jihad, what He has in mind is replacing the Arabs with the Turks. This author unquestionably sees the Ottomans as Turks, since he bills the capture of Constantinople in 1453 as their achievement. Thanks to their success in jihad, he tells us, the Turks have spread their language and religion and ethnically assimilated those they conquered, so that people who had been Greeks, Franks, and Russians have now become Turks. In the course of this discussion he shows his knowledge of Turkic antiquities, referring to Oghuz Khān and the twenty-four Oghuz clans that lived in Türkistān. The passage is all the more remarkable in that this author, Vānī Meḥmed Efendi (d. 1685), belonged to the distinctly fundamentalist Qāḍīzādeist movement, to which we will return.

The late Ottoman period

Heading into a time of troubles

The Ottoman Empire had had its share of troubles before 1566. No time had been more troublesome for the Ottomans than the early fifteenth century, with Tīmūr's invasion of Anatolia and the ensuing decade of civil war. Thereafter there had been major insurrections outside the state apparatus, such as that of Shāh Qulu in 1511, and costly succession disputes within it, most recently the rebellion of Süleymān's son Bāyezīd in 1558–59. But in the decades after the death of Süleymān troubles were to come thicker and faster. They did not start immediately. Süleymān's only surviving son and successor, Selīm II (ruled 1566–74), preferred drinking and hunting to ruling an empire, but he retained the services of Soqollu Meḥmed Pasha, his father's last and highly competent grand vizier, who held office from 1565 until his assassination in 1579. In fact, the reigns of Selīm II and his successor, Murād III (ruled 1574–95), were still noteworthy for the sheer geographical range of Ottoman intervention in the affairs of the world. In the east in 1567–68 the Ottomans sent two ships to Sumatra in response to a plea from the sultan of Aceh for help against the Portuguese. In the south in 1585 and 1589 an Ottoman corsair based in the Red Sea raided the East African coast, reaching ports south of the equator and stirring up the local Muslim enemies of the Portuguese. In the west in 1570 and again in 1574 the Ottoman central government was communicating with the rebellious Moriscos of Spain. In the north in 1569–70 the Ottomans attempted a bold strategic project, digging a canal to link the Don to the Volga; there had likewise been a plan for a Suez canal in 1568. Nothing much came of any of these initiatives, but they show a remarkable reach. So what was the problem?

There were in fact several looming problems, quite apart from the intrinsic fragility of so heavily centralized an imperial system. The first was a change in the pattern of succession that unfolded around the turn of the seventeenth century. Meḥmed III (ruled 1595–1603) was in two ways the key figure in this shift. First, he was the last sultan to have been sent out as a prince to govern a province and so the last to come to the throne with hands-on experience of the art of government and of the world outside the palace. No doubt the old fear of what a son with a provincial base might get up to was behind this change. Second, Meḥmed III was also the last sultan to kill his brothers on his accession—nineteen of them, it will be recalled. Here revulsion at the slaughter of 1595 may have been one factor at work when Aḥmed I came to the throne in 1603; as we saw, the killing of the nineteen brothers had called forth "the crying and weeping of the people of Istanbul," just as in 1669 they would protest vigorously when it was believed that another such fratricide was planned. A further factor was a very real fear of the extinction of the dynasty. In 1603 Aḥmed was a just a boy who might die without ever having a son, so there was a strong reason to keep his brother Muṣṭafā alive. In the event Aḥmed grew up to have three sons who, along with his brother, occupied the throne from 1617 to 1648. This was a very different pattern from the father-to-son succession that had hitherto been characteristic of the dynasty. From now on there would be an array of politically inexperienced princes stored in the palace—in the "cage," as later usage had it—and the succession would be determined by the political forces swirling around them, be it the factional conflicts of high officers of state, the demands of rebellious Janissaries, or the intrigues of the leading women in the palace. The power of these women is no surprise. The sultan's harem was a large and far from chaotic institution. By the late sixteenth century there were some 1,200 women in it, and despite the presence of several hundred eunuchs there was a formal hierarchy of female officials. In the course of their conflicts all the various political actors would install and depose sultans of their choice and on occasion even kill them, as in 1622 and 1648. The quality of rulers now depended significantly on luck: it so happened that Aḥmed's brother Muṣṭafā was a half-wit, whereas Aḥmed's son Murād IV turned out to be a chip off the old block. But the quality of the average Ottoman sultan was now well below what it had been in earlier times, when a Darwinian succession struggle had favored the survival of the fittest brother.

While this change was taking place at the center of the empire, something just as consequential was happening on its borders. Down to the later sixteenth century, the success of the Ottoman state was measured by the expansion of its territory. Even now this expansion was not entirely over. The Ottomans conquered Cyprus from the Venetians in 1570–72, just as they would eventually take Crete from them in a war that lasted from 1645 to 1669. But these Mediterranean islands were at least reasonably close to the Ottoman mainland. By contrast, the very success of the Ottoman expansion on land meant that the frontiers of the empire in eastern Europe and Iran had come to be inconveniently far away. Campaigns were now distant—a fact that the Ottomans noticed as early as 1536. They thus saw diminishing returns on their military effort. This was an age when the climate still dictated that in normal circumstances campaigning in the Balkans and the northern Middle East was a summer sport. An Ottoman army could not leave on campaign until the spring, and it had to be in its winter quarters by autumn. Since armies normally set out from Istanbul and moved at a pedestrian pace to accommodate the infantry, it could take them a couple of months to reach either frontier, and by the time they got there much of the campaigning season had already passed. Thus on the western front the Ottomans failed to take Vienna not once but twice, in 1529 and again in 1683. On the first occasion they did not reach Vienna until September 27. On the second they did better but were still slow, arriving on July 14, only to be routed by a relieving army. On the eastern front, as we have seen, they took Tabrīz more than once but never got a lasting grip on it. This was not just a problem at the level of grand strategy. Distant campaigns that failed to realize the rewards of fresh conquests were likely to impose a severe strain on fiscal resources and to give rise to discontent among the troops, as in the case of the war of 1593–1606 with Austria, which ended with neither side making substantial territorial gains; after that the Ottomans initiated no more wars on this front till the 1660s. Even temporarily successful wars on distant frontiers, such as that of 1578–90, which gained the Ottomans substantial territory in western Iran—including Tabrīz in 1585—were likely to prove unduly costly and give rise to disaffection among troops kept far from home. In any case these Iranian conquests were reversed in a new war of 1603–12. This problem of distance was intensified by the rise of infantry warfare. Writing to Süleymān I in 1547 about an upcoming campaign against the Ṣafawids, the Crimean Khān made the point frankly, if perhaps a little tactlessly: "Your military is a slow army (*aghïr cheri*), whereas the Qizilbāsh are fast cavalry, like the Tatars; they cover five of your stages in one."[31] The Qizilbāsh here are the Turcoman cavalry of the Ṣafawids. When it came to world conquest, the Ottomans were in no position to repeat what the Mongols had done.

At this point it may be worth pausing to get a sense of the logistical dimensions of Ottoman warfare. When we outline military history we tend to reduce it to battles—understandably, since battles combine the high drama of courage and carnage with outcomes that can be historically decisive. But if instead we slow down enough to watch the gradual unfolding of a campaign, it becomes obvious that battles are just the tip of the iceberg. In the everyday life of a military commander and his men, battles are few and far between. Instead, the daily round is the tedious business of assembling troops and moving them to where they are needed, all the while keeping them fed, equipped, and paid. This observation applies, more or less, to all the armies we are concerned with in this book—less to armies of nomadic cavalry like those of the Mongols, more to armies centered on plodding infantry like those of the Ottomans. What particularly distinguishes the Ottoman case is the relative richness of our sources, which allows us a much clearer picture of the logistics of campaigning. This potential has been realized in a study of the war of 1593–1606, in which the campaigns took place in the Hungarian borderlands.[32] We can take this war as an example.

With regard to assembling their troops for these campaigns, the Ottomans had a head start in that they possessed a large standing army located in their capital city; but during the winter preceding a campaign they had to decide which of the provincial Timariots they wanted to enlist and issue summonses instructing them when and where to report for duty. The journey to the frontier then took place in two parts. The first stage was from Istanbul to Belgrade and required around six weeks. Here provisions were accumulated at predetermined points along the road and sold to the troops at regulated prices. That meant transporting large amounts of grain and procuring a supply of sheep—unlike grain, sheep could at least be prevailed on to trot to their appointed destinations. Preparing the food then required the labor of an array of bakers, butchers, cooks, and the like. Along with food, a plentiful supply of water had to be ensured, which was easy enough near a river but could otherwise be a problem. Meanwhile, it was not just humans that needed to eat and drink: vast numbers of horses and other animals were es-

31. *Tāriẖ-i Ṣāḥib Giray H̱ān*, ed. Ö. Gökbilgin, Ankara 1973, 114.
32. C. Finkel, *The administration of warfare*, Vienna 1988.

sential to an army, not just for the cavalry to mount but also to pull wagons and artillery along unsurfaced roads. On the Austrian side of the fence it took sixteen horses to pull a mortar and twenty-six for a really large gun; things were probably no better for the Ottomans. This meant a massive amount of provender, and especially grass—an item as essential for an Ottoman army as fuel is for an army today. Moreover, all along the way a skilled labor force had to be sent ahead to clear the road of encumbrances, repair bridges or construct temporary ones, and make sure the route was marked for the troops with piles of earth. On the road beyond Belgrade the army relied on provisions collected there in advance, on local purchases as it went along, and on supplies accumulated in the castles of the region, including those of the frontier. Fortunately Hungary was particularly rich in grain, not to mention grass. The entire journey to the frontier lasted two months, or even three.

In all this the Ottomans had one great advantage over their eastern European enemies. Provided they did not goad their subjects into rebellion, they could commandeer what they needed without having to negotiate with uncooperative aristocrats or representative assemblies. But in another way they were significantly worse off. As a seventeenth-century European general remarked, the three things needed for war were money, money, and more money. There was never enough of it, and often it had to be borrowed. Creditworthy European rulers could get it in large quantities from bankers, but the Ottoman government had no such credit market to draw on and depended on more limited personal loans from members of the state apparatus. "Short of torture, there is no way to get a loan from anyone," as one Ottoman commander lamented to the sultan.[33] The single most crucial use of money was, of course, keeping the troops paid—and that meant paid in hard cash. Unpaid soldiers would raid the neighboring peasantry, eroding the long-term fiscal resources of the state; the Crimean Tatars, who came on campaign for the booty without being paid, were quite likely to do this anyway. Worse yet, the soldiers might refuse to fight. In fact, it was prudent not just to pay the troops but to keep them happy with sweeteners at various points in the campaign—again in cash. All this cash had to be transported from Istanbul by a force large enough to fend off bandits and trustworthy enough not to embezzle it. And the longer the distance to the frontier, the more pressing all these problems became, and the more likely it was that despite the best-laid plans something would go wrong.

In principle, of course, the problem of frontiers that were no longer within convenient walking distance could easily have been solved. Instead of setting out from Istanbul, as they so often did, the Ottomans could have stationed a large part of their forces in forward bases located, let us say, in Belgrade and Erzurum. With

33. Quoted in Finkel, *The administration of warfare*, 264.

the army regularly setting out from such a base at the beginning of the season, there would have been a much greater chance of achieving dramatic conquests in eastern Europe or Iran. Ottoman armies did sometimes winter in such places, but they were not stationed there permanently, and it is easy to see why. In the short run a grand vizier wintering with his army in Belgrade was well placed for an early departure to the frontier, albeit vulnerable to political intrigue behind his back in the capital. But in the long run political power would inevitably have shifted with military power; the forward bases would have begun to overshadow the capital, and the unity of the empire would sooner or later have been compromised. In this connection it is worth bearing in mind what happened in the early nineteenth century, not in Belgrade or Erzurum but in Cairo. At a time when the Ottoman central government was particularly weak, Meḥmed ʿAlī Pasha (ruled 1805–48) established his power in Egypt, used the wealth of the country to build up a modern infantry army, conquered himself an empire, and even threatened to take over the Ottoman heartland. He also built himself a navy and was the only ruler of Egypt ever to take possession of Crete. His descendants ruled Egypt until 1952, almost three decades after the last members of the Ottoman dynasty had gone into exile. That is the kind of thing that can happen when the strongest army in your empire is located in a faraway province.

Distance is not the only thing that can be problematic about military frontiers; just as important is the question who is on the other side of them. On the eastern front, as we have seen, dangerous neighbors were a matter of historical accident. Here the Ottomans could occasionally find themselves in trouble in the face of an idiosyncratically energetic ruler such as Shāh ʿAbbās. On the western frontier, however, the threat was more ominous because it came to be structural rather than personal. A key aspect of this was the rapid evolution of warfare in Europe. Ambassador Busbecq in the mid-sixteenth century had commented, favorably and unfavorably, on numerous aspects of Ottoman life. One of them was the Ottoman attitude to foreign technology. Here he wrote that "no nation in the world has shown greater readiness than the Turks to avail themselves of the useful inventions of foreigners, as is proved by their employment of cannons and mortars, and many other things invented by Christians."[34] He noted only two exceptions: printing and public clocks. But a Bosnian scholar, writing in the 1590s with reference to the Croatian borderlands, sounded a different note: "Our experience in our land over the last fifty years has been that our infidel enemies beyond the frontiers have the better of us every time they invent some kind of weapon and use it; then, when we adopt the like of it, we get the better of them, with the help of God, may He be exalted, thanks to the strength of Islam. But at the present time, our enemies

34. Thornton Forster and Blackburne Daniell, *The life and letters of Ogier Ghiselin de Busbecq*, 1:255.

are going to great lengths in using various new weapons, such as handguns and the like. Our army has been negligent in adopting and using things of this kind."[35] As he indicates, it was not hard for the Ottomans to keep up with such developments when they put their minds to it, though that would eventually change. There was a similar pattern at sea. One reason the Ottomans lost the battle of Lepanto in 1571 was that the Venetians now possessed a modified form of the galley known as the galleass. At the time of the battle the Ottomans had no galleasses, but from 1572 their use was a regular feature of the Ottoman navy. Yet just as our Bosnian commentator laments the recent failure of the Ottomans to keep up with European technological advances on land, so too they lagged well behind the Venetians in adopting the next development in naval warfare, the high-sided, sail-powered galleon—though here the North African corsairs were much quicker off the mark than the regular Ottoman navy. There is also an implicit assumption of our Bosnian that is worth bringing out into the open. He takes it for granted that it is for the infidels to invent and for the Muslims to imitate; he does not entertain the idea that the Muslims themselves might engage in technological innovation. Not that everyone thought this way. An Ottoman reformist of the late eighteenth century anticipated that "trained and able Muslims will not only learn all the European crafts but make a great many fine inventions."[36] Indeed, according to an early nineteenth-century Egyptian chronicler, technology transfer to Europe had already happened as a result of some European students studying geometry with an Egyptian scholar in the 1740s. But the gap was real, and it did not favor the Ottomans.

As the importance of firearms increased on the western front, so too did that of infantry. European armies now employed large numbers of foot soldiers equipped with handguns. An Ottoman commander against the Austrians noticed this at the beginning of the seventeenth century: "Most of the troops of these accursed ones are on foot and arquebusiers. Most of the troops of Islam are horsemen, and not only are their infantrymen few, but experts in the use of the arquebus are rare. For this reason, there is great trouble in battles and sieges."[37] The Ottomans obviously had to match this development, and the result was a continuing expansion in the number of Janissaries: eight thousand in 1527, thirteen thousand in 1567, thirty-nine thousand in 1609. In principle the need could have been met by intensifying the enslavement of Christians within the empire, but in practice the Devshirme largely fell into disuse in the seventeenth century, and increasing numbers of freeborn Muslims, including sons of Janissaries, were

35. Āqḥiṣārī, *Uṣūl al-ḥikam*, Amman 1986, 32 (Arabic version); M. İpşirli, "Hasan Kâfî el-Akhisarî ve devlet düzenine ait eseri," *Tarih Enstitüsü Dergisi*, 10–11 (1979–80), 268 (Turkish version).

36. Quoted in E. L. Menchinger, *The first of the modern Ottomans*, Cambridge 2017, 182.

37. Quoted in Imber, *The Ottoman Empire, 1300–1650*, 284.

allowed to enlist in the Janissary corps. This in turn meant that more revenue had to be collected to pay them, and an obvious way to do this was to downsize the Timariot cavalry, who were no longer needed in such numbers. Their lands could then be turned over to tax farmers, and the state could use the proceeds to pay its additional infantry. In military terms all this made sense, but it did not turn out so well. At the center, the Janissaries, as we have seen, had never been particularly well behaved. There were now more of them, and they tended to be more discontented because of the difficulties encountered by the state in raising enough revenue to pay them. It did not help that with the passage of time the Janissaries started to marry and have sons who themselves enlisted as Janissaries, and they were joined by complete outsiders. At the same time, they became more and more embedded in local economic life, not least in Istanbul. By the second half of the eighteenth century more than half of the Janissaries were so involved in making a living, whether honest or not, that they rendered no military service to the state. This reversal of the original character of the Janissaries enhanced their political power and made them more representative of the civilian population—in that respect they now joined the religious scholars—but it did so at the expense of their effectiveness as a fighting force. Meanwhile in the provinces, the loss of the Timariots had an adverse effect on the maintenance of public order. It had been part of their traditional role to keep order in their villages; it was a commonplace that public order deteriorated when the country was "empty," in other words when the Timariots were away on campaign. There were now fewer Timariots left to discharge this duty at any time of year.

The increasing efficacy of men on foot armed with handguns when pitted against cavalry had a further effect on the balance between order and disorder in Ottoman society. From the later sixteenth century onward handguns were being imported or manufactured in large numbers, and they were passing into the hands of a wide population outside the state apparatus. They were not cheap, but one could acquire two or three muskets for the price of a horse. As an imperial order of 1607 lamented, muskets and gunpowder had come to be "made and sold by anybody anywhere," and the result was that "the musket being available to people of evil intention, its spread became the main source of the disorders and banditry in the empire."[38] By definition, the age of the cavalry had been a time when men on horseback had the edge in conflict with men on foot, irrespective of whether they fought as soldiers, rebels, bandits, or marauding nomads. This edge did not eliminate those who fought on foot, but it did limit the scale of their activities. The

38. Quoted in H. Inalcik, "The socio-political effects of the diffusion of fire-arms in the Middle East," in V. J. Parry and M. E. Yapp (eds.), *War, technology and society in the Middle East*, London 1975, 197.

proliferation of handguns now removed that limit. We have already seen what this meant for Ottoman armies, especially those operating on the European front; our concern here is with its implications for rebels and bandits within the empire. The time-honored practice of equestrian insurrection and marauding—the *qazaqlïq* of the steppes—was now joined by a much-expanded pedestrian version of these activities, as they were taken up by a larger section of society and on a larger scale than ever before in Ottoman history. Old-fashioned Timariots on horseback were of little use against wandering bands of musketeers.

The most conspicuous component of the new phenomenon was a pattern of insurrection known as the Jelālī risings. The trouble began in 1596, initially among disaffected troops involved in the war on the western front, but it rapidly went beyond that to become a widespread and long-lasting conflagration in Anatolia; just how long it lasted depends on how broadly or narrowly one wishes to define the term "Jelālī." The result was massive disruption of the agrarian economy, as large numbers of peasants were killed or abandoned their fields, either fleeing to the cities in search of security or joining the marauders. But there were other variations on the theme, which was not confined to Anatolia. Many of the men with guns were would-be soldiers. Though on occasion employed by the state, they were far too numerous for the state to absorb them all into its armed forces on a regular basis. They wanted a world in which "no one would be cut off from his pay" and "no standard would be furled, no company abolished at the end of a campaign."[39] In its absence they marauded to make up for the fact that they spent most of their lives without being paid. Others were unemployed college students, others again were old-fashioned brigands. With a notable exception in Syria, none of these groups showed any interest in state formation, though one Jelālī leader claimed to be descended from the kings of the past. They showed equally little interest in being rebels with a cause. The tone is set by some of the nicknames by which prominent Jelālī rebels were known: "Infidel Murād" (Kāfir Murād), "Won't-fit-in-his-grave" (Qabre-ṣïghmaz), "Doesn't-recognize-God" (Tanrï-bilmez). The whole phenomenon posed an enormous challenge to the state while at the same time seriously depleting the fiscal resources without which the state could not respond effectively; more often than not, the government forces sent against the Jelālīs were defeated by them. All this was also manifestly bad news for Ottoman society. Nothing disrupts economic activity like insecurity, and getting the state off the backs of the people does not help them much if the alternative is having hordes of wandering gunmen on their backs. There is only one serious qualification to be borne in mind in all this. We don't have a good sense of the baseline,

39. Quoted in H. İnalcık, "Military and fiscal transformation in the Ottoman Empire," *Archivum Ottomanicum*, 6 (1980), 293 note 23.

that is to say the level of disruption that prevailed before the middle of the sixteenth century. We do have evidence of quite extensive disorder in 1559–60, and it is similar in character to what we encounter later.

It is nevertheless hard to shake off the view that things got a lot worse in the late sixteenth century and thereafter stayed bad for a long time.[40] For example, a study of the region of Amasya shows the size of the population declining by four-fifths between 1576 and 1643, while two-fifths of rural settlements disappeared, with the exposed villages in the plains doing worst. In this context the empire was perhaps fortunate in having more than its fair share of mountains. Yet it was not till the nineteenth century that rural society made up the lost ground. The various aspects of Ottoman history that we have been looking at in this period—the change in the pattern of succession, the diminishing returns on expansive military campaigns, the widening technological gap between the empire and its European enemies, the new style of infantry warfare, and the spread of firearms among the population—all contribute handsomely to the explanation of the Ottoman time of troubles. But there may be an underlying factor that intruded from outside the realm of human action: the Little Ice Age. Its reality was appropriately dramatized in 1621 when the Bosphorus froze over in the bitter cold of February, but in the eastern Mediterranean at large it brought long-lasting droughts as well as cold weather. This climatic aberration impacted the history of the period on a global scale. In the Ottoman heartlands it struck at a time when the population had been growing for a century or so, a rise that may have caused serious pressure on the available supply of arable land and hence an enhanced vulnerability to human or natural disaster. Under such conditions it is plausible that a climatic downturn could have seriously affected agriculture in the Ottoman Empire, devastating peasant society and bringing about both a substantial decline in the overall size of the population and a rise of nomadic pastoralism. Of course population decline, however catastrophic, must have relieved the pressure on arable land. What is striking here is that in comparison to other parts of the world that suffered much from the Little Ice Age, such as Russia and China, the Ottoman lands seem to have been significantly slower to recover. This relative lack of resilience, in turn, helps explain something we will come to: the low level of the equilibrium that characterized the empire after it emerged from the worst of its troubles in the late seventeenth century.

40. I am here endorsing the view that the Ottoman Empire underwent a significant decline. This view has not been mainstream for some decades, but there is substantial support for it in two recent studies on which I draw in this paragraph: S. White, *The climate of rebellion in the early modern Ottoman Empire*, Cambridge 2011, and O. Özel, *The collapse of rural order in Ottoman Anatolia*, Leiden 2016.

The upshot of the time of troubles

Such, then, were the main factors at work in the Ottoman time of troubles, and taken together they give a fair sense of the texture of the period. We can therefore dispense with a detailed narrative, but some larger aspects of the story are worth taking up. The first is the course taken by the political instability that came to characterize the central government from the early seventeenth century. There was a period of renewed stability in the latter half of the reign of Murād IV, once this tough-minded sultan had come of age, but thereafter the instability resumed until 1656, when it finally ended with the appointment to the grand vizierate of an iron-fisted octogenarian strongman, Meḥmed Köprülü. Members of his family then succeeded him in the office. At first this looked like the emergence of a new locus of stability, a dynasty of grand viziers playing a role similar to that of the Tokugawa shoguns in stabilizing seventeenth-century Japan. However, the continuity of Köprülü rule was ended by the disastrous outcome of the second siege of Vienna in 1683. And yet the period after 1683 did not see a reversion to the chaotic politics so typical of the first half of the century. Moreover, even the political instability of the time of troubles had not led to a fundamental rupture in the structural continuity of the Ottoman state and its institutions.[41] All the basic components survived. The idea that the dynasty could be replaced if necessary by putting a member of the Crimean royal family on the throne is an interesting indication that the Ottoman elite could think of the empire as a continuing institution even without the presence of the Ottoman dynasty. But in the event there was never a need to have recourse to such a measure, let alone to enthrone a woman—though there is said to have been talk of that in the early nineteenth century. One sultan entertained the idea of doing without a grand vizier, and another, whom we will come to in a moment, is believed to have wished to do without the Janissaries. But neither came to pass in our period. Some components, such as the sultanate, tended to lose power, and others, such as the religious scholars, to gain it—the chief Müftī was more likely now than he had been earlier to frustrate the wishes of the ruler. Meanwhile there were rebellions aplenty, but there was no revolution. In fact, the closest approach to a revolution was the alleged plan of the young sultan ʿOthmān II (ruled 1618–22) to rid himself of the Janissaries and recruit a new army in their place. He paid for his radicalism with his life when the Janissaries rebelled against him, and it was not till 1826 that an Ottoman sultan could finally rub out the Janissaries and start again. Until the end of our period the empire survived without radical change.

41. For a significant—and significantly different—view of what did change see B. Tezcan, *The Second Ottoman Empire*, Cambridge 2010.

A second aspect of the period concerns the fortunes of war on the frontiers of the empire. Given the troubles afflicting the state, together with the developments in warfare on the other side of the European frontier, the surprise is that the empire came through the period with relatively little net loss of territory. The Yemen, a distant outpost, was the site of a prolonged sectarian rebellion that evicted the Ottomans in the first half of the seventeenth century, and Ottoman Hungary was a casualty of the failure at Vienna in the second half; with Hungary went further territory in the northern Balkans, notably Transylvania. These losses were significant, and hardly balanced by the acquisition of Crete. But large-scale territorial contraction was still far in the future.

A third aspect of the period that is worth attention is the trajectory of the chaos in the provinces. Determined action by Murād IV and Meḥmed Köprülü had some effect in reining in the disorder, but it did not solve the fundamental problem: we still find the unemployed soldiers with their guns playing a major role in Ottoman politics in 1687–89. The hero or villain of these events was Yegen ʿOthmān Pasha, a commander of military vagrants who effortlessly combined the roles of brigand and high officer of state—something by no means unique in the seventeenth-century Ottoman Empire. The constants of the story are his widespread looting in the Balkans and Anatolia, his implacable hostility to the Janissaries, and threats to march on Istanbul that caused panic in the capital. The central government, by contrast, flip-flopped between co-opting him and suppressing him. In the end he was suppressed, but even after that there was no lack of disorder. Indeed, the worst outbreak of banditry in the Balkans took place late in the eighteenth century. And insofar as there was stabilization, it was the result not of a restoration of central authority but rather, as we will see, of the emergence of new and semiautonomous structures of power in the provinces.

How the Ottomans thought about their troubles

Those who endure troubles such as we have described can be expected to think seriously about them and to ask themselves what caused them, what could be done about them, and whether there was anything helpful to be learned from the experiences of others. Some members of the seventeenth-century Ottoman elite left written records of their thinking in one form or another, and what they had to say is worth attention. As might be expected, there was considerable variety in their views, and all had their particular concerns. One, who wrote in 1632–33, regarded the explosion in the numbers of Ottoman subjects claiming descent from the Prophet as a major issue. He cited the case of a Balkan village whose inhabitants in former times had not included a single descendant of the Prophet, but now all their descendants laid claim to that status. Such idiosyncratic concerns apart, three very different overall perspectives stand out.

We have already met the central idea of the first perspective, which we can call Qānūnism. As Qochu Beg told Murād IV in 1630, the good order of the polity depended on adherence to the Muḥammadan Sharīʿa and the Qānūns of the sultans of the past. In fact, it is clear that he mentioned the Sharīʿa largely in a display of due deference and that his more pressing concern was the Qānūn. His approach is typical golden-age thinking. The general drift is that in the good old days the Qānūn was scrupulously observed in the empire and things went well, whereas today it is regularly ignored and things are going badly. The implied remedy is obvious: a return to faithful observance of the Qānūn. But what would that have involved in concrete terms? Here one of Qochu Beg's central themes is the importance of security of tenure for the incumbents of offices. In the good old days, provincial governors would remain in their positions for twenty or thirty years, whereas these days they are hired and fired at the drop of a turban. This, for Qochu Beg, is a major cause of the prevailing disorder. Indeed, as we will soon see, he goes so far as to express a favorable view of hereditary office. Just what he could have cited from the Qānūns of the sultans of the past by way of chapter and verse to support his view is a tantalizing question. His concern with the secure tenure of offices was shared by a writer of the same period who, though not allergic to the idea of the Qānūn, was not much invested in it. This writer tells the sultan that his message to all judges should be to rest assured that they would not be fired. But it is Qochu Beg's hankering after hereditary office that is most striking here, and it brings us to a curious irony. One thing that had particularly impressed Busbecq in the mid-sixteenth century had been Ottoman meritocracy. Describing a large gathering around the sultan, he commented that none of those present owed their positions to anything other than their valor and merit: "No distinction is attached to birth among the Turks."[42] It was what a man made of himself, not what he was born to, that counted—in complete contrast to European society, where merit counted for nothing and birth was everything. The fact that Busbecq himself was the illegitimate son of a Flemish aristocrat by a lower-class woman may have colored his feelings, but the basic contrast he drew between the two systems was on target. Now we have Qochu Beg reversing Busbecq's valuation—a striking case of the grass growing greener on the other side of the fence.

But did Qochu Beg actually have the European example in mind? Qānūnism puts the focus on one's own past, not the pasts or presents of others. But it does not entirely exclude such sideways glances. Back in the early sixteenth century a Muslim traveler had written a book about China and presented it at the Ottoman court. At one point he praised the Chinese to the skies for their unfailing fidelity to the Qānūn of their past rulers and lamented that in the Muslim world such

42. Thornton Forster and Blackburne Daniell, *The life and letters of Ogier Ghiselin de Busbecq*, 1:154.

fidelity was not to be found—this in what for Qochu Beg was the golden age. Qochu Beg himself shows a similar, again limited, openness to foreign models. In a rather complex maneuver he tells a story about Shāh ʿAbbās, who was of course a damnable heretic in Ottoman eyes. The Shāh is perturbed that the Ottomans are doing so well and Iran so badly and demands that his officers of state and scholars come up with an explanation. They do that, and one of the things they explain to the Shāh is that among the Ottomans there is no short-term hiring and firing: "Officers are not fired unless they are guilty of wrongdoing." The Shāh takes this to heart: "He bestowed offices on his grandees for life, and after that he would give them to their sons."[43] The moral is that the Ottomans of the 1630s should imitate Shāh ʿAbbās imitating the Ottomans of the golden age. In another passage Qochu Beg is geographically vague, appealing to the example of the kings of the world at large, whether they are Muslim or belong to "the various other religious communities." Their Qānūns, he tells us, have no place for "hiring and firing, chopping and changing" in state offices. More than that, in some cases these offices "are passed on from fathers to sons and grandsons, whether adult or minor, in the manner of private property and real estate."[44] The result is that everything goes well for these states. But alas, that is not how things are in the Ottoman Empire, where respect for the Qānūn of the Ottoman rulers is no longer what it used to be. The non-Ottoman model Qochu Beg describes in this passage sounds very like the European *ancien régime* that was to be swept away by the French Revolution. It is understandable that he may have preferred not to make this invocation of a Christian European model explicit—he would have risked being denounced as an infidel-lover.

A very different kind of view is that of a man of letters known as Kātib Chelebī (d. 1657); we can call it conservative realism. Unlike Qochu Beg, he was not close to the sultan. He made a living as a minor official, but what mattered about him was his role as a major intellectual and scholarly figure in the Ottoman capital. At one point he wrote a short tract addressing the problems of the empire. In it he showed that he was familiar with the grand ideas of Ibn Khaldūn, whose conception of the dynastic life cycle he adopted. Dynasties, in this view, are like people: they are born and grow, they mature, and then they age and die. For both people and dynasties the timing can vary, since in each case a robust constitution lengthens the life cycle, whereas a weak one shortens it. Hence the signs of distemper apparent in the aging Ottoman state in the mid-seventeenth century were "in conformity with the nature of civilization and human society."[45] It follows that

43. Qochï Beg, *Risale*, 85, 86.

44. Qochï Beg, *Risale*, 114.

45. Kātib Chelebī, *Destūr ül-ʿamel*, in Ayn-ı Ali Efendi, *Kavânîn-i Âl-i Osman*, reprinted Istanbul 1979, 119.

a return to the golden age of dynastic youth is not an option for an aging dynasty, just as it is pointless for a graybeard to dye his beard black and then try to prevent it going gray again. By implication, he is telling us that the basic premise of Qānūnism is delusional. As Ḥüseyn Hezārfenn, a younger member of his circle, was to put it without mincing words, "The desire to make the custom of these days conform to that of the past is a false and stupid idea born of ignorant obsession."[46] It is not that there is nothing to be done—measures can indeed be taken to alleviate the aging process. But there is no way to reverse it. What we have here is an intellectually sophisticated conservative realism, in contrast to the somewhat naïvely moralistic reformism of Qochu Beg.

Like Qochu Beg, Kātib Chelebī makes reference to Iran. He recalls that when he traveled around the Ottoman lands for twelve years he found most of the villages to be in ruins, whereas in Iran, in the regions of Tabrīz and Hamadhān, he did not see a single ruined village over a distance of fifteen or twenty days' journey. But he does not explain this as Qochu Beg might have done as the result of different policies regarding the hiring and firing of provincial governors. Instead he ascribes it to the disparity in the relative age of the two states—that of the Ṣafawids still being in its phase of maturity. Beyond that he does not refer to foreign models in his tract, even as potential sources of palliative measures to ease the aging process. But elsewhere in his numerous works he displays a sharp awareness that a gap had emerged between the Ottomans and the western Europeans. Those wretched unbelievers had discovered the New World and seized the ports of India; they were busily seeking a northwest passage and were even reputed to have reached the North Pole. Meanwhile the Ottomans, with the partial exception of the Barbary corsairs, had done nothing of the kind. Kātib Chelebī saw in this a direct consequence of a difference between the two societies in their cultivation of the indispensable science of geography. Here the Muslims had shown themselves exasperatingly feckless, whereas the unbelievers were performing superbly. In fact, one of Kātib Chelebī's works was a Turkish rendering of the *Atlas minor* of the sixteenth-century Flemish cartographer Mercator, and this was not the only one of his works that involved translation from Latin. He did not make the translation himself, being fortunate to have as his assistant a French convert to Islam. But he used this translation as one of his basic sources for a cosmography he then started writing. Of course he referred to the infidels in a suitably derogatory fashion and omitted passages concerned with such distasteful matters as wine, pigs, and churches. But it is hard to resist the impression that in using such language he had his tongue somewhere in his cheek, and it fits that when Ḥüseyn Hezārfenn was exchanging views with a French friend—not a convert—in

46. Quoted in R. Anhegger, "Hezarfen Hüseyin Efendi'nin Osmanlı devlet teşkilâtına dair mülâhazaları," *Türkiyat Mecmuası*, 10 (1951–53), 390.

1675 and told him about his unorthodox belief in the transmigration of souls, he mentioned a wish to be reborn as a Frenchman in his next life. Such off-the-record conversations between western Europeans and members of the Ottoman elite were no doubt much more frequent than the sparse references in our sources—in this instance exclusively European—would suggest. In the same way, European printed books may have been more widely available in the Ottoman Empire than we tend to assume. Evliyā Chelebī tells us that when the library of the Khān of Bitlis in the wilds of Kurdistan was auctioned off in 1665, it included two hundred infidel-printed books, one of which was the same *Atlas minor*, and Evliyā himself seems to have had access to a copy of the book. Yet the picture of Europe offered by Kātib Chelebī in his works was not a particularly sharp or up-to-date one. For that discriminating Ottoman readers had to wait till they could read the publications of Ibrāhīm Müteferriqa (d. 1745–46), a Hungarian prisoner of war and convert to Islam who also brought them printing.

However different their views, neither Qochu Beg nor Kātib Chelebī put Islam center stage in their analyses of the problems of the empire. As we saw, Qochu Beg showed a proper piety in referring to "the firm bond of the Muḥammadan Sharīʿa" but went on to focus on the Qānūn. Kātib Chelebī was more direct. In one of his works he declared the pointlessness of golden-age thinking with reference to early Islam; that was then, and this is now. What today we call Islamic fundamentalism was in his view foolishly unrealistic: "Once an innovation has become firmly rooted among a people, to seek to prevent people from doing it . . . is the height of stupidity and ignorance."[47] But not everyone thought in this realist fashion. The first decades of the seventeenth century were the high point of the Qāḍīzādeist movement, named after a certain Qāḍīzāde Meḥmed (d. 1635) who was one of its leading proponents. It was very much a religious movement, directed at stamping out innovations that sullied the face of true Islam, particularly those found among the Ṣūfīs. Its tenor is caught in a skit in which a sophisticated man-about-town engages a member of the movement, highlighting the absurd implications that rejecting all innovations would have: "So you gentlemen want to strip everyone and dress them like bare-buttocked desert Arabs!"[48] More seriously, we know from a letter written by Qāḍīzāde around the age of thirty that one of the books he studied in his youth was a multivolume attack on the innovations of his time by a fourteenth-century Maghribī scholar. It must have been a perfect fit. But the Qāḍīzādeists, though they made political waves, seem to have lacked a political vision, if by that we mean a sustained analysis of the troubles the empire was going through and a prescription for curing them.

47. Kātib Chelebi, *The balance of truth*, trans. G. L. Lewis, London 1957, 89.
48. Naʿīmā, *Tārīkh*, Istanbul 1283 *hijrī*, 6:237.

There was, however, a remarkable moment in which we see the statesmen of the empire applying such a program. The political context was the completion of the conquest of Crete from the Venetians in 1669, while the legal context was the sixteenth-century dispute over the compatibility of Qānūn and Sharīʿa with regard to standard Ottoman practices of land tenure and taxation. Birgevī (d. 1573), the scholar whose views lay behind Qāḍīzādeism, had been one of those left unconvinced by the Sheykh ül-Islām's attempt to paper over the cracks. Now, on conquering Crete, the Ottoman authorities proceeded in a manner that would have ensured them Birgevī's approval, invoking the exalted practice of the Prophet as followed in the days of the Rightly Guided Caliphs. This was not just a rhetorical flourish: throwing tradition to the winds, they abolished a slew of traditional Ottoman taxes, not sparing such time-honored sources of revenue as title-deed tax, beehive tax, scarecrow tax, windfall tax, bride tax, and salt tax. This was bringing practice into line with principle with a vengeance. We do not have a record of the deeper thinking behind these measures, but it is quite likely that the inspiration came from the Qāḍīzādeists, or if not from them, then from some other milieu with a similar commitment to the rigorous application of the Sharīʿa. In any case, the mood did not last. When the Ottomans reconquered the Morea from the Venetians in the early eighteenth century and had to choose what fiscal system to establish there, it was the sultan's law, not God's law, that prevailed.

Of the three approaches, religious fundamentalism was the one least likely to be receptive to non-Muslim models. Even in the other cases, where we do see such receptiveness, it is still limited. Only near the end of our period would the gap between the empire and western Europe become so wide and the consequent pressure on the Ottomans so great that the adoption of European ways would begin to be a central issue. This is not surprising—having to imitate other people tends to be embarrassing. The traveler who praised the Chinese to the skies would have liked to see Muslims imitate Chinese fidelity to their Qānūn, but he made no suggestion that they should think about adopting the actual content of Chinese law. It was not till well after the end of our period that the Ottoman state began to import substantive law from European sources.

Low-level equilibrium: From the later seventeenth to the end of the eighteenth century

The renewal of stability at the center initiated by the Köprülü viziers in the mid-seventeenth century did not last. To make do with a single crude but telling index, between 1683 and 1730 the reigns of three sultans were terminated by deposition, as against two that ended in death from natural causes. But things were still much better than they had been in the first half of the seventeenth century: no sultan was killed in these years by rebellious Janissaries. And after 1730 no sultan was deposed, let alone killed, for the rest of our period (grand viziers were another matter). Selīm III (ruled 1789–1807) was to be deposed in 1807 and killed the next year, but by then times had changed drastically. Another index of stability, though a somewhat overlapping one, is the changing frequency of significant Janissary rebellions. In the seventeenth century there were six of them, whereas the eighteenth saw only two, in 1703 and 1730; thereafter there were none till the early nineteenth century. But the return to stability was not a renewal of the dynamism of the first three Ottoman centuries. Once again there was equilibrium, but at a much lower level. The obvious question is what sustained this equilibrium.

One precondition was undoubtedly a degree of stability on the borders of the empire. Catastrophic territorial losses to foreign invaders are the kind of failure that is likely to destabilize any imperial center; it is no mystery that the Köprülü regime did not survive the failed siege of Vienna and ensuing loss of Ottoman Hungary in the 1680s. It was therefore a key feature of the period that the balance of territorial gains and losses, though in the end unfavorable to the Ottomans, was only modestly so. On the eastern front they were engaged in extensive hostilities with Iran in 1723–46. This was a somewhat pointless repetition of a familiar story. In the first round, the Ottomans once again occupied Tabrīz and seized extensive territory in western Iran; in the second round they found themselves up against a warlike ruler, this time Nādir Shāh, and gave up these gains. On the western front their enemies were as usual the Venetians and the Austrians. In their hostilities with the Venetians, the Ottomans lost the Morea in the late seventeenth century and regained it in the early eighteenth. Against the Austrians, between the late seventeenth century and the end of the eighteenth the Ottomans lost and regained Belgrade three times—a wash, but it marked a worrisome shift in the balance of military power. In the south the rise of the Wahhābī movement in conjunction with the Saudi state posed a threat in the second half of the eighteenth century, but it was not until 1803 that the Saudis occupied the Ḥijāz, and ten years later they were expelled from it. Perhaps more worrisome was the fact that this victory was won not by the feeble forces of the central government but rather by those sent from Egypt by Meḥmed ʿAlī Pasha, the man who was to become a far greater threat to the empire than the Saudis until checked by the European powers. Yet if we stick to the eighteenth century, setting aside the prior loss of Ottoman Hungary, the hemorrhage of territory was limited.

The most threatening development of the century was not in any of these quarters, but rather in the north. Russia had long been a distant presence on the Ottoman military horizon, but it was not an enemy with the standing of Iran or Austria. In the first half of the seventeenth century the Ottomans had to put considerable energy into countering seaborne Cossack raiders who crossed the Black Sea in skiffs, even penetrating far into the Bosphorus. But they did not as yet have to reckon with Russian navies or armies. That changed as Russia began to modernize itself under Peter the Great (ruled 1682–1725), becoming a major military power on the margins of Europe with a territory extending from the Baltic to the Pacific. In 1695 the Ottomans suffered a rude awakening, and by the late eighteenth century it was clear that the Russians were more of a menace to the Ottomans than the Austrians were. This new danger issued in the definitive loss of the Crimean vassal state. Russia invaded it in the course of the hostilities of the early 1770s and formally annexed it in 1783. The Black Sea was no longer the Ottoman lake it had been since the fifteenth century, and one nightmare was now that the Russians, like the Cossack raiders, could penetrate the Bosphorus and threaten Istanbul itself—though in the event it was a British fleet that was to pose such a threat in 1807. Another nightmare was that the bond of a shared Orthodox Christianity that linked the Russians to most of the empire's Balkan Christian subjects would subvert Ottoman rule over them; Peter the Great was already talking of liberating these Christians from "the yoke of the infidels" in 1711.[49] By 1770 the threat was more concrete, for in that year a Russian fleet from the Baltic, having circumnavigated Europe, won a crushing victory against the Ottoman navy in the Aegean, at the same time encouraging the Greeks of the Morea to rebel against Ottoman rule. Yet the threat receded, and it was not till the nineteenth century that the relationship between Russia and the empire's Balkan subjects became a continuing problem for the Ottomans.

The provinces: The Balkans and Anatolia

A further precondition for the viability of the central government was the stabilization of the provinces. This, too, involved low-level equilibrium, since there was no question in this period of restoring the old centralization. In place of the chaotic marauding of the first half of the seventeenth century, intermediate structures of power emerged that were locally sustainable and maintained some degree of order. But at the same time such stability required at least a measure of central control over these structures—enough to ensure that the center could collect some revenue, raise some troops, and prevent local autonomy from taking the form of secession, as it had already done in the Yemen. For much of the later seventeenth and eighteenth centuries these modest but crucial requirements were successfully met. Thus the empire still had resources enough to maintain its armed forces in some fashion, and it lost no further territories to secession, as opposed to invasion from beyond the borders. But at the same time brigandage and other such disorders remained endemic and continued to disrupt economic activity. As a provincial administrator complained to ʿAbdülḥamīd I (ruled 1774–89), "If a

49. Quoted in A. N. Kurat and J. S. Bromley, "The retreat of the Turks," in V. J. Parry and others, *A history of the Ottoman Empire to 1730*, Cambridge 1976, 204.

governor goes to a locality, the inhabitants meet him with firearms."[50] Against this background we would not expect much uniformity in the intermediate structures of the period, and they were indeed as varied as local conditions were. But typically they were of two kinds: provincial dynasties at a higher level and local notables (*aʿyān*) at a lower level. These structures were in evidence in all the major regions of the empire, but on balance the notables were more prominent in the Balkans and the dynasties in Anatolia and the Arab lands. If we survey the regions in that order, we will see the scale of local or regional autonomy rise as we move from one region to the next.

In the Balkans, then, we do not usually find dynasties ruling over provinces. We can therefore concentrate on the local notables who came to occupy a position mediating between the central government and the population at large, thus assuming roles that in a more centralized polity would have been reserved for the state apparatus. For example, they collected taxes and maintained private armies, and in times of war or rebellion they could be asked to recruit and supply troops for the government. Becoming a notable in the Balkans (as also in Anatolia) was a hybrid process. On the one hand, a candidate needed strong local roots, or the local elite would not put him forward for the office; but on the other hand, he then had to be appointed by the relevant agent of the state, usually the grand vizier. The central government was not particularly happy with the institution, but it had to live with it; it was abolished in 1786, only to be reinstated in 1791. Yet the state was not without leverage. Being a notable was financially rewarding, so there was strong competition for appointment among the local elite. As often, the system comes into sharpest focus in our sources when things went wrong, as happened in 1784 in a town in what is now northwestern Bulgaria. Two prominent local figures, a certain Meḥmed and a certain Ḥüseyn, were competing for the office of notable, each with his local following and each claiming to have been duly chosen by the community for the role. Nearby Janissaries were involved on Ḥüseyn's side, whereas the provincial governor was said to favor Meḥmed, and in due course an official had to be sent from the center to take charge. The local judge, whose role it was to certify the assembled community's agreement on the notable to be appointed, told the official that he had certified Ḥüseyn, but a crowd assembled and called for Meḥmed to be appointed. Some of Ḥüseyn's supporters now attacked them, killing one of them and wounding another, while others threatened to emigrate if Meḥmed were appointed—indeed some had already done so. Meanwhile the two sides were lobbying in Istanbul, promoting their conflicting narratives there. The official was instructed that if necessary he should ascertain public opin-

50. Quoted in A. Yaycioglu, *Partners of the Empire*, Stanford 2016, 34, 149. This book is the source of much of what follows.

ion by visiting every settlement in the district. All this makes clear the importance of both local support and central action in the process of choosing a notable.

As mentioned, no significant and long-lasting dynasties emerged among these Balkan notables in the eighteenth century, but it is hard to avoid the sense that given time they could quite easily have done so. Consider the case of ʿAlī Pasha Tepedelenli (d. 1822), the long-term governor of Yanina in what is now northwestern Greece. His father and grandfather had held office in the region, and the central government gave him various positions, including the governorship of Yanina in 1787. Though it did not warm to ʿAlī Pasha's persistent tendency to expand the territories under his control, it obligingly conferred offices on his sons, one of whom he planned to have educated in western Europe. Meanwhile ʿAlī Pasha governed his territory in a conspicuously ruthless fashion, yet he provided his subjects, not least the Greek Christians, with a measure of security unusual in the Balkans at the time. In the same vein he made Greek, not Ottoman Turkish, the language of his court and at one point even announced his conversion to Christianity. By 1820, however, the sultan was in a centralizing mood and determined to end ʿAlī Pasha's career; after a two-year siege of Yanina he was killed in 1822. If instead things had continued in the old unreformed way in this part of the empire, ʿAlī Pasha might perhaps have been the founder of a dynasty comparable to that of Meḥmed ʿAlī Pasha in Egypt.

In Anatolia, intermediate structures involved similar combinations of local and central connections. One example is that established by Janikli ʿAlī Pasha (d. 1785). He was born in Istanbul, where his father was a palace official, but the family was from Janik, a region on the Black Sea coast to the west of Trebizond, and by the 1740s ʿAlī Pasha was active in this region. In the 1760s he held a major fiscal office there, and in 1770 he became governor of Trebizond. From there he extended his power into the interior of eastern Anatolia. His two sons succeeded him, but the power of the family was shaken when the central government executed two of its members in the early 1790s. In the first decade of the nineteenth century the ups and downs of the family were shaped by their hostility to the first Ottoman attempt to create a modern army under Selīm III and by their conflict with a neighboring dynasty, the Chapanids.

The Chapanids dominated the territory to the southwest of the Janiklis, and from their base in Yozgat they held sway over a large part of central Anatolia. They were of Turcoman stock and hailed from a part of Anatolia where nomadism was strong; their close relationship with one particular tribe suggests that they belonged to it. The family is first attested in 1704, but the founder of its political fortunes began to build up his position in the region only in the years after 1728, cultivating good relations with the central government and getting himself appointed to various local offices. Eventually he fell foul of the central government and was executed in 1765, after which the family held no office for three years. They nevertheless succeeded in restoring their fortunes, in part because the outbreak of war with Russia in 1768 meant that the government needed their services, and two of the founder's sons then held power in succession until the second died in 1813. One of the second brother's sons would have been a plausible successor, but the central government was by now determined to bring the line to an end and would only appoint him to offices in provinces far from the family's base. The story of the Chapanids could be said to mark the last fling of nomad power in the history of Anatolia. In the words of a ditty recorded in another part of the peninsula in the early twentieth century, "Pull the camel, push the sheep, and a day will come when you'll be a lord."[51] But the times were no longer propitious for Turcoman state formation. From Anatolia to Central Asia, the popular epic hero of the Turcoman world in the seventeenth to nineteenth centuries was Köroghlu, a fine, upstanding brigand who spends his life harassing and subverting the Ottoman and Ṣafawid states. One of his boasts is to have made Janissaries' heads roll. But he appears as a rebel, not as the founder of a state. The Turcoman background of the Chapanids should not, however, be taken to mean that they were uncivilized. By 1813 they possessed a well-appointed palace in Yozgat complete with clocks, a small organ, and a French physician. They were also strong supporters of the attempt to create a modern army under Selīm III.

A third family, the Qara ʿOthmānids of western Anatolia, was undoubtedly the most successful of the three. Like the Chapanids, the family seems to have been of Turcoman origin, but the founder, Qara ʿOthmān (d. 1706), was a sedentary native of Yayaköy, the family village near Maghnisa in western Anatolia. His father or grandfather, though buried in the same village, had been attached to the palace. Qara ʿOthmān launched the family fortunes by becoming wealthy when carrying out a commission for the central government. The outcome of his success was less a dynastic line than a broad family network that engrossed governorships and other offices over a large part of western Anatolia and continued to do so well into the nineteenth century. The Maghnisa region nevertheless remained the family's base, as is evidenced by the farms they owned there. On the whole the family's relations with the central government were good. However, one of its key members was executed in 1755, after which the family was kept out of office until 1758. Then another was ordered to be executed in 1766; he took refuge in Yayaköy with a force of two thousand men and then fled, dying in the course of his flight. Yet here, too, the war with Russia helped change the attitude of the government toward its overmighty subjects, and the Qara ʿOthmānids, like the Chapanids and unlike the Janiklis, were active supporters of Selīm's new army. In 1812 and 1816, however, the deaths of two powerful members of the family were an opportunity for the

51. Quoted in Kafadar, *Between two worlds*, 118.

central government to rein in the Qara ʿOthmānids, though the local power of the family took decades to fade out altogether. The overall pattern in Anatolia was thus one in which such families could exercise a great deal of power in their territories over long periods, but the central government retained the ability to interrupt and eventually terminate their sway. These, then, were significant structures of intermediate power, and more lasting than what we saw in the Balkans. Yet they were hardly incipient states.

Farther east, in the mountains of Kurdistan, the imposition of centralized government had made only limited progress since the days of the Carduchians. Sent to govern the province of Van in the mid-seventeenth century, an Ottoman grandee complained that "because it is Kurdistan, its pashas' authority does not extend beyond the territory below the cannons of Van castle."[52] He was exaggerating, but he had a point. Kurdistan was different: the Kurds were not Rūmīs, and Kurdistan was not Rūm. For the traveler Evliyā Chelebī, "Kurdistan" conjured up an image of truculence and rebellion. Since Bitlis is a city of Kurdistan, he tells us, its people fight each other day and night, with the result that everyone you find there is a surgeon. He also mentions that the Khān of Bitlis, accused of having raided the lands of a neighbor, responded, "This is Kurdistan," and alleged that a "law" (*qānūn*) of his dynasty prescribed that he raid his neighbors from time to time "in order to twist their ears."[53] And if the Kurdish mountains were unfriendly to empires seeking to control the region from outside, they were also unfavorable to the emergence of powerful states within it. Here, too, incipient states were scarcely to be found at more than a local level.[54]

The provinces: The Arab lands

In the Arab lands, by contrast, incipient states were more common.[55] Here intermediate structures were of two kinds. Some were Ottoman in origin, meaning that they tended to be the work of non-Arabs originally dispatched to the Arab provinces from the center. Others were of local origin, which is to say that they arose in general from the activities of the indigenous Arabs, particularly Arab tribesmen. Outside the Arabian Peninsula the Ottoman structures were much more conspicuous than the local ones, and it is with them that we will be

52. Quoted in R. Dankoff, *The intimate life of an Ottoman statesman*, Albany 1991, 147.

53. R. Dankoff, *Evliya Çelebi in Bitlis*, Leiden 1990, 175, 177.

54. For a survey of the Kurdish principalities under Ottoman rule see M. Atmaca, "Negotiating political power in the early modern Middle East," in *The Cambridge history of the Kurds*, Cambridge 2021.

55. For surveys of the Middle Eastern Arab lands under Ottoman rule see P. M. Holt, *Egypt and the Fertile Crescent, 1516–1922*, Ithaca 1980, and J. Hathaway, *The Arab lands under Ottoman rule, 1516–1800*, Harlow 2008.

concerned here. Geographically they fall into two groups, those of the Middle East and those of North Africa.

In the Middle East, the main Ottoman structures were centered on Baghdad, Damascus, and Cairo. In Baghdad the seventeenth century had been marked by the disorderly politics of the Janissary garrison, exemplifying a rule of thumb that although rebellious Janissaries could subvert a regime, they lacked the capacity to establish one for themselves; state formation was still an equestrian rather than a pedestrian activity. Times changed in Baghdad in the early eighteenth century with the emergence of the Mamlūk Pashalïq (1704–1831). Its story began when the central government installed a governor of Georgian origin who, despite having no local roots, held office for nearly twenty years, taking ownership of Baghdad and indeed of much of Iraq. He was succeeded by his son, who governed for just over twenty years. In the manner of the Ṣafawids a century earlier, father and son recruited for themselves a force of Georgian slave soldiers, and after the death of the son a succession of these Mamlūks—the actual Mamlūk pashas—held power until 1831. No doubt the central government tolerated this semiautonomous regime in part because it could ill afford chaos on the militarily sensitive frontier with Iran. It nevertheless retained a measure of control to the extent that it could exercise some leverage over the province when a pasha died and his successor was to be chosen; at such times it might even send in troops, as in 1831 when it brought the Mamlūk Pashalïq to an end. Baghdad was not, however, the only site of provincial state formation in Iraq. In the south, seventeenth-century Baṣra was ruled for several decades by a certain Afrāsiyāb, originally the holder of a local bureaucratic office, and his descendants after him. He acquired the city by purchase from the Ottoman governor who preceded him. The original Afrāsiyāb of Iranian legend was a Central Asian king, an enemy of Iran who came to be seen as a Turk, making the name an apt one for Turks, and the Afrāsiyāb who ruled Baṣra did indeed claim Seljuq ancestry. But he also had some Arab ancestors. The dynasty he founded ended with the rule of his grandson in 1668. In the north of Iraq, eighteenth-century Mosul was ruled by the Jalīlī family. ʿAbd al-Jalīl, the initiator of the family fortunes, is a somewhat elusive figure. On one account he was a Christian and an insider to the Ottoman power structure, being a servant in the governor's household. On another account he was a merchant from elsewhere who settled in Mosul, and a Muslim. His descendants were undoubtedly Muslims, and they held the governorship of the city most of the time from 1726 to 1834. Their moment of glory was their defense of Mosul against Nādir Shāh in 1743. In normal times they were a notably entrepreneurial family. They rose to office by making money and connections supplying the Ottoman military, and thereafter they continued to profit, not least at the intersection of business and power. They were also quite generous cultural patrons. Like the Mamlūk pashas, they fell victim to the nineteenth-century recentralization of the Ottoman Empire.

Damascus was different. It was closer to the center, and it was a key city on the annual pilgrimage route from the Ottoman heartlands to the Ḥijāz, with the result that the sultan's prestige was at stake in the running of the province. In the seventeenth century this did not seem to make much difference, and there was Janissary disorder in Damascus just as in Baghdad. The center responded by putting in a fresh Janissary force in 1658–59 and again in 1746. Inevitably the old and new Janissaries came into conflict with each other, and their clashes continued all through the eighteenth century. It was in that century that the divergence between the two provinces became more pronounced: Damascus, and Syria more generally, never developed a counterpart of the Mamlūk Pashalïq. What did emerge was a pattern whereby members of the ʿAẓm family—an Ottoman family of Syrian origin—were more likely than not to hold the position of governor of Damascus in the period from 1725 to 1757 and to a lesser extent to acquire other governorships in the region. Thereafter they had a comeback in the 1770s and were still in the running in the first years of the nineteenth century. Without one of the ʿAẓms as governor in Damascus things tended to go badly there; after the ʿAẓm governor was replaced in 1757 the pilgrimage met with disaster when a caravan that included the sultan's sister was attacked by the Bedouin, with the loss of some twenty thousand lives. But unlike the Mamlūk rulers of Baghdad, these governors could be hired, fired, or moved to another province at the will of the central government. As this suggests, Syria was not an inviting terrain for members of the Ottoman elite interested in establishing autonomous dynasties, though at the end of our period Aḥmad al-Jazzār (d. 1804) made a good start, despite showing no aspirations to break with the Ottoman order. This Bosnian had spent some time as a player in the messy politics of Ottoman Egypt, where his ferocity had earned him the nickname al-Jazzār, "the butcher." In 1775 he was appointed governor of Sidon and established himself in Acre. His fighting force was a mix of Bosnians, Albanians, and his own slaves. His ability to finance it reflected the existence of a thriving economy in northern Palestine based on the export of cotton to Europe. He was able to extend his power over Damascus and Lebanon and to withstand Napoleon's invasion of Syria in 1799. After his death in 1804 a member of his household succeeded him as governor till he in turn died in 1808, but that was as close as he came to founding a dynasty.

Cairo, and Egypt at large, were in material terms more important for the center than was either Baghdad or Damascus, thanks to the grain and revenue the province supplied. But from the start the Ottomans, though establishing a body of Janissaries and other troops in the country, had been willing to accommodate the continued existence of a Mamlūk elite, albeit in a modified form: while new recruitment from outside the country continued, the sons of Mamlūks were no longer excluded from serving as Mamlūks themselves. The survival of this military elite was a distinctive feature of the politics of Ottoman Egypt, and a remarkable one given that the Mamlūks were neither native Egyptians nor Ottomans. The pattern of provincial politics in Egypt thus consisted mainly of factional conflicts among and between the Mamlūks and the Ottoman troops. In a manner reminiscent of Baghdad and Damascus, Janissary politics provided the main theme in the struggle for power in the years 1676–94 and again in the major conflict that broke out in 1711, but they ceased to matter thereafter. On the whole, it was Mamlūk politics that dominated most of the seventeenth and eighteenth centuries. Chaotic conflict was often the order of the day, but sometimes a leading Mamlūk would hold power for an extended period. The center still cared about its supply of grain and revenue, but it allowed the Ottoman governors in Cairo to become little more than figureheads. The whole pattern looks like an invitation to the Mamlūks to nurse secessionist aspirations and seek to recover the independence that had been theirs before the Ottoman conquest. Indeed, a rebellion in 1609 seems to have had separatist aims, and there was a further hint of this in 1632, when a Mamlūk leader claimed descent from a fifteenth-century Mamlūk sultan. In the next century a Mamlūk potentate who held power from 1760 to 1772 clearly entertained secessionist ideas. We are told that he used to read about the Egyptian kings of the past and said to his intimates: "The kings of Egypt were Mamlūks like us; these Ottomans took Egypt through superior force and the treachery of its people."[56] Moreover, his ambitions extended well beyond the borders of Egypt. In 1770 he dispatched troops to the Ḥijāz and southern Syria, subverting the Ottoman order there. But the Ottomans could still crack the whip if they really wanted to, as when they sent an expedition to Egypt to get some respect from the locals in 1786; this was the kind of thing they would do about once a century. In this they were doubtless assisted by the fact that Egypt—unlike Iraq—was a long way from any significant military frontier, with the result that its military forces were not particularly formidable. This was something for which the Ottomans paid dearly in 1798, when in the course of the Napoleonic wars Napoleon himself invaded Egypt from the sea and the next year pushed on into Palestine. On Napoleon's part this was a wildly imprudent adventure, and the French were expelled in 1801, but it is telling that their expulsion owed as much to the intervention of the British as it did to Ottoman military forces, metropolitan or local.

When we move west to North Africa we enter the world of the Barbary states. As we saw, they had been established in the sixteenth century more through the private enterprise of the corsairs than through the efforts of the Ottoman state. Their livelihood derived primarily from their piratical activities on the sea, but they also extended their power over their hinterlands. The easternmost of these states, and the only one we have not previously encountered, was based in Tripoli, in what is now western Libya. Conquered by an Ottoman expedition in 1551, it had a some-

56. Quoted in Holt, *Egypt and the Fertile Crescent*, 96.

what chaotic history in the seventeenth century but settled down in the eighteenth under the dynastic rule of the Qaramānlī governors (1711–1835); they were no doubt a family of Anatolian origin, as their name implies. The province was in practice largely autonomous, though there were Janissaries present, and links with the center were maintained. Farther to the west was Tunis. After several decades of struggle for the city between the Spanish and the Ottomans, an Ottoman expedition seized Tunis in 1574 and Tunisia became an Ottoman province, initially under strong central control. Here, too, piracy was prominent, but there was much more of an agricultural hinterland. As usual the Ottoman establishment included Janissaries, but there were also other slave soldiers, and it was from the descendants of one of these—a Corsican in origin—that a first dynasty emerged in the mid-seventeenth century, to be replaced in the eighteenth by the long-lasting Ḥusaynids (1705–1957). Their founder was the son of a Greek convert to Islam. His dynasty recognized Ottoman overlordship, but the central government tended not to interfere in its affairs. The westernmost of the Barbary states was Algiers. It was also the first to be founded and the most notorious for its corsair activity—in 1627 its ships raided Iceland. The central government had played no part in its initial establishment in the early sixteenth century and was very far away, but at first it still appointed and removed governors; thereafter the corsairs continued to recruit from Anatolia and elsewhere in the eastern Mediterranean. The form of government of this state in its later history—an elected leader and a council whose members voted—was closer to that of a mercantile republic like Venice or Ragusa than to anything to be found in the rest of the Ottoman Empire, though a Janissary involved in the rebellion of 1703 in Istanbul made the imaginative suggestion that the Ottoman dynasty should give way to a collective government of this kind (*jumhūr jemʿiyyeti*). At the same time the corsairs of Algiers, in organizing their piratical enterprises, had recourse to arrangements resembling joint-stock companies, a European form of business activity otherwise absent from the Muslim world. This European tinge is not surprising. The corsairs of Algiers made a living off frequent if hostile interaction with Europe, they took large numbers of Christian captives, and they derived a significant fraction of their manpower from European renegades. Their maritime orientation did not, however, prevent them from extending their hegemony over a considerable hinterland. Indeed, they seem to have given serious attention to it: between 1790 and 1825 the leader in Algiers fired eight of his provincial governors and executed sixteen of them.

The looming crisis

Overall, what we see in the eighteenth century is a low-level equilibrium in terms of the stability of the central government, the alternation of territorial gains and losses, and the balance of central and local power in the provinces. Across three continents the Ottoman façade had largely been preserved, and the empire was now in considerably better shape than it had been in the first half of the seventeenth century. It was nevertheless a rather poor state sitting atop a rather poor society, one in which economic activity was frequently disrupted by brigandage and disorder. In short, the empire had proved remarkably good at surviving, but not at thriving. Toward the end of the eighteenth century this low-level equilibrium was beginning to be geopolitically dysfunctional. The empire had to respond to the continuing evolution of European warfare and the successful assimilation of the new techniques by Russia, and it had to do this with limited fiscal resources. Even in the early seventeenth century matching Europe in the field of firearms had not been a serious problem, but by the eighteenth century catching up with current military methods was significantly harder. To be state-of-the-art in a European context, an army now needed something quite new in military history: an educated officer corps familiar with the *science* of warfare. Acquiring this science required formal study in an institutional setting, not just experience in the field. So keeping up with Europe now required the Ottomans to do something they had never done before—to introduce a measure of European education into the training of the Ottoman military leadership.

Not everyone saw it this way. For example, Muṣṭafā III (ruled 1757–74) attributed the successes of the Europeans to their superior astrology and sought to tap European expertise in that field. But by the end of the eighteenth century the rulers of the empire had a clearer sense of their predicament. In fact, a school of geometry had been set up as early as 1734, though it soon fell by the wayside; a school of mathematics established for the navy in 1773 had shown more staying power. The eighteenth century also saw much discussion of more drastic measures of military Europeanization. Apart from sheer necessity, one of the arguments in support of this was of a kind that had a considerable future in the Muslim world: if the unbelievers had developed better military methods, that was because long ago they had borrowed the essence of them from the Ottomans. But as always talk is cheap; it was Selīm III (ruled 1789–1807) who finally took the bull by the horns. Perhaps significantly, he had not been forced to spend his early years in the "cage," and while still a prince he had corresponded with the French king Louis XVI (ruled 1774–92). Once on the throne, rather than seriously attempting to reform the recalcitrant Janissaries, he set about the creation of a new infantry army alongside them. This was in the spirit of a two-step proposal put forward by a distinguished Ottoman bureaucrat when Selīm convened a large gathering of notables soon after his accession to discuss what had to be done. The first step in this proposal was to recruit villagers and orphans without previous military experience, and the second was to have them trained by several dozen Prussian officers and organized just like a European army. This recommendation fed into a set of reforms enacted in 1792–93 that came to be known, in a phrase borrowed from the French, as the "New Order," Niẓām-i Jedīd—a term that in common parlance became the name of the new army. Both the idea of importing European officers to train Ottoman troops and the phrase "New Order" had already appeared in Ottoman texts of the first half of the century, but the sense of urgency was new. In the event Selīm opted for Ottoman officers to command his new army, but to educate them he created new schools in which Ottoman students studied with French officers and books. He was not the first Muslim ruler to adopt such a program. Shāhīn Girāy (ruled 1777–82 and 1783–87), the luckless last Khān of the Crimea, had tried to create a regular army dressed in European style and had obliged his military to study "in the infidel language."[57] But Selīm was the first to institute such a program in a major Muslim state, and as might be expected, his measures provoked considerable opposition—not least from the Janissaries, who refused to serve alongside the new troops. The rest of the story, including the deposition and subsequent killing of Selīm by the Janissaries and other opponents of the New Order in 1807–8, lies beyond the limit of our period and stretches far into the nineteenth century. What we should note in breaking off here is that the elite reformers who backed Selīm were by no means single-minded proponents of Europeanization. They had links to the Mujaddidī branch of the Naqshbandīs, a Ṣūfī order with a venerable ancestry in Central Asia and India. Moreover, the regulations of the New Order laid down that the troops were to be given religious instruction based on a short work by Birgevī, the scholar whom we met earlier as an uncompromising sixteenth-century pietist.

Muslims and Christians

Muslims and Christians: Demography

The famous Sinān is the dominant figure in the history of Ottoman architecture. One of the most imposing monuments of Istanbul, the Süleymāniyye, was his work, and he had hundreds of other buildings to his credit. The majority of them were located in Istanbul and its vicinity, but almost a third were out in the provinces. As we saw, Sinān was born a Christian and recruited into the service of the sultan through the Devshirme. The village he came from was Aghïrnas, some fifteen miles east-northeast of Kayseri. It was an overwhelmingly Christian village. The Ottoman survey of 1500, when Sinān must still have been a little boy in the village, showed just a single Muslim family, a father with his two sons; the other seventy-six adult males were all Christians, and it is a little tantalizing that we have no way to tell which of them was Sinān's father. Some of these villagers had names so transparently Greek that we can be assured that this was a Greek village rather than an Armenian one: Yani (John), Yorgi (George), Vasil (Basil), Nikola

57. Quoted in A. W. Fisher, *The Russian annexation of the Crimea*, Cambridge 1970, 129.

(Nicholas). But a fair number had straightforwardly Turkish names such as Yaghmur ("Rain"), Qar-yaghdï ("It-snowed"), Qara-göz ("Black-eye"), Ay-doghdï ("The-moon-rose"), and Tanrï-vermish ("God-gave"). This suggests a community in which Turkish was at the very least widely spoken, something that could have eased the transition for Sinān when he was taken from his family to serve the sultan. We happen to know that he did not lose touch with them—which may not have been as rare as one might imagine. When he was in his seventies the Ottomans conquered Cyprus, and orders were issued for a compulsory movement of population from the mainland to the island at a time when the village was still largely Christian. Sinān's Christian family could have been caught in the net had he not been in a position to ask the sultan for the favor of an exemption that would allow them to live out their days in Aghrïnas. So having a son taken to serve the sultan could be a cloud with a silver lining. Whether as a result of the forced migration to Cyprus or through a gradual shift in the demographic balance, by 1834 it seems that only a sixth of the population of the village was still Christian. This endpoint, though not the starting point, was fairly typical of Anatolia as a whole.

The Ottoman Empire contained a large number of Christians. Their distribution was uneven, but it made considerable historical sense. We can distinguish three broad regions—namely, the Arab lands, Anatolia, and the Balkans—though as might be expected there were significant variations within each of them. In the Arab lands, where the Muslim conquest went back to the seventh century, the Christian population was thinnest overall. Thus in Arabia, as in North Africa, there were no Christians at all, not even in the mountains of the Yemen, though there had still been Christians a little north of the Yemen in the early thirteenth century. In the Fertile Crescent there was a concentration in the mountains of Syria, as we might expect. The anomaly in the Arab lands was the relatively large minority of Coptic Christians found in Egypt, despite the flat terrain and the integrating role of the Nile. In Anatolia the Muslim conquest took place several centuries later—in the eleventh century for the plateau, in the thirteenth for the western plains, and not till the fifteenth for the Pontus. Here, then, the Christian population, Greek and Armenian, may have been larger, with Greeks by and large more numerous toward the west and Armenians toward the east. But by the time we begin to have data from the Ottoman fiscal surveys of the later fifteenth century Christians had been reduced to a minority. In the west, particularly in the plains, they were barely to be found outside the urban centers. Farther east, for example in the villages around Sivas, Tokat, and of course Kayseri, they were a significant minority of the population, and yet farther to the east there were larger numbers of Greeks in the Pontus and Armenians in Kurdistan. In the Balkans, Muslim conquest began only in the fourteenth century and was not completed until the sixteenth. Here Christians remained the majority of the population, despite the presence of a considerable Muslim minority. Chronology was not, however, the only factor in these outcomes. In the Arab lands much of the countryside was overrun by nomadic Arab tribes, and their presence is likely to have helped spread Islam (and Arabic) among the rural population. In Anatolia this role was played by the Turcoman tribes. In the Balkans, by contrast, Arab tribes were absent and Turcoman tribes were generally less prominent, though they had a considerable impact on the parts of the eastern Balkans where they settled. They must to some extent have been held back from moving into the Balkans by the difficulty of crossing the intervening sea, narrow as it was, with their tents and livestock. With regard to the urban population on the European side of the Straits, it is worth noting that as late as the first half of the nineteenth century Istanbul itself may not have had a Muslim majority.

Overall, this picture provides a reasonable approximation, but it does not take into account change over time. What was crucial here was the relative openness of Islam to converts and the fact that power was almost entirely in Muslim hands; non-Muslim rule under the Ottoman umbrella was found only in the mountains of Lebanon and the vassal states of the northern Balkans. We can infer from this that the predominant direction of conversion would be from Christianity to Islam, as may have been the case with the Jalīlī family in Mosul. But such conversion does not seem to have been enough under the Ottomans to bring about radical change in the overall picture. In the Arab lands, and in Anatolia from at least the late fifteenth century, the Christians were already a minority, though their numbers could have been further reduced under Ottoman rule. But in western Anatolia this was balanced by a flow of Armenian refugees seeking refuge from the depredations of the Jelālīs, together with an influx of Greeks from the late seventeenth century seeking economic opportunities. The one major change involving a whole region took place in the Pontus, where a largely Christian population was reduced to a minority by the nineteenth century. Thus the population of Trabzon, the former Byzantine city of Trebizond, was largely Christian as late as the 1520s, but it already had a slight Muslim majority by 1583 and a greater one by the nineteenth century. In the Balkans immigration of Muslims from Anatolia was considerable, and at the same time conversion was widespread. In 1520–35 about a fifth of the Balkan population under Ottoman rule was Muslim, while the eastern provinces already had a Muslim majority, as did many urban settlements, and Bosnia was approaching it. By 1831 the overall proportion of Muslims had risen to two-fifths, and in Albania, the only Balkan nation with a Muslim majority to emerge from the breakup of the Ottoman Empire, it was 70 percent. But Christians still accounted for three-fifths of the population of the Balkans at large. Perhaps with a few more centuries of uninterrupted Ottoman rule the Balkans would have become predominantly Muslim, but the events of the nineteenth century decreed otherwise.

Christians were not, of course, the only non-Muslims in the Ottoman Empire; there was also a significant Jewish community. Some of it was inherited from pre-Ottoman times, but much of it consisted of refugees from the expulsion of the Jews of Spain in 1492 and the forced conversion of the Jews of Portugal five years later. These immigrants continued over the centuries to speak a Spanish dialect, Ladino, writing it in the Hebrew script, and this language still survives. It was not that the Ottoman Empire was exactly a paradise for its Jewish population. Evliyā Chelebī, who himself clearly disliked Jews, mentions cities in which no Jews lived because, he says, had they attempted to settle there the inhabitants would have killed them. But not everything this traveler tells us is true, and large numbers of Jews from the Iberian Peninsula were able to settle in relative safety in the Ottoman lands, with concentrations in cities such as Istanbul and still more the Balkan port city of Salonica. There Jews were a majority of the population by 1520, much to the chagrin of the local Christians. Meanwhile, the Spanish decision to expel the Jews was severely criticized by fellow Christians: What sense did it make to throw away a population "so industrious and hard-working,"[58] or worse yet to donate it to the enemy? In pragmatic terms Christian loss was indeed Muslim gain, a point that was clearly not lost on the Ottoman rulers. A contemporary Jewish chronicler remarks that those refugees who reached the Ottoman lands were received kindly by the sultan, "as they were artisans." In other words, they were useful people whose hosts stood to benefit economically from their presence—and not just economically, if we trust a French commentator who observed that the Jews, to the great detriment of Christianity, "have taught the Turks divers inventions, crafts and engines of war." They also produced uniforms for the Janissaries. At the same time Jews could rise high in the Ottoman polity. They could serve as court physicians, and in the second half of the sixteenth century a Jewish banker governed some of the Aegean islands as duke of Naxos. It is telling that the major upheaval in Jewish history in the Ottoman lands came not from the host society but from within the community. This was the messianic movement initiated by Sabbatai Ṣevi, a Jewish scholar from Izmir who in 1666 headed for Istanbul with the intention of deposing the sultan. He billed himself as "the only son and first-born of God, messiah and savior of the world," engaged in what were known as "strange actions,"[59] and generated wild enthusiasm in the Jewish community. When the Ottoman authorities confronted him with a choice between conversion and a painful death, he chose to convert to Islam. The outcome was the emergence among his followers of the Dönmes, an unusual cross between a Jewish and a Muslim sect. But it is the interactions between Christians and Muslims to which we will devote the rest of this chapter.

58. For this and the quotations that follow see M. Mazower, *Salonica: City of ghosts*, London 2004, 47, 48, 73.

59. For this phrase see G. Scholem, *Sabbatai Ṣevi: The mystical messiah*, Princeton 2016, 147, 148, 159, etc.

Muslims and Christians rubbing off on each other

If Muslims and Christians lived side by side over long periods, it was inevitable that they would rub off on one another. Just as many—though not all—of the Christians living in the Arab lands forsook their Aramaic or Coptic dialects for Arabic, so many—but by no means all—of the Christians of Anatolia ceased to speak Greek or Armenian and spoke Turkish instead. Such populations often wrote in the language they spoke, whence the phenomenon of Arabic written in the Syriac script and Turkish in the Greek and Armenian scripts. But alongside Turkish-speaking Christians there were also Muslim populations that continued to speak their ancestral languages, as with the Slavonic-speaking Muslims of Bosnia and the Greek-speaking Muslims of the Pontus, Epirus, and Crete. We thus have Slavonic and Greek written by Muslims in the Arabic script; for example, Greek texts written in this way by the Muslims of Yanina in northwestern Greece survive from the seventeenth century. The peoples of the empire likewise exchanged loanwords on a large scale. The agricultural vocabulary of Anatolian peasants is full of borrowings from Greek, while the Balkan languages abound in Turkish words and expressions. The Turkish word *yoğurt* is the source of the Greek *yaourti* and the Bulgarian and Serbian *yogurt*—not to mention the English "yoghurt."

Alongside language, popular religion was a field in which this process of rubbing off was conspicuous. One form it took was the mixing of religions, commonly known as syncretism. As we have seen, in medieval Anatolia it was not uncommon for Muslims to have their children baptized. This practice is attested in the twelfth century and was alive in the sixteenth, when Ambassador Busbecq noted that he knew of instances of Turks having their children baptized in secret. It was not the only example he gave of such syncretism, but early twentieth-century ethnography provides us with a much richer picture of the phenomenon. For example, in response to a cholera epidemic in 1908 the Muslims of the Cappadocian town of Ürgüp asked the Christians to parade the body of a Christian saint around the Muslim quarters, which they did. This reflected the generous belief that "a saint is for all the world,"[60] not an asset to be selfishly monopolized by a single religion. There were likewise shared sanctuaries revered and visited by both Muslims and Christians. Alongside practices of this kind involving people unambiguously identifiable as Muslims or Christians, there were also small crypto-Christian populations who concealed an ancestral Christianity behind a veil of Islam. Such communities could be found in the Pontus, Cyprus, Crete, Albania, and Kosovo. There was no clear answer to the question whether such people were Muslims or Christians, though the phenomenon still presupposed a real distinction between Islam and Christianity. We could say the same of the way of life of the Albanian

60. Quoted in F. W. Hasluck, *Christianity and Islam under the sultans*, Oxford 1929, 1:72.

transhumants who were Muslims while down in the valleys in winter but Christians while up in the mountains in summer. Less drastic than mixed religion and concealed faith was an attitude of mutual benevolence, though this, too, could easily transgress the formal requirements of both religions. Börklüje Muṣṭafā, a dervish who in 1416 led a rebellion near Izmir on the west coast of Anatolia, is said to have combined two thoroughly heretical doctrines. One was a belief in the common ownership of property—though not of women. The other was the view that Christians were not unbelievers. He himself was a "simple and rustic Turk,"[61] and his followers are described as bareheaded and barefooted. Yet he seems to have been surprisingly well connected. He was a follower of Ibn Qāḍī Simāvuna, a respected jurist who at one point held a high judicial office but was also a Ṣūfī of a perhaps less reputable kind. He, too, rebelled in 1416, in his case in the Balkans, and was well disposed toward Christians. Yet another such heresy was the view attributed to Muslims preaching in Albania in 1650 that "everyone can achieve salvation in his own religion."[62] Two Catholic missionaries received an ecumenical welcome on presenting themselves at the door of a house in a village in Kosovo in 1637: "Come in, Fathers; in our house we have Catholicism, Islam, and Orthodoxy." As one of the missionaries commented sourly in his report, "They seemed to glory in this diversity of religions, as if they were wiser than the other peoples of this world." Whether or not they were wiser than the missionaries they shocked, they very likely believed that their whole family would find its way to heaven. Against this background we should perhaps not be surprised to hear of a bizarre practice described by Evliyā Chelebī, who was told that it was quite common in the Austrian frontier region. A Muslim and a Christian would establish a brotherly relationship by exchanging religions, whereby each committed himself to helping the other in the event that he was captured in the course of Muslim-Christian warfare. This is very much popular religion, for as Evliyā's informant tartly observed, "nothing of this sort is found in the books of the Muslims, or of the infidels."[63]

All these unorthodox ideas were no doubt much more widespread at a popular level than among the educated elite, but they were not an exclusively popular phenomenon. The elite, too, dabbled in syncretism. One Ṣūfī order, that of the Bektāshīs, preserved some obviously Christian practices: a ritual involving wine, bread, and cheese reminiscent of the communion service, and the confession of sins, followed by absolution. The order also reached out to Christians, allowing them to join without converting to Islam. Good relations were facilitated by identifying Muslim saints with Christian ones and by spreading legends about their secret conversion to Christianity. All this very likely originated as popular religion,

61. Quoted in Imber, *The Ottoman Empire, 1300–1481*, 84.

62. For this and the next quotation see N. Malcolm, *Rebels, believers, survivors*, Oxford 2020, 56, 60.

63. Dankoff, *The intimate life of an Ottoman statesman*, 250.

but it did not stay confined to it. Perhaps from the later fifteenth century and more assuredly from the late sixteenth, Bektāshism developed an intimate relationship with the Janissaries, the core of the Ottoman army and a major player in the politics of the empire. Of course the Janissaries were not exactly members of the polished cultural elite. But Jalāl al-Dīn Rūmī (d. 1273), the founder of the Mevlevī Ṣūfī order, certainly belonged to it. He has a poem whose message is that he has put away all binaries, so that he is not of the East nor of the West, not of the Land nor of the Sea, and so forth. In the first line of the poem he denies not a binary but a quaternary: "I am neither Christian, nor Jew, nor Zoroastrian, nor Muslim"[64]—a negative analog of mixed religion. There are also signs of a movement among Ottoman Muslims at a purely elite level that gave an unorthodox prominence to a cult of Jesus. For example, a scholar said to come from the east was executed in Istanbul in 1527 for maintaining that Jesus was superior to Muḥammad. An English ambassador who spent time in Istanbul in the mid-seventeenth century reported the existence of a secret sect among the elite that believed in the divinity of Jesus. Benevolence, too, could be found among the elite. The dissident Ṣūfī Niyāzī-i Miṣrī (d. 1694) was indignant at the maltreatment of the non-Muslims of the empire, pointing out that the taxes they paid provided the core of the funding of the oppressive Ottoman state. The grand vizier Rüstem Pasha (d. 1561), after failing to convert Ambassador Busbecq to Islam, confided to him his view that people who live virtuous lives "will be partakers of eternal bliss, whatever religion they may have followed." The ambassador comments that "such views are entertained by some Turks, but they are thought heretical."[65] They were likewise thought heretical in Christendom; the eighteenth of the Thirty-Nine Articles of 1562 commits Anglican Christians to the view that anyone presuming to say such a thing is "to be had accursed."[66] By the eighteenth century, it seems, members of the Ottoman and western European elites could find common ground in deism. Lady Mary Wortley Montagu (d. 1762) was a cosmopolitan elitist who spent some time in the Ottoman Empire in 1717–18 as the wife of a British ambassador and wrote spirited letters about it to her friends. In the course of her visit she and her husband spent a few weeks as the guests of a cultured Ottoman gentleman in Belgrade. At one point she was surprised to hear him inquire how Mr. Toland was doing. This John Toland (d. 1722) was a freethinker notorious among the Anglican faithful as a deist who corrupted young men with his "vile principles" and "wicked books."[67] In line with this, Lady Mary reassured a freethinking correspondent of hers that the Turkish cultured elite had no more faith in the divine

64. R. A. Nicholson, *Selected poems from the Dīvāni Shamsi Tabrīz*, Cambridge 1977, 125.
65. Thornton Forster and Blackburne Daniell, *The life and letters of Ogier Ghiselin de Busbecq*, 1:235.
66. *The book of common prayer*, London n.d., 619.
67. Quoted in R. E. Sullivan, *John Toland and the deist controversy*, Cambridge, MA 1982, 1.

inspiration of Muḥammad than it did in the infallibility of the pope. She could well have been exaggerating, but she is unlikely to have been inventing Ottoman deism out of whole cloth.

Alongside this variety of irenic views there was, of course, no lack of hard-line sentiment against Christians. Here a single vignette will suffice. An anonymous author of around 1560 highlights the problem posed for the Muslim public by impure bread. The issue arose from the fact that most of those who kneaded the dough in the bakeries of Istanbul were unbelievers who did not wash their hands and had the habit of stripping off their upper garments and headgear when they got to work. The result was that their sweat and lice poured into the tub and were mixed with the dough, soon to be consumed by Muslims as bread. Yet the owners of the bakeries refused to do the right thing and employ Muslims to knead the dough. If Muslims couldn't be found for the job, the author argues, the owners could at least make their workers keep themselves clean and have their hair shaved off, thereby solving the problem of the lice, if not that of the sweat. The author goes on to urge the grand vizier to take action, promising him a public relations bonanza in this life and great rewards in the next. But the chances are that the grand vizier turned a deaf ear to this advice, having other things on his mind. Likewise there was no lack of Christian hostility toward Muslims. Again to take a single example, this one from an extreme rural environment rather than metropolitan Istanbul, a mid-nineteenth-century traveler gave a description of the village of Varashós in Cappadocia, some fifty miles south of Kayseri. It was inhabited entirely by Greeks who, on account of its lonely position, ran wild, hated the Turks, went around armed with muskets, and paid no taxes. The only authority they recognized was that of some Turcoman chiefs with whom they would join to raid the luckless Turkish peasants in return for a share of the booty; the village priests were happy to participate in these raids. But as always, such evidence of communal hatred is not to be taken as the whole picture. In the Balkans and elsewhere, a characteristic Ottoman institution was the soup kitchen devoted to feeding travelers and the poor. It was not uncommon for these establishments to feed non-Muslims as well as Muslims. Evliyā Chelebī mentions some that would provide a meal to all comers, whether it was night or day, be they rich or poor, old or young, irrespective of their religions.

Muslims, Christians, and the Ottoman state

With the anonymous author's mention of the grand vizier we bring the power of the state into the picture. Other things being equal the average Muslim sovereign could be expected to rule his non-Muslim population in a fairly pragmatic fashion. Getting too close to them would be bad for his image among his Muslim subjects, but treating them too harshly would also be counterproductive—non-Muslims were useful people and, as the dissident Ṣūfī pointed out, they paid a lot of taxes, indeed more than they would pay should they convert to Islam. The Ottomans employed some Christian clerks, a practice to which one seventeenth-century preacher in Istanbul strongly objected; we have already encountered this centuries-old gripe of the Islamic scholars against their rulers. Back in the fourteenth century it was clear that the Ottomans were quite capable of getting along with Christians when they weren't actually fighting them. In the fifteenth century—in 1431, to be precise—an early Ottoman survey attests the existence of Christian Timariots in southern Albania, and they were likewise present elsewhere in the Balkans. This phenomenon survived into the early sixteenth century. Both the Christian clerks and the Christian Timariots invite comparison with what we will find in the Mughal Empire in the next chapter. But the effect of the Mughal comparison is also to underline the limited character of the integration of Christians into the Ottoman state apparatus. The one serious qualification to this would be the role of the Phanariots, the Greek community living around the Orthodox patriarchate in Istanbul toward the end of our period. They provided interpreters who handled relations with Christian powers, and they supplied governors for Walachia and Moldavia after their local dynasties had been terminated. At the same time, the Ottoman elite showed no great curiosity about the history and heritage of their Balkan subjects and no interest in translating texts from their literatures—both again points of contrast with Mughal India. Still less did they think of abolishing the poll tax paid by non-Muslims, as the Mughals did for a century. On the other hand, Ottoman statesmen were not about to force the mass conversion of their Christian population to Islam. Perhaps the wildest idea for radical change in the Ottoman Balkans was the recommendation of an eighteenth-century Ottoman bureaucrat that the Albanian language be abolished in favor of Turkish as a way to tame the unruly Albanians; but this was an ethnic, not a religious fantasy. Ottoman rule in the Balkans was thus compatible with the survival of a Christian majority, but the relationship of the state and the Muslim elite with its Christian subjects was not in general a warm one.

An Ottoman traveler

The number of travelers who have left us accounts of the Ottoman Empire is legion. Already during its first decades Orkhan received a visit from the Moroccan traveler Ibn Baṭṭūṭa, who presciently described him as "the greatest of the kings of the Turcomans and the richest in wealth, lands, and military forces."[68] In later centuries large numbers of European travelers wrote of what they had seen for the

68. Ibn Baṭṭūṭa, *Travels*, trans. H.A.R. Gibb, Cambridge 1958–2000, 2:451–52.

curious. Among them we have encountered Ambassador Busbecq in the sixteenth century and Lady Mary Wortley Montagu in the eighteenth. But the traveler who in his own idiosyncratic way best encapsulates the Ottoman experience was Evliyā Chelebī, whom we have already met several times.[69] Evliyā was a member of the Ottoman elite who spent some four decades on the road to get away from family obligations and the tedium of a regular job in the state apparatus; being cooped up in Istanbul was for him like being in prison. He was thus a rolling stone that gathered no moss, bar a massive account of his travels that survives to this day. His way of life went well with the fact that he was something of a dervish, which also gave him a good reason to travel to visit the tombs of Ṣūfī saints. But he was far from being a loner. On his travels he would have several slaves with him, not to mention a supply of horses. Moreover, he was sociable and had gifts that enhanced his sociability. He could get along with a wide range of people, including rebels and robbers. On one occasion the robbers included the Christian leader of a force of several hundred bandits in the Balkans, and on another occasion he made friends with seven Anatolian highwaymen—"We all kissed and became brothers."[70] He was also a well-trained Qur'ān reciter, which provided endless opportunities for admired performances. Not least, he had a talent for buffoonery, which stood him in good stead during the two years he spent in the entourage of the fearsome sultan Murād IV in an atmosphere very different from the cocoon of silence that had enveloped Süleymān. For Murād he played the role of the court fool—a figure widely attested at the courts of rulers east and west. For example, one of Murād's favorite pleasures when off duty was wrestling. Once when he emerged from his harem, Evliyā taunted him that he wouldn't be wanting to engage in this activity that day because of the exhausting wrestling matches with which he had already disported himself in his harem—an impudent reference to the sultan's sexual relations with his concubines. Murād's reaction was to demonstrate his vigor by picking up Evliyā and twirling him around in the air. Evliyā prevailed on the sultan to put him down only by pleading nausea and threatening to cover the sultan in vomit and worse, upon which, Evliyā tells us, the sultan almost died laughing. This episode netted Evliyā a gift of forty-eight gold pieces from Murād. He tells us that as soon as Murād would see him he would smile. To perform this role effectively required a fine sense of just how far he could go; a timid fool raises no laughs, but a reckless one is living dangerously. The role also required a certain bawdiness that comes out elsewhere, as in Evliyā's references to heterosexual sex as "the greater jihad,"[71] an edifying phrase properly used of the inner spiritual struggle against the temptations of this world. And when he reproduces phrases in his accounts

69. On Evliyā Chelebī see R. Dankoff, *An Ottoman mentality*, Leiden 2004; this book is the major source of what follows.

70. Quoted in Dankoff, *An Ottoman mentality*, 134.

71. Quoted in Dankoff, *An Ottoman mentality*, 118, 121.

of the languages he encounters on his travels, they are often obscene. More generally, he had the gift of the gab, which enabled him to attract patrons who possessed more than their share of wealth and power. That in combination with his independent means—his father had been chief goldsmith to a succession of sultans, and Evliyā owned a considerable amount of real estate in Istanbul and elsewhere—enabled him to spend much of his life as a traveler in and around the Ottoman lands.

Evliyā began his travels in 1640, the year Murād died, though the first was no more than an excursion to Bursa. But soon he was traveling most of the time, eventually covering the Balkans, Anatolia, and the Arab lands—his last years were spent in Egypt. In a number of directions he even went beyond the frontiers of the empire, visiting such regions as Austria, Circassia, the Qalmaq country, Azerbaijan, and the upper Nile valley. In some regions he participated in campaigns against the infidel—seventy-seven of them in all, he claims—though usually in the role of support staff rather than as a warrior. His reporting of all this varies on a broad spectrum from fact to fiction, with the proportion of fiction escalating in the peripheries. The factual information includes detailed and reliable accounts of the buildings he saw, particularly Muslim ones. He and his slaves would walk around buildings and fortifications counting the paces, if necessary using prayer beads to ensure the accuracy of the count; the paces, he notes, were those of a robust adult, not those of an opium addict. He understood the value of evidence and cited finds of seashells to prove his theory that the Black Sea had once extended much farther to the north than it now does. And yet the fiction includes some outstandingly tall stories, such as an account of a girl who gave birth to an elephant after a three-year pregnancy and a claim to have joined a Crimean Tatar raid that went as far as Amsterdam. His reports on the languages he encountered can be baffling, but also surprisingly informative. In one case, the numbers he quotes as representing the "Hebrew" of Sinnār on the Blue Nile turn out to be in Kanuri, an African language spoken in the region of Lake Chad.

As interesting as his accounts of what he saw are the attitudes he reveals. Evliyā was a Muslim, a Sunnī, and an Ottoman. So he was genuinely shocked to hear the caliph ʿUmar cursed in Shīʿite Iran—"I nearly went out of my mind."[72] When traveling in a remote part of the Morea he encountered a woman who had been born Muslim but after being carried off by Christians had adopted their religion, married one of them, and borne his child. Though she greeted Evliyā warmly, having known him in her Muslim days, she refused his offer to deliver her from captivity. He then wondered whether he should kill her (he didn't). On the other hand, he had learned to speak fluent Greek as a child, took an interest in Greek inscriptions, had a native speaker give him an oral translation of a Hungarian chronicle, and

72. Quoted in R. Dankoff and S. Kim, *An Ottoman traveller*, London 2010, 56.

found it easy to make friends with the Balkan bandit chief and other unbelievers. As a Muslim he was not fanatical or puritanical. He rejoiced in the punishment meted out to a Qāḍīzādeist who believed painting to be a sin and had vandalized the miniatures in a superb copy of the *Shāhnāma*. When a group of young men in Damascus persuaded him to join them in an expedition to a house of ill fame, he obviously felt uncomfortable and was lucky that on the way he was detained by a naked saint who frequented the Damascene marketplace—lucky since the brothel turned out to be a deathtrap for the young men. But however uncomfortable he felt, he was happy to regale his readers with the story of this off-color adventure. He likewise tells us he never drank wine but mentions that he had served it to his friends in his house, and of course he had seen Murād IV drink it. Occasionally we even get a whiff of relativism, something Ibn Baṭṭūṭa was so innocent of. After describing what strikes him as a pointless practice, he adds, "Nonetheless, every country has its own rites and traditions"; and after reporting behavior he regards as positively shameful, he comments, "But it is their custom, so we cannot censure it."[73] Altogether he was a man of wide horizons; he had sympathy for the predicament of the native population of the Americas in the face of European conquest. His one serious limitation was that he detested travel by sea—a mode of transportation that in the seventeenth century was becoming increasingly essential for anyone who wanted to see the wider world. Kātib Chelebī might well have seen this limitation as part of the Ottoman failure to keep up with the wretched unbelievers who had discovered the New World and seized the ports of India.

Here we leave the Ottoman Empire. It was a remarkably long-lived state. Its founders were contemporaries of the Īlkhāns, and its last rulers were contemporaries of the Bolsheviks. The Ottomans were indeed the only one of the world's imperial dynasties to rule an empire for six centuries. The ʿAbbāsids, the runner-up in the Muslim world, lasted only for five, and unlike them the Ottomans retained an empire almost to the end. In the course of its lifetime it encountered no small amount of adversity—the short, sharp invasion of Tīmūr and the subsequent civil war, the prolonged time of troubles that began in the late sixteenth century, and a very different set of problems that were already visible on the horizon by the end of our period. It was these problems that would eventually prove fatal, and we will touch on them in the last chapter of this book. But in its better days, the Ottoman state had shown more than just staying power. Against the wider background of Muslim history, it had also been unusually innovative, as with systematic fratricide, the Devshirme, and the religious institution. Its innovations, though not always pretty, proved strikingly effective in their day.

73. Quoted in Dankoff, *An Ottoman mentality*, 72, 73.

11

India

We come now to the Muslim expansion into India, by far the most momentous case of a territory that came under extensive Muslim rule but has since been largely lost to Islam. Up to this point we have encountered only the northwestern corner of the subcontinent, the part that the Arabs conquered. So we will need to get a sense of what India at large was like before the Muslim intrusion—a key point here being the absence of any large and powerful Indian state in the relevant period. We will then return briefly to the Arab conquest of the northwest and its aftermath.

Our main story begins with the Ghaznawids in the later tenth century. Like their successors, the Ghūrids, they were a dynasty from outside that expanded into India. Their activities led eventually to the formation of an extensive and long-lasting Muslim state within India, the Delhi Sultanate. Despite ruling the large and dense Hindu population of the northern plains, this sultanate was a fairly conventional Muslim state. There were Turkic slave soldiers, some of whom became rulers of the state, and there were Persian bureaucrats.

We then see a pattern of a kind familiar from the history of Iran: periods when a single large state dominates the scene alternate with periods of fragmentation. In India the large states are the Delhi Sultanate and the Mughal Empire.

The Mughals were in fact Tīmūrids, and they were in India only because they had lost out in Central Asia. But the state they created in India was considerably larger and grander than the Delhi Sultanate, and under the rule of Akbar in the later sixteenth century it responded to the problems and opportunities of ruling a Hindu society in ways that could be strikingly imaginative.

Like the Ottomans, the Mughals had the risky habit of deciding the succession to the throne by civil war, and in the early eighteenth century this led to a disastrous downturn in Mughal power and a period of fragmentation like that which had followed the decline of the Delhi Sultanate. There was, however, a contrast between the two periods: Hindu resurgence was marginal in the first period of fragmentation but conspicuous in the second. We leave India at the end of the eighteenth century with Muslim rule in some disarray and a new non-Muslim intruder, the British, beginning to take over.

The general tendency over the centuries was nevertheless for Muslim power to extend farther and farther south till very little of India was left to independent Hindu rulers. How Muslims and Hindus related to each other was thus a major issue over a large territory. As with Muslims and Christians in the Ottoman Empire, we will first look at the demography—considerably less favorable to Muslims than in the Ottoman case—and then at the ways in which the two populations rubbed off on each other, and finally at the role of the state. But most of our concern will be with a theme that was much more muted in the Ottoman case: the clash of views on the Muslim side about how best to live with the Hindus.

In previous chapters we have seen Islam spread over a remarkably large and diverse area in a politically and often demographically dominant form. To put it in terms of the imperial geography of late antiquity, this territory eventually came to include the whole of the former Persian Empire, the whole of the former Eastern Roman Empire, and the southern region of the former Western Roman Empire. Added to this were large areas in Arabia and northern Africa that had been outside the boundaries of the settled empires and now formed part of the Muslim world. Beyond that we saw the Arab conquests spread Islam into the northwestern corner of India in a form that was at least politically dominant. We have likewise followed its spread to parts of the eastern steppes, issuing in the formation of a small Muslim community in China and its delicate relations with the culture of its host society without the benefit of either political or demographic dominance. And we will come in later chapters to the spread of Islam around the rim of the Indian Ocean and across the Sahara deep into Africa, leading to the formation of Muslim societies in maritime Southeast Asia and the African savanna in which Islam became both politically and demographically dominant. There are, of course, substantial parts of the Old World—not to mention the New—that as of the twenty-first century have not become part of the Muslim world. Such regions include East Asia, continental Southeast Asia, much of Europe, and the whole of the New World. What that leaves us to account for is a set of regions that were once part of the Muslim world, at least in terms of the political dominance of Islam, but no longer belong to it. Here we are talking about territories such as Spain, the Balkans, Israel, certain parts of the Russian Empire, and what used to be Chinese Turkestan. But by far the most salient of these cases is India. It owes its salience to a number of considerations. One is its sheer size; the territory at issue dwarfs even the Balkans. Another is the fact that only in this instance was the fate of an entire Old World civilization at stake. A third is the drama of the encounter: almost the whole of India succumbed to Muslim political dominance, and in an alternative universe not so far removed from the one we live in, this might have led on to demographic dominance and the permanent incorporation of all of India into the Muslim world.

We begin this chapter with a section surveying the new environment in which the Muslim invaders of the subcontinent found themselves. The next section outlines the history of Muslim military and political power in India, with a concentration on the Delhi Sultanate and the Mughal Empire. The final section focuses on the interaction between Muslims and Hindus in the course of this long history.

The pre-Islamic background

The unity and diversity of India

In geographical terms we can think of India as a triangle bounded on two sides by the sea and on the third, the north, by massive mountain ranges—the Himalayas to the east and the Hindu Kush to the west, in other words the mountains of Tibet and Afghanistan. It is these boundaries that encourage us to separate India from the rest of the Eurasian landmass and call it a subcontinent. They make it a rather self-contained peninsula, in marked contrast to the Middle East, which despite the adjoining seas lies at the intersection of Africa, Europe, and Asia. India also differs from the Middle East in terms of the relative location of its highlands and lowlands. If we leave aside the towering mountains that mark its northern boundary, India's highlands, such as they are, have their place in the hilly south—the Deccan—starting with the Vindhya mountains, whereas India north of the Vindhyas is dominated by a vast plain. In addition to these physical differences between India and the Middle East there is a crucial climatic contrast. As we saw, thanks to the prevailing winds on the Indian Ocean the rain-bearing clouds of the summer monsoon bypass the Middle East; by the same token they bring an abundance of water to India. Much of this takes the form of direct rainfall. Here the southwest (Kerala) and the northeast (the Gangetic plain) are particularly well served. The northwest, however, suffers from the aridity so characteristic of much of the Middle East, and south of it Rajasthan is semiarid, as is the interior of the Deccan, particularly the northern Deccan. But the northern mountain ranges also bring down large amounts of rainfall that feed into the river systems of the north Indian plain: the Ganges with its tributaries in the northeast, and the Indus with its tributaries in the northwest. The Indus thus makes good the lack of rainfall in the arid northwest in the same way as the Nile does in Egypt. Both the northern Indian river systems are to a considerable extent navigable, which means that even under premodern conditions much of the northern interior was linked to the coasts by cheap transport.

Being well watered gave India the potential for great agricultural wealth, far greater than that of the Middle East. This, in turn, meant that it could support a much larger population. Around 1800 India's population may have been around two hundred million, perhaps eight times the size of that of the Middle East at the time. India thus provided a material basis for extensive political organization, an elaborately stratified society, and a ramified culture. Each of these deserves a look.

In political terms, the subcontinent was too large under premodern conditions to be brought together under the aegis of a single state. In fact the only state that has ever embraced the whole of India was the British Raj, and it did not do so until well beyond the end of our period. Before that there had been occasional states of imperial dimensions based in the northern plains: the Mauryas in the late fourth and third centuries BC, the Guptas in the fourth and fifth centuries, and the long reign of Harsha in the first half of the seventh century. But none of these states extended to the whole subcontinent. The normal condition of pre-Muslim India was thus division into a plurality of states. What India's geographically self-contained character helped bring about was not political unity but rather a certain homogeneity of political culture.

Something analogous can be said about social stratification in pre-Muslim India. Here the homogeneity consisted of two things. First, at the level of widely recognized principle, society was made up of a hierarchy of four classes (*varṇa*s). Three were "twice-born," meaning that their male members, having been born once at birth, were later born again through a rite of initiation into Aryan society. These three classes were the priestly class (the Brahmins), the military class (the Kṣatriyas), and the commercial class (the Vaiśyas). The fourth, the servile class (the Śūdras), was born only once and did not count as Aryan. Second, at the level of practice, over time society came to be divided into numerous castes (*jāti*s)—a process of considerable antiquity of which the early history is poorly known to us. But a Portuguese account of Kerala in the early sixteenth century already speaks of pretty much the same set of castes as are found there today, and it shows an acute awareness of the role of untouchability in the system. The two phenomena, class and caste, interacted with each other in ways that helped articulate a strongly hierarchical society. If the system as it emerged into the light of modern times is anything to go by, the rules of the castes, underpinned by the formal rules relating to the classes, determined with whom their members could intermarry, with whom they could eat, whom they could touch and be touched by, and in some cases even whom they could see and be seen by. Thus both class and caste were pan-Indian social phenomena. But this homogeneity was balanced by a large measure of diversity. Again judging by the system as it becomes visible in modern times, there could well have been some thousands of different castes in India, and most of them would have been local.

As these remarks on the political and social order may already have suggested, the unity of India was to a large extent vested in the religious and cultural phenomenon we know as Hinduism. Unlike the word "Muslim," the term "Hindu" was not indigenous; it was in fact largely the Muslims who brought it to India. But once it was there it gradually found acceptance among the indigenous population, with the result that in the sixteenth to eighteenth centuries we find people identifying themselves as Hindus and even speaking of their religion as Hinduism (*Hindu-dharm*). This term provides us with a convenient label for a complex that was already in place before the Muslims arrived and that in the course of the twelfth to sixteenth centuries went on to develop some sense of its own unity in response to that intrusion. Its core was a very ancient ritual tradition perpetuated by the Brahmins with their sacred texts, the Vēdas, and their sacred language, Sanskrit. But Sanskrit was not just an arcane ritual language like Avestan in pre-Islamic Iran. It was also the language of India's learned elite and the high culture associated with it, including an extensive philosophical literature produced by a variety of schools; the most successful of these schools in our period was Vēdānta. Alongside the punctiliously ritual and abstractly philosophical components of the Hindu tradition there was a third: theistic religion, of which the two main variants were Śaivism—the worship of Śiva—and Vaiṣṇavism—the worship of Viṣṇu. This kind of religion often took on a highly emotive and devotional form (*bhakti*) and was typically articulated in poetry in one or another of the vernacular languages of India. The elements of this tripartite complex were subject to a significant degree of local variation. Thus Brahmins came in many different flavors—for example, most were vegetarians but those of Kashmir were meat eaters—and the texts of a couple of the Vēdas might vary because different transmissions prevailed in different parts of the country. The grammar of Sanskrit was uniform enough, but both its pronunciation and the script in which it was written could depend on the region. Moreover, Śaivism and Vaiṣṇavism were far enough apart that one could well see them as different religions, though the degree of toleration between divergent Indian religious traditions was relatively high. The picture was further complicated by the presence of ancient and—in our period—highly literate non-Hindu forms of Indian religion. Buddhism was still a significant presence in Sindh when the Arabs invaded it in the early eighth century, and Jainism remains part of the religious landscape to this day. The overall balance of unity and diversity in the Indian tradition is nicely caught in a fourteenth-century Sanskrit inscription. On the one hand, it names the land stretching from the Himalayas to the southern ocean with the single term Bhārata-varṣa, but on the other hand, it goes on to describe this land as diverse in language and customs and divided into many regions. The linguistic diversity was indeed considerable: whereas the north spoke Indo-Aryan languages, the south spoke varieties of a quite different language family, Dravidian.

India and the wider world

That pre-Muslim India was unusually self-contained did not mean that it had no contacts with the wider world, but it did work to limit them in some key respects. We should glance at the military, religious, and cultural implications of this relative isolation.

In military terms, the borders of the subcontinent were such as to discourage both Indian expansion and foreign invasion. The presence of the Indian Ocean on two sides of the triangle was an effective barrier to the projection of Indian military power farther than Ceylon. In the first half of the eleventh century a South Indian ruler dispatched a naval expedition to Southeast Asia, but this was unusual. Likewise, if naval efforts played any part in foreign conquests of India before the eighteenth century, it was at most an auxiliary one; only at that time did the maritime empires of European powers begin to pose a serious threat to Indian territory. On the northern side of the triangle the mountain ranges had a similar effect. In the northeast no Indian ruler ever took possession of Tibet, and Tibet in turn never seems to have posed a sustained military threat to the Gangetic plain—in contrast to the aggressive expansion of the Tibetan kingdom of the seventh to ninth centuries in other directions.

In the northwest, however, the natural barriers to movement into or out of India, though real, were less formidable. As far as outward movement was concerned, Indian expansion never took a military form, though there was Indian emigration from time to time, whether voluntary or coerced. We know this from historical information about a turbulent people of Indian origin known as the Ẓuṭṭ who are widely attested in the Middle East in the seventh to tenth centuries. It is also apparent from the later existence of small populations speaking languages of manifestly Indian origin not just in the Middle East but also much farther to the west; the Gypsies were in Ireland by 1516. But it was the movement of invaders into India that made history, this military asymmetry being an abiding characteristic of Indian history. For these intruders there were two major routes across the northwestern frontier. The first led through the passes of the Hindu Kush to the region of Kābul and on down to the Indus valley. Here the discouraging effect of the Hindu Kush was reinforced by the presence of fierce mountain tribes. This was nevertheless the route taken by Alexander the Great (ruled 336–323 BC) during his invasion of northwestern India in 327–325 BC. The second route avoided the mountains of Afghanistan and their well-armed inhabitants by taking a more southerly course through the region of Makrān. But to follow this coastal route was to court disaster owing to the extreme aridity that prevailed in most of this territory. It was by taking this route in reverse that Alexander returned from his Indian adventure with a very thirsty army. A third, intermediate route led eastward from Sīstān to Kābul, bypassing Makrān on the south and the worst of the mountains on the north, but it played only a minor role in our story. For those who were determined to invade India, the mountain route was probably the best option. Irrespective of the route taken, between Alexander and the Arabs we can count no fewer than six foreign peoples or dynasties that established their rule in northwestern India. Significantly, three of the peoples concerned seem to have been of steppe nomad origin. The most recent of them were the Hūṇas, alias the White Huns or Hephthalites. They appeared in India around 450, were a menace to the Guptas, and ceased to matter around 530. These invasions must have been traumatic in their time, but none of them left a permanently distinct foreign population in India. Instead, the invaders were eventually assimilated by the Indian society around them.

In religious terms, we see the direction of movement reversed. India exported religion on a large scale, spreading Buddhism overland to Central and East Asia and both Buddhism and Hinduism overseas to Southeast Asia. It did not, however, export it westward. In pre-Islamic times Buddhism was a prominent feature of the religious scene in the eastern Iranian world, in other words on the first lap of the overland route to China, but it had no wider presence in the Middle East. Part of the explanation for this asymmetry may be resistance: the dominance of Zoroastrianism and Christianity in the Middle East must have worked to block the spread of Buddhism there. Another part of it is that the spread of Buddhism or Hinduism in Central and Southeast Asia came packaged with the adoption of literacy for the first time, in the form of imported Indian scripts; by contrast, Indian religion offered no such bonus to the Middle East, though the same is also true of China. Whatever the reasons, commercial contacts between India and the Middle East had far less religious impact than those between India and Central or Southeast Asia. In general, however, India was a net exporter of religion, importing it only to a very limited degree. Thanks to Indian Ocean seafaring, Nestorian Christian communities were well established in southwestern India by the sixth century at the latest, but they had little impact on the mainstream of Indian society.

Despite the weakness of religious interaction between India and the Middle East, there was a certain amount of cultural exchange. In one direction, a Middle Persian text tells us that Shāhpuhr I (ruled 240–70), the second Sasanian ruler, "assembled and united with the Avesta" books on a variety of scientific and philosophical subjects that had been scattered in India, Rome, and elsewhere.[1] In the other direction, there is manifest Greek influence on Indian astronomy, and probable Greek influence on Indian medicine. Other possible interactions have a more random look about them. Thus it is suggestive that the way in which the Ethiopic

1. Quoted in H. W. Bailey, *Zoroastrian problems in the ninth-century books*, Oxford 1971, 81.

script represents vowels is unique in the Middle Eastern context, but mainstream in India. One factor that may have encouraged such exchanges was the existence of a band of territory, located in what is today southeastern Iran and southern Afghanistan, that in cultural terms was extensively Indianized, despite the fact that neither the rulers nor the mass of the population seem to have been ethnically Indian.

Muslim conquest and Muslim rule in India

Before we start on the long history of the Muslim expansion in India, we should pause to take note of what the invaders called the country: they spoke of it as Hind in Arabic or Hindūstān in Persian. Etymologically these terms go back to Sindhu, the Sanskrit name of the river we know as the Indus and of the country around it that we know as Sindh. Phonetically, an old Iranian sound change turned the initial S into H, and the Greeks and Romans then dropped it altogether, whence our "Indus" and "India." Semantically, the ancient Persians used their form of the word, Hindush, to refer to their province of Sindh, but for peoples to the west of India the terms came to include a much wider territory. As one might expect from this background, both Hind and Hindūstān were somewhat slippery terms. Both could be used in a larger sense that extended even to Southeast Asia, but also in narrower senses: Hind tended to exclude Sindh, while Hindūstān could refer to a limited territory within northern India that did not even include Delhi. Yet Bābur, an invader of the early sixteenth century, reassuringly defines Hindūstān in essentially the same way as the Hindus defined Bhārata-varṣa—sea on the east, south, and west, mountains on the north. This is tantamount to India as it was before the partition of 1947.

The Arab conquest and rule of the northwest

The Arabs knew in advance what Alexander had learned the hard way. According to a report received by the caliph ʿUthmān (ruled 644–56), the gateway to Sindh was a region in which the water was just a trickle, the dates were bad, and the robbers were bold; "a small army would be lost there, and a large army would starve."[2] This did not entirely discourage the Arabs. At an early date there was an unauthorized naval expedition to Sindh, and around the middle of the seventh century a force was sent into Makrān. But the early caliphs were against an

2. Quoted in A. Wink, "The early expansion of Islam in India," in *The new Cambridge history of Islam*, Cambridge 2010, 3:83–84. The same author's three-volume work *Al-Hind*, Leiden 1990–2004, covers Muslim India to the fifteenth century.

invasion of India, and it was not until about 711 that Ḥajjāj, the energetic governor of the East, sent a small army to conquer Sindh. Being Arabs, these troops and their camels were no doubt better able to withstand the desert conditions of Makrān than Alexander's army had been. In any case they did not get lost, duly reached Sindh, defeated a local king, and conquered the country at least as far as the city of Multān in the Punjab. They also had the backing of a naval force that brought troops, weapons, and equipment by sea. Given the limited size of the invading force, this conquest was a considerable military achievement.

The result was the rule of a very small minority of Arab Muslims over a very large majority of native Hindus and Buddhists, the latter concentrated in lower Sindh. What was distinctive about Sindh was that so far as we know, none of the secondary processes that reinforced the Arab presence elsewhere was operative. The key factors behind this were the harsh climate of Makrān, the limited carrying capacity of shipping, and the marginality of Sindh from the viewpoint of the center. Thus there was little prospect of the original army of conquest receiving substantial reinforcements. At the same time, there was only a sparse tribal population in Makrān that could have been converted to Islam and integrated into the forces of the invaders; in other words, there could be no counterpart to the role of the Berbers in the conquest of Spain. In addition, there was no way that Arab nomads could reach Sindh with their livestock and bring about the spread of Arabic and Islam among the rural population. It would not, then, have been surprising if the Arab conquerors had gone the way of earlier invaders of northwestern India and gradually disappeared into the indigenous population, some of whom they were undoubtedly recruiting into their ranks. But this was not what happened. Around 800 the politics of Sindh were still dominated by the Arab tribal factions—Northerners and Southerners—and it remained a province under governors hired and fired from the center into the 830s. Thereafter its history is somewhat obscure. Meanwhile, the extent of the territory under Muslim rule in northwest India may have waxed and waned, but over the long run it seems to have been fairly stable between the Arab and the Turkic invasions.

We are not well informed about the history of Islam in Sindh under Arab rule. As we might expect, the Muslims seem to have been relatively tolerant. The general who commanded the army of conquest is associated with the view that idolatrous Indian temples have the same status as Christian churches, Jewish synagogues, and Zoroastrian fire temples—in other words, their existence can be tolerated. This was in line with the doctrine of the Ḥanafī law school, according to which the poll tax, which entitled the community paying it to toleration, could be taken from all infidels with the exception of idolatrous Arabs. This school was already present in tenth-century Sindh, and it was the one that would prevail among the majority of Indian Muslims down the centuries. The

Ḥanafī view contrasts with that of the Shāfiʿite law school, according to which those who have no scripture are not eligible to pay the poll tax in lieu of converting. In any case, Muslim rule in the region does not seem to have been threatened by large-scale Hindu rebellion. In fact the most subversive development in tenth-century Sindh was not a resurgence of Hindu power, let alone of Buddhism, but rather the spread of a Muslim heresy, Ismāʿīlism. As we have seen, an Ismāʿīlī leader in Yemen had sent an agent to Sindh in the later ninth century, and the sect was entrenched in tenth-century Multān, not to be suppressed until the coming of the Sunnī Turks. Indeed, in a kind of heresy within a heresy, the locally popular Ismāʿīlī leader provoked the ire of his Fāṭimid superiors in Tunisia by allowing non-Muslim converts—most likely Hindus—to retain un-Islamic practices from their former religion, and in the next century we know of an Ismāʿīlī leader with a strikingly Indian name. Meanwhile in lower Sindh, Buddhism—unlike Hinduism—seems to have disappeared rather rapidly in the aftermath of the Arab conquest; perhaps the Buddhists in that region converted more readily to Islam. But the Ismāʿīlī evidence of conversion from Multān fits with incidental mentions in the mainstream Arabic sources. They tell us about Indian kings and commoners converting to Islam, or at least describe them as apostatizing from Islam, which implies that they had previously converted to it. We also hear of typical intermediate situations, such as a king who kept his conversion secret for fear of compromising his authority in the eyes of his subjects, and another who affected to be a Muslim while the townspeople remained idolaters. In addition, there is some indirect evidence of conversion from the Hindu side. We read that a Hindu jurist was sitting at ease on the banks of the Indus when he was asked a difficult question: How could Brahmins and others who had been carried off by barbarians—very likely Muslims—be purified and restored to membership of their castes? The concern here was not with beliefs but with actions, since those enslaved by barbarians could have been forced to dine with them, or have intercourse with their women, or kill cows. But this is at least an indication that Hindus were being exposed to conditions in which they were at high risk of converting to Islam; as we saw, the enslavement of captives was a significant source of conversion in the early years of Muslim rule in the Middle East.

Between the Arab and Turkic conquests no one invaded India by either the coastal or the mountain route. There were, however, recurrent Muslim attacks on the culturally Indianized periphery in the northwest, especially what is now southern Afghanistan, and these incursions came mostly via the intermediate route. At first they were the work of the armies of the caliphs, but real success came only with those of the early Ṣaffārids (861–1003). In 870 the founder of this upstart dynasty of eastern Iran, Yaʿqūb ibn Layth (ruled 861–79), took possession of Kābul. These attacks did not, however, spill over into the Indus valley.

The Turkic conquest of the northwest: Ghaznawids and Ghūrids

When we traced the expansion of Turkic power in the Middle East, we saw two very different processes at work. One was the movement of nomadic Turcoman tribes complete with their women, children, and livestock; this was what led to the emergence of the Seljuq dynasties of Iran and Anatolia. The other process was the use of Turkic slave soldiers and their rise to political power; this was behind the cascade of dynasties that established Turkic domination in Syria and Egypt. The first process is nomadic conquest, whereas the second, though it started earlier, has aptly been described as postnomadic.

In the Indian case, nomadic conquest was almost irrelevant. The bulk of India was either too dry or too wet, and in either case too hot, to support the grasslands that were the basis of steppe nomadism. Admittedly there is some evidence of the presence of Turkic nomads in early Islamic times to the south of the Hindu Kush, in the territory that in those days was culturally Indian. Some of these Turkic nomads were Oghuz, while others belonged to an obscure Turkic people known as the Khalaj or Khaljīs who were eventually assimilated by the Afghans. The presence of these nomads in the region is attested long before the eleventh-century Oghuz invasion of Iran, and the Khalaj, in particular, are described as ancient immigrants. But there is little to suggest that these Turkic groups had spread their nomadic way of life any farther into India. It was not that the arid regions of India lacked pastoral nomads, but the terrain was unsuitable for horses.

Instead, the process whereby the Turks conquered much of India was more like what happened in Syria and Egypt. In the Indian case, however, there was no Seljuq starting point for the process. The first link in the chain was in fact the Sāmānid dynasty (819–1005), the Iranian rulers of Transoxania and, from 900 onward, Khurāsān.[3] They were a long way from India, but their position in the far northeast of the Muslim world of their day meant that they had an extensive frontier with the Turkic nomads of the steppes. Around 900 they began to use this location to acquire a force of Turkic slave soldiers. As often in such cases, these Turks came to play a prominent role in Sāmānid politics, and it so happened that in 961 one of their leaders found himself on the losing side of a succession struggle. He and his men decided to make themselves scarce, which they did by withdrawing to Ghazna on the southeastern horizon of Sāmānid territory. Once there, their successive leaders regularized their position by offering formal submission to the Sāmānid rulers, who responded by appointing them as governors. In due course one of their leaders, Sebüktigin (ruled 977–97), succeeded in establishing the dynasty we know as the Ghaznawids (977–1186). As Sāmānid power

3. For what follows see C. E. Bosworth, *The Ghaznavids*, Edinburgh 1963.

disintegrated, this dynasty became fully independent and took over a large part of the territory the Sāmānids had formerly ruled. In other words, we have here a dynasty that, like the Zangids, was founded by an ambitious and successful Turkic slave soldier. When Sebüktigin died, the ensuing succession struggle was won by his energetic son Maḥmūd of Ghazna (ruled 998–1030).

Much of the energy of the first Ghaznawid rulers was deployed in eastern Iran. Here Maḥmūd took advantage of the lack of serious competition to build himself an empire. In 1017 he added Khwārazm to his domains, and in 1029 his troops invaded western Iran, seizing Iṣfahān. But both Sebüktigin and Maḥmūd were also active on the Indian front. Sebüktigin was still operating in the adjacent frontier zone, but Maḥmūd broke through into the Punjab and in the course of some seventeen campaigns raided widely in northwestern India and beyond, becoming famous for this as far afield as Muslim Spain. There was a clear military complementarity here: the season for warfare in eastern Iran was the summer, whereas in India it was the winter. The point of these Indian campaigns was less to acquire territory, though that happened, than it was to seize booty, particularly by robbing temples. It was these spoils that enabled Maḥmūd to maintain the large army with which he conquered new territories in Iran. This army was distinctly heterogeneous; a Ghaznavid envoy is said to have boasted to the Seljuq sultan, "You have only one kind of troops in your army, whereas we have ten different ones."[4] When deployed in India, moreover, it would be accompanied by large numbers of volunteer fighters for the faith (*ghāzīs*). But Turkic slave soldiers were its core. A Ghaznawid poet of the later eleventh century lauds the Turks as "the backbone and the right arm of the kingdom" and as "proud and restless warriors, courageous and expert." In sum, up to this point in their history the Ghaznawids were a Turkic dynasty of eastern Iran with a lucrative Indian back yard.

This changed after Maḥmūd's death. Following the usual succession struggle he was succeeded by his less able son Masʿūd (ruled 1031–40). This ruler's misfortune was the Oghuz invasion of Iran, and in 1040 a decisive defeat at the hands of the Seljuqs stripped the Ghaznawids of most of their Iranian empire. Masʿūd's response to this setback was extravagantly defeatist: he abandoned even the heartlands of his empire around Ghazna and took refuge in India, only to be deposed there by his own troops and killed soon after. In the event the dynasty was able to retain its heartlands and govern from Ghazna well into the 1150s. But by now India inevitably meant more to them. The Ghaznawids continued to campaign there, and Lahore became in effect a second capital. Indeed, from the 1160s their Indian possessions were all that was left to the Ghaznawids. They nevertheless made no major territorial gains in India between 1040 and the fall of the dynasty

4. For this and the quotations that follow see C. E. Bosworth, *The later Ghaznavids*, Edinburgh 1977, 54, 60.

in 1186. For most of this period their Indian domains were made up of Sindh and the Punjab, and toward the end of the dynasty only the Punjab remained.

The reason the Ghaznawid dynasty fell is that it was overcome by the next link in the chain, a rival dynasty known as the Ghūrids (early eleventh century to 1215). Like the Ayyūbids, the Ghūrids stemmed from one of the numerous mountain peoples of the Iranian world, in their case the inhabitants of the region of Ghūr in the highlands of what is today northwestern Afghanistan.[5] It was a remote region and remained pagan well into the eleventh century. Unlike the Kurdish Ayyūbids, the Ghūrids were a family that developed from a chieftaincy into a state while still in their mountains; they had a capital at Fērōzkōh—today known as Jām—to the east of Herat. For military purposes their natural resource, so to speak, was the martial population of the mountains, who fought as infantry. But if they were to range further afield they needed cavalry, and one way in which they met that need was by acquiring Turkic slave soldiers like everyone else. There was a time when they were vassals of the Ghaznawids, but as their power grew and that of the Ghaznawids waned, the Ghūrids began to outstrip them. In a telling episode of 1150 or so they sacked Ghazna itself. Later they took over the Ghaznawid heartlands, which is why the last Ghaznawid rulers found themselves confined to India. Then, under the rule of Muʿizz al-Dīn Muḥammad (ruled 1173–1206), the Ghūrids went on to help themselves to the Indian possessions of the Ghaznawids, putting an end to the dynasty. They also made new Indian conquests, taking Delhi in 1193 and opening the way for Muslim raiding of the Gangetic plain as far east as Bengal. All this was matched by Ghūrid expansion in Iran.

Soon the Ghūrids, in turn, disappeared into the maelstrom of the early thirteenth century. The Khwārazm-Shāhs ended the dynasty in 1215, taking over all but its Indian territories, only to be swept away themselves by the Mongols a few years later. In the early 1220s the last Khwārazm-Shāh, in the course of his efforts to resist or flee from the Mongols, spent two years in the Indus valley, and Chingiz Khān visited the region in person in hot pursuit of him. But the Khwārazm-Shāh fled India, taking the desperate route through Makrān, and never returned, though a Khwārazmian presence remained in India for another six years. The Mongols, by contrast, were back in 1241, when they destroyed Lahore, and as we will see they long continued to pose a military threat. Yet they never established their rule in any part of India.

The result of these commotions was a crucial transition: the Turkic commanders of Muʿizz al-Dīn Muḥammad were now left to make what they could of northern India independently of any political authority based outside the subcontinent.

5. The alternative to Ghūr and Ghūrids would be Ghōr and Ghōrids, reflecting an archaism of the Afghan and Indian pronunciation of Persian, but I use the forms commonly found in current secondary literature.

In fact they had already been more or less on their own ever since the death of Muʿizz al-Dīn in 1206, and it was not till the sixteenth century that an invasion of India would once again reshape its political geography in a lasting fashion. In other words, the exclusively Indian future to which the despondent Ghaznawid sultan Masʿūd had reconciled himself in 1040 was now for real. This situation could have had a number of outcomes. One might have been the end of Muslim rule in India in the absence of external support. In most of India, as elsewhere, Turkic cavalry had a pronounced military edge over indigenous forces; Amīr Khusraw (d. 1325), the most famous poet of the Delhi Sultanate and a Turk himself, remarked that "the Hindu always falls prey to the Turk."[6] But good horses were not to be taken for granted, as they were expensive to import and hard to maintain in the Indian climate. For the price of a warhorse in early fourteenth-century Delhi a man could acquire two, three, or even four concubines. There was indeed a brisk trade that brought warhorses to India by land from Central Asia and by sea from the Middle East, and the land route at least could be monopolized by a Muslim state ruling the northwest. But horses were still expensive. And in any case, good cavalry was not always enough to guarantee victory. In 1178, for example, no less outstanding a commander than Muʿizz al-Dīn had suffered a stinging defeat at the hands of an Indian ruler of Gujarat. In short, it was questionable whether an isolated Muslim presence in India would have the military resources to sustain itself. A second possible outcome of the early thirteenth-century cataclysms might have been the survival of Muslim rule, but only in a fragmented form. Muʿizz al-Dīn's commanders were a peer group, and different commanders quickly established themselves in different parts of the former Ghūrid territories. It is not hard to imagine such fragmentation persisting indefinitely. A third possible outcome would have been the creation of a single state ruling over all the Muslim-dominated lands of India. What actually happened was a mixture of these three divergent outcomes: occasional elements of the first, a large dose of the second, and enough of the third to allow us to outline what happened as a single story.

The Delhi Sultanate

The state that now concerns us is the Delhi Sultanate, which was in fact a succession of dynasties that—until the sixteenth century—had in common a capital city in Delhi or its neighborhood.[7] Conventionally the dates of the Delhi Sultanate are given as 1206–1555, but for now we will deal only with its history over the two centuries down to Tīmūr's brief but destructive visit in 1398–99. Like the Mamlūk state in Egypt in roughly the same period, the Delhi Sultanate was the

6. Quoted in P. Jackson, *The Delhi Sultanate*, Cambridge 1999, 213.
7. For what follows see Jackson, *The Delhi Sultanate*.

last link in a chain that brought Turkic power to a land inhospitable to steppe nomads and did so through the familiar vehicle of slave soldiers who took over when a hereditary dynasty came to an end. But there were differences as well as similarities.

One difference is simply that we are much better informed about the Turks of Egypt than we are about those of India. Another concerns the ethnicity and status of the military elite as a whole. That of the Mamlūks was not exclusively Turkic, but it was largely so until the Turks were joined in large numbers by the Circassians. The elite of the Delhi Sultanate was considerably more heterogeneous. This reflected the fact that India was close to the regions where the Mongol invasions caused maximum disruption, Central Asia and Iran, with the result that the pull factor of opportunities for employment in a well-funded sultanate was reinforced by a powerful push factor. The Delhi sultans responded not just by seeking to purchase slaves in Central Asia but also by inviting free notables of all kinds to come and join them. The result was a more varied pattern of immigration than we saw in the case of the Mamlūk slave trade. Within the elite the slave component certainly mattered, and alongside Turks acquired as slave soldiers there were also some Ethiopian and Indian slaves. Indeed, one Indian slave was briefly sultan. However, there was no equivalent to the Mamlūk exclusion of the sons of slave soldiers from participation in the military elite. Alongside the slaves, many members of this elite were recruited as free men. Some of these were Turks, and many were from the Ghaznawid and Ghūrid heartlands. Some stemmed from the Khalaj, who played a major role in establishing Muslim rule in Bengal, and as we will see they provided the Delhi Sultanate with one of its dynasties. The Khalaj, however, were Turks only in a rather etiolated sense, and by the time of the Delhi Sultanate they may well have been closer in character to the mountain tribesmen of Afghanistan than to their steppe ancestors. There were also straightforwardly Iranian mountaineers, notably Ghūrīs and Afghans. These recruits from Afghanistan complemented the Turkic presence in India just as the Berbers had complemented that of the Arabs in Spain. Alongside them we even encounter a prominent Tājīk commander. Meanwhile, native Indians served in the infantry, though in the age of the cavalry there was no room for an Indian counterpart of the Ottoman Janissaries. Yet despite all this heterogeneity, the state remained broadly Turkic; a poet of the early fourteenth century testified to the importance of knowing Turkic for a career in government or the army. Another significant contrast between the armies of the Mamlūks and those of the Delhi sultans concerns numbers. As we saw, a generous total for the Mamlūk army might have been twenty thousand men, whereas if we can set any store by the figures we find in the sources, the army of the Delhi Sultanate must have been larger by an order of magnitude. The comparison is crude but significant. By the standards of the Middle East, India was extraordinarily wealthy.

A final difference is largely a consequence of the heterogeneity of the military elite in India. It was much rarer for Delhi sultans than for Mamlūk sultans to start their careers as slave soldiers. In the first segment of their history, from 1206 to 1290, there were only three rulers of servile origin, though admittedly they were the ones that mattered most. Five descendants of the second—including one woman—ruled after him, a pattern that invites comparison with the rule of the descendants of Qalāwūn in Egypt. The next segment, from 1290 to 1320, was made up of a Khaljī and his four descendants; even if we reckon them as Turkic, they were born free. The final segment, from 1320 to 1398 (or in some fashion to 1412) was founded by Tughluq Shāh, a soldier who may have been a slave but more likely stemmed from the Qara'unas, a composite Turco-Mongol tribe based in southern Afghanistan. He and his rather indeterminate number of successors can thus be classed as Turks, but we cannot say for sure whether he was freeborn.

The immigrant military elite was complemented by immigrant Tājīk bureaucrats. Though we tend to hear less of them, they had the misfortune to be in the headlines in 1236 when many of them were killed by mutinous Turks. As already mentioned, the traumas of the Mongol invasion of Central Asia and Iran did much to encourage emigration to India, and this no doubt helped provide the rulers of Delhi with a supply of well-qualified administrators. The influx of bureaucrats and others from Iran was a major factor in ensuring that Persian was to become the prime language of administration and culture in Muslim India to the end of our period. The result was that large numbers of people for whom Persian was not a mother tongue, be they Turkic immigrants or Hindu natives, acquired the ability to function in Persian. Already under the Delhi Sultanate Hindu clerks were a significant presence in the bureaucracy, just as Hindu infantry were a part of the army, and the clerks, at least, became proficient in Persian.

When the commanders of the Delhi Sultanate were not engaged in fighting each other—as they often were, not least in cases of violent succession struggles—they tended to be at war on one of two fronts. To the northwest they fought defensively against formidable invaders. As we have seen, there were Mongol invasions in the early 1220s and again in 1241, and around the middle of the century Mongol raids were an annual event. Though the pressure eased later in the century, it was renewed in the 1290s from the Chaghatay Khānate, with Delhi itself in danger. The defenders did not always fight the Mongol threat wholeheartedly: there were times when one faction would seek to use the Mongols against another. Such invaders could do a lot of damage, as was to be the case with Tīmūr's sack of Delhi. But fortunately the Mongols disliked the Indian climate, and until the sixteenth century no new invaders were to make themselves at home in India.

To the south and east, by contrast, the troops of the Delhi Sultanate fought aggressively against the Hindus, over whom on balance they continued to enjoy military superiority. At times they sought to conquer and hold new territory, but for the most part they raided for booty—the booty that provided them with the resources to confront the menacing invaders in the northwest. Yet in the long run the acquisition of territory was of more consequence than the raiding. It tended to happen in spurts. As we have seen, there had been one in the late Ghūrid period, in the years leading up to the foundation of the Delhi Sultanate, if we take 1206 as its starting date. This spurt had extended Muslim rule over considerable territories to the south and east—to Delhi and as far east as Bengal. But the first segment of the Delhi Sultanate was marked by a lull, and the next spurt came only under the Khaljī rulers. It was with ʿAlāʾ al-Dīn Khaljī (ruled 1296–1316) that the conquest of the Deccan began in earnest, and Muḥammad ibn Tughluq (ruled 1325–51), in whose time the Delhi Sultanate was more extensive than ever before or after, went so far as to adopt one of the cities of the Deccan as a second capital. By now only the deep south of India was still beyond the boundaries of Muslim rule. Thereafter there was another lull, together with increasing disarray in the internal politics of the Delhi Sultanate in the years leading up to Tīmūr's invasion.

Before we leave the first two centuries of the Delhi Sultanate, a couple of unusual episodes in its history are worth attention. One is an early departure from the normal deference of Indo-Muslim rulers to Islam. We are told that ʿAlāʾ al-Dīn Khaljī was an illiterate and uneducated sultan who was much impressed by the mark the Prophet Muḥammad had made on the world thanks to the efforts of his four companions, meaning the Rightly Guided Caliphs. He would rant at drinking parties about emulating Muḥammad's success with four companions of his own. In response to this he was firmly advised to limit himself to the job description of a ruler and to consider the case of Chingiz Khān. Despite the rivers of blood this ruler had caused to flow, had not most of the Mongols converted to Islam, whereas not a single Muslim had become a Mongol or converted to the Mongol religion? So far as we can tell, ʿAlāʾ al-Dīn's impious fantasy was in no way related to the practical problems of governing India—unlike the innovative religion of the Mughal sultan Akbar some centuries later.

The other unusual episode was the brief rule of a woman. Unlike Shajar al-Durr, who was to rule more briefly still in Egypt a few years later, Raḍiyya Begum (ruled 1236–40) had not begun life as a slave. But her father Iltutmïsh was a Turkic slave who rose to be sultan, ruling from 1211 to 1236, and it was his Turkic slave soldiers who subsequently put his daughter on the throne. Given what we know about the role of women among the nomads of the steppes, it is unlikely to be accidental that both Raḍiyya and Shajar al-Durr were of Turkic descent and enmeshed in a Turkic milieu. Raḍiyya was also popular among the people of Delhi, but in the event she alienated the Turkic commanders by bestowing too much favor on an Ethiopian slave. That led to a conspiracy in which the slave was killed and Raḍiyya herself imprisoned. In league with her jailer—likewise a Turk—she then attempted a comeback, but this venture ended in defeat, after which she and her jailer were killed—as it happened by Hindus. That her killers were Hindus was felicitous because it made her a martyr, and by the time Ibn Baṭṭūṭa visited India a century later her tomb near Delhi had become a place of pilgrimage. Meanwhile, a contemporary chronicler writing in Delhi had praised her to the skies. She was "endowed with all the admirable attitudes and qualifications necessary for kings," including a talent for war. But he then went on to ask a question as acid as it was rhetorical: Since she was not a man, "of what advantage were all these excellent qualifications to her?"[8] Not being a man was indeed a problem. Like any female monarch in a Muslim society, what she had to confront was not only common or garden male chauvinism but also the incompatibility of the public lifestyle of rulers with the seclusion of women. Her response was to take the bull by the horns: she discarded her female clothing, donned the cloak and headdress of a man, and allowed herself to be seen by all and sundry as she mounted an elephant. When we come to Southeast Asia we will encounter a very different solution to this awkward dilemma.

The first age of fragmentation

The disarray in the years leading up to Tīmūr's invasion of 1398–99 brings us to another theme in the story of Muslim political domination in India—namely, its tendency to fragment. There is nothing unusual about this. In physics entropy always increases; in history things are less assured, but there is no doubt that entropy does often increase, and it is the times when it decreases that we should think of as anomalous. Particularly under premodern conditions, fragmentation was a frequent, though not inevitable, affliction of large-scale political structures the world over. In the Indian case the sheer size of the subcontinent meant that the process was liable to affect even the plains of the north, not to mention the hill country of the south. Any weakening of power at the center was an opportunity for actors in the provinces to seek greater autonomy or to break away altogether. Tīmūr's visit to India, not unlike his visit to Anatolia, contributed handsomely to that opportunity.

The period between his incursion and the coming of the Mughals in the sixteenth century was thus one in which the simultaneous existence of a plurality of Muslim states was the norm in India. In Delhi itself, following the twilight of the descendants of Tughluq Shāh in the opening years of the fifteenth century, we can distinguish three successive dynastic regimes. The first of them was established

8. Quoted in W. Walther, *Women in Islam*, Princeton 1992, 121.

by a former governor of Multān who had treacherously sided with Tīmūr during his invasion. He took over Delhi in 1414, founding a dynasty known as the Sayyids that lasted until 1451. They ruled a much-reduced territory, acknowledged the overlordship of the Tīmūrids, and did not even pretend to be sultans, though they did claim to descend from the Prophet. The background to the second dynasty was an influx of Afghan immigrants into fifteenth-century India. Afghans made up much of the elite under the Sayyids, and in 1451 an Afghan tribal chief courteously put the last Sayyid ruler out to graze and founded the Lōdī dynasty (1451–1526). The Lōdīs were made of sterner stuff than their predecessors and recovered a fair amount of the former territory of the Delhi Sultanate; the second of the three Lōdī rulers once again took the title of sultan. But the last ruler was perhaps excessively stern and proceeded to alienate his military elite. As a result, his governor of the Punjab sided with Bābur, the Tīmūrid—or Mughal—who invaded India in 1526 and ended the rule of the Lōdīs in an abortive attempt to establish his own power. Amid continuing Afghan resistance to the Mughals, Shēr Shāh Sūrī, an able and energetic Afghan who had been in the service of the Lōdīs, was at first content to rule Bihar as a Mughal vassal. Soon, however, he made claims to independence and countered Mughal forces so successfully that he took over the center and founded the third dynasty, that of the Sūrīs (1540–55). He ruled much of northern India and made extensive use of muskets and artillery, but his dynasty, the last that is reckoned to the Delhi Sultanate, was short-lived. By now, however, the term "Delhi Sultanate" had long been something of a misnomer. The second Lōdī ruler had in fact moved his capital to Āgrā in 1505, and thereafter it was Āgrā rather than Delhi that served as the capital city for the Sūrīs and to a considerable extent for the Mughals.

If such were the fortunes of the center in this period, what of the provinces? We should begin by noting that fragmentation had dogged the Delhi Sultanate from the start. The first of the Delhi sultans in the conventional reckoning was Quṭb al-Dīn Aybak (ruled 1206–10), though in fact he was based in Lahore and may well not have claimed to be sultan. When he died in 1210, two rival warlords emerged, one based in Delhi and the other in Multān. It was the one in Delhi, Iltutmïsh, who was the real founder of the sultanate; he began his reign in 1211, but it was not until 1228 that he eliminated his rival. So we are looking at variations on a theme that had been prominent long before Tīmūr's invasion. The subsequent period was different only in that it was now easier for provincial dynasties to maintain long-term independence, particularly in regions far from the center. A standard handbook counts no fewer than fourteen Muslim dynasties that were established in India after the formation of the Delhi Sultanate but before that of the Mughal Empire. We can best sample them by concentrating on three outlying regions: Bengal in the east, the Deccan in the south, and Gujarat in the west. Besides distance from the center, each of these regions had immediate access to a potential source of revenue denied to the landlocked center: the commerce of the Indian Ocean.

Bengal was particularly prone to break away from the center. Its distance from Delhi, its rich agricultural resources, and its maritime commerce combined to provide a tempting foundation for independence. Indeed, it had a dynastic history reaching back several centuries before the Muslim conquest, the dynasty driven out by the Muslims being the Sēnas. Muslim rule was first established in 1204 by an Afghan adventurer who acted with the permission of Quṭb al-Dīn Aybak, then the leading Ghūrid commander in India, and formally recognized the authority of the distant Ghūrids. But soon Bengal drifted away, with a couple of its rulers claiming sovereignty, and it was not till the early 1230s that Iltutmish brought the region under the control of Delhi. Subsequently it can sometimes be hard to say whether at any given moment Bengal was the easternmost province of the Delhi Sultanate or an independent state. Raḍiyya at one point made a questionable deal with the then ruler of Bengal, conferring on him a ceremonial parasol, a symbol of sovereignty. Subsequently Bengal was clearly independent under the rule of a Turkic dynasty that held power from 1287 to 1324. Delhi then reasserted its power, but Bengal slipped away once more in the 1330s, to be taken over by an upstart dynasty of obscure origin, the Ilyāsids, who ruled it until 1414 and then again from 1437 to 1487. In the intermission from 1414 to 1437 a local Hindu lord, Rājā Ganēsh, seized power, and after 1487 the dynasty's Ethiopian slaves took over for a few years. This latter is a striking but by no means isolated testimony to the reach of the Indian Ocean slave trade; we are told that in 1494 five thousand Ethiopians constituted the bulk of the royal guard in Bengal. But throughout this later turbulence the region remained independent of Delhi, as it continued to be until conquered by Shēr Shāh Sūrī in 1538. Only in the 1570s did it become a Mughal province.

In this long and involved story the intermission of 1414–37 is just a minor episode, but a significant one nonetheless. It seems natural enough that some Hindus would take advantage of the fragmentation and disarray among their Muslim rulers to attempt to evict them from power, and it figures that this should have been particularly true of Bengal, which thanks to the delta of the Ganges was "a land for foot soldiers"[9] in which Muslim cavalry was relatively ineffective. Yet as a general rule in this period, once Muslim power had been established for some time in a sizeable region of India, it was there to stay. In this case it is striking that we have to wait over two centuries for a Hindu interlude, one in which the Hindu Rājā Ganēsh, described by a contemporary source as "a landholder of four hundred

9. Quoted in Jackson, *The Delhi Sultanate*, 90.

years' standing," became the ruler of Bengal[10] and a local Ṣūfī protested that "infidelity has gained predominance and the kingdom of Islam has been spoiled."[11] It is also noteworthy that we have no indication of the revival of the trappings of Hindu kingship at this time, such as the minting of coins with images of Hindu gods, and that in any case the interlude was so brief: the son of Rājā Ganēsh, who ruled from 1418 on, had already converted to Islam. In short, a Muslim-dominated region, even one as remote as Bengal, could break away from the center without incurring a serious risk of succumbing to a Hindu restoration.

Our second outlying region is the Deccan, the territory to the south of the Vindhyas but excluding the southern tip of the peninsula.[12] This is a much larger region than Bengal, and with the two coasts sandwiching a semiarid interior it did not lend itself to the rule of a single dynasty. At the time when the Muslims began to pay attention to the Deccan it was divided between four major Hindu kingdoms, two on the western side of the peninsula and two on the eastern side. Apart from a devastating raid in 1296, the Delhi sultans had left the Deccan alone until the opening years of the fourteenth century—very much in contrast to the early invasion of Bengal. The Yādavas, who ruled the northwestern Deccan (roughly today's Maharashtra), were the first of the four dynasties to be attacked. They were the target of the raid of 1296, and by 1318 they had succumbed to Muslim conquest. It was their capital city, Dēvagiri, that became a second capital for the Delhi Sultanate in 1327. Meanwhile in 1303–4 the Muslims had also started to campaign against the Kākatīyas, who ruled the northeastern Deccan (roughly Andhra Pradesh as it was until the division of the state in 2014); they went down to Muslim conquest in 1323. It was not long before the same treatment was meted out to the Pāndyas in the southeast (in part of today's Tamil Nadu) and the Hōysalas in the southwest (roughly today's Karnataka). In the course of the first decades of the fourteenth century the Delhi Sultanate had thus acquired a vast new territory in the south, but it failed to consolidate its hold on it, and the tide of Muslim conquest was partly reversed in the early 1330s by a massive Hindu rebellion extending over much of the Deccan. One outcome of this insurrection was the formation of a powerful new Hindu state, Vijayanagara (1336–1565), which expanded to occupy roughly the territory that had been held by the Hōysalas. Only in the northwestern Deccan did the Delhi Sultanate remain in control. Even this was soon to be lost, but in this case to Muslims rather than Hindus. It so happened that the officials in charge of the collection of taxes there learned that they were likely to be punished severely for having allegedly been remiss in their duties, so they rebelled rather than await the sultan's pleasure. The result was the establishment

10. Quoted in R. M. Eaton, *The rise of Islam and the Bengal frontier*, Berkeley 1993, 51.

11. Quoted in Eaton, *The rise of Islam and the Bengal frontier*, 53.

12. For what follows see K. A. Nilakanta Sastri, *A history of South India*, Madras 1966.

of the breakaway Bahmanid dynasty (1347–1527), based in the region over which the Yādavas had formerly reigned. It was not until the expansion of Mughal power in the late sixteenth and seventeenth centuries that the rulers of northern India once again held sway over the Deccan.

There are three features of the history of the Bahmanid dynasty that are worthy of note. The first is their considerable territorial expansion. At their height they possessed territory on both coasts, to the west and to the east. What is more, down to the late fifteenth century they remained, with a minor exception, the sole Muslim state in the Deccan. The minor exception was a small state in the far southeastern Deccan that was founded by a rebellious governor in 1334 and conquered by Vijayanagara around 1377—a rare but noteworthy example of Hindus conquering Muslims in this period.

The second feature concerns the domestic politics of the Bahmanids. There was of course plenty of the usual skullduggery, but one aspect of the discord is distinctive. For much of the fifteenth century the Bahmanid state was riven by tension between two groups among its servitors: the homegrown Muslims of the Deccan and the foreigners who had come to India to seek their fortunes. The foreigners were known as Āfāqīs, "people from the horizons," in contradistinction to Dakhnīs, "the people of the Deccan"; many of the Āfāqīs were also Shīʿites, whereas the Dakhnīs were Sunnīs. In such a case it can be difficult to determine which source of tension was primary, but the fact that contemporaries labeled the parties in geographical rather than sectarian terms encourages us to put more weight on geography. The tension went deep and could lead to the perpetration of massacres on both sides. Quite why this tension should have been more intense in the Bahmanid state than at other times and places in the history of Muslim India is not obvious, since the employment of talented foreigners in the state apparatus was nothing unusual.

The third feature is the way the dynasty ended. The background was a combination of intense factional conflict and an ineffective ruler, and the outcome was the breakup of the state into five separate fragments. Of these the state of Aḥmadnagar, for example, was ruled by the Niẓām Shāhī dynasty (1490–1636), and it held sway over much of what is today Maharashtra. To its south was Bījāpūr, ruled by the ʿĀdil Shāhī dynasty (1490–1686), and so on. Each of these fragments was in the possession an insider who took it over, though the origins of these insiders varied—one was a Turkic slave, another was a Hindu convert, and a third was a scion of the Qara Qoyunlu dynasty who had made his way to India. In religious terms two of the resulting states were Sunnī, two were Shīʿite, and the remaining one flip-flopped. These principalities, despite the rather adventitious way in which they had come about, showed remarkable durability. Only one of them lasted for less than a century, and two of them were still there the best part of two centuries later. Eventually each of them came to an end through absorption either by one of its peers or by the Mughals. The Bahmanid dynasty itself lasted in some manner till 1527, but its last rulers were puppets. Two things were significantly absent from the story of the breakup of the Bahmanid state. One was any attempt by the Delhi sultan of the day—one of the Lōdīs—to take advantage of the disorder to reclaim the Bahmanid territories for the center. In fact, the prime Muslim enemies of the Bahmanids were the provincial Muslim states immediately to their north—Gujarat and Mālvā—and not the Delhi Sultanate. The other thing that was absent was any move toward a Hindu restoration. In the 1330s, when Hindu rule was still a living memory all over the Deccan, restoring it was very much on the agenda, but a century and a half later the Bahmanid state could disintegrate without endangering Muslim supremacy. This is surprising. In comparison with northern India, the Muslim population of the Deccan had always been thin, with the result that Muslim states there had of necessity to employ large numbers of Hindus. And as we will see later in this chapter, the Hindus did not keep quiet forever.

Our third and last outlying region is Gujarat in the west. Though by no means as well watered as Bengal, it possessed rich agricultural plains to the east, and its Indian Ocean commerce was much more developed in this period. Like Bengal, it was a reasonably well-defined region that for centuries prior to the Muslim conquest had lent itself to the dominance of a single major dynasty. Here the counterpart of the Sēnas was the Caulukyas, who ruled Gujarat from the tenth to the thirteenth century. This dynasty included a Jain king of the mid-twelfth century who is said to have been so zealous an exponent of nonviolence that he fined people for killing fleas, but it was a later Caulukya monarch who inflicted that crushing defeat on a Ghūrid army in 1178. The Caulukya capital was then raided by Quṭb al-Dīn Aybak in 1197, at about the same time that the Muslims penetrated Bengal. Yet in contrast to Bengal, it was over a century before the Muslims conquered the lion's share of Gujarat, and in the interval between the raid and the conquest there had been a change of dynasties from the Caulukyas to a leading noble family of the kingdom, the Vāghēlās (ca. 1244–1304). The conquest of most of Gujarat was at their expense, and it followed a devastating raid in 1298 as part of the Khaljī expansion. Thereafter Muslim Gujarat was ruled for about a century by a tumultuous succession of governors appointed from Delhi. But in the last years of the fourteenth century the power of Delhi was weakening, and Tīmūr's invasion ended it for the foreseeable future. Hence the last of these governors—the son of a Punjabi convert to Islam—had the opportunity to found a dynasty that ruled independently of the center from 1403 to 1573. This dynasty was involved in frequent wars with its neighbors, both Hindu and Muslim, but surprisingly it was not till around 1470 that peninsular Gujarat (Saurāṣṭra) was taken from its Hindu rulers.

Meanwhile, the center played no significant part in the history of Gujarat until the coming of the Mughals. The Gujaratis lost a war with them in the 1530s, and the Mughals finally completed their conquest of Gujarat in 1573.

Two further features of the political history of the Gujarati sultanate are worth noting. One concerns the muted part played in it by Hindus. In contrast to Bengal, there was no figure like Rājā Ganēsh in the dynastic history of Gujarat, nor was there any parallel to the large-scale Hindu rebellion in the Deccan. Instead, resistance came only from neighboring Hindu rulers who had not yet been subjected to Muslim rule. The other feature concerns the role of the sea. Despite the importance of Indian Ocean trade, in the centuries before the Portuguese appeared in 1498 maritime violence was mostly a matter of endemic piracy—self-respecting territorial states made war on land, not at sea. But now naval warfare became the order of the day, as it had long been in the Mediterranean. The Gujaratis were on the winning side in 1508, when a fleet assembled jointly with the Mamlūks defeated the Portuguese, but the tables were turned in 1509. Thereafter the Portuguese were mostly left to rule the waves; as one sixteenth-century sultan of Gujarat memorably put it, "Wars by sea are merchants' affairs, and of no concern to the prestige of kings."[13] Yet the maritime power of the Portuguese directly affected only the coasts, where they sought to acquire strategic ports such as Goa to the south of Gujarat, which they seized in 1510, and Diu on the southern tip of peninsular Gujarat, which they took in 1535. There was as yet no serious threat to the interior, where the shifting capital cities of Gujarat were located and where Muslim sultans and Hindu kings continued to fight each other in traditional fashion. In this respect the Gujarati sultanate was typical of Indian states of any size, whether Hindu or Muslim: even if such a kingdom had a coast, it would rule it from the interior.

Before leaving this period of fragmentation it is worth underlining the absence of major Hindu rebellions outside the recently conquered south. The only instance of Hindu assertiveness we have encountered so far in the north is the rather indeterminate interlude of the rule of Rājā Ganēsh in Bengal. To this we could add a widespread peasant revolt in the 1330s closer to the center. Here in response to fiscal oppression the cultivators, who must have been predominantly Hindu, burned their crops, drove off their cattle, and took refuge in the jungle. This was a real peasant revolt of the kind we did not encounter in the Middle East, but in the event it was no parallel to the peasant movement that led to the expulsion of the Mongols from China and the establishment of the native Ming dynasty there.

13. Quoted in M. N. Pearson, *Merchants and rulers in Gujarat*, Berkeley 1976, 91.

The beginnings of the Mughal Empire

The period of fragmentation was ended by the formation of the Mughal Empire.[14] This was an unlikely occurrence, whether we look at it within a purely Indian context or in a wider framework that includes the Indian Ocean, Central Asia, and Iran.

In the Indian context, as we have seen, the authority of the Delhi sultans over such outlying areas as Bengal, the Deccan, and Gujarat had been short-lived. Only for a few years in the 1320s had the center ruled all three of them simultaneously, and after 1403 it had not ruled any of them. In other words, by the sixteenth century a plurality of Muslim states had for long been the normal pattern in India. Admittedly the course of Indian history both before and after the coming of the Muslims showed that the formation of states of imperial dimensions was a possibility, but it did not happen often enough to suggest that the chances of such an outcome were high.

Bringing in the Indian Ocean further reduces those chances. The sixteenth and subsequent centuries saw the sea play an increasing role in India's relations with the outside world. Fundamentally this was a matter of the gradual expansion of transoceanic commerce, but it was dramatized by a sudden change in the route by which military innovation reached India. Until the sixteenth century it did so exclusively overland, as in the days when invaders brought forms of cavalry warfare derived from the steppes. But from now on military innovation increasingly arrived by sea. This was mostly how muskets and artillery were imported to India, together with people who knew how to use them. There was still great agricultural wealth in the Indian interior, but the relative weight of the coasts and the interior was shifting in favor of the coasts. This was the trend that would eventually lead to a situation in which the three most dynamic cities of India were the upstart ports of Bombay, Madras, and Calcutta (today's Mumbai, Chennai, and Kolkata)—cities on or close to the Indian Ocean that did not exist as such before the Europeans appeared. Given that India has ocean on two sides, the enhanced maritime pull was likely to prove centrifugal, and under such conditions the formation and maintenance of an imperial state with its base in the center of the subcontinent became that bit less likely.

Of course, Indian empires did not have to arise from purely internal processes; they could also be the work of invaders. This is where Central Asia and Iran have an obvious relevance. As we have seen, the invasions of India that had lasting impact in Muslim times were driven by strong and expansive states based outside the subcontinent: first the Caliphate in the Middle East and then the Ghaznawids and their successors, the Ghūrids, in what is now Afghanistan. But in the sixteenth

14. For its history see J. F. Richards, *The Mughal empire*, Cambridge 1993.

century there were no such states in sight. The Özbegs in Transoxania repeatedly invaded Khurāsān, but they never invaded India, while the Ṣafawids were usually on the defensive on other fronts and showed no interest in expanding their territories beyond the region of Qandahār. And yet as we will see, both the Özbegs and the Ṣafawids were to play key roles in the formation of a new imperial state in India.

Bābur (ruled 1526–30), the founding figure of what came to be called the Mughal Empire, was the son of a Tīmūrid prince. His father, whom he describes as portly, pious, and a heavy drinker, ruled in Farghāna until he met his death by falling into a ravine at the age of thirty-nine, leaving the eleven-year-old Bābur to succeed him. Like any Tīmūrid worth his salt, Bābur was ambitious, and we soon find him competing with his kinsmen for the possession of Samarqand, a bigger prize than Farghāna. He held the city twice in his early years, but on the second occasion he lost it not to a rival Tīmūrid prince but to the Özbegs, who were henceforth to be the bane of his life. This misfortune led to a period of *qazaqlïq*, as we saw in an earlier chapter. In 1504 he nevertheless succeeded in establishing himself in Kābul—a reassuringly long way from the Özbegs—with the result that India was now on his horizon. Yet apart from some minor raids, until the last years of his life he showed more interest in recovering Samarqand and seizing Qandahār; he even went to the length of professing Shīʿism to secure Ṣafawid support against the Özbegs. But eventually he was invited to intervene in the internal struggles of the Lōdīs, invaded India, and won a crucial battle in 1526. He then took Delhi and Āgrā, and by the time of his death in 1530 he had conquered a large expanse of Indian territory. So in these years he achieved success on a scale quite different from that of any of his earlier efforts.

It was not, however, the success that he had craved. As he tells us in his memoirs, he found India dreary. "The cities and provinces of Hindūstān are all unpleasant. All cities, all locales are alike."[15] There was "no beauty in its people, no graceful social intercourse, no poetic talent or understanding, no etiquette, nobility, or manliness"—and worse yet, "no good horses, meat, grapes, melons or other fruit." Altogether, it was "a place of little charm." But it did have an undeniable merit: its economic productivity. "The one nice aspect of Hindūstān," he remarks, "is that it is a large country with lots of gold and money." He then generously adds a further nice aspect: "the unlimited numbers of craftsmen and practitioners of every trade." Though he died in Āgrā, his body was moved a few years later to a grave in a garden in Kābul. He would have liked that: Kābul was not home, but it was a cut above India, and in his opinion it had the most pleasant

15. For this and the following remarks of Bābur see *The Baburnama*, trans. W. M. Thackston, New York 1996, 334, 350, 351.

climate in the world. India might be a good place for a refugee prince to collect booty and taxes, but it was a terrible place to have to live, let alone die.

If the role of the Özbegs was to leave Bābur with nowhere to go but India, the role of the Ṣafawids was to help his son and successor Humāyūn (ruled 1530–40 and 1555–56) to return there. Humāyūn had joined his father in his invasion of India but had then gone off to Central Asia in a typical attempt to recover Samarqand—hope springs eternal. But he was back in India in time to succeed to his father's throne without incident in 1530. For several years he did well, winning a war against the sultan of Gujarat, but when he went east to challenge Shēr Shāh Sūrī he suffered disastrous defeats in 1539 and 1540. Like his father, he was now on the run, and like the Ottoman prince Bāyezīd a few years later, he ended up as a guest of the Ṣafawid ruler Ṭahmāsp. But he did better than Bāyezīd: though like his father he had to profess to be a Shīʿite, Ṭahmāsp left him alive, allowed him to leave, and even sent him on his way with a force of twelve thousand men. In 1545 Humāyūn was able to repossess Kābul, the city where he had been born, and after various alarms and excursions he mounted an invasion of India in 1554. At first it went well, and in 1555 he was enthroned in Delhi. But the next year he fell down the stairs of his library and died of his injuries. It was not a good time to die, as his son and successor Akbar was a mere thirteen years old.

For a couple of dispossessed princes in search of a kingdom, Bābur and Humāyūn had put on remarkable performances. Each had triumphed against all odds, but their roller-coaster careers had left them with little opportunity for state building. At the point at which Humāyūn fell down the stairs there was as yet no such thing as a Mughal Empire, and given the conjunction of an abundance of enemies with the accession of a ruler who was only just a teenager, the prospect that a Mughal Empire would emerge in the future was still slim.

The history of the Mughal Empire

As might be expected, the first years of the reign of Akbar (ruled 1556–1605) were troubled. Despite Humāyūn's military successes there were still Sūrī claimants and Afghan forces to mop up. Akbar was remarkably broadminded in his appreciation of diversity, but he never lost his dislike of Afghans, whom he was still fighting in the 1580s. More alarming was the rebellion of Hēmū soon after Akbar's accession. This Hēmū was a Hindu general who had been in the service of the Sūrīs, and he now claimed the throne, calling himself Rājā Vikramāditya and seizing Delhi. But for a stroke of good luck, his forces could easily have defeated the much smaller Mughal army. This was surprisingly late in the day for a counterpart of Rājā Ganēsh to appear at the center. It was also a notably strong assertion of Hindu restorationism: Vikramāditya was a legendary Hindu king who drove the Śaka invaders out of Ujjayinī in Madhya Pradesh and then ruled over the whole of a happy and prosperous India. Meanwhile, Akbar's loyal and able guardian Bayrām Khān, a Shīʿite scion of the Qara Qoyunlu who had recruited many Persians into the service of the Mughals, rocked the boat by appointing too many fellow Shīʿites to high office. The resulting tension is reminiscent of the factional conflict we saw at the Bahmanid court. Bayrām Khān fell from power in 1560, leaving the ship of state somewhat rudderless for the next few years. This could well have been disastrous, for between 1564 and 1567 Akbar confronted a dangerous combination of rebellious Özbeg nobles, a half brother who was supposed to be content to govern Kābul but was not, and a group of unemployed Tīmūrid princes who tried to seize Delhi. But thereafter affairs of state were in better shape, and the danger that Akbar would end up sharing the vagabond life of his father and grandfather receded. Instead he enjoyed a reign that proved longer than the checkered lifespans of either of them, and he seems to have felt pretty much at home in India. It was under his rule that an empire was created that would last into the early eighteenth century—and formally until 1858.

We can sketch the history of this empire in terms of three major themes: the expansion of the territory it ruled, the structure of the state that ruled this territory, and the way in which it managed—or omitted to manage—succession to the throne. In the case of the first two themes we can best start by looking at the reign of Akbar as the founder, and then at those of the three subsequent Mughal rulers who shared his imperial stature: Jahāngīr (ruled 1605–27), Shāh Jahān (1628–57), and Awrangzēb (1658–1707).

It was Akbar who expanded Mughal territory most dramatically. His main achievements were three. First, over the course of his long reign he brought all the Muslim states of northern India into his empire, including Gujarat in two quick campaigns in 1572–73 and Bengal in a long, slow slog beginning in the 1570s and continuing into the 1580s. Second, in 1567 he defeated the prestigious Rājpūt ruler of Mēvāṛ in southwestern Rajasthan—the Rājpūts being the archetypal Hindu warriors and rulers of Rajasthan and other parts of northern India. This opened the door to a general understanding with the Rājpūt rulers of Rajasthan whereby they joined the Mughal polity as accredited members of the Mughal aristocracy. Akbar was now in possession of the entire north of India. Third, he initiated the extension of Mughal power to the south. His demand in 1591 that the Muslim sultanates of the region submit to him had little effect, but between 1595 and 1601 he conquered a fair amount of territory in the northwestern Deccan. Altogether these were enormous gains, and there were no territorial losses to set against them. They were also profitable: Akbar never confronted a budget deficit. In this connection there is a certain prudence to be discerned in the limits of his efforts to expand on the northern frontier of India. He did not go beyond Qandahār, Kashmir, and the Rājpūt statelets of the Himalayan mountain valleys—and Qandahār was handed to him on a plate in 1595.

Akbar's successors continued to campaign vigorously over most of the seventeenth century, but with diminishing returns in both north and south. Their attempts to push further up the valley of the Brahmaputra in the far northeast involved costly campaigns in which territory would be gained in one war and lost in another. In the far northwest they lost Qandahār in 1622, recovered it in 1638, and lost it for good in 1648; over the next five years they mounted three fruitless campaigns to recover it. On the Central Asian front, ever the object of Tīmūrid daydreaming, they dispatched an army of sixty thousand to intervene in an Özbeg civil war. It occupied Balkh in 1646 but had to abandon it the following year—for one thing, the land around the city was too poor to supply so large an army with the food it needed. On the southern front, Jahāngīr, Shāh Jahān, and Awrangzēb were all active. In 1636 the two surviving Muslim sultanates of the Deccan agreed to recognize Mughal overlordship. The result was a temporary easing of Mughal pressure that gave them an opportunity to extend their own territories farther to the south at the expense of the Hindu rulers of the region. Thereafter, in the 1680s, Awrangzēb renewed the pressure, conquering both sultanates in 1685–87. As of 1689, the Mughal frontier was now as far south as the Muslim domination of India would ever reach. But this was not quite the triumph it sounds like. Awrangzēb was very successful in eliminating rival states, but despite the inordinate amount of time he spent in the Deccan, he failed to pacify the region. One aspect of the disorder there was particularly debilitating: a new Hindu adversary, the Marāṭhās, had appeared in the middle of territory long subject to Muslim rule. We will meet them again.

In sum, three things about the territorial record of the Mughals are noteworthy. The first is the unprecedented extent of the territory they possessed, ruling as they did the whole of India bar the far south. The second is the contrast between the profitable conquests of Akbar and the costly ventures of his successors. The third is that until the Marāṭhās began to make serious trouble in the later decades of the seventeenth century, the Mughals were not losing territory to others on any significant scale. In this respect there is a marked contrast with the unsteady trajectory of the Delhi Sultanate, where, as we saw, periods of expansion were followed by periods of contraction.

Let us turn now to the structure of the Mughal state, again starting with the reign of Akbar. Of several major components of this structure, the first was Akbar himself. He was by any standards a remarkable ruler. He possessed all the usual virtues of an effective monarch—he was intelligent, courageous, decisive, organized, attentive both to detail and to the larger picture, charismatic, likable, and accessible. A Portuguese Jesuit commenting on his death catches something of his personal style with the remark that Akbar was "the same to everyone, be they natives, foreigners, small or great. . . . Everyone felt they had him on their side."[16] In addition, he possessed in abundance the gift of imagination, and as we will see he made striking use of it in constructing his empire. He was also curious about many things. Like some other rulers we have encountered he was illiterate, though not for want of instruction—he may well have been dyslexic. But this disability did not stop him from taking an educated interest in books and their contents. He was one of the few rulers in the Muslim world of his day who had large numbers of European printed books in his library. He was also endowed with unfailing energy, and it is no surprise that early in his reign he decided to do without a vizier. Instead he dealt directly with four ministers, each of whom was assigned a distinct sphere of action. This quadripartite structure was replicated in the provinces. Something else that was absent from Akbar's court is the phenomenon of conspicuously powerful women. This was not, however, typical of the Mughals as a whole. Bābur had great respect for the political acumen of his maternal grandmother, and Akbar's son Jahāngīr deferred to his wife Nūr Jahān to the point of including her name on his coins.

Akbar's self-assurance owed much to his personal qualities, but not everything. He was also part of a dynasty that stretched back to Tīmūr and before that, albeit in the female line, to Chingiz Khān. This was a lineage that carried prestige even outside Central Asia and the steppes. A Tīmūrid was a prince born to be king, for all that his chances of attaining his royal destiny were often limited by mundane political realities—too many princes, not enough kingdoms. This sense of ancestral pride made the Mughal Empire very different from the genealogically scruffy Delhi Sultanate, where the most effective rulers of the thirteenth century began their careers as slaves, and none had plausible claims to descend from the great sovereigns of the wider world. Tīmūr accordingly featured prominently in the imagination of the Mughal dynasty, figuring in both the art and the texts it generated. So did the fantasy of reconquering the family's original possessions in Central Asia—Awrangzēb was still dreaming of it in the later seventeenth century. The same went for the old Tīmūrid fidelity to the Turco-Mongol customary law (*törä*) associated with Chingiz Khān. Bābur, as we saw, was no fundamentalist in his attitude to it, but his successors continued to refer to it into the seventeenth century. Yet another aspect of the Tīmūrid heritage was linguistic. Knowledge of Chaghatay Turkic, the language of Bābur's memoirs, was preserved in the ruling family into the nineteenth century, though from the late sixteenth century onward it seems to have been a language learned through study with a tutor rather than a mother tongue. A member of the royal lineage writing in 1810 considered

16. Quoted in M. Alam and S. Subrahmanyam, *Writing the Mughal world*, New York 2012, 161–62.

himself the only Mughal prince of his generation who had good Turkic; he had learned it from three teachers, one of whom attributed the decay of Mughal power to the declining use of Turkic in favor of the Persian that prevailed among the Mughal elite—and in which the prince himself was writing.

Below the princes of the blood, the next component was the Mughal aristocracy. It was a freeborn aristocracy—powerful military slaves of the kind so prominent in the Mamlūk and Ottoman states, not to mention the Delhi Sultanate, played no part in the Mughal Empire. As befits an imperial aristocracy, it was diverse in its origins. When Humāyūn returned to India in 1555, he had with him fifty-one nobles, most of whom belonged to one of two groups of unequal size. Twenty-seven of them were "Tūrānīs," that is to say men of Central Asian (and Sunnī) background, be it Chaghatay or Özbeg, who were the unrepentant heirs of a notoriously insubordinate political culture. Another sixteen were "Īrānīs," meaning that they came from Iran (and were Shīʿites), though they could well be of Turcoman background like Bayrām Khān. Their political culture tended to make them more dependable than the Tūrānīs. This was the elite that Akbar inherited, and he was clearly not very happy with it. By 1580 he had one that was more of his choosing. It was much larger; he had expanded it from fifty-one to 222. Within that total we can identify four major groups of roughly equal numbers: forty-eight Tūrānīs, forty-seven Īrānīs, forty-four descendants of Muslim families already established in India, and the best part of forty-three Rājpūts. The absolute number of Tūrānīs had thus increased significantly, but they no longer dominated the aristocracy as a whole. The old Muslim families later came to include a small but increasing number of Afghans, despite Akbar's dislike of them. One obvious feature of this elite was the immigrant background that many of its members shared. India was a place where a man of talent could seek his fortune—not that he was guaranteed to find it. But in comparison to most Muslim polities in India and elsewhere, the most striking feature of Akbar's elite was the unqualified integration of the Hindu Rājpūts into the aristocracy. This had begun with an isolated case in 1561, when the ruler of Āmbēr in eastern Rajasthan made an overture to Akbar, but by 1580 it was a pattern. The Rājpūts were not just convenient allies whose idolatry one could quietly overlook; it was part of the deal that in return for their submission to the Mughal emperor they got respect for their religious and cultural traditions, and when their daughters married into the royal family they were allowed to continue to practice their Hindu rites. This was new, and it was no small matter. Respect is one of the most precious commodities in human affairs, and its absence one of the most corrosive. Akbar also made the Rājpūts richer, which of course did no harm. The other major presence of Hindus in the state apparatus was in the lower ranks of the bureaucracy, which a number of literate castes more or less monopolized, except for the ministry that dealt with religious patronage. These petty bureaucrats did not get the same respect as the Rājpūt warriors, but

Hindus at large stood to benefit from Akbar's abolition of the poll tax payable by tolerated non-Muslims under Islamic rule.

Like many of the states we are concerned with in this book, the Mughal Empire did not pay the salaries of its nobles and their large military followings out of a central treasury. Instead, an aristocrat would be assigned revenues that he then collected for himself. Such an assignment was a *jāgīr*, the term used in Muslim India for a fief. In that way the central government outsourced the collection of some 90 percent of its revenues to its aristocracy. This sounds like a recipe for decentralization, with overmighty subjects striking deep roots in the provinces and turning them into more or less autonomous principalities. And eventually something like that did happen, as we will see. But this was not how Akbar set things up. His system was designed to keep his aristocrats on a tight leash in several ways. First, the right to collect taxes from a given territory was divorced from any other kind of authority over it. Second, the financial bureaucracy was aggressive in regulating and monitoring the amount of taxes collected and the manner of their collection. And third, the state could take back an aristocrat's fief and replace it with another. Alongside these arrangements regarding fiefs there were other mechanisms that worked to prevent subjects becoming overmighty. One was a practice that we are already familiar with from the rapidity with which caliphs and Ottoman sultans rotated their provincial governors: Akbar would not let his nobles serve too long in any one place. The other was a system of numerical rankings of the aristocracy that had partial precedents but in its comprehensiveness and complexity must have owed much to Akbar's imagination. There were thirty-three ranks (in principle sixty-six), and the system covered both the military and the bureaucracy. Members of the Rājpūt elite were included and got high rankings. These rankings were always subject to change upward or downward, and it was Akbar who changed them. A man could expect his son to be given a position in government service, but the son did not inherit his father's rank—he had to rise through the ranks for himself. In short, Mughal aristocrats were blessed with great wealth, great power, and the large retinues that go with them, but they were not left to engage in state formation at the emperor's expense. This was true also for the Rājpūts, for all that unlike other aristocrats they were allowed to retain possession of their ancestral lands; the Rājpūt kingdoms were deeply penetrated by the standard forms of Mughal provincial administration. Yet alongside all these well-calculated checks on wayward aristocratic ambition, there was also real warmth in Akbar's relations with his nobles. This, too, was institutionalized. In a move that was without precedent in the annals of Muslim rule in India, Akbar more or less invented a new religion for himself and his court, a kind of sun worship. He would initiate his nobles into this flagrantly un-Islamic cult as his disciples. The esoteric society that emerged from this may have come to include a majority of the aristocracy.

We shift now to a lower level of provincial society. Northern India was full of local elites (the *zamīndārs*, "possessors of the land," as the Mughals called them), and these elites played a major role in the affairs of their districts. They could mobilize sizeable military forces, though these would be made up almost entirely of infantry. The government made every effort to prevent them from acquiring muskets, but by the early eighteenth century it would seem that such efforts had failed. In other words, these local chiefs were not in the same league as the Mughal aristocracy, but if alienated they could make a lot of local trouble. When the state collected taxes from the localities, it did not normally go into the village and assess the amount due from each peasant. Instead, the long-standing practice had been to negotiate with the relevant chiefs for a lump sum. Akbar and his leading fiscal experts put a great deal of thought and energy into changing this system. They did not attempt to sweep away the local elites, a project that would have been quite impractical under the conditions of the time. But over a five-year period they mounted a thoroughly intrusive exercise in data collection, at the end of which they knew exactly what there was to tax in each village and how much they should be getting from it—even if the tax was still collected from the local chiefs. They had thus pushed the administrative frontier deeper into rural society, very likely further than any previous state in the region had ever done. But this did not, of course, apply to the entire territory under nominal Mughal rule. A European observer commented in 1620 that the emperor ruled only the plains and the royal highways; beyond that people barely knew that he existed. Fortunately for the Mughals the plains of northern India were unusually extensive.

Even then, we should not think of the plains under Akbar or his successors as cultivated by a pacific and docile peasantry and traversed by roads on which travelers enjoyed security for their goods and persons. There is abundant evidence of armed violence in the Mughal countryside. A caravan traveling between major cities in 1622–23 kept itself safe by employing several hundred Balūchīs, Jāṭs, and others, armed with firearms and swords. The Balūchīs were Iranian tribesmen from the northwest, but the Jāṭs were peasants from the Punjab. In 1717 a caravan was stopped by five thousand peasants, two thousand of them armed with muskets. An Italian observer describes the marital synergy with which villagers would defend themselves against Mughal tax collectors: "The women stood behind their husbands with spears and arrows. When the husband had shot off his matchlock, his wife handed him the lance, while she reloaded the matchlock."[17] Peasants would attack and kill troops, especially but not exclusively those fleeing from defeat. Things were not so very different in the cities. In 1761 three thousand defeated Marāṭhā soldiers were plundered by the "local vagabonds" of Delhi, before

17. For this and the next quotation see D.H.A. Kolff, *Naukar, Rajput and Sepoy*, Cambridge 1990, 7, 8.

fleeing south to be killed by peasants. But that was nothing to what had happened in the city in 1719, when the populace registered its displeasure at the deposition and killing of the current Mughal emperor. Then, too, they targeted a Marāṭhā army, but not a defeated one. A crowd of men and women attacked the Marāṭhā horsemen, grabbing the bridles of their horses, felling them with brickbats and staffs, and then stripping and killing them. The Marāṭhās, it was said, were "killed like dogs and cats," with the result that "more than three or four thousand infidels were dispatched to hell."[18] This time, at least, the dissidents were siding with their emperor, not rebelling against him. But in general the violence was rebellious. The emperor Jahāngīr lamented that despite the "frequent and sanguinary executions" inflicted by the authorities on the people of Hindūstān, "the number of the turbulent and disaffected never seems to diminish."[19] There was scarcely a province, he observed, in which at one time or another hundreds of thousands of rebels had not been slaughtered on the battlefield or subsequently executed. It was not till the consolidation of British rule in the nineteenth century that most of Indian society, and in particular the countryside, was at last demilitarized. But let us return to the Mughal Empire at the death of Akbar.

Much of the structure created by Akbar remained in place under his successors. The sultan continued to exercise real power at the apex of the system. Each ruler, of course, was different. Jahāngīr was the least effective: he was indolent, given to withdrawing from public life, and like his grandfather Humāyūn in the habit of consuming too much wine and opium. Shāh Jahān, the builder of the Tāj Maḥall, was a better fit for the job, being confident, competent, and aggressive. Awrangzēb had the same qualities and remained a vigorous ruler into old age, dying at the age of ninety, though he lacked the warmth, openness, and imagination of Akbar. Through all this the dynasty continued much as before—that is to say, in the traditional Tīmūrid style. There was nothing comparable to the radical change whereby the Ottomans started to isolate princes in the "cage"; instead, the ruler's sons continued to be given assignments that familiarized them with the exercise of political and military power.

The major change with regard to the aristocracy was simply that it grew larger. From 283 members at the end of Akbar's reign it had expanded to 445 in 1647, matching a large increase in revenue and in the size of the army. There were minor changes in composition, with the number of Afghans rising somewhat. The Rājpūts continued to be a part of the Mughal elite, though they were no longer as privileged as they had once been: Awrangzēb preferred Muslims, and as a result the Rājpūt nobles were now fewer, less highly ranked, and poorer—part of the background to a Rājpūt rebellion in 1679. But there was no major change in composi-

18. Quoted in A. Kaicker, *The king and the people*, New York 2020, 220.

19. Quoted in Kolff, *Naukar, Rajput and Sepoy*, 14.

tion until Awrangzēb's conquests mandated the admission of large numbers of Dakhnīs—both Muslim officers of the former sultanates of the Deccan who were easily assimilated, and Hindu Marāṭhā chiefs who were not. In 1647 there were only ten Marāṭhā officers in the imperial service, whereas in the later part of Awrangzēb's reign there were ninety-six, though they tended to be used only in the Deccan wars and thus not to be well integrated into the wider aristocracy. Over the aristocracy as a whole the ranking system was maintained, and nobles continued to dispose of an abundance of wealth and power. There was nevertheless a significant change in the political culture as it affected relations between the sultan and his nobles. Jahāngīr still initiated aristocrats into Akbar's cult, but Shāh Jahān no longer did this, nor did Awrangzēb. Less esoteric forms of interaction continued, but here Awrangzēb's Islamic piety threw a spanner in the works: he banned the drinking of wine, the essential lubricant of social life among the Mughal elite. On a more material level, however, things continued to look good. The revenue system established in the reign of Akbar remained robust into the late seventeenth century, and the extent of land surveyed and assessed by the bureaucracy increased markedly. For a long time, shortfalls in revenue and budget deficits were something Akbar's successors did not need to worry about any more than Akbar himself had done. Altogether, the empire continued to expand its territory and deepen its administrative reach until it reached its high point in 1689. Despite the armed violence in the countryside, it seems that the Mughal seventeenth century saw nothing like the time of troubles that afflicted and impoverished the Ottomans. Yet by 1689 trouble was not far away.

That brings us to our third and final Mughal theme, succession to the throne. In contrast to succession among the Delhi sultans, this was a game reserved for princes of the blood. But there was never any lack of them—into the eighteenth century every Mughal ruler after Bābur had a major conflict with a brother, a son, or both. Humāyūn fought an eight-year war against a brother prior to his return to India, and as we have seen, early in his reign Akbar had to deal with a half brother and later faced a rebellion by his son, the future ruler Jahāngīr. On Akbar's death Jahāngīr's succession was eased by the fact that two brothers had already died of alcoholism, but at that point he still had to contend with one of his own sons. Another son, the future Shāh Jahān, rebelled against him in 1622. When Jahāngīr died in 1627, there were two brothers in competition for the throne, a third having died of alcoholism. The vizier—by now there were no longer four of them—defeated one brother and secured the throne for the other, Shāh Jahān. But all this was nothing to what happened when Shāh Jahān fell ill in 1657. He had four sons, two of them serious contenders. One was Dārā Shukōh, who had the advantage of being at court and his father's favorite; the other was Awrangzēb, who was on bad terms with his father and served as governor of the Deccan. Of the other two, one was in Bengal and the other in Gujarat. The struggle lasted from 1658 to

1660, with the fighting spread widely over India. In the course of it Awrangzēb took his father prisoner, betrayed one brother, and defeated the other two. His three brothers naturally lost their lives, but at least Awrangzēb did not kill his imprisoned father, who survived until 1666. Twenty years later, in 1681, Awrangzēb's own son Akbar rebelled against him. When Awrangzēb eventually died in 1707, he left three sons and a will according to which the empire was to be divided between them—among the Mughals, as among the Ottomans, the idea of division was occasionally raised but never implemented. The princes ignored their father's will, and the winner of the ensuing succession struggle was Bahādur Shāh (ruled 1707–12). But there was a problem. Awrangzēb had lived too long, with the result that his successor was an old man. He died five years later, at the age of sixty-nine, leaving four sons who at the time of his death had already plunged the empire into yet another war of succession. By now the dynasty was falling apart.

The second age of fragmentation

The disintegration of the Mughal Empire had roots that went back into the later seventeenth century and were linked to the manner in which Awrangzēb had ruled it, in particular his religious policies. He had significantly eroded the bond between the dynasty and the Rājpūts, still a major component of the Mughal aristocracy. Among other things, he destroyed temples and reimposed the poll tax, which did not play well in Rajasthan. The ensuing sourness is reflected in the actions of one Rājpūt ruler upon Awrangzēb's death: he destroyed the mosques erected in his capital by the Mughals and forbade the performance of the Islamic ritual prayers there. At the same time, Awrangzēb's reign had seen the emergence of a new and formidable Hindu military antagonist, the Marāṭhās of the northwestern Deccan. As a result, this region, where Awrangzēb stayed from 1682 till his death to fight his unending wars, had proved to be a quagmire with heavy costs in terms of revenue and elite self-confidence. For the first time since the reign of Akbar, the resources of the empire were insufficient. Awrangzēb's rule had likewise increased the hostility of what would soon be another formidable Hindu enemy, the Sikhs of the Punjab. Altogether, his piety and policies were apt to fan the flames of religious conflict. There was to be some attempt to reverse Awrangzēb's policies during the brief reign of Jahāndār Shāh (ruled 1712–13), when the poll tax was abolished and concessions were made to the Rājpūts, but by then it was too late to make much difference. All these were real problems, but the chances are that they would not have issued in the disintegration of the empire without the train wreck of multiple wars of succession in the early eighteenth century. As already mentioned, this had a lot to do with Awrangzēb's unusual longevity. The chaotic events of these struggles were deeply destructive of both the power and the prestige of the center, and when the dust had settled with the inauguration of the long reign of Muḥammad Shāh (ruled 1719–48), the empire was not much more than one regional state among others. It could still secure some revenue by blessing arrangements made in the provinces, and it could occasionally field an army, but it was no longer in control. Throughout the seventeenth century the Mughals had done far better than the Ottomans, but in the eighteenth century the comparison was reversed. Unlike the residual Mughal state, the Ottomans Empire was still an empire in more than name, retaining as it did the ability to fight major wars and make decisive if intermittent interventions in the affairs of its provinces.

As might be expected, what happened in the periphery of the Mughal Empire bore some similarity to the breakup of the Delhi Sultanate centuries earlier. Once again insiders—members of the Mughal state apparatus—took over provinces and established virtually independent dynasties. This happened in Bengal, where a Shīʿite governor appointed by Awrangzēb in 1704 administered the province in an increasingly independent fashion until his death in 1725, after which his successors—the Nabobs—continued to rule it until defeated and sidelined by the British in 1765. One of them is worth picking out here for the way in which he responded to the British threat: Mīr Qāsim ʿAlī (ruled 1760–63). He sought stay clear of the British, setting up a new capital located well away from them in Bihar. At the same time he replaced his existing troops with new, European-style regiments—a parallel to the efforts of the Khān of the Crimea and the Ottomans later in the century. Something similar happened in the eastern Deccan, where a Sunnī Mughal governor appointed in 1720 became independent in 1724, establishing the dynasty known as the Niẓāms of Hyderabad. Unlike the Nabobs of Bengal, they became allies of the British and were thus able to retain a measure of power until 1948. A third case was Oudh (or Avadh), the territory around the city of Lucknow on the Gangetic plain. Here another Shīʿite governor, an immigrant from Iran, was able to establish himself as an autonomous ruler in 1722 and found a further dynasty of Nabobs. Thanks to a rather stifling alliance with the British this dynasty ruled until deposed by them in 1856, leaving as its legacy the largest concentration of Shīʿites in northern India. The tensions between this community and the Sunnīs of the city have been a source of sectarian violence since the eighteenth century. In all three cases these rulers continued to acknowledge the nominal authority of Delhi. Only one major Muslim state of this period, a short-lived dynasty in Mysore (1761–99), had a different origin. Here a member of a Hindu dynasty, itself a residue of the Hindu kingdom of Vijayanagara, retained the services of a Muslim general, Ḥaydar ʿAlī, in a succession dispute, and in 1761 the general took power for himself. Nominally he retained the dynasty, but later his son Tīpū Sulṭān (ruled 1782–99) dispensed with it altogether. Taking advantage of the presence of the European trading companies in India, these rulers allied with the French against the British. Ḥaydar ʿAlī had the French train his troops in modern warfare—yet another parallel to the Crimean and Ottoman reforms. Then in 1785 Tīpū reached out to the Ottoman sultan requesting military assistance. He wished to borrow an Ottoman army, whose expenses he would cover, and to have Ottoman gun makers come and settle in Mysore. In due course the British defeated Tīpū and restored the Hindu dynasty. One bizarre side effect of this was that the British now found themselves saddled with the task of relocating Tīpū's court and maintaining it for a while in some semblance of the style to which it had been accustomed. The meticulous bureaucracy this involved sheds an interesting light on the composition of the court, revealing that it included 601 women, many of them entertainers who had been born as Hindus and could not now return to their families.

Muslim states were not, however, the only ones that mattered in late Mughal India. This second age of fragmentation was marked by a phenomenon that was much less salient in the first age—namely, the revival of Hindu power. There were three significant cases of this: the Rājpūts, the Marāṭhās, and the Sikhs.

We have already encountered the high-caste Rājpūts. Theirs was a warrior culture with an aristocratic sense of honor. Seventeenth-century historical texts from this milieu are full of the names of men who "died fighting," a heroism matched by their womenfolk as they mounted the funeral pyres of their husbands. As we saw, the Rājpūts were becoming disaffected under Awrangzēb, and the collapse of central power was their opportunity to stretch their muscles. One example of this was Jai Singh II (ruled 1700–1743), the ruler of Āmbēr in eastern Rajasthan whose ancestor had been the first Rājpūt to join the Mughal aristocracy in 1561. He now enlarged his territories and in 1727 founded a new capital named after himself, the city of Jaipur. He was sufficiently diplomatic to secure Mughal recognition of it in 1733, but he consecrated it with a Hindu ritual of hoary antiquity, the horse sacrifice. Yet Rājpūt assertiveness in this period did not issue in fundamental change even for Rajasthan, let alone for India at large. The region continued to be divided into the same plurality of Rājpūt states, and these states continued to be characterized by long-standing tensions within Rājpūt society, notably conflicts pitting the bonds of kinship against the bonds of clientage.

Farther south, in the northwestern Deccan, the low-caste Marāṭhās were a force of a very different kind.[20] An Englishman who arrived in India in 1673 and spent the best part of a decade there describes them succinctly as "a warlike and troublesome nation, apt to dislike government, proud and brave."[21] These fractious, insubordinate, and disorganized Hindu warriors fought as light cavalry. They became prominent thanks to a circumstance noted above: the thinness of the Muslim population in the Deccan, including the territory of the Niẓām Shāhī dynasty (1490–1636) in what is today Maharashtra. In its last decades this state was defended against the assaults of the Mughals by Malik ʿAnbar (d. 1626), an

20. On them see S. Gordon, *The Marathas*, Cambridge 1993.

21. See R. P. Patwardhan and H. G. Rawlinson, *Source book of Maratha history*, Calcutta 1978, 302.

Ethiopian slave who had talent as a general, politician, and administrator. He had himself been purchased by another Ethiopian slave implausibly called Chingiz Khān, who was likewise in the service of the dynasty. In the absence of adequate numbers of Muslim soldiers, Malik ʿAnbar needed to find troops among the Hindu population of the region. He thus recruited numerous Marāṭhās, including the father and grandfather of the future Marāṭhā king Śivājī. At the same time he developed new tactics to exploit the superior mobility of Marāṭhā horsemen against the heavy cavalry of the Mughals. The trick was to avoid fighting pitched battles against Mughal armies and instead to harry them, cut off their supply lines, and create diversions by attacking soft targets deep inside enemy territory. A Mughal commentator had no trouble finding a familiar Central Asian term to describe this strategy: it was *qazaq* warfare. For similar reasons Marāṭhās were also retained in large numbers farther south in the state of Bījāpūr; Śivājī's father spent part of his career in its service.

In short, history had taken a turn that made the Marāṭhās a significant military resource for themselves and others. From the 1660s they proceeded to take advantage of their newfound strength by raiding mercilessly over large parts of India. Their depredations soon reached Gujarat, the eastern coastlands of the Tamil country, and eventually the Punjab and even Bengal. Their very disorganization made them irrepressible, as Awrangzēb learned to his considerable cost: Mughal heavy cavalry could defeat them in a pitched battle, but that did not suffice to bring them under imperial control. By the same token they were not natural state builders, since no one could count for long on the loyalty of the leaders of the Marāṭhā war bands. But they did establish a handful of states.

The first and most significant was formed by Śivājī (ruled 1674–80). He moved slowly but persistently toward the creation of an independent Marāṭhā—and Hindu—state. He had no serious problem doing business with the Mughals when convenient or necessary, and like earlier Hindu rulers, he welcomed Muslims into his service, even employing a force of seven hundred Afghans. But in 1674 he took a drastic symbolic step, though a genealogically problematic one, whereby he distanced himself sharply from the political culture of the Mughal Empire. The proceedings lasted several weeks and centered on the enactment of an ancient Hindu ritual through which he was crowned—or more precisely sprinkled with holy water—as an authentic Hindu king. What was problematic here was that if Śivājī was a Marāṭhā, he could not be a Kṣatriya, a member the twice-born class to which Hindu rulers were supposed to belong. It took some genealogical ingenuity on the part of a distinguished Brahmin of Benares to iron out this wrinkle. But ironed out it was, and the moment was experienced as a glorious one. It was also associated with intense anti-Muslim sentiment, at least at the level of public relations. A court poet wrote a Sanskrit epic celebrating Śivājī's exploits, and in one passage he has him declare the Muslims (styled Yavanas, a term originally referring to the Greek invaders of ancient India) to be "incarnations of demons" who seek "to flood the earth with their own religion (*dharma*)"; Śivājī's response will be to "destroy these demons" and fearlessly spread the true religion. In other passages the poet has the god Śiva identify Śivājī as an incarnation of Viṣṇu come down to earth to kill "all these Muslims" who "despise gods and Brahmins."[22] He tells us that Śivājī will establish independent rule (*svarājya*) and put his feet on the head of the Mughal emperor. Yet even this did not signal a total break with the coexistence of Mughal times. In an open letter that Śivājī wrote (or had ghostwritten) to Awrangzēb in 1679, he made apt use of the discourse of diversity to present Islam and Hinduism as complementary: they were pigments used by the Divine Painter to blend His colors and fill in the outlines of His painting. This image may not have gone down well with Awrangzēb, a ruler whose Islamic piety led him to fire his court painters by the dozen—an action that his great-grandfather Akbar would have regarded as a bigoted misstep. Meanwhile the ecumenical Śivājī is described in one source as telling his men that when engaged in looting they were not to desecrate mosques or Qur'āns; if he came by a Qur'ān he would pass it on to one of his Muslim servants. The Marāṭhās also continued to bestow patronage on Ṣūfī saints, and in 1752 a Mughal-Marāṭhā treaty went so far as to make the Marāṭhās the protectors of the Mughal throne. Even Śivājī's court poet thought that there were people worse than Muslims. Those were the Europeans, with their well-aimed cannons, clever fortifications, wealth, and near-invincibility on the high seas.

The dynasty founded by Śivājī was to reign in Maharashtra until 1848, but it only held real power—or disputed it in civil war within the family—for two or three decades. It then succumbed to an internal takeover by its own Brahmin viziers, known by a Persian term as the Pēśvās (*pēshvā*s). They effectively ruled the state from 1713 or so until the British in turn took over in 1818. Brahmins, it seems, were more organized than Marāṭhās—and undoubtedly better at bureaucracy. The Marāṭhās nevertheless established half a dozen further states in the later seventeenth and early eighteenth centuries, including one in Tanjore in the Tamil coastlands and another in Gujarat. The rest were closer to home, but one of them, based in Nāgpūr in eastern Maharashtra, conquered Orissa on the distant fringes of Bengal and ruled it from 1751 to 1803. Another, which ruled Gwalior, was uncharacteristic of the Marāṭhā states in the energy with which, in the last years of the eighteenth century, it adopted the new European style of infantry warfare, complete with French and other European officers; it also recruited large numbers of Muslim soldiers. A third of these states, Indore, was noteworthy for being ruled with great success by a woman for three decades in the second half of the eighteenth century. A point of interest here is that her role was eased by the absence of a tradition of female seclusion among the low-caste Marāṭhās.

22. *The epic of Shivaji*, trans. J. W. Laine and S. S. Bahulkar, Hyderabad 2001, 126, 236.

Meanwhile to the north, the Sikhs of the Punjab were likewise for the most part a low-caste Hindu community.[23] They came to be recruited increasingly from the Jāṭs, a hardy and bellicose peasant caste of the region that had already been making trouble for the early Arab and Turkic conquerors of India. From the sixteenth century to the early eighteenth the Sikhs were led by a succession of ten gurus. In the course of the seventeenth century the relations of the gurus with the Mughals became increasingly hostile. The fifth guru was executed in 1606, mainly for making a bad bet in a Mughal succession struggle; the ninth guru was beheaded in Delhi in 1675 when he refused to convert to Islam, after which a Sikh in Āgrā threw a couple of bricks at Awrangzēb; and the tenth guru was assassinated by an Afghan in 1708 in the camp of the Mughal emperor Bahādur Shāh. Meanwhile the gurus had begun to militarize the sect. The sixth guru encouraged martial activity among his followers and built a fort, and by 1688 the tenth guru could win a battle, though not against the Mughals. A more momentous event took place in 1699, when he proclaimed the establishment of the Khālsā, a militant religious order that became the core of the sect. This new development combined a strong emphasis on the "unity and friendship" that should prevail inside the community with a violent hostility toward its enemies: "The command of the Gurus is 'Fight the barbarians, destroy them all!'"[24] The "barbarians" are readily identifiable as the Muslims in this context; as another text tells us, "The true Khālsā is one who carries arms and slays Muslims."[25] There was thus a powerful resonance between the militant doctrine of the last of the gurus and the martial values of the Jāṭs. In addition there was an aspiration to form a Sikh state: "The Khālsā shall rule, no enemy shall remain."[26]

It took a while for this aspiration—or at least the first part of it—to be accomplished. In the year following the killing of the tenth guru a bloody Sikh rebellion broke out in the Punjab. The rebels destroyed mosques, and the rising and was not suppressed till 1715. After that the Sikh insurgency took the form of small mobile bands, like those whose raids destroyed the suburbs of Delhi in the aftermath of Nādir Shāh's invasion of 1739. It was out of the activities of these bands that scores of independent Sikh principalities gradually took shape. In the 1790s, in the context of resistance to Afghan invasions, one of these principalities emerged as the strongest and soon began to absorb the rest. The king of this Sikh state was Ranjīt Singh (ruled 1799–1839), and its capital was Lahore. This kingdom was in some ways a radically new phenomenon. Unlike Muslim sects, Hindu sects did not normally engage in state formation, and the divergence played a significant part in the process whereby the Sikhs eventually ceased to regard

23. For what follows see J. S. Grewal, *The Sikhs of the Punjab*, Cambridge 1990.
24. See W. H. McLeod, *The Chaupa Singh Rahit-nama*, Dunedin 1987, 150, 157.
25. See W. H. McLeod, *Textual sources for the study of Sikhism*, Chicago 1990, 79.
26. Quoted in W. H. McLeod, *Who is a Sikh?*, in his *Sikhs and Sikhism*, New Delhi 1999, 50.

themselves as Hindus. On the other hand, there were several aspects of the Sikh kingdom that were continuous with the old Mughal order. Substantial numbers of Muslims and non-Sikh Hindus were employed in the state apparatus, Hindu and Muslim religious institutions enjoyed the patronage of the state alongside those of the Sikhs, Persian remained the language of administration, and the king encouraged literary activity in Persian. We have already noted a typical Sikh coin, inscribed with its Persian couplet. These sectarians also resembled the Muslims of India in that even on their home territory they were a minority of the population. But in one way Ranjīt Singh departed sharply from Mughal precedent. Like Mīr Qāsim ʿAlī in Bihar, Ḥaydar ʿAlī in Mysore, and the Marāṭhā rulers of Gwalior, he was interested in Europeanizing his army, and to this end he employed some European officers. In short, the Sikhs, like the Marāṭhās, were a transformative force in a way in which the Rājpūts were not.

If we leave aside the brief reign of Rājā Ganēsh in Bengal, the only parallel to these three assertions of Hindu power in the first period of fragmentation would be the formation of the Hindu state of Vijayanagara in fourteenth century. In other words, the eighteenth century saw an unprecedented unraveling not just of the Mughal Empire but of Muslim military and political dominance as such. This should not, however, be taken to mean that the Muslims of India were confronting a high level of Hindu solidarity in this period. One of the most effective generals sent against Śivājī by the Mughals was the Rājpūt ruler of Āmbēr, Jai Singh I; conversely, the Rājpūts suffered extensively from the raids of the Marāṭhās and their demands for tribute. Meanwhile to the south, the Marāṭhās plundered the monastery of Śṛngērī, a venerable Hindu institution reputedly founded by the Vēdānta sage Śaṇkara (fl. ca. 700) and located in today's Karnataka. It was the Muslim ruler of Mysore, Tīpū Sulṭān, who despite a reputation as a Muslim zealot came up with funds to make good the damage. Similarly, a Marāṭhā invasion of the Punjab met with Sikh resistance, and in the far northeast the Hindu victims of Marāṭhā raiders in Bengal did not look kindly on their "foul and evil deeds."[27] This lack of fraternal spirit among Hindus was not a contravention of values enshrined in the Hindu tradition. There was no Hindu counterpart of the Islamic teaching that Muslims are brothers and should not be fighting each other. The Hindu threat to Muslim power in India was nevertheless significant enough for Shāh Walī Allāh Dihlawī (d. 1762), a famous and often rather uncompromising Islamic scholar in Delhi, to ask himself what it would be like if the Hindus came to rule India on a lasting basis. He came up with an answer that has turned out to be overoptimistic: God in His wisdom would inspire the leaders of the Hindus to adopt Islam, just as He had done with the Turks.

27. Quoted in P. J. Marshall, *Bengal: The British bridgehead*, Cambridge 1987, 72.

Another process that went much further in the second age of fragmentation was foreign invasion. Unlike the Delhi sultans, who confronted repeated threats on the northwestern frontier, the Mughals faced no danger in that quarter until well into the eighteenth century—which is why they could expend so much military energy in conquering the south. Back in the first age of fragmentation, as we saw, Tīmūr's invasion of 1398–99 and his sack of Delhi were a blow to a Delhi Sultanate that was already in serious trouble, but they had no lasting impact beyond that. Something similar could be said of Nādir Shāh's invasion and his sack of Delhi in 1739. Both these incursions were little more than large-scale smash-and-grab raids. But what followed in the Mughal case was different. Invasion now came from two quarters, the northwest and the Indian Ocean. The threat from the northwest was in the end less significant, and it was a variation on a familiar theme: the overland expansion into India of a state based in Afghanistan—a term that we can begin to use at this point without anachronism. When Nādir Shāh was assassinated in 1747, one of his leading generals, Aḥmad Khān Abdālī (ruled 1747–73), took command of his Afghan troops and used them to establish the Durrānī monarchy that ruled Afghanistan until 1973. In Iran Aḥmad Khān had far less of a presence than the Ghaznawids and Ghūrids once had, and for the most part he was content to be the patron of Nādir's grandson Shāh Rukh in Khurāsān. But he was much more active in India, which he invaded nine times between 1747 and 1769, sacking Delhi and Āgrā in 1757, defeating the Marāṭhās in 1761, and annexing Sindh, much of the Punjab, and Kashmir to his kingdom. A striking innovation of the Afghan invaders in the Indian context was their use of light artillery mounted on camels, a phenomenon we encountered a little earlier in Toqay Temürid Transoxania. The Afghan expansion could be seen as delivering the Muslims of India from the menace of the Marāṭhās, and it was in that vein that Shāh Walī Allāh invited the Afghan ruler to come to the rescue. But it also had a strong ethnic coloring. The Rōhilla Afghans, who already held considerable territory to the north and east of Delhi, made common cause with Aḥmad Khān; one of their leaders wrote to him saying, "I too am an Afghan, and you ought to preserve the honor of the Afghans."[28] But in the long run Aḥmad Khān's venture had little impact, as his successors failed to retain his Indian conquests in the face of the hostility of the Marāṭhās and Sikhs. The outcome was to underline an Afghan predicament that is still with us today: a country lacking the resources to support an effective state on its own must depend on foreign resources to survive, and if it cannot obtain them by conquest, as Aḥmad Khān did, it can do so only by becoming the client of a foreign power.

The invasion of India from the Indian Ocean was far more consequential. It was not a passing moment, and if it did not quite mean the end of Muslim power in

28. Quoted in I. Husain, *The Ruhela chieftaincies*, New York 1994, 87.

India, it left it severely constricted. It was also quite unlike anything that had happened before in Indian history. The intruders did not arrive overland from somewhere on India's doorstep, but rather by sea from Britain, an island halfway around the globe. Moreover, the fighting force built up by the British was not serving a ruler seeking imperial glory, but rather a commercial company in search of profits. There was, of course, precedent in the Mediterranean world for mercantile republics acquiring significant territories—Carthage in the south and east of Spain, Venice on Cyprus and Crete. So it is no great surprise that in the sixteenth century the Portuguese state sought to acquire key Indian ports and that the merchants of other European countries followed suit when they reached the Indian Ocean in the next century. But taking over a vast territory in northeastern India, let alone India as a whole, was something quite new. Such territorial conquest had traditionally been an activity pertaining to "the prestige of kings," and it was hardly to be expected that an organization of mere merchants like the East India Company would be able or willing to engage in it. It is true that in 1346 a Genoese joint-stock company had conquered the Aegean island of Chios, but in terms of size there is no comparison between Chios and Bengal. It is also telling that the initial antagonist of the British in the subcontinent was not an Indian state, be it Muslim or Hindu, but their western European neighbor France. One result of all this was a geopolitical oddity: for a long time the British ruled the subcontinent from its ports, and it was not until 1911 that they moved their capital to Delhi and became plausible successors of the Mughals.

At the end of our period most of this was still in the future, but the foundations of the British Raj had already been laid. The story begins in the seventeenth century, when the English, like their French rivals and the Portuguese before them, were still content with ports. On the English side the East India Company secured Madras in the 1630s, Bombay in the 1660s, and Calcutta in the 1690s; on the French side the Compagnie des Indes Orientales established itself in Pondicherry, to the south of Madras, in 1674. There was, however, a significant difference between the two companies, and it related to the degree of state control, which was much greater in the French case. The contrast helps explain the fact that the French were commercially considerably less successful in India than the British were. But seeing the Indian scene through the eyes of a state did arguably give the French one advantage, though it did not last very long. It was the French who were acute enough to discern how a commercial company could achieve military success in eighteenth-century India.

The starting point was the fact that foreign commercial companies, like the local elites of the Indian countryside, needed armed men to protect them; we have seen that caravans in the Mughal Empire could not move without them. Thus we find the East India Company hiring Rājpūts in Madras in 1664, in Bengal in 1682, and in Bombay in 1684. But the jump from such native guards to a European-style army was a large one, and there was a major obstacle in the way: it was prohibitively expensive to hire a large body of European troops trained in state-of-the-art infantry warfare, bring them all the way to India, and then maintain them there in the face of the ravages of tropical diseases. What the French realized was that hiring native Indian soldiers and training them in the new style of warfare could be a cheap and effective substitute. This strategy worked well for them when the wars between Britain and France brought the conflict to the east coast of India in the 1740s, and in 1746 the French were able to take Madras from the British. The problem was that within a few years the British had copied the French model. This led to the British acquiring some east coast territory that went well beyond a mere port, though territorial expansion on a grand scale did not begin until 1756. At that point the British traders in Bengal were confronting a Nabob whose policies posed a severe threat to their commercial interests, and indeed to everyone in the neighborhood. In 1756 the Nabob sacked Calcutta. Even then the British did not think of annexing Bengal. But at the end of that year they brought to Bengal a part of the army they had recruited farther south to fight the French, consisting of nine hundred European soldiers and twelve hundred Indian ones. In 1757 this force, somewhat expanded, won a decisive battle against the much larger army of the Nabob, and by 1765 what had started as an attempt to restore the *status quo ante* had escalated into the British conquest of Bengal, Bihar, and Orissa. The initial dynamic was in part at least a simple one. Those with commercial interests required troops to defend them but were reluctant to shoulder the burden of paying for them. Hence revenue had to be secured from the taxation of agriculture, and that meant annexing territory, which in turn meant a need for yet more troops to seize and defend it. So in addition to its European mercenaries the Company continued to recruit Indian troops, and their numbers rose from twenty-five thousand in 1768 to forty thousand in 1784. By the end of our period the British had begun to expand to the west of Bihar and had acquired extensive new territories in the far south of India. What they had not yet done was to push the administrative frontier any further down in rural society than the Mughals had extended it in their day. At this point the British were still content to deal with the local elites, not with the cultivators themselves. But the British Raj was in the making.

Muslims and Hindus

The Muslim predicament in India

Underlying the history outlined in the preceding section is a basic demographic fact: to the end of our period and beyond, Muslims remained a minority of the Indian population. A seventeenth-century French traveler estimated that for every Muslim there were five or six Hindus. There were, however, no firm figures to back this up until the British instituted their decennial census of India in 1871, so it is worth looking at the picture that subsequently emerges. Let us pick the census of 1891. At that date Muslims constituted 20 percent of the total Indian population, and we can take it that the proportion in our period was never higher than that, since we have good reason to think that conversion from Hinduism to Islam was historically far more frequent than conversion from Islam to Hinduism. One relevant factor here was the unequal distribution of political power. Historically it was much more common for Hindus to find themselves ruled by Muslims than for Muslims to find themselves ruled by Hindus, and this meant that in political terms converting to Islam was usually more advantageous than converting to Hinduism. Another factor was the very different character of the opposing religious communities. Islam made conversion easy and apostasy difficult; a pious Muslim ruler like Awrangzēb was out to encourage conversion. On the Hindu side, by contrast, the caste structure made it hard to absorb outsiders even if they wanted to join, and those who left tended to be written off rather than pursued. Thus we can safely think of the proportion of Muslims in the overall population as tending to rise over the centuries, so that in our period it would never have exceeded the level it had reached in 1891.

Of course, we also have to allow for geographical unevenness in the distribution of the Muslim population. At least in the early centuries, for example, the proportion of Muslims must have been higher in the cities that in the countryside, since it was primarily in the cities that Muslim immigrants settled. At the same time the proportion of Muslims must have been greater in northern India than in the center and south. This is as we would expect and fits the clear pattern of the 1891 census, which found that those parts of the country in which Muslims made up 13 percent or more of the total population were all in the north, whereas those in which they made up less than 13 percent were mostly in the south or center. Even within the north, only three regions had Muslim majorities: Sindh (77 percent), Kashmir (70 percent), and by the skin of its teeth the Punjab (51 percent); in the case of the Punjab the concentration of Muslims was in the west of the province. Whatever local factors may have been in play, the general location of these Muslim-majority regions makes sense. They form a band of territory in the northwest that adjoins the heartlands of the Muslim world, and with the exception of the mountains of Kashmir it was these regions that first succumbed to Muslim conquest—and in due course went on to become the Pakistan we know today. In the rest of India only one region had a Muslim minority that exceeded 30 percent. This was Bengal, where just under a third of the population—32 percent—was Muslim. Within Bengal this Muslim population was unevenly distributed: as the general report on the census of 1891 put it, there was a strong Muslim element "exceeding one half of the population, nearly all over the whole of the eastern division" of the province.[29] In fact, already by the early nineteenth century the British consensus was that in the eastern—but not the central or western—part of the province about half the population was Muslim. It is the emergence of a Muslim majority in eastern Bengal, so remote from the core regions of the Muslim world, that most needs to be explained.

The rather convincing explanation that has been proposed runs as follows.[30] Down to the late sixteenth century, it seems that we can think of much of eastern Bengal as an untamed jungle from which civilization, be it Indian or Muslim, was largely absent. The successive Hindu and Muslim capital cities of Bengal, for example, had clustered in the northwest; the east, by contrast, served as a refuge for rebels. Then, in the later sixteenth century, two things changed. The first was environmental. Manifesting the instability typical of many Indian rivers as they wend their way across the alluvial plains, the Ganges changed its course, swinging far to the east to discharge its vast supply of silt onto the lowlands of eastern Bengal and thereby creating a new agricultural opportunity there. The second change was military and political. When the Mughals conquered Bengal, their concern with hunting down rebels led them to select Dacca—well to the east—as their provincial capital. What we see, or at least glimpse, in the centuries that follow is a vast process of land reclamation taking place in eastern Bengal. The earliest attestation of the existence of a Muslim peasantry there dates from 1599. But the mode of colonization does not seem to have been one in which peasants settled on the land on their own initiative. Instead, the sources show us a process in which the key actors were intermediaries between the peasants and the state, or between the peasants and absentee landlords. It was crucial that these intermediaries were typically religious figures, such as Ṣūfī leaders (Pīrs). Among these religious figures, it seems that Muslims were much better represented than Hindus were—whether because they were more interested in the activity or because the state favored them. In one way or another, it appears that the religious allegiances of these intermediaries were mapped onto the newly settled peasantry of the reclaimed areas, despite the fact that many of these peasants seem originally to have been low-caste Hindus. Hence by the end of our period eastern Bengal may already have had a Muslim majority, as it undoubtedly did by the time the British instituted their censuses. This, of course, is why eastern Bengal is today the site of the Muslim country of Bangladesh. But it was an untypical region, and one that seems previously to have been effectively beyond the frontiers of traditional India, Hindu or Muslim.

29. *General Report on the Census of India, 1891*, London 1893, 174.
30. See Eaton, *The rise of Islam and the Bengal frontier*.

Because Indian Muslims at large were a demographic minority, their situation was very different from that of the Ottoman Muslims of the Balkans. The latter, too, lived alongside a non-Muslim majority, but while the empire lasted this was more than balanced by the Muslim predominance in the rest of the polity to which they belonged. Something analogous could be said about the Balkan Christians. They had numerous coreligionists beyond the frontiers of Muslim rule, whereas the Hindus had only a commercial diaspora. Matters were thus very different for both the Muslim and Hindu populations of India under Muslim rule, be it that of the Delhi Sultanate or the Mughal Empire. This situation ensured two things.

One was that in India the two populations would rub off on each other to an unusual degree. Hindus would be deeply influenced by Muslims because of Muslim political dominance, and Muslims would be deeply influenced by Hindus because of Hindu demographic dominance. We can see obvious examples of both in the shared language of northern India, the dialect of Delhi whose modern forms are known as Hindi for Hindus and Urdu for Muslims. For convenience we can call this language Hindi, as was common in our period. On the one hand, it is very much an Indian language, ultimately descended from Sanskrit or something close to it, and we can accordingly see it as a part of the Hindu heritage that has rubbed off on Muslims. Muslims did bring a variety of non-Indian languages to India—the word "Urdu" is itself a Turkic loanword—and of these languages, as we have seen, Persian became the formal medium of the military and political elite. But Hindi, or other vernacular Indian languages depending on the region, gradually became the mother tongue of most Indian Muslims. The Muslim elite was composing poetry in Hindi at least as early as the fourteenth century, and such poetry later found generous patronage at the Mughal court. It is significant in this context that, as we have seen, Persian has not survived as a vernacular in modern India, despite the fact that as late as the eighteenth century, when Shāh Walī Allāh wanted to make his translation of the Qur'ān accessible to the sons of craftsmen and soldiers as soon as they came of age, the language he chose for it was Persian. Yet the rubbing off has not, of course, been solely from Hindus onto Muslims. Even as spoken by Hindus in India today, in an era of Hindu nationalism, Hindi is full of Arabic and Persian loanwords—the term "Hindī" itself being one of them.

Other cases of Hindus and Muslim rubbing off on each other are not hard to find. The role of Persian in the Mughal Empire provides a remarkable example of Muslim influence on Hindus. As we saw, the Mughal bureaucracy was staffed by large numbers of Hindus, and to succeed in their careers they had to master Persian. That they worked hard at this is in itself is no surprise, despite the view of some Hindu jurists that one ought not to study a barbarian language; when it comes to making a living, people do many things they might otherwise choose not to do. What is remarkable is the degree to which these Hindu bureaucrats internalized the Persian literary tradition. Dozens of Hindus composed poetry in Persian, and one Hindu bureaucrat urged his son to assimilate not just the literary style of the Persian classics but also the values embedded in them. When an early eighteenth-century Muslim adventurer found himself ruling a minor state near Madras and wanted to have his glorious deeds celebrated in ornate Persian, he entrusted the task to an accomplished Brahmin. Another plausible instance of Muslim influence—this one unacknowledged—is the general development of Sikhism that we sketched above. Here the emphasis on communal solidarity, the religious militancy, and the aspiration to rule have the air of an effort on the part of Hindus to be more like Muslims. Turning southward, an instance of overt Muslim influence is the adoption of the Muslim title "sultan" by the Hindu rulers of Vijayanagara, as when they styled themselves "Sultan among Hindu kings."[31] This was associated with the abandonment—at least in public contexts—of the traditional nudity of southern Hindu rulers from the waist upward and the adoption of Muslim court dress, something much appreciated by a Muslim visitor to the court. At the same time, there is no denying the subterranean depth of Hindu influence on Muslim society. Shāh Walī Allāh wrote a testament for his children and friends in which, among other things, he urged them to avoid Hindu customs and in particular the utterly un-Islamic practice of not allowing widows to remarry. He urged them to oppose this custom in the wider society, or failing that within the family, or if even that was not possible by merely affirming the truth in their hearts. In other words, he had little hope that this high-caste Hindu reshaping of the family values of the Muslim elite could be eradicated.

The other thing that was assured by the continuing existence of a Muslim minority and a Hindu majority side by side was that relations between them would be a source of recurrent controversy. From a Muslim point of view—and it is the Muslim point of view that primarily concerns us—there were two very different conclusions that could be drawn from the fact that the Muslims of India were surrounded by vast numbers of Hindus. One was that the religious peril of this situation called for an unrelenting assertion of Islamic values as they had been brought to India from the heartlands of the Muslim world. In this view there could be no compromise with the Hindus, their idolatry, and their culture; those inveterate unbelievers had to be held at a safe distance and kept firmly in subjection. We could call this the monoculturalist view. The alternative conclusion was that it was essential for India's Muslims and their rulers, if only to secure their position in an alien environment, to come to terms with the Hindu majority and its traditions. In a strong version of this view, such terms could be more than just a matter of pragmatic accommodation and could rise to the level of shared values and mutual respect. We could call this the multiculturalist view. Both

31. On this phrase see P. B. Wagoner, "'Sultan among Hindu kings,'" *Journal of Asian Studies*, 55 (1996).

views are well represented in the literary record of the Muslim elite of India. In the Ottoman case, by contrast, the multiculturalist view, though present, is far less in evidence.

An eloquent spokesman for the hard-line view was Ḍiyāʾ al-Dīn Baranī, a courtier of the Delhi Sultanate writing in the 1350s. He had fallen out of favor and was trying to write his way back into it. He tells us that rulers must protect Islam, and that doing so requires uprooting unbelief, polytheism, and idolatry. He acknowledges, however, that it may not in practice be possible to achieve this lofty ambition, owing to the rooted character of unbelief and the large number of its adherents. In that case, "kings should at least strive to insult, disgrace, dishonor, and defame the polytheistic and idolatrous Hindus, who are the worst enemies of God and the Prophet." Rulers who protect Islam are easily recognized: "When they see a Hindu, their eyes grow red and they wish to bury him alive; they also desire to completely uproot the Brahmins, who are the leaders of unbelief and polytheism."[32] He was particularly angered by the public performance of Hindu rites in places where Muslims lived: "In the capital and in the cities of the Muslims the customs of infidelity are openly practiced, idols are publicly worshiped." He complains that "openly and without fear, the infidels continue their rejoicing during their festivals" to the accompaniment of drumming, singing, and dancing.[33] As we have seen, Baranī's view that it was the job of a ruler to uproot unbelief was out of line with the standard position held by the Ḥanafī jurists, whose doctrine prevailed in India. In their view Hindus had the option of paying the poll tax and retaining their religion subject to certain limitations, in the same way as Jews and Christians had. But a willingness to accept this tax from the Hindus and leave them to practice their idolatry did not entail any benevolence toward them. A case in point is the attitude of Shaykh Aḥmad Sirhindī (d. 1624), a Ḥanafī and a prominent adherent of a Ṣūfī order recently imported into India, the Naqshbandīs. He was very clear that the point of the tax was to put the infidels in their place: "The real purpose in levying poll tax on them is to humiliate them to such an extent that, on account of the fear of the poll tax, they may not be able to dress well and to live in grandeur. They should constantly remain terrified and trembling. It is intended to hold them in contempt and to uphold the honor and might of Islam."[34] There was, then, no question of Muslims showing respect for Hindus and their religious traditions: "The honor of Islam lies in insulting unbelief and unbelievers. One who respects the unbelievers dishonors the Muslims." His notion of the respect that had to be denied to non-Muslims was a broad one. He did not limit

32. Quoted in A. A. Rizvi, *Muslim revivalist movements in northern India in the sixteenth and seventeenth centuries*, Agra 1965, 9.

33. Quoted in A. Schimmel, *Islam in the Indian subcontinent*, Leiden 1980, 20–21.

34. For this and the quotations that follow see Rizvi, *Muslim revivalist movements*, 248–49.

himself to condemning such gestures as giving a Hindu a seat of honor in a gathering, since even keeping company with Hindus or showing consideration for them amounted to unacceptable respect. Instead, "They should be kept at arm's length like dogs." If there could be no respect for Hindus, there could obviously be none for Hinduism: "Unbelief and Islam are opposed to each other. The progress of the one is possible only at the expense of the other, and coexistence between these two contradictory faiths is unthinkable. To honor the one amounts to insulting the other." He had no patience for an irenic Hindu who expressed the view that Rām and Allāh were just different names of God; only Allāh was to be worshipped, he retorted, while Rām and the rest of the gods of the Hindus were the meanest of Allāh's creation. Nor did he look kindly on ignorant Muslims—especially women—who celebrated the Hindu festival of Dīvālī as if it were their own, giving presents to their daughters and sisters, coloring their pots, and filling them with red rice as gifts.

To sample the alternative view of Hindu-Muslim relations, let us turn to a couple of adherents of a very different Ṣūfī order that had entered India in the fifteenth century, the Shaṭṭārīs. One is Shaykh Muḥammad Ghawth of Gwalior (d. 1563). A contemporary chronicler, whom Akbar described as a bigoted follower of Islamic law, was disturbed to learn that this shaykh would rise to his feet to show respect for Hindu visitors. Among his works was a Persian translation of a Sanskrit text on Hindu asceticism from Bengal; a somewhat nervous biographer writing around 1600 was at pains to emphasize that the saint had freed the work from its origins among the misguided polytheists and rescued it for the true religion. The other Shaṭṭārī was Muḥammad Ghawth's disciple Mīr Sayyid Manjhan Rājgīrī, who in 1545 wrote a mystical romance, the *Madhumālatī*, in a tradition that went back to the fourteenth century and continued far into the eighteenth. He wrote it in Avadhī, the Hindi dialect of Oudh that would be used a few decades later by the Hindu poet Tulsīdās (d. 1623) for his vernacular version of the *Rāmāyaṇa*, the Sanskrit epic that recounts the life of the Hindu god and hero Rām. But unlike Tulsīdās, Manjhan was a Muslim. Early in his prologue he praises Muḥammad, and he goes on to speak of his four companions and successors, Abū Bakr, 'Umar, 'Uthmān, and 'Alī. In itself this is reassuringly orthodox, but there is also something a little odd: he describes Muḥammad as "king of three worlds." The idea that there are *three* worlds is Hindu, not Muslim. The opening couplet of the poem speaks of only two worlds, but it tells us that God created them "in the one sound Ōṃ."[35] In fact the poem is saturated with Hindu religious, historical, and aesthetic references. For example, the poet compares his patron to the legendary Hindu ruler Vikramāditya and refers repeatedly to the time he lives in as the Kali age. Just as

35. Manjhan, *Madhumālatī*, trans. A. Behl and S. Weightman, Oxford 2000, 3, 5.

his teacher's habit of standing to receive Hindu visitors showed respect for Hindus, so, too, the poet's rich invocation of Hindu traditions shows respect for Hinduism. That might suggest that this poet was someone on the periphery of Muslim society, but such an inference would be quite wrong: Manjhan was a court poet of one of the Afghan Sūrī rulers who held power while Humāyūn was in exile. And yet the poem must at some point have had a Hindu audience, for one of the four manuscripts of the work was copied in 1687 in Dēvanāgarī, the main Hindu script of northern India. Moreover, these Shaṭṭārīs were far from isolated. A Muslim poet in the Deccan wrote a commentary on a Hindu sacred text and was a devotee of the Hindu god Gaṇēś.

A point that emerges very clearly from all this is that Ṣūfism has no inherent bias for or against non-Muslims and their religions. Some Ṣūfīs could well be described as Muslim chauvinists. Sirhindī is the prime example, but he had a soulmate in fifteenth-century Bengal, as also in Bījāpūr around the time of the conquest, and we will meet yet another in Africa, in eighteenth-century Hausaland. Other Ṣūfīs looked at non-Muslims and their religions with a sympathy that could blossom into syncretism. Here our two Shaṭṭārīs are prime examples, and to them we can add a Ṣūfī of the Chishtī order in sixteenth-century Bījāpūr whose work is pervaded by Hindu thought, though he disliked his Hindu counterparts, the Yōgīs. In the next century his heterodox son borrowed a Hindu cosmology. Outside India we have already met Jalāl al-Dīn Rūmī and the Bektāshīs. And yet there is no rigid consistency here: even among the Shaṭṭārīs we find hard-liners, such as those who stood up to Ibrāhīm II of Bījāpūr (ruled 1580–1627), a syncretistic sultan who adopted the cult of the Hindu goddess Sarasvatī. What is true is that of all the major components of the Islamic mainstream, Ṣūfism had the greatest potential for warm relations with non-Muslims and their beliefs. But whether in any given context that potential was activated is another question. Quite often it was. Thus from the fifteenth century the Chishtīs of Bījāpūr were composing devotional poetry in the vernacular that was sung by women in the villages—a genre that had its Hindu counterpart. These women must have been converts or their descendants, and there is some evidence that it was by joining the order that Hindus converted. Of the heterodox son of the Chishtī Ṣūfī it is said that hundreds of thousands of Hindus came to worship him, thus adopting Islam—or at least Islam of a kind. Small wonder that his activities prompted raised eyebrows among the religious scholars of the day. Meanwhile, one of his disciples had such good relations with the local Hindu Lingāyat sect that they permitted him to wear the sacred emblem of Śiva on his left foot. Yet a Ṣūfī did not have to be heterodox to appeal to Hindus. In Delhi the Chishtī Shāh Kalīm Allāh (d. 1730), who had no use for antinomian heretics, nonetheless told a disciple not just to be at peace with Hindus but to be ready to train them in Ṣūfī practice in the hope that they would convert to Islam—as some did.

The policies of rulers

One reason these antithetical attitudes mattered historically is that they had champions at the highest political level. This was particularly so in the Mughal case. Here the policies of Akbar, the first ruler of imperial stature, sought to establish an empire that included Hindus alongside Muslims, whereas the last such ruler, Awrangzēb, moved sharply in the opposite direction.

We have already encountered some of Akbar's policies, such as his inclusion of the Rājpūts in the Mughal aristocracy and his idiosyncratic sun cult. This cult was in part the product of Akbar's own spiritual quest. In the 1570s he was in a phase of Islamic piety and Ṣūfī spirituality, but he was already staging religious debates at court, and toward the end of the decade he widened these to include adherents of non-Muslim religions, including Jesuits. In the course of this phase he moved away from any kind of Islamic orthodoxy and developed his eclectic sun cult. Predictably, this put him at odds with the Muslim religious scholars, especially when he added injury to insult by moving to limit their holdings of tax-exempt land grants. Just as naturally, his spiritual odyssey led to a benevolent tolerance of other religions, and in particular of Hinduism. He extended grants of tax-exempt land to the religious leaders of faiths other than Islam, and with a fine disregard for the provisions of the Sharīʿa he allowed Hindus to repair old temples and build new ones. He also permitted those who had been forcibly converted to Islam to apostatize. In 1579 he took the drastic step of abolishing the poll tax on non-Muslims. It is thus not surprising that an unsuccessful rebellion in that year was backed by a fatwa issued by a Muslim judge declaring Akbar an infidel. Moreover, he was not just a tolerant spectator of the religious activities of his Hindu subjects: he and his courtiers would celebrate Hindu festivals such as Dīvālī. Altogether, as his son and successor Jahāngīr was to put it, Akbar "associated with the good of every race, creed, and persuasion, and was gracious to all in accordance with their condition and understanding." The adherents of the various faiths thus "had room in the broad expanse of his incomparable sway."[36] Here Jahāngīr contrasted the situation in Iran, where there was room only for Shīʿites, and in Central Asia, where there was room only for Sunnīs. Akbar accordingly wanted his subjects to get along with each other despite their religious differences, and in this regard he had adopted the principle of "universal harmony" (*ṣulḥ-i kull*). His freethinking counselor Abū ʾl-Faḍl ʿAllāmī (d. 1602) tells us that Akbar wished to dispel "the fanatical hatred prevailing between Hindus and Muslims," which he believed (as many do today) to arise from mutual ignorance. To this end he initiated the translation of major Sanskrit texts into Persian by "competent impartial

36. Jahāngīr, *The Tūzuk-i-Jahāngīrī*, trans. A. Rogers, Delhi 1989, 1:37–38.

men of both communities."[37] Through this measure, Abū 'l-Faḍl continues, Akbar also intended to shake up the beliefs of both sides, showing the Hindus that "some of their errors and superstitions had no foundation in their ancient books," and at the same time convincing the Muslims of the foolishness of their view that the world had only been in existence for a mere seven thousand years. Thus even in criticizing the beliefs of his subjects he was evenhanded. In short, as an imperial edict had it in a different connection, "Hindus and Muslims are one in my eyes."[38] It would be hard to imagine such things happening at the court of the Ottoman sultan Süleymān. One Sanskrit scholar, the author of a grammar of Persian written in Sanskrit at Akbar's request, described him effusively as "born in order to protect cows and Brahmins."[39]

Akbar's inclusiveness survived for some decades after his death. His successor Jahāngīr had similar attitudes and continued his father's policies. Dārā Shukōh, the prime loser of the bloody succession struggle of 1658–60, was in the same tradition. He tells us that after he had learned "the secrets and subtleties of the true religion of the Ṣūfīs," he "thirsted to know the tenets of the religion of the Indian monists"—which we can understand as a reference to the Vēdānta philosophy of Śaṇkara. He spent a lot of time in discussion with these monists, at the end of which "he did not find any difference, except verbal, in the way in which they sought and comprehended Truth." He accordingly compiled a work that brought together "the truth and wisdom" of the Ṣūfīs and Vēdāntists. In a daring use of a Qur'ānic phrase, he entitled it "The meeting-place of the two seas" (Q18:60),[40] and for good measure he had it translated into Sanskrit. In an anticlerical vein he expressed a correspondingly low opinion of the Muslim religious scholars; Paradise, he averred in a poem, is where they do not exist, and his hope was that the world would come to be free of their noise. Unlike the prince himself, his writings survived well and had a considerable Hindu readership.

It was typical of what was to follow that Dārā Shukōh's brother Awrangzēb, the victor of the succession struggle, chose to frame their quarrel in religious terms. As the loser in such a struggle Dārā Shukōh was of course going to die, but Awrangzēb saw to it that he was executed for betraying Islam. Not content with unbelief and heresy, the accusation went, he "also showed an inclination towards the religion of the Hindus and institutions of those accursed ones." He spent his time with Hindu ascetics, regarded the Vēda as divine revelation, and had it translated (the reference is to the Upaniṣads). The conclusion was that if he were to succeed to the throne, "the pillars of the exalted Sharīʿa would be in danger" and

37. For these and the quotation that follows see Schimmel, *Islam in the Indian subcontinent*, 85.
38. Quoted in Richards, *The Mughal empire*, 90.
39. Quoted in A. Truschke, *Culture of encounters*, New York 2016, 39.
40. Quoted in Rizvi, *Muslim revivalist movements*, 356.

"the precepts of Islam" would give way to "the rant of unbelief."[41] The killing of Dārā Shukōh was undoubtedly the most dramatic moment in the transition from the policies of Akbar to those of Awrangzēb, but in fact the process had already begun in the previous reign, with the more conventionally Islamic attitudes of Shāh Jahān. For example, this ruler had all the recently built temples in Benares demolished, and he abandoned Akbar's sun cult. But he was not a zealot. It was Dārā Shukōh, not Awrangzēb, who was his favorite son and heir apparent. Awrangzēb was more consistent and took the change initiated by his father much farther. As we have seen, his Muslim piety adversely affected his ties with the Rājpūts and undermined his social interactions with the aristocracy. It also affected his relations with his Hindu subjects at large. In 1669 he issued a general order for the demolition of all temples recently built or repaired. A Sikh temple in a Punjabi town was duly destroyed and a mosque built in its place—except that the Sikhs then demolished the mosque. In 1679 he reimposed the poll tax, a century after Akbar had abolished it. This led to massive protests in Delhi and a strong rebuke from Śivājī in the letter mentioned earlier. Awrangzēb's ultimate objective was no less than the conversion of the Hindus to Islam. He was not, however, consistently fanatical; if he had been, he could not have ruled effectively. But he took a hard line where pragmatic considerations did not preclude it. This went down well with the Muslim religious scholars, particularly as they once again had their way with regard to grants of tax-free land. But Awrangzēb's policies were not universally accepted even among the Muslim aristocracy. There was a real sense in some quarters—including, of course, the Rājpūts, but also Awrangzēb's appropriately named rebel son Akbar—that his policies were unwise and courted disaster.

A noteworthy point about Śivājī's letter to Awrangzēb is that in addition to denouncing the reimposition of the poll tax he reminded the emperor of Akbar's "admirable policy of universal harmony."[42] Long after Akbar the idea was still remembered. Within a year or two of Śivājī's letter, a Muslim religious scholar in northern India was debunking "universal harmony" by pointing out that if God had wanted people to be left to their own beliefs, He would not have prescribed the duty of jihad, which inevitably leads to suffering and death for Muslims and unbelievers alike.

Similar tensions existed at other times and places in the history of Muslim India, though they did not usually manifest themselves with such high drama as in the Mughal case. The courtier Baranī has a story set in the early years of the Delhi Sultanate in which some religious scholars tell the sultan, Iltutmish (ruled 1211–36), that Hindus do not have the option of paying the poll tax and accordingly can only be offered the choice of Islam or death (this follows the teaching of the

41. Quoted in Rizvi, *Muslim revivalist movements*, 362–63.

42. Quoted in J. Sarkar, *Shivāji and his times*, London 1992, 251.

Shāfiʿites as opposed to that of the Ḥanafīs). The sultan wisely passes the buck to his vizier, who concedes the principle but urges pragmatically that it would be premature to apply it at a time when the Muslims of India are no more than a sprinkling of salt. In the next century, Muḥammad ibn Tughluq (ruled 1325–51) leaned toward a positive attitude to the Hindus, whereas Fērōz Shāh III (ruled 1351–88) inclined to a negative one, wishing to be remembered for the destruction of newly built Hindu temples. As might be expected, Muḥammad ibn Tughluq had bad relations with the Muslim religious scholars, whereas Fērōz Shāh was on friendly terms with them. The ʿĀdil Shāhī sultan of Bījāpūr Ibrāhīm II (ruled 1579–1626), whose army and administration were mostly staffed by Hindus, was deeply interested in Hindu thought and music. On the other hand, Aḥmad Shāh I (ruled 1411–42), the sultan of Gujarat who founded the city of Aḥmedābād, had a reputation for zealous discrimination against Hindus and ruthless iconoclasm; according to a chronicler of Gujarati history writing in the early seventeenth century, he overthrew temples and built mosques in their stead. As we saw, Tīpū Sulṭān was supportive of the Hindu monastery of Śṛngērī after the Hindu Marāṭhās had looted it. In writing to the abbot he made reference to the ills of the Kali age, quoted a Sanskrit verse to suggest that the raiders would suffer for their violation of such a holy place, and urged the abbot to reconsecrate the idol of a goddess that the raiders had absconded with. He ended by asking the abbot to pray for him. And yet this was a man who sought to force the Hindus of Kerala to convert to Islam. For Muslim rulers in India the issue was real and pervasive, and whatever they did, even if they could please themselves, they could never hope to please everybody. If they allowed the killing of cows, Hindus were outraged; if they forbade it, Muslims were outraged. Indeed, the sacred cow was a perennial irritant in Muslim-Hindu relations. On the Hindu side, the fourteenth-century Sanskrit inscription that remarks on the diversity of Bhārata-varṣa had this to say about the Muslim invaders, who were clearly not perceived as teetotalers: "To those despicable wretches wine was the ordinary drink, the meat of cows the staple food, and the slaying of the twice-born the favorite pastime."[43] On the Muslim side, one of Sirhindī's fulminations was manifestly directed against Akbar, though he was careful not to mention him by name: "The tyrant," he raged, "has forbidden the sacrifice of the cow, which is one of the most important rites of Islam in India."[44] In strictly religious terms there was no ground for holding that the animals sacrificed for the festival coinciding with the pilgrimage to Mecca had to be cows, but killing cows was one in the eye for the Hindus.

43. See N. Venkataramanayya and M. Somasekhara Sarma, "Vilasa grant of Prolaya-nayaka," in *Epigraphia Indica*, 32 (1957–58), 241, 261.

44. Quoted in Y. Friedmann, *Shaykh Aḥmad Sirhindī*, Montreal 1971, 33.

Even the stalwart Maḥmūd of Ghazna appears to have been affected by these tensions. In 1027 a coin was minted in India under his rule. On one side it looks like a generic Muslim coin, with the Islamic profession of faith prominently displayed in Arabic: "There is no god but God; Muḥammad is the messenger of God." The other side of the coin is more arresting. Inscribed in Sanskrit in an Indian script, it reads: "The Unmanifest (*avyaktam*) is One, Muhammad is the Incarnation (*avatāra*), Mahamūd is the King."[45] The mention of Maḥmūd's being the king would suggest that he approved this message. But leaving that aside, what we have here is a rendering of the Islamic profession of faith into Sanskrit. Yet it is a very odd one, quite unlike the more or less literal rendering into Middle Persian found on a coin of 691–92 from Sīstān. Instead of the standard Sanskrit word for "god" (*deva*) we have the term "the Unmanifest"; since the word is grammatically neuter, it has to be understood as referring to an abstract metaphysical entity rather than a personal god. And instead of referring to Muḥammad with the ordinary Sanskrit word for "messenger" (*dūta*), the coin describes him with a term normally used for the ten incarnations of the Hindu god Viṣṇu. From any remotely orthodox Islamic viewpoint, the result is not the translation of the profession of faith so much as its utter subversion—and this from Maḥmūd of Ghazna, who made a point of being seen as a champion of Islamic orthodoxy. We have no way to reconstruct what could have happened here. Was the coin the work of a wayward Muslim at the mint who already thought like Dārā Shukōh? Or was it the artifice of a malicious Brahmin who was out to ensure that the Muslims failed to get their message across to his fellow Hindus? Or do we have to do with nothing more than an innocent collapse of cross-cultural communication in a context in which there was no one to hand with an adequate knowledge of both Arabic and Sanskrit? What is clear is that either Maḥmūd or someone with authority in his entourage felt a need to convey some kind of understanding of Islam to the Hindus, and not just to plunder them.

A less enigmatic spin-off from Maḥmūd's campaigns in India was the encounter with Indian culture of the eleventh-century Khwārazmian scholar Bīrūnī, whom we met in an earlier chapter disparaging the Persian language. He could also be quite disparaging about the Hindus, characterizing their mathematical and astronomical literature as a mixture of pearls and dung. But two things were remarkable about him. First, he went to the length of learning Sanskrit—a notoriously difficult language—because he was curious about the elite culture conducted in it. In other words, he learned the language not because he wanted to adopt the culture of the Hindus in the manner of a convert, nor because he wished to persuade them to adopt his own in the manner of a missionary, but because he wanted

45. S. Goron and J. P. Goenka, *The coins of the Indian sultanates*, New Delhi 2001, xxvi, coin GZ2.

to know what they had to say. This is something for which we have no parallel among writers on exotic peoples in the ancient or medieval world; Bīrūnī apart, this phenomenon makes its first appearance in early modern Europe. Second, he did indeed discern pearls as well as dung in the Hindu literature he studied. He saw the Hindu philosophical and scientific heritage as one that invited comparison with that of the ancient Greeks. It was, of course, the elite heritages of both peoples that elicited some respect from him; he had no use for popular superstition and would have had no sympathy for subaltern studies or anthropological fieldwork among primitive tribes. In short, he was a cosmopolitan snob. He was also vividly aware how much Muslim incursions into India, and especially the campaigns of Maḥmūd, had stimulated Hindu hatred of Muslims.

Bottom lines

As this discussion has shown, it is easy to find evidence of hostility and distance between Muslims and Hindus, and just as easy to match it with evidence of closeness and comity. On the one hand, since Akbar was concerned about fanatical hatred between the two groups, it is reasonable to suppose that such hatred existed. So it is not surprising, for example, to find that the pattern of Hindu-Muslim communal riots familiar in modern times is already anticipated in our period. It is reported that in the reign of a king who ruled from 1094 to 1144, Zoroastrians in Cambay incited the Hindus to attack the Muslims; a minaret was destroyed, a mosque was burned, and eighty Muslims were killed. Ibn Baṭṭūṭa describes recurrent violence between Hindus and Muslims in the west coast port of Mangalore. The Hindu spring festival known as Hōlī could mean trouble: in Sūrat in 1644 drunken Hindus rioted and killed a descendant of the Prophet who tried to stop them, and in Aḥmedābād in 1714 there was another riot between Hindus and Muslims. The first half of the eighteenth century also saw communal clashes in Āgrā, Kashmir, and Delhi, and in 1789 it was the turn of Calcutta. Some rioters had pistols and cobblers used their rasps, but anyone could hurl their iron-heeled shoes at the enemy. On the other hand, since Sirhindī was so incensed about Muslims celebrating Hindu festivals, that too must have been happening. What, then, was the balance of hostility and comity? It stands to reason that it must have varied greatly over space and time and that a vast amount of real-life experience must have been situated somewhere between the extremes articulated in the views we have examined. One factor that could have helped here is that by today's standards communications were glacially slow, which meant that local accommodations were easier to reach and preserve. But they could, of course, be very unequal accommodations. In any case, while the overall balance must have been somewhere between the extremes, just where it was is anybody's guess.

An underlying assumption in all this, and probably a correct one, is that however close Muslims and Hindus came to each other they hardly ever fused. Crypto-

Hindu sects—Muslim in public and Hindu in private—do not seem to be an Indian phenomenon, and it was almost always clear who was a Muslim and who was a Hindu. An interesting figure in this connection, and a possible exception, is the mystic poet Kabīr. He was a low-caste weaver of Benares and probably lived in the first half of the fifteenth century. But was he a Ṣūfī—and so a Muslim—or was he a devotee of the god Viṣṇu—and so a Hindu? According to a Hindu source he gave religious instruction to Hindus and Muslims alike, while a Muslim source relates that when he died the Brahmins wanted to cremate his body and the Muslims to bury it. His poetry was likewise recited by both Hindus and Muslims, and his followers, the Kabīr-panthīs, were divided into Hindu and Muslim branches. The oldest testimony has it that he was born a Muslim, but it would be hard to infer this from his poetry, where he trashes the standard forms of both religions with evenhanded contempt. The deeds of the All-merciful are indeed wonderful, but the Vēda and the Qur'ān are worthless, as are the law of the Qur'ān and the sacred thread of the Brahmins. To talk of the two religions is folly; when we set aside false dualities, "there is neither Hindu nor Turk"[46]—where "Turk," as in early modern English, means "Muslim." On the one hand, Kabīr rejects Hindu notions of caste—despite caste marks, no one is lowborn. And on the other hand, he has no use for the Muslim practice of circumcision—if God wanted you to be circumcised, why didn't He circumcise you in the womb? What Kabīr does affirm is his devotion to his god, Allāh-Rām—exactly the interfaith equation that Sirhindī excoriated. Symmetrically, this deity is at once his guru and his Pīr—his Hindu mentor and his Ṣūfī guide. Yet he often breaks the symmetry by referring to his deity simply as Rām, one of the incarnations of Viṣṇu. All in all, we have good reason to be uncertain whether to classify Kabīr as a Hindu or a Muslim. Yet everyone else who was connected with Kabīr—the Hindus and Muslims he instructed, the Hindus and Muslims who wanted to take charge of his mortal remains, the Hindus and Muslims who recited his poetry, the Hindus and Muslims who belonged to the Kabīr-panth—all these are described in a way that takes it for granted that however much they had in common, they belonged unambiguously to one religion or the other.

On a different front, it could be argued that the continuing existence of a large Hindu majority, together with the somewhat parvenu status of Indian Islam, carried a significant opportunity cost for the role of India in the Muslim world. But for these factors, the resources of India might well have made it the center of gravity of the wider Muslim community and given it a corresponding cultural predominance. As it was, it was rare for the Muslims of India to have a major influence on the Islam of the heartlands. Perhaps the main exception concerns the legacy of a familiar figure, Aḥmad Sirhindī, here in his role as a Ṣūfī. The Ṣūfī order he

46. Translated in C. Vaudeville, *A weaver named Kabir*, Delhi 1993, 217.

founded, the Mujaddidī branch of the larger Naqshbandī order, spread widely in the Ottoman Empire from the late seventeenth century onward. It was also not unknown for individual Indian scholars to move to the heartlands and acquire outstanding reputations there. The scholar and Ṣūfī Muttaqī al-Hindī (d. 1567), who moved from Gujarat to Mecca, produced a new version of a vast inventory of traditions from the Prophet and others. The lexicographer Murtaḍā al-Zabīdī (d. 1791) was born on the Gangetic plain and in 1753 settled in Cairo, where he composed a ten-volume Arabic dictionary. It took him fourteen years, but thereafter, he states, it became so famous that he received requests for copies from the Ottoman ruler, the king of Morocco, and the sultan of Dār Fūr (the region of Africa known today as Darfur). Here, then, we have an Indian Muslim who achieved celebrity status; a North African scholar even held him up as an example of the point that later scholars can be superior to earlier ones. Both his book and that of Muttaqī al-Hindī became standard works of reference at the center of the Muslim world. And yet the cultural influence India exerted in the heartlands was far from being in proportion to its resources.

12

The Indian Ocean

By the time the Portuguese had circumnavigated Africa, Muslims were to be found around the greater part of the Indian Ocean rim. This success was unique. On the one hand, no earlier religious community had spread so widely around this ocean, and on the other, the Muslims themselves did not achieve anything like it around either the Atlantic or the Pacific. They did reach some parts of the coastlands of both, but their presence there did not issue in any larger diffusion of Islam around the rims of either.

In some ways the spread of Muslims around the Indian Ocean is surprising. Although the heartlands of Islam extended to its shores, the coastal populations found there were demographically thin. Moreover, the ocean itself served as a barrier to military conquest, ensuring that the primary agents of the propagation of Islam would be merchants. Islam was nevertheless the first religion to achieve primacy around the Indian Ocean rim as a whole.

Apart from the shores of the heartlands, we can divide the Indian Ocean rim into three sectors: East Africa, India, and Southeast Asia.

The East African sector was made up of three regions: the island of Madagascar, the East African littoral, and the Somali coast and hinterland. The seaboard of Madagascar saw persistent Muslim settlement over the centuries, but to little cumulative effect. Along the East African coast Muslim settlers, often on islands close to the mainland, joined with native converts to produce the Swahili culture, a ribbon development down the coast with little penetration inland. The Somali case was different: here mercantile activity on the coast led to the conversion of the camel nomads of the interior.

The Indian sector was distinctive inasmuch as Islam reached the Indian interior through military conquest. But its presence on the coasts, as also on Ceylon, was largely the work of merchants, who unlike conquerors needed to come to terms with the Hindu or Buddhist states that held power there. Moreover India, with its vast population, was inevitably the economic center of gravity of the Indian Ocean.

Turning to the Southeast Asian sector, the Muslim presence on the mainland was limited. There were Muslims in Arakan thanks to overland links with Bengal, and there were brief periods of Muslim political prominence in seventeenth-century Cambodia and Siam. But the only people of the region who converted to Islam in significant numbers were the Chams of what is now southern Vietnam.

There was a much greater Muslim presence in maritime Southeast Asia, on the Malay Peninsula and the islands. This initially followed the normal Indian Ocean pattern, with the coasts turning Muslim; the surprise, as in the Somali case, is that the religion went on to penetrate the interior, especially on Java. Farther east there was Muslim activity as far as the edge of the Pacific.

The forms of Islam that took root around the Indian Ocean showed considerable variety. In general, as might be expected, the mercantile spread of Islam worked in favor of accommodation with local cultures. We will see notable cases of this on the southwest coast of Madagascar, on the southeastern coast of India, among the Chams, and in the Javanese interior. But less accommodating forms of the religion were also present in the region.

The spread of Islam, as we have seen it in the preceding chapters, was in the first instance a matter of conquest.[1] It was through military expansion that new lands were subjected, forcefully bringing Islam to the notice of the conquered peoples and setting the terms of their interaction with their new rulers. The result was to place these peoples in a situation in which the benefits of joining the ruling community could decisively outweigh the costs of breaking with their own communities. In this chapter, however, we come to a major region, and not the only one, in which there was a massive geographical barrier to such external conquest. This does not mean that conquest as such was irrelevant to the spread of Islam in these regions: once the religion was sufficiently well established there, nothing prevented its followers from waging war on their infidel neighbors to secure their subjection to Islam. Indeed, instances of such internal conquest are by no means rare. But the process by which Islam first crossed the barrier could not involve conquest. So what kind of geographical barrier would have this effect?

The one that concerns us in this chapter is an ocean. There were in fact three oceans that set limits to Muslim conquest: the Atlantic in the west, the Pacific in the east, and the Indian Ocean in the south. The first two require only brief treatment because they effectively blocked almost all human communication until the inception of the European voyages of discovery in the late fifteenth century. In the case of the Atlantic, the seventh-century Arab conqueror of North Africa is said to have ridden his horse into the ocean on reaching the Moroccan coast, telling God that but for the sea he would have continued farther in order to defend His religion and fight those who disbelieved in Him. But there was no maritime

1. An earlier and shorter version of this chapter was published as "The spread of Islam around the Indian Ocean," *Proceedings of the Israel Academy of Sciences and Humanities*, 9 (2019), no. 7.

follow-up to this dramatic gesture. Despite the later presence of Muslim states along this coast, Muslim seafaring on the Atlantic was so limited that Islam did not even establish itself on the Canary Islands, the closest of which lies less than sixty miles off the Moroccan shore. On the east side of Africa, by contrast, Islam had reached the Comoro Islands by the fifteenth century and very likely long before, despite their being about three times as far from both the African coast and Madagascar. Returning to the Atlantic, we will see in a later chapter that after the Christians of Spain and Portugal had opened up the ocean, a Moroccan sultan of the later sixteenth century showed a passing interest in transatlantic colonization. But nothing came of this, and most of the Muslim migrants who reached the New World in our period did so involuntarily as slaves. Meanwhile, there did indeed come to be a significant amount of Muslim seafaring on the Atlantic thanks to the piratical activities of the Barbary corsairs, who were based in the southwestern Mediterranean. For example, they raided Iceland in 1627, and an Ottoman scholar of the day mentions a report that Muslim corsairs had sailed close to the North Pole. But these corsairs, many of them European renegades, did not settle the lands they raided and left no converts behind there. In the case of the Pacific there is even less to report. This ocean was almost twice as far from the Muslim heartlands as the Atlantic was, and to reach it Islam had to start by crossing either Inner Asia or the Indian Ocean. In the event, as we will see, the Muslim presence on the shores of the Pacific was very limited.

The Indian Ocean was different. Like the Atlantic and the Pacific, it blocked the movement of Muslim armies. Neither the Arabs nor the Turks could project any significant amount of military power across it, and no large-scale transoceanic conquests took place in this part of the world until well into modern times. But like the Mediterranean, the Indian Ocean did not prevent the movement of merchants, since the combination of sea and wind made it relatively cheap to move people and goods over long distances. It nevertheless differed from the Mediterranean in significant ways. The most obvious of them is that where the Mediterranean is small, the Indian Ocean is vast—the best part of thirty Mediterraneans would fit into it. Likewise, where the Mediterranean is closed except for a break of less than ten miles at the Strait of Gibraltar, the Indian Ocean is open. More precisely, its coastlands consist of an arc that is wide open to the south, where its two ends are separated by nearly five thousand miles. This fact, in turn, affected the history of the human understanding of the two bodies of water. Whereas a knowledge of the overall shape of the Mediterranean was widely available already in ancient times, it was not until the exploration of the Indian Ocean by the Europeans that the two ends of the arc came within the horizon of geographical knowledge. At the same time, the shores of the Mediterranean are on average more supportive of human habitation than are those of the Indian Ocean. Around the Mediterranean only some parts of the coasts of Libya and Egypt are desert; the rest can support agrarian societies that provide a foundation for cities and states. Although certain parts of the Indian Ocean rim are equally fortunate, a large share of it is either desert or tropical jungle. A final point worth noting here concerns the religious affiliations of the mariners and merchants who dominated the two commercial scenes. Already in the tenth century the Mediterranean was beginning to revert to what it had been in late antiquity, a sea dominated by Christians, whereas on the Indian Ocean Muslims came to play the leading role until the arrival of the Portuguese at the end of the fifteenth century. These points are enough to suggest that the maritime scene on the Indian Ocean would be very different from that of the Mediterranean.

For convenience we will divide this scene into a number of sectors, starting with the coastline of the Muslim heartlands. But before we begin, a point needs to be made about our sources. Medieval chroniclers usually occupy themselves with events that concern the prestige of rulers, not the profits of merchants, and this tendency seriously limits what we can know about the history of the Indian Ocean before the arrival of the Europeans. Nor does it help that Muslim sources tend to be much less interested in the actual processes of conversion than Christian ones are. It is only with the coming of the Portuguese that we begin to be much better informed. The Portuguese state had a voracious appetite for information about distant lands, its rulers were deeply interested in the doings of merchants, its bureaucrats preserved relevant archival documentation, and the literate public of Europe at large developed a strong interest in accounts of the wider world. For earlier centuries, however, our information is often scant. We do in fact possess a considerable number of letters and documents relating to Indian Ocean trade that date from the eleventh and twelfth centuries, but they concern Jewish, not Muslim, merchants.

The coast of the heartlands

Geography and its implications

The Indian Ocean coast of the Middle Eastern heartlands is a long one, and it is made even longer by the presence of the Persian Gulf and the Red Sea. Their mouths constitute two of the three chokeholds of the Indian Ocean, the third being the Strait of Malacca. But unlike the Strait of Malacca, the Persian Gulf and the Red Sea are dead-end waterways—they give ships no access to the Mediterranean. The stretch of the littoral that concerns us here starts in the northeast with the coast of Makrān, after which we have in succession the southern coast of Iran, the eastern, southern, and western coasts of Arabia, and the western coast of the Red Sea. In ethnic terms the main element in the coastal population was Arab. Even along the southern coast of Iran a Dutch report of 1756 tells us that all places "capable of receiving vessels" were "inhabited by Arab colonies."[2] This was nothing new: medieval terminology divided the Iranian coast of the Persian Gulf into three parts, each named for an Arab tribal group that had established itself there. But the Arabs did not monopolize the coastlands. Along the western coast of the Red Sea there were non-Arab nomads such as the Beja. They are described in the tenth century as camel nomads who neither lived in villages nor practiced any form of cultivation, and we are told that an early Arab governor of Egypt had decided that their land was not worth attacking. Farther south the Ethiopians had a maritime presence at the beginning of our period. As might be expected of a coastline extending from Makrān to Ethiopia, there is considerable variation in the natural environment along its length. But in one crucial respect it is much of a muchness: it is part and parcel of the arid zone of the Middle East. The exceptions are few and far between. One region on the southern shore of Iran receives a bit of rainfall as do parts of the coast of Oman, and the region of Dhofar is grazed by the monsoon. But the only major divergence from the overall aridity is the irrigated agriculture made possible in the hinterland of Baṣra by the rivers of Iraq and Khūzistān. Yet even Baṣra was never a capital like Rome or Constantinople, and it was only a great city when times were good, as in the early Islamic period. By the twelfth century it was in ruins. Ottoman Baṣra, though no longer in the same location and inhabited by fewer than six thousand households in 1689, was not a ruin, but it could be cut off from the Persian Gulf by the local tribesmen and even seized by them. With this partial exception the coastlands were mostly desolate, precluding the large-scale agricultural production that could support a dense peasant population or a major city. In short, the Middle East had its back to the Indian Ocean.

This meant that urban life on these coasts had more to do with long-distance trade than with local agricultural resources, making for a marked instability in the location of major settlements. The Red Sea coast abounds in what have aptly been called "ghost towns." A sixth-century Gallo-Roman historian explains that Qulzum—the ancient Clysma near Suez—was built where it was "not because of the fertility of the site, for nothing could be more sterile, but for its harbor,"[3] adding that ships from the Indies unloaded their goods there; it has been a ruin since the eleventh century. Farther to the south, the medieval port of ʿAydhāb was located more or less opposite Jeddah. It declined in the fourteenth or fifteenth century and today only its ruins remain, yet a twelfth-century traveler described it as one of the world's busiest ports thanks to its trade with India and the Yemen, together with the annual pilgrim traffic. He went on to say that it was located in a barren wilderness, and that all its food had to be imported. The Dahlak Islands, located off the African coast about a quarter of the way up the Red Sea, were similarly

2. Quoted in W. Floor, *The Persian Gulf: The rise of the Gulf Arabs*, Washington 2007, 24.
3. Gregory of Tours, *The history of the Franks*, London 1974, 75 (1.10).

unpromising. They had little rain or vegetation, offering only wretched grazing for goats and camels, and the main town was described by a thirteenth-century geographer as hot and cramped. Yet the islands were well placed to benefit from long-distance trade. We know from their gravestones that there were people there with ancestors from as far afield as Morocco and Khurāsān and that in the eleventh to thirteenth centuries there was a ruling dynasty. Jewish documents show that there was a customhouse and that the town was frequented by Jewish merchants—and no doubt Muslim ones too. As late as the seventeenth century the Ottoman traveler Evliyā Chelebī, whom we last met in the Morea, reported the presence of six hundred houses at the time of his visit. But by the end of our period the islands were of little interest to anyone, though a visitor in 1804 commented that "the port still exhibits many vestiges of its former consequence."[4] Likewise Aden, on the south coast of the Yemen, is an excellent port that played a major part in the commerce of the Indian Ocean, but it was separated from the mountains of the Yemen by an arid coastal plain, and when the British seized it in 1839 it was a mere village. Typically these ports were bedeviled by the arduous overland travel that separated them from any major population centers. Thus the journey from ʿAydhāb to the Nile valley took seventeen days, including a stretch of three or four days with no possibility of finding water.

The Persian Gulf was no different. Sīrāf on the south coast of Iran was a wealthy commercial city in the early centuries of Islam, but tellingly it had no permanent supply of running water; the inhabitants dug wells, built conduits into the hinterland, and constructed dozens of reservoirs. It is thus no surprise that Sīrāf ceased to be a significant center of Indian Ocean commerce after the eleventh century. The silver lining to this collapse was that it made the site a boon to archaeologists: when they came to excavate it there was no modern city impeding their access, just a small village occupying a fraction of the medieval site. Meanwhile Sīrāf lost its commercial role to Kīsh—an island that did at least support a measure of agriculture, but in turn lost its primacy to Hormuz in the fourteenth century. The island of Hormuz, at the mouth of the Persian Gulf, was just as barren as the environs of Sīrāf. Even its drinking water had to be brought by boat, and in 1512 an interruption of its rice supply from India threatened famine. It lost its commercial role when captured and destroyed by the Ṣafawid ruler Shāh ʿAbbās in 1622, and it is almost uninhabited at the present day. Its place was taken by Bandar ʿAbbās, which sat on an empty windswept plain. It was a flourishing port in the 1640s, but a mere village by the 1750s. Conversely, Bushire was a minor port that started to matter only in the eighteenth century; in 1787 a traveler remarked that the surrounding country was "naked, and without verdure," exhibiting "a dreary and

4. George, Viscount Valentia, *Voyages and travels*, London 1809, 2:41.

unpleasant prospect."[5] What these ports had against them was not, however, just their lack of robust local resources to support urban life. Here again, it was also the forbidding terrain that separated them from the cities of the interior where the major consumers of Indian Ocean merchandise lived. The journey from Bushire on the coast of the Persian Gulf to Shīrāz, a mere hundred miles away on the Iranian plateau, was so difficult that in the 1830s the British deemed it impossible to send an army into Iran by that route.

All this, in turn, had implications for the political geography of the region. No large and powerful states were ever based on this coastline. The nearest substantial states tended not to exercise much control over it and to engage in naval activities only intermittently. One example of such activity was the naval component of the conquest of Sindh under the Umayyads, another was a major maritime raid mounted by the ʿAbbāsids on an Indian city in the 770s—but this was a raid, not a conquest. For a time the Ottomans were active on the wider Indian Ocean in response to the challenge of the Portuguese, who worried about "what it will mean to have the Ottomans for neighbors."[6] Indeed, the Ottomans flexed their muscles as far afield as Aceh on Sumatra, but they ended up doing little more than securing the entry to the Red Sea. In the case of Iran the short-lived attempt of Nādir Shāh (ruled 1736–47) to develop a powerful navy stands out as exceptional. His priorities are shown up by the fact that this remorselessly military ruler never visited his fleet, and by the time of his death most of his ships were wrecked or rotting. A Dutch report of 1756 anticipated the passing of many centuries before Persia was likely to be ruled by another king like Nādir and held out little hope of ever again seeing a Persian fleet in the Gulf. It is this absence of major naval powers that explains the ease with which distant European counties such as Portugal were able to range freely on the Indian Ocean from the late fifteenth century onward. Indeed, one European analyst of the early fourteenth century, the author of a tract on how to defeat and "extirpate all the Saracens from the Indian sea and its coastal cities,"[7] argued that a fleet of three or four galleys manned by 1,200 Genoese could destroy Egyptian trade by blocking the mouth of the Red Sea.

Lesser states could be more active if they had immediate access to the sea and depended on maritime commerce for their livelihoods. As with larger states, their rulers might own ships and profit from their commercial activities, as was the case with Hormuz, and likewise with the Rasūlids (1228–1454), who ruled the southern Yemen and were thus in a position to control the entrance to the Red Sea. Merchants may not have appreciated such competition, but they could do little to stop it; as a sixteenth-century jurist of Aden put it, "If the sultan applies

5. Quoted in Floor, *The Persian Gulf*, 310.
6. Quoted in G. Casale, *The Ottoman age of exploration*, Oxford 2010, 28.
7. William of Adam, *How to defeat the Saracens*, Washington 2012, 117.

himself to commerce, he annuls the commerce of merchants."[8] But in the Rasūlid case the rulers did not limit themselves to commerce. A remarkable document from the 1290s shows the dynasty dispensing largesse to more than sixty judges and preachers of the Muslim mercantile communities residing in the coastal cities of India. Obviously the ruler of the Yemen must have derived some benefit from these arrangements. No doubt this included good relations with merchants whose activities enriched the royal treasury and the prestige of having his name mentioned in the Friday prayers of Muslim communities far away across the ocean. Yet even the Rasūlids made no attempt to project naval power across the sea to India. Smaller states could be more waspish: around 1135 the ruler of Kīsh sent fifteen ships from the Gulf to attack Aden, and he was not above using his fleet to discourage merchants from taking their wares to rival ports. But the fact that in general states of any size tended to be absent or only weakly present on these coasts meant that until the coming of the Europeans, commercial opportunities were to a large extent left to private enterprise. Such enterprise was real enough, but it lacked the backing of powerful states. Prior to the arrival of the Europeans, this general lack of engagement on the part of the larger states left Muslim merchants in a situation no worse than that of their competitors. Even after the Europeans had demonstrated that their combination of commerce and sea power could be effective, there was little attempt to emulate it on the part of the larger Muslim states. The one state in the heartlands that did that, and with considerable success, was Oman in the last two centuries of our period, but Oman was a second-tier state.

The aridity of the region had two other effects that worked against merchants from the heartlands. One was a lack of timber for shipbuilding. Here again Baṣra had the potential to be something of an exception, despite not having timber resources of its own, since a power like the Ottoman Empire could have floated timber down from eastern Anatolia by river. But for most inhabitants of the coastlands the nearest accessible source of suitable timber was the west coast of India—and it was not easy to get there to build a ship unless you had one already. When Nādir Shāh created his abortive navy he showed his awareness of the problem by employing three strategies to overcome the scarcity of timber. One was borrowing, buying, or seizing ships from the English and the Dutch. Another was getting his ships built at Sūrat on the west coast of India. And the third was having timber transported overland from the Caspian coast. This latter was a task only a tyrant such as Nādir would have imposed on his unhappy subjects. The other negative effect of aridity for Arab and Persian merchants was demographic: the thinness of the coastal population lessened local demand, with the result that in

8. Quoted in E. Vallet, *L'Arabie marchande*, Paris 2010, 695.

comparison to the Mediterranean, short-distance trade carried less relative weight in the overall commercial mix, and the same tended to be true of trade in bulk goods. But bulk goods were by no means absent, as is shown by the rice trade. While no one in their right mind would have thought of shipping rice from one side of the Indian Ocean to the other, it was still transported over long distances. So too were marble tombstones for Muslims produced to order in Gujarat and shipped as far afield as East Africa and northeastern Java in the thirteenth to fifteenth centuries.

A final implication of geography concerns the slower pace imposed on Indian Ocean navigation by the powerful monsoon winds. On the Mediterranean sailing was subject to seasonal constraints—it was a summer, not a winter activity. But in the course of a long summer there was nothing to stop a ship making multiple trips to the same destination. This was not so on the Indian Ocean. It had been discovered in ancient times that the best way to reach India from the Middle East was not to hug the coast but rather to venture out into the ocean and cross with the summer monsoon; a ship could then return home in the same way with the winter monsoon. This meant that one could travel to India and back only once in a year. The farther east the journey extended the longer the turnaround time, so a trip to southern China and back meant a year and a half at sea.

Muslim merchants from the heartlands

Despite all this, merchants from the Middle Eastern coastlands seem to have done well on the Indian Ocean, at least until the arrival of the Europeans. They were already prospering long before the rise of Islam. There is a short Greek work dating from the first century that describes the coasts of the Indian Ocean from East Africa to Bengal; it mentions the prominence in the trade with Azania on the East African coast of Arabs who "are familiar through residence and intermarriage with the nature of the places and their language."[9] We do not know whether this Arab activity continued into the seventh century, but it is quite likely that it did, since Roman coins of the fourth century have been found on the northern coast of Kenya. Our Greek text likewise refers to ships sailing from Egypt to the west coast of India, mentioning the presence of Greek ships there, and indeed considerable numbers of Roman coins have been found in India. Meanwhile we have a remarkable account, also in Greek, of the commerce of Ceylon from the mid-sixth century. It notes the existence of a community of Persian Christians on the island, speaks of ships from Persia and Ethiopia frequenting it, and tells a story in which two ships arrive there at the same time, one from Persia and one from Ethiopia.

9. *The Periplus of the Erythraean Sea*, trans. G.W.B. Huntingford, London 1980, 30.

So it may well be that the rise of Islam involved no major structural change and that many of the merchants who had previously plied the trade now quietly converted to Islam and carried on doing what they had done before.

There is, however, some reason to think that their activities now extended farther. To the south, as we have seen, the ancient Greeks had some familiarity with the East African coast. According to our first-century source its southernmost trading post was a place called Rhapta. This was a possession of an Arabian ruler, though located in the middle of an anarchic territory in which each locality had its own chief; beyond that the ocean was unexplored. We do not know exactly where Rhapta was, but ancient sources show no awareness of the existence of Madagascar, which as one of the world's largest islands is hard to miss for anyone in the vicinity. In Islamic times, by contrast, the horizon had shifted southward. By the tenth century the East African coast was known as far as Sofala in today's Mozambique, that is to say well to the south of the northern end of Madagascar, and Muslim references to this island, though initially foggy, eventually come to be unambiguous. By the time the Portuguese arrived Muslim settlements extended over a hundred miles south of Sofala. At the same time there seems to have been a comparable extension of the horizon to the east. We have no good evidence that in pre-Islamic times either Persians or Arabs were trading by sea with southern China. But we know that in 671 Persians (perhaps Zoroastrians) were present in Canton, since a Chinese Buddhist pilgrim tells us of a Persian ship that was there in that year. In the next century the presence of Arabs (perhaps including Muslim Persians) is attested in both Chinese and Arabic sources, and for a while the two groups became the main players in the overseas trade of southern China. Later, at the point at which the Europeans arrived, even merchants from Ottoman Anatolia seem to have been casting a wide net. Thus in 1510 the Portuguese reported their presence on Sumatra, and in 1587 the English found four of them on the island of Ternate in the Moluccas, as little as sixty miles from the Pacific rim.

We have no reason to think that these merchants played much part in the early spread of Islam within the heartlands from which they came. Here Arab political and military power was paramount, even if it may have taken time for its full effects to reach parts of the thinly populated coastlands. The only region where merchants are likely to have played some role would be the western coast of the Red Sea, among pastoral nomads like the Beja. However, such indications as we have do not suggest that the Beja owed their conversion to maritime commerce. The beginnings of Beja conversion seem rather to have been linked to mining activities on their territory. Here as elsewhere in the Red Sea hinterlands, the mountainous terrain associated with the rifting that opened the way for the sea also ensured the presence of mineral resources, notably gold. These were not as abundant as in the northern Middle East, but in compensation the aridity of the region made them easier to find—and also helps archaeologists today rediscover mines worked in ancient and medieval times. In a way the exploitation of these mines seems to have resembled the early stages of oil production in the eastern Middle East in modern times: where the local tribesmen were too proud or too lacking in technical skill to operate the mines, enclave economies emerged in which outsiders took charge, provided the workforce, brought in food to feed it, and sold what they produced to richer and more densely populated societies located elsewhere. Hence in the ninth century there came to be a significant presence of Arabs in the territory of the Beja, who resented the fact that these interlopers were taking over resources located on their lands. Although their relationship was largely antagonistic, this meant that pagan Beja were now interacting on a daily basis with Muslim Arabs. The interaction resulted in the conversion of a Beja tribe, though even these Beja are said to have become Muslims only in name. As late as the first half of the fifteenth century, an Egyptian polymath described the Beja at large as having no religion; he excepted the same Beja tribe but qualified the faith of the tribesmen as weak. Indeed, the full conversion of the Beja has been linked to the establishment of the Funj Sultanate on the Blue Nile in the sixteenth century, and if that was indeed the case, then here again Indian Ocean merchants would have been irrelevant. In general, the importance of Muslim merchants for the spread of Islam lay in the results of their presence in sectors of the Indian Ocean coastlands outside the heartlands.

What kind of Islam would result from the activities of the merchants in these distant sectors would naturally depend in part on the conditions that obtained in the various ports to which they sailed. But it would also be affected by the kind of Islam with which the merchants set out. Here the coasts of the heartlands were far from homogeneous. Shīʿism of more than one kind was politically dominant in Egypt under the rule of the Fāṭimids (969–1171), in the Yemen under their Ṣulayḥid co-sectarians (1047–1138), and in Iran under the Ṣafawids (1501–1722) and their successors; it rose to power again in the Yemen when the Zaydī imamate became strong enough to control the coast in the seventeenth century. Ibāḍism was politically dominant in Oman, where Ibāḍī rulers had firm control of the coasts in the eighth to ninth centuries and again from the seventeenth century onward. It also had its day in Ḥaḍramawt between the eighth and eleventh centuries. Sunnism was politically dominant in Egypt before and after the Fāṭimids and demographically at all times, as it likewise tended to be in the southern Yemen, in Ḥaḍramawt after the eleventh century, in Dhofar, on parts of the southern coast of the Persian Gulf, in Iraq until the conversion of the southern tribes to Shīʿism in recent centuries, and on the coast of Iran before the rise of the Ṣafawids. Even then, Sunnism remained prominent on the Iranian side of the Persian Gulf, particularly among the Arabs. The Dutch report of 1756 notes that as "followers of the sect of ʿUmar" the Huwala Arabs "feel a deadly hatred for the Persians," who are adherents of the sect of ʿAlī[10]—in other words, Shīʿites. Thus Sunnism, though widespread, was far from exercising a monopoly. Shīʿism and Ibāḍism were nevertheless only marginally represented in the Islam that the merchants implanted elsewhere around the rim of the Indian Ocean. Shīʿism had a long-term constituency in northwestern India, is mentioned in Kerala, and made minor and doubtful appearances in East Africa. Ibāḍism was present on the island of Kilwa on the East African coast around the twelfth century and arrived in force with the Omani conquest of the later seventeenth century. Yet overwhelmingly it was Sunnī Islam that spread to the coastlands of East Africa, India, and Southeast Asia. Moreover, it was just as overwhelmingly a particular form of Sunnī Islam: Shāfiʿism, the school of Islamic law that follows the doctrines of Shāfiʿī (d. 820). Ḥanafīs and Mālikīs play only bit parts in this story, and Ḥanbalīs none at all. It is obviously relevant here that Shāfiʿism came to be dominant in the Egyptian delta, the lowlands of the Yemen, Ḥaḍramawt, and Dhofar, and was well represented in much of Iran before the rise of the Ṣafawids. Of these regions it was, rather surprisingly, Ḥaḍramawt that from the sixteenth century became the source of a continuing migration of Arabs to India and on to Southeast Asia. But again Shāfiʿism did not hold a monopoly, even among Sunnīs. Mālikism was prominent in early ninth-century Egypt and maintained its dominance in Upper Egypt, which in turn was linked to ports such as ʿAydhāb and Quṣayr—another of those ghost towns on the Red Sea coast. It was also well represented in medieval Iraq, whence its presence in Kuwait and other parts of the southern coast of the Persian Gulf to this day. In short, it is by no means obvious why Shāfiʿism was so successful elsewhere on the Indian Ocean rim, but there is no doubt that it was so. Something that sooner or later tended to accompany this spread was Ṣūfism. For example, the Ḥaḍramī descendants of the Prophet who migrated eastward took with them a Ṣūfī order of their own. The Islam of the Indian Ocean, like Islam in general, could take on a marked Ṣūfī coloring.

There is another aspect of mercantile Islam that is worth attention here. To make their profits merchants need at least three things in their interpersonal relations. One is to be able to trust each other, even when they may not know each other personally. Here a small and closed ethnic, religious, or caste group that has little in common with its surroundings can provide a favorable basis for developing a high degree of internal trust—as with the North African Jewish merchants of the medieval Indian Ocean or the Julfan Armenian traders of early modern times. The disadvantage of such groups is, of course, that they are small. The trust that can be generated by large and open groups such as Shāfiʿites is likely to be significantly weaker, but the advantage is that it includes a much larger number

10. Quoted in Floor, *The Persian Gulf*, 30.

of people. We should perhaps think of the general Shāfiʿite sense of community as providing broader support for more specific mercantile networks. We can tentatively identify one such network, a certain Ṣūfī order. As we saw in connection with the religious history of Iran, the founder, Abū Isḥāq al-Kāzarūnī (d. 1033), was mainly interested in converting the Zoroastrians of his native Fārs, but by the fourteenth century the order he founded had a wide presence around the shores of the Indian Ocean and as far afield as China, providing hospices at which travelers such as Ibn Baṭṭūṭa were welcome to stay. The order would also provide spiritual solace to merchants at sea in accordance with an apt business model. If a ship was in danger, a Kāzarūnī agent on board would collect from the terrified passengers written promises of donations they would make if delivered to land. Should the ship then reach its destination, the staff of the local hospice would come aboard and collect; if it did not, the promises presumably went down with the ship. Such an order could well have played a role in generating trust. But besides trusting and being trusted by his peers, another thing a trader has to do is to get along with people in the lands he visits who are not members of his in-group. This is something merchants have to worry about far more than soldiers. We owe to a twelfth-century source an account of merchants based in a town not far from Ghazna who traded with India. They were Khārijites claiming descent from none other than the ferocious Azāriqa, but by now they were peaceable, and in their relations with the princes of India each of their chiefs assumed an Indian name alongside his Arabic one. The soldiers of armies of conquest do not act like that. Here, then, the pursuit of profit went well with a measure of tolerance for religious diversity. A mid-fifteenth-century Muslim visitor to the island of Hormuz remarked that "people of all religions, and even idolators, meet in the city of Hormuz and nobody permits any hostile gesture or injustice against them."[11] Indeed, in the mid-sixteenth century there were Hindu holy men living in caves on the island, not to mention the sacred cows that wandered around. The diverse residents of the port did not even segregate themselves into separate quarters. All this was abnormal in the heartlands of the Muslim world, but it made good sense: Hormuz depended entirely on trade for its livelihood, and anything other than a generous tolerance would have been bad for business. Yet this did not mean that merchants were free to go native without cost. A third thing merchants typically needed to do was to retain good relations with the societies into which they were born, particularly if they continued to be based there. These three conflicting pulls made for rather unpredictable outcomes.

In all this, it does not seem that Shāfiʿism, conceived as a set of beliefs and practices as opposed to a community, had any particular elective affinity for Indian

11. Quoted in V. F. Piacentini, "Salghur Shāh, malik of Hormuz, and his embargo of Iranian harbours," in D. Couto and R. M. Loureiro (eds.), *Revisiting Hormuz*, Wiesbaden 2008, 8.

Ocean trade. Certainly the Islamic tradition in general enshrines attitudes favorable to merchants and their activities, but Shāfiʿism does not stand out here. In fact, Shāfiʿite law regarding a key form of mercantile partnership was less sensitive to the interests of merchants than the Ḥanafī stipulations were. In one respect Shāfiʿism did have the edge: it allowed its followers to eat seafood, undoubtedly a perk for maritime traders. But its dietary provisions were far from antinomian. A vegetarian meal provided by polytheists was not in itself a problem, but their meat was forbidden, and polluted dishes were a concern. Moreover, Ibn Baṭṭūṭa makes it clear that the rules had real-world consequences. He describes a road on the Malabar coast of southwestern India that was equipped all along the way with Muslim-owned houses where passing Muslims could buy what they needed and have food cooked for them. Without these safe houses, he adds, no Muslim could have traveled this route. Likewise Shāfiʿite stipulations regarding marriage to non-Muslim women are discouraging. Marrying polytheists is in any case forbidden in the Qurʾān, and unlike the Ḥanafīs, the Shāfiʿites stigmatize even marriage to Jewish and Christian women, which the Qurʾān allows. Presumably the native wives that Muslim merchants acquired around the Indian Ocean rim underwent at least nominal conversion.

We are now ready to embark on a survey of the various sectors of the rim to which Islam came through commerce. Let us start in the far southwest with Madagascar and gradually work round toward Australia.

The western sector

Madagascar

Remarkably, this large island seems to have remained without any human inhabitants until perhaps as little as sixteen hundred years ago; the earliest evidence of significant settlement is from the ninth century. Although Madagascar lies only some 250 miles off the shores of Africa, it appears that there was no indigenous tradition of seafaring on the East African coast to bring settlers to it. Both genetic and linguistic evidence indicate that the initiative came instead from southeastern Borneo, where the Austronesian languages closest to Malagasy, the language of Madagascar, are still spoken. In the course of their travels these Austronesian migrants must also have reached the East African coast, carrying off Africans to Madagascar, very likely as slaves. The result of this mixing is a population that in genetic terms is about two-thirds East African and one-third Southeast Asian on the coasts, but evenly balanced in the interior. The two elements came together to speak Malagasy, an Austronesian language marked by Bantu loanwords from Africa. Just when these migrations took place is uncertain in the absence of historical accounts. It seems that they happened before Islam reached Madagascar, though not before Indian cultural influence became noticeable on Borneo, since traces of it are to be found in the presence of Sanskrit loanwords in Malagasy. One estimate would see the migration begin in the seventh century and issue in the settlement of Madagascar in the eighth.

This was the background against which Muslim mariners and merchants seem to have arrived on Madagascar. As always in historical research we are at the mercy of our sources, and in the case of Madagascar they do not even begin to be merciful until late in the day. The result is that down to the nineteenth century we perceive much of the history of the island through a glass darkly. There are nevertheless three relevant bodies of source material. The earliest are medieval Arabic (and occasionally Chinese) works that offer usable accounts of the island from the twelfth century onward. Then come the reports of European observers, in particular the Portuguese who reached Madagascar in 1506, and the French who had a presence on the island in the mid-seventeenth century. These accounts, and especially those of the French, are much richer than the Arabic (or Chinese) sources. Finally, there are collections of Malagasy oral traditions, rarely known to have been assembled before the nineteenth century but containing material relating to much earlier periods. Some of this material reaches us in written form, recorded in Malagasy in the Arabic script.

The picture that emerges from this material appears to be something like the following.[12] Down to the sixteenth century Madagascar was divided between a large number of petty chiefdoms; there was as yet no major state on the coast, and until the middle of the seventeenth century no sign of the existence of one in the interior. Individual Muslim traders on the coast would presumably have had to reach accommodations with the local chiefs. One practice we hear of toward the end of our period is contracting with a chief for the erection and protection of a warehouse. But from at least the twelfth century onward there were whole settlements of Muslim merchants on the coasts of northern Madagascar, and later the Portuguese found them on the northwest coast and down the entire east coast. Most likely they had arrived via East Africa. Such groups of merchants could reach collective accommodations with chiefs, or they could establish politically independent settlements at convenient points on the coast—or better still, on small islands just off it. Thus the Portuguese reported two independent settlements of Muslims from the African mainland on the northern coast in 1556. In this way Muslims, and hence Islam, found some perches on the island, mainly but not exclusively in the north.

From that point Islam could become part of the Malagasy scene through either or both of two processes. One was the conversion of members of the native

12. For much of what follows see R. K. Kent, *Early kingdoms in Madagascar*, New York 1970, and S. Randrianja and S. Ellis, *Madagascar: A short history*, Chicago 2009.

population to Islam, and of this there is some evidence. For example, in the early seventeenth century Malagasy rulers on the northwest coast had Swahili merchants and scribes in their service, and it appears that in this setting many of these rulers and their subjects became Muslims. The other process was the assimilation of the progeny of foreign Muslims into Malagasy society, leaving only memories of foreign origin. Of this, too, we have some evidence, and we will come to it shortly. In either case a likely outcome was a form of Islam heavily mixed with native elements. One factor that may well have helped both processes is the tendency for long-distance traders to leave their wives behind at their points of origin and acquire new ones at their destinations. Here we are not reduced to pure speculation. Around 1800 there is attestation of a practice on Madagascar whereby a merchant would acquire a native wife for the duration of the trading season. She doubled as his commercial agent and would travel into the interior to trade on his behalf. Conversion could come easily in such settings; even chiefs who formed alliances with Swahili traders might become Muslims. Moreover, there is genetic confirmation of sexual asymmetry in the case of one of the most assimilated foreign communities of Madagascar, the Antemoro of the southeastern coast. Among the elite groups of this population, which claims a Meccan origin, some Middle Eastern ancestry does indeed show up in the Y-chromosomes of the male line, but none in the mitochondrial DNA of the female line. And if second-generation Muslims had indigenous mothers, together with fathers who were often away at sea, then the immigrant heritage was more than likely to be diluted in the absence of continuing reinforcement from across the ocean. Here a key factor may have been the disruption of Muslim trading patterns through the arrival of the Europeans, first the Portuguese and then the pirates. Their impact must have been considerable in the case of an island as remote as Madagascar—particularly on the southeastern coast, as opposed to the northwestern coast with its easy links to East Africa. In the northwest there was in fact some recovery of the Muslim settlements and their contacts with Arabia and India toward the end of our period. Thus around 1650 the port of Mazalagem Nova was the most flourishing on the island. Its population was Muslim, and it was ruled by a Muslim sultan until conquered by one of the most powerful pagan kings of the period, along with other Muslim settlements on this part of the coast, to form the Sakalava kingdom of Boina. But southeastern Madagascar was not part of this scene, and to the extent that its Muslim population had lost touch with the wider Muslim scene, it would have become increasingly vulnerable to the pull of assimilation into the native society. A late sixteenth-century traveler said of the Muslims of Sofala under Portuguese rule that "they are become neither utter pagans, nor holding to the sect of Mahomet."[13] This could be an apt description of the condition of the Antemoro.

13. Quoted in M. N. Pearson, *Port cities and intruders*, Baltimore 1998, 58.

Here it is worth pausing to look more closely at the curious case of this group. We can perhaps think of the ancestors of the Antemoro, or some of them, as reaching the north of the island around the twelfth century and later moving south to their present location. There one of them founded a kingdom that lasted into the nineteenth century. We are told that it was the practice of his descendants to visit the founder's grave every "Friday year" (this being a particular year in a seven-year cycle that was doubtless of Southeast Asian origin). None of this sounds in the least Islamic, and indeed the descendants of the founder of the kingdom seem to share a dearth of recognizably Muslim names like Aḥmad or Yūsuf. Nor did they have mosques or perform the obligatory ritual prayers. Although it seems that their calendar had lunar months, it appears that they intercalated an extra month every three years to keep it in phase with the seasons of the solar year—a most un-Islamic practice. In 1741 the Dutch witnessed a bizarre ritual performed on the seashore involving a pig and large amounts of alcohol; the Antemoro reputedly assured the Dutch that this was central to their observance of Islam. Yet we are also told that they considered themselves to be good Muslims, and indeed that they prayed. Their restriction of the public role of women may also have been a part of their Muslim heritage. For example, it was the general custom of Malagasy ruling families to allow their princesses to acquire and discard male consorts at will, and the Antemoro stood out in not sharing this practice. What is more, they possessed books that were partly in Arabic and partly in Malagasy written in the Arabic script. This latter manner of writing later came to be known as *sorabe* or "big writing" (in contrast to the little letters of the Latin script). There is some slight reason to think that the Arabic script as it arrived on Madagascar had been filtered through Southeast Asia. We are told that the books written in it were jealously guarded by the religious elite. Hundreds of these books survive, containing prayers and magical material, though unfortunately for us it was only belatedly that historical information began to be recorded in this fashion. At least one manuscript is likely to date from the sixteenth century, since it was already in French hands in the early seventeenth. It consists mainly of ritual texts in Arabic with an interlinear Malagasy translation, and it is unquestionably an Islamic text. Thanks to their literacy and their esoteric knowledge, the Antemoro scholars could render services to pagan societies in other parts of Madagascar. Thus in the eighteenth century the non-Muslim Sakalava rulers of western Madagascar employed them as scribes, and the Merina kingdom likewise made use of them in the early nineteenth century. The young Merina ruler Radama I (ruled 1810–28) learned the script as a teenager, and there are examples of it in his own hand.

There is no indication of any significant spread of Islam into the interior of Madagascar in our period. The myriad local chiefs of the hinterland did not convert on any scale, and the situation did not change when in the seventeenth century larger kingdoms began to take shape. In particular, the Merina kingdom, which was just beginning the process of extending its power over the island as a whole under King

Andrianampoinimerina (ruled 1778–1809), showed no interest in adopting Islam. The question was rather whether the kingdom would adopt Christianity, as it eventually did in 1869. So it is to be expected that the Muslim population of contemporary Madagascar is a small one. There are no census data, but as of 1977 there were estimated to be some fifty thousand Malagasy Muslims in a total population of over eight million—well under 1 percent, and concentrated in the northwest. Likewise, Arabic loanwords are not salient in mainstream Malagasy, with the conspicuous exception of the names of the days of the week.

This meager harvest from a millennium of interaction with Muslim merchants is puzzling, and it would be satisfying if we could be more definite about the history of Islam on Madagascar. Yet some of the key themes that have appeared here are worth retaining as more or less typical of the mercantile spread of Islam around the Indian Ocean rim. First, relations between foreign merchants and the native society show a spectrum ranging from individual arrangements with local chiefs to collectivities making such arrangements and from that to fully independent settlements. Second, the arrival of these Muslim merchants could and did lead to a measure of native conversion to Islam, despite the later erosion of the mercantile settlements in the northwest and the tendency to de-Islamization in the southeast; both processes likely reflect the pronounced vulnerability of the Muslims of Madagascar to the arrival of the Europeans. Third, in the absence of continuing contact with metropolitan forms of the religion, Islam was likely to reach accommodations with the local culture that would strike a European as exotic and a pious Muslim as outrageous. Finally, the spread of Islam began and ended on the coast, without leading on to the conversion of the interior. We can keep these themes in mind as we proceed to other parts of the Indian Ocean rim.

East Africa

Crossing to the mainland opposite Madagascar, we find ourselves in Sofala on the coast of what is today Mozambique. This takes us close to the southern horizon of medieval Muslim knowledge of the east coast of Africa, at least insofar as the information available locally reached the literary sources at our disposal. It was only in the later seventeenth century that Muslims reached the Cape of Good Hope, and that was because the Dutch were bringing them from Southeast Asia. These involuntary migrants were either slaves or exiled grandees deported to the Cape to keep them out of mischief. Our most interesting account of Sofala comes from Masʿūdī (d. 956), a purveyor of wide-ranging geographical and historical information who had himself visited East Africa. He gives an account of an early Zanj kingdom with its capital in Sofala, in the course of which he includes words in the indigenous language. Thus he tells us that the ruler had the title *waflīmī*, which can readily be identified with a Bantu word for "king" or, more precisely, "kings" (*wafalme* in Swahili). This incidentally provides early linguistic confirmation that speakers of Bantu languages had reached the east coast in the course of their migrations across sub-Saharan Africa. Masʿūdī also tells us that in the absence of horses the ruler had an army of three thousand men mounted on cattle. This figure suggests a larger scale of political organization than appears to have characterized early Madagascar. That the king's troops rode on cattle is entirely credible, since this practice is ethnographically attested later in the history of southern Africa; similar horse envy appears among the reindeer riders of northern Eurasia. It is a pity that Masʿūdī tells us nothing about the role of Muslim merchants in this polity, though he mentions that the ships of the Sīrāfīs and Omanis sailed as far as Sofala. Muslim merchants must indeed have been there, or we would not know of the existence of this kingdom; presumably they had reached some arrangement with the ruler. But if their presence had led to any conversion among the native population, it must have been marginal, since Masʿūdī describes the kingdom as pagan. The Zanj, or their kings, he tells us, "have no religious law to which to refer, but rather some customs of their kings and some political traditions according to which they rule their subjects."[14]

What was special about Sofala was the existence of gold in the interior. The presence of plentiful gold was already mentioned by Masʿūdī, and it remained Sofala's key export. The political configuration supported by this trade was, however, subject to change. By the twelfth century the indigenous kingdom described by Masʿūdī had disappeared, and Sofala was controlled by a governor appointed from the Muslim city-state of Kilwa farther north. When the Portuguese arrived in 1505, they soon replaced Sofala as their main port with the island of Mozambique farther up the coast. But this did not prevent a lively Portuguese interest in the region where the gold came from. By this time the gold trade was providing the basis for the emergence of significant African states in the interior. The first, known to us only archaeologically, is represented by the elaborate stone ruins of Great Zimbabwe, which date from the fourteenth to fifteenth century. That this state was linked to the coastal trade is shown by the presence of high-quality Chinese and Persian ceramics, found nowhere else in the African interior south of Egypt. The second of these states, known as Monomotapa, flourished in the sixteenth century and was described by the Portuguese. From what they say it is clear that Muslims from the coast were present in the interior in considerable numbers. Very likely they made converts among the indigenous population, but if so, this had no lasting impact. In particular, the Muslims had not converted the ruler to Islam, though they reacted sharply when a Portuguese missionary persuaded him to adopt Christianity.

14. Masʿūdī, *Murūj al-dhahab*, ed. C. Pellat, Beirut 1965–74, 2:125 §872.

The East African coast north of Sofala was characterized by a different pattern. Here there is little evidence of penetration of the interior, and indeed much of the hinterland of the northern part of the coast is a wilderness barely worth penetrating. Moreover, merchants were not dealing with indigenous authorities like Masʿūdī's king of the Zanj, in whose interests it was to attract foreign traders by providing for their security. Instead we find them establishing independent settlements, typically on offshore islands, sometimes quite inhospitable ones. This preference for islands is significant: it means that the merchants feared enemies on land more than they did enemies at sea. Ibn Baṭṭūṭa remarks that the people of Kilwa were constantly engaged in warfare with the pagan Zanj whose territory lay next to theirs. In a variant on this theme, a later Portuguese source describes the Arabs living on the coast near Mombasa as being "like prisoners" of the local pagan tribe "because they have to pay them a large tribute in cloth in order to be allowed to live in security."[15] But worse dangers than this loomed in the interior. In 1588 the Zimba suddenly appeared in the hinterland of Sofala and proceeded to Kilwa, reputedly killing and eating some three thousand people. They planned to make a similar meal of Malindi but were driven off and disappeared. A key role in driving them away was played by the Segeju, a pagan people of the mainland whose activities were not always so helpful. What we do not encounter in the hinterland is states.

The Muslim coastal settlements were ruled by dynasties whose ancestors may well have come from the heartlands, though claims to such ancestry could always be fabricated. Thus the island of Kilwa was ruled from the tenth century to the fifteenth by two successive Muslim dynasties, one of which came to be known as "Shīrāzī," suggesting an origin in Iran. That the medieval East African elite had a considerable admixture of Iranian blood was unexpectedly confirmed by a genetic study published in 2023; much as in the case of the Antemoro of Madagascar, this admixture was overwhelmingly on the male side. The second dynasty claimed descent from the Prophet, implying that ultimately it originated in Arabia. Farther to the north the island of Pate was ruled by a dynasty apparently of Omani origin. The beginnings of these dynasties may lie in the tenth century or so, as in the case of Kilwa—it is about then that the minting of coinage seems to have begun in East Africa. But they could also be much earlier. In an account of the island of Qanbalū—identifiable as Pemba to the north of Zanzibar—Masʿūdī describes a Zanjī-speaking Muslim population living alongside pagan Zanj. He explains that some Muslims had conquered the island in the middle of the eighth century, enslaving the Zanj who were already living there. This account is not to be dismissed out of hand. If we can rely on it, it gives us an early date for Muslim settlement on

15. See G.S.P. Freeman-Grenville, *The East African coast*, Oxford 1962, 180.

the coast and also provides a significant counterexample to the otherwise plausible assumption that the spread of Islam there took place through peaceful commerce. At the other end of our period we have a case where the fact of conquest is beyond question: the seizure of the island of Zanzibar by the Omanis in the course of their overseas expansion. In this case, at least, there can be no doubt about the foreign origin of the rulers; indeed, they were and remained so foreign that in 1964 they were overthrown in a revolution that targeted Arabs and Asians.

The chief exports from this part of the coast were ivory, a perennial, and slaves, particularly in the early centuries of Islam and again toward the end of our period. Zanj slaves appear in the heartlands in the late seventh century, providing evidence that Muslim trade with East Africa was already active at that time. In 749–50 we hear of a force of four thousand Zanj sent to suppress a revolt in Mosul, and by the ninth century the trade was so vigorous that it fed a formidable Zanj rebellion in Iraq; as we saw, this broke out in 869 and took fifteen years to suppress. Zanj slaves must also have been exported all the way across the Indian Ocean, since Zanj are attested in ninth-century Java and even earlier in China. But not all the Zanj who appear in these distant lands seem to have been slaves, since the Chinese sources mention Zanj embassies to China in the later eleventh century.

Toward the end of our period there is some evidence of Muslims engaging in missionary efforts to spread Islam in the region. In the eighteenth century Dominican friars on Mozambique Island complained of Muslims going to "great excesses in the propagation of their false sect," and in 1726 a Muslim functionary was "sending to Mozambique many people of his sect to teach the dogmas of his belief and exercise public ceremonies under the pretext of them being traders."[16] It may well be that the Muslims of the East African coast engaged in such activity more energetically once exposed to Christian competition. But after our experience of Madagascar we would not expect these efforts to result in the large-scale conversion of the hinterland. And indeed Islam seems to have made little headway there. Thus Ibn Baṭṭūṭa, as we have seen, describes the people of Kilwa as at war with the pagan Zanj whose territory adjoined theirs. Likewise a late fifteenth-century source contrasts Muslim rule on Zanzibar with the unbelief that prevailed on the mainland. By 1753 a king in the hinterland of Mozambique at least claimed to be a Muslim and dressed as one; he even recruited teachers from the coast to instruct his subjects in Islam. But this did not go very far. The Yao, a matrilineal people of the southern interior who were already trading with the coast in the sixteenth century, are today overwhelmingly Muslim, but they did not begin to convert until the later nineteenth century.

16. Quoted in R. J. Barendse, *Arabian seas 1700–1763*, Leiden 2009, 1:159–60.

Though it may have been small in numbers, the Muslim community that emerged on the East African coast was nonetheless a remarkable one. At its heart lay an unusual linguistic development, the formation of the Swahili language (the term derives from the Arabic *sawāḥil*, appropriately meaning "coasts"). There is scant written documentation of the history of Swahili before the first half of the eighteenth century, when we have the first Swahili texts written in the Arabic script: letters dating from 1724 found in the archives of Goa, followed by poetry preserved in manuscripts of 1728 and later. For earlier periods we are lucky to possess just a two-line song recorded by a Portuguese missionary in southern Mozambique in 1568. This means that any reconstruction of the history of the language necessarily relies on more or less indirect and speculative inferences. But these inferences can generate a fairly plausible account of what must have happened. Here one thing we know about the language is that before the nineteenth century it was the mother tongue of an exclusively coastal population, which suggests that already in its formative period its speakers had taken up a way of life that was to a significant extent maritime. A seventeenth-century observer remarks that "almost all inhabitants have little boats with which they trade in all parts along the coast," and he adds that this "was always their way of life."[17] There is, however, as yet no archaeological evidence of such a maritime culture in pre-Islamic times, and far into the Islamic period we do not find the Swahili population engaged in long-distance seafaring other than as passengers. So it would make sense to think of the speakers of Swahili as having acquired their coastal maritime skills through interaction with Muslim traders. We can easily assume that this interaction will have included such intimacies as intermarriage, already attested in the first century for pre-Islamic Arabs. An early Portuguese observer, Duarte Barbosa writing in 1516, describes the skin colors on the coast as black, white, and tawny.

Another thing we know is that within the vast and ramified Bantu language family, Swahili is closer to some languages than it is to others. This can help place the formation of Swahili in both time and space. As to time, the extent to which Swahili diverges from its closest living relatives gives linguists at least an idea how long ago it must have separated from them. The answer—by the year 800 according to one reckoning that mixes in the findings of archaeology—can only be vague, but it does overlap comfortably with the early centuries of Muslim commerce in the region. In other words, the inference would be that Swahili became an independent language in an early Muslim commercial context, many centuries before we have any texts written in the language. As to space, Swahili's closest relatives are a group of languages in the far north of the region in which Swahili is currently spoken, reaching from Kenya into southern Somalia. The inference from that is that Swahili took shape in the north and then spread southward down the

17. Quoted in Barendse, *Arabian seas 1700–1763*, 1:112.

coast as far as Mozambique, in a ribbon well over a thousand miles long. A major part of this spread was doubtless the work of speakers of Swahili who themselves migrated southward. Thanks to their interaction with Muslim traders they had a culture that effectively filled a niche on the East African coast. That they may have faced little competition in occupying that niche is suggested by the fact that there is virtually no archaeological evidence for any coastal settlements at all before the eighth century. Against this background it is perhaps worth noting two things that did not happen. First, the arrival of Arab merchants did not turn the indigenous population into Arabic speakers—though when the Portuguese arrived they found Arabic being spoken as far south as Sofala. Second, and perhaps more surprisingly, it was not the case that at each latitude there emerged a coastal dialect based on the neighboring language of the interior. This fits with the impression that the emergence of Swahili was at the same time an ethnogenesis, the formation of a Swahili people, despite the fact that the term "Swahili" does not seem to have been used in this way before the nineteenth century. The ethnic bond was, of course, reinforced by a religious one. The Swahili population of the coast had in common not just Sunnī Islam but more specifically Shāfiʿism, and its prominence was already remarked on by Ibn Baṭṭūṭa.

The violent and disruptive arrival of the Portuguese was bad news for the Muslim city-states of the East African coast. The mission of the newcomers was not a friendly one. Dom Manuel I (ruled 1495–1521) instructed the commander of a fleet he dispatched to the Indian Ocean to make war on the Muslims "and do them as much damage as possible as a people with whom we have so great and so ancient an enmity."[18] In 1528, for example, the Portuguese took Mombasa and wrecked it. Decades later, when given the opportunity in 1585, the somewhat recovered city was to declare for the Ottomans. But for several reasons the Portuguese intrusion was not as bad as it might have been. For one thing, the intruders made Muslim friends as well as Muslim enemies. Thus their attack on Mombasa had the support of the kings of Malindi and Zanzibar, and after the Ottoman threat had passed they installed the king of Malindi as ruler of Mombasa; he obviously found it expedient to ally with the infidel intruder against the local Muslim bully. For another thing, the prime interest of the Portuguese was in key commodities of long-distance trade, so they were not much concerned with the local activities of Swahili society. Finally, the Portuguese in this period were looking for select ports to seize and defend, not for extensive territories that could be conquered and annexed. Underlying all these points was the plain fact that Portugal was a very small country trying to dominate a very large ocean from very far away, and this disparity meant that many things fell through the cracks. That the ruler of Mombasa had been free to side with the Ottomans is an example; it was only in the 1590s that the Portuguese

18. Quoted in S. R. Prange, *Monsoon Islam*, Cambridge 2018, 222.

built themselves a fort there. They also went to the lengths of bringing up an heir to the throne as a Christian, but a few years after they had installed him he reverted to Islam and rebelled in 1631. When the Portuguese eventually repossessed Mombasa they found it empty and had to repopulate it—and inevitably, in part at least, they did so with Muslims. All in all, the Portuguese presence, followed by that of other European powers, carried significant costs for East African Muslims, but it did not threaten their collective survival. Muslim trade continued on the Indian Ocean, and Swahili Islam in 1800 was not so far from what it had been in 1500. One index of this is mosque building. Though there are many ruins of sixteenth-century mosques, and almost none seem to have been built in the seventeenth century, construction resumed in the eighteenth century—albeit still confined to the coast. Moreover, there was an unexpected revival of Muslim power starting in the middle of the seventeenth century, though from a Sunnī point of view it was a heretical one. As already mentioned, the Ibāḍīs of Oman took to the seas and established a colonial empire in East Africa. Their raids began in 1652, reached Mozambique in 1669, and issued in the capture of Mombasa in 1698. Later it was Zanzibar that served as the center of Omani power in East Africa. It seems that the Omani hegemony was recognized as far south as the Comoros, whence in 1750 the sultan of the island of Anjouan composed a letter to the ruler of Oman begging him to excuse his people from a demand for men and money; the reasons he gave were poverty and lack of population—"We are obliged to keep our youths and get them married and have them live with their wives."[19] Overall the main damage inflicted by the Portuguese on Islam was perhaps an opportunity cost: the loss of potential Muslims who might otherwise have converted. Significant numbers of pagans became Christians rather than Muslims thanks to the European presence and the somewhat more organized missionary activity that went with it.

The Somali coast

North of the Swahili settlements we come to what is today the southern coast of Somalia, with the city of Mogadishu. This stretch of the coast may once have had a larger Bantu-speaking population than it has now, but if so, it was largely displaced by Somali pastoralists pushing south at a date we cannot determine, perhaps starting in the tenth century and continuing until the seventeenth. Mogadishu itself was not a Somali city for most of our period—Barbosa describes it as Arabic-speaking. It was only in the early seventeenth century that it was conquered by Somalis, and thereafter it was ruled by them. One feature of medieval Mogadishu is of some comparative interest. In the early thirteenth century the city enjoyed a nonmonarchical form of government, something that we occasionally see

19. See M. R. Bhacker, *Trade and empire in Muscat and Zanzibar*, London 1992, appendix I, 199.

in Muslim city-states despite the lack of a formal republican tradition in the world of Islam. Specifically, the author of a geographical dictionary writing in 1224 says that the people of Mogadishu have no king and that their affairs are in the hands of the leading citizens. Mogadishu was not alone in this. Brava, a bit to the south on the Somali coast, is described by Barbosa as having no king and being ruled instead by elders who were also its leading merchants. Yet farther south, Pate had a sultan, but its sovereign institution in the 1730s was a small assembly.

Just as in the East African hinterland, there is no indication of the existence of a sizeable state in the Somali interior. But at some time in our period a significant change took place: the Somalis converted to Islam. Merchants based in Mogadishu are quite likely to have played a part in this development, but the fact is that we do not know when or how the conversion came about. There is nevertheless an obvious contrast between the Islamization of the Somali hinterland and the absence of such a process in the Bantu-speaking hinterland to the south. Perhaps three points are worth making by way of a speculative explanation. First, the Somalis were geographically closer to the Muslim heartlands, so they may have been that bit more exposed to Islam. Second, their exposure may have been enhanced by the fact that the land of the Somalis, unlike that of the Zanj, has the shape of a triangle of which two sides are coasts. Third, despite the presence of some cultivators, the Somalis overall resembled the nomads of Arabia in the way of life they practiced in their desert, possibly under Arabian influence. Both were largely stateless peoples, both combined patrilineal kinship with a strong awareness of genealogy, and both were camel nomads—this latter as much a fact about their cultures as it was about their economies. Perhaps, then, they shared an elective affinity for Islam that we can also see in some measure among the nomadic peoples of the Sahara.

To sum up our findings on the western sector of the Indian Ocean rim, the main conclusion is that the spread of Islam by merchants was extensive but one-dimensional—it rarely penetrated the interior. That apart, three specific phenomena are worth keeping in mind for comparison as we move eastward: the Somali exception to the confinement of mercantile Islam to the coasts, the emergence of Swahili, and the highly assimilated culture of the Antemoro.

The Indian sector

Geography and its implications

Bypassing the coast of the heartlands, we now move east to India. Here the terrain at first seems only too familiar. Just as the aridity of the heartlands extends southward into Somalia, so too it spills over from the desert of Makrān eastward into Sindh. The saving grace of Sindh is the Indus, just as that of Iraq is the twin rivers, the Tigris and the Euphrates. Even Karachi, now the largest city in Pakistan, began as an upstart port of the eighteenth century and was initially more like the transient ports of the Red Sea and Persian Gulf than those of India at large. It remained so until it was linked to the agricultural hinterland by rail in the second half of the nineteenth century. As we move farther south, however, we start to encounter a very different geographical environment, one increasingly shaped by abundant rainfall and thus supportive of dense populations, agricultural wealth, teeming cities, powerful states, and timber for shipbuilding. This is the India we met in the preceding chapter, and there was nothing to compare with it behind the East African coastline, or indeed anywhere else around the Indian Ocean rim. In purely material terms India was the unquestioned center of gravity of the Indian Ocean, and on that basis one might have expected that India, rather than the Middle East, would be the source of any religion that spread to all its sectors. The only downside of India was the relative scarcity of good ports. For the most part the coast lacks the islands and bays that give shelter to seafarers elsewhere on the Indian Ocean rim, though there are exceptions such as Diu just off the south coast of peninsular Gujarat.

One implication of this geographical environment was that the scale of commercial activity around the coasts of India would be far greater than it was along the shores of East Africa, or indeed anywhere else around the rim. The economy of India possessed by far the largest and densest concentration of producers and consumers; to match it we would have to go outside the Indian Ocean altogether, to China or Europe. The Indian economy was also unusual in the Indian Ocean context for the extent to which its exports consisted of manufactured goods, above all textiles. The disparity between India and the rest was reflected in the sheer number of Indian ports. Indian merchants played a prominent role in maritime trade, and not just in the immediate neighborhood of India itself. Thus in the seventeenth century many Indian merchants would have their agents in the ports of the Middle East and Southeast Asia. Hindu and Jain merchants from Gujarat maintained settlements in Iran, Arabia, and East Africa, while the Tamil Muslim merchants of the southeastern coast did the same in Ceylon and Southeast Asia. These wide horizons were nothing new: Indian merchants were already to be found in Alexandria in the first century.

Another implication of the Indian environment was that here, as not in East Africa, merchants—particularly foreign ones—had to reach accommodations with territorial states that held sway over the coasts. On the upper west side much of the coast tended to be in the hands of major dynasties, even if they did not live there themselves. When Mas'ūdī visited the port of Cambay in Gujarat in 915, the Muslim community was under the authority of a Brahmin governor with a taste for interfaith debates; he represented a powerful Hindu ruler based in the interior. When the Portuguese arrived it was in the hands of the sultan of Gujarat, who again ruled from the interior. Under the Mughal emperors Sūrat came to serve as the leading port of Gujarat. All such rulers had good reason to make overseas traders welcome, but they did not lack leverage in setting the terms of the relationship. Farther south the narrowing of the coastal plain by the modest yet persistent mountain chain known as the Western Ghāts could have the effect of sheltering the coast of Kerala from the larger states of the interior. In such an environment merchants might find themselves in the relatively advantageous position of reaching accommodations with less powerful rulers who were more dependent on revenue from commerce. It is telling that the capitals of these rulers—unlike those of the larger states of India and the Indian Ocean world in general—were located on the coast. The effect may have been enhanced by the political traditions of Kerala, where royal power seems to have been seriously constrained by the ancient rights of local lords, temples, and assemblies. Thus the Portuguese report that in Calicut on the Malabar shore the foreign merchants had a leader who "governs and punishes them" with scant reference to the local ruler.[20] They also enjoyed the rare privilege that if one of their ships was wrecked on the coast of the kingdom, the goods aboard it would not be seized by the state. But this may have been wisdom as much as weakness, since we know that the ruler was strong enough to require as a condition of residence that cows be protected and not eaten. Under these conditions, establishing fully independent mercantile communities was rarely an option until the Portuguese brought with them sufficient military force to override the wishes of Indian rulers and seize strategic locations such as Goa. There was nevertheless a sixteenth-century Muslim takeover of the Hindu state of Cannanore in northern Kerala. Here what began as a Hindu monarchy developed into a dual polity in which the Hindu ruler of the land coexisted tensely with a Muslim ruler of the sea. In the course of several decades of maneuvering the Muslim ruler emerged supreme and established a dynasty, while his Hindu counterpart was banished to the hinterland. But this was exceptional.

The example of Cannanore might suggest that Indian states were not given to asserting themselves at sea, and on the whole this was true. Quite a few of them, including the Mughals, engaged in maritime commerce, and the ruler of seventeenth-century Calicut operated a commercial fleet. Yet the only Indian dynasty known for large-scale naval activity was that of the Cōḻas, Hindu rulers of the Tamil south who conquered the Laccadive Islands in the tenth century and dispatched a major maritime expedition to Southeast Asia in the eleventh. Meanwhile on the west coast, in the region between Bombay and Goa, there are thousands of medieval memorial stones for those killed at sea; these sculptures provide evidence of frequent sea battles, though they do not reveal the forces behind them, whether small states or large piratical enterprises. Either way,

20. Quoted in M. N. Pearson, *Merchants and rulers in Gujarat*, Berkeley 1976, 17.

when the Muslim merchants of the west coast were first exposed to the Portuguese menace around 1500, it was to the Mamlūks of Egypt that they appealed for help, not to the sultan of Gujarat or any other Indian ruler. Likewise when the Muslim ruler of Aceh on Sumatra was in need of assistance in the middle decades of the sixteenth century, he sought it from the Ottomans, not from any Indian Muslim state. In each case we see the Muslims of the Indian Ocean looking to a distant Mediterranean power rather than one based in India. The most serious enemies of the Portuguese in Indian waters proved to be their European rivals, and no Indian state ever projected naval power across the western Indian Ocean onto the Middle East until the coming of the British Raj.

The geographical environment of India was significant in another way: as we have already seen, it made the subcontinent well worth conquering. While Muslim merchants were bringing Islam to the coasts, Muslim soldiers were bringing it to the interior—and eventually reaching the coasts as well. No such process of large-scale overland conquest brought Islam to the African or Southeast Asian interior. This made the spread of Islam in India a more complex process, but fortunately there came to be a way to tell mercantile and military Islam apart. What the soldiers brought to the interior was above all Islam according to the Ḥanafī law school. They brought Shāfiʿism too, but it did not take root. On the coasts, by contrast, mercantile Shāfiʿism predominated. The differences between the two schools for the most part related to points of detail that need not concern us, though they did sometimes have practical implications—as with the question whether one could take the poll tax from the Hindus and on that basis tolerate their idolatry with a clear conscience. But this was of more consequence for soldiers than it was for merchants. In practice, differences of cultural background probably counted for more than differences of law school. Allegiances to rival law schools can nevertheless be useful to us, since they often provide a prima facie indication of the provenance of the Islam of any given Indian Muslim community.

The Malabar coast

Muslim trade with India began early. Already in the late seventh century we have evidence that Muslim merchants were active on Ceylon. This implies that they must also have been frequenting the Malabar coast—and very likely the southeastern coast as well. In general, the outcome of the Muslim mercantile presence on the west coast of India was a ribbon development comparable to what we saw in East Africa. Here, too, when Muslim merchants arrived and acquired local women as wives or concubines, the likely result was to spread Islam. Barbosa remarks that foreign Muslims would have several wives and concubines and that they made Moors—meaning Muslims—of their offspring. They are also described as collecting money for converts and competing in making donations to them. Such attitudes could well be expected to propagate Islam, though also, in the absence of reinforcement, to dilute it; but reinforcement was far more readily available on the Malabar coast than it was in the remote southeast of Madagascar. As in East Africa, we can easily imagine this process leading to the formation of increasingly indigenous Muslim communities. But in one way the outcome was very different: there was nothing resembling the emergence of Swahili. That would have meant, let us say, the formation of a Muslim Sindhī dialect through the interaction of Muslim merchants with the native population of Sindh, followed by its southward spread down the coast. That did not happen, or if it did, then only on a very limited scale. Instead, the rule of thumb seems to be that the communities emerging from such interactions spoke the language of the region where they lived. Let us then start from Sindh and proceed down the west coast to Kerala.

It is not unlikely that there were at one time Shāfiʿite mercantile communities in Sindh, but if there were, they seem to have left no trace in the face of the dominance of Ḥanafī Islam. Farther south, there was a large and very successful community of Muslim merchants in Gujarat, though for the most part we seem to lack evidence as to whether they were Shāfiʿites. Around 1500 they were the single most prominent group on the core trade routes of the Indian Ocean. They also had some presence inland and will undoubtedly have spoken Gujarati. A bilingual pair of inscriptions of 1264 from the coast of peninsular Gujarat sheds an interesting light on the way they may have related to their Hindu neighbors. The inscriptions record the munificence of a rich merchant from Hormuz who sponsored the building of a mosque. The one in Arabic is unremarkable, but the one in Sanskrit is couched in notably Hinduized terms; for example, it applies to the Muslim God an epithet of the Hindu god Śiva, "Viśvanātha." It also discreetly omits a sentence in the Arabic expressing the pious hope that God would make Somnath "one of the cities of Islam,"[21] banishing unbelief and idols from it. This inscription further provides evidence that the local Muslim community was substantial and divided into caste-like groups.

South of Gujarat we come to the Shāfiʿite Muslims of the Konkaṇ, on the coast of Maharashtra, who were no doubt speakers of a Marāṭhī dialect. Masʿūdī visited a large mercantile settlement on this part of the coast, a little south of the modern city of Bombay, in 916. He found migrants from Oman, Sīrāf, and Iraq who had married and settled there, together with their Indian-born offspring, and he reports that the Hindu king would appoint a leading member of the community to exercise judicial authority over them. To their south, on the coast of what is now Karnataka, was another Shāfiʿite maritime community, the Navāyats, who spoke

21. Quoted in V. K. Jain, *Trade and traders in western India*, New Delhi 1990, 77.

Konkaṇī, a coastal language distinct from Marāṭhī but closely related to it. That they spoke Konkaṇī rather than Kannaḍa, the language of Karnataka, might suggest that they had moved southward from the region where they originally settled—a small-scale hint of the Swahili pattern. The earliest reference to this community may go back to 1059, when the ruler of Goa granted a deserted village to a maritime Arab (*Tājiya*) to enjoy as long as the sun and moon should last. Later the omnipresent Ibn Baṭṭūṭa describes what is likely to have been a settlement of Navāyats in this region. He says that they lived from maritime trade, having no cultivated land, and that they were ruled by a Muslim sultan who, though recognizing a Hindu overlord, could project a degree of military force on both land and sea—an unusual case of Muslim power emerging on the coast. Ibn Baṭṭūṭa was also mightily impressed by the women, who combined beauty, virtue, and knowing the Qur'ān by heart; there were thirteen schools for girls in the town, something he notes that he had not seen elsewhere. In the sixteenth and seventeenth centuries the Navāyats figured in commerce. Modern ethnography reports that they practice matrilocal marriage, with the wife's family continuing not just to house but also to maintain her. If this pattern is ancient, it would have been an excellent fit for an itinerant Arab merchant, who could visit his wife when in port without having to concern himself with arrangements for her welfare in his absence. All this sounds blissfully symbiotic, but Ibn Baṭṭūṭa also speaks of frequent violence between Hindus and Muslims in the port of Mangalore just north of Kerala. Here he estimated the Muslim population at some four thousand. The Hindu ruler, who needed the merchants, would make peace between the two sides. As usual, the extent to which we get a view of the processes by which such communities were formed is very limited. But one very distinctive west coast community provides a vivid illustration, if not of the process itself, then at least of one possible outcome: the Moplahs.

The Moplahs (or Māppiḷas) make up most of the Muslim population of Kerala today,[22] and like everyone in the region they speak Malayāḷam. The Muslim mercantile community in Kerala may go back to the ninth century or even earlier. At the time the Portuguese arrived it was particularly well established in the kingdom of Calicut, but Barbosa remarks that the "Mapuleres" were found throughout Malabar, which could suggest that they were not confined to the coast. As long as the community retained its predominantly mercantile character it seems to have been on reasonably good—if appropriately distant—terms with its host society; a Muslim scholar of the sixteenth century looked back to the good old days of harmonious relations before the intrusion of the Portuguese. And indeed the activities of these newcomers proved particularly disruptive on the Malabar coast.

22. For their history see S. F. Dale, *Islamic society on the South Asian frontier*, Oxford 1980.

This was where pepper came from, and pepper was high on the list of the spices for which the Portuguese had gate-crashed the Indian Ocean. The result was that the Muslim merchants of Malabar lost possession of most of this very lucrative trade. Soon many of them were gone, no doubt emigrating to lands where conditions were better—merchants can always move. As usual there were complexities. The ruler of Cochin welcomed the Portuguese to balance his unwanted overlord, the ruler of Calicut, just as Malindi allied with them against Mombasa. But the Portuguese hit the rulers of Calicut particularly hard, and it was in their lands that most of the Moplahs lived. So the departing merchants left behind them a community that could no longer hope to make much of a living from trade and was now in competition with its Hindu neighbors for land. Relations deteriorated, and the Moplahs, who had rapidly developed a robust religious militancy in the unsuccessful struggle against the Portuguese, now turned it against the Hindus. Their tactics included strikingly suicidal attacks. The nadir came in the later eighteenth century, when the Muslim rulers of Mysore invaded Kerala in 1766 and 1773. When not rebelling against them the Moplahs sided with the invaders, engaging in massacres of the Hindu population and facing the inevitable reprisals when the armies of Mysore withdrew. In 1792 they came under the rule of the British. Though they first rebelled against them in 1800, and small-scale risings peppered the nineteenth century, the bloodiest confrontation did not take place until 1921, when it was accompanied by forced conversions of Hindus. This grim story nonetheless had an unexpectedly happy ending: relations between Muslims and Hindus in Kerala in recent decades have by Indian standards been unusually good.

Against this rather toxic background it may come as a surprise that the Moplahs held fast to several noteworthy features of their largely Hindu roots. Traditional Moplah wooden mosques looked somewhat like Hindu temples. The men dressed in a local fashion that by mainstream Islamic standards was indecent. Despite the fact that they were Muslims and seem to have felt a considerable degree of Muslim solidarity, the Moplahs were divided into two main castes. One was rather aristocratic and believed to descend from high-caste converts, whereas the other consisted of commoners thought to be the offspring of converts from a lower caste. On top of this, the Moplahs of northern (but not central) Kerala retained a matrilineal kinship system. This fits well with their surroundings: among the Hindus of the region, such a system was practiced by both the high-caste Nāyar warriors and a major low-caste group. Barbosa tells us that in the ruling family of Calicut "royal descent is through the women, and the first son born to the king's eldest sister is heir to the throne."[23] Such a system does not, however, fit well with Islamic law, which assumes a kinship system that is resolutely patrilineal. We thus

23. *The book of Duarte Barbosa*, trans. M. L. Dames, London 1918–21, 2:11.

have the spectacle of a community that on the one hand was zealously devoted to Islam, but on the other hand was divided into castes and observed the norms of a matrilineal society. Yet despite this social continuity with Hindu society, the Moplahs were culturally isolated from it. Though they spoke Malayāḷam, they wrote it only in the Arabic script, creating a literature sealed off from that of their Hindu neighbors and playing no part in the wider literary scene of Kerala. At the same time they may have suffered a degree of involuntary isolation from the wider Muslim world, leading to a certain attenuation of their Islamic heritage. A Yemeni Zaydī chronicler of the seventeenth century gives the Muslims of Malabar full credit for the courage they showed in fighting the infidel, but against that he notes that they "have but few scholars among them, and no more of Islam than the merest name."[24] Scholars, like merchants, can easily move, taking their talents and erudition with them.

The southeastern coast

Rounding Cape Comorin we leave behind Kerala and the Malabar coast, reaching the Tamil country and eventually the Coromandel coast.[25] In some ways the scene on this coast resembled what we saw on the coast of Kerala. Here, too, there was a considerable Muslim population. Barbosa mentions "many Moors, natives of the land" in the ports.[26] As in Kerala, they had undoubtedly been there a long time—there is a Muslim inscription dating from 875. Moreover, in cultural and historical terms Kerala and the Tamil country had a lot in common. Malayāḷam is basically a Tamil dialect that broke away to form its own literary language in the Middle Ages, and for a long time the people of Kerala still called their language Tamil. But if the building blocks were similar, for a number of reasons the edifices were very different. One reason was simply that the Tamil scene was larger, more heterogeneous, and more complex. In Kerala we encountered just a single Muslim community, the Moplahs, but among the Tamils we meet two major communities, the Maṟakkāyars and the Labbais, and we could add at least one smaller community, not to mention several Muslim groups that lived in the Tamil country but do not concern us because they originated in the Deccan or farther north.

If we are looking for descendants of Arab merchants and local women on the southeastern coast, the Maṟakkāyars undoubtedly fit the bill. They are Shāfiʿites who claim Arab descent, and they practice a matrilocal marriage system like the

24. Quoted in R. B. Serjeant, *The Portuguese off the South Arabian coast*, Oxford 1963, 117.

25. In what follows I draw extensively on S. Bayly, *Saints, goddesses and kings*, Cambridge 1989; S. Subrahmanyam, *Improvising empire*, Delhi 1990; and D. D. Shulman, *Tamil: A biography*, Cambridge, MA 2016.

26. *The book of Duarte Barbosa*, 2:126.

Muslim communities of the west coast. Again, such a system is good for merchants, but also for women since they retain the support of the families they were born into. There could be a link between this and the fact that by the early nineteenth century each quarter of a typical Maṟakkāyar settlement possessed a network of women's lanes running behind the houses, giving them freedom of movement outside their homes and access to their own prayer halls. As usual there is a lack of direct evidence of the emergence of the community, so we have no idea when it was first formed; one Tamil port has a mosque going back to 1331. When we begin to hear about Maṟakkāyars in the sixteenth century, we find them heavily engaged in maritime trade out of the ports of the Tamil coast. What is more, they were able to sustain this activity despite the arrival of the Portuguese. This resilience contrasts with what we saw in Kerala, and it reflects the fact that the impact of the Portuguese on the Tamil coast was far less disruptive. On the Malabar coast they were prepared to go to any lengths to seize the export trade in pepper, but they had no such interest in taking control of the export of textiles from the southeastern coast. As a result, the form taken by the Portuguese presence there was largely unofficial. The organs of the Portuguese state maintained only a feeble establishment, while private traders from Portugal settled in the port cities in considerable numbers and conducted their business alongside their native competitors. This was, in fact, the situation not just on the southeastern coast but in the Bay of Bengal at large. Here the Portuguese were prepared to make serious efforts to retain control of the direct route to Malacca on the Malay Peninsula, but they tended to leave the rest of the bay to its own devices. The Maṟakkāyars were thus able to continue their mercantile way of life with what seems to have been considerable success. They come across in our sources as confident and accomplished patricians.

Alongside their mercantile activities, they engaged in other elite pursuits. One of these was politics. In the later seventeenth and early eighteenth centuries a Maṟakkāyar family was prominent in the service of a local Hindu state, that of the Sētupatis of Rāmnād. The family was much disliked by the Dutch, who did everything they could to persuade the Sētupatis to remove them from office, but the Sētupatis valued their services, and it took several decades and the devolution of the leadership of the family onto a young and inexperienced heir before the Dutch could get their way. The other elite activity in which this family involved itself was the patronage of mainstream Tamil literature. A leading member of the family, Cītakkāti (d. 1715), alias Shaykh ʿAbd al-Qādir, was a patron of Hindu poets and literati and was lauded by them in traditional Tamil style. He was also a patron of Tamil Muslim literature. Like the Moplahs, the Tamil Muslims wrote religious texts in the Arabic script, but unlike them, they also created a substantial literature in the Tamil script that took its models from the wider Tamil culture. Cītakkāti was a patron of Umaṟuppulavar, ʿUmar the Poet, who also counted among his patrons the Hindu ruler who was Cītakkāti's employer, as well as a second Maṟakkāyar who took over Cītakkāti's role as patron after his death. 'Umar may not himself have been a Maṟakkāyar, but he is described as a Cōṉakar, implying a mercantile ancestry mixing Arab and Tamil blood; his father was a merchant trading in scents and spices. Because of his close ties to his Maṟakkāyar patrons and his similar background, a glance at his major work will give us at least an indirect sense of Maṟakkāyar culture in relation to that of the surrounding Hindu society.

According to tradition, it was 'Umar's patron Cītakkāti who requested that he compose a poem on the life of the Prophet. 'Umar knew all he needed to know about poetry, having studied with a Hindu court poet, but he may not have been well informed about the life of Muḥammad. He therefore went to consult a learned Tamil Muslim scholar, who initially sent him packing him because he was dressed like a Hindu and wearing gold rings—something Hindus do and Muslims don't. The title of 'Umar's poem, *Cīrappurāṇam*, is a remarkable Muslim-Hindu hybrid: the first part derives from the title of the standard Arabic work on Muḥammad's life, the *Sīra* of Ibn Hishām (d. 833), while the second is the Hindu term *purāṇa*, used in the titles of a relatively late stratum of religious writings. The poem is in literary Tamil—no longer intelligible to the average Tamil speaker at the present day—and it observes conventions that go with the language. Its model is in fact a Tamil version of the Hindu *Rāmāyaṇa* dating from the twelfth century or so. With appropriate humility 'Umar defers to "the exalted Tamil poets" of yore.[27] At one point he mentions the caliph 'Umar's standardization of the text of the Qur'ān, but he does not use the word, preferring to refer to the Muslim scripture as the Sacred Vēda. In the same spirit he portrays the women of Arabia as if they were bare-breasted Tamil women at work in the rice paddies: "Mud splashes on their breasts that soar like the tusks of a lusty elephant"—an image that might have raised eyebrows in the heartlands of the Muslim world. When he comes to describe Mecca, he begins with the large lakes that he imagines to grace the town. Likewise the Prophet's birth there is his incarnation (*avatāra*). Much of this is reminiscent of Manjhan's *Madhumālatī*, which we encountered in the preceding chapter. The difference is that Manjhan evokes the Hindu tradition from the outside, whereas in literary terms 'Umar the Poet is fully inside it. The whole story would have been unimaginable in Kerala—though there would seem to be nothing about Malayāḷam literature as such that would make it less accessible to Muslims than was that of the Tamils.

The other major Tamil Muslim community were the Labbais. If the patrician Maṟakkāyars absorbed male converts, one suspects that they would have come from fairly high-caste backgrounds, like Nāyars entering the Moplah community.

27. For this and the next quotation see V. Narayanan, "Religious vocabulary and regional identity," in D. Gilmartin and B. B. Lawrence (eds.), *Beyond Turk and Hindu*, Gainesville 2000, 82, 86.

The Labbais, by contrast, look like the product of conversion to Islam among less exalted castes. Unlike the Maṟakkāyars, they are not thought to have had much Arab ancestry, and despite the fact that some Labbais did very well for themselves there are indications that they were looked down on. Thus in a Tamil Muslim ballad about a hero who is eventually executed at the command of the Nabob of Arcot—ironically a fellow Muslim—the hero goes out of his way to insult his enemy: "You son of a washerwoman, you dry fish-selling Labbai!"[28] But in our period we know less about the Labbais than we do about the Maṟakkāyars because they were much less prominent. When we get more of a sense of them under British rule and after, we find them in the region of the coast, but not as firmly established on the seashore as the Maṟakkāyars. They live partly by trade, but not in general long-distance trade, and they also have other ways of making a living, including agriculture. They abstain from eating beef and seem open to mainstream Tamil culture, though hardly grand enough to act as its patrons. In the countryside they dress like Hindus—just as 'Umar the Poet did. How much of this we can read back into our period is hard to say, but we know at least some things about the Labbais in those days. They cultivated betel vine, they served as divers in the annual pearl fishing, and many of them were carpet weavers. Some of them owned ships trading as far as Aceh on Sumatra, though in general they seem to have been more at home in the coastal trade. We can also say a bit about individual traders. The Dutch had a great liking for a certain Ādam Labbai, who played a major role in the pearl fishing. The scholar whom 'Umar the Poet went to consult, or perhaps a pupil of his, was a Labbai. The Nabob of Arcot in the second half of the eighteenth century appointed a Labbai as chief judge of Madras. From all this it is clear that the Labbais were not the dregs of society, but they do seem significantly less patrician than the Maṟakkāyars. To that extent, it is as if the two main sources of the community that came together in the case of the Moplahs—Arab merchant settlers and native converts—had formed distinct communities in the Tamil case. Perhaps this reflects the absence of the bitter confrontations with infidel enemies that put such a premium on Muslim solidarity in Kerala; hostility to infidels, be they European or Indian, does not seem to have saturated the worldviews of either the Maṟakkāyars or the Labbais.

So who among the various Muslim communities of the Tamil country was Shāfi'ite and who was Ḥanafī? As we would expect, most of those that had come overland were Ḥanafīs, like the Afghans who arrived with the Muslim conquest of the south. The one exception here is easily explained. A fair number of Navāyats had moved into the region in the same period, and while some continued to make a living from commerce, others went into service with Muslim rulers. In other

28. Quoted in Bayly, *Saints, goddesses and kings*, 215.

words, this latter group now lived like Ḥanafīs but nevertheless remained Shāfiʿites. Coming to those whose Islam had arrived on the southeastern coast by sea, the Maṟakkāyars are no problem: they were Shāfiʿites, just as we would expect. The problem is the Labbais. They look very much like a product of the arrival of Islam by sea, and yet they are Ḥanafīs. Why this is so does not seem to be known.

From Ceylon to Bengal

Before proceeding farther up the east coast we should pause to look at Ceylon. Then as now, it was populated by Sinhalese Buddhists in the center and south and by Tamil Hindus mainly in the north. But there was and is a Tamil Muslim minority, said to be made up mostly of Labbais; the 1971 census showed Muslims as 7 percent of the total population. This community seems to have arisen in the usual fashion from the settlement of Muslim merchants in the ports, where, as often, they were allowed autonomy. As we have seen, there is evidence for the presence of Muslim traders on Ceylon as early as the late seventh century, and from at least the eleventh century they played a prominent role in the island's commerce. According to Barbosa, many Muslims lived in large towns on the coast. They were subject to the king of the island but enjoyed great liberty. A Portuguese source from the 1680s states that after the arrival of the Portuguese the number of Muslims actually increased, and that they lived not just in the ports but also in the interior—where indeed they could still be found in the twentieth century. The Muslims of Ceylon were Shāfiʿites. It is noteworthy that their presence did not give rise to an analogous community of Sinhalese Muslims. It may be that the Thēravāda Buddhist tradition, of which Ceylon was the metropolis, was ideologically or organizationally better equipped than Hinduism was to resist the encroachments of foreign religions.

Returning to the mainland, we proceed up the east coast toward Bengal. The middle stretch of this coast seems to be more or less a blank in the story of the spread of Islam around the Indian Ocean rim, with an absence of any significant Muslim settlements. The last one noted by Barbosa before Bengal is Pulicat, still in the Tamil country, though there is a stray statement in a late Persian source that Masulipatnam on the Āndhra coast farther north was founded by Arab traders in the fourteenth century. Moving north again, Barbosa describes Orissa as having "but few seaports and little trade,"[29] and despite his eagle eye for Muslims he makes no mention of their presence there. Bengal, of course, had a large Muslim population, but like that of Sindh it was overwhelmingly a product of Ḥanafī Islam spreading overland, not of Shāfiʿite Islam spreading by sea. Barbosa reports Mus-

29. *The book of Duarte Barbosa*, 2:133.

lims living in the ports of Bengal and a great Muslim city with its own Muslim king, but he was not sensitive to the distinction between Shāfiʿites and Ḥanafīs. For practical purposes it seems that in Bengal, as in Sindh, the noise of military Islam drowned out the signal of mercantile Islam. Geography, too, may have played a part in this. The riverain character of Bengal meant that there was no sharp division between maritime and inland zones, which is why Calcutta was to serve as a seaport despite being located sixty miles from the coast.

To sum up, there are perhaps three main points to take away from this survey of the coming of Islam to the coasts of India by sea. First, it makes a big difference to have a real economy and real states in the hinterland. Second, the evolutions that led to the alienation of the Moplahs and the integration of the Tamil Muslims are instructive as a lesson in contrasts. And third, the gap in the settlement of the rim that we see on the upper east side of India tells us something about the limits of Muslim mercantile activity on the Indian Ocean.

The eastern sector

Geography and its implications

By now we are in Southeast Asia, and here we encounter a major geographical asymmetry. Before the opening of the Suez Canal in 1869, a ship wending its way from the Indian Ocean to the Atlantic had to head for the far south of the western sector and circumnavigate Africa. By contrast, a ship in transit from the Indian Ocean to the Pacific did not need to mirror this detour and circumnavigate Australia. The first stretch of the coast of the eastern sector is indeed unbroken; it comprises the Burmese coast, the southern part of which was in some periods the west coast of Siam, plus the Malay Peninsula. But farther south there are crucial breaks in the rim. The first and most important of these is the Strait of Malacca, a narrow channel some twenty-five miles wide between the Malay Peninsula and the island of Sumatra. This break gives easy access from the Indian Ocean to the rest of Southeast Asia, both continental and maritime, and hence to the ports of southern China and beyond. To the south of this break lies island Southeast Asia. For our purposes, however, it will be convenient to think in terms not of island Southeast Asia but rather of maritime Southeast Asia, thereby including the Malay Peninsula with the islands and excluding it from the mainland. A peninsula, after all, is etymologically "almost an island," and the narrow strip of land that joins the Malay Peninsula to the mainland is at one point a mere forty miles wide.

We need not spend long on the relatively simple geography of continental Southeast Asia, a region that in any case will concern us less than its maritime counterpart. We are dealing with a wide peninsula jutting out to the south between northeastern India and southwestern China. Here the major states of the present day were already in place in the valleys of the major rivers in the centuries that concern us—notably Burma (Myanmar), Siam (Thailand), Cambodia, and Vietnam. Of these, two have shown themselves more apt to expand their territories than the others have. One is Burma, which has engrossed the kingdom of Arakan, the Mon kingdom, and what was the west coast of Siam. The other is Vietnam, which has expanded south to overwhelm the Chams.

The geography of maritime Southeast Asia is more complicated. Life would be simpler in an ice age, when thanks to the lower sea level the northern break would disappear and most of the islands would become part of the Asian mainland. But life would also be the poorer for the disappearance of the Strait of Malacca. The west coast of Sumatra is on the whole agriculturally unproductive and unfriendly to mariners, so most of what happens in lowland Sumatran history takes place on the east side of the island, with its long and lazy rivers flowing into the sheltered Strait. The disparity between the two coasts is even more pronounced in the case of Java. Historically very little happens on the south coast of the island, and almost the only role it plays in the history of Muslim Java arises from the offshore presence of the mythical figure of the Goddess of the Southern Ocean, whose interactions with actual and potential rulers we will come to. So without the existence of the northern break, this part of Southeast Asia with its forbidding coastline would play a much-reduced role in the history of the Indian Ocean. But since we live in an interglacial, we need a schematic way to organize the confusing mass of islands that currently occupies much of the space between continental Southeast Asia and Australia. One way to think of these islands is as forming two major chains, with some further islands in between. The chain that concerns us most runs from west-northwest to east-southeast and constitutes a three-thousand-mile segment of the Indian Ocean rim, with mostly narrow gaps between the individual islands. In this chain we have Sumatra, with the Malay Peninsula immediately behind it, and then Java, then a series of smaller islands stretching as far as the western end of New Guinea. The other chain runs roughly from north to south and marks the western rim of the Pacific. It starts with the Philippines, a cluster of islands of which the two largest are Luzon in the north and Mindanao in the south, continues through Halmahera, and again terminates off the western end of New Guinea. There the two chains come together in the Moluccas, the famous Spice Islands. In between the two chains are Borneo and Sulawesi (Celebes). Leaving aside New Guinea, which plays very little part in our story, the largest islands are Borneo, Sumatra, Sulawesi, and Java, in that order. Smaller islands are legion but need not detain us.

There is no lack of rainfall in maritime Southeast Asia. This news is not, however, as good as it might sound to someone from the heartlands, where the problem is almost always aridity. One thing to notice is that we are much farther south than we usually find ourselves in this book: the equator runs through the middle of Sumatra and Borneo, the Malay Peninsula is just to north of it, and Java is entirely in the southern hemisphere. This means that the natural vegetation cover of most of maritime Southeast Asia is tropical jungle, and the soils of tropical jungles tend not to be particularly fertile. The largest example of this is Borneo, while the crucial exception is Java, which benefits from the residue of its eighty-five past and present volcanoes. It thus has substantial amounts of highly fertile land and can support a much larger population than the other islands. At the present day as much as 62 percent of Indonesia's population lives on Java, and for our period it has been estimated that around 1600 the island was comparable to India and China in population density, and more densely settled than other Southeast Asian islands by an order of magnitude—the single exception being Bali, Java's even more densely settled eastern neighbor. So while Java comes in fourth among the larger islands in terms of surface area, it easily ranks first in economic and demographic terms. Alongside Javanese agriculture, trade had a considerable potential for generating wealth in the region. Quite apart from the products—notably spices—that it could export, anyone trading between India and China by sea had no choice but to take a route through Southeast Asia.

To the south of the islands marking the Indian Ocean rim is another major break, this one separating maritime Southeast Asia from Australia. The best part of three hundred miles across, this gap is much wider than the one between the Malay Peninsula and Sumatra. The existence of this substantial gap is undoubtedly a major reason Australia lay beyond the horizon of geographical knowledge until discovered by the Dutch in the seventeenth century.

Continental Southeast Asia

When we looked at the Indian coast between Cape Comorin and Bengal, we saw that evidence of Muslim commercial settlements was scarce to nonexistent. The same is true of much of the Burmese coast. Barbosa says of the kingdom of Burma that "there are no Moors therein inasmuch as it has no seaport which they can use for their traffic." He also remarks of the coastal kingdom of Arakan, a complex of islands and estuaries, that it "possesses no port on the sea."[30]

There was in fact a Muslim population in Arakan, but it was a spillover from neighboring Bengal and so part of the overland—not the maritime—expansion of Islam. It was the only case of this kind anywhere in Southeast Asia. Until conquered by the Burmese in 1785, Arakan was an independent Buddhist kingdom. But in the early fifteenth century a Burmese invasion drove the king into exile in Bengal. Eventually, it is reported, he was restored to his kingdom thanks to a

30. *The book of Duarte Barbosa*, 2:149, 150.

Muslim army supplied by his hosts. Thereafter there was a significant presence of Muslims in the state apparatus, and relations with Bengal, though often hostile, were close. For a long time the rulers of Arakan adopted Muslim titles along with their Arakanese ones, and prominent Muslim officials there patronized a seventeenth-century efflorescence of Bengali literature. The high point of Muslim power came near the end of that century, when the Muslim soldiery took over the government of Arakan for twenty years. How far this presence gave rise to a Muslim population outside the state apparatus, through either Bengali immigration or Arakanese conversion, is hard to say. We know that there was persistent raiding of eastern Bengal to supply Arakan with slaves, at least some of whom would have been Muslims. The best of them were taken by the kings for service in the palace, but most were used for hard labor. We also learn of the presence of an Arakanese Muslim minority after Burma came under British rule in 1824–25; in 1842 its size was estimated at twenty thousand. It was believed to have arisen from willing or unwilling immigrants from Bengal who had been ethnically assimilated while retaining their religion, rather than from the conversion of native Arakanese Buddhists. Thus a British observer described the Muslims of the island of Ramree as "now so assimilated to the rest of the population in dress, language, and feature, that it is difficult to conceive a distinction ever existed."[31] He added that each of them had two names, one presumably Muslim and the other Arakanese, and that they wished to be known by the second. By the twentieth century there were considerable numbers of Arakanese converts. But as already indicated, this is not part of the story of the maritime expansion of Islam.

When we continue south to the Mon kingdom of Pegu in lower Burma we are back with mercantile Islam. Here Barbosa speaks of three or four harbors "where there are rich merchants and great towns inhabited as well by Moors as by the heathen,"[32] and he states that every year many Muslim ships come to trade, bringing textiles from Gujarat. Moving farther south to what was then the west coast of Siam, he reports the presence at Tenasserim (doubtless meaning its port of Mergui) of "many merchants both Moors and heathen" and the comings and goings of "many Moorish ships from divers regions." He speaks of a similar presence of Muslim shipping at Kedah (then ruled by Siam, though now part of Malaysia). But he tells us that Muslims were not permitted in the interior, or if they did enter it, they were not allowed to bear arms. His next port of call is Malacca on the Malay Peninsula, which we will leave aside until we come to maritime Southeast Asia.

For this stretch of the coast we do not have much to go on before the arrival of the Portuguese, but there is no lack of evidence of Muslim ships and merchants trading with it thereafter. For example, in 1625 ships belonging to Muslim mer-

31. Quoted in J. P. Leider, *Le royaume d'Arakan, Birmanie*, Paris 2004, 32.

32. For this and the quotations that follow see *The book of Duarte Barbosa*, 2:153, 164.

chants from the Coromandel coast were trading with Pegu and Kedah, while in the same period Ḥājjī Bābā, a prominent merchant based in Arakan, traded with Masulipatnam. But north of the Malay Peninsula none of this maritime activity seems to have led to the formation of significant Muslim populations—in contrast to the overland spread of Islam into Arakan from Bengal.

Through the Strait of Malacca Muslims from the Indian Ocean could reach the South China Sea, giving them access to the southern and eastern coasts of continental Southeast Asia and beyond that to the ports of China and even Korea. We know that Muslim merchants were active in this region very early, for as we saw, they appear in Chinese sources already in the eighth century. On the coast of southern China, Muslim traders had presumably reached an accommodation with the T'ang authorities; one source has it that the Chinese ruler would appoint a Muslim as judge over the community. This is a widespread theme. A tenth-century Arab geographer remarks of regions under non-Muslim rule that "Muslims do not accept that any but a Muslim shall judge over them,"[33] and he mentions other examples of such arrangements on the west coast of India, among the Khazars north of the Caucasus, in the Caucasus itself, and in West Africa. But whatever accommodation was reached in southern China, it does not seem to have worked reliably: in 758 the Muslims sacked Canton and sailed away. At some point they returned, but that, too, ended badly, for China in the later ninth century was suffering from a plague of bandit gangs reminiscent of the Jelālī rebels whom we encountered in the Ottoman Empire. In the course of an extraordinary rampage through China, an army of such gangs sacked Canton in 879, and there was massive slaughter of foreign merchants, including Persians and Arabs. In any case there is no indication that this mercantile presence in China led to the formation of a lasting Muslim community among the native Chinese of the coastlands. It was only in the aftermath of the overland conquest of China by the Mongols that Islam acquired a significant Chinese following—and as one might expect, a Ḥanafī one.

Of more interest to us is the spread of Islam in Champa (Campā), the land of the Chams. This people has almost disappeared, but in earlier times it occupied much of what is today central and southern Vietnam. Unlike the other peoples of continental Southeast Asia, the Chams had capital cities on the coast and spoke a language that, though akin to Malay, was yet more closely related to Acehnese. They maintained strong links to maritime Southeast Asia, and indeed the linguistic evidence indicates that they must have originated there. Like many other peoples of Southeast Asia they adopted an Indian—primarily Hindu—elite culture; their earliest surviving Sanskrit inscription is likely to date from the fourth century or so. Thereafter they had a long history, but in 1471 the main Cham

33. N. Levtzion and J.F.P. Hopkins, *Corpus of early Arabic sources for West African history*, Cambridge 1981, 52.

kingdom went down to Vietnamese conquest from the north. Only the minor kingdom of Pāṇḍuranga in the far south, today's Phan Rang, was able to survive into the 1830s as a vassal of Vietnam. The earliest references to Champa in Arabic sources date from the middle of the ninth century. They refer to the country as Ṣanf and describe it as offering freshwater and aloeswood. That we have this information means there must have been early contacts between Muslim merchants and the native Chams on the coast of Champa, but these do not seem to have engendered an enduring Muslim community. When Barbosa came to describe the Chams in the early sixteenth century, he characterized them as heathen and made no mention of Moors, and indeed his contemporary Tomé Pires states explicitly that "there are no Moors in the kingdom."[34] Yet in the later sixteenth century conversion to Islam was proceeding apace among the Chams. A Spanish source of 1604 comments that "those who newly profess it are numerous."[35] The king himself was still a Hindu, but he was encouraging his subjects to convert, and mosques were being built. By the 1670s the bulk of the population had converted, and so had the king. However, it is not until the late nineteenth century that we begin to have detailed accounts of the beliefs and practices of the Muslim Chams. At that point it is evident that their Islam had deviated spectacularly from metropolitan standards. For example, they had a mother goddess and priestesses, abstained from sex on Mondays because they believed God to have been born on that day, and held Nosirwan—the sixth-century Sasanian ruler Anūshirwān—to be God's son. This is the only case of conversion to Islam on the part of a continental Southeast Asian people, or at least a significant fraction of one. It must surely have been Muslim merchants who first brought Islam to Champa, but the later receptiveness to it on the part of the Chams calls for a different explanation. One factor was no doubt the pervasive conflict between Christians and Muslims that broke out across the Indian Ocean with the arrival of the Portuguese. The din of this conflict must have raised awareness of Islam as something more than just a religion of foreign merchants, and in the ensuing polarization it could have provided a ready basis for seeking alliances with Muslim rulers of maritime Southeast Asia. Thus at one point the Cham king had an alliance with a Muslim ruler on the Malay Peninsula against the Portuguese and Spanish; loyalty to Hinduism would have paid no such dividends in this situation. Another factor may have been the desperate straits in which the Chams now found themselves. The one success of mercantile Islam in continental Southeast Asia was thus with a singularly ill-starred people.

34. Tomé Pires, *The Suma oriental*, London 1944, 1:114.

35. Quoted in A. Reid, *Southeast Asia in the age of commerce*, New Haven 1988–93, 2:187. This work is a major source of my treatment of Southeast Asia.

While the Cham conversion was exceptional, two major continental polities went through passing flirtations with Islam in roughly the same period. These were Siam and Cambodia. The other major continental polities, those of the Burmese, the Mons, and the Vietnamese, did not even flirt.

Let us start with what happened in Siam. One circumstance in the background to the story was that from 1629 to 1656 the country was ruled by a usurper, Prasat Thong; after his death his son Narai (ruled 1657–88) prevailed in a violent succession struggle. To usurp is by definition to ride roughshod over the traditional norms of a polity. This inevitably creates tension between the ruler and his subjects and pushes him to look for allies from outside the system. The other feature of the background was the presence of a rich array of foreign groups in Ayutthaya, the inland capital of Siam. This was significantly different from the old-fashioned presence of merchants going about their business in ports along the coast. Rulers naturally find accomplished foreigners to be useful people to have at hand, since they have skills not available locally and lack connections to the polity's indigenous stakeholders. In this period the array was unusually rich and diverse thanks to the higher degree of maritime mobility that characterized the Indian Ocean after the coming of the Europeans. There was thus a variety of Christian and Muslim groups in Ayutthaya. On the Muslims side there were Sunnīs from Champa, Macassar, and elsewhere, but also numerous Persian Shīʿites, including a merchant, Āqā Muḥammad Astarābādī, who became for a time the most influential man in the country. This Persian presence is not as serendipitous as it sounds: Persian merchants were active in Indian Ocean trade, not least in Siam's maritime backyard, the Bay of Bengal. A ruler who is firmly in control can readily make use of such groups without succumbing to their machinations, as in the end Narai was able to do. But he did not get off to a good start. He needed support in his bid for the succession, and he got it from the Persians.

For several years thereafter the Persians dominated affairs of state. There were Persian provincial governors, Persian and Indian Shīʿites were recruited into the standing army, and embassies were exchanged with Ṣafawid Iran. All this had some impact on the native population. A European observer reported in 1686 that in Ayutthaya "a great many Siamese men and women" had converted to Islam,[36] and there are also reports of ten thousand converts in Tenasserim on the west coast. But by now the Persian merchant had died and Narai was showing that he had a mind of his own. He had had his fill of the Persians and their culture and was becoming enamored of the French. At this point, in 1686, a few hundred Muslims led by aristocratic refugees from Macassar and Champa mounted a rebellion. They were suppressed by the European soldiers who were another element in the

36. Quoted in Reid, *Southeast Asia in the age of commerce*, 2:191.

ethnic cocktail of Ayutthaya, and thereafter the Muslims no longer played so prominent a role. If it was any comfort to them, the French in turn overreached and paid for it at the time of Narai's death in 1688. What is striking about this whole story is what didn't happen: at no stage was there an intervention by any Siamese noble. One reason for this was that for the last few decades the kings of Siam had been putting considerable effort into getting rid of the Siamese aristocracy. But an indigenous actor of a different kind eventually played a part in the downfall of Narai's regime. Siam had long before adopted the Thēravāda Buddhism of Ceylon, and it had come to be deeply embedded in Siamese society. The Buddhist monastic community, the Sangha, expected a close relationship with its king and had no wish to see him flirt with Islam or Christianity. Moreover, the Sangha was by now a unified order and a popular force. Its strength helps explain why Narai's flirtation with Islam came to nothing.

The Cambodian story is a variation on the same themes. Here, too, there was a background of political disarray, with a succession of usurpers issuing in the seizure of power by a certain Cau Bana Cand (ruled 1642–59). There was again a rich soup of foreigners, including Japanese from Nagasaki. And once more, those who brought the new king to power were Muslims. Soon they were his only supporters, and in 1643 the king was so badly in need of his Muslim allies that he converted to Islam, styling himself Sultan Ibrāhīm and setting up a court in Malay style. He is said to have insisted that everyone in his employ should convert to Islam or leave the royal service. His reign ended in 1659 after some dissident princes called in a Vietnamese invasion, and this was effectively the end of Cambodian Islam. The royal chronicle comments that the monks of the kingdom were much annoyed by the king's attitude to them and that everyone, high and low, was against a king who turned his back on Buddhism.

In short, continental Southeast Asia proved more or less impermeable to the large-scale spread of Islam. That leaves us to wonder why the story of Islam in maritime Southeast Asia should have turned out so differently.[37]

Maritime Southeast Asia

In maritime Southeast Asia, as on the continent, prehistory lasted until the early centuries of our era—rather late by the standards of China, India, or the Middle East. At that time the islanders, like so many other peoples, were engaged in agriculture, but they also did a lot of seafaring. It was this maritime activity that eventually led them to the settlement of Madagascar. Yet at the turn of our era the islanders were still untouched by the literate civilizations of the Eurasian

37. For a survey of the history of the regions that now make up Indonesia see M. C. Ricklefs, *A history of modern Indonesia since* c. *1200*, Stanford 2008.

mainland, and they showed no disposition to develop a civilization of their own. What gradually ended prehistory in maritime Southeast Asia was the rise of long-distance trade with India and the territorial expansion of China. These developments exposed Southeast Asians to the economic, cultural, and political stimuli of both India and China. Of the two, it was Indian influence that set the tone in most of Southeast Asia, including the Malay Peninsula, Sumatra, and Java. The result was a reception of Indian culture that seems to have been closely associated with state formation. Thus by the time of the rise of Islam, there was a well-established literate culture of Indian origin not just in continental Southeast Asia but also on the Malay Peninsula and the western islands, in particular Sumatra and Java. This region was ruled by native dynasties, but they patronized Indian culture, wrote inscriptions in Indian scripts, and adopted Indian religions. If they chose to establish Hindu cults they imported Brahmins, and if they preferred Buddhism they presumably imported monks; one difference here was that Brahmins initially needed the natives to supply them with wives, after which they could reproduce themselves locally—just as Muslim merchants were to do. In other words, India offered Southeast Asians what Islam offered East Africans: a literate civilization for peoples that had previously been without one.

Islam must have reached maritime Southeast Asia in the same way as Hinduism and Buddhism had done—through maritime commerce. But the accounts of its arrival given in a standard Malay source, the "Malay Annals," are so obviously legendary that over a long period we are reduced to inference. It stands to reason that if there were Muslim merchants on the south coast of China in the eighth century, they must already have been active in Southeast Asia. Moreover, the pattern of the winds dictates that ships cannot pass through Southeast Asia without spending a significant amount of time there. If Muslim merchants were present, then no doubt they made some local converts. Yet it is not until the last years of the thirteenth century that we have unambiguous evidence to back up such inferences. In 1295 the Italian traveler Marco Polo reported the presence of Islam in northern Sumatra, saying of the kingdom of Pĕrlak: "Its inhabitants are for the most part idolaters, but many of those who dwell in the seaport towns have been converted to the religion of Mahomet by the Saracen merchants who constantly frequent them."[38] In 1345–46 Ibn Baṭṭūṭa visited this coast; he tells us that at Pasai the ruler and his subjects were Shāfiʿites and loved to fight the infidel. Between then and the arrival of the Portuguese in 1509 we have further cases. One is Malacca on the west coast of the Malay Peninsula, a port city that seems to have emerged around 1400 with Chinese support, though the first ruler's conversion to Islam may have taken place only toward the end of his reign. Here, too, rulers

38. Marco Polo, *Travels*, London 1954, 338.

might own ships and profit from their commercial activities. Another case is Aceh, like Pĕrlak located at the north end of Sumatra. This sultanate seems to have taken shape around 1500, and as we have seen it was to reach out to the Ottomans around the middle of the sixteenth century. In each case we most likely have to do with an independent city-state that lived off the opportunities provided by long-distance trade but had only a limited relationship to its hinterland—a phenomenon that presupposes the absence in the interior of strong states whose existence would have precluded the evolution of coastal mercantile settlements into independent polities. In this way, some of the ports of Southeast Asia are reminiscent of those of the heartlands, though less extreme in their deprivation. A Chinese source of the mid-fifteenth century says of Malacca that "the infertile fields yield little rice, so that the people are not greatly concerned with agriculture,"[39] and according to a Portuguese source of the early sixteenth century, 90 to 95 percent of the revenues of Malacca came from dues levied on commerce. On the other hand, a Portuguese observer reported more than a thousand orchards in the territory of Malacca—a luxury that the inhabitants of Hormuz would have appreciated.

This pattern of mercantile city-states is, of course, already familiar to us: it is what we saw on the East African coast, in contrast to the coasts of India. It may therefore be worth pausing to make some comparisons between the city-states of East Africa and those of Southeast Asia. The first relates to the origins of the rulers. As in East Africa, Southeast Asian rulers could be either foreign or native in origin. In the case of Aceh, one late report has it that the founder was an Arab, and for sure there were three Arab rulers between 1699 and 1726. In the case of Malacca, the founder is reputed to have been a prince from Palembang in southern Sumatra who, prior to his conversion, was known by the manifestly Hindu name or title Paramēśvara. In the case of Dĕmak on the north coast of Java, the rulers were of Chinese Muslim descent; this was a significant case because Dĕmak played a central part in spreading Islam on Java. More obviously mythical claims abound. Many Malay dynasties of the seventeenth and eighteenth centuries claimed Turkic ancestors. A more extravagant claim, made by the dynasty of Malacca, was descent from Alexander the Great in his Islamic guise of Iskandar Dhū 'l-Qarnayn. Whether factual or fanciful, these accounts echo an ancient theme: the earliest Indianized polity we know of in Southeast Asia was reputedly founded by a Brahmin who disembarked on the seashore and married the naked queen of the region.

A second comparison concerns the form of the polity. Again, as in East Africa, the standard model was monarchical. But in East Africa we saw an occasional republican tendency, and this, too, had parallels in maritime Southeast Asia.

39. Quoted in P. Wheatley, *The Golden Khersonese*, Kuala Lumpur 1961, 321.

Around 1600 the Dutch found that in some of these polities no important decision could be made except in the presence of an assembly of notables, each of whom would have his say. In eighteenth-century Sulu—the archipelago in the southwest of the Philippines—there was a system of this kind with formal rules. The sultan had two votes, fifteen councilors had one each, and the crown prince had two votes if he sided with the sultan but only one if he voted against him. In Macassar a kind of dual monarchy emerged and was formalized in 1593: one lineage provided the king, the other the chief minister. In Aceh we can perhaps see a functional equivalent to such arrangements at work. In the half century after 1589, two of its rulers had behaved in a crudely despotic fashion, which was undesirable from a mercantile point of view. Thereafter, from 1641 to 1699, Aceh was consistently ruled by virgin queens. A Persian observer deemed this unmanly, as did the "insolent highlanders" of the hinterland,[40] but an English commentator clearly thought it a wise solution to the problem of despotism, as no doubt it was. With a touch of cynicism the device could be seen as providing a female monarchical front for male oligarchy. It fits with this that the Acehnese queens had a very different strategy from that adopted by the thirteenth-century Delhi sultan Raḍiyya when it came to the problem of combining female rulership with seclusion. Like the ancient Egyptian Pharaoh Hatshepsut in the fifteenth century BC, Raḍiyya in effect impersonated a man and showed herself in public dressed like one, but the queens of Aceh, though able to move around by boat, did so without ever being seen, thereby surrounding themselves with an air of mysterious modesty. But of course by metropolitan Islamic standards neither style of female rule was a respectable way to run a state, and it is said that a letter from Mecca denouncing the practice as contrary to Islam was instrumental in enabling its opponents to end it in 1699. The rule of queens was not unheard of elsewhere in maritime Southeast Asia. The Chinese had already reported the good governance of a Javanese queen in 674, and Patani on the east side of the Malay Peninsula had a succession of queens that lasted from 1584 to 1688; the motivation here was similar to what we saw in Aceh.

A final comparison between East Africa and Southeast Asia relates to the role of language. If that of the East African commercial scene was Swahili, its Southeast Asian counterpart was Malay, which seems to have been the common language of most if not all of these city-states. Yet the deeper history of the two languages is probably different. It makes sense to think of Swahili as developing through the interaction of East Africans with Muslim merchants. By contrast, long before it became associated with Islam, Malay was the language of a non-Muslim commercial hegemony, that of Śrīvijaya in the seventh to thirteenth centuries. The earliest

40. A. Reid, *Witnesses to Sumatra*, Kuala Lumpur 1995, 104.

Malay inscriptions come from near Palembang at the center of Śrīvijaya in southern Sumatra. They date from the late seventh century and are written in a script imported from the south of India. It is thus likely that Malay was already a widespread language of mercantile activity under the aegis of Śrīvijaya.

It is unfortunate that our sources tell us nothing of the existence or otherwise of Muslim commercial city-states in maritime Southeast Asia before the thirteenth century. There are, of course, two ways to interpret such a silence. We could assume that the city-states that begin to appear then were a new phenomenon, or we could take it that they had been there for centuries, and that the change lies in the availability of evidence. Two things tend to suggest that the change was a real one. First, it is the view of those who study these things that the volume of trade in or through Southeast Asia was increasing substantially at the time when we start to hear about the city-states. Second, there is a loose correlation with the appearance on the islands of Muslim tombstones with inscriptions. The earliest is perhaps one in northern Sumatra, reputedly dating from the early thirteenth century, but we are on somewhat more solid ground with one from 1326, which graced the tomb of a Muslim ruler on the north coast of the island and is the start of a long tradition. There are others dating to the fifteenth century in Sumatra and the Malay Peninsula, and one from 1419 on the Javanese coast—again the tombstone of a Muslim ruler. Alongside these Arabic inscriptions we also have one in Malay dating from the fourteenth century—our earliest Malay text in the Arabic script. This is the Trengganu Stone, the work of a Muslim ruler on the east coast of the Malay Peninsula, and we will come back to it. Very likely Malay was already being written in the Arabic script on perishable materials, though the earliest surviving manuscripts date only from the late sixteenth century. But all this looks like a change on the ground, not just a change in the extent to which evidence has reached us.

What this early evidence does not show is significant penetration of Islam beyond the coastlands. Yet this too was changing, though unevenly, and eventually the result would be a major divergence between maritime Southeast Asia and the rest of the Indian Ocean rim outside the heartlands—with the single exception of the Somali hinterland. At the point at which the Portuguese reached Southeast Asia, however, this momentous process had barely begun. Barbosa speaks of the "city and realm" of Malacca, stating that many foreign Muslims established there had become so rich that "they turned the people of the land into Moors"[41] and on that basis achieved independence of the ruler of Siam. This description suggests a city-state with some neighboring territory, though not necessarily in the interior. Of Sumatra he says that the ports are mostly occupied by Muslims, while

41. *The book of Duarte Barbosa*, 2:169, 171–72.

the heathen mostly dwell inland. He goes on to describe Java in the same terms: its inhabitants are "heathen in the inland regions but Moors in the sea-havens."[42] Yet in all three of these territories Islam went on to penetrate the interior in varying degrees. The case of the Malay Peninsula seems the most obscure. Here the bulk of the interior was tropical rain forest, but there were some alluvial flood plains that could be cultivated. What is clear is that the non-Malay indigenous population of the peninsula remained almost untouched by Islam far into the twentieth century. As of 1969 this population numbered some 53,000; of these, only some 1,600 were Muslims, and all but 200 of them belonged to a group of historically recent immigrants to the peninsula who may already have been Muslim when they arrived. So it would not be rash to assume that as of 1800 the entire indigenous population was non-Muslim. What we would like to know is how far inland Muslim Malays had moved by the end of our period. Turning to Sumatra, many of the Minangkabau in the west-central highlands had converted to Islam by the early seventeenth century, and some coastal states, notably Aceh, had put considerable military effort into enforcing the religion on their up-country neighbors. This zeal may have been political, but it fits with a tendency to intolerance in disputes around orthodoxy that marked Ṣūfism in Aceh in the second quarter of the seventeenth century, complete with the burning of books and the execution of the disciples of their authors. It likewise went with a liking for the more drastic criminal punishments of Islamic law. Otherwise most of the highlanders stuck to their paganism into the nineteenth century and beyond—and this at a time when the majority of Sumatra's population still lived in the highlands. In 1823 a British visitor commented that "there are yet hundreds of thousands, perhaps millions, in Sumatra, who at this moment possess no religion at all."[43] The case we are best informed about, however, is Java.

On Java the last major Hindu state was Majapahit in the late thirteenth to early sixteenth centuries. Its capital was in eastern Java, inland from Surabaya, and a tantalizing set of tombstones have been found in the district. Typically they have appropriate Qur'ānic material in Arabic script on one side, though with many mistakes in the vocalization, while on the other side they give a dating using Old Javanese numerals and the Indian Śaka era. Translated into our era, the dates range from 1376 to 1475. These tombstones show beyond doubt that Muslims were present at the center of Majapahit—albeit Muslims who either did not know what year of the Muslim era they were in or felt the Śaka era to be more prestigious. The inscriptions tell us nothing about the deceased, so there is no sure way to know whether they were Javanese or foreign and whether they were merchants, soldiers, or bureaucrats. But their presence does suggest that the

42. *The book of Duarte Barbosa*, 2:190.
43. Quoted in Z. Rais, *Against Islamic modernism*, Jakarta 2001, 18 note 12.

rulers of Majapahit were already finding it desirable to have Muslims around them. By the later fifteenth century, however, Majapahit was beginning to fall apart, and from the sixteenth century it was primarily Muslim states that ruled Java. There were around ten of them strung out along the north coast, and further ones in the interior. At first the most powerful of them was Dĕmak on the north coast, but in the long run by far the most successful one was based a long way to the south. This was Mataram, which lasted from around 1575 to 1755, at which point it divided into two kingdoms, those of Surakarta and Yogyakarta, both of which formally outlasted Dutch rule over the island. To go back to the history of the undivided kingdom, after a long struggle Mataram extended its power over the north coast and conquered all of central and eastern Java. It did not, however, rule western Java, where the state of Bantĕn prevailed, converting to Islam in response to an invading Muslim army in the 1520s and going on to eliminate the last significant Hindu state of the Javanese interior. Under the rule of Mataram and its successor dynasties, full-blooded Hinduism became a thing of the past on Java outside the remote southeastern highlands of Tengger, though much of the spread of Islam at the eastern end of the island took place only in the late eighteenth century. The reception of Islam did not, however, mean that Mataram had become a common or garden Muslim state. At this point a single detail is enough to illustrate the gap: the role of professional female soldiers at court in the mid-eighteenth century. They were experts in the use of artillery, firearms, and other weapons, guarded the palace at night, and at the same time served as scribes and concubines. This is not something we would expect to find in the heartlands of the Muslim world. Nonetheless, Islam had been very successful in penetrating the interior of Java—though as we will see, that success was a matter more of quantity than of quality. But whatever the qualifications, by the end of our period Islam had reached into the interiors of Sumatra, Java, and perhaps the Malay Peninsula to an extent that it had not done in the countries of continental Southeast Asia. As in East Africa and along the coasts of southern India, the Islam that prevailed was Shāfiʿite. Muslims from China appear to have contributed to the conversion of Java and might thus have been expected to bring Ḥanafī Islam to the island, but the evidence that they did so is minimal.

Why were the maritime and continental outcomes so different? One reason is geographical. On the continent, with its higher ratio of interior to coastline and its greater agricultural wealth, maritime trade is likely to have counted for less than it did on the islands. A continental country was certainly exposed to the pull of coastal Islam, but it was not surrounded by it, as the populations of the insular interiors tended to be. Only on Java could a ruler in maritime Southeast Asia afford to agree with the sultan of Gujarat that "wars by sea are merchants' affairs, and of no concern to the prestige of kings"—or as Sultan Agung (ruled 1613–46) of the Javanese state of Mataram put it with studied contempt, "I am a prince and a soldier, not a merchant like the other princes of Java."[44] The merchant princes he despised had perforce to take commerce seriously, though an aggressive ruler, like the tyrant who governed Aceh from 1589 to 1604, was more likely to seek to monopolize trade than to promote it as a public good. At the same time, the effect of being on an island was enhanced by a simple point of physical geography. The Malay Peninsula, Sumatra, and Java are all elongated in shape and thus very unlike continental Southeast Asia—or indeed Borneo, which is not only the largest Southeast Asian island but also unusually compact. For anyone living deep in the massive interiors of continental Southeast Asia or Borneo, the call of Islam was likely to be far less audible than it was for those hemmed in by coasts. A further reason for the contrast is that the mutual support of state and religion may have been better articulated on the continent, where Buddhism of the Thēravāda variety as developed on Ceylon had taken hold in Cambodia, Siam, Pegu, and Burma—in contrast to maritime Southeast Asia.

At this point it may be worth extending our comparative horizon beyond Southeast Asia to include the other large islands of the Indian Ocean. One contrast that easily comes to mind pits the eventual success of Islam in the interiors of the Malay Peninsula, Sumatra, and Java against its failure on Ceylon. Here two of the points already made have some purchase: Ceylon is a fairly compact island, and its Buddhism is of the Thēravāda variety. We can also contrast the success of Islam in maritime Southeast Asia with its failure on Madagascar, the only other large island in the Indian Ocean. Again physical geography helps: compared to the islands of the Southeast Asian rim, Madagascar is large and relatively compact. What it did not have was Thēravāda Buddhism. Moreover, there is a reason one might have expected the Malagasy to show more interest in Islam than the islanders of Southeast Asia did. Islam was effectively the first literate culture to reach Madagascar, whereas in Southeast Asia it had been preceded by a literate Indian culture that was widely adopted. Yet for a long time there was no demand for literate culture from states on Madagascar because there were no states, and insofar as nonstate actors adopted it, they tended to do so while more or less forgetting about Islam. Perhaps the key point here is again a geographical one: Southeast Asia was on the way from India to China, whereas Madagascar, until the Portuguese rounded the Cape of Good Hope, was on the way to nowhere. Muslim merchants did not ignore it, but they would have been unlikely to give it the attention they gave to Southeast Asia even if its resources had been comparable.

What of the rest of maritime Southeast Asia? One obvious point is that the islands behind the rim were more remote—more remote, that is, with regard to any form of literate culture coming to Southeast Asia from across the Indian Ocean.

44. Quoted in Reid, *Southeast Asia in the age of commerce*, 2:284.

There was, of course, an obvious alternative. When Southeast Asians began to upgrade their cultures by importing foreign scripts and practices in the early centuries of our era, they had a choice between two major brands, Indian and Chinese. Yet only the Vietnamese, who had experience of being ruled by China, opted for its elite culture. The peoples of the Philippines imported Chinese ceramics in considerable quantities, but this taste was not matched by an enthusiasm for Chinese characters or values, any more than it was in the many other societies of the Indian Ocean importing Chinese pottery. If it had been, the Philippines would have enjoyed a geographically more advantageous position than the islands of the Indian Ocean rim did. But as things were, the cultural history of the islands behind the rim was shaped by their relative remoteness. This is not to say that Indian culture had no impact on the remoter islands. Despite the lack of imposing ruins of Hindu or Buddhist temples on Borneo, it is there that we find the oldest inscriptions known on any Southeast Asian island. Still less are such ruins to be found in the Philippines, and yet on the island of Mindoro just south of Luzon folk scripts of Indian origin were still in use in a tribal society in the second half of the twentieth century. But there is an obvious geographical imbalance. The inscriptions we possess are heavily concentrated on or near the Indian Ocean rim—on the Malay Peninsula, Sumatra, Java, and its immediate neighbor Bali. The significance of this distribution is that if the influence of Indian culture diminishes as we move away from the rim, we can expect the same to be true of Islam; it, too, came to maritime Southeast Asia from the west.

Such a gradient is already discernible in Barbosa's survey. East of Java, Sumbawa is a heathen island; then follow other islands, including Timor, which are "inhabited by heathen with some Moors,"[45] then some small islands with both, and then some heathen islands that are raided by Moors. Finally, in this eastward progression, he comes to the Moluccas. There our geographical pattern comes somewhat unstuck: Barbosa reports both heathen and Moors but specifies that the kings are Moors. This relative salience of Islam nevertheless makes some sense, since these five islands lay at the source of the enormously lucrative spice trade and were thus of intense interest to maritime Muslims. But Barbosa proceeds to add some details suggesting that the Muslim presence in the Moluccas was as yet a shaky one. The greatest of the five kings, he tells us, though a Moor, is almost a heathen. He has a Muslim wife whose children are Muslim, but she is in reproductive competition with four hundred heathen maidservants whose children by the king are heathen. The impression of shakiness is reinforced by the account of the islands given by Tomé Pires in the same period. The kings are indeed Muslims, but "not very deeply involved in the sect."[46] Overall he estimates a quarter of the

45. *The book of Duarte Barbosa*, 2:195.
46. Pires, *The Suma oriental*, 1:213.

population to be Muslim, but on two of the islands this proportion falls to a tenth, two have almost entirely heathen populations, and one is purely heathen. He reports that Islam was said to have reached the islands only fifty years before his time, and he remarks that many of the Muslims are not circumcised. In other words, the Portuguese are giving us a vivid snapshot of a population still in the early stages of Islamization. By now we are within a couple of hundred miles of New Guinea. Some Portuguese, such as Pires, had already heard of this vast island, but they had yet to visit it, and it clearly lay beyond Barbosa's geographical horizon. So after completing his account of the Moluccas Barbosa doubles back and comes to Sulawesi, where he mentions cannibals but no Muslims, then continues through a couple more heathen islands to end up on Borneo, which he describes as having a heathen population and king; he says nothing about the sultanate of Brunei on the northwest coast of the island, where the rulers were Muslim from at least the early sixteenth century. He likewise knows nothing of the Philippines and the Muslims who had recently established themselves there. Overall, Barbosa leaves us with the definite impression that Muslims were present only on a minority of the islands behind the rim and constituted a minority even where they were present.

How far had this balance shifted by the end of our period? On the one hand, the processes set in motion by the arrival of mercantile Islam continued, but on the other hand, the coming of the Europeans brought Christianity as an alternative backed by the naval and military power of the newcomers. To get a sense of the outcome as of around 1800, let us follow in Barbosa's tracks, updating his account. Immediately to the east of Java, Bali remained staunchly Hindu, despite some Muslim settlement on the coast. The Islamization of Lombok had begun in the first half of the sixteenth century, but it remained superficial and was not helped by the fact that from the early eighteenth century the island was dominated by a Balinese kingdom. Sumbawa, a heathen island for Barbosa, was conquered by the Muslim sultanate of Macassar in the first half of the seventeenth century. On the islands farther to the east the Muslim impact was still slight. Timor, for example, became overwhelmingly Christian. Turning northward to the Moluccas, the competition between Islam and Christianity following the arrival of the Portuguese led to a differentiation between a north that was more Muslim and a south that was more Christian. Sulawesi was, on balance, a success for Islam. In the early sixteenth century Muslim traders were settling there, though it was not till 1605–7 that the rulers of the two kingdoms of Macassar in southwestern Sulawesi converted to Islam, whereupon they formed a single sultanate and embarked on an aggressive expansion that included much of Sulawesi, together with neighboring islands. In the north of the island, however, there was considerable conversion to Christianity, and there were still resilient heathen, as Barbosa would call them, in the interior—even though the island seems too straggling in shape to have much of one. The Dutch conquest of Macassar in 1669 may have done something to check the spread of Islam, and it undoubtedly caused a fair number of Macassarese Muslims to abandon their island for a lifestyle that we could best describe as maritime *qazaqlïq*; but the earlier gains of Islam were not reversed. Borneo, in contrast to Sulawesi, has its large and compact interior, and despite the extended presence of Islam—as also of Christianity—on the coasts, the interior remained almost entirely pagan.

The Philippines were a very different case, contrasting not just with the other outer islands but also with the Malay Peninsula, Sumatra, and Java. As a general rule, European powers and their commercial companies showed little appetite in our period for conquering and administering extensive Southeast Asian territories. On the Malay Peninsula the Portuguese seized Malacca in 1511, but they had no aspiration to annex the peninsula as a whole. Indeed, a Portuguese commentator of the early seventeenth century felt that even conquests such as that of Malacca were too much, since the Portuguese presence in the region "was intended for trade and not for conquests"; it was not as if such overseas territories were "a province bordering on Portugal."[47] Likewise on Java, the Dutch seized Jayakĕrta (now Jakarta) in 1619, renaming it Batavia, but had no ambition to rule the island as a whole. By 1800 the Portuguese were in any case barely a stakeholder: they had lost Malacca to the Dutch in 1641 and retained only a tenuous hold on the eastern part of the island of Timor. The Dutch were a heavier presence, given to playing a hegemonic role in the affairs of Java and the Moluccas and investing much military effort to that end. But they were not yet interested in the direct administration of large native populations, and their increasingly bankrupt United East India Company—in business since 1602, but fated to be taken over by the Dutch state in 1800—would have lacked the resources to undertake it. The Dutch did eventually come to rule some territory outside Batavia directly, especially on the north coast of Java, but as of the end of the eighteenth century the extent of their control was still limited, and in practice they were ruling through local lords. The only other European power that showed a serious interest in Southeast Asia before 1800 was Britain. In 1786 the British, or more precisely the East India Company, did something that in Southeast Asian terms was very traditional. They secured possession of the island of Penang off the west coast of the Malay Peninsula, acquiring it from the sultan of the nearest of the Malay coastal states and for a while building it up as a commercial entrepôt. Then in 1795, in the context of the wars precipitated by the French Revolution, they took Malacca from the Dutch to preempt its acquisition by the French. But they had no interest in taking over the minor sultanates of the Malay Peninsula. All this meant that however disruptive

47. See P. Cardim and N. G. Gonçalo Monteiro (eds.), *Political thought in Portugal and its empire*, Cambridge 2021, 171.

the activities of the Portuguese, and still more those of the Dutch, may have been for the Muslim merchants of Southeast Asia, they had relatively little impact on the size of the existing Muslim population. This European aversion to direct rule over large native populations was to change drastically in the very different conditions of the nineteenth century, but as yet there was no Southeast Asian parallel to the dramatic territorial expansion of the East India Company that we saw in eighteenth-century Bengal, and by the time things had changed, imperialism was tending to become an increasingly secular pursuit.

Against this background, the experience of Spanish rule in the northern and central Philippines after the conquest of 1565 stands out as an exception. Unlike the Portuguese or the Dutch, the Spanish had the means to hold and rule a large territory in some fashion, and they continued to do so until they lost the Philippines to the United States in 1898. Such control, however imperfect, was essential for a program aiming to Christianize the entire population. It cleared the way for the work of the Jesuits and other religious orders, with their organized and systematic efforts to convert the native population. Such efforts had no real parallel on the Muslim side, where the Ṣūfī orders tended to be more like networks than organizations. And unlike the Portuguese and the Dutch, the Spanish were in deadly earnest in seeing the triumph of Christianity and defeat of Islam as their objective. The missionary effort and intermittent wars against the Moros (the Moors or Muslims of the Philippines) were enough to check and—to an extent—reverse the spread of Islam. On Luzon there seems to have been little more than a vague awareness of Islam when the Spanish arrived. An account of 1572 affirms that the natives "do not know or understand the commandments of Muḥammad."[48] In some coastal towns, as a result of contact with Brunei, people could be found who did not eat pork, though it was believed that anyone who had not been to Brunei was free to consume it. A few who had been there knew more and could read some words of the Qur'ān. We have a similar account of the Moros of Cebu, a smaller island north of Mindanao, where Islam was a recent arrival. It describes families in which the husband is a Moro, the wife a pagan, and the parents seek baptism for their son; "they do not at all object to each one living according to the belief that he likes best."[49] The outcome in the northern and central Philippines was already clear in 1604: as a Jesuit put it, the population had moved from "I will become a Christian as soon as the rest do" to "We desire to become Christians because all the rest are Christians."[50] Things were different farther south, as in

48. Quoted in I. Donoso, "The Ottoman Caliphate and Muslims of the Philippine archipelago during the early modern era," in A.C.S. Peacock and A. T. Gallop (eds.), *From Anatolia to Aceh*, Oxford 2015, 127.

49. Quoted in J. N. Crossley, "Dionisio Capulong and the elite in early Spanish Manila," *Journal of the Royal Asiatic Society*, 3rd ser., 28 (2018), 701.

50. Quoted in J. L. Phelan, *The Hispanization of the Philippines*, Madison 1959, 57.

the Sulu archipelago to the southwest, where Islam is attested as early as 1310, and on Mindanao, which we will come back to below. In these regions the Spanish had no success in eradicating Islam. The Moros are still there today, numbering some five million, though that is only about 6 percent of the overwhelmingly Catholic population of the Philippines as a whole. As we would expect, the Moros are Shāfiʿites, but located as they were on the edge of the pre-Islamic Indian cultural sphere, they would call an Islamic scholar a pundit (*pandita*, from the Sanskrit *paṇḍita*). Like many other non-Arab Muslim peoples, they had traditions of writing their languages in the Arabic script.

The character of Islam in maritime Southeast Asia

What was Southeast Asian Islam like? One feature worth mentioning, though it is nothing unusual, is the presence of Ṣūfism; we have encountered it in seventeenth-century Aceh, and we will meet it again among the Minangkabau. When the Ṣūfī orders first reached Southeast Asia is anybody's guess—the earliest evidence we have relates to the late sixteenth century, and mass followings are not attested before the nineteenth century. A more interesting question is how the Islam of the islands compared to that of the heartlands. As might be expected, there is a spectrum, and in a rough and ready fashion we can divide it up as follows. At one end, there are cases where the basic religious and social norms do not look very different from what we might expect to find in the heartlands. In the middle are cases where the religious norms look familiar but the social norms look strange by metropolitan standards. Then at the far end of the spectrum there are cases where both religious and social norms, even among the elite, look weird from such a perspective. As this makes clear, distance from the heartlands is not the only factor at work.

As an example of the first category, consider what a French priest had to say in 1688 about the unimaginable "exactness" with which the Muslims of Macassar performed their religious duties: "They are far more devout than all other Mahometans; because they observe an infinite number of ceremonies that are not in use among the Turks, nor among the Indian Mahometans; because they believe them to be practised at Mecca, which they look upon as the center of their religion, and the pattern which they ought to follow."[51] A local chronicle says of the first Muslim ruler of Macassar that from the time he embraced Islam in 1605 until his death he never once missed the ritual prayer. We might contrast this rigorism with the attitude of the first ruler of Patani on the east coast of the Malay Peninsula. We are told that on converting he gave up eating pork and worshipping idols,

51. Quoted in M. Laffan, *The makings of Indonesian Islam*, Princeton 2011, 21.

but apart from that he did not alter any of his infidel habits. The unflinching acceptance of key Islamic norms is somehow what we would expect of the Macassarese and their neighbors. They were serious people, and whatever they did, they did properly. Thus the archaeological record suggests that upon adopting Islam they promptly gave up an ingrained social practice of burying the dead with appropriate grave goods. Similarly, two years after the king converted, a visitor reported that pigs had become difficult to obtain, and forty years later another visitor remarked that they no longer existed. Something similar seems to have happened with regard to female dress, for the second visitor described women as covered from head to foot, with not even their faces visible. But the same purposiveness also shows up in a quite different context. The Macassarese stand out as the only people of maritime Southeast Asia who had the acumen to make translations of European texts on firearms—a distinction that may be linked to the fact that a chief minister in the mid-seventeenth century possessed a library of Spanish and Portuguese books. It is also among the Bugis, one of the peoples of southwestern Sulawesi, that we find an unusually aggressive and explicit commitment to political freedom. But in the present context what matters is that the exactness of the Macassarese in performing their religious duties was matched by a drastic adherence to some social practices that would have met with full approval in the heartlands. And yet this did not prevent them from retaining their pre-Islamic script, their epics, their court ritual, and their aristocratic mythology.

Perhaps a more run-of-the-mill case to consider here would be a few pages from an autobiographical account written in Malay by a Muslim of Malacca, a certain Abdullah. He was born in Malacca around the time when it passed from the Dutch to the British, which happened in 1795. His great-grandfather was a Yemeni who had migrated to India and died there; his sons had moved farther east, and one of them settled in Malacca, where he married a Labbai. Their son, Abdullah's father, grew up there and became a merchant trading between Malacca and the hinterland. Alongside his commercial activities, he spread knowledge of the Qur'ān to the up-country people and told them how to perform the Muslim prayers. No doubt many Muslim merchants had done this before him when they found the natives receptive, but here for once we get a glimpse of it actually happening. Abdullah's parents, however, had a problem. His four elder brothers all died in childhood, and he himself was a sickly child. For us there is a silver lining to this: the stress of sickness can reveal a lot about a culture. Unsurprisingly, his parents were ready to try anything in the hope that it might save their son from the fate of his brothers. They spent large sums buying medicines indiscriminately from Indians, Malays, and Chinese—only very pious Muslims would respond to sickness by confining themselves to remedies transmitted from the Prophet. But people also recommended that Abdullah's parents have recourse to a flagrantly un-Islamic Malay practice, and they did so: they sold him for a pittance to six or seven people who had many children of their own. According to custom, the new owners would rename the child, and the parents, while continuing to care for it, would pretend that it was not their own. Presumably the point was that malign spirits had a track record of causing the sickness and death of any child of Abdullah's parents, but they had no such animus against those of his purchasers. If the spirits could be fooled into thinking that he was the child of those who had bought him, they would leave him alone. It seems to have worked—Abdullah survived into adulthood. The deviation from metropolitan Islamic standards here is significant, but so also is the embarrassment from which Abdullah suffers in recounting it. It was, he says, "a foolish custom of our forefathers," "entirely wrong and foolish,"[52] with no basis in the teachings of God or His Prophet. While fully appreciative of his mother's good intentions, he makes the religiously correct observation that it was with the help of God that he was restored to health. In contrast to this embarrassment, Abdullah feels nothing but pride in the fact that his grandmother had been a very successful teacher. She taught all the children of Malacca; two hundred boys and girls learned the Qur'ān from her, and she instructed all kinds of people. We would not expect to find a woman playing so prominent and public an educational role in the heartlands of the Muslim world. But Islam in Malacca had come a long way since the fifteenth century, when the Arab navigator Ibn Mājid gave this unflattering description of it: "These are bad people who do not observe any rules, the infidel marries a Muslim woman and the Muslim the infidel woman; and when you call them infidels, are you sure they are really infidels? And the 'Muslims' that you talk of, are they really Muslims? They drink wine in public and do not pray before beginning a voyage."[53]

An obvious example of the second combination—religious conformity and jarring social deviance—would be the Minangkabau in the highlands of west-central Sumatra.[54] This was a geographically remote region, but it was also a relatively wealthy one with a long history of linkage to the outside world. The reason was that the land of the Minangkabau was unusually well endowed with both agricultural and mineral resources. Agriculturally it supported enough wet rice cultivation for a dense population to feed itself, and it could also grow cash crops for export if there was sufficient external demand. On the mineral side it could keep itself in iron and export gold. In both respects its resources were much greater than those of the highland regions to its north and south, as also of the adjoining coast. Gold, in particular, was a commodity in which the outside world had an unfailing interest,

52. Abdullah bin Abdul Kadir, *The Hikayat Abdullah*, trans. A. H. Hill, Kuala Lumpur 1970, 37.

53. Quoted in L.F.F.R. Thomaz, "Melaka and its merchant communities," in D. Lombard and J. Aubin (eds.), *Asian merchants and businessmen in the Indian Ocean and the China Sea*, New Delhi 2000, 34.

54. For what follows see C. Dobbin, *Islamic revivalism in a changing peasant economy*, London 1983.

and since medieval times foreign merchants had been prepared to brave the dangerous waters and inhospitable shores of the west coast in pursuit of it. This trade made it possible for the region to support a royal family, or in other words a state. So it is no mystery that Islam came early to this part of the Sumatran highlands. The process had begun even before the Portuguese arrived—the king and a hundred of his men were already Muslims. By the mid-seventeenth century all the centers of the gold trade had converted to Islam, and by 1800 we no longer hear of paganism among the Minangkabau. At this time the gold mines were becoming exhausted, but by good fortune this coincided with the rising importance of coffee as a cash crop, again reinforcing external links. One further feature of this scene is worth noting. We usually think of Islamic scholars as a characteristically urban phenomenon, and usually we are right. But there were exceptions to this pattern, and the villages of the Minangkabau highlands supported one of them.

In narrowly religious terms there was not much to complain about in the Islam of the Minangkabau. It is true that the most prominent Ṣūfī order among them was the Shaṭṭāriyya, which we have already encountered in India, where we saw two of its followers showing a marked sympathy for Hinduism. But there is no comparable record of Shaṭṭārī syncretism in the Sumatran context. What made the Minangkabau socially deviant by metropolitan standards was above all their kinship system, which was matrilineal. They were not, of course, alone in this. We have already encountered the combination of devotion to Islam with matrilineal kinship among the Moplahs of Kerala, and we will meet it again when we come to West Africa. Though our knowledge of the history of the Minangkabau before the early nineteenth century is very limited, it would seem that the combination of religious conformity and social deviance remained stable down to the end of our period.

The destabilization of this highland society that set in soon after was a result of the rapid intensification of its links to the outside world. These enhanced links led to two things. One was economic and therefore social change, as new economic opportunities meant new tensions within the society. The other was a greater awareness of religious trends in the wider Muslim world. In particular, more Minangkabau were now making the pilgrimage to Mecca and returning with what they found there. In our period pilgrims were not likely to pick up anything wildly subversive while in Mecca, but in 1803 the city was taken over by the Wahhābīs, a radical Islamic reform movement, who held it until evicted by Egyptian forces in 1811. Returning pilgrims in 1803 brought back to their Minangkabau homeland a whiff of this new form of metropolitan Islam and went on to start a reform movement of their own. The reformers, who became known as the Padrīs, do not seem to have taken matrilineal kinship as their central target, but they took great exception to the traditional sport of cockfighting. Indeed, this became such a signature issue that their opponents, when they had the power, would taunt the Padrīs by building cockfighting rings in front of their noses; one such ring staged its fights to coincide with the Friday prayers in the neighboring Padrī mosque. But abolishing cockfighting was not the end of it. Men were to grow their beards and cover their knees, and women were to cover their faces. Prayer discipline was to be enforced, a distinctive form of dress was to be adopted, and tobacco was to be banned. All this resulted in an explosion of violence, billed on the Padrī side as jihad, and eventually led to hostilities with the Dutch. These began in 1821 and did not end until the final defeat of the movement in 1837.

That leaves the case in which both religious and social norms exhibit a high level of deviance from the Meccan standards to which the French priest referred. The obvious example is Java, but before we try to characterize its hybrid culture, it is worth pausing to sketch the historical context in which it arose. With its regions of wet rice cultivation, Java was agriculturally wealthy enough that the interior was a viable basis for a reasonably strong state. The Hindu kingdom of Majapahit had been such a state, and it had been powerful enough to dominate the coasts from the interior. For some decades after its fall it looked as if political power on Java had shifted north to the coast. This was the period in which the most dynamic state on the island had its center in the port of Děmak. But the rise of the Muslim state of Mataram in the later sixteenth century restored the primacy of the interior for a while. Mataram, however, eventually lost its grip on the coast and fell into weakness. Sultan Agung failed to evict the Dutch from their port of Batavia in 1628–29. Then his successor, the erratic Amangkurat I (ruled 1646–77), sought domestic security by moving to close the country in a manner reminiscent of the Tokugawa shoguns of Japan. He forbade Javanese merchants to trade abroad, closed the ports for long periods, and in 1655 requisitioned or destroyed his subjects' ships. Finally, in the middle of the eighteenth century, the dynasty relinquished the north coast to the Dutch. The interior nevertheless retained the resources needed to maintain its political culture. Moreover, Amangkurat I had moved to sever rather than strengthen his links to mainstream Muslim piety, which was strongest on the coast. This was not just a matter of symbolism. Soon after his accession he assembled two thousand Muslim religious scholars and had them massacred, along with their women and children. Subsequent rulers did not repeat this measure, but neither did they open the door to the radical Islamization of the interior. This made it possible for much of the pre-Islamic culture of Java to survive into the nineteenth century in a hybrid form.

It was in this context that the rulers of Mataram were seeking to boost their legitimacy. Kings in need of this precious commodity have to take it where they can find it. New dynasties require it because they originate in usurpation, and the later rulers of Mataram soon came to need it because despite their resources they proved ineffective against the Dutch, so much so that they came to be thoroughly dependent on them. Thus Amangkurat II (ruled 1677–1703) owed his throne to the Dutch, who suppressed a rebellion that would otherwise have swept the dynasty away. He sometimes dressed like a Dutchman, and it was rumored that he was actually the son of the Dutch governor-general. In the quest for legitimacy one potential source the rulers of Mataram could tap was Islam. Senapati (ruled ca. 1584–1601), who effectively founded the dynasty, waged war on his infidel neighbors, who were stubbornly refusing to accept the new religion, and this gave him a claim to the glamour of jihad. His grandson Agung sent to Mecca in 1641 to secure for himself the Islamic title of "sultan"—though the idea that Mecca had the power to mint sultanates was not one current in the heartlands. The other available source of legitimacy, not to be set aside lightly, was indigenous Javanese tradition.

This is where we come to the Goddess of the Southern Ocean, whose palace lay beneath the waves off the south coast of Java.[55] Before making his bid for power, we are told that Senapati spent three days—and, we are given to understand, nights—with the Goddess. Later Sultan Agung, too, enjoyed her favors. She was still part of the political seascape in the early nineteenth century. Dipanagara (d. 1855), a disaffected prince whose rebellion was suppressed by the Dutch in the Java War of 1825–30, had close links to pious circles through his mother's family and saw himself very much as a member of the wider Muslim community; his military arrangements included echoes of Ottoman terminology. Yet while practicing asceticism in a cave on the south coast he, too, had an encounter with the Goddess. In a concession to pious sensibilities we are assured that he did not succumb to her blandishments, but she did promise to help him when the time came—a good sign, because it was a promise she would make only to a king, which Dipanagara aspired to become. The Islamic and Javanese elements that came together in this pursuit of legitimation may well strike the logically fastidious as incompatible. There is, however, a way to reconcile them. The existence of genies (the *jinn*) is a well-established Islamic doctrine, so why should not the Goddess be one of them? In our own time this suggestion has been taken up by her friends, though her more orthodox enemies will have none of it. But in the real world nothing beats having one's cake and eating it, and this is what the Javanese continued to do into the nineteenth century without undue worry about logic. Just how much the Goddess appealed to the Javanese royal imagination was shown by a literary event of 1774. In that year a Yogyakarta prince and future king composed a long narrative poem on the occasion of the beginning of a new century according to the Śaka era. The story is set in a mythical past that is a thinly disguised version of the present, and the hero is rather transparently the prince himself. He has good relations with pious Muslims and wages jihad against the infidel foreigners who have

55. For what follows see M. C. Ricklefs, *Mystic synthesis in Java*, Norwalk 2006.

destroyed the cities of the coast. Yet at the same time he has the full cooperation of the Goddess and her army of spirits. In a particularly elegant touch, victory comes when she orders the Javanese to recite the Qur'ān and pray to God. They do as the Goddess tells them and win. This naturally leads to a happy ending. When the hero besieges the defeated infidels in their capital city, he calls on their king to convert to Islamic monotheism, and the king duly does so. Now that the mission of the Goddess is accomplished, the hero orders her to withdraw from the former infidel capital with her army, which she does, and they all live happily ever after. What more could Islam reasonably ask of the Goddess of the Southern Ocean?

We shift now to the wider culture that took shape around this meshing of Islamic and Javanese strands. To start with, one of the most visible accompaniments of the retention of indigenous traditions in Mataram was the continued use of the pre-Islamic Javanese script, which, like so many other Southeast Asian scripts, was of Indian origin. Thus mainstream Javanese did not follow the example of the Trengganu Stone when they converted to Islam, though the more pious, as among the Tamil Muslims, would use the Arabic script to write their language in religious contexts. This general retention of the pre-Islamic script is a phenomenon for which we have only isolated parallels in Malay, such as a tombstone of 1380 from northern Sumatra on which everything is Islamic bar the script.

Turning now to the content of the elite culture of Muslim Java, we can best illustrate it with a few sample themes. If we go to a Javanese court chronicle of 1738, one point of interest is the way in which the chronicler dates events. As we have seen, the era to which the Javanese were accustomed was the Indian Śaka era, which had an epoch of AD 78. In 1633 Sultan Agung promulgated a very Javanese calendar reform following a rebellion with a Muslim religious leadership. In accordance with this reform the Javanese retained their Śaka era and continued to count years in it. But in deference to Islam, from that point on their year was to be the Islamic lunar year, without intercalation. (Mataram did not, of course, rule the whole island, so the mountaineers of Tengger ignored the reform and continued to intercalate as before.) Alongside this absolute count the Mataram calendar also made use of a cyclic one, similar in that respect to the animal cycle of East Asia and the steppes, but here it was an eight-year cycle, not a twelve-year one. In Southeast Asia such cycles are commonplace; we already encountered a seven-year cycle on Madagascar that no doubt originated in Southeast Asia, and in the Tengger highlands they used a five-year cycle. But the Javanese were at pains to Islamicize their eight-year cycle, so the years were named with letters of the Arabic alphabet—the first was Alip (Arabic *alif*), and so forth. As indicated, the Islamicizing elements in the new calendar have plausibly been seen as a response to a rebellion led by religious figures. Though the rebellion was suppressed, there was reason to placate some of the sentiment behind it.

Let us now consider a religious text originating in the same court milieu, an eighteenth-century version of a work from 1633—the very year of Sultan Agung's calendar reform. Here we encounter a similar mix. There are a good many Arabic loanwords for key religious conceptions, as we would expect in an Islamic text, but also no lack of Sanskrit ones. Thus *agama* (Sanskrit *āgama*) is used for "religion"—a central concept for which many Muslim languages would use the Arabic *dīn*. Considerable liberties are taken with what we, like metropolitan Muslims of the day, would regard as matters of fact. Jesus and Muḥammad are presented as contemporaries, and they dine together, along with Jesus's wife (in this version of his biography Jesus could hardly have done without a wife, or at least a concubine, since all his descendants were to be kings). Jesus tells Muḥammad that he will install him as king, and his palace is to be built in the terrifying forest of Medina, which is full of such wild beasts as the rhinoceros, the tiger, and the elephant. This last liberty is not arbitrary. The writer is superimposing on the Arabian desert the idea that the foundation of a new Javanese capital involves taming the surrounding forest. This text also rewards us with an explicit reference to the relationship between the Arabic and Javanese heritages. After declaring Jesus to be a king (using the Sanskrit *narēndra*), Muḥammad adds that Jesus is bilingual—his two languages being Javanese and Arabic.

Our text does not explain why this bilingualism is so crucial, but here a work plausibly ascribed to king Pakubuwana II (ruled 1726–49) can help us out. The king, if the work is indeed his, compares the two heritages to the two eyes. Arabic literature is the right eye and Javanese literature the left eye (the word he uses for "literature" being *sastra*, from the Sanskrit *śāstra*). Arabic literature is a vision of God: if you don't know Arabic, you don't know the order of life, and you will have lived in vain. Javanese literature, by contrast, is a vision of the self: if you don't know Javanese, "your speech is confused" and vitiated.[56] This kind of dual allegiance was not new on Java. An Old Javanese text of the fourteenth century has this to say: "The sage of the Buddhist denomination will fail, if he does not know about the way to Śivahood, which is the highest reality, and likewise the excellent sage who follows the yoga of Śivahood, if he does not know about the essence of Buddhahood, which is the highest reality."[57] But to return to the king's concern with confused speech, what he has in mind is a specific feature of Javanese usage. In any society the way people speak to each other depends in some measure on their perception of their relative status; you do not address a Supreme Court judge as "hey, dude!" or "hey, babe!" unless you are going out of your way to show disrespect. What is unusual about Javanese is the extent to which an elaborate

56. See M. C. Ricklefs, *The seen and unseen worlds in Java*, St. Leonards, NSW 1998, 219.

57. Quoted in J. Ensink, "Śiva-Buddhism in Java and Bali," in H. Bechert (ed.), *Buddhism in Ceylon and studies on religious syncretism in Buddhist countries*, Göttingen 1978, 184.

systematization of such hierarchical tendencies is built into the language. And "the proper manner of speaking," as the king informs us, "is founded upon Javanese literature." In sum, if you do not know both heritages you will be unable to make use of the teachings of your father and grandfathers, and "you will be weighed down in your heart."[58] Unlike Jesus, you will be at best a courteous worldling or a pious boor. Pakubuwana II has been rated as probably the most foolish king of the entire dynasty, but we can thank him for an unusually explicit articulation of the synthesis of Islamic and Javanese traditions that had come to prevail in the polite society of Java.

A final example of this synthesis relates to law, and we can treat it very briefly. As one would expect, there was no move on the part of the rulers of Mataram to make the Sharīʿa the law of the land, but neither did Old Javanese law books remain in use unchanged, as they did on Bali. Instead, Old Javanese legal literature was adapted by removing material relating to the Hindu priesthood and letting in elements of the Sharīʿa.

As emerges from these examples, what was involved was not a full survival of the pre-Islamic Javanese literary heritage. Indeed, there is some reason to think that after the 1730s the Javanese elite—unlike that of Bali—was losing touch with that heritage and no longer able to read or understood it; most of the Old Javanese texts that survive today were preserved on Bali and Lombok, not on Java itself. But Javanese culture still gave strong expression to a stance in which a zealous Islamic monoculture based on rigid adherence to metropolitan Islamic standards would have been felt as profoundly alienating. In fact, in the nineteenth and twentieth centuries some Javanese felt sufficiently alienated by the demands of Islamic reformers to renounce Islam altogether. If, as reformist Muslims claimed, Javanese traditions were incompatible with Islam, then in this view it was Islam that had to go. The highlands of Tengger were a hotbed of such sentiment, but it affected the wider society, which in the nineteenth century began to split into a majority of "reds," who were nominal Muslims, and a minority of "whites," who were pious Muslims.

We should not think of the Javanese synthesis as inherently novel or unique. The Javanese themselves had done such things before. The Old Javanese text of the fourteenth century quoted above was devoted to reconciling two divergent Indian religions, and its punch line was "Buddhahood is one with Śivahood, they are distinct, yet they are one."[59] Now it was Islam and Javanese tradition that were to be distinct and yet one. Likewise we have already encountered the elective affinity of Hindu and Islamic mysticism in India and the generous mixtures of elements drawn from Islamic and non-Islamic religious traditions that are to be found at a

58. Translated in Ricklefs, *The seen and unseen worlds in Java*, 219–20.
59. Quoted in Ensink, "Śiva-Buddhism in Java and Bali", 182.

popular—and not only popular—level in the Muslim heartlands. Nor should we think of the Javanese synthesis as isolated within Southeast Asia. The fourteenth-century Trengganu Stone, from a part of Malaysia known today for its fundamentalist piety, is a good example. This somewhat fragmentary Malay inscription, the work of a Muslim ruler, refers to Muḥammad as *Rasūl Allāh*, which is good Arabic, but to God as *Dēvata Muliā Rāya*—"the Great Noble Godhead"—which is two-thirds Sanskrit and one-third Malay. Though the inscription is in the Arabic script, the term used for law is not *sharīʿa* but *dĕrma*, the Sanskrit *dharma*, which means "religious law" as much as "religion." As regards the substance of the law, we can turn to a longer and better-preserved text dating from about a century later, the "Laws of Malacca." This code begins by announcing in ungrammatical Arabic that it is an exposition of the ruler's law (*qānūn*) in the land of the great king—the sultan of Malacca—and his viziers. It then switches to Malay and in this language repeatedly juxtaposes the ruler's law (or the "custom of the country") with the law of God, without ever telling us which one we should go by. The punishment of the adulterer is a case in point: he is fined under the ruler's law but stoned under God's law. Seeking a peg on which to hang its ruler's law, the code ascribes it to Sultan Iskandar Dhū 'l-Qarnayn, alias Alexander the Great. This makes sense, since he was at once the ancestor of the dynasty and a monotheist worthy thanks to his inclusion in the Qur'ān. Even the female warriors of the court of Mataram had a parallel at the seventeenth-century Mughal court, and even the love life of the Goddess of the Southern Ocean has its parallels elsewhere in maritime Southeast Asia. Thus according to a foundation legend for the state of Johor on the Malay Peninsula recorded in the 1770s, Iskandar dived into the sea and there married the daughter of the king of the ocean. The difference is that outside Java such submarine romances were a feature of the legendary past, not part of the political present. But perhaps we do not need to be surprised that the wider literature of the Muslim Malays includes versions of ancient Indian epics, notably the *Rāmāyaṇa*. The Sasak Muslims of Lombok had something analogous to the culture of the Javanese interior, though on a smaller scale, while the Islam of the Chams, as we have seen, was if anything even more distant from the mainstream. At the same time, we should not think of the Javanese synthesis developed in Mataram as something to which all Javanese subscribed. As a pious Javanese tract shows us, there were Javanese Muslims for whom it was unbelief even to ask the question "Which is better, the religion of Islam or the religion of Java?"[60] For them, a Muslim who respected unbelievers and went along with their doings had himself become an unbeliever. So also had anyone who preferred to settle a dispute in an infidel court rather than according to the Sharīʿa. No doubt such uncompromising pietists

60. Quoted in Ricklefs, *Mystic synthesis in Java*, 25.

tended to be more common on the coast than in the interior. And yet even the author of our pious tract was comfortable referring to Muslim scholars as pundits; modern Javanese would use the term *ulama*, from the Arabic *'ulamā'*. The bottom line is that what made the Javanese synthesis distinctive was not its nature but rather how far it went, how long it lasted, and how firmly it set the tone among the elite.

The last of the rim and the edge of the Pacific

Once we leave maritime Southeast Asia and proceed farther round the rim, we no longer find much to attend to. The Muslim presence on the Indian Ocean barely touched Australia. The only qualification here is that in the eighteenth century there is attestation of annual expeditions from Macassar on the island of Sulawesi to Arnhem Land on the north coast of Australia. Their purpose was to collect sea slugs for the Chinese market—the slugs being used to make soup and as an aphrodisiac. These expeditions had contact with the nearby aboriginal population. Since, as we saw, Macassar had converted to Islam early in the seventeenth century, those who manned these expeditions must have been Muslims. But we have no record of this contact leading to any aboriginal conversions to Islam, and these Muslim mariners did not settle in Australia.

While we are in this faraway region, we can take the opportunity to consider the presence of Islam on the Pacific rim at the easternmost edge of the Muslim world. We would not expect to find much there, since, as already noted, the western shore of the Pacific is almost twice as far from the Muslim heartlands as the eastern shore of the Atlantic. There was nevertheless a small Muslim sector on the Pacific rim, largely made up of two islands. One was Halmahera in the Moluccas, to the northwest of New Guinea, and the other, yet farther to the north, was Mindanao, the southernmost of the larger islands of the Philippines. Islam came to Halmahera from the sultanates of Ternate and Tidore, two small neighboring islands located just to the west of Halmahera, leading to a west-facing Muslim presence on Halmahera itself. Yet we also find Muslims on the island's east coast, on smaller islands yet farther to the east, and very marginally on the western coast of New Guinea. Thus by the end of our period there had been at least a limited and superficial spread of Islam to Papuans in or close to this region. The character of this eighteenth-century Papuan Islam has aptly been compared with that of sixteenth-century Moluccan Islam. But this was not a dense presence, and Islam did not spread farther. Today there are about a quarter of a million Muslims on Halmahera, roughly half the population. The case of Mindanao involves a much larger Muslim population, some five million at the present day. Islam arrived there with the establishment of the Maguindanao Sultanate in the agriculturally richest part of Mindanao, perhaps a little before the Spanish invaded the Philippines.

Again, the Muslim population was concentrated on the western side of the island. Yet Muslims did make it to the Pacific, reaching and even ruling the southeastern coast, not to mention establishing a slave market on a small island immediately to the south of Mindanao. Moreover, the population was maritime and the sultans could mobilize hundreds of boats. The Spanish, however, made efforts to prevent the eastward spread of Islam on the island, and Davao, the major port on the Pacific coast, though at one time under Muslim rule, is today an overwhelmingly Catholic city and was so already in the late nineteenth century. All in all, to compare the Pacific rim with the Atlantic seaboard, we have here a considerably smaller Muslim population, though a much more maritime one. The result was no different: Muslim seafaring did not spread Islam significantly farther around the Pacific rim.

To this account of Muslim activity on the Pacific Ocean we should add a pendant. By far the largest and most powerful state on its rim was China. In general, this state was not much interested in projecting power across the sea, but between 1405 and 1435 an idiosyncratic Ming emperor and one of his successors mounted no fewer than seven massive and enormously expensive maritime expeditions. They set sail from the Pacific coast of China, but they did not explore the Pacific. Instead, their destinations were Southeast Asia and the Indian Ocean, where they visited the coasts of Kerala, Arabia, and East Africa, not to mention the island of Hormuz. Thereafter the expeditions stopped as suddenly as they had started. China was not, of course, a Muslim state, but by this time, as we have seen, there were significant numbers of Muslims in the country. One of them was the eunuch Cheng Ho. A member of the Ma clan in Yunnan, far from the nearest coast, he was seized as a boy and castrated for service at the Ming court. He did well there and was put in charge of the maritime expeditions. Nor was he the only Muslim involved: there were Muslims among his leading officers, one of whom visited Mecca, and some of his soldiers and mariners were Muslims.

The small islands of the Indian Ocean

In addition to the large islands of Madagascar, Ceylon, Sumatra, and Java, the Indian Ocean has a considerable complement of small islands located at a distance from its coasts. The more notable clusters are the Comoros between the northern tip of Madagascar and the east coast of Africa, the Laccadives to the west of the Malabar coast, and the Maldives to their south. To these we might add the Nicobar Islands to the northwest of Sumatra and the Andaman Islands to their north. But the nude inhabitants of the Nicobars and the cannibals of the Andamans, as they are described in our sources, did not convert to Islam. Likewise, it was Christianity rather than Islam that prevailed on the islands that had remained uninhabited until the arrival of the Europeans, such as the Chagos and the Seychelles. The one rather insignificant exception here is the Cocos Islands, some seven hundred miles southwest of Sumatra. They acquired their majority population of Malays, now a few hundred strong, only in the nineteenth century; in 1857 the British annexed the islands by mistake. Mauritius, which also falls in this category, currently has a significant Muslim minority who were brought to the island by the British in the same century, but tellingly they are Ḥanafīs and thus ultimately a product of the overland expansion of Islam, not of its maritime spread. Thus our concern here is only with the first three clusters named above: the Comoros, the Laccadives, and the Maldives.

As might be anticipated from their location, the population of the four islands that make up the Comoros represents a mixture of East African and Malagasy elements, together with an Arab leavening. We do not know to what extent the original African immigrants were Muslim when they arrived, or when they or the Malagasy immigrants converted, but they must have done so by the fifteenth century. The first mosques date from the mid-sixteenth century. As we would expect, the Comorians are Shāfiʿites. Their language—Comorian—has been categorized as a sister of Swahili, which would imply that the original African immigrants came from the same northern region.

The twenty-seven islands making up the Laccadives lie some two hundred miles off the Malabar coast and were settled from it by speakers of Malayāḷam in the centuries before the rise of Islam. They remained closely connected to the mainland. A South Indian kingdom invaded the Laccadives in the tenth century, and another had sovereignty over them at the time the Portuguese arrived. Around the thirteenth century the population of the islands converted to Shāfiʿite Islam, thus establishing a bond with the Moplahs of Kerala. Like them, they retained a caste system from their Hindu past, together with matrilineal kinship and matrilocal marriage; a husband had no authority over his wife. Only the few descendants of the Prophet adhered to a strictly patrilineal system in harmony with Islamic law. The women were not secluded and had mosques of their own.

The Maldives, made up of some twelve hundred islands, have a different background. The language of the inhabitants is most closely related to Sinhalese, suggesting that at some unknown date the islands were settled from Ceylon—despite the fact that even the closest of them is more than twice as far away from Ceylon than the Laccadives are from the Malabar coast. Originally, like the Sinhalese, the people of the Maldives were followers of Thēravāda Buddhism, and one thing they seem to have retained from their Buddhist past is a reluctance to take human or animal life. They must have had ample opportunity to interact with Muslim merchants. Masʿūdī mentions traders and mariners from Oman, Sīrāf, and elsewhere frequenting the islands. So it is not surprising that at some point the population adopted Islam, and according to an early eighteenth-century Maldivian chronicle the conversion took place in 1153. This conversion had an unusual twist: the Islam the islanders initially embraced was not Shāfiʿite but Mālikī. This was naturally noted by Ibn Baṭṭūṭa, a Mālikī himself, when he visited the islands in the 1340s and served as a judge there. His explanation was that the man who persuaded the islanders to accept Islam was a North African, and therefore a Mālikī. An alternative hypothesis would be that Mālikism reached the Maldives through the Mālikīs of the Persian Gulf. But today the people of the Maldives are Shāfiʿites. The change seems to have been a result of the coming of the Portuguese, who occupied the islands in 1558 and provoked fierce resistance, in the face of which they withdrew in 1573. In the interval Portuguese repression had apparently taken a heavy toll on the religious scholars of the islands, and after the Portuguese left no Mālikī scholar could be found to take on the position of judge. Just then a Maldivian returned from South Arabia, where he had spent fifteen years studying with Shāfiʿite scholars, and he proceeded to fill the vacuum, thus bringing the Maldives into line with the Indian Ocean rim at large. But as so often happens, there were aspects of the indigenous way of life that could strike observers with more metropolitan standards as inappropriate. Unlike the people of the Laccadives, the Maldivians did at least have a patrilineal kinship system, and according to Ibn Baṭṭūṭa they were pious and upright. But there was something that bothered him about their women: they went around topless. He made every effort to instill a sense of Islamic decency in them, but with no more success than poor Ibn Faḍlān had enjoyed in his campaign against nude mixed bathing in the Volga. The islanders also had queens, despite the admonition of the Prophet against the rule of women. Ibn Baṭṭūṭa noted that the reigning monarch at the time of his visit was a queen, and Masʿūdī, writing before the conversion, states that according to the ancient custom of the Maldivians only queens could rule.

In the grand scheme of things the Comoros, Laccadives, and Maldives do not matter very much. The contemporary populations of the three archipelagoes add up to about a million and a half, less than a tenth of a percent of the current population of India. But their conversion raises interesting questions. Why did the Comoros, the Laccadives, and the Maldives convert to Islam, while Madagascar and Ceylon did not? The simplest answer to this question is probably the best: it is a lot easier to convert a small island than a large one. We can compare this to the way in which small islands may see their populations wiped out and replaced from time to time, as large islands do not. But then how do we explain the fact that the Nicobar and Andaman islanders did not convert? Were the Nicobarese and Andamanese just too averse to contact to engage in such interaction with outsiders?

We have seen in this chapter that interposing an ocean between Muslim and non-Muslim territories can filter Islam through the negotiations of merchants rather than the depredations of warriors. Over the course of Islamic history as a whole, the warriors were on balance more successful in spreading Islam than the merchants were. They opened up much more territory for Islam, they got more attention for it, and on average the style of Islam adopted by the people they conquered was closer to that practiced in the heartlands. Such were the strengths of a forcefully top-down approach. But there were places that warriors could not reach and merchants could, and given the general absence of a systematic Muslim missionary enterprise, Islam would reach such places through the activities of merchants or not at all. In one sense merchants did indeed disseminate the religion widely: the Indian Ocean rim extends for many thousands of miles. But some of it was not covered at all, and over most of it the spread of Islam was an intermittent coastal phenomenon that did not extend into the interior. Somalia and the western part of maritime Southeast Asia were the exception—though by no means a trivial one, inasmuch as Indonesia today has the largest Muslim population of any country in the world. At the same time the process of cross-cultural negotiation between relative equals that must have accompanied the mercantile spread of Islam could produce results that were both colorful and significant, however much they might appear to a pietist from the heartlands as deviations from the true religion. Thus we have encountered instances of matrilineal societies, matrilocal marriage customs, topless women, queens, and female soldiers—phenomena that tended to be rare or nonexistent in the Middle East. Remoteness from the heartlands only partly explains this phenomenon. In the Antemoro case the effect of being remote was enhanced by not being on the way to anywhere, and in the Javanese case the agricultural wealth of the hinterland was crucial. In each case the effect was to place such exotic developments beyond the effective reach of metropolitan Islam. Today such deviant forms of the religion are under siege, but that does not make them any less interesting or historically significant.

It is worth noting that one widespread pattern found in the spread of religions is conspicuously absent in the case of Islam around the Indian Ocean. In a society that possesses a state but no writing system, a literate religion can be distinctly attractive to a ruler and his elite because the new information technology can be used to make them more powerful. This seems an obvious way in which a coastal religion brought by merchants could gain acceptance in the interior. And yet we have encountered no instance of this. In the western sector the main reason was the general absence of indigenous states. Even the successful penetration of the interior in the Somali case seems to have taken place without one. In the Indian and eastern sectors there was no lack of states, but they were already in possession of writing systems at the time Islam arrived, and the conversion of the Malay Peninsula and the islands of Sumatra and Java took place despite this fact. Thus the only part of the Indian Ocean world where such a conversion could have happened was the far southwest, where states without writing appeared first in the hinterland of Sofala and then in the interior of Madagascar. At least in the case of

Madagascar we know that rulers valued the literacy Islam could provide, but in the event no large-scale conversion ensued there.

Another thing we do not see in East Africa, coastal India, or maritime Southeast Asia is the emergence of Islamic scholars or movements authoritative enough to carry weight in the heartlands. To put it bluntly, these regions remained provincial. This was by no means the fate of all geographically peripheral territories of the Muslim world. As we have seen, there were scholars in eleventh-century Muslim Spain whose books became standard works in the heartlands. It took longer for Morocco to escape from provinciality, but manuscripts of a fifteenth-century Ṣūfī work by an author from the Sūs in the far west were plentiful in the Middle East, where the work was also printed several times in nineteenth-century Cairo and Istanbul. Indeed, manuscripts of the work can readily be found on Java, and one such manuscript has an interlinear Malay translation. By contrast, manuscripts of works by Southeast Asian scholars are not to be found in Morocco. In a world like that of Islam with a strong sense of metropolitan prestige, provinciality can be hard to escape.

What the world of the Indian Ocean did give rise to was perhaps the most cosmopolitan scene to be found anywhere on the planet in our period. In this chapter we have seen endless comings and goings between geographically and culturally distant lands. We can perhaps sum them up in the figure of a remarkable eighteenth-century tourist. This Sayyid Muḥammad was, or claimed to be, a descendant of the Prophet and a prince of the royal family of the island of Anjouan in the Comoros. We should not think of eighteenth-century Anjouan as the back of beyond. The aristocrats of the island took an interest in news of the kings of Britain and France, sported aristocratic titles in the English manner, and liked to wear British naval uniforms; ordinary people joked that relations between Anjouan and the island of Mayotte, its supposed dependency, resembled those between Britain and its North American colonies. These islanders also had fun expressing themselves in English doggerel verse: "Englishman very good man, drinkee' de punch, / Fire de gun, beatee' de French, very good fun."[61] Not that this prevented them being just as warm to the French. Coming from a background like this, Sayyid Muḥammad was well prepared for his travels on the eighteenth-century Indian Ocean. In 1729 he was welcomed at the Dutch factory in Mocha on the coast of the Yemen. He told his hosts that he had toured India and Persia for nine years and that his motive was not commercial or religious, but rather "curiosity to see at least part of the world."[62] He spoke an array of Indian Ocean languages: English, Arabic, Swahili, French, and Portuguese. His next destination was the land of his ancestor,

61. Quoted in J. Martin, *Comores*, Paris 1983, 1:37.
62. Quoted in Barendse, *Arabian seas 1700–1763*, 1:501.

the Ḥijāz. Perhaps this princely tourist had finally woken up to his Islamic duty of pilgrimage, or perhaps, as ever, he was just curious.

In short, the story of the spread of a maritime and mercantile Islam around the Indian Ocean was not just unprecedented; it was unique. There was no such Muslim expansion around the Atlantic or the Pacific, and the spread of Islam around the eastern and southern coastlands of the Mediterranean was a victory of military, not mercantile, Islam. Its spread around the rim was also unique in the sense that, despite political fragmentation, it gave to the Indian Ocean of medieval and early modern times a degree of cultural unity it had never had before. In the centuries prior to the rise of Islam we could perhaps think in terms of the coexistence around the Indian Ocean of two overlapping cultural zones, one to the west, where Christianity was prominent, and the other to the east, where the most widespread religion was Buddhism. But this was still a culturally divided Indian Ocean. Islam brought to it a degree of unity that it did not have before and that it has since lost.

Meanwhile, an intriguing question arises from our survey of Indian Ocean Islam. If we were to substitute desert for ocean as a barrier, would it have the same effect?

13
Africa

In the last decade of the sixteenth century a small army just made it across the Sahara. But in general the Sahara desert, like the Indian Ocean, was a formidable barrier to armies. It did have the potential to be inviting to merchants seeking profits from trade with the lands to the south, but it was not until Islam reached the Mediterranean coastlands of Africa that this potential began to be realized on a significant scale. Now, for the first time in history, we begin to get a sense of what was happening in the societies of the savanna, on the far side of the desert. What was it about Islam and its bearers that brought about this change?

Before we get to the savanna we have the nomads of the Sahara to consider. In essence the desert was occupied by three indigenous peoples, who were joined after the rise of Islam by the Arabs. The indigenous peoples were the Tuareg in the central Sahara, the Tubu to the east of them, and the Beja, whom we already know, on the eastern side of the Nile. No doubt their ancestors had been there since pre-Islamic times. The rest of the desert came to be populated by Arab nomads, such as the Moors of Mauretania, who largely absorbed or replaced the old Berber population of the western Sahara. The political organization of these desert peoples was weak, and serious Ibn Khaldūnian state formation appeared only once in their history. Ethnographically the non-Arab peoples were often colorful, not least with regard to relations between men and women; the Arabs, by contrast, were closer to Islamic norms.

To the south, in the savanna, we find a band of black peoples and their states stretching from the Atlantic to the borders of Ethiopia. Sooner or later all these peoples converted to Islam, and toward the end of our period violent conflict broke out between rigorists and those practicing more relaxed versions of the faith. Although we will briefly survey each of the savanna states, we will also take advantage of the fact that two of them are described in detail by medieval Arabic authors. One of these is eleventh-century Ghāna (in today's western Mali and southeastern Mauritania, some hundreds of miles from the country that calls itself Ghana today). The other is fourteenth-century Mālī (partly coinciding with the modern country of Mali).

That will leave us with some major gaps to fill. One is Ethiopia, where warfare between Muslims and Christians is historically a major theme; here a couple of chronicles will give us a vivid sense of how the two sides regarded it. Another is Nubia on the upper Nile, where Christian kingdoms went down to Muslim conquest thanks to the efforts of the Mamlūks and the Arab tribes. A third is the region to the south of the western savanna, where there was significant Muslim penetration of the tropical forest toward the end of our period.

We will end the chapter with a global view of two themes that have run through it. One is the spread of Islam in Africa, and the other is the role played in the region by differences of skin color.

The barrier blocking the spread of Islam into the African interior by conquest was the world's largest desert, the Sahara. Whether or not we call all of it the Sahara, this desert effectively extends all the way across Africa from the Atlantic to the Red Sea, and indeed the Arabian desert is in effect a further extension of the Sahara, separated from it only by the geologically recent rifting process that led to the opening up of this arm of the Indian Ocean. Moreover, the Saharan barrier is a wide one, over a thousand miles from north to south. It was, of course, possible to bypass the Sahara on the west by taking to the sea. But as we have noted, this did not happen until the voyages of the Christian Portuguese in the fifteenth century. The Judāla Berber tribesmen, in the hinterland of Awlīl in the far southwest of the desert, were camel nomads whose territory included a stretch of the Atlantic coast, and according to an eleventh-century geographer they benefited from it as a source of ambergris and salt, which they could trade, and of giant turtles, which they would eat. But they were not seafarers. Even fishermen made little or no use of boats. Farther north the lack of maritime activity is yet more striking. As we have seen, Islam never established itself on the Canary Islands. When in the fourteenth century European Christians sold natives of these islands as slaves on the Moroccan coast, it transpired that the islanders had not been reached by any missionary activity and knew no religion other than prostration to the rising sun. Ibn Khaldūn, our source for this information, tells us that the islands could only be reached by chance, there being no way to set a course to them. A case in point is an earlier account of a ship that was blown onto one of the islands by a storm; the islanders told the crew that they had never before known anyone reach them from the east. There is evidence for such occasional contacts in medieval times, but none for regular voyages to the islands, least of all the kind of exploration that was carried out under the Mauretanian king Juba II (ruled 25 BC to ca. AD 23). The absence of Arabic loanwords in what we know of the languages of the Canaries fits well here, not to mention the fact that technologically the islands were still in the stone age. There were reasons for this absence of developed maritime activity. The winds, currents, and reefs make it hard to round the coast of West Africa and return, and the barren shore of what is now Mauritania lacks drinkable water. Our concern in this chapter will accordingly be the African interior.[1] For the most part we will divide it into a series of bands stretching west to east. The first is the Sahara itself. We will then cross the southern "coast" (Arabic *sāḥil*) of the desert into our second band, the savanna. In northeast Africa, however, the existence of the Ethiopian highlands disturbs the regular pattern of climatic bands, so we will give separate consideration to Ethiopia and Nubia. Finally we will venture into a third band, the tropical rain forest to the south of the savanna. As we will see, the spread of Islam was extensive in the Sahara, the savanna, and Nubia and considerable in Ethiopia, but limited in the rain forest.

The Sahara desert

The Sahara as a barrier

Physically the Sahara and the Indian Ocean are quite different, but from a human point of view they have something fundamental in common: the extreme scarcity of freshwater.[2] This scarcity meant that people crossing the desert, like those crossing the ocean, had to take very deliberate steps to avoid dying of thirst. When Ibn Baṭṭūṭa was making his way southward on the two-month journey through the Sahara in 1352, the caravan he had joined stopped at a point where he and his fellow travelers filled their waterskins as usual before continuing their journey. But this time they would not be able carry enough water to get them to the next supply, which was at Walāta on the southern edge of the desert. The solution was for a messenger belonging to a local Berber tribe, the Masūfa, to go on ahead and alert the people of Walāta—likewise Masūfīs—that a caravan was on its way. When he arrived and announced the caravan, they would travel for four nights into the desert to meet it, bringing water with them. This was an ingenious arrangement. The Masūfa were a deep-desert tribe of veiled Berber warriors with an uncanny sense of direction; a Masūfī on his own would be able to find his way to Walāta much faster than a lumbering caravan could. The arrangement was also expensive. The messenger who went ahead of Ibn Baṭṭūṭa's caravan was paid about fifteen ounces of gold, worth some $25,000 at today's prices. But however ingenious and expensive, the arrangement fell short of being foolproof. Ibn Baṭṭūṭa tells us that sometimes the messenger would perish on the way; when that happened, no one would come out to meet the caravan, and most if not all of its members would die of thirst

1. For a succinct survey of much of the ground covered in this chapter see R. A. Austen, *Trans-Saharan Africa in world history*, New York 2010.

2. For the view that the Sahara has never been a barrier see G. Lydon, *On trans-Saharan trails*, Cambridge 2009.

amid the shifting sands. Yet if thirst was the most acute danger for desert travelers, hunger was not far behind. Here again the Sahara was in practical terms not so different from the Indian Ocean: in the Sahara agriculture was confined to occasional highlands and oases, just as on the Indian Ocean it was confined to scattered islands. Hunting could provide some relief in the Sahara, just fishing might on the Indian Ocean, but the thin vegetation cover of the desert was not enough to support an abundant fauna. In addition, there was no equivalent to the wind power that made traveling long distances on the Indian Ocean relatively effortless. All travel in the Sahara was ultimately on foot—whether the feet of the travelers themselves or those of the animals that pulled or carried them. Under these conditions, getting an army across the Sahara that could conquer territory on the far side was almost impossible. As we will see, one ruler of Morocco did succeed against all odds, but this was a unique case in the millennium and more of history covered in this book.

Merchants, too, risked death when crossing the desert, as was dramatized in 1960 when the remains of an ill-fated medieval caravan were discovered in the Sahara west of the Aïr massif. They could die of hunger or thirst, but they also faced a danger to which armies were somewhat less sensitive: the predatory habits of the Saharan tribesmen, who unless paid off were the desert counterparts of the pirates infesting the Indian Ocean. The Roman historian Tacitus describes one Saharan people of his day, the Garamantes, as "a wild race incessantly occupied in robbing their neighbors."[3] This characterization would apply well to the Saharan nomads of Islamic times. Muḥammad Bello (d. 1837), the son of the religious reformer ʿUthmān ibn Fūdī, alias Usuman dan Fodio (d. 1817), described the Tuareg as "a people who are by nature bloodthirsty, who loot and pillage goods and possessions and wage war."[4] And yet, whereas only one small army ever crossed the Sahara in our period to conquer territory on the other side, merchants regularly made the journey in pursuit of gain. Many, perhaps most, of Ibn Baṭṭūṭa's traveling companions must have been merchants. The prospect of gain arose above all from two commodities that the world to the north wanted from the far side of the desert: gold and slaves. In return, the settled peoples to the south of the Sahara prized the horses and manufactured goods of the north, especially textiles—Ibn Baṭṭūṭa describes the sultan of Mālī as being in the habit of dressing in a velvety red tunic made of a European fabric. The people of the savanna were also heavily dependent on Saharan salt, the residue of what in the geological past was a shallow ocean, and this salt could likewise be exported to the north. Thanks to this pattern of trade, we can make the assumption that it was Muslim merchants who brought Islam to the savanna. This does not, of course, mean that all Muslim

3. Quoted in Austen, *Trans-Saharan Africa*, 13.
4. Quoted in H. T. Norris, *The Tuaregs*, Warminster 1975, 102.

merchants were zealous propagators of their religion. There is a famous scene in which a Berber tribal chief from the Sahara explains the religious ignorance of his people to a distinguished jurist of eleventh-century Qayrawān; in one version he avers that "nobody reaches us but a few ignorant merchants whose business is buying and selling and who have no learning."[5] But even this limited contact with a few ignorant merchants had apparently been enough to instill in the chief and his people a desire to know Islam better.

In some respects this long-standing commercial pattern would be disrupted once the Europeans reached the shores of West Africa in the fifteenth century and trade routes opened up between the western savanna and the coast to the west and south. Three-quarters of the gold produced in West Africa would eventually find its way north by sea rather than across the desert. The slave trade was less of a zero-sum game, since the Atlantic trade dealt disproportionately in males for plantation slavery and the Saharan trade in females for domestic slavery; returning home at the end of his West African trip, Ibn Baṭṭūṭa joined a caravan that included around six hundred slave girls. But as we will see, Islam was by this time firmly rooted in the savanna.

Before we proceed to the savanna, however, we should look harder at the Sahara. It accounts for a significant fraction of the area of the Muslim world, if not for much of its population. We can best begin with some geographical fundamentals. Just as in the arid heartlands of Islam, the presence or absence of rivers was crucial for the Sahara. Rivers originate in rainfall, which in the Sahara is at once scant and irregular. Nor are the coastlands of northern Africa sufficiently well watered to feed large rivers flowing south, though there may be a slow trickle of North African groundwater in that direction. Thus any river big enough to make a difference to the Sahara would have to start from the south, and two of the world's major rivers in fact do that. One is the Niger, which rises in the hinterland of Guinea and flows northeast toward the Sahara for some seven hundred miles, almost reaching the desert near Timbuktu. But thereafter it gradually turns away to the southeast and then due south, so that it ends in a delta on the coast of Nigeria. The other river is of course the Nile. It has two main tributaries: the White Nile, which rises in Uganda, and the Blue Nile in Ethiopia. They come together at Khartoum, on the northern edge of the savanna, and from there the Nile flows more or less steadily northward through the desert, ending in a delta on the Mediterranean coast. Unlike the Niger, the Nile thus cuts through the desert, dividing it into two very unequal parts: a vast expanse to the west and a relatively narrow strip between the river and the Red Sea coast to the east.

5. N. Levtzion and J.F.P. Hopkins, *Corpus of early Arabic sources for West African history*, Cambridge 1981, 311. This book contains translations of all significant medieval Arabic sources for West African history.

This asymmetry makes the eastern Sahara a very different place from the central or western sectors of the desert. Over much—though not all—of its course the Nile engenders a long, thin strip of green. In combination with the delta this makes possible a dense and easily taxed peasant population providing a solid basis for state formation. Small wonder, then, that Egypt has five thousand years of statehood behind it. The asymmetry also means that as long as the resulting states function reasonably well, it should be possible for a traveler on the Nile to cover long distances by boat without undue fear of thirst, hunger, or rapine. There is, however, a downside to this bliss: since the Nile valley is rich, it is also worth conquering. Egypt experienced an isolated foreign conquest in the second millennium BC, and since the eighth century BC it has been conquered repeatedly by outsiders. The rulers of Egypt have likewise occasionally expanded southward into Nubia. But the presence along the Nile of a dense peasant population, as opposed to a scattered nomadic one, had a countervailing demographic implication: even if conquest led to large-scale linguistic, cultural, and religious changes, in genetic terms the core of the population was likely to remain largely unchanged. One particular aspect of this phenomenon concerns us here. Conquest by Egypt of the southern Nile valley meant the domination of the light-skinned people of the north over the dark-skinned people of the south. But the southerners retained their color. The Nubians today, together with most of the people of Sudan, are black, just like the Nubians of Pharaonic times. Such differences of skin color will crop up repeatedly while we are in Africa, and we will return to the phenomenon at the end of the chapter.

The other fundamental geographical fact about the Sahara is the uneven distribution of such water as there is. Here elevation is crucial in two antithetical ways. First, there are a number of highland areas in the Sahara with mountains reaching heights of up to ten thousand feet or so. A chain of such massifs, a product of volcanic uplift resulting from hot spot activity, extends diagonally from the southeast toward the northwest. The chain starts with Dār Fūr in the savanna and continues in the Sahara with the Tibesti, followed by the Ahaggar; an outlier is the Aïr to the south of the Ahaggar. Because these mountainous regions attract the lion's share of what rain does fall, some agriculture can be practiced in and around them, and consequently somewhat denser populations can survive there. Second, there are the oases. They are distributed across the Sahara with less appearance of rhyme or reason, but strings of them are typically found in long and narrow depressions where groundwater accumulates on or close to the surface. Here again we have conditions that allow some cultivation. The main crop is dates, thanks to the relatively high tolerance of date palms for salinity, and again they make it possible to have denser populations than are to be found in the desert at large. Both the highlands and the oases have the further effect of making the Sahara a bit less of a barrier, since they can serve as stepping-stones for travelers seeking to reach the far side of the desert.

The Sahara: History

The extent to which the Sahara is a barrier has changed over the last few thousand years owing to two main developments that have worked in opposite directions. The first, which for the most part took place long before our period, saw the Sahara become the desert it is today through increased aridity. There was a time some thousands of years ago when the water supply in and around the highland regions of the Sahara was quite generous, and many of its inhabitants could make a living by fishing. But these much wetter conditions ended around 3000 BC, and since late antiquity things have been more or less what they are today, though with historically significant variations. Thus conditions in the fourth to tenth centuries seem to have been somewhat wetter, whereas in recent centuries the desert has been eating its way into the savanna. This aridity has meant less scope for agriculture and hence a thinner population. It may also have led to a significant demographic change. The northern limit of the black population in the Nile valley is well to the north of the southern border of Egypt. If this is not just a local idiosyncrasy, it may well be that much of what is now the Sahara was once occupied by dark-skinned populations of which those found in the oases today are a residue. If so, it is noteworthy that their reaction to desiccation was to huddle in the oases, for the most part leaving the nomadic option to light-skinned intruders from the north.

The second and more recent development, which worked in the other direction, was the impact of Arabia on the Sahara. There were several aspects to this influence. One was the spread of the domesticated camel to Africa. Although there is isolated evidence of camels in Nubia around the ninth century BC, their presence in the Mediterranean coastlands of Africa dates from not much earlier than the first century BC, suggesting that Saharan nomads would have acquired them only a few centuries before the rise of Islam. In Islamic times camel nomadism was widespread in the Sahara. Whenever the change took place, it must have made a major difference to the nomads' command of the desert. Unlike equines and humans, camels can go as much as ten days without needing to drink, and they can carry heavier loads.

Another aspect of the Arabian impact was the coming of the Arabs themselves, first as conquerors and later as nomadic tribes. Like other imperial powers of premodern times, the Arab conquerors of the seventh century made no effort to incorporate the Sahara into their empire, despite launching raids deep into the desert. But their presence in Egypt and North Africa may well have reinforced the impact of the camel. They undoubtedly had much longer experience of using camels to survive in desert terrain, and it is plausible to see this advantage as contributing to the subsequent success of Arab tribes in gradually displacing or assimilating the populations of much of the Sahara. At the same time, the Arab conquerors of North Africa were less oriented toward the Mediterranean than their Roman predecessors had been; their capital city was Qayrawān, not Carthage.

A third aspect of the Arabian impact was the coming of Islam. The trans-Saharan slave trade was to a significant degree the consequence of an Islamic norm that in itself was distinctly benign. By way of background we should start by noting that despite the high demand for slaves in the societies of the ancient Mediterranean, we have no evidence of a large slave trade across the Sahara in antiquity. Nor is this surprising. For most of their history these societies could conveniently meet their needs for unfree labor through such processes as the enslavement of debtors and prisoners of war, the purchase children sold by impoverished parents, and the importation of slaves across more convenient frontiers. Under these conditions, organizing the transport of large numbers of slaves across the Sahara would have been an expensive and unrewarding logistical nightmare. A twelfth-century Ibāḍī author describes the miseries endured by an exhausted merchant taking his consignment of slaves through the desert: "This woman had grown thin, this one was hungry, this one was sick, this one had run away, this one was afflicted by the guinea-worm."[6] But things could be much worse for both the slaver and the slaves. An Ottoman document of 1849 mentions that a caravan crossing the Sahara from Bornū had come to grief that year for lack of water, resulting in the death of sixteen hundred black slaves. We can be sure that this was not the first time such a thing had happened, though the arrival of the camel and the desert skills of the Arabs may have reduced the difficulty and cost of the trade. At the same time, Islam is likely to have increased significantly the demand for imported slaves. The reason is that Islamic law forbids the enslavement of free Muslims, as also of poll tax–paying non-Muslims living under Muslim rule, and this prohibition, though often disregarded, seems to have been sufficiently widely observed to bring about a substantial increase in the demand for slaves from outside the Muslim world. Here a key change may have been the drying up of the supply of slaves from the Berber population of North Africa owing to the spread of Islam, a development that was already perceived as a problem at the beginning of the ʿAbbāsid period. A trans-Saharan slave trade now became feasible, and it was to prove remarkably long-lasting.

There was another way in which Islam must have made a difference to commercial life. It is perfectly possible for merchants and rulers of differing religious loyalties to coexist and cooperate. This point is eloquently articulated in a twelfth-century story about a governor of Sijilmāsa, the city in southern Morocco that served as the northern terminus of the trans-Saharan trade with Ghāna: "We are neighbors in benevolence even if we differ in religion," he wrote to the king of Ghāna; "we agree on right conduct and are one in leniency towards our subjects." The governor added a very pragmatic reason for this high-minded disregard of

6. Levtzion and Hopkins, *Corpus of early Arabic sources*, 90.

religious particularism: "The coming to and fro of merchants to a country is of benefit to its inhabitants and a help in keeping it prosperous."[7] The chronology of this story is problematic because by this time the ruler of Ghāna had converted to Islam, but the point is clear enough. Yet it goes without saying that a shared religion makes long-distance mercantile activity, and the trust that it requires, considerably easier to sustain. Islam helps merchants network.

All this gave rise to a vigorous trans-Saharan commercial scene in Islamic times. A plausible suggestion on the basis of our historical sources would be that it dates from the eighth century, though there is sporadic archaeological evidence of some trans-Saharan trade in late antiquity. The development of this trade in Islamic times explains the fact that Islam and its culture spread to the savanna, as Christianity—and ancient Mediterranean culture in general—had never done. Roman goods had reached the Garamantes of the central Sahara but are barely to be found farther south. The rise of trans-Saharan trade in the early centuries of Islam also explains the remarkable change in the quality of our knowledge of the savanna between late antiquity and the Islamic period. Our abundant Greek and Latin sources tell us almost nothing of this region, whereas medieval Arabic literature offers numerous descriptions of trans-Saharan societies from the ninth century onward. It is as if the Sahara, so opaque in antiquity, had now become transparent.

The Sahara: Peoples

Despite the relative richness of the Arabic sources, it is easier to provide an overview of the major peoples of the Sahara at the end of our period than when it begins, and even then it is hard to do so without incorporating ethnographic information from more recent times, as I will do where there is no obvious reason to suspect recent change. The tense I employ will usually indicate what kind of source I am relying on—past for historical sources relating to our period, present for ethnographic accounts of the nineteenth and twentieth centuries—but my use of the ethnographic present does not imply that these accounts describe the situation as it is today. Our concern here is more with the nomads than with the sedentary populations of the oases.

In the western Sahara at the end of our period it was the Arabs who dominated. These Arabs, also known conveniently as the Moors and more narrowly as the Awlād Ḥassān, had begun to displace, subjugate, or assimilate the Berber population of the region in the fourteenth century. By the mid-seventeenth century they had reached the valley of the Senegal River. The Zenāga Berbers succeeded in

7. Levtzion and Hopkins, *Corpus of early Arabic sources*, 372.

holding on to a corner of their old territory in the southwest, where they retained their language, but their attempt at military resistance against the Moors in the 1670s was a failure. These Moors are camel nomads. A well-to-do family among them may have something like twenty-five camels, together with sheep and goats. Theirs is, however, a steeply stratified society. At the top are the aristocratic warrior lineages, the Arabs proper. Next come the Zawāyā, lineages supplying the society with its religious scholars and specialists. Some are independent of the warriors, while others rely on their protection. Their genealogies point to a Berber background. One of the largest of these tribes today, the Kunta, claims descent from an Arab, a Qurashī who played a central role in the conquest of North Africa, but the earliest genealogical evidence makes it clear that they were Berbers. Below the Zawāyā tribes are lineages that pay tribute to the aristocrats, and they, too, have a Berber background. Finally there is the dark-skinned servile population, whose members work as cultivators and herdsmen. This pattern of stratification—sometimes termed a caste system, since it links occupation to inherited status—is more Saharan than Arabian and thus looks like something the incoming Arabs acquired from their new environment. It is not their only borrowing. Their dialect contains loanwords from Zenāga Berber, and an unusual concern with educating girls seems to have had a precedent among the Berbers of the region. Indeed, one woman in this milieu, Khadīja al-Daymāniyya (d. 1834–35), went on to write on logic. In the Berber context, as we will see, this concern was matched by the unusual freedom with which women interacted with men, but the Moors did not borrow either this degree of freedom or the matrilineal kinship system of the Saharan Berbers that accompanied it. And yet one nineteenth-century Mauritanian jurist made the argument that the full application of the rules regarding the segregation of the sexes was virtually impossible for nomads. In political terms, despite the relative homogeneity of their social structure, the Moors had no overarching organization. This is not surprising given the extreme aridity of their territory—they possessed no highland regions elevated enough to match those of the central Sahara. Instead they had a plurality of emirs, whose authority must have varied considerably in extent. Here regular commercial relations with European traders were clearly a significant asset, as in the case of the coastal emirate of Trārza, despite its fractious politics.

Meanwhile in the central Sahara, it was the Tuareg, a Berber people, who were the major nomadic group. This, too, is a society in which camel nomadism is very salient. Indeed, it is a key part of Tuareg culture—for example, skillful camel riding at social gatherings is one way for young men to impress young women. The territory of the Tuareg extends to the edge of the savanna in the south but leaves a wide band of Arab nomads to the north. The Tuareg are veiled Berbers, like the Masūfa of earlier times, and their society is stratified in the Saharan manner. Thus the aristocratic Tuareg do not allow their dark-skinned vassals to breed camels, and they refer to them pejoratively as "sheep people." The gap is wide enough to invite the speculation that the system was originally the product of one society subjugating another, just as in the case of the Moors. Among the Tuareg, too, there are lineages of religious scholars and specialists, known here as the Ineslemen, in other words Muslims, suggesting a time when as yet nobody else was Muslim. They do not participate in warfare and rely on the warrior tribes for protection. In contrast to the Moors to their west, the Tuareg are in possession of the largest highland region of the Sahara, the Ahaggar. It is in keeping with this environment that the Ahaggar Tuareg used to recognize a single overall political authority, known by a Berber title, the Amenūkal (whereas a local Tuareg ruler in the Aïr styled himself sultan from the early fifteenth century). The powers of the Amenūkal did not amount to much in peacetime, but he was a leader in war. The position was passed down matrilineally, though the appointment was subject to the approval of an assembly of tribal notables. Such a pattern of matrilineal succession to office was old. For example, Ibn Baṭṭūṭa reports a suggestive case from an oasis in the region of the Aïr. The practice reflects the fact that Tuareg society in general is to a large extent matrilineal, unlike that of the patrilineal Moors, and thus the head of a Tuareg family is not the father of the children but rather the mother's brother. Traces of matrilineal descent likewise appear in medieval inscriptions found in the region. We have already encountered matrilineal societies in India and Southeast Asia, and one thing about them is that they can be beneficial for women (not to mention itinerant merchants). Here Tuareg society is no exception. That this feature, too, is old is suggested by a set of inscriptions of the early twelfth century found a few miles east of Gao and marking the tombs of queens. We will return to the role of Tuareg women when we come to the character of Islam among the Tuareg.

To the east of the Tuareg were the Tubu (alias Tēda), though for the most part they did not range as far north. Their territory includes the highlands of the Tibesti, where the loftiest peak of the entire Sahara is found. They are neither Arabs nor Berbers, though they match them in their nomadic lifestyle and propensity for raiding their neighbors. Their language is related to Kanuri, a major tongue of the savanna in the neighborhood of Lake Chad, and they are very dark-skinned. Perhaps related to this is the fact that the Tubu were already playing a role in the history of the savanna state of Kānem from at least the eleventh century. But we know little of the Tubu of the Tibesti until the seventeenth and eighteenth centuries, when we find them raiding the Fazzān in the north and Bornū—southwest of Lake Chad—in the south. These Tubu resembled the Tuareg of the Ahaggar in having a supreme authority with a native title, the Derde, though again his control over his tribesmen was limited—even more so in the case of the Tubu thanks to the surly insubordination with which they regularly confront pretensions to authority. In principle the Tubu are inegalitarian in the manner of the Moors and the Tuareg, divided into nobles and common people, but in practice this hierarchy seems less rigid among them, perhaps reflecting their greater poverty, and we hear nothing of a caste of religious specialists. Tubu society is patrilineal and patriarchal, with men responsible for public affairs and almost anything to do with camels. But as we will see, this does not seem to have made Tubu women submissive.

Beyond the Tubu lies the eastern Sahara, where Arab tribes again prevail. They most likely arrived from the Nile valley. In Cyrenaica, to the west of Egypt, they were already present in the ninth century, and in the early eleventh they participated in a rebellion against the Fāṭimids, though Berber tribes were also involved. In essence they have the same tripartite hierarchy that we saw among the Moors and the Tuareg. Farther south, we know that Arab tribes reached the eastern savanna between the White Nile and Lake Chad at about the time when the Moors were taking over the western Sahara, and in due course some of the tribes spread far enough south to become the cattle nomads known as the Baqqāra (*baqqār* being the Arabic for "cowboy"). In 1391–92 a letter from the ruler of Bornū arrived in Cairo with a complaint about the depredations of the neighboring Arabs, primarily those of the tribe of Judhām, who were enslaving the ruler's subjects to export them to Egypt and beyond; very likely these were camel nomads expanding westward through the eastern savanna. Sooner or later Arab tribes presumably moved into the part of the eastern Sahara that lies south of Cyrenaica and north of Kordofān—insofar, that is, as this region had any human population at all. But Ibn Khaldūn in the later fourteenth century still speaks of a Berber band that is continuous from the Atlantic coast to the banks of the Nile, whereas today the only survival of Berber in the eastern Sahara is in the oasis of Sīwa.

On the far side of the Nile, as we already know, were the Beja, with more Arab nomads to their north. This is likely to represent a continuation of a pre-Islamic pattern. In antiquity there were enough Arabs in the northeastern desert of Egypt for the region to be known as "Arabia," and indeed there is some attestation of an Arab presence in the core territory of Egypt itself in pre-Islamic times. Meanwhile the Blemmyes to the south of this "Arabia" are likely to have been the ancestors of the Beja. There is, however, a noteworthy contrast in orientation between these Arabs and the Beja. The Arabs of the northeast have more in common with those of Sinai and Arabia than with those to the west of the Nile, and some of them are historically recent arrivals from farther east. In particular, they lack the typically Saharan hierarchy. By contrast, the Beja belong to the same world as the Berber tribes of the Sahara. We find noble and vassal lineages among them, their kinship system is already described in medieval sources as matrilineal, and—to anticipate—adultery is a far less serious matter for them than it is for the Arab tribes. Why Arabian and Saharan nomads, who live in such similar environments, should have such contrasting social structures is, incidentally, a puzzle for the curious. Another intriguing finding, this time about Saharan prehistory, is that the Beja and the Tuareg are genetically close to each other—in fact closer than the Tuareg are to other Berber-speaking populations.

The overall picture we thus form of the peoples of the Sahara is in a way a rather simple one. From west to east, leaving aside the continuous band of Arab tribes in the north, we have the Arabs, the Tuareg, the Tubu, the Arabs again, and finally the Beja on the far side of the Nile. Each group occupies a territory comparable in size to that of the Arab nomads of Arabia. This is not surprising. The openness of the Saharan landscape and the mobility of camel nomads are conducive to the formation of large-scale ethnic homogeneities. In this respect life will prove more complicated once we leave the Sahara for the savanna. Of a piece with this relative simplicity is the fact that all Saharan languages are related to those of larger populations outside the Sahara. Arabic is of course the language of the entire Arab world, Berber is best represented in North Africa and was dominant there in the first centuries of Islam, Tubu's closest relative is Kanuri in the eastern savanna, and Beja is likewise classified with languages spoken to its south, including Somali. The Sahara, in short, is nothing like the Caucasus with its four dozen languages, many of them unrelated to anything spoken elsewhere.

The Sahara: States

The strongest of the states that influenced the history of the Sahara were mostly located outside it. There was certainly some penetration by such outside powers, but it was limited. It was neither feasible nor rewarding in premodern times for a sedentary state to conquer and administer a desert. Even on the edge of the Sahara the terrain hollowed out the power of states. Consider, for example, an early sixteenth-century account that describes how a conflict played out between the ruler of Timbuktu and the chief who controlled Walāta over 250 miles to the west, in a region where windblown sand was a climatic hazard. When the king arrived with his army, the chief fled into the desert where his kinsmen lived, and the king came to see that he could not hold the territory as he wished because of the trouble the chief and his kinsmen could make for him, so he settled for a fixed tribute. Once the deal was done, the chief returned to Walāta and the king returned to Timbuktu. Deeper in the desert there was to be no large-scale subjugation of Saharan territory until the coming of the French in the nineteenth century. This did not, however, preclude the launching of more modest expeditions for one reason or another and the exercise of looser hegemonies. The Romans twice dispatched troops into the Saharan interior to attack the Garamantes of the Fazzān and later ventured farther south in their company—just as they once sent an expedition through the Arabian desert to the Yemen. In the Islamic period there was a stronger motive for such activity: the importance of the trans-Saharan trade. As early as the middle of the eighth century the Umayyad governor of North Africa was investing in trans-Saharan infrastructure by digging wells along the way. On the other side of the Sahara the kingdom of Mālī, at the height of its power in the fourteenth century, flexed its muscles in the desert to the north. Ibn Khaldūn tells us that it imposed tribute on the veiled nomads and recruited them into its armies. In the sixteenth century, possession of Taghāzā, a major salt pan in the western Sahara, was disputed between the rulers of Morocco and the savanna kingdom of Songhay, and in 1544 the conflict led the ruler of Songhay to send a force of two thousand Tuareg to raid the Darʿa region in the far south of Morocco. Farther to the east, from the eleventh to the end of the thirteenth century, Kānem-Bornū exercised a hegemony that extended even to the north of the Fazzān. Here it had a decided geopolitical advantage over Mālī. Across the Sahara from Mālī lay a region liable to be controlled by strong states based in either Morocco or Tunisia, whereas Kānem-Bornū faced the one extended stretch of the Mediterranean coast where the desert reaches to the sea, or comes close to it. It was consequently easier for Kānem-Bornū to project its power and influence northward than it was for Mālī to do so. Thus Kanuri is the lingua franca all over the Tubu region, and it has, or had, some presence as far north as the Fazzān. But for the most part the states outside the Sahara prudently left the desert alone or contented themselves with occasional raids, as even the Arab conquerors of the seventh and early eighth centuries had done.

This left plenty of room for such state formation as was possible in the Sahara, but in general this was limited in scope. A tenth-century geographer states that the Berbers of the desert have kings, as well as chiefs and headmen. "These kings," he goes on to say, "give commands and are not disobeyed."[8] The Garamantes already had their king in antiquity, and in due course the Tuareg and Tubu had their supreme leaders, while the Moors had their emirs. Such states, if we can call them that, were inevitably lightweight, but they did make a difference.

What then of explosive state formation, the kind that leads to the conquest of lands beyond the desert, as in the case of the rise of Islam? To the north, Egypt and North Africa look like inviting targets for an expansion out of the Sahara, and our historical sources are good enough that we would not miss a major event of this kind. Yet in the entire history of our period we know of only one instance of such a conquest. This was a classic episode of Ibn Khaldūnian state formation brought about by the activities of a religious leader, Ibn Yāsīn (d. 1059), who went to work among the Berber nomads of the western Sahara. The movement he founded went on to conquer much of North Africa and Muslim Spain, issuing in the Almoravid dynasty (1062–1147). The main Berber tribe behind it was the

8. Levtzion and Hopkins, *Corpus of early Arabic sources*, 48.

Lamtūna, but the Judāla and Masūfa were also involved. We will come back to the history of the Almoravids in the next chapter. Whether they also conquered territory in the savanna to the south is harder to say because our sources here are far less comprehensive. There are, for example, somewhat threadbare reports of an Almoravid conquest of Ghāna. Moreover, we should probably take seriously the occasional indications that some of the dynasties we know of in the savanna were established by Saharan nomads, in line with the role of nomads in state formation in the Middle East. Back in the tenth century we hear of a powerful Berber ruler of Awdaghust in the southwestern Sahara who collected tribute from more than twenty kings in the land of the blacks. Likewise at the very end of our period we encounter a major example of a religious movement that conquered territory in the savanna; led by ʿUthmān ibn Fūdī, its ethnic core consisted of Fulānī cattle nomads. But these were pastoralists of the savanna, not of the Sahara. There was indeed some Tuareg participation in the movement, but the Tuareg themselves never launched a massive conquest of this kind. In short, the nomads of the Sahara do not seem to have made a habit of conquering territories outside their desert, and their military energy never achieved anything on the scale of the Arab conquests.

The Sahara: Islam

By 1800 the tribes of the Sahara must have been largely Muslim—though the Kawār region was still partly pagan in the early nineteenth century, and the Bideyat of the Ennedi, a minor highland region of the southeastern Sahara, converted only in the twentieth. But a general acceptance of Islam did not mean that the Saharan nomads ranked as good Muslims by the standards of the Islamic scholars of the heartlands of the Muslim world. Here we can use modern ethnographic testimony in good conscience, since it is historically unlikely that the nomads were more observant Muslims in our period than in the more recent past.

To take the case of the Tuareg, they are described as lukewarm in their religious devotions and generally failing to observe the fast of Ramaḍān. They also have practices that are notably un-Islamic. They are, as we have seen, to a large extent matrilineal: a man belongs to his mother's tribe, not his father's, and he inherits from his mother's brother, not from his father as Islamic law would require. The incompatibility of such inheritance with the Sharīʿa had long been plain. When the ruler of Songhay consulted a Moroccan jurist about this ancient practice of the Sahara and savanna toward 1500, the response was that anyone who regarded it as lawful was an unbeliever. Nor do a couple of Tuareg peculiarities concerning dress sit well with Islam. A boy ceremonially takes the veil at the age of eighteen, thereby becoming a man, while among the southern Tuareg women often go topless. Still worse, young men and women, as yet unmarried, interact freely and throw parties where they get together. Indeed, free interaction between men and women is attested among the Tuareg already in the early sixteenth century, and it makes for a society that is distinctly lacking in puritanical attitudes to sex. For example, no particular significance is ascribed to a bride's virginity. Sometimes it can be hard not to be reminded of the extravagant sexual customs described by Herodotus in the fifth century BC in his account of the "Libyan" tribes of his day ("Libya" for the Greeks being a term for most of northern Africa). The contravention of the Sharīʿa is hard to miss, and a Tuareg scholar who led a jihad in the early nineteenth century is reputed to have attempted to impose strict seclusion on Tuareg women, but his jihad was a failure.

Another intriguing feature of the culture is the use the Tuareg make of a non-Arabic script. Known as Tifinagh, it must derive from some ancient Libyan script, and its name suggests, perhaps correctly, that the Libyan script in turn had its origin in the Phoenician script brought to North Africa by the Carthaginians. Knowledge of Tifinagh is passed on by the women; it is used, among other things, in brief exchanges of love letters. It has been said that every second Tuareg seems to know the script, especially the women, or even that it is hard to find an adult Tuareg who does not know it. As with the Indian scripts of Mindoro mentioned in the previous chapter, and a similar one in southern Sumatra, one reason such scripts can survive without any institutional support could be their association with flirtation. It is perhaps this association that renders unnecessary the coercive primary school systems through which civilized societies inflict literacy on children who would much rather run away and play.

The Tubu, too, are reported to be bad Muslims, not having really broken with their pre-Islamic ancestor cult. Their observance of the fast of Ramaḍān is described as discontinuous and occasional, and into the nineteenth century it seems that they were burying their dead in a seated position—a practice attested by Herodotus for a Libyan people known as the Nasamonians. As usual, their deviation shows up in what by mainstream standards is the inappropriate conduct of their womenfolk. Tubu women are unusually aggressive. They observe female segregation only at mealtimes, speak up, engage in domestic violence against their husbands, and carry weapons for use against either men or women as the occasion demands. Should a husband be unwise enough to insult his wife in public, she humiliates him by stripping off her clothes, throwing them on the ground, and stalking off stark naked to her tent.

Because ignoring Islamic norms regarding the role of women makes a society so conspicuously un-Islamic, we do not have to depend entirely on the modern ethnographic record to document it. Ibn Baṭṭūṭa, as we know by now, was an assiduous commentator on such matters. Thanks to the fact that his caravan survived the journey to Walāta, we have his sketch of the manners and customs of the Masūfa Berbers who lived there. Their culture was clearly related to that of the Tuareg, if not ancestral to it. These Berbers, Ibn Baṭṭūṭa tells us, are Muslims who pray, study Islamic law, and memorize the Qur'ān. And yet they are matrilineal—a man's heirs are the sons of his sister, leading Ibn Baṭṭūṭa to make an apt comparison with Kerala (he was not aware of the Minangkabau). But there is more to it than just this deviant kinship system. The men, he observes, lack sexual jealousy, and the women lack modesty in the presence of men. Though they pray assiduously, they do not wear veils, and they get more respect than their menfolk. As if to dispel any suspicion that he is merely peddling stereotypes, Ibn Baṭṭūṭa goes on to give us a couple of concrete examples. He describes going to the house of the man who had been the leader of his caravan across the Sahara, only to find that his host was allowing his wife to have a friendly chat with another man. It is striking that despite his extensive travels Ibn Baṭṭūṭa seems never to have acquired an ounce of cultural relativism. He accordingly rebuked his host, who should have known better: "Do you acquiesce in this when you have lived in our country and become acquainted with the precepts of the Sharī'a?" His host was unrepentant: "The association of women with men is agreeable to us and a part of good conduct to which no suspicion attaches." And as if that was not bad enough, the man went on to take a swipe at Ibn Baṭṭūṭa's pride in coming from a land where Islam was properly observed, saying appreciatively of the local women: "They are not like the women of your country."[9] Shocked, Ibn Baṭṭūṭa made a point of not visiting the man again. His other example concerns what happened when he went to see the judge of Walāta, that is to say to a man who by profession was committed to the implementation of Islamic law. Ibn Baṭṭūṭa was invited to enter, but on doing so he realized with embarrassment that a young and attractive woman was present with the judge, so he naturally made to withdraw. The woman reacted by laughing at him without the slightest bashfulness, while the judge urged him to stay and introduced his girlfriend. That year, Ibn Baṭṭūṭa was told, the judge wanted to have his girlfriend—either this one or another one, it was not clear—accompany him on pilgrimage to Mecca, but the ruler would not allow it. Ibn Baṭṭūṭa does not tell us why the ruler put his foot down, but it is likely that his concern was not with the sanctity of Mecca but rather with the rights of the woman and her family. According to Ibn Baṭṭūṭa, the women of Walāta did not travel with their husbands, and even if they wished to do so, their families would not permit it. This suggests a matrilocal society in which a woman remains firmly anchored in her own family, just as we saw on the southern coasts of India and the Maldives. Indeed, there is a pattern here that, as was clear in the Indian context, could suit a foreign merchant very well: Ibn Baṭṭūṭa says of the women that anyone who wants to marry one may do so, though she will not travel with him. Three centuries earlier Ibn Yāsīn seems

9. Levtzion and Hopkins, *Corpus of early Arabic sources*, 286.

to have flourished in such a setting, enjoying the novelty of several new wives each month before divorcing them; despite this binging, he was no doubt punctilious in never having more than four at a time. Ibn Baṭṭūṭa also remarks that the foreign men of Walāta had local girlfriends, just as the local men did among the foreign women. The presence of these foreign women is the surprise here, but he does not tell us who they were.

Such flagrant deviance from Islamic norms with regard to the role of women is rare among the Arab tribes of the Sahara. The Rgaybāt, for example, are Moorish camel nomads of the northwestern Sahara whose women are kept out of public space and out of sight, largely confined to their tents. Something similar would be true of women among the Moorish tribes in general. Likewise among the Arab tribes of Cyrenaica, though the women could hardly be described as repressed, they are excluded from the company of men in public. For a young couple in love to meet each other in secret, even without the slightest sexual activity, is to court death.

Despite all this, the scholarly lineages of two major nomadic peoples of the Sahara maintained a surprisingly high level of Islamic religious learning. This is a phenomenon that to the best of our knowledge had no parallel in the pre-Islamic Sahara: no Saharan nomads cultivated the scholarly traditions of ancient Egypt, Carthage, Greece, or Rome. Even within the Muslim world, the Saharan nomads seem to be exceptional. Elsewhere we can certainly find examples of religious scholarship outside the cities, be it in mountains or oases, or among the Berbers of the Sūs. But we do not encounter it among nomads. Here the Tubu were no exception, but the Tuareg undoubtedly were, and at the end of our period some of their scholars played a significant part in the movement of ʿUthmān ibn Fūdī. Yet it is the tribes of the western Sahara that stand out most for the strength of their scholarly tradition. It cannot have been easy for them to achieve this, since nomadism and libraries do not go well together. Muḥammad al-Yadālī, a scholar of the first half of the eighteenth century who belonged to one of the Zawāyā tribes of the southwestern Sahara, is said to have lamented that if he had been a city dweller and not a Bedouin, he would have written as many books as Suyūṭī (d. 1505). Suyūṭī was indeed very much a city dweller. Born and domiciled in Cairo, he counted as the last great polymath of Mamlūk Egypt. He was much sought after in his lifetime by West African scholars and even by one of the rulers of Songhay, who was passing through Cairo on a pilgrimage to Mecca. We have a text in which he responds to queries—about matrilineal inheritance, the mixing of men and women, and other matters—that seem to have been sent to him by a scholar of the Aïr. He was thus a towering figure in Yadālī's world, an apt benchmark for comparison, and Yadālī's bibliographical information about him was correct: Suyūṭī is credited with a little short of a thousand works. Poor Yadālī's total was fewer than sixty. This nomadic scholarly tradition did, of course, have its origins in an urban setting—namely, the sixteenth-century cities of the Niger Bend, and in particular Timbuktu—but after the end of the sixteenth century it became self-sustaining. It could even be notably innovative in the way it went about securing the material interests of the scholars vis-à-vis the rest of society. Although these scholars tended to belong to lineages with a Berber background, they wrote exclusively in Arabic. In fact Moorish society was very prolific in Arabic poetry, including verses extemporized as occasions arose, and the poets of pre-Islamic Arabia were part of the educational curriculum. Altogether, this scholarly tradition is a remarkable refutation of the view of Muḥammad al-Jaylānī, a militant Tuareg scholar of the early nineteenth century, that "the desert is the ruin of religion";[10] by the same token it confutes the traditional Islamic disparagement of the religious observance of the Bedouin.

What is harder to say is just when in the course of our period the various peoples of the Sahara converted, let alone how it came about. The sources—as much through their silences as anything else—convey the impression that conversion, whatever its limits, came fairly easily to the Saharan nomads. And yet there is good reason to believe that they took their time. Here a significant point arises from the finding that the earliest merchants of the trans-Saharan trade seem to have been not Sunnīs but Khārijites. They belonged to two distinct Khārijite groups, the Ibāḍīs and the Ṣufrīs, each of which became active in North Africa in the mid-eighth century (we can ignore the Shīʿites of North Africa in this context, as they are not known to have played a part in trans-Saharan trade). And yet we have no indication that any Saharan population south of the Fazzān converted to either Khārijite persuasion. Thus if we take the Berber tribesmen who were to be recruited into the Almoravid movement, what we learn is not that they were heretics, but simply that they were not good Muslims—a man might marry ten wives, far above the legal maximum of four. As their tribal chief indicated to the distinguished scholar of Qayrawān, they were ignorant Muslims, knowing little or nothing of their religion because they lacked the opportunity to learn. There was also an element of recalcitrance, as when they told Ibn Yāsīn that they would accept what he said to them about prayer and alms but would have no truck with the Islamic punishments for murder, theft, and adultery—suggesting that they were happy to accept Islam as just a religion but did not appreciate its intrusive claim to be a more comprehensive way of life. We thus seem to be dealing with people who had previously been nominal Muslims, though a twelfth-century source states that the relevant tribes adopted Islam only in 1043, soon after Ibn Yāsīn arrived among them. In any case, there is nothing here to suggest early involvement with the Khārijites. But if we ask at what point between the eighth century and the

10. Quoted in Norris, *The Tuaregs*, 149.

eleventh these nomads had become nominal Muslims, we have only a stray statement of Ibn Khaldūn's placing their conversion in the ninth century.

Elsewhere in the Sahara the evidence is much thinner but could perhaps be used in support of two rather uninteresting generalizations. The first is trivial, namely that different populations converted at different times. The second, though not trivial, is obvious: other things being equal, people in the north tended to adopt Islam earlier than those in the south. Thus the people of the Fazzān, just a third of the way across the desert, were known as pagans in the eighth century, though even then Ibāḍī Islam had a presence among them. By the late ninth century Islam was well established in at least part of the Fazzān, and from the tenth century to the twelfth there was an Ibāḍī principality there. By contrast, some of the people of the Adar, to the south of the Aïr, were still pagans until forcibly converted by Muḥammad al-Jaylānī in a jihad of 1814. But these were laggards: the Aïr itself had a Muslim population by the mid-fourteenth century, and in the later fifteenth century a fatwa of Suyūṭī's describes Agades, its main settlement, as entirely Muslim. Two-thirds of the way across the Sahara, northeast of the Aïr but south of the Fazzān, lay the oases of the Kawār; this region is described as Muslim already in the later ninth century, but as we have seen the population was still partly pagan at the end of our period. North of the Kawār and south of the Fazzān, but much farther to the east, was the oasis of Kufra, already reckoned as Muslim in the eleventh century. Meanwhile, late ninth-century Awdaghust in the southwestern Sahara was still ruled by a king who had no religion or law, but in the next century its people are described as Muslims who, though previously sun worshippers, now had mosques and studied the law of Islam. Looking more broadly at the major non-Arab ethnic groups, the Tuareg in general seem to have adopted Islam around the fifteenth century. The Tubu are described by a thirteenth-century source as unbelievers, and those of the oasis of Kufra were still pagan in the eighteenth century. At some point the Tubu became at least nominal Muslims, but they were as yet no more than that in the nineteenth century. Yet the Saharan nomads, like the Somalis, perhaps felt a degree of elective affinity for Islam. In contrast to the sedentary Nubians of pre-Islamic times, few of them apart from the Garamantes seem previously to have shown much interest in Christianity. But here, as usual, we need to make some allowance for the extent of our ignorance of the earlier history of the Sahara. It is a tantalizing fact of etymology that the Tuareg word for sin (*abekkadh*) is a loanword from Latin (*peccatum*).

The savanna

We now cross the southern "coast" of the Sahara to enter the savanna, a belt of territory a few hundred miles wide extending all the way across Africa. At its eastern end, however, its geography is complicated by a couple of irregularities: first the White and Blue Niles, and then the Ethiopian highlands. We will accordingly reserve this eastern region, including the whole of Nubia, for a later section of this chapter. That leaves us with a band of territory whose components we can identify in a more or less linear fashion. Between the Atlantic coast and the western bank of the White Nile, we have Takrūr, Ghāna, Mālī, Songhay, Hausaland, Bornū, Kānem, Wadai, Dār Fūr, and Kordofān. These ten regions of the savanna had much in common. In particular, they were populated by black Africans, and they had enough rainfall for agriculture. There was, however, a catch. The rainy season in the savanna is in summer, not in winter as in the lands to the north of the Sahara, with the result that northern crops could not be introduced here. The consequent need to develop new crops by domesticating local plants was associated with a much later onset of cultivation in the savanna. But by Islamic times this was water under the bridge, and the savanna had already entered its iron age. Savanna societies were thus able to support states more substantial than those of the Sahara, and in at least some cases they are likely to have been doing that even before the coming of Islam, perhaps benefiting from somewhat wetter conditions in the fourth and succeeding centuries. Moreover, these states were on balance centered closer to the northern than to the southern edge of the savanna, so that they faced toward the Sahara and the Mediterranean, rather than toward the rain forest to the south. As this orientation would lead us to expect, once the Sahara had opened up, all of them at one point or another would adopt Islam. We will start with a quick survey of each of the ten with particular reference to two themes, state formation and conversion. After that we will look in more detail at two parts of the belt: Ghāna and its neighbors in the eleventh century, and Mālī in the fourteenth. These happen to be the places and times that we know most about in the medieval savanna, but they also matter historically.[11] We now begin our survey in the western savanna, starting with Takrūr.

The savanna belt: The western states

The term Takrūr is related to the name of a sedentary people who live on the Senegal River, the Tukulor; the nomadic Fulānī, of whom we will hear more when we reach Hausaland, were closely related to them. The Arabic sources use Takrūr in two very different senses: as the particular name of the westernmost part of the savanna and as a general term for West Africa. We can ignore the general usage, which is secondary. The main things we know about the early history of Takrūr are that there was a kingdom there in the first half of the eleventh century, that the king and his people had been idolaters, and that this had changed when a king

11. For these West African states see N. Levtzion, *Ancient Ghana and Mali*, London 1973; also M. A. Gomez, *African dominion*, Princeton 2017.

who died in 1040–41 converted to Islam and imposed the religion on his people. To our knowledge he was the first ruler in the savanna to do so. Thereafter Islam took root, and by the thirteenth century it had penetrated all the towns along the river, though there was still a pagan presence in the capital. Later, however, there seems to have been considerable backsliding in the region. For the Wolof of what is now northwestern Senegal, we have an early sixteenth-century European account of the Jolof kingdom. It describes the king and the aristocracy as Muslims who retained the services of literate white clerics, whereas the people at large figure in this account as only partly Muslim. At the same time, there was little continuity to the political history of Takrūr. The kingdom was doing well in the twelfth century but was later absorbed by the more powerful kingdom of Mālī, based farther to the east. The subsequent history of the region was turbulent, with political fragmentation being the norm. One destabilizing factor was the rise of the transatlantic slave trade and the proclivity of the states of the region for selling their own subjects into slavery in order to profit from it. The 1670s saw a rebellion against this practice led by a religious scholar; this was another face of a movement we have already encountered in the form of Berber resistance to the Moors. As a percipient French slave trader articulated the message of the rebels, "God in no way permits kings to pillage, kill, or enslave their people." On the contrary, they are there to protect their subjects from their enemies, "the people not being made for the kings, but the kings for the people."[12] The rebellion was suppressed, but a century later another reformist movement took shape in the region, by now known as Fūta Toro, and achieved a longer-lasting success. It began in the 1770s when religion, politics, and defense came together and issued in a dynasty that lasted into the late nineteenth century. The defense was again directed against the sale of subjects into transatlantic slavery and the raids of nomads from the north. But the Wolof kingdoms withstood these pietist challenges.

We now move east to Ghāna, a kingdom we are comparatively well informed about thanks to its role as a major terminus for trans-Saharan trade in the early centuries of Islam. We first hear of it in a bare list from the first half of the ninth century, but by the end of that century we know that Ghāna was ruled by a powerful king, that there were subordinate rulers under him, and that the country could supply gold. As with Takrūr, we have no real evidence as to when the kingdom had been founded. If we are willing to wait till the seventeenth century, a chronicler in Timbuktu provides a fanciful tradition according to which twenty-two kings ruled Ghāna before the Hijra of the Prophet, and another twenty-two after it. Back in the tenth century, however, our pool of credible information expands a bit. One thing we learn is that the wealthy—clearly the native elite—were accom-

12. Quoted in R. T. Ware, *The walking Qur'an*, Chapel Hill 2014, 104.

panied in death by their slave girls. This is representative of a historically widespread custom, most familiar in modern times from the Hindu practice of suttee, and it is a strong indication that the elite of Ghāna were as yet untouched by Islam. On the other hand, Muslims—presumably foreign merchants—were already a significant presence there. We are told that they had judicial autonomy just as Muslims in other pagan lands such as India, the steppes, and the Caucasus did. It is not, however, until well into the eleventh century that we have a source rich enough to give us a real picture of what Ghāna was like; it is this source that we will take up when we look more closely at the kingdom. Soon after, if we go by the testimony of Ibn Khaldūn, Ghāna was conquered by the Almoravids, and many of its people converted to Islam. A twelfth-century source dates the conversion to 1076–77, adding that this formerly pagan people now had eminent scholars, jurists, and Qur'ān reciters, and that their leaders performed the pilgrimage to Mecca and spent large sums on waging jihad against the pagans. This indicates that any semblance of Almoravid hegemony must have evaporated by the time of this source. Another twelfth-century source raises the question whether the dynasty of the day might have had a northern origin: the king of Ghāna, it reports, is said to descend from ʿAlī, the cousin of the Prophet. But in this form at least, the claim is easily dismissed as genealogical climbing. From the thirteenth century onward we no longer have attestations of Ghāna as an independent kingdom. One fourteenth-century source has it as a kingdom under the hegemony of Mālī, while another simply describes it as part of the kingdom of Mālī.

Mālī was indeed the next powerful state to emerge in the western savanna. We barely hear of it until the late 1330s, but a few decades later Ibn Khaldūn provided an account of its early history based on the oral testimony of West African scholars he had met. Most of this evidence is close enough in time to deserve some credence, and it is tied into the well-established chronology of Mamlūk Egypt thanks to the fact that several rulers of Mālī passed through while on pilgrimage to Mecca; during his stay in Cairo one of them took the opportunity to buy himself a bodyguard of thirty Turkic slave soldiers. In essence we learn two things from this information. First, at an unknown date a king of Mālī had converted to Islam, and the people at large did so too. Second, the expansion of Mālī began under a king who must have ruled in the mid-thirteenth century, and it was continued by one who most likely ruled in the early fourteenth. In the west this extended the rule of Mālī to the Atlantic coast. The next major ruler went on pilgrimage to Mecca in 1324—giving us our first exact date in the history of Mālī. The journey must have enabled him to see for himself how things were done in the metropolitan Muslim lands, and it may help explain his reputedly fluent Arabic and the conspicuous presence at his court of a small number of Turkic slaves. Meanwhile territorial expansion continued, and in the 1370s and 1380s the eastern frontier was extended beyond Gao. In short, for the first time in the history of West Africa we are looking at an empire. But by now the dynasty was no longer what it had been. The eastern conquests were the work of an all-powerful vizier who had seized control from the ruler, and thereafter Ibn Khaldūn reports a time of troubles with three rulers in as many years. His narrative ends in 1390, leaving us with no coherent account of the subsequent history of Mālī, though we know enough to infer that later Mālī must have been seriously diminished from what it had been in the fourteenth century. Much about the history of the kingdom is obscure even for the period covered by Ibn Khaldūn. Thus we do not really know where Mālī was located prior to its expansion, though there is some reason to place it on the upper Niger to the south of Ghāna. Nor do we know where its capital was, though it has been assumed that it was in the same region—and not, as we might have expected, in one of the major cities of the Niger Bend, be it Jenne, Timbuktu, or Gao. We nevertheless have a vivid sense of what Mālī was like from Ibn Baṭṭūṭa's account of his visit in 1352–53, and we will take it up later in this section.

The successor to Mālī was Songhay, marking an eastward shift of the political center of gravity in West Africa.[13] As we saw, Mālī seems to have started on or near the upper Niger and to have expanded eastward to dominate the Niger Bend. Songhay, by contrast, began on the lower Niger and expanded westward to bring the Niger Bend under its rule. As a people, the Songhay were a riverain population, and by the early seventeenth century—if not before—they were entirely Muslim. Prior to their expansion in the later fifteenth century there is no mention of them in our sources, but it is likely that they had been living in the region of Gao for a long time. And indeed we know that Gao was the center of a major state as early as the ninth century, since a Muslim author of the time describes it as the paramount state of the blacks: "All the kingdoms obey its king."[14] Yet despite traditions ascribing a hoary antiquity to the Songhay state, the first ruler to have more than a local impact was Sonni ʿAlī (ruled ca. 1464–92). Depicted by the scholars of Timbuktu as an energetic tyrant and conqueror, he extended his sway to cover about a thousand miles of the Niger, including Timbuktu and Jenne. But he failed to establish a dynasty, and shortly after his death one of his generals took over. This was Askiyā Muḥammad (ruled 1493–1529), who enlarged the kingdom away from the river and dispatched expeditions as far afield as Fūta Toro and the Aïr. His success extended to founding a line of Askiyās that lasted almost a century; their capital, as might be expected, was Gao. But in 1588 there was a debilitating civil war, and in 1591 a Moroccan army equipped with firearms effectively ended their rule, despite some lingering resistance in the far southeast.

13. For the history of Songhay see J. O. Hunwick, *Timbuktu and the Songhay empire*, Leiden 1999, especially the introduction.

14. Levtzion and Hopkins, *Corpus of early Arabic sources*, 21.

The Moroccan invasion of Songhay did not exactly make world history. The conquerors put an end to the indigenous imperial tradition of West Africa and set up in its place what was to be a smaller and much weaker state of their own. It was based in Timbuktu, though this did not do the city much good. The ruler of this state was known as the Bāshā, the Arabic version of the Turkish "pasha," a testimony to Moroccan emulation of the Ottomans. The ruling group were known as the Arma, from an Arabic term meaning musketeers. At the same time an attempt was made to secure some local legitimacy by appointing Askiyās as puppet rulers. After a few decades the Bāshās were no longer answering to Morocco, and in 1660 they formally claimed independence. They also tended to assimilate to the local environment—the second generation of the conquerors naturally had local mothers. But they were not strong rulers: between 1591 and 1832 the average tenure of a Bāshā was less than a year. The result, as a seventeenth-century chronicler of Timbuktu lamented, was chaos. In the good old days of Songhay rule, he tells us, the region had been "one of God's most favored countries in prosperity, comfort, security, and vitality." But with the Moroccan conquest all that had changed: "Over the length and breadth of the land people began to devour one another, raids and war spared neither life nor wealth. Disorder spread and intensified until it became universal."[15] He may have exaggerated, as is the wont of chroniclers lamenting the evil times in which they live, but levels of security do change dramatically in human societies. Ibn Baṭṭūṭa, who as we will see was not particularly enthusiastic about West Africans, had still felt bound to compliment them on "the security embracing the whole country, so that neither traveler there nor dweller has anything to fear from thief or usurper."[16] By the eighteenth century the enfeebled Arma found themselves exposed to repeated harassment by the Tuareg, and then, from 1775 to 1794, there was a prolonged interregnum without Bāshās. A brief chronicle of the affairs of the city in the second half of the eighteenth century shows how the Bāshā would be appointed when there was one. The Arma would assemble to discuss the question and make the decision—except that in 1794 a local office holder brought in the descendants of the Prophet, the jurists, and the local judge to break a deadlock among the Arma. The bright spot in all this is that we now have indigenous West African chronicles, starting with two from seventeenth-century Timbuktu. These chronicles are the work of scholars, so their language, of course, is Arabic—though at least in one case notably bad Arabic.

If the Moroccan invasion of Songhay did not make world history, it was still very much a product of it. As we will see in the next chapter, from 1578 to 1603 Morocco was ruled by a powerful and ambitious sultan, Aḥmad al-Manṣūr. This

15. Quoted in Levtzion, *Ancient Ghana and Mali*, 91.
16. Levtzion and Hopkins, *Corpus of early Arabic sources*, 296.

was a ruler with wide horizons. He was well aware of the overseas activities of the Christian powers of the Atlantic seaboard to the north of Morocco, and he wanted a piece of the action. In 1600 he even tried an approach to Queen Elizabeth of England, proposing a joint English-Moroccan venture to colonize the New World, though nothing came of it. But if he could not send his conquistadors across the Atlantic, he could always try dispatching them to the other side of the Sahara, and that was what he had done in 1590–91. No doubt he hoped that the gold of West Africa might match the silver of Peru—as to an extent it did. His prudent advisers had strongly discouraged him from so quixotic a venture; no previous rulers of Morocco, they argued, had ever attempted to send an army to the far side of the desert. But the sultan highlighted the enormous revenue such a conquest would secure in support of the armies of Islam—armies that were then to be employed in a reconquest of Spain. In a more realistic geopolitical vein he pointed out that Moroccan expansion to the north and east was blocked by the Christians and the Turks, so the only way to go was south, against blacks who had nothing but spears and javelins to pit against Moroccan muskets. The sultan got his way and set about preparing his expedition. We know the composition of his army from a contemporary Spanish source. It was notably small, and largely Spanish-speaking. Most of the troops carried firearms. There were 2,000 infantrymen and 500 cavalry, Moriscos from Spain and renegade Christians. The commander himself was a blue-eyed renegade from Granada, and he had with him seventy professed Christians who had fallen into Muslim hands. For the rest there were 1,500 Arab horsemen armed with lances, no doubt recruited from the Arab tribes of Morocco. Alongside these 4,000 fighters there were 600 sappers and 1,000 camel drivers, for a grand total of 5,600 men. This human force was considerably outnumbered by the animals they took with them, 8,000 camels and 1,000 packhorses. In addition there was plenty of gunpowder and lead, and a modest number of field guns. The preparations took months and revolved around ensuring a supply of food and water for the desert crossing. The army finally left in mid-October 1590 and arrived at the end of February. Only a madman would have set an army to cross the Sahara in summer, but even the winter crossing was a severe trial. If the army that left Morocco was small, the army that reached the north bank of the Niger was smaller still, having lost almost half its men to hunger, thirst, and sunstroke in the desert. Those who survived were so exhausted that had the ruler of Songhay been paying attention he could easily have disposed of them despite their firearms. That al-Manṣūr's conquistadors were so few in number helps explain the unsteady outcome of the conquest. After their initial victory they lacked the manpower to establish their rule in a solid fashion, despite a further force of five thousand men that crossed the desert late in 1591. The result, as we have seen, was to turn order into chaos—much as was the case with the Spanish conquest of Peru.

We now move yet farther east to Hausaland. This part of the savanna lies to the northeast of the lower Niger, in what is today northwestern Nigeria. More than that of any other region of the savanna, its history came to be shaped by the vision of a single man, the religious reformer 'Uthmān ibn Fūdī (d. 1817).[17] Insofar as his movement established the Sokoto Caliphate, he brought into existence a new political order that was to last until the inception of British rule in 1904, and to an extent even beyond that. What is problematic for us is that he also set his stamp on the history of Hausaland before his time: given the lack of independent sources, it is hard for us to avoid seeing the past of the region through his censorious eyes. For the most part Hausaland lies beyond the horizon of the external Arabic sources that are crucial for our knowledge of early West African history, and it offers no internal sources dating from before the reformist jihad. Two points are nevertheless reasonably clear. One is that Hausaland differed from the regions of the savanna we have examined so far in having had no tradition of large-scale state formation. We know of nothing in its past resembling the states of Takrūr, Ghāna, Mālī, or Songhay. Instead the Hausa states were small, typically no more than city-states notable for their city walls, and they fought among themselves. The other point is that the coming of Islam was late and patchy in comparison to its trajectory in those larger states. Thus it does not seem to have reached Kano, the major city of Hausaland, in a significant way before the fourteenth century, and very likely we should correct that to the fifteenth. Yet later in the fifteenth century the ruler of Kano was already listening to the counsels of Maghīlī (d. ca. 1504). This zealous Moroccan scholar had shown his mettle by picking a fight with the Jews of the oases of Tuwāt, and after crossing the Sahara, he went on to spend some time in Kano. It may well have been on Maghīlī's advice that the ruler introduced his subjects to the segregation of men and women, and it was on Maghīlī's orders that he had the sacred tree overshadowing the city's mosque cut down. Such rigorist thinking did not die with Maghīlī. The view of the Saharan Ṣūfī al-Mukhtār al-Kuntī (d. 1811) was that "the land of the blacks is a land in which unbelief prevails among the majority of its people,"[18] a sentiment 'Uthmān ibn Fūdī quoted with approval. And in any case, whatever we make of the aspersions he cast on professed Muslims among the Hausa, it does seem that full-blooded pagan populations could still be found in the region. The political disunity and the shakiness of Islam among the Hausa are plausibly linked, and there is nothing to suggest that had they been left to themselves, they would have acted to change their situation.

But the Hausa were not left to themselves. Instead, 'Uthmān ibn Fūdī stepped in, together with large numbers of Fulānī, the ethnic group to which he belonged. The Fulānī were a people of the western savanna, but an unusual one. They spoke

17. For what follows see M. Last, *The Sokoto Caliphate*, London 1977.

18. 'Uthmān ibn Fūdī, *Bayān wujūb al-hijra*, trans. F. H. El Masri, Khartoum 1978, 51.

a language related to those of the black agricultural population, yet unlike them they were relatively light-skinned cattle nomads with a caste system somewhat reminiscent of what we saw in the Sahara. Genetic evidence likewise points to a northern origin. Their cattle nomadism seems to have provided them with an ecological niche across the savanna, for in the centuries before ʿUthmān ibn Fūdī's jihad they had spread eastward from Fūta Toro all the way to Dār Fūr, and eventually, in the twentieth century, they would reach the Ethiopian border. As a result of this expansion they were well established in part of Hausaland, living alongside the Hausa agriculturalists and sometimes clashing with them. Many of the Fulānī were Muslims, and like the Moors and the Tuareg they had scholars, who may have played a significant role in the spread of Islam among the Hausa. At the same time, being nomads, they were relatively easy to mobilize for war and thus a potential resource for Ibn Khaldūnian state formation. Indeed, the eighteenth and nineteenth centuries were a period in which the Fulānī showed a partiality for jihads. They were involved in one that we have already noted in Fūta Toro, in another to the south in Fūta Jalon, and in a third in Massina on the upper Niger.

Yet for a long time ʿUthmān ibn Fūdī showed no interest in mobilizing the Fulānī. He started preaching in the 1770s, and by the late 1780s he was successfully demanding that the sultan of the Hausa state of Gobir not obstruct his reformist movement. As yet he had no recourse to violence. In 1794, however, he had a vision in which the Prophet instructed a twelfth-century Ṣūfī saint to invest him with the sword of truth. This saint was the founder of the widely disseminated Qādirī order, which had been spread in the region by the Kunta and to which ʿUthmān ibn Fūdī himself belonged. Three years later he and his followers resolved to take up arms, following the example of the Prophet. Even then hostilities did not begin until 1804. But by 1808 he had conquered the Hausa states and turned to attack Bornū. A work he wrote in 1811 articulated the core of his doctrine: people who mouth the confession of faith without performing any of the actions that go with it are without any doubt unbelievers, and waging jihad against them means killing their men, taking their women captive, plundering their property, and enslaving all of them. But he was not power-hungry, and in 1812 he handed over his political role to his son Muḥammad Bello and his brother ʿAbdallāh, himself withdrawing to teach Ṣūfism, to worry about whether he had caused the death of Muslims in the course of his jihad, and not least to write more. In all, he was the author of some hundred and fifty works, including religious poetry composed mainly in Fulfulde, the language of the Fulānī. This choice of language was no accident. Although the movement mostly ignored ethnicity in its rhetoric, it was obvious that one of its major effects was to establish the power of the Fulānī at the expense of the Hausa. This went well with the contempt of light-skinned nomads for black peasants that the Fulānī shared with the Tuareg, and indeed we find Muḥammad Bello lamenting the presence of such Fulānī chauvinism in the movement. The Hausa, of course, had their own brand of ethnic chauvinism: they distinguished the seven Hausa states from the seven "worthless" states found in their neighborhood—worthless in the sense that they were not Hausa.

This completes our survey of the western states of the savanna belt. Hausaland, as is clear, stands out as the exception within this set, the one case of a major state formed in Ibn Khaldūnian style; and as we will now see, it is in fact an exception in the savanna at large.

The savanna belt: The eastern states

Our first stop in the eastern savanna is around Lake Chad, a shallow lake fed by rivers flowing into it from the south and west. Here the largest role in state formation was played by two regions: Kānem to the northeast of the lake and Bornū to its southwest. Despite being separated by the lake, the two came to share a language, Kanuri, and tended to belong to a single kingdom, conveniently referred to as Kānem-Bornū. This kingdom displayed remarkable staying power. The entries in a laconic indigenous chronicle of its history down to the nineteenth century are at first obviously mythical—the dynasty is said to descend from Sayf ibn Dhī Yazan, a celebrated Yemeni of the sixth century, and of one of his descendants we are told that "the length of his reign was 250 years, or it has been said 300 years."[19] But an Arabic source of the late ninth century mentions a kingdom of Kānem and even provides the ruler's name—though it is not to be found in the chronicle. By then Kānem must have been in contact with the Muslim world for some time, since we hear of a Berber in the hinterland of Tripolitania, already a prestigious figure in 811, who knew not just Berber and Arabic but also the language of Kānem. Thereafter the chronicle seems to provide authentic information about the rulers of the kingdom from at least the eleventh century, and in the second half of that century we have a monarch with the obviously Muslim name of ʿAbd al-Jalīl. So by then, we can infer, Islam must have begun to make converts. A thirteenth-century source then informs us that the population of Kānem was now Muslim except in some outlying districts. Returning to the chronicle, another thing it tells us in a matter-of-fact way is that a ruler of the later twelfth century was "very black in color," whereas all previous rulers had been "red like an Arab nomad"; "red" in the Arabic vocabulary of skin color is tantamount to white. This, far more than the legend of descent from Sayf ibn Dhī Yazan, raises a serious possibility that the dynasty was founded through an incursion from the Sahara. In general, we face a problem of interpretation when we encounter such statements. Although it is entirely plausible that nomads would conquer sedentary people, it is also plausible that

19. For this and the quotations that follow see D. Lange, *Chronologie et histoire d'un royaume africain*, Wiesbaden 1977, 65, 71.

sedentary people would claim prestigious but spurious nomadic ancestry. In this case at least, the specificity of the evidence favors nomadic conquest rather than genealogical fabrication. Despite occasional changes of dynasty, the major discontinuity in the subsequent political history of the state was geographical: in the late fourteenth century a local rival forced the ruling dynasty to move from Kānem to Bornū, for a while relinquishing control of Kānem. The intrusion of Arab nomads coming from the east may have added to the pressure to move. But as we have seen in the Saharan context, Kānem-Bornū was a powerful state at times, for example in the thirteenth and sixteenth centuries. Moreover, its sixteenth-century rulers, unlike those of Songhay, realized the importance of firearms. As we know from an indigenous chronicle, they procured Turkish musketeers and trained foreign slaves in the use of muskets. Yet they were unable to withstand a major threat from the west at the end of our period, when the jihad of ʿUthmān ibn Fūdī swept away the quarreling Hausa states and put in their place the formidable Sokoto Caliphate. In 1808 the dynasty's capital in Bornū was sacked by a Fulānī force. The ruler then fled to Kānem and there found help against the Fulānī from a locally powerful scholar who defended him with both pen and sword, but the cost was relinquishing the reins of government to this savior. After the failure of a plot to escape from this stifling protection, the main line of the dynasty came to a bloody end in 1846.

East of Kānem-Bornū the next significant region of state formation was Wadai. But in comparison to other parts of the savanna, it was a poor relation. Though it did have an ethnic core, the Maba or Borgū, the mildly elevated region of Wadai was not anchored in any pronounced geographical feature. Nobody is quite sure how to spell its name, it is well beyond the horizon of the early Arabic sources, and there are no indigenous chronicles for our period, only belatedly recorded traditions. Altogether, Wadai was clearly a late starter. We know of no state formation there before the sixteenth century, when the region was apparently invaded from the east by an obscure people known as the Tunjur, who proceeded to rule Wadai from Dār Fūr. Around this time Arab nomads were likewise moving into Wadai from the east—part of the same migration that impinged on Kānem-Bornū. It is only after this that we see anything approaching indigenous state formation in Wadai, and even then the founding figure, ʿAbd al-Karīm ibn Jāmiʿ, was of Arabized Nubian stock. Probably in the first half of the seventeenth century he repudiated the rule of Dār Fūr, founding a well-organized savanna state with Wāra as its capital and Maba as its court language. The dynasty he established was a successful one, lasting to the end of our period and beyond. At first its energies were taken up with a century of warfare in which it withstood the expansionist state of Dār Fūr. But when peace came in the second half of the eighteenth century, the effect was to leave Wadai free to expand westward as far as Lake Chad. Just as Wadai seems to have come late to state formation, so too it came late to Islam. Tradition associates the advent of the religion with the same ʿAbd al-Karīm, and here for once we have a contemporary source, a marginal note of 1657–58 in a manuscript, describing Wadai as recently converted. The dynasty nevertheless persisted in its pagan rainmaking rituals.

Dār Fūr has a much more definite geographical profile.[20] Its core is the region in and around the highlands of the Jabal Marra, with a peak rising to ten thousand feet; this is a domain of cultivators. To the north lies "the land of the wind," a place for camel nomads, while to the south is a marshy region of high rainfall, suitable for cattle nomads. Most of the nomads in both north and south are Arabic-speaking. Here the presence of camel nomads is no surprise, but the black Arab cattle nomads of the Baqqāra Belt represent an unusual adaption of desert nomads to a very different environment. This belt extends westward from the White Nile to what is now northeastern Nigeria. These nomads are likely to have arrived from the east after Nubia was overrun by Arab nomads in the fourteenth century, to have been forced south by rival camel nomads, and to have learned cattle nomadism from the Fulānī, with whom they were intermarrying in the seventeenth century. Indeed, their skin color points to extensive interbreeding with local populations. But despite this more differentiated geography, as far as sources are concerned we are not much better off in Dār Fūr than we were in Wadai. Though Dār Fūr is closer to the White Nile, it was still largely beyond the horizon of the medieval Arabic authors, and again it has no indigenous chronicles. It is clear, however, that the historical basis of state formation in Dār Fūr was the agricultural core, a region we know as inhabited by the Fūr, the black people after whom Dār Fūr is named. Tradition, however, tells first of the rule of a people called the Dājū, perhaps around the twelfth century, followed by the same Tunjur that we encountered in Wadai. In Dār Fūr, just as in Wadai, Tunjur rule seems to have been brought to an end through the formation of an indigenous state among the Fūr, perhaps in the first half of the seventeenth century. The earliest historical ruler of this state was a certain Sulaymān Solong, who may have ruled around 1660–80. His clan was the Keira, which remained the royal clan throughout the kingdom's existence, and was part of the Fūr, though there are also traditions to the effect that it was of Arab descent. For a century this Dār Fūr Sultanate put energy into expanding its territory, threatening its neighbors on both sides. To the east Kordofān was conquered and held for the best part of forty years, but in 1821 it was lost to the expansionist ruler of Egypt, Meḥmed ʿAlī Pasha, in a battle in which a modern army equipped with firearms destroyed the traditional heavy cavalry of Dār Fūr. That this army did not go on to conquer Dār Fūr was a matter of luck: the invaders had to turn

20. For the history of Dār Fūr see R. S. O'Fahey and J. L. Spaulding, *Kingdoms of the Sudan*, London 1974, and R. S. O'Fahey, *The Darfur Sultanate*, London 2008.

away to deal with fierce resistance in Nubia. Thus the rule of the Keira dynasty was not finally extinguished till the British conquest of 1916.

Like ʿAbd al-Karīm ibn Jāmiʿ in Wadai, Sulaymān Solong is credited with introducing Islam to his kingdom. But this cannot be right since a document from 1576 mentions a pious endowment established in Medina by a Tunjur ruler. Thereafter the trend was, as often, toward greater Islamization. But around the end of our period the influence of Islam on the political culture of Dār Fūr was still limited. Like the Mongol and post-Mongol states and the Malay sultanates, Dār Fūr was bilegal: there was God's law and there was the sultan's law. The first ruler of the kingdom was reputed to have codified its laws and customs in a book, and there was a tendency for God's law to be sidelined by pagan observances. For example, on the sultan's death the sacred fire in the palace would be allowed to go out, not to be lit again until the new sultan came to the throne; at this point the new ruler would disappear into a week of seclusion. Likewise, in the course of an annual festival, sacrifices would be offered at the tombs of the previous rulers of the dynasty. Yet even here Islam was asserting itself. The pious sultan ʿAbd al-Raḥmān (ruled from 1787–88 to 1803) refused to go into seclusion on the ground that the custom was a bad one, having no authorization from God or His Prophet. His piety nevertheless provoked a backlash. Angered by his practice of spending all his time with scholars, his viziers vowed never again to have a ruler who could read. Meanwhile, the annual ritual at the tombs came to include the recitation of the Qurʾān for the Muslim rulers of the past—though not for the pagan ones, who still enjoyed their sacrifices. Another practice in tension with Islamic norms was the formal standing of women at court. The roles of the sultan's mother, favorite sister, and leading wife were not just a political fact; they were officially recognized through the titles bestowed on these women. We do, however, have to wait until the mid-nineteenth century to hear of a royal sister who roamed the country at the head of a band of armed men. She rode with her skirt hitched up, plundering and looting as she went. Yet even here there was a touch of Islamization—this rapacious princess was named Zamzam after the sacred spring of Mecca. Among the common people of Dār Fūr pre-Islamic customs remained strong into the nineteenth and twentieth centuries, especially among the women. Muḥammad al-Tūnisī (d. 1857), a descendant of the Prophet who arrived in Dār Fūr from Egypt in 1803 as a teenager and spent almost eight years there, had a lot to say about the mixing of boys and girls, and subsequently of men and women, among the indigenous population and the range of sexual activity to which this gave rise. ʿAbd al-Raḥmān, the pious sultan who refused to go into seclusion, tried hard to rein this in and also targeted the consumption of millet beer, but the efforts of his eunuch police force met with little success, and his ban on beer was flouted by his own womenfolk. Just as we have seen with other indigenous populations of the Sahara and savanna, the role of women generally was very different in Dār Fūr from what it was in the core regions of the Muslim world. Tūnisī comments that the women of Dār Fūr participated in all decisions except making war. Dār Fūr was still a remote region of the Muslim world, "so far from civilization," as Tūnisī put it.[21] When he visited the Jabal Marra large crowds of blacks gathered to stare at him, amazed at his ruddy color. One view was that he must have failed to ripen in his mother's womb, and another that he was not a human at all, but rather an edible animal in human form—it being unthinkable that a human being could have a white or red complexion. Nevertheless, people in Dār Fūr had muskets and English cloth, and at the very end of our period there was even some interaction with the French during their occupation of Egypt from 1798 to 1801.

Our last region of the savanna before we reach the White Nile is Kordofān, though we do not need to spend long on it—it is if anything an even poorer relation than Wadai. Like Dār Fūr, it had a tripartite structure: camel nomads in the north, cultivators in the center, and cattle nomads in the south. In both north and south the nomads were predominantly Arab. But there was a major geographical difference between Kordofān and Dār Fūr—namely, the location of the region's highlands. The center of Kordofān is a vast plain, which helps explain why pastoralism loomed large here alongside rainfall agriculture. The Nūba Mountains, by contrast, are located in the southeastern corner of Kordofān, adjoining the territory of the cattle nomads. The open terrain of the center had an obvious implication for state formation. It meant that this region, unlike the highlands of Dār Fūr, did not provide shelter for a state, so that whoever sought to establish one there was likely to be buffeted by stronger neighbors in Dār Fūr or southern Nubia. To an extent the Nūba Mountains provided a counterpart to the highlands of Dār Fūr, but their physical and human geography was very different. Instead of being a single massif, the Nūba Mountains consist of a number of isolated highlands, each rising from a plain through which cattle nomads move freely, and whereas the mountains of Dār Fūr are dominated by a single ethnic group, the population of the Nūba Mountains is fragmented in the extreme—as is indicated by the presence of some thirty different languages. These highlanders in fact played little part in the wider history of Kordofān. A small state, Taqalī, did arise in the eastern part of the mountains in the sixteenth and seventeenth centuries, and it was or became Muslim, but it was overcome by the Funj kingdom of southern Nubia in the mid-seventeenth century. In the north of Kordofān a persistent family and its followers, the Musabbaʿāt, attempted to establish an independent state in the later eighteenth century, but in the end they were unable to withstand the hostility of the neighboring states. Before them the region had been under the partial hegemony of the Funj from the later seventeenth century, and after them, as we have

21. Muḥammad ibn ʿUmar al-Tūnisī, *In Darfur*, trans. H. Davies, New York 2018, 2:195.

seen, it was ruled by Dār Fūr until the Egyptian conquest of 1821. In short, of all the sites for savanna state formation that we have considered, Kordofān was arguably the least promising.

The savanna belt: Comparisons and contrasts

As is clear from this survey, the various regions of the savanna had much in common. They were similar in climate and vegetation. They all had black populations making a living from agriculture, they were all exposed to Muslims—merchants and others—crossing the Sahara from the north, and they all had more or less indigenous states that could exercise considerable agency in the process of Islamization. Sooner or later they all adopted Islam, whether nominally or substantively, but not in general as a result of conquest. This last point may help explain why heretical forms of Islam—resistance Islam—had little abiding appeal here, in contrast to their enthusiastic reception among the Berbers of North Africa. It also does something to account for the extensive survival of pagan customs among the Muslim populations of the savanna, though there was undoubtedly a long-term trend toward deeper Islamization. For example, Mansā Mūsā in early fourteenth-century Mālī enjoyed a custom of his people whereby anyone with a beautiful daughter would offer her to him as a concubine, and this despite his personal piety and the general adoption of Islam. On being told that this indulgence was not permissible for Muslims, his surprised response was "Not even for kings?"[22] But once he had been informed that in this matter even kings were not entitled to a special deal, he pleaded ignorance and said he would abandon the custom; this, after all, was a ruler who sent students to study in Fez. There must have been many moments like this in the history of the savanna over the centuries. Another feature shared by the states of the savanna was their exposure to a similar cast of enemies: the neighboring kingdoms, the camel nomads of the desert, and the cattle nomads of the savanna, be they Fulānī or Arab. Likewise they all relied on long-distance trade with the lands on the other side of the Sahara. An early sixteenth-century visitor to Timbuktu reported that the ruler had given two of his daughters in marriage to two merchant brothers because of their wealth. Here the constant was the slave trade. A typical savanna state would busy itself raiding its southern neighbors with a view to seizing and exporting captives to satisfy the demand for slaves on the northern side of the desert. Less constant, but at times vital to the interests of all the savanna states, was the return trade in horses—large horses fit for cavalry warfare, in contrast to the small horses characteristic of the savanna in the early centuries of Islam. Such horses were worth a lot more than the

22. Levtzion and Hopkins, *Corpus of early Arabic sources*, 268.

average human. According to a Portuguese traveler of the late fifteenth century, the rate of exchange at the western end of the savanna was one horse to ten or fifteen slaves, and scattered data suggest that this was not untypical of the savanna as a whole. The importation of such horses may have begun in the thirteenth century and is well attested in the fourteenth. The army of Mālī in this period is said to have included ten thousand cavalry, the ruler being a determined importer of horses.

There were also some noteworthy contrasts within the savanna. One concerns the scale of political organization. As we have seen, the pattern of small states that typified Hausaland until almost the end of our period was relatively untypical in the savanna, though at home farther south, as among the Yoruba of what is now southwestern Nigeria. Another contrast concerns the date at which Islam was established in different parts of the savanna. In the west, Takrūr and Ghāna are two of the three regions where we have reason to date conversion to Islam as early as the eleventh century (the third being Kānem-Bornū). In the east, Wadai, Dār Fūr, and Kordofān are three of the four regions to which Islam seems to have come the best part of half a millennium later (the fourth being Hausaland). At first sight this contrast seems counterintuitive, since the eastern savanna was considerably closer to the heart of the Muslim world than was the western savanna. It nevertheless makes a certain sense. First, before the fourteenth century the riverain route from Egypt to the eastern savanna went through Christian Nubia. Thus until then the Nile did not offer an easy route for Muslims traveling to and from the savanna—though no doubt it was possible to cross from Dār Fūr to Egypt through the Sahara, bypassing Nubia by following what was later known as the Darb al-Arbaʿīn, the "forty-day trail." Second, perhaps a weightier argument concerns exports from the savanna. In the western savanna, as we have seen, there was a vigorous gold trade. In the eastern savanna, by contrast, only Kordofān had gold, and not much of it at that, as Meḥmed ʿAlī Pasha learned to his chagrin after his troops had conquered the region. Slaves apart, the main export of Kordofān was gum arabic, a versatile and valuable commodity but not one in the same league as gold. It thus figures that the gold of the western savanna would attract more vigorous attention from the north. A final contrast concerns the reactions of the kingdoms to global changes in warfare consequent on the development of firearms. We have seen two kingdoms, Songhay and Dār Fūr, lose crucial battles against invaders from the north who came armed with such weapons. But we have also seen Kānem-Bornū adopt them—and do so at a time when there had as yet been no northern attack making use of the new technology. This was a remarkable step, and it is a pity that our sources give us little insight into the thinking of the rulers who were responsible for it.

A final theme worth taking up across the savanna is the writing of indigenous languages in the imported Arabic script—a widespread practice in the Muslim world that we looked at most closely in the case of Persian. The oldest and best-documented example from the savanna concerns Kanuri, the language of Kānem-Bornū. By 1669 Old Kanembu, a very archaic written form of the Kanuri of the northeastern side of Lake Chad, was being used alongside Arabic in the context of religious instruction in Bornū. We know this because an old copy of the Qurʾān has marginal notes in both Arabic and Old Kanembu. The Arabic annotations are dated 1669, and their placement on the page shows that the Old Kanembu annotations were already in place when the Arabic was added. A less archaic form of this language is still used in religious teaching in Bornū. We have no indication that either form was used for more secular purposes, but another form of Kanuri, this one from Bornū, was employed in the late eighteenth or early nineteenth century for lists of the rulers of Kānem-Bornū over the course of nine centuries—probably the closest parallel we can hope to find to a Kanuri *Shāhnāma*. The question is whether what we see here is something exceptional, or just the tip of an iceberg. Had Old Kanembu been written for centuries before 1669? The extreme archaism of this literary language and the fact that it was based on a form of Kanuri spoken on the other side of the lake do indeed suggest that it had taken shape long before it is first attested. Were there similar phenomena elsewhere in the savanna? Here we can at least say that Mandinka, the language of a West African mercantile diaspora, was being written in the Arabic script by the 1680s, Fulfulde by the late eighteenth century, and Hausa by the early nineteenth century. There is also a parallel to the east of Ethiopia, where Arabic-script texts in the Semitic language spoken in the city of Harar go back at least to the seventeenth century. But when it was that these languages first began to be written is anybody's guess.

Back to eleventh-century Ghāna and fourteenth-century Mālī

By far our richest source on Ghāna and its neighbors is a geographical work by a Spanish Muslim author writing in 1068. This was Bakrī (d. 1094), who never visited West Africa but assiduously and intelligently collected information from earlier written sources and from travelers—most likely merchants—who had been there. He was sufficiently up to date in his reporting to know that just five years previously a new king had come to throne at the age of eighty-five. The result is an account that provides a remarkable snapshot of a region in uneven transition from paganism to Islam.

A good place to start is Bakrī's account of the capital city of Ghāna. It had two centers that were six miles apart. One was the royal town, which he describes as almost entirely pagan in character, surrounded by temples and mysterious groves. In it were found the pagan priests, their idols, and the tombs of the former kings. Here the reigning king, decked out with jewelry, would give audience in a domed pavilion around which stood ten horses, obviously there to impress, and there were guard dogs at the entrance to the pavilion. Any pagan approaching the king would fall on his knees and sprinkle dust on his head. When the king died, he would be laid to rest under an enormous wooden dome with appropriate grave goods—his jewelry, his weapons, and his bowls and cups filled with food and drink. The men who used to serve his meals would be with him, presumably to serve him in the afterlife. The dome would then be closed, a mass of earth heaped over it, and a ditch dug around it. Though Bakrī does not spell this out, we can assume that in due course the king's servants would perish in the tomb. Ibn Baṭṭūṭa describes such a practice on the death of a pagan ruler in fourteenth-century West Africa, though in that case it was not just servants who suffered, and the victims had their hands and feet broken, presumably to ensure that they could not dig their way out. Returning to Ghāna, the other center was the Muslim town, which Bakrī describes as a large one—there were no fewer than twelve mosques. All the personnel needed for a proper Muslim life could be found there: muezzins, prayer leaders, jurists, scholars. As to what people did in the Muslim town, he has little to say beyond a mention of the ritual of the Friday prayer in one of the mosques and a reference to the cultivation of vegetables; it was the royal town, not the Muslim town, that stood in need of description for Bakrī's readers. This binary arrangement was by no means unique. Bakrī provides a close parallel when he comes to Gao: here, too, there were twin towns, the royal town and the Muslim town. Separate political and commercial centers are well attested elsewhere in the savanna, though usually without the difference of religion.

The six-mile gap between the two towns of Ghāna served to ensure that both pagans and Muslims had space to live their lives in the manner to which they were accustomed, but it did not seal them off from each other. While Bakrī says nothing about the presence of pagans in the Muslim town, he is informative about the role of Muslims in the pagan town, where there was in fact a mosque in which visiting Muslims could pray. These Muslims were far from marginal, for the king's interpreters, his treasurer, and most of his ministers were Muslims. In other words, the pagan king regarded Muslims as useful people to have in his kingdom and at court; indeed, Bakrī praises the reigning king for his friendliness toward Muslims. They had the gift of literacy in a society that lacked it, they knew how things were done in the wider world on the far side of the desert, and they were presumably free of politically undesirable ties to the indigenous pagan elite. It is unfortunate that Bakrī omits to tell us the ethnicity of these Muslims.

Elsewhere in West Africa Bakrī's reporting is less detailed, but it shows paganism and Islam coexisting in a bewildering variety of ways. One kingdom has no Muslim residents but treats Muslim visitors with respect. Two towns are inhabited by Muslims but surrounded by pagans. A king converts to Islam in return for the assistance of a Muslim visitor in ending a prolonged drought, after which the nobles convert while the common people remain pagan. Another king is said to be Muslim but to conceal his religion. At a certain point on the Niger Muslim Berbers live on one bank and pagan blacks on the other. Even Gao is not quite like Ghāna: despite the thoroughly pagan—and public—ritual observed each time the king has a meal, the pagans of Gao will only have a Muslim as their king, and at his accession he is handed a copy of the Qur'ān. By contrast, Bakrī reports no more than two cases of solidly Muslim kingdoms. One is Takrūr, where as we saw the king converted in the first decades of the eleventh century and imposed Islam on his people. The other is Silā on the Senegal River, which Bakrī describes as a large neighboring kingdom that converted under the influence of Takrūr.

One other point is worth picking out from Bakrī's account of Ghāna. Like many people socialized into patrilineal societies, he found matrilineal inheritance sufficiently exotic to be worth highlighting. So he tells us that when the king of Ghāna died, the new king would be the son of the king's sister, not his own son. He adds a comment of a kind that comes easily to members of patrilineal societies encountering matrilineal inheritance, remarking that the old king "has no doubt that his successor is a son of his sister, while he is not certain that his son is in fact his own."[23] There may in fact be something to this view of the matter, in the sense that in a matrilineal society female infidelity is by no means as consequential as it is in a patrilineal one: a new king's claim to the throne would not turn on who his father might be. By now we have encountered matrilineal inheritance often enough not to be surprised at it. But in the savanna, as in the Sahara, it was far from being universal. Although a tenth-century Arab geographer calls it "a custom of all the blacks,"[24] Bakrī at one point describes a people among whom the eldest son inherited all his father's property. Likewise in his account of the history of Mālī, Ibn Khaldūn notes one instance of matrilineal succession "according to the custom of these non-Arabs"[25] but also mentions five cases of sons succeeding to the throne. In the eastern savanna, succession among the rulers of Kānem-Bornū was patrilineal, just as it was in Dār Fūr, though not, as we will see, in Nubia.

We turn now to Mālī as described by Ibn Baṭṭūṭa. Unlike Bakrī, he had direct experience of West Africa, and especially of Mālī, thanks to his journey of 1352–53. His very personal account is informative about the logistics of the journey and especially revealing with regard to his view of the economics of tourism. We take it for granted today that tourism is financed by the tourists: it is for them to unload hard currency onto the host society in return for local services. Ibn Baṭṭūṭa, by contrast, expected the host society, and in particular its rulers, to unload hard currency onto him, together with other forms of hospitality and largesse, and he clearly assumed that his readers would share his view. When his expectations were

23. Levtzion and Hopkins, *Corpus of early Arabic sources*, 79.
24. Ibn Ḥawqal, *Ṣūrat al-arḍ*, Leiden 1967, 57.
25. Levtzion and Hopkins, *Corpus of early Arabic sources*, 333.

not met, he was capable of responding ruthlessly. Thus he tells us that the ruler of Mālī at the time of his visit, Mansā Sulaymān (ruled 1341–60), was notoriously stingy. This was Ibn Baṭṭūṭa's judgment, but it was shared, he informs us, by the ruler's subjects. By contrast, a recent predecessor, Mansā Mūsā (ruled 1312–37), had been generous and virtuous and had a liking for white men. But Ibn Baṭṭūṭa arrived in Mālī too late to benefit from his patronage, and the gift the current ruler sent after their first meeting was derisory. Thereafter two long months passed without any further gift. By now this lack of royal largesse was becoming too much for Ibn Baṭṭūṭa to bear; it was time for a shakedown. He accordingly explained to Mansā Sulaymān that as a confirmed traveler he was the kind of person who met and spoke to many rulers. He followed this up with a sharp rhetorical question: "What shall I say of you in the presence of other sultans?"[26] This threat to sabotage the ruler's reputation with his peers finally had the desired effect, and as Ibn Baṭṭūṭa was leaving Mālī he was presented with some fifteen ounces of gold. This parting gift must have been a welcome boost to his finances, and it helps explain why on his way back across the Sahara he was looking to splash out on a rare and expensive commodity, an educated slave girl. But even fifteen ounces of gold did not suffice to dissuade him from bad-mouthing Mansā Sulaymān when he came to narrate his travels, thereby tarnishing this ruler's reputation down the centuries. Mansā Mūsā, after all, had been known to hand out gold in amounts thirty or forty times larger than what Ibn Baṭṭūṭa received from Mansā Sulaymān. Of course, complaints about the stinginess of royal patrons were not confined to Ibn Baṭṭūṭa or West Africa. A discontented historian who spent time at the Ottoman court in the early sixteenth century made a similar effort to shake down his patrons and complained that they had fobbed him off with trifles, "as one gives walnuts and raisins to a child."[27]

Fortunately Ibn Baṭṭūṭa's problems with the miserly ruler do not seem to have distracted him from observing the manners and customs of the people of Mālī. Being nothing if not judgmental, he arranged his observations under two headings: what he approved of about the blacks, and what he disapproved of. Some of their good qualities had no necessary connection to Islam: their country was not ravaged by the law of the jungle, there was no insecurity, and no attempt was made to seize the property of deceased whites. The same could be said of some of their bad qualities: the poor quality of their food, their incivility, and their disrespect for whites. But several of the things that elicited Ibn Baṭṭūṭa's praise or blame had a lot to do with Islam, at least from his more metropolitan point of view. Among the virtues of the blacks was that they were assiduous in performing the ritual

26. Levtzion and Hopkins, *Corpus of early Arabic sources*, 290.

27. Quoted in C. Markiewicz, *The crisis of kingship in late medieval Islam*, Cambridge 2019, 93–94.

prayers in congregation, they dressed in fine white clothes for the Friday prayer, and they were eager to memorize the Qur'ān. Moreover, they showed a commendable zeal in passing on these good qualities to their children. They would beat them to make them pray and would fetter them if they were dilatory in learning the Qur'ān by heart. In these respects, then, they were notably good Muslims. And yet in some other respects they were very bad ones. As usual, the conduct of women was a leading target of Ibn Baṭṭūṭa's disapproval, but in this case his complaint was not that they were sexually depraved like the Berber women of Walāta, but rather that they went around without any clothes on. Little girls and slave girls appeared in front of men completely naked, and when breaking the fast in the evening during Ramaḍān, the grandees would proceed to the sultan's palace, each bringing food carried by a score or more of naked slave girls. Women went into the sultan's presence naked, and two of his daughters were to be seen topless. Other practices were perhaps less deeply shocking, but still quite un-Islamic. One was eating forbidden flesh—carrion and the meat of dogs and donkeys. Another was the tenacious custom of throwing dust on one's head as a sign of deference. We met this practice already in eleventh-century Ghāna, and it was still being condemned by 'Uthmān ibn Fūdī at the end of our period. More idiosyncratic was the fancy dress worn by the court poets of Mālī, which made them look like birds, combining feathers with a wooden head and a red beak. To Ibn Baṭṭūṭa the bizarre appearance of the poets was more ridiculous than shocking. He did not share the modern tourist's taste for the exotic.

Two things emerge from these lively details. One is an interesting dichotomy. Though their customs may seem foreign to us, it is as if the people of Mālī had a general view of things that was not altogether different from a modern Western perspective. They were happy for Islam to be their religion, but—like the Berbers who broke with Ibn Yāsīn and those whom Ibn Baṭṭūṭa encountered in Walāta—they do not seem to have wanted their religion intruding into other parts of their lives. As a religion, Islam was well and good, but it was to mind its own business; it was not, for example, to pose as a dress code or a law of inheritance. In this attitude the people of Mālī seem to have been fairly persistent, despite eventual indications of segregation. A century and a half after Ibn Baṭṭūṭa's visit we find Askiyā Muḥammad, the pious ruler of Songhay, consulting Maghīlī about such issues. In the city of Jenne, this ruler lamented, a girl would wear nothing as long as she was a virgin, so that the most beautiful young women of the city would appear in public stark naked, even the daughters of judges—who as usual ought to know better. The other point of interest that emerges from Ibn Baṭṭūṭa's comments on West Africans is that although he did not particularly like them, he did not link their faults to their blackness. Given his cultural heritage, he could very easily have done so. He came from a part of the world where as a matter of social fact blackness was quite closely linked to slavery. As an educated Muslim he was no doubt familiar with the controversial idea of the curse of Ham, with its genetic understanding of racial differences. According to one tradition, Ham begat all those who are black and curly-haired, while Shem was the ancestor of everyone with a handsome face and beautiful hair; their father Noah prayed that wherever the descendants of Ham met those of Shem, the descendants of Shem should enslave them. Ibn Baṭṭūṭa may also have been familiar with the more sophisticated environmental explanation of racial differences, an idea that Muslims inherited from Mediterranean antiquity: too little sun makes the people of the north pale-skinned and stupid, too much of it makes the people of the south dark-skinned and silly, whereas the people in the middle—the people who invented and perpetuated this schema—are of course just right. Here blackness, like whiteness, is sensitive to latitude: after seven generations, blacks who live in a land of whites will turn white, and vice versa. But Ibn Baṭṭūṭa, like Masʿūdī in his sympathetic account of the Zanj of Sofala, does not present the blacks of West Africa through either of these cultural prisms. At the same time, he has no difficulty giving good grades to individual blacks, like the judge of the capital city, whose noble virtues found apt expression in his gift of a whole cow to Ibn Baṭṭūṭa. Mansā Sulaymān's gift, by contrast, included no more than a single cut of beef.

Northeast Africa

The Ethiopian highlands: Background

The main reason northeast Africa breaks with the pattern we have seen farther west is that here the savanna gives way to the Ethiopian highlands. These highlands are part of the East African rift system, forming a large, uneven plateau at around 7,000 to 8,000 feet. They are thus on a quite different scale from the occasional mountainous regions we have encountered in the Sahara and savanna. One result of this is that Ethiopia attracts considerably more rainfall than does the savanna, let alone the Sahara, and it loses less of it to evaporation. Some of the water stays in the highlands, but a large amount leaves them in the form of rivers. Here a crucial feature of the highlands is that they reach their greatest elevation in the east, where they rise sharply above the lowlands of the Horn of Africa. This creates an escarpment running roughly north to south, interrupted only by a spur of the southern highlands that juts out into the eastern lowlands. West of this escarpment the highlands descend unevenly toward the lowlands of the upper Nile. What this means is that a disproportionate share of the water leaving Ethiopia goes to feed the Nile, thus making possible dense agricultural societies downriver in Nubia and Egypt—but not in the coastal lowlands of northeast Africa. More particularly, there would be no Nile flood without the existence of the highlands. Awareness of this dependence led the ruler of Ethiopia in 1326 to threaten the Mamlūk sultan that he would dam the Nile if the Copts were not treated better in Egypt—a threat that was ridiculed at the time. We will accordingly start our survey in Ethiopia and then move downstream to Nubia. But before we begin, there is a basic point about contemporary political geography that needs to be made. The highlands—and in particular the northern highlands—are the historical core of Ethiopia, and they are largely contained within the borders of the country as it is today. But as a result of an Ethiopian expansion that began in the late nineteenth century and was only partly reversed by the secession of Eritrea in 1993, these borders also include extensive lowland territory to the east of the highlands. This territory impinges on our story from time to time, but when we speak of Ethiopia it is the highlands that we have in mind.

Highlands in general are more resistant than lowlands are to processes of ethnic, religious, and cultural homogenization. But in the Ethiopian case the effect is enhanced by a peculiar feature of the landscape. Although the country has its share of peaks, which can rise to over fifteen thousand feet, a more characteristic formation in the highlands is the "amba" or tableland (Amharic *ambā*), a plateau with almost sheer sides. Once established on an amba, a population can make a living from cultivation and pastoralism while easily defending its plateau against attempts to invade it. The highlands are thus a refuge, or rather a whole set of refuges, for populations differing in one way or another from those of the lowlands. Even ambas are not, of course, impregnable, but penetrating them is an uphill task for people and ideas alike. This feature tends to make Ethiopia a kind of palimpsest, in which from time to time the old is overwritten to a greater or lesser extent by the intrusion of the new but nevertheless continues to survive in its mountain fastnesses.

The most ancient intrusion that concerns us took place around the eighth century BC and involved the arrival of settlers from South Arabia. They must have begun by entering the lowlands immediately across the Red Sea from their land of origin, but we first become aware of their presence at the northern end of the highlands. Their arrival is not, however, a process of which we have any direct historical record; we know that it must have happened only because of its aftermath. The intruders brought with them a culture of manifestly South Arabian origin, as is shown not least by the inscriptions associated with it, in a language and script that are alike of South Arabian provenance. The language is a Semitic tongue more or less ancestral to Geʿez, the classical language of Ethiopia, and ultimately to Amharic, its major language today. But although Semitic languages came to be well established in the highlands, the indigenous Cushitic languages did not disappear there, as is attested by the scattered pockets of Agaw speakers in the northern and central highlands at the present day. Moreover, it is enough to eyeball the contemporary population of the highlands, in comparison to that of the Yemen, to conclude that there must have been extensive interbreeding between the new arrivals and the indigenous population. By the first century of our era this hybrid society was also a polity, with a monarchy based in the city of Aksum in the northern highlands.

The next significant intrusion took place over a millennium after the first and involved ideas rather than settlers. This was the Christianization of the kingdom of Aksum in the fourth century. The initiative came from a Syrian, but it is clear that his work was supported by the Aksumite state. From this point on there is considerable continuity in Ethiopian history. Linguistically, Geʿez became and remained the literary language of Ethiopia down to modern times. The Bible was translated into it, and the chronicles that record the history of the country from the fourteenth century onward are written in it. Religiously, the Ethiopian church has maintained a continuous existence down the centuries, free of lasting schism if not of internal conflict. In doctrinal terms it was aligned with the Monophysite churches of Armenia, Syria, and Egypt, and its primary link to the outside world was with the Coptic patriarch of Alexandria, who appointed the head of the Ethiopian church, subject to the permission of the rulers of Egypt. Politically the tradition of the Ethiopian monarchy, if not the monarchy itself, seems to have survived more or less continuously from the first century to the later twentieth. A significant shift was that over the course of Ethiopian history the center of power moved several hundred miles to the south, but even in later centuries kings would sometimes be anointed in Aksum. The whole complex was strongly identified with Christianity. An early sixteenth-century Ethiopian king wrote pointedly to his Portuguese counterpart wishing peace to all the inhabitants of his great cities "that are not Jews or Moors, only to those who are Christians."[28]

There were nevertheless major periods of discontinuity in the history of the country. The first is obscured by a prolonged information blackout. We know remarkably little about what was happening for half a millennium following the rise of Islam, from the seventh century to the twelfth. A significant part of what we don't know about this period doubtless concerned relations with the Muslims of the lowlands to the east. We can assume that over the long term the Islamization of the Red Sea coastlands worked to reduce Ethiopian contacts with the wider world. We also know that Muslims must have had some kind of presence in the highlands in this period, since inscriptions in Arabic have been found there that date from the eleventh and twelfth centuries. Moreover, we can at least suspect that the period was one of massive cultural loss. Although the church survived, with Geʿez as its literary language and the Geʿez translation of the Bible as its fundamental text, any wider Geʿez literature disappeared. The second period of discontinuity came in the sixteenth century, when the Ethiopians in their

28. Quoted in A.H.M. Jones and E. Monroe, *A history of Ethiopia*, Oxford 1955, 81.

highlands were deeply shaken by invasion, first by the Muslims of the eastern lowlands and then by the initially pagan Oromo pastoralists who now dominate much of the southern highlands. We will take up the Muslim invasion but pay less attention to the movements of the Oromo, who were historically known as the Galla. Finally, the third period of discontinuity saw the monarchy effectively collapse in the eighteenth century, not to be revived as a center of real power until 1855. It was in the late eighteenth century that a militant Islamic reformer, the Qādirī Ṣūfī Muḥammad Shāfī (d. 1814–15), was active in Ethiopia. His concerns and methods were reminiscent of those of his contemporaries 'Uthmān ibn Fūdī in Hausaland and Muḥammad ibn 'Abd al-Wahhāb in Arabia, but his activities were on a smaller scale.

The Ethiopian highlands: Muslim-Christian warfare

The background to the Muslim invasion of the early sixteenth century was the emergence of a set of Muslim states, typically small and rather weak, in the eastern lowlands and the southern highlands. Late medieval Egyptian sources list seven such states in this region. The struggle between these states and the much larger Ethiopian kingdom was already under way in the reign of the Ethiopian ruler 'Āmda Ṣeyōn (ruled 1314–44), who in 1329 mounted a campaign against the Muslim state of Īfāt (1285–1415) that is vividly recorded by an eyewitness in a Christian chronicle written in Ge'ez. This state was relatively extensive, stretching from the edge of the plateau to the Gulf of Aden, and the Ethiopian king's objective was not to destroy it but rather to reduce it to the status of a vassal. Indeed, it was common for the Muslim states of the region to be subject to the hegemony of the more powerful Christian monarchy. But in the first half of the sixteenth century the tables were turned by Aḥmad Grāñ—"Left-handed Aḥmad," as the Ethiopians correctly called him. Many of his campaigns are recorded in detail in a Muslim chronicle written in Arabic, likewise the work of an eyewitness. At some point he had seized power in the Muslim state of 'Adal. This state was essentially a continuation of the earlier state of Īfāt, and by 1520 its capital was located in Harar, a Muslim city on the spur jutting out east from the southern highlands. Once in power, Aḥmad Grāñ refused to pay tribute to the Ethiopian monarch, thus precipitating war. He won a major victory in 1529, and in the years that followed he conquered most of the highlands. But in 1543 he was killed in battle and his invasion collapsed. A key element in these dramatic reversals was the role of firearms: Aḥmad Grāñ initially made very effective use of Ottoman musketeers, but Portuguese musketeers—and an impregnable amba—helped turn the tide. It was during this prolonged invasion that Ethiopia came closest to succumbing to Islam. At one point the Muslim chronicler estimated that all but a third or a quarter of the country had been conquered, and this resulted in large-scale if often temporary conversions, forced or otherwise. But an attempt to repeat the conquest in the second half of the century came to nothing, and thereafter there was no significant Muslim challenge to Ethiopia. Christian Ethiopia thus survived in the northern and central highlands, albeit eventually bordering on Muslim populations on most of its periphery. But this survival did not mean an absence of Muslims even in the core territory of Christian Ethiopia. For example, the speakers of a minor Semitic language known as Argobba, a close relative of Amharic, are Muslims living on the eastern edge of the central highlands, and they may have converted under Muslim rule as long ago as the early twelfth century. There is also a small Muslim population, mainly artisans and merchants, scattered throughout the Christian highlands. Another component of the spread of Islam in the highlands was the belated conversion of many of the pagan Oromo. This had its beginnings in the eighteenth century but was mostly a nineteenth-century phenomenon, and even then a very incomplete one. As might be expected from these rather heterogeneous origins, the Islam of Ethiopia, though entirely Sunnī, is varied in terms of law schools: there are Ḥanafīs, Shāfiʿites, and Mālikīs. Within the present borders of the country Muslims make up a third of the population.

All in all, it is unlikely that Ethiopia, situated as it was in a region so close to the cradle of the Muslim world, would have survived as a Christian country but for geography. Indeed, geography came to the rescue in two distinct ways. First and most obviously, the Christian highlands were by nature far more defensible than were the lowlands to the east. Second, despite the obstacles that mountains pose to rulers, the resources for state building were in far more generous supply in the well-watered highlands than they were in the arid lowlands. In the absence of Ibn Khaldūnian state formation it is perhaps this that explains why the Muslims of the lowlands do not appear to have posed a serious threat to the Ethiopian highlands before the first half of the sixteenth century, and why they never did so again. Aḥmad Grāñ himself was very conscious that his war on Ethiopia was a departure from precedent: in the past, he told the Ethiopian ruler, the Muslims had raided and left, but now they planned to conquer and stay. Just why they were able to mount what came so close to a definitive subjugation of Ethiopia in that limited period is a fair question. A significant part of the answer is no doubt to be found in the qualities that made Aḥmad Grāñ so effective as a leader. For example, the Muslim chronicle describes numerous occasions on which he consulted with his commanders, each time soliciting their views and adopting the one he thought best—a powerful combination of openness and decisiveness. In engaging in such consultation he was of course following the example of the Prophet, but he consulted his subordinates far more often than Muḥammad is recorded to have done.

As is evident, conflict between Muslims and Christians is a major theme in the history of Ethiopia. Before we leave the country, it may therefore be worth looking at the two eyewitness chronicles mentioned above for what they tell us of the rhetoric—and beyond that the grim realities—of this conflict.

Naturally the Ge'ez chronicle recording 'Āmda Ṣeyōn's campaign of 1329 is staunchly Christian. Other things being equal, and they usually are, Christians are good and Muslims are bad—"all the Muslim people were rogues."[29] The king and his army lay waste to the lands of the Muslims, destroy their mosques, kill their men in large numbers, at times extending the slaughter to old men, women, and children, and accumulate booty and captives. The religious antagonism thus manifested is backed up with quotations, paraphrases, or evocations of bellicose passages from the Bible: "Two can repel ten thousand!" (cf. Deut. 32:30). Hostility to unbelievers is the overwhelming message of the chronicle, summed up in an apt quotation from another Christian source: "Slay the infidels and renegades with the sword of iron, and draw the sword on behalf of the perfect faith!" And yet there is a significant qualification to be made. The chronicler has at his disposal an alternative to his religious perspective, what one might call a secular conception, in which the enemies of the king are seen as rebels against their lawful sovereign. There is in fact a pervasive ambiguity here: the term the chronicler regularly uses to refer to the Muslims on whom the king makes war could mean either "rebel" or "infidel." Thus the narrative begins with 'Āmda Ṣeyōn hearing that the ruler of the rebels—or infidels—has revolted. Immediately afterward we are told that this ruler was full of arrogance toward his "lord" 'Āmda Ṣeyōn. Here the reference to the lordship of the king goes better with the rendering "rebels." The implication is that there is in principle a legitimate order—legitimate in this world if not in the next—under which Muslim princes rule their Muslim subjects while accepting the rightful overlordship of the Christian king; as the king himself puts it, he is "king of all the Muslims of the land of Ethiopia." So when some Muslim princes belatedly offer to submit to him, he tells them that had they done so in a timely way "there would have been friendship between me and you." As it is, however, he declares to them his intention to continue his attacks until "your land has been made a desert." The chronicler nevertheless gives us a concrete example of what such amicable relationships might look like. Once he has overthrown the rebellious Muslim ruler, the king has a vacuum to fill. We could easily imagine him appointing a Christian governor backed by a substantial military force, but instead he installs the brother of the defeated ruler, thereby showing his respect for dynastic continuity in a Muslim state. Unfortunately for the king, the new ruler, despite his initial professions of loyalty, proves as rebellious as his predecessor. But even that is not the end of the road, for the king proceeds to appoint yet another brother in his place. Such relationships could also be cemented with

29. For this and the quotations that follow see *The glorious victories of 'Āmda Ṣeyon*, trans. G.W.B. Huntingford, Oxford 1965, 59, 67, 69, 92, 101, 102.

marital ties. We have no indication of this in our chronicle, but Queen Helen (d. 1522) is a conspicuous example from a later period. A daughter of the Muslim ruler of the state of Hadiyya in the southern highlands, she was given in marriage to the Ethiopian king, becoming a pious Christian and a promoter of close relations with the Portuguese. Handing over a Muslim girl to an infidel, and worse yet one who would make a Christian of her, was a serious violation of Islamic norms, as Aḥmad Grāñ would insist when he met the ruler of Hadiyya. Yet Helen's preference for staying close to her homeland suggests that despite her conversion she had continuing links to her family.

A mirror image of the Christian chronicler's perspective pervades the Arabic chronicle recording the campaigns of Aḥmad Grāñ—the Imām, as the chronicler refers to him. Here in the normal course of events Muslims are good and Christians are bad, though the chronicler makes a bit of an exception for one leading Christian who was a just man according to the standards of the Christians. The campaigns are similar in style to that of ʿĀmda Ṣeyōn. The Muslim armies lay waste to the countryside, never passing by a village in the land of the infidel without obliterating it. They burn churches, slaughter men, kill monks, take women and children captive, and amass booty, seizing so much of it that they sometimes have a hard time transporting it. Yet alongside the overall similarity there are some noteworthy differences. In the Arabic chronicle the Muslim burning of churches is systematic, whereas Christian demolition of mosques makes only one appearance in the account of the campaign of ʿĀmda Ṣeyōn. And despite the rhetoric of the Christian chronicler—"gold and silver and fine clothes and jewels without number"[30]—one has the impression that the booty seized by the troops of ʿĀmda Ṣeyōn pales in comparison to that accumulated by the Muslim conquerors; but this, of course, may reflect the simple economic reality that the highlands were rich while the lowlands were poor. At the same time, there are no clear references in the Muslim chronicle to the killing of women and children. Instead, they are regularly captured alive and enslaved. Indeed, on one remarkable occasion Christian women are taken prisoner by Muslim women. At a more rhetorical level, where the Christian chronicler appeals to the Bible to articulate his religious militancy, the Muslim chronicler naturally quotes the Qurʾān: "Count not those who are slain in God's way as dead, but rather as living with their Lord, by Him provided, rejoicing in the bounty that God has given them" (Q3:169–70). The banner of the Imām as he describes it is a veritable anthology of appropriate Qurʾānic verses. So just as in the Christian case, religious militancy is the overwhelming message of the chronicle. We read of one heroic horseman who had to be forcibly restrained when he saw infidels; he was like a camel in heat, and his godly anger

30. *The glorious victories of ʿĀmda Ṣeyon*, 60–61.

and passion for jihad in the way of God were so great that his nose would bleed. What is different here is that the Muslim chronicler is able to make repeated references to the formal Muslim duty of jihad, a concept explicitly articulated in the Islamic tradition of which the Christian chronicler—who does not share the Catholic notion of a crusade—lacks an equivalent. Thus a Muslim who has been captured by the Christians cries out "Jihad in the way of God!" and thereby terrifies his Christian captors.[31] In another passage the Imām invokes the doctrine of jihad when he praises God for ennobling the Muslims with Islam and making it lawful for them to plunder the polytheists—the term regularly used by the chronicler to refer to the Christian enemy. It fits well with this that the Muslim chronicler seems not to have an equivalent of the alternative conception of Muslim-Christian relations that is available to his Christian counterpart, where a Muslim ruler rules over Muslims under Christian hegemony—despite the fact that historically many Muslim rulers have had such non-Muslim vassals. What the Muslim chronicler does possess is the familiar Islamic principle that certain kinds of unbelievers—notably Christians and Jews—may be tolerated under Muslim rule provided they pay the requisite poll tax and are humbled. Aḥmad Grāñ naturally brought this principle to his campaigns, but it seems that he also entertained a less formal one. His idea was to create marital ties that would bind the Ethiopian royal family to him. Thus at one point he offered the king peace in return for the hand of an Ethiopian princess, and at another he sought to marry a captive Ethiopian prince, who had presumably converted, to a daughter of his own.

None of this suggests much empathy, let alone sympathy, on either side. But the two sides readily impute to their respective enemies a rhetoric that often mirrors their own. According to the Christian chronicler, the Muslim ruler wanted to conquer the Christians: "I will rule the Christians according to my law, and I will destroy their churches."[32] Or more conservatively, "I will make the Christian churches into mosques for the Muslims," and more ambitiously, "I will convert to my religion the king of the Christians together with his people." In the same vein the chronicler has the rebels at large tell each other: "When the Christians kill us we become martyrs, and when we kill the Christians we gain paradise." On the other side of the fence, the Muslim chronicler describes how a leader of the Christians—the one who is described as just according to their lights—wrote to the Imām: "You are the Muslims and we are the Christians. We used to come to your country, lay it waste and burn it; now God has given you a turn"[33]—but of course this turn will soon be over. The Muslim chronicler likewise tells us that this same leader later upbraided some of his coreligionists for their cowardice in the

31. ʿArab Faqīh, *The conquest of Abyssinia*, trans. P. L. Stenhouse, Hollywood 2003, 21.
32. For this and the quotations that follow, see *The glorious victories of ʿĀmda Ṣeyon*, 54, 55, 69.
33. For this and the quotations that follow see ʿArab Faqīh, *The conquest of Abyssinia*, 169, 182, 207.

face of the enemy: "Are you afraid of death? Your fathers and grandfathers died for their religion!" He then tells them that he himself will die fighting for his faith. Apart from his unfortunate allegiance to the wrong religion, he thinks and acts as a true believer should do, and the chronicler clearly respects him for this. Aḥmad Grāñ himself at one point speaks in this vein, saying to an aristocrat who unlike others declines to convert to Islam: "You are better than those who have converted to Islam, and firmer in faith than they are."

A topic on which the Muslim chronicler is notably silent is the potential relevance of the early history of Muslim relations with the Christians of Ethiopia. As we saw, the Islamic tradition relates that some of the first Muslims took refuge in Ethiopia to escape the persecution to which they were exposed in Mecca. This was a kindness not matched by the Byzantines or the Persians, and it led to the belief that the Ethiopian king who gave the refugees this sanctuary had responded to the call of Islam and died a Muslim. At the same time, the Ethiopians were distinguished from other peoples of early Islamic times in the same manner as the Turks were, for the Prophet was reputed to have told his followers: "Leave the Ethiopians alone as long as they leave you alone."[34] And indeed the Arabs did just that at the time of their conquests. But such abstention did not have to be understood as an expression of gratitude; a later scholar explains that it was because of the forbidding geography of the country that the Muslims were spared the obligation to conquer it. When a Yemeni Zaydī ruler of the mid-seventeenth century wrote to his Ethiopian counterpart, he duly evoked the memory of the king's Muslim predecessor, but not with any warmth. Instead, he used it to admonish the king that it was his duty to respond to the call of Islam just as his predecessor had done.

Nubia

Nubia is the Nile valley south of Egypt. Its northern border is the first cataract, a little upstream from Aswān, but there is no consensus as to where its southern border is to be drawn. Geographically the territory we are concerned with consists of two parts, with the division falling at the confluence of the White and Blue Niles, where the upstart modern city of Khartoum is located. North of that point the Nile is a single river until it reaches the delta, though it receives a final tributary, the Atbara, which like the Blue Nile rises in Ethiopia and contributes to the annual flood. Over this whole northern stretch the Nile makes its way through desert; the river apart, we are in the Sahara. During our period the main urban center in this part of Nubia was Dongola (more precisely Old Dongola), the

34. ʿAbd al-Razzāq ibn Hammām al-Ṣanʿānī, *Muṣannaf*, Beirut 1970–72, 5:136 no. 9177 and note 4.

capital of a medieval Christian kingdom and subsequently a Muslim city. The capitals of the ancient kingdom of Kush, namely Napata and Meroe, were no longer in evidence. The other part of our territory lies to the south of Khartoum. Here the White and Blue Niles have their separate courses, and these rivers apart, we are in the savanna. If we continue yet farther to the south up the White Nile we eventually enter a land of swamps beginning some three hundred miles south of Khartoum, but for now we can ignore it. In the southern part of Nubia there were two main urban centers in our period. One was Sōba, located on the Blue Nile a bit south of Khartoum, and again the capital of a medieval Christian kingdom. The other was Sinnār, likewise on the Blue Nile but some 150 miles farther south, and the capital of a Muslim state that took shape in the early sixteenth century. Overall, Nubia is by no means as flat as Egypt, as is indicated by the fact that between Khartoum and Aswān the placid flow of the Nile is interrupted six times by cataracts that limit navigation. Nor is it as fertile. In parts of Nubia the river has carved out a course so deep that its banks are barren. In the 1170s an Ayyūbid emissary was assigned the task of spying out Nubia with a view to conquering it, and he reported that it was not worth the effort: "a narrow country, with no crops other than millet and with small palm trees."[35] But in contrast to Ethiopia, Nubia is emphatically a lowland territory.

As with the ancient Kush, the main external influences on the Nubia of late antiquity came from or through Egypt. Sixth-century Nubia was divided into three kingdoms, all of which converted to Christianity and used Old Nubian as their literary language, writing it like Coptic in an adapted form of the Greek alphabet. These kingdoms were Nobadia—in Arabic Marīs—in the north, Alodia—ʿAlwa—in the south, and Makuria—Maqurra—between them. But this political division was not written in stone, and Nobadia and Makuria were soon brought together into a single state with its capital at Dongola. In this two-state form Christian Nubia continued to exist for several centuries after the rise of Islam despite significant Muslim penetration of Marīs, not to mention the presence of Muslims farther south. Already in the tenth century Sōba possessed a large Muslim quarter, in part no doubt a commercial diaspora, and in the same period we hear of a vassal of the king of ʿAlwa who ruled over seminomadic pastoralists, was a Muslim, and spoke Arabic. As might be expected, there was also Muslim cultural influence, despite the fact that Nubia already possessed a literate culture: at the beginning of the eleventh century the ruler of Dongola introduced a new, Iraqi style of palace. When we factor in the absence of mountain fastnesses and the geographical continuity of the Nile valley, the prolonged survival of Christian Nubia may surprise us, but it is not inexplicable. Part of the explanation concerns Egypt. Until Saladin

35. See G. Vantini, *Oriental sources concerning Nubia*, Heidelberg 1975, 370.

took over the country in the twelfth century, Egypt tended to lack an army commensurate with its economic resources, and its rulers were in any case likely to be preoccupied with aspirations and challenges on other fronts. Another part of the explanation concerns the Nubians themselves. Muslim historiography of the early Islamic period depicts Nubian infantrymen as phenomenally good archers, and this seems to have acted as a serious deterrent to Muslim expansion to the south. Taken together, these two factors make it easy to understand why after a couple of early raids into Nubia the Arabs in Egypt were ready to settle for a treaty (*baqṭ* or pact), under whose terms they received an annual tribute of 360 slaves and left the Nubians alone. An Arabic document of 758 shows the governor of Egypt complaining about tribute arrears and the shoddy quality of the slaves the Nubians were palming off on him—the one-eyed, the lame, and the like. But such infractions did not lead to military responses. There was also a third factor behind Nubian survival. The quality of life of the settled Nubians of the Nile valley was always affected by the behavior of the desert nomads, particularly those to the east—the extremely arid desert to the west of the Nubian stretch of the Nile was largely uninhabited. But even the Eastern Desert has only sparse vegetation, so the pasture is poor and can support only a small nomadic population. In the early Islamic period, moreover, the nomads of the region were familiar ones, whether we think of them as the Blemmyes of antiquity or the Beja of later times. A sixth-century source describes the nomads of the desert east of Upper Egypt not only as "not subject to the authority of the Roman Empire" but also as receiving "a subsidy on condition that they do not enter or pillage Egypt."[36] No doubt the Nubians reached similar accommodations. Such nomads were a threat, but one the Nubians had lived with for centuries. If these had continued to be the nomads they confronted, there was no obvious reason their uneasy coexistence should not have continued indefinitely. In short, as long as Nubian society was effectively governed by Christian Nubian rulers, mass conversion to Islam was unlikely.

Against this background, it is not hard to see why Nubia fell apart half a millennium later. The coming of Turkic military power under the Zangids, the Ayyūbids, and above all the Mamlūks meant that Egypt now had an army to match its economy, and the Turks may have been less vulnerable to the archery of the Nubian infantry than the Arabs had been. So invading Nubia was not a formidable task for a Turkic cavalry army, and when the Mamlūks began doing so in earnest in the second half of the thirteenth century, they met with no effective resistance. In 1276 they took advantage of a succession dispute to invade the country, defeating the army of the incumbent king and putting another member of the royal family on the throne on terms advantageous to themselves; this time we

36. Vantini, *Oriental sources concerning Nubia*, 8.

hear nothing of Nubian archery. In 1316 the Mamlūks for the first time installed as king a member of the royal family who was a Muslim, and the year after that the cathedral of Dongola became a mosque. Just when the northern Nubian kingdom finally came to an end is not clear, but it does not seem to have survived the fifteenth century. Its disappearance did not in itself entail the extinction of Nubian Christianity—in Egypt, after all, Christianity has survived a millennium and a half of Muslim rule. But in Nubia the impact of another factor is likely to have been crucial: the Arab nomads.

As we will see in the next chapter, Arab nomads showed a capacity to displace or assimilate non-Arabs over large parts of northern Africa. The northern Nubian kingdom is an example. The collapse of Nubian military power in the face of the Mamlūk challenge opened the way for the Arab tribes to overrun the country, and this they did very effectively. Not that this was the intention of the Mamlūks, who had no love for the Arab tribes and would have preferred to keep them out of Nubia. When they placed a puppet ruler on the Nubian throne in 1276, they made him swear not to allow any Arab nomads to enter the kingdom. Ibn Khaldūn characteristically comments on the rapine and disorder with which the nomads filled the land, leaving no vestige of central authority. He also identifies an interesting mechanism that led to the subversion of the Nubian kingdom at the hands of the Arabs. Seeking to co-opt them, the Nubian kings would offer them their daughters in marriage, and the Muslim sons of these marriages would then succeed to the throne by virtue of Nubian matrilineal inheritance. More generally, a factor that weakens matrilineal polities is their tendency to diffuse power rather than concentrate it. In ethnic terms the Nubians survived as a people in the northern part of the country, where Nubian is spoken to this day. Farther south most of the Nubian population was assimilated by the Arab nomads, resulting in a Muslim population known as the Jaʿalīs, who claim Arab ancestry and now speak Arabic. This, of course, is geographically counterintuitive: we would have expected the Arab impact to be stronger in the north and to fade out as we go south. But for whatever reason, Nubian ethnic identity survived only in the north. Meanwhile, Nubian Christianity vanished altogether from what had been the northern kingdom, along with Nubian political independence.

Yet farther south, in what had been the kingdom of ʿAlwa, the story was somewhat different. Here, too, Christianity disappeared, though it was still in evidence in the 1520s, at a time when the kingdom had already come to an end. What was striking was the extent of the Arabization of the region, a process that extended well to the south of Khartoum. This again seems counterintuitive in comparison to what happened in northern Nubia. One would have expected a two-dimensional savanna population to be less vulnerable to ethnic change than a one-dimensional riverain population was. That this was not so suggests that the Arab nomads had adapted well to the conditions of the savanna, leaving the aridity of their ancestral desert behind them. Yet non-Arabs long retained a robust grip on political power in this southern region. The prime example is the Funj kingdom,[37] which was centered on Sinnār and lay to the south of the domain of the ʿAbdallāb dynasty, an Arab lineage with which the Funj developed a curious relationship of competition and symbiosis. In good times, moreover, the rule of the Funj expanded northward to include Maqurra and westward into Kordofān. The first attestation of their kingdom in a contemporary source dates from 1523. It appears to have been established by cattle nomads from farther up the Blue Nile. The dynasty seems to have converted to Islam at an early stage; a ruler who held power in the mid-sixteenth century already bore the Muslim name ʿAbd al-Qādir. Yet the Funj long retained some conspicuously pagan customs, such as the idea that the king's subjects should not see him eat—a notion with a Nubian precedent that we likewise encounter in Dār Fūr and Mālī. There are also indications of matrilineal kinship in the background. Yet it was predictable that the dynasty would come under the influence of the Muslim culture that prevailed to the north, and in this vein we find it adopting an Arab genealogy that boasted of descent from the Umayyads. The Ottoman traveler Evliyā Chelebī, who was in Sinnār in 1672–73, gave a mixed report of the kingdom. On the one hand, he noted the lack of a coinage and was struck by the absence of stone buildings of the kind one would see elsewhere—no stone hostelry, no bathhouse, no covered market, no soup kitchen feeding the poor, no fountains, no school. On the other hand, the king had a small arsenal, a depository for gunpowder, and fifty cannons, and he could hand out gifts of Indian and Chinese goods. By the eighteenth century the rulers were coming under increased pressure to observe Islamic norms, and some of them did. A king killed in 1769 is described by the chronicler of the dynasty as "a lover of books, a man of religion, and a calligrapher"[38] who died with a Qurʾān at his right hand and a foundational text of Mālikī law at his left. But irrespective of the shifting balance of pagan and Muslim traditions, the Funj state was never a highly centralized one. Particularly in the north, it tended to look more like a loose collection of subkingdoms than like a unified polity, and some of its components might break away altogether. Starting in 1762 the Funj experienced a time of troubles that continued until the Egyptian conquest of 1821, when the dynasty was pensioned off. From the late 1780s on the kings had been of such little consequence that, as the chronicler of the dynasty remarks, "no list of them was kept."[39] Nevertheless it is only for the twilight decades of the dynasty that his chronicle offers anything approaching a detailed record of its history.

37. For this kingdom see O'Fahey and Spaulding, *Kingdoms of the Sudan*.

38. P. M. Holt, *The Sudan of the three Niles*, Leiden 1999, 20 (the book is a translation of the Funj chronicle).

39. Holt, *The Sudan of the three Niles*, 31.

South of the savanna

We are now ready to make our last move south. If we leave aside the anomalies of the eastern side of the continent, the overall map of the African climate is dominated by bands that are roughly symmetrical about the equator. In the north we have the Mediterranean coast, followed by the desert, the savanna, and the rain forest; in the south we have the continuation of the rain forest, followed by a southern savanna, a southern desert, and finally a Mediterranean climatic zone around the Cape of Good Hope. Of these, the bands to the south of the forest are of no concern to us in this chapter. In other words, it would seem that the rain forest acted as a barrier to the overland spread of Islam into southern Africa, and in the absence of a Muslim maritime scene on the west coast this barrier could not be circumvented. Farther to the east, but still well short of the coast, the forest ended. But here two further barriers took its place: the marshes of the upper White Nile, and the Ethiopian highlands. These, too, posed obstacles to the overland spread of Islam. That left the east coast. There, as we saw, Islam reached much farther to the south; but except in the case of the Somali lowlands, it barely penetrated inland. The result was that Islam did not reach the southern interior. A more intricate question, and one we will try to answer here, is the degree to which Islam established a limited presence within the barrier zones themselves. Let us take them from east to west.

In Ethiopia we have already seen that Islam had only a limited impact on the Christian highlands of the north and center. At this point, however, our focus is on the highlands of the south, where Muslims were more likely to encounter pagans than Christians. We have already taken note of one Muslim state in this region in late medieval times, namely Hadiyya, the homeland of Queen Helen. There were several others. This early process of Islamization must have been seriously disrupted when the region was overrun by the pagan Oromo in the sixteenth century, but as we have seen some of the Oromo themselves began to convert to Islam toward the end of our period. The net result as of the middle of the twentieth century was to turn the southern highlands into a patchwork of religions, combining the presence of Muslims and Christians with a massive persistence of paganism. The Muslim presence, significant though it was, did not suffice to carry Islam farther south into northern Kenya.

West of the Ethiopian highlands lie the marshes that impede travel around the upper course of the White Nile and its tributaries. This swamp is known as the Sudd, an Arabic term (*sadd*) that appropriately means a barrier. Its role in impeding the spread of Islam may have been reinforced by a human factor. Among the cattle nomads of the region the largest people today are the Dinka, and in the course of the nineteenth and twentieth centuries this people, for whatever reason, displayed a remarkable imperviousness to Islam. We lack the evidence to trace this disposition back into our period. The Funj chronicle records hostilities with a related people, the Shilluk of the upper White Nile, in the later seventeenth century, but it is not till the nineteenth century that the Dinka begin to figure in the chronicle. Nor are we told who were the victims of the annual Funj slave hunt that is attested around 1800, though the Dinka could well have been among them. It is only over the course of the nineteenth century that the history of the Dinka and related peoples comes into focus. The absence of a Dinka Muslim community at that time and their strong resistance to Islam are good indications that there had been no significant Dinka conversion in our period.

We come now to the rain forest, the most extensive of the three barriers that we could expect to impede the southward expansion of Islam. As we move south through the savanna there is a gradual transition from dwarf shrubs to low trees to tall trees, the latter characteristic of what is known as the "savanna woodland," but the boundary between the savanna woodland and the rain forest itself is usually a sharp one. This forest was undoubtedly much more extensive in the past than it is today. A good part of the savanna woodland immediately to the north of it appears to be former forest degraded by human activity, not by changing climate, though what exactly this means for our period is hard to say. In any case we can conveniently divide the forest into two parts. In central Africa it extends over both sides of the equator, whereas in West Africa its southern boundary is the coast. The width of the central African forest would undoubtedly have impeded any spread of Islam to the southern savanna. The West African forest was less formidable. But did Islam penetrate the forest at all? Here we are not much helped by our sources. We are dealing with an area that is largely beyond the horizon of premodern Muslim writers, and written sources of any kind barely penetrate the rain forest before the nineteenth century.

In the central African sector, the primary link between the states of the northern savanna and the peoples to the south was the slave trade. Here a familiar provision of Islamic law is likely to have had some historical impact. As already mentioned, once a population had converted to Islam, its members could no longer be enslaved in good faith. This certainly did not guarantee their freedom, bad faith being endemic in human affairs. But the most famous scholar of Timbuktu, the Berber Aḥmad Bābā (d. 1627), felt the need to take a strong stand against the enslavement of free black Muslims. Being enslaved, as he observed, was a demoralizing experience: "The mere fact of being owned generally breaks people's hearts because of the dominance and subordination associated with this condition, especially when one is far from home."[40] He cites the example of one Hausa city raiding another, despite their common language and way of life—an interesting

40. Aḥmad Bābā, *Miʿrāj al-ṣuʿūd*, trans. J. Hunwick and F. Harrak, Rabat 2000, 35.

indication that alongside the formal religious prohibition of enslaving Muslims there was also an informal sense that members of the same ethnic group should not be doing it to each other. All in all, such violation of the law, together with protests like Aḥmad Bābā's, seems to have generated enough embarrassment to make a difference, and at the same time the rulers of well-ordered states do not usually kidnap their own subjects to export them as slaves. Hence the tendency was for the raiding grounds that fed the trade to move southward, to regions where non-Muslim populations still abounded. The states of the settled lands of the eastern savanna accordingly had in common a concept of pagan peoples of the south whom it was appropriate to enslave, though in each case the term they used was different. In Dār Fūr, for example, these southern pagans were known as the Fartīt. Whether the net effect on such populations of being raided for slaves was likely to favor the spread of Islam is hard to say. What is clear is that the southern savanna in our period did not see the emergence a second tier of Muslim or Muslim-influenced states on the fringes of the forest, let alone inside it. Instead the region remained pagan into the nineteenth century. Only early in that century did a Muslim state appear in Adamawa, in what is now northern Cameroon, well to the north of the forest; and it resulted not from indigenous state formation but rather from a Fulānī conquest of previously pagan and stateless tribes. It was in fact an extension of ʿUthmān ibn Fūdī's jihad. Against this background we can take it that no spread of Islam into the forest itself took place in our period.

The West African sector is less straightforward. As late as the early eighteenth century a pagan Bambara kingdom was present on the middle Niger in the region of Segu, only a bit over a hundred miles to the west of the long-established Muslim city of Jenne. It was not till 1861 that a Muslim conquest of this predatory state brought Islam to the region as more than the religion of a mercantile diaspora. Turning to the south, as far as the early centuries are concerned the external Arabic sources are well aware of the existence of peoples living beyond the states of the northern savanna, but their information about them is slight. This is not just because they were farther away. A significant factor here is that the trade across the Sahara and the trade farther south seem to have been in different hands. Just as West African merchants rarely crossed the Sahara, North African merchants do not seem to have traveled south of the savanna. We know from Bakrī that there was already an indigenous kin group of merchants active in the south in the eleventh century. When the picture comes into focus in later medieval times, the routes to the south are dominated by a particular West African Muslim ethnic group, the Wangara. Another factor was the gold trade. Although the external sources were intensely curious about it, they knew almost nothing of the location of the goldfields. There is reason to believe that this was not accidental, and that those involved made a point of denying the information to outsiders. Thus a Portuguese account of the early sixteenth century states that only the Wangara were allowed to travel to the gold mines. Our sources are consequently unaware of the existence of the major goldfields of the Akan forest to the west of the Volta River. In short, they have little to report of the peoples of the south bar rumors of cannibalism.

The result is that until European seafarers began to appear on the West African coast in the mid-fifteenth century, much of the testimony we do have derives from indigenous oral traditions—a tricky source to use. These point to the emergence of states well to the south of the Niger Bend around the fourteenth or fifteenth century. These states, notably Dagomba and Mamprussi in the north of what is now Ghana, had close relations with Wangara merchants. As a result they came under Muslim influence, and the outcome was a phenomenon reminiscent of eleventh-century Ghāna: pagan states whose rulers regarded Muslims as useful people to have at hand. This pattern seems to have been established in Dagomba early in the eighteenth century, but as it happens our first hard evidence comes from Kumasi, the capital of the kings of Ashanti who ruled in the forested south of modern Ghana from the seventeenth to the nineteenth century. We owe this evidence to the testimony of two British envoys who visited the city in the early nineteenth century, one in 1817 and the other in 1820. The second described the reigning king as "somewhat religiously inclined towards the followers of Mohammed, from a reverential awe of the universal God," but he went on to add that this ruler chose "to adhere faithfully to his pagan rites in all their manifold horrors and enormities," while noting that he "does not neglect to supplicate the Muslims for their prayers, particularly when oppressed with anxiety."[41] The Muslims felt the same way about the horrors and enormities, but part of the price they had to pay for their influence at court was attendance at these rituals, including human sacrifice. In addition to their spiritual powers, their literacy made them useful as bureaucrats. This scene was a fairly recent one in Kumasi. According to what the Muslims told the British envoy in 1820, they owed their position at court to the benevolence of a king who had ruled in the last quarter of the eighteenth century. This king was reported to have taken his liking for Muslims a bit too far, becoming "a believer at heart"[42] and eventually being deposed for his attachment to them. The immediate result was a reaction against the Muslims, some of whom were executed. But the pattern of pagan rulers patronizing useful Muslims soon stabilized, and it lasted until the British took over Ashanti around 1900. Islam nevertheless remained marginal in Ashanti, as it did in the Akan forest in general. Farther north the pattern does not come into focus until later, and there are local variations, but the general character of the relationship between Muslims and rulers is similar. For example, the ruler of the Mossi state of Wagadugu to the north

41. Quoted in N. Levtzion, *Muslims and chiefs in West Africa*, Oxford 1968, 187.
42. Quoted in Levtzion, *Muslims and chiefs in West Africa*, 186.

of Dagomba was expected to fast in the Muslim holy month of Ramaḍān, though it is also said that he would hire someone else to do it for him; or the ruler himself would pretend to fast, and the Muslims would pretend to be taken in. Southwest of Dagomba, in the state of Gonja, Muslims were sometimes referred to as "wives of the chief,"[43] highlighting the intimate dependence of the relationship. There would be some converts in these states, mostly among the chiefly lineages, but no mass conversion among their subjects.

There were also large territories to the east and west of these states where variant patterns prevailed. To the east let us take the Yoruba of what is now southwestern Nigeria. We already have evidence of the presence of Islamic scholars among them in the later seventeenth century, and in the later eighteenth century Islam had reached the coast at Lagos. It is said that in 1780 the ruler of Lagos was deposed for allowing Islam to be practiced at his court, and by the end of the century this controversial religion had become a major factor in the violent politics of the Yoruba. Large-scale conversion was nevertheless still in the future.

To the west we encounter a long stretch of coast, today divided between the Ivory Coast, Liberia, Sierra Leone, and Guinea. Here the closest approach of Islam to the Atlantic shore in 1600 was nowhere much less than two hundred miles. In 1850 the situation was unchanged for the eastern part of this coastline, but starting from the far northwest of Liberia Islam was now a significant influence on or near the coast, playing a part in the lives of such peoples as the Vai on the border between Liberia and Sierra Leone and the Susu of southwestern Guinea. Ironically, the key to this spread was the presence of European traders. Where they established footholds on the coast, their settlements would act as magnets attracting Muslim merchants from the interior, and the presence of these merchants would in due course lead to the spread Islam among the local population. Naturally, due course might be a long time. A traveler on the coast of Sierra Leone in the 1720s remarked on the missionary zeal of the Mandinka but added that the natives "believe themselves to have enough of one religion without burdening themselves with yet another."[44] Thus the Vai, who hosted Muslim Mandinka traders closely related to the Wangara merchants whom we met above, were still described as non-Muslim in the early eighteenth century, though the presence of Muslims, presumably Vai, is attested later in that century. Farther to the northwest the Susu were exposed to an eighteenth-century Mandinka settlement that took the form of a petty kingdom. At the end of the eighteenth century a man claiming to be the Mahdī—the Islamic redeemer who is to appear toward the end of time—appeared among the Susu and Mandinka and ruled over them for three years until

43. See Levtzion, *Muslims and chiefs in West Africa*, 58.

44. Quoted in J. F. Hopewell, "Muslim penetration into French Guinea, Sierra Leone, and Liberia before 1850," Columbia University PhD 1958, 106.

killed by a Susu chief. This suggests that a significant fraction of the Susu had already converted, and an observer in 1803 noted that the Mandinka had spread their religion among the Susu with much success. Christianity did, of course, compete with Islam in this region. An eighteenth-century king in northern Sierra Leone had his three sons look into the three religions on offer—Catholicism, Protestantism, and Islam—but himself died clutching a large pagan fetish. Jihad, by contrast, did not pay good dividends in this part of Africa. The Dialonke of Fūta Jalon—closely related to the Susu—had been allies of the Fulānī, but at one point they were attacked by them. Before this falling out they had dressed as Muslims, but thereafter, we are told, it was "the fashion to appear as different to their enemies as possible, in dress as well as religion."[45] Their king was in fact a Muslim, but he kept his faith to himself and prayed only in the strictest privacy. Even today the old contrast between the two stretches of coast still shows through: in the Ivory Coast and Liberia Muslims are a minority of the population, whereas in Sierra Leone and Guinea they are a majority.

The spread of Islam in Africa

At this point we can pause to review the overall picture of the spread of Islam in Africa. What, if anything, should surprise us about the ground we have covered in this chapter? Historians are not in the high-risk business of predicting the future, but it does no harm to engage in a mild analog of this, looking back on the past to see where our narrative flows easily and where it enters the rapids and maybe even capsizes. No major cataracts call for our attention in the account we gave of the spread of Islam in the three major climatic bands: the Sahara, the savanna, and the rain forest. Given that sooner or later the peoples of the Sahara were likely to adopt the elements of what used to be called a higher religion from the lands to the north if they did not invent one for themselves, it makes sense for reasons we have noted that it should have been Islam rather than Christianity. The spread of Islam in the savanna likewise seems fairly straightforward. We have here a classic case of iron-age peoples with elites and states, both of which had obvious uses for a religion associated with the skills of literacy; Islam was effectively the first such package that history had offered them. That does not, of course, explain why in such contexts Islam could spread beyond the ruler and elite to the mass of the population. But the old Arabic adage that "people follow the religion of their rulers"[46] counts for something in the savanna. So, too, does the ability of a religion such as Islam to make sense of the wider horizons that accompanied the opening up of the Sahara. The only puzzle, if it is one, is the fact that Christianity did not

45. Quoted in Hopewell, "Muslim penetration", 74–75.
46. See, for example, *Ghazālī's book of counsel for kings*, trans. F. R. C. Bagley, London 1964, 62.

spread into the eastern savanna from southern Nubia prior to the arrival of Islam. As for the rain forest, given the difficulty of penetrating it and the limited rewards of doing so, it was to be expected that even at the end of our period the Muslim presence there would be sporadic and that there would be no spread yet farther to the south—except, of course, in the East African sector of the Indian Ocean rim.

Turning to the geographically very different environments of the eastern interior, there is nothing very mysterious about the Ethiopian case. Ethiopia already possessed a Christian cultural and religious package, and it was geographically well endowed to resist Muslim conquest. So it need not surprise us that despite the crisis of the first half of the sixteenth century, it held out. The complication here is that while Ethiopia could resist invasion by the armies of Muslim states and was not in danger of being overrun by lowland nomads such as the Beja, the Arabs, or the Somalis, its Achilles' heel was its vulnerability to highland nomads, in other words the Oromo. Turning to Nubia, there is nothing very puzzling about the trajectory of the northern kingdom. As with the Sasanian Empire and the southern provinces of the Byzantine Empire, the Muslims conquered it and sooner or later conversion followed. The difference was that in northern Nubia the Muslim conquest came several centuries later, and again we have seen some reasons for this. The territory of the southern Nubian kingdom, by contrast, did not experience a northern conquest until Meḥmed ʿAlī Pasha's invasion of 1821. This was centuries after the Nubian kingdom itself had disappeared, overrun by Arab tribes. We have here a good example of what Arab tribes can do—a theme we will return to in the next chapter.

Another question we might ask is how the Sahara and the Indian Ocean compare as barriers. In the African interior west of the Ethiopian highlands, just as around the Indian Ocean outside the heartlands, Islam was filtered through a barrier that was almost impermeable to military force, but not to merchants. In the case of the African interior, however, the success of Islam was much greater. The Somalis and some of the islanders of maritime Southeast Asia apart, mercantile contacts around the rim of the Indian Ocean gave rise only to a discontinuous Muslim coastal ribbon. In the African interior, by contrast, conversion extended over much larger areas, encompassing most of the Sahara and the northern savanna. Only well to the south did Islamization assume a spotty character reminiscent of the coastlands of the Indian Ocean. One obvious reason for this contrast lies at the intersection of politics and culture. The Indian Ocean rim, as we saw, lacked states in need of literate culture: either there were no states or the states had it already. By contrast, the savanna west of southern Nubia was characterized by states sufficiently developed to appreciate the uses of literacy but not yet blessed with it at the time when they first encountered Islam. More broadly, literacy was just one aspect of the novel cultural trappings that the savanna states and their elites imported from the north with the growth of trans-Saharan trade in these centuries, along with Ṣūfism, warhorses, Turkic slaves, firearms, and other necessities of civilized life as practiced in the core regions of the Muslim world. But even with all this, conversion was not a foregone conclusion. In Africa as elsewhere, loyalty to one's forebears mattered, and breaking with them was politically risky—as King Ethelbert of Kent had well understood. When the Songhay ruler Askiyā Muḥammad sent to the ruler of the Mossi inviting him to accept Islam, the ruler replied that he would have to consult his ancestors. He did so, and their response was negative.

The relationship between the savanna states and the Muslim heartlands was, of course, asymmetric. The African interior imported numerous items of high culture from the north but did not export any to the north in return. The early sixteenth-century visitor to Timbuktu whom we met above reported that no trade was more profitable there than the importation of books from North Africa, but there is no sign of a return trade in books written or copied in the savanna. And despite the considerable development of Islamic scholarship in the region, with the obvious exception of Aḥmad Bābā few of its scholars were read in the heartlands of the Muslim world. A Fulānī scholar of the occult sciences from Katsina, in what is now northern Nigeria, could move to Egypt in the eighteenth century and be well received there by a scholar of Ethiopian descent. Another eighteenth-century Fulānī, this one from Fūta Jalon, seems to have been a successful teacher in Medina and wrote a reformist tract that won him readers and admiration as far away as India. But no migrant from the Sahara or the savanna became a celebrity in the manner of the Indian Murtaḍā al-Zabīdī. The other side of the coin was that the mercantile filter gave African Muslims a degree of license in picking and choosing their imports that would have been much more elusive if Islam had arrived by conquest. We have seen the populations of West Africa exercising this license in early Ghāna and Mālī, and much later in the states below the Niger Bend as far south as Ashanti. Despite the presence of learned Islamic scholars such as those of sixteenth-century Timbuktu, it could well be that these examples are more broadly typical of Islam in sub-Saharan Africa from its beginnings until the religious landscape was transformed by the unleashing of the Fulānī jihads around the end of our period.

Race in the African context

In this chapter I have hitherto made little explicit use of the category of race, but implicitly it has been there all along. Of all the frontier regions of the Muslim world, Africa was the one where the genetic differentiation of human populations was most obvious to the naked eye. Even today, peoples to the north of the Sahara are predominantly light-skinned, whereas those to the south of it are predominantly dark-skinned. The sheer visibility of this difference of pigmentation made it very unlikely that human societies would ignore it. If we go back to a time before the rise of Islam when trans-Saharan contacts—and consequently gene flow—must have been relatively rare, the picture was no doubt sharper than it is today: overwhelmingly light-skinned people north of the desert, overwhelmingly dark-skinned ones to the south, with a coexistence of lighter-skinned camel nomads and darker-skinned oasis dwellers in the Sahara itself. In Islamic times interactions across the Sahara increased dramatically, bringing light-skinned and dark-skinned people together, with the inevitable result that sooner or later they mated, producing offspring with a pigmentation somewhere in between. This outcome is most obvious in the north, where over the centuries the slave trade meant a significant influx of dark-skinned people, especially women, into a region whose native population was light-skinned. But there was an analogous situation in the south, even in the absence of a significant reverse slave trade—blacks, it was said, preferred their own women. There were light-skinned Saharan camel nomads, Berber and Arab, pressing south from the desert, and at the same time originally light-skinned cattle nomads were spreading through the savanna, the Fulānī from the west and the Arabs from the east. None of this is likely to have been enough to bring about a major shift in the gene pool of the savanna population at large, but it made for a continuum of skin colors ranging from light to dark within the same societies, both in the Sahara and on either side of it. What, then, would these societies make of this continuum?

An obvious thing for them to do was to develop ways of describing shades of skin color. For example, the Arabic dialect of the Moors distinguishes yellow, red, green, and jet black. An anecdote from a seventeenth-century chronicle from Timbuktu reveals a similar concern with precise description. A holy man had come to Timbuktu to visit the tomb of someone who had appeared to him in a dream, and in conversation with the local scholars he was asked about the skin color of this mysterious figure. Addressing himself to a distinguished scholar of Wangara origin, he responded, "You are darker than him." Then, turning to another scholar, who seems to have belonged to the Berber or Arab population of the city, he said, "You are lighter than him." At this point he was able make a match, pointing to third scholar who was of Berber origin: "His color was like the color of this man."[47] So far, all we see here is ways of describing gradations of skin color—the saint was simply looking for a practical way to convey the complexion of the man he had seen in his dream. But humans being what they are, a way of describing skin color readily becomes a way of evaluating it, and it can thus provide the underpinning of a social hierarchy. One way to realize this potential is to link gradations in social status to gradations in skin color by tying them to the balance of light-skinned and

47. Translated in Hunwick, *Timbuktu and the Songhay empire*, 266–67.

dark-skinned ancestors in a person's background. Such a system, or the idea of it, is attested in the colonial New World and has been called graded pigmentocracy. As an eighteenth-century author put it with regard to the parts of the Americas that fell under Spanish rule, "a Quateron will hardly keep company with a Mulatto; and a Mestize values himself very highly in comparison with a Sambo"[48]—each of these terms representing a different mixture of black and white ancestry.

In the part of the world we are concerned with there would have been two problems with this schema. First, although the influx of slaves from south of the Sahara undoubtedly led to some darkening of average skin color at the bottom of society, it could have the same effect at the top thanks to the disproportionate prevalence of concubinage among the elite, royalty included. This meant that a ruler in a dynasty that made liberal use of black concubines could well be darker in complexion than many of his subjects were. The Fāṭimid caliph al-Mustanṣir (ruled 1036–94) had a black mother, as did the ʿAbbāsid caliph al-Muqtafī (ruled 1136–60) and the Moroccan Mawlāy Ismāʿīl (ruled 1672–1727). Likewise, several of the imams of the Imāmī Shīʿites are reported to have had Nubian mothers or to have been very dark-skinned. Any system of social stratification that closely followed gradations of skin color would thus have verged on subversion. Second, such a system would have been a bad fit with Arab genealogy as it developed after the rise of Islam. In this genealogical culture, mothers came to matter less and fathers more in determining the social identity of the child: "The mothers of men," it was said, "are but vessels."[49] It was by virtue of having a father who was caliph that al-Mustanṣir was eligible for the caliphate. Similarly, when Arab tribes moved into Nubia and male tribesmen mated with Nubian females, their darker-skinned offspring could nevertheless claim Arab descent thanks to their patrilineal genealogy. (Analogous disparities could doubtless arise within matrilineal societies.) Perhaps the most extreme case is that of the Baqqāra Arabs of the far south, who in terms of skin color could hardly be darker but who still identify strongly as Arabs.

What, other than egalitarianism, could be an alternative to a system of graded pigmentocracy? If we go back to the dialect of the Moors, we find that alongside the vocabulary for describing gradations of skin color we also have a simple binary schema based on two terms that it will be appropriate to capitalize here since they make something like a distinction between castes: Whites (*bīḍān*) and Blacks (*sūdān*). The Moors are the Whites. These terms tell us about a person's social status, but despite their literal sense they may well fail to correlate with skin color, since a White by patrilineal descent may have many Black ancestors. If we go back to our seventeenth-century chronicle we find the same binary usage. By way of background, Timbuktu entered the fifteenth century under the control of Mālī,

48. E. Long, *The history of Jamaica*, London 1774, 2:261.
49. Quoted in I. Goldziher, *Muslim studies*, London 1967–71, 1:118.

so it was then under the rule of Blacks; but in the 1430s it was taken over by Berbers whom the chronicler refers to as Tuareg, thus passing under the rule of Whites. Speaking of those who held the office of prayer leader in the great mosque of the city, the chronicler tells us that at first, under the rule of Mālī, all the prayer leaders were Blacks, but under Tuareg rule the last of the Blacks was succeeded by the first White to hold the office. We can assume that the Black prayer leaders were indeed dark-skinned, but what about the White? Very likely he was light-skinned, but the only indication here is that our author tells us that he had come to Timbuktu from Fez.

As we have seen, visible differentiation between human populations, however construed, is an invitation to hierarchical thinking. As an eighth-century Shīʿite polemist—one whose views on the superiority of Arabic we encountered earlier—boldly remarks, "When anything God has created is varied, there will be distinctions of merit." He then gives the example of the recognized superiority of the Persian to the Zanjī "by virtue of descent and color."[50] So Whites and Blacks were not equal, and it was better to be White than Black. Here, of course, we are seeing things through the eyes of the Whites, and there is no lack of evidence that they regarded themselves as not just different from Blacks but also better. Not that White attitudes were uniform. They could be sympathetic, as in the case of Masʿūdī's reporting on the Zanj, or mixed, as in the case of Ibn Baṭṭūṭa, or derogatory, as with the genetic and environmental theories of blackness. Ibn Baṭṭūṭa, as we have seen, combines a generally dim view of Blacks with a willingness to recognize exceptions; this is perhaps the default human attitude to aliens. White superiority is likewise assumed as background when Ibn Ḥazm states that since all Muslims are brothers, "a son born to a Zanjī prostitute is not forbidden to marry the daughter of the Hāshimite caliph."[51] He chooses this particular example because the gap between the potential mates couldn't get any worse. Altogether, we can take a sense of White superiority for granted among Whites in the regions of the Sahara and the north where Whites had Blacks as slaves.

But how did Blacks see it? We have very little evidence to go on, since in our period it was Whites who wrote almost all of the sources. Sub-Saharan Africans who came into contact with Whites must have been aware that many of them looked down on Blacks. The Fulānī scholar from Katsina who spent time in Egypt also traveled to the Ḥijāz, where his experience was that the inhabitants did not like anyone, and especially not people from the land of the Blacks, though he did encounter an exception. His experience could have been fairly typical on both counts. He also attacked the environmental theory of blackness and associated deficiencies. But as a Fulānī he may not have considered himself Black, and indeed

50. Zayd ibn ʿAlī, *Ṣafwa*, Baghdad 1967, 23.
51. Ibn Ḥazm, *Muḥallā*, Beirut n.d., 10:24.

at one point in his argument he notes that the Fulānī complexion is brown. How, then, might Black slaves living in White households north of the Sahara have seen things in a society where Whites were politically and socially dominant? As we saw Aḥmad Bābā point out, being enslaved is a demoralizing trauma exacerbated by homesickness, and the brutal journey across the Sahara can only have reinforced the effect on those who survived it. On the other hand, nineteenth-century European testimony suggests that once slaves had been marketed to consumers in Morocco, their experiences were often relatively benign—this was not the kind of slavery that led to the massive rebellion of the Zanj in ninth-century Iraq. But what the net effect of these experiences would have been on their attitudes to race we cannot say. We are no better informed about the Black populations of the savanna, where despite some extension of nomad power from the desert and the eventual Moroccan invasion, the normal state of affairs was the political dominance of Blacks. There could well have been a sense among the Blacks that the Whites brought with them better goods and a better religion. But did Blacks under Black rule really think that the Whites themselves were better? It seems unlikely—it goes against the grain of human nature. Here we have at least the testimony of Ibn Baṭṭūṭa describing his arrival in Walāta, where he had his first exposure to the Blacks of the savanna in the shape of an arrogant and ill-mannered deputy of the sultan of Mali. This official, he tells us, spoke to the assembled merchants through an interpreter to show his disrespect for them. At this point Ibn Baṭṭūṭa was moved to regret his journey "because of their ill manners and their contempt for White men."[52] So Ibn Baṭṭūṭa was convinced that the Blacks of Mālī looked down on the Whites who came to their country. But as so often happens there was an exception: as we have seen, he reports that the former ruler Mansā Mūsā had liked Whites and treated them well.

More fancifully, Ibn Baṭṭūṭa tells a story about a White who was banished to the land of the cannibals and spent four years among them without being eaten. This happy outcome, he tells us, arose directly from his skin color, but it was not an expression of respect on the part of the cannibals. On the contrary, the omission arose from their belief that a white man would be inedible because he wasn't yet ripe—perhaps a plausible theory in the circumstances, but one that works better for eggplants than for humans. If there is any truth in the story, the White in question was singularly lucky in the antiwhite prejudice to which he was exposed. But the idea that light skin color results from a failure to ripen could reflect a genuine belief. As we have seen, Tūnisī describes an encounter with it in the Jabal Marra of Dār Fūr. So does Evliyā Chelebī in the context of his excursion up the Blue Nile. After setting eyes on Evliyā and his entourage, he tells us, the brother

52. Levtzion and Hopkins, *Corpus of early Arabic sources*, 284.

of the Funj ruler exclaimed to those around him, "Have you ever seen uncooked men like these?"[53] One possibility he entertained was that some malefactor had flayed the skin off the faces of his visitors, in which case he stood ready to punish whoever had done this foul deed. But someone who had visited Egypt patiently explained to him that people farther north remain raw because the sun is not so hot there. Do we have here expressions of an indigenous theory of skin color, or just an idea imputed to blacks by whites?

53. See R. Dankoff and others, *Ottoman explorations of the Nile*, London 2018, 276.

14

The Arabs

This chapter is mostly about the history of the Arabs from the eleventh to the eighteenth century. But by this time just who were the Arabs? We will work with two understandings of the term, both of which appear in our sources. First, there is a broad sense in which all those who speak Arabic as their mother tongue qualify as Arabs; and second, there is a narrow sense in which only members of Arab tribes merit the ethnic label.

More specifically, one aspect of the history of the Arabs with which this chapter is concerned is their role in state formation. To that end we will start by surveying the potential sites for the formation of major states in the Arab lands and picking out the role of the Arabs—if any—in each. These sites were Iraq, Egypt, Tunisia, Spain, and Morocco. To the extent that the rulers of these lands were Turks we will have little to say about them, since we have already dealt with this aspect of their history in earlier chapters. But to the extent that they were Berbers and have not been considered earlier, we will take our time, despite the fact that they were manifestly not Arabs. The upshot of the discussion is that the only Arab state in this league was Morocco, and only from the sixteenth century onward.

We will then descend to midlevel state formation and look for the part played by Arabs in it. We will go first to Arabia, where the Arab role predominates, and consider the Yemen, Oman, the Ḥijāz, Aḥsā', and finally Najd, where toward the end of our period the Saudi state made its first appearance with its rigorist Wahhābī religious message. Following that we will move on to two regions where after the eleventh century the Arab role in state formation was only intermittent: one is the Fertile Crescent, and the other is Africa.

A quite different aspect of Arab history with which this chapter is concerned is the expansion of the Arab tribes, which displaced or assimilated earlier populations in several regions. We will trace this expansion, and the linguistic Bedouinization that often went with it, both in Asia, where it transformed the character of much of Iraqi society, and in Africa, where it greatly expanded the territory populated by speakers of Arabic.

We will then come back to the nontribal Arabic speakers. One question to be taken up is their ethnic identity and the resentments that went with it—were they Arabs, non-Arabs, or something in between? And how did they feel about Turks? Another question is the geographical distribution of the nontribal Arabic-speaking population, both urban and rural. Finally, we will touch on the issue of the impact of nomads on peasants and the possibility that the last centuries of our period were a time of demographic contraction.

Islamic history began with the Arabs. On his deathbed in 644, the caliph ʿUmar is remembered to have described them as "the very substance of Islam."[1] But as we saw, the success of their enterprise soon had the effect of diluting their demographic presence outside Arabia, and in our time the people whom we call Arabs make up only about a fifth of the world's Muslim population. Yet the role of the Arabs in Muslim history has always remained a considerable one. Just how considerable turns in part on a question of definition: Who counts as an Arab? Historically this ethnic label has been used in two very different senses. The narrower sense restricts it to members of Arab tribes, many though by no means all of them nomadic. The broader sense extends it to a much larger population of native speakers of Arabic. This latter is the usage that prevails at the present day, and it has a long ancestry. A Damascene scholar who died in 1731 wrote that "what is meant by an Arab (*al-ʿArabī*) in our age and others, past and future, is someone who speaks the Arabic language naturally and fluently,"[2] and in affirming this view he had the authority of the Prophet behind him. What was at stake here was whether nontribal Arabic speakers were to be deemed Arabs. One consideration that tended to exclude them was that they were likely to be descendants of non-Arab populations that in the course of the centuries had been Arabized. That there had been extensive Arabization of non-Arab populations was not an insight vouchsafed only to modern academics. The famous Syrian scholar Ibn Taymiyya (d. 1328) remarked that most people in his time were of unknown origin, unaware whether their ancestors had been Arabs or non-Arabs. We can return to the ambiguity of their status later. But at this point it is more convenient to adopt the inclusive usage in order to demarcate the population, and hence the territory, with which this chapter is concerned.

The lands that at the end of our period were Arab in this wider sense consisted in the main of a large band of territory extending continuously for some four thousand miles from east to west and partially divided by the Red Sea. On the Asian side of the Red Sea lay Arabia and the Fertile Crescent; on the African side lay the Nile valley, North Africa, and the western Sahara. Despite the survival of non-

1. *The history of al-Ṭabarī*, Albany 1985–2007, 14:92.
2. Quoted in M. Cook, *Ancient religions, modern politics*, Princeton 2014, 13.

Arabic tongues in each of these regions, Arabic came to be the dominant spoken language over this enormous area. In addition to that core territory, there were three peripheral regions that will occasionally claim our attention. One is Khurāsān, where scattered pockets of Arabic speakers survived into modern times. On the evidence of their dialects they would seem to be a residue of Arab settlement at the time of the conquests, and they are still found today—or were until recently—in parts of Iran, Afghanistan, and Uzbekistan. Another is the Baqqāra Belt, the territory inhabited by the Arab cattle nomads of the eastern savanna whom we met in the previous chapter. The third, separated from the core territory by the sea, is made up of Spain and some of the islands of the western and central Mediterranean, notably Sicily. Here Arabic was widely spoken in medieval times, though today it is confined to the island of Malta, where it takes the form of the Arabic dialect we know as Maltese. Spain and Sicily aside, none of these peripheral regions have carried much weight in the history of the Arabs in the last thousand years, but they are nevertheless a historically significant phenomenon.

Before we begin this survey, a few things need to be said about the structure, content, and approach of this chapter. First, it would be logical to begin by mapping out the Arab population of these lands, distinguishing between its tribal, peasant, and urban components at different times and places in our period. With such a demographic foundation firmly in place, we could then move on with some confidence to the political history of the Arabs. But in practice we may be better served by taking the two assignments in reverse order. The reason is that our sources tell us much more about the political role of the Arabs in our period than they do about the underlying demographic phenomena. The long section that follows is therefore concerned with Arab state formation—or the lack of it, as the case may be. We will begin at the more ambitious end of the spectrum, looking for states that ruled sizeable countries, if not quite empires.

Second, Arab tribes were in contact with non-Arab tribes in both Asia and Africa. But in Asia, Khurāsān apart, interaction with Iranian and Turkic tribes came to be limited to the northern fringe of the Arab lands, and the location of this borderland was fairly stable. In Africa, by contrast, Arab and non-Arab tribes rubbed shoulders over a much larger territory, and the borderlands kept shifting. Thus in North Africa, where the proportion of Berbers to Arabs rose as one went from east to west and from the lowlands to the highlands, the territory inhabited by Berbers tended to contract over time; our period begins with islands of Arab population in a Berber sea but ends with Berber islands in an Arab sea. When we come to North Africa we will thus find it harder to separate the activities of Arab tribes from those of their Berber counterparts, and as a result we will often pay as much attention to Berber as to Arab state formation in this region.

Finally, this chapter outlines the history of a substantial part of the Muslim world over a period of some eight centuries by focusing in the main on the fortunes of a particular ethnic group. This is by no means the only way to approach this segment of Muslim history. Although no adequate account of it could ignore ethnicity, it does not have to be central. Yet using it as an organizing principle can illuminate significant features of the period that would otherwise remain obscure.

The political history of the Arabs

Potential sites for large-scale state formation: Iraq, Egypt, Tunisia

The vast region that concerns us in this chapter had only a limited number of sites with agrarian resources adequate to support substantial states, let alone empires. In the early centuries of Islam, if we set aside the peculiar case of Umayyad Syria, the only such site on the Asian side of the Red Sea was Iraq. After the ninth century there were none, though Iraq could still provide some resources for less ambitious states. To the west of the Red Sea things looked better. The north coast of Africa possessed three plausible sites—Egypt, Tunisia, and Morocco—and for a while southern Europe provided a fourth, Spain. All these sites at one time or another in their histories supported states of imperial dimensions. We will pass each of these sites of large-scale state formation in review, considering Iraq, Egypt, and Tunisia in this subsection but leaving Spain and Morocco to subsections of their own. Only after that will we consider midscale state formation in the Arab lands.

As we have seen, the lowlands of Iraq had a long history of providing the fiscal basis for empires whose military manpower derived from the uplands of Iran. But the early ʿAbbāsid Caliphate constituted the last chapter in that history. Here the dynasty itself was unquestionably Arab, so that however ethnically varied its political and military elite might be, the caliphs were a living link to a time when Arabs ruled the world. But after the early tenth century there was no mistaking the fact that the ʿAbbāsid caliphs had ceased to be imperial rulers. It was now their fate to reign rather than rule, with the lion's share of the power passing to the Iranian Būyids in 945 and the Turkic Seljuqs in 1055. There was to be a limited restoration of ʿAbbāsid power in the twelfth and early thirteenth centuries, but even at its height this was confined to Iraq and western Iran; we will glance at it later under the more modest rubric of midscale state formation.

Thereafter non-Arabs ruled Iraq into the twentieth century, insofar as anyone did. In this period the region usually formed part of the Mongol or Turkic empires of the northern Middle East. Most of these were based in Iran, as in the case of the Īlkhāns, the Qara Qoyunlu, the Aq Qoyunlu, and the Ṣafawids, all examples of the long tradition whereby rulers of western Iran would help themselves to Iraq. But in the long-lasting case of the Ottomans, Iraq found itself part of an empire based in Anatolia and the Balkans. The Ottomans nevertheless had to maintain a significant military force in Iraq to ward off threats from Iran, a danger dramatized by the Ṣafawid recovery of Iraq in 1623–38. At times states based within Iraq were significant enough to occupy the center of the local stage, as with the Mongol Jalāyirids of the fourteenth and early fifteenth centuries and the Georgian Mamlūk Pashas who took advantage of Ottoman decentralization in the eighteenth and early nineteenth centuries. But none of these rulers were Arabs, nor is this surprising. Iraq still had the resources to support either a measure of provincial government within an empire or a weak but more or less autonomous local state, and thanks to its location on the northern edge of the Arab lands there was usually no lack of powerful non-Arabs on hand to appropriate its resources in one way or the other. In this story the Arab tribes figure repeatedly as dissidents, the targets of endless military expeditions dispatched by Ottoman governors. Thus for several years in the later eighteenth century the ʿUbayd were making their presence felt on the outskirts of Baghdad. The Muntafiq, a formidable tribe of southern Iraq in the seventeenth to nineteenth centuries, took possession of the city of Baṣra in 1694 and held it for several years; in 1787 they took it again. But despite the fact that the idea of taking over Iraq seems to have occurred to them, the tribes showed no capacity to unite and establish a wider dominion of their own. A British traveler who made the journey from Aleppo to Baṣra in 1745 was struck by this, commenting that "the greatest unhappiness of the Arabians immediately under the Ottoman tyranny is their disagreement amongst themselves." Uniting, he argued, would both secure them from "the insults of the Turks" and "render them a powerful people," but as things were, the Turks were in a position to "constantly play the different tribes and petty bodies one against another to their utter destruction."[3]

From the tenth century onward, Egypt was a much more desirable economic prize than Iraq. As at most times in its history, it combined agricultural wealth with a commercially strategic position athwart the shortest land crossing from the Mediterranean to the Indian Ocean. With the decline of Iraq it now had a fiscal potential unmatched by any other site in the Arab lands. Hence the country could not fail to attract the interest of outsiders, and indeed it had already been ruled by foreigners for a millennium prior to the Arab conquest. The Arabs, as we have seen, took Egypt from its Byzantine rulers in the seventh century but lost control of it in the ninth. For several centuries thereafter Egypt was ruled by foreigners based inside the country: the Turkic Ṭūlūnids and Ikhshīdids, the Fāṭimids, the Kurdish Ayyūbids, and the Turkic and Circassian Mamlūks. Most of these dynasties used the fiscal resources of Egypt to build themselves empires, though these tended to be smaller than those of the northern Middle East—no doubt because Egypt lacked

3. See H. Halm, *The Arabs: A short history*, Princeton 2012, 245–46.

adequate pastureland for a large cavalry army. But of these imperial rulers, only the Fāṭimids (969–1171) claimed Arab descent; indeed, several members of the dynasty bore names of hoary Arab antiquity, such as Maʿadd and Nizār. But there is no strong reason to believe their genealogical claims, and whatever their origins they came to Egypt as foreigners with a largely Berber following. The line of foreign dynasties ruling from inside Egypt ended with the Ottoman conquest in 1517. Thereafter, as we have seen, Egypt was a province of the Ottoman Empire until the French occupation in 1798. During the long period of Ottoman decentralization in the seventeenth and eighteenth centuries Egypt had the resources and the distance from the center to support local state formation, and there were moves in this direction, but nothing much came of them, and in any case the natives of the country played no part in them.

This is not to say that the indigenous population, and particularly the Arab tribes on the Egyptian periphery, were content with their situation. A Sharīf—a descendant of the Prophet—who led the tribes in revolt in 1253, soon after the start of Mamlūk rule, challenged it in no uncertain terms: "We are the owners of the country, and are more entitled to rule it than the Mamlūks."[4] A century later a powerful chief leading a large tribal coalition in Upper Egypt went so far as to set up a royal court for himself. A similar sense of ownership is imputed to the Arabs of Egypt by a Venetian merchant in the early fifteenth century. As in Iraq, these tribes could make a lot of trouble. Some elected to cooperate with the state, which was anxious to co-opt tribal leaders with titles and fiefs, but even these tribes might still do great damage to the agricultural economy. Nor was the threat limited to the countryside. An Ottoman visitor to Egypt in 1599 commented on the Bedouin horsemen who robbed and plundered on the outskirts of Cairo, on occasion entering the city, and we hear of armed bands of youths being formed on the edges of the city for defense against such attacks. But as in Iraq, the tribes had no ability to combine their considerable forces. The same visitor remarks that it was thanks to this disunity that a mere ten thousand salaried soldiers were able to hold Egypt for the Ottomans despite the presence of many hundreds of thousands of Arabs. Were the Arabs to join together, he said, it would take an army of a hundred thousand to hold them in check. But disunity was not the only bar to an Arab revolt that might have overwhelmed the Turkic rulers of Egypt. As the Arabs of Upper Egypt put it in the late fourteenth century, when declining an invitation to participate in a Mamlūk civil war, they were not up to fighting Turks, though they had no problem fighting other Arabs. Altogether the idea of the Arab tribes uniting and taking over Egypt may have been a fantasy, but a source from the first half of the sixteenth century tells us that it was entertained by the Arabs themselves: the

4. Quoted in Y. F. Ḥasan, *The Arabs and the Sudan*, Edinburgh 1967, 100.

Bedouin boasted that they would unite and become masters of the country. A French observer at the end of the eighteenth century still took the prospect seriously. The Arabs, he wrote, considered themselves "born to rule on the banks of the Nile,"[5] and they regarded Egypt as their property; only their disunity saved the country from them.

Tunisia, like Egypt, had a certain maritime significance: it dominated one of the two passages from the eastern to the western Mediterranean. As we have seen, it also enjoyed agricultural wealth thanks to its plains, though in the absence of a river like the Nile far less so than Egypt. Its resources were nevertheless enough to ensure that it attracted foreign rulers, and this ancient pattern continued in Islamic times. The Aghlabids (800–909) were Arabs and as such could be seen as perpetuating the order established by the conquest, but Fāṭimid rule over Tunisia was the achievement of a Berber army from what is now eastern Algeria. The Zīrids (972–1148), who succeeded the Fāṭimids in Tunisia, were likewise Berbers from farther west. Their rule was ended by the Almohads (1130–1269), Moroccan Berbers who for some time ruled Tunisia from Morocco. The Ḥafṣids (1229–1574), who succeeded them in Tunisia, were likewise Berbers, and this long-lived dynasty ended only with the definitive Ottoman conquest of Tunisia in 1574. The decentralization of the Ottoman Empire later made possible the establishment of the Ḥusaynid dynasty (1705–1957) with its Greek origin. In short, we can sum up the history of post-Aghlabid Tunisia as six centuries of Berber rule and three under the Ottoman umbrella. Of the dynasties based in the country itself, the Fāṭimids had a claim to rule an empire, the first to be based in Tunisia since that of the Carthaginians—though for the Fāṭimids, Tunisia was in effect a stepping-stone on the way to the greater riches and more central location of Egypt. The only other Tunisian dynasty that could make a plausible claim to imperial status would be the Ḥafṣids, and we should look more closely at them here.[6]

This Berber dynasty had a curiously hybrid origin. We are used to the idea that some dynasties come to power through religious mobilization, while others do so through the normal processes of worldly politics. In the North African context the Almoravids (1062–1147), who mobilized the Berber tribes of the Sahara, were a straightforward example of the first process, and the Aghlabids, provincial governors who became effectively independent, are just as clear-cut an example of the second. The Ḥafṣids contrived to belong in some degree to both sets. They emerged from the Almohad movement, a religious mobilization of Berbers from the mountains of Morocco in which the ancestor of the Ḥafṣids played a leading

5. E. Jomard, "Observations sur les Arabes de l'Égypte moyenne," in *Description de l'Égypte*, Paris 1809–29, État moderne, 1:574.

6. For the Ḥafṣids see M. Fierro's chapter on the Almohads and Ḥafṣids in *The new Cambridge history of Islam*, Cambridge 2010, vol. 2.

role. This Abū Ḥafṣ was a close companion of Ibn Tūmart, the religious leader who founded the movement, and the most active supporter of the Mu'minid dynasty that emerged from it to rule from Morocco. Yet the process that led from the insider status of Abū Ḥafṣ to dynastic power for his descendants was rooted in provincial government. The Almohads had taken Tunis in 1159, and in due course a son of Abū Ḥafṣ held the position of governor there from 1207 to 1221. A few years later the governorship was being disputed between two of his grandsons; the winner founded the dynasty by asserting his independence of the Mu'minids in 1229, claiming fidelity to Almohad doctrine at a time when the Mu'minid ruler had disowned it. The founder's successor then went on to claim the caliphate. In fact the Ḥafṣids never entirely renounced their allegiance to the Almohad cause, though they soon came to terms with the Mālikism of the great majority of their subjects. Thus on balance they were not so different from the regular run of dynasties of their day.

In geopolitical terms the Ḥafṣids, like most dynasties, had their ups and downs. The first two reigns, spanning the years 1229–77, were very successful, marked by conquests in eastern and central Algeria and overlordship in western Algeria, northern Morocco, and even Spain. Here, then, was something that could be called a Ḥafṣid empire. But this period was followed by some four decades of weakness and disorder. From this time on the Ḥafṣid domains were often divided between rival lines of the dynasty, with one based in Tunis and another farther to the west. Meanwhile, states in western Algeria and Morocco that had previously accepted Ḥafṣid overlordship now turned the tables and attacked. The Marīnids (1217–1465), based in Morocco, invaded Tunisia and occupied it in 1348–50 and again in 1357–58. The end of the fourteenth century nevertheless saw the Ḥafṣid dynasty enter a renewed quasi-imperial phase that lasted into the late fifteenth century. Algiers was retaken, overlordship was restored in western Algeria and even Morocco, and the Ḥafṣid navy was active against the Portuguese. But once these good times were over, they did not return, and the last decades of the dynasty were undignified—the Ḥafṣid ruler depended on the Spanish to save him from the Ottomans, and it was the Ottomans who finally triumphed and ended the dynasty in 1574.

What, then, was the role of the Arab tribes in all this? From the eleventh century onward they were prominent—and often disruptive—actors in the affairs of Tunisia, but they never formed a state that ruled it. The main thing we hear about is their dissidence. Like the Turcomans of Anatolia, they readily appeared on the side of rebel princes and other such contenders for power. If the rebel they supported was successful, they could have revenues assigned to them, just as in Egypt. In fact, the practice of giving the Arab tribes such grants was already in evidence on a small scale from the beginning of the Ḥafṣid dynasty, but during its time of troubles in the late thirteenth and early fourteenth centuries it became much more widespread. Thus in the late thirteenth century a rebel prince who established his power in the western part of the Ḥafṣid domains rewarded his Arab supporters with grants of land and revenues. Later attempts to reverse such grants provoked Arab rebellions. These arrangements obviously implied that the Arab tribes would play some part in the Ḥafṣid army. At least until the end of the fourteenth century the core of the army was made up of Berbers from Morocco, but already in the thirteenth century there was a significant Arab tribal component. These Arab troops were troublesome and unreliable, and also part-time—after participating in a summer campaign they were in a hurry to get back to their nomadic lifestyle. Just as in Iraq and Egypt, the Arab tribes never came close to taking over Tunisia and governing it for themselves. Their one attempt at creating an alternative polity close to the center was a local affair: in mid-sixteenth-century Qayrawān a miniature state briefly took shape around a certain Sīdī ʿArafa, the leader of a Ṣūfī order known as the Shābbiyya that had a strong following among the Arab tribes.

Potential sites for large-scale state formation: Spain

We now move to Spain,[7] where the early centuries of Islam had been marked by an unusually long survival of Arab power. Like the ʿAbbāsids, the Spanish Umayyads were an incontestably Arab dynasty, and to a far greater degree than the ʿAbbāsids they were associated with the continuing existence of an Arab elite. When the Spanish Muslim scholar Ibn Ḥazm (d. 1064) wrote a compendium of Arab genealogy in the mid-eleventh century, he had no trouble updating his source material to inform his readers of the whereabouts of members of this or that pre-Islamic Arab tribe in contemporary Spain. For example, he remarked that the members of the tribe of Balī still resided in a place to the north of Cordoba, where they preserved their genealogies. As we have seen, they spoke only Arabic, even their women being unable to speak the Romance vernacular. This points to a certain archaism about Muslim Spanish society. In the east descent from the Prophet and a few of his most prominent followers never ceased to be prized and recorded, or alternatively invented; but it is unlikely that an eleventh-century genealogist in one of the cities of Iraq could have traced so many links between the leading families of the settled population of his day and the tribes of pre-Islamic Arabia. The Spanish Muslim elite of these centuries was not, of course, purely Arab. In addition to imported Slavs there had been a significant Berber presence in Muslim Spain from the start, and the role of these two elements became particularly obtrusive in the last decades of Spanish Umayyad rule. Yet the degree to which the Arab elite survived into the eleventh century made Spain unique among the sites we have so far surveyed. Thus when the Umayyad Caliphate broke up into some

7. This period of Spanish Muslim history is covered in H. Kennedy, *Muslim Spain and Portugal*, London 1996.

three dozen local principalities in the first half of the eleventh century, several of them were ruled by Arab dynasties, including the most powerful of them, that of Seville. More of them, however, were ruled by Slavs and Berbers, and as we will soon see, within a few decades newly arrived Moroccan Berbers had taken over. Yet even then families of Arab descent could resurface locally when Berber rule was weak, and as late as the fourteenth century leading families in Granada—including the Naṣrid rulers themselves—still had their Arab genealogies.

Meanwhile the re-Christianization of Spain—the process that from the late eighteenth century came to be known as the Reconquista—was proceeding apace. The geographical potential for it had been there from the start: Spain is separated from North Africa by sea, even if only by ten miles of it, and it is joined to the rest of Europe by land, even if much of the border is mountainous. Almost from the time of the Muslim conquest there had been a fringe of unrepentant Christian power in the north, and over the course of the eleventh to fifteenth centuries the frontier between Christian and Muslim rule moved southward until the entire peninsula was in Christian hands. On the Christian side this was partly due to the efforts of the rulers of what began as small states in the north of Spain, but it also owed a lot to the increasing military effectiveness of European Christendom on the far side of the Pyrenees. On the Muslim side the process was given a head start by the fragmentation of the Umayyad Caliphate in the first half of the eleventh century. The debilitating effect of this development is shown by the fact that most of the new Muslim principalities were paying tribute to Christian rulers. But in the long run these rulers were not content to leave the Muslim principalities in place and levy tribute on them. A Muslim source reports the assertive Christian irredentism of the period in the form of a speech made by Ferdinand I of Castile (ruled 1035–65) to a deputation from Toledo, which until 1085 was still in Muslim hands: "We seek only our own lands which you conquered from us in times past at the beginning of your history. . . . So go to your own side of the Strait and leave our lands to us, for no good will come to you from dwelling here with us after today."[8] And indeed in the long run, no good came to them unless they were willing to endure the humiliation of conversion. One Muslim in Murcia in 1243, invited by the conquering Spanish king to become a Christian, replied that he had hitherto performed so poorly in the worship of a single god that his failure would only be compounded were he to attempt to serve three. But as we will see, even those who converted often did not do well. Moreover, the Christian reconquest took as long as it did only because two great Berber dynasties of Morocco came to the rescue of the Muslims of Spain, the Almoravids in 1086 and the Almohads in 1145. This staved off the worst of the reconquest until the thirteenth century. But even at their

8. Quoted in D. Wasserstein, *The rise and fall of the party-kings*, Princeton 1985, 250.

most successful their campaigns still left much former Muslim territory in Christian hands, and Almohad power in Spain disintegrated in the decades following a disastrous defeat in 1212. Cordoba fell to the Christians in 1236, Seville in 1248. The next Berber dynasty of Morocco, the Marīnids, sought to follow in the footsteps of its predecessors, but five expeditions mounted in the years 1275–91 failed to effect any significant reconquest of Spanish territory.

From the mid-thirteenth century Muslim rule in Spain was for the most part limited to the homegrown Naṣrid dynasty (1232–1492), which was able to carve out a kingdom centered on Granada in the southeast of the peninsula, with access to the sea. This was in some sense an Arab dynasty. The founder claimed a Medinese companion of the Prophet as an ancestor, and Ibn Khaldūn was fully convinced of the Arab descent of his line. On the other hand, the backbone of the army was Berber. The founder was also some kind of a religious leader, but this soon wore off. The greatest achievement of the dynasty was to survive for two and a half centuries in a very exposed location, and it did this by more or less deft, not to say cynical, maneuvering through unstable alliances with and against the nearby states, Muslim and Christian; the Marīnids figured on both sides. Often the Naṣrid ruler had to pay tribute to the king of Castile, and in 1248 he helped him conquer Seville from his fellow Muslims. But in the long term the Naṣrid enclave of Muslim power was unsustainable, particularly so once the two major Christian kingdoms, Aragon and Castile, were brought closer together through a royal marriage in 1469. The Naṣrids, themselves disunited, suffered repeated losses of territory in the 1480s and finally lost Granada itself in 1492. Their chief claim to subsequent fame is the palace they left behind, the Alhambra. Though it must have been modest by the standards of the major dynasties of the day, it is the only truly medieval Muslim palace to survive, and it is ironic that it owes its unique preservation to the Christian conquerors of Granada.

The thirteenth-century reconquest and the fall of Granada placed large numbers of Muslims under Christian rule. In the parlance of the time, they were Mudéjars. They had three options. One was to emigrate to a region such as North Africa that remained under Muslim rule. This was what the Muslim scholars said believers should do in such a situation, and it could work for those who had portable skills or capital they could take with them. In 1468 a Muslim from Toledo, who rather remarkably identified himself as a Goth (Qūṭī), had the means to buy himself an expensive manuscript in the oasis of Tuwāt while on his way across the Sahara to the land of the blacks; unlike many refugees he clearly was not destitute. Another option was to convert to Christianity and do whatever it took to assimilate. This was doubtless quite widespread, but in the nature of things successful conversion often left no paper trail behind it, and where we do have evidence it can be hard to interpret. The third option was to stay on as Muslims under Christian rule, practicing their religion as best they could and hoping that the

Christians would keep the promises of toleration that they regularly made on conquering Muslim populations. Such toleration could be long-lasting: after the Muslims of Navarre came under Christian rule in 1119, they freely practiced their religion until 1516 and enjoyed the right to bear arms. Yet toleration could fade away or end suddenly in the event of a Muslim rebellion, with the result that there was no longer a public space for Islam. If, in the face of such denial of toleration, Muslims were still not ready either to emigrate or to convert, their only course was to hide their Muslim faith under an outward show of Christianity. They would then be crypto-Muslims, and by 1526 this had become the situation of virtually all Muslims in Spain. This is the population we know as Moriscos. As one of them put it, "They were serving two religions: the religion of the Christians openly and that of the Muslims in secret."[9] It was not an easy way to live. Quite apart from the internal emotional conflicts it led to, the authorities were liable to regard converts—whether sincere or insincere—with suspicion. The Spanish Inquisition, established around 1482, made a handsome living out of this suspicion of converts and their descendants. Whereas Old Christians—people whose ancestors had been Christian as far back as anyone could remember—were credited with purity of blood (*limpieza de sangre*), people with impure blood in their veins—be it Muslim or Jewish—could easily find themselves in trouble, with the Inquisition or otherwise. In one way purity of blood was very much a populist notion. Commoners could relish the fact that aristocrats were at much higher risk of impurity—they had so many more known ancestors than ordinary people did. The idea was also wide open to abuse, since anyone with a grudge could denounce an enemy as a secret Muslim or Jew. For these and other reasons, there was both principled and practical opposition to the whole idea of purity of blood in several quarters of Christian Spain. Meanwhile, the workings of the Inquisition led Moriscos not just to fear it but to mistrust each other. Despite this, the Inquisition signally failed to eliminate secret adherence to Islam among the Moriscos, a fact that was not lost on the rulers of the country.

By the early seventeenth century the Spanish authorities had reached the conclusion that the struggle to make good Christians of the Muslims of Spain was hopeless. "It is not just that nothing has been achieved, but that every time some effort has been made, their stubbornness and ill will has only increased," as one commentator put it.[10] When the Moriscos of the Alpujarra in the former kingdom of Granada rose in rebellion in 1568, the first thing they did, we are told, was to declare themselves to be Moros—Moors, Muslims—who had nothing to do with the Catholic faith that their fathers and grandfathers had professed—at least outwardly—for so long. When a Portuguese army intervening in a Moroccan suc-

9. Aḥmad ibn Qāsim al-Ḥajarī, *Kitāb nāṣir al-dīn*, Madrid 1997, 64.

10. Quoted in L. P. Harvey, *Muslims in Spain, 1500–1614*, Chicago 2005, 307.

cession dispute was destroyed in a battle of 1578, the Moriscos of Cordoba openly rejoiced at this Muslim triumph. As a bishop in eastern Spain noted in 1587, the mediocre results of missionary work among the Moriscos were in stark contrast with the magnificent harvest among the Indians of the New World. But the obvious inference that missionary efforts were best directed overseas was open to challenge: Why, someone asked around 1570, do we "go off to convert the infidels of Japan, China, and other remote parts," in the manner of someone hunting lions or ostriches in Africa while leaving his own home "full of snakes and scorpions"?[11] So in 1609–14 the Spanish government at long last expelled the Moriscos. By this time the rationale for doing so, though still highly controversial, was plain enough, and it was enhanced by a fear that Moriscos were reproducing faster than Old Christians. In all, some three hundred thousand Moriscos were expelled from the country—with predictably disastrous results for the finances of the Inquisition. The French statesman Cardinal Richelieu (d. 1642) described the expulsion as "the most barbarous act in human annals,"[12] and many in Spain would not have disagreed with him. Even the official representatives of the Inquisition in Valencia favored resettlement of their Moriscos within Spain rather than outright expulsion from the country on the ground that "after all they are Spaniards like ourselves," thereby affirming that ethnicity could trump religion—an attitude that might have been harder to match in the public values of the Muslim world of the day.

Even after the expulsion was over, some vestiges of Islam still remained on Spanish soil. The Ottoman traveler Evliyā Chelebī reports that one of his patrons received greetings from two crypto-Muslim Ṣūfīs living in Spain in the 1650s. In 1690–91 a Moroccan ambassador spent some time in Madrid. He was descended from a Spanish Muslim family, so most likely he was a fluent speaker of Spanish, like many in the Morisco diaspora. He reported that during his visit many people of Muslim ancestry came to see him. They were no longer Muslims, but they wanted to hear about Islam. One man who accosted him in the street expressed a nostalgic sense of lingering Muslim identity: "We are of Muslim stock (*jins*)."[13] Even this was not quite the end of Islam in Spain. As late as 1727–28 the Inquisition was proceeding against scores of suspected Muslims who still passed as Christians in Granada.

But after 1614 the bulk of the Morisco population lived outside Spain as a diaspora. Although most Moriscos settled in North Africa, others were widely scattered around the shores of the Mediterranean. There were even some who crossed the Atlantic to the New World, often as slaves, despite the concern of the

11. Quoted in Harvey, *Muslims in Spain*, 110.
12. For this and the next quotation see H. Kamen, *The Spanish Inquisition*, London 1997, 228.
13. Muḥammad al-Ghassānī al-Andalusī, *Riḥlat al-wazīr fī 'ftikāk al-asīr*, Abu Dhabi 2002, 53.

Spanish authorities to prevent such contamination of their magnificent harvest; this was already happening in the sixteenth century. Some of these Moriscos did well, at least in worldly terms, particularly if they were women and made it as far as Peru. A certain Juana was auctioned in Lima in 1541, and a witness in a subsequent court case testified that he had been present at the sale of other Morisca slaves "as beautiful as the said Juana and even more so."[14] The silver lining was that in the absence of an adequate supply of Old Christian women from Spain in early colonial Peru, such Moriscas might be bought, manumitted, and married by men rich enough to afford them. One Morisca, a certain Beatriz who arrived in Peru in 1532, became the wife of a high official. Because as an official he was not permitted to engage in trade, she acted as his business manager. But by and large, Morisco refugees did not have an easy time of it. In Tunisia they received a warm welcome, but in western Algeria many were despoiled after their arrival by the Arab tribesmen of the region. Perhaps unluckiest of all were the members of Morisco families who over the years had become committed to Christianity and now risked their lives to maintain this commitment in the face of Muslim hostility in North Africa. Yet the members of one Morisco community succeeded in combining political autonomy with a measure of revenge against their former Christian rulers. In 1627 they established a tumultuous piratical republic at Rabat on the west coast of Morocco, where they were well placed to attack Spanish transatlantic shipping. However, this polity lasted only a few decades, and ironically the hostility of these Moriscos to Spain was not unremitting. They were homesick. In 1631 they proposed a deal under which they would surrender their base, complete with its cannons, to Spain in return for being allowed to return home. In this connection they told the Spanish that they were "more Christian than Moorish"[15] and were prepared to accept the presence in their town of the priests and friars who would instruct them, though not of any other Old Christians. In the event they remained in Rabat, becoming entirely Muslim but leaving a heritage of Spanish family names—Vargas, Moreno, Lopez, Perez, Molina, and the like—that was still locally conspicuous in the twentieth century.

If unlike them we return to Spain, a vivid sense of the cultural erosion to which the Moriscos were increasingly subject toward the end of their time there is conveyed by a translation of the Qur'ān dating from 1606, just a few years before the expulsion. The language of the translation is Spanish, with a flavoring of Aragonese dialect, but what is telling about it is that the scribe who copied it made extensive

14. I owe this quotation and my other information on Moriscas in early colonial Peru to Rukhsana Qamber, who kindly shared with me her work on Moriscas who crossed the Atlantic. The remarkable story of Juana's time in Peru is told in the second chapter of her forthcoming monograph, provisionally entitled *Moriscas in sixteenth-century Latin America.*

15. M. García-Arenal, "The Moriscos in Morocco," in M. García-Arenal and G. Wiegers (eds.), *The expulsion of the Moriscos from Spain*, Leiden 2014, 326.

use of what he aptly called "Christian letters"[16]—in other words the Latin script—in place of the Arabic script that was typically used by Moriscos to write Spanish. For this he asked his readers' indulgence, explaining that he had to make the copy in a hurry. We thus have a clear indication that he was more at home writing with Christian letters than with Muslim ones. He went on to cite a further justification of what he had done: Muslims who knew only Christian letters would be able to read the translation. So there were literate Muslims who had lost the ability to read the Arabic script. It is no surprise that the scribe's Arabic is poor—Arabic is, he says, the perfect language, and he mentions that he is studying it, but he makes some awful mistakes in his colophons. There he also gives dates in both the Muslim and Christian eras, but not quite evenhandedly. He can give the Christian date in full, but when it comes to the Muslim date he supplies only the month and the day of the month—information he would need for Muslim ritual purposes—but makes no mention of the year; no doubt he had lost track of it. In this cultural twilight any hope of a Muslim restoration in Spain was long gone, short of an invasion from Morocco that never happened. Throughout the Iberian Peninsula—in both Spain and Portugal—the formation and maintenance of states was now a Christian monopoly.

Potential sites for large-scale state formation: Morocco and its Berber dynasties

Like the sites we have already considered, Morocco possessed considerable agricultural resources. But it also labored under a couple of disadvantages. One was maritime. Most of the Moroccan coast faced the Atlantic, where, as we have seen, not much was happening before the rise of European sea power. There was also a stretch of Mediterranean coast, but it was shorter and did not give as good access to the hinterland. The other—and greater—disadvantage was terrestrial. Despite the existence of significant plains, particularly on the Atlantic coast, Morocco had a massive mountainous backbone that favored tribes and disfavored states. One effect of this was to make it hard for an empire based elsewhere to integrate Morocco as a province. As we have seen, the Romans ruled Mauretania Tingitana for two centuries but then abandoned most of it. Neither the Arab conquerors nor the Fāṭimids achieved more than transient success in ruling Morocco: Arab rule did not outlive the eighth century, and that of the Fāṭimids did not survive the tenth. Even the Ottomans acquired no territory west of what is now Algeria, though in 1557–58 some Janissaries who after entering the service of a Moroccan ruler had been involved in his assassination were able to hold out

16. C. López-Morillas, "'Trilingual' marginal notes (Arabic, Aljamiado and Spanish) in a Morisco manuscript from Toledo," *Journal of the American Oriental Society*, 103 (1983), 500a.

for a few months in the Sūs, in the far southwest of the country. The other implication of Morocco's physical geography was that it did not seem destined to be the site of a single state of its own. There had indeed been an ancient kingdom of Mauretania, a large though most likely shallow polity, in the decades around the turn of our era. But in Muslim times, from the eighth century through to the eleventh, the normal condition of Morocco had been fragmentation, with different dynasties ruling in different regions. This was now to change. Although no external power was again to conquer Morocco until the French established their protectorate in 1911–12, a pattern of indigenous Moroccan statehood gradually emerged.

For a long time this process was dominated by Berbers. Two of the three dynasties of this phase emerged from religious movements that swept up Berber tribes, the first being the Almoravids (1062–1147).[17] We have already seen that this movement originated in the mission of Ibn Yāsīn (d. 1059), a native of the Sūs recruited by a tribal chief to bring a more rigorous form of Mālikī Islam to the Berbers of the western Sahara. Those who joined his movement were known by an Arabic term suggesting their devotion to jihad (*al-murābiṭūn*, whence—through Spanish—the English "Almoravids"). Their jihad was successful and soon spilled over into the conquest of richer territories beyond the borders of the desert. As already noted, there is some reason to think that the Almoravids conquered Ghāna. But their major conquests were in the north, in North Africa and Spain. It was in a campaign against the Barghawāṭa in western Morocco that Ibn Yāsīn himself was killed in 1059. It had not, however, been his practice to lead his army in person. That task he delegated to a leading figure of the Lamtūna tribe—the Lamtūna Berbers being the core of his support and of the Almoravid army, accompanied by a leavening of such imported elements as blacks and Christian mercenaries. When this leader died, his brother took over the role and led the invasion of Morocco. There he soon found himself handing over the substance of power (together with his beautiful and politic wife) to his ambitious and able cousin Yūsuf ibn Tāshufīn (ruled 1061–1107). The result was a relatively smooth transition to a political leadership based in Morocco. At some point Ibn Tāshufīn defined his position by taking the title "Commander of the Muslims" (*amīr al-muslimīn*). Among other things, this choice of title was a way of not quite claiming to be "Commander of the Faithful" (*amīr al-mu'minīn*), thus conveying recognition of the distant suzerainty of the ʿAbbāsid caliph. Such niceties could matter. In the eyes of many of their subjects the Almoravids were uncouth desert nomads, all the more conspicuously so thanks to their bizarre Saharan practice of male veiling. Indeed, they clung to the veil so tenaciously that an Almoravid offshoot established in the Bale-

17. For the Almoravids and their successors, the Almohads, see A. K. Bennison, *The Almoravid and Almohad empires*, Edinburgh 2016.

aric Islands still maintained it years after the main dynasty had fallen. We know this because when they seized the port of Bougie in eastern Algeria in 1184, the judge of the city contemptuously refused to accept the authority of the veiled intruders on the ground that he could not tell if the person to whom he was being asked to give his allegiance was a man or a woman. But the Almoravid recognition of the ʿAbbāsids, like their Mālikism, may have helped reduce tensions between them and their new subjects. Meanwhile, under the rule of Ibn Tāshufīn what began as a military camp became the city of Marrakesh and the Almoravid capital; it was to serve two later Moroccan dynasties in the same role. The Almoravids went on to conquer the rest of Morocco. Fez fell to them in 1070. Thereafter they extended their sway eastward till in 1082 it passed beyond Algiers and bordered on the lands of the Ḥammādid dynasty (1015–1152) in eastern Algeria. Finally they intervened in Spain in 1086, winning a major victory against the Christians and eventually taking over most of the remaining Muslim territory there. But things started to go badly for the Almoravids from about 1120. In Spain they were no longer sufficiently effective against the Christians of the north to retain the loyalty of their Muslim subjects. As their power decayed, the local Muslims rebelled and recreated something like the fragmented political landscape of the previous century, which in turn invited further loss of territory to the Christians. "We will throw you back into your Sahara and cleanse Spain of your filth," a bombastic bureaucrat from Muslim Spain declared to the Almoravids.[18] In North Africa, meanwhile, they proved unable to withstand the attacks of a new religious movement to which we will come shortly—that of the Almohads, who put an end to Almoravid rule in 1147.

The Almoravids nevertheless marked a watershed in the history of Morocco, and this in two ways. One was political. At the time they conquered it, there was no significant state in North Africa west of the Ḥammādids. Of the minor states of the early centuries—those of the Barghawāṭa, the Idrīsids, and the Midrārids—only the Barghawāṭa remained, and any authority the Fāṭimids and their successors in Tunisia had ever exercised over Morocco had evaporated, leaving little more than a sea of Berber tribes. Against this background the emergence of a single state based in Morocco, and in some fashion ruling the whole country, was a major novelty. The other way in which the Almoravids left their mark on Morocco was religious. Morocco in early Islamic times had been as religiously diverse as it was politically fragmented: alongside Christians, Jews, and Sunnīs there were Khārijites, Shīʿites, and adherents of Berber prophets—indeed it was not till the thirteenth century that the last Berber prophet had his say. But the Almoravids played a major role in making Morocco the overwhelmingly Sunnī, and more

18. Quoted in M. J. Viguera-Molins, "Al-Andalus and the Maghrib," in *The new Cambridge history of Islam*, 2:42.

specifically Mālikī, country that it is today. No doubt this homogeneity in turn made it more amenable to the rule of a single state.

Like the Almoravids, the Almohad dynasty (1130–1269) came to power through the mobilization of Berber tribes by a religious leader, again a rigorist preacher.[19] Two things, however, were different. One concerned the tribes: this time it was the Berber tribesmen of the Moroccan countryside, particularly the mountains of the High Atlas, and not those of the Sahara, who provided the movement with its military manpower. The other concerned the religious leader. In personal terms, Ibn Tūmart (d. 1130) comes across as a more sinister figure than Ibn Yāsīn does. Where Ibn Yāsīn was conspicuous for the number of his short-term marriages, Ibn Tūmart stood out for the number of people he killed. In doctrinal terms, whereas Ibn Yāsīn represented a more zealous and activist form of the Mālikī tradition that was already established in parts of North Africa, Ibn Tūmart rejected that tradition, and while remaining broadly within the Sunnī fold, put together a curiously eclectic religious message of his own. Its most salient feature was his claim to be the Mahdī, the redeemer who is to come toward the end of time, and what is more to be infallible (*maʿṣūm*)—a quality that Sunnīs, as opposed to Shīʿites, normally reserve for prophets. His main doctrinal platform was the condemnation of anthropomorphism (*tashbīh*). He accused the Almoravids of this heinous error and accordingly denounced them as infidels against whom jihad was to be waged. His own followers, by contrast, were believers in the unity of God (*al-muwaḥḥidūn*, whence—through Spanish—the English "Almohads"). He took the propagation of his message among them seriously, composing creeds not just in Arabic, the language of the scholars, but also in the Berber vernacular. These texts were to be memorized by his followers, and in one instance we are told that this obligation extended to men and women, be they free or slave.

The institutional arrangements he made for his nascent community were similarly eclectic, not to say creative. Like the founders of other Muslim religious movements in tribal societies, in some ways he modeled his career on the archetypal figure of the Prophet. In 1124 he moved his base from the village of his birth in the mountains south of the Sūs to Tīnmāl, an impregnable location in the High Atlas to the north. This move to Tīnmāl was designated Ibn Tūmart's Hijra, on the analogy of the Prophet's move to Medina—though the analogy was imperfect, not least because Ibn Tūmart had already begun to fight his enemies in 1121. Another way in which he departed from the Prophetic model was by setting up two councils with defined memberships, a Council of Ten and a Council of Fifty; he declared the inhabitants of the territories he conquered to be slaves of the members of the Council of Ten. The Prophet had indeed made a point of consulting his fol-

19. For the Almohads see Bennison, *The Almoravid and Almohad empires*, and M. Fierro, *ʿAbd al-Muʾmin*, London 2021.

lowers on occasion, but he had no such formal councils, and though he had ten companions to whom he had promised Paradise, they did not assemble as a body. Ibn Tūmart's councils are thus more likely to reflect Berber custom than Prophetic precedent. And unlike the Prophet, Ibn Tūmart was quite capable of turning on his own followers and having them killed. At one point he instituted a massive purge known as the "Distinguishing" (*tamyīz*). In doing so he was invoking verses of the Qur'ān according to which God will "distinguish the corrupt from the good" (Q3:179, Q8:37). His claim was apparently that one of his more suspect followers had been vouchsafed the ability to see into people's souls and discriminate between the saved and the damned—a faculty that not even the Prophet had claimed for himself. Meanwhile the war against the enemies of the movement continued. In 1130 an attack on Marrakesh led by the same follower ended disastrously, and three months later Ibn Tūmart died—having announced he was going on a journey alone. At this point the most likely outcome of his life's work was that the tensions within the movement he had put together would lead to its rapid disintegration.

Just how problematic the situation of the Almohads was at this juncture is indicated by the fact that the inner circle of the movement concealed the death of Ibn Tūmart from his followers for the next three years. The man who took over the running of affairs and is reckoned the first caliph of the Almohad dynasty was a long-term disciple of Ibn Tūmart named ʿAbd al-Mu'min (ruled 1133–63); hence the alternative name of the dynasty, the Mu'minids. Ibn Tūmart had encountered him while on his way home from a journey to the east in 1119. ʿAbd al-Mu'min had the requisite political and military skills, but he was at a disadvantage in that he did not belong to the group of tribes that accounted for the majority of Ibn Tūmart's followers. As one chronicler put it, he was an alien in the middle of these tribes and "had neither a family on which he could rely, nor a tribe that he could trust or depend on."[20] It is thus no surprise that in 1149–50 we find him implementing the second great purge of Almohad history and that in 1154 he was still dealing with trouble made by Ibn Tūmart's brothers, brutally suppressing their rebellion. Altogether, he faced some forty rebellions in the course of his reign. What helped establish his position in the face of such obstacles was his military success, culminating in the capture of Marrakesh in 1147. This city now became the capital of the Almohads, as it had been for the Almoravids. At the same time, the Almohads conquered themselves an empire extending well beyond Morocco. To the north they invaded Spain in 1147 and acquired considerable territory there, much as the Almoravids had done. To the east they achieved something no other Moroccan dynasty ever did—a long-term conquest of the whole of North Africa, with Tunis taken in 1159. Within this empire they adopted a systematic policy that was unusual

20. Quoted in R. Le Tourneau, *The Almohad movement in North Africa*, Princeton 1969, 66.

in the Muslim world: Jews and Christians had to convert to Islam, depart, or be killed, no poll tax being accepted from them. But by the middle of the thirteenth century the Almohads had lost their empire. Spain was now in the hands of the Naṣrids and the Christians; Tunisia was ruled by a rival claimant to the Almohad heritage, the Ḥafṣids; and as we will see, even western Algeria had fallen away under an independent dynasty, the ʿAbd al-Wādids. Meanwhile after 1213, and still more after 1224, the Almohads were doing poorly in Morocco itself, though the end did not come till the fall of Marrakesh in 1269. Political instability apart, the disarray of these last decades was manifested in two telling symptoms. One was religious: in 1229 the Almohad ruler repudiated the legacy of Ibn Tūmart, reinforcing this unsettling message with a massacre of Almohad chiefs. The other was ethnic: rather than cultivating the Berbers who had formerly constituted the core of the Almohad army, the rival contenders were increasingly seeking the military support of the Arab tribes. Employing Arab tribal troops in Morocco was by now a well-established practice whose beginnings went back at least to the 1160s. These Arabs were not just an exotic element like the Turks, black slaves, and Christian mercenaries who came to be part of the Almohad army. But prominent as the Arab tribes may have been by the thirteenth century, politically their time had not yet come. The next dynasty to take possession of Morocco was still a Berber one, and Berber rule remained the norm in North Africa into the sixteenth century.

The third and last major Berber state of Morocco was the Marīnid dynasty (1227–1465). It originated among Berber nomads of eastern Morocco and remained linked to them through a council of tribal chiefs. The Marīnids took Fez in 1248, making it their capital, and in 1269 they seized the Almohad capital, Marrakesh. Unlike the Almoravids and Almohads, their rise to power did not depend on any form of religious mobilization. Such a secular path to statehood was, of course, common enough in the Muslim world at large, but it was a significant novelty in the history of Muslim Morocco. Territorially the Marīnids were no less ambitious than their predecessors, but much less successful. Though a major dynasty, their wider imperial ambitions came to nothing. As we have seen, their interventions in Spain failed to repeat the conquests of the Almoravids and Almohads, and their dramatic campaigns in mid-fourteenth-century Tunisia had no lasting impact. Thereafter the dynasty was no longer what it had been, and it suffered an internal takeover by the Waṭṭāsid family. These were fellow tribesmen who at first served the Marīnids as administrators and regents. But eventually the Waṭṭāsids (1472–1549) became a dynasty in their own right, ruling a much-diminished state around Fez. Despite all this, the Marīnids were in one key respect a sign of things to come. To a greater extent than the Almohads had done, they sought good relations with Arab tribes, marrying the daughters of prominent tribal chiefs. Thus in southern Morocco the Marīnids were heavily dependent on the help of the Maʿqil Arabs, rewarding them with grants of territory, and their army included large numbers of Arab tribesmen. This did not, however, prevent them from continuing to employ a variety of troops from outside Morocco, including Christian mercenaries, black slaves, and Turks. Moreover, the core of their army was still its Berber cavalry.

One inadvertent but significant result of the territorial history of the Marīnids was a closer approximation to a Moroccan state than any that had previously appeared. Provided it held together, Morocco was a well-defined country in the north and west thanks to the sea, and in the south thanks to the Sahara. The ill-defined frontier was the eastern one, so much so that in place of the three-state configuration of modern North Africa, it would be easy to imagine two states, one based in Morocco and the other in Tunisia, with what is now Algeria divided between them. Thus the region of Tlemcen in western Algeria was conquered by both the Almoravids and the Almohads. In the days of the Marīnids and the Waṭṭāsids, however, it came to be ruled by a local Berber dynasty, the ʿAbd al-Wādids (1236–1555), who headed a nomadic tribe of the region. Like the Ḥafṣids, the ʿAbd al-Wādids endured for over three centuries, significantly longer than the Marīnids. But they were forced to expend much of their energy in attempting to defend themselves against repeated attacks from the Marīnids in the west and the Ḥafṣids in the east. In their last decades they became the object of a contest between the Spanish and the Ottomans, which the Ottomans won. The last ruler took refuge with the Spanish in Oran and died a few years later, leaving a son who was baptized and given the name Carlos. The generally defensive posture of this state reflects the fact that in terms of its resource base it was not in the same league as the Marīnids or the Ḥafṣids, let alone the Spanish or the Ottomans. As of 1500 there was thus no particular reason to think that the long-term future of Tlemcen would be divorced from that of Morocco. It was the establishment of the corsair state of Algiers as an Ottoman outpost in the early sixteenth century that made the separation of Marīnid and Waṭṭāsid times definitive. As we have seen, the business of this Barbary state was primarily maritime, but it proved capable of projecting sufficient power into the interior to block any eastward expansion by the rulers of Morocco, thereby defining the eastern limit of that country more or less as we know it today.

As we prepare to leave behind the long centuries of Berber domination in Morocco, we should take a look at expressions of Berber identity in this period. One theme is less prominent here than it had been in the days before the Almoravids: Berber self-assertion in religious terms. We barely hear of Berber prophets, and despite the marginal survival of the Ibāḍīs, the sectarian diversity of early Muslim North Africa had largely disappeared. The future of the Berbers thus lay overwhelmingly within the Sunnī tent, however capacious or cramped it might be. But within this tent the Almohads, as we have seen, laid considerable emphasis on the use of the Berber language in religious contexts, and it is perhaps no accident that it was in 1145 that a certain Ibn Tūnārt composed the first Arabic-Berber dictionary we know of. One Mālikī jurist held that someone who is ignorant of Arabic may use Berber in performing the ritual prayers—God, after all, knows all languages—but we are not told where in the western Muslim world he lived, nor when, except that it was not later than the fifteenth century. We know, however, that Berber phrases in the call to prayer were still in use in Granada, where much of the army was Berber, into the fourteenth century. We also encounter the assertion of Berber pride in explicitly ethnic terms. A work compiled in 1312 and preserved in a manuscript in Morocco brings together a considerable amount of material about the Berbers from a variety of sources. The texts collected here relate to the genealogy of the Berbers, to their history (or pseudohistory), and to the points in which they can take pride (*mafākhir*). The unknown author explains that many people have a low opinion of the Berbers, and he seeks to counter this disdain. Thus he starts his book with an anecdote set at the Fāṭimid court in Cairo. One of those present quotes a disparaging saying to the effect that the world is shaped like a bird and the Maghrib is its tail. To this someone from the Maghrib aptly retorts that the saying is correct, and the bird in question is a peacock. A characteristic motif of the work is the claim that the Berbers saw the truth of Islam before, not after, they were conquered by the Arabs. Unfortunately, we have little beyond the date and provenance of the manuscript to point us toward the milieu in which the compiler worked or the character of his intended audience. It would be easy—perhaps too easy—to imagine that he was responding to the rising presence and power of the Arab tribes in Marīnid Morocco.

Potential sites for large-scale state formation: Morocco and its Arab dynasties

The early sixteenth century saw the rise of the first of two Sharīfian dynasties that have dominated the history of Morocco ever since.[21] This was the Saʿdid dynasty (1510–1659), which emerged in the Sūs. We are now in a period in which the Christian reconquest of Spain was complete, and the question was whether it would carry over into a reconquest of North Africa. In the event, despite considerable naval and military activity, the Mediterranean was largely to block the extension of Christian rule in this direction until the nineteenth century and after. The Portuguese and Spanish were nevertheless able to establish themselves at some points on the North African coast for varying periods. Thus the Portuguese held the port of Tangier from 1471 to 1671. Farther south they were also interested in Āgādīr on the coast of the Sūs, where a wooden castle was built by a Portuguese

21. For these dynasties see S. Cory, "Sharīfian rule in Morocco," in *The new Cambridge history of Islam*, vol. 2.

aristocrat in 1505 and sold to the king of Portugal in 1513. This incursion provoked a strong response from the Berber tribes of the Sūs, and from 1510 they were led by Sharīfs belonging to the local Saʿdī family. Jihad and descent from the Prophet gave religious legitimacy to their activities, and in 1541 they finally recovered Āgādīr from the Portuguese. Their rise to power as rulers of Morocco was a by-product of this local struggle against the infidel. In the 1520s they had already taken Marrakesh, adopting it as their capital. In 1549 they went on to take Fez, putting an end to the incumbent Waṭṭāsid dynasty and becoming the sole rulers of Morocco; some members of the fallen dynasty now left for Spain and turned Christian. But Saʿdid sway over Morocco was beset by turbulence. Rebellions, succession conflicts within the ruling family, and foreign interventions were the order of the day. In Fez, for example, a Waṭṭāsid pretender was warmly welcomed in 1554. On this occasion a scholar of the city with an ear for rhyme remarked laconically that killing a Sūsī was tantamount to killing a Majūsī—in other words, a Zoroastrian. The ensuing repression was savage, and the scholar in question was beheaded after a defiant exchange with the Saʿdid ruler. The Ottomans came as far west as Fez in 1554 and 1576, and in 1578 the Portuguese king mounted a disastrous invasion in which he lost his life. Against this chaotic background one reign stood out as a prolonged period of strong government: that of Aḥmad al-Manṣūr (ruled 1578–1603). We met him in the previous chapter as the ruler who defied the Sahara by dispatching an army across it to conquer Songhay and who later wanted to join with the English to colonize the New World. But after his death in 1603 the turbulence resumed, and from then until the end of the dynasty in 1659 Saʿdid rule was more or less ineffective.

We could easily imagine such turmoil issuing in a fragmentation of Morocco into a plurality of states floating uneasily on a sea of tribes. This would have meant a return to the state of affairs before the rise of the Almoravids, though without the religious diversity. In this vein it would not be hard to imagine Morocco's two major political centers, Marrakesh and Fez, settling down as the capital cities of two mutually independent states, and indeed it is said that on his deathbed al-Manṣūr prescribed just such a division of Morocco between two of his sons. But the eventual outcome was not fragmentation but rather the emergence of a new Sharīfian dynasty once more ruling Morocco as a whole—or as much of it as was possible given the ubiquitous military capacity of the Berber and Arab tribes. This was the ʿAlawid dynasty, which was established in 1666 and still rules Morocco today. Though it, too, was a Sharīfian dynasty, the story of its rise was rather different from that of the Saʿdids. The family lived in the Tāfīlālt on the edge of the Sahara and did not initially seem likely to become a serious competitor in the struggle to replace the Saʿdids. A far more formidable contender at the time was the leader of a Ṣūfī order strategically based among the Berber tribes of the Atlas mountains. Its headquarters—its Zāwiya, in some ways the counterpart of a Christian or Buddhist monastery—was located in the countryside at Dilāʾ. The leader of the order proclaimed himself sultan of Morocco in 1651, and his military expansion reached as far as the Tāfīlālt. Here, then, was a religious mobilization among the Berber tribes that could have returned Morocco to a Berber hegemony reminiscent of the days of the Almoravids and Almohads. But this incursion into the Tāfīlālt was to prove the undoing of the movement. Like Morocco in general, this region was originally Berber (any word in a North African context that both begins and ends with a *t* is more than likely to be Berber). But with the arrival of the Arab tribes it now had a mixed population. To resist the invaders from Dilāʾ the people of the Tāfīlālt threw their support behind the local Sharīfian family who were to become the ʿAlawid dynasty. They, too, were the possessors of a Zāwiya, though a far less famous one. At first their horizons remained local, but in due course a member of the family established himself in northeastern Morocco with Arab and Berber support; the Arabs in question belonged to the Maʿqil tribe, which was also present in the Tāfīlālt. In 1666 he seized Fez, which initially served as the new dynasty's capital, and in 1668 he destroyed the Zāwiya of Dilāʾ and took Marrakesh. The ʿAlawid dynasty had thus extended its rule over Morocco as a whole.

Here, then, we find confirmation that since the early centuries of Islam something had changed in the character of Moroccan history. Morocco was by now a country and not just a region. Just why this change had taken place is hard to say. In part it was perhaps endogenous and linked to increased urbanization in Morocco. But the Almoravids, the first dynasty to rule Morocco as a whole, were a product of the Sahara, a region utterly devoid of cities. In any case the change was to be confirmed in a backhanded way in the eighteenth century, when the state once again fell apart. Just as in the Saʿdid case disorder followed the reign of an unusually determined and vigorous ruler, Mawlāy Ismāʿīl (ruled 1672–1727). This opinionated sultan disliked Fez so much that he established a new capital in Meknès. He balanced his Arab troops with a large black slave army, much of it improperly recruited within Morocco by enslaving free members of the local black population—a violation of Islamic law comparable to the Ottoman Devshirme. And just as energetically, by 1704 he was reputed to have sired six hundred sons (in this he had the assistance of five hundred concubines). But this time the chaos following the ruler's death lasted only three decades, not six, and the claimants to the throne were all sons of Mawlāy Ismāʿīl. The outcome of the eighteenth-century succession struggle was thus the continuation of the ʿAlawid dynasty, not the advent of a new one, let alone a reversion to the chronic fragmentation of the pre-Almoravid period. Once the turbulence of the struggle was over, Muḥammad III (ruled 1757–90) struck a modest but more sustainable balance between the forces order and disorder, showing himself content with less taxes and a smaller army than rulers such as Aḥmad al-Manṣūr and Mawlāy Ismāʿīl had insisted on. Sure enough, there was another period of chaos following his death, but this time it lasted only a few years. There was thus a marked trend toward increased structural stability in the history of Morocco. By 1800 the country itself was a given, and as of today no other dynasty in its history has lasted as long.

That Sharīfian rule in Morocco endured from the early sixteenth century to the end of our period and beyond suggests that the pattern was widely seen as legitimate. This legitimacy was in large measure religious. It is true that fully Ibn Khaldūnian movements in the style of the Almoravids and Almohads were no longer much in evidence in Sharīfian times, though they were not entirely absent. When in 1610 the Saʿdid ruler disgraced himself by handing over a port to the Spanish, a scholar and Ṣūfī named Abū Maḥallī not only mobilized a mass following by calling for jihad against the Spanish and the overthrow of the Saʿdids but also claimed to be the Mahdī. He mounted his venture in state formation with an army composed primarily of Arabs from the Moroccan Sahara and was killed by a chance bullet in a battle of 1613. But after an early flirtation with Mahdism in the context of their jihad against the Portuguese, the Saʿdids left this style of politics behind them, and the ʿAlawids never took it up. Yet neither did the Sharīfian rulers of Morocco resemble the Marīnids and Waṭṭāsids, or the Ottoman rulers of Algiers or Tunis, or even the Ottoman sultans themselves. Such rulers had little claim to religious legitimacy beyond the fact that they were Muslims who happened to hold political power and, in some cases, used it to fight bravely against the infidel. By contrast, the Saʿdid and ʿAlawid Sharīfs were intrinsically religious figures who could claim the caliphate by virtue of their descent from Quraysh, the tribe to which their ancestor the Prophet had belonged. This was an idea available anywhere in the Muslim world, but Morocco became particularly fertile ground for it with the increasing prominence of its Sharīfian families in late medieval times. The trend was associated with the formation of an image of the Idrīsid dynasty in which religious heterodoxy played no part. Allegedly the tomb of Idrīs II (ruled 803–28) was rediscovered in Fez in 1437–38, and in 1465–71 a Sharīf of Idrīsid descent ruled there for a few years. Thereafter the idea of an Idrīsid restoration had a continuing place in the political imagination of Morocco. The Saʿdids and ʿAlawids were not Idrīsids themselves, but they shared a wider Sharīfian culture, and to this extent they had more in common with the Zaydī imams of Yemen than with most of the Sunnī rulers of the day. There was indeed a certain sense of rapport between the two societies despite the sectarian and geographical distance between them. When an Idrīsid Sharīf from Fez visited Yemen in the late sixteenth or early seventeenth century, he got a warm welcome from his Zaydī kinsmen, among whom his ancestor Idrīs I (ruled 789–91) was recognized as an imam, and he in turn evinced a strong interest in Zaydī literature. Overall this pattern leaves the Marīnids isolated as the only major Moroccan dynasty that had no special religious legitimacy. And even the Marīnids claimed the caliphate, an instance of North African title inflation that could raise eyebrows in the east.

Whatever its importance, religious legitimacy did not ensure the substance of Sharīfian power. Effective Sharīfian rulers had to be organizers, politicians, diplomats, and generals. For this they had indigenous models, but they could also look beyond the borders of Morocco to the changing world outside it. No realistic ruler of the country in this period could fail to be aware that the Ottoman state was far more powerful than his own, and the result was a tendency to Ottomanization that was entirely compatible with hostility to the Ottoman presence on Morocco's eastern frontier. We already see this in the case of the ruler who first established the Saʿdid dynasty as more than a local presence, Maḥammad al-Shaykh (ruled 1517–57).[22] On one occasion he was so ill-mannered as to refer to the Ottoman sultan as "Sultan of the Fishermen."[23] His attitude failed to endear him to Süleymān the Magnificent, and he was killed by assassins sent from Algiers. What is significant is the reason these assassins were able to get close to him without being detected. He had surrounded himself with an entourage of Janissaries whom he had taken into his service—a measure that invites comparison with the Almohad acquisition of Turkic troops in the late twelfth century. The trend was even more pronounced in the case of his son ʿAbd al-Malik (ruled 1576–78), who got to know the Turks while in exile in Algiers and Istanbul before he came to the throne. He dressed like an Ottoman, Ottomanized his army and administration, and adopted Ottoman titles for his officials. According to a bureaucrat and historian who wrote toward the end of the century, down to the mid-1570s the Saʿdid caliphs ran a plain Arab state that dealt with issues as needed, unconstrained by elaborate rules and regulations. Then ʿAbd al-Malik came to the throne and forcefully moved the state away from the Arab way of governing toward the non-Arab way—in other words, the Ottoman way. The result was a lot of resentment. Yet his brother and successor, Aḥmad al-Manṣūr, shared his experience of exile and was likewise something of an Ottomanizer; as we have seen, his expansion across the Sahara spread the Ottoman title "pasha" to the banks of the Niger. In 1599 his chamberlain subjected an English merchant who had lived in the Ottoman Empire to over six hours of intensive questioning about his experiences there. A later Saʿdid ruler, Zaydān (ruled 1603–27), issued coins modeled on those of the Ottoman sultans.

The other power that rulers of Morocco were keenly aware of was naturally Spain. Of course, the fact that the Spanish were unbelievers made overt Hispanization problematic, but Aḥmad al-Manṣūr's aspiration to colonize the New World was a clear case of emulation of a successful non-Muslim power. There were also religiously acceptable channels through which Moroccan rulers could monitor and even learn from Spain: Christian renegades and Morisco refugees who fled to Mo-

22. "Maḥammad" is not a misprint. Like the Turkish "Meḥmed," originally "Meḥemmed," it is a respectful way to evoke the name of the Prophet without fully reproducing it.

23. Quoted in Cory, "Sharifian rule in Morocco," 457.

rocco bringing with them their knowledge of Spain and Spanish. One Morisco translated a Spanish or Portuguese work on medicine into Arabic, sanitizing the contents by entitling it [*A book that*] *enables the physician to dispense with the books of the enemies of the Prophet*. Another had served as a cannoneer in the Spanish army and was familiar with developments in his field in Europe and the Americas. He wrote a work on the subject in Spanish, and a fellow Morisco translated it into Arabic in 1638; the translation survives in many manuscripts. The Moroccan ambassador who was in Madrid in 1690–91 included in his report on Spain careful accounts of the postal system and the dissemination of news through gazettes. The rulers of Morocco thus had access to such information, whether or not they did anything with it. While the Moroccan state may have been relatively weak, it was by no means isolated.

What we have yet to consider is the sense in which the Sharīfian dynasties that came to power in Morocco were Arab. All descendants of the Prophet were of course Arabs by genealogy, though in itself this did not mean very much—even a Berber like ʿAbd al-Mu'min, the founder of the Almohad dynasty, had laid claim to Arab ancestry. It is not as if the Saʿdids rose to power as Arab tribal chieftains backed by their fellow tribesmen. Nevertheless, the rhetorical potential of the Arab ancestry of the Saʿdids was not left unexploited. Here the historian Ibn al-Qāḍī (d. 1616) provides a striking example. A man of letters from Fez, he was a faithful follower of Aḥmad al-Manṣūr—he owed him, as this ruler had ransomed him at great expense after he was taken captive by Christian pirates while returning from a trip to the east. One of Ibn al-Qāḍī's works is accordingly an extended panegyric celebrating the virtues of al-Manṣūr. Though Ibn al-Qāḍī had been born into an old and prominent Berber family, at least when he was in Egypt he seems to have felt like an Arab. Thus in one passage of his panegyric he describes a run-in he had with some Turks at the entrance to a mosque. Unlike the submissive Egyptians, he showed his contempt for them, and predictably the Turks reciprocated—one of them spat in his face. The point Ibn al-Qāḍī is making here is that Turks considered Arabs to be of no account, and he may not have been entirely wrong. An Ottoman visitor to Egypt in 1599 cited an extravagant tradition about the doings of Satan in the country as showing that "most of the people of Egypt are of a devilish nature and not fit to associate with the human species."[24]

The same ethnic tension recurs in a purple passage in which Ibn al-Qāḍī describes the overwhelming popularity of al-Manṣūr in the eastern Arab world. Our author had been present at elite gatherings in Cairo, Alexandria, Upper Egypt, Jeddah, Mecca, and Medina, it would seem at a time when news had arrived of the victory over the Portuguese that placed al-Manṣūr on the Moroccan throne

24. A. Tietze, *Muṣṭafā ʿĀlī's description of Cairo of 1599*, Vienna 1975, 39.

in 1578. People swore to Ibn al-Qāḍī that if even a slave girl of al-Manṣūr's were to come and ask for their allegiance, they would immediately proffer it and join her with thousands of horsemen. He also passes on a problematic but interesting report from someone he trusts who had been in the Upper Egyptian town of Jirjā, the seat of the emirate of the Banū 'Umar, the Bedouin potentates of the region under late Mamlūk and early Ottoman rule. According to this informant, the chief of the Banū 'Umar told him that he had heard the news of al-Manṣūr's victory while he was a captive of the Christians on the island of Rhodes (an anachronism, since the Ottomans had held Rhodes since 1522). It seems that he shared his captivity with some Turks, who were beside themselves that such a glorious victory should have gone to an Arab emir; while the Turks were filled with anger, the Arabs were filled with joy. In fact, Ibn al-Qāḍī tells us, this joyful reaction was widespread: Arabs in every region took pride in al-Manṣūr's achievement, and did so at the expense of the Turks. All the people of the east—he means the eastern Arabs—thus looked to al-Manṣūr because of the maltreatment they experienced at Turkish hands. Ibn al-Qāḍī then continues with his complaints about the humiliation the Arabs endure from the Turks, including what the Turks do to their women and boys. We should not, of course, take anything Ibn al-Qāḍī tells us as hard evidence of the state of public opinion among the Arabs under Ottoman rule. Although his testimony has the support of a Moroccan ambassador who was in Istanbul in 1589–90, that could be just as tendentious. Yet in the light of other evidence of tensions between Arabs and Turks, the gist of Ibn al-Qāḍī's account it is by no means implausible. In all this, be it noted, he has not yet said a word about the Berbers, from whom, as we saw, he himself descended. But he now ends this section of his panegyric with a reference to God's aid to al-Manṣūr against the rebels who abound in Morocco. That these rebels are so numerous he attributes to a simple cause: the irrationality of the Berbers high up in the mountains. Curiously, or perhaps not so curiously, he makes no mention of any such rebelliousness among the Arab tribes of the plains. Ibn al-Qāḍī is not an isolated figure in the Moroccan context. Ifrānī (d. ca. 1744), the author of the main chronicle of Sa'did history and likewise of Berber descent, has a comparable tendency to speak of Moroccans as Arabs when juxtaposing them with the Turks.

Even official diplomacy was not free of ethnic slurs. In an exchange of letters preserved in Moroccan chronicles, the father of the first ruler of the 'Alawid dynasty, already a powerful figure in eastern Morocco, traded insults with the Ottomans around 1655. A letter addressed to the Moroccan, apparently by the governor of Algiers, complains that the Moroccan side disparages the non-Arabs (*'Ajam*) as ignorant, boorish, and rude. He hits back by praising God for telling people to resist thieves and assailants irrespective of whether they are descendants of the Prophet. The Moroccan responds in a letter in which he in turn praises God, but for favoring Arabs over non-Arabs. He mentions that he has been raiding the Bedouin, and he has some unflattering things to say about them. They are like birds on branches, which can be raided to good effect only at dawn; he also compares them to locusts, which never remain in any one region. And yet, he says, there is an ethnic bond between him and the Bedouin: they are brethren in ancestry. Clearly this was a brotherhood that excluded the Turks.

In more concrete terms, how Arab was the Sharīfian state? What, for example, of the army? Here things are more complicated. In the first place, both Sharīfian dynasties had some Berber support. The Saʿdids began their rise to power by leading the Berber tribesmen of the Sūs, in part at least against the tribal Arabs of the region. The ʿAlawids likewise had Berbers behind them in their rise to power, and near the end of our period the winner of a succession struggle in 1792–96 enjoyed Berber backing—though rebellious Berbers were later to take the same ruler captive. Such support is hardly surprising. The Berbers of Morocco had not been demographically marginalized like those of Tunisia. They were still the majority of the population, and as arms-bearing tribesmen they retained much of the military potential they had possessed in the days of the Almohads. But Berbers did not constitute the core of the army for the Saʿdids and ʿAlawids as they had done for the Almoravids and Almohads. In the second place, both Sharīfian dynasties, like so many others, had a tendency to recruit troops among outsiders, in this case populations that lacked ties to powerful Moroccan tribes. The Saʿdids valued renegades and Moriscos in this role, as is apparent from the story of Aḥmad al-Manṣūr's expedition to West Africa; we can compare this with the employment of overtly Christian mercenaries by the Almoravids, Almohads, and Marīnids. As we have seen, the ʿAlawid Mawlāy Ismāʿīl preferred black slaves, who whatever their geographical origins stemmed from outside the ranks of the Moroccan elite, and these troops were still there at the end of our period, numbering eighteen thousand, it is said, in 1808. This, too, had ample precedent in North Africa. The Aghlabids had initiated the practice, and the Almoravids and Almohads had returned to it. But once the Arab tribes began to spread in North Africa, they were a further option. When Hilālī Arabs arrived in Tunisia in the mid-eleventh century, the response of the Zīrid ruler was to try to co-opt them for his army. In the same way the Almohads and Marīnids recruited from the Arab tribes. It would thus have been odd if the Saʿdids and ʿAlawids had not done the same. In the case of the Saʿdids, already in the Sūs they had the support of a clan of Maʿqil, a tribe that had arrived in North Africa toward the middle of the eleventh century. This was more than just a mercenary relationship, as Aḥmad al-Manṣūr took a wife from this clan. In fact, the core of the Saʿdid army, known as the Jaysh, came to be made up of certain Arab tribes, including the Maʿqil of the Sūs. Moreover, it was members of these tribes who became the highest officers of the state. Turning to the ʿAlawids, we likewise find Mawlāy Ismāʿīl recruiting Maʿqil tribesmen, this time from the oases of the northern Sahara. His mother belonged to a subtribe of Maʿqil that became a key component of his army. Here again the Arab tribesmen were not just one of several elements of a diverse ʿAlawid army; they belonged to its core. When the state fell apart once more, these tribes—along with the black slave troops—played a central role in the commotions that followed. Altogether, the prominence of the Arab tribes in the ruler's army made Morocco in this period very different from the Ottoman outposts in Tunis or Algiers, where the core of the armed forces continued to be imported from the heartlands of the Ottoman Empire—a system that survived in Algeria till the French conquest of 1830 and remained in operation in Tunisia even after the ruler suppressed a rebellion of his Janissary troops in 1811, with many of the rebels being killed by his Arab troops. More broadly, Morocco was the only major state in the Muslim world that relied primarily on Arab tribesmen for its army. So it was not just their descent from the Prophet that made the ʿAlawids an Arab dynasty.

As our survey of the Arab lands from Iraq to Morocco has shown, Arab power was not much in evidence in the context of large-scale state formation in the eleventh to eighteenth centuries. In Iraq, Egypt, and Tunisia, it was entirely absent, and as of the sixteenth century all three were ruled by an empire based outside the Arab lands. Arab power survived uniquely long in Spain, but without achieving imperial dimensions, and in any case the eleventh century saw its demise. Thereafter it was to make a unique if qualified appearance in Sharīfian Morocco, but not until the sixteenth century, and again without giving rise to an empire, unless we are to count the few decades during which the possession of Songhay gave the rulers of Morocco a semblance of imperial power. Sharīfian Morocco apart, just who it was that held power in place of the Arabs varied over time and space. In the west it was Berbers, who long ruled as far east as Tunisia. In the east it was Turks, whose sway eventually extended as far west as what is now western Algeria. And in Spain it was either Berber intruders from the south or Christian intruders from the north. Overall the negative pattern is surprisingly consistent, though it may be hard to find a single explanation for it.

This is one of several points in this book where we could pause to consider the costs and benefits of being a province of an empire. What, in this instance, did the Arabs of the Ottoman lands gain or lose from being ruled by an empire based elsewhere, rather than by states located within the Arab lands, as had been the pre-Ottoman pattern before power shifted to the north?

Let us start with an obvious benefit of being part of an empire, even if it is someone else's, at least if the imperial rulers are able to ensure a modicum of security. The rule of a single state means that life within its borders is not disrupted by the wars that a plurality of states sharing the same territory would wage against each other. The absence of conflict, in turn, is good for economic activity. But if an imperial state fails to deliver security, as was the case with the Ottoman Empire after the sixteenth century, an empire may not be much better in this respect than a plurality of states would be. Meanwhile, the most obvious downside of being ruled from a distant capital is that empires tend to exploit their provinces. There can, of course, be exceptions. A poor but strategically vital region may gain more resources from the center than it loses to it, and the same goes for a poor but religiously prestigious region such as the Ḥijāz. But by and large empires exist to exploit their provinces, not to bankroll them. Thus significant resources that would have been enjoyed by rulers and elites based within the Arab lands and that would in some measure have trickled down to the mass of the population there were instead routed to an imperial center. This, in turn, meant less political and cultural patronage in the provinces. For the Egyptian elite and its culture, and to an extent for its common people, it was clearly an adverse change that under Ottoman rule there was no longer a dynasty in Cairo and that large amounts of Egyptian grain and revenue were appropriated and redistributed by the central government in Istanbul. This point also applies in some measure to Damascus, which had long been a kind of second capital for the Mamlūks. On the other hand, it hardly applies to Baghdad: savagely destroyed by the Mongols in 1258 and again by Tīmūr in 1401, the city had not been the seat of even a minor dynasty since 1410, so that by the time of the Ottoman conquest in 1534 it had long forgotten what it had been like to be a capital city. In this perspective the decentralization of the seventeenth and eighteenth centuries should have worked in favor of local societies in the Arab lands, and to an extent it probably did. It must have increased the proportion of local wealth spent locally—even if the total amount of available wealth was reduced by disorder. As we saw, the Jalīlīs in Mosul had a reputation for cultural patronage. However, the political structures that arose in the period of Ottoman decentralization do not seem to have generated a level of patronage comparable to that dispensed by the pre-Ottoman states. There is no mistaking the fact that the monuments of Cairo today are of Mamlūk rather than Ottoman vintage, just as the great scholars of Cairo under the Mamlūks are vastly more prestigious figures than those of Ottoman Cairo and had access to early Arabic texts that have since been lost. As we have seen, a sense that the Arabs were getting a raw deal from the Ottomans found lively expression at the time. The antagonism we see here does not, of course, mean that Arabs and Turks could never get along. They had to if they were to live together, however bumpy and unreliable the process of mutual accommodation may have been. This imperative applied as much to formal institutions as it did to informal interactions. One of the formal institutions of eighteenth-century Damascus, for example, was the office of Naqīb al-Ashrāf, the official in charge of the affairs of the local descendants of the Prophet, the Ashrāf. He would be appointed by his metropolitan counterpart, the Naqīb al-Ashrāf of Istanbul, but the appointee would nonetheless be a local, not an intruder from the capital. Informal interactions included the evening gatherings of the cultured elite of the city, where in one respect at least the local Arabs were likely to have the edge on their political masters: they were better equipped to prevail in the competitive arena of polite conversation in Arabic.

A significant factor in all this is the extent to which provincial populations share their ethnic and religious identity with the people most closely linked to the imperial center—the "Herrenvolk," as German has it. In the case of the Arabs under Ottoman rule the ethnic distinction was clear: Arabs were not Rūmīs, and both of them knew it. But two things served to mitigate this exclusion. One was the fact that the majority of the Arabs shared with the Rūmīs their allegiance to Sunnī Islam, even if they differed in their schools of law. The other was that the Arabs were the bearers of a literary culture that the Ottomans had to respect, even if the lion's share of their literary patronage, particularly of poetry, tended to go to non-Arabs composing in Persian and Turkish. In both these respects, despite Arab complaints, the situation of the Sunnī Arabs was significantly better than that of the Christians of the Balkans. For them, and particularly for those living under direct Muslim rule, the effect of being part of someone else's empire was exacerbated by the deep religious cleavage and the lack of comparable cultural respect. As we have seen, the situation of the Hindus in India was somewhat better. For the most part the Muslim states that ruled them were based inside India, and some Muslims had respect for—not to say a fascination with—Hindu culture that has no Balkan parallel. This comparison would, of course, have been moot had the conversion of the Balkan Christians and the Hindus of India to Islam proceeded rapidly enough to create a Muslim majority comparable to those of Anatolia and the Arab lands.

Midscale state formation in Arabia

Once we descend from large-scale to midscale state formation, it becomes much easier to find examples of Arab agency in the process. Roughly speaking, we are looking for sites that satisfied two conditions. In material terms, they had to be endowed—if not permanently then at least temporarily—with sufficient resources to make state formation possible, but not enough to make lasting foreign conquest inevitable. And in strategic terms, the farther they were from powerful non-Arab states, and the weaker those states became, the better the prospects for Arab state formation. This combination of factors, material and strategic, makes broad sense of most midscale Arab states that we find. As we might expect, Arabia provided some promising sites for such activity, and we can best begin there.

One such site, and the best of them, was the Yemen. Strategically located at the entrance to the Red Sea, as we have seen it combined maritime frontage with enough rainfall for an agricultural economy. Its mountainous terrain nevertheless made the region unlikely to come under the long-term rule of a single state, and it posed a massive obstacle even to more limited state formation. It thus makes some sense to think of the default condition of the Yemen as tribal anarchy. In the early seventeenth century an Ottoman governor asked a gathering of local notables if the country had ever been in such a state of disorder as it was then, and he was told that it had often been so. Of course, tribal anarchy was also a kind of tribal order, and mountains—in contrast to deserts—helped make some elements of it remarkably long-lasting. Two key tribal groups, Ḥāshid and Bakīl, were present in the Yemen two millennia ago, and they are still there, though not in quite the same places, even today. But this stability did not make the country governable. As a fifteenth-century Egyptian historian put it, "In the Yemen, under almost every stone there is a troublemaker, and a rebel in the shade of every tree."[25]

Against this daunting background, the most persistent tradition of state formation in the Yemen was the Zaydī imamate, with its core of support among the mountain tribes of the northern highlands. Intermissions aside, this Shīʿite tradition endured from 897 to 1962. One reason for its longevity was the close fit that developed between the Zaydī imamate and the social structure of the region. In the northern Yemen, as elsewhere in the country, the mass of the population was made up of tribes that in the grand scheme of Arab genealogy were solidly southern. Alongside them lived an aristocracy of descendants of the Prophet, the Sayyids; they cultivated learning, often in rural surroundings, and provided candidates for the imamate. These Sayyids, as descendants of the tribe of Quraysh, were genealogically Northerners, which meant that despite their sanctity they could be seen by the southern tribesmen as alien and unwelcome. But they could also benefit from the fact that as outsiders they started from a position of neutrality with regard to the endemic tribal conflicts of the Yemen. There is a certain analogy here with the role played by the Sharīfs of Morocco, first in the days of the Idrīsids and then again under the rule of the Saʿdids and ʿAlawids. And much as in Morocco, it was only toward the end of our period that the Zaydī imamate proved capable of extending its rule to the country as a whole, first briefly in the sixteenth century and then in a more continuing fashion for something like a hundred years in the seventeenth and eighteenth centuries.[26] This latter was a period in which the Zaydī imamate even expanded eastward into Ḥaḍramawt and acquired such trappings of a regular state as a small standing army, one that included imported slave soldiers. Parallel to this was a shift in religious orientation. The Zaydī imams now ruled over the large Sunnī population of the southern Yemen, and this circumstance stimulated a marked movement in the direction of Sunnism in the Zaydism of the day. Two developments of the seventeenth century made possible the belated evolution of the imamate into a real state. One was the success of the

25. Quoted in E. Vallet, *Arabie marchande*, Paris 2010, 650.

26. For the history of the Zaydī imamate in this period see B. Haykel, "Western Arabia and Yemen during the Ottoman period," in *The new Cambridge history of Islam*, vol. 2.

Zaydī imams in eliminating the Ottoman presence, a struggle that lasted for decades and was concluded only in 1635. The other was an unprecedented commercial opportunity. The period from the beginning of the seventeenth century to the early eighteenth was the only one in the history of the Yemen when the highlands had a cash crop to export, namely coffee. Though a precarious monocultural basis for a state, it was good while it lasted. But from the 1720s the Yemen was to lose much of its market share as coffee production developed elsewhere.

Prior to the days of the coffee imamate a large if fluctuating part of the Yemen was mostly beyond the reach of the Zaydī imams. This was particularly true of the southern lowlands and the western coastal plain—the Tihāma. The result was the existence of an alternative region for state formation; indeed, coffee apart, it was a better one. Between the decay of ʿAbbāsid power in the ninth century and the Ayyūbid conquest in the twelfth, a variety of more or less indigenous actors occupied this space, often competing with the Zaydī imams for possession of Ṣanʿāʾ. One of them, the Ṣulayḥid dynasty (1047–1138), represented a rival religious movement, Ismāʿīlism. Though aligned with the Fāṭimid rulers of Egypt, this was essentially an indigenous state founded by a member of the ancient Yemeni tribe of Hamdān. The dynasty held sway over a larger territory than was subject to the Zaydī imams at any time before the sixteenth century, and it included in its domains the major port city of Aden. The founder was even powerful enough to intervene militarily in Mecca. The dynasty was also remarkable in that for several decades its ruler was an able and determined woman, the Sayyida Arwā (d. 1138), who moved her capital southward from Ṣanʿāʾ to Dhū Jibla. Her motivation for the move was straightforward: if you assembled the people of Ṣanʿāʾ you saw nothing but the lightning flashes of drawn swords and lance blades, whereas if you did the same in Dhū Jibla you saw men leadings rams or carrying pots filled with clarified butter or honey. But though more powerful than the Zaydī imamate of its day, the Ṣulayḥid state could not match its longevity. The same was true of the other dynasties of this period, most of which were more or less secular in the sense that whatever their religious allegiances, they were not seeking to mobilize the tribes in support of a religious cause.

The later twelfth century saw a significant change in the origins of these secular dynasties. A fourteenth-century administrator took the view that the king of the Yemen slept well because he had no enemies, being "protected by a vast sea and a land remote from all countries."[27] There was some truth in this, but not enough. Though the resources of the Yemen were hardly abundant, they could still trigger foreign interest, and as we have seen the remoteness of the country provided only partial protection from this hazard. There had been Roman, Ethiopian,

27. Quoted in Vallet, *Arabie marchande*, 495.

and Sasanian incursions, though these had not resulted in the implantation of foreign dynasties. In Islamic times the Yemen was a province of the Caliphate from the seventh century to the ninth. Thereafter it was not invaded until the twelfth, when a foreign conquest of 1173 installed a branch of the Ayyūbids (1174–1229) that ruled in the southern lowlands. Their Turcoman successors, the Rasūlids, lasted until the mid-fifteenth century. Then in the early sixteenth century a threat of a new kind appeared, that of the Portuguese maritime empire. This in turn led the Mamlūks to seize Zabīd in 1516. One reason for their success may have been the presence within the Mamlūk force of Ottomans with firearms, which were new to the Yemen. The Ottomans themselves followed suit in 1538, taking Aden and going on to occupy a large part of the country. Although the Zaydī imams evicted them in the seventeenth century, the Ottomans would be back in the nineteenth. In short, from the twelfth century onward coastal and southern Yemen was often in the hands of foreigners. But the mountainous terrain of the northern highlands, though inimical to the formation of a strong state, enabled the Zaydī imamate to survive these invasions, and its success in ending the Ottoman presence enabled it to reap the benefit of the unprecedented commercial opportunity of the seventeenth century. All told, from the later twelfth century to the end of our period the Yemen was for the most part ruled either by the Zaydī imams or by foreigners. There were minor indigenous potentates on a local scale, as when the Zaydī imamate began to lose territory in the eighteenth century, but the only significant indigenous dynasty of the lowlands in this period was that of the Ṭāhirids (1454–1517); they inherited the Rasūlid state but lost out to the Mamlūks.

A second site of Arabian state formation was Oman.[28] As we saw, Oman was similar to the Yemen in combining a commercially advantageous maritime frontage, here at the mouth of the Persian Gulf, with a certain agricultural potential. The only significant changes in Oman since the First Imamate were the arrival of the Europeans in the late fifteenth century and the displacement of Ṣuḥār by Muscat as the major port of Oman. As before, the resources of the region provided a basis for indigenous state formation while at the same time inviting foreign invasion.

Just as in the Yemen, the most persistent contender for power in Oman was a sectarian tradition, in this case a Khārijite one, that of the Ibāḍī imamate. In fact, this imamate lasted from 750 to 1955, even longer than its Yemeni counterpart, though probably with longer intermissions than in the Yemeni case. Unlike the Zaydī imamate, the Ibāḍī imamate enjoyed not one but two extended periods of relative success, the first from 793 to 893 and the second from 1624 to the end of our period. As we have seen, in the first period the imamate was not

28. For what follows see J. Wilkinson, *The imamate tradition of Oman*, Cambridge 1987.

dynastic, though most of the imams belonged to a particular tribe, and the polity was characterized by mechanisms that made for limited government. In the second period no such mechanisms are in evidence. Instead there were two successive dynasties, one being the Yaʿrubids or Yaʿāriba (1624–1743) and the other the Āl Bū Saʿīd (ruling since 1754). Somewhat as in the Yemen, the imamate thus became more like a sultanate. A telling moment came in 1719, when the deceased imam was succeeded by a minor—a typical hazard of common or garden dynasties, but unthinkable in the case of an imamate. Indeed, the Āl Bū Saʿīd no longer even claimed to be imams after the late eighteenth or early nineteenth century. What the two extended periods had in common was that success turned on combining rule over the interior with control of the coast and its agricultural and commercial resources. Though the second period was roughly contemporary with the era of the coffee imamate in the Yemen, Oman had no comparable cash crop to export. Instead, as we have seen, the Omanis benefited from the growth of world trade by engaging in commerce and acquiring a small but valuable maritime empire. In this enterprise they made liberal use of the services of Portuguese captives and renegades, along with Dutch and English navigators and gunners. Between the two periods the imamate tended either to lose control of the coast or to be in abeyance altogether, thus leaving space for secular dynasties of the usual kind, notably the poorly known Nabhānids (ca. 1100–1624). Ibn Baṭṭūṭa encountered one of them, an Ibāḍī ruling in Nizwā. Though he refers to him as a sultan, this ruler was not surrounded by the pomp of royalty: he had no chamberlain or vizier, and anyone could come to see him. In those respects he sounds like an imam without the title.

All this presupposes that Oman was left to itself. In fact, however, the resources that made indigenous state formation possible also made Oman at least somewhat attractive to outsiders, just as the Yemen was, though until the coming of the oil industry in the middle of the twentieth century their interest stopped short of the interior. At the same time, the maritime scene around the Persian Gulf was much livelier than that around the Red Sea, so that Oman was more easily accessible than the Yemen was to outside powers. In Islamic times no foreign dominations lasted as long in Oman as those that characterized the Yemen from the twelfth century onward, but incursions were much more frequent. Any land power throwing its weight around in the region of the Persian Gulf tended sooner or later to appear on the Omani coast; even the Khwārazmians, whose homeland was over a thousand miles from the ocean, showed up in the Omani port of Qalhāt. So, too, did the Portuguese, who sacked it and took possession of some of the Omani ports, including Ṣuḥār in 1507. It was evicting the Portuguese that set in motion the Omani overseas expansion under the Yaʿrubids, somewhat as the expulsion of the Ottomans from the Yemen led to the coffee imamate. An agreement reached with the British in 1798 in the context of the Napoleonic wars was a sign of future foreign entanglement: Oman was destined to become in effect a British protectorate in 1891.

A third Arabian site that could provide more or less continuous support for some kind of state or states in Islamic times was the Ḥijāz. As we saw in surveying its history from the ninth century to the eleventh, there were three alternative configurations of power in the Ḥijāz. It could be under the direct rule of an outside power; it could be abandoned by the wider Muslim world; or it could be ruled by local ʿAlid dynasties with an outside power serving as overlord. In the period we are now concerned with we no longer hear much of the first two configurations. No outside power again sought to rule the whole Ḥijāz directly till the Saudi conquest of 1924–25, and the region was not left to go to rack and ruin again. Instead, dual rule was more or less continuous from the later tenth century to the early twentieth. Once their external support was assured, the Sharīfs of the two cities could extend their geographical reach to the mining resources of the hinterland or to ports such as Jeddah on the Red Sea coast. These ports were of poor quality, but levying customs duties at Jeddah offered a way to take a cut from the profits of the long-distance trade between the Indian Ocean and the Mediterranean, as seems to have been done in late medieval times. Something else that made for stability was the fact that for most of the time in these centuries there was just a single outside power seeking to exercise hegemony in the Ḥijāz, rather than competing powers resorting to violence against each other or the local population. For obvious geographical reasons the outside power would normally be whoever ruled Egypt, be it the Fāṭimids, the Ayyūbids, the Mamlūks, or the Ottomans. At first there had been competition between the Fāṭimids and the Seljuqs, and in this unsettled period Seljuq forces plundered Mecca twice in the 1090s. But thereafter military competition involving multiple patrons was rare, and absent such violence, the Ḥijāz stood to benefit from peaceful competition between rival donors. Particularly beneficial was the rise of wealthy Muslim states in India. These states made no attempt to project hard power across the Indian Ocean, but they were generous with their soft power. This brought a supply of Indian rice to supplement the continuing import of Egyptian grain.

These conditions left space for local Sharīfian dynasties to emerge and take root. As a Sharīfian ruler put it to his sons in the early thirteenth century, "God has protected you and your country through its inaccessibility."[29] By 940 one such dynasty had been established in Medina, and it proved remarkably long-lived, surviving until the late seventeenth century. This Imāmī Shīʿite dynasty was no

29. Quoted in C. Snouck Hurgronje, *Mekka*, The Hague 1888–89, 1:78.

doubt associated with the presence in Medina of a once-dominant Imāmī community that survives to this day; since the later seventeenth century they have been known as the Nakhāwila. Around 967 a counterpart dynasty emerged in Mecca. Whereas the initial Meccan dynasty came to an end in 1061, the third, established in 1201, lasted until 1925, thereby taking its place among the longest-lasting dynasties of Muslim history. The Sharīfs were not, or course, fully independent rulers. They depended too much on the charity of the outside world, and hegemonic powers would readily intervene in their turbulent internal affairs. The effect of their dependence is evident in some obvious contrasts between the Ḥijāzī Sharīfs and the imams of the Yemen and Oman. First, the Sharīfs did not make a habit of claiming the imamate—in other words, the caliphate. Second, whereas until the later fourteenth century they were Shīʿites—Zaydīs in Mecca and Imāmīs in Medina—from the fifteenth century onward, in Mecca at least, they were Sunnīs in line with the hegemonic powers and the majority of Muslims. As sectarians they could resist the external pressure to conform, but they could not do so forever. Third, despite their claim to religious legitimacy as descendants of the Prophet, they did not come to power through any kind of Ibn Khaldūnian religious movement. All in all, the system was to prove remarkably stable: at least in Mecca the outside powers did not impose direct rule, the Sharīfs rarely claimed independence, and their recurrent quarrels among themselves did not lead to the collapse of their polity. As before, Sharīfs could be known for conspicuously bad behavior. A twelfth-century Damascene poet who was robbed by Sharīfs between Medina and Mecca complained loudly in verse about his experience, only to have a dream in which Fāṭima, daughter of the Prophet and ancestress of all Sharīfs, explained to him, likewise in verse, that her descendants were not evil, just unfortunate.

Apart from Oman, the Yemen, and the Ḥijāz, no region of Arabia had a record of persistent state formation in our period. There were nevertheless a couple of sites that supported significant states for a while, one at the beginning of our period, the other at the end. The first site was Aḥsāʾ, known in earlier times as Baḥrayn. It was located in the northeast of the peninsula with easy access to the coast, and it contained the most extensive oasis in Arabia. Here the Ismāʿīlīs had been active since the late ninth century. As we saw, their activity led to the establishment of a state that was ruled by the breakaway Qarmaṭī sect and lasted into the later eleventh century. We possess a vivid description of this state from a traveler who visited it in 1051. Two things stand out. First, this polity was not a monarchy. Instead, it was ruled by a council of six descendants of the founder of the state, together with their six viziers. This arrangement is not an altogether isolated case. Nonmonarchical rule is an occasional feature of remote city-states in the Muslim world, as we have seen in the case of early thirteenth-century Mogadishu. Another example would be the Saharan oasis of Ghadāmis in the tenth century, of which we are told that "they have no chief, but are governed by their elders."[30] Second, the Qarmaṭī state treated its citizens with unusual generosity. They paid no taxes, had ready access to credit, and led an easy life thanks to the presence of thirty thousand East African slaves. The puzzle is how the rulers could have financed so expensive a welfare state from the revenues available to them; the economic rent from oil production that makes such things possible in the Persian Gulf today was still far in the future. In the tenth century the military power of the Qarmaṭīs had given them a substantial income from raiding and extortion, and the eleventh-century traveler reports that they still had twenty thousand men able to bear arms. But in this period they were no longer mounting raids in the old way.

The subsequent history of the region is not well known, but in recent centuries it has been notable for its Imāmī Shīʿite population. A good guess would be that over the intervening period the Qarmaṭīs had retained their Shīʿism but shifted their sectarian allegiance within it. Meanwhile the agricultural resources of the oasis had not gone away, and after the demise of the Qarmaṭī state in the later eleventh century we hear of a succession of minor secular dynasties in the region—the ʿUyūnids (eleventh to thirteenth centuries), the ʿUṣfūrids (thirteenth to fifteenth centuries), the Jabrids (fifteenth and sixteenth centuries), and the Banū Khālid (seventeenth and eighteenth centuries). The Banū Khālid, in turn, fell victim to the Saudi expansion in the last decade of the eighteenth century. The Saudis were not the only eighteenth-century invaders from the interior to conquer parts of the eastern Arabian coast. The ruling groups of some of today's Persian Gulf states have their origins in migrations of this period; this is the background to the current Sunnī dominance over the indigenous Shīʿite population of the island of Bahrain. But whether we would want to describe these various later entities as states rather than tribal chieftaincies is arguable. The region could also attract some interest from outside Arabia. Thus the Persians were there in pre-Islamic times, the Portuguese arrived in the early sixteenth century, and the Ottomans established a presence in the middle of that century.

The second site, the one that supported a state only toward the end of our period, was the region of Najd in the eastern Arabian interior. Here the Saudi state had its beginnings in the oasis of Dirʿiyya in the mid-1740s. Najd was a land of scattered oases. None of them were of any size, and each was accustomed to being an independent polity, pursuing its own violent internal feuds and often at war with its neighbors. Moreover, Najd, unlike the other Arabian sites we have looked at, lacked access to the sea. This denied it the benefits of maritime commerce, though

30. N. Levtzion and J.F.P. Hopkins, *Corpus of early Arabic sources for West African history*, Cambridge 1981, 199.

also giving it limited protection against foreign intrusion. All in all, Najd was an unlikely site for the emergence of a state. If we scrape the barrel for a precedent, it would have to be a minor Sharīfian dynasty of the ninth to eleventh centuries that ruled only the southern part of the region.

In the absence of a credible material basis for a state, faith was the wild card, and the Saudi state was indeed the result of an Ibn Khaldūnian process of religious mobilization in a tribal society. But this state differed from the Arabian states established by the Zaydīs, Ibāḍīs, and Qarmaṭīs in its allegiance to Sunnism. The leader of the movement, Muḥammad ibn ʿAbd al-Wahhāb (d. 1792), was a Sunnī, and like the inhabitants of Najd at large he was a follower of the Ḥanbalī law school. An earlier member of this law school, the Damascene scholar Ibn Taymiyya (d. 1328), had been strongly opposed to what he saw as polytheistic practices among Muslims. Ibn ʿAbd al-Wahhāb proceeded to revive his thinking, labeling those he deemed polytheists as infidels against whom the true believers had the obligation to wage war. According to his opponents he had adopted Ibn Taymiyya's teaching without properly understanding it. They went on to label his cause with the derogatory but convenient epithet "Wahhābī" and saw it as a deviation from true Islam. At the same time, the Wahhābī movement differed from those of the Arabian sectarians in another respect. Among the sectarians there was no differentiation between religious and political leadership, and the Ibāḍī and Zaydī imams combined these roles, just as the Prophet had done. The alternative, as we have seen, was to separate the two roles in the manner of Saul and Samuel, and it was an arrangement of this kind that emerged in the Wahhābī case. After a failed attempt to implant himself in the oasis of ʿUyayna, Ibn ʿAbd al-Wahhāb succeeded in Dirʿiyya. Here in the mid-1740s he reached an agreement with the local chief, Muḥammad ibn Suʿūd. This chief had been pressed to back Ibn ʿAbd al-Wahhāb by his wife, who saw an opportunity worth seizing. Religious authority was thus vested in Ibn ʿAbd al-Wahhāb and, after him, his descendants, whereas political authority was exercised by Ibn Suʿūd and his descendants—which is why we speak of the Wahhābī movement but the Saudi state.

The military expansion of this state was initially so slow that it took the Saudis decades of warfare to bring the entirety of Najd under their sway. But from about 1785 things went faster. In 1793 they conquered Aḥsāʾ with its relative agricultural wealth, in 1802 they raided Iraq, in 1803–5 they conquered the Ḥijāz, and in 1810 they raided Syria. In the Ḥijāz they effectively closed down the pilgrimage for most Muslims—whom of course they considered to be unbelievers. This was too much for the Ottomans, for whom even Bedouin attacks on caravans of pilgrims were a public relations disaster. As we saw, the Ottoman sultan delegated the task of destroying the Saudi state to the upstart ruler of Egypt, Meḥmed ʿAlī Pasha. The invasion that followed ended Saudi rule in 1818, but it did not issue in a permanent conquest of Najd. The Wahhābī movement survived, and within a few years the Saudi state was restored. Despite a further discontinuity in the later nineteenth century, it is there to this day.

Overall, the Arabs did rather well as rulers in their Arabian homeland during the eleventh to eighteenth centuries. As indicated, this reflected the coincidence of two factors. On the one hand, there were several sites that had enough resources to support midscale state formation, but not so much as to pose an irresistible temptation to foreign powers. And on the other hand, all these sites had at least a degree of strategic insulation from such powers by virtue of intervening sea or desert. As we will now see, Arabia was in fact the only region in the Arab world that satisfied both conditions. We will indeed find midscale Arab states elsewhere, but in no other region will they be either so numerous or so durable.

Midscale state formation outside Arabia

As we saw, the period around the turn of our era witnessed the establishment of a set of Arab principalities in the Fertile Crescent. They owed their existence to the weakness of the outside powers, a window of opportunity that closed once the Romans had replaced the Seleucids in the west and the Sasanians had overthrown the Arsacids in the east. The Arab frontier principalities of late antiquity, the Ghassānids and Lakhmids, were very different: they owed their existence more to imperial policy than to imperial weakness. It was not until the later tenth century that a window of the Arsacid type reopened in the Fertile Crescent with the decay of ʿAbbāsid power and the absence of other strong states until the coming of the Seljuqs. In this interval the cat was away and the mice could play. We have already examined some aspects of this phenomenon, and will confine ourselves here to a closer look at the Bedouin dynasties of the period. There were four of them: the Mirdāsids (1024–80) based in Aleppo, the Mazyadids (ca. 961–ca. 1150) in Ḥilla, the Numayrids (990–ca. 1081) in the Jazīra, and the ʿUqaylids (ca. 990–1169), whose branches ruled at various times and places in the Jazīra and northern Iraq. These four dynasties shared two features. First, they were not just of Arab tribal background; they also retained a marked tribal and nomadic character, living in camps rather than cities. A Mazyadid ruler bore the unusual title "King of the Arabs," and Arab tribesmen seem to have remained the basis of the military power of these dynasties throughout their history. In this respect they differed from the roughly contemporary Ḥamdānids of Mosul and Aleppo. But this did not mean that the ways of sedentary states were unknown to them. One ʿUqaylid ruler knew enough to place an intelligence agent in each of the villages under his control, and the temporary encampment (*ḥilla*) from which at one stage the Mazyadids ruled eventually blossomed into the city of Ḥilla thanks to their efforts. The second feature of these dynasties—here including the Ḥamdānids—was that they tended to be Shīʿite. This was a time when it was by no means obvious that the core of the Muslim world had a Sunnī future. The demise of these Arab dynasties of the Fertile Crescent came in various ways, but a key factor was the arrival of the Seljuqs.

To get a more vivid sense of what these dynasties were like, let us take a closer look at the Mirdāsids. They belonged to the tribe of Kilāb, which had long been established in northern Syria but was reinforced in 932 by the arrival of large numbers of fellow tribesmen from Najd. It was these Kilābī tribesmen who until the last years of the dynasty provided the military basis of Mirdāsid power; on occasion they could win a pitched battle against a Fāṭimid army. The geographical basis of the dynasty was the region around Aleppo, strategically located at a reasonably comfortable distance from each of the main centers of power at the time—Fāṭimid Cairo, Būyid Baghdad, and Byzantine Constantinople. The Mirdāsids were nevertheless obliged to maneuver between these powers. Of the three, they were politically closest to the Byzantines, who at one point granted titles to the Mirdāsid ruler and his wife. The history of the dynasty was an eventful one. The founder, Ṣāliḥ ibn Mirdās (ruled 1024–29), was the courageous survivor of a banquet to which the then ruler of Aleppo had invited a thousand Kilābīs, plying them with drink and then massacring most of them. A few years later the Fāṭimids were able to install a governor in Aleppo. Ṣāliḥ then put together an anti-Fāṭimid alliance comprising the three main Arab tribes of Syria—his own Kilābīs in the north, the Kalbīs in the center, and Ṭayy in the south. The Ṭayy chief, in turn, reached out to one of the Arab tribes of Cyrenaica, on the other side of Egypt, in a remarkable exercise of Arab geopolitical imagination. Against the background of this transitory edifice of Arab unity, Ṣāliḥ was able to seize Aleppo in 1024, and it became—with some intermissions—the Mirdāsids' capital. It was there that they now established their state, complete with a vizier. Yet they did not lose touch with their nomadic background. The first Mirdāsid ruler was known as "Emir of the Arabs of Syria,"[31] and he preferred to live in the tribe's encampment on the outskirts of Aleppo. A later ruler, one of his sons, saw fit to send his wife to negotiate with the Fāṭimid caliph, who found her utterly charming. On another occasion, however, the couple quarreled, and she absconded to the tribal encampment in high dudgeon. She was by no means the only politically prominent woman in the history of the Arab dynasties of the period. But with the coming of the Turcomans and their Seljuq rulers this kind of Arab power, whatever its desert charm, was no longer viable. The end came when the Seljuq Tutush (ruled 1078–95) set about establishing his rule in Syria. As he was besieging the last Mirdāsid ruler, Sābiq ibn Maḥmūd (ruled 1076–80), in Aleppo, Sābiq made a desperate appeal to two of his brothers, who in a typical pattern of fraternal conflict were siding with the

31. See S. Zakkar, *The Emirate of Aleppo*, Beirut 1971, 104.

enemy: "If this city falls into the hands of Tutush, he will demolish the rule of the Arabs."[32] He made a similar appeal to the Kilābī tribesmen and invoked ties of Arab blood in seeking the help of the ʿUqaylid ruler of Mosul. The latter responded, thus staving off Seljuq rule, but only for another six years. Here again, appeals to Arab solidarity were clearly meaningful, even when they fell on deaf ears. But by now the good times were over for Arab rule in the Fertile Crescent.

There was nevertheless one familiar Arab dynasty in the Fertile Crescent that was to have some success in the twelfth and early thirteenth centuries: the ʿAbbāsid caliphs in Baghdad.[33] As we have seen, after the early tenth century they were no longer imperial rulers. Indeed, from 945 they were reduced to sharing even their city of Baghdad with intrusive Būyid rulers and Seljuq governors. This was when the astrologers summed up the situation by remarking that all that was now left to the caliph was a religious authority to the exclusion of a secular one—he was now a mere "head of Islam." The caliph himself was not in disagreement with this assessment. Deflecting a Būyid request for funding for jihad, al-Muṭīʿ (reigned 946–74) explained that he had neither the money nor the troops with which to discharge this or any other duty of a Muslim ruler; the world, he pointed out, was not in his hands, but rather in those of the Būyids and their likes. Conditions were initially no better under the Seljuqs, who tended to take the view that the caliph should leave the affairs of this world to the sultans. The Seljuq sultan Masʿūd (ruled 1134–52) put it bluntly: "I want someone on the throne who will meddle in nothing but religious matters, and will not raise an army."[34] But such a division of labor was not one that a caliph could accept with any enthusiasm. After the Būyid ruler of Iraq deposed the reigning caliph in 991 by having him dragged from his throne, the new caliph, al-Qādir (reigned 991–1031), had an understandable desire to repair the authority of his office. Tellingly, the most salient way in which he was able to do this was by acting precisely as the head of Islam: he promulgated an orthodox creed. Or at least it was orthodox by the standards then prevalent in Baghdad—a significant alignment, since one of the few quarters to which the caliph could look for a measure of dependable support was the Sunnī, and specifically Ḥanbalī, populace of the city, to the exclusion of its large Shīʿite community. As one contemporary expressed it, the caliphate was like a tent with the Ḥanbalīs as its ropes; if the ropes failed, the tent would collapse. But when it came to the affairs of this world, the bottom line was the question Stalin is said to have asked about the pope: "How many divisions has he?" Like the pope, the caliphs in this epoch had none, having been stripped of what was left of their army in the 930s.

32. Quoted in Zakkar, *The Emirate of Aleppo*, 194.

33. For ʿAbbāsid history in this period see T. El-Hibri, *The Abbasid caliphate*, Cambridge 2021, chs. 5–6, and E. J. Hanne, *Putting the caliph in his place*, Madison 2007.

34. Quoted in C. Hillenbrand, *A Muslim principality in Crusader times*, Leiden 1990, 73.

It was not until the withering of Seljuq power after 1092, particularly in western Iran, that a window of opportunity opened up for a more muscular reassertion of caliphal authority. The first caliph to step through the window was al-Mustarshid (ruled 1118–35). Though his reign ended badly, this ambitious ruler was able to do two things. He extended his rule over enough of central Iraq to secure a viable source of revenue, and he recruited a large enough army to make him a regional contender. Each of these achievements presupposed the other, and it is unclear how he reached the point at which his efforts could be sustained, but reach it he did. One of his assets in the struggle was the continuing loyalty of the Sunnī populace of Baghdad—he did not hesitate to arm them in response to military danger. Two subsequent caliphs were able to sustain or recreate his success: his brother al-Muqtafī (ruled 1136–60) and the latter's great-grandson al-Nāṣir (ruled 1180–1225). The first can be seen as a more successful version of al-Mustarshid. For his army al-Muqtafī recruited Greek and Armenian slaves (he considered Turks unreliable), and he used them to such good effect that he came to rule over most of Iraq. Like his brother he was ready to arm the people of Baghdad in an emergency. In some ways al-Nāṣir was in the same tradition. His powerful symbolic gesture of demolishing the Seljuq palace in Baghdad in 1187 would have warmed the heart of his great-grandfather. He, too, had an army, and unlike al-Muqtafī he had no objection to Turkic slaves. He, too, used his forces to extend his rule in Iraq. But al-Nāṣir also set about developing a novel form of soft power. He cultivated a religious profile that, though inimical to philosophers, was friendly to Shīʿites, to Ṣūfīs, and to groups practicing a kind of male youth culture (*futuwwa*). Above all, he sought to weld all this into an organization extending far outside Iraq, with himself as its supreme leader. Like al-Qādir, he was staking out a role as the head of Islam, though in a very different vein. But the window that made possible these late revivals of ʿAbbāsid power closed abruptly when the Mongol conquerors sacked Baghdad and ended the dynasty's rule in 1258. In any case, as the role of al-Muqtafī's Greek and Armenian soldiers makes clear, it was the dynasty rather than the state that was Arab. Not that Baghdad was immune to the charms of the Bedouin moment in the Fertile Crescent, as the case of a poet of the city known as Ḥayṣa Bayṣa (d. 1179) makes clear. He did, of course, have a real name, but he had acquired his nickname from a recondite Arabic phrase that he used in his speech, something the Arabs—meaning the pre-Islamic Arabs—reputedly used to say. In line with this he cultivated a Bedouin manner of speaking and dressed in the style of the Arab rulers of his day. He also claimed descent from a famous sage of the ancient and prestigious tribe of Tamīm. However, a literary antagonist told him—in verse, of course—that he lacked even a single hair of Tamīm, and suggested he eat lizard, an animal that the Bedouin were notorious for savoring, though everyone else considered it disgusting. Ḥayṣa Bayṣa's affectations were an expression of ethnic nostalgia, not of Arab power.

Thereafter Arabs continued to play some part in state formation in the Fertile Crescent, but less frequently than they had done before the coming of the Seljuqs, and on a smaller scale. One such dynasty was known as the Musha'sha'. This family claimed descent from the Prophet and professed highly heterodox Shī'ite beliefs. In the fifteenth century they established their rule among the Arab tribes around Ḥuwayza in Khūzistān, or 'Arabistān as it was now appropriately called. The rise of the Ṣafawids clipped their wings, but they were able to maintain a local presence among the turbulent Arab tribes of the region down to modern times. Meanwhile in Mamlūk Syria, the Bedouin—including the familiar tribes of Kilāb and Ṭayy—still roamed the desert to the east, and they still mattered. The sultan would appoint an "Emir of the Arabs" from a leading chiefly family, an arrangement indicating a symbiotic relationship between the nomads and the state that we do not encounter in Iraq after the disappearance of the Mazyadids. Sultan Baybars (ruled 1260–77) put real effort into cementing these ties in the context of the wars between the Mamlūks and the Īlkhāns. This military relationship is reminiscent of the link between the Byzantine rulers and the Ghassānids in late antiquity. But when it came to actual state formation, the more successful Arab protagonists in Syria now tended to stem from mountain clans rather than desert tribes. Such was the case of Mount Lebanon from the sixteenth century onward. Here, under an Ottoman aegis, first the Druze Ma'nids (sixteenth and seventeenth centuries) and then the Sunnī—later Christian—Shihābids (1697–1842) ruled an emirate whose material basis was initially European demand for Lebanese silk. Elsewhere in Syria we find ourselves scraping the barrel. In Palestine a tent-dwelling Bedouin family already prominent under Mamlūk rule made a successful transition to the new Ottoman order, providing governors for the northern province of Lajjūn for much of the sixteenth and seventeenth centuries. As we have seen, something closer to an autonomous state emerged in the same region in the middle decades of the eighteenth century, based on cotton production for the European market. But it did not outlast the lifetime of its founder, Ẓāhir al-'Umar (d. 1775), and the next strongman to establish himself in the region was not a local Arab but a Bosnian pasha. Meanwhile, the 'Aẓms who governed Damascus at various times in the eighteenth century were in some sense Arabs, whatever their ultimate origins; that is to say, they were part of the Arabic-speaking rural population of northern Syria. But they rose to power and exercised it within the framework of Ottoman provincial government. In short, Ottoman decentralization opened a window for Arab state formation, but a considerably smaller one than that of the tenth and eleventh centuries. Turkish power was still crowding out Arab power.

Leaving Asia for Africa, we find ourselves in a vast region in which there is relatively little to detain us. Most of the African territory occupied by speakers of Arabic was either too poor to support passable states or too rich to be left to the rule of Arabs in this epoch. We nevertheless encounter cases of midscale Arab state formation here and there. Let us start with the coastlands of northern Africa to the west of Egypt. We come first to Cyrenaica, a peninsula of sorts with a modest mountain chain behind the coast that endowed it with some agricultural resources. Its main settlement was Barqa (now al-Marj) northeast of Benghazi and a few miles inland. The region attracted some foreign rule but saw no significant indigenous state formation. Farther to the west was the port of Tripoli, the capital of modern Libya. It lies on a coastal strip where, as in Cyrenaica, some Mediterranean agriculture can be practiced. Usually it was ruled by outsiders from various parts of the Mediterranean world, and after 1551 these were the Ottomans and their governors. Since the ninth century Arab tribes had been a significant presence in the region, but they never came to form a state there. At some times the city was ruled by local figures; one in the twelfth century seems to have claimed Arab ancestry, but he did not found a dynasty.

We do a little better when we move on to Tunisia. As we have already seen, political power in the core of the country was never in the hands of its indigenous inhabitants, Arab or other, but the power of the incumbent states did not necessarily extend to the periphery. Thus Qābis in the south was a rich and extensive oasis with a major port, and at times it was politically independent. In one of those periods—from the end of the eleventh century until well into the twelfth—it was ruled by an Arab dynasty, the Banū Jāmiʿ, in alliance with nearby Arab tribes. One member of the dynasty made a formal claim to sovereignty by minting his own coins.

Moving west from Qābis, we find ourselves in the transition zone between the North African mountains and the Sahara desert. In general this zone has little agricultural potential, but the region of eastern Algeria known as the Zāb is an exception thanks to its soils and water resources.[35] Since the twelfth century its main urban center has been Biskra, and by that time Arab tribes were present in the region. In 1293–94, after a prolonged struggle, a family of settled Arabs, the Banū Muznī, was able to seize Biskra from its non-Arab rulers with the help of the Ḥafṣids. They went on to establish a prosperous and to a considerable extent autonomous state. They had, of course, to maneuver between the various major dynasties of North Africa, to whom they paid tribute as necessary. Their relations with the Arab tribes of the Zāb were mixed. Sometimes they paid the Arabs to fight on behalf of their current dynastic patron, whoever that might be, but on one occasion the tribesmen kidnapped the ruler and extracted a small fortune in ransom. The dynasty was also challenged by a religious movement directed against fiscal oppression, but these pietists had no success in setting up a state of their own. In the end the Banū Muznī succumbed to the Ḥafṣids in 1402. Theirs was the most

35. For what follows see M. Brett, "Ibn Khaldūn and the dynastic approach to local history," *Al-Qanṭara*, 12 (1991).

notable Arab statelet of the late medieval Zāb, but it was by no means the only one. When the Ottomans reached Biskra in the mid-sixteenth century, they turned over local power to another chiefly family, the ruling member of which was known as the "Chief of the Arabs" (*Shaykh al-ʿArab*). But in general, state formation in the region between Tunisia and Morocco was dominated first by the Berbers and then by the Ottomans. Geopolitically the two were very different. Under the Berbers there was a tendency for western and eastern Algeria to be ruled by different dynasties: the ʿAbd al-Wādids in the west, the Ḥammādids and western Ḥafṣids in the east. The Ottomans changed that. Without their intervention in Algeria, and their selection of the more centrally located Algiers as their capital, it is unlikely that Algeria would be a country today. But the key point for us here is that between Berber and Ottoman rule Algeria saw no intervening phase of Arab state formation. Yet farther to the west, in Morocco, the success of the larger dynasties tended to leave little space for midscale Arab state formation. Beyond Morocco we come to the Moors of the western Sahara. As we saw in the previous chapter they had their emirs, but none of them stand out as rulers of plausible states. Nor did the Moors engage in state formation in the settled lands of the western savanna.

If we now return to Egypt and head south, a plausible example of midscale state formation would be the Banū 'l-Kanz, a clan based in the Eastern Desert of Upper Egypt between the ninth and the fifteenth centuries. They exercised considerable power from the eleventh century onward. If they qualify as a state, it would be because they exploited two resources not usually available to desert Arabs: the gold mines of the region and proximity to the northern Nubian kingdom, where at one point in the fourteenth century their incursions led to the rule of a member of the family. Farther south, as we have seen, the Funj coexisted with the Arab ʿAbdallāb dynasty based at Qerrī, a bit north of the confluence of the White and Blue Niles. If we now move westward into the eastern savanna, we have already noted a tendency to claim Arab descent among major settled dynasties. But there is no indication that the Arab nomads of the region, be it the camel nomads of the north or the cattle nomads of the south, engaged in state formation.

The analysis of the role of Arabs in state formation in this section has been a rather loose one, largely because my categorization of dynasties as Arab or non-Arab has been somewhat crude—it is, after all, uncommon for a Muslim dynasty and its supporters to belong exclusively to a single ethnic group, and if we looked into matters more closely we would soon encounter gray areas. Moreover, I have made no attempt to develop precise criteria for distinguishing large-scale from midscale state formation, or for that matter midscale from small-scale, a category I have in practice ignored, though it would not be hard to find examples. The minor dynasties that held power in Aḥsāʾ after the Qarmaṭīs could well belong here. Another example might be the Jarrāḥids. This family belonged to the tribe of Ṭayy and exercised some power around Ramla in Palestine during the later tenth and eleventh centuries, maneuvering energetically between the neighboring powers. But being too close to Fāṭimid Egypt to be in a position to carve out a real state for themselves in the manner of the Mirdāsids, they tended to raid their territories rather than govern them and were not above threatening caravans of pilgrims. A later example from the eastern Fertile Crescent would be the seminomadic Banū Kaʿb, who held considerable territory in ʿArabistān in the late seventeenth and eighteenth centuries. In the 1760s they dominated the estuary of the Tigris and Euphrates with forces that included a navy, which put them in a position to cut off Baṣra from access to the Persian Gulf. That we are looking at an incipient state and not just a powerful tribe is suggested by a contemporary comment on their chief that "within his domains thieves and footpads have become as rare birds as the ʿAnqāʾ"[36]—the ʿAnqāʾ being a fabulous bird resembling the phoenix that no one has ever seen. In North Africa the statelet that existed briefly in sixteenth-century Qayrawān might well qualify as a further example. But ambiguities of classification do not affect the general conclusion that the Arab role in state formation in the eleventh to eighteenth centuries was—or soon came to be—a limited one outside Arabia, the one region where the religious mode of state formation remained very much alive.

The demographic history of the Arabs

The Arab tribes

Between the eleventh and eighteenth centuries the Arab tribes showed a marked tendency to expand their territory. This was nothing new. As we have seen, the Arabs had already spread into the northeastern corner of Africa in antiquity, with the result that by the turn of our era this region had come to be known as "Arabia." We have also had occasion to note the Arab penetration of the Fertile Crescent in ancient times. Indeed, such expansion did not cease even with the end of our period. For example, the nineteenth century saw the Awlād Sulaymān, who boasted never to have paid tribute to any ruler, migrate from the Fazzān to Kānem in 1842–43; they left the Fazzān because they had been defeated by the Ottoman pasha of Tripoli, but in their new territory they were once again the dominant element. An example that dates from the late twentieth and early twenty-first century and is set in a context of modern ethnic conflict is the role of the Arab tribal militia known as the Janjawīd in the destruction of the sedentary black population of Dār Fūr. At the same time, we seem to have no cases where Arab tribes lost significant territory to non-Arab populations in the course of our period. Arab expansion was, then, a very persistent process. In any given region a major role

36. Quoted in J. R. Perry, "The Banū Kaʿb," *Le monde iranien et l'Islam*, 1 (1971), 135.

must have been played Arab nomads arriving from elsewhere, since settled tribal cultivators are much less likely engage in long-distance migration. But the arrival of new tribal populations cannot be the whole story. It is clear that the assimilation of local non-Arab populations by the newcomers must also have played a prominent part.

We have already met a couple of examples of such assimilation. There are telltale signs of a Berber substratum among the Moors of the western Sahara, and the Baqqāra, the cattle nomads of the southern savanna, are as black as anyone in Africa. Another example comes from the Fayyūm, the depression a little to the west of the Nile valley that has been a focus of irrigated agriculture since the third century BC.[37] In the first half of the eleventh century the villages of the Fayyūm were still populated overwhelmingly by Copts—that is to say, nontribal Christian peasants. By 1245, as we know from the fortunate survival of a fiscal survey, the presence of Coptic peasants was residual, and almost all the rural cultivators were now "Arabs," that is, Muslim tribesmen. There is nothing to suggest that the old population had been violently displaced by a new one. Indeed, the survival of the old Coptic names of the villages points in the opposite direction—in contrast to the heavy mortality of Greek village names in large parts of Anatolia. What we lack is direct evidence of the way in which the transition took place, but there are a couple of points worth making here. One is that already in the eleventh century we find instances of tribal Arabs playing the role of protectors of the local population. These men were Kilābīs, members of a tribe that had become powerful in the region. The other point is that the crisis of the Fāṭimid state in 1066–74 is likely to have had an adverse effect on the Fayyūm, among other things by making it easier for the Arab tribes to expand their power. One source tells us that the Lawāta tribesmen took advantage of the chaos to raise their profile in the Egyptian countryside. If we move on to the twelfth century, a geographer, speaking of a settlement in the Fayyūm, laments that "the Lawāta Berbers and other vile Arabs" have taken it over and ruined it.[38] We come then to our fiscal survey of 1245, and sure enough we find the Lawāta (by now very likely Arabized) occupying ten of the 102 villages of the Fayyūm. Another fifty-one villages were inhabited by Kilābīs—the tribe to whom the eleventh-century protectors belonged. The few remaining Coptic peasants were clients of the Arabs, who saw keeping them in their place as part of their way of life. From such fragmentary evidence it would seem that the tribalization of the Fayyūm resulted from the exposure of the Coptic peasants to the increased power of the Arab tribes and the consequent need to secure their

37. For what follows see Y. Rapoport, *Rural economy and tribal society in Islamic Egypt*, Turnhout 2018.

38. Quoted in Rapoport, *Rural economy and tribal society*, 49.

protection. At the same time it reflected the decreased ability of the state to provide such protection for its subjects.

In outlining the part of the larger story that took place between the eleventh and eighteenth centuries we can conveniently deal first with Asia and then with Africa. In Asia there are two main regions worth considering. One is southern Arabia, where the presence of Arabs from the north is already well attested in pre-Islamic times; here the Arabization of the indigenous population may have been largely complete by the eleventh century, if not before. Today the residues of pre-Arab populations are slight. They include the survival of some non-Arabic Semitic languages as islands in a sea of Arabic—though surprisingly, the mountains of the Yemen have been completely Arabized. Beyond the southern coast of Arabia Arab nomads could spread no farther. They were not usually seafarers, and even when they were, they could not easily transport their pastoral economy across the ocean to such places as Somalia or Sindh—environments that might otherwise have been attractive to them. The other region is Iraq, where a far-reaching transformation took place over the course of our period. Its starting point is encapsulated in a dictum of the caliph ʿUmar (ruled 634–44). He is said to have urged the Arabs of his day to cultivate their tribal genealogies and not to be like the natives of Iraq, then known as Nabateans: "When one of them is asked about his origin, he says: 'From such-and-such a village.'"[39] In other words, the Nabateans were peasants, and they were known for their servility. By the end of our period, thanks to the immigration of nomads from northern Arabia, what had once been a land of peasants was mostly a domain of Arab tribes, partly nomadic and partly settled. The chronology of the process is unclear, but a considerable movement of Arab tribes into Iraq had already taken place in the tenth century, and there was another peak in the seventeenth and eighteenth centuries. What Arab nomads did not do on any significant scale was spread north of the boundary separating the lowlands of the southern Middle East from the highlands of the north, where languages other than Arabic were spoken. Though attractive to Iranian and Turkic nomads, the northern Middle East was inhospitable to their Arab counterparts. What happened in Iraq seems also to have happened on a smaller scale in Syria. Thus in Palestine the coastal plain became Bedouin territory, and in the Euphrates valley in what is now Syria the cultivators were tribal.

The impact of this transformation is again evident linguistically. Long ago Ibn Khaldūn made a basic distinction between two kinds of Arabic dialects spoken in his day, those of the city dwellers and those of the Bedouin—the Arabs, as he put it. As a sure way to distinguish them he highlighted a difference in the pronunciation of a phoneme corresponding to the letter *qāf* of literary Arabic. This

39. Ibn Khaldûn, *The Muqaddimah*, trans. F. Rosenthal, Princeton 1967, 1:266.

may sound trivial, but it could become a matter of life and death. When the Mamlūks were suppressing an Arab rebellion in Upper Egypt in 1298, they went about it by killing Bedouin while sparing the nontribal population. The shibboleth they used to distinguish the two populations was the Arabic word for flour, *daqīq*: whoever said *dagīg* in Bedouin fashion was killed. Ibn Khaldūn's categories still apply to Iraqi dialects as we know them today. On the one hand, there are dialects that descend from those of the sedentary population of ʿAbbāsid times, in which *qāf* is an unvoiced *q*; this would originally have been the speech of the city dwellers, and of the peasants to the extent that they had come to speak Arabic. And on the other hand, there are the Bedouin dialects, brought to Iraq in later centuries by immigrant nomads, among whom *qāf* is a voiced *g*. What is historically significant is the extent to which the Bedouin dialects have driven out those of the old sedentary population of Iraq. By modern times, perhaps as a result of immigration from the countryside late in our period, even the Muslim population of Baghdad had come to sound more like nomads, with only the Jews and Christians of the city continuing to speak dialects of the old sedentary type. Farther north, as in Mosul, Muslims could still be found speaking the older dialects, but they survived as pockets surrounded by Bedouin dialects or by Kurdish. A similar though less sweeping process must have been at work in parts of Syria.

In Africa, too, we encounter the division between Bedouin and sedentary dialects, with the same contrast between *q* and *g* that was so consequential in Upper Egypt in 1298. In Egypt as a whole the mass of the population of the Nile valley has retained its sedentary dialects despite extensive Bedouin penetration, which in the eastern delta can be dated to late medieval times. In Libya Bedouin dialects prevail even in the cities—no surprise given the lack of a solid agricultural population to shield the urban populations from Bedouin influence. Across North Africa Bedouin dialects are widespread, dominating the plains. Nevertheless, many cities—such as Tlemcen, Fez, and Rabat—retain their old sedentary dialects, though others, such as Oran, do not. A similar conservatism is found in an extended mountain region of Morocco whose Berber inhabitants adopted the Arabic of the neighboring cities, and such regions are also to be found in Algeria. Thanks to a medieval geographer we know that to the south of Fez this process of early Arabization had already begun by the twelfth century. But in the plains outside the cities Bedouin dialects came to prevail.

Just as in Iraq, the spread of Bedouin dialects in Africa was a result of the arrival of nomadic Arab tribes. As we saw in the previous chapter, there were two main migratory movements here, both starting from Egypt, and in the end they led to the spread of Arab tribes to regions far beyond the limits of the original Arab conquest. One movement, beginning on a large scale as early as the ninth century, involved their spread westward from Egypt to Cyrenaica, Tunisia, Morocco, and eventually what is now Mauritania. Some even reached Spain, where despite the military use of Arab tribesmen and the abundance of pasture, the sea once again posed a significant barrier to the immigration of whole tribes with their livestock. The history of late medieval and early modern Spain might have looked very different if the sheep owners of the Mesta had been Arab nomads. As it was, their expansion to the west was primarily at the expense of the Berber tribes of North Africa and the western Sahara. For the most part this movement of nomads is not well known to us—it usually failed to make headlines in the chronicles of the day in competition with reports of kings and battles. But we have already encountered a major exception: the arrival of the tribes of Hilāl and Sulaym in Tunisia in the mid-eleventh century. This, as we saw, had a background in high politics. The Zīrid governors of Tunisia had thrown off their allegiance to their Fāṭimid patrons in Egypt, and the Fāṭimids retaliated by urging two predatory tribes of Upper Egypt to invade Tunisia. These tribesmen defeated the Zīrid ruler in a crucial battle in 1052 and devastated the country, even sacking Qayrawān. We have a contemporary attestation of their depredations: Ibn Ḥazm (d. 1064), in his genealogical handbook, identifies the Banū Riyāḥ—a subtribe of Hilāl and the leading group among the invaders—as "those who ruined Ifrīqiya,"[40] in other words Tunisia. These Banū Riyāḥ spread widely in North Africa. Soon after the invasion one of their chiefs established himself amid the ruins of Carthage, on the east coast of Tunisia, and a century later the Almohad ruler moved some of them to the Atlantic plains of Morocco. In between, in what is now Algeria, they remained powerful down to the sixteenth century. Ibn Khaldūn describes the plains of eastern North Africa as former Berber territory now occupied by Arab tribes who had subjugated the remaining Berbers, resulting in their loss of their native language and assimilation to Arab culture. Meanwhile in the fourteenth century, as we have seen, the Awlād Ḥassān, a part of the tribe of Maʿqil, moved on from Morocco to Mauritania to become the nomadic population we know as the Moors, likewise subjugating and assimilating the Berber population. Altogether this westward movement of the Arab tribes was an extraordinary expansion, but it had its limits, quite apart from the blocking effect of the sea. One was the survival of significant Berber populations in northern Africa, albeit pretty much surrounded by Arabs. The size of these populations increases as one goes west, from the isolated Berber population of the oasis of Sīwa in the western desert of Egypt to the large Berber populations of the Moroccan highlands. Another limit was the continued domination of the central Sahara by the non-Arab Tuareg and Tubu. A third was the fact that the Moors never established themselves in the western savanna. There was thus no western analog to the Arab interaction with the Fulānī cattle nomads that engen-

40. Ibn Ḥazm, *Jamharat ansāb al-ʿArab*, Cairo 1982, 275.3. For a different and more benign view of the arrival of the Arab tribes see S. Garnier, *Histoires hafsides*, Leiden 2022, 331–35.

dered the Baqqāra in the eastern savanna, perhaps because the Fulānī population was much larger in its western homeland.

The other movement, starting around the thirteenth century, saw a comparable spread of Arab nomads southward from Egypt into Nubia and then westward into the savanna. Here, as we have seen, some of them were pushed so far to the south that to survive they had to make a drastic shift from camel to cattle nomadism, thereby giving rise to the Baqqāra. Again, there were limits. Thus the Arab tribes in our period did not displace or assimilate either the Beja nomads of the eastern desert or the black agricultural populations of the eastern savanna. Nor, as we have just seen, did they establish themselves in the western savanna: the Baqqāra Belt ends in what is now northeastern Nigeria.

At this point it is worth widening our perspective to include the isolated Arabic-speaking communities of Khurāsān. They are small—a few villages here and there—and thus a minor feature of the current ethnic landscape, and they developed no symbiotic relationship with Turkic nomads to produce a Central Asian counterpart of the Baqqāra. Their dialects are of an Iraqi type, but so archaic with respect to both types of Iraqi dialect today that they must have been brought to Khurāsān at the time of the conquest or soon after. They are thus linguistic fossils that have been cut off from the mainstream of spoken Arabic for well over a thousand years. We know little of their history in the intervening period, though a tenth-century geographer mentions the presence of Arabs scattered throughout Khurāsān, the richest of them being a group of twenty thousand in the steppes north of Jūzjān that possessed numerous sheep and camels. It is accordingly not a trivial fact that these communities have continued to identify themselves as Arab and their language as Arabic. The same is true of the speakers of the most remote of Arabic dialects on the other side of the Arab world, those of the Nigerian extremity of the Baqqāra Belt. In linguistic terms what goes for both these outposts applies also to the tribal populations of the vast Arabic-speaking region in between. There is an obvious contrast here with the way in which speakers of Romance have for many centuries seen themselves as peoples with distinct ethnic identities speaking different languages, and the same would go for speakers of Germanic or Slavic. One factor that must surely have been at work here is Islam, whose special relationship with the Arabs and Arabic is reflected in the widespread prestige of Arab descent and literary Arabic among non-Arab Muslim peoples. With regard to Arab descent, we have already met the claims of the Kunta, a Berber tribe of the Sahara, to a Qurashī genealogy. The Albanians are another example: the seventeenth-century Ottoman traveler Evliyā Chelebī tells us that they boast of descending from Quraysh. As to literary Arabic, the case of Maltese is highly suggestive. Malta, as already mentioned—and unlike Spain, the Balearic Islands, Sardinia, Sicily, or Crete—has retained its Arabic dialect. But this dialect had no continuing contact with literary Arabic or Islam, and the result is that the Maltese, unlike the remotest Arabs of Uzbekistan and Nigeria, do not identify themselves as Arabs or their language as Arabic. The other question that arises as we leave the Arab tribes is why they have been so successful in expanding their territory—why, when Arab tribesmen come up against non-Arab tribesmen, it is the Arabs who on balance prevail, whether by displacing, subjecting, or assimilating the non-Arabs. The prestige of Arabs in the Islamic context may be part of this, but it would be satisfying to have a more materialistic explanation.

Nontribal Arabic speakers

What, then, of nontribal Arabic speakers, be they peasants or city dwellers? Two questions are central here. One concerns identity. Did they count as Arabs, as for the most part they do today? The other concerns the extent and social character of this population.

With regard to identity, we have seen that there were two ways in which the term "Arab" could be used. One included nontribal Arabic speakers, as when our scholar in Ottoman Damascus affirmed that anyone who speaks Arabic naturally and fluently is an Arab. The other usage excluded them, as when Ibn Khaldūn contrasted the pronunciation of contemporary Arabs with that of the people of the cities. Despite the rise of Arab nationalism, which favored inclusion, the exclusive usage persisted even in modern times. Thus in the language of a caste system found in the Upper Egyptian countryside, the dominant tribesmen are Arabs, while the subordinate peasants are not. Likewise in the Persian Gulf, Arabs are speakers of Bedouin as opposed to sedentary dialects. In short, we have a gray area, and at least in Egypt and Syria in Mamlūk and Ottoman times there was a term for it: such nontribal Arabic speakers were "sons of the Arabs" (*abnā' al-ʿArab* or *awlād al-ʿArab*), not quite Arabs and not quite non-Arabs. Yet at times they were referred to simply as Arabs.

One likely example of this, from the same eighteenth-century Damascene scholar, provides an indication that such people had a sense of a distinctive ethnic identity vis-à-vis their Ottoman rulers, and what is more an identity with political undertones. He tells us that one of his teachers, the Palestinian Muḥammad al-Khalīlī (d. 1734–35), had a dream in which he spoke to the Ottoman sultan. The sultan complained to him about the state of the empire; Khalīlī responded by advising him to rely on the Arabs, since they alone would help him. In the same way a Meccan chronicler of the first half of the sixteenth century speaks of Arabs and Rūmīs (meaning Ottomans) in describing events in the city. On one occasion, he tells us, the Arabs were shortchanged in the distribution of largesse from Gujarat. On another, a confrontation over some unpopular construction work undertaken by a Rūmī scholar outside his house led him to launch into a derogatory outburst against the Arabs. In a third incident the Arabs were offended by the partiality shown by the Rūmī judge of the city in assigning roles in a ritual Qur'ān recitation. As we have seen, the inclusive usage of the term "Arab"—and the theme of Arab resentment—was shared by the Moroccans, who saw themselves as Arabs in contradistinction to the Turks and used the term in the same way when they traveled to the east. A later example is found in a work by Abū 'l-Qāsim al-Zayyānī (d. 1833), a Moroccan scholar and diplomat who was in Istanbul in the late eighteenth century. He reports a debate that allegedly took place among the religious scholars of the city in the late 1730s and revolved around the complaint of the Arabs among them that the non-Arabs—in other words, the Ottoman scholars—were keeping the best positions for themselves and leaving the Arabs at the bottom of the hierarchy. The Arabs contrasted this selfishness with the generosity they had shown to the non-Arabs while Arab rule lasted, a generosity that they claimed had reached the point of reverse discrimination. The response of the Ottoman scholars was that the Arabs had indeed made a good start at the beginning of Islamic history but had failed to maintain it, with the result that Islam itself was endangered and was saved only by the actions of the non-Arabs, most recently the Ottomans. Whether such a debate actually took place may be open to doubt, but the story articulates the same Arab resentment that we see in Khalīlī's dream, and the patronizing and disparaging character of the Ottoman response to the Arab scholars is quite credible. As we have seen, a Qāḍīzādeist writing in 1679–80 comments brazenly on a Qur'ānic verse in which the believers are warned that if they fail in their duty of jihad God will "substitute for you a different people" (Q9:39): "This people is the Turks," he says, "who are completely different from the Arabs."[41] He goes on to glory in the achievements of the Turks in boosting the fortunes of Sunnism, winning the battle of Manzikert, and taking Constantinople. We also see a sharp sense of the difference between Arabs and Persians in the politics of the Persian Gulf, and in particular those of the commercial city-state of Hormuz. On the Persian side, in the course of a fourteenth-century struggle for hegemony between the islands of Hormuz and Kīsh, we hear of a refusal by the people of Hormuz to submit to the Arabic speakers (*Tāzīgūyān*) and a rejection of Arab oppression; the merchants and the common people, we are told, were rooting for the Persians. On the other hand, the grandees of Hormuz in 1475–76 preferred a prince who had lived in Arabia and had acquired the manners of the Arabs, while the people of Baḥrayn disliked being colonized by Persians. But the Arabs in question here may well be tribal, whereas in the Ottoman context the term is clearly used more broadly.

41. Vānī Meḥmed Efendī, *'Arā'is al-Qur'ān wa-nafā'is al-Furqān*, ms. Süleymaniye, Yeni Cami 100, fol. 542b.

The extent and character of the nontribal Arab population are likewise topics that could benefit from more research, so the remarks that follow are impressionistic. But wherever we have cities in the Arab world we can assume the presence of such a population—even if, as in the case of Baghdad, the dialect of the Muslims of the city had been Bedouinized. Obvious examples of cities that were populated by gray-area populations of this kind are Damascus and Cairo. Small towns, however, might well be inhabited by tribal populations or exhibit a clan structure intermediate between tribal and nontribal society. Turning to the countryside, where the bulk of the population was to be found, there were likely to be peasants in villages located in the immediate vicinity of the cities, but a large part of the rural population was tribal, and where nontribal groups existed they were liable to be subject to tribal domination. In the case of Iraq at the end of our period, and no doubt for quite some time before it, the countryside was overwhelmingly tribal. The Syrian countryside was less homogeneous. As might be expected from the long-standing Bedouin presence in the desert to the east, some of Syria's cultivators were of Bedouin origin, or strongly Bedouinized, just as in Iraq. In the highlands, however, the characteristic social formation was the clan rather than the tribe. There were also some real peasants, lovers of the soil who had neither clans nor tribes. They were to be found near such cities as Damascus, Ḥimṣ, and Ḥamāh, as also in the northern coastal plain near Latakia. With Egypt we come to an authentic peasant society on a much larger scale, particularly in the Nile delta. In Upper Egypt, too, we can find peasant populations, but they were subject to the social domination of the tribesmen. To the west of Egypt the only region where we might have expected to find a peasantry was Tunisia. It must have had one in antiquity, and no doubt it was still there in the early centuries of Islam, but little if any of it was left by the nineteenth century. In Algeria and Morocco the rural population consisted initially of Berber tribes, and as we have seen, outside the mountains these came to be replaced over large areas by Arab tribes.

Unlike the tribes, such populations were too much under the thumb of existing states, and too lacking in solidarity, to engage in state formation. They could always resist existing states, but peasant revolt is conspicuous for its absence from the history of the premodern Arab lands. City dwellers were different in this respect, aided by their demographic concentration and the relatively greater sensitivity of rulers to their discontents. As we saw in previous chapters, urban militias (*aḥdāth*) could play a significant role in political events when states were weak. A visitor to Aleppo in 1057 described the members of the local militia as the real masters of the city. When Ṣāliḥ ibn Mirdās seized the city in 1024, it was not just the grand tribal alliance against the Fāṭimids that enabled him to do so: the Aleppine militia opened the gates to him. They did the same for the ʿUqaylid ruler in 1080 as Mirdāsid power was collapsing, thereby helping avert Seljuq possession of Aleppo until 1086. Once the Seljuqs had taken over the city, however, the future of the militia was in doubt, and the reign of Zangī (ruled 1127–46) brought down the curtain on the militias of Syria. But the decentralized Ottoman Empire saw a revival of urban militia activity in later eighteenth-century Aleppo on the part of the local Sharīfs. Their enemy was the local Janissaries, to whom they eventually lost out. Yet even urban populations that could not hope to participate in politics in the manner of these militias, let alone to form states, could still make trouble for their rulers. The Cairene populace of the seventeenth and eighteenth centuries is a case in point. It could react noisily and violently to the price of food or the burden of taxation, and students at the Azhar—Cairo's largest college—might engage in conspicuous protests when their interests were affected or join the wider populace in revolt. But such popular disturbances led to the emergence of powerful leaders only under the extreme conditions brought about by Napoleon's invasion of 1798, and even then these leaders seem to have had no real impact on the outcome of the elite struggle for power.

All this suggests that the spread of the Arab tribes and the elusiveness of peasant populations in the Arab world outside Egypt go hand in hand. In other words, here as in Iran, what was good for the tribes was bad for the peasants. We do not hear as much in our sources about attacks on villages as we do about attacks on pilgrim caravans, as in the case of the tribal chief who in 1530 caused many pilgrims to die of thirst by sabotaging the pools of water along their route with felled palm trees, ground colocynth, and the carcasses of animals. But peasants, though less newsworthy than pilgrims, probably suffered more. In early nineteenth-century Syria we hear of powerful tribes sacking villages by the dozen. There is thus some reason to take seriously Ibn Khaldūn's view that in the absence of religious leadership, Arab nomads were a force that tended to erode the foundations of sedentary civilization: "A nation dominated by the Arabs is in a state no different from anarchy. . . . Such a civilization cannot last and goes quickly to ruin."[42] Nomads such as the Bedouin have a built-in military advantage in any conflict with peasants, and in the absence of a restraining authority they are likely to use it, perhaps with least inhibition when they move into a new region. At such moments they approximate to a pure case of the roving bandit. Of course, the Bedouin and the peasants have some overlapping interests and may eventually reach an accommodation. But even then the military balance means that the terms are likely to be unequal: protection money is regularly paid by peasants to nomads, not by nomads to peasants. The alternative is that Bedouin raids lead to the long-term attrition of the settled population, and there is evidence of this. In the nineteenth-century Syrian interior, abandoned villages were legion. Likewise archaeological evidence shows considerable destruction accompanying the tenth-century spread

42. Ibn Khaldûn, *The Muqaddimah*, 1:307.

of the tribes into the Fertile Crescent. There is reason to think that the coming of the Seljuqs was from this point of view beneficial, at least initially. But there were no Seljuqs in North Africa, where it was not just the mid-eleventh-century invaders of Tunisia who had a reputation for destructiveness. From the late twelfth century the Arab tribes overran the plains in the interior of the central Maghrib, resulting in an extensive decline of agricultural and urban life, and once established in Morocco the Maʿqil tribesmen engaged in widespread plundering, reducing the Sūs to anarchy.

This leads to a larger point. Though we have no reliable data, estimates of the size of the population of the Arab world around 1800 are smaller than those for India, China, or Europe by an order of magnitude. In part this is undoubtedly a reflection of the much more limited water resources of the Arab lands, but it is also likely that over the centuries the size of the population had fallen in tandem with the spread of the nomads. In Iran and Central Asia, too, and to a lesser extent in Anatolia, nomadic tribes may have been associated with a similar if less drastic contraction in the size of the population; but it is in the Arab lands that the phenomenon is most striking. Thus in Iraq, as also in Syria, we hear of vast tracts of land that by the mid-eighteenth century had been abandoned by their cultivators. In Palestine, comparison of the Ottoman fiscal surveys of the sixteenth century with maps of the later nineteenth century shows a substantial decrease—smallest in the hills, greatest in the plains—in the number of villages in various parts of Palestine and Transjordan. Even in the agricultural lowlands of Tunisia nomads outnumbered villagers around the end of our period. What is obscure is whether the fundamental change was the work of the nomads or rather one they took advantage of. And whether long-term climatic change is also part of the story it is too early to say.

PART III

Epilogue

15

The Muslim world and the West

This chapter addresses two major gaps in the coverage of the history of the Muslim world in the first fourteen chapters of this book.

The smaller gap, though still a significant one, is the interaction of the Muslim world with western Europe before 1800. Although we touched on this from time to time, particularly in the Spanish context, the fact that the two regions were largely separated by the Mediterranean made it relatively easy to leave the gap unfilled. But here we will also go behind the Mediterranean façade of western Europe to take cognizance of the background to the global power of the region in the nineteenth and twentieth centuries.

The larger gap is, of course, the history of the Muslim world since 1800. To cover that history adequately would require a massive volume in itself, one that would tell the story by region and period in the manner of the preceding chapters. This chapter is no substitute for such a treatment, but it does try to link the history of the Muslim world as covered in this book to the present state of the region. It does this by providing a rough and ready account of what has changed in the Muslim world over the last two centuries, what has not changed, and why. Here we look in turn at territory, population, communications, the economy, society, and the state. Key actors in this drama, alongside those belonging to the Muslim world itself, have often been Europeans, or more broadly Westerners. Their actions, and Muslim responses, have brought change to almost every aspect of life, but they have by no means erased the links between the Muslim world as it was in 1800 and what it is today.

Much of the response of the Muslim world to the incursions of the West has of necessity involved imitating it—a course inevitably in tension with traditional values, not least Islamic ones. Here we will outline the history of Muslim views of western Europeans, and of Muslim attitudes toward imitating them, from medieval to modern times.

We will end by comparing and contrasting the two great transformations that bookend the history of the Muslim world as laid out in this book: the initial transformation brought about by the rise of Islam, and the more recent transformation resulting from the rise of the West. What this chapter does not cover is what the reader is most likely to be curious about: the future. We will nevertheless end with a thought or two about the prospects for a non-Western modernity in the Muslim world.

Charles of Anjou was a crusading Christian king who ruled Sicily from 1266 to 1285, long after the Normans had conquered the island from its last Muslim rulers. But this did not prevent him from contacting the Muslim ruler of Tunisia to ask for a copy of an Arabic medical work. The author of the work was Abū Bakr al-Rāzī (d. around 930), a Persian alchemist, physician, and philosopher who became famous in Christian Europe as Rhazes. The Muslim ruler graciously provided his Christian counterpart with a copy, and in 1279 Charles ordered that the book be translated. This was part of a long story that went back to the late eleventh century and continued into the fourteenth, issuing in a substantial transfer of philosophical and scientific learning from Arabic to Latin. The story played out under Christian rule, first in southern Italy and then in Spain, where Toledo, despite being lost to the Muslims in 1085, retained an Arabic culture into the thirteenth century. The translations involved both Greek works that had been rendered into Arabic a few centuries earlier and new works by Muslim authors in the same tradition—though Abū Bakr al-Rāzī, who dismissed the Qur'ān as full of contradictions, was arguably too much of a freethinker for us to count him as a Muslim. This whole development was based on a widespread—though by no means universal—belief among the Christian intellectual elite of western Europe that the Muslims were in possession of intellectual resources that the Christians desperately needed. As a translator working in Aragon in the first half of the twelfth century put it with regard to astral science, the Arabs were people "whom it is especially befitting for us to imitate, being as it were our teachers and predecessors in this art."[1] The Muslims, for their part, seem scarcely to have been aware of the attention their culture was getting from these avid intellectual clients; the work was taking place beyond the frontiers of Muslim rule, and the Italian translator of Rāzī's book, like many of the translators in Spain, was a Jew.

In this chapter, however, we will be concerned mainly with a period in which this civilizational hierarchy was sharply reversed. The background to this reversal was long in the making. By 1800, as we have seen, the Muslim world's relations with western Europe had become a historically significant theme, and not just in neighboring regions: as far away as India and Southeast Asia, Europeans had emerged as major players whose activities impacted large numbers of Muslims. This, however, was just the beginning of an encounter that has made the history of the Muslim world in the last couple of centuries very different from what we

1. See C.S.F. Burnett, "A group of Arabic-Latin translators working in northern Spain in the mid-12th century," *Journal of the Royal Asiatic Society*, 1977, 91.

could otherwise have expected it to have been. The present chapter is largely about that difference. It does not attempt even to outline the narrative history of the various regions of the Muslim world, but it does seek to provide a succinct thematic account of what has changed about it—and just as importantly, what has not changed—since 1800. But before that we need to do something by way of background—namely, to trace the main lines of the relationship between the Muslim world and western Europe over the preceding millennium. In the first instance, this means focusing on the frontier of the Muslim world in the western Mediterranean. Here our immediate concern will be more with commercial and military exchanges than with the movement of books.

Background

The western Mediterranean frontier

On Malta, "No smoking" signs read TPEJJIPX, meaning "Don't smoke." This bizarre word, weighed down with an abundance of consonants and a paucity of vowels, may strike most readers as resistant to analysis. But it has a story to tell, and one readily intelligible to anyone familiar with both English and Arabic. We can rewrite the word more helpfully as *t-peyyip-sh* and start in the middle: *peyyep* is the Maltese verb meaning "to smoke." It does not look in the least like Arabic, since Arabic notoriously lacks a *p*, and it is in fact a close relative of the English noun "pipe" in the sense of "tobacco pipe." What the English have not done is to make a verb of the noun—they don't use "to pipe" in the sense of "to smoke." But the Italians and Sicilians do just that: *pipa* is "pipe" and *pipare* or *pipari* is "to smoke a pipe," which is no doubt the source of the Maltese usage. But where does that *-eyyi-* appear from? Here we are up against the fact that Maltese is an Arabic dialect, though one long severed from the wider world of Arabic. Malta had been conquered by the Muslims in the early centuries of Islam, perhaps in 869. But it lies considerably closer to Sicily than to Tunisia, and in 1090 they lost it to the Norman conquerors of Sicily. For some time Muslims were still permitted to live on the island under Christian rule, but in 1249 they were expelled. So by the time the tobacco habit reached the Maltese following the discovery of the Americas, their commercial and cultural links were with the Christian world to the north rather than with the Muslim world to the south. Yet they retained their Arabic dialect, as they still do today. So when they borrowed the word *pipa* from the Italians or Sicilians, and like them made a verb of it, they assimilated it to a grammatical pattern typical of Arabic: *peyyip* is what Europeans call the second form of the Arabic verb (the verbal noun, for those familiar with Arabic, being *tipyip*). The *t* and *sh* on either side of *peyyip* are likewise Arabic: the *t-* marks the masculine second person singular, while the *-sh* is what is left of the negative.

This example is typical of Maltese, but in the wider context of the islands of the Mediterranean, Maltese is quite exceptional. Recent immigration from North Africa apart, no Arabic dialect is spoken on the Balearic Islands, Corsica, Sardinia, Sicily, or Crete. There is one on Cyprus, but it results from the migration of Maronite Christians from Syria at an uncertain date, not from Muslim expansion. Beyond this Maronite dialect and Maltese, it is only on small islands close to the southern or eastern seaboard of the Mediterranean that Arabic is spoken offshore, as in the case of Jerba off the coast of Tunisia and Aradus off the coast of Syria. This situation points to a far-reaching maritime extinction of Arabic, not to mention Islam, despite the success of both in spreading thousands of miles overland. From the perspective of the early Middle Ages, this is a surprising outcome. All the major islands of the Mediterranean were subject to significant Muslim incursions in the early centuries, and some of them, including the Balearics, Sicily, and Crete, experienced long periods of Muslim rule. Thus Majorca in the Balearics was under Muslim rule from at least the tenth century to the thirteenth, Sicily from the ninth to the eleventh, and Crete from the ninth to the tenth. In the Sicilian case, at least, we have indications that Arabic spread widely. These centuries also saw extensive Muslim raiding of smaller islands, particularly those of the Aegean, and beyond that of the northern coastlands of the Mediterranean. Thus in 838 and 848 Marseilles was attacked; in 846 the Basilica of Saint Peter was sacked in a Muslim raid on Rome; in 904 it was the turn of Salonica, and in 934–35 that of Genoa. In Provence Muslim raiders from Spain established a base near Saint-Tropez around 887 and used it to raid far and wide until 972. Yet farther to the west, the Muslim governors and rulers of Spain at first posed a threat deep into France. Indeed, some parts of the Mediterranean coastlands of western Europe were not just raided but conquered on a significant scale. The major and most long-lasting example was of course Spain, or a substantial part of it. But Muslim rule was also to be found in southern Italy in the ninth and tenth centuries, though here it was a less enduring phenomenon, and as fragmented as the Christian political landscape of the region. Yet the religious legacy of these early expansions was everywhere erased, and loanwords apart, so too was the linguistic legacy—except in the unique case of Maltese.

At a later stage, as we have seen, a Muslim presence was reestablished on the islands of the eastern Mediterranean thanks to a major resurgence of Muslim sea power at the hands of the Turks. This was closely linked to the process by which the two eastern peninsulas on the north side of the Mediterranean came under Muslim rule: Anatolia permanently thanks to the Turkic expansion of the eleventh to thirteenth centuries, and Greece until the nineteenth century thanks to the Ottoman conquest of the late fourteenth and fifteenth centuries. Given the very considerable investment of the Ottomans in naval power, it is not surprising that the islands of the northeastern Mediterranean likewise fell to them, including

Cyprus and eventually Crete. But here, too, the tide of Muslim sea power eventually began to ebb. In demographic terms the change became evident only after 1800, but the net result is that the Turkish and Muslim presence on the islands of this part of the Mediterranean—not to speak of the Greek mainland—is today very limited. Outside the boundaries of Turkey Muslim speakers of Turkish are a substantial minority of the insular population only on Cyprus, and the Mediterranean has no population of Turkish-speaking Christians to match the Maltese. Altogether the erasure is not as complete as it proved in the northwestern Mediterranean—as might be expected from the fact that these developments are more recent—but it is still quite sweeping.

What we see here reflects above all a couple of massive shifts in the balance of sea power on the Mediterranean.[2] To understand them we should start by identifying a few of the factors that normally contributed to naval strength in the premodern world. One was the possession of timber, whose uneven distribution around the Mediterranean gave the north a certain advantage over the south. Another was general economic resources, above all the potential for a taxable agricultural economy, possession of which made it possible for a territorial state to bear the considerable burden of building and manning a fleet. Here, too, the north had the advantage, though the two factors were very much at odds with each other in the case of Egypt, with its combination of agricultural wealth and dearth of timber. Yet another factor, and a crucial one, was the presence of strong states; agricultural potential was close to being a necessary condition for this, but it was not sufficient. Until about the tenth century these are really the only factors we need to keep in mind. After that a very different phenomenon was to come into play.

What is most striking about the first centuries of the Islamic era is the success with which the Muslim south continued its overland expansion by taking to the sea at the expense of the Christian north. As we have seen, Muslims were raiding throughout the Mediterranean, helping themselves to its islands and even conquering territory on parts of the northern mainland. These centuries, then, were an era of Muslim naval dominance. This went against the grain of the overall distribution of timber and agricultural resources and reflected the asymmetrical distribution of strong states in this period. In the southeast there were the Umayyad and then ʿAbbāsid Caliphates, both active on the Mediterranean. They were followed by less powerful but still formidable successor states based in Egypt, Tunisia, and Spain. Thus the Ṭūlūnids put effort into strengthening their navy and the Aghlabids mounted a conquest of Sicily across some hundred miles of open sea, while the Fāṭimids in North Africa and the Umayyads of Spain engaged in naval

2. For much of what follows see D. Abulafia, *The great sea*, London 2011.

hostilities against each other. In the north, by contrast, the resources of what was left of the Byzantine Empire were ravaged by Arab raiding in Anatolia and Slav marauding in the Balkans. The only other significant Christian state, that of the Carolingians, was based too far to the north in Aachen and was on balance too little interested in the sea to become a serious Mediterranean power. There was nevertheless a flurry of Frankish naval activity around the early ninth century, when several expeditions were mounted—one to the Balearic Islands in 799 to protect them from Muslim pirates, further expeditions to Corsica in 806 and 807, and even a failed attack on the Tunisian coast in 828. But the Carolingians had no permanent naval base on the shores of the Mediterranean. All in all, the early Islamic centuries were a period in which the Muslims of the Mediterranean could not quite have claimed it as "our sea" (*mare nostrum*) in the manner of the ancient Romans, but they came closer to it than anyone else.

Around the tenth century two things changed. The first development was a familiar one: the revival of Byzantine power. A state that had been weak was once again strong for a while, and what this meant for its naval reach was shown by its recovery of Crete from the Muslims in 960–61. Farther to the west, however, no strong territorial states had yet emerged on the coasts of the Christian Mediterranean. The second and more remarkable change was in fact predicated on the absence of such states. This was the reemergence of a form of sea power that had been a prominent feature of the ancient Mediterranean but had disappeared with the rise of Rome. A key feature of the Phoenician city-states of the Syrian coast and of the Phoenician colony of Carthage in North Africa had been their potent combination of maritime commerce with sea power. It was this combination that reappeared around the tenth century among some of the city-states of Italy. The classic examples are the mercantile republics of Venice and Genoa, but the phenomenon was also in evidence at an early date in Amalfi. For these mercantile republics to flourish, it was essential that there be no strong state in their vicinity threatening to stifle them. Here their independence was reinforced by their tendency to establish themselves in locations not easily accessible by land—Venice on its islands; Genoa and Amalfi, like the later Ragusa in Dalmatia, with their backs to coastal mountains. Like the emporia of the Red Sea and the Persian Gulf, such ports were dependent on imported food, though not on imported water. There were no ports of this kind on the Muslim shores of the Mediterranean. The medieval lagoon cities of the eastern Nile delta, Tinnīs and Damietta, were similarly dependent on provisions from afar, but they were in no position to escape the clutches of the Egyptian state and evolve into mercantile republics.

We have already seen the naval potential of this development in the Genoese raid on Mahdiyya in 1087, and it was dramatized by the way in which the Italian city-states both assisted and took advantage of the Crusaders. This happened in Syria at the time of the First Crusade at the end of the eleventh century, and more brazenly when the Venetians diverted an army of Crusaders intended for Egypt, shipping them instead to Constantinople, which they sacked in 1204. For the rest of the Middle Ages, these city-states played a central role in ruling the waves of the Mediterranean. This did not, of course, mean that they held a monopoly of sea power. Both Christian and Muslim territorial states retained the ability to will navies into existence, provided they had the resources to pay for them. On the Christian side, the twelfth-century Sicilian monarchy was a case in point. On the Muslim side, in 1340 a Moroccan fleet defeated its Castilian counterpart in a sea battle off Gibraltar. In the eastern Mediterranean we see the same phenomenon with the Fāṭimids, to a lesser extent with the Mamlūks, and to a far greater extent with the Ottomans. But in late medieval times the balance still favored the Italian city-states. The sullen acceptance of this fact by the Ayyūbids, and still more the Mamlūks, is poignantly expressed in the drastic steps they took to dismantle rather than strengthen ports and fortifications on the Syrian coast after capturing them from the Crusaders. Indeed, the Mamlūk Sultan Baybars I (ruled 1260–77) made an epigram of the disparity when he wrote to the Christian king of Cyprus, following a disastrous Mamlūk naval expedition that targeted the island in 1270, that "your horses are ships, while our ships are horses."[3] He was certainly right about the Mamlūk side of this comparison, but the Franks had at their disposal both ships and horses. In the sixteenth century, however, the sheer scale of the Ottoman naval effort could at times be overwhelming. At the same time, Muslim piracy was on the rise. As we have seen, some Turcoman principalities on the coasts of late medieval Anatolia had made a remarkably smooth transition from raiding on land to raiding at sea. It was, however, the Barbary corsairs of North Africa who took the prize in the early sixteenth century, mounting a ramified and long-lasting piratical enterprise out of the ports of North Africa. Yet neither the Ottomans nor the corsairs restored the Muslim dominance that had marked the Mediterranean in the early centuries of Islam. They were thus unable to prevent the Spanish and Portuguese from continuing to hold ports on the coasts of Muslim North Africa; the Spanish, for example, held Oran from 1509 to 1792. In addition, the piracy of the Barbary corsairs was rivaled on the Christian side by the depredations of the Knights of Malta. The Muslim maritime presence had nevertheless greatly expanded.

What was not to be found on the Muslim side was the symbiosis of naval and commercial activity that characterized Venice and Genoa. Moreover this symbiosis was eventually to take a new turn on the Christian side, one that had no precedent in antiquity. From the thirteenth to the fifteenth century, Catalonia was both a territorial state with a navy and a set of commercially active cities of which

3. Quoted in D. Ayalon, "Baḥriyya, II" in *The Encyclopaedia of Islam*, 2nd ed., Leiden 1960–2009, 1:945b.

Barcelona was the dominant member. The interests of the count of Catalonia, who was also the king of Aragon, converged with those of the urban patricians of Barcelona. It was not just in the western Mediterranean that the Catalans were active at sea in this period. In 1353, for example, they sent a fleet to the Bosphorus, and they were full participants in the trade with the eastern Mediterranean. The next development was that the Catalan pattern began to be replicated in one form or another by states on the Atlantic seaboard. First it was the Portuguese, and then it was two peoples of northwestern Europe, the Dutch and the English, whose forceful intrusion into the Mediterranean began in the late sixteenth century. Prior to this, only Mediterranean states had competed for sea power on the Mediterranean. In part this new development reflected a change in technology: galleys powered by rowers were out, and sailing ships were in. Sailing ships were, of course, nothing new in themselves, but an improvement in metallurgy meant that they could now be equipped with large numbers of cheap cast-iron cannon, in contrast to the expensive bronze cannon traditionally used by Mediterranean galleys. With their heavily armed sailing ships the Dutch and English had no trouble gate-crashing the Mediterranean and thereby contributing to the obsolescence of both Italian and Ottoman naval power. That they did not immediately do the same for the Barbary corsairs was somewhat ironic. Northwestern Europe was increasingly the source of the naval technology of these nests of Muslim pirates and a significant share of their manpower was European, albeit reflagged as Muslim through capture and conversion. The process of changing sides was not necessarily coercive. A French observer in 1667 commented acidly that men from Provence, if allowed to disembark at Algiers, would don a turban as easily as a nightcap, and the English consul in Tripoli wrote in 1680 that voluntarily "turning Turks" was "no uncommon accident to our drunken hard-headed sailors."[4]

The share of Mediterranean sea power in the hands of the European Christians was nevertheless disproportionate, and it was more than matched by their role in commerce. It is, of course, easy to imagine Muslim merchants regularly making their way to and from the Christian ports of the Mediterranean on Christian ships; nothing compels a merchant in pursuit of profit to travel in a vessel owned and run by a coreligionist, though he might well prefer it. Indeed, the Spanish Muslim pilgrim Ibn Jubayr (d. 1217), on his way from Granada to Mecca and back in 1183–85, showed himself a confirmed traveler on Genoese ships, boarding them during both his outward and his return journey across the Mediterranean. And he was not alone: he had Muslim fellow travelers and at one point encountered yet another Genoese ship bearing pilgrims returning from Mecca. This did not mean that Muslim passengers had any liking for the company of Christians. With regard to

4. See C. R. Pennell, *Piracy and diplomacy in seventeenth-century North Africa*, Rutherford 1989, 133.

one leg of the journey, Ibn Jubayr notes that the Muslim passengers kept to themselves. But the discomfort of traveling in the company of Christians on Genoese ships was clearly something that could be endured. Likewise in 1728 a French observer remarked that Turkish merchants of the Levant (the coast of greater Syria) and the Barbary coast, when trading from one city to another, would always travel on French ships, since these gave them protection against the attacks of Christian pirates. Yet despite this convenience, the presence of Muslim merchants in the ports of Christian Europe seems to have been relatively rare. Occasional cases are attested in the high Middle Ages, but we hear most about the phenomenon on the east coast of Italy in a later period, above all in Ancona in the first half of the sixteenth century and in Venice over an extended period. In the Venetian case we have a precise figure for 1570, when war broke out with the Ottoman Empire and seventy-five Muslim merchants were arrested in the city. From 1579 on, such merchants were housed in a separate residence, the Fondaco dei Turchi, comparable to the Fondaco dei Tedeschi that provided for German merchants in Venice and to the analogous establishments that housed Christian merchants in Muslim lands. But even here the Muslim presence was small in comparison to the Christian presence in Muslim ports. It is thus makes sense that the Lingua Franca, the mixed contact language of the Mediterranean spoken by Christians and Muslims alike, was at root a form of Romance, not of Arabic or Turkish. "Signor Consule, per que non restar à casa tova quando ti estar sacran?" a pasha of Tripoli in Libya asked the English consul; "Mr. Consul, why don't you stay in your house when you're drunk?"[5] Here only the word for "drunk" is of Arabic origin (*sakrān*). All in all, what we see is that the frontier of the Muslim world in the Mediterranean was a markedly asymmetrical one. As with all frontiers people crossed it, but those who did so were disproportionately Christians from the north and west, rather than Muslims from the south and east. This made the Mediterranean frontier unique among the major border regions of the Muslim world. Elsewhere Muslim merchants readily ventured into non-Muslim lands, as we have seen in the African savanna, around the Indian Ocean, in continental Southeast Asia, in southern China, and in Inner Asia. Why, then, was the Mediterranean different? Perhaps it was because the imbalance of sea power was reinforced by a convergence of negative attitudes on both sides.

On the Muslim side the jurists at large had serious reservations about the desirability of Muslim merchants traveling to infidel lands and residing there to engage in trade. What is significant for our purposes is that opposition to such activity was particularly strong among the Mālikīs, in contrast to the Shāfiʿites and the Ḥanafīs. Whereas the Shāfiʿites predominated around the Indian Ocean and

5. Quoted in J. Dakhlia, *Lingua franca*, Arles 2008, 219.

the Ḥanafīs in the Indian interior, Central Asia, and the northern part of the Ottoman Empire, the Mālikīs came to have something close to a monopoly in the western Muslim world. Their negative attitude went back to Mālik (d. 795), the Medinese founder of the school. We are told that he strongly disapproved of a merchant traveling to the lands of the unbelievers inasmuch as he would be subject to "the laws of polytheism"; in another version he says, "I don't like it and don't think it's right for him."[6] Such wordings left two possible loopholes. One was that even severe disapproval fell short of outright prohibition. But Ibn Rushd the Elder (d. 1126), a distinguished Spanish jurist and the grandfather of the famous Averroes, unhesitatingly plugged this gap: he explained that Mālik as a good jurist avoided expressing himself too categorically, but that what he meant was that such conduct was forbidden. Indeed, another early source states that in the view of Mālik and his followers not only was such travel forbidden to individual merchants but it was the duty of the ruler to prevent it, and one ninth-century Mālikī jurist, speaking of trade to the land of the blacks, insisted that it was forbidden because a merchant would be subject to the laws of unbelief. Ibn Ḥazm (d. 1064), whom we met as an expert on the genealogies of the Arabs of Spain and a propagandist for the excellence of his Spanish homeland, was not a Mālikī, and he liked nothing better than to pick holes in Mālikī legal doctrines. Yet on this issue he toed the line. It was, he said, unlawful to trade in the lands of the infidels when the merchants would be subject to their laws. But these jurists did not consider another possible loophole. What if the unbelievers did not in fact impose their polytheistic laws but instead allowed the Muslim merchants legal autonomy? Something like this was indeed to be found on several frontiers of the Muslim world. We met it, for example, in eleventh-century Ghāna, where the Muslims lived and practiced their religion in a town of their own. By that time most of the merchants crossing the Sahara must have been Mālikīs. By contrast, we hear little of Muslim merchants enjoying legal autonomy in Christian Europe. A rare case in point might be the Fondaco dei Turchi in Venice, but the merchants from the Ottoman Empire residing there would almost certainly have been Ḥanafīs, not Mālikīs.

Meanwhile on the Christian side, a rather high level of religious intolerance was in play. One of the conditions on which Spain relinquished Gibraltar to the British in 1713 was that no Jews or Moors—that is, Muslims—should be allowed to live there. The Spanish state was, of course, notorious in Europe for its intolerance, but even in cosmopolitan Venice the very idea of a Fondaco dei Turchi had been opposed in 1602 on the ground that it could lead to the construction of a mosque and the worship of Muḥammad—a worse scandal even than the presence of Jews

6. Saḥnūn, *Mudawwana*, Beirut n.d., 4:270; Ibn Rushd, *al-Bayān wa'l-taḥṣīl*, Beirut 1991, 4:171.

and Protestants. The objection did not prevail, but popular intolerance of Muslims in Venice was a continuing problem for the Venetian authorities, not to mention the Muslims themselves. Of course, Christian intolerance was by no means uniform. In 1534 it was none other than the pope who allowed "all merchants of whatever nation, profession or sect, even if Turks, Jews or infidels," to reside and trade in Ancona.[7] Here the "even if" is significant—we are perilously close to the outer edge of papal toleration. In 1572, when the ruler of Savoy wanted to welcome Jews, Turks, Moors, and Persians to Nice in the same way, it was the pope who, with the king of Spain, successfully objected to the scheme. Then again, when the Moriscos were expelled from Spain in 1609–14, one option open to them was to settle in the domains of the grand duke of Tuscany, who saw them as an economic asset. It was in fact his predecessor who in 1591 invited merchants from a profusion of ethnic and religious groups to settle in his free port of Leghorn, and he, too, included Jews, Turks, Moors, and Persians. But these were special arrangements. Overall, Christian Europe was significantly less welcoming to Muslims than were the non-Muslim lands beyond the other frontiers of the Muslim world. Moreover, the outcome of such arrangements on the Christian side does not suggest that Muslim merchants would have flocked to a more welcoming Europe in large numbers. Leghorn developed a significant Jewish community—numbering some three thousand in the later seventeenth century—but not a Muslim one, despite the fact that "even our enemies the Turks"[8] were entitled to enjoy the freedom of the port. We nevertheless hear of occasional Muslims who did go so far as to take advantage of this offer, including one described as "perfectly fluent in the Italian language."[9] A few intrepid Muslim traders even made their way to Marseilles, where they were distinctly unwelcome. Thus in 1620 two merchants from Tunis were jailed by the French authorities to protect them while rioters were killing some forty-five Muslim galley slaves and others. In the next century we hear of isolated arrivals of Muslim merchants in 1757 and 1759, and in 1767, quite exceptionally, merchants from Tunis arrived on Tunisian ships. Unwelcome though they were, these Muslim merchants had a reputation for good faith in commercial matters. But they were outliers.

Before we leave this maritime domain of encounter between Muslims and Christians, we should pause to weigh the significance of religious allegiances in their interactions. As is evident, such ties were not everything, but neither did they count for nothing. A much more conspicuous phenomenon than the presence of Muslim merchants in Christian ports is worth considering here: the role of mercenaries of the wrong faith in medieval Spain and North Africa. Christian rulers

7. Quoted in M. Greene, *Catholic pirates and Greek merchants*, Princeton 2010, 28.
8. Quoted in C. Tazzara, *The free port of Livorno*, Oxford 2017, 79.
9. Quoted in F. Trivellato, *The familiarity of strangers*, New Haven 2009, 82.

employed Muslim mercenaries, just as Muslim rulers employed Christian ones. Yet to see these arrangements through a rigorously cynical lens might be a mistake. Ibn Khaldūn makes the point that in his day the Muslim rulers of North Africa would not use their Christian mercenaries against other Christians for fear that they might defect. Likewise the Christian rulers of Aragon would employ their Muslim mercenaries against other Christians, but not against Muslims. Such limitations were not always observed, but they were taken seriously enough to be built into treaties between Muslim and Christian rulers. In the same way, religious allegiances could have practical, though not always predictable, consequences for merchants. There are indeed times when cynicism is entirely in place. We should not underestimate the capacity of people in those and other centuries to engage in interfaith enterprises that were deeply shocking to their more right-thinking contemporaries. A fleet of Barbary corsairs spent the winter of 1543–44 in the port of Toulon, where the French authorities made them welcome and generously handed over the local cathedral for use as a mosque. In terms of religious allegiances the arrangement was an embarrassment, but it made perfect geopolitical sense: the parties were united in their hostility to Spain. Likewise the crews of pirate ships might mix Christians and Muslims indiscriminately. One ship had a crew of Englishmen, Turks, and Moors, plus a Maltese pilot; another mixed Englishmen with Turks from Tunis in equal numbers, a clear mark of an equal-opportunity employer.

Western Europe beyond the Mediterranean

The Mediterranean maritime frontier between the Muslim world and western Europe was just one of several Muslim frontiers, but it was to prove far more indicative of the future than any of the others. Perhaps the first manifestation of this future outside the Mediterranean was the fate of the Canaries. These islands were separated from the coast of Morocco by less than sixty miles of open sea, whereas they lay over seven hundred miles from the Iberian Peninsula. And yet, as we have seen, they had never been part of the Muslim world, whereas now, in the course of the fourteenth and fifteenth centuries, they became fully part of the Christian world. The conquest and colonization of the Canaries was a multiethnic venture, or series of ventures, involving Genoese, Portuguese, Spanish, and French. Muslims from the African mainland were also present, but only as slaves brought to the islands by the Christians to serve them alongside the native population. There was thus no Muslim parallel in the Atlantic to the role once played by the Carthaginians beyond the Pillars of Hercules.

Of all those involved in the conquest of the Canaries, it was the Portuguese and Spanish who were now taking over from the Italian merchant republics the role of the prime Christian sea powers. In the last years of the fifteenth century the

Portuguese circumnavigated Africa and appeared on the Indian Ocean, soon after which they were sailing well beyond it to China and Japan. We already know what this meant for the Muslim world: trouble for the Mamlūks and Ottomans, together with varying degrees of disruption for the Muslim populations of northwestern Africa and the Indian Ocean rim. Meanwhile, as the Moroccan sultan al-Manṣūr was so well aware, the Spanish had reached the Americas. There they conquered Mexico and Peru and continued westwards across the Pacific to the Philippines, where they checked and to a degree reversed the spread of Islam. Dramatic though it may have been, this early phase of western European expansion was in one way rather limited. Outside the Americas, and with the partial exception of the Philippines, it involved sea power rather than land power. The result was that Christian gains were mostly confined to seizing a limited number of strategic islands and coastal enclaves, very much as in the Mediterranean in the same period. The Reconquista had, of course, involved significant territorial conquest, but it had by now been completed on the Iberian Peninsula—in Portugal with the conquest of the Algarve in 1249, and in Spain with the fall of Granada in 1492. There was to be no continuation of the Reconquista into the North African interior, despite the fact that in 1578 a Portuguese king lost his life in a battle over the Moroccan succession. The same pattern held good for the Muslim lands farther down the African coast and around the Indian Ocean.

This relative immunity to territorial conquest, or at least the appearance of it, continued long after Portuguese and Spanish sea power had been upstaged by that of the Dutch and the English. As late as 1800, the Dutch had yet to make a move to conquer the bulk of the Javanese interior. This was not because they were peaceful merchants. As early as 1614 the Dutch governor on Java had written home that "trade cannot be maintained without war, nor war without trade,"[10] and the period between then and 1800 saw much military activity on the island and the spread of Dutch rule along the north coast. But the large-scale acquisition of territory by the Dutch still lay in the future. Things were different with the British in India, or more precisely with their East India Company, but even here the expansion of British rule over the subcontinent began only in the second half of the eighteenth century. The Levant Company, the counterpart of the East India Company in the eastern Mediterranean, never played such a role at the expense of the Ottomans. Yet the last years of the eighteenth century saw a short-lived but ominous French incursion into the very heartlands of Islam. In 1798 Napoleon invaded and occupied Egypt in the course of a war against Britain and other European powers. France was not a maritime power on a par with the British, which is a major reason its Egyptian adventure lasted only three years. But it was a formidable

10. Quoted in G. Parker, "Europe and the wider world, 1500–1700," in J. D. Tracy (ed.), *The political economy of merchant empires*, Cambridge 1991, 180.

continental power, particularly in the aftermath of the French Revolution of 1789. In the course of the eighteenth century it had been able to muster sufficient naval resources to mount challenges to the British in India and North America, and now it was in effect attempting to do the same in Egypt.

France was not the only continental power in Europe that showed an interest in acquiring territory from the Muslim world before 1800. So, too, did Austria and Russia. The Austrians were already expanding at the expense of the Ottomans in the Balkans in the later seventeenth century. The Russians, a marginally European power well positioned to expand in Asia, had already absorbed the Muslim Khānates of Kazan and Astrakhan in the sixteenth century and went on to take the Crimean Khānate from the Ottomans toward the end of the eighteenth century. Meanwhile the Manchus, a very un-European power, had conquered eastern Turkestan. Such territorial losses were still limited as of 1800, but the tide was turning against the Muslim world.

The mention of the French Revolution should remind us that all these encroaching countries had their own internal histories. The one that concerns us most, however, is not France but Britain. In 1848 Lord Macaulay (d. 1859) began to publish his history of England. This was a work of national self-congratulation, but a perceptive one. Among the themes he undertook to treat in telling the story of his country was "how her opulence and her martial glory grew together."[11] He had a strong sense of the long-term economic development that lay behind the rise of British naval and military power. For at least six centuries, he remarked, the "national wealth" had been "almost uninterruptedly increasing," and from the middle of the eighteenth century this progress had become "portentously rapid," continuing with "accelerated velocity" in the nineteenth. He associated this trend with rapid population growth—the size of the English population had more than tripled since 1685—and with the spread of agriculture to parts of the countryside that were formerly "nothing but heath, swamp, and warren." He described the transformation as particularly striking in the north of England. Beyond the river Trent, he wrote, a large part of the country was "in a state of barbarism" down to the eighteenth century. The gentry and the larger farmers lived in fortified residences; judges and their entourages moved around "armed and escorted by a strong guard" and had to carry provisions with them because the country was "a wilderness which afforded no supplies." He described one region close to the Scottish border as "peopled by a race scarcely less savage than the Indians of California." But the transformation Macaulay was describing was not just agricultural. Though he did not use the phrase himself, the decades since 1760 had seen an industrial revolution—a development in which the north of England was

11. For this and the quotations in the rest of this paragraph see Lord Macaulay, *The history of England*, New York 1898, 1:2, 322, 323, 327, 329, 358.

to play a conspicuous role. All in all, since 1685 the country had undergone "a change to which the history of the Old World furnishes no parallel."

What made this fundamental economic transformation possible? The factor Macaulay invoked most strongly was security. Thus the old north was "often the theater of war," and even under conditions of nominal peace it was "constantly desolated by bands of Scottish marauders,"[12] whereas now, "in the train of peace," industry and "all the arts of life" had finally reached this unhappy region. More generally, England had come to be "exempt from the evils which have elsewhere impeded the efforts and destroyed the fruits of industry": the "bloody and devastating wars" that had affected every part of the Continent from Moscow to Lisbon and the violent political instability that was "all around us." Here, then, was a crucial precondition for sustained economic growth: "Every man has felt entire confidence that the state would protect him in the possession of what had been earned by his diligence and hoarded by his self-denial." This idea is simple enough, and already familiar to us. In the premodern Muslim world there was no shortage of regions that Macaulay would have described as being "in a state of barbarism," and it is a safe bet that just about anyone trying to make a living from economic production in those regions understood the value of security. It was a fragile good even when the state was delivering it, and often it was absent altogether.

What Macaulay did not share was the assumption, so widespread in the premodern world and far from forgotten even today, that the only antidote to anarchy is some kind of despotism. Instead, he saw the settlement that emerged in England from the Glorious Revolution of 1688 as one under which "the authority of law and the security of property were found to be compatible with a liberty of discussion and of individual action never before known."[13] To many in the premodern world this compatibility would have seemed counterintuitive, and its emergence was indeed highly contingent, not to say chancy. Yet it was from this "auspicious union of order and freedom" that there sprang "a prosperity of which the annals of human affairs had furnished no example." Nor was this all. A key part of the story was the unprecedented role of science under the "benignant influence of peace and liberty." Not only did science flourish; it did so with dramatic consequences: it was "applied to practical purposes on a scale never known before." At the same time, wealth and power—"opulence" and "martial glory"—grew together. Thus "a gigantic commerce gave birth to a maritime power," one that had no rival in the past or present.

12. For this and the quotations in the rest of this paragraph see Macaulay, *The history of England*, 1:322–23, 327, 329.

13. For this and the quotations in the rest of this paragraph see Macaulay, *The history of England*, 1:1–2, 323.

Macaulay's account of the rise of his country was nothing if not rhetorical, and he tended to look on the bright side of things. He shared the pride of the poet William Blake (d. 1827) in "Englands green & pleasant Land," but unlike him he did not speak of "these dark Satanic Mills."[14] The larger phenomenon he identified was nevertheless very real, and however reassuring for Macaulay, its implications for the rest of the world were ominous. The most obvious was that it placed other societies on the receiving end of a severe disparity of power. As long as Britannia ruled the waves, not to speak of increasing expanses of adjacent land, and practiced a "gigantic commerce," others had abundant reason to fear the potential consequences for them. A further implication was that the needs of self-defense, if nothing else, would give them a strong incentive to seek to appropriate those features of the English development in which Britain's looming power appeared to be grounded. As might be expected, some societies fared better than others in this. Overall, those that did well fell into three groups. One was made up of the continental societies of western and central Europe, though not their southern and eastern fringes. Another consisted of the northern European settler societies of the New World and the Antipodes. The third, to the initial surprise of many, was the Japanese—a people described by one nineteenth-century Western commentator as "a happy race" who "being content with little are not likely to achieve much."[15] These societies proved capable of competing with Britain and even overtaking it. The rest did not do so well, though there was great variety in how badly they did. Some occupied a gray area between the winners and the losers, the leading example being Russia. By the standards of western and central Europe, Russia was a notably backward country, and it was not a mere accident that in 1917 it went down to a revolution that was to blight its economic development for decades. But Russia was also to prove a far more formidable enemy on the extended northern land frontier of the Muslim world than Austria was. No Eurasian power since the Mongols had operated on so wide a territorial front—indeed, by the 1630s the Cossacks had reached the Pacific. Many other societies did much worse, with some suffering loss to the point of extinction, as in the case of the Tasmanian aborigines.

How readily different societies responded to the challenge depended on many things, but two are worth picking out here. One is the part played by cultural proximity or distance. In 1776 Adam Smith (d. 1790) published his *Inquiry into the nature and causes of the wealth of nations*. This was the fundamental text of modern political economy, and for a long time it was compelling reading for anyone interested in "the discovery of the secret of the wealth of nations," as a Russian

14. G. E. Bentley (ed.), *William Blake's writings*, Oxford 1978, 1:318.

15. Quoted in C. Issawi, "The Japanese model and the Middle East," in his *The Middle East economy*, Princeton 1995, 168.

author put it in 1818.[16] A German translation of the book appeared in the same year as the English original, and before the end of the century Smith could be read in French, Danish, Italian, Spanish, and Dutch; by 1812 this stretched to Swedish, Russian, and Portuguese. Moreover, the availability of the book in European languages was not limited to the Old World. The Portuguese version was published in Rio de Janeiro, and there were early printings of the original English in Philadelphia. At times the spread of the book in foreign languages could be bumpy. The translations might be incomplete or inaccurate, and in the case of the Spanish version of 1794 the text was cleansed to satisfy the Inquisition, which meant the elimination of "various impious proposals," together with an unacceptable passage advocating "tolerance on points of religion."[17] Yet overall, the rapid diffusion of the work in European languages is in striking contrast to its belated appearance in non-European tongues: Japanese in 1870, Chinese in 1901, Turkish in 1948, Korean in 1957, Arabic in 1959, and Persian in 1978–79. That Japanese comes first in this list is significant.

The other major factor shaping reactions to British power was whether a society possessed sufficient resources and organization to respond effectively. Translating Adam Smith did not need very much of either, but constructing a railroad of any length called for a large measure of both. Railroads had antecedents stretching back long before Adam Smith, for example to German mining technology of the early eighteenth century, but it was well into the nineteenth century before this development came to fruition with the opening of the Liverpool & Manchester Railway in 1830. Within a decade, the technology was well established in Europe and North America. By contrast, work on the first railroad in the Muslim world did not begin until 1851. Completed in 1856, this railroad linked Alexandria to Cairo and was soon extended to Suez. As we will see, it was no accident that Egypt was in this respect ahead of other Muslim lands. In the rest of the Ottoman Empire a start came in 1857, with two railways in western Anatolia finished in 1866, but the line linking Istanbul to Vienna was not completed till 1888, and the brunt of the expansion of the network came after 1890. Farther east the Trans-Iranian Railway was begun only in 1928, to be completed ten years later. Meanwhile in sub-Saharan Africa, North Africa, Central Asia, India, and Southeast Asia, it was overwhelmingly the European imperial powers that invested in railroads, not the indigenous states that had previously ruled there. And even where indigenous states did preside over the effort, as in Tunisia in 1876, they tended to be heavily dependent on European capital and expertise. A partial exception was the Hijaz Railway linking Damascus to Medina, built in 1903–8. For symbolic reasons the Ottomans engaged in a major effort to make this a purely Muslim enterprise, but

16. See H. Mizuta (ed.), *Adam Smith: Critical responses*, London 2000, 5:149.
17. Quoted in C. Lai, *Adam Smith across nations*, Oxford 2000, xix.

even here they proved unable to do without European experts, and in any case the line ceased to function within a few years.

One thing that emerges from the history of railroads is that Macaulay's account tends to exaggerate the degree to which the history of England was a singularity. The English readily borrowed from their continental neighbors, and these neighbors in turn readily borrowed from the English, as did populations of western European origin overseas. Thus the industrial revolution had reached parts of continental Europe as early as 1815. The more lasting gap, in other words, was not between the English and everyone else, but between the larger entity we call the West and much of the rest of the world. Against this background we can now turn to a survey of what has—or hasn't—changed in the Muslim world since 1800. We start with a crude but significant bottom line: the extent of Muslim territory.

What has changed since 1800?

Territory

Aḥmad ibn Qāsim al-Ḥajarī, a Morisco writing in Arabic in 1641, was proud to survey the vast extent of the Muslim presence in Europe, Africa, Asia, and the East Indies—what we would call Southeast Asia. Such broad awareness of the extent of the Muslim world was of course nothing new. Ibn Ḥazm (d. 1064), who lived in Spain, celebrated the conquests of Maḥmūd of Ghazna (ruled 998–1030) in India, and the end of the ʿAbbāsid caliphate in 1258 was lamented from India to Spain. But it was a sign of the times that in conducting his survey Ḥajarī was partly dependent on Christian sources, particularly for the islands of the East Indies, where he relied on the testimony of a Dutch diplomat he had met in Morocco. He nevertheless concluded his survey by rejoicing that, praise be to God, most of the inhabited world belonged to the Muslims, whose sovereignty would endure to the end of time. It was, he added, no surprise that those eastern islands were in Muslim hands, since God had ordered Muslims to make war on infidels and polytheists. His belief in the global demographic dominance of the Muslims was undoubtedly somewhat exaggerated, and his view of the reason for the spread of Islam in maritime Southeast Asia underestimated the role of trade. But what we should attend to here is his faith that Muslim sovereignty would endure to the end of the world. As of the early twenty-first century this prediction has not proved altogether wrong, but it needs considerable qualification. Let us therefore trace some of the very different territorial trajectories of the Muslim lands in modern times.

The worst-case scenario was for a Muslim-majority society to be subjected to non-Muslim colonization on a scale that marginalized or eliminated the Muslim population. As we have seen, there were occasional precedents for this in premodern times. We saw it happen in the Arab-Byzantine frontier lands in the tenth to eleventh centuries, though this loss was soon made good thanks to the arrival of the Turks. There were similar adverse developments in Spain with the Reconquista and on some of the major islands of the Mediterranean. Meanwhile in Eurasia, the Khānate of Kazan was heavily colonized after it fell to the Russians. But such losses of Muslim lands to full-scale colonization were relatively rare before the eighteenth century and continued to be so in modern times. There are, in fact, only four conspicuous modern cases. Three were continuations of the Russian and Manchu imperial expansions of the eighteenth century. The Russians colonized the Crimea after conquering it in the later eighteenth century and did the same with nearby Circassia—in the northwestern Caucasus and the adjacent coastlands—in the course of a decades-long war of conquest that climaxed in the early 1860s. Yet in most of Russia's Muslim territories the settler population, though considerable, was not enough to tip the demographic balance. Meanwhile the Manchus had conquered eastern Turkestan—alias Xinjiang—in the eighteenth century and already then adopted a policy of moving in colonists, but large-scale Chinese settlement of the region, especially the eastern part of it, came only in the second half of the twentieth century. These cases are not particularly puzzling. Each region was, so to speak, in the backyard of the major power that was the source of the colonists, and in each case the process was facilitated by contiguity—neither armies nor settlers had to face the logistical difficulties of crossing an ocean. Elsewhere the absence of these conditions is at least part of the explanation for the failure of the attempt of the French to colonize Algeria after they began to conquer it in 1830, and of the Italians to do the same in Libya after they invaded it in 1911.

The final case was distinctly surprising: the Jewish settlement of a large part of Palestine that gave rise to the state of Israel. The Zionist project that lay behind this—the aspiration to establish a Jewish state in Palestine—is unique in modern history, but it can be seen as a combination of two rather commonplace ones: national liberation and colonization. Looking at it in this way shows why it seemed unlikely to succeed. National liberation is typically successful when the nation-to-be starts with demographic dominance in the prospective national territory, as in the case of the Greeks under Ottoman rule in the 1820s. The Jews, by contrast, enjoyed no such dominance in either eastern Europe or Palestine. Colonization is typically successful when the settlers are backed by their home state, as in the case of the British colonists in nineteenth-century New Zealand, but there was no Jewish home state to back the early Zionists in Palestine. Moreover, the Zionists were trying to realize both these projects at once. The enterprise would almost certainly have failed but for the somewhat halfhearted backing of the British state that the Zionists adventitiously secured in the course of the First World War and its aftermath. There was, however, one feature of the demography of Palestine in the late nineteenth and early twentieth centuries that worked in favor of Zionist settlement: the relative depopulation of the plains, as opposed to the hills. This was a widespread feature of the Mediterranean coastlands at the time, the result of a long-term process of environmental degradation whereby the deforestation and erosion of the hillsides led to the spread of malarial swamps in the plains, a syndrome readily accentuated by chronic insecurity in the absence of strong government. Under modern conditions the swamps could be drained, malaria brought under control, and public order established, with the result that the plains could once again fill up with dense populations. A prime example is the Cilician plain in southeastern Anatolia. At the start of the nineteenth century it was a poorly drained, malarial wasteland, but by the early 1880s it was rapidly being brought under cultivation, and today it is one of Turkey's richest and most productive agricultural regions. What, then, was to be the source of the new population in such cases? The obvious answer was peasants from the neighboring hills, and there were signs of this starting in Palestine. But there were other possibilities. In Italy as late as the 1920s the Pontine Marshes to the southeast of Rome were inhabited only by a small population of nomadic pastoralists. The Fascist government then proceeded to drain the marshes and move in settlers; these were indeed Catholic Italians, but they were not from the neighboring hills. Zionist settlement in Palestine was a more extreme case. Here the newcomers came overwhelmingly from eastern Europe and shared neither ethnicity nor religion with the indigenous population.

Thin populations do not have to be vulnerable to colonization, and in this respect the Mediterranean coastal plains were exceptional. Large parts of the Muslim world were thinly populated because they were desert, an environment generally unattractive to colonists. Things are different only if the desert possesses valuable subsoil resources. We saw a medieval example of this effect in the case of the mines located in the territory of the Beja. The modern equivalent is the presence of oil underneath the Arab tribes of eastern Arabia, resulting in a demand for labor so great that the immigrant populations outnumber their hosts in Kuwait, Bahrain, Qatar, and the United Arab Emirates. But this is labor migration, not colonization. As we will see, these states have continued to be ruled by their Arab dynasties, with citizenship largely confined to the indigenous Arab population and immigrants denied a right of permanent residence.

The Crimea, Circassia, Xinjiang, and Palestine are not, of course, the only territories largely lost to the Muslim world. But the others, though much more extensive, were lands under Muslim rule in which the majority of the population was non-Muslim. The two major examples of this in modern times are the Balkans and India. Over most of the Balkans, several centuries of Ottoman rule had not issued in the conversion of the majority of the Christian population to Islam. Under nineteenth-century conditions, in a world now dominated by European Christian powers—two of them neighbors—the rule of a Muslim minority over a Christian majority was no longer sustainable. The eventual success of the Greek rebellion of

1821 thus initiated a domino effect that deprived the Ottoman Empire of its most prosperous and modern provinces. Within a century, if we leave aside the corner of European territory retained by Turkey today, the only Balkan country that still belonged in some sense to the Muslim world was Albania, where the majority of the population was Muslim. With the breakup of Yugoslavia it has since been joined by the entity known as Bosnia and Herzegovina, a conflicted state reckoned to have a slight Muslim majority. Elsewhere much of the Muslim population that survived the end of Ottoman rule left for territory still under Muslim administration. But survival was far from assured for either Muslims or Christians. For example, during the Greek rebellion, the fall of Tripolitsa in the Morea in 1821 led to the killing of thousands of Muslim civilians, and the next year on the island of Chios, Ottoman irregular troops massacred thousands of Christian men and enslaved an even greater number of women and children. In the Indian case, too, the majority of the population had not converted to Islam despite prolonged Muslim political dominance. Moreover, in this case Muslim rule had already been much reduced long before the subcontinent was partitioned into independent countries in the mid-twentieth century; as we have seen, this reduction was the work of the Rājpūts, the Marāṭhās, the Sikhs, and the British. When the British finally left India in 1947, this had the effect of confirming the demographic outcome over the bulk of what had been British India, leaving only two Muslim-majority territories in the northwest and northeast to be ruled by Muslims—today's Pakistan and Bangladesh. Within the borders of what was now India, the remaining Muslim states, such as that of Hyderabad, had no chance of survival. Much as in the Balkans, the process of partition meant death and displacement on a large scale. The Indian outcome again is no surprise. Irrespective of religious allegiances, modern political conditions have made the rule of minorities over majorities far less stable than it was in premodern times—a major reason even European rule over non-European majorities barely survived the mid-twentieth century. This general destabilization of minority rule has also led to successful non-Muslim separatist movements within Muslim countries. It doomed Indonesian rule in East Timor in 1999 (though not, as yet, in western New Guinea) and Sudanese rule in southern Sudan in 2011.

Yet the major story in the Muslim world over the last two centuries has not involved either the limited loss of Muslim-majority territory through colonization or the more extensive forfeiture resulting from the empowerment of preexisting non-Muslim majorities. A far more widespread pattern was for a Muslim land to be subjected to a longer or shorter period of European imperial rule. This rule would be established in the face of variously brief or sustained resistance. What is noteworthy here is that the most effective defiance tended to come not from the rulers of conventional states, such as Egypt in 1882 or Morocco in 1911–12, but rather from leaders of tribal followings in geographically forbidding regions. One example is the resistance led by ʿAbd al-Qādir al-Jazāʾirī (d. 1883), who fought against French rule in Algeria from 1832 to 1847; another is the struggle of Shāmil (d. 1871) against the Russians in the northern Caucasus from 1834 to 1859; a third is the rebellion of Muḥammad ibn ʿAbdallāh Ḥassān (d. 1920) against the British in Somaliland in the first two decades of the twentieth century. Once established at some point in the nineteenth or early twentieth century, European rule would typically last into the middle years of the twentieth century—or until its last decade in the case of Muslim-majority regions conquered by the Russian Empire. But the duration of imperial rule could also be very short, as in the case of Albania. Then the only Muslim-majority country in Europe, Albania was ruled by Italy from 1939 to 1943, followed by a brief German occupation. Whatever the duration of European rule, sooner or later the imperial power would depart, leaving behind a newly independent Muslim country. In general, it did not require insurrection to bring this about; the massive violence accompanying the establishment of Pakistan in 1947 was not directed against the British. But there were conspicuous exceptions. It took several years of vicious fighting before the French accepted that they could not continue to rule Algeria and left in 1962.

As all this suggests, European rule in the non-European world was by no means a homogeneous phenomenon. One significant variable was what the imperial power did with the existing political order when it took over a territory. There might already be a state there, as in Morocco, Tunisia, and Egypt, almost all such states being monarchies at the time. Or there might be no state, as was the case in much of the Sahara. Leaders such as ʿAbd al-Qādir al-Jazāʾirī in the mountains of Algeria and Shāmil in the northern Caucasus were engaged in abortive processes of state formation in the face of European invasion, not in defense of existing states. In cases where a state already existed, the new imperial rulers might decide to erase it and start afresh. This was what the French did with the Barbary state of Algiers when they invaded it in 1830, what the British did with the Mahdist state in the Sudan when they conquered it in 1898, and what the Dutch did in Aceh between 1873 and 1907. But in other cases imperial rulers found it expedient to preserve existing states, formally and even substantively. The French did this in Morocco and Tunisia, the British in Egypt and Brunei, and the Russians, though only initially, in the Khānates of Bukhārā, Khīwa, and Khoqand. Sometimes the European intruders would accept the existence of a plurality of indigenous states within a single imperial territory. The British did so in northern Nigeria, along the southern and eastern coastlands of Arabia, in parts of India, and in Malaya, while the Dutch did so in parts of Indonesia. In some instances an imperial power might even elect to install an indigenous ruler or accept an indigenous intruder soon after it had taken over a territory. In the aftermath of the First World War this was the case with the British in Iraq and Transjordan (the future Jordan). But in general we are concerned here with states that already existed before the imperial takeover. Those that survived it then faced a second ordeal when the territories over which they reigned became independent. Many monarchies now went down to reform or revolution, as was the case in parts of Indonesia in 1950, in Egypt in 1953, in Tunisia in 1957, in Zanzibar in 1964, and along the southern coast of Arabia west of Oman in 1967. Only a limited number of Muslim monarchies survived both the inception of imperial rule and the coming of independence, notably those of Morocco, the smaller states of the Persian Gulf, and Brunei, to which we could add the titular monarchies of Malaysia and Java. In Jordan, too, where the monarchy was established only after the inception of imperial rule, it survived independence.

That leaves a small number of Muslim states that did not succumb to European rule. They are a mixed bag: Turkey, Iran, Afghanistan, Saudi Arabia, and Yemen. All five have suffered from at least some degree of occupation by foreign armies in modern times. In the case of the first three, these armies were Western or Russian. Thus parts of what became Turkey were occupied in the course of the dissolution of the Ottoman Empire after its defeat in the First World War; these included Istanbul, then the capital city and still the economic center of the country. Iran suffered varying degrees of occupation in the years around the First World War and again in the Second World War. The turn of Afghanistan came in the late twentieth and early twenty-first centuries, with first a Russian and then an American occupation. Yemen and Saudi Arabia were different in that no non-Muslim armies were involved. In each case the occupying forces were Egyptian, in the first half of the nineteenth century in the case of Saudi Arabia and in the 1960s in the case of Yemen. Either way, none of these five countries was formally subjected to Western or Russian rule, though Iran in 1919 came close to becoming a British protectorate. The reasons for this relative immunity varied. In the cases of Afghanistan and Yemen a severely mountainous terrain and a lack of significant resources discouraged imperial annexation—though these features did not prevent the Russian conquest of the Caucasus. Forces of a more geopolitical character could also be at work. In the century before the First World War it suited the British and Russian Empires to have Iran and Afghanistan as buffer states between them. In the Ottoman case geopolitics merged with a strong element of historical contingency. Defeat in the First World War opened the door to a drastic partition of the empire, and yet a fairly large and genuinely independent Turkey emerged from the wreckage. This was due to a number of things. One was the collapse of Russia into revolution in 1917, which made possible the presence of an undefeated Ottoman army on the Caucasian front and rendered the claims of Russia to Ottoman territory moot. Another was that in the absence of Russian imperial expansion the war-weary British and their allies had little interest in direct intervention in what was left of Ottoman territory. A third was a Greek invasion of western Anatolia in 1919, which galvanized Ottoman resistance around a new leadership that went on to establish the Turkish Republic. Saudi Arabia is a rather different case. Prior to the discovery of oil in the eastern region of the country, there was little about its desert landscape to attract the territorial ambitions of a Western power, which, given the British hegemony on the eastern and southern coasts of Arabia, would almost inevitably have been Britain—although the very similar landscape of the Sahara failed to deter the French. After the oil began to flow the country did indeed have a major resource to offer, and it used it to secure the alliance and protection of the world's most powerful country, the United States. Here the timing was of the essence: had the oil wells been developed in the first half of the nineteenth century, the British might simply have seized the territory around them, as they did the port of Aden in 1839.

In sum, most of the Muslim world survived the rise of Western and Russian power in the nineteenth and early twentieth centuries. There were, as we have seen, a limited number of cases in which territories populated by Muslim majorities were lost to the Muslim world, and on a larger scale most territories in which Muslims ruled over non-Muslim majorities went the same way. But by and large the Muslim lands that experienced Western or Russian rule reemerged from it, and a few were never subjected to it. What Muslims did not do in this period was extend their share of the world in the manner of the Europeans in the last few centuries, creating new societies with large settler majorities in the hitherto thinly populated regions of the Americas and the Antipodes. As we have seen, at the time of the Spanish overseas expansion some Moriscos did succeed in crossing the Atlantic despite the official prohibition of such migration. The caused consternation—Moriscos were learning Nahuatl, putting them in a position to transmit their hidden beliefs to the Mexican Indians. But whatever the dimensions of this migration, it was clearly too limited to create lasting Muslim communities in the emerging societies of the Americas.

So also, in the end, was the importation of slaves to the New World from West Africa. Going by their provenance, there must have been significant numbers of Muslims among these slaves from the sixteenth century onward, though explicit evidence of their retention of Islam can be hard to come by before the nineteenth century. In early nineteenth-century Bahia, in northeastern Brazil, there was a considerable population of Hausa Muslim slaves. This arose from a combination of two factors. On the demand side the sugar producers of Bahia needed large amounts of labor, and on the supply side the Fulānī jihad meant the large-scale enslavement of Hausas who were then available for export (their Muslim enslavers did not, of course, regard them as Muslims). These slaves were able to practice Islam fairly openly, and they made their mark on the history of Bahia through their participation in a series of rebellions that began with an abortive conspiracy in 1807 and culminated in a major revolt of 1835 in whose leadership Muslims played a prominent role. There were likewise Muslims among the African slaves imported by the British settlers in North America, but the Black Muslim communities in the

United States today reflect a process of conversion that began in the twentieth century through the activities of a Druze salesman. So just as in the case of the Moriscos, the African slave trade did not lead to the presence of enduring Muslim populations in the New World.

Today there is nevertheless a diaspora of emigrants from the Muslim world extending far beyond its borders, though we can do no more than cite some random examples of it here. In the non-Western world a large component of this diaspora stems from emigration from the Levant—Lebanon and Syria. Initially most but not all of the migrants were Christians. They typically began their new lives as itinerant peddlers and rose through commercial success. Because they came from the Ottoman Empire, Latin Americans called them "Turcos," often disparagingly; in Brazil "Turco" could serve as a playground insult among schoolchildren. A considerable number of these immigrants headed for Argentina. They began to arrive there as early as the 1860s, and in the first decade of the twentieth century Muslims joined the Christian flow. There were significant numbers of Levantine immigrants even in the remote northeastern province of Tucumán thanks to the economic opportunities afforded by its sugar monoculture. Here the year 1929 saw the establishment of a Panislamic Cultural Association. In the late 1970s its executive committee included members with obviously Muslim names, but also an Eduardo and a Pedro, suggesting a degree of assimilation. This was not a new phenomenon: an Emilio who married in 1935 had been born a Mahmoud. Another and more pointed Argentinian case of assimilation was Carlos Menem (d. 2021), president from 1989 to 1999 and widely known as "el Turco." He was born into a Muslim family a couple of hundred miles south of Tucumán and became an aspiring politician. Until 1994 the Argentinian constitution required that the president of the republic be a Catholic, and Buenos Aires was undoubtedly worth a mass. Menem, however, is said to have become a Catholic as far back as the 1960s, and in his memoirs he gracefully lays an even earlier foundation for this politic change of religion. In the course of an illness following his birth, his Muslim mother had a vision in which the Virgin Mary spoke to her, and thereafter she became more and more devoted to her cult. So once a year the family would visit the shrine of Our Lady of the Valley in nearby Catamarca. Nor was this all: at some point, he tells us, a Catholic neighbor had taken the initiative of having little Carlos secretly baptized. This whole account is indeed "molto ben trovato" in that it also highlights the strategic roles in the spaces between religions that women can often play more easily than men can do. Another phenomenon illustrated by Menem's career is the remarkable success of Levantine immigrants as politicians in Latin America, as, for example, in Ecuador, where the Bucaram family has played a prominent role in the politics of the country.

Elsewhere the Muslim diaspora can look very different. For example, a large South Asian diaspora resulted from the migration of Indian coolies in the nineteenth and early twentieth centuries to such islands as Mauritius, Réunion, Fiji, and Trinidad, together with the Guyanas on the South American mainland. Again, most of these immigrants were not Muslims, but there has been a continuing presence of Muslim minorities in each of these territories. There is likewise a Muslim diaspora in the United States and Europe. The United States has well over three million Muslims, three-quarters of them of immigrant background, mostly South Asians and Arabs, but these Muslims make up only a little more than 1 percent of the total population. By contrast, Muslims in European countries number some twenty-six million, or about 5 percent of the population, and in the case of France, where most Muslims are of North African origin, the proportion approaches 9 percent. Moreover, many of the Muslims of Europe, unlike most of the Muslim diaspora elsewhere, are stuck at the bottom of the economic pyramid. These factors help explain why continuing Muslim immigration has become a major issue in European politics.

Returning to the relative territorial integrity of the Muslim world in modern times, it did not mean that any part of it came through the last two centuries intact. The changes were far-reaching, and almost without exception, they would not have taken place without the rise of European power. In principle, of course, it might make just as much sense to inquire about changes arising from interactions with parts of the world other than the West, but in practice their impact so far has been far less salient. It would likewise make sense to ask about developments that happened, or would have happened, through processes purely internal to the Muslim world. There is, after all, no reason to believe that the Muslim lands, if left to themselves, would have been no different today from what they were in 1800. But the further we move into the nineteenth and twentieth centuries, the harder it becomes to identify such changes with any assurance. So for the most part our concern here, as above, will be with developments arising from interactions with the West and, to a more limited extent, with Russia in its Tsarist, Communist, and post-Communist incarnations. We can consider these changes under the rubrics of population, communications, the economy, society, and the state.

Population

Perhaps the single most dramatic change that calls for our attention is demographic: the enormous increase in the population of the Muslim world, as of the world at large. Today there are some two billion Muslims—a quarter of the world's population—with most of them living in Muslim-majority countries. What might that figure have been in 1800? Medieval Muslim writers would say about large populations that only God could count them, and that was still a plausible view in 1800, a date well before the European-style census had become a standard instrument of government in the Muslim world. A guess based on only slightly more than thin air might be that the total Muslim population as of 1800 was well under a tenth of what it is now. Egypt, which today has a population of a hundred million, had a bit less than ten million in 1897, the year of its first fully modern census, and an informed guess for 1800 comes in at a bit less than four million; if we go by that figure, Egyptians are now some twenty-five times as numerous as they were then. The case of Java is even more extreme. The island is estimated to have had a population of between three and five million in 1800. By 1890 this had become twenty-four million, and today it is around 155 million. That would indicate that the population of Java is now thirty to fifty times what it was in 1800. The basic process involved in such population increase is simple enough. We start in a premodern world where both birth and death rates are high; then death rates fall while birth rates remain high, and the result is population growth that continues until such time as birth rates fall to levels commensurate with death rates. A corollary of this development is a doubling in the expectation of life. In the Muslim world as elsewhere, the fact that death rates fell for most of the nineteenth and twentieth centuries can be attributed to the abatement of major causes of premodern mortality: the devastation wreaked by warring armies living off the land, varieties of domestic disorder ranging from endemic banditry to episodic revolt and occasional civil war, the horrors of famine, and the ravages of epidemic disease. Much of this abatement arose directly or indirectly from developments initiated in the West. Modern transport made the provisioning of troops less dependent on looting, enabled states to repress disorder more effectively, and rendered it easier to compensate for a failed harvest by bringing food from elsewhere. Meanwhile, the impact of epidemic disease was reduced by public health measures, notably the imposition of the quarantine system and the provision of clean water. Urban civilization no longer stinks as much as it did in premodern times. All this, of course, applies in large measure to the world at large. But comparatively speaking, the increase in the population of the Muslim world seems to have been on the high side. The population of the world as a whole is reckoned to have increased only about eightfold since 1800, less than the growth suggested above for the Muslim world and far less than what we saw in the cases of Egypt and Java. Two factors could be involved here: a lower baseline for the size of the population in the Muslim world in 1800 and higher Muslim fertility rates sustained until recent decades. The increase could thus be seen as too much of what was initially a good thing. That is to say, if we think in terms of an optimal population size for a given set of resources, it seems clear that on average the Muslim world was well below it in 1800 and is well above it today.

A second fundamental demographic shift has been the increase in the proportion of the population that is urban as opposed to rural. In contrast to the trajectory of the total population size, the baseline here seems to have been relatively high in comparative terms, at least in some parts of the Muslim world, with much of the transformation being rather recent. Estimates of the urban fraction of the population of the Middle East in 1800 put it at between 10 and 20 percent, in any case not more, but enough to make the region more urbanized than France was at the time. Today the only Muslim country in that range is Niger, which consists mostly of a thankless expanse of Saharan desert. Disproportionate urban population growth in the Muslim world appears to have begun in the middle decades of the twentieth century, but since then it has been rapid. In the Middle East and North Africa just under two-thirds of the population was urban in 2018, while for Turkey and Iran the proportion was as much as three-quarters. In the two Muslim countries of South Asia the urban population was only a little over a third of the total, but in Indonesia, where in 1930 it had been a mere 4 percent, it had risen to 55 percent. As might be expected, most of this increase has been a result of migration from the countryside, where the supply of cultivable land has not kept pace with rapid demographic growth. The result has been a teeming landless population even in countries in which the state expropriated large landowners and redistributed their estates to the peasants. Landlessness, in turn, led to migration to the cities in search of economic opportunity, leading to the formation of extensive slums around major cities and often swamping the traditional urban populations.

Communications

While these demographic changes were taking place, a far-reaching adoption of modern Western technologies for the transportation of people and goods was in progress. We have already seen how railroads came to the Muslim world in the second half of the nineteenth century. In British India serious road building had begun in the 1840s, but in the Middle East good roads were mainly a development of the twentieth century. As late as 1890, for example, the roads around Aleppo were so bad that carriages preferred to avoid them by following tracks through the fields on either side. It was the coming of motor vehicles that was the major stimulus for better roads. Over the half century from 1966 to 2012, the length of roads in Indonesia grew sixfold, at the same time as the number of cars grew almost sixtyfold. What these two technologies—rail and road—had in common was that they required massive investment along every mile of the route linking a starting point to a destination. Ships and airplanes, by contrast, did not need this, since the sea and the air could be left to take care of themselves. Here investment was mostly limited to the vehicle and the facilities at either end of the journey. The exception was the construction of canals to enable shipping to take shorter routes—notably the Suez Canal, completed in 1869. Steamships began to visit the Middle East in the second quarter of the nineteenth century, leading to the enlargement of ports. On Java a steamship was built with local labor as early as 1825, which was also the year when the first steamship made the journey from Britain to India.

However, it was not until midcentury that the technology became really efficient, and it was only in the 1860s that the use of steamships became widespread in maritime Southeast Asia. Air transport arrived in the early twentieth century. The airport that served Istanbul for decades began as a military airport in 1912, during the last years of the Ottoman Empire. In the 1920s the new technology was brought to the European-ruled territories of the Muslim world by the British, French, Russians, and Dutch, and it reached Iran thanks to a German company. All this amounted to a revolution in the means of transport. At the same time, as the example of the Ottoman military airport suggests, these new technologies often had major uses in warfare, a context in which they were deployed in the first instance by European powers.

It was not just people and goods that now circulated faster and more cheaply; it was also information. The first major development toward its instantaneous transfer was the coming of the electric telegraph. Already in use in Europe in the 1840s, it was brought to the Ottoman Empire a decade later by the British and the French in the context of the Crimean War (1853–56). The Ottoman government quickly saw the value of the invention: the Directorate of Ottoman Telegraphs was established in 1855, and the first telegram in Turkish was sent in 1856. The telegraph reached other parts of the Muslim world in roughly the same period, and in due course it was joined by the telephone. Invented around 1876, this novel contraption spread to the Ottoman Empire, Egypt, India, and the Dutch East Indies as early as 1881–82. The late nineteenth century also saw the early development of radio transmission, with radio broadcasting becoming significant from the 1920s and television from the 1930s. Both were adopted across the globe. Television first came to the Muslim world in 1954 and thereafter spread so rapidly that by 1980 only a few countries still lacked it. Then came the internet. Developed in the last four decades of the twentieth century, its use exploded in the first two decades of the twenty-first, with the social networking sites Facebook and Twitter acquiring hundreds of millions of users. The Muslim world was now deeply enmeshed in the World Wide Web. All these changes in communications are most palpable in the cities, but they also penetrate the countryside, making the villages of the Muslim world far less isolated than they used to be.

The economy

As we would expect, these changes in demography and communications were closely linked to economic developments.[18] One of them was commercial. The rapid growth of the Western economies provided a ready market for many exports of Muslim countries and a major source of imports, and it was now much

18. For much of what follows see C. Issawi, *An economic history of the Middle East and North Africa*, London 1982.

easier—and cheaper—for these countries to export what they produced and import the products of others. The result was a dramatic expansion of their foreign trade. Its growth was uneven, subject to occasional reversals, and in general rather less than that of world trade as a whole. But the foreign trade of the Muslim world has increased many times over since 1800. One obvious manifestation of this development, direct or indirect, has been a tendency for coasts to rise at the expense of hinterlands. We see this at the western end of the Muslim world in the case of Casablanca. This settlement on the Atlantic coast of Morocco was not much more than a fishing village in 1834, but it is now the largest city in the country, and its economic capital. It has a population of well over three million, dwarfing Fez and Marrakesh, the historic Moroccan capitals in the interior. Meanwhile, at the eastern end of the Muslim world power shifted from inland Javanese capitals such as Yogyakarta and Surakarta to the Dutch port of Batavia, now Jakarta, the capital city and economic center of Indonesia with a population over ten million. In between are two telling cases where the creation of an inland political capital in the twentieth century failed to end the economic primacy of the major coastal city. One is Turkey, where Istanbul has about three times the population of Ankara, and the other is Pakistan, where the population of Karachi is about fifteen times that of Islamabad. Not surprisingly, the rise of global commerce has touched every sector of the economy in the countries of the Muslim world, though in different ways.

In premodern times the dominant sector of any large economy had to be some combination of agriculture and animal husbandry. This was slow to change. As late as 1970, in the majority of the larger countries of the Middle East and North Africa, half or more of a now much larger labor force was still engaged in agriculture. This sector of the economy has seen a major increase in production across much of the Muslim world over the last two centuries. Behind this expansion three familiar factors were at work. One was greater security in the countryside thanks to the growing power of the state. Another was the increasing size of the population; whether it remained in the countryside or migrated to the cities, it had to be fed. The third was, of course, the rise of foreign trade, in which agricultural exports were prominent.

These exports varied from country to country, but in the Middle East and Central Asia the single most important of them was cotton. As we saw, cotton was already a cash crop in northern Palestine around the middle of the eighteenth century, but it now played this role on a far larger scale. The most striking case was that of Egypt, where in 1818 a French engineer discovered a long-staple variant of the plant that was particularly attractive to the dark satanic mills of England's textile industry. Although the dependence of this development on European expertise and demand was obvious, it was Meḥmed ʿAlī Pasha, the very Ottoman ruler Egypt from 1805 to 1848, who employed the engineer and seized the opportunity to give the country a major role in the world economy, just as it was the Egyptian peasants who provided the hard labor, often unwillingly. This precocious development of a major cash crop is the background to the early adoption of the railroad in Egypt. What the pasha had started was continued by the subsequent rulers of the country, including the British after they occupied it in 1882, and on the eve of the First World War cotton accounted for over 90 percent of Egypt's exports. The main contribution to increased production in Egypt came not from expanding the area of agricultural land—though this too was significant—but rather from cultivating it more intensively thanks to radical change in the irrigation system.

Elsewhere, an increase in the amount of land under cultivation was doubtless the more salient factor. Thus in the early nineteenth century foreign observers of the Javanese countryside saw its problem as a scanty population amid an abundance of good land that was left uncultivated, whereas a century later the Dutch saw the problem as a growing population pressing on a limited supply of agricultural land. Once this latter stage was reached, the pull of the world market and the need to feed a growing population could, of course, be at cross-purposes. Many Muslim countries that formerly exported food have found themselves having to import it to feed their growing populations. The mismatch between population and resources in the agricultural sector is also indicated by a notable disparity: the contribution of agriculture to gross domestic product has tended to be much lower than its share of the labor force.

Manufacturing is a very different story. Here there were two phases. In the first, largely coterminous with the nineteenth century, the effect of rising foreign trade was not to increase demand for the manufactures of the Muslim world but rather to reduce it, sometimes drastically. Textiles produced by European factories were cheaper if not better, and they tended to crowd out those produced locally. The result was a process of deindustrialization in which these lands became suppliers of raw materials to industrial economies located elsewhere. An official Russian source of 1914 bluntly described Central Asia as "a purveyor of raw material for the metropolis and a consumer of its manufactures."[19] Despite some exceptions—notably carpets—the effect was to kill off much of the traditional handicraft production of the Muslim world, especially in the cities. The second phase, largely coterminous with the twentieth century, saw the reception of Western methods of industrial production and the consequent emergence of an industrial sector and a working class within Muslim countries. Some of this reindustrialization reflected the advantages of local production over importation from far away, as with the Egyptian beer industry. But much of it arose from the aspirations of states. Already

19. Quoted in G. Wheeler, "Russian conquest and colonization of Central Asia," in T. Hunczak (ed.), *Russian imperialism from Ivan the Great to the Revolution*, New Brunswick 1974, 280.

in the first half of the nineteenth century Meḥmed ʿAlī Pasha sought to create an industrial sector in Egypt, though with little success. What made a major difference was the coming of independence to many Muslim countries in the twentieth century. Economic development was high on the agendas of the new nationalist rulers, and they now had the ability to protect domestic industry by imposing tariffs on imports of manufactured goods. The danger was, of course, that the industries fostered or even run by the state behind these tariff walls would be too inefficient to compete internationally. Since the 1960s several Muslim countries, including Tunisia and Turkey, have nevertheless seen a major change in the goods they export, with the share of manufactured goods rising from less than a tenth to more than two-thirds. Malaysian industry has also been a significant success story, and it may not be a coincidence that in 2019 Malaysia was the only Muslim country to be ranked in the top fifteen for ease of doing business. Meanwhile, the Russian invasion of Ukraine in 2022 highlighted the military effectiveness of drones manufactured in Turkey and, perhaps more surprisingly, Iran. Yet no country in the Muslim world has yet created a manufacturing sector comparable to those of the industrialized countries of Europe, North America, or East Asia.

The remaining sector that calls for our attention is the exploitation of subsoil resources. A variety of minerals were mined in the Muslim world before modern times, and overall this activity has grown a lot in the last two centuries. But the single most prominent subsoil resource has been oil. This fuel was known in the Middle East long before modern times; the seventeenth-century Ottoman traveler Evliyā Chelebī described its wide distribution from the region of Bākū. Yet oil came into its own only in the nineteenth century. The first major success of the modern oil industry took place in the New World, in Pennsylvania in 1859, but its second was the oil of Bākū in the 1870s. This was not, however, an enterprise shaped by the local Muslims. Bākū, today the capital of the independent republic of Azerbaijan, had been part of the Russian Empire since 1806, and the key entrepreneurs in its nascent oil industry were Swedes. Considerable numbers of Muslims were involved, but they were concentrated at the bottom of the labor hierarchy. The next major success was again in the Muslim world, in northeastern Sumatra in the early 1890s. Here, too, Europeans were the prime movers, and at least part of the labor force was Chinese, but this time it was a local Muslim ruler under the Dutch umbrella, the sultan of Langkat, who granted the concession that allowed the enterprise to proceed. Thereafter the action moved back to the United States with the development of new oilfields in Texas and Oklahoma, but it returned once again to the Muslim world with the discovery of oil in the lowlands of southwestern Iran in 1908. As usual, many of the key actors were Western, in this case British, and after much internal dissension they included the British government. But despite the fact that the oil industry—unlike cotton production in Egypt—

could easily take the form of a self-contained Western enclave, indigenous actors played a number of parts in the Iranian story. On this occasion the original initiative for the concession came from the cash-strapped Iranian government in Tehran. Other actors were local. While the Bakhtiyārī tribal chiefs at the wellhead proved exasperatingly difficult to do business with, the shaykh of Muḥammara in nearby ʿArabistān facilitated the establishment of a refinery on his territory. With this discovery began the exploitation of one of the world's largest concentrations of oilfields, a region centered on the Persian Gulf but stretching far into the lowlands of Iraq to the north and Oman to the south. Several other countries, large and small, became significant producers in this region: Iraq in 1927, Bahrain in 1932, Kuwait in 1938, and Saudi Arabia in the same year, to be joined in due course by Qatar, the future components of the United Arab Emirates, and Oman. Other Muslim countries in which oil was discovered in large quantities were Algeria in 1956, Libya in 1959, and Kazakhstan, which despite a history of oil production that began under the Russian Empire became a significant producer only in the 1960s. Toward the end of the second decade of the twenty-first century, the Muslim world as a whole produced just under half of the world's total oil supply and possessed significantly more than half of its total proven reserves. Within the Muslim world it is the complex of fields around the Persian Gulf that constitutes by far the largest concentration of oil. In the same period this region produced over a third of the world's oil supply and possessed about half of its proven reserves.

One way in which the oil industry in the Muslim world has changed since its beginnings is that it no longer has the look of a Western enclave among populations otherwise untouched by the modern world. As late as the 1950s the oil companies prospecting on the territory of Abu Dhabi, now the core of the United Arab Emirates, were dealing with a ruler who insisted on being paid in Indian rupee notes, which he counted himself and stored in his strong room. Even this, however, could be seen as progress: his ancestors would likely have insisted on payment in Maria Theresa dollars, the silver coins displaying a rather décolleté Austrian empress of the eighteenth century that were a leading currency of nineteenth-century Arabia. But by the 1950s most rulers in the Persian Gulf were more sophisticated in their dealings with oil companies. The ruler of Kuwait in 1934 had already proved himself a tough negotiator, having done his homework on the terms of concessions in neighboring countries. More broadly, two structural changes overtook the industry. First, the share of the profits accruing to the states in which the oil was located grew much larger. A fifty-fifty arrangement, pioneered in Venezuela, was standard by 1952. The end point of this redistribution of the profits of the industry was nationalization, which excluded the Western oil companies from production altogether. This, too, began in the Americas, with Mexico in 1938. It could be friendly, as in Saudi Arabia in 1980, or unfriendly, as in Kuwait in 1975, or downright hostile, as in Iran in 1951 and Iraq in 1972. The second structural change was the increasing presence in the industry of modern-educated citizens of the producing countries. By the early 1980s Western expatriates were limited to a few of the highest positions, and large numbers of indigenous professionals had been trained abroad.

It is worth pausing at this point to ask how the current prominence of the Gulf region relates to its past. As we saw, the Middle East as a whole is marked by a steep aridity gradient: in rough and ready terms, it is wettest in the northwest and driest in the southeast. The result is that the two naturally occurring liquids that matter most in its modern history, freshwater and crude oil, are in complementary distribution: the northwest has the lion's share of the water supply, whereas the southeast has the lion's share of the oil supply. This matters because an abundant supply of freshwater is historically associated with agriculture, dense populations, cities, and states, whereas its scarcity correlates with nomadism, thin populations, the nonexistence of cities, and the absence or weakness of states. In the distant past a major qualification to this picture was the agricultural wealth of Iraq, made possible by the supply of freshwater delivered to it through its rivers. This had once provided the fiscal foundation for recurrent state formation on an imperial scale. But as we have seen, the degradation of this resource from the later ninth century onward created a situation in which a large and stable empire was no longer viable in the eastern Middle East. This, in turn, has had a major geopolitical consequence for the world we live in. Had there been a state on the footprint of the Sasanian Empire in modern times, it would have held sway over the entire Gulf region and would have been in a position to assert ownership of all its oilfields. As it is, the region is politically fragmented, with the oilfields divided between three middle-sized states and five smaller ones; of these smaller states the United Arab Emirates is itself a federation of seven chieftaincies brought together in 1971–72. All the small states owe their survival in the first instance to British maritime hegemony in the Gulf in the nineteenth century and after. The prime concern of the British was freedom of navigation at sea, which meant ending the piratical activity of the coastal Arabs, but once that objective was secured, they had little interest in the internal affairs of the tribes. The effect was to freeze in place an archaic political geography that looks bizarre in the modern world. Since the 1970s the British role has been inherited by the United States. Today the typical Gulf state is made up of a royal family, a citizen body, and an imported labor force. By normal standards the royal family and the imported labor force tend to be on the large side, and the citizen body on the small side. The oil revenues disbursed by the state mean that its citizens—historically the wellhead tribal population—benefit from rates of gross domestic product per capita that are among the highest in the world. This, in turn, is a powerful incentive to the beneficiaries not to make political trouble. There is only one other state of this kind in the world: the sultanate of Brunei. Located on the northwestern coast of Borneo, it likewise owes its survival to a former British presence in the region and its affluence to its combination of oil revenue and the small size of its citizen population.

Figures for gross domestic product per capita have something to tell us about the Muslim world at large. Today there are the best part of two hundred countries spread over the globe. If we take the top thirty-three of them, we can divide them into three groups: twenty Western countries, six East Asian countries, and seven Muslim countries. The Western and East Asian ones are normal First World countries, but the Muslim ones are not. All but Brunei are located in the Persian Gulf region, all but Saudi Arabia are small, and all with the partial exception of Bahrain depend heavily on oil production. Unlike the citizens of the Western and East Asian countries, those of the seven Muslim ones do not come by their wealth through economically productive labor. Instead, they live on largesse that the state is able to distribute thanks to its oil revenues. The wealth of the seven is thus based on the serendipitous presence of a natural resource that is in global demand, not on what Macaulay called diligence and self-denial. But the most significant point here is that no other Muslim country ranks in the top thirty-three. The highest-ranking Muslim country without significant oil production is Turkey, which comes in fifty-fourth, and twice as many Muslim countries are below the world average as above it. These rankings are subject to change and give a false air of precision, but they make a basic point: even today there is no Muslim country that can claim First World economic status in the manner of the Western and East Asian groups.

Society

Moving from economic to social changes, we enter a field in which it is harder to identify large-scale generalizations that are also have the merit of being true. Here we will make do with two major developments that have undeniably contributed to reshaping society across the Muslim world in quite intimate ways.

The first is that slavery has more or less disappeared. Slavery is a historically widespread institution that Muslim societies, like most others, took for granted until modern times. As we have seen, a basic step taken by Islamic law was to ban the enslavement of free Muslims and protected non-Muslims, thereby encouraging the importation of slaves from beyond the frontiers of the Muslim world. Once imported, some might be used in ways that compare with American plantation slavery, such as the four thousand slaves who cultivated Muʿāwiya's estates in Yamāma or the slave labor force of the East African coastal plantations of the nineteenth century. Others, as we have seen repeatedly, were employed as military slaves. But the great majority were absorbed into Muslim households as servants and concubines, and this was undoubtedly the most pervasive and continuous form of slavery in the Muslim world. Creating concentrations of slaves in large-scale economic enterprises and armies carried with it a serious risk of rebellion, particularly if the slaves shared an ethnic identity, as in the case of the Zanj rebels in the marshes of ninth-century Iraq. But dispersed domestic slaves were in no position to rebel and in any case less likely to want to, so the history of slavery in the Muslim world is to a large extent a quiet one. This is not to say that relations between slaves and their owners were reliably harmonious. From time to time there were cases of people being killed by their own slaves. Less drastic disharmony figures in a scene that played out in an Arab tribal setting in what is now southern Jordan in 1910. A tribe was about to move, so one of its leading chiefs needed his tent taken down. But his slaves did nothing. He shouted abuse at them, but no one listened, and in the end the chief was reduced to pulling out the poles and rolling up his tent for himself.

By this time slavery was on its way out in the Muslim world, thanks in the first instance to European pressure and influence. As might be expected, the pressure met with strong reactions from conservative Muslims. In 1842 the ruler of Morocco told the British consul general in no uncertain terms that the legality of enslavement and the slave trade was confirmed by the Qurʾān and the practice of the Prophet and that there was unanimity among the religious scholars regarding the issue. In 1855 the efforts of the Ottoman authorities to end the slave trade provoked a rebellion in Mecca; it was initiated by a fatwa denouncing the Turks as apostates who could lawfully be killed and whose children could be enslaved. In the Philippines the sultan of Maguindanao was asked to give up his slaves in 1861 and replied that "he would rather give up his wife and children than his slaves, for lacking the latter he simply would cease to be a sultan."[20] But alongside European pressure there was also European influence. This led many Muslims to internalize the rejection of slavery, whether by adopting the relevant European values or by seeking an alternative rationale for abolitionism in the Islamic heritage. It was a telling moment when in 1864, in an exchange of letters with the American consul general in Tunis, a Tunisian official recommended the abolition of slavery to his American correspondent. Here Tunisia was some two decades ahead of the United States. The Tunisian reforms of the 1840s had been the work of Aḥmad Bey (ruled 1837–55), who undertook them under European influence, but not under strong European pressure. Altogether the pattern across the Muslim world was a prolonged and unsteady process that issued in the ending of the large-scale traffic in slaves and eventually more or less eliminated slavery itself. By 1981 slavery had been abolished as a legal institution in every Muslim state, though not always as a social fact. In this way a practice that had contributed in a fundamental way to the texture of Muslim society over the centuries effectively disappeared. The short-lived revival of

20. Quoted in W. G. Clarence-Smith, *Islam and the abolition of slavery*, London 2006, 122.

slavery by ISIS in the teens of the twenty-first century did not herald any wider reversion to it in the Muslim world at large.

The second change we will take up here is the coming of mass literacy. Adult literacy is by no means universal in the world today, but for the most part it is now the rule rather than the exception. Only thirteen countries currently have literacy rates below 50 percent. Of these thirteen, one is Afghanistan, a Muslim country with a very troubled history in recent decades. The other twelve cluster in Saharan or sub-Saharan Africa. Six of them are Muslim-majority countries, and six are not. Clearly we are looking at a predominantly regional phenomenon. The state with the lowest literacy rate in the world is Niger, the Muslim country we picked out earlier for its low level of urbanization; only 19 percent of its adult population is literate. By contrast, the Muslim countries that were formerly part of the Soviet Union have near-universal literacy, reflecting a benign aspect of the Soviet legacy not matched by British, French, or Dutch imperial rule. Several other Muslim countries now have literacy rates over 90 percent, including Turkey, Saudi Arabia, and Indonesia. No Middle Eastern country falls below 70 percent, and even the Muslim countries of South Asia have rates around 60 percent. How then might the picture have looked around 1800? In the absence of census data it is, of course, impossible to be sure, but one estimate of the world literacy rate in 1820 is 12 percent, well below the current rate even for Niger. Early census data for the Muslim world would suggest that the rates may in fact have been considerably lower there. The Egyptian census of 1907 showed a literacy rate of 7 percent, and the Indian census of 1911 revealed a literacy rate among Muslim males that was also 7 percent (the Hindu rate was 13 percent). The Indonesian census of 1930 likewise put literacy at 7 percent. It is unlikely that these rates had fallen since 1800; the Ottoman literacy rate at that time has been estimated at 1 percent. Another indication of the magnitude of the change that has taken place in the Muslim world is the discrepancy in recent literacy rates between the young and the old. The young typically have rates in the eighties and nineties (71 percent in Pakistan), whereas the old tend to have rates in the thirties, twenties, and even teens (25 percent in Pakistan). This transformation reflects a major—and on the whole surprisingly successful—attempt by states and societies to school their children. Significantly, the children affected have typically included girls as well as boys.

A related change that took place on a more limited scale but was nevertheless of great significance was the formation of modern-educated elites. In premodern times a robust and rather homogeneous institutional framework for religious education extended across the Muslim world, but there was no comparable system for secular education—that is to say, for the production of a literate elite outside the ranks of the religious scholars. Such an elite did, of course, exist, and it acquired its cultural skills in a variety of ways. Students destined for it might participate in the religious system, which could include some coverage of secular topics in its curriculum; or they might be educated at the court of a ruler, something we encounter in the Ottoman case in the sixteenth and seventeenth centuries; or they might learn much of what was required of them either within their families or as apprentices on the job. The first option—the education of future bureaucrats in religious colleges—was behind the overlap of religious scholars and bureaucrats that we saw in later medieval Egypt. That this overlap could have been culturally rather stifling is by no means an idle thought. But since 1800 there has been a sea change not just in the size of the nonreligious elite but also in what its members need to know and how they get to know it. A large part of the content of their education is now of Western origin, and the entire institutional framework within which they receive it is an import from the West. As we have seen, this change had its beginnings in the Ottoman Empire and the Crimean Khānate in the later eighteenth century. But these early attempts were fits and starts, and more sustained efforts began only in the early nineteenth century. It was in 1826 that Meḥmed ʿAlī Pasha sent a group of forty-four young men from Egypt to study in Paris. The Ottoman central government followed suit, sending students to Europe the next year. At the same time, both governments set up technical schools at home, at first with European instructors. Universities on the European model came later. If we leave aside those established in the Muslim world by Western agency, the earliest modern university in the Middle East was a product of Ottoman Westernizing reform. There had been an Ottoman plan to create a university as early as the 1840s, but after an abortive effort in 1870, what became the University of Istanbul was founded only in 1900. This time it was Egypt that followed the Ottoman example. Remarkably, the Egyptian initiative that led to the creation of a university in Cairo in 1908 came from what would now be called civil society, not from the state—a testimony to the prominence already achieved by the country's modern-educated elite. But many Muslim countries established their first universities only around the 1950s. Today their numbers in the Muslim world are legion, and at the same time numerous students from Muslim countries still study at universities in the West. The problem now is not a shortage of universities in the Muslim world, but rather the fact that they produce too many graduates for the jobs available. A further downside of the system from the point of view of the state, already manifest in the nineteenth century, is that a Western-style education can give people access to subversive Western ideas. In Muslim lands under Western imperial rule this danger was compounded by the fact that such an elite could plausibly seek to take over the jobs of Western officials in the name of nationalism.

The state

The last topic we need to take up before closing this section is the state. There are currently some fifty Muslim-majority states in the world. Very likely the number was higher in 1800, though this would depend heavily on what we choose to count as a state. Yet despite such consolidation, the Muslim world in our time is politically fragmented. Not least, it lacks any single state large enough to dominate it. Giant states such as Russia, India, China, the United States, or Brazil are a major geopolitical reality today, but they have no counterpart in the Muslim world. This absence is, of course, a modern development. In 1700 there were two such states, the empires of the Ottomans and the Mughals. By 1800 the Mughals no longer ruled an empire, but the Ottomans still did. From the late eighteenth century onward, however, the Ottoman Empire was hemorrhaging territory, and with the abolition of the Ottoman Caliphate in 1924 its last institutional residue was ended by the government of the Turkish Republic, causing a reaction across the Muslim world that was not unlike the response to the fall of the ʿAbbāsid caliphate in 1258. The states that since then have developed aspirations to lead the Muslim world have not been well placed to do so. The Islamic Republic of Iran has been hamstrung by its Shīʿism in a Muslim world that is overwhelmingly Sunnī, while Saudi Arabia, despite its wealth, is a weak state that long depended for its survival on its American alliance and may well continue to do so. Interstate organizations, such as the Organization of the Islamic Conference, formed in 1972, are no substitute.

If the Muslim world today lacks a giant state, it has many middle-sized countries and a scatter of small ones. Over the course of the nineteenth and still more the twentieth century, the overall tendency was for the state apparatus in these countries to wax larger and stronger relative to the society it ruled. In terms of sheer size, the number of state functionaries increased by an order of magnitude. In terms of strength, the most obvious enhancement of state power has been the creation of public order, ending or at least reining in the predatory activities of nomads, bandits, rebels, and local strongmen. This went hand in hand with the formation of an increasingly centralized administration that penetrated deeper into society and farther out into the provinces. Whether the work of imperial rulers or indigenous states, the process was highly intrusive and often violent. It could be particularly unpleasant for ethnic or religious minorities, as also for tribal populations, which were now vulnerable to bombardment from the air. But it did have one assured benefit: as always, the single most effective thing a state can do to promote economic growth is to provide security. Of course, the timing and extent of these developments varied from country to country. Here a dramatic contrast is provided by the constitutional revolutions that took place in both the Ottoman Empire and Iran in the first decade of the twentieth century. In each case the revolution was followed by a counterrevolution, and in each case the counterrevolution in turn was reversed by an armed intervention in 1909. But there the similarity ends. In the Ottoman case it was a modern army from Salonica, the empire's most advanced city, that marched on Istanbul, whereas in the Iranian case it was a force of Bakhtiyārī tribesmen that rode on Tehran from the hills of southwestern Iran. Indeed, the tribes still counted for something in Iranian politics as late as the Second World War, and they remain significant players in such countries as Iraq and Yemen to this day. Another example of uneven development stems from farther west. From 1958 to 1961 Egypt and Syria merged to form the United Arab Republic. When looking back on this unsatisfactory experience in 1963, President Nasser of Egypt disparaged the administrative machinery of the Syrian government as scarcely worthy of a grocer's shop. A comparison of the execution of the Egyptian and Syrian land reforms shows that Nasser had a point.

By that time the Egyptian state was going well beyond providing its subjects with the security they needed to go about their economic activities. The land reform of 1952, to be extended in 1969, had been implemented in such a way as to bring about a major expansion of the role of the state in the economy of the countryside. Meanwhile, nationalization did the same for much of the urban economy, creating a large state sector. These twin processes, land reform and nationalization, were imitated or paralleled in other Middle Eastern countries. Extensive nationalizations also took place farther afield, as in Algeria in the 1960s, Pakistan in the 1970s, and Bangladesh in 1972. Nationalization, in particular, tended not to have optimal economic outcomes, but irrespective of their economic effects, such measures worked to the benefit of the state. Especially in the Middle East, they increased its power by sidelining the old social elite of landlords and businessmen and bringing in a new state middle class of bureaucrats and army officers. In many such countries the state now dominates both the society and the economy. There are indeed Muslim countries where the private sector is prominent, as in Turkey and Indonesia. In the Turkish case the massacre of the Armenians in the course of the First World War and the deportation of the Greeks in its aftermath, in combination with the influence of the Soviet model, led to the formation of a large and inefficient state sector in the interwar period. The decades following the Second World War then saw the energetic liberalization of the Turkish economy and the rapid growth of the private sector, though the state sector showed itself to be remarkably persistent. In the Indonesian case, too, the starting point was the domination of the urban economy by minorities, especially the immigrant Chinese. But despite their exposure to considerable and sometimes violent native hostility, Chinese entrepreneurs continued to control a significant part of the economy. In neither Turkey nor Indonesia has a more favorable attitude to the private sector served as a guarantee of political openness, and in general authoritarian rule has proved remarkably resilient in the Muslim world. In short, the rising power of the state could free society from local tyranny, but often at the cost of subjecting it to centralized tyranny.

Alongside a bureaucracy, a state apparatus almost invariably maintains an army. Armies played their part in taming the domestic enemies of the state, but they were also intended to deter its foreign enemies. Not surprisingly, it was in response to the military challenge of European warfare that the first steps toward Westernization were taken in Muslim societies. There were several attempts in the Muslim world of the late eighteenth century to create armies on the European model, though none of them lasted; we saw examples of such efforts in the Crimea, the Ottoman Empire, Bihar, and Mysore. The new army created by Meḥmed ʿAlī Pasha in early nineteenth-century Egypt lasted considerably longer, and for a while it made him the most powerful ruler in the Middle East. But when the British occupied Egypt in 1882 they defeated and later disbanded it. Meanwhile, the Ottomans had spent much of the early nineteenth century without an effective military force. It was only after massacring the Janissaries in 1826 that the state was once again free to pursue the project of forming a modern army. Even then it took time. But Ottoman troops were to perform unexpectedly well in the First World War, and as we have seen an Ottoman army that survived the war undefeated was to play a key role in the creation of the modern country of Turkey. Iran, of course, lagged far behind the Ottoman Empire. A British observer who spent time there in 1889–90 commented that "a more irregular army, in the most literal sense of the word, does not exist on the face of the globe."[21] In fact, the only effective military formation in Iran was the Persian Cossack Brigade, a small force established in 1879 and made up of Iranian troops commanded by Russian officers. After the Russian officers left in 1920, a Persian Cossack force of three thousand or less was enough to enable its new commander, Riḍā Khān, to take power in a coup d'état of 1921. In 1925 he went on to depose the last Qājār ruler and make himself Shāh. His Cossacks became the core of his new army. But this army, though effective internally against provincial and tribal resistance to the central government, mounted no serious resistance to the renewed occupation of Iran by the British and Russians in the Second World War. It was not till the Iraqi invasion of 1980 that an Iranian army mounted a successful, if very costly, defense against a foreign enemy.

What we have seen in Egypt, the Ottoman Empire, and Iran are cases of Muslim states that were still independent and were responding—precociously or belatedly—to the threat posed by the new European style of warfare. Matters were different in cases where Muslim countries became independent only after a period of European rule. At that point there were typically two possible sources for the formation of a national army. One was the legacy of the imperial rulers, who had often recruited indigenous troops to keep order in the territories they administered. The other was rebel forces that had been mobilized by independence movements engaged in violent struggles to end imperial rule. The Persian Cossack Brigade was in effect a variant of the first source. A more straightforward case of it was Syria, where the French had enlisted a force of a few thousand Troupes spéciales du Levant, and this became the Syrian army when

21. G. N. Curzon, *Persia and the Persian question*, London 1892, 1:609.

the country became independent in 1946. These men had been recruited disproportionately from ethnic and religious minority populations—as opposed to the Sunnī Arab majority—and especially from the ʿAlawīs, a mountain population on the far fringes of Shīʿism. The role of the army in the subsequent history of Syria meant that this sectarian imbalance has had a profound impact on the politics of the country, leading to the empowerment of the ʿAlawī minority over the Sunnī majority. Likewise when British India was partitioned in 1947, Pakistan inherited just over a third of the British Indian Army, initially retaining the services of almost five hundred British officers. This, too, had a long-term effect on the politics of the country: the British had recruited Punjabis in disproportionate numbers, and this initially helped cement the domination of the new country by the Punjab. If Syria and Pakistan were at one end of the spectrum, Algeria was at the other. Unlike Syria, Algeria under French rule was home to a million European settlers and had formally been part of metropolitan France since 1848. It thus took a prolonged insurrection beginning in 1954 to bring about Algerian independence in 1962. The rebels—including many who had been based outside the country and so were not directly involved in the fighting—now became the Algerian army, while large numbers of Harkis—roughly, Algerian counterparts of the Syrian Troupes spéciales recruited by the French during the insurrection—were killed or fled to France. Indonesia was a curious hybrid. There were the indigenous forces recruited by the Dutch rulers of the country, and there were more irregular forces recruited by the Japanese while they occupied it during the Second World War. When Indonesia became independent in the later 1940s, the Indonesian army took the form of an uneasy merger of the two. There were also countries that became independent with neither locally recruited imperial forces nor rebel movements to draw on; such was the case with the republics of Soviet Central Asia in 1991. Irrespective of their origins, many of the armies that took shape in the modern Muslim world sooner or later manifested a tendency to take power from civilian governments. They have also tended to be expensive: if we take the ten countries in which military spending eats up the largest proportion of gross national product, Muslims are the majority of the population in no fewer than eight of them.

The development of modern communications was by and large a force making for stronger states. When the Ottoman government moved with alacrity to adopt the telegraph, it may not have been thinking of the potential benefits of this technology for its subjects. As a rather sour British observer put it in 1900, the Turks were "great patrons of the telegraph, because it is the most powerful instrument for a despot who wishes to control his own officials." Rather than leaving a governor to administer his province as he pleased, it was now possible to "order him about, find out what he is doing, reprimand him, recall him, instruct his subordinates to report against him, and generally deprive him of all real power."[22] Of course, rulers had been doing this kind of thing to the best of their abilities long before they acquired the use of the telegraph, but it was now much easier for them. And it was not just Ottoman provincial governors who lost out. The French ambassador in Istanbul at the time of the Crimean War cursed the invention of the telegraph because it limited his freedom of action and ability to make policy on the spot. Indeed, everywhere the advent of the telegraph marked a major change in the relationship between governments and their local agents. But it could also enable members of the elite outside the state apparatus to communicate with each other, and the telephone later did much to enhance that effect. By contrast, both radio and television tended to be very much organs of the state. The internet initially redressed the balance, greatly expanding the agency of subjects; social media figured conspicuously in the popular risings against authoritarian governments that constituted the Arab Spring of 2011. Just how threatening social media can be for a state is shown by the costs currently shouldered by the Chinese government in order to isolate and censor the country's internet.

But states do not always become stronger. The strengthening of states was indeed the major trend of the nineteenth and twentieth centuries, but in recent decades a significant countertrend has also been in evidence, an increased tendency for at least some states to wither away. An interesting—if somewhat controversial—source that identifies and ranks states that are dangerously weak is the Fragile States Index, a somewhat euphemistic renaming of the former Failed States Index. If we take the states ranked highest for fragility in 2019, two points are readily apparent. The first and most salient is geographical. The great majority of fragile states are located in Saharan or sub-Saharan Africa; this is the case for seven of the top ten, and for twenty-one of the top thirty. The second point is that a disproportionate number of fragile states are Muslim: six of the top ten and thirteen of the top thirty. Many of these Muslim states are also African, but a significant number are not: Yemen, Syria, and Afghanistan are in the top ten, joined by Iraq, Pakistan, and Libya in the top thirty. By contrast, if we search for states that are neither Muslim nor African, we find none in the top ten, and only three in the top thirty. This general picture is reinforced if we go instead to the other end of the list. Here, if we take the sixty least fragile states, only one of them is African. Seven are Muslim, but of these seven, five are small oil monarchies, and the remaining two are Albania and Malaysia. Only one of the seven, the United Arab Emirates, makes it into the thirty least fragile states, and only just.

What explains this pattern? Fragile states are, of course, unlikely to be a homogeneous category, and what places non-Muslim African states among the most

22. Quoted in B. Lewis, *The emergence of modern Turkey*, London 1961, 183.

fragile thirty could be significantly different from what places non-African Muslim states there. So let us take this latter group—Yemen, Syria, Afghanistan, Iraq, Pakistan, and Libya—and consider what they have in common. It is not the varied circumstances that initiated their descent into some kind of chaos. The surge of enthusiasm for democratization during the Arab Spring of 2011 triggered the process in Yemen, Syria, and Libya, but in the other three cases the weakening of the state was already under way well before that date. Nor is foreign intervention likely to be the key precipitating factor, though it is conspicuous in all but Pakistan; fragile states invite intervention. Perhaps more significant is something all six have in common. Earlier or later, a central role has been played in their troubles by militant Islamist groups of one sort or another, whether attacking regimes or defending them. By contrast, this feature does not recur with the same reliability in the case of the Muslim African states, where (with the exception of Somalia) fragility tended until recently to have more to do with ethnic than religious animosities, much as in the non-Muslim African countries to the south. In the last few years, however, there has been a significant convergence between the two groups of fragile Muslim states, with jihadism becoming more salient in several countries of the Muslim African group. The convergence is nevertheless as yet incomplete: as of 2023, jihadis are still absent from the politics of Guinea. In causal terms, the key point is that whereas all fragile states invite foreign intervention, only ones with significant Muslim populations invite jihadism.

This brings us to ideology, or more broadly to professed political values. In the Muslim world, as elsewhere, these come in a variety of brands, but the option most widely adopted in modern times has been nationalism. In one way nationalism is an import from the West. The idea of a world made up of nations—each equipped with an ethnic identity, a historical past, and a sovereign state—is a product of western European history, though one that has particularly strong resonance in the case of premodern East Asia. But in another way nationalism tends to have strong indigenous roots. Ethnic identities, animosities, and memories were widespread in the premodern Muslim lands, as in most of the world; Iran, as we have seen, had existed in the mind of its people since antiquity. What changed with the advent of nationalism was that old ethnic ties now provided a basis for new claims to territory and statehood—claims that in the past might have been articulated primarily in dynastic or religious terms, if at all. For example, in premodern times there was no idea of a state uniting all Kurds, but by 1919 a popular poem circulating among them lamented that if only they had a king, they would share in his good fortune, and "Turk and Persian and Arab would all be our slaves."[23] A much more successful example is the reflagging of what was left of the Ottoman Empire

23. Quoted in G. R. Driver, *Kurdistan and the Kurds*, Mount Carmel 1919, 96.

as Turkey in the aftermath of the First World War. Europeans had been speaking of Turkey ever since the Middle Ages, but the term was not current in Ottoman circles till the last decades of the empire's existence, and it became the official name of a country in the form "Türkiye" only in the early 1920s. The redefinition of the political community as the Turkish nation had the advantage of tying it to a real ethnic identity, but a political idiom that excluded the Kurds and sidelined religion would lead to major problems down the line. Other nationalisms in the Muslim world have tended to give rise to analogous problems, if not in so acute a form. But the chief limitation of nationalism as a political value is that it is better at inspiring people with a sense of who they are than it is at telling them what they should do to solve their problems.

When it comes to deciding what to do in the face of an unrelenting blizzard of troubles, states—and politicians in general—spend much of their time muddling through in an opportunistic and eclectic manner. But they may not be content with this. Instead they may commit to some grand unified theory of politics and aspire to implement it, particularly if they seek to change the world in a radical fashion. In the twentieth century a prominent ideology of this kind was Marxism—a doctrine of central European origin, but a dissident one that could be invoked not just against incumbent elites in the Muslim world but also against the West. Thus Marxist parties played a major role in Iran in 1941–53, in Iraq in 1941–63, and in Indonesia in 1950–65. But it was rare for Marxists to come to power in the Muslim world outside the lands forming part of the Soviet Union and the People's Republic of China, whose communist parties were of course dominated by non-Muslims. One of the rare cases where Marxists held power elsewhere in the Muslim World was Albania from 1944 to 1992, reflecting geopolitical realities on the periphery of eastern Europe at the end of the Second World War. Another case was South Yemen while that country lasted between 1967 and 1990; from 1970 this corner of Arabia called itself the People's Democratic Republic of Yemen. Neither country became a model for others to emulate. This limited harvest is at least in part a reflection of a widespread Muslim allergy to the antireligious stance of Marxism. When in 1965 a Syrian Communist gave a speech in Sudan in which he declared belief in God and the Prophet to be an anachronistic superstition, his irreligion was invoked to justify the banning of the Sudanese Communist Party. But in the more diluted form of socialism, leftism had a much wider currency in the Muslim world in this period. Around the 1960s, for example, socialism was formally adopted by the Egyptian regime, by the Ba'th Party in Syria and Iraq, and by the newly independent Algerian regime. It even had a moment of a sort in Pakistan. The Ba'th Party, for example, was at core an Arab nationalist movement, but in 1963 it was talking about democratic centralism, the socialist revolution, the revolutionary intelligentsia, collective farms, and revolutionary vanguards (all of them good things), together with the petty bourgeoisie (an ally for now), the bourgeois middle class, and state capitalism (both bad things). Such socialism did not have to share the antireligious stance of hard-line Marxism, particularly when imbued with a local ethnic coloring. Thus commitment to "Arab socialism" could be paired with commitment to Islam, or the two could be compounded in "Arabo-Islamic socialism." As an Egyptian journalist put it in 1962, "Our socialism believes in God."[24] But it was not so clear that God believed in Arab socialism.

The 1960s may have been the heyday of communism and socialism in the Muslim world, but this same period saw the rise of a new ideology that would largely reduce leftism to a back number. It goes by various names, but we can conveniently call it Islamism. An Islamist is someone who responds to the distemper of the times by constructing a political ideology out of Islam, to the exclusion of other ideologies. As might be expected, Islamism is not a homogeneous movement. Most obviously it comes in two very different—and mutually antagonistic—sectarian flavors, Sunnī and Shīʿite. One significant difference is that the Shīʿite version has a certain continuity with leftism that the Sunnī version largely lacks.

Leaving the differences aside, we can conveniently see the whole phenomenon in terms of a pyramid. At its base lies the Islamic revival, a marked increase in piety and observance that has affected very large numbers of Muslims in the last few decades. This revival is not in itself Islamism, but it has done much to make Muslims receptive to it. In the middle of the pyramid we have Islamic politics, embracing a significantly smaller but still large subset of Muslims and itself a complex phenomenon. One component of it is the politics of Muslim identity, conspicuous in the movement that led to the formation of Pakistan in 1947 as a state for Indian Muslims. Another is the politics of Muslim values, exemplified in the policing of female attire that was practiced until recently in the cities of Saudi Arabia and Iran. A third is the politics of the Islamic state, where the point is to create a polity that is intrinsically Islamic, and not merely one run by Muslims or used to impose Islamic values. Finally, at the apex of the pyramid, we have a much smaller number of Muslims who engage in violence not just as part of the general human propensity for mayhem but in fulfillment of the Islamic duty of jihad against unbelievers. Each element in this complex has at least one modern parallel outside the Muslim world, but the complex as a whole does not, and in that sense Islamism is unique in the world today.

Although Islamism has resonated throughout the Muslim world, its political success has been limited. Its pan-Islamic appeal has by no means overcome the stubborn ethnic divisions within the Muslim community. For example, diversity has proved problematic for al-Qāʿida just as it has for American corporations. One operative described ungrammatically to his interrogators how he and others had

24. A. Abdel-Malek, *Égypte, société militaire*, Paris 1962, 281.

complained to the leadership that "we have people from Nigeria, from Tunisia, from Siberia, why is Egyptian people got more chance than other people run everything?"[25] Moreover, Islamism, though it has been widespread in the Muslim world, has not come to power in much of it, having powerful enemies both domestic and foreign. The largest and most lasting Islamist state to date is the Islamic Republic of Iran, where it is of course the Shīʿite version of Islamism that prevails. The Sunnī form has been less successful. The Ṭālibān ruled Afghanistan from 1996 to 2001 and returned to power in 2021. In Egypt an Islamist government came to power in 2012 through an election rather than an insurrection but was overthrown the next year by a military coup. Starting in 2014, ISIS ruled a territory comprising large parts of eastern Syria and western Iraq, but it sustained this for only three or four years. During those years it showed itself lethal to the point of being genocidal. But in this respect the larger fact is that Islamists, however violent some of them have been, have as yet killed far fewer people than have the proponents of secular ideologies such as Nazism and communism.

Even in the case of these Islamist polities, states in the modern Muslim world have been extensively modeled or remodeled along Western lines. As a Tunisian statesman wrote in 1868 in a liberal vein, "The countries that have progressed to the highest ranks of civilization are those that have established the roots of liberty and the constitution";[26] what state would want to be anywhere but in the highest ranks? A striking index of the strength of this Western influence is the changing balance of republics over monarchies in the Muslim world. In 1800 virtually all Muslim states were monarchies, and virtually all Muslim political thinking was monarchical, though by no means absolutist. In the meantime a shift had begun in the West, where an ancient republican tradition had been revived in the late eighteenth century with the formation of the first modern republics, those of the United States and France. By the middle of the twentieth century this change of constitutional fashion had reached the point at which monarchies had become a discontinued line: if a new state was created or an old one succumbed to revolution, the result would now be a republic. The Muslim world has participated fully in this trend. Today the only Muslim states ruled by monarchs are Morocco, Jordan, the cluster around the Persian Gulf, and Brunei. The preservation of this archaic form of polity was largely the work of the British and, in the case of Morocco, the French. The rest of the states of the Muslim world—some forty of them—are republics. At least one of them, Iran, is in a serious sense an Islamic republic, but it, too, has a Western-style constitution. Adopted in 1979, the document was drafted by French-educated lawyers and drew extensively on the French constitution of 1958. Overall, the adoption of Western political forms in

25. F. A. Gerges, *The far enemy*, Cambridge 2005, 104.
26. Khayr al-Din al-Tunisi, *The surest path*, Cambridge, MA 1967, 164.

the Muslim world has been far-reaching. But despite the liberal sentiments of the Tunisian statesman, it has not in general been accompanied by the more benign features of Western states. Many Muslim states have succumbed to longer or shorter periods of military rule, and few rank as electoral democracies. In 2010, by one count, there were only eight electoral democracies among forty-six Muslim-majority states, and it was telling that not one of the eight was in the Arab world. The Arab Spring of 2011 led to the emergence of just one electoral democracy, Tunisia, and it lasted only a decade.

Despite the fact that the various regions of the Muslim world differ greatly among themselves, the changes we have surveyed in this section have for the most part affected all of it. But with the exception of the rise of Islamism, these transformations are by no means unique to the Muslim world, most of them having numerous parallels outside it. By the same token, Islam has so far played only a limited role in this survey. It has nevertheless been there in the wings, and it is now time to bring it center stage.

Imitating non-Muslims

Ethelbert's dilemma

Imitating others can be fun, as when Westerners experiment with chopsticks in a Chinese restaurant. In a Persian painting of around 1500 everyone looks a bit Chinese, whereas in one dating from a couple of centuries later everyone looks a bit Italian. Though such a change of fashion did not mark a profound spiritual transformation, novelties of this kind could help keep the Persian elite from getting bored. But imitating others is not always so lighthearted. Muslim societies over the last two centuries, like many societies at different times and places in history, have faced a daunting challenge. If you find yourself doing badly in competition with other people, one very real possibility is that they, unlike you, are doing something right. In that case your best bet may be to imitate them, even if they are people you have always looked down on. Here, too, Ovid's dictum was in place: "It is proper to learn even from an enemy." Faced with rising Western power, the Japanese did just that in the later nineteenth century, whereas the Koreans did not, and early in the next century found themselves being colonized by the Japanese. Something rather similar nearly happened in the Middle East. As we have seen, in the early decades of the nineteenth century the most modern army in the region was that of Meḥmed ʿAlī Pasha. In the age of the infantry the old ceiling on the size of an Egyptian army no longer applied, cotton provided the pasha with plentiful funds, and European instructors were readily available. The pasha responded to the opportunity by doing something very European—namely, conscripting the peasants of his country in large numbers. This Egyptian army fought for him in Arabia, the Sudan, Greece, Syria, and Anatolia. Meanwhile, the Ottoman Empire, despite the challenges it faced, was lagging behind in military reform, and twice in the 1830s the pasha looked set to take it over. It was only the intervention of the European powers that saved it, a favor they did not extend to Korea. Under such conditions, Westernization was inevitably going to happen sooner or later. States will do almost anything to escape defeat, just as individuals will do almost anything to regain their health. The alleged Mamlūk view that firearms were to be rejected as an unmanly invention of the European Christians had never cut much ice. So in the face of the inevitability of Westernization, the chief religious authority of the Ottoman Empire in the 1850s is said to have told a high official: "Sir, don't ask our opinion on everything. If we are not asked, we do not interfere with what you are doing."[27] A more direct response was to argue from necessity. Ḍiyā' al-Dīn Baranī, whom we met as a courtier of the Delhi Sultanate writing in the 1350s, claimed that the only way a Muslim ruler could be effective in upholding the cause of Islam was to adopt the political style of the pre-Islamic kings of Iran, forsaking that of the Prophet and his immediate successors. He justified this stance by invoking the analogy of the starving man for whom the prohibition of eating carrion is waived. Necessity was just as relevant when the infidel European model replaced that of the infidel Persians. As an Ottoman statesman put it in 1912, "Either we Westernize, or we are destroyed."[28]

Although necessity can do a lot to justify the imitation of an alien model, it still sets up an unsettling dilemma. How far can you go in adopting the ways of others and still remain true to yourself—your culture, your ancestors, your gods, or indeed—if you are a monotheist—God? The dilemma is an old one. As we saw, King Ethelbert of Kent confronted it in 597, when he told the missionary Saint Augustine that he liked the sound of Christianity but could not accept it and "forsake those beliefs that I and the whole English race have held so long." The pagans described in the Qur'ān respond to the monotheistic message in similar terms: when the ancient Arabian prophet Hūd preaches to his people, they answer, "Why, hast thou come to tell us that we should serve God alone, and forsake that which our fathers served?" (Q7:70). Now it was the Muslims themselves who were under pressure to forsake that which their fathers had served. Nor had their Prophet made it easy for them, for he was credited with saying that "he who imitates a people is one of them."[29] Of course, like everything he said, this was subject to interpretation. A sixteenth-century scholar from Herat held that the saying applied only to

27. U. Heyd, "The Ottoman 'ulemā and Westernization," in U. Heyd (ed.), *Studies in Islamic history and civilization*, Jerusalem 1961, 89.

28. Quoted in Lewis, *The emergence of modern Turkey*, 231.

29. See, for example, Abū Dāwūd, *Sunan*, ed. M. M. 'Abd al-Ḥamīd, n.p. n.d., 4:44 no. 4031.

the markers of difference that distinguish a community from its rivals, whereas an Egyptian contemporary took the view that it covered a much broader range of everyday practices involving food, dress, domestic life, marriage, social activity, travel, and other things. In any event, the plain sense of Muḥammad's pronouncement lent itself to the purposes of religious conservatives opposed to the increasing adoption of modern European ways in the Muslim world.

Meanwhile, Europeans did not make things easier by censoriously exhorting Muslims to adopt Western ways. As a British observer of the Ottoman scene described it in 1900, the last half century had seen "the determination of Europe to impose its civilisation on uncivilised and half-civilised nations all over the world."[30] His point was that the Turks were not going to like it. There was, moreover, a further reason for them to dislike it: the prominence of non-Muslim minorities, especially Christians, at the economic interface between the Ottoman Empire and Europe. The same observer recounts a conversation he had with an Ottoman governor on a rainy afternoon in 1897. At one point the governor asked him, "Who profit by all these concessions for railways, harbours, and quays?" He went on to answer his own question: "Franks, Jews, Greeks and Armenians, but never a Muslim." As the observer tactfully abstained from pointing out, this ignored the handsome bribes that Muslim officials received from negotiating such concessions. But the governor's point about the role of the minorities was a pertinent one. Unlike such broadly Muslim minorities as the ʿAlevīs, the local Christians and, to an extent, Jews had easy access to Europeans, and their interactions with them were relatively free of cultural inhibition—though more so for the Catholics than for the Orthodox, for whom Russia was religiously closer than central or western Europe. Imitation thus came more easily to the Christians, and it enabled them to play a disproportionate role in the most modern—and profitable—sectors of the economy. The effect was compounded by the tendency of European powers to intervene on behalf of their coreligionists and demand reforms to improve their lot. This, in turn, made Westernizing reform an uncomfortably ambivalent project: Was the object to render the empire better able to stand up to the Europeans, or was it rather to appease them? In 1856, at a time at which it was particularly important for the empire to look good in European eyes, the sultan issued a decree that included the following provision: "Every distinction or designation tending to make any class whatever of the subjects of my empire inferior to another class, on account of their religion, language, or race, shall be forever effaced from administrative protocol."[31] A widespread Muslim reaction was to lament that "the Islamic community, which was the ruling community, has now been de-

30. For this and the quotations that follow see Odysseus, *Turkey in Europe*, London 1900, 3, 14 ("Odysseus" is Sir Charles Eliot).

31. J. C. Hurewitz, *The Middle East and North Africa in world politics*, New Haven 1975–79, 1:316b.

prived of this sacred right."[32] (Meanwhile the Christians, instead of being happy, expressed their resentment at being made equal with the Jews.) This minority problem was particularly salient in the Ottoman Empire. In North Africa, in the absence of an indigenous Christian population, the role of intermediary was played by the Jews, but not to the same extent; in Iran it was Armenians and Jews, but again to a lesser degree. Farther east the phenomenon was largely absent. Thus in maritime Southeast Asia minorities did indeed play a conspicuous role in the economy, but they were mainly Chinese, Indian, or Ḥaḍramī and as such culturally more distant from the Europeans.

As if all this was not enough, the challenge forced on Muslims a jarring change in their view of Europe and its culture. As of the eighteenth century, they had had little experience of looking up to a dominant but alien culture. There were exceptions, but they were rare and tend to strike us as engagingly exotic, as in the cases of the Chinese and Tamil Muslims. So let us take a look at some Muslim attitudes to Europeans down the centuries. We will mostly be concerned with modern times, but the Middle Ages are a good place to start.

Muslim attitudes to Christian Europe

Usāma ibn Munqidh (d. 1188) belonged to an Arab clan, the Banū Munqidh, who came to be based at Shayzar in northern Syria. He was a man of affairs in the turbulent politics of the twelfth century—a warrior, a politician, a diplomat, and an author who left us his memoirs. In this context he interacted with Frankish Crusaders in ways that were sometimes friendly, and his memoirs include an account of them. In general he had a low opinion of the Franks, describing them as "animals possessing the virtues of courage and fighting, but nothing else."[33] To illustrate their lack of sense, he recounts how one of them, a friend of his, proposed to take Usāma's fourteen-year-old son on a trip to the land of the Franks, where he would see the knights and learn wisdom and chivalry before returning to Syria. To Usāma this was an astoundingly bad idea; nothing could have been a worse misfortune for his son than being taken off to the land of the Franks. But how was he to extricate the boy from a fate worse than death without giving offense to his senseless but well-intentioned Frankish friend? Fortunately Usāma was not a diplomat for nothing, and he aptly fielded a cross-culturally valid excuse for declining the invitation. The boy's grandmother, he explained, was so fond of him that she had made Usāma promise to return him to her. Even a senseless Frank could understand the appeal to family values and the force of a promise.

32. Cevdet Paşa, *Tezâkir*, Ankara 1953–63, 1:68.
33. See P. K. Hitti, *An Arab-Syrian gentleman and warrior*, Princeton 1987, 161.

As might be expected, Usāma's views on Frankish culture were not in general favorable. He gives vivid examples of medical malpractice among the Franks and its fatal consequences, though also reporting cases where their treatments worked; one was a cure for scrofula that he himself adopted to good effect. His opinion of Frankish judicial procedures was entirely negative—he describes a judicial duel and an ordeal by water, procedures of a kind that were beginning to attract criticism even in Europe itself at the time. Nor did he have anything good to say about the absurd lack of sexual jealousy among the Franks. A husband, he tells us, may be walking along with his wife when another man meets them and takes her aside to talk to her, while the husband waits patiently for the conversation to end—the kind of behavior that had shocked Ibn Baṭṭūṭa among the Berbers of Walāta. The rest of what Usāma has to say on this score is considerably more graphic. Such observations led Usāma to formulate the grand paradox of Frankish culture: the Franks lacked sexual jealousy and yet had great courage! But not being a social scientist in the manner of Ibn Khaldūn, he did not attempt an explanation. The accessibility of European womenfolk is in fact a recurrent theme of Muslim commentary on Western Christians. The Ottoman prince Jem, who spent thirteen years in Europe in the late fifteenth century, was able to relieve the tedium of exile with occasional amorous encounters. In recording these our Turkish source gives us a succinct account of the girls of Nice: unveiled, proudly kissing and embracing, sitting on the knees of their lovers, and of course very décolleté. Ḥajarī, the Morisco whose views on the extent of the Muslim share of the world we examined earlier, likewise spent some time in France and met unveiled French girls. In one case there was clearly strong mutual attraction, but unlike the Ottoman prince, Ḥajarī was too pious to seize the opportunity. Muslim observers obviously took this accessibility as an indication that extramarital sex was much more prevalent in European society than in their own. They were probably right, though Lady Mary Wortley Montagu, whom we met as an acute English observer of a somewhat naughty disposition, was struck by the anonymity that elite Turkish women gained from veiling and commented that "the Turkish ladies don't commit one sin the less for not being Christian." They were, she opined, "the only free people in the empire."[34]

One thing Usāma said nothing about was any kind of literate culture among the Franks. He was no Bīrūnī. But with the passing of the centuries this silence slowly began to be breached. To throw in a few details of a long and complex history, Ibn Khaldūn had heard that in his time the philosophical sciences were thriving in the lands of the Franks. Skipping from the fourteenth century to the seventeenth, we have seen the exasperation of the Ottoman polymath Kātib Chelebī (d. 1657) at

34. Mary Wortley Montagu, *Letters*, New York 1992, 115–16.

the contrast between the ignorance and fecklessness of Muslim writers on geography and the attentiveness and skill of Christian practitioners of this science. Moving on to the end of the eighteenth century, the Egyptian historian Jabartī (d. 1825) was a witness to the French occupation of Egypt in 1798–1801. In some ways little had changed since the days of Usāma ibn Munqidh. The French were still outstanding fighters—single-minded, disciplined, and content with the bare necessities of life. On this score Jabartī compared them to the early Muslims and contrasted them with the irresolute, divided, and self-indulgent troops that the French confronted on the Ottoman side. Likewise relations between the sexes had not changed: the women had no modesty, and the men were promiscuous. But Jabartī highlighted two aspects of French life that make no appearance in Usāma's account. One was a literate culture that included the sciences and extended to a lively interest in Muslim culture. There was nothing new about the idea that some non-Muslim peoples were good at science; the surprise was that the French should have joined this exclusive club. By contrast, their interest in Muslim culture clearly struck Jabartī as odd. They had a large, illustrated book on the life of the Prophet and possessed copies of standard works of Muslim piety. Some of them even knew parts of the Qur'ān by heart. He was clearly impressed by their library, which he visited many times. He comments on its organization and the silence in which those consulting its books did their work—suggesting that Egyptian libraries of the day were disorganized and noisy. The other novelty he reported lay in the political values of the French. Their polity was nonmonarchical, and they believed in liberty and equality. Jabartī had no trouble understanding what equality meant, but he had a hard time making sense of the French conception of liberty. Overall, it is evident that he had a low opinion of the French in some respects and a high opinion in others. But whatever he may have been thinking, one thing he did not do was point to features of the French way of doing things that Muslims should adopt.

This was soon to change. As we saw, in 1826 Meḥmed 'Alī Pasha dispatched a group of forty-four young men—their average age was twenty-six—to study in Paris. This time a trip to France, far from being seen as a fate worse than death, was a privilege coveted for their sons by the leading families of the Turkish-speaking elite of Egypt. Among the few native Egyptians included in the mission was Rifā'a Rāfi' al-Ṭahṭāwī (d. 1873), a member of a family of religious scholars in Upper Egypt. Thanks to his teacher's recommendation, he was appointed to accompany the mission as one of its prayer leaders, and he was the one member of the mission to leave us a written account of his experiences. None of the group had any prior knowledge of French, and most of them seem to have been rather halting in acquiring it. In this they contrasted with a group of six black slaves, mostly from Kordofān, who were brought to France at ages of between nine and twelve in 1828; they acquired fluent French and made rapid progress in the study of geography and natural history. Yet despite a clumsy performance in his final oral examination, Ṭahṭāwī showed himself to be a talented translator, then and subsequently. His translations included works on such practical and relatively value-free sciences as mineralogy and geography, but they also extended to natural law, to what the French call political law (*droit politique*), and to the history of the manners and customs of the various nations. Back in Egypt he was appointed director of a school of translation in 1837.

Ṭahṭāwī was firmly rooted in two cultures, the Muslim culture he inherited in Egypt and the French culture he acquired during his stay in Paris. He was well aware that there could be tensions between them. Anyone wishing to delve into the French language, he wrote, needed to have a firm grounding in Islam to prevent his faith from being eroded. In the same vein he was careful not to endorse Copernican astronomy, reassuring his readers that the Europeans would eventually see the light and return to the Ptolemaic system. His commitment to his inherited culture is also shown by the fact that alongside his memoirs of Paris and his translations of French texts he also wrote a life of the Prophet. That might seem remote from his Parisian activities, but there was a link. In the course of his narrative he came to the Battle of the Khandaq in 627. As we saw, this battle took its name from the trench (*khandaq*) that Muḥammad dug with his companions to prevent the enemy cavalry from penetrating Medina. In the version that concerns us, the digging of the trench was proposed to Muḥammad by his Persian companion Salmān al-Fārisī, who told him: "Prophet, when we were in the land of Persia and in danger from cavalry, we used to dig a trench to protect ourselves."[35] Muḥammad immediately approved the idea. After telling the story, Ṭahṭāwī underlined the moral: "The fact that the Prophet ordered the digging of a trench around Medina on the advice of Salmān the Persian . . . is proof that it is commendable for Islam to acquire useful technologies that are found in foreign lands, as is the practice in Islamic countries today."[36] Here, then, was a Prophetic precedent for adopting something from a foreign culture without thereby betraying one's own.

The problem was that what Ṭahṭāwī wanted his fellow Muslims to take from the French went well beyond useful technologies. Near the beginning of his account of his experiences in "a land of infidelity and obstinacy,"[37] he seeks to explain why he and his companions were sent to study in such a place. One point he makes is that the Muslim countries had neglected the philosophical sciences and thus had need of the Western countries to fill the gaps in their knowledge. As

35. Wāqidī, *Maghāzī*, London 1966, 445.
36. Ṭahṭāwī, *Sīrat al-Rasūl wa-ta'sīs al-dawla al-islāmiyya*, Beirut 1977, 259.
37. For this and the quotations that follow see Ṭahṭāwī, *An imam in Paris*, London 2004, 101, 105, 109, 125.

if to avoid wounding the pride of his Muslim readers, he soon adds that the Europeans acknowledge "that we were their teachers in all sciences and that we had an advance on them." Yet he makes no bones about their current superiority: "Their scholars exceed all others in the area of the philosophical sciences." Indeed, they have surpassed even Aristotle and Plato: "Their philosophy is purer than that of the ancients." Fortunately, this incomparable alien wisdom is not as scary as it might sound, since "they construct proofs of the existence of Almighty God, of the immortality of the soul, and of the reward and punishment," meaning heaven and hell. This is news that Ṭahṭāwī's Muslim readers could be expected to find reassuring.

If we move to the Ottoman Empire at a somewhat later date, we encounter a trend of thought that was prepared to ride roughshod over Islamic sensibilities, rather than handling them with kid gloves in the manner of Ṭahṭāwī. A good example is a newspaper article of 1883–84 by the Ottoman Albanian Shemseddīn Sāmī Frashëri (d. 1904). The objective, he said, must be to save the Muslim peoples from ignorance and "once again bring them to civilization."[38] They had indeed possessed a civilization long ago, but by now it was obsolete: to rely on its literary remains was like "trying to benefit from the wick of an oil lamp in the presence of sunlight." "The duty we owe to those lamps today," he told his readers, "is simply to cherish and respect them for their role in getting us out of the darkness" in former times. What mattered now was the light of the sun, and that sun was modern European civilization. So "if we wish to become civilized, we must do so by borrowing science and technology from the contemporary civilization of Europe, and leave the study of the works of Islamic scholars to the students of history and antiquity." The problem, as he saw it, was that Muslims associated modern civilization with Christianity. He scorned the attempts of well-intentioned people to get around this obstacle by exaggerating the indebtedness of European civilization to the Muslims, and blamed these people for encouraging a new kind of fanaticism that saw European civilization as an inferior imitation of their own. Europe, too, had experienced fanaticism as "an obstacle on the road to civilization," and European intellectuals had solved the problem by waging war on it "with axes, crowbars, and gunpowder." In the same way Muslim nations had to declare war on fanaticism and crush it with force. This was an impious proposal if ever there was one. Frashëri did not, however, want it to appear that in targeting fanaticism he was attacking Islam itself. Quite the contrary. Fanaticism, he wrote, is the rust of religion, and left unchecked it corrodes it. Religion must therefore be purified of this rust "so it shines with its true and essential luster."

38. For this and the quotations that follow see Şemseddin Sami Frashëri, "Transferring the new civilization to the Islamic peoples," in C. Kurzman (ed.), *Modernist Islam*, Oxford 2002, 149b, 150a, 151b.

From 1893 Frashëri was under house arrest in Istanbul, so he was in no position to wield an axe or a crowbar against fanaticism, let alone bring on the gunpowder. But matters were different with Muṣṭafā Kemāl Pasha, alias Atatürk (d. 1938), the founder of modern Turkey and effectively its ruler from the early 1920s till his death. This was the man who in 1934 evicted Islam from Aya Sofya—the greatest mosque of Istanbul, once a Byzantine church—and turned it into a museum. A characteristic measure that directly affected the lives of many more people was a law of 1925 that criminalized the wearing of the fez and imposed the European hat in its place. The fez itself had been adopted by the Ottoman government from North Africa in a reform of 1829 in the face of some opposition. At the time it was essentially a compromise. Whereas the turban that it replaced was by European standards absurdly exotic—suggestive of "walking toadstools," as one observer uncharitably expressed it[39]—the simple fez had a more modern look about it. But at the same time it could be accepted by the pious: thanks to the absence of a brim, it was compatible with the prostrations required by the ritual of Muslim prayer. A hat, by contrast, has a brim, as Atatürk spelled out in no uncertain terms. To wear one is tantamount to a public statement that one does not pray. In a six-day speech of 1927 celebrating his achievements, Atatürk justified this jarring reform as follows: "Gentlemen, it was necessary to abolish the fez, which sat on the heads of our nation as an emblem of ignorance, negligence, fanaticism, and hatred of progress and civilization, to accept in its place the hat, the headgear used by the whole civilized world."[40] In the same speech he took credit for the abolition of Ṣūfī religiosity, which he equated with the "superstitions and prejudices" of a "primitive nation."[41] One might have thought that at this point he would have made the same rhetorical move as Frashëri, distinguishing the folly of fanaticism and superstition from the true and essential luster of religion. Instead, he went on to describe the new Turkey as a modern state "founded on the latest results of science." In a final emotional peroration he entrusted the future of the country to "Turkish youth," speaking of the external and internal dangers they might confront. In this highly emotive context he did not so much as mention Islam. We see here the way in which disinvesting from a Muslim identity and investing instead in a Turkish one could help justify the wholesale adoption of European ways. As the Turkish nationalist Ziya Gökalp (d. 1924) put it in 1923, "Civilization is the clothes of nations." The moral was clear: "Just as individuals change their clothes so nations may do."[42] Literally and figuratively, Atatürk's hat law was the prime example.

39. Quoted in N. Berkes, *The development of secularism in Turkey*, Montreal 1964, 123.

40. *A speech delivered by Ghazi Mustapha Kemal*, Leipzig 1929, 721–22, as quoted in Lewis, *The emergence of modern Turkey*, 263.

41. For this and the quotations that follow see *A speech delivered by Ghazi Mustapha Kemal*, 722, 723.

42. Ziya Gökalp, *Turkish nationalism and Western civilization*, London 1959, 266.

It is true that Atatürk did not go as far as Enver Hoxha (d. 1985), the Albanian dictator who in the late 1960s saw fit to abolish religion altogether. It is nevertheless unsurprising that the irreligious tendencies of people such as Frashëri and Atatürk should have led to a considerable backlash. Yet this backlash, at least in its twentieth-century form, was not a call for a simple return to the way things had been before Europe had started the trouble. On the contrary, the backlash itself was profoundly affected by the encounter with the West. An Ottoman conservative writing in 1908–9 held that "if we ever run our affairs according to European principles, the moral degeneration that has fallen upon them will be inevitable for us." But he still conceded the need "to benefit from European civilization, industry, and knowledge."[43] Ḥasan al-Bannā (d. 1949), the Egyptian founder of the Muslim Brothers, dismissed Western civilization as bankrupt but nevertheless invoked the authority of Bernard Shaw. Abū 'l-Aʿlā Mawdūdī (d. 1979), the Indian and later Pakistani intellectual who played a key role in the emergence of Islamic fundamentalism, deplored the fact that two militant Indian Muslim leaders of the early nineteenth century had not thought of sending a delegation of scholars to Europe "with a view to investigating and inquiring into the causes of the material superiority of her people."[44] What Muslims needed in his own time, he argued, was "a comprehensive universal ideological movement"—a very Western notion. Sayyid Quṭb (d. 1966), an Egyptian who was likewise a major fundamentalist thinker, spoke frequently of "liberation," a European political value introduced into the Muslim world in the nineteenth century. It had become a regular part of current political vocabulary, but it lacked the Islamic precedent that one might have expected a fundamentalist to insist on. Osama bin Laden (d. 2011) in 2004 remarked that Spain—once al-Andalus and now an infidel country—had an economy stronger than that of the entire Arab world and opined that the reason was that "the ruler there is accountable,"[45] again using a Western term. In the mid-2010s ISIS, an organization from which one might have expected an uncompromising rejection of Western culture, set up a bureaucracy larded with Western terminology. There was a Delegated Committee, an Office of Research and Studies, a General Committee, a Central Office for Overseeing the Departments, an Office for Methodological Inquiry, and a Department of Research and Fatwas; this latter was later to become the Committee for Research and Fatwas and then the Office of Research and Studies. None of these administrative entities had any precedent in the governance of the Prophet or his Rightly Guided successors, and only the word fatwa reminds us that ISIS had something to do with Islam.

43. Quoted in Berkes, *The development of secularism in Turkey*, 354.

44. For this and the quotation that follows see Abul Aʿla Maududi, *A short history of the revivalist movement in Islam*, Lahore 1963, 113, 114.

45. Osama bin Laden, "Resist the new Rome," in J. Howarth (trans.), *Messages to the world*, London 2005, 227.

The extent and limits of imitation

As the preceding discussion suggests, the adoption of Western practices has had a pervasive influence on the way people live in the Muslim world today, often reaching the point of what might be called hyper-Westernization, the adoption of Western practices for no other reason than that they are Western. But just how pervasive have Western practices been? Where, if anywhere, can we draw the line between the indigenous tradition and the imports from the West?

Let us start by considering something concrete and visible—namely, cityscapes. In many respects a Muslim city of the early twenty-first century would look more familiar to a contemporary European than to one of its eighteenth-century denizens. There would be buildings large and small inherited from the premodern past, many of them of continuing religious significance. But for the most part the squares, avenues, side streets, office blocks, apartment blocks, and private houses surrounding such monuments would look quite different, and not in general as a result of indigenous architectural development. This would be true in different degrees for such cities as Rabat, Fez, Tunis, Cairo, Damascus, Baghdad, Tehran, Lahore, and Malacca. Of course, there are limits. In most of these modern cities we would not look to find an opera house such as the Khedive Ismāʿīl (ruled 1863–79), the grandson of Meḥmed ʿAlī Pasha, built in Cairo for the first performance of Verdi's *Aida*. This was a ruler who went to the extreme of boasting (in French) that "my country is no longer in Africa; it forms part of Europe."[46] But the general picture applies just as much to Mecca, a city whose very existence turns on its role in the Islamic past. It is not just the modern traffic, with its endless streams of cars and buses. The Kaʿba today is dwarfed by the neighboring high-rise buildings, the tallest of which, the Royal Clock Tower completed in 2012, runs to 120 stories. The style and engineering of this edifice is Western, with only a crescent at the top of the building to reflag it as Islamic. Indeed, the very idea of a clock tower was an import from Europe, perhaps first attested in seventeenth-century Albania, and it spread widely in the late Ottoman Empire.

Another example of such saturation is the pervasiveness of Western information technology: newspapers, telephones, radio, television, the internet. Even books with their long indigenous history have changed significantly under Western influence. If we leave aside the assimilated Muslims of China, who participated in Chinese print culture, the printing of books (as opposed to the medieval block printing of good-luck charms and the like) came late to the Muslim world: in the Ottoman Empire it was not adopted till the eighteenth century, and elsewhere not until the nineteenth. But it is now universal. So, too, are such details as page numbers, spaces between words, modern punctuation, and a table of

46. Quoted in I. Gershoni and J. P. Jankowski, *Egypt, Islam, and the Arabs*, New York 1986, 43.

contents laid out in Western style. This latter is placed either at the beginning of the book on the English model, or at the end of it on the French model (in the nineteenth century and well into the twentieth, civilization for many Muslims was the way things were done in Paris, not in London or New York). If the book is a work of scholarship there will be footnotes rather than marginal annotations, and at the end the unprecedented convenience of an index. For emphasis, Western-style underlining has replaced the more elegant indigenous tradition of overlining—a clear case of hyper-Westernization. All this increasingly applied even when the text being published was not some translation of a European work but rather a forgotten treasure of early Arabic literature. Indeed, the urge to seek out and publish "the books of the ancients" that had "not been read for centuries" was itself a product of the nineteenth-century upheaval.[47]

As this last point makes clear, much still remains from the past. A more obvious example would be the languages of the Muslim world. For the most part they are those that were already there in 1800: Arabic, Turkish, Persian, Swahili, Urdu, Malay, and a host of lesser-known tongues. They have, of course, been affected by major cultural changes. Knowledge of Arabic and Persian is now far less widespread than it used to be among educated Muslim speakers of other languages. For many of them the language of wider horizons today is not Arabic or Persian but English, a profound cultural reorientation. Just as drastic a change, but a geographically more limited one, is the fact that for the most part Turks and Malays no longer write their languages in the Arabic script. Likewise all Muslim languages that serve as modern literary media have undergone strong Western influence, with the result that their vocabularies are full of direct borrowings and loan-translations of Western terms. For example, two direct borrowings into Arabic are *intarnit* and *wāy fāy* for "internet" and "Wi-Fi," while an example of an Arabic loan-translation is *ʿarḍ al-niṭāq*, literally "breadth of the belt," which is of course the Arabic for "bandwidth." As a result of such changes, eighteenth-century Cairenes resurrected today would be distinctly puzzled by some of the chatter on the streets of Cairo, though they could still understand far more of it than a foreign tourist could. Particularly striking is the fact that Classical Arabic has retained its hegemonic role as a literary language, albeit in the guise of Modern Standard Arabic. In this remarkable survival it contrasts strongly with the fate of such venerable competitors as classical Chinese, Sanskrit, Greek, and Latin.

The situation with regard to the ethnic identities of the Muslim world is somewhat similar. For the most part those that are there today were present in some form in 1800. There were and are Berbers, Arabs, Turks, Persians, and so forth. But there have been changes, many of them arising from the adoption of the

47. See the quotation from Aḥmad al-Ḥusaynī (d. 1914) in A. El Shamsy, *Rediscovering the Islamic classics*, Princeton 2020, 113.

European notion of nationalism. Some of these are a matter of names: many speakers of Arabic who in the eighteenth century would have been styled "sons of the Arabs" are now unambiguously "Arabs," while the speakers of Turkish who in the high Ottoman period called themselves "Rūmīs" would now identify unhesitatingly as Turks. Other changes are a result of the ways in which old ethnic groups have been repackaged in new polities billed as nation-states. There is now a Pakistani identity alongside Sindhī or Punjabi identities, and likewise Malays are Malaysians if they live in Malaysia rather than Indonesia or Brunei. But again, we should not exaggerate the changes. In general people resurrected from the eighteenth century would not find it too hard to pick out their ethnic kin in the world today.

Undoubtedly, what has survived best as of the early twenty-first century is neither language nor ethnic identity but rather the crown jewel of Islamic civilization, the religion of Islam. One aspect of this is demographic. Even in the often adverse conditions of the last two centuries, Islam seems likely to have gained more converts from other religions than it has lost to them. One thing this reflects, in addition to the ease of conversion to Islam, is the high apostasy threshold that characterizes the religion. As we have seen, the period from the sixteenth to the eighteenth century was marked by the prolonged resistance of the Muslims of Spain and the former Khānate of Kazan to forced conversion at the hands of their Christian rulers. In Algeria in 1885, after more than half a century of French rule, the governor commented that the native population was "impermeable to the Christian faith."[48] This contrasts strongly with the low apostasy thresholds characteristic of East Asian societies. Here the most striking case is South Korea, where a quarter of the population has converted to Christianity, mostly in recent decades, without provoking any serious backlash among the other three-quarters—and this despite the fact that the country has never been under Christian rule. At the same time, Islam has not suffered from the tendency for religion to wither away that has affected some other major religions in the modern world. In South Korea and Britain roughly half the population no longer claims any religious affiliation, and both eastern Europe and the United States have been moving toward rather than away from this pattern of religious indifference. Meanwhile, modern communications have enhanced the role of Islam as a conduit of sympathy between diverse Muslim populations. They also facilitated a dramatic growth in the number of pilgrims attending the Ḥajj, the central cultic event of the Muslim year. The number rose from 50,000 in the mid-nineteenth century to over 300,000 in the years leading up to the First World War, and by 2019 it had swollen to the best part of two and a half million. (The drastic reduction that has taken place since then,

48. Quoted in C.-R. Ageron, *Les Algériens musulmans et la France*, Paris 1968, 305.

whether or not it lasts, of course reflects another feature of modern communications—their potential to enable the rapid spread of viruses.) Through all this, the substance of Islam has been well preserved. The Qur'ān, for example, retains its prestige as divine revelation, and its text reads exactly as it did in premodern times. Likewise the standard Sunnī collections of traditions transmitted from the Prophet continue to be authoritative.

We nevertheless encounter frequent cases of hybridization. Even in the core components of the religious tradition we often see an admixture of Western coloring. In line with the adoption of Western information technology, the scripture is now printed and the 114 chapters (Sūras) into which it is divided are now numbered, as are the individual verses within each chapter. Something similar applies to the collections of Prophetic traditions. For example, good editions now number the thousands of traditions contained in each collection, something we never see in manuscripts. These are matters of packaging, but in other areas the Western influence can be substantive, as with Sayyid Quṭb's inclusion of liberation among more traditional Islamic values. Another such case is Islamic banking. In the Muslim world banks are an import from Europe, so Islamic banking is not a revival of an indigenous institution but rather an innovation intended to customize the modern banking system in a way that is compatible with the Islamic prohibition of interest. An interesting case is conflicting attitudes to the compatibility of democracy and Islam. The religiously ultraconservative Salafīs are supposed to be adamantly opposed to Western democratic practices, and often they are. According al-Qā'ida, "He who believes in the concept of democracy, or who calls to it or supports it or rules by it, is an apostate regardless of his affiliation to Islam or his claim to being a Muslim."[49] Democracy, in a pithy formulation of one of its leaders, Ayman al-Ẓawāhirī, is "a new religion that deifies the masses."[50] Yet in 2011 an Egyptian Salafī spoke out in defense of constitutions, elections, and representation: "The West took it from us. They wrapped it and canned it and re-exported it to us."[51] So in this view Salafī democrats were just reclaiming a part of their own heritage that had wandered abroad; like monotheism for the seventh-century Arabs, it was their birthright. A more sustained argument in favor of democracy—Islamic democracy, to be precise—was advanced by Mawdūdī, who reckoned the political system of Islam to be "a perfect form of democracy—as perfect as a democracy can ever be."[52] In this conception political authority travels downward from God to the individual believers, each of whom is thus a deputy

49. B. Haykel, "On the nature of Salafi thought and action," in R. Meijer (ed.), *Global Salafism*, New York 2009, 53 no. 21.

50. R. Ibrahim, *Al Qaeda reader*, New York 2007, 130.

51. *The New York Times*, December 11, 2011, 12.

52. Abul A'la Mawdudi, *Human rights in Islam*, Lahore 1977, 7.

of God. The believers then delegate their authority upward to whomever they choose as caliph. In examples such as these we see the balance of the Islamic and the Western shifting from case to case, but they are consistently hybrid.

We find similar effects if we look at the attitudes of those we call fundamentalists to the traditional inequality of men and women. This inequality is explicit in the Qurʾān: one verse states that men are a step above women (Q2:228), another that they are in authority over them (Q4:34). In premodern times there was nothing problematic about this, at least not to the men who composed our sources. Thus a fourteenth-century Damascene commentator devotes no more than a couple of lines to the first verse, listing without further comment seven respects in which men are manifestly superior to women. He has more to say about the second verse, stating among other things that the reason for male authority is that men are better than women, which in turn explains why women cannot be rulers or judges. In a similar vein, a twelfth-century Khwārazmian exegete explains that men command and forbid women just as rulers do with their subjects. When he goes on to list the ways in which men are superior he starts with their rationality; here he could have cited a tradition attributed to the Prophet according to which women are deficient in intellect. But perhaps the most interesting item on the commentator's list is his statement that in general it is men who have the ability to write. A larger point is that there is nothing unusual about premodern Muslim attitudes to the inequality of women. Aristotle, the Bible, the Laws of Manu, and Confucius were in full agreement on the basic principle of female subordination.

How well has this principle fared in the modern Muslim world? There are indeed fundamentalists in our time for whom nothing has changed. Ayman al-Ẓawāhirī, in an attack on the democratic idea of equality, averred that it cannot be accepted because it is incompatible with man's domination over woman. Yet his fellow leader of al-Qāʿida, Osama bin Laden, does not seem to have taken female intellectual deficiency very seriously: the women of his household played a key role in vetting the drafts of his public statements. And if we take the two founding fathers of Islamic fundamentalism, the Indian Mawdūdī and the Egyptian Quṭb, we encounter a tone very different from Ẓawāhirī's. For Mawdūdī, "None can deny the fact that as human beings man and woman are equal."[53] Likewise for Quṭb women enjoy "complete equality" except in some "specific situations connected with natural and recognized capacities" that do not affect "the essential nature of the human situation of the two sexes."[54] As Quṭb's somewhat guarded wording makes clear, he does have reservations about unqualified female equality. But he has no wish to confine women to the harem—an institution that, in typical Arab fashion, he blames on the Turks. Mawdūdī, in fact, has considerably

53. Abul Aʿla Maududi, *Purdah and the status of woman in Islam*, Lahore 1983, 112–13.
54. W. E. Shepard, *Sayyid Qutb and Islamic activism*, Leiden 1996, 61.

more reservations. He denounces the "wrong concept of equality"[55] according to which women are free to hold the same kinds of jobs as men, and unlike Quṭb he believes in enforcing the seclusion of women: "Let us not weaken Purdah, which is a bulwark against the sex anarchy, especially of the present age."[56] So instead of being straightforwardly unequal, women are now equal but, with due respect, different. As one Iranian Āyatullāh explains, they are blessed with a stronger capacity for tender emotions and thus possess "superiority in feeling," whereas men are superior in "strength of thought."[57] It is easy to be cynical about such wordings, but the break with the old, unthinking assertion of male superiority is nevertheless a drastic one. It is undoubtedly linked to the direct appeal of intrusive Western values, but it also arises indirectly from the way in which a Western educational paradigm has led, as we have seen, to the spread of literacy among women. The ability to write is no longer the male characteristic that it was in twelfth-century Khwārazm, and even fundamentalists have to reckon with the fact that what they publish today is going to be read by women tomorrow—and very likely read critically. This a point well understood by the Ṭālibān in Afghanistan and Pakistan when waging war on the schooling of girls: if your objective is to keep women in their place, educating them is a disastrous mistake.

One thing we see here is an undoubtedly significant survival of attitudes from premodern times, attitudes that may not always have much to do with Islam. They clearly loom large behind the reservations of Mawdūdī and Quṭb regarding female equality. Another area in which we can plausibly see such survival at work is the low level of female participation in the labor force. If we order the countries of the world according to this metric, using data from 2019, several things stand out. First, the highest reported rates are found not—as one might have expected—in advanced Western or East Asian countries, but rather in the non-Muslim countries of sub-Saharan Africa. Second, no Muslim countries figure in the top two dozen, and when they do start to appear, they belong to one of two categories: sub-Saharan African or ex-Soviet. Third, of the ten countries with the lowest rates of female participation, eight are in the Middle East or North Africa, and of these eight, seven are Arab. To the extent that this is likely to reflect people's values, it suggests that a strongly negative attitude to female participation prevails in the Arab countries, affecting either the reality itself or the reporting of it, or both. And indeed such attitudes are real: if a woman in the Arab world works outside the home after her marriage—and marriage is often early—it suggests that her husband is unable to provide for her needs. This contrasts with parts of the Muslim world that have a pre-Islamic African heritage or a more recent Soviet one. Yet

55. Maududi, *Purdah*, 12.
56. Maududi, *Purdah*, 218.
57. K. Bauer, *Gender hierarchy in the Qur'ān*, New York 2015, 223.

another plausible case of the survival of premodern values is the strong approval seen in parts of the Muslim world for punishments that in the West would be deemed cruel and unusual. A survey of 2010 showed 82 percent of Muslims in Egypt favoring the stoning of adulterers and 84 percent agreeing with the death penalty for apostasy from Islam; the figures for Pakistan were similar. In Turkey, by contrast, the relevant figures were 16 percent and 5 percent. This is a huge difference. Although we do not have eighteenth-century surveys with which to compare the data for 2010, this looks like a case in which an attitude has survived in Egypt and what is now Pakistan but has been eroded in Turkey as a result of a twentieth-century experience of aggressively Westernizing rule.

A final example, and a lurid one, is the obstinate survival of sectarian animosity. As we have seen on more than one occasion, there was endemic hostility between rival Muslim sects in premodern times, just as there was among Christian or Hindu sects—Catholics against Protestants, Śaivas against Vaiṣṇavas. The difference is that with few exceptions virulent sectarianism has largely faded out in the modern Christian and Hindu contexts, whereas on balance this has not been the case in the modern Muslim world. There did indeed emerge a sense among the Western-educated elite that medieval sectarian disputes had no place in a modern society, and even someone as religiously committed as Ḥasan al-Bannā could take an irenic view of sectarian differences: "Let us cooperate in those things on which we can agree and be lenient in those on which we cannot."[58] But the overall effect of the Islamic revival of the later twentieth century was to restore the prestige of a world view in which sectarian issues, far from seeming archaic and irrelevant, were of the essence. Wahhābism, a major contributor to the revival, had been strongly sectarian from the start: its eighteenth-century founder, Muḥammad ibn ʿAbd al-Wahhāb, regarded the Shīʿites as "the first to bring polytheism into this [Muslim] community."[59] It was in this spirit that ISIS—very much a Wahhābī movement—celebrated a suicide bombing in eastern Saudi Arabia that killed twenty-one Shīʿites at a mosque in 2015: "They are apostate unbelievers, whose blood and property it is licit to take. It is obligatory for us to kill them, to fight them, and to drive them away, nay but to cleanse the land of their filth."[60] ISIS is a fringe movement, but sectarian conflict has been widespread in the recent history of the Muslim world. Iraq, Syria, and Yemen have been ravaged by sectarian civil wars, and tensions between sects can and do turn lethal in Turkey, Iran, Lebanon, Bahrain, Saudi Arabia, Afghanistan, and Pakistan. A significant factor in this has been the export of sectarianism by the rulers of two particular countries: Iran, which has exacerbated sectarian conflict by reaching out

58. R. P. Mitchell, *The society of the Muslim Brothers*, London 1969, 217.
59. Quoted in C. M. Bunzel, *Wahhābism*, Princeton 2023, 210.
60. See C. Bunzel, "Appendix B," in F. Wehrey (ed.), *Beyond Sunni and Shia*, London 2017, 309.

to Shīʿite minorities in Sunnī-majority countries, and Saudi Arabia, which for a long time was funding the spread of Wahhābism. But the successful exploitation of sectarian divisions by governments would not be feasible without the prior existence of sectarian animosities waiting to be exploited.

Returning to the aspects of Western culture that are now well entrenched in the Muslim world, one final point is worth a mention. The process of adopting the ways of another culture is far more wrenching than is having adopted them at some time in the past. Once they are there, the universal human capacity for getting used to things comes into play. Take a second look at the page you are currently reading with a view to acknowledging of your cultural debts. You see a piece of paper courtesy of the Chinese, letters belonging to an alphabet courtesy of the Phoenicians, numerals courtesy of the Indians, and movable-type printing courtesy of the Germans (and behind them perhaps the East Asians—this is plausible but has yet to be proved). The language of the present sentence belongs to the English, but it is larded with words borrowed from the French. It is unlikely that you count all the seven peoples implicated in the making of this page among your ancestors, and quite probable that you do not claim descent from any of them. Has the burden of your historical indebtedness to so many foreigners ever bothered you? Does it really bother you now that I point it out? To this we could add a geopolitical consideration. A major reason the adoption of Western ways has been so contentious for the Muslim world in the last two centuries has been the steep power gradient it has faced in its relations with the West. How might the optics change if at some time in the perhaps not so distant future the hegemonic role were to be assumed by East Asia?

Another major trend that has had a strong effect on the character of Islam today is homogenization. In part this is a development that in modern times has affected all societies, bringing local diversity under increasing pressure from wider uniformity. Much of this is a result of the workings of modern society irrespective of the grander purposes of its rulers and elites. But the effects of such workings have often been exploited and enhanced by the purposive action of those who hold the reins of political, economic, social, and cultural power, especially those who are ideologically committed to a single right way of doing things. In the secular domain the most comprehensive example of this has been communism, but there is no lack of more disparate instances from capitalist societies. Whether coercive or voluntary, the process has been hard at work in the religious life of contemporary Muslim societies. The most far-reaching example—though by no means the only one—is the propagation of Salafism. There is, of course, nothing new among monotheists about the idea that there is just one true form of religion and all else is false. But modern conditions have worked to make it much easier to spread such forms. Thus the divergent types of Islam that we encountered among the Cham Muslims of mainland Southeast Asia and the Sasak Muslims of Lombok are now under siege. Among the Muslim Chams, only a tenth of the community still adheres to its traditional script and religious heritage; the rest have undergone "Jawization," which means assimilation to a more mainstream form of Islam. In the same way only a tiny minority of the Sasak Muslims has yet to be Jawized. The evolution among the far larger population of Muslims on Java has been in the same direction. Here, however, traditionalist foot-dragging has been stronger. In one instance, for example, the Goddess of the Southern Ocean was defended against the inroads of fundamentalism with the claim that although she had possessed no religion in the past, she had now become a Muslim and was able to read Arabic. The same overall trajectory has been in evidence in South Asia, where in Pakistan there has been a series of violent attacks on Ṣūfī shrines. In Turkey ethnographical work on popular Islam done a century ago would be utterly misleading as a guide to current realities. It is not that all inhomogeneities have disappeared in Islam today, but a lot of effort has gone into ironing them out.

The bulk of this book has been concerned with the history of the Muslim world between two profound discontinuities. The first was the emergence of Islam in the seventh century and its spread over a vast territory that eventually extended all the way across the Old World. The second was the rise of Europe in the nineteenth century and the extension of its power, technology, and much of its culture to the world at large. Both processes were deeply intrusive and often accompanied by considerable violence. Both led to radical transformations of the societies affected by them. By contrast, nothing in the intervening period can quite compare. The coming of the steppe peoples was no small matter, but it was geographically less far-reaching and structurally less momentous. Yet drastic as they were, neither of the two great discontinuities changed everything. Each reshaped some things radically while leaving others largely untouched. Moreover, the two were significantly different in the aspects of life they affected most. At one extreme, the rise of Islam fundamentally changed the religious allegiances of large populations from Morocco to Mindanao, whereas in this respect the rise of the West had only a marginal impact on the Muslim world. At the other extreme, the Western impact had massive consequences for the material conditions prevailing in the Muslim world, transforming them in ways that the rise of Islam never did. To a degree, then, the two discontinuities could be seen as complementary. From that point of view we could argue that since the Muslim world has retained its identity despite assimilating numerous material and organizational features of the modern West, we are approaching a new equilibrium. Yet in between the two complementary zones there is a large area of overlap and thus of contention, particularly in the realm of social and political values. Not surprisingly, this overlap has engendered considerable tension between the Muslim world and the West and within the Muslim world in modern times. To the extent that Western ways have prevailed in this overlap, we could argue that the very existence of Islamic civilization—as opposed to Islam—is in question in the world today. Undoubtedly it was still there as late as the early nineteenth century, providing a comprehensive framework of values, institutions, and roles within which Muslims lived out their lives. But since then, we could well argue, the hurricane of Western modernity has swept away large parts of this overarching structure, leaving something more like an ancient ruin.

These are teasing historical issues, but whether they matter for the future remains to be seen. To speak of Western modernity is to imply that modernity could also exist in other, non-Western forms. It is difficult to think clearly about this, not least because the word "modernity" tends to be both slippery and somewhat talismanic. But in a widespread usage it points to certain aspects of Western society in the last few centuries that led to the development of the disproportionate power and influence of the West. These features, if conceived in the abstract, are not intrinsically Western, though if taken together they have hitherto been Western in contingent historical fact. Just what they are is hard to say at all precisely, though it is not difficult to form at least an intuitive notion of them—as Macaulay did in his somewhat lyrical celebration of the dawn of English modernity. Under close study the individual features frequently turn out not to be unique to the modern West; that is to say, they often have precedents in older layers of the Western tradition or parallels in premodern non-Western traditions. So the idea of a non-Western modernity makes at least conceptual sense, even if claims to its realization have so far been implausible.

Perhaps in the more distant future we could indeed imagine the emergence of such a thing as a convincing non-Western modernity. Though historically downstream of the Western form, it might in other respects be sufficiently distant from it to qualify as non-Western. The least implausible sites for such a development currently seem to be China and the Muslim world. But China, though it has the best material preconditions for it, largely destroyed its premodern tradition in the decades following the collapse of its last imperial dynasty. The result is that there has been little substance, either culturally or politically, to the Confucian revival of the late twentieth century. Meanwhile, the Muslim world, while remaining in possession of the premodern non-Western tradition that has retained the greatest continuing relevance in the world today, has lacked the material preconditions for success in such a venture. What we have seen there so far has consisted essentially in the formation of hybrids in which the load-bearing timbers of modernity remain essentially Western but are combined with the symbolic resources—identities and values—of the indigenous tradition, often vetted for compatibility (or incompatibility, as the case may be) with Western modernity. ISIS provided a striking example—or perhaps caricature—of this phenomenon with its combination of Western-style armaments and committees with the revival of the caliphate and the premodern Islamic law of slavery, the latter at once a seductive convenience for its male fighters and a flaunting of its radical rejection of Western values. What, then, would it take to get beyond such a hybrid in which modernity remains manifestly Western and instead develop something that would unambiguously count as a non-Western modernity? The opacity of the future makes it virtually impossible to say anything perspicacious in answer to this question. Assuming the continued survival of the human race, perhaps such a modernity will make an appearance within a few centuries. Or perhaps the very categories that we invest so much in today—categories like modernity, the West, China, and the Muslim world—will have lost all meaning in the eyes of our distant descendants.

INDEX